the Blues of Summer

The True Story of Baseball in Daniels County, Montana

Joe Puckett

Aubade Publishing
Ashburn, VA

Copyright © 2025 Joe Puckett

All rights reserved. No part of this publication may be reproduced, stored in a retrieval system, or transmitted in any form or by any means, electronic, mechanical, photocopying, recording, or otherwise, without the prior written permission of Aubade Publishing.

This work is a true story, based on old scorebooks, research in newspaper articles and other sources, interviews and letters received, and the author's memories of the people, events, conversations, and locales at that time of his life. At times during the story, the author's and others' memories of the people, conversations, events, and locales might not be perfectly accurate, but the attempt was made to be faithful to the historical events. Except for some entries that are clearly fictional for storytelling purposes, no names, places, or events have been changed, invented, or altered.

Cover design and book layout by Cosette Puckett

Cover photo courtesy of the *Daniels County Leader*

Back cover watercolor painting by Dianne (Puckett) Beesley

Library of Congress Control Number: 2025938878

ISBN: 978-1-951547-38-7

Published by Aubade Publishing, Ashburn, Virginia

Printed in the United States of America

To the veterans of The United States American Legion:

Not only have you defended our country and kept us safe,

You gave us the opportunity to play baseball.

Thank you.

Table of Contents

Prologue	1
The Homesteaders and Early Town Teams (1900–1924)	6
The Scobey Giants (1925–1929)	18
The Sons of the Pioneers (1930–1945)	34
Baseball is Back in Daniels County (1946–1956)	52
The Baseball Renaissance (1957–1968)	88
The Doc Norman Championship Era (1969–1982)	150
The Don Lekvold Era (1983–1991)	430
The Ken Meyer / Mike Lee Era (1992–1997)	510
The Last Years (1998–2003)	580
The Long Winter (2004–2015)	628
The Revival (2016–2019)	638
The Froid Bulls (2020–2024)	662
Epilogue	671
Acknowledgements	674
References	676
Index	682

Prologue

When I told my wife Vonda I was going to write a memoir about playing baseball like I had done with basketball, she said, "Do you lose in this one, too?" I replied, "No, we don't lose. Scobey won eight state American Legion Baseball championships!" Vonda jokingly asked me that because my high school team lost the Montana state championship game in the basketball book, *The Dream: The Story of the 1978 and 1979 Peerless Panthers*.[1] (You have to understand my wife: she has a wonderful sense of humor and keeps me an honest man.)

In the prologue to *The Dream*, I wrote, "Life for me growing up in the 1960s and '70s in the small farming and ranching community of Peerless, Montana, was very simple. Eat, sleep, play all day, and go to church on Sunday—that was about it. About the only thing that changed in this cycle was what game I played, which depended on what time of year it was. But the particular sport I played that this story revolves around is basketball—a game for which I still have a tremendous passion and love."

Substituting the sport "baseball" for "basketball," we have the same opening for *The Blues of Summer*.

What prompted me to write *The Dream* was the closure of Peerless High School (PHS) in June 2009. I wanted to keep the memory of PHS and the memory of the Peerless community alive. Several other high schools in our conference also closed due to the declining population in northeastern Montana. Like *The Dream*, the folding of the Scobey Blues American Legion Baseball program for the second time after the 2019 season (it had shut down from 2004 to 2015) prompted me to write *The Blues of Summer*. I wanted to keep the memory of the Scobey baseball tradition alive. As with basketball, several other American Legion Baseball teams in northeastern Montana have also gone the way of the dodo bird, primarily due to declining population, and this book honors their memory, too.

My dad, George "Tiny" Puckett,[1] taught me to play baseball. He coached my twin brother Jon and me in Peewee, Little League, and Babe Ruth from 1967 to 1976, when we were six to 15. Baseball during the summer months in northeastern Montana was our life. My memories of playing baseball with Jon and all my friends in Peerless for the Peerless Pirates are some of the best memories I have. Beginning in 1973, when I was 12 years old in Little League, I played on all-star teams with players from other towns in Daniels County, and those all-star teams later became the American Legion Baseball teams I played on during my high school years. Thanks to the United States American Legion, to whom this book is dedicated, I was lucky to be able to continue playing baseball during my high school years for legendary coach Clyde H. "Doc" Norman and the Scobey Blues American Legion Baseball team, playing on four Montana state Class B American Legion Baseball championship teams from 1976 to 1979. This book is partly a memoir of my childhood and teenage memories playing baseball in Peerless and Scobey in small-town America.

But it is much more than that. *The Blues of Summer* tells the story of all the men and boys who played baseball those summers in northeastern Montana. It also contains a section on the women and girls who played softball, who were as much a part of the story as anything. *The Blues of Summer* forever memorializes the storied baseball tradition of Daniels County, Montana.

Scobey hosted seven state American Legion Baseball tournaments in its history. I watched four of them and played in two. When the tournament came to Scobey, I would often skim through the State Class B Tournament program pages and come across the "Area Baseball" section of the program. In it, it talked about the homesteaders who brought the game to the area in the early 1900s, the 1925 Scobey Giants team which had Swede Risberg and Happy Felsch from the Chicago White Sox on it, Scobey's first American Legion team in 1930, the championship Scobey Plainsmen town teams in the late 1950s and early 1960s, through the current day American Legion Baseball teams. When I read it, I had this sense that Scobey and Daniels County had a rich historic baseball tradition and that I was part of it. It made me feel proud. To tag the tradition with a name, The *Daniels County Leader* christened

---

1 Dad got his nickname by playing Tiny Tim in Charles Dickens's *A Christmas Carol* when he was a little boy.

Daniels County as "Baseball Country" in an article for the first state tournament Scobey hosted in 1969.

Aware of this history, I owed it to the town of Scobey and Daniels County to write not just a memoir about the years I played, but the entire baseball story, because the four years I played for the Blues were a mere blip in a long, storied tradition. When I called my friend and former teammate Kelly Norman to tell him I would undertake the project, he said, "The book will be fun, but the process will be the best part." Boy, was he right. I have reconnected with many of my old teammates and made many new friends with players from teams that came before and after the years I played. I did my best to approximate the incredible story of Scobey's and the surrounding towns' baseball tradition. I needed everyone's help to do that. After almost three years of research in newspapers and archives and interviews with former players and coaches, I have attempted to tell that story in my most difficult at-bat. The legacy of the historical tradition of baseball in Scobey and broader northeastern Montana has been written, and the memory of those glorious summers will be preserved forever.

In October 2022, not long after I began this project, I was hiking alongside the Great Falls of the Potomac River in Great Falls, Virginia, then further on to a gorge where the river got wild with rapids. The river became more serene as it got closer to the Chesapeake Bay, which widened before it flowed gently into the Chesapeake Bay, then out to the Atlantic Ocean. As I was hiking, I thought about the history of Scobey, Montana, baseball, and its surrounding communities in Daniels County, how the sport of baseball has changed over time, but in its essence has remained the same. Just as the Potomac River changes form, from its source in the Allegheny Mountains of West Virginia as it winds its way forward to Chesapeake Bay, its essence—the water—remains the same.

What is the "essence" of Scobey baseball? Beginning with the origins of baseball in the Scobey and surrounding communities in northeastern Montana in the early 1900s when the homesteaders brought the game to the area, it is very evident that there was a passion for the sport of baseball, from the businessmen to the managers and coaches to the adult players to the fans to the parents and to the kids who played the game. That passion and commitment the homesteaders brought with them remained strong through the generations, as it continued through the 1920s, when Charles "Swede" Risberg and Oscar "Happy" Felsch—shortstop and center fielder for the Chicago White Sox who were banned for life from professional baseball in 1920 for throwing the 1919 World Series—were lured by Scobey businessmen to come to play for the Scobey Giants, a semiprofessional town team. It carried forward to Scobey's first American Legion Baseball team in 1930, which won the northeastern district in its first two years of existence. The passion led to the development of the Scobey Ball Park in 1957, the hosting of several National Baseball Congress (NBC) tournaments at Scobey Ball Park, the Scobey Plainsmen town team Montana state championships in 1958 and 1960—both hosted at Scobey Ball Park—and the Plainsmen seventh-place finish in the United States at Nationals in Wichita in 1960.

Further downstream, as the baseball river wound its way forward in time, the spirit remained the same, although its form changed significantly. The arrival of legendary American Legion Baseball coach Doc Norman in Scobey in 1959 would prove to be lightning in a bottle. Doc's passion and commitment to the sport would ignite with that of the Scobey area's players and fans. The lightning bolt and ensuing clap of thunder reverberated across four decades, spawning eight American Legion Baseball state championships between 1969 and 1982, four hosted at Scobey Ball Park. The passion led to three Legion Baseball third-place finishes at State in 1985, 1990, and 1996, and the revival of the American Legion Baseball program in 2016, after the program had folded in 2004. Sadly, the program folded again following the 2019 season. The primary culprit was the declining population.

If a picture is worth a thousand words, the cover photo might be worth ten thousand. It contains the entire book in one image. Several symbolic themes are represented. This photo was taken at the trophy presentation following Scobey's first state American Legion Baseball championship over Havre in 1969, which was won in dramatic fashion. The state tournament was hosted in Scobey for the first time that summer. In the photo, Larry Bowler, at the far right on the microphone, symbolizes our nation's veterans and American Legion Post 56 in Scobey. Larry was also the editor of the *Daniels County Leader*, the local newspaper whose detailed coverage of the Scobey town teams and Legion teams through the years made this book possible. Jack Reiner, who is presenting the trophy, represents the Scobey Plainsmen town team (he played for the Plainsmen for over 20 years) and the community. He symbolizes the passing of the baton of the Greatest Generation to the Baby Boomers, when American Legion Baseball replaced the town teams as the hottest baseball ticket in town after Junior Legion raised the playing age to 18 years old in 1961. Then there is the 1969 Scobey Legion baseball team to the left, symbolizing success, the commitment and dedication to winning that Doc instilled in all his players. Also to the left are the batboys, who saw the excellence of the first team to win and were inspired to follow the path of winning state championships, and they did. Head Coach Doc Norman, the reason for all of it, is standing just behind the ball player receiving the trophy, proudly surveying the championship moment he created. Dick Puckett from Peerless is receiving the trophy. Dick symbolizes how Doc recruited young players to play Legion, as Dick was in his fifth year of Legion ball, having started playing when he was 14 years old in 1965. He also symbolizes the all-county team formed only a year earlier in 1968, when players from Flaxville, Peerless, and Scobey joined the team for the first time. It had to be an all-county team to win it. Dick also represents the talent that Doc lured to Scobey and developed, as he started at second base for four years for the South Dakota State Jackrabbits and was team captain his senior year. Standing just behind Jack Reiner's left shoulder is second baseman Danny "Charlie" Wang, and to Danny's right in the back is third baseman Rick Danelson. Danny and Rick have both recently passed on: Danny in 2020 and Rick in 2025. Pete Dickson and Dennis "Doc" Miller from the 1969 team have also passed away. These ball players symbolize the passage of time, of love and loss, and the end of the era when baseball was king in Daniels County. But we honor and remember them, as we honor and remember all the Blues who have passed before us. Finally, the championship game date was August 10, 1969, just three weeks after Apollo 11 and Neil Armstrong landed and walked on the moon for the first time. Doc and Scobey's first state championship had also been a decade in the making, as Doc started coaching in 1959. The 1969 state championship opened up the floodgates for many state championships to come.

A note on the book's title. I always wondered where the phrase "The Boys of Summer" came from. It has always rolled off my tongue so easily, a visceral part of me since I was a little boy. Dad used to say it when he talked about Major League Baseball players, so to me, it was always synonymous with baseball players in the summer. I thought it was probably "boys of summer" instead of "men of summer" because the professional baseball players I saw play on TV played the game with the joy of little boys rather than men working to earn a paycheck and make a living. They were having fun playing a game and getting paid for it. I thought it was also because baseball has the stage in summer; football is in the fall, and basketball is in the winter, and the summer months are reserved for baseball.

The first time I remember hearing the phrase from someone other than my dad was when Vin Scully said it on the air while broadcasting the 1984 World Series between the San Diego Padres and the Detroit Tigers. I distinctly remember Vin saying, "I see the boys of summer *in their ruin*" (italics mine). I can't remember the exact context, but it seemed to do with a player approaching the end of his career, and his best baseball-playing days were behind him.

What Vin Scully said puzzled me. Why did he say, "I see the boys of summer *in their ruin*"? What did he mean by that? I use italics for *in their ruin* because he emphasized those three words when he said it. He also seemed very familiar with the saying, as if it had been a part of him for a long time. But I set the puzzlement aside and didn't give it another thought after the series.

Later that fall, Don Henley released a single titled "The Boys of Summer," which I remember listening to on the radio often and watching the MTV video. I liked the song and still do. The song's music, as did the lyrics, had a "nostalgic" feeling. It seemed like the man in the song longed for his youth and the nostalgic theme of summer love. Whenever I hear it, the song still takes me back to those summer days of playing baseball in Scobey because of its nostalgic theme and the title, "The Boys of Summer," which always meant baseball to me.

Then, several years later, I picked up my wife's book from a literature class she was taking in college and started reading some of the stories and poems. To my surprise, I found a poem titled "I See the Boys of Summer" by Dylan Thomas. I read the first line of the poem: "I see the boys of summer in their ruin."

There it was! It was the same line Vin Scully said during the World Series.

I read the poem, but it wasn't easy to decipher. I read it over and over, but still couldn't grasp it. I still really can't. It seemed a nostalgic poem about boys who were destructive in summer, lived a slash-and-burn life, wasted their youth, thinking it would last forever, and ruined harvests and relationships. It wasn't what I thought it would be, but I picked up on the nostalgia. That part I got. I thought it would be about baseball. But then, why would it be about baseball? Dylan Thomas was from Wales, and the poem was written in 1934. I don't think they played much baseball in Wales in 1934.

Before writing the book, I thought about a title. What would capture the spirit of the book? It had to be nostalgic because the story would be about a bygone era when "baseball was the king" in Scobey, as Ryan Linder and Morgan Oie said in their interviews. I considered "The Boys of Summer" because I remembered my dad saying that all the time when I was a boy, and Vin Scully saying it on air during the World Series. Don Henley's song and Dylan Thomas's poem were nostalgic.

Wanting to learn more, I searched the internet about "The Boys of Summer" and discovered why Vin Scully said what he did.

Roger Kahn wrote a book titled *The Boys of Summer* in 1972 about the Brooklyn Dodgers of the 1950s.[2] Kahn was a young boy and a Dodgers fan who could walk to Ebbets Field to watch them play, then became a sportswriter and covered the team. In his book, Kahn recalled his childhood as a Dodgers fan, the team he covered as a sportswriter in the early 1950s, then examined the same players' lives—sometimes not so happy—after baseball. The players' baseball careers were fleeting; the summers in Brooklyn were transitory. Kahn's nostalgic book captures the passion of the Brooklyn Dodgers players and fans while the franchise was in Brooklyn. However, the Brooklyn Dodgers left Brooklyn for Los Angeles for the 1958 season, and Vin Scully was their announcer in Brooklyn starting in 1950. I think that is why Vin Scully emphasized the words in their ruin—baseball careers and summers are fleeting. The Dodgers were gone from Brooklyn, and Ebbets Field was torn down to make brick apartment buildings.

Like the Brooklyn Dodgers, the Scobey Blues American Legion team is no more. Many former players I've interviewed talk about how the Scobey Ball Park is now in ruin. That's when I thought of the title *The Blues of Summer*. It's the same story, except it's about the Scobey Blues. The word "Blues" fits nicely because that was the American Legion's name beginning in 1977, and the book is a little bluesy, remembering a bygone era.

Since Dylan Thomas was from Wales, I wanted to see if they played baseball in Wales. I had to smile at the irony that the title of Roger Kahn's book about baseball in Brooklyn was taken from a poem written by a Welsh poet, and Don Henley's song was taken from the baseball book. It turns out they do play baseball in Wales—sort of. In 2021, the Welsh Baseball Union Cup final was played between Grange Albion and Newport City, the first men's final played since 2016. Baseball was trying to make a comeback in Wales.[3]

Who knows, maybe Dylan Thomas played this version of baseball in 1934?

Picking up on this nostalgia theme, the seventh commissioner of Major League Baseball, A. Bartlett Giamatti, talked about baseball and America's obsession with it in several speeches before he died in 1989. One of his themes was, "Baseball is About Going Home." He said, "Baseball is of course entirely about going home. And to that extent, because it is the only game you ever heard of where you want to get back to where you started (all the other games are territorial; you want to get his or her territory; not baseball). Baseball simply wants to get you from here back around to here, and that I think is why baseball is its own long poem, its own endless epic."[4]

He then talked about how the journey home in baseball is nostalgic. "Baseball is about going home, and how hard it is to get there and how driven is our need. It tells us how good home is. Its wisdom says you can go home again but you cannot stay. The journey must always start once more, the bat an oar over the shoulder, until there is an end to all journeying. *Nostos*; the going home; the game of nostalgia, so apt an image for our hunger that it hurts."[5]

The Blues of Summer is a nostalgic baseball story about going home to one small town and county in northeastern Montana. It is the story of our nation and its love affair with our National Pastime. Hop in the Wayback Machine with me, travel back in time, and make it home safely again.

And take your time reading it. Relax, enjoy. There are a lot of pictures—time-collapsing windows to the past. Sit back and watch the ball game on a nice, warm, breezy Sunday afternoon. There is no pitch clock with *The Blues of Summer*. Why rush a game you wish could last forever?

SECTION NOTES

1. Joe Puckett, *The Dream: The Story of the 1978 and 1979 Peerless Panthers*, (Aubade Publishing, 2010).
2. Roger Kahn, *The Boys of Summer* (Harper & Row, 1972).
3. "Men's baseball returns to Wales with Welsh Baseball Union Cup final," *BBC Sports*, August 5, 2021.
4. A. Bartlett Giamatti, "Going Home," 1989, taken from James Preller Blog, April 15, 2015.
5. Giamatti, "Going Home."

The Homestead Town Teams
1900 – 1924

1930 – 1945
The Sons of
the Pioneers

1957 – 1968
The Baseball
Renaissance

The Scobey
Giants
1925 – 1929

Baseball is Back
in Daniels County
1946 – 1956

The D
Cham
1969 –

ers and Early

1983 – 1991	1998 – 2003	2016 – 2019
The Don	The Last	The
Lekvold Era	Years	Revival

...rman	The Ken	The Long	The Froid
...hip Era	Meyer/Mike	Winter	Bulls
	Lee Era	2004 – 2015	2020 – 2024
	1992 – 1997		

1900–1924
The Homesteaders Bring the Game to Daniels County

> *Baseball was taken seriously in northeastern Montana in the early 1900s. A good baseball team was a badge of civic progress and activity.*
>
> —From the article, "Baseball Club of 1913 Was Fast Aggregation," The Glasgow Courier, August 6, 1953

The success of the Scobey American Legion Baseball and Scobey Plainsmen teams was built on the foundation of the people who settled Daniels County when they brought the game of baseball with them to the area in the early 1900s. The homesteaders worked hard; it was a tough life, but when they played, they played baseball. When the first settlers came to the area, baseball was *the* sport. Most of the smaller communities formed baseball teams, and the game was also a pastime, played recreationally, often the focal point of social events in the summer, including picnics on Sunday. However, for one family, Sunday baseball was a problem. Fern Wiley Sandon wrote about the Jesse Wiley homesteader family from Whitetail in the *Daniels County History* book published by the Daniels County Bicentennial Committee in 1977: "Activities consisted of visiting, dancing, and Sunday afternoon baseball games. Sunday baseball was a sore point in our home, as my mother was reared to honor the Sabbath and keep it holy. Her father was a minister as well as a farmer."[1]

The *Daniels County History* book is replete with entries written by people in the early 1900s who talked about playing baseball on Sundays with picnics and other social events. Their love of baseball in the area in those early years leaps off the pages, and their passion was passed down to us through the generations.

The *Daniels County History* book wrote this summary about baseball in Daniels County in the early 1900s:

> *Baseball, during the time that the county was first being settled, often was a spontaneous affair. Teams were of a temporary arrangement, put together for a local celebration or picnic. During the ball season players would switch from one team to another as the occasion demanded. Later many teams did play regularly scheduled games. Old-timers state that Smoke Creek, south of Flaxville, had one of the first teams in the area and that, in 1911, that team played games in Old Scobey. One of the players, Olson by name, had only one arm but this did not seem to affect his ability.*
>
> *During the summer of 1913, ball games were played at Orville.*
>
> *The year 1914 saw the Smoke Creek team in the field again. That year also saw the rise of a ball team in the new town of (East) Scobey under the managership of Lou Boyd, early day saloon keeper. It won sixteen games and lost five, although accounts do not record the opponents.*
>
> *Flaxville's 1914 team was managed by Ed Molden, also a saloon keeper.*
>
> *The ball team from Police Creek, south of Four Buttes, was organized in 1916. Throughout the years of play team members pooled money to buy gasoline for a Model T truck which carried them to games with Pleasant Prairie, Flaxville, Scobey, Ossette, Mineral Bench, Benrud, Peerless and Lustre. One of the original players recalls that Lustre, Police Creek's toughest opponent, had eight brothers on its nine.*[2]

The writers wrote numerous anecdotes about playing baseball in the early 1900s in the book. Here are just a few:

- "Every third cow pasture had a corner dedicated to baseball."[3]
- "One year some Indians from Brockton were hired to provide the crew, teams and bundle racks for the threshing rig. Four Indians with their families came from Brockton with their teams and bundle racks and pitched their tents in the pasture. They enjoyed a game

of 'burnout'* catch with a baseball. No baseball gloves were used, and the idea was to see who could catch the hardest thrown baseball."[4] This story can be traced to future Scobey Legion baseball players in Daniels County—the Higgins family from Flaxville. I asked John "Jack" Higgins, who played Legion ball from 1965 to 1969, if he knew about the story. He said, "That was Grandpa Jack. Grandpa Jack homesteaded 20 miles south of Flaxville in 1915 and moved to the last farm about 10 miles south of Flaxville in 1927, which is where I grew up. The homestead place was located on the reservation, and Grandpa Jack was good friends with a group of Indians. They came up every year to do his threshing and maybe twice if snow interrupted their work. Pretty sure the book refers to the original homestead, and the burnout game would have been somewhere between 1916 and 1926." He added, "I think there might have been a little firewater involved!" I have played burnout before, but sober and with a glove!

- "Through the years, with helping on the farm, there were baseball games on Sundays when the neighboring young folks came to play ball."[5]
- "In the early years, Jimmy Dorwin kept in shape playing baseball, first for the old Smoke Creek team and later for some of Flaxville's good teams. He is one of the few fellows around here to have played ball in England and Wales! A World War I veteran, Jimmy was one of the servicemen chosen (after the Armistice was signed) to travel around the British Isles and show them how the famous American game was played."[6]
- "Fred Hanson played on baseball teams in the early years in and around Flaxville. When the Chicago Cubs ended one of their seasons several of their players came to Scobey, and Fred had the opportunity to play ball with them."[7]
- "During the early years in the Julian community Juy [Robertson] played third base and shortstop for some of the local baseball teams. This was during the time of the great emphasis on baseball in northeast Montana, with some of the teams employing major league players, such as those involved in the Black Sox scandal."[8]
- "At the Line Coulee School, popular recess and noon hour games were baseball, pum, pum pull away, tag, and after snowfall, fox and geese."[9]
- "During my stay in Madoc, I played third base on the baseball team, and I did help to win a few games."[10]
- "Early day activities included dances in the haylofts of newly built barns before the entertainment hall was built. Mother often played. Everyone always brought all their kids, and they slept in the hay and the straw at the sides. Branding time was always exciting. People came from all over to the Yuill ranch. Baseball was a great sport then, too. We often went seven miles and stayed all day."[11]
- "All was not work. Those first few years found Carl [Jacobson] playing first base on the Madoc baseball team."[12]
- "Dad [Herbert Grant] pitched baseball for a local team in the Redstone, Flaxville area, and I remember he hung a horse blanket in the barn door with a bull's-eye marked on it, for target practice. We kids would return the balls to him. I thought that he was a good pitcher."[13]
- "Claude Hanrahan played for Bengough. Claude played baseball for many years, and at one time hired out to the Bengough, Saskatchewan team, thus augmenting the family's income."[14]
- "In those days (1915) we had a rodeo every Sunday, and I played on the baseball team. We were called The Sod Busters and we even played Outlook. Those were the good days!"[15]

Although the *Daniels County History* book summary wrote, "Baseball often was a spontaneous affair. Teams were of a temporary arrangement, put together for a local celebration or picnic," several country and town teams were formed after the communities started to form:

- **Coal Creek (Calbert)**: Coal Creek was about 12 miles north of Peerless. "All was not work in this community, and the Coal Creek neighbors formed a baseball team that played other teams on both sides of the International Boundary. Members of the team varied but at the time of the picture taking the team was composed of Mark and Roll Larson, Clint Richardson, Bob Humbert, Lee McCann, Dick McConnon, Joe Hershkivitz, Al Beamer and Jack Carney."[16]
- **Moe Brothers**: "Moe Hill" is named after Peder Moe, who homesteaded south of Flaxville in 1915-16. He came from the Red River Valley in North Dakota in 1911 to the Archer-Plentywood area. He came from a family of ten boys and two girls. Nearly all worked on Moe Hill at one time or another. From 1913 through

---

* "Burnout" is a game in baseball where two players line up opposite in each at a distance, make a hard throw to the other, take a step in, and the process continues until the two players are so close that one of them can't handle the throw from the other. The player who can't handle the throw loses the game. I played burnout a lot when I was a kid.

1917, the Moe Brothers baseball team played in the area. Brother Sig Moe recalls that he heard his first World Series baseball game on radio in the old Sparling Hardware Store in the fall of 1924. He played baseball on the Flaxville team in 1924 and especially remembers pitching against Scobey that year.[17]

- **Four Buttes**: "At various times, the community has had baseball and softball teams. The Little League team won first place one year, and the men's softball team won second place in county competition. Uniforms for the Little League were donated by Selmer Nelson in memory of his son Richard, who was killed in an automobile accident. Richard and his family lived in Four Buttes for a few years and he ran the gas truck for the elevator."[18]
- **Police Creek Baseball Team**: Police Creek was south of Four Buttes. "The Police Creek Baseball Team was organized in 1917. They were a lively bunch of young farmers in the area around Lekvolds and Four Buttes. The team members were Marion LaMotte, their manager and first baseman; Bob Rhodes, pitcher; Jim Rhodes, center field; Rex Rhodes, shortstop; Sherd Wilcoxon, catcher; Elmer Olson, left field; Ted Rustebakke, right field; B. J. Lekvold, second base and Ernie Gampp, third base. At various times later on, Joe Beauchamp, Richard Veis, Chris Veis, Ozro Brown and Harry Wilcoxen also played with them. The main baseball diamond was at the Rex Rhodes homestead about six and a half miles northwest of where the Silver Star Hall now stands. Many good games and arguments took place on that diamond. Games were played with Volt, Benrud, Mineral Bench, Scobey, Ossette, Butte Creek, Pleasant Prairie and Big Flat, the Gilchrist school field. Jim Penrose was their 'colorful' official umpire. He had a large barn on his homestead where they had Saturday night dances. Oscar Shipstead and Jim Penrose furnished the music, both played violins. The families of the baseball players usually went with them and made a picnic day of it. The Police Creek Team had a 1948 reunion with all the members present. Three members of the team were left for the reunion: Ted Rustebakke, Marion LaMotte, and B.J. Lekvold."[19]
- **Orville**: Orville was about seven miles southwest of Flaxville. "Orville got to be a pretty good town as by 1914 we had two grocery stores, a bank, a barber shop, blacksmith shop and restaurant. We had a good baseball team, with big crowds to watch us play."[20]
- **Middle Fork**: "There were baseball games, with much talent, and cheering could be heard at the games at great distances."[21]
- **Madoc**: "I remember that in 1912 we organized a baseball team in Madoc and Herman Forbregd was our catcher."[22] "The spring of 1915 was cold and almost all summer. After getting the crop in, on the Fourth of July Madoc put on its one and only celebration, baseball, rodeo and dance. People were wearing heavy coats and at times snowflakes were flying around, but that was our best crop ever. I played baseball and basketball with the Madoc town team from 1915 on.[23]
- **Peerless**: "July 3 will open with the boom of cannon at 7 o'clock. It is planned by the committee to invite the Whitetail and Peerless baseball clubs to contest for honors and the gate receipts sometime before the noon hour. These teams are evenly matched and their last meeting resulted in a 3-2 score in favor of Peerless."[24]
- **Flaxville**: "Flaxville was known as a good baseball town through the years—even before there was a town team there were country teams in Smoke Creek, Orville, etc. There were many good ball players back in the early years, one who was outstanding was Milo Kingsley, who managed the local lumber yard. He was a pitcher and played some professional ball in Canada. Some of the early players in the '20s were George Holmes, Frank Hewitt, Harry Barnhart, Stan Milford, Layton Galloway, the Giles brothers, and Jim Dorwin—a very good athlete."[25]
- **Smoke Creek**: "Old-timers state that Smoke Creek, south of Flaxville, had one of the first teams in the area and that, in 1911, that team played games in Old Scobey."[26] The years 1912–1914 saw Smoke Creek teams in the field again.
- **Whitetail**: "Jim Trower was a baseball enthusiast. He managed the Whitetail team and umpired many games around the area and across the Canadian border. His loud, clear voice boomed out so all could hear the calls, even though he was a small man. Some of the players on the Whitetail ball team that I recall were Donald Trower, Hayden Thomas, Bill Northelfer, George Holmes, and Art Wilkes."[27] One interesting note is that on Christmas Day in 1928, a baseball game was played in Whitetail by two teams from that town. Whitetail had two teams! One of those freak spells.

Whitetail Ball Team, 1928, after a game on Christmas day. *1913-1948 Anniversary Album.*

1900-1924

Smoke Creek Team, 1913. Kneeling, Walt Seiler, Art Dorwin, Frank Hewitt, Jimmy Dorwin; sitting, Harry Vandenberg, Stan Milford, Harry Barnhart, Elmer Gile, Layton Galloway. *1913–1948 Anniversary Album.*

Orville Baseball Team, 1914. Front row, Art Gord, Alvin Ryerson, Tony Swenson, Fred Hanson; second row: P.R. Kurtz, Vick Merell, unknown, Thrunson, L. V. Hanson; Ed Molden, manager at back. *Daniels County History.*

Smoke Creek Team, 1914. Sitting, Walt Seiler, Elmer Gile, Harry Barnhart, Stan Milford, Paul Milford, Frank Hewitt, Layton Galloway, Dick Seiler, Harry Vandenberg, Art Nelson; standing D. J. Martin and Gene Lapke. Art Hagen's car. *1913–1948 Anniversary Album.*

Coal Creek Baseball Team, circa 1915. Standing, L to R: Mark Larson, Clint Richardson, Bob Humbert, Lee McCann, Dick McConnon; seated, L to R: Joe Hershkivitz, Jack Carney, Al Beamer, Roll Larson. *Daniels County History.*

Moe Brothers Team, 1914. Peder Moe is in the center back row. *Daniels County History.*

Police Creek Team, 1917. *Daniels County History.*

Moe Brothers Team, circa 1915. *Montana Baseball History.*

Ball Team, 1922. Standing L to F, Chief Manning, Humbert, "Toots" Morrison, Keith Whipple, Joe Walker, Patterson; kneeling L to R, F. Working, Mitchell, McIntyre, Wilson. *1913–1948 Anniversary Album.*

Baseball was the top draw recreationally and competitively in all northeastern Montana counties in the early 1900s, not just Daniels, as Valley, Sheridan, and Roosevelt Counties had baseball tales told by their homesteaders, too. In addition to Scobey's traditional rival, Plentywood, town teams were forming in all the young towns that were taking shape in northeastern Montana. The baseball teams were a source of pride and a symbol of status for the towns. Here are some additional photos showing other towns in northeastern Montana that were playing baseball during the early 1900s.

Sheridan Baseball League, 1917. Plentywood on a day when a baseball game was scheduled. In 1917, Scobey, Froid, Outlook, Dooley, Flaxville, and Plentywood made up the Sheridan Baseball League. *Ronan Pioneer, June 8, 1917.*

Plentywood Team, 1910. Valley League Champions. *Montana Historical Society.*

Wolf Point State Champions, 1919. George Eastman, who played on the 1925 Scobey Giants team, is fifth from the left. *Photo from Marvin Presser's book Wolf Point: A City of Destiny.*

This article from the *Glasgow Courier* tells the story of the 1913 Glasgow team and how seriously baseball was taken in Glasgow in 1913:

Baseball Club of 1913 Was Fast Aggregation

Baseball was taken seriously in northeastern Montana 40 years ago. It was long before the day of surfaced highways, a multitude of cars and other distracting entertainment events. When there was a contest at the local park, most of the town was there.

Excitement reached fever heat in contests with such other towns as Malta, Wolf Point and Culbertson, and sometimes boiled over into fisticuffs. A good baseball team was a badge of civic progress and activity.

The 1913 team in Glasgow cleaned up most of the nearby opposition, although the newspaper records of that day are a bit sketchy as to details.

One highlight early in the season came when the Glasgow club met the "All Nations" club of

Froid Baseball Team, circa 1915. *Montana Picker.*

Flaxville-Outlook Game at Flaxville, May 28, 1916. Flaxville playing against Outlook in the Sheridan League in Flaxville in 1916. *Photo provided by Ken Christensen of Flaxville.*

Glasgow Baseball Team, 1913. Left to right, Coach Bucko Knowles, Chet Grace, Pete Brien, Johnny Gritz, Leo Hurly, catcher; unidentified player; DeHaven, Crawford, Lee Chouinard, Dutch Altman, George Sagen, Crawford, Lou Bretzke, and Manager H. M. (Orpheum) Wilson. Johnny Illman is the batboy. *Photo provided to Glasgow Courier by C. F. (Chet) Grace.*

Des Moines, Iowa, a team that might be compared with the present traveling House of David team. Glasgow took the first game, 5-3, in July 1913, but then bowed 6-1 to the All Nations in the second game.

The season wound up with a five-game series with Great Falls. The Electrics of that day were champions of the old Union association of organized baseball, and came here with little anticipation of trouble. But the Glasgow team, perhaps with some outside talent to bolster the lineup, was set to make the series a real contest. It won the first two of three games. But Great Falls took the next three for three out of five.

The leaguers didn't do it the easy way, though, and had to score the game-winning home run in the tenth inning of the final game to take the series title. The home run was the only score of the game.[28]

And not to be outdone, the women in Glasgow were playing baseball too!

Glasgow Women's Baseball Team. *Photo by J.H. Polberg.*

Scobey's first town team was formed in 1914. Scobey and Plentywood were traditional baseball rivals, and the rivalry started in 1914 when Scobey recruited pitcher Clifford Rule and catcher Charlie Emming from the Pacific Northwest League to play for Scobey to beat Plentywood. Cliff Rule returned to Scobey to visit in 1949, and the *Daniels County Leader* caught up with him, not missing the opportunity to capture his memories of that season. The following article resulted from the interview:

Former Pitching Star Revisits Scobey Scene[29]

Last Friday a gentleman by the name of Clifford Rule was a visitor in Scobey, from Alton, Illinois. It was his first visitation in 35 years. Remembrance of things long past came rushing into minds of many old-timers when they saw him again.

In the spring of 1914 a couple of young men, Clifford A. Rule, promising young pitcher, and Charlie Emming, his catcher, were trying out at Vancouver, B. C., with the then Northwestern Baseball league.

About a year previous to that, old Ed Burton, pioneer Scobey restaurant man, had seen the two lads in action. There was fierce rivalry then between the baseball teams of Scobey, Plentywood and other surrounding towns—especially with Plentywood. Burton tried to interest the two young men to come up to Scobey.

Aided by other baseball enthusiasts in the very new town of Scobey, Burton was successful in getting Rule and Emming up here in that spring of 1914. Their salary was $150 a month and part of their board, for about one game a week. The main idea was to beat Plentywood and its all-salaried club.

That year Scobey also built itself a ballpark and new grandstand (the latter blew down in 1946). Irving Davis pitched the first game on the new diamond. Irving, still a resident of Scobey, was switched to third base when the new battery arrived. There were a number of other good players around town. Lou Boyd was named manager, and he was a man who put his money where his mouth was.

Scobey met Plentywood and shut their rivals out, 5-0. Rule was a pitcher and a good one. During the course of that season of 1914 the Scobey team played 25 games and lost 5. They won two of the four games played with Plentywood.

Manager Lou Boyd offered a side bet of $1,000 that Scobey would win the fifth game, if Plentywood cared to play it off at Culbertson. The game was never played.

Fairview that year also had an ambitious team, supported by rabid rooters. Scobey accepted a challenge to go there for a 3-game series. In the first game Scobey pulled its team off the field in an early inning when the umpire called Charlie Smith out at first on what was alleged to be a rather raw decision. The second game was called on account of rain in the 4th inning with Scobey leading 5-2. In the third game Pitcher Cliff Rule stepped up and knocked a ball clean out of the park, with two men on base. Rule jogged around. The umpire said he didn't touch second base, and called him out. Scobey lost that game, 3 to 2.

As old-timers around here say, those were the days—hard fought, by rooters as well as players, and the long green rode heavy on each favorite.

Rule, in his visit here, was accompanied by his wife whom he married a couple years after leaving Scobey. They now have one son. Cliff Rule played just the one season with Scobey, moving on in '15 to Crosby and then to Williston in '16, the year Williston had a great team. On his visit here, the former pitching star looked fit enough to go out and pitch another game. He has lost track of his old battery mate, Charlie Emming.

Scobey's First Baseball Team, 1914. Left to right: Manager Lou Boyd, Rule, Shook, Paulson, Dudley, Dupuyer, C. Smith, Irving Davis, Emming, Tip, Michels, Mullen. *1913–1948 Anniversary Album.*

⚾ ⚾ ⚾

SOME KEY HISTORICAL EVENTS DURING THIS TIME ARE CENTRAL to the story of American Legion Baseball in Daniels County. In 1919 Congress chartered The American Legion as a patriotic veterans' organization. The organization was founded by a group of war-weary World War I veterans and focused on serving veterans, servicemembers, and communities.[30] On November 29, 1920, the Scobey American Legion Post 56 charter was issued at National Headquarters. Montana Department officials countersigned it on December 4, 1920.[31]

In 1924, another Legion Post in Daniels County was founded when American Legion Post No. 121 was organized in Whitetail. It was named after Ancel Fassett, the first member of the armed forces from that community to be killed in action in France in World War I. It first consisted of World War I veterans of the Whitetail area, but in the following years, the membership included the additional towns of Flaxville, Madoc, Navajo, and Redstone, Montana, and Big Beaver and Buffalo Gap, Saskatchewan. Like other Legion posts, it later included veterans of World War II, the Korean War, and the armed conflicts to follow. The Whitetail Post 107 Ladies' Auxiliary Unit was organized in 1927 and was active in community affairs. The fundraisers for an extensive baseball program were earmarked, as American Junior Legion, Little League, and Babe Ruth teams were sponsored.[32]

Peerless American Legion Post 107 was not founded until after World War II. The post was named the "Elwood Lien Post" in memory of Staff Sergeant Elwood Jacob Lien (1919-1945). SSgt Lien, a soldier returning home after serving almost 35 months overseas in World War II, died in a tragic train crash in North Dakota on August 9, 1945. Most of the victims in the crash had served their country during the war and were on their way home to

1924 Scobey Baseball Team. Left to right: Manager Tom Conboy, Porky Dallas, unknown, Joe Walker, unknown, Delno Cottingham, Joe Lupe, John Myers, unknown, unknown. *Daniels County History.*

their families and a return to civilian life.[33] The Peerless Legion Auxiliary charter was issued on June 1, 1954. My mom, Faustine (Sparagno) Puckett, was a charter member, along with Dorothy Ethier, Norma Puckett, Ruth Machart, Jennie Grove, Majorie Fladager, Doreen Bingham, Virginia Machart, Helen Trangsrud, Bernice Machart, and Marion Howard. The Peerless Auxiliary was always active in community activities and veterans' projects.[34]

⚾ ⚾ ⚾

THE BASEBALL RIVALRY BETWEEN SCOBEY AND PLENTYWOOD and the recruitment of talented players that began in 1914 continued into 1925. In the early 1920s, Plentywood consistently dominated Scobey in town-team baseball. In 1924, Plentywood beat Scobey 5-2 and trounced them 13-4. Plentywood claimed "the Championship of Northeastern Montana" by pounding Bainville 10-1 to end the season. The table was set for the wild 1925 season, when Scobey sought its revenge on rival Plentywood.

The Homesteaders and Early Town Teams

SECTION NOTES

1. Fern Wiley Sandon, "J. L. Wiley," Whitetail, *Daniels County History*, 1977, 978.
2. Charles Cassidy, Scobey, "Baseball," *Daniels County History*, 88–93.
3. Ruth A. Hanrahan, "Enjoying Life – Pioneer Style," adapted from Richard C. Davids, in *Farm Journal*, Scobey, *Daniels County History*, 153.
4. "John (Jack) and Nettie Higgins," Smoke Creek, *Daniels County History*, 822.
5. "George and Ruth Severson," Eagle Creek, *Daniels County History*, 332.
6. Jimmy Dorwin, Flaxville, "Flaxville 1975, 81-Year-Old Man Digs Own 105-ft. Sewer Ditch," *Daniels County History*, 361.
7. "Fred and Evelyn Hanson," Eagle Creek, *Daniels County History*, 321.
8. Mrs. Hilda Robertson, Julian, "M. M. Robertson," *Daniels County History*, 444-45.
9. Laverne Holmberg Hellickson, Line Coulee, "Line Coulee School in the Late 20s," *Daniels County History*, 470.
10. William Middlebrook, Madoc, "William T. Middlebrook," *Daniels County History*, 497.
11. Grace Yuill, Madoc, "A.B. Yuill Family," *Daniels County History*, 545.
12. H.J. Jacobson, Madoc, "The Life and Times of the Carl Jacobson Family," *Daniels County History*, 526.
13. Bob Grant, Whitetail, "Herbert Grant," *Daniels County History*, 924.
14. "Claude and Alice Hanrahan," Whitetail, *Daniels County History*, 927.
15. Glenn Ring, Whitetail, "Glenn Ring," *Daniels County History*, 957.
16. Randall Thorpe and B. Christianson Family, Carbert or Coal Creek, "Carbert Store and Post Office," *Daniels County History*, 282.
17. Sig Moe and Ida Erickson, Flaxville and outlying areas, "Peder Moe," *Daniels County History*, 382.
18. Norman and Hilda Johnson, Four Buttes, "Four Buttes," *Daniels County History*, 393.
19. "Police Creek Baseball Team," Kahle-Silver Star, *Daniels County History*, 449-50.
20. Orville Lockrem, Orville, "The Henry & Orville Lockrem History," *Daniels County History*, 591.
21. "Gullick and Anna (Horvick) Fadness," Pleasant Prairie, *Daniels County History*, 723.
22. Sam Montgomery, Madoc, "Sam Montgomery," *Daniels County History*, 522.
23. Horace J. Bourassa, Madoc, "Mr. and Mrs. Horace Bourassa, Sr.," *Daniels County History*, 507.
24. "Plans Completed for July 3 and 4 Celebration Here," *Daniels County Leader*, June 17, 1926.
25. Alice Brenden, Flaxville and outlying areas, "Flaxville Baseball Teams," *Daniels County History*, 342.
26. Charles Cassidy, Scobey, "Baseball," *Daniels County History*, 88–93.
27. Fern E. Trower, Whitetail, "James A. (Jim) and Rosa Trower," *Daniels County History*, 974.
28. "Baseball Club of 1913 Was Fast Aggregation," *Glasgow Courier*, August 6, 1953.
29. "Former Pitching Star Revisits Scobey Scene," *Daniels County Leader*, Aug 04, 1949.
30. American Legion website, legion.org, retrieved on 28 Feb 2025.
31. Charles Cassidy, Scobey, "Scobey Post 56, American Legion," *Daniels County History*, 86–87.
32. Phyllis Southland, Whitetail, "American Legion Post," *Daniels County History*, 883-84.
33. "Services held Thursday for Sgt. Elwood Lien of Peerless," *Daniels County Leader*, August 16, 1945.
34. "History of Peerless Auxiliary," Peerless, *Daniels County History*, 613.

The Scobey

1925 – 1929

1900 – 1924
The Homesteaders and Early Town Teams

1930 – 1945
The Sons of the Pioneers

1957 – 1968
The Baseball Renaissance

Baseball is Back in Daniels County
1946 – 1956

The D
Cham
1969

Giants

1983 – 1991
The Don Lekvold Era

1998 – 2003
The Last Years

2016 – 2019
The Revival

rman hip Era

The Ken Meyer/Mike Lee Era
1992 – 1997

The Long Winter
2004 – 2015

The Froid Bulls
2020 – 2024

1925–1929

Baseball in Scobey During the Roaring Twenties

1925 Scobey Giants. Left to right: Batboy Charles Smith, Porky Dallas, Wally Hinden, Honey Guyer, Delno Cottingham, Happy Felsch, George Eastman, Joe Lupe, Johnny Meyers, Steve Mattick, and Swede Risberg. In the upper left-hand side of photo at Ticket Taker Jack Conboy's Model T, stand Joe Walker and Keith Whipple. *Daniels County Museum.*

THE RECRUITMENT OF FORMER CHICAGO WHITE SOX players Charles "Swede" Risberg and Oscar "Happy" Felsch to play in Scobey cannot be understood without some context: the purpose for assembling the crack 1925 Scobey Giants team was to compete with archrival Plentywood, who had also formed a strong team that year with semiprofessional players. It is hard for us to appreciate the intense rivalry between Scobey and Plentywood. Dave Walter, former research historian at the Montana Historical Society and author of six books, wrote an excellent article titled "Pitched Battles on the Diamond, 1925-26,"[1] which provides some context for the rivalry and some eye-opening incidents related to the baseball games between Scobey and Plentywood in the 1920s. At the beginning of his article, he wrote,

Through the years, Montana has seen some rabid town rivalries: Cut Bank vs. Shelby; Butte vs. Anaconda; Whitefish vs. Columbia Falls; Baker vs. Ekalaka; Wolf Point vs. Poplar. None, however, have generated more gut-level opposition than the clash between Scobey and Plentywood. These two communities in far northeastern Montana—separated by forty miles and Flaxville—have squared off for decades. High school football, basketball, and track meets proved especially contentious and fed the controversy.

The creation of Sheridan County in 1913 placed both communities in the same county. But then the Great Northern pushed its branch line west to Scobey, and the homestead boom filled up western Sheridan County with dryland wheat farmers. By 1920 locals could demand a separation from Sheridan County—creating Daniels County, with Scobey its county seat.

Politics fanned the town rivalries into flames. Socialists had dominated early Sheridan County, and then the Nonpartisan League gained widespread support from distraught farmers looking for agrarian relief and reform. But it took Charlie "Red Flag" Taylor to throw gasoline on the blaze. Nonpartisan League organizers had sent Taylor to Plentywood in 1918 to create a farmer-owned newspaper, the PRODUCERS NEWS. Folks in Scobey countered with Burley Bowler, the flamboyant editor of the DANIELS COUNTY LEADER. Week in and week out, these two newspapermen stood toe-to-toe and slugged it out.

In a journalistic era that knew no libel, Taylor regularly assailed Bowler and his paper, calling it the Scobey Poker Chip. For example, "Red Flag" railed: Take Burley. In Plentywood and Antelope and Flaxville, where he has operated, he is known as a cheap, a saloon rounder, a bum, and a tinhorn gambler. He lived in each of these towns as long as he could make a living, [until] he had to get out... [Every] dreg of the gutter has more prestige than he has.

Bowler responded in kind, referring to Taylor as that impractical, ridiculous editor of the PRODUCERS NOOSE.

In summer, baseball encounters between the towns' two amateur teams drew boisterous crowds and elicited heavy betting. It was all about "bragging rights" and perceived superiority.

In the early 1920s, Plentywood's town team consistently had dominated Scobey's. In 1924 the two teams had squared off twice, with Plentywood winning the contests 5-2 and a humiliating 13-4. Moreover, Plentywood had claimed "the Championship of Northeastern Montana" by thumping Bainville 10-1 to end the season.

Daniels County residents felt deeply each of the defeats to Plentywood. Losses to Wolf Point or Culbertson or Medicine Hat were unfortunate; defeats to Plentywood were absolute catastrophes!

Former Scobey resident Gary Lucht also wrote about the Scobey-Plentywood rivalry: "It was a rivalry that ran the gamut from politics to sports, particularly baseball. Local favorites of the diamond were often praised into superhuman proportions. Quite often, when all the boasting was finished and the two teams met on the dusty arena, a player who didn't live up to advance billing quietly left town on the first eastbound freight."[2]

The dominance of Scobey by Plentywood in the early 1920s, culminating with the two losses in 1924, set the stage for 1925. The formation of the 1925 Scobey Giants team was the result of Scobey businessmen and the Scobey Commercial Club paying Swede Risberg and Happy Felsch of the 1919 Chicago White Sox—banned from organized baseball for life for allegedly throwing the 1919 series—to come to play in Scobey to beat Plentywood. In addition to Risberg and Felsch, other good players were paid to play for Scobey, including George "The Indian" Eastman, formerly of the St. Louis Browns; "Porky" Dallas, a Winnipeg boy who had played the infield for St. Paul; Bob Marshall, who "had a cup of coffee" with the New York Giants, and Johnny "Chief" Meyers, one of the stars of the Boston Braves a decade earlier. Local Scobey boys rounding out the roster were Delno Cottingham, Joe Walker, and Keith Whipple. The batboy was Charlie Smith. Harry Hansen was the manager.

The Scobey businessmen who got Risberg and Felsch to come to Scobey were the same businessmen who made Scobey the "Primary Wheat Market of the World." Melvin Nelson, in the *Daniels County History* book, honored some of those Scobey businessmen: "I want now, therefore, to add to the list those businessmen whose good faith and credit—and courage—did so very much to help farmers, stockmen and all others to help Scobey to become, as it boasted, the largest 'Primary Wheat Market of the World.' These were some of the people who took such active parts in bringing baseball to the area in the 1920s. Happy Felsch and Swede Risberg from the Chicago Red Sox and also the great negro pitcher John Donaldson will long be remembered by the old-timers. Nor were our home boys neglected on the playing field, Joe Walker among them. Yes, I wish they were all still alive and in Scobey to accept the honors for their long years of great effort, namely Knapp and Crandell, Davis and Shook, Battleson-Peterson, Hanson, Rasmus Nelson, Vic Hillstrom, Pat Murphy, and H.C. Nelson."[3]

Not surprisingly, several old-timers in Daniels County remembered the wild season in 1925 when the two former White Sox came to Scobey to play. Here is a small sample of those memories from *Daniels County History*:

- "Sports have always been an important part of Scobey's heritage, with baseball boasting the most colorful past, beginning with teams almost as soon as there were enough young men around and hitting national sports magazines with the hiring of some of the infamous 'Chicago Black Sox' of 1919. During the prosperous '20s, archrival Plentywood decided to put a team together that could beat powerful Scobey. They hired some players, including a noted black pitcher, John Donaldson. Scobey, not to take this lying down, hired some former big leaguers, including members of the 'Black Sox' who had been banned from organized ball for life after allegedly 'throwing' the 1919 World Series. Swede Risberg, Happy Felsch, Honey Guyer, Johnny Meyers, Porky Dallas, George Eastman and Wally Hinden were former professional players on the Scobey team. They were a bit out of shape and did too much partying, but were still one of the best and certainly the most colorful group of ball players ever assembled in Montana. Large amounts of money reportedly were bet on two games between Scobey and Plentywood as businessmen supported the fellows they had hired to play ball. Scobey cleaned up... winning both games by narrow margins... in spite of the extreme effort of Plentywood sportsmen of flying a pitcher in from Missouri just in time for one game and then immediately flying him back again in a private plane. This was in 1925. Scobey had three years of this high-priced baseball, with the team barnstorming around a large area, as far east as Minnesota, winning almost every game. In order to encourage sportsmen from other towns to bet on the game Scobey would sometimes agree to pitch a different man each inning."[4]

- "Because of rumors, in 1925, that Plentywood had engaged John Donaldson, noted colored pitcher, and to provide some real competition, the Scobey manager, H.J. Hansen, and other interested persons began to look for players for the Scobey team. A group of Chicago White Sox, who had been barred for life from organized baseball, were discovered to be available. Swede Risberg, shortstop, was signed up at $600 a month plus expenses. Happy Felsch, center fielder, Honey Guyer, Johnny Meyers, Porky Dallas, George Eastman, Wally Hinden and others were signed. The businessmen of Scobey subscribed over $3000 to start the team, the Giants. Home games grossed as high as $1200. The team barnstormed east to Minnesota, west to Havre and north into Canada. This venture was costing Scobey businessmen $4,300 a month to meet the team payroll and expense; this was kept up for three months. Scobey had about three years of high-priced baseball and glamorous as it was it was not worth the price."[5]

- "Joe Walker loved baseball and he and several other boys from Scobey played on the famous baseball team of 1925. He also played several seasons of semiprofessional baseball as a catcher and center fielder on teams in North Dakota, Montana, Utah and Canada."[6]

- "During the early '20s Harry Hansen served as a manager of the famed Scobey Professional baseball teams. A well set-up fellow of dogged determination Harry broke up quarrels among the team members from time to time by the simple expedient of physically yanking them apart. This was a task of no mean proportions at times, particularly when the participants included such toughs as Swede Risberg and Happy Felsch, former Chicago White Sox starts, who were capable barroom and street fighters of no small repute."[7]

- "George Johnson worked in the lumber yard until 1924 when he was appointed town constable of Scobey. Those were busy times for a policeman at night in Scobey. Numerous speakeasies were operating, and the product sold stimulated plenty of excitement in the alleys and on the streets. Some of the hard cases from the standpoint of peace disturbances were a few of the professional baseball players, like Swede Risberg and Hap Felsch. Frequent street brawls were the rule; streetlights would get knocked out."[8]

- "Jim McIntyre served as manager of the Scobey baseball team in the 1920s. This was a very successful period due to the intense rivalry between the town teams of Scobey and Plentywood. Many a dollar changed hands on the outcome of those games. At one time the roster of the Scobey team included two former players who were banished from organized baseball as a result of the Chicago Black Sox scandal of the World Series (that scandal led to the establishment of the Office of Commissioner of Baseball)."[9]

- "Delno Borchgrevink pitched for the Regina Balmorals. Delno worked part-time at the Scobey post office and graduated from high school in Scobey. During those years, he also played baseball on the Scobey team, leaving about 1925 to pitch for the Balmoral Baseball Club in Regina, the 1929 Saskatchewan champions."[10]

- "Tom Conboy was manager of the 1925 baseball club and was also manager of the American Legion Baseball Club, when it was first formed in 1930."[11]

⚾ ⚾ ⚾

A SIGNIFICANT HIGHLIGHT OF THE RAUCOUS 1925 SCOBEY Giants baseball season was a matchup between archrivals Scobey and Plentywood, played on June 14, 1925, in Plentywood. The game was a pitcher's duel between Swede Risberg (who played shortstop for the White Sox) and John Donaldson (who pitched for the All Nations team and the Kansas City Monarchs of the Negro League).

1914 All Nations Team. John Donaldson is sitting third from the left. *J.L. Wilkinson's publicity photo for the All Nations baseball team.*

Scobey won 4-1 in 10 innings. According to several newspaper accounts, around 3,500 fans attended the game, and there would have been more had there not been rain. In looking at the picture of the game, a hit over the cars lining the outfield was a homer, but a hit into the autos netted only a ground rule double.

There were several accounts of the game in the major Montana newspapers, but the *Scobey Sentinel* in Scobey, Montana, wrote the most interesting one:

Scobey Beats Plentywood 4-1
Scobey and Plentywood Battle for Ten Frames—Big League Ball All the Way Through. Game a Pitcher's Duel.[12]

The fastest game of baseball ever seen in the northwest was staged at Plentywood last Sunday, in a ten-inning game resulting in a score of 4-1 in Scobey's favor.

It was a little tough for the boys to play on a back yard lot but nevertheless they came out on top.

"Swede" and Donaldson fought hard for 10 innings with a score of 1 to 1 until the first of the tenth the Giants pushed three over the pan. The last half of the ninth looked bad for Scobey. One man down and bases full, a short liner to second then completing a sensational double play at first stopped them from scoring.

In the tenth Myers went to first and succeeded in reaching third on pass balls. Eastman's single brought Myers home. Eastman was forced at second on an infield grounder. Dallas walked and both advanced a base on a wild pitch. "Swede" clouts out a single bringing in two scores. Plentywood failed to score in the last of the tenth and the game ended with a final score of 4-1 for Scobey.

One of the longest two base hits and the largest crowd for an eight-hundred-dollar gate ever seen on any ballpark, fans saw them that day. Had it not rained, there might have been a few more dollars taken in at the gate, but the rain prevented many from reaching the game.

Last Monday Plentywood again went down to defeat at the Scobey park by a score of 7-2. Cottingham was on the mound for the locals.

Fishie's "fish" used to wish,
To fish from Scobey's brook.
Now Fishie's "fish" don't care to fish,
Since Scobey has a "hook."

Naturally, much has been written about the former Chicago White Sox coming to Scobey to play baseball, but no account is more entertaining than the story about the Scobey-Plentywood game at Plentywood on June 14, 1925, as told by Burley Bowler in his article titled "The Off Colored Scobey Sox." Burl's article about the game appeared in the *Daniels County History* book, published in 1977. Here is the colorful article in its entirety:

THE OFF COLORED SCOBEY SOX by Burley Bowler[13]

It was springtime, 1925, and prospects for a good ball team at Scobey were looking up. Plentywood, a traditional rival, also had the makings of a club considerably better than in past years.

The teams had their opening contest at Scobey and fans noted a number of new faces on both line-ups. Scobey edged its Sheridan opponents 4-3.

Before the scheduled return game at Plentywood, the grapevine had it that Plentywood had engaged John Donaldson, the noted colored hurler of whom John McGraw of the New York Giants is reported to have said, "If he could be whitewashed I would give a million dollars for him."

Donaldson was getting along in years. He claimed to be in his late 30s, but some claimed he was past 40 years. But all agreed he was a pitcher who could still do a good job in the major leagues.

The Scobey manager, H.J. Hansen, and others interested in local baseball began looking around. It was then that someone thought of the 1919 Chicago White Sox outcasts. Where are they? Swede Risberg, the "Black Sox" shortstop who, with Cicotte, Felsch, Jackson and others had been barred for life from organized baseball, was located in Rochester, Minnesota. He was signed up at $600 per month and expenses. Honey Guyer, Johnny Meyers, Porky Dallas, an Indian boy by the name of Eastman, a big first baseman by the name of McLaughlin (of whom more later), and a ski-jumping Finn from St. Paul, Hinden by name, all of whom had at some time or other played in the minor leagues, were signed.

Between 300 and 400 Scobeyites journeyed to Plentywood for the game. It was by far the biggest crowd a ball game had ever attracted in northeast Montana.

The Scobey Giants

The players had their workout and the umpire issued his "play ball" order. On the mound, beaming with confidence, John Donaldson was the focus of attention.

On the Scobey lineup, batting fourth, was an outfielder listed as Jackson. Donaldson's control was too good for the first two men facing him. Then Risberg stepped to the plate.

Donaldson, realizing he had stiffer opposition now, all at once diverted his gaze from Risberg to the batter on deck.

The crowd was tense and then above the stillness Donaldson's voice was heard in a rather surprising tone, "So they've got Happy Felsch, too."

That announcement was as much of a surprise to the majority of Scobey fans at the game as it was to Plentywood. Felsch, coming at Risberg's invitation, had been picked off the Oriental Limited at Bainville and driven by car to Plentywood, arriving only a few minutes before the game. He changed into a Scobey uniform in the dugout.

Undaunted, Donaldson began pitching. Swede got a single and stopped at first. Happy, who hadn't swung at a ball in two years, he said, stepped into the batter's box. Neither pitcher or batter had ever faced each other before. Happy took three mighty swings and was out, ending that part of the inning.

Plentywood also failed to score in the first inning. It was the third inning before Swede came to bat again. Donaldson walked Swede to get at Happy again. With his first pitch Happy swung and there was a ringing smack.

The ball was a little above Donaldson's head as it began its climb. It kept on going and climbing and it was still going strong when it passed over the tiers of parked cars which surrounded the outfield—on, on to the other side of the racetrack on which the diamond was located. Swede and Happy jaunted home. Then the rhubarb began. Ground rules said a ball hit into the cars around outfield was an automatic two-bagger. The fact that the ball sailed completely over the cars—an entirely unanticipated event—left room for argument. But the umpire ruled it was a two-base hit, so Swede went to third and Happy to second base. Donaldson was still the old master on the mound and no scores were made in that inning.

It was on their next turn at the plate, two innings later that the "Black Sox" pair showed the "bush leaguers" a new angle.

Before Swede went to the plate Happy told Swede to get on base even if he had to take a Donaldson curve in the ribs. But Swede again singled. When Happy stepped to the plate wielding his mighty willow, Donaldson waved a pitchout to his catcher. Just as soon as the fourth "ball" was called, Felsch lowered his head and made first in record time, but didn't stop there. Swede was automatically on second. The infield called for the ball and the catcher threw it to the bunched infielders who began their attempt to get Hap.

To be brief, Happy, who was a fast man on his feet despite his waddling walk, kept the

Scobey vs. Plentywood, June 14, 1925. *Daniels County History.*

infield busy until Swede had crossed home plate and Happy ended up safe back at first.

In the meantime, Donaldson stood on the mound, his high-pitched voice heard by everyone but the busy infielders, crying, "Give me that ball, throw it here, please give me that ball."

The game ended 4 to 1. Practically everyone from Scobey had wagered every dollar for which they could find takers. No definite count was made, but some of those who were in a position to estimate fairly accurately, said that Scobeyites came home with about $6,500 of Plentywood money. Plentywood was then headquarters for a group of gamblers and they went all out for more than peanuts on their team.

Happy Felsch, Milwaukee Dutchman who still holds some kind of record as an outfielder for the great 1919 White Sox,* spelled the difference between defeat and victory for the Scobey club.

Scobey couldn't lose that season, whether they played at Plentywood, Havre, Moose Jaw, Regina, Minot or what have you. And on more than one occasion a majority of the players carried more beer under their belts when they went on the diamond than Volstead had any idea existed in the Treasure State.

The initial game at Plentywood attracted sufficient attention so that a federal internal revenue man was at the gate to see that Uncle Sam got his share of the admission money. The teams were playing on a percentage basis, 60-40, and the gate was reported at $1,100. It didn't matter that a Scobey checker said there were enough paid admissions to mean a gross of at least 50% more. The gross still set a record for those days in eastern Montana. With a similar crowd at a return game in Scobey the gate was reported at $850.

Scobey businessmen were putting up $4,300 per month to meet the team payroll and expenses, and they kept it up for three months.

That year Scobey had also won renown as the biggest primary wheat market in America, something more than 2,500,000 bushels of spring wheat being loaded into cars at Scobey for shipment.

Some record yields were evident in the fields in the northern part of the county along the Canadian line. The Scobey customs officer, who later became a plainclothes man for the department with territory ranging from British Columbia to Mexico, said some fields must have produced more than 100 bushels per acre.

At any rate Scobey made wheat and baseball history in 1925.

Scobey played their archrival, Plentywood, seven times in the summer of 1925, winning six games. The one game Scobey lost to Plentywood was at Scobey "when the roistering Scobey team took the field still groggy from dissipations of the evening before."[14]

Heavy drinking was the norm for the rowdy 1925 team. Keith Whipple told a story about when the Giants stayed overnight in a Canadian hotel and Porky Dallas got drunk. Porky was the smallest Giant, but that didn't affect his capacity for booze. In his interview with Gary Lucht, Keith said, "The club had been drinking most of the night, except

Scobey vs. Plentywood, June 14, 1925. *Daniels County History.*

---

* Felsch held the major league record for most outfield assists in a single game, tying his own record with four assists on August 14, 1919.

Joe Walker and me. We had gone to bed early. The next morning, we went looking for the rest of the team. We stopped at Porky's room and when we opened the door, it was a sight to behold. There were beer caps all over the floor and Porky was in his underwear, barefooted and drunk, running around hollering, 'Who put these damn rocks in the infield?'"*

Happy Felsch, 1919 Chicago White Sox. *Chicago Historical Society.*

Swede Risberg, 1919 Chicago White Sox. *Chicago Historical Society.*

⚾ ⚾ ⚾

- The competitive craze to get talented players to come to Scobey and Plentywood didn't end with the 1925 season. In 1926, Happy Felsch returned to Scobey to captain the Scobey team, and many other talented players were also lured back. Swede Risberg returned to his team in

Happy Felsch baseball card playing for the Scobey Giants.

Rochester, Minnesota, but not before he left the Rochester team on July 21 (citing a sore arm), then appeared a week later pitching for Plentywood against Scobey in a big-money tournament in Regina, Saskatchewan.

- The 1925 Giants' record of 65-9 (6-1 against Plentywood) allowed them to claim the "All-Montana Championship." Local Scobey backers nicknamed the 1926 Giants "Happy Felsch's All-Stars" and surrounded him with quality semipro talent. The *Scobey Sentinel* wrote: "Scobey enters the season as undisputed champions of 1925, having swept everything before them in the vicinity of home and, like Alexander the Great, had to travel abroad to conquer the world."[15]

- The 1926 season would be different, but one thing remained the same: the Scobey-Plentywood rivalry was raging. Plentywood won the first two games against Scobey (18-10 on May 29 and 8-0 on May 30). Plentywood had six-foot, six-inch Davie Davenport, a pitcher released by the St. Louis Browns, and "Porky" Dallas, Scobey's second baseman, who they had lured away with more money.

- The 1926 season was not without its drama, too. In another wild game, played in Plentywood on June 6, the Giants were leading 3-1 in the seventh inning, but Plentywood loaded the bases, and the batter hit a ball down the first-base line into foul territory and the automobiles surrounding the field. Happy Felsch argued with the umpire that this should be a ground rule double, but Plentywood umpire Blaine Dean (who the

---

* Lucht, *Montana The Magazine of Western History*. Gary said of his article, "Northeastern Montana had its share of colorful characters and events, but very few stories ever got into print. As a boy, I listened to the old men spin yarns about Scobey's fabulous ball team of 1925 and I was determined that one day I would write about it."

Daniels County Leader referred to as "Blind Man Dean") allowed each Plentywood base runner three bases, putting Plentywood ahead 4-3. An argument raged at home plate, and Dean finally called the game a forfeit, with Plentywood winning 9-0. The Plentywood team immediately left the field.

- Bedlam ensued. The *Scobey Sentinel* wrote: "As the game was called, the crowd surged onto the field and, for a time, a riot was threatened as angry partisans of both teams argued, gesticulated, cussed, and pleaded. . . Arguments were free on the streets of Plentywood, and the excitement kept many people away from the stampede, which closed its exhibition that afternoon."[16]
- Word leaked that a Plentywood baseball promoter might not give Scobey any portion of the gate. This promoter then got into an altercation with Scobey's business manager, Bill Stephens, who was livid that Scobey might go home penniless. After several punches were landed, Bill had the Plentywood promoter on the ground, but people watching the fight pulled him off, and Stephens was finally given Scobey's share of the gate.
- And there was more off-the-field drama in 1926. Dave Walter wrote, "On July 13, 1926, 'a person or persons unknown' burgled and fire-bombed Burley Bowler's *Daniels County Leader* office. The Scobey sheriff tracked the criminal's Matter Six Buick sedan all the way back to Plentywood, where it proved to be an automobile stolen in Williston. Bowler concluded that the fire bombers were in the employ of Charlie 'Red Flag' Taylor, manager of the *Producers News*. He contended further that their actions were condoned by the sheriff of Sheridan County, Rodney Salisbury Strangl; however, no one ever was brought to justice for this crime, or even charged with its commission."[17]
- The Scobey Giants repeated as "The All Montana Champion" in 1926, winning two out of three games against the Havre Hillers, the first-place team in the Montana Northern League, managed by Herb Hester. The best-of-three series was played in Glasgow. Jim Thorpe—the famous all-around Indian athlete who played six years in the major leagues—played for the Havre team.
- The Giants played one final game in 1926 against Plentywood on July 25 at the Brush Lake Amusement Resort near Dagmar. The stakes were high for this game, as whoever won would win the 1926 series between the two teams and take home all the gate receipts. Plentywood jumped on top 7-0 early, but Scobey came back to win 9-8.
- At the end of 1926, Hap Felsch joined the Regina Balmorals and barnstormed western Canada. In 1927, Felsch played for the Balmorals, and Risberg was in South Dakota and North Dakota.
- The intensity of the baseball rivalry between Scobey and Plentywood continued strong in 1928. After playing for the Regina Balmorals in 1927, Happy Felsch returned to northeastern Montana to put on the Plentywood uniform in 1928, playing against his former Scobey Giants. It was rumored earlier in the spring that Felsch would play for Havre,[18] but apparently, the Plentywood businessman gave him a better offer to play in Plentywood.
- Felsch faced his former Scobey team several times during the season, and some wild events ensued. What else could be expected? Perhaps the most bizarre event between the two rivals occurred in a game in Scobey during the 1928 season. Scobey had played Plentywood multiple times, with Plentywood winning every game, so Scobey took extreme measures to prevent another loss at home in Scobey their next game, but it didn't work—Scobey lost anyway. The Helena *Independent Record* wrote, "The services of Chief Sealy, star Indian hurler, were valued so highly by the Scobey ball club that he was brought to Scobey by airplane in a vain effort to avenge a recent defeat at the hands of the Plentywood team. Chief Sealy, who was in Albert Lea, Minn., was scheduled to pitch for Scobey in the Decoration Day game, but missed train connections. A phone call to R. J. Coughlin, president of the Westland Oil company, Minot, N. D., followed, and the Chief was taken from Great Northern train No. 3 at Minot at 1:25 p. m., whisked into the Westland plane and deposited at the Scobey ball park in time to start the game at 3 o'clock. In spite of an all-night ride on the train and a two-hour ride by plane, the Indian pitched a big-league game, but due to poor support, the game went to Plentywood by a 5 to 3 score."[19]

After Sealy "dropped out of the clouds onto the ballpark,"[20] he impressed the locals in Scobey with his pitching, but the hometown crowd of 1,200 people witnessed Scobey's three errors lead to four unearned runs and cost them the game. Referring to Sealy's impressive performance, the *Leader* wrote, "Good things were expected of Sealy, and he disappointed no one. Cool, always in control, Sealy proved his mettle. Ball players and fans alike quickly recognized the smoothest, finest pitcher ever seen in action here, barring none."[21]

In other matchups between the two rivals, Plentywood beat Scobey 9-3 in Bainville, with Chief Sealy again taking the loss for Scobey. Scobey then beat Plentywood 6-1 in Plentywood. Then—more drama for the two old rivals in Scobey on the Fourth of July. Just when you thought it was safe to go in the water, another brouhaha erupted in front of the largest crowd to ever see a game in Scobey, as "fully 3,000 fans crowded into the park to witness the battle and battle it almost turned out to be."[22] Chief Sealy was again on the mound for Scobey, and things started badly for Plentywood, as Sealy struck Hap Felsch out looking in the first inning, but Felsch wasn't happy about the call, and he protested bitterly. "It was the first time this season that Plentywood hadn't got all the breaks of the game, and from there on in, the visitors were outclassed at the great national game."[23] Scobey proceeded to pound Plentywood pitching for 12 hits and 14 runs, and ran away with the game, 14-5. Johnny Meyers and Walt Keistling homered for Scobey, and Hans Wagner hit two singles, a double, and a triple in five trips to the plate. Chief Sealy went the distance, pitching a four-hitter and striking out 10.

Scobey won the battle on the field, but the "battle it almost turned out to be" the *Leader* referred to happened when the crowd rushed the diamond late in the game. Plentywood, embarrassed in front of Scobey's large hometown crowd, started to show signs of frustration. The *Leader* wrote, "During a heated part of the game, with Scobey ten runs in the lead, Plentywood's third baseman threw the ball out of the park. Scobey's captain, Chief Sealy, objected to the caddish stunt and soon half the crowd was on the diamond, and heated words passed. Plentywood's catcher, Jackson, ordinarily a very fine fellow, made the mistake of calling Sealy a name which usually means trouble, and Sealy, who had previously started to walk back to the dugout to end the argument, turned and smacked him on the whiskers. A scuffle followed, and the crowd separated them. Prevented from starting a row to end the game, and with a new ball in play, the Plentywood club was no match

1928 Plentywood Team. Happy Felsch is standing in the front row, fourth from the left.

for the Scobey boys."[24] In the end, Scobey "trounced its old rival, 14-5, before more than 3,000 fans."[25]

Just another day at the ballpark for Scobey and Plentywood on our nation's 152nd birthday.

In 1929, Felsch and Risberg would rejoin each other to play in Manitoba.[26] And, after four seasons of loaded lineups with paid players from out of town, things reverted to normal for Scobey in 1929, as the Scobey town team consisted only of local players. The *Leader* wrote that the team had an "exceptionally strong nine for all home products."[27] L. P. Lane managed the team, and Cliff Peterson was chosen captain. Plentywood, Opheim, Grenora, Flaxville, Whitetail, Peerless, Glasgow, and Medicine Lake also put town teams together with local players, and Scobey played some of these teams during the season.

The reason for the change to an all-local team was that money was running out. The *Leader* wrote, "Scobey's experiences in the semiprofessional attempts have proven interesting but costly for the sponsors, and this year a purely amateur team will supplant the former big-league material which made Scobey famous for its national sport events."[28]

Yes, we can safely say that Scobey's experiences in semiprofessional baseball had proven "interesting." What a wild ride it was. It was fitting that this tumultuous run of baseball in the quiet northeastern corner of Montana coincided with the Roaring Twenties. The craziness with baseball in Scobey and Plentywood matched the craziness of the decade. But in the end, Scobey and Plentywood's rivalry endured, as did the game of baseball, after the thrill was gone.

⚾ ⚾ ⚾

KEITH WHIPPLE WAS AN OUTFIELDER ON THE SCOBEY town teams in the 1920s, including the 1925 team. In the upper

1928 Scobey Giants.

left-hand side of the 1925 team photo, you can see Keith Whipple standing next to Joe Walker at ticket-taker Jack Conboy's Model T. In September 1988, 63 years after Keith played with Swede Risberg and Hap Felsch for the Scobey Giants, the movie *Eight Men Out* was released. The film, written and directed by John Sayles, was based on Eliot Asinof's 1963 book *Eight Men Out: The Black Sox and the 1919 World Series*. The movie dramatized the Black Sox scandal. Most of the movie was filmed at the old Bush Stadium in Indianapolis, Indiana.[29]

Edgar Richardson brought the movie to the Cinema Centre in Scobey in December 1988. Keith was the theater owner's guest of honor for dinner at the Silver Slipper and later for the movie showing at the Cinema. For a while before and after the showtime, Keith was given a seat in the theatre lobby, meeting folks who visited with him and viewing the display of memorabilia from the Daniels County Museum archives on the lobby walls about Scobey's famous town baseball team in 1925.

Luckily, Keith's memories of playing for the Scobey Giants were captured in an excellent article written by Dorothy Rustebakke titled "Prairie baseball in the 1920s

Edgar Richardson got the baseball memorabilia together at the theater. BORDERLAND photo.

Keith Whipple in the Cinema Center lobby before showtime with **Larry Bowler**. BORDERLAND photo.

featured pro players," which appeared in the *Billings Gazette* on March 24, 1987. Dorothy interviewed Keith Whipple in the article, who provided many anecdotes about playing with the 1925 team. Many articles have been written about the Black Sox in Scobey, but a Daniels County resident wrote this one, which includes stories told from the perspective of a player from Scobey who played on the team. The article is included here in its entirety.

Prairie baseball in 1920s featured pro players[30]

Editor's note—There may be snow on the ground, but some people's thoughts are already on summer—and baseball. With those thoughts in mind, here's a look back to the heyday of baseball in Eastern Montana.

By Dorothy Rustebakke for the *Gazette*

Many people in northeastern Montana remember the 1920s as a time of violent politics, illegal moonshine, big gambling—and baseball.

Eight-six-year-old Keith Whipple of Scobey especially remembers the baseball—and playing alongside of Swede Risberg and Happy Felsch on the high-rolling Scobey ball team of 1925 and 1926.

"I don't think you ever get baseball out of your blood," he said.

Scobey's traditional rival is Plentywood, 42 miles to the east. In the 1920s this rivalry was a serious matter. Editors of the newspapers of those two towns hurled insults at each other with front-page editorials hot enough to scorch the newsprint. On one occasion some hitmen from Plentywood burned the Scobey newspaper office.

There were back-room rumors that Plentywood was hiring big-time ball players in order to beat Scobey. Scobey retaliated. Local businessmen pooled $3,015 to bring together a team that would put Plentywood to shame.

"They got Swede Risberg and Happy Felsch up here," Whipple said. "They were both kicked out of professional baseball because they were said to have thrown the World Series for the Chicago White Sox in 1919."

Risberg was the former White Sox shortstop, and Felsch was a center fielder whose name made the record books for the most putouts at first base from center field.

Montana fans didn't care who the players were or where they came from, as long as they could do the job. Other team members were recruited from baseball leagues from Minnesota, Wisconsin, Ohio, Washington, the Dakotas, other Montana towns, and Canada.

"There were three of us from Scobey. They were Delno Cottingham, Joe Walker, and myself. The batboy was Charlie Smith, who lives in Great Falls now. Harry Hansen was manager.

"The out-of-town players got salaries. Risberg and Felsch got $600 a month, which was a lot of money in those days. We three hometown boys got $5 a game, and that was pretty good wages because we played pretty near every day," Whipple said.

To meet its competition, Plentywood began gathering some top-notch players of its own. John Donaldson was the most powerful. He was a noted pitcher with the All-Nations League.

"Donaldson would have been a big-league pitcher if colored men had been accepted in those days," Whipple said.

One time he was contacted by a touring Cuban team. They wanted to know if he could pass for a Cuban, so they sent a letter asking his color. He put an ace of spades in an envelope and mailed it back to them.

Scobey's regular pitcher was hometown Delno Cottingham. Risberg did some relief pitching now and then.

The team also had its cantankerous moments north of the border.

"At Moose Jaw, Sask., one fan was using abusive language and it got to Felsch. He spit on his hand, rubbed the top of his bat in it, and hollered to the fan that he was going to give him a tonsillectomy with the bat if he didn't shut up. He and the fan started for each other, but a couple of Mounties moved in and threw the fan out of the ballpark.

"Later that night at the hotel Felsch and Johnny Meyers met this fellow, and they had it out right there. Hap hit him first, and then Johnny Meyers clobbered him. News of this got around town and a few irate Canadians started gathering to clean house on those bums from across the border. The whole team had to pack up and leave town for Regina in order to prevent a riot," Whipple said.

Larry Bowler, Scobey's newspaper editor, remembers seeing Felsch and Risberg having some pitching practice on Scobey's main street, using rocks instead of balls, and the streetlamps as targets. Nobody stopped them.

The old Scobey ballpark, north of the railroad tracks, was on barren prairie soil. Whenever a game was interrupted by a quick rain shower, ball players and fans gathered onto the field. Scoops and buckets hauled off any rain that collected in puddles. Mudholes were sopped dry with the aid of blankets, and greasy spots were saturated with gasoline and set afire to dry them off.

Life was hazardous for the ever-present prairie gophers whose holes happened to be in the playing arena.

A finance committee made up of E.W. Battleson, Harry Shook, and Otto King handled a monthly payroll and expenses totaling $4,300.

Scobey-Plentywood games were sell-out affairs, often with local stores closing so everyone could watch the games. One home game took in $1,200, and more than 3,000 fans attended.

According to Whipple, 40 or 50 players were involved with the Scobey team in 1925 and 1926, some of them playing for a game or two and then leaving. Some even left before their first game.

Swede Risberg left the team after the 1925 season to sign up with Medicine Hat, Alberta. Happy Felsch remained for the 1926 season and then moved on to play for Plentywood.

⚾ ⚾ ⚾

JUMPING BACK TO THE 1925 SEASON, THE 1925 SCOBEY Giants disbanded in Milbank, South Dakota, on September 14, 1925. It was uncanny that earlier that summer, in stark contrast to the tumultuous 1925 Scobey Giants, American Legion Baseball was quietly founded in Milbank, South Dakota. Even more amazing is that the founding of American Legion Baseball in 1925 and the 1919 Chicago White Sox scandal were strangely connected. The synopsis for William E. Akin's book, *American Legion Baseball: A History, 1924-2020*, reads, "In the wake of the 1919 White Sox scandal and the suspension for life of eight players, baseball saw a precipitous decline in popularity, especially among America's youth. To combat this, a group of World War I veterans who were members of the newly formed American Legion created an organization to promote teenage interest in baseball."[31]

Regarding the decline in baseball's popularity among the nation's youth, Akin wrote, "Before the Great War, boys of all ages joined in pickup games, playing until darkness sent them home. Country boys might play barefooted in pastures without fences, backstops, or real bases. Town kids found vacant lots on which to play. City boys in knickers played in streets where fire hydrants and manhole covers served as bases. Following the Great War, the thinking went, boys were not playing those informal games that developed skills and instilled a passion for the National Game. That drop-off appeared in high school and college baseball, both of which showed sharp decline beginning in 1922. John L. Griffith believed it would take a nationwide organization to adopt and sponsor the effort to restore baseball to its pre-war eminence. He imagined an organization, which he termed a 'league,' whose play culminated in a national tournament to crown a sandlot champion of the entire United States."[32]

Akin writes in his book that the founding of American Legion Baseball for America's youth was a collaborative effort between former Army Maj. John L. Griffith, commissioner of the Big Ten Conference, and Frank McCormick, Commander of the South Dakota American Legion. Before the South Dakota Legion convention in the summer of 1925, Griffith and McCormick agreed that The American Legion would be the best organization to develop a program to revive declining interest in baseball among teenage boys. On July 17, 1925, Frank McCormick took the proposal to the 1925 South Dakota American Legion convention meeting in Milbank, South Dakota, where he asked the state group to pass a resolution urging the national American Legion to create a summer baseball league for young boys. Griffith also spoke at the convention and asked the South Dakota Legion Department to "assist in the training of young Americans through our athletic games," that such a program would "teach courage and respect, sportsmanship and citizenship." The South Dakota convention approved the proposal with little debate. After the approval by the South Dakota Legion convention, McCormick took his proposal to the Minnesota State Legion convention to approve and support the program, and the convention agreed.

At The American Legion's 7th National Convention in Omaha, Nebraska, in October, the Americanism Commission proposed organizing a National Junior All-American Baseball League for boys ages 14 to 16. Its purpose would be to promote "citizenship through sportsmanship." The proposal was approved, establishing Junior Legion Baseball at the national level.

In South Dakota, Legion baseball got underway in 1925, but Legion Junior Baseball officially began in 1926, when 2,000 teams from 15 states played Legion ball. Playoffs determined local champions, then state, regional, and sectional champions. At the end of the 1926 season, over 2,000 teams were narrowed down to four, who played in the first American Legion Junior Baseball World Series in Philadelphia from October 11–15, 1926. A team from Yonkers, New York, won the first tournament.

Due to a lack of financing, no tournament was held in 1927, but in 1928, Major League Baseball and Commissioner Kenesaw Mountain Landis agreed to support Legion baseball. Each league provided $25,000 to support sectional, regional, and national tournaments. State championships were played in 44 states, including Montana, whose state tournament was won by Great Falls over the Butte Belmonts. By 1929, teams from every state and the District of Columbia participated. Scobey's first Legion team was fielded in 1930.

It is ironic that the two players from the Chicago Black Sox, who tainted the professional sport of baseball and contributed to the founding of American Legion Baseball, would play in Scobey, a town that would go on to have one of the most successful Legion Baseball programs in the history of Montana American Legion Baseball.

SECTION NOTES

1. Dave Walter, "Pitched Battles on the Diamond, 1925-26," *Montana Magazine*, May/June 2001.
2. Gary Lucht, "Scobey's Touring Pros: Wheat, Baseball & Illicit Booze," *Montana The Magazine of Western History*, Vol. 20, No. 3, Summer 1970.
3. Melvin Nelson, Daniels County, "Melvin Nelson recalls early homesteaders," *Daniels County History*, 24-25.
4. Milton Gunderson, Scobey, "Scobey, Pioneer Country," *Daniels County History*, 66-67.
5. Charles Cassidy, Scobey, "Baseball," *Daniels County History*, 88–93.
6. "M.J. and Auget Walker," Scobey, *Daniels County History*, 260.
7. "M.J. and Auget Walker," Scobey, "Harry J. and Laura M. Hansen," *Daniels County History*, 198.
8. "George W. Johnson Family," Scobey, *Daniels County History*, 208.
9. "History of the James R. McIntyre Family," Scobey, *Daniels County History*, p. 228.
10. "Harry and Mayme Cottingham," Westfork, *Daniels County History*, 840.
11. "The Conboy History," Carbert or Coal Creek, *Daniels County History*, 287.
12. "Scobey Defeats Plentywood 4-1," *Scobey Sentinel*, June 19, 1925.
13. Burley Bowler, Scobey, "The Off Colored Sox," *Daniels County History*, 148-49.
14. *1913–1948 Anniversary Album of the Scobey Community, Daniels County, Montana: A Picture Story of Its Pioneers, Its Progress, Its Present*, Junior Chamber of Commerce of Scobey Montana, 1948.
15. "Happy Felsch and Several Players Already in Town," *Scobey Sentinel*, April 30, 1926.
16. "Plentywood Pirates Would Pilfer Game When Pitcher Fails," *Scobey Sentinel*, June 11, 1926.
17. Walter, *Montana Magazine*.
18. "Happy Felsch Says He Plays with Havre This Year," *Havre Daily News*, May 10, 1928.
19. "Rush Pitcher by Plane in Effort to Score Victory," Helena *Independent Record*, June 1, 1928.
20. "Sealy Stars on Mound," *Daniels County Leader*, May 31, 1928.
21. Ibid.
22. "July Fourth Brings Biggest Crowd Ever Seen At Scobey," *Daniels County Leader*, July 5, 1928.
23. Ibid.
24. Ibid.
25. "SCOBEY SLUGGERS WIN," *Great Falls Tribune*, July 7, 1928.
26. This paragraph was consolidated from several newspaper articles, but mostly from the *Daniels County Leader* and the *Scobey Sentinel*.
27. "Baseball Boys Organize Club; All Home Team," *Daniels County Leader*, May 2, 1929.
28. Ibid.
29. *Eight Men Out*, directed by John Sayles, Orion Pictures Corporation, September 2, 1988.
30. Dorothy Rustebakke, "Prairie baseball in 1920s featured pro players," *Billings Gazette*, March 24, 1987.
31. William E. Akin, *American Legion Baseball: A History, 1924-2020* (McFarland, December 6, 2021).
32. Akin, *Legion Baseball*.

The Sons of

1930 – 1945

1900 – 1924
The Homesteaders and Early Town Teams

1957 – 1968
The Baseball Renaissance

The Scobey Giants
1925 – 1929

Baseball is Back in Daniels County
1946 – 1956

The D... Cham...
1969

The Pioneers

| 1983 – 1991 | 1998 – 2003 | 2016 – 2019 |
| The Don Lekvold Era | The Last Years | The Revival |

| ...rman ...hip Era | The Ken Meyer/Mike Lee Era 1992 – 1997 | The Long Winter 2004 – 2015 | The Froid Bulls 2020 – 2024 |

1930–1940

The Homesteaders Pass the Game Down to the Next Generation

> *Whoever wants to know the heart and mind of America had better learn baseball, the rules and realities of the game—and do it by watching first some high school or small-town teams.*
>
> —Jacques Barzun, God's Country and Mine, 1954.

Some sons of the pioneers at play, circa 1930. Roy "Jiggs" Humbert with the big bat, Harry Larson catching, and his brother, Ken Larson, umpiring. The parents of these boys were among the early settlers and homemakers of the Scobey area. *1913–1948 Anniversary Album of the Scobey Community.*

Whittier School (near Dagmar), circa 1920. Boys playing baseball at Whittier School (near Dagmar) in Sheridan County.

Leaving the Roaring Twenties and the raucous Scobey Giants behind, these two photos paint a more enduring picture of baseball in northeastern Montana, showing how the game of baseball was passed down from the homesteaders of the early 1900s to the "Sons of the Pioneers" in the next generation. The first photo—the three boys playing baseball—would have been taken circa 1930 and looks like it came straight out of a Norman Rockwell painting. In his book about Legion Baseball, Akin wrote that "country boys might play barefooted in pastures without fences, backstops, or real bases."1 Except for the bare feet, this photo shows that to be true. These boys played baseball through their adult years in Scobey, as Roy "Jiggs" Humbert, the batter, later played on and managed the 1949 Northeastern Montana Baseball League championship Scobey Plainsmen team, and the other two boys—Harry Larson (catcher) and Ken Larson ("umpiring")—played second base and pitched on that 1949 Plainsmen team. The second photo is from Whittier School (near Dagmar, Montana), in Sheridan County, circa 1920. (I love the catcher!) These photos illustrate how the game of baseball had been passed down to the next generation in the early 1920s and 1930s, and the game would in turn be passed down to the sons and daughters of the next generation in Daniels County as well.

1930

Scobey's First Legion Team

The founding of American Legion Baseball in 1925 gave these Sons of the Pioneers the chance to move off the pastures and play for coaches in an organized league, and Scobey's first Post 56 American Legion team was fielded in 1930. The team was coached by Preston McLoughlin and managed by Irving Davis, who played on Lou Boyd's 1914 team.[2] Here was the roster for Scobey's first American Legion team:

- Bob Schaefer, pitcher
- Myron Johnson, catcher
- Sidney Smith, 1st base
- Larry Fjeld, 2nd base
- Willard Peterson, shortstop
- Raymond Waller, 3rd base
- Larry Bowler, left field
- Oscar Jacobson, left field
- Harrison Conboy, center field
- Taylor Crum, center field
- Ross Seger, right field
- Paul Henry, right field

REGULAR SEASON AND DISTRICT PLAYOFFS

Five of the 12 teams that entered the state Legion playoffs in 1930 were from small towns in northeastern Montana, showing how prominent baseball was in that corner of the state in the early years of Montana Legion baseball. The five Legion posts competing in the northeastern district were Scobey, Outlook, Plentywood, Medicine Lake, and Wolf Point. Scobey's first conference game was played on July 20, 1930, and Scobey went undefeated during the regular season. Scobey hosted the first northeastern district tournament, where they beat Plentywood in their first game. Wolf Point beat Medicine Lake to set up the championship game between Scobey and Wolf Point.

Coach Preston McLoughlin started ace pitcher Bob Schaefer in the district championship game, while Wolf Point coach R. L. Boe countered with Ervin.[3] The championship game was a seesaw affair from start to finish, and the going was rough for the Scobey nine as Wolf Point got to Schaefer for some early runs. The *Leader* wrote, "Victory seemed lost to Scobey in the early session when the stiff breeze played hob with Schaefer's curves and he had to resort to his straight, fastball, which was fairly met by visiting stickers often enough to cause the locals to worry"[4]

With ace pitcher Schaefer struggling with his curveball in the wind, it took two dramatic half-innings late, the bottom of the ninth and eleventh, for Scobey to avoid defeat and claim victory. Scobey was clinging to a 6-5 lead in the top of the ninth, but Wolf Point scored three runs to go ahead 8-6. Scobey tied it with two in their half when Harrison Conboy drove in the tying runs to tie the score at eight. Bob Schaefer, still on the mound for Scobey in extra innings, settled down from then on, as the *Leader* wrote, "The breeze subsided, and Schaefer then began to shut out the visitors, and it became just a matter of time until Scobey could score."[5] Neither team scored in the 10th, although the Wolves got two men on. In the bottom of the 11th, Scobey got a baserunner on, and catcher Myron Johnson's two-out hit brought him home to walk it off for Scobey 9-8.

The extra-inning eastern divisional championship game between Scobey and Wolf Point foreshadowed many future championship games between these two Legion posts, as Scobey and Wolf Point would be the two most dominant teams in the northeastern corner of the State throughout the history of the district.

EASTERN DIVISION CHAMPIONSHIP

Scobey's dramatic 9-8 walk-off win over Wolf Point in 11 innings allowed Scobey to claim its first northeastern district championship in its first opportunity, and the win advanced Scobey to play Billings for the eastern division championship in Billings. The championship game was played at Athletic Park in Billings, which later became Cobb Field in 1948.

There was a lot of excitement in Billings as the city anticipated the arrival of the country boys from the north. The winner of the Billings-Scobey semifinal would play undefeated Butte a few days later at Bozeman during the State Legion convention for the state championship. The state champion would then travel to Baker, Oregon, for the

Northwest Regional Tournament championship, and the regional champion would play for the western divisional championship at Colorado Springs, Colorado. The Junior World Series, which would determine the championship of the United States, would be played in Memphis, Tennessee. Thanks to The American Legion, these boys competed in an organized national championship tournament.

Scobey jumped on Billings in the top of the first inning. After Billings's lean southpaw Ken Linville retired leadoff hitter Fjeld, he walked the next two hitters, and Scobey catcher Myron Johnson blasted a three-run home run to stake pitcher Bob Schaefer and Scobey to an early 3-0 lead. The *Gazette* wrote that Johnson's home run "was one of the longest poled at Athletic Park this year."[6] His home run was only a foot off from winning him a brand-new Elgin wristwatch, which was in the days when very few boys had a watch of any kind.

Meanwhile, the "determined youngster named Schaefer started like the proverbial streak and kept Billings well in hand with his fast-breaking hook" for the first two innings, but Billings power-hitting outfielder Luke Cook clubbed two-run home runs in consecutive at-bats in the third and fifth innings, driving in four runs and bringing Billings from behind. Scobey's defense made some mistakes in the fifth, as the fielders "got a little excited, making a couple of costly errors which let in two more."[7] After five complete innings, Billings led 8-4, but Schaefer and Linville settled down the remaining four innings, and the game ended with the same score.

Both teams committed five errors in the game, but the costliest error for Scobey that day was not in the field; it was on the basepaths. First baseman Sidney Smith smashed an extra-base hit with two outs and the bases loaded, but he missed second base, and as a result, three runs, and potentially his own, were voided on appeal. Many years later, the *Leader* interviewed coach Irving Davis about the game, and the *Leader* wrote, "Scobey had the ball game won, except for the late 'Smitty' [Sidney Smith], whom they claimed did not touch second base when he drove in what would have been the winning run and was on his way to score."[8]

The Gazette article stated that Myron Johnson of Scobey was "easily the best junior league catcher in the state," and that Bob Schaefer, Scobey pitcher, "was second to none in the league." It also stated that Paul Henry, Scobey outfielder, was the only Chinese boy in the organization.[9]

In the box score for the Billings-Scobey game, the name "Bayne" for Billings appears, who batted third and played third base. This was Eddie Bayne, a friend of Doc Norman's in Billings. Ed Bayne and Doc Norman later became legendary coaches in Montana American Legion Baseball, Bayne in Class A and Doc in Class B. Their friendship continued through their legendary coaching years. Ed Bayne first got involved in Legion baseball at the age of 12. He played in the Billings Legion Baseball program for more than five years. After beating Scobey for the eastern divisional championship, Billings and Bayne went on to win their first Montana American Legion state championship in Bozeman.

Even though Scobey lost, the *Leader* was positive for the next season: "While our boys were defeated, the experience will help them. It is their first defeat this season, but it puts them out of the running for the state championship. Scobey has a splendid team and, even though the boys got no farther than the district championship this year, they will have had coaching and experience which will put them up with the best for next year."[10]

EXTRA INNINGS

Joe Walker, a Scobey native who played for the Scobey Giants, umpired the eastern divisional championship game in Billings.

Fifty-five years later, at the last State Legion Tournament Scobey hosted in 1985, third baseman Raymond "Whitey" Waller (from Whitetail), second baseman Larry Fjeld, and left fielder Larry Bowler from this inaugural 1930 team were honored in a ceremony at the tournament in Scobey.

1930 Billings Legion Team, State champions. *Billings American Legion Baseball photo gallery.*

1930 Billings-Scobey Box Score. *Billings Gazette.*

1931

Scobey Repeats as Northeastern District Champions

In 1931, American Legion Baseball was only beginning to catch fire across Montana—and the nation. In 1930 and 1931, only four districts existed in Montana, and 12 teams entered the tournament. The following year, 1932, eleven districts were formed with over 40 teams in the tournament. A good quote that captures this was in the *Wolf Point Herald* following the Scobey-Poplar decisive play-off game, which stated, "Junior league teams are composed of boys of seventeen years of age or under and the brand of ball displayed by these youngsters is indicative of the new life that is being instilled in this grand old national pastime throughout the entire United States. Walter Johnsons and Babe Ruths of the future are assured, with nationwide activities in this line as portrayed by the zest and ability of these two junior teams Sunday."[11]

REGULAR SEASON AND DISTRICT PLAYOFFS

On July 4, 1931, in a regular season game against Poplar, ace pitcher Bob Schaefer hurled a no-hit shutout and struck out 20 Indians in a 10-0 Scobey win. This was the first no-hitter thrown by a Scobey American Legion pitcher in the program's history.[12]

Poplar and Scobey met twice during the regular season, splitting their home-and-home matchups. The two teams finished 1-2 in the league standings, so a "rubber" match was scheduled on a neutral field in Wolf Point to determine the northeastern district champion. In the rubber match, Scobey scored four runs in the first inning to take a 4-0 lead, and led 8-5 lead in the sixth, but Poplar scored four runs to take a 9-8 lead. Scobey came from behind in the seventh when Poplar pitcher Hall, "the peewee pitcher who had hurled excellent ball thus far," ran into control problems and allowed four runs, walking three of them in. Scobey went on to win 16-12 and claim their second consecutive district championship.

STATE TOURNAMENT

In 1931, there were four districts in the state, so by winning the northeastern district, Scobey advanced to the state tournament in Helena. (There was only one division in the state then, as the Class A and Class B divisions were not formed until 1949.) The winner of the Helena tournament would advance to play in the Northwest Regional, hosted at Billings, with the winner advancing to the Junior Legion World Series in Texas. However, due to a lack of financing (during the Great Depression), Scobey did not have the funds to make the trip to Helena and was forced to forfeit their semifinal game against Miles City, who went on to win the Montana state championship against Great Falls.

EXTRA INNINGS

The American Legion Auxiliary, Scobey Post 56, was organized on February 25, 1931. The charter members were Lavina Babb, Blanche Brunet, Fay Brunet, Lillian Bystrom, Amelia Bystrom, Ruth Chelgren, Hulda Chenoweth, Catherine Conboy, Agnes Conboy, Lura Dahl, Laura Davis, Elsie Eichhorn, Estelle Davis, Gertrude England, Selma Funk, Bertha Greengard, Pearl Generud, E. Helen Hansen, Madeline Hauge, Mable James, Molly Kronick, Mary Davis, Laura Lekvold, Hazel LaRoche, Grace Morrow, Anna Thompson, Olive McDaniel, Lydia McIntyre (Knight), Selma McLaughlin, Korab Millar, Hazel Nash, Victoria Olson, Florence Peters, Lydia Scarseth, Hazel Shaw, Cora Shumacher, Margaret Smith, Ella Sullivan, Kate Von Kuster. The first officers were president, Fay Brunet; first vice president, Bert Greengard; second vice president, Ruth Chelgren; secretary, Olive McDaniel; treasurer, Victoria Olson.

At the time, the American Legion Auxiliary was Scobey's largest women's organization and one of the most active. It grew from 39 charter members to 127 members in 1974. Its varied activities included veterans' affairs, community service, education and scholarship, children and youth, civil defense and national security, girls' state, and many other projects. An auxiliary singer's group was formed in 1970, and they entered the national competition at three National Legion Conventions and placed at two of them. Selling poppies for veterans and helping with the Veteran and Memorial Day programs were other projects the Auxiliary participated in.[13]

1932–1940

Baseball in Daniels County During the Dirty Thirties

After Scobey won the first two northeastern district championships in 1930 and 1931, Havre beat Scobey for the district title in 1932 and 1933. Havre beating Scobey for the district title in 1932 and 1933 and Havre and Scobey winning the first four district titles anticipated a state-level rivalry decades later, as these two Legion programs would dominate Class B American Legion Baseball in the state of Montana in the late 1960s through the early 1980s. The seeds of baseball were planted in these two towns, and they would later germinate and grow into Legion powerhouses when two legendary coaches took over the programs—Tom Nielson in Havre and Doc Norman in Scobey. Interestingly, a pitcher named "Kato" beat Scobey for the district championship in 1933 and pitched against Miles City for the Eastern championship. The excellent Kato baseball players from Havre who played against Scobey in state tournaments in the late 1960s and early 1970s were descended from this Kato.

At the state Junior American Legion baseball level, a Junior Legion champion was crowned every year during the Great Depression and World War II, with Miles City dominating the state of Montana, winning nine titles. As dominant as Billings would become in the 1950s and 1960s, Miles City was king in the 1930s and 1940s. In 1940, Denton Field (now called Denton Field at Connors Stadium) was built to the specifications of professional minor-league baseball by the Work Projects Administration as part of President Franklin Delano Roosevelt's Second New Deal. In 1943, Miles City was selected to host the American Legion World Series, primarily because of the war and to keep the tournament out of a large city, especially if that city was in a congested war area.*

There were three increases to the Junior Legion age limit during this period. Between 1930 and 1935, the age limit was increased by six months so that any player who did not turn 17 before July 1 of the season could play. This allowed players to play who turned 17 in July or later of the calendar year. Before this, if a player turned 17 during the calendar year, he could not play. In 1936, the age limit increased by three months so that all boys who had not reached their 17th birthday before April 1 of the season were eligible to play—a player needed to be 16 on March 31. In 1939, the age limit increased by another three months so all 17-year-olds could play.

The Great Depression limited town team and Scobey Legion Baseball, like it did so many other aspects of life. The *Area Baseball History* states, "Legion baseball went into a slump until about the time of the Second World War, when Bob Tande took up the coaching duties. He coached for several years, and upon his retirement, Don Christensen and then Babe Holyk took over the Legion teams."[14] But one constant during the bleak period was the undying support of the Scobey community: "Since 1930 the minutes of the Legion Post are replete with references to Legion baseball—the problems and vicissitudes with money, transportation, players and coaches, but during those years the community has faithfully encouraged and supported the program."[15]

However, it wasn't a complete shutout, as some town-team baseball was played during the "Dirty Thirties." In 1934, Outlook played Bengough for the league title in Flaxville. The *Leader* wrote, "Harry Seiler of Flaxville was in Scobey Wednesday getting advertising for a classy ball game at Flaxville on Sunday, August 26, when Outlook and Bengough will settle the season's dispute for prowess. The diamond will be put in good shape for a fast game."[16]

As the Great Depression wound down and before World War II started, town-team baseball reappeared. In 1938, a new league, the Northeastern Montana (NeMont) League, was formed with eight teams: Brockton, Culbertson, Flaxville, Froid, Plentywood, Poplar, Medicine Lake, and Wolf Point. To help Flaxville's team get off the ground, several local businessmen supported the team's revival. Gene LaRoche donated the ballpark, and the county donated snow fences. Wilbur Swenson was the secretary-treasurer, and Bert "Stinky" Cossette the team captain. The lineup includ-

---

* Denton Field has one of the northwest region's deepest center fields (438 feet). It is 312 feet to left and 321 feet to right. Denton Field received its name in 1966 from American Legion Coach Doug Denton for his prominence in baseball and other Miles City athletic circles. His teams won six state titles and runner-up seven times from 1936 to 1950. (Miles City Youth Baseball Association website.)

ed Don Mohn, Harvey Hicks, Phil Hexom, Burnie Mohn, Jim Haugen, Clifford Cossette, Loyal Brenden, Adolph Hexom Al French, Harvey Hewitt, D. Bunse and "a number of other players available if needed."[17]

Don Mohn, the playing manager, had 25 strikeouts in his first two games in the NeMont League, and he continued to dominate the league with his fine pitching as the season progressed. In a game that gave Flaxville the undisputed lead in the league, he was one hit away from pitching a perfect game, as he hurled a one-hit shutout to lead Flaxville over the Wolf Point Wolves 7-0. He faced only 28 hitters in the game (one over the minimum), as he didn't walk a batter and Flaxville played errorless ball in the field. The win ran Mohn's record to 5-0, and Flaxville's record to 6-0 in the league. Chappie Courchene took the loss for Wolf Point. Stub Fjeld, shortstop, was leading the team in hitting with a .400 average, with first baseman Phil Hexom (.371), Loyal Brenden (.360), and catcher Bert Cossette (.320) also hitting over .300. Bill Morrow was the second starting pitcher for Flaxville, and he had the other win as Flaxville won the first half of the NeMont League season.

But perhaps the highlight of Flaxville's banner 1938 season was a game against the highly competitive Notre Dame University Hounds from Wilcox, Saskatchewan. The Hounds were coached by Father James Athol "Père" Murray, who was assigned to St. Augustine's parish in Wilcox, Sask., where he began the high school program known as Notre Dame of the Prairies College. He was the inspirational force behind the famous Notre Dame Hounds hockey team, influencing generations of Canadians and the development of Canadian hockey. Father Murray said, "I love God, Canada, and hockey—not always in that order." He was inducted into Canada's Sports Hall of Fame (1972) and Hockey Hall of Fame (1998).[18]

But in the summer, Father Murray could have said he loved "God, Canada, and baseball—not always in that order," as his team played an average of five games a week and led the first half of the Regina League. The Hounds were undefeated (Flaxville had one loss) when they rolled into Flaxville for the highly touted game. But they had one loss when they left, as "speed-ball" pitcher Don Mohn hurled a three-hitter and struck out 15 Hounds to lead Flaxville to a 3-1 victory.[19] The Hounds scored their only run of the game in the third inning on two singles, but Don Mohn shut them out the rest of the way, yielding only one more hit. Larry Fjeld scored Flaxville's first run after he singled, advanced to second on Bert Cossette's walk, and then scored on a fielder's choice by Phil Hexom. The pitcher's duel between Mohn and his counterpart on the mound for Notre Dame, Reynoldson, was tied 1-1 in the bottom of the eighth, when Flaxville pushed across two runs to win it. Bert Cossette and Adolph Hexom reached base on errors, and Stub Fjeld's sacrifice advanced both runners. Bill Morrow then delivered the clutch game-winning base hit, and Mohn held the Hounds in the ninth for the 3-1 win. Mohn's counterpart on the mound, Reynoldson, "Hound twirler," only gave up two hits and fanned seven, but the difference in the game was in the field, as Flaxville committed only one error while the Hounds made six. I would not have wanted to be one of the fielders who made those six errors at confession to Father Murray on Sunday. "Bless me, Father, for I have erred."

In September, Flaxville became the undisputed Northeastern Montana Baseball League champions with a 10-1 victory over Poplar in Poplar. Don Mohn and Bill Morrow pitched a combined two-hitter, one off each pitcher, and struck out 12.[20] Flaxville won every game in the second half and lost only one in the first, a 1-0 loss to Poplar, when Chief Crow pitched a shutout to outduel Don Mohn.

Flaxville, 1938 and 1939, Northeastern Montana League Champions. Left to right, back row: Larry Fjeld, Pete Kurtz, Adolph Hexom, Umpire Bill Notholfer, Bill Morrow, Art Stafne, and Manager Harold Hewitt, L. Haroldson, Joe Haugen, Wilbur Swenson, Phil Hexom, and Burnie Mohn. Front row: Alvida French, Don Mohn, Stub Fjeld, Loyal Brenden, and Bert Cossette. *Daniels County History.*

Flaxville's crack team in 1938 continued to play ball in September after the NeMont League was over. They played Nashua, the champions of the Milk River Baseball League, another new league formed in 1938. The other teams in the new league included New Deal, Glasgow, Malta, Hinsdale, and Zortman. Arthur Wilkes of New Deal was president of the new league.[21] The NeMont champions were beaten by Nashua, 6-3. Molnor, Nashua's "star hurler," struck out 14 Cardinals in the seven innings that he pitched.[22] Don Mohn was not his normal—that would mean perfect—self, as he "gave his first walks of the season." It is incredible to go through an entire season without walking a batter. After the two walks, "he retaliated by fanning the next two men and retiring the side." The loss was only Flaxville's second of the season. Their only other loss was a 1-0 loss to Poplar in the first half of the NeMont League. They finished the season 26-2.

The 1938 Flaxville team had some high averages. A. Hexom, .386; L. Brenden, .354; P. Hexom, .346; L. Fjeld, .346; D. Mohn, .326; C. Fjeld, .317; R. Cossette, .306; B. Morrow, .300 all batted over .300. The statistics were submitted by Art Stafne, official scorekeeper for the Flaxville team.[23]

Flaxville won the NeMont League championship in its first two years of existence in 1938 and 1939. Flaxville was always a prominent baseball town. In *Daniels County History*, Alice Brenden wrote about the Flaxville teams of the 1930s: "In the 1930s, John and Elvin Mollerstuen, the French brothers—Omer, Chic, Dona, Alvida and Wilfred—Loyal Brenden, Harold Hanson, Emil Morvik, Phil and Adolph Hexom, Bert and Clifford Cossette, Larry Fjeld (who played on Scobey's first Legion team in 1930) and Stub Fjeld, Don, and Burnie Mohn and Harold Hewitt played. Some of our Canadian neighbors were team members too: Bill Morrow, Orris Monson, Erling and Marlowe Hicks, and Harrison. Artie Stafne was the team manager in the 1930s and 1940s. In 1938 and '39, the Flaxville team was the champion of the Northeastern Montana Baseball League—this was a very competitive group of teams, enthusiasm ran high locally, both among players and fans. Large crowds attended each game, with cars more than surrounding the park."[24]

Alice also mentioned Flaxville's baseball supporters: "Mention should be made of a few of Flaxville's most ardent baseball fans of yesteryear: Harry Seiler, Pete Johnson, Pete Kurtz and Earl Randall, who still enjoy a good ball game and a visit about the good teams that Flaxville had. George Tryan, another baseball fan, continues to follow all of Flaxville's ball teams. The local business people were great contributors, as well as many other local folks, even during the depression. The team sponsored an annual dance in the Flaxville Hall to raise money for uniforms, etc."[25]

Scobey did not play in the NeMont League in 1938, but they played a rambler schedule, which included a 16-3 win over rival Plentywood, which was the runner-up to Flaxville in the NeMont League. Scobey also played Wolf Point, led by Chappie Courchene, who was rated "as one of the best pitchers in the league." Scobey's rambler schedule included several games against Canadian teams, as they traveled to Rockglen and lost 6-3. Lloyd Scholtz held "the heavy-hitting Canucks"[26] scoreless until the sixth when they scored two runs. Rockglen added four more runs in the seventh. Scobey scored its three runs when Freeze and Conboy singled, and Howard Schaefer drove them in and scored on Gray's single. Scobey threatened with two on base in the ninth, but a "circus catch"[27] of Smith's long drive finished the game. Scobey filled the bases several times but lacked good cleanup hitters.

In 1939, Flaxville played Father Murray and the Notre Dame Hounds again. In the first game at Bengough, Flaxville won 3-2, but in the rematch in Flaxville on July 4th, the Hounds earned a season split with a 5-1 win, beating ace pitcher Don Mohn. There was so much baseball being played in Flaxville that summer that Flaxville fielded a second-string team called Hexacola's. In the game before the Notre Dame game on the 4th of July, Hexacola's beat Redstone 9-5.

Flaxville repeated as Northeastern Montana League champions in 1939, winning both the first and second halves of the season standings.

Don Mohn, one of Flaxville's best players in the 1930s, wrote about his baseball playing days: "Some of my most enjoyable memories are my baseball days in the years past. I played at Bengough as a teenager, and later with Scobey in 1935. For every game I pitched for Scobey I received $5.00. That $5.00 looked mighty 'big' in those days. In 1935 and 1939, I pitched for the Flaxville team in the Northeast Montana baseball league. If I remember correctly, we won 26 games out of 28. In 1940 and 1941, I played with the shipbuilders' team at Tacoma, Washington, in the city league. Several times, we were invited to play an exhibition game at the penitentiary on McNeil Island. We usually lost those games. After one game, I told the manager of the team that they really had a good team, and he replied, 'Well, we have the advantage over you boys on the outside as our boys usually stay around year after year.' I ended my baseball career in 1948 at Sandy, Oregon."[28]

In western Daniels County, Peerless, Butte Creek, and other communities were playing baseball at this time, too. Lalon Jones from Peerless remembers a funny story about Gus Jensen, who used to pitch for the Butte Creek baseball team, north of Peerless. Lalon wrote, "Gus Jensen used to pitch baseball for the Butte Creek Club. He had one of the best windups I believe I have ever witnessed, and was a horrible pitcher. I shall always remember that windup."[29]

Another funny baseball story during this period is about a game between the Peerless and Flaxville town teams: "In a pre-World War II game between the Flaxville and Peerless town teams, the Flaxville pitcher walked the first three Peerless players in the first inning. Flaxville's capable catcher threw the three outs, one after another, as he caught them attempting to steal second. On the third out, the pitcher

> **BASEBALL**
>
> ***Flaxville vs. Peerless***
>
> **Flaxville Ball Park**
>
> **2:30 P.M.**   Sunbay, June 9

Flaxville vs. Peerless Flyer, June 9, 1940. *Daniels County Leader.*

flung his glove down and allegedly stated, 'If I can keep pitching like this, I can win the game!'"[30]

In 1940, all three Daniels County town towns were actively playing baseball, with Flaxville by far having the most experienced club. In a game in Ossette, Peerless beat Ossette, 10-1, as Ric Halvorson, pitching to my uncle Angelo Sparagno, scattered five hits. Peerless batters had ten hits.

Scobey's town team, managed by Bob Tande, had not fielded a team since 1938, and the *Leader* wrote that "the team has a battery, but the locals lack experience, practically the whole team is new."[31] Art and Sam Johnson were the battery the *Leader* was referring to. "The former North Dakota league brothers will be two of the too few men that have played in fast competition. Manager Bob Tande is a good infielder, but an old injury hampers his ability."[32] Scobey opened its season against the Halvorson brothers and company (Peerless), and this "will be an indication of Scobey's strength and possibly uncover a number of potential ball players."

The matchups between Scobey and Peerless in 1940 were great games, with the two teams splitting two close games, both games going 10 innings. In the 6-5 Peerless win in 10 innings, Ric Halvorson hurled six-hit ball for his victory while losing pitcher Kenny Larson allowed scattered five hits and struck out 14 batters.[33]

Peerless and Flaxville played each other in 1941, too. Flaxville won a "free-scoring frolic" 13-10 at Peerless.[34] With neither team having its regular pitching staff, the game turned into a heavy-hitting affair. The *Leader* wrote, "Peerless threatened Flaxville all the way. Flaxville would pile up what it thought was a safe margin, only to have Peerless start blasting short singles."[35] After two innings of play, Flaxville led 6-0, when Al French, Larry Fjeld, and Bert Cossette scored in the first, and French and Fjeld came in in the second on Bert Cossette's double. Phil Hexom scored on brother Adolph's single.

But Flaxville's sloppy play in the last half of the second, when they committed five errors, allowed Peerless to get back in the game, as the Pirates scored four unearned runs. Indy Halvorson reached first on an error and scored on another. Andy Oie did the same. Ernie Halvorson reached first on an error with Martin ahead of him. Martin scored on an error at the plate. My uncle Gussie Whipple's triple scored Ernie Halvorson.

The game went back and forth from there, as Phil Hexom tripled in the fourth to score Fjeld and Cossette. Phil came home on Adolph's fielder's choice. Whipple scored one for Peerless in the fifth on a single, an error, and a bases-loaded walk.

The scoring continued in the sixth, as Adolph Hexom scored Cossette and Phil, who had reached first on errors with another double in the sixth. Adolph scored on an error. Bradley singled to score Hewitt, who had reached first on an error.

Peerless countered with three runs in the sixth, when John Martin, Jimmy Kasseth, and Lester Estenson came around to score. Peerless ended the wild-scoring affair with two runs in the eighth when Lester Estenson and Ernie Halvorson came around to score on two doubles and a single.

Later in the summer, Peerless won a pitcher's duel over Ossette 3-1, "in a nip and tuck baseball game at Peerless."[36] Pitcher Indy Halvorson allowed only four hits and struck out eight while his Pirates had nine. Ossette scored their only run in the second inning when catcher Berg tripled and scored on a fielder's choice, but Peerless tied the score in the last half when Reese Puckett Sr. scored on Martin's single with the bases loaded. Angelo Sparagno scored in the second after reaching base on an error to come home on a scratch hit by Coram. Ossette's Belling bobbled a ball at first base to let Friess score. That ended the scoring for both teams. Willison from Ossette pitched well, fanning seven. Both pitchers only allowed two bases on balls. H. Harsager of Ossette got the only double play of the game, and that was unassisted. The game was well played, as Peerless made only one error while Ossette committed three.

Peerless won another one-run game over Scobey, this time 9-8, when pitcher Indy Halvorson scored the winning run on an error with two outs in the bottom of the ninth inning. The walk-off win for Peerless at Pirate Field happened when Scobey's Chris Veis, playing first, muffed the throw to first on Lester Estenson's infield grounder after Indy had singled, stole second, and advanced to third on brother Ernie's sacrifice.

Bob Tande playing first base for the Scobey town team in the early 1940s. *Family photo.*

Bob Tande, first baseman. *Family photo.*

The game was close all the way through, with the score tied three times. Indy relieved starting pitcher Angelo Sparagno in the seventh. He faced only 10 men in the last three innings. Peerless outhit Scobey 13 to 10 while both teams made five errors, the last one being the costliest for Scobey.

The rivalry between Scobey and Plentywood flared up again in 1940, as the two old rivals split their head-to-head games. Scobey won the first game in Scobey 16-2, but in "the game of revenge" in Plentywood, the locals won 13-5. It was another contentious affair, as the *Leader* wrote, "The game nearly ended in a free for all, as usual, with players, spectators, and umpires haranguing. The umpires changed decisions several times."[37] The two rivals met again in 1941, with Plentywood winning 5-4 in 11 innings in Scobey. The fans were in rare form again in this game: "The crowd was more than vociferous at times, some of the fans recovering old-time form for the occasion."[38] Good to see some things never change.

In the 11-inning game in Scobey in 1941, Bob Tande made 13 putouts at first base for Scobey.

While it was difficult for Scobey Legion Post 56 to field Legion teams during this period, the post remained active, as this photo of the Scobey Legion Post's parade entry at the at the Montana State Legion Convention in Glasgow in 1940 shows

Scobey Legion Post's parade entry at the Montana State Legion Convention in Glasgow, 1940. W.E. Rowe at the wheel; B.J. Lekvold in the co-pilot's seat; Ralph Greengard at the typewriter; probably Irving Davis next to him; Alvah "Slim" Shaw, standing next to auto. *Daniels County History.*

1941-1945

Two Future Coaches Volunteer to Serve in World War II

I HAD TWO COACHES IN MY BASEBALL CAREER: MY DAD AND Doc Norman. Dad coached me in Peewee, Little League, and Babe Ruth Baseball from when I was six years old in 1967 to when I was 15 in 1976, and Doc coached me in American Legion Baseball from 1976 to 1979 when I was 15 to 18. My dad and Doc were both born in 1920, so they were teenagers during the Great Depression and young men during World War II. Both enlisted to serve in World War II and became members of The American Legion after their service. Practically all my teammates' dads from the 1976 to 1979 American Legion Baseball teams I played on were also World War II veterans. We were shaped by these men who fought for our country's freedom and came home to raise families and contribute to their communities after serving their country. This book is dedicated to these veterans of The American Legion, who defended our country and gave us the opportunity to play baseball.

When I was younger, I did not have the perspective to appreciate my dad's and all the veterans' military service, nor did I appreciate that The American Legion had given us the opportunity to play baseball. I took it for granted. I was a spoiled Baby Boomer. Now that I'm older, I have a better appreciation of the sacrifices that he and all the veterans made, and I am grateful.

Dad enlisted in the United States Army Air Forces on November 21, 1941, 16 days before Pearl Harbor. He trained at

Sergeant George Puckett, U.S. Army Air Forces (USAAF), Key Field in Mississippi, before deploying in May 1943 to Algeria. *USAAF photo.*

Staff Sergeant George Puckett (second from left) Marseille, France, October 1945, in charge of detail overseeing loading and protecting supplies on dock at Marseille, France, and shortly to embark for home after two and a half years overseas. *USAAF photo.*

Will Rogers Field in Oklahoma and Key Field in Mississippi before deploying in May 1943 to Algeria in North Africa with the 526th Fighter-Bomber Squadron of the 86th Fighter-Bomber Group, 12th Air Force. He served in North Africa, Sicily, Italy, Corsica, France, and Germany from 1943 to 1945.

In April 1942, while Dad was training at Will Rogers Field, his dad, my grandfather, Forgey, Principal of Peerless High School, suddenly died of a heart attack at the age of 55. For the remainder of Dad's military service in World War II, he sent part of his paychecks home to provide for his mom, my grandmother, Bessie (Moody) Puckett. She was listed as a dependent on his military records. That was Dad, and that was that generation.

Dad told me a few "war stories," but only when I asked him about it. There was one story that he had trouble relating to me. While he was in the desert of North Africa, Dad was directed by his commanding officer to drop a fellow soldier off for night guard duty around the base. The soldier pleaded with Dad not to drop him off, as he feared for his life in the desert at night. But dad had his orders. The soldier was killed that night while on guard duty. Dad looked down in sorrow after he told the story.

My American Legion Baseball coach, Doc Norman, enlisted as a United States Marine during World War II and was a member of "Carlson's Raiders," 2nd Marine Raider Battalion.* Doc volunteered to join Carlson's Raiders while he was a first-year medical student at Northwestern University in Evanston, Illinois, in 1942. All my Legion Baseball teammates—including Kelly Norman, Doc's son and my teammate on the 1976-79 teams, whose dads fought in World War II—told me their dads never talked much about the war with them. But one story about Doc and his time with Carlson's Raiders made the *Billings Gazette*, as Doc was a Billings native, so we get to hear Doc tell his Carlson's Raiders story in the papers.

Local Marine Found Japs, Sharks Both Troublesome in Yank Raid on Makin Island[39]

San Francisco, Oct. 8. - "I don't know whether it was the sharks or the Japs that gave us the most trouble."

It was Private Clyde H. Norman speaking, as he celebrated his twenty-second birthday chattering with a marine corps combat-correspondent at a Pacific base to which he had returned safely after the raid in which a picked marine corps unit wiped out the Japs on Makin Island.

The story of the raid in which Norman, son of Mr. and Mrs. C. L. Norman, 501 North Thirtieth street, Billings, Mont., played a part was related Saturday by the public relations section of the Marine Corps recruiting division here.

The Billings marine dropped his medical course at Northwestern University, from which he had graduated a year before, in order to join the leathernecks.

He was among those picked men—volunteers selected from among 7,000 eager applicants—who were designated as "Carlson's Raiders," after their commander, Lieutenant Colonel Evans F. Carlson, and were specially trained for months in anticipation of the bloody work to come.

Norman learned to handle a rifle, a submachine gun, automatic rifle and pistol with equal facility, as well as other less orthodox weapons of raiders—including knife and bayonet.

In August the raiders waded ashore from landing barges early one morning, to catch the startled Japs at Makin by surprise.

"After we had effected [sic] our landing," Norman says, "we stalked up the beach as if we

Private Clyde H. Norman, U.S. Marine Corps (USMC), island hopping from Makin Island to Guadalcanal Island in the South Pacific, August 1942 to February 1943. *USMC photo.*

---

* Carlson's Raiders, officially the 2nd Marine Raider Battalion, were a pioneering US special operations unit formed during World War II under the command of Lieutenant Colonel Evans "Tex" Carlson. They were known for their innovative tactics and successful hit-and-run raids against the Japanese in the Pacific. ("Carlson's Raiders," National World War II History Museum.)

Private Clyde H. Norman, USMC, safely back at a base in the Pacific for his birthday on August 26, 1942, following Carlson's 2nd Raider Battalion raid on Makin Island, August 17-18. *USMC photo.*

Hundreds of athletes gave up their baseball careers to serve in the armed forces. Sixty-nine veterans from the Civil War, both World Wars, and the Korean War are in the Baseball Hall of Fame, 14 of whom were former American Legion Baseball players. Dad's favorite player in Major League Baseball was Ted Williams, which was why he became a Boston Red Sox fan. I never asked him why he liked Ted Williams so much, but other than the fact that he was the greatest hitter in MLB history, it might have been because of his military service. Ted was drafted in 1942 and served for five years in the United States Navy and the United States Marine Corps as a fighter pilot in World War II, returning to the Red Sox in 1946. Six years later, Williams was called to active duty again, this time to serve in the Korean War. He is the only Hall of Famer who fought in two wars. The American Legion recognized Williams's accomplishments with the "Graduate of the Year" award in 1960.

Bob Feller, another Hall of Famer, started playing baseball on his family farm and by age 12 was good enough to play Legion Baseball. He played Legion Baseball through 1934 and reached the Major Leagues as a 17-year-old before even graduating from high school. Two days after the bombing of Pearl Harbor, he enlisted in the Navy, becoming the first Major Leaguer to join the war effort. He sacrificed nearly four seasons of baseball in the prime of his career. In 1962, Feller became the first American Legion player inducted into the Hall of Fame.

Feller was a member of Variety American Legion Post 313 in Ohio and served as a Legion Baseball chairman in Cleveland. Of American Legion Baseball, he said, "What impresses me most about the Legion's baseball program is that it is so truly American. It contains all the principles which are basic to democracy. Here are grown men, soldiers and sailors who have been through wars, handing bats and balls to youngsters so they can play a fun game."[40]

Two of those veterans who "handed bats and balls to youngsters so they could play a fun game" were Doc Norman and Tiny Puckett. Doc was a Marine; Dad was a soldier. Doc was in the Pacific Theater; Dad was in North Africa and Europe. But these two World War II veterans' coaching philosophies were the same—they were both hell-bent on winning, whether fighting in a world war or on the baseball diamond. Doc and Dad kept the practices fun, but they demanded the best out of their players, and they got it. The result was normally a W.

```
were hunting ducks back home. Suddenly the Japs
cut loose and everyone hit the deck.

"We moved in on them slowly and snipers gave
us trouble all the way. One sniper was shooting
at me for what seemed about a half hour, but I
guess he was a bum shot.

"Meanwhile, we were blazing away at every-
thing we could see moving.

"During our advance across the island we
encountered natives." (Previous reports of the
Makin raid reported that 1,700 Polynesians on
the island welcomed the marines as deliverers
and helped them locate snipers. The natives
also brought Che hot and tired raiders coconut
milk to drink as they pushed through the jungle
growth in relentless pursuit of the Japanese.)

"The toughest part of the entire raid was get-
ting off the beach to return to our ship. The surf
was rough, and in all, we made six attempts before
reaching the ship. On one of these attempts our
boat capsized and the water was full of sharks,
which miraculously failed to catch any of us."

The raid in which Norman took part brought
death to every one of some 350 Japanese on
Makin, blew up installations, radio stations,
supplies and gasoline dumps and accounted for
two Jap planes and as many ships.*
```

---

* The attack on Makin Island took place on August 17-18, 1942. The raid had several objectives: destroy Japanese installations, gather intelligence, capture prisoners, and divert Japanese attention away from allied landings on Guadalcanal that occurred on August 9th. The raid also was an initial test of the raiding tactics and capabilities of the Marine Raider units. There is historical debate as to the effectiveness of the raid: "The Raiders' first test on Makin Island, though celebrated by the media at home, received mixed results. They had proven themselves effective in battle (killing 83 Japanese soldiers and losing 14 Marines) but ultimately failed to redirect Japanese attention from the Solomon Islands—one of the main goals of the mission." (Stephanie Hinnershitz, Contributor, World War II Museum, New Orleans, Louisiana, July 4, 2022.)

During his temporary return to the U.S. in 1943, Doc married "a cute, spunky Montana gal, Marge Sampson, in Los Angeles." My dad married my mom, beautiful Faustine Sparagno, on December 7, 1945, (the anniversary of Pearl Harbor) less than a month after returning from overseas—he always joked that "another war started the day we got married." *Family photo.*

I was bred to win by Dad from an early age. Playing baseball for Dad was always fun, but competing and winning were part of that fun. I could share many stories of how he coached us that way, but one that stands out is after a win. We were playing Outlook in a doubleheader at home when I was 10 years old. We won the first game 10-8, but I gave up a lot of runs as pitcher. I was happy after the win, but not Dad. He had seen Jon and me playing a lot of Wiffle ball with the Chapmans that summer, and in Dad's eyes, I was a better Wiffle ball pitcher than I was a baseball pitcher. After the game, he communicated to me very clearly that I needed to practice pitching a baseball, not a Wiffle ball. Throughout the entire second game, which we lost, mustering only two hits and nearly being shut out by Outlook pitcher Randy Wangerin (he was good though), Dad was in the third base coaching box growling, "the Wiffle-ballers, the Wiffle-ballers," to all of us. In Dad's mind, we could hit a Wiffle ball but not a baseball. I knew at that moment that my Wiffle ball career was over at 10 years old.

One of my teammates from Peewee through American Legion Baseball was first baseman Ray Chapman. We played together from when we were six years old to 18 and played on three state Legion championships together from 1977 to 1979. Ray shared a letter with me that includes his most vivid memory of playing for Dad:

I have one particular memory of Tiny I must relate because it ties in with something I told you years ago which wasn't quite true. I said then that Tiny was great with us kids who weren't his own because, unlike with you and Jon, he never really got angry at us. Fortunately for us, he saved most of his ass-chewing for you two. But there was one time I now remember that he really let me have it. It's a memory that sticks, of course, because I don't ever remember his getting mad at me like that, before or after. I remember at practice one day, Tiny was hitting grounders to the infield and I let one go right between my legs and out into the outfield. Big mistake. Tiny yelled at me and spent the next few minutes drilling grounders at me that had a bit of spice on them. Scorcher after scorcher came my way and the only thing I could do was either glove them or, at the very least, knock them down with my chest. It was either that or face Tiny's wrath. I chose the former. I mention this episode because I'm not one who normally responds well to anger being directed at me like that. But, even at the time, I knew I could get through this test because I knew deep down, on some sort of fundamental, visceral, and unconscious level, that Tiny loved me and that I could do what he was asking of me. And I did it. And, years later, the skills that Tiny taught me stood me in extremely good stead during my Scobey Blues playing days.

Dad was no-nonsense when it came to selecting players to play. He basically coached a select team from the beginning. One spring, I remember around 18 players showing up for Little League practice. In previous years, we had maybe 11 kids on the team. Dad knew he couldn't take 18 kids, so during the practice, Dad was tough on all the players. He swatted ground balls hard and demanded a high standard of play from each player. The same with hitting. He didn't cut anyone, but the next day at practice, only 11 kids showed up, the same 11 he had been coaching the previous years. There was no recreation league with Dad.

Doc could be a hard-nosed coach at times, too. I have memories of watching Doc Norman conduct Legion Baseball practices before I started playing for him in 1976. In 1973, I was 12 years old and was in the dugout watching with my Scobey friends. Rick Danelson, Scobey's regular third baseman for five years, from 1969 to 1973, was playing third base. Doc slapped a grounder to Rick at third. He pulled his head, and Doc went off on him, like my dad did with Ray. Doc started spiking hard ground balls at Rick— one-hoppers, line shots, right at him, one right after the other. The rest of the team stood and watched with jaws dropped as Doc continued to drill hard grounders at him with his fungo. I was amazed at how Rick stood in there and never flinched, even as my eyes grew wider and wider with each successive hard-hit grounder that came his way. His head stayed down every time, like a Catholic drops their head after receiving Holy Communion. One grounder was hit so hard that Rick had to jump straight up like a startled cat to field it. This activity went on for several minutes. Rick was a good third baseman; he was better after that.

That same season, I remember another incident at Scobey Legion practice. It was during batting practice, and Jack Tryan was in the outfield. Jack loped after a fly ball hit in front of him and let it drop. There was a lot of "grab ass"—as Doc called it—going on. Doc sauntered out of the dugout and summoned Jack to come to see him just inside the third baseline, where he met him face to face. I was in the grandstand, so I couldn't hear what was being said, but it was very clear Doc was not impressed with Jack's effort on that fly ball. After a few minutes of Doc in his face, Jack sprinted back to the outfield to take his position. I had never seen a Tryan run so fast, and Tryans were quick. But I saw Jack run even more quickly on a ball hit over his head in straightaway center field just moments after that. He made a fantastic basket catch on it over the shoulder, as Willie Mays did at the Polo Grounds in the 1954 World Series. My takeaway from both incidents was how well Doc's players performed for him when he demanded it. I was only 12 then, but I knew I would be playing for him in a few years. I will never forget those two incidents. I watched many Legion practices in those summers before my rookie Legion season in 1976. Jay Hagfeldt, who played for Doc from 1972 to 1974 and was a teammate of Rick and Jack, was at practice both times. He said, "I remember both of those events. Doc could get right to the point when he needed to."

The competitive juices really flowed when Doc coached Scobey and Dad coached Peerless when I played Little League and Babe Ruth. Those were some intense games. Dad coached players from Peerless, Glentana, and Opheim, and the players he coached on the Peerless Pirates teams were key to all eight of Doc Norman's state American Legion Baseball championship teams.

While this section only honors the two World War II veterans I played baseball for, it honors all who served, and I say "thank you" to all for your service. And thank you to The American Legion for giving us the opportunity to play baseball. The United States Armed Forces and baseball are woven into the fabric of our nation's history, and the American Legion stitched the quilt together.

SECTION NOTES

1. Akin, *Legion Baseball*.
2. Charles Cassidy, Scobey, "Scobey Post 56, American Legion," *Daniels County History*, 86–88.
3. R. L. Boe, "Scobey Beats Wolves 9-8," *Wolf Point Herald*, August 1, 1930.
4. "Juniors Win an Exciting Game Sunday," *Daniels County Leader*, July 31, 1930.
5. Ibid.
6. "Junior Legion Club Defeats Scobey 8-4," *Billings Gazette*, August 1, 1930.
7. "Scobey Loses to Billings 8-4," *Daniels County Leader*, July 31, 1930.
8. "Old Cronies," *Daniels County Leader*, August 5, 1965.
9. "Junior Legion Club Defeats Scobey 8-4," *Billings Gazette*, August 1, 1930.
10. "Scobey Loses to Billings 8-4," *Daniels County Leader*, July 31, 1930.
11. "Scobey Legion Juniors Down Poplar Rivals," *Wolf Point Herald*, July 31, 1931.
12. Cassidy, "Scobey Legion."
13. Else Daniels, Scobey, "American Legion Auxiliary No. 56," *Daniels County History*, 86.
14. "Area Baseball History," State Class B Legion Program, 1971.
15. Milton Gunderson, Scobey, "Scobey, Pioneer Country," *Daniels County History*, 66-67.
16. "Baseball at Flaxville Sunday, August 26th," *Daniels County Leader*, August 23, 1934.
17. "State Corner Ball League Starts Play," *Daniels County Leader*, June 2, 1938.
18. "Monsignor (Père) Athol Murray 1892-1975," Heritage Toronto, archived from the original on August 19, 2019.
19. "Mohn's Speed Paces Flaxville; Notre Dame University Hounds Fall Prey to League Leaders," *Daniels County Leader*, July 14, 1938.
20. "Flaxville Undisputed Title Holders; Drub Poplar 10 To 1 On Foreign Diamond; Win Both Halves," *Daniels County Leader*, September 1, 1938.
21. "New Baseball League Is Organized," *The Nashua Messenger*, June 16, 1938.
22. "Molnor Upsets Flaxville; Nashua Hurlers Speed ball, Hooks And Drops Halt Flaxville Hopes," *Daniels County Leader*, September 15, 1938.
23. Ibid.
24. Brenden, "Flaxville Baseball Teams."
25. Ibid.
26. "Locals Lose; Wolves Here for Sunday," *Daniels County Leader*, July 7, 1938.
27. Ibid.
28. Ellen R. Mohn, Smoke Creek, "The Thomas Mohn Family," *Daniels County History*, 826.
29. *Daniels County History*, p. 267, "Butte Creek Community," Lalon Jones, Butte Creek.
30. "Area Baseball History," State Legion Tournament Program, 1971.
31. "Scobey Opens Play Sunday on Peerless Diamond," *Daniels County Leader*, June 13, 1940.
32. Ibid.
33. "Peerless Gets Revenge Sunday; Beats Scobey 6-5; Second Game Goes Ten Innings At Scobey Park" *Daniels County Leader*, July 4, 1940.
34. *Daniels County Leader*, "Peerless Seeks Revenge Over Flaxville," July 11, 1940.
35. Ibid.
36. *Daniels County Leader*, "Peerless Beats Ossette Sunday on Pirate Field," August 1, 1940.
37. *Daniels County Leader*, "Scobey Loses at Plentywood," July 18, 1940.
38. *Daniels County Leader*, "Scobey Loses in 11 Innings to Old Rivals," July 31, 1941.
39. "Local Marine Found Japs, Sharks Both Troublesome in Yank Raid on Makin Island," *Billings Gazette*, October 9, 1942.
40. Jeremy Field, "In 1925, American Legion Baseball was born of a need to strengthen young people and the nation," *The American Legion Magazine*, July 18, 2019.

Baseball is Ba[seball] County

1946 – 1956

1900 – 1924
The Homesteaders
and Early Town Teams

1930 – 1945
The Sons of
the Pioneers

1957 – 1968
The Baseball
Renaissance

*The Scobey
Giants
1925 – 1929*

*The D[...]
Cham[...]
1969 –*

k in Daniels

1983 – 1991	1998 – 2003	2016 – 2019
The Don	The Last	The
Lekvold Era	Years	Revival

...rman	The Ken	The Long	The Froid
...ip Era	Meyer/Mike	Winter	Bulls
	Lee Era	2004 – 2015	2020 – 2024
	1992 – 1997		

1946

Scobey Legion Wins the District for the First Time Since 1931

> " *The boy wonders, more than half of whom have never seen a baseball game until they started playing this year, are the new champions of Junior Legion baseball in District No. 3.*
>
> —"Scobey Junior Legion Wins District Title," Daniels County Leader, July 18, 1946 "

1946 Scobey American Legion Team, District champions. Front row, left to right: Clay Gilchrist, Ramon Trower, Donald Christensen, Harvey Eide, Vern Veis, Dick Conboy, Ron Fjeld; back row left to right: Len Dallas Foanes, Don Brayko, Alfred Schammel, Gordon Vanderpan, George Cornwell, Richard Roland, John Nelson. *Daniels County History Museum.*

PRESEASON

THE GREAT DEPRESSION AND WORLD WAR II TOOK their toll on all aspects of life, including baseball, as there were long stretches of time in the late 1930s and 1940s when Junior Legion and town teams were not fielded in Daniels County. The 1930-1931 District 3 Legion championship teams and 1932-1933 runner-up teams seemed but a distant memory. It had been so long that the *Billings Gazette* referred to Scobey's 1946 team as their first organized Junior Legion team.[1]

But baseball was back in 1946. Tom Conboy, who managed the Scobey town teams in the 1920s, worked hard to put a postwar Junior Legion Baseball team together, and he planned for Scobey to play a full schedule of games. Tom was chairman of a Legionnaires committee that supervised the organization and management of a newly formed Junior Legion Baseball team. Because money was still tight, there were no plans to solicit funds from people, but businesses were asked if they would sponsor a uniform with their firm name on it. In the end, Tom Conboy, Charles Eichhorn, and Mons Tonjum each contributed $200 for new uniforms and baseball equipment for the team.

Tom Conboy, 1946 Team Manager. *Daniels County History.*

Even by Junior Legion Baseball standards, Scobey's first postwar Junior Legion team was young, as the roster had only three players—Gordon "Dike" Vanderpan, Richard "Rip" Roland, and Quentin Karlsrud—who were 17. American Legion Baseball had increased the age eligibility limit from 16 to 17 years old in 1939. This was still young—the league was called *Junior* American Legion Baseball for a reason. When 18-year-olds wanted to play baseball, they suited up for the town teams with the older men in the summer of their junior and/or senior years in high school.

The 1946 team was also inexperienced, as more than half the players had never seen a baseball game before, let alone play in one. In addition to three players already mentioned, Scobey's young and inexperienced roster included Don Christensen, Dick Conboy, George Cornwell, Harvey Eide, Ronnie Fjeld, Len Dallas Faanes, Clay Gilchrist, Fred Leibrand, John Nelson, Al Schammel, Ramon Trower, Don Brayko and Vern Veis.

Tom Conboy managed the team. Bob Tande was the head coach, assisted by Chris Veis.

Rod Tande, c. 1947-48. "Guess you're never too young to be a baseball icon! Scobey start 'em early!" —Rod Tande. *Family photo.*

Bob Tande, 1946 Head Coach. *Family photo.*

In 1946, there was still only one class of Junior Legion Baseball in Montana, as Class A and Class B had not yet been formed. There were eight districts in the state. The winners of each district tournament played against winners of other districts in their region, eventually crowning a state champion.

REGULAR SEASON

BASEBALL WAS BACK ACROSS THE ENTIRE COUNTY IN 1946. In addition to Scobey's Junior Legion team, Peerless had a town team, and Flaxville had a town team and a Junior Legion team. Flaxville's Junior Legion team did not participate in the league, so Flaxville and Peerless played Scobey in nonleague games. Flaxville's Junior Legion team, coached by Phil Hexom, beat Scobey 10-9. Scobey Junior Legion also played Flaxville's town team, but that didn't go so well, as the *Leader* wrote that the Juniors "found they do better in the junior league."[2]

Against the Peerless town team, Scobey won the first matchup 4-3. Gordon Vanderpan pitched a four-hitter, walked four, and struck out 16 Pirates to get the win. My uncle, Angelo Sparagno, who once showed me how he threw his curveball, pitched a three-hitter for Peerless, walked three, and struck out 16 hitters in the loss. Indy Halvorson for Peerless had two hits, with Trang and Lester Estenson getting one each. Harvey Eide, Vanderpan, and Ken Larson had the hits for Scobey. Peerless beat Scobey 11-5 in the rematch. The *Leader* wrote that the "boys from the west end were just too heavy on the hickory," as Peerless gathered 12 hits off Vanderpan, Roland, and Christensen. Peerless pitchers Angelo Sparagno and Indy Halvorson scattered eight hits, but it was Scobey's fielding that cost them the game. The *Leader* wrote that Scobey's "lack of experience caused the locals to falter in defense a few times when bases were loaded and the pressure was on."[3]

In another nonleague game, Scobey played a newly formed Opheim Junior Legion team and won 47-2.[4] John Nelson, Harvey Eide, Richard Roland, Quentin Karlsrud, and Don Christensen all homered for Scobey. The 47 runs scored by Scobey set the record for most runs scored in a game, but it (unbelievably) would not stand. Opheim would come back in the following seasons with older players and a much better team.

Scobey won six league games against only one loss. Dike Vanderpan was the go-to pitcher for Scobey in most of their wins, as he struck out 14 Wolves in a 19-6 win over

Wolf Point and was the winning pitcher in most of the other wins. Scobey's one loss came at the hands of Poplar, 12-6. Their inexperience hurt them in the field, as Scobey outhit Poplar seven to five, but "booted the ball" several times to lose the game.

DISTRICT TOURNAMENT

THE DISTRICT 3 TOURNAMENT WAS HELD AT GLASGOW. THE SIX teams were Wolf Point, Glasgow, Saco, Poplar, Malta, and Scobey. Scobey faced Malta ("the strongest other team in the district") in their first game and won 5-3 on a three-hitter by Dike Vanderpan. Vanderpan struck out nine and didn't walk a batter. Malta's pitching also only gave up three hits but issued seven walks. George Cornwell led Scobey with two hits and an RBI. Len Dallas Faanes got the other hit.

Scobey beat Poplar, the only team that beat them in league play, 10-6 in the final. George Cornwell again led his teammates with three hits and two runs batted in to lead Scobey's nine-hit attack. Poplar managed five hits off Dike Vanderpan. Scobey had some fine defensive plays to help win the game, as center fielder Don Brayko robbed Poplar of a hit and score in the fifth when he ran way back and pulled down a long drive, and shortstop John Nelson snuffed a Poplar rally out when he snared a hard line drive and tossed it to second for an inning-ending double play. Vanderpan got the win on the mound for Scobey again, and Scobey won their first district championship in 15 years.

Considering how young and inexperienced the Scobey team was, winning the district championship was quite an accomplishment. Of course, the other teams were just getting started after the war, too, but still. The *Leader* called the championship team the "boy wonders, more than half of whom have never seen a baseball game until they started playing this year."[5]

EASTERN DIVISIONAL PLAYOFFS

THE SEVEN OTHER DISTRICT TOURNAMENT WINNERS IN 1946 were Missoula, Fairfield, Helena, Stanford, Butte, Billings, and Miles City. Scobey traveled to Miles City to play District No. 8 champion Miles City in a one-game playoff on beautiful Denton Field, a field described by the *Leader* as "a miniature big league ballpark."[6] More than 25 Scobey fans traveled to Miles City for the game. The winner of the one-game playoff would face off against Billings for the Eastern division championship. Scobey was jittery in the field, which was the primary reason for their 10-2 loss. But Scobey played hard: "A frightened, but scrappy group of American Legion juniors from Scobey fought every minute to hold the local Legion club here, but 13 errors handcuffed the visitors."[7] The *Leader* wrote, "The lack of experience under tension led to many errors by Scobey and determined the score."[8] Dike Vanderpan pitched to Don Christensen for all nine innings for Scobey and scattered five hits, all of them singles. Scobey had four hits in the loss.

Miles City went on to defeat Billings two out of three to win the east, then lost to Butte for the state championship in Miles City.

SEASON SUMMARY

THE *LEADER* CLOSED THE BOOKS ON THE 1946 TEAM BY writing, "Scobey's showing in the season was very good. Next year they aim to better it." Their performance was good considering the team's youth and inexperience. The Scobey Juniors were 9-2 in games they played against Junior Legion teams and 4-3 in games played against older ball players of other clubs like Peerless and Flaxville.

Bob Tande kept meticulous season statistics, including fielding percentages, which Scobey needed to improve on if they were to get better in 1947. The *Leader* referred to statistics as "dope for the hot stove league sessions during the winter evenings when baseball fans hash over last season's results and prepare predictions for the next."[9] The hot-stove dope for Scobey in 1946 was that Harvey Eide led the team in hitting with a .382 average and was also the team's leading run-producer, driving in 23 runs. Dike Vanderpan was second in both categories with a .379 average and 20 runs batted in.[10]

Looking ahead to 1947, ace pitcher and second-leading hitter Dike Vanderpan, second baseman and pitcher Rip Roland, and outfielder and pitcher Quentin Karlsrud would be lost to age eligibility. These players would be missed, but with everyone else returning, Scobey's "aim to better" the 1946 season was promising.

EXTRA INNINGS

THE FIELDING ERRORS SCOBEY MADE AGAINST MILES CITY ARE significant because I remember when I played against Class A (now Class AA) competition for the first time, I was tense when fielding. It didn't seem to bother me so much pitching or hitting, but for some reason, fielding a ground ball against a Class A team affected me, and I would sometimes make errors on balls I would normally make plays on. Later, after playing against that level of competition more often, I became more confident and relaxed and was able to make plays. This is thanks to Doc, who would schedule regular season games against Class A competition so we would become comfortable playing against that level of competition and learn that we could stay on the field with them, and even win.

Ron Fjeld, who was only 15 years old in 1946, remembers playing Little League during World War II, and how important Tom Conboy was in keeping baseball alive in Scobey during the war, and getting the Legion program started up again in 1946. He also remembers Bob Tande on the baseball field coaching, and Chris Veis. Ron said, "Tom's son Dickie Conboy was a baseball player, and Tom wanted him to have the chance to play." His contribution to the team gave everyone the chance to play.

In order to keep a baseball program going, the pipeline for ballplayers has to start at an early age, and in 1946, John O'Meara was the key man in Scobey for that. He organized a baseball league for boys 12 years old and under, which is what we would now call Little League. At the first practice, he had six boys, but the number grew to 17 later in the season. The *Leader* wrote, "John thinks all little boys should play baseball. They turn out every night to play. Many of the boys never had tried the national game before." John's goal was to have enough players for four teams by the end of the season. There was no Babe Ruth baseball then, so the boys would make the jump from Little League to Junior Legion, where John hoped the boys he was training would "enjoy three or four years of the sport."[11]

John O'Meara, along with Claude Tande, Selmer Nelson, and Oscar Matternach, was one of the group of Scobey supporters who attended the regional baseball playoff at Miles City.

Known more for its basketball rivalry in later years, the Peerless and Flaxville town teams squared off on the baseball field in 1946, with Flaxville winning a 14-13 slugfest in 10 innings.

Dad picked a great player to root for in Ted Williams, but the Boston Red Sox did not achieve the same success as the Splendid Splinter did. Dad (and the rest of his family until 2004) would experience a lifetime of heartache with the Red Sox, starting with their World Series loss to the Saint Louis Cardinals in seven games in 1946. My older brother Bill recalls, "Dad used to talk about Ted Williams all of the time. He talked a lot about the 1946 World Series when the Red Sox lost to the St. Louis Cardinals in seven games. He said that shortstop Johnny Pesky made an error that cost them the series. Dad never lived to see the Red Sox win a World Series."*

---

* Red Sox shortstop Johnny Pesky's hesitation on a relay throw home on a double to center by Harry Walker allowed Enos Slaughter to score what proved to be the winning run in bottom of the eighth inning in game seven of the 1946 World Series. (Gregory H. Wolf, "Country's Mad Dash: Enos Slaughter scores winning run for Cardinals in Game 7," Society for American Baseball Research.)

1947

Scobey Repeats as District Champions

> *Unusual interest in junior ball has been noted all over northeastern Montana this year. Plentywood, which had no team last year, now has sixty juniors out for practice sessions. Wolf Point is expected to be much stronger this season.*
>
> —Daniels County Leader, "Legion Baseball Starts Monday," May 15, 1947

PREASON

Junior Legion Baseball had a sluggish postwar reboot in northeastern Montana in 1946—it was hard to restart an engine that had been idle for over a decade. But things picked up in 1947, as the towns shook off the Great Depression and World War II and started to rev up their baseball engines. Plentywood now had a Legion team, and Wolf Point returned with a stronger team in 1947.

Scobey, coached again by Bob Tande, returned all but three of their players from the 1946 team, and players who had never seen a baseball game before—let alone played in one—now had a year of baseball experience under their belt. Pitchers included Don Christensen, Johnny Nelson, Don Brayko, Vern Veis, and Ron Fjeld, with Len Faanes catching/second base, George Cornwell at first, Don Christensen at second/catcher; Harvey Eide at short, Ron Fjeld on third, and Jim Sorte, Al Schammel, Ramon Trower, and Don Brayko in the outfield.

REGULAR SEASON

The Scobey Juniors lost only one game again in 1947, dominating the eight teams in District 3. In one dominant regular-season game against Plentywood, Johnny Nelson pitched a three-hitter and struck out 15 in an 11-2 win. Len Faanes went 4-for-4 with a triple to lead Scobey's hitting, Harvey Eide added a single and a double, and Don Brayko "stole bases with abandon."[12] All but one Scobey regular got a hit in the game.

In the Daniels County Junior Legion games, Scobey came from behind to beat Peerless 10-9 on the Fourth of July in Scobey, but Flaxville handed Scobey their only league loss in a wild 20-19 game later in the week.

DISTRICT TOURNAMENT

Eight teams—Malta, Glasgow, Peerless, Scobey, Poplar, Plentywood, Wolf Point, and Flaxville—competed in District 3 in 1947, but only the top four teams in the standings played in the district tournament in Scobey. Those teams were league-champion Scobey, Plentywood, Saco, and Malta.

Scobey played Plentywood in their first game and trailed the Sheridan County boys 2-0 in the third inning, but Scobey scored eight runs in the third and the game ended in a rout for Scobey. Malta won over Saco, and Scobey beat Malta 11-7 for the title, winning their second consecutive district championship. This would be Scobey's last district title for 12 years. The next one would be in Doc Norman's first year coaching the Scobey Legion team in 1959.

PLAYOFFS

After winning the district, Scobey traveled to Denton Field in Miles City to play the Cowboys in a best-of-three inter-district playoff. The Cowboys won the first game 22-0. Scobey's John Nelson kept Miles City in check for the first four innings, but "wildness and errors" led to runs in the later innings, when Miles City scored runs in bunches. Cowboy Pitcher Gary Anderson gave up only two hits and fanned 15 Scobey batters in his shutout. One of the 15 strikeout victims was Scobey's Ron Fjeld, who remembers looking at "three straight fastballs right down the middle."

Miles City ran away with the second game, too, winning 19-3, and went on to win the eastern division against Billings, then won the state championship against Great Falls.

EXTRA INNINGS

At that time, Miles City was the dominant Junior Legion program in Montana, as this was Miles City's 10th state championship between 1928 and 1947. During that same 20-year period, Billings won only one state championship (1930). Following their state championship in 1947, Miles City has won only one state title (1996).

Ed Bayne, who played on Billings's only state title in 1930, began getting involved with the Billings Legion program at this time, and Billings would soon become the uber-dominant team in Montana Legion baseball. Between the years 1950-1971, Billings won *all but two* state Class A championships, including *14 in a row*.

In a game at Plentywood between Westby and the State Line Night Club team during the Fourth of July celebration, Bert Shepard, a former Washington Senators southpaw, played for State Line. Shepard played one season with the Washington Senators with the aid of an artificial right leg. He was a member of the White Sox farm team prior to the war and lost his leg when his airplane blew up over Germany. He was a prisoner of war for eight months before returning to the United States, where, at Walter Reed hospital, he received his artificial limb on March 10, 1945. Five days later, he began playing ball with the Washington Senators, where he remained the rest of the season as player and coach. He pitched his first game following hospitalization against Brooklyn in a war relief game, winning 4 to 3. He served as relief pitcher against the Boston Red Sox for five and one third innings, allowing one run and three hits. He was also a member of Earl Mack's All-American All-Stars, who toured the West. Because of a reamputation in 1946, he was unable to play in the major leagues again and played with the State Line team.[13]

1948

The Scobey Plainsmen Win the Northeastern Montana League

TALK ABOUT BASEBALL BEING BACK IN DANIELS COUNty in 1948! Scobey fielded a high school baseball team (referred to as the "Scholars" by the *Leader*), a Junior Legion team, and a town team (the Plainsmen) in 1948. The Peerless Pirates and Flaxville Cardinals also fielded town teams.

This was the first season for high school baseball in Montana. Scobey was one of about 40 high school teams that pioneered prep baseball in the spring. The chief purpose of the high school baseball program was to give boys over the Junior Legion age of 17 the opportunity to play baseball, as many juniors and seniors were not eligible to play baseball their last two years in high school. The high school team was coached by Bill Cullen and played under the rules of the Montana High School Association (MHSA). Great Falls, Glasgow, Roundup, Kalispell, and Forsyth won their districts and competed in the state tournament in Great Falls. Great Falls beat Kalispell 10-4 for the state championship.

At the end of the season, the *Great Falls Tribune* summed up the "experiment" of prep baseball in 1948: "Despite the cool reception given baseball by most of the larger schools in the state, the program made tremendous progress this spring. Class B schools [Scobey was one], many of which have no hope whatsoever of winning in track, found baseball much to their liking. Good teams or not, more youngsters participated and got more enjoyment from baseball than they ever did from track, which is largely a sport for individuals rather than teams."[14]

For town team baseball, Scobey competed in the revived Northeastern Montana League (NeMont) in 1948. The league had previously existed in 1938 and 1939 (Flaxville won it both years) but folded during World War II. Teams included Scobey, Outlook, Plentywood, Wolf Point, Whitetail, Alkabo, North Dakota, Ray, North Dakota, and Big Beaver, Sask. Flaxville, which had players from Canada on their roster, did not field a team in the league as the league rules contained a player clause which stated that no player out of the league area was eligible for any of the league teams and that all players must maintain an amateur standing.

This was the first season the *Daniels County Leader* dubbed the Scobey town team the "Plainsmen," and they would carry that moniker with them for the remaining history of the team. The Scobey town basketball team would also later be called the Scobey Plainsmen.

REGULAR SEASON

THE SCOBEY PLAINSMEN, MANAGED BY JIGGS HUMBERT AND wearing new uniforms purchased by Scobey businessmen, went undefeated to win the NeMont League in its first year. Several former Legion players who played on Scobey's 1946 and 1947 district championship teams (many of them just 18 years old) were on the roster, including Don Christensen, Quentin Karlsrud, Harvey Eide, Don Brayko, Dike "Fireball" Vanderpan, Rip Roland, Ramon Trower, Al Schammel, George Cornwell, Quentin Karlsrud, Len Dallas Faanes, and Johnny Nelson. The Plainsmen were loaded in 1948, as the roster also included Bob Tande, Indy Halvorson, Elmer Gilchrist, Ken and Harry Larson, Bob Clemens, Bob Willard, Dallas Gaines, and catcher Jack Reiner, who had recently moved to northeastern Montana from Missouri.

The strong Plainsmen team started strong. In their league-opener at Alkabo, North Dakota, the Plainsmen won 12-2, as Don Brayko pitched a five-hitter and nearly tossed a shutout, losing it on a "fluke" in the later innings. The Plainsmen then pounded the Plentywood Cubs 25-12 in their home opener, as Bob Clemens and Harvey Eide led a barrage of Scobey hits with Clemens getting two triples and a pair of singles, and Eide getting one triple, a double, and three singles. Dike Vanderpan got the win in relief of Ken Larson.

The Plainsmen continued their winning ways throughout the season, as they rode a six-game winning streak into the Fourth of July weekend. Dike Vanderpan pitched a five-hitter and struck out 14 Outlook hitters in seven innings in an 11-2 win, and for their sixth consecutive win, the Plainsmen beat Assiniboia, Sask., 6-5 in 10 innings. After Assiniboia tied the game 5-5 in the ninth, the Plainsmen walked it off on "a perfect squeeze play" by Dike Vanderpan in the bottom of the 10th. Vanderpan's squeeze bunt down the first base line scored Bob Clemens with the winning run. John Nelson pitched a hell of a game for Scobey, going all 10 innings to get the win.

The Plainsmen's undefeated season and winning streak came to an end in a 12-team tournament in Rockglen, Sask., as the Plainsmen lost 3-2 to Fife Lake, Sask. All the runs were scored in the first inning. Dike Vanderpan, after surrendering a three-run double in the first inning, did not allow another Laker to score, but Scobey couldn't push across a third run to tie the game. This time, a suicide squeeze attempt by the Plainsmen in the last inning was not successful. Other than the nonleague loss to Lake Fife, the Scobey Plainsmen sailed through the NeMont League undefeated, and Plentywood finished second. In the game on Riba Field in Plentywood that decided the regular season championship, the *Plentywood Herald* recalled the old rivalry between Scobey and Plentywood that was still going strong: "The much-improved Cubs will be out to knock the vaunted Scobeyites out of first position. The ever-present Scobey-Plentywood rivalry will be burning brightly as the two teams slug it out for league leadership."[15]

Turning to other teams in the county, the Peerless Pirates hosted a non-league tournament in Peerless that summer, with Rockglen, Scobey, Ossette, and the Pirates participating. Peerless beat Rockglen 3-2 and Scobey won 12-2 over Ossette to set up the championship game between the Plainsmen and Pirates. While the Peerless Pirates dominated the Plainsmen on the basketball court (that would be another book), the Plainsmen got the best of Peerless 7-6 in the championship game on Peerless's home field. Rockglen beat Ossette 12-5 for the consolation.

Flaxville did not participate in the NeMont League but played plenty of baseball that summer. They did not lose many games, if any. In a 6-2 win over Wolf Point, the *Leader* wrote, "The game was a hard one and Flaxville says it was about their most difficult this season."[16] But I would say the most difficult game the Cardinals played that summer was against Bengough, not Wolf Point. The Cardinals beat Bengough in a nailbiter, 8-7. Flaxville scored five runs in the first inning and one in the second to lead 6-0, but Bengough rallied to come from behind and took the lead in the 8th inning, 7-6, on a two-run triple. Flaxville walked it off in the bottom of the ninth when Canadian Bill Morrow connected on a 3-2 pitch to drive home Hexom and Barth with the tying and winning runs. It was Morrow's second triple of the day.

As they had done in 1938, Flaxville again hosted the Notre Dame Hounds of Wilcox, Sask., coached by Father Athol Murray. There is no record of the results, but how could I miss the opportunity to write about the Notre Dame Hounds again? I would have paid money just to see their uniforms.

Notre Dame Hounds vs. Flaxville, July 18, 1948. *Leader.*

It was the season for new leagues for the town teams in 1948, as Peerless, Richland Ossette, Glentana, and Opheim formed their own five-team town team league. The Peerless Pirates won their league opener 14-8 over Richland, then beat them later in the year 13-9. The two teams had identical league records, but with their two wins over Richland, the Pirates won the league, and Richland finished second.

The Scobey Junior Legion team struggled in 1948, having lost a slew of regulars from their 1946 and 1947 district championship teams. Had the Legion age been 18 at the time, they would have been stronger, but as it was, those boys (young men) were playing for the Plainsmen. Pitchers Ronnie Fjeld and Vern Veis, now in their third and final year of Legion baseball, led manager Chris Veis's team on the mound, but their strong pitching was not enough for the Juniors to win their third consecutive district championship. In addition to Veis and Fjeld, the 1948 Scobey Junior Legion roster included Clay Gilchrist, Dorence "Doug" Bundren, Tony Lamotte, Bill Wright, Clayton Swenson, Gerald Pittenger, Burnell Rhodes, Tommy Hayes, Jim Sorte, Cliff "Finley" Hagfeldt, and Young Hueseman. Terry McIntyre was the batboy.

The Juniors lost their league opener to rival Plentywood, 11-8, and that was indicative of the remainder of their season. One highlight of the regular season for the Juniors was beating Wolf Point 11-10 on the Fourth of July in Scobey, but the Juniors finished behind Plentywood and Fort Peck in the eastern division of the District 3 standings, so they did not qualify for the postseason district tournament.

TOURNAMENT

The NeMont League concluded its first year with a season-ending tournament on Riba Field in Plentywood. Scobey finished the season unbeaten in league play and was looking to complete a perfect run by winning the tournament.

Five NeMont League teams—Alkabo, Ray, Outlook, Plentywood, and Scobey—participated in the tournament. In first-round games, Alkabo beat Raymond, 4-1, and Outlook edged the host Plentywood Cubs, 3-2. Scobey received a first-round bye, then Johnny Nelson pitched a shutout to lead the Plainsmen to a 6-0 win over Alkabo to set up the championship game between Scobey and Outlook.

Outlook's upset of Plentywood had spoiled a championship game between the two old rivals, but the Scobey-Outlook game turned out to be a barn burner. Outlook had the tying and winning runs on second and third in the ninth inning when Johnny Nelson "reared back and fired his last high hard one past the Outlook batter to end the game 5-4 in favor of the Plainsmen." Ken Larson pitched the first six innings and was relieved in the seventh by Nelson. The most spectacular play of the day was made by Plainsmen center fielder Elmer Gilchrist when he went deep into center field to make a going-away, back-handed stab of a long drive by Ole Fiske.[17]

In the Junior Legion postseason, Fort Peck won their first District 3 championship, 7-2 over Plentywood. To reach the finals, Fort Peck beat Opheim 5-4, and Plentywood beat Glasgow 16-10. Fort Peck then lost in a playoff to Lewistown.

EXTRA INNINGS

The Police Creek Baseball Club had a banquet in 1948 to remember their first team in 1917. With the exception of Rex Rhodes, who died in 1945, all members of the old, original Police Creek baseball team met with their wives to reminisce about the old days. Former players present were James Rhodes, Robert Rhodes, B. J. Lekvold, Elmer Olson, Ted Rustebakke, Sherd Wilcoxon, M. A. Lamotte, and Ernie Gampp. Ozro Brown, who played with the Police Creek team during the early 1920s, was also there. The 1917 Police Creek ball team was managed by Marion LaMotte, and Jim Rhodes was the captain.

1917 Police Creek Team reunion. Seated: B. J. Lekvold, Bob Rhodes, Ernie Gampp, Marion LaMotte; standing, Sherd Wilcoxon, Elmer Olson, Jim Rhodes, Ted Rustebakke. *1913-1948 Anniversary Album.*

In 1948, Montana Junior American Legion split into A and B Divisions, but there was still only a single state championship tournament. It wouldn't be until 1949 that the first state Class B champion would be crowned. In 1948, the winners of the western and eastern A and B divisions played in a four-team tournament for the state championship. In Class B, Bozeman won the western division, and Lewistown won the eastern division, but Bozeman and Lewistown were both disqualified from playing at State as they did not provide birth certificates for all the players on their rosters. So, Havre and Fort Peck—runners-up in the West B and East B Divisions—played against Great Falls and Billings at Cobb Field in the state tournament. Great Falls won the championship 12-2 against Billings.

Tournament flyer for the first State Legion tournament on Cobb Field, 1948. *Billings Gazette.*

The year 1948 was the inaugural season of Cobb Field in Billings. Can you imagine what a special experience it must have been for the Havre and Fort Peck players to play on Cobb Field in August 1948?

Originally named Athletic Park when it was built in 1932, Cobb Field opened on May 4, 1948, after substantial renovations. I am sure many readers have special memories of Cobb Field. I saw the Billings Mustangs play there many times in the 1970s with Dad, Mom, and Jon. That field was dripping with rich tradition and character.

Cobb Field had a natural grass surface and seated 4,200. The dimensions were 335 feet to left, 405 feet to center, and 325 feet to right. The field was named after Bob Cobb, who was responsible for bringing the Mustangs to Billings.[18]

Cobb Field was the home of the Billings Mustangs, a rookie affiliate with several organizations in the Pioneer League from 1948-2007. The Mustangs were named by Marge (Sampson) Norman's dad, L. R. Sampson of Billings, as Mr. Sampson won the team-naming contest. For winning the contest, he received season tickets to the Mustang games. The Sampsons were lifelong Mustang fans. Here is the history of the Billings Mustangs affiliates on Cobb Field:

- Brooklyn Dodgers (1949–1951)
- Pittsburgh Pirates (1952–1956)
- St. Louis Cardinals (1957–1963)
- Seattle Pilots (1969)
- Kansas City Royals (1970–1973)
- Cincinnati Reds (1974–2007)

Construction of a new stadium at the Cobb Field location began in the spring of 2007, and Cobb Field was torn down after the 2007 season. The new stadium opened as Dehler Park on June 29, 2008. A documentary film—*Cobb Field, A Day at the Ballpark*—was shot about Cobb Field during the final weeks of its existence in 2007. It gives a view of the world of minor league baseball from the eyes of the ballpark. The film won Mid-America Emmys in three categories.

Here are just a few special moments for Scobey and Northeastern Montana baseball on historic Cobb Field through the years:

- In 1930, the first Scobey Junior Legion team lost to the Billings Legion team 8-4 at Athletic Park, which became Cobb Field in 1948. Prior to 1930, baseball games in Billings were played at North Side Field.
- In 1966, Scobey beat the Billings Scarlets 4-3 on Cobb Field. Dan Smith, Scobey catcher, had four hits—a triple and three singles—to lead Scobey's hitting. He also scored the winning run in the ninth. Phil Audet went the distance for Scobey, scattering eight hits.
- In 1969, Scobey lost to the Billings Royals 4-1 on Cobb Field, but Craig Audet's "towering" home run over that 335-foot left field fence in the ninth broke up Jerry Schuster's bid for a Royal shutout. The home run was a "towering blast [that] carried over the 335-foot marker just inside the left field foul pole."[19] It was the first ball hit out of the park in Legion action at Cobb Field that year. And 14-year-old "Little Terry Puckett" yielded only two earned runs in eight innings for Scobey.
- In 1971, David Fanning—after outdueling Terry Puckett 1-0 in Scobey to lead Havre to the State B championship a week earlier—struck out 25 Billings Royals in 12 innings, and Havre went on to beat the Royals 3–2 in 14 innings at the state tournament.
- In June 1974, Scobey came back from a 3-0 deficit to beat the Billing Scarlets 4-3 on an error made by the

Cobb Field being constructed in the late 1940s. *Western Heritage Center.*

North Side Field, c. late 1920s. *Courtesy photo.*

Scarlets on a suicide squeeze called by Doc in the 11th inning. Jay Hagfeldt pitched to Dana Audet the entire 11 innings to earn the win, pitching 10 straight shutout innings after yielding three runs in the first. The Scarlets later won the State B championship that year and then took third at the State A. They moved up to the A Division the following year in 1975 and won their first State A championship in 1976.

- In 1979, Dan Danelson pitched a one-hitter against the Billings Royals to lead Scobey to a 2-1 win at the Billings IGA tournament. Scobey also beat the Billings Scarlets 16-9 at that same tournament.
- In 1987, the Wolf Point Yellowjackets, coached by Michael Neubauer, won the State A Tournament on Cobb Field. Wolf Point also won the sportsmanship trophy. This was the first year Montana Legion transitioned from A and B Divisions to AA and A Divisions, although for one year (1969), Montana Legion did split into AA and A Divisions. Scobey's first state championship in 1969 was actually in the A Division.
- In 1996, the Scobey Blues, coached by Ken Meyer, played on Cobb Field in the State A Tournament. After losing to Libby 8-7 in the opener, Scobey went on to win four consecutive games before being eliminated by the Bitterroot Red Sox to take third place in the tournament. Scobey won the sportsmanship trophy, and Spencer Frederick was named MVP.

1949

The Scobey Plainsmen Repeat as NeMont League Champions

> *The Scobey Plainsmen reaffirmed their leadership in the Northeastern Montana League by emerging undefeated in tournament play.*
>
> —**"Plainsmen Show Excellent Wares at Ball Meet,"** Daniels County Leader, **September 8, 1949**

There were three flavors of baseball in Scobey again in 1949: high school (the Spartans), Junior American Legion (dubbed the "Legionnaires" for the first time by the *Leader*),* and the town team (the Plainsmen).

The Junior Legion team played in District 4, which consisted of Scobey, Plentywood, Glasgow, Opheim, Fort Peck, and Wolf Point. The roster for the Juniors included Tommy Hayes, Donnie Brasen, Clay Gilchrist, Tony LaMotte, Doug Bundren, Ken Lekvold, Clayton Swenson, Kenny Tonjum, Howard Farver, Llewellyn Kestin, Terry McIntyre, Ralph Tkachyk, and Cliff "Finley" Hagfeldt.

SCHOLARS

The Scobey High School team was again coached by Bill Cullen. Bill Cullen also coached the Scobey Junior Legion teams in 1948 and 1949. Forty-five boys from Scobey High School signed up to play high school baseball for Bill Cullen in the spring. The team included seniors in high school, and eighth graders were eligible to play, too. The high school league Scobey played in was called League 6, and consisted of Scobey, Antelope, Poplar, and Wolf Point in the north, and Circle, Terry, and Wibaux in the south. Opheim also had a high school team but played in a different league.

---

* The first reference to the Scobey Junior Legion team as the "Legionnaires" appeared in an article in the June 2, 1949, *Daniels County Leader* with the headline "Legionnaires Hold Scoring Spree in Plentywood Game." The *Leader* referred to the Scobey Junior Legion team as the Legionnaires after that, but the team was not formally given a team name until 1977, when they became the Scobey Blues.

The Spartans, led by pitchers Vern Veis and Ron Fjeld, won the north section of League 6. Three hitters—Freddie Leibrand, Tony LaMotte, and Ron Fjeld—batted over .400. Scobey won 4-2 over Poplar to win the north and played off against the Terry Terriers, the champion from the south, for the League 6 championship in Scobey. Vern Veis struck out 19 of 21 Terriers in seven innings, but 10 Scobey errors, three walks, and a hit batsman led to several Terry runs, and Terry won 8–5. High school baseball was a gift to 18-year-olds like Vern Veis and Ron Fjeld, who were ineligible to play Junior Legion Baseball at the time. The Glasgow Scotties, led by Bunky Sullivan, then beat Terry for the Eastern championship and played at State in Great Falls.

1949 Scobey Plainsmen, Northeastern Montana League champions. Seated, Dallas Gaines, lf; Indy Halvorson, 3b; Vern Veis, p; Don Brayko, p; Ken Larson, p; Harry Larson, 2b; Jack Reiner, c.; standing, Elmer Gilchrist, cf; Harvey Eide, ss; Jiggs Humbert, mgr.; Alfred Schammel, rf; Tom Wright, 2b; Don Christensen, ss.

LEGIONNAIRES

In a 12-3 win over Outlook, Scobey Junior Legion pitcher Donnie Brasen hurled seven innings of hitless ball in relief of Doug Bundren to lead Scobey to the win. When Coach Cullen motioned for Donnie to come in from left field to pitch, "the little wiseacre looked at him and said, 'Are you crazy?'"[20] He then went on to pitch seven innings without yielding a hit or a run.

Scobey won the regular season league but couldn't play in the District 4 tournament because several players were ruled ineligible as their birth certificates were not submitted on time. Opheim, led by pitchers Andy Stolen (who later became my pitching coach) and Leo Zimmer, won the Junior Legion District 4 championship, played at Plentywood. Plentywood, Fort Peck, Glasgow, and Opheim were in the tournament.

In Opheim's 8–2 win over Plentywood in the District 4 semifinals, *The Plentywood Herald* wrote, "Little Andy Stolen, picked two years in succession as all district pitcher, limited Plentywood to three hits as Opheim took the locals in the first-round competition."[21] Opheim then won the title game 10–9 against Fort Peck. Opheim lost to Forsyth for the Eastern championship, and Anaconda beat Forsyth for the first State B Legion championship in Montana.

PLAINSMEN

The roster for the Plainsmen included Dallas Gaines, Indy Halvorson, Vern Veis, Don Brayko, Ken Larson, Harry Larson, Jack Reiner, Elmer Gilchrist, Harvey Eide, Jiggs Humbert, Alfred Schammel, Tom Wright, and Don Christensen.

The Plainsmen repeated as champions of the eight-team Northeast Montana Baseball League in 1949 by winning 11 of 14 conference games. The Plentywood Cubs won 10, finishing one game behind the Plainsmen. Outlook and Big Beaver, Saskatchewan, tied for third. Other teams in the league were Raymond, Antelope, Whitetail, and Redstone-Archer. The league had been in operation for two years, and all the players were required to be residents of their team's locality. Flaxville had players from out of the area, so they did not participate in the league. The *Leader* wrote that the Scobey Plainsmen showed that Scobey can have "a good baseball team without hired players."[22] No doubt this was in reference to the 1925–28 teams, where players from the Chicago White Sox and other professional players came up to Scobey to play. (And perhaps a jab at Flaxville, who had players from Canada on their team.)

The Plainsmen played the Flaxville Cardinals in a highly publicized nonleague game in Scobey on July 4, 1949. Flaxville won the game 16–5. The Cardinals were not permitted to play in the NeMont League as they had players from north of the border, one of them a 24-year-old farmer named Bushwright from Wilcox, Sask., who "could not only pitch well, but was a deadly hitter."[23] The NeMont League rule was that all players must be residents of the locality their respective teams represent. Later in the season, the Plainsmen got their revenge on the Cardinals, winning 15-5 in Flaxville.

Following the NeMont League season and tournament, the Plainsmen were challenged by the Outlook Old-Timers (ages 40 to 50) to a best-of-three series, where the winner would take 60% of the gate. Scobey won the series by winning both games, 9–5 in Outlook and 11–2 in Scobey.

The season-ending games for the Plainsmen were played in an "exceptionally well-attended"[24] eight-team invitational tournament in Outlook over Labor Day weekend. Scobey swept the tournament in three games. Ken Larson pitched a one-hit shutout in Scobey's 3-0 win over Outlook in the first game. In the semifinal, Don Christensen scattered six hits to get the win over Big Beaver, Sask., in 10 innings, as Jack Reiner singled to score Ken Larson and win the game, 4-3.

The Outlook Old-Timers challenged the **Plainsmen** to a home-and-home series. Youth prevailed over experience, as the Plainsmen swept the series.

Scobey then crushed their old rival, Plentywood, 15-7 in the final, as winning pitcher Don Brayko led a 17-hit attack for the Plainsmen by hitting the tournament's only home run.

EXTRA INNINGS

Jiggs Humbert and Ken and Harry Larson of the 1949 Plainsmen were the three boys in the "Sons of the Pioneers" photo from circa 1930 that looked like it was a Norman Rockwell painting. The three boys were having fun playing baseball and winning championships for the town team 20 years later.

Coach Bill Cullen passed up an offer to play baseball with Butte in the Mines League to coach the Scobey Junior Legion team that summer. He had played with Butte in previous summers.

The original season for Montana high school baseball in 1948 had almost 40 teams, and in 1949, there were 60 teams. One thing that was helping high school baseball was that spring football had been discontinued by the MHSA. Due to the smaller schools not being able to compete with the larger schools, the MHSA would create two leagues, Class A and B, for high school baseball in 1950. But now that spring football had ended, the argument against baseball was its competition with track and field. In answer to that argument, Bill Johnstone, state high school baseball chairman, said: "Baseball should not be ruled out under the mistaken idea such action will build up track. The number of boys who wish to compete in both programs is small now and probably will be even smaller after the two sports have operated side by side for a few years. There is no justification for discontinuing a sport which could show 35 schools participating its first year and 60 its second year. No other high school sport can show a two-year record of growth to compare with this, either as to numbers of schools or numbers of persons competing."[25]

1950

The Scobey Spartans Win the District 6 High School Title

> *The 'Good ol' days of baseball' appear to be returning to this area; and in Scobey, with its history of baseball greats, the renaissance of baseball here may not at first be as glamorous, but prospects for continued success are on a much more sound basis.*
>
> —*Daniels County Leader*, April 27, 1950

THERE WERE HIGH EXPECTATIONS FOR SCOBEY baseball in 1950, with three flavors of baseball in play for the third consecutive year: the Spartans, Legionnaires, and Plainsmen. Bill Cullen coached the high school team, Don Christensen coached the Legionnaires, and Keith Whipple (who played for the 1925 Scobey Giants) managed the Plainsmen.

SCHOLARS

THE SCHOLARS WERE LED BY EXPERIENCED SENIORS VERN Veis and Doug Bundren and were looking to win their first District 6 championship. Flaxville also fielded a high school baseball team in 1950. In addition to the two Daniels County teams, Outlook, Plentywood, Westby, Brockton, Antelope, and Medicine Lake fielded high school teams that season. The district was split into two divisions, east and west, with the winner of each division playing one game for the championship.

The Scobey-Plentywood rivalry assumed three forms in 1950, as the Spartans and Wildcats squared off against each other, adding to the Junior Legion and town teams' rivalries. The "Scholars" won a close game at home despite "a strong invasion by the Plentywood Wildcats." Plentywood took an early 3-0 lead on "erratic play" in the infield by Scobey. But with two outs and the bases loaded in the bottom of the fourth, Scobey's version of "Mighty Casey," big Doug Bundren, the Scholar's first baseman, came to bat. The *Leader* wrote, "The noise of the crowd burst into a sudden crescendo as big Doug put his well-coordinated mass behind a good one and sent a very hard, low fly ball into deep center field for a home run." With Doug's mighty swing, Scobey took the lead 4-3, and there was joy in Scobey, as that was all the scoring in the game, although the Wildcats threatened several times after Doug's home run. Vern Veis pitched a four-hitter to garner the win, and Pat Gallagher from Plentywood also only yielded four hits, but one of them was the grand slam to Bundren. The *Leader* wrote that Gallagher pitched well, "except for that one he grooved for Bundren."[26]

The Scobey Spartans played the Flaxville Cardinals in high school baseball in 1950, resulting in a 14-3 win for Scobey. Donnie Brasen pitched the first four innings for Scobey, and Vern Veis handled the last three.

Scobey went undefeated in the western division, and Medicine Lake won the eastern division, setting up the championship game between the Spartans and the Honkers. Vern Veis pitched a three-hitter and recorded 11 strikeouts to lead Scobey to a 4-3 win. Scobey trailed 3-1 but plated three runs in the sixth inning to come from behind and win it, with Vern Veis driving in the tying and winning runs. Coach Bill Cullen commented on the come-from-behind win. "In one of those games, anything can happen, and it happened right for us."

There was no further play beyond the eight district championships in Montana high school baseball that year.

LEGIONNAIRES

THE JUNIOR LEGION TEAM HAD MANY EIGHTH-GRADERS ON it the previous year, but the team was now getting a little older. The *Leader* was optimistic about the Legionnaires' fortunes, writing, "Prospects are excellent for a number of good baseball teams in the community this season. One of the brightest is that for the Scobey Junior Legion team, many of whose 'feather merchants' from last year have added inches, weight, and know-how."[27] Don Christensen's "feather merchants" included the following team members: Larry Wangrud and Terry McIntyre in the catching assignments; Clayton Swenson at first, Cliff "Finley" Hagfeldt at second, Tommy Hayes at shortstop and pitching, and Howard Farver and Ken Tonjum at third. Outfielders were Earl Oldenburg, Duane Overby, Ordean Wangrud, and Ralph Tkachyk, with several general utility men in Dallas Hagfeldt, Eddie Brooks, Art Fredriksen, Richard Audet, and Wasyl Adkins.

District 4 was split into two divisions that year, with the winner of each division meeting in a one-game playoff for the championship. Scobey competed in the eastern division of the district with Outlook, Plentywood, Culbertson, Bainville, and Poplar.

The Legionnaires battled with rival Plentywood during the regular season, losing the first game to Plentywood 16-15 on an error in the bottom of the ninth inning, but getting their revenge in Scobey, winning 9-7.

After a 19-6 win over Bainville and a 14-6 win over Poplar, the Scobey Juniors moved into a tie with Poplar for the eastern division lead. Poplar's loss to Scobey was their first of the season, and Scobey only had one loss to Plentywood. Tom Hayes pitched a complete game for Scobey against Poplar, scattering six hits, striking out five, and walking four.

The winner of the eastern division of District 4 was decided on the final game of the regular season on Independence Day in Poplar. It doesn't get any more American than that. Scobey and Poplar each had one loss, so the winner would advance to play in a one-game playoff with the western division champion, which would either be Fort Peck or Glasgow. The stage was set for a dramatic finish.

It is rare for a championship baseball game to be decided on our nation's birthday. Could the two teams match the moment in Poplar? Yes, they could. For five complete innings, the game was a pitcher's duel between Engles of Poplar and Donnie Brasen of Scobey. With the score tied 0-0 in the top of the fourth, Scobey touched Engles for an unearned run when Kenny Lekvold singled, stole second, and came all the way around to score on a wild throw to second. Then in the bottom half of the fourth, Poplar scored twice when Nordwick singled and Nees tripled to drive home Nordwick, then Nees scored on a bad throw to home to give the hometown boys a 2-1 lead.

But with Scobey trailing 2-1 in the sixth, the Legionnaires got to Poplar ace Engles and broke the game open, exploding for nine runs. Larry Wangrud started the rally with a single. Adkins got to first on an error, Overby flew out, then Swenson loaded the bases with an infield single. Brooks walked, forcing in the first run; Brasen forced in another when he was hit by a pitched ball. Ordean Wangrud was safe on an error. Bases were still loaded when Farver got a walk for another run. Lekvold again singled, driving home two runs. A double by Larry Wangrud and a single by Adkins produced three more. Nine runs had now crossed the plate for Scobey in the barrage. Nees for Poplar was then sent in to replace Engles on the mound. He struck out Overby and Swenson to end the inning, but it was too late, as Scobey now led 10-2.

Poplar made an attempt at a comeback in the bottom of the seventh, as Brasen, who had pitched a fine game for six innings, started to weaken. He gave up three base hits and walked two, enabling Poplar to score four runs before the fire was put out. The final score was 10-6 for Scobey, the new eastern division champions.

The Legionnaires traveled to Glasgow to play in a one-game playoff to decide the District 4 champions. The winner of the game at Glasgow would meet Forsyth in a three-game series at a site to be determined. The game in Glasgow would be played under the lights at Glasgow's field. This would be the first time the Scobey Legion team played under the lights.

Both Scobey and Glasgow had only one loss. Scobey's only loss came to Plentywood, and Glasgow lost 1-0 to Fort Peck, but Glasgow handed Scobey its second loss of the season and won the game 8-0. Donnie Brasen pitched for Scobey, allowing only five hits, striking out seven, but he yielded seven walks, and his teammates committed six costly errors behind him. But it didn't matter, as Scobey ran into a buzzsaw in the form of pitcher Bob Gilluly of Glasgow, who tossed a two-hitter and struck out 13 Legionnaires. Gilluly allowed only five baserunners during the game. Glasgow got three runs in the second inning, three in the third, one in the fourth, and one in the 6th. This championship would be the first of three consecutive District 4 championships for Glasgow, coached by "Sully" and "Bunky" Sullivan.

Following their district championship, Glasgow played a best-of-three series against Forysth in an interdistrict playoff. The winner would advance to face another interdistrict champion for the eastern division title. Glasgow swept Forsyth, winning 5-3 and 3-0, with Bob Gilluly winning the first game and Chuck Sternhagen pitching a one-hit shutout in the second. Glasgow then lost to Laurel for the eastern division championship, and Laurel went on to win their first state championship over Fairfield.

Glasgow Legion Team, 1950 District champions. Standing, left to right, Coach B. T. (Sully) Sullivan, Bernard Combs, Jim Sullivan, Jim Kaneski, Nick Gamas, Chuck Sternhagen, Duane Jager and Bernard (Bunky) Sullivan, assistant coach; kneeling, left to right, Bob Gilluly, Jerry Edwards, Dan Schellinger, Jerry Luckman, Tommy Farrell, Walter Dahl and Bob Beardsley. *Glasgow Courier*.

PLAINSMEN

THE PLAINSMEN WERE LOOKING TO THREE-PEAT AS NEMONT League champions, and they had the horses to do it. Their roster was strong again, including pitchers Ken Larson, Vern Veis, Don Brayko, and Ronnie Fjeld; catchers Jack Reiner and Clay Gilchrist; infielders Doug Bundren, Indy Halvorson, Harry Larson, and Don Christensen, and outfielders Dallas Gaines, Bob Willard, Chet Brooks, Babe Holyk, and Ober Spear.

The Northeastern Montana League had twelve teams in 1950, with an eastern and western division. The six teams in the west were Scobey, Peerless, Whitetail, Flaxville, Big Beaver, Sask., and Bengough, Sask. The six teams in the east were Redstone, Archer, Outlook, Raymond, Plentywood, and Antelope.

The Scobey Plainsmen were tested by a good Peerless team that year, beating the Pirates 4-2 in a close game at Peerless. Leo Zimmer, pitching for Peerless, scattered seven hits and held Scobey to their lowest run total for any game as the Plainsmen dominated the league. Ken Larson went the distance for Scobey and struck out seven Pirates for the win. Larson carried a shutout into the ninth but lost it after Lien singled and Larson doubled to bring him home. Leroy Ackerman then got to second on an error, and Larson scored. With Ackerman still on second and the tying run at the plate, Larson put out the fire by striking out Ackerman and getting my uncle, Reese Puckett Sr., who already had two hits, to pop up to second to end the game. Zimmer got three strikeouts against the league-leading Plainsmen.

The Plainsmen won their second league game against the Pirates in Scobey by an 8-3 score. Scobey scored eight runs on 10 hits and three Peerless errors. Don Brayko pitched a four-hitter, struck out eight Pirates, and walked three. After the Peerless game, the Plainsmen hopped in their cars and hurried to Glasgow to play their first game under the lights, losing that one, 14-3. Maybe the lights affected them, as the Plainsmen committed eight costly errors to lose the game.

In other intercounty games, the Plainsmen beat the Flaxville Cardinals 15-12 in a slugfest, as the Plainsmen gathered 16 hits off Flaxville's Hansen, and the Cards got to Scobey's Brayko for 14 hits. The score stood at 11-all in the eighth, when the Plainsmen scored four runs to put the game away. Scobey won the second league game against Flaxville in Scobey, 14-5.

In other league games of note, Ron Fjeld pitched a masterful game against "a determined Whitetail team" to lead the Plainsmen to a close 4-1 win in Whitetail. The game was a pitcher's duel. With Scobey holding a slim 2-1 lead in the ninth, Dallas Gaines got on base on an error, stole second, and then came home on Indy Halvorson's single. Indy advanced to second on an error, then Jack Reiner drove Halvorson home on a single, making a 4-1 score for Scobey. Ron Fjeld got in trouble in the ninth but snuffed out the rally. After Safty hit a double, Fjeld settled down and struck out the last two batters to end the game. Ron pitched a four-hitter and struck out 10.

In a nonleague game, Scobey trailed Wolf Point 2-1 in the bottom of the eighth in Scobey, but the Plainsmen rallied for the win. Halvorson singled, then Doug Bundren—the Plainsmen's leading hitter for power, average, and runs batted in—homered to give the Plainsmen a 3-2 lead, and the rally continued. Harry Larson got to first on an error, Don Brayko singled, then Reiner smashed a double, driving home Larson and Brayko. Reiner came in on Field's

Flaxville and the **Plainsmen** faced off frequently through the years. *Leader*.

grounder to first, making the score 6-2 for Scobey. The Leader wrote that Doug Bundren "was the big man in the game, both literally and figuratively." He was 4-for-4 with a double and the home run. Ken Larson was the winning pitcher for Scobey, scattering eight hits, striking out four Wolves, and walking none.

In their rematch against Glasgow at home in Scobey, the Plainsmen again played shoddy in the field, and the visiting Glasgow won 6-2. Scobey had seven errors, three of which accounted for two unearned runs in the first inning. The highlight for Scobey that day was again Doug Bundren, who hit a booming home run over the fence that went onto the racetrack.

The Scobey Plainsmen won the western division handily, and Plentywood won the eastern division of the NeMont League, setting up a possible showdown between the two rivals in the 12-team postseason tournament in Redstone. But Scobey lost their first game to Bengough 4-2 and was eliminated as it was single elimination. Flaxville made it to the championship by beating Peerless 6-2, Redstone 14-5, but then lost to Plentywood 14-5.

The Plainsmen, champions of the western division, were extremely unhappy with how the tournament was run, as it was a single-elimination tournament and they were pitted against the second-place team in their own division, Bengough, in the first game. This led to complications with the Plainsmen participating in the NeMont League the following season.

EXTRA INNINGS

First baseman Doug Bundren, who played tackle on the Scobey football team, was a big boy. When high school baseball coach Bill Cullen was having trouble finding a uniform that would fit him, he joked, "It may be necessary to contact a tent and awning company to cover his outsize frame." A special uniform for him (size 46) was ordered so that "the big boy, who hits homers, will not be restricted in his actions by lack of suitable yardage in his uniform." The special uniform worked, as Doug was the triple-crown leader for the Plainsmen as a rookie first baseman after he played high school baseball earlier that spring and Junior Legion ball in 1948 and 1949. He led the Plainsmen in hitting with a batting average of .425, and he also led the team in home runs and RBIs. He could not play Junior Legion ball that summer because he was 18 years old. Other Plainsmen hitters over .300 were Indy Halvorson at .349, Dallas Gaines .341, Harry Larson .333, Jack Reiner .324, and Don Brayko .307.[28]

The 1950 season was special for both the Legionnaires and the Plainsmen, as it was the first time playing under the lights for both teams at the fairgrounds in Glasgow. However, the Legionnaires and Plainsmen would have to wait seven years to play their first home game under the lights, when the new Scobey Ball Park opened in 1957.

In 1950, after 25 years of the American Legion Baseball program, a monument was erected in Milbank cementing the town's distinction as "The Birthplace of American Legion Baseball." On the monument, it reads, "In this city, on July 17, 1925, by action of the South Dakota Department of The American Legion, the nationwide organization of Legion Junior Baseball was first proposed as a program of service to the youth of America."

1951

The Plainsmen Withdraw from the Northeastern Montana League

Eight teams—split into League One and Two—competed in high school baseball in the northeast, and 10 teams—split into western and eastern divisions—competed in District 4 Junior American Legion in 1951. The Scobey Plainsmen withdrew from the Northeastern Montana League due to the fiasco of the previous season's seeding in the season-ending tournament, where they won the western division but were seeded against the number two team (Bengough) in the opening game of the tournament at Redstone and were eliminated in the single-elimination tourney's first round.

SCHOLARS

The Scholars competed in District 1 in 1951, which had eight teams and was divided into two leagues: League One (Scobey, Plentywood, Flaxville, and Outlook); League Two (Westby, Medicine Lake, Culbertson, and Brockton).

For the fourth consecutive year, the Scholars were coached by Bill Cullen. Coach Cullen's roster, which he anticipated would be stronger in the field and at bat, included Donnie Brasen, Glenn Stahl, Tom Hayes, Burnell Rhodes, Terry McIntyre, Kenny Tonjum, Cliff Hagfeldt, Larry Wangrud, Duane Overby, Garry Leibrand, Howard Farver, Eddie Fossen, Kenny Lekvold, Ordean Wangrud, Clayton Swenson, Richard Audet, Eddie Brooks, and Donald Fossen. "Oil Can" Oldenburg was the batboy.

Scobey opened its season at home against Flaxville. The game was played in a driving dust storm with Flaxville seeming to navigate the wind and dust early as the Flyers led 6-3 going into the bottom of the fourth. But Cardinals pitcher Donald Unsworth "lost his stuff," and Scobey broke it open with 10 runs. The dust storm was unrelenting, and the game had to be called at the end of five innings with the score 13-6 for Scobey. Donnie Brasen started on the mound for Scobey, but due to wildness had to be relieved by Burnell Rhodes. Larry Wangrud led Scobey's hitting attack by belting two home runs.

The Scholars traveled to Plentywood to play their rival and suffered their only loss of the season, 7-3 to the Wildcats. It was a costly loss, however, as Plentywood also lost only one game in League One, so they won the tiebreaker over Scobey to win the league. Don Brasen pitched well for Scobey, yielding only six hits, striking out 10 and issuing no walks, while his Wildcat counterpart, Ronnie Christensen, gave up seven hits, struck out nine and issued three walks. The difference in the game was fielding, as Christensen had excellent fielding behind him, whereas Brasen's runs were the result of several Scobey errors. It was so bad that the *Leader* wrote, "The Scobey boys found it difficult to hold on to the little pop flies of the infield variety."[29]

In another conference game, the Scholars routed Outlook 21-6. The surprising performance of this game was the relief pitching of Glenn Stahl, who relieved starting pitcher Tom Hayes in the fourth and struck out the first three men to face him. Stahl went on to get three strikeouts in the fifth, but only after three errors had allowed three runs. Brasen then retired the side in order in the sixth and seventh innings to close the game for Scobey.

Against Medicine Lake, Scobey ace Don Brasen battled with Allen Nielsen of the Honkers in a pitching duel. Brasen scattered six hits and had 14 strikeouts while Nielsen pitched a three-hitter and struck out 11. The score was tied at 5-5 going into the top of the seventh inning when Clayton Swenson put it on ice for the Scholars by blasting a grand slam home run. In the bottom of the seventh, Brasen loaded the bases by giving up two hits and a walk but then mowed down the next three men on strikeouts to seal the 10-5 win.

After winning League One, Plentywood played Culbertson, the winner of League Two, for the District 1 title. Ronnie Christensen of Plentywood, who had a no-hitter to his credit against Outlook earlier in the season and had beaten Scobey, tossed a two-hit shutout to lead Plentywood to its first district baseball title. Chalk one up for the rivals.

The Scobey High School baseball players would take two paths following the season. Most would play for the Legionnaires, but the 18-year-olds would try out for the Plainsmen.

LEGIONNAIRES

The Legionnaires, coached by Babe Holyk, competed in District 4, which consisted of 10 teams, divided into the eastern half (Plentywood, Bainville, Poplar, Outlook,

Culbertson, and Scobey) and western half (Opheim, Fort Peck, Glasgow, and Wolf Point). The roster for the Legionnaires included Keith Sell, Clayton Swenson, Tom Hayes, Cliff Hagfeldt, Leland Bummer, Larry Wangrud, Terry McIntyre, Kenny Lekvold, Howard Farver, Kenny Tonjum, Don Hansen, and Robert Girard.

The Legionnaires started their season with an extra-inning win over Culbertson, 5-4. The Juniors had six hits, but it was the pitching of Tom Hayes and Keith Sell that won the game for Scobey, as the two pitched a combined two-hitter for Scobey.

Scobey went through the eastern division, losing only three games, but two of them were to Poplar, which eliminated them from the postseason. Poplar beat Scobey 10-8 in Scobey. Engles from Poplar yielded only two hits and struck out 15 Legionnaires while his teammates hammered out 10 hits. Keith Sell pitched well for Scobey, striking out nine, but Scobey only managed two hits off Engles, both by Lekvold.

As was the case a year earlier, the championship of the eastern division again came down to the final game of the regular season with Scobey against Poplar, but this year Poplar won a 1-0 pitcher's duel. Keith Sell pitched a four-hitter and gave up only one run, but was outdueled by Poplar's Engles, who pitched a two-hit shutout. Engles had almost beaten Scobey the previous year for the eastern division championship when he carried a 2-1 lead into the sixth, but Scobey got to him for nine runs. Not this year. Head Coach Babe Holyk of Scobey stated in the *Leader*, "We wuz robbed,"[30] referring to a close call at the plate where a Scobey runner was called out and Poplar won 1-0.

The Glasgow Juniors, coached by Bunky and Sully Sullivan, won the western division in District 4, then won their second consecutive District 4 title by thumping eastern division champion Poplar 24-6 in the championship. Glasgow then lost to Forsyth in a best-of-three playoff. Fairfield beat Laurel to win their first state Class B championship.

PLAINSMEN

THE PLAINSMEN PLAYED A "RAMBLER SCHEDULE" IN 1951 AS they did not join the Northeastern Montana League due to what happened in the postseason tournament a year earlier, when they won the western division but were seeded against the second-place team in their division, Bengough, in the 12-team postseason tournament in Redstone. However, the Plainsmen were "in favor of league play and had not closed the door on the possibility of getting back in the league next year."[31] The teams who did participate in the NeMont League that summer were Flaxville, Whitetail, Raymond, Redstone, Archer, and Wanso in the western division, and Plentywood, Bengough, Big Beaver, and Outlook in the eastern division.

The Plainsmen had another loaded roster, consisting mostly of former Scobey Legionnaires and some seasoned veterans. The roster included Jack Reiner, Indy Halvorson, Babe Holyk, Don Brasen, Don Christensen, Don Brayko, Bob Willard, Doug Bundren, Dallas Gaines, Harry Larson, Ken Larson, Clayton Swenson, Larry Wangrud, Al Schammel, Ken Lekvold, and Tony LaMotte.

The Plainsmen's rambler schedule included playing many teams in the NeMont League, but the games did not count in the standings for either team. Early in the season, the Plainsmen played a doubleheader in Whitetail against the Whitetail Oilers and the Flaxville Cardinals. They won the first game against Flaxville, 8-7. Chick French pitched for the Cardinals, and Don Brayko hurled for Scobey. Whitetail won the second game, 11-10, with Donald Unsworth on the mound for the Oilers. Don Brasen tossed for the Plainsmen.

One of the most dramatic games for the Plainsmen was a walk-off win over Wolf Point in Scobey. The game featured several tie scores and lead changes. Scobey led 3-0 in the fifth, but Wolf Point scored three in the sixth to tie the score. The Plainsmen scored three more in the seventh, but the Wolves tied it 6-6 in the eighth with three runs. Wolf Point scored two in the top of the ninth, but Plainsmen walked it off in the bottom of the ninth with three runs on three hits and an error to win 9-8. Don Brayko got the win for Scobey, while Loendorf took the loss for Wolf Point.

Almost matching the drama of the previous game against Wolf Point in Scobey, the Plainsmen traveled to Wolf Point the following weekend for a rematch, and the Plainsmen pulled off another one-run win, this time 5-4 in 10 innings. With one out in the bottom of the ninth, Wolf Point came from behind to tie the score, 4-4, and had the winning run on third, but the Plainsman strategy paid off. Rather than bring their infield in to peg the runner at home, Ken Larson intentionally walked the next hitter, and the middle infield stayed back to play for the double play. Larson then forced the next hitter to ground into an inning-ending double play to short, and the Plainsmen got off the field. With one out in the top of the tenth, Don Brayko doubled, and Jack Reiner followed with another double to drive home the tie-breaking run. The Plainsmen then held off the Wolves in their half of the 10th to escape with the 5-4 win.[32]

The Plainsmen won the Peerless Pirate Invitational Tournament by winning two games in Peerless. By winning first place, the Plainsmen won the $60 prize money. The tournament in Peerless featured some stellar pitching by all four teams, as the Plainsmen won their first game over Peerless 3-2 behind the pitching of Ken Larson, who gave up only one hit, while Witschen and Leo Zimmer pitched for Peerless and scattered six hits. Rockglen shut out Opheim 2-0, as Andy Stolen and Chote held Rockglen to six hits and two runs, but they couldn't score a run against Rockglen. In the consolation game between Opheim and Peerless, the game had to end in an 8-8 tie when time expired on the game. Leo Zimmer and Ackerman pitched for Peerless, while Eliason and Chote pitched for Opheim. The Plainsmen got another well-pitched game in the championship game as Don Christensen scattered five hits and pitched a shutout against Rockglen, leading the Plainsmen to a 3-0 victory. Jack Reiner caught all 18 innings of the two well-pitched games for Scobey. In addition to the Plainsmen's 3-2 win over Peerless in the tournament, Scobey beat the Pirates 18-5 and 8-1 to earn a season sweep.

A historical game was played in 1951 when the Plainsmen traveled to Opheim to play the "Opheim Radars," a baseball team consisting of United States Air Force Airmen from the Opheim Air Force Station, a radar detachment located about four miles west of Opheim.* The Radars consisted mostly of Airmen who were assigned to Opheim from Malmstrom Air Force Base in Great Falls. As if the historical significance of the game wasn't enough, the game turned out to be a thriller, as the Plainsmen trailed the Radars 9-0 headed into the eighth inning, but tied the game, then won it in extra innings! Andy Stolen, a Glentana native who was recruited by the airmen to pitch for them, handcuffed the Scobey Plainsmen with his nasty drop curve and sneaky fastball for the first seven innings. Andy Stolen apparently had the game all wrapped up until the Plainsmen exploded in the eighth inning with eight earned runs. They went on to score again in the ninth, to tie up the ball game, and in the 10th, pushed two more runs across to blitz the radar men, 11-9. The "three Dons"—Brasen, Brayko, and Christensen—pitched for Scobey, with Christensen holding the Radars hitless in the last five innings to get the win.[33]

On the return trip to Scobey, Scobey won a 15-7 decision in a game that saw five home runs hit. The Radars' big first baseman, a master sergeant, slammed out two homers. Scobey's Jack Reiner, who led the Plainsmen in hitting in 1951 with a .400 average, got two homers and a double, and Doug Bundren also homered. Ken Larson pitched the first six innings for Scobey, followed by Don Brayko, who "had the satisfaction of striking out the home-run hitting first baseman for the servicemen."[34]

The Plainsmen finished their rambler season with a 13-5 record, with their only losses coming to Poplar, Opheim (not the Radars), Bengough, Westby, and Glasgow (under the lights again in Glasgow). So far, the Plainsmen were 0 and 2 under the lights.

NORTHEASTERN MONTANA LEAGUE

MEANWHILE, THE NEMONT LEAGUE CONTINUED WITHOUT the Plainsmen, and the Flaxville Cardinals had a good season in 1951. Following their 8-7 loss to Scobey, they rattled off three consecutive wins by beating Redstone 12-11, Archer 22-2, and Wanso 26-4. Wanso, a small community south of Redstone, was a new team in the NeMont League that year. The Cards' pitching staff consisted of Ronnie Guy, Irv Jacobson, and Chick French. Bert French and Lional Demieux were the catchers. Infielders were Bob Mollerstuen, Roy Robinson, Donnie Tryan, with Chick French and Guy alternating at shortstop. The outfielders were Don Higgins, Herman Ruud, Bob Kurtz, and Eddie and Leo Legare. Bob Hardy was the team manager.

But it was Whitetail, not Flaxville, who owned the western division of the NeMont League in 1951. After knocking Flaxville out of the undefeated ranks by beating them 4-2, the Whitetail Oilers remained undefeated and led the western division of the NeMont League at the season's midpoint, and they finished tops in the standings at the end. Paul Berger, an ardent Whitetail baseball fan, said, "They really got spirit" when talking about the Whitetail team. Manager Oscar Grendal hoped to keep that spirit alive and win a championship in the tournament. Pitchers for Whitetail were Ron Fjeld (Ron pitched for Whitetail while he was teaching there), Don Unsworth, and Pete Wiley. The rest of the roster included Ron and Delmer Safty, Merle and Skeg Wiley, Emil Morvik, Jimmy Holle, John Scott, Fred Hall, and Alvin Edwards.

After the brouhaha in the postseason tournament in 1950—and the Plainsmen's subsequent withdrawal from the league in 1951—the NeMont League changed the postseason format in 1951: there would be separate postseason tournaments for the western and eastern divisions of the league, not a combined tournament, and the tournament would be double-elimination. The western division tournament—consisting of Redstone, Wanso, Archer, Raymond,

---

* The 779th Radar Squadron was originally activated on February 23, 1951. Radar equipment began arriving in January 1952 and the installation effort began. On March 14, 1952, the first Search Radar became operational, and radar operations personnel maintained a daily average of 12 operational aircraft tracks during the first month of operation. The Opheim Air Force Station remained operational until Opheim AFS ceased operations on June 1, 1979, as part of the inactivation of Aerospace Defense Command. The 779th Radar Squadron (SAGE) was inactivated on September 29, 1979. (Air Force Historical Research Agency. U.S. Air Force. Maxwell AFB, Alabama.)

Flaxville, and Whitetail—was originally scheduled to be hosted by Redstone the third week in September, but a late harvest postponed the tournament twice, pushing the tournament to the middle of October. Ada Nash of Redstone wrote, "It seems that the late harvest has put a halt to our little 'series' here, for it has twice been postponed. We may still get it in, though, if it doesn't snow too soon."[35]

But the harvest—and tournament—beat the snow, and a western division championship of the NeMont League was crowned in mid-October in Redstone.

And what an exciting tournament it was.

After six games were played in the tournament, Wanso and Archer were eliminated, and four teams were left standing, setting up one semifinal between Flaxville and Raymond and the other between Whitetail and Redstone. Raymond beat Flaxville 12-1 in the first semifinal. In the other semifinal game, Whitetail defeated Redstone in a tight pitcher's duel 1-0. Jesse Bedwell pitched for Redstone, struck out eight men, and allowed only two hits, both triples by Barkovick. Ron Fjeld, Whitetail pitcher, struck out 10 and allowed only one hit, a single by Nash in the second inning. Whitetail got their only run in the third inning. Bedwell and Nash were the battery for Redstone; Fjeld and Skeg Wiley for Whitetail.

In the championship game between Raymond and Whitetail, Raymond jumped on Whitetail pitcher Ron Fjeld—pitching his third game of the tournament—for four runs in the first inning, but Whitetail countered with three runs in the bottom of the first. Raymond scored one run in the third, but Whitetail scored two in their half to tie the score at 5-5 as it started to get dark. Raymond went scoreless in the fourth, and Whitetail scored two runs to take a 7-5 lead after four. It looked bad for Raymond as it was getting darker by the minute, but in the top of the fifth, Raymond came back to score three runs to take a one-run lead into the bottom of the fifth, which would be the last at-bat for Whitetail as it was getting dark. With two out in the bottom of the fifth, Fjeld got to third base, but Symes struck Potter out to win the game 8-7. Due to the darkness, it was almost impossible for the fans to see the ball in play. Symes was pitching his fourth game in two days, and Fjeld his third for Whitetail, with Skeg Wiley catching every inning.[36]

So, as the October sun set on the longest baseball season in Daniels County history, Whitetail was denied its first NeMont League championship, but it was a fine season for the Oilers, winning the regular season standings and coming within ninety feet of tying for the championship.

Finally, I will hand the pen to Ada Nash of Redstone to proudly write about the exciting tournament for the hometown Redstone nine in mid-October 1951. It is a fine example of small-town pride in rural America and how baseball was woven into the fabric of the small communities.

Redstone[37]

We finally had the baseball tournament this weekend and was lucky enough to have two fair days. Sunday, it threatened to rain, but it was nothing serious, and the game went on. It had twice been postponed because of harvest.

One sight which is always inspiring to see during the tournament is the American flag proudly waving on top of the Petty Hill.

I'd just like to do a little bragging about our team here. For we all feel as though our team did very well. Each of the three pitchers, Sonny Jensen, Shorty Timmerman and Jesse Bedwell, allowed only two hits apiece. In the three games that our team played, the opposing teams picked up only one score. That was in the game with Whitetail when they won 1-0. In that game, Willard Nash made the only hit for Redstone.

The Parent-Teachers Club women were at it again at their stand, selling those luscious barbecued hamburgers, plain hamburgers, hot dogs, hot coffee, and pop throughout the day. That food really tasted good and helped to warm people up, for it was chilly most of the time. Not that we needed warming up at some of the games. Talk about excitement!

It was at it's peak in the last game, and many times, you couldn't hear the loudspeaker at all. Our little Redstone cheering section was in full voice again as you have probably heard.

The crowd wasn't as big as last year, but there weren't as many teams taking part this year, and then, too, the tournament was called on short notice. Considering all that, the crowd was pretty big.

Raymond went home feeling tired but very good. Our men are so tired and stiff that they can hardly move Monday. They hadn't played a game since early this fall so they were really out of practice.

There were several injuries received by our players, but it appears that they weren't too serious—leastwise no bones broken. Dut Loucks carries his left arm very carefully after being hit in the elbow, and Phil Loucks has a couple of mighty sore fingers, but apparently, they aren't broken as was first thought. Willard Nash got by lucky this time for he's usually getting his fingers banged up at every game. Jesse Bedwell's knee behaved O. K. this time too.

EXTRA INNINGS

WHITETAIL FAN PAUL BERGER'S COMMENT THAT "THEY REALLY got spirit" when describing the Oilers certainly applied to catcher Skeg Wiley. Whitetail pitcher Ron Fjeld recalls several "spirited" incidents with his fiery batterymate. Ron said, "In one game, Skeg threw down his catcher's mitt and caught my fastball bare-handed and said, 'Come on, you can throw harder than that!' Afterwards, he said he had never hurt so bad, and it left a picture of a seam on his hand."

The Big Muddy League (BML), another town-team league in northeastern Montana, was formed in 1951. The newly formed league was made up of teams that previously competed in the Montana-Dakota League, but the league folded when the North Dakota teams dropped out. In its first year, the Big Muddy League consisted of Medicine Lake, Reserve, Froid, Culbertson, and Dagmar, who played a 20-game schedule.

The 1951 baseball season was the longest in Daniels County history. The Scholars played the first game of the season against Outlook on May 2, and the last game of the season was the NeMont League championship played on October 14, so the season lasted almost five and a half months. Game Six of the 1951 World Series between the New York Yankees and New York Giants was played on October 10, so the NeMont League outlasted MLB in 1951, thanks to the late harvest.

One of the highlights of the Legionnaires and Plainsmen seasons in 1951 was that Scobey fans could watch both teams play at doubleheaders at home, where each team would play one game. This happened several times during the season, including on Memorial Day.

Following his baseball career in Scobey, Don Christensen played college football and baseball for the Carroll College Fighting Saints in Helena. He played baseball at Carroll with Bunky Sullivan from Glasgow, another northeastern Montana baseball player and coach of the Glasgow Junior Legion team.

1952

Glasgow Wins Its Third Consecutive Junior Legion District Title

THE NORTHEASTERN DISTRICT OF JUNIOR LEGION WAS again divided into two divisions, east and west. Babe Holyk managed the Legionnaires, and Keith Whipple managed the Plainsmen, who played a rambler schedule against the following teams: Plentywood, Opheim, Peerless, Plentywood, Rockglen, Bengough, Wolf Point, Ogema, and Assiniboia. Scobey also fielded a high school baseball team, but there is only a record of them playing one game against Outlook.

LEGIONNAIRES

THE 1952 LEGIONNAIRES CONSISTED OF LELAND BUMMER, Keith Sell, Mouse Girard, Ordean Wangrud, Dave Anders, Don Hansen, Richard Leibrand, Terry McIntyre, Ken Tonjum, Cliff "Finley" Hagfeldt, Richard Audet, Eddie Brooks, and Pete Hagfeldt. Bobby Roland was the mascot.

1952 Scobey Legionnaires. Standing: Leland Bummer, Keith Sell, Mouse Girard, Ordean Wangrud, Dave Anders, Don Hansen, Richard Leibrand, Mgr. Babe Holyk. Kneeling: Terry McIntyre, Ken Tonjum, Finley Hagfeldt, Richard Audet, Eddie Brooks, Pete Hagfeldt. Bobby Roland, mascot, in white sweater in the immediate foreground. *Leader.*

The highlight of the regular season was a game against Culbertson at Culbertson. The Legionnaires won 50-4 in seven innings, which broke the previous record for runs scored by a Scobey Legion team set in 1946 against Opheim when the Legionnaires beat Opheim 47-2. Pete Hagfeldt, Terry McIntyre, Ordean Wangrud, and Donny Hansen all hit home runs for Scobey, and Keith Sell pitched six innings of one-hit ball. Cliff Hagfeldt pitched the seventh, in what was decidedly not a save opportunity.

Scobey won the Legion eastern division, and Glasgow won the western division. The district championship game was played at Bob Cross Memorial Park in Glasgow, with Glasgow prevailing in a 10-0 shutout. Kenny O'Brien from Saco pitched a one-hitter for Glasgow. This was Glasgow's third consecutive district championship under Bunky and Sully Sullivan, and the fifth consecutive title for Valley County. Two years earlier, Glasgow also shut out Scobey for the championship, 8-0.

Glasgow then went on to sweep two best-of-three series against Forsyth (8-7 and 7-1) and Project (9-1 and 6-0). Glasgow's pitching was dominant in both series, with Kenny O'Brien pitching a no-hitter in the 6-0 Project game. Glasgow then faced Fairfield for the State B championship, with Fairfield sweeping the best-of-three series for the state championship, 4-3 and 10-3. Glasgow has one other second-place finish at State (2012), where the Reds, after winning four straight games to go undefeated, lost two consecutive games to Mission Valley for the championship. Glasgow is still looking for its first state Legion baseball championship.

PLAINSMEN

The Plainsmen did not rejoin the NeMont League and played a sparse 13-game "rambler" schedule in 1952, winning roughly half their games. The roster included pitchers Ken Horn, Ken Larson, Rip Roland, Don Brayko, and Gordon "Dike" Vanderpan; catchers Jack Reiner and Ken Lekvold; infielders Rip Roland, Dallas Gaines, George Perkins, Larry Wangrud, Harry Larson, Gene Martin and Babe Holyk; and outfielders Bob Willard, Tony LaMotte, Ray Trower, Warren Wilson, Dallas Gaines and Harold Shortle.

NORTHEASTERN MONTANA LEAGUE

The Northeastern Montana League had seven teams in 1952: Whitetail, Flaxville, Outlook, Mineral Bench, Big Beaver, Buffalo Gap, and Raymond. Outlook, led by pitcher Roald Selvig, dominated the league in 1952, going undefeated in the regular season and sweeping the postseason tournament (hosted by Flaxville) to win its first NeMont League championship.

EASTERN MONTANA LEAGUE

The Eastern Montana League (EML) was formed in 1952, making it the third town-town league in the northeastern corner of the state. The inaugural season for the EML consisted of Plentywood, Wolf Point, Poplar, Sidney, Culbertson, and Savage. The Plentywood Cubs won the regular season and swept the postseason tournament. Outlook and Plentywood, the champions of the NeMont League and the EML, faced off against each other three times that year, with Outlook winning all three games. Known more for its basketball prowess, Outlook had the best baseball team in northeastern Montana in 1952.

EXTRA INNINGS

For the first time, the Plainsmen played the Legionnaires in an exhibition game in 1952. When Doc Norman came to Scobey and started coaching the Legionnaires in 1959, the Legion game against the Plainsmen in the early season was not considered an "exhibition" game to him—the games were competitive. Doc would pitch his best pitcher against the Plainsmen, which typically consisted mostly of his former players, to beat them.

There was a vote for batboy for the 1952 Plainsmen that was announced in the *Leader*. The ballot box was located at the Battleson garage. On the "ballot" were Kevin Sell and Bobby Roland. Keith Whipple, Plainsmen manager, told the *Leader* the batboy voting would last for about ten days, and only boys between the ages of 9 and 13 were eligible to vote. Kevin Sell beat Bobby Roland for the Plainsmen batboy vote, but Butch Wangrud received some write-in votes. Couldn't they just have two batboys?

The Scobey Plainsmen showed a group of three World Series films as a fundraiser at the Methodist Hall in Scobey. The films featured the 1946 World Series between the St. Louis Cardinals and the Boston Red Sox, and the 1948 and 49 series between the New York Yankees and the Brooklyn Dodgers. There was no charge for the viewing, but a collection was taken for the benefit of the Scobey Plainsmen.

1953

Whitetail wins the NeMont League championship and Fort Peck Wins the State Junior Legion

The Scobey Plainsmen were the only show in town during the summer of 1953, as Scobey did not field high school or Junior Legion teams. The Plainsmen, after two seasons not competing in a league, joined the Eastern Montana League with Outlook, Poplar, Plentywood, Brockton, Wolf Point, and Culbertson. Flaxville and Whitetail each fielded teams and competed in the Northeastern Montana League with Big Beaver, Buffalo Gap, Raymond, Mineral Bench, and Redstone. The Big Muddy League continued its second season with Froid, Antelope, Reserve, Medicine Lake, Wanso, Zahl, Dagmar, and Grenora, North Dakota. That's 22 small towns in northeastern Montana, southern Saskatchewan, and northwestern North Dakota playing in three different town-team baseball leagues in 1953.

JUNIOR LEGION

Fort Peck won the district championship 8-5 over Glasgow, ending Glasgow's streak of three consecutive district championships but extending Valley County's streak of six consecutive district championships. Fort Peck then went on to win a best-of-three playoff series against Baker and Columbus and the best-of-three series against Libby to win the State B championship, the first for northeastern Montana.

1953 Fort Peck Legion Team, State Class B champions. Back row, left to right: Coach Johnny Hahn, John Ramsbacher, Tom Burns, Art Masters, Bill Black, Udell Miller, Darrel Hueth, Jim Johnston, Dan Burns, Gus Lightfoot, Leon Squires, and Clayton Linebarger. Front row, left to right: Tom Graham, Kenny Neiskens, Roger Miller, Charles Ramsbacher, Marvin Pischel, and Chuckie Johnston.

PLAINSMEN

As there was no Junior Legion team in 1953, some of the players eligible to play Junior Legion, like 15-year-old pitcher Keith Sell, played for the Plainsmen. The Plainsmen roster included Ken Lekvold, Howard Farver, Dallas Gaines, Eddie Brooks, Chet Brooks, Jack Reiner, Ordean Wangrud, Ken Tonjum, Keith Sell, Babe Holyk, Dave Anders, Cliff Hagfeldt, Ken Larson, Pete Kowcun, Fred Walker, Gene Dawson, and Pete Hagfeldt.

In their first game in the EML, the Plainsmen were fittingly pitted against their old rival, the Plentywood Cubs, on Riba Field in Plentywood. Scobey, "composed chiefly of inexperienced players," squeezed out a 4-3 victory, as 15-year-old Keith Sell pitched a complete game for the Plainsmen, scattering six hits to get the win. Jack Reiner of Scobey had two of Scobey's four hits against Plentywood's tough pitcher, Bob Painter.

Scobey's inexperience was exposed in their second game in the EML when the Wolf Point Wolves "chewed up the Plainsmen" 17-9. Keith Sell started and was relieved by Ken Larson after the Wolves shelled him, as Wolf Point pounded 19 hits in the game. An interesting note in the box score for Wolf Point was a Puckett (most likely Reese) playing center field. But Keith got his revenge on the Wolves later in the season, when he pitched the Plainsmen to a 6-2 win in Wolf Point.

The Plainsmen handed the ball to young Sell a lot that summer. After getting roughed up by Wolf Point, he pitched a one-hitter against Bengough to lead the Plainsmen to a 5-3 win. In their next game against Brockton, the 15-year-old pitched a four-hit shutout to lead the Plainsmen to an 8-0 victory. In the Brockton game, catcher Jack Reiner hit a home run, described by the *Leader* as "a drive which cleared the left field fence and stirred up the bullfrogs in the reeds over by the tracks to a course of applause."[38]

But Keith Sell wasn't the only pitcher the Plainsmen had that summer. Ken Larson was a great pitcher, and Gene Dawson, summer recreational director and athletic director at Scobey schools, pitched a three-hitter to lead the

Plainsmen to a 7-0 victory over defending NeMont League champion Outlook, who was playing in the EML this year. Dawson, "a big, congenial Missourian," was particularly anxious that mention of this game appear in the paper so he could send a clipping to his father-in-law, a pitcher for 10 years (1920-30) for the St. Louis Browns. Gene said, "That guy talks baseball all the time, and this is the first time I've played baseball. Softball was my game before, and I want to show my father-in-law that I can pitch a good one, too."[39]

The Plainsmen finished third in the six-team EML that summer. Wolf Point won it, and Plentywood finished second. Keith Sell won several games as a pitcher, including the one-hitter.

NORTHEASTERN MONTANA LEAGUE

Whitetail finished first in the standings in the NeMont League, winning the league on the final game of the regular season by edging second-place Mineral Bench 4-3. The winning battery for Whitetail was Pete and Skeg Wiley. But the excitement of Whitetail's one-run win over Mineral Bench in the regular season finale was no match for the drama that was to follow in the postseason tournament, hosted this year by league-champion Whitetail.

In perhaps the most dramatic finish to a baseball season in the history of northeastern Montana baseball, Whitetail came from behind with a six-run rally in the bottom of the seventh inning to defeat Mineral Bench 11-10 for the Northeastern Montana Baseball League championship. Going into the bottom of the seventh, Norgaard, the Mineral Bench pitcher, tired and gave up a series of hits. With four runs in, two out, and the bases loaded, Tony Volosick, Whitetail's shortstop, singled sharply to left field, scoring Pete Wiley and Ron Fjeld with the winning runs.

Safty led Whitetail's 14-hit attack with three hits, while Volosick, Borkovick, and Skeg Wiley contributed two hits each. For the losing Mineral Bench nine, Don Tryan and Norgaard had two hits each. Fjeld relieved Pete Wiley on the mound for Whitetail and pitched shutout ball for the last three innings to get the win, as well as scoring the winning run on Volosick's two-out single to left. Ron recalls scoring the winning run. "I got caught in a hot box between third and home and decided to go back to third and when I slid in I looked up and I saw the ball fly over the third baseman so I headed home again, so pooped out by then that I crawled as fast as I could and made it safely home."

The town of Whitetail played a baseball game between two teams from that town on Christmas Day in 1928, but baseball Christmas came early for Whitetail in 1953, in the form of its first NeMont League championship. Two years earlier in Redstone, as the chilly mid-October sun set on a late harvest, Whitetail was denied its first NeMont League tournament championship when Ron Fjeld was stranded on third base with Whitetail trailing Raymond 8-7, but Potter struck out to end the game. But not this year. This was Whitetail's year, as Ron Fjeld crawled safely home with the winning run.

EXTRA INNINGS

Doc Norman's Junior Legion coaching career began in Columbus, Montana, in 1951, where he started his first medical practice and helped establish a Legion baseball program with Gene Brown. In 1953, Gene Brown and Doc's Columbus team hosted Fort Peck on the new Gates Field for the eastern division championship. Fort Peck won the best-of-three series. Columbus would have hosted the state championship on Gates Field the following week if Columbus had won. In her interview, Ann (Norman) Lee recalls Doc helping build Gates Field with Gene Brown. Ann said, "My first memory of baseball I was four or five, probably five, and we lived in Columbus, and my dad and his best friend, Gene Brown, who was a highway patrolman, built the baseball fields in Columbus. I remember going out there and watching Dad on this front loader, or whatever it was, excavating this field, and I think the kids still play on that field, but it's probably been embellished a great deal."

I asked Ann if she ever remembered playing baseball as a little girl. She said, "I sure do. Mike would pitch to me, but I was littler by two years, and he threw hard. I had a glove, but it was probably not a very good one, and it hurt my hand. I started crying one time and he said, 'You cry, and I won't *ever* let you play with me again,' so I didn't cry, and I just kept catchin'." (Ann learned at an early age that there was "no crying in baseball.")*

During those years in Columbus, when Doc helped coach the Legion team, Ann's older brother Mike was the batboy for the Legion team. I asked Mike if he recalled his first baseball memory in Columbus. He said, "Yeah, I do. I was seven or eight years old, but my dad wanted me to . . . he thought I would be a good catcher [Doc was a catcher when he played], so he had one of the high school kids come throw pitches at me. I wanna say the guy's name was Alex Lofing, and he was in high school, and I was like in second or third grade. Dad said, 'Just see, you just catch the ball, no problem.' All I got was a sore hand out of that." (Alex Lofing lettered in football, basketball, and track and field—he threw the javelin and discus—at Columbus High School and was the ace pitcher on the Junior Legion team that played for the eastern division championship in 1953

---

* Quote from Manager Jimmy Dugan, played by Tom Hanks in *A League of Their Own*, directed by Penny Marshall, Columbia Pictures, 1992.

and 1954.) So, Doc had the biggest stud at Columbus High School and the best pitcher on the Junior Legion team come and fire fastballs at his son to teach him how to catch at seven years old. That was Doc: at six and eight years old, Ann got a sore hand catching older brother Mike, and Mike got a sore hand catching Alex Lofing.

In an early indication of Doc's commitment to youth sports and bighearted generosity, he, along with Coach Gene Brown, took 26 boys from the Columbus Peewee, Little League, and Junior Legion baseball teams on a five-day camping and fishing trip in the Beartooth Mountains following the baseball season. The time was coming (1959) when Doc's knowledge of baseball and his commitment and generosity would be coming to Scobey, and the Scobey Junior Legion baseball team would be the beneficiary of his largesse, with their fortunes changing forever.

The Korean War had been ongoing since 1950, and in 1953, Vern Veis, former Legionnaire and Plainsmen pitcher, was a corporal stationed with Company C, 369th Engineer Amphibious Support Regiment (EASR), Fort Worden, Washington. He was playing baseball for the Fort Worden army team. He wrote home to his parents, Mr. and Mrs. Chris Veis, that he had played with Doug Hansen, a second baseman, who was with the Cleveland Indians in 1951 before entering the service and was back playing in the Indians organization. The highlight for Vern playing baseball in the army came when Fort Worden played Fort Lewis in 1952. He relieved the starting pitcher in the fifth inning and, for the rest of the game, pitched no-hit, no-run ball. Pitching against him was Kenny Lehman, who later that year saw action as a relief pitcher for Brooklyn in the World Series. Fort Worden lost that game, 4-3, to Fort Lewis, but Vern said, "It felt good to be in there against that kind of mound opposition."[40]

The Butte Miners won their third State Class A Junior Legion title in 1953. It would not be until 2022, when Jim LeProwse, former Scobey Blue (1983–85), led the Miners back to another state title.

1954

Whitetail Repeats as NeMont League Champs and Plentywood Wins Junior Legion State

> " *Whitetail was a deserted town Saturday and Sunday when most of the people attended the baseball tournament held in Flaxville. Whitetail took first place.*
>
> —Plentywood Herald, *August 12, 1954* "

THE SCOBEY PLAINSMEN, MANAGED BY FRED WALKER, played in the eight-team Eastern Montana League, consisting of Opheim, Opheim Radars, Wolf Point, Plentywood, Culbertson, Poplar, and Outlook. The Northeastern Montana League had Flaxville, Whitetail, Raymond, Redstone, Big Beaver, Mineral Bench, and Buffalo Gap. Scobey and Flaxville did not field high school or Junior Legion teams in 1954, but Peerless had a high school team in the spring of 1954 that morphed into a Legion team that summer. Jim Hawbaker from Peerless remembers how Peerless's first Junior Legion team came about. He said, "Pre-Legion baseball was the spring of 1954 when a teacher/coach, Andy Anderson, started a high school team in Peerless and convinced the local Legion post to buy the uniforms. The high school program lasted only one year but morphed into the Legion program. I was a member of that team."

My cousin, Gordon "Gordie" Puckett, and Robert "Bobby" Machart, pictured here in Uncle Ed Puckett's backyard in Peerless, were original players on that first Peerless Junior Legion team. They were young; Gordon was 14 and Bobby turned 13 that summer, but with the maximum Junior Legion age of 17 and no Babe Ruth teams at the time, Junior Legion was the only option after Little League in the early 1950s.

Gordie Puckett (left) and Bobby Machart (right), 1954 Peerless Junior Legion Team. *Family photo.*

PLAINSMEN

THE 1954 SCOBEY PLAINSMEN WERE SPONSORED BY THE Scobey Lions Club. Their roster included Vern Veis, Keith Sell, Indy Halvorson, Don Brasen, Don Christensen, Gene Dawson, Jack Reiner, Howard Farver, Cliff Hagfeldt, Clay Gilchrist, Ken Tonjum, Ordean Wangrud, Eddie Brooks, and Babe Holyk.

The Plainsmen got off to a great start in league play, as Vern Veis pitched a no-hit shutout and struck out 18 to lead Scobey to a 10-0 win over Mineral Bench. Vern's no-hitter was the first for the Plainsmen, and the first of three no-hitters Vern would pitch for the Plainsmen in his career, with Jack Reiner calling the signals in each of them. Keith Sell had three hits to lead Scobey's hit parade, Jack Reiner had two, and Clay Gilchrist walloped a home run.

In a 4-3 loss to Ogema, Keith Sell took a tough loss on the mound, as he scattered six hits and struck out 15 Ogema batters; he also got two hits, leading his team in that department for the game. In this game, Cliff Hagfeldt was removed for unsportsmanlike use of his spikes. A team apology was given to the visiting Canadians following the game.

Scobey had great matchups with the Opheim Radars again in 1954, losing in 11 innings in Opheim despite a complete-game effort by Don Brasen on the mound for Scobey, who struck out 18 and only gave up three runs. Opheim walked it off in the bottom of the 11th after a single, an error on a sacrifice bunt, followed by another single to drive home the winning run. In the return game in Scobey, Opheim blew the Plainsmen out 8-1. Manager Fred Walker had some colorful comments about Scobey's dismal performance in the game. Walker paraphrased the late Mike Jacobs, prize-fight promoter who once said in disgust over a situation, "I should have stood in bed." Then he added, "We threw the ball all over, then kicked it for a while, but we did not hurt the ball much with our bats."[41]

But the worst drubbing the Plainsmen took that summer came against Outlook, not the Opheim Radars. In front of the hometown faithful in Scobey, the Plainsmen managed only one hit—a single by Indy Halvorson in the third inning—against pitcher Roald Selvig of Outlook and took the blank end of a 10-0 score. Selvig "had the Plainsmen baffled" throughout the game with his one-hitter, but apparently the Plainsmen had engaged in some heavy drinking the night before and were not quite up to snuff. The *Leader* wrote, "Manager Walker did not need to call in the services of a psychiatrist to figure this one out. 'Just a little too much extracurricular activity during the excitement of the festive weekend,' he commented morosely as the black raven of defeat rested on his left shoulder. But being an ol' army man, with the typical ground-pounder's philosophy that gives new promise to each succeeding day, he added, 'The boys can play mighty nice ball when they feel up to it. With Plentywood visiting this Sunday, perhaps we'll handle the situation better.'"[42] To be fair, Vern Veis pitched well for Scobey into the ninth inning, as the score was only 3-0 in the ninth when Outlook exploded for seven runs to make the game a rout. Keith Sell was missing from this game, as the talented youngster had been working out that week with the Williston Greasers in the Mon-Dak League. Sell would be back for mound duty against Plentywood later in the week. (Scobey lost that game 7-6 when Plentywood scored two runs in the bottom of the eighth. Sell took the loss.)

In other regular season highlights for the Plainsmen, Howard Farver, playing in his second year for the town team, hit his first home run of the season in an 18-13 slugfest win over Circle. Howard also pitched six innings in a game earlier in the season against the Opheim Radars, as Fred Walker was developing a fourth pitcher to add to his three-man starting staff of Vern Veis, Keith Sell, and Don Brasen.

The Plainsmen played .500 ball during the regular season, but there was no postseason tournament for the EML. Outlook dominated the league and won it going away.

NORTHEASTERN MONTANA LEAGUE

IT WAS WHITETAIL'S YEAR AGAIN IN THE NEMONT LEAGUE, although Raymond won the NeMont League regular season standings, with Whitetail second and Flaxville third. Whitetail's season started auspiciously with Ron Fjeld pitching a shutout against Coronach to lead the Oilers to an 8-0 win, and it ended with him on the mound in the postseason tournament, but it was quite a story about how Ron ended the season pitching for Whitetail.

Flaxville hosted the season-ending tournament. Whitetail was looking to repeat as NeMont League Tournament champions, and the Oiler faithful traveled to Flaxville to watch the Whitetail nine get it done. "Whitetail was a deserted town Saturday and Sunday when most of the people attended the baseball tournament held in Flaxville."[43]

And the Whitetail nine got it done, as the Oilers repeated as NeMont League tournament champions with a 12-7 win over Raymond, despite three Wileys—Jesse, Skeg, Merle—getting tossed out of the game by home plate umpire Jim Worthington from Plentywood. The fireworks started in the fourth inning when Worthington called catcher Skeg Wiley for attempting to delay the game to wait for a pitcher and using "vulgar language" to him. Ron Fjeld, who was the pitcher Skeg was trying to delay the game for in the fourth inning, later showed up at the field for the game. Then, in the sixth inning, Skeg's brother Merle was ejected by Worthington after Merle vulgarly protested a call made by Worthington, leaving Whitetail with only eight players. Raymond could have forced Whitetail to forfeit the game when they were down to eight players, but Raymond, in a sportsmanship gesture, allowed the Whitetail "eight" to utilize the services of an ineligible player to finish the game and go on to win the tournament.[44]

Ron Fjeld remembers that crazy day in Flaxville. "The Wileys called me that morning and said there was a game, and I was in Minot when they called. I was going to college, but on weekends I usually went home to play. I was late getting there that day, and they were waiting for me. The old man Jesse got kicked out first, then Skeg, and then Merle. I had to have a uniform to play, so I put on Skeg's uniform pants that were size 38, and I wore a size 32. Someone gave me some clothesline rope to cinch it up. It was hard playing and pitching with that rope, but we won the game."

The 1954 NeMont League championship roster for Whitetail included Ronnie Fjeld, pitcher; Skeg Wiley, catcher; Merle Wiley, first base; Selmer Safty, second base; Harry Larson, shortstop; Irv Prough, third base; Irv Brokevic, left field; Pete Wiley, center field; Ronny Safty, right field; and Johnny Scott and Elmer "Junior" Cole. Jesse Wiley was the manager, and Gerry Owen was instrumental in keeping the Whitetail baseball field in good condition.

JUNIOR LEGION

DISTRICT 4 JUNIOR AMERICAN LEGION TEAMS INCLUDED Glasgow, Opheim, defending champion Fort Peck, Wolf Point, Poplar, Plentywood, and Peerless.

Plentywood, coached by Jack McGowan, dominated the regular season and won the District 4 championship. Plentywood was led by right-handed pitcher Darrell Benson from Outlook. During the regular season, Benson pitched a perfect game against Poplar, striking out 20 of the 21 batters he faced. Peerless fared a little better against Benson, managing one hit, and Benson only struck out 17 Panthers on Riba Field in Plentywood. Peerless threatened to score in the second inning, when they loaded the bases on two walks and a single with none out but were stopped there with a strikeout, a force at the plate, and another strikeout. Benson shut the door from then on and pitched a shutout to lead Plentywood to a 21-0 win. In Peerless's other matchup with state-champion Plentywood, the Sheridan County nine got the best of the Panthers again, this time by a score of 15-1. Plentywood's Craig Christensen had his no-hitter broken up on a single by Lonnie Sterrett of Peerless with two out in the bottom of the sixth. After failing to score in the sixth, Peerless came back in the seventh when Baldry doubled and scored their lone tally when Jim Hawbaker singled. Christensen struck out twelve while walking two and allowed one run on three hits. Leo Zimmer was on the mound for the home Peerless team and struck out seven.

After winning the District 4 championship, Plentywood beat Wibaux 4-1 and 14-5 in the first inter-district playoff best-of-three series, then they played Columbus, coached by Doc Norman and Gene Brown, for the eastern division championship on Gates Field in Columbus. Plentywood beat Columbus 10-5 and 9-8 to win in a best-of-three series to make it to the championship series against Conrad, where Plentywood won its first—and only—State B baseball championship by beating Conrad in the best-of-three championship series in Conrad. Plentywood won the first game 8-6, lost the second game 7-3, then won game three 9-4 behind the four-hit, 14-strikeout performance by winning pitcher Darrell Benson, who had also won game one of the series. Plentywood rode the strong arm of big right-hander Benson from Outlook throughout their state championship run, as he was the winning pitcher in five of their six wins in the postseason and got the save in the other.

As was always the case in Junior Legion ball in those years, the State B champion received an automatic bid as the fourth seed in the four-team State A Tournament. Plentywood traveled to Anaconda to face the host, the Anaconda Athletics, in the first game. And they came very close to beating Anaconda, as they were leading 6-2 with two outs in the bottom of the ninth inning. Darrell Benson had handcuffed the Anaconda hitters for eight and two-thirds innings, allowing only two runs. But in one of the greatest comebacks in Montana Junior Legion Baseball history, Anaconda scored five runs with two outs in the ninth to walk

1954 Plentywood Legion Team, State Class B Champions. Kneeling (L-R): Truman Stageberg, Jr., Plentywood (of); Larry Ferguson, Westby (ss); Gordon Klofstad, Plentywood (batboy): Gary Knudsvig Plentywood (1b), and Dick McNulty, Plentywood (of). Second row standing (L-R): Bucky Wirtzberger, Westby (2b): Harvey Anderson, Plentywood (3b); Lyle Ekness, Westby (c): Don Benson, Outlook (if & of), and Les Anderson, Plentywood, (c and of). Top row: Truman Stageberg, Sr. Plentywood (mgr and American Legion representative): Ogden Hanson, Westby (of); Craig Christensen, Plentywood (p): David Ferguson, Westby (of); Darrell Benson, Outlook (p); Ron Heppner, Plentywood (of), and Jack McGowan, Plentywood recreation director and Jr. Legion coach and Westby high school athletic coach. *Plentywood Herald.*

off with a 7-6 win at Washoe Park in Anaconda. Plentywood was then ousted 8-6 by the Helena Senators in their second game. The Billings Royals, coached by Ed Bayne, won their first of 14 consecutive State Class A Legion titles in 1954 in Anaconda. Not even the Yankees can boast that many consecutive World Series championships.

EXTRA INNINGS

THERE WERE EIGHT WILEY BROTHERS FROM WHITETAIL, SONS of Jesse Lee Wiley, and they were uncles to Lee Cook from Flaxville, who played first base for the Scobey Legionnaires from 1972 to 1974. Lee remembers hearing the story about his grandpa Jesse Wiley and his uncles Skeg and Pete delaying the game for Ron Fjeld that day so he could pitch, but he also remembers other baseball stories told by the Wileys. Lee said, "The Wiley family used to get together with the Warken family from the Buffalo Gap and Big Beaver, Saskatchewan, area and play friendly baseball games in the summer. The Warken family had 27 kids, and there were 13 Wileys. It was a big social event between the two families, and the girls would sometimes get on the field and play baseball too." Lee added, "Every place had their little team. That's how big baseball was back in the 1950s." The friendly baseball games between the Warken and Wiley families led to a wedding, as Dallas Wiley married Rita Warken in 1959.

Lee told me another zany story about his uncle Skeg Wiley. Skeg taught his nephew Jesse Cook, Lee's younger brother, that if he ever needed to pee when he was outside on the prairie to find a gopher hole, lie down on top of it, unzip his pants, and pee inside the gopher hole. One day at a Little League baseball game, Jesse was playing center field, and suddenly everyone saw Jesse lying down on the ground in center field in the middle of the game. "Hey, what's that center fielder doing out there?" someone asked. Jesse was just doing what his uncle taught him to do when he had to pee on the ballfield. Lee added, "Our mom and dad, Calvin and Jean (Wiley) Cook, along with the rest of the amused or mortified Little League game crowd, were the beneficiaries of the event."

Several people in Scobey remember how colorful Skeg Wiley could be with his speech. Don Paulson (Scobey Legionnaires 1963–65), worked for Skeg and said, "I could see where foul language could get Skeg in a bit of hot water." John Murphy (Legionnaires 1962–64) added, "He could string them out, but would get very embarrassed if a woman or preacher accidentally heard him." Ron Fjeld, Skeg's teammate for several years in Whitetail, said, "Skeg may have had a fetish for using foul language, but he had a heart of gold. Floyd "Skeg" Wiley was very much a family man. He raised two wonderful daughters and had two sons who had Muscular Dystrophy. He devoted his life to them. His one son, Huck, was a baseball fan but was confined to a wheelchair. Skeg saw to it that Huck got to some Major League games and to meet some of the players. When I was teaching in Whitetail, we taught some of the kids Ham radio, and Huck was one of them. There is a lot more to Skeg than meets the eye!"

Whitetail pitcher Ron Fjeld was also playing baseball in North Dakota that summer. He pitched warm-up for the Minot Mallards in the Man-Dak League. The Mallards were managed by player-coach Zoonie McLean, who was coaching at Plentywood High School at the time. Ron was scouted by the Cleveland Indians organization and was offered a contract, but he turned it down. In 1951, he pitched baseball in Seattle until he went into the Air Force.

Plainsmen manager Fred Walker, "Scobey's Casey Stengel,"[45] had a private flying license and flew to Omega, Saskatchewan, to meet with their manager to arrange a game. The *Leader* wrote that Walker "is one manager who can keep his bearings if he gets up in the air. On rough decisions from an umpire, the license might come in handy."[46]

In 1954, the first Little League Baseball team in Peerless was organized by my dad. Dad and my Uncle Ed Puckett coached the Peerless Little League teams from 1954 to

1958. Some of the members of the team those five years were Reese Puckett Jr., Harland and Levi Hawbaker, two girls, Marcia Hawbaker and Gerri Puckett, Dennis Gilchrist, Jim Dighans, Bill Puckett, Bruce Fladager and Dick Puckett. For the four years the league was active, the team compiled a record of 43 wins and 6 losses.[47]

My sister Dianne remembers tagging along with Bill and Reese while Reese practiced pitching. She said, "They made me be a fake batter. I was very little and terrified 'cuz Reese had a wicked fast ball. (I had no helmet, of course.) But I felt it was a very important job and proud to be included!"

Girls were not allowed to play Little League Baseball in the 1950s, so Marcia Hawbaker and Gerri Puckett would put their hair in ponytails and tuck it under their jerseys. One time at a game in Scobey, Marcia's ponytail came out of her jersey, and a Scobey player yelled, "Hey, look, they have a girl playing on their team!" My sister Dianne also got to play with the team with her hair up in a baseball cap. She said, "I didn't play much as I was a few years younger, but I remember playing once, so we had enough to field a team!" Those girls, Marcia and Geri, were part of the reason the 1954-58 teams were 43 and 6.

At the end of 1954, Doc Norman moved his family from Columbus to Missoula, where he started a new practice. He was slowly making his way to Scobey through Missoula. While in Missoula, he would pick up where he left off coaching Little League Baseball and Junior Legion Baseball in Columbus, as we shall see.

For the third consecutive year, Scobey was not able to field a Junior Legion team in 1955. The *Leader* stated that the motion was brought up at a meeting, but no one volunteered to handle the project. This was likely the low point for Junior Legion Baseball in Scobey. There was a high school team, and six of those high schoolers played for the Scobey Plainsmen, described by the *Leader* as a team of "six high schoolers plus three veterans." Peerless, coached by Buck Baldry, fielded a Legion team again in 1955.

1955

Whitetail Three-Peats as NeMont League Champions

SCHOLARS

Coach Gene Dawson's high school team had the following players: Keith Sell and Larry Schaefer as pitchers; Duane Knight and Gary Farver as catchers; Robert Girard and Peter Voight at first base; Moose Sheron, second; Larry Schaefer doubling at short; and Gary Davies at third. In the outfield: Richard Leibrand, Gary Shuman, Larry Brasen, Russell New, and Gordon Hillstrom.

There were only two high school games recorded in the *Leader* in 1955, written by Keith Sell, Scobey's ace pitcher. The Scobey Spartans first game of the year was a pitcher's duel between Keith Sell of Scobey and Dick Correll from Circle. With the score tied 0-0 late in the game, Circle scored two unearned runs on two successive Scobey errors and a walk to load the bases, followed by catcher's interference on Scobey catcher Duane Knight and another Scobey error, which left the final score 2-0.

Scobey lost a second game to Poplar, 12-2, as "Scobey's fielding was very poor and committed many errors and allowed many pop-ups to fall in for hits which should have been easy outs."[48] Meanwhile, Poplar pitcher Renz took a no-hitter into the sixth inning, but Robert Girard broke it up with a base hit.

JUNIOR LEGION

The District 4 Junior Legion league consisted of eight teams: Glasgow, Fort Peck, Culbertson, Wolf Point, Plentywood, Opheim, Poplar, and Peerless. In the only record of a Peerless game, Fort Peck beat Peerless 22-4 in Peerless. Plentywood, defending State B champions, repeated as district champions, then lost in a playoff to Wibaux to advance to the State playoffs. Libby won the State B championship.

PLAINSMEN

The Plainsmen were not affiliated with any league in 1955 and played an independent schedule. Their roster consisted of young high schoolers and some savvy veterans. The demographic of the roster with all the high schoolers was indicative of the Junior Legion age, capped at 17 years old, where high schoolers would play with the town team the summer of their junior or senior year in high school. The roster for the 1955 Scobey Plainsmen included Keith Sell, Gary Farver, Duane Knight, Robert Girard, Fred Walker, Indy Halvorson, Cliff Hagfeldt, Ordean Wangrud, Eddie Fossen, Don Brasen, Larry Schaefer, Richard Leibrand, McIntyre, and Gary Davies.

Scobey won their season-opener 15-14 in a slugfest over Wolf Point, with Keith Sell getting the win in relief of Gary Farver, who homered for Scobey. But the season's highlight for the Plainsmen was taking second place at the Coronach, Sask. Tournament. They won their first two games (10-2 over Big Beaver and 8-4 over Coronach) to make it to the championship against Bengough, but ran out of pitching and lost to Bengough 13-3. For taking second place, the Plainsmen received the second-place purse of $70. During the entire tourney, Indy Halvorson and Fred Walker played good ball, as did Robert Girard, but "Scobey's hustle and a will to win were really their greatest assets for the tournament."[49] Sell was the winning pitcher in the first two games, and a relief pitcher for the third game would have made the game a tougher one for Bengough.

In other games of note, the rivalry with Plentywood in 1955 saw the Cubs get the best of the Plainsmen, as Plentywood trounced the Plainsmen 9-0 on Riba Field in Plentywood. Powers from Plentywood pitched a two-hit shutout and struck out 12 Plainsmen. Don Brasen took the loss for Scobey. The Plainsmen also lost to the Crane Valley Orioles, a "top-notch Canadian team," 3-2 in Scobey. The game was a 0-0 pitcher's duel for the first six innings, but Crane Valley scored an unearned run in the top of the seventh to take a 1-0 lead. Scobey tied the score in with a run in the bottom of the seventh, but Crane Valley scored two in the top of the ninth, and Scobey could only counter with one run and came up short. Keith Sell went the distance for Scobey on the mound, pitching well against the strong Canadian team.

In notable wins, the Plainsmen beat Richland 6-5 as Keith Sell outdueled Zimmer, pitching for Richland. The Plainsmen finished their season by winning a tournament hosted by Richland, with Opheim, Ossette, Scobey, and Richland.

NORTHEASTERN MONTANA LEAGUE

Seven teams—Outlook, Flaxville, Whitetail, Redstone, Coronach, Buffalo Gap, and Big Beaver—competed in the NeMont League in 1955, as Outlook rejoined the league but Raymond left to join the Big Muddy League. Whitetail three-peated as NeMont League champions, creating the league's first dynasty. The league tournament was hosted in Flaxville again, "and both days were perfect baseball days, bright sun and very hot."[50] Whitetail beat Flaxville 12-8, Big Beaver 18-1, and Outlook 15-9 in the championship.

BIG MUDDY LEAGUE

The Big Muddy League was going strong in 1955, with Medicine Lake winning the tournament hosted over Labor Day weekend in Dagmar. Medicine Lake also won the regular-season standings. The league consisted of Raymond, Medicine Lake, Froid, Dagmar, Antelope, and Reserve.

EXTRA INNINGS

Andy Stolen pitched for the Opheim Radars that summer. He would later pitch for the Plainsmen teams of the late 1950s, including the 1958 and 1960 Montana state semipro championship teams, traveling to Wichita, Kansas, to play in the 1960 National Baseball Congress (NBC) World Series. But he came within one bad inning of making it to the NBC World Series in 1955, as the Opheim Radars narrowly lost the Montana state semipro championship game to the Great Falls AFB Jet Liners at Bob Cross Memorial Park in Glasgow. With the "underdog Skysweepers" leading 3-2 in the bottom of the eighth inning of the championship game and Andy pitching, "the roof fell in on Opheim."[51] Great Falls scored four runs on two singles, a triple, and two costly errors and went on to win the state championship 6-3. Andy would have to wait five years to make it to Wichita, but he did, playing for the Plainsmen. Andy is in the center row, far left in the picture.

Junior American Legion Baseball increased the age limit by four months for the 1955 season. Boys who did not reach their 18th birthday before September 1, 1955, were now allowed

Opheim AFB Radars, 1955 Montana State AAU Runners-up.
Back Row (L–R): W. D. Buchanan (official), Doug Weaver (2b), Jere Sheppard (lf), Bill Goosevski (p), and Harold Steele (mgr). Center: Andy Stolen (p), Ed Lawson (cf), Ralph Young (of), Jim Oliver (of), and Willie Werleu (of). Front: Scott Castle (c), Wilfred Morganthaler (rf), Pete Healy (3b), Bill Sylstine (ss), Earl Vinson (1b), and Virgil Webb (ss-of). *Glasgow Courier.*

to play. Previously, boys who turned 18 during the calendar year could not play. With the four-month increase, the eligible age to play was still 17 years old. The age eligibility still restricted boys who were seniors in high school from playing.

The 1955 Scobey Spartans (Scholars) baseball team was the last high school team fielded in Daniels County.

Doc Norman, who, with Gene Brown, coached the Columbus Junior Legion team to the eastern division championship series in 1953 and 1954, moved his family to Missoula to start a new practice there at the end of 1954. Doc began coaching Pony League (13–15-year-olds) in 1955, and his city championship Missoula Pony League team played in a season-ending championship tournament in Helena.

After three consecutive years of not fielding a Legion team, Scobey fielded a Junior Legion team in 1956, and the Plainsmen rejoined the Northeastern Montana League, along with Flaxville-Whitetail and Peerless in Daniels County. Peerless Legion was coached by Dave Hawbaker. With the Baby Boomers becoming Little League age, youth baseball in Scobey was also picking up steam, as more than fifty 10-13 agers signed up to play, with Fred Walker, Dallas Gaines, Clip Zieske, and Chris Veis coaching the four teams.

Sheehan Bros. & Hober, 1955 Missoula Pony League champions. Kneeling, from left: Billy Dobner, Tracy Cuplin, Walt Hoefler, Tom Stage, Mike Burke, James Forman, Mike Norman (batboy), Dale Huber, Dennis Hill, Terry Hober, James Pramenko, William Chumrau and Howard Sickels. Standing, from left: Pony League President Floyd Hober, Team Coach Dr. C. H. Norman, Allen Sularz, Mike Dishman and Dan Krumm. *Missoulian.*

1956

The Plainsmen End Whitetail's Streak of Three Consecutive NeMont League Championships

JUNIOR LEGION

THE SIX TEAMS COMPETING IN THE NORTHEASTERN district in 1956 were Scobey, Outlook, Plentywood, Peerless, Flaxville-Whitetail, and Culbertson. Plentywood edged Outlook, coached by Roald Selvig, to finish first in the standings, then lost a 7-6 one-game playoff in extra innings with Wolf Point for the northeastern district title. Wolf Point then hosted the eastern division championship in Wolf Point. Laurel and Wibaux played in the round-robin tournament at Wolf Point to see who would qualify for the state tournament. Laurel won the round-robin tourney by beating Wibaux 10-6 and Wolf Point 9-6, and the state tournament (hosted by Laurel) by beating Libby and Conrad.

The highlight for the Scobey Junior Legion team in 1956 was a no-hitter pitched by Gary Davies in a 6-1 win over Flaxville-Whitetail. This was the second no-hitter by a Scobey Legionnaire, as Bob Schaefer pitched the first no-hitter in 1931 against Poplar.

NORTHEASTERN MONTANA LEAGUE

FIVE TEAMS—SCOBEY, CORONACH, BIG BEAVER, OUTLOOK, and Whitetail—competed in the NeMont League in 1956. After a "mediocre season of play" (according to the *Leader*), the Scobey Plainsmen won the NeMont League Tournament in Coronach, Sask., ending Whitetail's string of three consecutive NeMont League championships. In their first game, the Plainsmen won a 17-16 slugfest over host Coronach in extra innings. The game had to be called on account of darkness with the Plainsmen on top. Scobey pitcher Chuck Bowman gave up 14 hits, while his teammates racked up 17 hits in the slugfest. Scobey drew a bye for the second round, and in the third, they met Whitetail for the championship and won, 5-3, for the league championship, with Bowman again on the mound for Scobey as the winning pitcher. Chuck Bowman was the winning pitcher in both games, with Howard Farver and Vince Zimmer leading the hitters. Manager Ken Lekvold accepted the Great Falls Brewery trophy for the title.

The 12-man roster for the 1956 Plainsmen, managed by Ken Lekvold, was the following: Ken Lekvold, 2d base; Howard Farver, 3d base; Ordean Wangrud, 1st base, Harry Larson ss, Chuck Bowman p, Jack Reiner c, Fred Walker cf, Vince Zimmer rf, Leo Zimmer lf and p, Tom Hayes rf, Richard Roland 1st base, Doc Hawbaker 2d base.

The 1956 Scobey Plainsmen were sponsored by the Scobey Athletic Club, which encouraged and supervised "one of the most active summer seasons of sport this community has known."[52] Baseball was heating up in Scobey, and the Scobey Athletic Club was fanning the flames.

SECTION NOTES

1. "Miles City Eliminates Scobey; To Meet Billings in Semifinal," *Billings Gazette*, July 22, 1946.
2. "Junior Leaguers Wallop Opheim," *Daniels County Leader*, June 20, 1946.
3. "Early Dope for the Hot Stove League," *Daniels County Leader*, August 29, 1946.
4. "Juniors Wallop Opheim," *Leader*.
5. "Scobey Junior Legion Wins District Title," *Daniels County Leader*, July 18, 1946.
6. Ibid.
7. "Miles City Eliminates Scobey; To Meet Billings in Semifinal," *Billings Gazette*, July 22, 1946.
8. "Juniors Downed in Regional Contest," *Daniels County Leader*, July 25, 1946.
9. "Early Dope for the Hot Stove League," *Daniels County Leader*, August 29, 1946
10. Ibid.
11. "Little Scobey Boys Are Learning To Play Baseball," *Daniels County Leader*, July 16, 1946.
12. "Juniors Trample Plentywood Nine," *Daniels County Leader*, June 19, 1947.
13. "War Amputee to Hurl Game," *Billings Gazette*, June 22, 1947.
14. "Sports Chatter," *Great Falls Tribune*, May 23, 1948.
15. "P'Wood Juniors Win Second in District Meet, *Plentywood Herald*, July 22, 1948.
16. "Flaxville Beats Wolf Point, 6-2," *Daniels County Leader*, July 15, 1948
17. "Plainsmen Win Plentywood Tournament," *Daniels County Leader*, September 9, 1948.
18. "Billings has had baseball since the 1880s. Here are some of the city's ballparks," 406mtsports.com, June 18, 2017.
19. "Schuster Fans 15; Tops Scobey," *Billings Gazette*, July 30, 1969.
20. "Juniors Defeat Outlook 12-3," *Daniels County Leader*, June 9, 1949.
21. Robert Carbone, "Opheim Cops First in Junior Legion Tournament," *Plentywood Herald*, July 14, 1949.
22. "Champion Plainsmen Play Here Sunday," *Daniels County Leader*, August 11, 1949.
23. "Flaxville Club Brings Strong Team Here," *Daniels County Leader*, July 7, 1949.
24. "Plainsmen Show Excellent Wares at Ball Meet," *Daniels County Leader*, September 8, 1949.
25. "High School Baseball Will be Played in Two Classes Next Year," *Havre Daily News*, May 18, 1949.
26. "Bundren's Homer with Bases Full Beats Wildcats," *Daniels County Leader*, May 18, 1950.
27. "With People Making News," *Daniels County Leader*, April 13, 1950.
28. "Late Rally by Peerless Is Not Enough," *Daniels County Leader*, July 27, 1950.
29. "Scholars End Season Sunday with Plainsmen," *Daniels County Leader*, May 17, 1951.
30. "Poplar Wins East Division," *Daniels County Leader*, July 5, 1951.
31. "Double Bill Is Schedule Here this Sunday," *Daniels County Leader*, June 14, 1951.
32. "Plainsmen Win In Overtime From Wolves," *Daniels County Leader*, August 9, 1951.
33. "Plainsmen Win Thriller from Opheim Radars," *Daniels County Leader*, July 19, 1951.
34. "Opheim Radars Bow 15-7 to Plainsmen," *Daniels County Leader*, July 26, 1951.
35. Ada Nash, "Redstone," *Plentywood Herald*, October 11, 1951.
36. Ada Nash, "Raymond Is the Winner of BB Tourney," *Plentywood Herald*, October 18, 1951.
37. Ada Nash, "Redstone," *Plentywood Herald*, October 18, 1951.
38. "Plainsmen Win Over Brockton," *Daniels County Leader*, July 2, 1953.
39. "Plainsmen Win from Outlook," *Daniels County Leader*, August 13, 1953.
40. "With People Making News," *Daniels County Leader*, May 14, 1953.
41. "Scobey Splits Sunday Tilts, Loses Tuesday," *Daniels County Leader*, June 17, 1954.
42. "Outlook Wins Here Sunday Over Scobey," *Daniels County Leader*, June 24, 1954.
43. "Whitetail," *Plentywood Herald*, August 12, 1954.
44. "Two Players Ejected as Whitetail Wins," *Plentywood Herald*, Special Correspondent, August 12, 1954.
45. "Doubleheader Baseball Game this Sunday," *Daniels County Leader*, June 10, 1954.
46. Ibid.
47. George and Faustine Puckett, "Peerless Little League Baseball 1954–58," *Daniels County History*, 1977, 614.
48. Keith Sell, "Poplar Trounces Scobey 12-2," *Daniels County Leader*, May 19, 1955.
49. "Plainsmen Place 2nd at Tourney in Coronach, Sask.," *Daniels County Leader*, May 26, 1955.
50. "Whitetail Cops NeMont Ball Event," *Plentywood Herald*, August 4, 1955.
51. "Radar Players Lost to GFAB in Fatal Eighth," *Glasgow Courier*, August 4, 1955.
52. "Plainsmen Cop League Trophy," *Daniels County Leader*, August 9, 1956.

The Baseball

1957 – 1968

1900 – 1924
The Homesteaders
and Early Town Teams

1930 – 1945
The Sons of
the Pioneers

The Scobey
Giants
1925 – 1929

Baseball is Back
in Daniels County
1946 – 1956

The
Chan
1969

Renaissance

| 1983 – 1991 | 1998 – 2003 | 2016 – 2019 |
| The Don Lekvold Era | The Last Years | The Revival |

| ...rman ...hip Era | The Ken Meyer/Mike Lee Era 1992 – 1997 | The Long Winter 2004 – 2015 | The Froid Bulls 2020 – 2024 |

1957

Scobey Athletic Field Opens and the Baseball Renaissance Begins

Grand Opening

Presentation of Scobey Athletic Field to Mayor N. C. Wolfe, in behalf of City, by Victor Luft, Scobey Athletic Club President.

AFTERNOON

Flag Ceremony with Color Guard at 1:15
JUNIOR LEAGUE GAME: SCOBEY vs. WHITETAIL
NE LEAGUE GAME: SCOBEY vs. WHITETAIL
AFTERNOON ADMISSION: Adults 50c; Students 25c

Scobey Athletic Field

Sunday, June 2

EVENING: (Under the New Lights)
OPENING SPONSORED BY SCOBEY ATHLETIC CLUB

8:00 P.M: Lights will be presented to City after the Flag Ceremony. This will be followed by two games of Little League Baseball — Class A and B.

EVENING ADMISSION: Everyone 25c

Scobey Athletic Field Grand Opening, June 2, 1957. *Leader.*

THE SCOBEY ATHLETIC CLUB[*] HAD UNDERTAKEN A major project to improve the baseball field, including land leveling, fencing, installation of water, bleachers, lights, and grass seed planted on the field. The major improvements began in 1956 and were completed in late spring 1957 (the grandstand in 1958), and Scobey Athletic Field[†] was handed over to the town of Scobey on June 2, 1957, when Major N. C. Wolfe accepted on behalf of the town of Scobey in an afternoon and evening ceremony. The afternoon session featured a flag-raising ceremony by the American Legion color guard and the playing of the national anthem, followed by the presentation by Vic Luft, Athletic Club president, of the field to the mayor. This was followed in the afternoon by two baseball games: the Flaxville-Whitetail Junior Legion team played the Scobey Legionnaires, and the Whitetail Oilers town team played the Scobey Plainsmen. The second ceremony in the evening saw the Athletic Club present the new lighting system to the mayor, and was followed by two Little League games under the lights. The ceremonies on June 2 officially opened the field.

The two afternoon baseball games that officially opened the ballpark did not disappoint. Flaxville-Whitetail won the Junior Legion game 3-2, as Tommy Rasmussen from Flaxville-Whitetail outdueled Scobey's Kevin Sell for seven innings. In the town team game, another pitcher's duel unfolded for seven innings, as Ron Fjeld from Whitetail held Scobey scoreless for six innings, and Vince Zimmer pitched a complete game one-hit shutout for the Plainsmen. The only hit Vince surrendered was a single to Whitetail pitcher Ron Fjeld, who was relieved by Pete Wiley in the seventh when the Plainsmen broke the game open by plating four runs, eventually winning 5-0. The four teams in the county matched the moment with solid pitching and fine defensive play. It was a fantastic beginning to the historic moments that were to follow at Scobey Ball Park.

The need for the new ballpark had been growing each year as the Baby Boomers were growing up and becoming Little League age. It was the kids who wanted to play baseball, their parents, and the community of Scobey that drove the development of the park. Two years later, in 1959, Al Funderburke wrote a wonderful article in the *Billings Gazette* titled "Little League Craze in Scobey Is Spark for Town Action."[1] The entire article is printed here because it captures the spirit of the Scobey community, a small town that came together to build not only a pristine ballpark, but

---

[*] The Scobey Athletic Club came into being in the 1950s, and it was this organization that played a key role in building the Scobey Ball Park, complete with grandstand, lights, and underground watering facilities. The Club promoted Peewee, Little League, Babe Ruth, Legion, softball as well as sponsoring the Plainsmen. (Cassidy, "Baseball," *Daniels County History*).

[†] The opening ceremony christened the new ballpark as "Scobey Athletic Field," and it was frequently referred to by that name, but the name most often was used was the "Scobey Ball Park."

a curling rink, swimming pool, and sand-green golf course for the benefit of all who lived in Daniels County.

Little League Craze in Scobey Is Spark for Town Action (Curling Too)

By Al Funderburke

SCOBEY —Perch a town just 9 miles below the Canadian line out of the direct east-west traffic flow, add a sizable number of energetic youngsters without sports facilities, and you have the formula for a community headache.

Three years ago, this northeast Montana town dozed on weekends while its sports-minded residents headed south and east to ball games in other communities or north into Canada to curling games.

Today, youngsters congregate at one of the best ball parks of its class, or gather at a top-notch swimming pool. Adults head for one of the best sand green golf courses in the state, or bundle up for an evening at the only covered curling rink in the state.

Start Little League

The spark firing the town's latent energy came from Little League enthusiasts. Parents of the youngsters launched a campaign for a ball park and were promptly overwhelmed by offers of help from every side. A bulldozer from the U.S. Soil Conservation district levelled an area north of the business section, members of construction and utility firms erected lights for night playing, installed plumbing, and built an up-to-date grandstand, including locker room and press box. In a short time, the field was the center of attention, with local teams flocking back home, and neighboring towns asking for permission to use the ball park. This year practically every night was taken up with either scheduled games or ball practice. During the month of August only two nights were open.

Build Swimming Pool

The next step was installation of a top-notch heated swimming pool in the city park. Again by community effort the pool was built at a minimum cost. The heating unit, normally costing $5,000, was installed for only $1,100 by a local plumber.

The Canadian enthusiasm for curling—a sport centering around an ice rink, using 40-pound rocks in much the same manner as shuffleboard—spread to Scobey. Residents tired of driving across the international line to watch and take part in matches, so a drive was kicked off for a new curling rink. The new rink was completed in two weeks in 1958 and promptly put to use. A total of 26 curling teams took part in play before the balance of the season was over, playing on the 42-by-172-foot covered rink. Scobey turned out en masse each night of the week to watch their favorite curling teams compete. Although other state towns are considering curling, Scobey now has the only covered rink in the state.

Golf Is Popular

During summer months golf is a favorite pastime, with 50 to 60 members of the Scobey Golf Club playing on the sand green course. In line with the sports boom came rapid growth of the Scobey Athletic Club and Saddle Club. With both adults and youngsters now staying home, the town's growth spread beyond the sports field. Population in today's energetic Scobey has climbed to more than 1,700, with 150 new homes built in the past six years. As a necessary adjunct to the new boom came reorganization of the Scobey Commercial Club in 1957.

Several residents of the town were there in 1913 when the town of Scobey was formed. Originally, business establishments were located on the Poplar River flats, a mile and a half from the present townsite, as homesteaders moved in following the Homestead Law of 1900. Railroads, attracted by the growing need of transportation for the spring wheat, canvassed the area, and in 1913, the first rail line pushed across the eastern plains from North Dakota. The railhead located north of Poplar River Flats, and an immediate move started to develop a townsite at the new location. Homesteaders and businessmen approved, and the town of Scobey came into being on Thanksgiving, 1913.

But although the official beginning of Scobey dates from 1913, the real spirit of the town was born three years ago as "the town that sports built," found fresh meaning in working together toward a common goal.[2]

Rod Tande, who played for Doc Norman's first Junior Legion team in 1959, remembers the new park being built. "It was volunteer work. There were volunteers there who had skills. One guy who comes to light is Vic Luft. Vic worked for the telephone company; I think it was Mountain Bell at the time. He was a pole climber who helped with the lights. Vic and a lot of other skilled people put those lights up, basically by hand. What are they, 60 feet tall? I remember the guys putting the fence up, tamping the fence posts, and putting the sheets on the fence. And then the lights going up, that was quite something. Bud Jensen, who was a staunch advocate of the ballpark, pretty much took control because he operated big machinery. He and his son-in-law, Art Holum, helped a lot. Bud built the pitcher's mound."

Rod also remembers the nonstop activity at the ballpark once it opened. "The Madoc teams, the Whitetail teams, and the Peerless and Flaxville teams, there were some real good athletes that came into Scobey, because there were Little League games starting at five o'clock. Then there was a huge league of women's fast-pitch softball, and then there were the men's fast-pitch softball games, all on the same night! It was practically every night of the week with the lights on. It was a marvelous time for the entire community."

With the opening of the new ballpark, the year 1957 marked the beginning of the renaissance of baseball (and men's and women's fast-pitch softball) in Scobey. Baseball and softball flourished. Everyone in Daniels County—men and women, and boys and girls of all ages—enjoyed the park. Over 70 boys aged 8 to 14 signed up to play baseball in Scobey alone, and Peerless, Four Buttes, Flaxville, and Whitetail also fielded Little League teams. Six men's fast-pitch teams and four women's slow-pitch softball teams competed in new leagues started in 1957, all facilitated by the new park, which allowed for play under the lights. My older brother Bill told me my dad played fast-pitch softball on that field that same year, and I didn't even know my dad played fast-pitch softball.

Bill Puckett remembers playing Little League in 1957, the first summer the ballpark was open, along with my older cousin, Reese Puckett Jr., who was a really good pitcher. My dad and Uncle Ed Puckett coached the team. My cousin Gerri Puckett, daughter of Ed Puckett, played Little League baseball for Peerless that year, along with Marcia Hawbaker. The Peerless Little Leaguers finished first in the standings, and the Peerless men's fast-pitch team placed third out of six teams. The point of mentioning the Peerless men and women, and kids coming to play in Scobey on that field was that the park served the entire county, not just the community of Scobey. Everyone in the county now had a sparkling new park to play in, with lights and everything, including the Scobey Junior Legion team and the Scobey Plainsmen.

JUNIOR LEGION

It was fitting that in the year of the renaissance of Daniels County baseball that Scobey (coached by Jack Reiner), Flaxville-Whitetail, and Peerless all fielded American Legion teams in 1957. The eastern division of the district also included Outlook, Plentywood, and Poplar.

But the Sheridan County teams dominated the Daniels County teams in 1957, as Plentywood and Outlook finished top two in the standings, with Plentywood winning the eastern division of the Junior Legion district. Plentywood then won the inter-district Junior Legion title by beating western division champion Fort Peck in a best-of-three playoff, but lost to Roundup in a best-of-three playoff for the chance to play at State. Cut Bank won its first State B title.

PLAINSMEN

The Plainsmen roster in 1957 included Howard Farver, Gary Davies, Bud Jensen, Cliff Hagfeldt, Harry Larson, Gary Farver, Duane Knight, Vern Veis, Vince Zimmer, Charles Van Gorden, Ordean Wangrud, Fred Walker, Kenny Lekvold, and Jack Reiner. Batboys were "Turk" Forchak and "Baldy" Sell.

Seven teams—Scobey, Outlook, Flaxville, Plentywood, Whitetail, Big Beaver, and Coronach—competed in the NeMont League that summer. The season started off with a bang for Scobey, as in their first game of the season against rival Plentywood, Vern Veis tossed a 3-0 shutout and struck out 12 Cubs to lead Scobey to victory. The Plainsmen won the regular season standings in the NeMont League, with Plentywood finishing second.

The Plainsmen hosted the season-ending tournament at the new Scobey Ball Park. The eight-game tournament was well-attended, particularly the championship game between the Plentywood Cubs and the Scobey Plainsmen. It was fitting that the two old rivals would face each other for the title in the inaugural year of the new Scobey Ball Park. But there was no storybook ending for the Plainsmen in 1957, as Plentywood won the NeMont League championship tournament 7-1 over Scobey. Craig Christensen was the winning pitcher, and Vince Zimmer, the loser. Coronach and Outlook played a tight game for third and fourth, with the Canadians winning 5-4. The champion Plentywood team had depth from former Junior Legion players who won the state championship in 1954 and had strong Legion teams following that year.

FAST-PITCH SOFTBALL

THE FOUR WOMEN'S FAST-PITCH SOFTBALL TEAMS—THE Peerless Wranglerettes, Plentywood Ed's Girls, Scobey Greenhorns, and Scobey Slick Chicks—battled for the women's league fast-pitch championship, with Peerless upsetting the Slick Chicks 12-9, coached by Clarence "Clip" Zieske, in the semifinals and losing to Ed's Girls from Plentywood in the championship to take second place. The Wranglerettes, the first girls fast-pitch softball team in Peerless, were started and coached by Ed Puckett and assisted by George Larson, and included Audrey Kaiser, Millie Larson, Patty Prewitt, Frances Drummond, Illa Mae Forberg, Helen Trangsrud, Lorraine Fladager, Helen Fouhy, Mae Hames, AnnaBelle Fouhy, Grace Crandell, Norma Puckett, Betty Carney, Leona Richardson, Helen Dighans, and Lauretta Puckett."[3]

Some daughters of the Wranglerettes, who became known as the Pansies the following season, remember their mothers playing, or talking about playing. Gerri Puckett, Ed Puckett's daughter who was playing Little League baseball that summer, was the batgirl. Gerri said, "I was pretty young, but remember being batgirl for this team. Dad coached them, and I remember how I loved being in the dugout with them and getting to be involved." Mary Kay Fouhy added, "I was told (or remember?) the women's softball games with the young kids playing in the dirt by the cars as the men kept an eye on the kids and the field at the same time!"

1958

The Scobey Plainsmen and Flaxville-Whitetail Junior Legion Teams Win Championships

> *Baseball seems to be definitely dominating the news in this area, and justly so. Imagine that just within a week, there should be first a Junior Legion championship of eastern Montana game with Flaxville-Whitetail as a leading contestant; and this followed within a few days by the Scobey Plainsmen winning the AAU amateur baseball championship of Montana. That totals up to heady stuff!*
>
> **—Daniels County Leader, August 14, 1958.**

THE SCOBEY ATHLETIC CLUB CONTINUED ITS WORK on the new Scobey Ball Park in 1958 as a new grandstand was built and dirt work was completed around the fence where the cars park. The dirt work around the fence was on a terraced design so that two rows of cars could park and use their cars for seating with good viewing of the games on the field. Cars parked around the ballpark were a unique feature of the Scobey Ball Park, as the fans would sit in their cars (or on the hood) and watch the games, and when a good play was made, the cars would cheer by honking their horns. The cars were the best fans at the game. They could get pretty noisy!

After the successful inaugural season of the new Scobey Ball Park in 1957, the ballpark was in full swing in 1958. The Plainsmen, now managed by Joe Anderson, competed in the revamped Northeastern Montana League, which Joe registered as an official league with the National Baseball Congress (NBC).* Scobey, Flaxville-Whitetail, and Peerless

---

* The National Baseball Congress (NBC) World Series is an annual collegiate and semipro baseball tournament held in Wichita, Kansas. It has been held annually in Wichita, Kansas, since 1935. When the national tournament started in 1935, participants were primarily town teams (like the Scobey Plainsmen) and industrial teams. Team rosters featured aging former minor league and major league ballplayers and players ineligible for major league baseball. In the mid-1960s team rosters transitioned to collegiate players, including Major League Baseball prospects. The series now features amateur and collegiate teams competing for a national championship. Satchel Paige, Don Sutton, Tom Seaver, Ozzie Smith, Tony Gwynn, Barry Bonds and Roger Clemens are just a few of the Major League Baseball stars who have played in the tournament. (Bob Broeg,

all competed in the nine-team District 4 Junior American Legion league. The first Babe Ruth team in Scobey was formed, 10 Little League teams competed in the county, and the men's and women's fast-pitch softball leagues picked up steam from the previous season. There was not an idle minute at the Scobey Ball Park in 1958, and the season saw two teams in the county crowned as champions.

Flaxville-Whitetail Junior Legion Team, 1958 District Champions. Front Row, L-R: Arnie Burnett, Doug Holle, Gary Duval and Gail LeMieux. Center Row, L-R: Doug Krassin, Dennis Marriage, Dallas Hackmann, Dennis Baker. Back Row, L-R: Gerry Owen, manager and Legion representative, Gary Brenden, Dennis Kurtz, Tom Rasmussen and Mike Klos, coach. *Leader.*

JUNIOR LEGION

THE NORTHEASTERN JUNIOR LEGION DISTRICT 4 WAS SPLIT INTO northern and southern divisions, with Scobey, Peerless, Opheim, Flaxville-Whitetail, and Plentywood in the north, and Glasgow, Fort Peck, Wolf Point, and Poplar in the south. Flaxville-Whitetail dominated the northern division regular season, losing only one game (to Plentywood) in District 4. Of the 1958 Flaxville-Whitetail team, the *Leader* wrote, "The Flaxville-Whitetail Junior Legion baseball team this year certainly is one of the best this county has seen in many years. They had a good team last year, and it's better this year."[4]

During the regular season, the strong Flaxville-Whitetail team, managed by Gerry Owen and coached by Mike Klos, played a nonconference game against Glendive, which was competing in the Eastern Class A Division with teams like Billings and Miles City, and beat them 3-2. Tom Rasmussen hurled a four-hitter, and Gail LeMieux collected the game-winning hit in the eighth inning to give Flaxville-Whitetail the win. In intra-county play in the northern division, Flaxville-Whitetail beat Scobey so badly that the *Leader* simply wrote that Scobey "took a drubbing from the stout Flaxville-Whitetail club" without listing the score. Peerless fared much better, losing only 8-5 to Flaxville-Whitetail.

With only one regular season loss to Plentywood, Flaxville-Whitetail won the northern division, then played off with southern division champion Wolf Point in a best-of-three series for the district championship. Flaxville won the first game 6-5, lost the second game 9-8, and then won the rubber match 5-2 to win their first district championship and earn the right to host Roundup in a best-of-three series at Scobey Ball Park for the eastern division title. The winner of the series would travel to Sunburst to play Sunburst, with the winner facing Whitefish for the state title.

In the best-of-three playoffs against Roundup at Scobey Ball Park, Flaxville-Whitetail lost the first game 11-5 but "the doughty Flaxville-Whitetail team" bounced back to win the second game, 10-5, setting up the final for the Eastern Montana Class B Junior Legion championship.

The visitors from Musselshell County "unlimbered their artillery" and pounded out 21 hits to win the deciding game, 23-13. The game was a slugfest, lasting more than three hours with a total of 33 hits and 36 runs, as well as eleven recorded errors, many of them costly for Flaxville-Whitetail. Flaxville-Whitetail was in the game early, as starting pitcher Dennis Marriage kept the Roundup hitters at bay and his team only trailed 3-0 after three and a half innings. Then, F-W scored two runs in the bottom of the fourth when Tom Rasmussen reached base on an error, Doug Krassin singled sharply, scoring Rasmussen, and Krassin later scored on Gary Duval's long sacrifice. It was 3-2 for Roundup, and the F-W Juniors trailed by only one run after four.

But Roundup "caught fire" in the top of the 5th, scoring 10 runs on hits and errors. Dallas Hackmann relieved Marriage to put out the fire, but it kept burning into the sixth when Roundup tacked on three more runs to make it 16-2.

But the boys from eastern Daniels County with "indomitable spirit" were not done. In the bottom of the sixth, F-W "pulled up their socks and whaled away spiritedly," scoring seven runs and closing to 16-9. That was as close as Flaxville-Whitetail got, however, as Roundup scored six more runs in the top of the seventh inning and went on to win 23-13.

The *Leader* recognized the strong 1958 Flaxville-Whitetail team, as this was the first Daniels County team to play for the eastern division title since Scobey's first Junior team in 1930. Scobey had also won district Legion titles in 1931, 1946, and 1947, but had not played for the eastern division championship in those years. The *Leader* wrote,

"MLB Alumni," *NBC Baseball*, January 1989, and *Baseball's Barnum*. Wichita State University. 144.)

"Although defeated, they [F-W] nevertheless had the best season seen by any Junior Legion team in this county since about 27 years ago when a Scobey team played Billings for the eastern title, losing 8-4. The game saw a courageous Flaxville-Whitetail team go for a full nine innings without let-up, and still score a total of 13 runs; and it is not hard to imagine how doggedly their spirits had to be maintained when at one time in the game, against a superior Roundup team, they were faced with a 16-2 score against them. The contest ended 23-13, but it was a whale of a contest, and with due credit to Roundup, we also take off our respective hats to the scrappy F-W Legion juniors."

Roundup went on to win the state B championship by beating Sunburst 7-6 and Whitefish 12-2.

PLAINSMEN

AN ASSOCIATED PRESS ARTICLE REFERRED TO A "NEWLY formed" Northeastern Montana (NeMont) League in 1958,[5] but a league by this name in northeastern Montana was first formed in 1925 when the Scobey Giants competed against their rival Plentywood in the league. In 1938 and 1939, Flaxville won the Northeastern Montana (NeMont) League, as did the Plainsmen in 1948 and 1949, and Whitetail from 1953 to 1955, then the Plainsmen again in 1956. Teams from Sheridan County, including Plentywood, Outlook, and Raymond, had also won the league. What changed throughout the years was the teams in the league and the charter. In 1958, the five teams in the league were the Wolf Point Stampeders, Scobey Plainsmen, Poplar Oilers, Glasgow Highlanders, and the Circle Cowboys. In addition to the new teams, the new charter was different in that the league was registered with the National Baseball Congress, which meant that the winner of the league qualified to participate in the NBC World Series in Wichita, Kansas, as the Montana champion.

The first game of the league for the Scobey Plainsmen was a slugfest for the ages, as the Plainsmen lost to the Wolf Point Stampeders 33-27 on the Tule Creek diamond near Wolf Point. The Stampeders, managed by Roger "Swede" Johnson and Jim Burt, consisted of players from Wolf Point and Tule Creek. The game was hosted at Tule Creek diamond, where nine home runs were hit by both teams as strong winds boosted several home runs over the fence.[6] The players, coaches, and fans at the game were wondering if some sort of record had been set with the total number of runs scored (60) in the game.* The Associated Press article on the game referred to it as a "fielder's nightmare," as outfielders vainly attempted to chase down fly balls that repeatedly escaped their reach, but it was really a "pitcher's nightmare," as Andy Stolen took the loss for the Plainsmen.

After the slugfest at Tule Creek, other regular-season Plainsmen highlights featured fine pitching, as Chuck Bowman pitched a one-hitter in a 4-2 win over Glasgow and Andy Stolen, with calmer winds and a longer fence, pitched a five-hit shutout to lead the Plainsmen to a 3-0 win against the same Wolf Point team that had plated 27 runs in the season-opening slugfest. It took Andy's remaining career with the Plainsmen for his ERA to recover from that fateful blustery day at Tule Creek.

Scobey Plainsmen, 1958 Montana AAU Champions. Standing, L–R: Fred Walker, Larry Wangrud, Leo Zimmer, Ordean Wangrud, Cliff Hagfeldt, Chuck Bowman, Howard Farver, Gary Farver. Kneeling: Harry Larson, Joe Anderson (mgr), Jack Reiner, Andy Stolen, Ken Triplett, Dallas Gaines, Ron Fjeld, Batboy Alan Luft. Bill Richardson (batboy) in front. *Leader.*

---

* The 60 total runs scored by the Plainsmen and Stampeders would be a record in Major League Baseball. The largest two-team score ever recorded in MLB was played at Wrigley Field on August 25, 1922, when the Cubs beat the Philadelphia Phillies 26-23 for the all-time record two-team score of 49 runs. (Ron Liebman, "The Highest Scoring Games," *Baseball Research Journal*, 1980.)

At the end of the regular season, the Glasgow Highlanders and Scobey Plainsmen tied for first place in the standings, as each team had 12 wins and four losses. The two teams split their four regular-season games, so a one-game playoff game was scheduled to determine the league champion and the right to participate in the NBC World Series in Wichita. Prior to the one-game playoff, a round-robin league tournament was played in Glasgow, but the tournament had no bearing on league standings. Glasgow won a 4-0 decision over the Plainsmen in the round robin tournament, but the result would be different a week later in Scobey.

It was a dramatic finish to the first year of the newly formed NeMont League, as the Scobey Plainsmen hosted the Glasgow Highlanders at the new Scobey Ball Park on a Sunday night in a one-game playoff to determine the Northeastern Montana Baseball League pennant. The new grandstand and the terraced parking around the ballpark enabled over one thousand fans from all over northeastern Montana to enjoy the game under the lights, and the two teams met the moment, with a storybook nail-biting ending for the Plainsmen. And it was pitching that did it, as Chuck Bowman hurled a two-hitter and struck out 19 Highlanders and hometown Scobey boy Ron Fjeld—who had pitched Whitetail to three NeMont League championships (crawling home with the winning run in one of them)—came on with one out in the ninth with runners on base to record the final two outs and earn the save for Scobey in their 4-1 win over Glasgow for the State NBC championship.

Unfortunately, due to an administrative error, the Plainsmen were not allowed to compete in the national NBC World Series in Wichita. Earlier in the season, Montana Amateur Athletic Union (AAU) officials failed to notify national authorities that there would be a team from Montana competing nationally, so the national AAU playoff schedule did not include a Montana entry. The Plainsmen were recognized as champions of amateur baseball in Montana, but could not compete in the NBC World Series. Manager Joe Anderson said, "It is a disappointment, but we certainly want to thank all those fans whose generosity from here and around the state made it possible to complete the financial arrangements for Scobey to attend. We can know with a great deal of satisfaction that it is not due to any fault of our team, nor the fans, that Scobey is not competing at Wichita in the national competitions."[7]

FAST-PITCH SOFTBALL

THE PEERLESS PANSIES (WHO WERE CALLED THE WRANGLERETTES the previous year) won the women's fast-pitch softball league championship in 1958. The Pansies, coached by Ed

Peerless Pansies, 1958 Women's Fast-Pitch League champions (Or this could be the runner-up 1957 Peerless Wranglerettes.) Back row, L-R: Helen Trangsrud, Lorraine Fladager, Annabelle Fouhy, Grace Crandell, Lauretta Puckett. Front row, L-R: Audrey Kaiser, Millie Larson, Patty Prewitt, Frances Drummond, Illa Mae Forberg. *Family photo.*

Puckett, had finished second a year before after they upset the Scobey Slick Chicks in the semifinals. Peerless won the title from a field of five teams—the Pansies, Slick Chicks, Greenhorns, Fergusons, and Does. The Slick Chicks and Greenhorns were from the Scobey area; the Fergusons were from Plentywood, and the Does from Antelope-Reserve. The Pansies, led by pitchers Audrey Kaiser and Millie Larson, won the championship by beating the Greenhorns 12-10 and the Slick Chicks 16-14. The *Leader* noted "outstanding improvement in the general quality of play" in the league's second season.

This was the second league championship for a Peerless adult team in softball or baseball in history. The Peerless Pirates, managed by Leo Zimmer, won the five-team baseball league with Ossette, Richland, Glentana, Opheim, and Peerless in 1948. This was also the first softball championship for Coach Ed Puckett, who would lead Peerless softball teams to many more tournament championships in the years to follow, when the Wranglerettes-turned-Pansies became the Peerless Belles, then the mighty Peerless Hellcats of the late 1960s and 1970s. More to follow on Coach Ed Puckett and the Peerless Hellcats in a later chapter.

EXTRA INNINGS

IN AN INDICATION OF THINGS TO COME FOR SCOBEY AND Scobey Ball Park hosting big tournaments, the visiting Roundup team and fans were "loud in their praise" of how well they were treated in Scobey and remarked that Scobey Ball Park was one of the most outstanding in Montana. Scobey became famous across the state of Montana for its well-run tournaments.

The Umpires for the eastern division championship series in Scobey were Leo Zimmer, Melvin Buckles, and Cliff Hagfeldt.

G. J. (Gus) Waller, an ardent Scobey baseball fan, donated the uniforms to the 1958 Scobey Plainsmen. He was one of over a thousand fans who saw the Plainsmen beat the Highlanders for the Montana AAU championship. He had an anxious moment during the game when his son-in-law and business associate, Jack Reiner, was beaned by a fastball in the fourth inning, but Jack dusted his pants off and accounted for some important Scobey runs later in the game.

The Junior Legion Baseball maximum age in 1958 was still 17 years old, as boys who turned 18 years old before September 1 that year were not eligible to play. There had been talk of raising the age limit to 18, but no change had been made to the age eligibility since 1955, when the age limit was increased by four months. In an article titled "Should Boost Legion Age Limit," sportswriter Clausie Smith of the *Ottawa Herald* (Kansas) made a compelling case for raising the age limit.[8] Although the age limit would not increase to 18 until 1961, this article shows that sportswriters and coaches were discussing that possibility:

```
American Legion baseball as a whole would be
better off if the age limit were raised by one
year. Boys were eligible to play Legion ball this
summer if they were born after Sept. 1, 1940.
Following the established pattern, to be eligible
next season, they would have to be born after
Sept. 1, 1941. In other words, boys who are 17
are the oldest players in Legion ball, now.

A large group of youngsters, who have just
turned 18, and still have a year of high school
left, are cut out of Legion competition. The
baseball program on a nationwide basis would
be much better if the age level were moved back
one year.

With the declining popularity of town-team
baseball, most boys of mediocre ability are
left out after graduating from Legion programs.

Legion baseball would be a better game, more
professionally played, if 18-year-olds could
participate. Another year of growth and matu-
rity would make a tremendous difference in many
ball players.⁹
```

Doc Norman assisted Gene Thompson in coaching the Missoula Junior Legion team in 1958. Gene Thompson would later assist Doc on Scobey's first American Legion championship team in 1969, when Gene Thompson was superintendent of Peerless Schools.

On July 20, 1958, the following ad appeared in the *Missoulian*:

26 Help Wanted, Men

```
DOCTOR, who is thoroughly experienced in
general practice, is urgently needed at Sco-
bey, Montana, immediately. Single physician in
practice here is required to minister to the
needs of approximately 4,000 people. Unlimited
opportunity for the right man. For further
specific information, write to Box 584, Scobey,
Montana. All replies are confidential.¹⁰
```

Missoula Legion Team. Standing on the far left is Coach Gene Thompson, who assisted Doc on Scobey's 1969 state championship team. Doc, who assisted Gene in 1958, is standing on the far right. *Missoulian.*

But there had to be more to the story than an ad in the paper that Doc saw in the *Missoulian* while he was practicing medicine in Missoula. I asked Doc's daughter, Ann, who was 12 years old at the time, if she remembered how it happened that Doc moved his family from Missoula to Scobey. She said, "The reason he moved was he had a direct detail man that came through every month or so. The man was from Scobey, and he kept telling my dad, 'There's this little town in northeastern Montana that needs you, Doc, they need you really badly.' And Daddy's goal was always to be somewhere where he was really needed. He always wanted to be in a community that just really needed him. The detail man's name was Indy Halvorson. It was really funny because I came home from school and mother was out cooking dinner, and I went into the bedroom to get something for her and on the mirror, written in lipstick, because Dad could not find a piece of paper and a pen evidently, 'GONE TO SCOBEY, CALL YOU LATER, LOVE YOU.' And I said, 'Mama, what's a Scobey?' and she said, 'I don't know.' And that is the story of us moving to Scobey."

Ann added, "Daddy had done his medical schooling at Northwestern University, and he had the opportunity to stay there and be an OB/Gynecologist because he liked to deliver babies, and he was really good at it. They wanted him to stay there, but he wanted to go back to Montana. He had a chance to practice in Billings, but he wanted to be in a place where he was really needed, and even in Missoula, there were doctors all over the place, because it's beautiful there and people want to live there."

I asked Mike Norman what he thought about moving to a "Scobey." He said, "Well, I wasn't very excited about moving there either because I was in the middle of my 8th grade. And you know, I'd grown up in Missoula, and all my friends and I went to the same grade school. And I was gonna be going to high school the next year and then get pushed to some place I didn't know a soul. Yeah, that wasn't very much fun. I revolted against it at first, but you know, it doesn't do much good to do that because wherever dads say we're going, we're going, so that was that." But Mike would soon make friends in Scobey, and he became the starting first baseman on the Legion team his first year there.

Doc returned from his trip to Scobey, and Marge, Mike, and Ann soon learned what a "Scobey" was. I asked Ann if Scobey's sparkling new ballpark might have tipped the scales for Doc to decide to uproot his life in Missoula and move his family to northeastern Montana. She said, "Oh, he saw the ballpark, you can bet he did!" She paused to laugh. "He came back and he said, 'Oh, and they got a great ballpark there.'" Ann added Scobey also had a new hospital, because the hospital was new too.

So, thanks in part to the nudging of Indy Halvorson and the appeal of Scobey Ball Park, Dr. C. H. Norman, M.D., applied for and got the vacant physician position in Scobey and began practicing medicine in Scobey on November 3, 1958. What happened next forever altered the course of American Legion Baseball in Scobey, as the following year, 1959, would be Doc's first as head coach of the Scobey Junior Legion team. There was a new "sheriff" (doctor and coach) in town, and while Doc started practicing medicine in Scobey in November 1958, he started practicing baseball in April 1959. Over the next 25 years, it could be debated which part of his contribution to the community was greater—practicing medicine or practicing baseball.

1959

The Doc Norman Era Begins: The Legionnaires Win Their First District Title in 12 Years

Scobey Legionnaires, 1959 District Champions. Back row L–R: Head Coach Doc Norman, Randy Smith, Terry Veis, Bill Thompson, Al Luft, Bob Roland, Kevin Sell, Assistant Coach Bob Tande. Front row: Bink Sheron, Terry Forchak, Rod Tande, Baldy Sell, Phil Baker, Carl Tande, Mike Norman, Larry Veis. Sitting: Batboy Dan Smith. *Leader.*

DOC'S FIRST SEASON COACHING JUNIOR LEGION BASEball in Scobey was remarkable, as he molded an incredibly young team into the northeastern Montana district champion, their first in 12 years. The Plainsmen, with team manager Joe Anderson and field manager Harry Larson, repeated as NeMont League champions, were the State runners-up, and the NeMont Baseball League was registered with the National Baseball Congress. Flaxville and Peerless fielded Legion teams, too, and the Little League and men's and women's fast-pitch leagues continued steaming ahead with league schedules and tournaments.

JUNIOR LEGION

DOC'S FIRST JUNIOR LEGION COACHING ACTION WAS TO PURchase new uniforms for the team, both home and away. The Scobey players who wore those new uniforms were Alan Luft, Bob Roland, Kevin Sell, Bill Thompson, Randy Smith, Larry Veis, Mike Norman, Rod Tande, Dwain Sell, Terry Forchak, Carl Tande, Bink Sheron, Phil Baker, and Terry Veis. Dan Smith was the batboy. This was a very young team, as only Kevin Sell and Bob Roland were 17 years old. Almost everyone else on the team was 14, including Doc's son Mike, who had just completed 8th grade. Mike expected to play Babe Ruth that summer, but Mike recalls Doc saying to him, "You're plenty big enough to play ball, so just get out there and play. So I did. We ended up doing really well, much to the surprise of everyone in town. How can you take a bunch of 8th-graders and freshmen and win the district and playoffs, you know?" The roster consisted mostly of Babe Ruth–eligible players who played Legion ball because Doc "called them up." This was Doc's method—developing younger players in his system early and building strong teams as the players matured. But Doc built a championship team in 1959, even with his younger players.

Bob Tande, who coached Scobey to its last district titles in 1946 and 1947, was Doc's able assistant coach.

The district was again split into a northern and southern division, with Opheim, Peerless, Scobey, Flaxville-Whitetail, Outlook, and Plentywood in the north, and Poplar, Wolf Point, Fort Peck, and Glasgow in the south. The winners of the northern and southern divisions would playoff in a best-of-three series for the northeastern Montana district championship.

Early in May, Doc scheduled his first practice game for his Legionnaires against a Flaxville High School team, which allowed 18-year-old Flaxville High School seniors to play baseball who were not eligible to play later that summer under Junior Legion rules. The Flaxville team had Junior Legion players on it from the previous year's championship team, too. Flaxville pounded Doc's first Scobey team in the practice game, 24-8. Dallas Hackmann, "horsehide chucker" from Flaxville, pitched the win for Flaxville, while Randy Smith, relieved by Bill Thompson, took the loss for Scobey. Flaxville pounded the ball on their home field, as "home runs by Flaxville predominated the latter part of the event."[11]

Doc's second practice game in early May saw his Legionnaires travel to Circle, where they lost 5-3 to the Circle Cowboys town team, who competed in the NEMont League. Fourteen-year-old Randy Smith took the loss again, but "showed considerable improvement over his last casualty"—he only gave up two hits—but Scobey committed several errors, which led to Circle's runs. Kevin Sell, Doc's best pitcher, was not pitching early in the season due to a sore arm. After two early-season practice-game losses, Printer Bowler assessed Doc's young Legionnaires: "This sportswriter predicts that within the season, when the young Legion team gets a few more games under its belt, Dr. Norman will have his ace in the hole." Printer was right—Scobey lost only one game in conference play, went on to win its first district title since 1947, and then played off against Laurel to go to the state tournament.

Notwithstanding his young roster, Doc immediately began his method of scheduling stronger opponents during the season to build the team, as he organized an early-season four-team tournament in Scobey with Class A teams Williston, Regina, and Missoula, the first interstate and international Junior Legion tournament in Scobey. When talking about the tough competition in the tournament, Doc was his typical marine "gung ho" self: "Our boys may as well meet them during the season because they'll be meeting some of them anyway, in the finals." Printer Bowler wrote, "With that kind of spirit at the helm, plus plenty of know-how in the coaching, the boys have been responding, with the results that the squad has changed from a very mediocre aggregation at the beginning of the season to a spirited, hard-trying club. No matter what happens this weekend in the tournament, Scobey Juniors will be able to learn the measure of skill attained by their contemporaries in the much larger towns."[12]

Regina did not show, so the three remaining teams played a round-robin. Missoula won the round-robin by beating Williston, 11-1, and Scobey, 9-1. Against Williston, the young Scobey team "suffered first-inning jitters" in which they gave up seven runs, then rallied several times, but lost the game 10-8. Printer Bowler summed up Scobey's historic tournament against Class A competition this way: "Dwain 'Baldy' Sell, pint-sized fielder and second baseman, set an enviable record in the game here against Williston when he hit four for four. His older brother, Kevin, and Larry Veis, with assists from Randy Smith and Bill Thompson, take care of the mound duties. Against a sharp, hard-hitting Missoula team last Sunday, Larry Veis, except for two bad innings, showed plenty of moxie on the mound."[13] Playing against tougher competition, the young Legionnaires were improving. Printer Bowler was right again.

Terry Veis, Scobey's 14-year-old left fielder, remembers Missoula coming to Scobey to play. "They had that Pokey Allen,* you know, on the team, and oh gosh, it was quite an affair. The Missoula boys had bongo drums, wore cut-off beach pants, flip flops, and you know we'd never seen anything like that before. So that was quite a deal." The Missoula boys stayed with the Scobey boys, and the same when Scobey traveled to Missoula later in the season.

Not satisfied with hosting Class A teams at the tournament in Scobey, Doc then took the team on a barnstorming tour of Montana to play Class A teams Havre, Helena, Butte, and Missoula. In a season of many firsts historically, this road trip was another new experience for the Scobey Legionnaires. Rod Tande, 14-year-old shortstop for Scobey, remembers how special the road trip was for the young Scobey team and how it made them better. "In Butte, we were getting skunked 20-0, and Bob Roland was on second base. Someone got a base hit, and Bob rounds third and crosses the plate. Yes! He's safe. Okay, we're on the board, we got a run. Guy throws to third and steps on the bag. Bob failed to hit the bag, so we're back down to 20-0. Boy, you talk about breaking the spirit. We got beat badly that game, but Doc was positive. In his own mind, he never lost a game; it was always the umpire, and it went a little far sometimes. In Helena, when we walked into that stadium,

---

* Pokey Allen was a tremendous all-around athlete. He lettered in football, basketball, and track and field at Missoula County High School. Following his prep career, he played college football for the University of Utah Runnin' Utes and then played professionally for the BC Lions and the Edmonton Eskimos of the Canadian Football League (CFL) in the 1960s. After retiring as a player in 1968, he went on to a successful coaching career in college and professional football. He led Portland State to consecutive appearances in the Division II championship game in 1987 and 1988 and guided Boise State to the Division I-AA title game in 1994. ("Pokey Allen," Wikipedia, May 4, 2025.)

I kid you not, the grass was immaculate. We played on that beautiful field, and it was a true experience. We didn't do well on that trip, but we got some seasoning, and that's basically what Doc had in mind. We played the big boys, and we took our lumps, but later on, we gave the lumps. That's pretty much the story."

While the young Legionnaires got roughed up against the Class A competition on the trip, the Scobey nine almost got a win against Gene Thompson's Missoula team in Missoula, who had come to Scobey to play earlier in the season. Doc had assisted Gene in Missoula the year before, and Missoula had taken second in the State A Tournament, losing twice to Ed Bayne's Billings Royals in the championship games after beating them earlier in the tournament. Kevin Sell pitched a gem, allowing only one hit and no runs through five innings. Scobey scored single runs in the third, fourth, and sixth innings to take a 3-0 lead on RBI singles by Kevin Sell, Bob Roland, Phil Baker, and Larry Veis. But Missoula, held to one hit through five innings, got to Sell for four runs in the bottom of the sixth on two walks, two errors, and a wild pitch. The only hit in the inning was a bunt single. Scobey tied it in the top of the seventh on two walks and two hits, including a bunt single by Baldy Sell. The game, scheduled for seven innings, went two extra innings and ended in a thrilling ninth-inning finish as Missoula's Don Krumm singled to drive the winning run to beat Scobey 5-4. Although Scobey lost, pitcher Kevin Sell and the team had proven they could hang with tough competition. Were it not for the rough sixth inning, Scobey could have pulled it out. The Legionnaires also turned a defensive double play in the game to get out of an inning. Scobey performed well on Doc's former stomping grounds, and the *Missoulian* wrote, "Kevin Sell gave Missoula only four hits, throwing well throughout, and Scobey looked good in the games here. A fair little ball club, that Scobey outfit."[14]

A second game was played against an alternate team from Missoula in Missoula after the well-played 5-4 first game ended. This was the last game Scobey played on the road trip, and after playing Havre, Helena, Butte, and Missoula in successive days, the Scobey pitching arms were exhausted. So, Doc had to reach deep in the second game for pitching, and Terry Veis said he got his one pitching opportunity in his Legion career. Terry remembers it well. He said, "We weren't doing too well in the second game, so Doc said, 'Terry, get in there and pitch.' Well, I hadn't done too much pitching, and I went in there, and Bobby Roland was the catcher. I wound up and let 'er go, and it went over Bob's head and into the stands. That was the only pitch I delivered for the Scobey Junior Legion team. After that, Doc came in to pitch. I was the last resort, I threw it into the stands, and then Doc came in to pitch." So, with Missoula leading 13-2 in the bottom of the sixth, Doc—perhaps after deciding against bringing batboy Dan Smith in from the dugout to pitch—slowly walked to the mound to take Terry out. Instead of calling on another Legionnaire—Bill Thompson, Randy Smith, Al Luft, and Terry had already pitched—Doc stayed on the mound and recorded the last out to retire the side. To this day, Doc holds the record for the lowest ERA in Scobey Blues Legion team history with a 0.00 ERA in one-third of an inning pitched.

Within Daniels County, Peerless and Flaxville-Whitetail fielded Legion teams that year, too. It's important to note that Flaxville-Whitetail was the defending district champion and had several strong players returning from that championship team. Peerless had some excellent players too, like power-hitting Arden Nelson, speedy center fielder Sam Belling, and 14-year-old pitcher Reese Puckett, Jr., who might have been the best pitcher to come out of the Reese Puckett family in Peerless (my brother Bill recalls Reese pitching a five-inning perfect game in Little League in 1957), but he never played baseball past 15 years old. Coach Bob Tande and Doc Norman recruited Reese to come pitch for the 1959 Scobey Legion team. Bill was with Reese when Bob Tande asked Reese, "Would you like to come and give the ball a whirl?" But Reese wouldn't go. Meanwhile, Doc tried in vain to convince Flaxville-Whitetail to combine forces with Scobey but was not successful. A story goes that Doc was so frustrated with not being able to get Flaxville to combine with the Scobey Legion program in 1959 that he told the Flaxville-Whitetail Legion manager on the phone, "The next time one of your Flaxville boys gets sick, maybe they can drive to Plentywood to see the doctor; you should just run them over to Plentywood." When push came to shove, Doc would have treated the boys, of course, but the story does show how badly he wanted to recruit talented players to win.

The reason Doc Norman and Bob Tande were not able to successfully recruit Flaxville-Whitetail and Peerless kids to play in Scobey in 1959 was that the two small towns fielded Legion teams. It was understandable why Peerless and Flaxville-Whitetail resisted the calls from Doc to combine—the Legion posts Peerless and Flaxville fundraised so their boys in the community would have the opportunity to play Junior Legion baseball, and there was pride in the local community with the teams.

But even if the Legion posts of the two small towns had agreed to combine with Scobey, it would have been difficult to get the kids to come to Scobey to play. There was more of a boundary between the small towns and Scobey in the county then. I remember my mom talking about this phenomenon when I played baseball in Scobey in the late 1970s. She told me that when she went to Peerless High School in the late 1930s, there was a separation between Scobey and Peerless (and other small communities) that wasn't there as much when I was a teenager. She said the kids in Peerless were looked on as "hayseeds," "backwards," and "country kids." When she told me this, she focused her eyes on me and nodded her head up and down, emphasizing that this was really a thing when she was young. It was still a thing in the late 1950s, but it was getting better. It wouldn't be until nine years later in 1968 when the first all–Daniels County Legion Baseball team was formed, and Scobey won its first state Legion title a year later. Joining forces made sense from a winning perspective, but the time wasn't right in 1959. Beginning in 1968, the Scobey Legion team effectively became a select team of the best athletes in Daniels County, which is what it took to win the state championships.

In Legion action within Daniels County, in the first game between Scobey and Peerless, Scobey won 8-4 at Scobey Ball Park, as left-hander Bill Thompson went all nine innings for Scobey to get the win, despite giving up an inside-the-park home run to Peerless's Arden Nelson in the first inning. The following week, Scobey suffered its only conference loss to Peerless, 5-4, at Peerless. In the top of the ninth, Peerless was trailing 4-1, and Peerless center fielder Sam Belling made what might have been a game-saving catch off the bat of a long drive by Rod Tande to keep the score close for Peerless. The *Leader* referred to Belling's catch as a "sensational (in any league) running, diving catch."15 With Peerless trailing Scobey 4-1 in the bottom of the ninth and Randy Smith pitching for Scobey, Arden Nelson of Peerless hit his second home run against Scobey in two games to tie the game. Bill Puckett, who was 12 years old, remembers Arden's booming home run in Peerless: "I believe that the ball hit Pete Kleeman's driveway and then bounced off of his garage door. I don't know how far that would be, but it could have been close to a 400-foot drive. It was the hardest hit ball that I have ever seen in Peerless."*

Ben Haagenson followed with a long ball down the right-field line that umpire Ed Puckett called fair, and ended up on third. Then Sam Belling, who had made the outstanding play in center field in the top half of the inning, after missing a suicide squeeze bunt, hit a pop fly over the shortstop, and Haagenson scored from third for the win.

Rod Tande said, "Reese Puckett would have been the Peerless pitcher that day. He was such a good athlete all the way around. He was a lot like his dad, you know. His dad was soft-spoken. Reese had that way about him, and maybe that's why he didn't come in to play with us. We would have had one more really, really strong arm. Plus, he could play anywhere you put him. I'd have to rank him the best of anyone of that era. He really was that good."

Scobey committed five errors in the game, while Peerless committed none. Peerless's 5-4 come-from-behind win over Doc Norman's previously undefeated Scobey Legionnaires—handing them their only conference loss of the season—was the highlight of the Peerless Post 107 Legion program, and the Elwood Lien Post played clean baseball to do it.

In other exciting intra-county Junior Legion action, Scobey came from behind to beat Flaxville-Whitetail, 6-5. Carl Tande, Scobey's third baseman, beat out an infield single with the bases loaded to give the Legionnaires their 6-5 win, after the Cardinals had jumped to a 5-2 lead in the third inning. Kevin Sell was credited with his second win in conference play in relief of Bill Thompson, while Dallas Hackmann took the loss for Flaxville.

No season would be complete without mentioning how Scobey fared against its old rival, Plentywood. Kevin Sell pitched a one-hitter against Plentywood in a 3-0 Scobey win, and Scobey played errorless ball to back up Kevin's stellar pitching.

Scobey clinched the northern division when the Legionnaires beat defending champion Flaxville-Whitetail 7-0 on Flaxville's home field. Kevin Sell pitched a no-hitter to lead Scobey to the win. The Legionnaires picked up their seven runs on eight hits off Dallas Hackmann, Flaxville-Whitetail's star right-hander. Scobey finished 15-1 in conference play to win the northern division of the district, its only loss coming to Peerless.

The Legionnaires then hosted southern division champion, Fort Peck, in a best-of-three series at Scobey Ball Park to determine the northeastern Montana district champion. Scobey lost the first game 17-9 in 11 innings, with Kevin Sell taking the loss. Needing to win two straight games to take the series, the Legionnaires came roaring back to win games two and three, 22-12 and 11-7. Randy Smith was the winning pitcher in game two, and Kevin Sell won game three. In the third game, Scobey jumped to a 4 to 1 lead, which they built to an 11 to 1 score, going into the ninth inning, when Fort Peck staged a six-run rally but fell short on an 11 to 7 score. Phil Baker, Randy Smith, and Rod Tande were the leading hitters for Scobey.

Doc had led Scobey to its first district title in 12 years.

---

* Pete Kleeman's house was behind the road at the ballfield next to our house.

Scobey then traveled to Laurel to play the Laurel Dodgers in a best-of-three series for the right to determine the eastern division champion and the right to enter the state championship finals. In his first year at Scobey, with two 17-year-olds and a Babe Ruth roster, Doc had taken Scobey further in the postseason than the Legion program had been since 1930, when Scobey played Billings for the eastern division championship. The postseason run for Scobey ended in Laurel, however, as the Dodgers won the first game, 10-4, and the second game, 25-9. Scobey had some tough luck in the series when ace pitcher Kevin Sell was beaned by a pitch, which severely limited Scobey's chances, as he was unable to continue pitching in the series. But the young Scobey team made an impression on the Laurel crowd, as the *Laurel Outlook* wrote this about Doc's young team: "Scobey is the team to watch. Young and inexperienced, Scobey showed promise of turning into a fine ball club as soon as they gain a little size and experience. In the next three years, they will lose only two players."[16]

In the photo of the game between Scobey and Laurel, Scobey is in the field and Laurel is batting. That is likely Bob Roland catching and Kevin Sell pitching in the first game before he got injured. You can also see the Scobey third baseman, shortstop Rod Tande, and the left fielder. Rod tells me that Kevin Sell might have been playing third if he wasn't pitching and that Baldy Sell and Larry Veis also played infield that year.

Scobey playing at Laurel in the first game of the best-of-three series for the eastern division championship. *Laurel Outlook.*

Laurel was, and still is, a great baseball town. I called the *Laurel Outlook* to inquire about obtaining an original of this photo and had a great conversation about baseball with Editor Jaci Webb. I told Jaci that Scobey had played Laurel for the 1979 state championship in Scobey (we won 11-0) and that Laurel is the only team to have more state championships (nine) than Scobey (eight), and what a great baseball town Laurel is. She then told me a story about a man who applied for a job at the refinery there in the 1940s, but he couldn't get a job because he wasn't a good enough baseball player. This was not for the Junior Legion team but for their adult independent team, Laurel's version of the Plainsmen.

It is true that some towns just have an amazing baseball tradition that goes back a long, long time. Scobey is one of those towns. So is Laurel. Any town that has more state championships than Scobey must be a baseball town.

The *Leader* mentioned that the 1959 team prompted Assistant Coach Bob Tande to recall the 1946 and 1947 district champion teams he coached who played off against Miles City each year after winning the district championship. It had been a long time since Scobey had been this far in the postseason. Bob recalled that in 1946 and 1947, Johnny Nelson and Gordon Vanderpan had a combined win-loss record of 27-4 games, and Miles City was the only team that beat them. But looking back even further, the *Leader* correctly recalled that Doc's 1959 Legionnaires had gone further in the postseason playoffs than any Scobey Junior Legion team since Scobey's first Junior Legion team in 1930: "The most active Scobey Junior Legion baseball club in history is shooting to better the mark of Scobey's Junior Legion best. It was more than a quarter of a century ago when a Scobey team played Billings there in the semifinals of Junior Legion baseball for Montana. That team, coached by Irving Davis and P. R. McLaughlin and with ace pitcher Bob Schaefer, now of Chinook, had the Billings Club on the hip in that crucial game but lost out when the late Sidney Smith was claimed not to have touched second on a three-base hit. Myron Johnson, son of Jim Johnson of Scobey, was the star of the game when he hit a home run out of the Billings ballpark. The current Junior Legion team is playing a rambler schedule in addition to its regular district games, and before the season is over, the boys will have played more baseball in a season than any other previous Junior Legion team in this area."[17]

Doc's 1959 Scobey team made quite an impression on the state, and the success of the young team was an early indicator of things to come for Scobey Junior Legion baseball. The team played more games than any previous Junior Legion team in Scobey, hosted a tournament with Class A teams from Canada and North Dakota, went on a state-wide barnstorming tour against Class A teams, won the district championship for the first time in 12 years, and came the closest to making it to the State finals since the 1930 Legion team. The former Carlson Raider brought the same gung-ho spirit with him to Scobey that he brought to Makin Island.

What a special experience it must have been for all those young boys playing for Doc in his inaugural season in Scobey. Kevin Sell, one of only two 17-year-olds on the team, remembers the special experience well. His last year of Legion ball was playing for Doc Norman. I asked him to share a letter about playing for Doc that first season in 1959, and he shared this letter:

Baseball was always on the menu at our home. There were three of us brothers and we all played baseball. Keith the oldest, class of 1955, was the best and he was a pitcher. He played for the Scobey Legion and later for the Plainsmen our town team. His catcher on the town team was Jack Reiner another Scobey star. During this time Keith was given a tryout by the pro team The Williston Oilers. Later, after leaving Scobey, Keith played several years of baseball in the Navy. He also played in Helena with the East Helena Smelter team along with country music legend Charlie Pride. Later Keith managed the Helena Legion team for many years, and now has the annual "Keith Sell Invitational Tournament" named for him. Dwain, class of 1962, and I played locally in Scobey in the Little League, Babe Ruth, and American Legion programs. Prior to 1959 I had played under both Jack Reiner and Reid Grayson.

However, for Dwain, and for me, 1959 was our first year under Doc Norman. It was actually my only year playing for Doc. As in many small towns, none of the activities, including baseball, would survive for long without total support and loyalty from the parents and townspeople. My parents spent many hours at the ballpark selling tickets, umpiring, working concessions, keeping score and getting the field ready for play. I say "Thank You" to all the good folks who so willingly supported Scobey baseball.

I graduated from Scobey High in 1959 at 17 years old. I recall that at that time 17 was the maximum age allowed for players in legion baseball, so 1959 was my last year as a player. It was, of course, my only year playing for Doc. Bob Roland, our catcher, was a year younger at 16 or just 17. The rest of the team was either 14 or 15 and had just finished grades 8 or 9 in school. Despite being young these guys were all very athletic and very competitive. None of my classmates had played baseball for several years, so the young guys were able to play right from the get-go. I am proud to have played baseball with them. Our team in 1959 was also blessed to have Marge and Ann Norman and Lillian and Lona Rae Tande on our traveling unit. Best cheerleaders you could ever hope for. Doc was the Manager and Bob Tande was the everything-else coach and trainer. These two guys did it all and did it well. In later years Flaxville and Peerless were part of the team, but in 1959 they were the district competition along with teams from Outlook and Plentywood.

Doc and Bob trained us with lots of practice and drills. Both Doc and Bob had regular and demanding careers that they worked at all day as well. One of the really big changes was our new uniforms. These included caps and stockings and we looked sharp. That probably gained us a little advantage against our rivals. We dressed for success.

And we won. I think we won all of our league games except one against Peerless. I was a fairly good local pitcher. I'm sure my top speed barely approached the low 80s, but Doc taught me an effective slider and a change-up. So we won locally, but Doc also scheduled us against much bigger towns like Williston ND, Helena, Butte, and Missoula. I do not think we won these games, but they made us even hungrier to win locally.

Probably the highlight of our summer was taking a road trip to play Helena, Butte, and Missoula. We went pretty much first class staying in motels with pools and eating in restaurants. There were few, if any, cold-cut sandwiches on the hoods of our three travel cars, one of which I drove. Most of us had not traveled much beyond staying at the hotel in Wolf Point for the district basketball tournament. I think our only really close game on the trip was against Missoula on the last day, but we had fun. One of my not-so-fun memories of that trip was leaving my uniform in the locker room at either Helena or Butte. Bob Tande let me wear his uniform. It would have been large, but it worked. That was typical of Bob. He was always kind, caring and helpful. Doc was kind too, but in more of a tough-love kind of way. Doc called me "Keev" the only person to do so, but it was alright coming from him. Marge was like a mother to all of us and Ann was everyone's little sister tomboy to the max. She was always happy and welcomed by our entire team. Mike Norman our first baseman was a soft-spoken, but competitive guy. Doc's expectations were always that everything was done with the well-being of the team in mind. With Doc you never had to guess how you were doing. Doc was firm and direct, but fair.

One of the memories I have of the trip involved an unexpected car repair on the road home. Somehow a rock flew up beneath one of our cars and knocked a small hole in the oil pan. We made it to the next town and into a service station. It was necessary to get home that night as I recall. So while the team had supper at a nearby café some of us were able to patch and seal the small hole. We were able to drive home that night. End of trip. Funny the small details you remember years later.

So we won our district and next faced Nashua/Fort Peck in a 3-game playoff. They had some kids the same age as me against whom I had played high school basketball. Winning this meant a trip to the next level of the state playoff system. We lost game 1 and won game 2. I had pitched game 1 and came back two days later for game 3. I had nothing left and was really struggling. Our guys scored runs however, so we were in the game. Doc brought in Larry Veis and he pitched the game of his life. He shut them down, so we won and advanced.

Our next games were against Laurel in Laurel. This was another 3-game playoff to advance to the state finals. We lost. They were just bigger and better that weekend. I unfortunately was beaned while batting in the early innings in the first game. I was hit at the bottom of my helmet near my temple, but not on it. Doc checked me out, gave me some encouragement, and I stayed in for a few more innings. I don't think my well-being was a factor, but I do remember it happening. We lost the next game and our season was over. One of my good memories from that trip was eating pizza for the first time ever at a place in Billings called Ron George's Restaurant. It may have been the first for others too, but it makes me realize just how much I still had to learn. And I did at Eastern Montana College in Billings where I went to school. I played baseball at Eastern for two of my four years. One of my teammates was Gary Brenden from Flaxville.

One final memory involves oranges. Marge would buy oranges for us to eat during the games. However, Terry Veis and some of his pals would have a contest to see who could peel the orange with the fewest peels. By the third inning the oranges were usually gone. Needless to say, this was not a highly encouraged team-building exercise. We have kidded Terry about this for all the years since then. It still brings a lot of headshakes and laughter.

After almost 64 years, that summer of 1959 remains, not just a good baseball memory, but a great life memory. And at the center of it all is my mentor, my manager, and my lovable friend, Doc Norman.

Kevin Sell, Meridian, Idaho (2023)

Kevin's younger brother, Dwain "Baldy" Sell, was one of the 14-year-olds on Doc's 1959 team. I asked him what it was like playing for Doc the first year he got to Scobey in 1959. He said, "I was only 14 years old on that first team Doc coached in 1959. We had a lot of really good athletes in Scobey at that time, football players, basketball players, but not baseball. There was me, Randy Smith, Larry Veis, Carl, and Rod Tande. Our pitchers were my older brother Kevin Sell, Randy Smith, Bob Roland, Larry Veis, and Bill Thompson."

"Doc taught us how to play baseball. He taught us how to get down on one knee to field balls in the outfield and throw balls from the outfield to the infield. He taught us how to bunt, hit the cutoff man, and how to do double steals. We all had jobs, so we couldn't have practices at a certain time. Randy and I, and others, had jobs so we might have one practice at seven in the morning and one at six at night. Doc came there and he just showed us how to play baseball the right way. One of my first memories of Doc coaching in a game was when Doc told us, 'I don't want you razzing the other team. I want you guys to promote our team.' He also told us, 'You keep making mental errors, I'll say something, but not physical errors.

"Our Babe Ruth team the year before in 1958 was good and was coached by Bob Tande. When Doc came in, he assessed our talent and put us in the best positions. I thought I was the best player in my class. I wanted to be a shortstop or second base, but Doc told me, 'Baldy, I got to tell you something. You can't play in the infield if you're not going to keep your head down, so he put me in right field. Then I realized he put players where they should play. Doc just knew how to win, but he made it fun for us.

"In our first year in 1959, Doc took us on a barnstorming trip to Havre, Helena, Butte, and Missoula. The last game we played was against Missoula, where the year before, in 1958, Doc was the assistant coach to Gene Thompson, who was still head coach at Missoula in 1959. We went ahead 3-0 but lost the game in the bottom of the ninth, 5-4 on a walk-off single when a runner scored from second. Kevin pitched well, throwing a four-hitter against a really good Missoula team.

"Doc always played his best players to win. He immediately established a culture of winning. When we played in Wolf Point at the start of the season, he played his best players. At practice, he would hit just bullets to his son Mike Norman at first base. Right away, we won. He really had us playing the right positions. Rod Tande played shortstop. We beat the hell out of Wolf Point and Plentywood during the season. The only loss we had was to Peerless. We beat Nashua (Fort Peck) two out of three games to win the district championship. Then we played against Laurel for the Eastern championship. We lost in two games in the best-of-three series. Kevin got beaned by a pitch in the first game, which really hurt him (and us).

"The year we had our first team in 1959, Flaxville had a team. When you guys played in the 1970s, the Flaxville and Peerless kids were playing for Doc, but it wasn't that way then. In 1959, we could have had Dennis Baker, Doug Krassin, and the best of all was Gary Brenden from Flaxville. They would have started and really made a difference. They had three kids who could really play. Doc tried to get all of them to come to Scobey to play; he almost begged 'em in Flaxville to combine. Bob Tande and Doc also recruited Reese Puckett Jr. in Peerless to come and play with us, but he didn't."

I asked left fielder Terry Veis, one of Doc's many 14-year-olds on the 1959 team, what his first impression was of Doc and to share any memories he had of playing for Doc that first year. He said, "It was nice to have someone like

Doc, learning a lot of things, and he just taught us things like when you're in the outfield, and a ground ball comes at you, if you have a chance, make sure you block it, get down on one knee. Just little things like that; he taught us the fundamentals. And it was just so fancy, you know, we got new uniforms, away and home uniforms, sliding pads, stuff like that. We had things I hadn't heard of."

Bob Tande's son Rod, who played shortstop for Doc in 1959, also has special memories of that magical first season playing on the district championship team for his dad and Doc. I asked Rod if he recalled his first memories of Doc. He said, "Sure. The first time I met Doc, I had heard that he was moving to town and that he was a baseball guy. He had a small medical practice just off Main Street, and I had some kind of an injury, a scrape or whatever, so my dad brought me in to see this guy. And so, as per Doc, the first thing he did, he looked at whatever was wrong with me, and he says, 'So I hear you play baseball.' I said, 'Yeah, yeah, I do.' 'Well,' he says, 'I want you and your boys to come down to practice'—and this was before the season, it had to have been winter at that point. So we're excited, you know, and we think we know how to play baseball. Well, one of the first things I can remember is that Doc asked, 'Does anyone know how to slide properly?' Well, of course I raised my hand. 'Okay,' he says, 'Rod's gonna show us how to slide.' Well, I took a run at it and slid, and wiping the dirt off my knee, Doc says, 'Well, I'm gonna show you something else.' That's one of my first memories because—not that my dad didn't know baseball—but it was just, how shall I say, a step up. The people who coached us and encouraged us no doubt played a good brand of baseball, but technically, Doc was the man. He had us doing drills in the gym in the winter. Somehow, he got hold of the superintendent of the chairman of the school board, and we were throwing balls in the gym prior to our spring practice. He was ready to go, and he taught us the techniques, not only at first, but he also kept developing us. He had a mind for details. He taught the proper way to throw a curveball, a slider, how to hold the balls, how to move to first, a lot of that, and so technically, Doc excelled."

PLAINSMEN

THERE WAS NO ADMINISTRATIVE ERROR IN THE FILING OF THE Northeastern Montana (NeMont) Baseball League with the National Baseball Congress in 1959, as in early April, the Associated Press announced the official franchising of the NeMont Baseball League in Montana into its 1959 national association. Joe Anderson, still heavily involved with the Plainsmen as general manager, was the state NBC commissioner that year and ensured the league was properly registered this time. The five NeMont League teams were Scobey, Poplar, Circle, Glasgow Air Force Base, and the Glasgow Highlanders. Vic Luft of Scobey was the league president, and Kenneth Hansen of Poplar was secretary. The NeMont League was one of several leagues in Montana for players of unlimited age aimed at the 24th annual Montana state tournament, which was to be hosted on July 30 at Scobey Ball Park. The winner of that tournament would qualify for the NBC World Series in Wichita.

The pitching staff for the 1959 Scobey Plainsmen during the regular season included Mike Dishman (from Missoula), Andy Stolen, and Ron Fjeld. Jack Reiner did the catching, backed up by Ken Lekvold, who also played second base. Infielders were Ken Triplett, Leo Zimmer, Cliff Hagfeldt, Ron Wangrud, Marvin Torgerson, Gary Davies, and Howard Farver. Outfielders were Gary Farver, Ordean Wangrud, Dallas Gaines, and Larry Wangrud. Harry Larson, a veteran ball player of past Scobey teams, was the 1959 season manager and pilot for the Plainsmen.

The Plainsmen repeated as champions of the NeMont League. Here were some highlights—mostly featuring fine pitching—of the 1959 regular season:

- Andy Stolen pitched a three-hitter and struck out 15 to lead Scobey to an 8-3 win over Poplar.
- Mike Dishman, newly acquired pitcher from Missoula who had pitched Legion ball for Gene Thompson and Doc while he was there, scattered six hits and gave up four runs in an 11-4 win over Glasgow AFB.

Scobey Plainsmen. Top, standing, L–R: Ordean Wangrud, Leo Zimmer, Mike Dishman, Cliff Hagfeldt, Dave Wensloff. Kneeling: Jack Reiner, Ken Triplett, Ron Fjeld, Gary Davies. Seated: Howard Farver, Batboy Paulson, Buzz Torgerson, Batboy Richardson, Andy Stolen, Dallas Gaines. Team manager Harry Larson not shown. *Leader.*

- Mike Dishman beat Norm Anderson of Circle in a pitcher's duel, as the Plainsmen beat Circle 3-2 under lights at Scobey Ball Park. Dishman tossed a four-hitter, struck out 18 Wildcats, and only walked two. He was a little better than his opponent on the mound, Norm Anderson of Circle, who also chucked a four-hitter, struck out nine, and walked four.
- Scobey's top three pitchers combined on a one-hitter to beat Glasgow AFB 6-4, and Scobey clinched first place in the NeMont League. Mike Dishman started and won his fourth game of the year, despite being tossed out of the game for arguing balls and strikes. Andy Stolen pitched middle relief to get the hold, and Ron Fjeld came in to close it out and get the save, preserving Scobey's 6-4 win.

The nine-team, double-elimination NBC State Tournament was hosted at Scobey Ball Park, with the winner qualifying for a trip to Wichita, Kansas, for the NBC World Series. Teams from across the state of Montana came to Scobey, including the Lewistown Jaycees, Sidney Gems, Glasgow Air Force Base, Glasgow Highlanders, Poplar Oilers, Westby Nitehawks, Flaxville Cardinals, Baker, and the host Scobey Plainsmen, defending state NBC champions. Team rosters were not limited to regular-season players, so teams—including the Plainsmen—beefed up their rosters (especially pitching), for the tournament, hoping to qualify for the nationals in Wichita. Scobey added John Freeman from and Norm Anderson from Circle to its pitching staff. Most teams built up strong clubs for the tourney by recruiting top college and seasonal ball players from throughout the state.

The Sidney Gems, "an alert, hard-hitting team," managed by Bill Sharp and composed mostly of former Sidney Junior Legion players, won its first Montana state amateur championship, winning five straight games. The Gems beat Poplar, 16 to 9; Glasgow AFB, 22 to 5; Scobey, 8 to 7; Lewistown, 12 to 3 in the semifinals (Sidney pitcher Ed Williams had a no-hitter through seven), and Scobey, 6 to 3 in the championship game.[18]

Here were some tournament highlights:

- In a 6-0 loss to the Lewistown Jaycees, Don Tryan of Flaxville had all three of Flaxville's hits off Jim Neal from Lewistown. Neal struck out 12 Cardinals in the shutout. Barth from Flaxville struck out seven Jaycees in the loss.
- Scobey won their first game over Baker, 7-1, but the game was tied 1-1 after six innings. Pitcher Freeman for Scobey got 14 strikeouts.
- In Sidney's 8-7 win over Scobey, the Plainsmen had two men on base in the bottom of the 9th inning but were unable to push a run across to tie the game. Andy Stolen and Mike Dishman pitched for Scobey, sharing 12 strikeouts between them. Sidney's starter pitcher Erwin Schmitt and relief pitcher Ed Williams had only three strikeouts, but Sidney's tight fielding, with John Carranza's hitting and stellar play in the infield, gave them the margin of victory. Dick Wilson and Stolen led the hitting for Scobey with three hits each. Carranza got three hits for Sidney.
- Scobey pounded Baker for fifteen hits to win 12-5. The Plainsmen's Norm Anderson had four hits, with Buzz Torgerson and Mike Dishman adding three each. Pitcher Mike Dishman had 17 strikeouts, but had control problems, as his 10 walks led to five Baker runs.
- The Plainsmen, "Scobey's iron men," had to play in all three of the tournament's 18 games on Sunday, beating Westby and Lewistown before losing to Sidney in the championship. In their 8-6 win over Westby, Plainsmen starting pitcher Ron Fjeld got the win, and Andy Stolen earned the save for Scobey. Ron and Andy got seven strikeouts between them and gave up four walks. Norm Anderson led the hitting for Scobey with two hits. The Plainsmen then defeated Lewistown, 6-3, with Norm Anderson ("Anderson the Great") getting the win on the mound for Scobey. Norm also got three of Scobey's 13 hits to lead his team in batting. Andy Stolen relieved Anderson in the 7th inning for Scobey to earn his second save of the day.
- Scobey then faced Sidney in the nightcap for the championship, but they would have needed to beat Sidney twice to repeat as state champions. Stolen, who had relieved Anderson against Lewistown, continued for Scobey against Sidney in the final. The "well-rounded" Sidney ballclub was too strong for the "weary" Plainsmen, and they beat Scobey 6-3. Stolen was relieved by Dishman, and between the two, they held Sidney to seven hits while Scobey gathered six hits with Anderson getting three of them. Larry Henderson was the winning pitcher for Sidney and also led his team in hitting.

Sidney's young team was credited with winning its first state tournament with good pitching, solid defense, and speed. Their three pitchers were Ed Williams, Larry Henderson, and Erwin Schmitt, with Jim Haugen handling the staff behind the plate. The Gems' infield included Tom Quilling at first, John Carranza at second, Craig Price at shortstop, and Wolff at third base. A speedy outfield in-

Scobey Greenhorns, 1959 Fast-Pitch Champions. Muriel Grayson, Della Hartgrove, Lillian Wahl, Carol Grotjohn, Leverne Waller, Alphild Doucette, Mae Kessler, Lorraine Jerome, Millie Poyner, Ruth Goller, Alice Halvorson, Ada Whitlow, Edith Grayson, Edna Hedges, and Coach Reid Grayson. *Leader.*

cluded Ron Quilling in center, pitcher Erwin Schmitt, Ernie Olness, pitcher Larry Henderson, Jack Marman, and Delmar Nesper alternating in right and left fields. The Sidney Gems added only "lanky fastballer" Ed Williams, formerly of the Williston Oilers of the Man-Dak League, to their regular-season roster for the tournament.

FAST-PITCH SOFTBALL

WITH THE BASEBALL (AND FAST-PITCH SOFTBALL) RENAISSANCE now in its third year, the Scobey Greenhorns, coached by Reid Grayson, dominated the regular season, outscoring their opponents by 411 to 191 to win the league. The Greenhorns had 11 batters hitting over .300, led by Carol Grotjohn and Lillian Wahl at .576 each and Alice Halvorson at .532, with Ruth Goller, Edna Hedges, Ada Whitlow, Allie Doucette, Leverne Waller, Edith Grayson, Della Hartgrove, and Lorraine Jerome all hit over .300. Other squad members, Mae Kessler, Millie Poyner, Christine Shennum, Joyce McCann and JoAnn Vandeberg also played during the season, but had limited at-bats.

After winning the regular-season title, the dominant Greenhorns then sought to win their first postseason league tournament championship. The six teams in the tournament were the Scobey Greenhorns, the Scobey Slick Chicks, the Plentywood Jaguars, the Antelope Fauns, the Reserve Starlets, and the Peerless Belles. (It didn't seem like Ed Puckett's Peerless women's fast-pitch team could settle on a team name, as this was the third team for Peerless in three years: they were known as the Wranglerettes in 1957 and the Pansies in 1958.) The Greenhorns won their first postseason tournament behind the pitching of Edna "Fireball" Hedges, as she beat defending champion Peerless 14-3 in the semifinals and the Plentywood Jaguars 20-7 for the championship. The Greenhorns were the third different team to win the tournament in three years, as Ed's Girls from Plentywood won it in 1957 and the Peerless Pansies in 1958.

Coach Ed Puckett organized the first women's fast-pitch invitational softball tournament in Peerless in 1959, with the Scobey Slick Chicks defeating the Scobey Greenhorns 14 to 6 in the championship. Host Peerless beat Plentywood 7 to 3 for third place. This would be the first in a long line of big softball tournaments hosted in Peerless, when the small town became the epicenter of women's softball in northeastern Montana in the late 1960s and early 1970s.

EXTRA INNINGS

ROD TANDE, WHO MOSTLY PLAYED SHORTSTOP IN 1959, remembers catching Kevin Sell a few times. He said, "He's probably the best pitcher I caught in Legion. He had a zip on his ball and was such a force. It's too bad that he wasn't a year or two younger, because he faced down Laurel; he was just a marvelous pitcher."

Not to be outdone by rival Scobey, Plentywood built a sparkling new ballpark in 1959 named "Sportsman Park," replacing the old Riba Field. The *Williston Herald* sponsored its 3rd Annual Herald Amateur Tournament, with Saturday's games played at Municipal Park, home of the Williston Oilers, but all Sunday games were played at the new Sportsman Park in Plentywood. Tournament manager Harry E. Polk of the *Williston Herald* said, "Plentywood's new field is one of the finest in this area, and the splendid cooperation of the Athletic Club there couldn't have been finer."[19] The Plainsmen lost the championship game in a pitcher's duel between "Big Ed" Williams of the Williston Herald Headliners and Scobey's John Freeman. Scobey lost the game in the bottom of the ninth when the Headliners had a runner on third and put on the suicide squeeze. The bunter missed, and the baserunner was caught in a rundown, but third baseman Leo Zimmer's throw to Jack Reiner was wide of the plate, allowing the winning run to score.

The Scobey-Plentywood rivalry was not exclusive to baseball, as the Scobey Greenhorns and Plentywood Jaguars women's fast-pitch softball teams had an incident at the new Sportsman Park in Plentywood at a tournament later in the season that led to bad blood between the two teams. The Greenhorns won the championship game 16-15 over Plentywood, but ran into some confusion. At the start of the game, the Plentywood rules committee stated that any time one of the two teams got ahead by 10 runs, the game would be over. The Greenhorns led 16-5 Plentywood in the 6th inning and thought the game was over, but then the rules committee changed its mind and made the two teams play on through the seven innings. The let-down suffered by the Greenhorns on this occasion almost lost them the contest, as the Plentywood team, "getting its fourth strike, so to speak, came on strong," but the Greenhorns eked out a 16-15 victory. The *Leader* stated, "It is this sort of horseplay that will not be seen again on the part of officials as it causes needless bad feelings."[20]

Mike Norman started at first base for Doc's first team in Scobey in 1959. He had converted from catcher to third base in Little League in Missoula because he was the only boy who could throw the ball across the infield, but Doc played him at first. It was the summer of his 8th-grade year, as he was a year behind most of the other 14-year-olds, like Rod Tande and Baldy Sell, who were freshmen. He was yet another one of Doc's 14-year-olds on the team. Mike did not want to leave Missoula to move to Scobey, as all his friends were there, and he was a teenager. Interested in his teenage transition, I asked Mike how he fared assimilating into the Scobey scene that first year. He told me this story: "Academics were easy for me. I got mostly A's and some B's in school, so that created some problems because sometimes back then you'd get made fun of for being smarter, guys in my class like Ben Lee Danelson and Turk Forchak. I wasn't much of a basketball player, but I went out to play basketball anyway in the wintertime. After practice, I took a shower and went to put on my clothes, and I found that someone had thrown all my clothes in the shower, and it was 20 below zero out. So I put all my clothes on, and they were frozen by the time I got home. That sort of ticked me off, so the next week, the basketball coach, who was also the PE teacher, announced that we were going to have boxing for PE. I had taken boxing lessons, and my dad had taught me a lot about boxing. Ben and Turk were harassing me, so Turk says, 'Well, I'll box Norman.' And I said, 'Okay.' Turk was a fairly small guy; I wasn't big, but I was quite a bit bigger than him. So we put on these big boxing gloves, and Turk came out, and he didn't know anything. He came out just trying to swing big roundhouse swings, so I just blocked every one, and then he got a little closer and I just gave him two left jabs and a right uppercut, and I knocked him out cold in the gym. So they had to take him to my dad's office. Anyway, after that, Turk and I actually became good friends, and Ben became very friendly after that. So I sort of fought my way into there." Nothing like a couple left jabs and a solid uppercut knockout punch to make some friends in a new town.

In a sign of the generosity of the Normans, and how their contribution went far beyond the baseball field, Doc and Marge showed the Scobey boys the beauty of western Montana on the road trip. "Following their rambler playing schedule, the Normans took the team up to a mountain lake resort over the July 4th weekend, where some of the boys saw mountains and the tall trees for the first time in their lives. It was a memorable trip for a Scobey Junior Legion team, and they were also able to sample the standard of baseball being played on the Class A Junior Legion circuit."[21]

The Scobey Junior Legion team took their knocks on the road trip—literally. Terry Veis recalls an incident in the Helena game. "We were playing in Helena and they were broadcasting it on the radio and they went, 'Oh, routine ball hit to so-and-so from Scobey, routine fly ball, oh, it hit him in the head.'"

The baseball renaissance that began in 1957 with the building of the Scobey Ball Park was flourishing in 1959. It is hard to imagine how busy the Scobey Ball Park was in those days. Rod Tande remembers how active the field was when he played Junior Legion in 1959. "There were Little League games starting at five o'clock. Then there was a huge league of women's fast-pitch softball, then there were men's fast-pitch softball games, all on the same night. It was practically every night of the week, you know, with the lights on. When the lights were put up and the ballpark was built the way we know it now, it was a marvelous time for the entire community." As an example of how active the field was in 1959, here was the schedule for the week of June 18 to June 25:[22]

- June 18: Cubs vs. Flaxville, Little League B; Whitetail vs. Peerless, Little League A; Peerless vs. Stags, Men's Fast-pitch
- June 19: Braves vs. Indians, Little League B; Slick Chicks vs. Greenhorns, Women's Fast-pitch; Falcons vs. Mechanics, Men's Fast-pitch
- June 20: Scobey vs. Outlook, Junior Legion, at 8 p.m.
- June 21: Scobey vs. Flaxville Whitetail, Junior Legion, at 8 p.m.
- June 22: Peerless vs. Giants, Little League A; Peerless vs. Four Buttes, Little League A; Butte Creek vs. Four Buttes, Men's Fast-pitch
- June 23: Braves vs. Flaxville, Little League B; Yanks vs. Whitetail, Little League A; Whitetail vs. Stags, Men's Fast-pitch
- June 24: Scobey Plainsmen vs. Glasgow Highlanders, NEMont Baseball League, at 8 p.m.
- June 25: Four Buttes vs. Indians, Little League B; Four Buttes vs. Yanks, Little League A; Greenhorns vs. Peerless, Women's Fast-pitch.

Junior Legion Baseball was growing in Montana in 1959, as 34 American Legion posts fielded junior baseball teams. There were 12 class A teams and 22 class B teams. Of the 22 Class B teams, 10 of them (almost half) came from the northeastern part of the state, as Scobey, Peerless, Flaxville-Whitetail, Plentywood, Glasgow, Opheim, Poplar, Fort Peck, Wolf Point, and Outlook Legion posts all fielded teams. Northeastern Montana was where baseball was played in Class B Junior Legion baseball in 1959.

It was a historic season for the Scobey Junior Legion program in 1959, but the Missoula Junior Legion program also established its own history that year—thanks to Scobey. Their 585-mile road trip to Scobey—bringing their bongo drums, flip flops, and cutoffs with them across the state—was a record trip for any Missoula Junior Legion club. The *Missoulian* mentioned Scobey baseball tradition in the same breath as the record road trip: "Scobey is historic in Montana baseball in that in the early '20s, just after the Chicago World Series scandal, three of the Black Sox barred for participating came to Scobey and played baseball for the team assembled by the wheat-rich, diamond-enthusiastic farmers of the area. That was when the whole world heard of Scobey, when Felsch, Risberg and Co. were there."[23]

1960

The Plainsmen Win Their Second State Championship and Doc Flies Too Close to the Sun

> *We are happy to be in the State A competition this year. It will do our boys good and acquaint them better with higher standards of baseball and sportsmanship. Win or lose, our opponents will find tough picking. We intend to win.*
>
> —Doc Norman, Daniels County Leader, April 7, 1960

After Doc's blockbuster first year in Scobey in 1959, in which Doc led the fledgling team to its first district championship in 12 years, Doc, the gung-ho marine ever hitting the beachhead, decided to move the young team up to the Class A division. This was classic Doc—aggressively charging forward with complete abandon like he did as a marine on Makin Island—but he moved too fast, too soon in this case, flying too close to the sun. "The move up to Class A," as Baldy Sell said, "was a mistake." Because the Junior Legion age limit at the time was 17 years old, Kevin Sell, the ace pitcher of 1959, had aged out of eligibility, as had his batterymate Bob Roland. The young, inexperienced team of 1959 was now just one year older but was still a very young team, even by the 17-year-old age limit standard. The team competed in the Eastern A Division with Miles City, Glendive, and Billings, with home-and-home doubleheaders scheduled with each. Billings had won 9 of 10 state A championships and was coached by Doc's friend Ed Bayne. The 1960 Billings team included Dave McNally in his final year of eligibility. They won the regional and took second in the national tournament, the best finish ever for a Montana team.

LEGIONNAIRES

The Scobey Junior Legion team roster—even by the 17-year-old age limit at the time—was still incredibly young, as there was not a 17-year-old on the roster. The team consisted of 16-year-olds Bink Sheron, Terry Veis, Larry Veis, Carl Tande, Randy Smith, Phil Baker, and Pete Darchuk; 15-year-olds Baldy Sell, Rod Tande, Mike Norman, Bill "Oscar" Thompson, Don Oie, Charlie Mueller, and John Downs; and 14-year-olds Terry "Turk" Forchak, Gordon Cornwell, and Al Luft. Doc was assisted by Jack Reiner (catchers and infield) and Gordon "Butch" Goddard.

Doc stated in the *Leader* at the start of the year, "We are happy to be in the State A competition this year. It will do our boys good and acquaint them better with higher standards of baseball and sportsmanship. Win or lose, our opponents will find tough picking. We intend to win."

To prepare for the step-up to Class A, Doc purchased new uniforms, "the monster"—a brand-new pitching machine—as well as a team bus, which the team used for a barnstorming tour of North Dakota and eastern Minnesota, playing Devils Lake, Crookston, Grand Forks, Moorhead, Fargo, Bismarck, Dickinson, and Jamestown, then played Fargo, Minot, and Williston separately in the season. Terry Veis recalls the famous "red bus" for their barnstorming road trip. "Doc bought a bus, it was this old

Scobey Legionnaires. Standing, L–R: Bud Veis, Larry Veis, Rod Tande, Don Oie, Pete Darchuk, Terry Veis, Alan Luft, Randy Smith, Billy Thompson, Coach Clyde Norman. Kneeling, left to right: Bink Sheron, Charlie Mueller, Dwain Sell, Bob Thompson, Mike Norman, Terry Forchak, John Downs, Gordie Cornwell, and (in front of kneeling row) batboy, Curtis Luft. *Leader.*

bus, and the team sanded it off, and we painted it red, and that was our touring bus. Because we were impressed by the Missoula boys, the big city boys, we ended up getting some bongo drums and stuff like that, too, and watermelon, we had watermelon floating around the floor of the bus."

Charlie Mueller remembers the zany barnstorming road trip to North Dakota and Minnesota. "On our barnstorming trip, we actually ended up in Eau Claire, Wisconsin, for a ballgame. And guess who was on their roster? Joe Torre. It was either Joe Torre or his brother. Here we are, from little ol' Scobey, Montana. That was quite a trip. Doc Norman's red school bus, that old bus, was somehow going to take us to Minnesota. We had a watermelon, and we're tossing it around on the bus, and all of a sudden, somebody dropped it. Now we've got watermelon going back and forth on the bus. We pull into Devils Lake, North Dakota, and Doc is pretty upset with us. Baldy, Pete Darchuk, and I didn't even get close to our room until we had that bus washed out. Doc would always have us run, and Pete Darchuk, who was a big boy, says to Doc, 'Well, Doc, now that I cleaned out the bus, do I have to run?' Later on, we stopped in Fargo, North Dakota, and Doc didn't hold back on the old checkbook, you know, so we go to this really nice restaurant to eat, like a night club. Doc says, 'Okay boys, order whatever you want, whatever you want. When we got done eating, they handed Doc the check, and Doc's going down through the check, and he says, 'Hmm, who ordered filet mignon?' Bink Sheron raised his hand. Then Doc says, 'Well, who else ordered filet mignon?' Bink raised his hand again and said, 'Doc, I ordered two.'"

The young Legionnaires had difficulty competing with the Class A competition, but dominated any Class B competition they played, as they beat Fort Peck 20-8 and 10-9, then beat Wolf Point—eventual district B champion—8-7 and 6-5. Later in the season, they also beat Wolf Point 10-2. They lost to Lewistown in two close games, 7-5 and 7-6. Had they remained in Class B in 1960, Scobey would have likely repeated as district champions and perhaps made some noise in the playoffs.

After previous doubleheader losses to Glendive and Miles City and following a doubleheader loss to Miles City over the Fourth of July weekend, Scobey canceled the following weekend's doubleheader against Billings in Scobey. The boys finished the season following the Miles City games, resuming play against Glendive the following weekend. They played well, losing in extra innings in the first game, then 16-15 in the second game slugfest.

Later in the season, the team played Minot at home. For all the difficulties in the step-up to Class A, the young team

Scobey Plainsmen, regular-season and state tournament team. Front row, L-R: Wally Sinner, Jack Reiner, Ken Lekvold, Vince Zimmer and Ed Teller. Second row, left to right: Dick Wilson, Buzz Torgerson, Andy Stolen, Ken Hansen and Gordon Skjerven. Standing, left to right, manager Joe Anderson, Ronnie Fjeld, John Austin, Tom Rasmussen, Norm Anderson and Jim Peterson. Not pictured are Cliff Hagfeldt, Tom Quilling, and Ron Quilling. *Leader.*

played more games—and a tougher schedule—than any Scobey Junior Legion team in history to that date. It was a frustrating season for Doc, the parents, and the community, but the boys played through the end of the season and became better baseball players.

Wolf Point, coached by Bobby Lowry, won the northeastern district championship—its first of five consecutive district championships—then lost to Laurel 11-5 and 6-5 (in eleven innings) in a best-of-three series for the eastern division championship at Wolf Point. Laurel went on to win the state B championship in a best-of-three series against Sunburst.

I asked Baldy Sell, who was only 15 years old in 1960, what his memories of that season were, moving up to Class A. He said, "We weren't good enough to compete in Class A. We couldn't compete against the likes of Glendive, Miles City, and Billings (with Dave McNally). If Doc would have kept us in Class B, we would have had a chance. Mike [Norman], Larry [Veis], Rod [Tande], we were all good players. At the start of the season, he took us on a barnstorming tour through North Dakota to play A teams. We were in over our heads. We played Williston, Dickinson, Bismarck, Mandan, Fargo, and Jamestown on the trip. Phil Jackson was pitching for Williston. We weren't able to beat those teams.

"When we were coming back from our trip to North Dakota, Bink Sheron and I had peashooters and were shooting them on the bus. Doc said, 'Baldy, Fink you're outta here!' I got out and I rode in Marge's car. When my mom and dad found out what happened, they told me, 'We're not asking you. Get your butt over there and apologize to Doc and Marge.' I did, and they appreciated the apology. Later that season, we lost to Glendive and Miles City, then canceled against Billings, where Dave McNally was playing his last season."

PLAINSMEN

WHILE DOC AND THE JUNIOR LEGION TEAM STRUGGLED IN their move up to Class A in 1960, the Scobey Plainsmen reached their zenith. The Plainsmen, managed by Joe Anderson, three-peated as the NeMont League champions, winning the regular-season schedule, which consisted of Scobey, Fairview, Plentywood, Outlook, and Culbertson.* They then proceeded to win the State NBC championship hosted at Scobey Ball Park, beating Culbertson 2-1 in the final, qualifying the Plainsmen to play in the NBC World Series in Wichita, Kansas, as the Montana champion. The winning pitcher for Scobey in the championship game was Wally Sinner.† He pitched 22 and two-thirds innings in two days in the tournament.

After area fundraising and strong community support, the Plainsmen were able to travel to Wichita to play in the 1960 NBC World Series. Manager Joe Anderson stated that under the National Baseball Congress rules, the league champion could add up to six all-star players in the competing local area for the World Series, so he beefed up his roster for nationals. Making the trip to Wichita for the Scobey Plainsmen were Gordon Skjerven, Ken Lekvold, Allan Lowes, Wally Sinner, Andy Stolen, Cecil McCarrow, Bob Beatty, Norm Anderson, Kenneth Hansen, Tom and Ron Quilling, Larry Ferguson, Paul Feser, and Cliff Hagfeldt. Accompanying the squad as assistant manager was Luverne Hansen, who said, "I don't imagine I'll be of much use in the strategy, but with the new station wagon of mine, I'll be able to help get the boys down there in good shape."[24]

The loaded Plainsmen team played well at nationals, winning three games and taking seventh place. In their first game, they beat the Mississippi state champions, the West Point Packers, 7-6. Then, "in a stunning upset," the Plainsmen knocked off the third-seeded Cherokee Oklahoma Chiefs, 5-2. They were then defeated by the number one seed and eventual NBC World Series champions, Grand Rapids, Michigan, 8-0. The Plainsmen bounced back and won their third game of the tournament over the National Negro champs from College Park, Georgia, 8-6. They lost their next game to the Kansas state champions, the Wichita Wellers, 2-0. This eliminated the Plainsmen from the tournament, but they had made a mark in being the first Montana team to have ever won a game at the National Tournament, finishing better than any Montana team at the national amateur tournament. Wally Sinner pitched all three wins. "It was thought by many that the Plainsmen were of a caliber to have been able to compete in either of the two professional leagues in the area—the Class C Pioneer League or Class D Man-Dak League, or with any of the other semipro leagues of the Northwest."[25]

Manager Joe Anderson receives the seventh-place trophy the Plainsmen won at the National Baseball Congress World Series in Wichita, Kansas. *Great Falls Tribune.*

Manager Joe Anderson came back with plans for future Montana entries in the tournament. He said, "I would like to see the state get a little more interested in this tournament. I am sure with the right backing, Montana could place pretty high in this tournament, if we could pick the cream of Montana ballplayers." But like the 1925 Scobey Giants, the 1960 Plainsmen model of bringing in outside talent to compete nationally was not sustainable. Soon,

Scobey Plainsmen, team that played at the 1960 NBC World Series in Wichita, Kansas. Front row, L–R: Gordon Skjerven, Ken Lekvold, Allan Lowes, Wally Sinner and Andy Stolen; middle row (from left), Cecil McCarrow, Bob Beatty, Norm Anderson, Kenneth Hansen and Tom Quilling; back row (from left), Larry Ferguson, Paul Feser, Cliff Hagfeldt, Ron Quilling and Manager Joe Anderson. *Daniels County Museum.*

---

* The Culbertson team that Scobey beat for the championship consisted mostly of college baseball players from Colorado State University. Rosters for the NBC teams often did not consist only of local players.
† Wally Sinner from California signed a contract to play with the Billings Mustangs in the Pirates organization in 1952 and was 9-6 with the Mustangs (including a no-hitter against Boise in May) before leaving for the Korean War in July of that season. He rejoined the Mustangs in 1954-1955 and later pitched for the Worland Indians semipro team in Wyoming.

the Plainsmen (and town-team baseball in Daniels County) reverted to the style of baseball in which town teams were put together for special events or tournaments, as the Daniels County town-team baseball leagues ceased to exist, and most of the games were played against Canadian teams. But the decline of town-team baseball in northeastern Montana was countered by the rise of Legion baseball, as we shall see.

FAST-PITCH SOFTBALL

IT WAS ANOTHER BUSY SEASON AT SCOBEY BALL PARK. BEFORE "the season of lights and action nearly every night at the Scobey Ball Park passed into limbo, marking the end of another successful summer of varied athletics at that center," the Scobey men's softball Stags and women's softball Greenhorns, both defending champions of 1959, repeated as champions in 1960. To win their respective titles, the Stags beat Madoc, 25-0, Four Buttes, 14-8, lost to Four Buttes, 11-8, and then won the rubber game from Four Buttes, 21-12. Albert Nickola pitched a no-hitter in the Madoc game. The Greenhorns repeated by beating Flaxville, 35-23, losing to the Slick Chicks, 10-9, beating Flaxville again, 13-12, beating the Slick Chicks twice: 24-22, and 14-3. Peerless lost 20-12 to the Slick Chicks and was eliminated by Flaxville, 13-12.

Scobey Greenhorns, 1960 Women's Fast-Pitch League Champions. Standing, L–R: Phyllis Hanger, Lillian Wahl, Alice Halvorson, Donna Stoe, Alphild Doucette, Christine Shennum, Millie Poyner, Edith Grayson, Coach Reid Grayson. Kneeling: Ruth Goller, Dixie Jensen, Edna Hedges, Lorraine Jerome, Ada Whitlow, Karen Linder, Frances Paulson, Arletta Kjensmo. Sitting in front: Madonna Michel, Muriel Grayson. *Photo by Ernie.*

LITTLE LEAGUE

TWO LITTLE LEAGUE DIVISIONS (A AND B) WERE PLAYING WITH 11 teams, along with a Babe Ruth team. The Whitetail White Sox, coached by Dennis Marriage, won the Little League championship. All the Little League games were played at the Scobey Ball Park, many of them under the lights. Rocky Ware, a future Legionnaire and Plainsman, remembers playing Little League under the lights at Scobey Ball Park. "We used to play our Little

Scobey Stags, 1960 Men's Fast-Pitch League Champions. Standing, left to right: Don Hughes, Albert Nickola, Clip Zieske, Reid Grayson, Curley Weidner Larry Fjeld. Kneeling, left to right: Larry Willard, Bud Jensen, Bob Willard Sr., Buddy Willard, Alvida French, Kenny Larson. In front: Alan Willard. *Photo by Ernie.*

League games on the big field under the lights. I was playing second base and somebody hit a pop fly, and I'll never forget looking up in the air and not being able to see that ball, but somehow, I ended up catching it." I did not get to play under the lights at Scobey Ball Park until I was 13 years old, playing Babe Ruth. But I did get to play "under the lights" in Peerless several times in Peewee and Little League, because when it got late at night, and an intense game was still in progress, the coaches, players, and fans wanted to complete the games, so the cars parked around the ballpark would turn their lights on and shine them on the field. I remember playing shortstop one night, and the umpire was guiding cars parked behind the backstop to reposition and shine their lights at certain angles on the field. It didn't work that well. If the car was parked just right so the hitter, umpire, and catcher could see, the lights would shine right in my face at shortstop. It didn't matter to me, though—I was playing "under the lights"!

EXTRA INNINGS

ANN LEE REMEMBERS HOW ASSISTANT COACH GORDON "Butch" Goddard became part of the Norman family. Butch was another beneficiary of the generosity of Doc and Marge Norman. Ann said, "When I was a very little girl, we had a boy live with us, because he came from a great big family, and they didn't do anything but make him work. He came and lived with Mom and Dad so he could play football in Columbus when we lived there. And Mom and Dad continued to be a mentor to him all his life." In addition to helping Doc with the Junior Legion team, Butch was the Scobey High School athletic director and was hired by the Scobey Athletic Club as the custodian of the Scobey Ball Park that summer.

The trip to Wichita was more expensive than the Plainsmen originally budgeted for, as they had not counted on staying so long, winning three games. The team ran into some financial difficulties, as hotel bills came to $1,600. To help cut expenses, Mrs. Luverne Hansen and Carol Stolen did much of the laundry for the team.

Peerless fielded its last Junior Legion team in 1960. Dave Knudson from Peerless remembers the team was coached by Buck Baldry. Flaxville would continue to field Legion teams on and off through 1967.

1961
Junior Legion Baseball Raises the Age-Limit to 18

THE YEAR 1961 BROUGHT MORE CHANGE TO THE COMmunity of Scobey and the Scobey Junior Legion program. After practicing medicine in Scobey for two and a half years and coaching the Legion team for two years, Doc moved his family back to Missoula in May 1961. Mike Norman had moved back to Missoula for his second school term in the 1960-61 school year. Doc stated in the *Leader* that the move back to Missoula was more to keep the family together than for any other reason, but it is also rumored that Doc and the hospital board had several disagreements that couldn't be reconciled. Baldy Sell said, "We were all very disappointed when Doc left, of course. Doc's departure with his family to Missoula was a blow to the Scobey community, both in terms of losing his direly needed medical practice and his contribution to the Junior Legion program. The boys on the 1959 and 1960 teams had had a taste of elite coaching and supreme commitment from the best, and now it seemed like the rug was suddenly pulled out from underneath them. Almost as soon as he got there, he was gone. It was difficult for the 1959 and 1960 boys to recover from that.

But an even bigger change came at the national level in Junior Legion Baseball for the 1961 season: American Legion Baseball increased the age-eligibility from 17 years old to 18 years old. Before 1961, the maximum eligible age was 17 years old: a player could not play if they reached the age of 18 before September 1st of the season. This eliminated all seniors in high school from playing, and some juniors. The new eligibility moved the date back eight months so that players who turned 18 or after January 1st of the playing season could play. This greatly increased the capability of the Junior Legion teams, as boys who were another year older and stronger could play, while at the same time, it accelerated the decline of the town teams, as they lost many potential 18-year-olds on their roster the summer after their senior year. Junior Legion's gain was the town team's loss. With the increase in age to 18, Junior Legion Baseball became known as Legion Baseball.

LEGIONNAIRES

Scobey Legionnaires. Back row, L-R: Walt Ware, Larry Veis, Bill Thompson, Pete Darchuk, Don Oie, Terry Veis, Dwain "Baldy" Sell, Coach Bob Tande. Kneeling: Gary Linder, Smokey Grendal, John Downs, Phil Baker. Seated: Jim Schaefer, Rod Tande, Charles Mueller, Randy Smith, batboy Rocky Ware.

SCOBEY'S 1961 LEGION TEAM WAS MANAGED BY WALT WARE and coached by Bob Tande, who welcomed back 12 players with two or more years of experience. The Legion team competed in the Eastern B Division, consisting of Glasgow, Wolf Point, Fort Peck, Poplar, Plentywood, Outlook, and Scobey.

Scobey was the only town in the county to field a Legion team in 1961, which hadn't been the case for a while, as Peerless and Flaxville had both been fielding Legion teams. Note the addition of Gary Linder from Flaxville on the Scobey roster. Veteran members of the team returning in 1961 were Rod Tande, Larry Veis, Randy Smith, Bill Thompson, Phil Baker, Smokey Grendal, Arnie Burnett, Baldy Sell, Carl Tande, Terry Veis, Charlie Mueller, Gordon Cornwell, and Don Oie.

In a regular-season game against Glasgow, which Scobey won 3-0, Randy Smith pitched five innings of scoreless, no-hit ball, but was forced to leave the game after the fifth inning due to a pulled muscle. Since the score was tied at 0-0 after the fifth, Smith effectively pitched a no-hitter but was not credited with the win or the no-hitter. Bill Thompson earned the win in two innings of relief and preserved the shutout. Scobey played errorless ball in the game.

Bill Thompson, Larry Veis, Randy Smith, and sometimes Baldy Sell shared most of the pitching duties during the season.

The Bob Tande-coached Scobey Legion team did very well in the regular season, winning big over Fort Peck, and had conference wins over Outlook, Glasgow, Plentywood, and Poplar. However, Wolf Point won the regular season standings and, therefore, won the district title. Scobey finished a fine season with a 13-7 record. Four players for Scobey Legion finished with batting averages over .300: Rod Tande, .382; Baldy Sell, .355; Charlie Mueller, .333; Smokey Grendal, .318.

Following their second consecutive northern district title, Wolf Point once again played off against Laurel, the southern district champs, to go to the state tournament. This time Wolf Point traveled to Thompson Park in Laurel and lost in the best-of-three series in two games, losing the first game on a walk-off sacrifice fly in the bottom of the ninth, 3-2, then the second game 7-3, after giving up three runs in the top of the ninth to break open a close game. Laurel then went on to win its third consecutive state championship, once again against Sunburst, by sweeping the best-of-three series 6-5 and 5-0.

Meanwhile, in Missoula, Doc was awarded a one-year contract to be the county doctor. When Doc arrived in Missoula in early June, Gene Thompson—who Doc had assisted coaching the Missoula Legion team in 1958 and who later assisted Doc on the 1969 Scobey state championship team—resigned as head coach of Missoula due to "health reasons" after four seasons. Doc was named head coach of the Missoula Legion team and led the team to a second-place finish in the western division, but the team was not able to compete in the state tournament, as Helena was the host team and had finished below Missoula in the standings. Mike Norman played first base for Doc during the season.

PLAINSMEN AND FLAXVILLE TOWN TEAM

THE 1961 SCOBEY PLAINSMEN roster included DAVY HAYES, Harlan Stahlecker, Andy Stolen, Gordon Skjerven, Jack Reiner, Kenny Hansen, Cliff Hagfeldt, Norm Anderson, Norm Kampsher, Kevin Sell, Kenny Lekvold, McCarren, Henry Butzlaff, Howard Farver, Gary Farver, Vince Zimmer, Gary Davies, and Dick Wilson. Joe Anderson was the general manager, Leo Zimmer field manager, and Louis Lekvold was the treasurer.

Following their third consecutive NeMont League championship, their second state NBC championship, and seventh-place finish at the NBC World Series in 1960, the Plainsmen had another tremendous season in 1961, going 24-4, playing a nonleague rambler schedule against teams from Saskatchewan and North Dakota, including the Regina Red Sox, Regina Braves, the Estevan Maple Leafs, and the Williston Headliners. Likely due to an early harvest, the 25th annual state of Montana semipro tournament scheduled for July 27-30 at Scobey Ball Park was never held, so Scobey did not have a chance to repeat as state NBC champions. The tournament's cancellation was a reminder that the harvest was more important than baseball.

The rambler schedule the Plainsmen played in 1961 included hosting a two-game series with the "renowned quasi-pro"[26] Dixie Rebels from Fort Worth, Texas, managed by W. R. Morris, a former Pittsburgh Pirates baseball player. This was a historic series for the town of Scobey and the Plainsmen, as the Rebel players were Cubans from Cuba. They had left Cuba months earlier when the Castro Regime was reaching the peak of its power and were smuggled out of Cuba by friends of the anti-Castro cause, coming to the United States. Being foreigners, they were faced with making a living once they got here. Since the only thing they all knew for sure was baseball, they formed a team and began touring the country to earn a living, arriving in Scobey for a two-game series. It was reported that the Dixie Rebels were working for something like three dollars a day, plus hamburgers.

Due to a transportation problem, the Rebels were unable to bring their full team on time for the first game. As a result, Rod Tande and Randy Smith of the Junior Legion and Ordean Wangrud were selected to put on the Dixie uniforms and play for the Rebels in the Saturday night game.

Rod Tande remembers playing for the Cubans against the Plainsmen. "They were a very, very good team, but so were the Plainsmen. Randy Smith and I played outfield; they just kind of stuck us in there. Andy Stolen was pitching; I remember he had that big, sweeping curveball. I think he walked me intentionally out of sympathy. So I'm on first base, and one of the Cubans hit a single, so I get to second, and I'm thinking, *I'm fast, I can get to third*, and I made it. I rounded the base with a pretty big lead, and I recall taunting Plainsmen first baseman Norm Kampsher, who was clear across the diamond on first base with the ball, when

I realized I was probably three steps too far according to his arm. I dove back into third, and he had me by a mile at third base—he nailed me."

Rod getting picked off third base by Norm Kampsher might have cost the Cubans a run, and the Plainsmen won the game, 8-5. "Ironsides" Andy Stolen went the distance to get the win for the Plainsmen. The remaining Cubans showed up for the second game on Sunday night, with Harlan Stahlecker pitching the Plainsmen to a 3-1 win. Norm Anderson, Vince Zimmer, and "Renaissance" Jack Reiner (batting .500 in the series) led the Plainsmen in hitting.

Since Rod played against the Plainsmen with the Cubans that night in Scobey, I asked him if he remembered some of the players from those Plainsmen teams of that era. He said, "There were a lot of players I could name on that Plainsmen ballclub. Andy Stolen came in from Opheim. There was a guy named Gordon Skjerven who would come down from the Coronach area. He was a terrific infielder. He would field the ball, and he had a little hop to him when he would throw to first. Kind of a showman but very good. And there was Kenny Hansen, who came in from Glasgow. Kenny was a terrific hitter. And from Scobey, catcher Jack Reiner, second baseman Kenny Lekvold, Cliff Hagfeldt at first, and Ordean and Larry Wangrud played. Then there was a big ol' boy from somewhere else named Paul Feser.* Terrific player. A pitcher, and could he ever hit. He knocked a lot of balls out of Scobey Ball Park playing *against* the Plainsmen. But probably the best ballplayer to ever hit northeastern Montana was Norm Anderson. He was the best ballplayer I ever saw play who wasn't playing organized ball. He came up from Glendive. He farmed in that Circle-Glendive area. And he brought a kid with him from Glendive, Norm Kampsher, who played first base and had a tryout with the Yankees. He was the one who threw me out when I overran first base. And he was a hitter. He and Norm Anderson would come up, and they filled a lineup all by themselves. It was pretty spectacular to watch. It was good ball."

Major League Baseball scouts attended the games at Scobey to see the highly touted Dixie Rebels, but they were not the major league-type ball players the scouts were looking for. Vic Luft, State NBC Commissioner from Scobey, said, "The scouts were looking for younger stuff, ballplayers between the ages of 17 and 21."[27] The Cubans were good, but older, and not major league caliber.

In other rambler schedule action with the Canadians, the Plainsmen beat the Regina Red Sox, semifinalists in the Southern Baseball League, 6-3, then split a two-game series with the Regina Braves, winning 5-4 and losing 13-8. Gordon Skjerven, "pitching against his Canadian brothers," scattered nine hits to get the win in game one, and Vince Zimmer took the loss in game two after relieving Andy Stolen in the fifth.

The Plainsmen weren't the only town team playing baseball in Daniels County in 1961, as Flaxville's town team was still going strong. They hosted the third annual Flaxville Invitational Tournament in Flaxville. The double-elimination tournament featured town teams from Bengough, Sask., Fortuna Air Base, Flaxville, Plentywood, and the Scobey Plainsmen. Flaxville took third in their own tournament, beating Bengough and Fortuna but losing to Plentywood twice. Don Tryan hit three home runs in the tournament for Flaxville. The Plainsmen won the tournament by "climbing all over a highly touted Plentywood team," 9-3 in the championship game. Crafty left-handed veteran pitcher Andy Stolen had command the entire way for Scobey, until it appeared he got tired in the last of the ninth. But when manager Leo Zimmer made a trip to the mound to chat with Andy, "Leo came away grinning," and Andy kept Plentywood's rally from getting out of hand. The Plainsmen hitters teed off early on the fastball pitcher Aubrey Ferguson had brought from Minneapolis for his Blue Mooners for the tournament.[28]

Craig Price, Sidney Gems shortstop on the 1959 NBC state championship team, who later coached the Richland County Patriots Legion team in the late 1970s, remembers the Flaxville Invitational Tournament. Craig said, "Aubrey Ferguson of Plentywood called me to come up to Flaxville and play. He brought in a couple of strong arms from Minneapolis to pitch. We played the Plainsmen for the championship, and I was playing for Plentywood Blue Moon. I knew the Plainsmen team because I'd played against 'em that summer, and those guys—a bunch of farm guys that would get off their tractors and play ball on the weekends—they could hit the livin' daylights out of a fastball, you know. So I told this young pitcher from Minneapolis, 'You gotta mix it up against these guys, because they do hit the fastball *really* well. They don't look it, but they will.' And so, this young guy got on the mound, and before you know it, we were behind big early, and these Scobey guys just continually hit line drives. I was playing shortstop, and they hit the ball over my head, 10 in a row it seemed like. So the pitcher settled down and eventually we started playing pretty good ball, but what a lesson he learned about, 'Ooh man, you can't underestimate these guys. They love baseball and they can't wait to hit it, you know.'" Craig also

---

* Paul Feser played high school ball in South Dakota but was teaching and coaching at Culbertson at the time.

mentioned how big town-team baseball was in northeastern Montana at that time, adding, "Everyone had a town team then. Circle, Wolf Point, Culbertson, Plentywood, Scobey, Flaxville, everyone, and we had plenty of ball to play."

Although the NeMont Baseball League was dormant in 1961, the Big Muddy League in Sheridan County was going strong, as Raymond, Reserve, Antelope, Froid, Medicine Lake, and Dagmar played a full schedule and postseason league tournament.

FAST-PITCH SOFTBALL, BABE RUTH, AND LITTLE LEAGUE

The renaissance that had started with the opening of Scobey Ball Park in 1957 was now blooming in full force in 1961, and Reid Grayson, Scobey Athletic Club Director, had a problem—he needed coaches. Babe Ruth (for boys aged 13 to 15) started in Scobey in 1958, but now that the Legion age had been raised to 18, more younger boys would be playing Babe Ruth and not making the leap directly from Little League to Junior Legion, as many had done before. Due to the increasing number of boys in the Little League and Babe Ruth system—an average of 20 8-year-olds were coming out every year—the Scobey Athletic Club decided to increase the number of Little League teams to 10 or 12 and Babe Ruth teams to three or four. Reid Grayson said, "In the past, we have not had enough boys in the 13 through 15-year age group to make up more than one Babe Ruth team at best. But now we have 48 boys who have been active in baseball through the Little League, and who are now old enough for Babe Ruth competition. We hope to be able to have three or four teams."[29]

At the season-ending women's softball tourney in the Scobey Ball Park, a "full house turned out" to see the "heavy-hitting" Scobey Greenhorns defeat the Slick Chicks, 15-9, in the championship game. This was a three-peat for the Greenhorns, as they won the title in 1959 and 1960. Lillian Wahl and Edna Hedges shared the win, and Darlene Henderson took the loss, pitching for the Slick Chicks. The single-elimination one-day tournament was composed of teams from Saskatchewan and northeastern Montana: the Greenhorns and Slick Chicks of Scobey, Peerless, Flaxville, Westby, Plentywood, Killdeer, and Rock Glen, Sask. Peerless beat Westby 6-3 in their opening game, and Flaxville won their first game 12-8 over Killdeer, setting up four Daniels County teams in the semifinals, and both were close games. The Slick Chicks beat Flaxville 9-6, and the Greenhorns narrowly edged Ed Puckett's Peerless Belles, 7-6.

A ton of fun was had at the packed Scobey Ball Park for the women's tournament, as local Scobey merchants donated novelty prizes to the players and teams for novelty events. A straw hat from the Woman's Shop was given to Sherry French, Flaxville, for hitting the first home run of the tournament. Karen Mahler won a floor waxer from Coast-to-Coast Store for the most hits (four) in one game. Edna Hedges won a jewelry set from Ware's Style Shop for pitching the most strikeouts (eight). Four girls were each given a pillowcase set from the Federated Store for hitting the most home runs of the tournament: French, Dakker, Nuhring, and Weidner. Each hit four home runs. Lorraine Jerome, with the most hits (eight) of the tournament, was given a bathroom set by Anthony's. The losing team with the highest score in the first round (Rockglen, 14) received a 12-pack of beer from the 201 Club. The team scoring the most runs in one inning (Greenhorns, 12) was given a 12-pack of beer from the Club 109. The team losing the closest game (Peerless 6 against Greenhorns 7) was given a 12-pack of beer from Ginger's Bar. Joan Buer received two chicken dinners from Bill & Betty's Drive-in for the most put-outs (seven) by an outfielder. Edna Hedges, pitcher with the most strikeouts (five) in one game, received a snack tray from Paus-Strom Hardware. The 201 Club gave a six-pack of beer to all players (10) who hit a home run.[30]

Reid Grayson later took his championship Greenhorns team barnstorming to Canada in September and won a season-ending tournament at Rockin Beach Park on the shores of Fife Lake, Sask., winning 14-4 from Kildeer and 10-4 over Rockglen.

In men's fast-pitch, Flaxville beat Four Buttes 10-9 to win the six-team men's fast-pitch softball league championship tournament. Dallas Gaines won three games as pitcher for Flaxville, leading them to the title. Other teams participating were Peerless, Madoc, Scobey Stags, and Ken Lekvold's Team.

Scobey Greenhorns, 1961 Women's Fast-Pitch League Champions. Standing, L–R: Reid Grayson, Edith Grayson, Lorraine Jerome, Lillian Wahl, Anna Mae Nuhring, Madonna Michel, Frances Paulson, Muriel Grayson; front row: Alphild Doucette, Dixie Jensen, Edna Hedges, Arletta Kjensmo, Ada Mae Whitlow, and Ruth Goller. Missing from the picture is Millie Poyner.

The men's and women's softball season-ending championship tournaments capped the most active season yet for Scobey Ball Park. At one period during the summer, there were 43 consecutive days (nights) of baseball at the park. Reid Grayson reflected on another busy summer. "It's been a very good season. We're all getting our money's worth watching those kids develop into fine athletes and future Plainsmen."[31] It is noteworthy that Reid used the phrase "future Plainsmen" and not "future Legionnaires," because the hottest baseball ticket in town in 1961 was still the town team, but that was about to change. Part of the reason for that was the increase in the Junior Legion age to 18, but an even bigger part was that the first wave of Baby Boomers, who had been swarming the baseball diamond in droves since the new Scobey Ball Park opened in 1957, were now becoming Legion age. It was now time for the fathers and mothers of the "Greatest Generation" to pass down the game to the sons and daughters of the next generation.

I was a late Baby Boomer, born in 1961, so I never got to watch my dad play basketball or baseball in his prime. But I heard the stories. Mom told me that the hottest ticket in town when she was younger was the Peerless Pirates basketball team in Peerless. She said the Pirates games were the major social event during the cold winter months from the late 1930s through the 1950s. The same held true for the Scobey Plainsmen in baseball during the summer. And in 1961, the women's fast-pitch softball tournament in Scobey was played before a "full house." As a young boomer, it was hard for me to comprehend that at one time the town teams were the show, because when I played, it was all about us, my generation. But there was a time when the town teams were it. I do remember watching my mom play softball once. I loved it. She was playing second base in Peerless. She had her hand over her eyes, shading the sun. I thought, *What if a ground ball gets hit to her? She won't be ready!* She needed a cap!

EXTRA INNINGS

BASEBALL AND SOFTBALL BROUGHT EVERYONE TOGETHER FROM the small communities of northeastern Montana, southern Saskatchewan, and northwestern North Dakota in those days, but at a women's fast-pitch softball tournament in Peerless over the Fourth of July weekend, two people connected in a deeper way than most of those friendly tournaments. Carole Beliveau, playing for the Rockglen Rockets, met her future husband Bernie Dighans while playing in the tournament on the Fourth of July. Bernie and Carole were married in October. Now that's international relations!

1962

Legion Raises the Age Limit by Another Four Months

FOLLOWING THE EIGHT-MONTH AGE-LIMIT INCREASE IN 1961 to 18 years old, American Legion Baseball again increased the age eligibility by an additional four months in 1962, making a boy born on or after September 1, 1943, eligible to play in 1962. This age limit must have been switched to August 1 at some point, as that is the age limit we are all familiar with. The new rule also allowed 18-year-olds who had graduated from high school the previous year to return to play Legion Baseball after they attended college. The rule changes allowed several of the current Scobey Legionnaires to play baseball in 1962, who would have been ineligible only two years earlier, like Kevin Sell in 1960, whose last year was in 1959 when he was 17. He could not play when he was 18, so he played for the Plainsmen. If you think 17 years was a young age limit, the original age limit for Junior Legion was 16. This was the age limit Bob Schaefer and his team played in 1930 and 1931.

For the first time since 1947, the Scobey Plainsmen did not field a team in 1962. There is no record of any games.

LEGIONNAIRES

MANY EXPERIENCED AND OLDER BOYS—ESPECIALLY NOW THAT the age limit had been increased to 18 years old—were back for another season in 1962, some in their fourth year of Legion ball, and many who had played for Doc in 1959 and 1960. Once again, Walt Ware managed, and Bob Tande coached the team, but Baldy Sell sometimes would have to coach. Baldy said, "Bob Tande was having some health problems that year, so he really couldn't coach the team, so I would have to coach the team sometimes, including making out the lineup. Sometimes it was hard to get players to come to practice and to get enough players to games. During these years, it was hard; we all felt a little let down because Doc wasn't there."

Flaxville-Whitetail also fielded a Legion team in 1962. Sidney, who had not fielded a Legion team in 1959-61, was a significant new addition to baseball in northeastern Montana.

In February 1962, in Missoula, Doc and Marge adopted a baby boy into the Norman family. In his general practice as the county physician in Missoula County, Doc delivered the baby, whom the mother planned to put up for adoption, then called Marge and asked her, "Do you want a baby boy?" Marge said "yes," and the rest is history. Kelly Gene Norman is named after Kelly Baggs, a friend Doc had served with in the United States Marine Corps in World War II; his middle name, Gene, is after Eugene Thompson, Doc's friend and baseball coach, whom Doc assisted in Missoula in 1958, replaced as head coach in Missoula in 1961, and later assisted Doc in Scobey in 1969. Rumor has it that Doc immediately began grooming Kelly for his rookie batboy season in 1967 by having Kelly crawl toward a baseball bat on the living room floor and then return it to him.

After one year of practice as the county physician in Missoula, Doc returned to Scobey and resumed his general practice there on July 2, 1962. Doc and the hospital board had reconciled their differences, and Doc was persuaded into returning to Scobey. Doc did not want to leave Scobey in the first place. It was too late in the season for Doc to resume any coaching duties.

For the 1962 Scobey Legion team, Baldy Sell, Bill Thompson, Charlie Mueller, and Larry Veis shared most of the mound duties, with Rod Tande, Charlie Mueller, Baldy Sell, Smokey Grendal, and Phil Baker heavy on the bat. This was an experienced team, many of them with four years of Legion experience now, and they were good.

The northeastern district consisted of Scobey, Sidney, Wolf Point, Glasgow, Westby, Outlook, Fort Peck, and Flaxville-Whitetail. At the end of June, Scobey had regular-season wins over Glasgow, Fort Peck, Westby, Flaxville, and Outlook, with their only district loss to Outlook 9-5. In a doubleheader with Fort Peck and Glasgow, Scobey scored 47 runs in two games, winning 29-3 over Fort Peck and 18-14 over Glasgow. At this point in the season, Scobey was tied for the northeastern district lead with Wolf Point, as each team had only one loss. Scobey's season was careening toward a crucial game against Wolf Point with district title implications. The game was to be played in Scobey on the Fourth of July.

In the Wolf Point-Scobey game at Scobey on the Fourth, multiple Scobey errors led to an early 8-0 Wolf Point led after three innings, and Wolf Point went on to win the game 13-7. The following week, Wolf Point again beat Scobey 4-3 at Wolf Point, then beat Sidney 7-2 to take sole possession of first place.

Scobey later dropped a decision to Sidney, and Wolf Point went on to win the northeastern district. By all accounts, Scobey would have finished second—perhaps tied with Outlook—in the league standings behind Wolf Point. There was no season-ending district tournament at this time, so how a team fared in the regular season sealed their fate for any hopes of playing in the postseason. Outlook also had a good team in 1962, with Clair Garrick and Jerry Tange sharing the bulk of mound duties, including pitching multiple shutouts.

Wolf Point, coached by Dick Wilson, played off against Laurel for the third consecutive year to determine who would represent the eastern division at State. This time, it was a single, sudden-death game in Miles City, rather than a best-of-three series on a home field. The game, referred to in the *Laurel Outlook* as an "action-packed thriller,"[32] was won by Wolf Point. Jim Olson was the starting pitcher for Wolf Point and allowed only one run until the seventh inning, when Laurel erupted for five runs. Olson was replaced by Cliff Page on the mound. With Laurel leading 6-5 in the ninth, Wolf Point had a baserunner reach first on an error, followed by a base hit. Then, on another error, Wolf Point scored to tie the game at 6-6. The game then went into extra innings, and Wolf Point won it in the 10th, as Doug Schillinger doubled in the winning run for a 7-6 Wolf Point win.

At the state best-of-three series in Sunburst, Wolf Point lost to Sunburst 7-0 in the first game. Jim Olson started for Wolf Point, then was relieved by Cliff Page, then Doug Schillinger relieved Page in the second inning. Sunburst scored all their runs in the first two innings, and then the game was scoreless from that point on. Wolf Point won the second game 17-13, but Sunburst came back to take the clincher 12-6 to win State. Bob Parsley hit a home run for Wolf Point in one of the Sunday games.

FASPITCH SOFTBALL

WOMEN'S FAST-PITCH SOFTBALL WAS STILL GOING STRONG IN 1962. Rather than participating in a league, the three Daniels County teams—the Scobey Greenhorns, Scobey Slick Chicks, and Peerless—played mostly in big tournaments against Canadian teams. Following the Legion game on the Fourth of July between Scobey and Wolf Point, four women's fast-pitch softball teams played a mini tournament at Scobey Ball Park. The Greenhorns beat Coronach, and the Slick Chicks beat Peerless. The Greenhorns then beat the Slick Chicks for the $15 championship prize.

Peerless hosted its fourth annual fast-pitch invitational tournament in late July, with a "huge crowd"[33] in attendance. The event was sponsored by the Peerless Community Club, and they presented the winners with a percentage of the gate receipts. Seven teams participated. Killdeer, Sask, beat Wood Mountain, Sask., for the championship. The Scobey Greenhorns beat Peerless in the consolation game. The other teams participating were the Scobey Slick Chicks and two teams from Opheim.

Later that summer, the three Daniels County women's softball teams—the Greenhorns, Slick Chicks, and Peerless—traveled to Killdeer, Sask., to play in the tournament, where the Slick Chicks took second place, losing 8-5 to host Killdeer in the championship game. The roster for the runner-up Slick Chicks included Donette Tryan, Charlotte French, J. Flint, Marla Teigen, M. Suess, LuAnne French, Lorraine Spoonheim, Marge Hagfeldt, and Jen Robinson.

EXTRA INNINGS

BILL "OSCAR" THOMPSON, IN HIS FIFTH YEAR OF LEGION BALL in 1962, had a live fastball, but his curveball was just as deadly. Bill remembers who taught him how to throw his curveball and the grip. He said, "Andy Stolen taught me how to throw his special curve. This lefty threw the curve with the Andy Stolen grip, that being with the ball resting on the thumb surface from the knuckle to nail. Then, during the delivery, with a mere flick of the thumb, the ball usually did its thing. It worked great!"

Catcher Rod Tande, whose last year playing Legion ball was 1962, remembers catching Bill Thompson. Rod said, "Bill Thompson, by far, had the heaViest ball I ever caught. His ball was so heavy you'd swear he was throwing a shot put. I remember catching those super lefty sliders and live fast balls."

But perhaps the deadliest of Bill's pitches wasn't a pitch at all—it was the left-hander's pickoff move to first base. Several players commented on how deceptive the move was, including his catcher, Rod Tande. Rod said, "Oscar had the greatest left-hand pickoff move in the business. His pickoff move would rival any pro that played the game. When Doc came to town in 1959, he taught us the little things, the details. He taught Oscar the left-hand pickoff move that *never* failed. And Doc taught me the one-step throw to second. You don't hop, you just stand up and fire that thing and flip that wrist. Because of Doc, we were *technically* sound. I do not recall anybody stealing on Oscar and me."

Lillian Wahl, who played several seasons for the Scobey Greenhorns, played on the state women's softball championship team in Great Falls in 1962. Apparently, the Greenhorns' loss was Great Falls's gain.

1963

Doc Norman and the Scobey Plainsmen Return to Scobey Ball Park

Scobey Legionnaires. Back row, L–R: Don Paulson, Charlie Mueller, John Hudyma, Bill Thompson, Dwain "Baldy" Sell, Terry Gilbertson, Bud Veis. Second row. L to R: Glen Halvorson, Tom Shuman, Jim Downs, Phil Audet, John Murphy, Randy Peck. Front: Batboy Rocky Ware.

PRESEASON

The roster for the 1963 Scobey Legion team consisted of three seasoned veterans who were now in their fifth year of Legion ball and were returning a year after they had graduated from high school—Bill Thompson, Charlie Mueller, and Baldy Sell. (Rod Tande missed the age cutoff by a week.) In addition to Rod, gone from the Legion team were Randy Smith, Carl Tande, Larry Veis, Terry Veis, Phil Baker, and Pete Darchuk. The three experienced players were joined by a heavier mix of younger players. One of the younger players was 14-year-old Phil Audet, who played with the team when he could during the regular season, then joined the team permanently later in the season after getting "called up" from the Babe Ruth team.

The Babe Ruth team—the Scobey Giants (ring a bell?)—was coached by the man himself, Doc Norman, who had returned to the Scobey baseball fields after a two-year absence in 1961 and 1962. Doc was teaching Phil Audet, John Morrison, and others how to pitch and play baseball in Babe Ruth, but Doc would also join the Legion team on the field, coaching at the season-ending district tournament in Glendive, where Phil and three other dual-rostered Babe Ruthers also traveled. Also on the 1963 team were Don Paulson, John Hudyma, Bud Veis, Glen Halvorson, Tom Shuman, Jim Downs, John Murphy, Randy Peck, and Terry Gilbertson. Rocky Ware was batboy.

The head coach of the Legion team was Bob Tyler, assisted by George Lake, who was working at the Victoria

Scobey Giants Babe Ruth team. Back row, L–R: Coach Doc Norman, Reid Grayson Jr., Carl Darchuk, Barry Harmon, John Morrison, Randy Peck. Front row, seated: Ernie Anderson, Jimmy Tkachyk, Steve Sprague and Glen Halvorson. Not pictured: Phil Audet, Bill Dale, Ray and Ralph Lystad, Curtis Luft, Ron Montgomery, and Paris French.

elevator in Scobey. Jim Hellickson, Legionnaire committeeman and immediate past commander, was also involved. But Baldy Sell said he did a lot of team management and organization, and Larry Veis did a lot of coaching of the team until Doc's return later in the summer.

Terry Gilbertson from Flaxville joined the Scobey Legion roster in 1963, as Flaxville did not field a Legion team. In 1961, Smokey Grendal and Gary Linder broke the "intra-county barrier" by joining the Scobey Legion roster when Flaxville did not field a Legion team. This was the first inkling of an all–Daniels County baseball team, but it wouldn't be until 1968 when that would happen. At this time, no one from Peerless had ever played for Scobey, although Bob Tande had tried unsuccessfully for several years to recruit Reese Puckett Jr. to pitch for Scobey.

REGULAR SEASON

THE YOUNG LEGION TEAM HAD A ROUGH BEGINNING TO THE season, losing six consecutive games—three to Weyburn, Sask., and one each to Glendive, Plentywood, and Glasgow. However, the cavalry arrived in the form of Bill Thompson, who joined the roster in June after a year at Concordia College, and Baldy Sell, who had returned from his first year of college at Western. Until that time, veteran Charlie Mueller was having trouble holding down the fort.

After Thompson and Sell returned from college, and as the younger players on the roster began to develop, the results got better for the Legion team. Scobey broke into the win column with wins over Outlook (19-10), Fort Peck (18-3), Westby (10-1), and Outlook again (15-6) but then lost to Wolf Point 21-3. A season highlight saw Bill Thompson pitch the third no-hitter in Scobey Legion history in a 4-3 win over Sidney. Phil Audet led Scobey in the hitting department in that game. In July, four of the Babe Ruthers came up to play Legion, with Phil Audet seeing some action on the mound against Wolf Point in another 20-3 Wolf Point win.

Doc, following the Babe Ruth season, joined the team on the field as a coach at the season-ending district tournament in Glendive, reuniting with some of his former players from the 1959 and 1960 teams in the process. Scobey did well, winning two games and losing two, finishing fourth out of eight teams. Scobey lost 11-3 to Plentywood in their opener. Thompson pitched a 2-hitter but was the losing pitcher in the game, as all 11 Plentywood runs were unearned, exposing the inexperience of the Scobey defense. Scobey actually outhit Plentywood 11 to 2 in the game. Scobey then beat Laurel 5-4 in their second game. In the bottom of the ninth with Scobey trailing 4-3, Laurel intentionally walked Baldy Sell with runners on second and third to load the bases, and Charlie Mueller hit a game-winning double. Charlie was also the winning pitcher in that game. Baldy Sell remembers Charlie's big hit. "He bounced it off the wall. He could really hit. He hit a rocket to the left-center field wall, and it bounced and hit the fence. The two runners scored from second and third, and he rounded the bases, and the game was over. Charlie taunted the Laurel coach and players by pointing his finger at their dugout and shouted, 'No one, *no one*, walks the hitter in front of me with the game on the line, *no one*!' Doc said, 'Charlie, knock that shit off.'" Baldy added, "Charlie was our best hitter during those years. He hit over .600 his last season in 1963 and hit a couple of home runs over the left field fence at Scobey that bounced off the highway. He was also a good outfielder."

Scobey then won their next game against Plentywood 9-3, with Thompson getting the win this time as Scobey shored up their defense in the field.

In their next game, Scobey led Glasgow 7-2 but ran out of pitching innings and eventually lost 14-8.

Wolf Point continued their steady ramp up to their 1965 state championship and was once again the class of the northeastern district, winning their fourth consecutive district title, both the regular season and—for the first time—the season-ending eastern divisional tournament with southern district teams. They swept four straight games in Glendive to win it, with Jim Olson pitching a four-hit shutout to beat Lewistown 7-0 in the final.

Wolf Point then met Cut Bank in a best-of-three series for the state championship on a neutral field, Meissner Memorial Field in Glendive. Cut Bank won the first game 3-2, then Wolf Point came back to win the second game 11-2, setting up the deciding final game on Sunday, which turned out to be a "wild one."[34] In what became the first of several heartbreaking late-inning comebacks against Wolf Point in state tournament final games, Cut Bank put up back-to-back four-run innings in the sixth and seventh to overcome an 11-6 deficit and take the lead 14-11. Wolf Point scored two runs in the top of the ninth, but the rally fell short, and Cut Bank won the state championship game 14-13.

It was poetic that Doc rejoined Charlie Mueller, Bill Thompson, and Baldy Sell on the field at the season-ending district tournament in Glendive. Baldy and Bill were two of the 1959ers who played for Doc on the district championship team in his inaugural season. Charlie, Bill, and Baldy played for Doc on baseball fields ranging from Eau Claire, Wisconsin, across the entire states of Minnesota and North Dakota, to Glendive, Miles City, and all the way to Missoula, Montana. And while the Glendive district tournament in

1963 closed the chapter on the 1959 players, it opened a new chapter with the emergence of a talented crop of younger players, whom Doc would mold into the team that earned Scobey its first trip to the state tournament in 1967. That chapter began being written the following spring in 1964, when Doc once again took the reins as head coach of the Scobey Legion team and resumed the grand march toward a Montana Legion Baseball dynasty (although no one could have predicted it at the time) that eventually would become known as the Scobey Blues.

PLAINSMEN

THE PLAINSMEN PLAYED A VERY ACTIVE "RAMBLER" SCHEDULE that summer, but they did not participate in a league or a postseason tournament. Baldy Sell covered the team in the *Leader*, and the team played a very active schedule. Scobey had a good pitching staff with Kevin Sell, Vince Zimmer, Larry Veis, Andy Stolen, and Randy Smith. Some highlights of the season: Kevin Sell struck out 15 Opheim batters in a 6-3 win; Cliff Hagfeldt hit a three-run home run to lead Scobey to a 10-9 comeback win over Bengough, with Rod Tande contributing some clutch hits as well; Andy Stolen pitched a complete game win over Bengough 5-4; Randy Smith got the win in relief of Andy Stolen in a 9-7 over the Notre Dame Hounds of the South Saskatchewan League. Tracking all results, the Plainsmen ended the season with a 12-3 record. The roster for the Plainsmen included Kevin Sell, Buzz Torgerson, Don Tryan, Rod Tande, Clay Dunlap, Randy Smith, Kenny Lekvold, Cliff Hagfeldt, Vince Zimmer, Bobby Machart, Jack Reiner, Doug Krassin, Norm Anderson, Andy Stolen, and Gordon Skjerven. Doc Norman assisted with the scheduling.

While the Plainsmen were active in 1963, the time was coming soon when town-team baseball in Daniels County would end. The raising of the Legion age to 18 and the declining population in that part of the state, which began in earlier decades and was starting to accelerate at that time, was a one-two punch that town-team baseball in Daniels County was not able to recover from. Also, the parents of the Baby Boomers were aging, and it was time for them to step aside and watch their kids play Little League, Babe Ruth, and Legion baseball.

But town-team baseball in broader northeastern Montana was not dead just yet. While the NeMont League folded in Daniels County, the Big Muddy League (BML) in Sheridan County continued through the 1960s and into the early 1970s. The six regular teams in the BML were Reserve, Antelope, Raymond, Froid, Dagmar, and Medicine Lake. The six teams participated in a full regular-season

The 1963 Big Muddy League Tournament was hosted in Reserve. *Plentywood Herald.*

schedule and an annual postseason tournament hosted at alternating towns. Randy Pederson from Plentywood, who played for the Scobey Blues in 1982, remembers watching his older brother Gary play in the Big Muddy League in 1971. Randy said, "I watched two games: one in Raymond and the other in Reserve. It may have only gone one more year; not sure."

FAST-PITCH SOFTBALL

THE PEERLESS COMMUNITY CLUB SPONSORED THE ANNUAL fast-pitch softball tournament in Peerless. The "large crowd witnessed some close and well-played games."[35] The Scobey Greenhorns beat Peerless for the championship, with third place going to the Glasgow Air Base Blue Devils, who edged the Glasgow Base Misfits. Other participating teams were King Springs Trailer Court Women from near Glasgow, the Glasgow women's team, Opheim women, and Killdeer, Sask.

Peerless and the Greenhorns played each other several times during the summer, but the women's fast-pitch league that had started in 1957 with the opening of the Scobey Ball Park was no longer going. Most of the games consisted of tournaments.

EXTRA INNINGS

PRIOR TO THE EASTERN DIVISION CHAMPIONSHIP GAME BEtween Wolf Point and Glasgow in Glendive, the formal dedication of Meissner Memorial Field took place. The project began with the late Steve Meissner's interest in and dedication to sports and athletics. Part of his will bequeathed some lots on the south side of Glendive for the purpose of the establishment and perpetuation of baseball there. The dedication of the field was the culmination of six years of work, with many business firms, organizations, and individuals in the Glendive community contributing equipment, machinery, and man-hours toward the successful completion of the project.[36] Meissner Memorial Field's hosting of the 1963 Eastern Divisional Tournament became the first of many memorable games and tournaments to be played on that field.

Baldy Sell played Legion Baseball from 1959 to 1963. His career was "interesting": playing for Doc at the beginning and the end and for several different coaches in between; playing both in Class B and Class A; seeing the Junior Legion age eligibility increase twice, allowing him to play the summer after his freshman year in college; helping organize the team and doing a little coaching himself—he about saw it all. But nothing is more interesting than Baldy's stories, and he shared a few with me.

Baldy recalls his umpiring "career" in Scobey after his playing days. "When I was in law school in college, I came back to Scobey in the summers. Charlie Mueller was calling games behind the plate. Terry Puckett and Danny Wolfe were playing for the Scobey Legion team. Charlie Mueller was a really good umpire and was umpiring behind the plate, and I was umpiring first base, but had an attitude problem. When I played, I felt the umps made a few bad calls when we played on the road, so I was going to make up for it. I was umpiring first base, and I called every close call in favor of Scobey. After the game, Doc said, 'Baldy, all those calls were close and they all went Scobey's way.' I said, 'When we played Wolf Point and other teams, we got some bad calls.' Doc said, 'Baldy, I can't have you on first anymore. You still have a little chip, and I can't have you umpiring first base.' The only time he ever used me at first again was when he thought the game was not going to be close."

I asked Baldy to talk about his relationship with Doc and Marge. He said, "I just had such a good relationship with Doc and Marge. They were like second parents to me. After high school and American Legion, I would come back to Scobey all the time. My son Derrick's middle name is Harrington after Doc. Marge even provided me advice on relationships. Marge was a special woman, and she worked so hard. Here is a funny story about Doc and Marge. While at college one year, I came back to Scobey for Christmas. Terry Veis, John Downs, Mike Norman, and I were going to Regina for a hockey game, but Doc invited his way in. At this time, Marge had Doc on a strict diet and wouldn't let him smoke. As we were leaving their house, Marge said to me, 'Now Baldy, you don't let Doc smoke. It's okay if he has a beer or two, but you don't let him smoke.' Doc sat in the back seat by the window, and before we got to Flaxville, he rolled the window down and started smoking. He smoked all the way up and all the way back!"

Baldy shared another funny story about Doc. "When Dad [Ernie Sell] was sheriff, Doc was the doctor in Scobey. There was a young woman out in Flaxville someplace. Doc told her she needed to get to town because she was going to have a baby; the baby was due. He told her to come, but she didn't come. There was a huge blizzard, so they called Doc on the phone, and Doc went out to the farm to deliver the baby. So, Dad drove Doc in some type of police vehicle that was four-wheel drive and had some kind of a phone in it, but they couldn't get all the way through to the house, the roads were blocked. They were about a mile away from the farm. Doc could walk on the road, but they couldn't drive the car any further. Doc walks through the blizzard, delivers the baby, and calls Dad to tell him he was heading back to the car. Dad could see him coming because as he got closer, he could see the little cigarette light shining through the blizzard. Doc was smoking a cigarette in the blizzard! Marge didn't like Doc smoking, you know. And when he got back to the car, Dad or Doc had one of those little pints of peppermint schnapps, so on the way back to Scobey, Dad and Doc, the town sheriff and doctor, shared that little pint of peppermint schnapps in the police vehicle."

1964

Doc Asserts Control of the Scobey Legion Program

PRESEASON

Doc Norman (with the bat on the left) runs a drill he called "Situations" in a practice at Scobey Ball Park in spring 1964. *Leader.*

IN APRIL 1964, DOC WAS BACK ON THE FIELD AS HEAD COACH of the Scobey Legion team, where he could be found every April from 1964 until 1983. The photo shows Doc in early April conducting a drill he called "Situations." It was amazing that there was a photo of Doc conducting this drill, because it was my favorite part of practice. The 1964 Scobey Legion team was young; this was very much a developmental year for the team and the program.

1964 Scobey Giants. Back row, L-R: Assistant Phil Audet, Craig Audet, Ernie Anderson, Bill Dale and Coach Charlie Mueller. Front row: Rocky Ware, Danny Audet, Larry Thompson, Mark Reiner, John Nelson. Others not in picture are Ralph Lystad, Dan Smith, Jim Tkachyk, Alan Willard, Dick Puckett, Bernie Maher and Dennis Nieskens. *Leader.*

And speaking of development, Charlie Mueller was head coach of the Scobey Babe Ruth team which included three players—Rocky Ware, Craig Audet, and Dick Puckett—who would play on the 1969 State championship team, as well as Dan Smith. Rocky Ware was dual-rostered as a 13-year-old on both the Legion and Babe Ruth teams. Fifteen-year-old Phil Audet was also the assistant coach for the Babe Ruth team. Phil was still eligible to play Babe Ruth but was playing Legion and *coaching* Babe Ruth. This was Doc's method in action: playing young Babe Ruthers in Legion to develop them in his system, have them gain valuable experience, and get them accustomed to tougher competition at a young age. Flaxville did not field a Legion team in 1964, so Dan Tryan and Terry Gilbertson played for Scobey. The roster also included Randy Peck, Barry Harmon, Bob Thompson, Ray Lystad, Al Wrona, Bud Veis, Terry Gilbertson, Don Paulson, Tom Shuman, John Murphy, Jim Downs, and Glen Halvorson.

There was a new format in postseason play for Class B Legion. There would be a postseason tournament where the top three teams in the east would advance to play against the top three teams from the west in a state tournament. Previously, there were postseason playoffs, but only the top team in the east advanced to play in a best-of-three series with the western division champion.

LEGIONNAIRES

THE EASTERN DISTRICT IN 1964 CONSISTED OF SEVEN TEAMS: Scobey, Wolf Point, Glasgow, Plentywood, Poplar, Sidney, and Glendive. Scobey played a 17-game schedule and competed in the postseason tournament in Plentywood.

Scobey played its opener against another tough Wolf Point team and lost 19-4; however, in a game later in the season, 15-year-old Phil Audet pitched against Wolf Point again and yielded only three hits in a 6-0 loss. Phil became the ace of Doc's staff, and Doc would call on Phil every time to pitch the biggest games.

Some regular season highlights for Scobey: Tom Shuman made a triple play against Wolf Point in the 6-0 game; Dan

---

* In "Situations," Doc would set up the field with different scenarios in a game, with number of outs, score of game, and inning, then hit the ball or square to bunt with live baserunners to the right of him on the first base line. I learned more about baseball in this drill than any other thing we did in practice, and it was my favorite.

1964 Scobey Legionnaires. Back row, L-R: Phil Audet, Randy Peck, Barry Harmon, Bob Thompson, Ray Lystad, Al Wrona. Front row: Rocky Ware, Bud Veis, Terry Gilbertson, Don Paulson, Tom Shuman. Not pictured are John Murphy, Jim Downs, and Glen Halvorson who were at the state musical festival. Also missing is Dan Tryan from Flaxville. *Leader.*

Tryan and Terry Gilbertson from Flaxville pitched Scobey to a 9-5 win over Grenora; later in the regular season, Scobey played Wolf Point tough in a 6-5 loss, showing the team's steady improvement over the season.

At the district tournament in Plentywood, Scobey lost out in two games, losing to Wolf Point 9-0 and Glasgow 6-2, but as the *Leader* stated, "The Scobey team was a young one this year and most of the boys will be in action next season."[37] Not to mention some good players who would begin their Legion careers the following season.

Glendive won the district tournament in Plentywood, with Wolf Point finishing second and Sidney third. These three teams would also finish 1-2-3 at State in Laurel. In the state championship game between Glendive and Wolf Point, the first inning lasted 35 minutes, as Wolf Point scored five runs in the top half and Glendive scored seven in the bottom half.

Glendive went on to win 15-13 in another high-scoring loss for Wolf Point in a state championship game. This was Glendive's first state championship, while Wolf Point was runner-up for the third year in a row. Wolf Point would cease to be the bridesmaid the following season when it won its first state championship.

PLAINSMEN

THE PLAINSMEN HAD A UNIQUE ARRANGEMENT IN 1964. Waller Funeral Home supplied them with materials and equipment, but the players got all gate receipts, in turn paying all other expenses. Jack Reiner said in the *Leader*, "If the fans want to see a real bunch of hustling capitalists, this should be it. They will be splitting up at season's end, either a surplus or a deficit."[38]

The roster included many local players, "as well as a number of those who, in the past, have shown a marked preference to cast their lot with the Plainsmen." Some players who donned the Plainsmen uniform that summer included field manager Dwain Sell, Jerry Ginger, Phil Baker, Gary Brenden, Doug Schillinger, Jim Olson, Randy Smith, Dave Hayes, Bill Thompson, Charlie Mueller, Henry Butzlaff, Cliff Hagfeldt, Ken Hansen, Andy Stolen, Ken Lekvold, Clay Dunlap, Larry Veis, Mike Norman, "plus whatever other potential playing stockholders may present themselves."[39] Mike Norman had played first base for the University of Oregon Ducks earlier that spring and was home from college for the summer.

The Plainsmen competed in the revived NeMont Baseball League, which included rival Plentywood, the Williston Herald Headliners, and the Wolf Point Stampeders. This would be the last season the Plainsmen competed in an organized league, as town-team baseball was fading. There was a little nostalgia for the heyday of town-team baseball and the Plainsmen, as the *Leader* wrote, "For some, there is an old sentiment of the days when the Plainsmen were eminent in the National Baseball Congress competitions, which included two state championships and one 7th place in the national congress."[40]

After losing their first game of the season to the Moose Jaw Astros of the South Saskatchewan League, the Plainsmen stockholders won nine games in a row, the last two coming against the Williston Herald Headliners in a doubleheader, winning 8-6 and 14-6. In the first game, Randy Smith hit a bases-loaded triple, and in the second game, Gary Brenden hit a grand slam homer. Bill Thompson, Jim Olson, Randy Smith, and Baldy Sell shared the pitching duties.

Their nine-game winning streak was snapped by the visiting Minot AFB Jet Stars, who beat the Plainsmen 12-9 at Scobey Ball Park. The Jet Stars were winding up a four-state tour. They played a rambler schedule in addition to the NeMont League, including the Assiniboia and the Minot Jet Stars from Minot AFB.

1964 Scobey Plainsmen. Back row, L-R: Dwain Sell (mgr), Charlie Mueller, Larry Veis, Ken Hansen, Bill Thompson. Front row: Gary Brenden, Doug Schillinger, Mike Norman and Jim Olson. Many players who played during the season are missing from the photo. *Leader.*

The Plainsmen lost their second game in a row to the Assiniboia Aces, 8-3, despite Mike Norman knocking one out of Scobey Ball Park. In the rematch at Assiniboia, Scobey edged the Canadians 3-2, but then dropped the nightcap, 7-2. In the first game, Wolf Point's Jimmy Olson pitched a gem for Scobey, and Charlie Mueller doubled to drive home Mike Norman for the winning run, who had just singled. In the second game, the Aces got to Scobey for seven runs in the first inning but were held scoreless the rest of the way. Scobey tried to come back, but Baldy Sell's solo home run needed more runners on base to pull the Plainsmen closer. Randy Smith, Bill Thompson, Doug Schillinger, and Charlie Mueller shared eight innings of pitching. Phil Baker caught both games.

The Plainsmen hosted a round-robin tournament with the South Saskatchewan All Stars and the Wolf Point Stampeders to end the season. The Plainsmen won both their games, beating South Saskatchewan, 8-7, and Wolf Point, 14-7. The Plainsmen won the NeMont League in its last year of existence and completed a successful season, ending with a 12-4 record. But more importantly, did the stockholders make money? I asked Charlie Mueller if he remembered a surplus at the end of the season for the "hustling capitalists." He said, "Surplus? Not a chance!"

FAST-PITCH SOFTBALL

THE SCOBEY GREENHORNS AND PEERLESS SOFTBALL TEAM continued playing their top-brand of fast-pitch softball in the county in 1964, mostly in tournaments, as league play had discontinued. The Peerless Community Club sponsored the seventh annual Peerless Invitational Tournament, with Killdeer, Sask., the Greenhorns, Opheim, and Peerless. Killdeer won the tournament with three wins, the Greenhorns were second, Peerless third, and Opheim fourth. As with all softball tournaments hosted at Peerless, the games were well attended.

The Greenhorns and Peerless traveled to play in a big eight-team tournament in Glendive, which the Greenhorns won, sweeping three games, but having to get by Peerless in a tough semifinal game. LuAnne French from Flaxville was the winning pitcher for the Greenhorns in all three of their victories. They won 21-4 from Terry, 15-10 over Peerless in the semis, and 8-6 over the Miles City Sports Center in the championship. Other teams in the tournament were Williston, two Glendive teams, and one other from Miles City. Reid Grayson, who had been coaching the Greenhorns for seven years, said in the *Leader*, "The gals were really sharp, and in that final game against the Miles City Sports Center, they could have beaten just about anybody."[41]

1964 Scobey Greenhorns. Standing, L–R: Karen Demick, Diane Urquhart, Lynette Halvorson, Muriel and Edith Grayson, Karen (Mahler) Pearce, Lorraine Jerome, and Coach Reid Grayson. Kneeling: Allie and Karlene Doucette, Charlotte French, LuAnne French, Marsha Winkler, and Ada Whitlow. *Leader*.

Since their formation in 1957—the year the new Scobey Ball Park opened and women's fast-pitch softball started in the county—the Scobey Greenhorns had established themselves as the elite fast-pitch softball team in northeastern Montana, winning the league championship three times, and finishing in the top two in almost every tournament they played. Charter team members for the Greenhorns playing at Glendive included Allie Doucette, Edith Grayson, Ada Whitlow, and Lorraine Jerome. Also playing in Glendive were Muriel Grayson, Karlene Doucette, Lena Lystad, Lynette Halvorson, Charlotte French, LuAnne French, Donnette Banko, Diane Urquhart, and Marsha Stroh. Other Greenhorns in 1964 who did not travel to Glendive to play were Donnette Handy, Norma Johnson, Sharon Wagar, and Rosie Nuhring.

Following a 16-14 win at home against the Rockglen Rockets the first week of August, it appeared the Greenhorns' season was over, but Reid planned to take the team to a big Labor Day Weekend tournament in Williston to

1964 Scobey Greenhorns following Rockglen game. Back row, L–R, Coach Reid Grayson, Lorraine Jerome, Edith Grayson, Allie Doucette, Muriel Grayson, Donnette Handy, Lynette Halvorson, Front row, Charlotte French, Karlene Doucette, Luanne French, Ada Whitlow, Rosie Nuhring. *Leader*.

close out the season. To prepare for the tournament, Reid Grayson had the Greenhorns practicing three times a week to keep in shape.[42] At Williston, they competed against Bismarck, Minot, Glendive, Miles City, two teams from Williston, and a team from Canada.

The "skilled and durable"[43] Greenhorns played six games and took second place They won their first game 19-7, against Corky's of Williston; lost to Bismarck, 12-7, then won from Miles City, 15-14; won 14-13 from Tioga; avenged their loss to Bismarck, 11-0, and in the championship (their sixth game), bowed 7-4 to the Williston New York Lifers.

Similar to the fading of town-team baseball and the Plainsmen in the early 1960s, the 1964 season was the end of the golden era for the Greenhorns and the women's fast-pitch softball league in Daniels County, as the Greenhorns' run of fielding teams would end in 1965. Women's softball in Daniels County would soon transition to slow-pitch softball, and the epicenter of the top brand of softball in the county would shift to Peerless. Ed Puckett had been coaching the Peerless fast-pitch softball team—known variously as the Wranglerettes, Pansies, and Belles—since 1957, and Peerless had been hosting big invitational tournaments since 1958, always with huge crowds. Ed and Peerless had fielded competitive fast-pitch softball teams, as they took second in the league in 1957 and won the league championship in 1958. In 1964, Ed's daughter Gerri was his power-hitting, slick-fielding shortstop who had a cannon for an arm and could throw runners out from deep in the hole. I remember watching her play after she left Peerless and played for Chinook when her team would come to Peerless to play. Ed's presence on the Peerless ball field every summer would attract the next generation of softball players, a talented group of girls in Peerless who would become known as the Peerless Hellcats slow-pitch softball team in 1967. More on the Hellcats later.

EXTRA INNINGS

Ann (Lee) Norman recalls riding with Marge to all the road games with players in the car with them in the 1960s. She shared a funny story about playing poker with the boys on one road trip. "Butch Goddard taught me how to play poker when I was about five years old when we lived in Columbus. I was pretty lucky, and I understood this game. So the boys are playing poker in the backseat, and I said, 'Whatcha playin?' and they said, 'Oh, it's poker,' and I said, 'Oh, will you teach me?' And my mother gave me a dirty look because she knew I knew how to play. I just cleaned up on 'em. I think I won two dollars and fifty cents. (You know, they were playing for nickels and dimes.) My dad made me give it all back. He said, 'You're a ringer. You know how to play poker. That wasn't fair!'"

1965

Wolf Point Legion Team Wins Its First State Championship

Don Paulson pegs throw from third over to **John Morrison** at first. **Dick Puckett** from Peerless is at second. *Leader.*

PRESEASON

Several rookies joined the 1965 Legion team, along with veteran Don Paulson (now in his final season) and other players with Legion experience, like Phil Audet, Randy Peck, and Carl Darchuk. This year was historically significant in that it marked the first time a player from Peerless—14-year-old Dick Puckett—played for Scobey, which paved the way for so many other boys from Peerless to follow. Dick had played Little League in Peerless for my dad and Ed Puckett, and one year of Babe Ruth in Scobey for Charlie Mueller. Dad provided the logistical support for Dick (and later Terry and Don) to practice in Scobey by having them ride with him on the mail route from Peerless. Randy Smith, Craig Audet, John Morrison, Rocky Ware, George Heath, Paris French, and Jim Hansen were also new on the roster. An early season photo in the *Leader* shows Don Paulson, Dick Puckett, and John Morrison practicing on the Scobey field in early April. Doc was now building the team that would get Scobey to State for the first time in 1967 and win it in 1969.

And in Flaxville, coached by Dallas Gaines, two young 14-year-olds—Randy Legare and Jack Higgins—would play their first year of Legion ball. Randy and Jack would join the Scobey Legion team in 1968. This year also marked the first time Scobey hosted the district tournament,* which consisted of seven teams: Scobey, Poplar, Outlook, Wolf

1965 Scobey Legionnaires. Standing, L–R: Dick Puckett, Carl Darchuk, Randy Peck, Danny Smith, Phil Audet, Don Paulson, John Morrison. Kneeling: Paris French, Bill Dale, Jack Carney, Jim Hansen, Craig Audet, and Coach Dr. C. H. Norman. Not pictured are Rocky Ware, George Heath, and Glen Halvorson. *Leader.*

1965 Flaxville-Whitetail Legion Team. Kneeling, L–R: Mike Barstad, Leon Cantrell, Larry Dickman, Jim Frasier, John Higgins, Mitch Higgins, Ralph Kanning. Standing: Randy Legare, Rick Marriage Bruce Owen, David Owen, Van Southland, Coach Dallas Gaines and Manager Gerry Owen. *Leader.*

---

* Scobey hosted the eastern division playoffs between Flaxville and Roundup in 1958, but this was the first tournament.

Point, Sidney, Glendive, and Flaxville-Whitetail. (Plentywood was in the league, but they did not play in the tournament as they hosted the state tournament.)

REGULAR SEASON

Home-Opener at Scobey. Scobey and Phil Audet came back from a 7-0 first-inning deficit to beat Wolf Point, 8-7. *Leader.*

THE SEASON-OPENER FOR SCOBEY AGAINST WOLF POINT HAS to be the most remarkable Legion season-opener ever. Wolf Point, described by Phil Audet in his interview as "men among boys" that year, jumped on Phil and Scobey for seven runs in the top of the first inning and led 7-0 after the frame, but then Phil and the Scobey defense held Wolf Point scoreless for the next eight innings, and Scobey came back to win the game 8-7. Phil struck out 12 and yielded 12 hits, but most of them in the first inning. Wolf Point, coached by Lenny Loendorf, had an incredibly talented and strong team that year and won the district and state championships, but Scobey and Phil had their day in that opener.

Some other regular-season results for Scobey in district play:

- Flaxville 10-6 (W)
- Plentywood 6-3 (L)
- Outlook 20-11 (W)
- Outlook 10-7 (W)
- Wolf Point 24-3 (L)
- Wolf Point 7-0 (L)

Phil Audet and Don Paulson did most of the pitching, with Danny Smith and Glen Halvorson catching when Paulson pitched. George Heath and John Morrison also got some innings on the mound. For Flaxville, Dan Tryan, Rick Marriage, Van Southland, and Mitch Higgins pitched, and Owen and Southland did most of the catching.

DISTRICT TOURNAMENT

THE DISTRICT TOURNAMENT AT SCOBEY WAS HIGHLY ANTICIpated, as this was the first Legion event of this magnitude hosted by Scobey, with seven teams participating. The *Leader* dedicated two issues to previewing the tournament, then covered it extensively, including photos of each of the seven teams in the tournament. Scobey also provided detailed game results to the major Montana newspapers. This district tournament in 1965 was only a small sampling of what was to come, as Scobey would host state tournaments in 1969, 1971, 1973, 1975, 1977, 1979, and 1985, along with several divisional tournaments through those years and following. The American Legion Post 56, parents, and volunteers in the community all made it happen.

Wolf Point was heavily favored in the district tournament, and they didn't disappoint. After their first-round bye, they steamrolled over Glendive 10-1 and Sidney 16-3 in the final to win it. Bob Loucks pitched a four-hitter and struck out 14 batters in the final against Sidney. Glendive challenged Sidney and won 15-5, so Wolf Point and Glendive advanced to the state tournament in Plentywood the following weekend.

But the big story of the tournament was the play of Scobey and Flaxville. Each team played four games in the tournament, winning two and losing two, and they played each other. Scobey won its first game 4-3 over Outlook, with Don Paulson the winning pitcher over Kenny Selvig. In Flaxville's first game, Glendive scored 13 runs in the seventh, eighth, and ninth innings to win 19-2. Dan Tryan started, and Rick Marriage relieved, with David Owen catching.

Scobey lost 10-0 against Sidney in their second game. Phil Audet and George Heath pitched for Scobey. Scobey made six costly errors in the game. Bob McChesney almost hit for the cycle for Sidney, with a single, a double, and a triple. Flaxville beat Poplar 13-4 in their second game, with David Owen getting the win for Flaxville. Flaxville then won their next game 7-5 over Outlook. Van Southland and Dan Tryan pitched for Flaxville, with Tryan getting the win. Flaxville scored five runs in the top of the seventh to overcome a 5-2 deficit.

That set up the game between Scobey and Flaxville, which the *Leader* described as "easily the best game of the tournament."[44] The game was tied 2-2 after nine innings and went into extra innings. Then, in the bottom of the tenth, 14-year-old George Heath knocked in the winning run and Scobey walked it off 3-2. Phil Audet pitched eight innings for Scobey, and Don Paulson pitched the ninth and tenth for the win. Rick Marriage pitched for Flaxville and was relieved by Mitch Higgins, who took the loss. Scobey then lost 18-8 to Glendive to finish their season.

The *Leader* recognized Randy Peck for his fine hitting in the tournament, going 8-18 with several extra base hits, and referred to Don Paulson as "the iron horse of the tournament."[45] Don caught most games he didn't pitch, pitched one full game and relieved two others, and also played one game in the outfield. Randy Smith caught the game where Don played in the outfield.

Randy Peck led Scobey in hitting at the district tournament. *Leader.*

At the state tournament at Sportsman Park in Plentywood the following weekend, Wolf Point swept it in three games, but the going wasn't always easy. Plentywood, playing on their home field, beat the Billings Scarlets* 4-1, then played Wolf Point tough, losing 3-2, as Dennis Lee pitched strong for Plentywood. Plentywood stranded 15 baserunners in the game. Wolf Point then shut out Cut Bank 4-0 and then beat them again in the championship 13-1, as Tony Welzenbach led a 14-hit Wolf Point attack with three doubles. Plentywood, coached by Leo Froelich, had a fine showing as host, winning two games over the Scarlets and losing to Wolf Point 3-2.

Following their 13-1 state championship win over Cut Bank in Plentywood, Wolf Point played off against Bozeman

Wolf Point Legion Team, 1965 state champions. Back row as heads appear, L–R: Jim Dwyer, Bob Loucks, Ron Loendorf, Don Schillinger, Tony Welzenbach, Roger Schillinger, Larry VanAtta, Wayne Bergen, Rick Whittelsey, Henry Hamill. Kneeling: Coach Lenny Loendorf, Dave Parsley, Carl Hotvedt, Jack Shamley, Barry Kurokawa, Dave Ahlberg, Doug Mair. *Wolf Point Herald.*

to get into the State A Tournament and lost 8-4, but not before 260-pound catcher Tony Welzenbach broke the Bozeman bench in half when he stepped on it chasing a foul ball.

Catcher Tony Welzenbach tapes up with team captain and pitcher Roger Schillinger before the Bozeman challenge game. *Glyn Deem photo.*

Wolf Point Coach Lenny Loendorf looks over his team's lineup with his pitchers Larry VanAtta, left, and Bob Loucks, right. *Glyn Deem photo.*

PLAINSMEN

The Plainsmen did not participate in a league but played a few games in 1965. A "pickup team" of Plainsmen was put together for a Fourth of July doubleheader between the Plainsmen and the Assiniboia Aces† at Scobey Ball Park, which saw brilliant pitching and fielding on both sides of the field. Fans were treated to two pitchers' duels, and only one walk was issued on the day. Scobey lost the first game 3-2, with Jimmy Olson from Vida pitching a complete game and taking the loss for the Plainsmen. In the second game, Keith Sell, who was home from Helena for his 10-year class reunion, pitched for the Plainsmen, and Rube "Lefty" Erfle, a left-hander, pitched for Assiniboia. Both pitchers pitched 10 innings of shutout ball, but Assiniboia finally got to Keith for a run in the top of the eleventh. Scobey failed to

---

* The Billings Scarlets were formed as a "B" team for the Post No. 4 Billings Legion team, who became known as the Billings Royals in 1965.
† The Assiniboia Aces were the Southern Baseball League (SBL) champions and Saskatchewan provincial champions in 1965.

score in the bottom half, so Assiniboia won 1-0. The fine pitching in the second game was matched by solid defense, as both teams recorded two double plays. Playing for the Plainsmen that day were Gary Brenden, Mike Norman, Jim Olson, Terry Gilbertson, Keith Sell, Doug Schillinger, Larry Veis, Charlie Mueller, Larry Ferguson, and Dwain Sell. On the roster for the Aces was Gordon Skjerven,* who played for the Plainsmen from 1960 to 1963 and traveled to Wichita to play in the 1960 NBC World Series. The *Leader*, recognizing good ball when it saw it, wrote this about the doubleheader: "A pickup team of baseball players upheld the name of the Scobey Plainsmen in a credible fashion when they played a doubleheader with the visiting Assiniboia Aces, a seasoned Canadian team. Fans saw some excellent baseball. Both ball games were played in a total of four hours and 10 minutes. Officiating was crisp and fair. Don Paulson did the 20-inning stint behind the plate and did it well. It was obvious to everyone in the Scobey Ball Park that both teams thoroughly enjoyed the concentrated and hard play. Fans found it contagious and consequently respected it, with a minimum of the customary vulgarity and invective that so often characterizes a crowd watching an American sporting contest. Altogether, it was a rare and tensely interesting afternoon of baseball."[46]

EXTRA INNINGS

JACK REINER COACHED BABE RUTH TWO TEAMS—THE Mosquitoes and the Bed Bugs—that summer in a developmental league in Scobey. There were no scheduled games. Jack said, "We're just going to have some interclub games, some fun, and along the way teach the kids something about the game."[47]

1966

Scobey Qualifies for Its First State Tournament—But is Disqualified

PRESEASON

WHILE THE 1966 SCOBEY LEGION TEAM WAS still young by the 18-year-old Legion age limit (19 after August 1), it could not be said that they were inexperienced. Seventeen-year-old Phil Audet was now in his third full year of Legion and had been rostered on the Legion team for four years, and many other players now had at least one year of Legion ball under their belts. These same players had all played a lot of ball in Little League and Babe Ruth, but this team was still being developed by Doc. A couple notable rookie 14-year-olds added to the roster were Danny Wang—who would become Scobey's starting second baseman for the next five years—and Jerry LaPierre, a young left-handed pitcher and outfielder. And Doc, after taking over as head Legion coach again in 1964—and who had coached some of the boys in Babe Ruth in 1963—was now in this third full year with this team. So, when Doc got the boys on the field in early April, as he always did, expectations were growing, and the talented young team delivered, qualifying for the state tournament for the first time in Scobey American Legion Baseball history. But they were disqualified for having an ineligible player on the roster and were not able to compete at State. Flaxville-Whitetail would again field a Legion team in 1966,

1966 Scobey Legionnaires. Standing, L–R: John Nelson, George Heath, Danny Wang, John Morrison, Craig Audet, Dick Puckett, and Phil Audet. Kneeling: Paris French, Carl Darchuk, Rocky Ware, Larry Thompson, Jerry LaPierre. Batboy (front) is Dana Audet. Not pictured is Dan Smith. *Leader.*

---

* While playing for the Assiniboia Aces, Skjerven won the SBL most valuable player award in 1955; struck out the first seven batters he faced and finished with a total of 18 strikeouts in one SBL game; had a 15-year batting average of .378 and was a member of the 1965 SBL and provincial championship team and the SBL champions of 1966.

and many of the talented players from Flaxville—whose players would begin playing for Scobey in 1968 after their Legion program was discontinued—were gaining valuable Legion experience playing for Dallas Gaines.

REGULAR SEASON

THE FORMAT FOR THE REGULAR AND POSTSEASON CHANGED again in 1966: the eastern division was split into northern and southern districts, with Scobey, Flaxville-Whitetail, Glasgow, Wolf Point, Plentywood, and Poplar competing in the north, and Sidney, Glendive, and Circle competing in the south. The top two teams from the north and south would compete in a four-team tournament in Glendive, where the top two teams would advance to State, to be hosted at Cobb Field in Billings by the Scarlets.

A notable participant playing Legion baseball in Montana in 1966 was Havre Post No. 11, whose Junior Legion program had been on life support since 1948, as they had not fielded a Legion team since 1963 and had only fielded one team since 1959. Havre played in the state tournament on Cobb Field in 1948, but only as the runner-up in the B division in the west, because Bozeman, the champion in the west, was disqualified for not providing birth certificates for its roster. Havre's Legion program was in shambles in 1966, but, as in Scobey, everything changed with the arrival of a new coach. Doug Shepphard, who played second base that year, recalls how things turned around in Havre: "The year 1966 was a rebirth of Legion Baseball in Havre with the hiring of Tom Nielson and support of many other fans and parents." Havre did not play in a district that year but played a rambler schedule mostly against Class A competition, like the Great Falls Electrics and Williston Keybirds. Coach Tom Nielson was stealing a play out of Doc's playbook, playing tougher competition to get better. Doug Shepphard added, "We lost all those games, but stuck with it as the next years would show!" The slumbering giant, eventually known as the Havre Northstars, would soon awaken.

And Scobey's Legion Baseball program was on the rise, too. Tom Nielson and Doc Norman. Havre and Scobey. The two emerging Legion programs were on a collision course for some classic matchups in the years to come. There was something about these two programs, dating back to when Scobey won the district championship in 1930 and 1931, and Havre followed in 1932 and 1933. A new era was coming when these two Legion programs would dominate State Class B Legion Baseball in Montana like no two teams had previously done.

The highlight of Scobey's regular season play was a classic road trip Doc took the team on before the eastern

John Morrison, Scobey first baseman, belts a single Saturday night in Cobb field. Scobey edged the Billings Scarlets 4-3. Scarlet catcher is Pat McCann. The ump is Warren Frazee. *Gazette photo by Carl Kubo.*

divisional tournament, this time to play on Cobb Field in Billings and Denton Field in Miles City. As the *Leader* wrote, "The young team gratified the fondest wishes of Coach Norman on the tour by coming from behind on both occasions."[48] In their game against the Billings Scarlets, Scobey won 4-3. Dan Smith, Scobey catcher (and batboy for Doc's first Scobey team in 1959), had four hits—a triple and three singles—to lead Scobey's hitting. He also scored the winning run in the ninth on Paris French's single to right. Phil Audet went the distance and got the win for Scobey, scattering eight hits. "Phil Audet went the distance" was a familiar phrase during his Legion career.

The talented young Scobey team, many of them still Babe Ruth–age, was beginning to turn some heads. The baseball-savvy fans on Cobb Field in Billings took notice of the young team: "Dick Puckett's performance at third base and at bat, in addition to Smith, brought much favorable comment from the Billings crowd. The boys all looked good."[49] Scobey then won their next game the next day at Denton Field in Miles City, winning 9-6. In that game, Craig Audet started on the mound but had control problems, so he was relieved by George Heath in the third inning. The game was tied 4-4 in the top of the fifth, when Scobey erupted for five runs to take a 9-4 lead and held on to win 9-6. Heath got the win.

EASTERN DIVISIONAL TOURNAMENT

THE 1966 EASTERN DIVISIONAL TOURNAMENT ON MEISSNER Memorial Field in Glendive featured the top two teams from the northern district—Plentywood and Scobey—and the top two teams from the south—Glendive and Sidney. Bob Weinberger, Glendive head coach and tournament director, stated that "Sidney was favored to win the tournament," but any team could win it. For example, Plentywood had won nine consecutive games going into the tournament and had a good team. But this tournament would turn out to be the most bizarre and controversial divisional tournament in the history of Montana American Legion Baseball. The tournament affected Doc so deeply that it would almost take him off the baseball field the following year—having him walk away from the team he had been grooming to be a champion and the game he loved—and it took the parents of the players and the community of Scobey to coax Doc into to returning to coach the team.

Scobey opened against Glendive and won 6-4, with Phil Audet going the distance to get the win. Sidney beat Plentywood 8-3. In the loser's bracket, Glendive eliminated Plentywood 6-5. In the winner's bracket, Sidney beat Scobey 10-7. Glendive then bounced Scobey from the tournament 9-3. Glendive then won the championship 10-3 over Sidney to win the title. (There was not a second game as at this point Glendive and Sidney each had one loss.) So, it was Glendive (2-1) and Sidney (2-1) headed to State, and Scobey (1-2) and Plentywood (0-2) returning home.

But what happened next—both on and off the field—would shake all of that up.

Following the Glendive-Sidney championship game, Doc, in his role as district commissioner, filed a protest with state commissioner John Russell, stating that Glendive had used an illegal player, Jim Peters. The protest was based on legal residence because Peters' parents had moved to Casper, Wyoming, earlier in the year. The rule stated that if a Legion player's parents move prior to the season to a town that has a Legion program, that boy must play in that program, and Casper had a Legion program. The state commissioner upheld the protest, so Glendive was forced to forfeit its championship to Sidney, which was awarded the championship. But who now—Plentywood or Scobey—was to be awarded second place and a trip to State? Since Scobey and Plentywood had not faced each other in the tournament, it was decided that they would play each other on a neutral field—Moose Memorial Park in Sidney—on Tuesday night, with the winner earning a berth to State.

In the Tuesday night matchup, Plentywood had a strong team, but Scobey was favorably situated to do well, as ace pitcher Phil Audet, who got the 6-4 win over Glendive in the tournament opener, got his innings back and had a couple of days' rest. In 1966, Scobey didn't really have a pitching staff; it was just Phil. This weakness was not an issue during the regular season, when there would often be days between games. The battery for almost every game read, "Audet and Smith." But in the tournament this chink in Scobey's armor was exposed. I remember when I was a kid, my dad told me this catchy phrase: "Spahn and Sain and pray for rain." He explained to me what it meant: the 1948 Boston Braves had two really good starting pitchers, Warren Spahn and Johnny Sain, but nothing after that, so after each of them pitched, the team needed a rainout so they could get rest and pitch again. The corollary to that for the 1966 Scobey Legion team was, "Phil and sun and Scobey's done." Ironically, in my interview with Phil, he identified this game as the best game he ever pitched in Legion—he had a slew of them.

But it was all for nought.

Phil pitched a gem—a three-hitter with seven strikeouts and gave up only two earned runs—and Scobey won the game 4-2, ostensibly qualifying Scobey for its first state tournament appearance. Gary Pederson, Phil's counterpart on the mound for Plentywood, only allowed five hits to take the loss. Phil Audet recalls the hard-fought game. "It was really a battle," he said. "They had Gary Pederson, and he'd burned us a couple of times during the season. He was a very good pitcher. The Glendive people and some of the players were over there, and they gave Doc a heck of a bad time the whole game. They didn't bother any of the players, but they sure harassed poor Doc because of the disqualification. But through all of that, we won the game, and we were going to State." There was joy in Scobey.

The headline in the *Billings Gazette* on Wednesday read, "Scobey Earns Tourney Berth."[50] But hold the press. A footnote to the article on Scobey's tournament berth in the *Gazette* on Wednesday morning was, "Scobey withdrew from the Class B Montana Legion tourney in Billings."[51] Why? Following Scobey's win over Plentywood, Coach Bob Weinberger and Glendive had filed a protest that Scobey had used an ineligible player—Dan Smith—whose parents had moved to Havre from Scobey in 1966. The state commissioner never actually ruled on the protest, as Doc decided not to fight it and forfeited the game to Plentywood. So, Plentywood—who had lost to Sidney 8-3, Glendive 6-5, and Scobey 4-2 and was now 0-3 in the tournament—was awarded second place and a state tournament berth. The headline the next day in the *Gazette* read, "Plentywood Nine Bewildered,"[52] and it went on to explain how it came to be that Plentywood—after losing three games in the tournament—was headed to State.

It is hard to imagine thinking you've qualified for the state tournament for the first time in program history, you're packed and ready to go, then find out you're not going. Phil Audet, who had pitched Scobey to State (or so he thought), recalls the morning he and Craig found out they were not going to State. He said, "I remember Mom coming downstairs saying, 'No, we can't go to State.' She was waking us up because we were supposed to leave that day. So, that was kind of a tough year for us." Dana Audet, batboy for the 1966 Scobey Legion team and the younger brother of Phil and Craig, said, "I remember beating Plentywood, everyone was excited, really great game, we went back to Scobey, go to bed, and all of a sudden the lights come on, and there's this commotion and uproar in our house. Phil and Craig are angry. I remember hearing my folks saying, 'We're not going to go to State . . . declared ineligible.'" That was not a great memory.

Meanwhile, both Glendive coach Bob Weinberger and Doc Norman published statements in the *Billings Gazette* providing their side of the story following the tournament. Doc's statement in the *Gazette* was in response to Weinberger's statement. There was also a lot of press on the disqualifications written by other sportswriters, and most of the press was bad for Doc and Scobey, siding mostly with Glendive. The ugliest part of the entire situation occurred at the neutral field in Sidney in the game between Plentywood and Scobey on Tuesday. Many Scobey players attested to the negative conditions under which that game was played. In Doc's letter, he referred to the "vicious and vulgar heckling that the claque from Glendive instituted and continued at Sidney (with megaphones) . . . against Scobey's team and the coach personally."[53] In the same letter, Doc openly criticized the umpiring in Glendive, mentioning that ground rule decisions made by the all-Glendive umpire crew cost Plentywood its game with Glendive, and that he had a signed statement from the Plentywood coach "protesting unwarranted decisions by Glendive umpires."[54] For the reader to hear both sides of the story, both letters are reprinted here in their entirety. I am partial to Doc's side of the story, of course, but Glendive Coach Weinberger made some good points in his statement in the *Gazette*. Coach Weinberger's statement appeared first, followed by Doc's the next day.

Glendive Coach Issues Statement[55]

GLENDIVE – Bob Weinberger, coach of the Glendive American Legion baseball team, in a signed statement to The Billings Gazette Wednesday, asks "How important is winning."

The Glendive team was disqualified from the state Class B tournament after winning the district tournament, following a protest by Scobey that Glendive used an ineligible player.

Later Scobey, winner of a playoff with Plentywood for the right to replace Glendive in the state tourney in Billings, was also charged with using an ineligible player. Scobey then withdrew in favor of Plentywood, rather than fighting the protest. Weinberger's statement, in part, follows:

"The Glendive team has been accused of recruiting 'a ringer' to win the district tournament in Glendive.

"The protestor, Dr. C. H. Norman, district commissioner, filed a protest with the state commissioner, John Russell, stating Glendive used an illegal player in the Eastern Legion Tournament and consequently must forfeit the right to participate in the state tournament. The protest is based on the question of legal residence. Where does this boy live? Where has he played baseball? This young man has played 4 years of organized baseball, all of which has been played in Glendive. Three years in the Glendive Babe Ruth League and one in the Glendive American Legion League. If this doesn't establish intention and residence of this young man I can't imagine what more can be done.

"This same boy has played 18 of the 21 games Glendive Legion team has played this year. Three times he has played against the Legion team Dr. Norman coaches, and nothing has been said about being ineligible.

"I contacted Russell about our team being qualified and he told me July 11 all our papers were in order and we could participate in the tournament.

"Doctor Norman contacted the state commissioner July 21 and was told that the Glendive team was qualified, so why now do we find ourselves disqualified? Why too wasn't this technicality discovered prior to tournament play? Why aren't the team rosters checked prior to team play so this type of maneuvering can't happen? We teach, above all things, sportsmanship and this type of action destroys the whole season's work. How can we be eligible on the 11th of July and again on the 21st and not adding or changing our roster in any way be ineligible on the 25th of July?

"Another thing that puzzles me is what is really meant be the term 'ringer'? Let me tell you that the boy in question is a fine young Glendive boy, has a very good reputation in our community and is a good baseball player. He is a boy that the rest of the team enjoys as a teammate, has an average to good record in the playing scorebook, but, in all honesty to both the boy and myself, could not be classified as outstanding except in character. It would appear to me that the Glendive American Legion team has been viciously insulted and I must assume that WINNING has become so important that the future of organized youth baseball programs is being threatened. I hope for the future success of Montana athletic programs, something more promising can be developed."

The next day came Doc's rebuttal:

Scobey Commissioner Blames Technicalities[56]

SCOBEY - Confusion about a technicality resulted in the elimination of the Glendive and Scobey American Legion baseball teams from the Montana Class B tournament, Dr. C. H. Norman, eastern district commissioner and coach of the Scobey team, said in a statement to the *Billings Gazette* Friday. Dr. Norman's statement, in part, follows:

"Flurries of charges and counter charges seem to be clouding the picture of Junior Legion baseball in Eastern Montana.

"It is indeed unfortunate that those who spend the time working with the boys in the game find themselves involved in a maze of technicalities and rulings that complicate rather than clear up areas of confusion," he said.

"The matter of Glendive's disqualification after the district tournament was a technical one and was discovered just before the filing of the rosters for the state tournament, and not before. However, it was a technicality that could not be ignored. I refer specifically to the matter of one Glendive player being listed under two different names, and that he also was from a high school in Casper, Wyo.

"During season play I think it is fair to assume that all of the team coaches presume the players on opposing teams are eligible, and that they try to see that players on their own teams also are. I also believe that the player in question was eligible likely through some oral communication with state authorities on the matter.

"I believe this to be true because the Scobey team has had a similar experience in regard to one of its players—a boy raised here, who played all of his Babe Ruth and Junior Legion baseball in Scobey, but whose folks, in between seasons, moved to Havre even though they are still registered voters in Scobey, that, and the fact that Havre had no Junior Legion team for several years until this year.

"Normally, a boy is not allowed to play in another place when his high school town has a Junior Legion team. However, in a ruling March 20, 1965, at the annual baseball meeting in Bozeman, it was clearly ruled and stated that in a city or town that renews Junior Legion baseball activity, it shall have no prior claim to a boy that wants to continue playing with a team he has played with the year before, regardless where he lives.

"In the matter above we certainly understood from state authorities that he was eligible here.

"But here was where both Scobey and Glendive fell down—on a technicality. Both of us should have had a formal letter on the matter from the state commissioner before July 10, final deadline on registrations. This we did not do, and likely Glendive did not do it for the same reason that we did not—there had been oral assurances of no problem in each matter.

"In the subsequent necessary challenge that could not be overlooked (in regard to Glendive's player appearing under two different names and from a high school in Wyoming) when the rosters for the state tourney had to be recorded, all this could have been avoided by a ruling that held up the previous oral affirmation. But this was not done by the State Commissioner. Thus, Glendive was disqualified for state tournament play, and Scobey, even though winning a playoff game with Plentywood, found itself also challenged in eligibility.

"We could have invited an airing and investigation on this, in the knowledge that we had every reason to believe our player was eligible. I am sure Glendive feels the same way about its player.

"However, instead of furthering the tempest, we decided to withdraw and let things die down. Yet, in view of the foregoing, and recent published statements in *The Billings Gazette*, this must be answered. "I did not care to go into the questionable conduct of the tournament by Glendive there in the recent district tournament. But I will do so now. I have in hand a written and signed statement by the Plentywood coach protesting unwarranted ground rule decisions by Glendive umpires. Anyone in baseball knows it is highly illegal to make ground rule decisions in matters in which the visiting teams have not been advised on previously. "These cost Plentywood its game with Glendive.

"I had not intended to go into the base umpiring at the tournament—particularly at crucial times for Glendive. Moreover, it has not been considered good practice in a tournament for the host town, with a team in the tournament, to have all umpires from the host town. Such, however, was the case at Glendive. There were in fact a number of Glendive people who volunteered the fact that it was too bad Glendive had to win that way. I had not intended to go into the vicious and vulgar heckling that the claque from Glendive instituted and continued at Sidney (with megaphones) during the playoff game between Plentywood and Scobey, against Scobey's team and the coach personally. . . .

"It becomes apparent in reviewing all this, the Class B Junior Legion Baseball is considered by state authorities as an ugly stepchild. Rulings are made and then rescinded; eligibilities are resolved orally and then reversed. This sort of thing is not stood for in the Class A setup. I see no reason why it should not be the same in Class B.

"I hope this statement will answer some of the loose ends left hanging, after previous appearances of the matter in *The Billings Gazette*, and which could not go unanswered."

> Signed:
> C. H. Norman, M.D.
> District Commissioner.
> Scobey

1966 State Class B American Legion Tournament flyer.

STATE TOURNAMENT

AT THE STATE TOURNAMENT ON COBB FIELD, SIDNEY—KNOWN as the Majestics at the time—swept it in three straight games for their first state championship, winning over each team in the tournament: 3-2 over the Scarlets, 6-5 over Cut Bank, and 10-1 over Plentywood in the championship. Dale Thomas and Ervin Frank combined to pitch a two-hitter for Sidney in the championship. After losing its opener 10-2 against Cut Bank, Plentywood clawed its way back through the loser's bracket to beat the Scarlets 5-1 and Cut Bank 12-2 to get to the championship game.

So, in three successive years, three eastern Montana baseball towns had won their first state championship: Glendive in 1964, Wolf Point in 1965, and now Sidney in 1966. Fort Peck won in 1953 and Plentywood in 1954. When would Scobey's turn come? The power was in the east for Legion Baseball in 1966, but Havre would soon have its say about that.

EXTRA INNINGS

THE IRONY IN THE REVIVAL OF HAVRE'S LEGION PROGRAM IN 1966 is that it ultimately cost Scobey a trip to State. Dan Smith's parents—Dale and Billie Lou Smith—had moved from Scobey to Havre in 1966. Legion rules state that if a town has a Legion program, the player must play for the town where the parents are residents. Since Havre had restarted its Legion program in 1966, Dan was required to play Havre. But Doc's letter to the *Gazette* rebutted that by identifying a special ruling made by Montana Legion at the annual baseball meeting in Bozeman on March 20, 1965, where it was "clearly ruled and stated that in a city or town that *renews* [italics mine] Junior Legion baseball activity, it

1966 Sidney Majestics, State Class B Champions. Back row, L–R: Dick Norden, Dale Thomas, LeRoy Amundson, Jim Ausk, Ervin Frank, Bob Rollnis and Coach Leo Schlenker. Front row: Jim Thogerson, Tim Sampson, Bob McChesney, Dave Riley, Mike Gear, Tom Carranza, Perry Miller. Not pictured are Marshall Olson and Bill Price. *Sidney Herald.*

shall have no prior claim to a boy that wants to continue playing with a team he has played with the year before, regardless where he lives." Since Havre *renewed* its Legion program in 1966, this special ruling should have allowed Dan to play in Scobey that summer.

In 1966, the Great Falls Electrics would often split their Legion team into two squads and play games on the same day or weekend. The Great Falls Sparkies would form the following year, compete in the western B division, and host the state tournament. Billings and Great Falls would now each have one B team competing.

1967

Scobey Qualifies for Its First State Tournament—For Real This Time

> *For Doc Norman, team coach and indefatigable enthusiast for young sportsmen—who over the years has spent thousands of dollars in handling the teams, plus a great deal of expensive time—getting the team into the state tournament this season was an extra and unexpected dividend. And those who are fans of the game, in what always has been a baseball community, can thank Doctor Norman, a personified bundle of energy who also has one of the busiest general practices in Montana. They can also thank his chief of staff, Marjorie Norman, who has a way of making it look easy.*
>
> **—Daniels County Leader, August 3, 1967**

FOLLOWING THE BIZARRE END TO THE 1966 SEASON—where both Scobey and Glendive were disqualified from competing at State due to ineligible players—the beginning of the 1967 season began strangely as well. The parents of the Scobey Legion players had to talk Doc into returning to coach the team. According to the *Leader*, Doc had "definitely decided not to handle the team due to pressure on his time, but when no one came forward to handle the Juniors, parents of the eligible boys drafted him."[57] Also, the stress from the season-ending disqualifications and the toxic conditions under which the game against Plentywood at Sidney was played at the end of the previous year might have also had something to do with Doc's resistance to continue coaching in 1967.

But Doc and Chief of Staff Marge said yes to the parents, and Scobey had Doc back for their push for their first-ever trip to State in 1967. As Phil Audet, now in his final season, said in his interview, "We had a little extra incentive in 1967 to get back there to State after the incident [in Glendive] in 1966." And boy, would Scobey's first-ever berth in a state tournament come in the most dramatic fashion.

The year 1967 was also a milestone season for Flaxville, but in an era-ending way. This season would mark the final year that American Legion Post No. 121 (Whitetail) would field a Flaxville-Whitetail Legion team. Flaxville had a strong team in 1967, but star player Rick Marriage was seriously injured in an automobile accident, which

The Baseball Renaissance

1967 Flaxville American Legion Team. Front row, L–R: Danny Tryan, Dale Fishell, Greg Kurtz, Jim Miller, Mitch Higgins, and Mike Barstad. Standing: Don Higgins, Dennis Miller, Jack Higgins, Royce Fishell, Randy Legare, and Coach Larry Getts. In front, Craig Miller, batboy. *Leader.*

hurt their chances to qualify for the district tournament in Plentywood. Peerless's last Legion team was fielded in 1960.

The 1967 Scobey American Legion roster now consisted of players with several years' Legion experience, and the middle infield for the 1969 state championship team had already settled into Dick Puckett at short and Danny Wang at second. Rocky Ware played third with George Heath at first. As catcher Dan Smith's family had moved to Havre, Craig Audet took over all the catching duties. Bill Dale, Jerry LaPierre, and Paris French played in the outfield. And of course, 18-year-old right-hander Phil Audet anchored the pitching staff, with Dick Puckett and Jerry LaPierre picking up most of the other innings.

DIVISIONAL TOURNAMENT

1967 Scobey Legionnaires. Standing, L–R: Coach Norman, Craig Audet, Paris French, Phil Audet, Jim Hansen, Jerry LaPierre, Dick Puckett, Harvey Bush. Second row: John Nelson, Bill Dale, Jim Nelson, Rocky Ware, George Heath, Danny Wang. In front, Kelly Norman and Dana Audet, batboys. *Leader.*

THE FOUR-TEAM EASTERN DIVISIONAL TOURNAMENT—HOSTED by Plentywood—consisted of the top two teams in the northern district and the top two teams from the southern district, with the top three teams in the divisional tournament advancing to State in Great Falls. Wolf Point won the north, but because of a delay in getting their birth certificates in on time, they were disqualified from competing in the divisional tournament before it started. Plentywood had taken second and Scobey third, so Plentywood bumped up to the number one seed and Scobey slipped in as the number two seed in the north.

Scobey's competition in the 1967 Eastern Divisional Tournament was strong. Glendive and Sidney had tied for first in the South and had a combined record of 28-6 between them. Their programs were both strong year-over-year, as Glendive had won State in 1964 and Sidney won it in 1966 and was third in 1964, and Glendive had won the eastern divisional in 1966 but was disqualified from going to State. Plentywood was strong too, with athletes like Kenny Selvig and Zoonie McLean Jr. on the team. Plentywood had only lost to Wolf Point in the regular season in the north, and they had Scobey's number. Plentywood also had taken third in State in 1965 and was runner-up to Sidney in 1966. All of this led up to Scobey being considered the "Cinderella" team in the tournament—they were not expected to win a game and advance, which makes the story of their first berth in the state tournament even more remarkable.

Scobey's first game in the tournament was against Glendive, the number one seed in the south, and the favorite to win the tournament. Scobey needed one win in the tournament to advance to State, so Doc put ace Phil Audet on the mound for Scobey in that first game, and what a game it was! The game turned out to be a pitcher's duel between Phil Audet of Scobey and Russ Evinrude of Glendive. Scobey scored one run in the bottom of the first inning to take a 1-0 lead, and the score remained 1-0 until the top of the ninth inning. Phil Audet had pitched eight shutout innings against Glendive, and, after yielding but one run in the bottom of the first, Evinrude had pitched seven consecutive shutout innings against Scobey.

That would all change in a wild ninth inning. With Scobey leading 1-0 and three outs away from the win—and Phil Audet on cruise control for a shutout—Glendive shocked Phil and Scobey by pushing across three runs to take a 3-1 lead entering the bottom of the ninth. And Scobey, only moments before on the edge of their seats for their first state tournament berth, now faced a two-run deficit in their last at bat, and the looming prospect of elimination the next day against Plentywood, a team they had yet to beat that year.

But the game—and Scobey's hopes for its first state tournament berth—was not over. With baserunners on first and second, Paris French doubled in a run to cut the deficit to 3-2. Scobey now had runners on second and third but was down to its final out. With two outs, the next hitter hit a routine ground ball to shortstop, and it looked like the game was over, but Glendive's shortstop threw wild to first, and two runs scampered across the plate to give Scobey a 4-3 win on a walk-off two-run error! But make no mistake about it, Scobey was headed to their first state tournament since the program began in 1930,* and they were not done in the eastern divisional tournament.

After the first-game pitcher's duel, the next day Scobey upset Sidney 12-9 in a slugfest. Trailing 5-0, Scobey came back to score three runs in the second and added four more in the fourth to take the lead, adding five runs later. Rocky Ware had a triple and two singles and Dick Puckett had three singles to lead Scobey's hitting, and Paris French got the win in relief of Jerry LaPierre. This put Scobey in the championship against Plentywood, who had come back from an opening game loss to make their way to the championship.

Scobey, an underdog going into the tournament, was starting to garner attention for its play. The *Gazette* headlines for their wins against Glendive and Sidney were "Scobey Upsets Glendive"[58] and "Scobey Stuns Sidney."[59] Prior to the championship game against Plentywood, the *Gazette* referred to the team as "surprising" and "upstart" Scobey.[60] In the championship, Plentywood beat undefeated Scobey 11-2 to force a second game, which turned out to be another dramatic game, but this time not in Scobey's favor. Phil Audet was back on the mound for Scobey in the final game, and pitched well again, but Zoonie McLean Jr. scored the winning run from third base in the sixth inning when the throw to the plate was wild, giving Plentywood a 6-5 win and the eastern division championship. But little matter for Scobey—they were headed to Great Falls to play in their first state tournament, along with Plentywood and Sidney.

STATE TOURNAMENT

The state tournament, hosted by the Great Falls Sparkies, consisted of Cut Bank (top seed), Havre, and Great Falls from the West; Plentywood, Scobey, and Sidney from the east. In its first-ever state tournament game, "the tough Scobey team"[61] won 10-3 against Great Falls, with Phil Audet scattering seven hits to get the win. Scobey only led 4-3 going into the top of the ninth but scored six runs to break the game open. Leading Scobey's hitting was Dick Puckett with two hits. Jerry LaPierre had a triple, and Paris French had a double. In its second game, Scobey lost to Plentywood 17-5. (The *Leader* referred to Plentywood as Scobey's "jinx," which they were at that time.) Scobey then eliminated Havre 7-3 to stay alive in the tournament. Dick Puckett scattered six hits against Havre to get the win. This would mark the first time Scobey and Havre played in a state tournament and would begin the classic matchup that would become an annual event at state tournaments for years to come. Scobey then bowed to the Great Falls Sparkies 10-5 to be eliminated from the tournament, finishing a very respectable fourth place in its first appearance. Cut Bank went on to win the tournament by beating the Great Falls Sparkies 7-5 in 10 innings in the championship game. This was Cut Bank's third and final state championship.

Another notable quote in the *Leader* referred to the hosting of the state tournament by Great Falls: "The conduct of the tournament left quite a bit to be desired. In previous Class B tournaments, the teams have had to get to the tournament site, but once there were provided room and board. Not so in Great Falls. Scobey will likely be placing a bid for the State B Tournament next year."[62] This was the beginning of Scobey's eventual run of hosting state tournaments, as Scobey would host its first tournament in 1969, its first of seven.

The *Leader* summed up the great season for Doc and his team this way: "For Doc Norman, team coach and indefatigable enthusiast for young sportsmen—who over the years has spent thousands of dollars in handling the teams, plus a great deal of expensive time—getting the team into the state tournament this season was an extra and unexpected dividend. And those who are fans of the game, in what always has been a baseball community, can thank Dr. Norman, a personified bundle of energy who also has one of the busiest general practices in Montana. They can also thank his chief of staff, Marjorie Norman, who has a way of making it look easy."[63]

And it was onward and upward for the Scobey Legion team in 1968. The program was still ascending, and qualifying for state tournaments would become an annual routine. Beginning in 1967, Scobey would qualify for the state tournament for 16 consecutive years, winning eight of them. And it all started with Phil Audet, who pitched Scobey to the state tournament—twice—and was the winning pitcher in Scobey's first state tournament game.

EXTRA INNINGS

Phil Audet's Legion career spanned from 1963 to 1967. Since 1963, Doc had built the foundation of his Legion program on Phil—specifically, his right arm. In Holy Scripture in *The Book of Blues*, Doc said unto Phil, "Thou art Phil, and upon this rock I will build my Legion team; and the gates of hell shall not prevail against it." After five years

---

* Scobey had qualified for the State playoffs in 1931, as Bob Schaefer once again pitched Scobey to the District title over Havre, but Scobey couldn't travel to state due to lack of financing, it being the Great Depression.

of Legion ball, Phil's heavily used right arm, weary from throwing the curveball that Doc had taught him how to pitch in Babe Ruth in 1963, had finally gotten Scobey to the promised land, a berth in the state tournament. But Phil also played a mean shortstop and was a good hitter—he was a good all-around baseball player. I asked Phil if he remembered any funny stories about playing Legion ball, and he recalled one about his battery mate of several years, catcher Dan Smith. Phil said, "He caught me quite a bit. Smitty didn't really rip it back to ya so you could catch it every time. A few were skipping off the ground. One game, he threw one back to me, and it hit one of the stones on Scobey Ball Park, and bounced up and hit me in the chin and chipped my tooth. So I spit this out and look at it and look back down there, and Smitty's sitting back there laughing behind the mask. I still have that chipped tooth." I asked Phil if Dan ever said he was sorry. Phil said, "No! He just went and looked at it and laughed."

Something about Coach Doc Norman that was a thing when he coached was "the needle." Doc always had a little black bag with him in the dugout for medical purposes. The two most frequently used treatments that Doc pulled out of that little black bag and administered for games were the needle (which contained a shot of cortisone) and an ointment called DMSO.* There are a lot of famous stories from former Legion players about Doc and the needle, so it's appropriate that the first one should come from Phil, his ace pitcher, who likely threw well over 200 pitches in a game several times during his Legion career.† I asked Phil if he remembers "getting the needle." He said, "Oh yeah. I experienced the needle a few times over my career. One time, I got a shot in the arm *and* the back at the same time before one game."

I was six years old in 1967, and my first memory of watching the Scobey Legion team play was in Plentywood at the first Divisional championship game on Sunday. Dad was excited to bring Jon and me to the game because our older cousin Dick Puckett was playing, and Scobey was playing for the Divisional championship. This was a *big* deal. Phil Audet was pitching the championship game, but my first memory is not of the players on the field; rather, it is of watching five-year-old Kelly Norman as a batboy. With several years of experience, Dana Audet was also a batboy that year, too. Dana and Kelly had different batboy styles: Dana's was structured, measured, focused, all business; Kelly's, precisely the opposite!

As 1967 was the last year Flaxville fielded a Legion team, I asked Dan Tryan, who played on that last Legion team, to share his baseball memories of growing up in Flaxville and how his dad, Don Tryan, passed the game down to him and his brothers. Danny shared this letter with me:

> *Baseball, the word that resembles most every family in the small towns that we grew up in . . . My baseball story goes back a long way. My dad, Don Tryan, played a lot of baseball when I was just a young child.*
>
> *My first recollection of me getting involved was when Dad said I was old enough to be the batboy for his team. He and other local guys played for Mineral Bench, which was a small community south of our farm (south of Flaxville) that had a baseball diamond. Dad played a lot of baseball games on the Poplar baseball field, which I believe was the first baseball field to have lights installed and with a grass infield. I just know that it was neat to go down and watch.*
>
> *Even before I was old enough to play Little League, I was already playing catch with Dad after he would come out of the fields at night. He taught me the basics over and over before I even hit my first practice. Our Little League team in Flaxville was made of both town kids and country farm kids, and we all could not wait for the next ball game.*
>
> *One of my fondest memories was when Miles City invited Flaxville to play in a tournament in Miles City. We went in two cars with Patty Legare and my mom, Phyllis, driving the two oldest cars in the community. Sure enough, our car heated up before we got to Miles City and had to wait for water. As we pulled into the Miles City sports complex, I looked at the towering facility. It was quite amazing. As impressive as the*

Don Tryan with his son, Danny, early 1950s. Family photo.

---

* DMSO (dimethyl sulfoxide) is a nonsteroidal anti-inflammatory drug used in horses, primarily for its anti-inflammatory and antioxidant properties.
† There was no pitch count in American Legion Baseball then. American Legion Baseball did not institute a pitch count until the 2017 season. Prior to then, the only limitation was the number of innings per day or over a three-day period. Both were 12 innings.

Danny Tryan as the batboy for the Mineral Bench baseball team that his dad, Don Tryan, played on. *Family photo.*

Danny Tryan with younger brother, Gord, around 1964 or 1965. *Family photo.*

outside was, the best part was inside.* We walked to the back entrance and up the ramp only to see the most beautiful field and seating for five hundred fans. It was our first time ever to play under the lights. I remember it being a calm and beautiful evening playing ball.

My dad also coached us kids on the Babe Ruth team. I remember Dad taking me over to the shop and going to show me how I could become a better pitcher. He took an old peach crate and nailed it to a piece of plywood and leaned it up against the back of the chicken coop, then measured off the required distance for a pitcher's mound, built me a little 2 × 4 pad to pitch from. Dad always took care of all the leagues, baseballs, and bats; he dumped out about 20 baseballs next to me and said, "Keep throwing at that peach basket until you can hit inside of it every time." That's control, and that's where he taught me how to throw a real curveball.

My most memorable Babe Ruth experience was being selected to the All-Star team to play in the Babe Ruth World Series, which was held in Glendive. Some of your folks will remember the Babe Ruth diamond in Glendive . . . a beautiful sunken field with lights and a grassy sloped area all the way around the outfield for people to sit and enjoy.† It was cool.

The American Legion post was in Whitetail, and we had quite a few good ball players from Whitetail and Flaxville. As I look back, it was quite humorous, thinking about the first uniforms that we had. I believe they were all men's uniforms, and none of us were very big guys, some of them were gray, some of them were off-white, and hardly any of the uniforms fit anybody. I remember our moms taking it in here and taking it in there and making them fit a little better. But then we got some new duds. We did not need new duds to play better because, my recollection, we were pretty darn good as a Legion team. I do not recall how many games we won or how many games we lost, but we played together, grew up together, laughed together, and had a lot of fun with a very competitive spirit. My brothers Gordon and Michael also played from the time they could walk and run, I guess. Both played on some great Scobey teams. As I said in the beginning. Baseball was a way of life for us, and I am so thankful for that wonderful opportunity.

—Dan Tryan (alias Danny Tryan)

Joey Girard from Scobey, who played for the Blues from 1981 to 1984, remembers Don Tryan coaching on the baseball field. "He was one of the classiest guys I remember in Little League would approach players on the opposite team. He always had something nice to say to the youngsters who would make a good play."

---

* The baseball park Dan played in was Denton Field in Miles City.
† The Babe Ruth field Dan played on was Whipkey Park in Glendive.

1968

The North Star Rises in the West for the First Time

> *We believe this is a vintage year for the Scobey Legion team.*
>
> —*Daniels County Leader*, August 1, 1968

The year 1968 marked the beginning of a new era for State B American Legion Baseball in Montana and in Scobey and Daniels County. At the state level, the perennial dominance of Havre and Scobey as state champions began, as between 1968 and 1980, Havre and Scobey would win 12 of 13 state B championships. The Billings Scarlets in 1974 were the only team to break the run. In Daniels County, 1968 was the first year players from all three Daniels County high schools would play for Scobey, as Jack Higgins and Randy Legare—who had been playing Legion ball in Flaxville since 1965—joined the team after Flaxville discontinued its Legion program. Dick Puckett from Peerless had been playing in Scobey since 1965.

A gaping hole to fill in the roster was the loss of ace pitcher Phil Audet, who had been the go-to pitcher for four years and had twice pitched Scobey to the state tournament, with one of those years negated by a disqualification. Three key rookies to join the 1968 team were Rick Danelson and Terry Puckett (both 13-year-olds), and Danny Wolfe, who was 15.

REGULAR SEASON

A significant home win for the Legion team against Plentywood was captured in a headline by the *Leader*: "Scobey Lads Break Plentywood Jynx." Dick Puckett doubled in the tying run for Scobey in the bottom of the ninth, and Scobey—despite yielding four unearned runs in the game—walked it off in the bottom of the tenth for the 5-4 win against Plentywood. In the previous year, Plentywood had beaten Scobey in both regular-season games, twice in the district tournament to win the championship, and then had eliminated Scobey at State. The last time Scobey had beaten Plentywood was in the last game of 1966, when Phil Audet pitched Scobey to the 4-2 win.

But an even more significant win for Scobey during the regular season was a 2-0 nonconference win over the Billing Scarlets at Cobb Field. According to the *Gazette*, the Scarlets had "their best team in years,"[64] and Dick Puckett pitched a three-hit shutout against them. Both teams played errorless ball in the well-played game. In 1968, Dick had emerged as

1968 Scobey Legionnaires. Back row, L–R: Doc Norman, Clarence Zieske, Dan Wang, Rocky Ware, Jim Hansen, Dick Puckett, Craig Audet, John "Jack" Higgins, Jerry La Pierre. Front row: Randy Legare, Lloyd Bantz, Brad Murray, Rick Danelson, Jim Darchuk, Danny Wolfe, John Nelson, Pete Dickson. Not pictured are Terry Puckett and George Heath. Batboys: Pat Anderson and Kelly Norman. *Leader.*

Dick Puckett drives in the game-tying run with a double in the bottom of the ninth inning to knot the score at 4-4 against Plentywood and force extra innings. Scobey won 5-4 in the tenth. *Leader.*

the new ace of Scobey's pitching staff, although his glove at short was sorely missed when he was on the mound.

STATE TOURNAMENT

THE FORMAT FOR THE POSTSEASON TOURNAMENT CHANGED again in 1968, as it seemed to do almost every year. The state was partitioned into three divisions—northern, eastern, and western—with the top two teams in each division qualifying for the state tournament, to be played in Glendive. Plentywood again won the northern division, with Scobey placing second; in the eastern division, it was the Billings Scarlets (undefeated) and Sidney; in the west, it was Havre number one and defending champion Cut Bank second. Glendive hosted the state tournament, but their Legion team did not compete as the Scarlets and Sidney were the top two teams in the east. The following season would correct this, where the team that won the east would host.

As Cut Bank attempted to defend its state title at the state tournament in Glendive, the three division champions—Havre, Plentywood, and the Billings Scarlets—were considered pre-tourney "co-favorites" according to the *Gazette*.[65] Scobey was considered a "dark horse" because they were the only team in the tournament to beat the Scarlets during the regular season.

Havre had the best record at 14-4, but the Scarlets were 16-8, with most of their losses coming from out-of-state competition. However, the tournament was wide open for anyone to win it.

Coaching the six teams were Ben Zeidler from Plentywood, Doc Norman from Scobey, Chuck Miller from Billings, Mike Gear of Sidney, Tom Sheridan from Cut Bank, and Tom Nielson from Havre. In just three short years, Coach Tom Nielson had revived Havre's program, as they entered the 1968 state tournament as the Western division champion and a state title co-favorite. That's a meteoric rise to the top.

With the benefit of hindsight, it seemed predestined that the Havre-Scobey era would begin with the two teams playing each other in the tournament's opening game. In the previous year, Scobey had eliminated Havre 7-3 from the state tournament on a six-hitter by Dick Puckett, and Doc would hand Dick the ball for the first game of the 1968 tournament against Havre. And, as all of us who play sports know, the pre-tournament hype goes out the window once the teams take the field. Scobey jumped on Havre for eight runs in the first inning, and Havre was never really in the game, as Scobey went on to win in a 12-2 rout. Dick and Terry Puckett combined to hurl a two-hitter at Havre. Doc put thirteen-year-old Terry Puckett on the mound in the later innings to get him some state tournament experience and save Dick some innings. Jack Higgins had an incredible day at the plate in his state tournament debut for Scobey, going 5-for-5, hitting for the cycle with a three-run home run, a triple, two doubles, and a single, and driving in four runs. The *Leader* wrote that Jack "likely has the best batting average of any Class B ball player in Montana this year."[66]

In other opening-round games, Sidney beat Plentywood 6-3, and the Billings Scarlets won over Cut Bank 2-1 in 10 innings when Cut Bank's pitcher Mike Harris, who struck out 16 Scarlets, balked in the winning run. In the winner's bracket game with Scobey and the Scarlets, the Scarlets came away with a 6-4 win. Four errors by Scobey and several successful bunts by the Scarlets doomed Scobey. Continuing in the winner's bracket, Sidney walked it off against the Scarlets on a triple by Tim Sampson—who earlier had hit a three-run inside-the-park home run—in the bottom of the ninth.

But the story of this tournament was the resilience of Havre. After their humbling 12-2 loss to Scobey in the first game, Havre clawed its way through the loser's bracket to win five consecutive games and the championship. They came back from a 3-1 deficit against Plentywood to win 6-4, then returned the favor against Scobey by shutting them out 12-0, although this game was only 1-0 Havre after five innings. Havre scored 10 runs in the seventh, eighth, and ninth innings to blow it open after Dick Puckett ran out of innings for Scobey. Havre pitcher Barry Damschen had a no-hitter through seven and two-thirds innings but lost his no-hit bid after a dropped third strike would have been the final out of the eighth inning. The next hitter, Dick Puckett, then singled to break up the no-hitter. Damschen finished with a two-hit shutout, and Scobey's season was over.

After the Scobey win, Havre still needed three more wins to win the championship. Trailing the Scarlets 6-5 in the top of the ninth, they scored two runs to win it 7-6. Catcher Bruce Nelson drove in the winning run with a single. Barry Damschen earned the win in relief. That left Havre needing to beat undefeated Sidney twice to win the tournament.

The first Havre-Sidney game was an excellent one—a fantastic win for Havre but a heartbreaking loss for Sidney. With Havre batting in the top of the 14th inning and the score tied 4-4, Havre won the game when Hank Tweeten got to first on an error, was sacrificed to second, then scored the winning run on a two-out throwing error by the second baseman. Sidney fought back in the bottom half of the 14th, but with one out and runners on second and third, relief pitcher Doug Shepphard came in for Havre and choked off the rally. Shepphard struck out the first man he faced, then got the final out on a ground ball to shortstop to save the game for Havre and force the second playoff game.

After losing to Scobey in their opening game, Havre won its fifth consecutive game 9-2 over Sidney to complete their incredible backdoor run and first state championship. Bruce Nelson delivered a bases-loaded triple in the first inning, which would be the fatal blow for Sidney. Havre used four pitchers in the game, with Dennis Kuntz earning the win. After scoring four runs in the first, Havre added runs in the fifth and sixth innings.

STATE A PLAYOFFS

THINGS WERE MESSED UP BACK THEN FOR STATE B CHAMPIONS and how they had to immediately play off against Class A teams to get into the State A Tournament. After Havre played its sixth game in four days and 59th inning on Monday to win the State B championship, they had to travel from Glendive to Helena to play the Senators on Tuesday night. Even Havre's batboys were out of pitching innings, not to mention how tired the entire team had to be. After winning its first state championship the following year, Scobey would experience the same thing.

Scobey's first state championship? Most people in the United States think of the year 1969 as the first year man set foot on the moon, but people in Daniels County and Scobey remember it for a different reason.

EXTRA INNINGS

CENTER FIELDER JACK HIGGINS RECALLS A FUNNY STORY ABOUT Doc, his first year playing for Scobey in 1968. He said, "I think everyone has a favorite Doc story—mine came from a 1968 game played at Plainsmen Field in Scobey. I was on first base and decided I was going to steal second base. As I was sliding into second base, I felt a pain in my groin area. I stood up and motioned to Doc, who was coaching at third base, that something was wrong. Doc came over to second base and asked me what was wrong. I told Doc I had felt a pain in my groin when sliding into second. He said, 'Jack, honey, drop your pants and I'll check it out.' I told Doc I was not going to drop my pants in the middle of the infield in front of everyone at the game. Doc motioned for all the opposing team members who had congregated around second base to come closer and form a circle so folks in the crowd couldn't see what was going on. Now, Doc said, 'Drop your fucking pants so I can check you out!' And I dropped my pants!!

"Turns out I had an inguinal hernia, which happened when I was sliding into second base. This was typical Doc Norman, and an incident that I will always remember from my time playing Legion Baseball in Scobey. Doc was one of a kind and so beloved by his players."

Terry Puckett remembers a funny story that happened on the practice field in 1968. Terry said, "Doc challenged George Heath to a race between home and first because Doc was so pissed at George because he was slow. Doc was ripping down the first baseline—he could run fast for a big guy—and was handily winning the race when he tripped and went down hard. It's the maddest I've ever seen Doc the whole time I played for him."

Dana Audet, who was a batboy in 1968, also remembers the incident. (Everyone who was there remembers it!) Dana's version goes like this: "George Heath was an incredibly slow runner and very well may have been the origination of Doc screaming 'Unhook the piano!' every time he ran the bases. He was so slow that one night at practice Doc challenged him to a race from home to first. George was not in a position to say no lest the humiliation from his teammates, but I think he wanted to. They lined up at home, and someone said go. Everyone was hootin' and hollering, and they were neck and neck about 45 feet in when Doc started to get a lead. He could move quite well for a big man. With a slight lead at about the 80-foot mark, Doc stumbled and fell straight down on his frontside and slid a few feet. It was not a pretty sight as George tumbled the last few feet with the win. Doc was a bit embarrassed, it seemed, and the guys withheld any comments as best they could. Without the stumble and scraped-up belly he may just have won it. At least that's the way I remember it. I'm sure there are varying memories of the details because it was about 58 years ago."

Rocky Ware, who was 17 in 1968, added, "That had to be one of the funniest things I've ever seen. Doc was quite a ways ahead of George when he went to stumblin', and he would have easily won the race. George was pretty slow." Then, Rocky provided some context for the story. "That race came about because George came into home plate one time, standing up, and got tagged out. Doc was so damn mad at him he said, 'George, why didn't you slide?' and George said, 'Doc I was running too fast!'"

Terry remembers his rookie season with the Legion team. "I started to play Legion as a 13-year-old in 1968. I didn't play very much. It was kinda scary being around all the big studs. I got to pitch against Havre in the state tournament in Glendive, though. Dick was pitching and we had a big lead, so I don't think Doc felt he had anything to lose by putting me in. About all I remember is Craig [Audet] was throwing the ball back to me so hard as a catcher, my hand couldn't take it!

"I didn't really know why I was on the team at 13, but now I realize it was because Doc wanted to make us mentally tougher at a young age. He instilled in us a confidence to win, and we expected to win. He built us up mentally that we were good and that we were better than the opponent. Later in Legion, we knew the only way we were going to lose was if we made the mistake. Doc gave us that confidence.

"I did get to play a little bit of Babe Ruth in 1968 when I was 13, when Doc would allow it. I pitched the district championship game against Froid at Froid. I think I struck out 20 or 21 hitters in seven innings. I still have the baseball for that game. After pitching in Legion that season, it was like I was playing against kids in Babe Ruth!"

SECTION NOTES

1. Al Funderburke, "Little League Craze in Scobey Is Spark for Town Action (Curling Too)," *Billings Gazette*, September 14, 1959.
2. Funderburke, "Little League Craze."
3. *Diamond in the Rough Jubilee*, Peerless, Montana, 1987.
4. "With People Making News," *Daniels County Leader*, July 31, 1958.
5. Associated Press, "NeMont League Opens Regular Season May 18," *Great Falls Tribune*, May 5, 1958.
6. Associated Press, "Possible Record in 33-27 Game," *Great Falls Tribune*, May 24, 1958.
7. "Plainsmen not in National Competition," *Daniels County Leader*, August 21, 1958.
8. Clausie Smith, "Should Boost Legion Age Limit," *Ottawa Herald*, August 23, 1958.
9. Smith, "Boost Age Limit."
10. "Help Wanted, Men," *Missoulian*, July 20, 1958.
11. "Legionnaires Drop Two To Flaxville, Circle," *Daniels County Leader*, May 14, 1959.
12. "Junior Legion Meets Big-Time Competition," *Daniels County Leader*, June 11, 1959.
13. Printer Bowler, "Scobey Legion Seeing Plenty of Action," *Daniels County Leader*, June 18, 1959.
14. "Legion Juniors Beat Scobey, 5-4 and 13-2," *The Missoulian*, July 3, 1959.
15. "Legion Retains Lead; Splits Weekend Games," *Daniels County Leader*, June 11, 1959.
16. "Division Champs to Host Legion B," *Laurel Outlook*, August 5, 1959.
17. "Scobey Junior Legion Seeing Plenty of Action," *Daniels County Leader*, June 18, 1959.
18. "Sidney Defeats Plainsmen for Montana Title," *Daniels County Leader*, August 6, 1959.
19. "Williston Takes Tournament; Scobey 2nd; Blue Moon is 3rd," *Plentywood Herald*, September 3, 1959.
20. "Greenhorns Win Championship at Plentywood," *Daniels County Leader*, September 3, 1959.
21. "Junior Legion Series for N.E. Title Here July 17," *Daniels County Leader*, July 16, 1959.
22. "At The Scobey Ball Park," *Daniels County Leader*, June 18, 1959.
23. *Missoulian*, "Sport Jabs," Ray T. Rocene, June 7, 1959.
24. "Plainsmen Will Play Exhibition with Regina Here; Benefit for Trip to National Finals," *Daniels County Leader*, August 11, 1960.
25. Cassidy, "Baseball."
26. "Plainsmen Win Two Games; Rebs Leave Hungry," *Daniels County Leader*, July 20, 1961.
27. "Rebs Leave Hungry," *Leader*.
28. "Plainsmen Win Ball Tourney," *Daniels County Leader*, July 6, 1961.
29. "Athletic Club Plans Expanded Babe Ruth, L-L," *Daniels County Leader*, March 9, 1961.
30. "Greenhorns Are Softball Champs," *Daniels County Leader*, August 31, 1961.
31. "Season Ends," *Daniels County Leader*, August 31, 1961.
32. "Laurel Legion Team Takes Second Place," *Laurel Outlook*, July 25, 1962.
33. Lois Fladager, "Peerless News," *Daniels County Leader*, August 9, 1962.
34. "Cut Bank Wins B Junior Title," *Billings Gazette*, July 22, 1963.
35. "Peerless Softball Tournament," *Daniels County Leader*, August 1, 1963.
36. "Meissner Memorial Field Dedication Slated Tonight," *Glendive Ranger-Review*, July 14, 1963.
37. "Juniors Have Heavy Going at Tourney," *Daniels County Leader*, July 23, 1964.
38. "Plainsmen This Year, New Arrangement," *Daniels County Leader*, July 2, 1964.
39. Ibid.
40. "Plainsmen Open Here Sunday Night," *Daniels County Leader*, June 11, 1964.
41. "Greenhorns Win First at Glendive," *Daniels County Leader*, July 16, 1964.
42. "Greenhorns Will Play in Tourney in Williston," *Daniels County Leader*, August 27, 1964.
43. "Greenhorns Runners-up at Tourney," *Daniels County Leader*, September 10, 1964.
44. "Wolves Win Class B Tourney," *Daniels County Leader*, July 22, 1965.
45. Ibid.
46. "Fans See Some Good Baseball," *Daniels County Leader*, July 8, 1965.
47. "Scobey Ball Park Scene of Lively Action," *Daniels County Leader*, May 13, 1965.
48. "Scobey Juniors Enjoy Tour; Nip Billings, Miles City," *Daniels County Leader*, July 21, 1966.
49. Ibid.
50. "Scobey Earns Tourney Berth," *Billings Gazette*, July 27, 1966.
51. Ibid.
52. "Plentywood Nine Bewildered," *Billings Gazette*, July 28, 1966.
53. "Scobey Commissioner Blames Technicalities," *Billings Gazette*, July 30, 1966.
54. Ibid.
55. "Glendive Coach Issues Statement," *Billings Gazette*, July 29, 1966.
56. "Blames Technicalities," *Gazette*.
57. "Cinderella Juniors in State Play," *Daniels County Leader*, July 27, 1967.
58. "Scobey Upsets Glendive," *Billings Gazette*, July 22, 1967.
59. "Scobey Stuns Sidney," *Billings Gazette*, July 23, 1967.
60. "Scobey Handed 1st Loss," *Billings Gazette*, July 24, 1967.
61. "Cut Bank, Sidney, Scobey Win Legion B," *Great Falls Tribune*, July 29, 1967.
62. "Scobey Gets 4th in 'B' State Play," *Daniels County Leader*, August 3, 1967.
63. Ibid.
64. "B Legion Tourney Set," *Billings Gazette*, August 2, 1968.
65. Ibid.
66. "How It Went at Tourney," *Daniels County Leader*, August 8, 1968.

The Doc Norm Championship

1969 – 1982

1900 – 1924
The Homesteaders
and Early Town Teams

1930 – 1945
The Sons of
the Pioneers

1957 – 1968
The Baseball
Renaissance

The Scobey Giants
1925 – 1929

Baseball is Back in Daniels County
1946 – 1956

n Era

1983 – 1991
The Don Lekvold Era

1998 – 2003
The Last Years

2016 – 2019
The Revival

The Ken Meyer/Mike Lee Era
1992 – 1997

The Long Winter
2004 – 2015

The Froid Bulls
2020 – 2024

1969

Scobey Wins Its First State Championship

> *Scobey is a calm, disciplined team, looking like a championship club.*
>
> —Bob Davis, "Scobey – A Team to Watch," Billings Gazette, July 30, 1969

PRESEASON

Preparations for the first state tournament hosted by Scobey in August 1969 began in the spring when new concrete dugouts were installed, a new turf infield was established, and the lighting was renovated at Scobey Ball Park. But what was already healthy and didn't need much renovation was Scobey's veteran-laden roster. Several players, including Dick Puckett, Craig Audet, Rocky Ware, Jack Higgins, and Randy Legare, were now 18 and in their fifth year of Legion ball. Earlier in the spring, Dick Puckett started at second base for the North Central Conference champion South Dakota State Jackrabbits and Craig Audet started in the outfield for the Eastern Montana Yellowjackets. Danny Wang and Jerry LaPierre were in their fourth seasons, and talented 14-year-olds Rick Danelson and Terry Puckett were in their second year. Danny Wolfe provided strength at the catcher position when Dick and Craig pitched, and left-handed pitcher Jim Hansen provided depth on the pitching staff. As if that were not enough, joining Randy Legare and Jack Higgins from Flaxville on the roster in 1969 were Don Higgins and Jim and Dennis "Doc" Miller. Larry Grayson and Pete Dixon rounded out the roster.

But a significant addition to the 1969 roster was not a player but a coach—Gene Thompson, who was the superintendent and head basketball coach at Peerless High School. Doc had assisted Gene at Missoula in 1958 and took over the head coaching job from him in Missoula in 1961. Gene's contribution to the team was working with the pitchers. Jack Higgins remembers, "Gene was a great pitching coach and helped the pitchers. He was a good part of them knowing how to pitch and not just throw." Terry Puckett also remembers working with Gene Thompson. He said, "Doc was a really good pitching coach, and so was Gene Thompson. Doc really liked left-handed pitchers. When I played, there were a lot of left-handed pitchers on the staff." While there had been a lot of talent on Scobey's roster in previous seasons, what set this team apart was depth on the pitching staff, as Dick and Terry Puckett, Jerry LaPierre, Jim Hansen, Craig Audet, and Danny Wang (when needed) could all get on the mound and help the team win. This depth would prove to be critical at the state tournament. State championships cannot be won without depth at pitching, and Scobey had it in 1969.

Kelly Norman, Dan Danelson, Pat Anderson, and Don Puckett were batboys.

REGULAR SEASON

The format for the regular and postseason in 1969 was the same as in 1968. There were three Divisions—northeast, southeast, and west—with the top two teams in each division qualifying for the state tournament. Scobey won the northeast—their first championship since 1959, when Doc started coaching in Scobey—with a 16-2 record, with Wolf Point second. In the southeast, Glendive won it with Baker second. In the west, it was the Great Falls Sparkies first, with Havre—the defending State champions—in second. One change in 1969 was that the names of the Montana State American Legion divisions were changed from Class A and B to Class AA and Class A. The same teams competed in each division; just the names were changed. The following season, the divisions would revert to the familiar Class A and B divisions until 1987, when they changed again.

Two notable regular-season games were against the "high-flying" Missoula AA team, which traveled to Scobey to play the tough Scobey team. Missoula was coached by Terry Hober, who had played under Doc as a catcher during his Legion years in Missoula. Scobey won both games, with the first one ending in an unbelievable fashion. With Scobey leading 7-4 in the top of the ninth, Missoula loaded the bases with two outs. Missoula pitcher Mark Stanley hit a drive down the right-field line that the first-base umpire ruled fair, but according to the *Missoulian*, just as the tying run was about to cross the plate, the home plate umpire ruled it foul! Stanley was retired on the next pitch, and the game was over. Scobey won the next game 8-5 to sweep an excellent AA Missoula team in Scobey.[1]

After winning the northeastern championship, two weeks remained until the state tournament, so Doc, as was his model, took the team on a barnstorming tour of Montana to play some strong AA opponents—including the Billings Royals—to toughen the team up and prepare them for the tournament.

The Royals game was set up by a phone call by Doc to his old schoolmate and friend Ed Bayne, the legendary coach of the Billings Royals. While Scobey had played the Scarlets several times previously, this was the first game Scobey had played against the Royals, although Bob Schaefer and the 1930 team had played Billings for the eastern division championship, losing 8-4. It must have felt good for Doc to take a team to Cobb Field that he thought could stay on the field with the Royals, a team that, until the previous season, had won 15 consecutive State AA titles.

When I interviewed Terry Puckett, I couldn't wait to ask him about this Royals game because it was long-remembered in Peerless baseball lore (at least Puckett baseball lore), Terry's pitching performance as a 14-year-old that day against the Royals in 1969. In his interview, Terry told me that before the game, everyone wondered who Doc would announce as the starting pitcher: "No one knew who Doc would start. Just an hour or so before the game, Doc told me I was going to start, and he handed me the ball. I was only 14 years old. I about shit my pants! At that age, I couldn't get my fastball past the Royals hitters, so I relied on my roundhouse curveball." The *Gazette* referred to him as "14-year-old little Terry Puckett,"[2] and he pitched into the eighth inning, yielding only two earned runs. Terry came out of the game and Scobey eventually lost 4–1, but Craig Audet's "towering" home run over the 335-foot left field fence in the ninth broke up Jerry Schuster's bid for a Royal shutout. The *Billings Gazette* described Craig's home run as a "towering blast that carried over the 335-foot marker just inside the left field foul pole."[3] It was the first ball hit out of the park in Legion action at Cobb Field that year.[4]

On that same barnstorming tour, Scobey next lost to Missoula 9-2, then got a gem of a game pitched by left-hander Jim Hansen against Kalispell, losing 2-1. Hansen yielded only six hits and went the distance as Scobey played errorless ball. Craig Audet hit another booming home run for their lone run in that game. In the finale against western division leader Libby, which Scobey won, the *Billings Gazette* wrote that pitcher Dick Puckett "impressed statewide observers with a 4-2 victory over Class AA power Libby."[5] Libby went on to win the western AA division.

STATE TOURNAMENT

THE WEEK OF THE STATE TOURNAMENT, ANTICIPATION AND excitement were running high in Scobey and Daniels County. "It could be the best ever," tournament co-director Jack Reiner told the *Daniels County Leader*. "We have one of the finest ballparks in Montana, and with the improvements which continue to be made, it makes a proper site for a state tournament." Of course, it took a lot of volunteers to make it happen: N. C. Wolfe headed the housing committee for teams, coaches, and officials; Else Daniels headed the meals committee; Frank Reemsnyder, American Legion Post 56 commander, headed the gate committee with Charlie Cassidy; Joe Anderson, manager of the championship Plainsmen in the late 1950s and early 1960s, led the grounds committee; Vern Veis, assisted by Cliff Hagfeldt, had announcing and official scorekeeping; Marge Norman, with Ann Norman and Clara Ofstedal helping, headed up the concessions; Leendert Vink was in charge of parking; and Charlie Cassidy headed up the programs committee. Seven umpires in platoon-spacing handled the games: Andy Stolen, umpire in chief, of Glentana, Dennis Casey of Wolf Point, Airman Arthur Buck of St. Louis (Opheim AFS), Charlie Mueller of Wolf Point, Roald Selvig of Outlook, Billy Richardson, and John Murphy of Scobey. "With all these people," Jack Reiner said, "I don't see how we can help but have a successful tournament that will be enjoyed by everyone." He added, "We're going to see some very good ball games. You can be sure of that. After all, this is

Jim Hansen dives back to first base as Royals pitcher Jerry Schuster throws to first in Scobey's 4-1 loss to the Royals at Cobb Field. *Billings Gazette.*

'baseball country.'"[6] Jack could not have had any idea how much of a prophet he would prove to be. In the 1969 State Class A Tournament program, an article titled "Baseball Country" was included. The pride in the Scobey baseball tradition was on full display as the teams prepared to play the games on the first day.

Despite having never won a state tournament, Scobey—due to its 16-2 record in the northeastern division and the eyebrows they had raised on their Class AA barnstorming tour—was favored to win the 1969 tournament. "Scobey: Legion Team to Beat,"[7] ran the headline in the *Billings Gazette* the day before the tournament began. But Doc was not so sure. "We really don't know what to expect," Doc said. "We haven't played any teams in the tournament except Wolf Point." He went on to say that he rated his ace Dick Puckett (7-0) as one of the top players in the state and that his leading hitters were Jack Higgins and Randy Legare, each hitting around .500 for the season. The article concluded by saying that "championship baseball is nothing new to Scobey" and cited the championship Plainsmen teams of the late 1950s and early 1960s.[8] Again, the tradition.

Scobey's first game of the tournament was against Baker. A seismic shift in Doc's pitching strategy in tournaments manifested in 1969. Instead of starting his ace in the first game, as he had always done with Phil Audet, he would start another pitcher and save his ace's innings for later in the tournament. Doc started Jerry LaPierre against Baker, and everything was going well until the bottom of the fifth inning. Scobey scored eight runs in the top of the fifth—including a grand slam home run by Randy Legare—to take a 12-1 lead, but Baker rallied for seven runs in the bottom half to close the score to 12-8. Doc brought in Terry in the inning but then had to relieve with Dick, who would remain in the game until the ninth when Danny Wang closed it out. Scobey eventually won the slugfest 17-10, but they were only ahead 12-10 in the top of the ninth when they plated five runs. Jack Higgins went 4-for-6, Craig Audet went 3-for-6, and Legare drove in six runs with a grand slam and a double. Dick Puckett got the win in relief for his eighth win against no losses. Brian Bechtold drove in three runs for the heavy-hitting Baker team, who plated 10 runs against Scobey pitching. Baker had three more earned runs than Scobey in the game.

In other first-round games, Havre, aided by Glendive errors, beat Glendive 17-3, and Great Falls beat Wolf Point 16-3, with a pinch-hit, inside-the-park grand slam by Larry Ivers providing the major blow for Great Falls. In the Havre game, Barry Damschen pitched the first five innings to get the win, and Scott Kato pitched the final four. They combined for 14 strikeouts and didn't walk a batter between them. This was Damschen's third win against no losses in the last two state tournaments. Recall that he had a no-hitter going against Scobey with two outs in the eighth inning the previous year until Dick Puckett broke it up with a single. He was also 4-for-7 and drove in five runs. Micky Williams was 3-for-5 with a double, and Hank Tweeten was 3-for-6.

Scobey's second-round game was against the western division champion, the Great Falls Sparkies, who were, according to one paper, a co-favorite in the tournament as they had won the western division and had a 20-3 record. Jim Hansen pitched a five-hit complete game, and Dick Puckett went yard in a three-run fifth to lead Scobey to an 8-3 victory. Randy Legare doubled in two runs, and Rocky Ware had an extremely rare two-run sacrifice fly to drive in two more. Jim Hansen "showed grit" when struck by a hard line drive toward his head in the seventh. He brought up his bare hand to cushion the blow to his jaw and, after a brief pause, resumed pitching with his bruised hand and completed the final two innings of the game. It's not known if Doc's needle was employed in this situation or not.

Havre had a second-round bye, so this set up the critical semifinal between Scobey and Havre on Friday afternoon. The winner of this game would need only one win to claim the championship on Saturday, whereas the loser would need to win three more games. Doc sent Dick Puckett to the mound, and Havre started left-hander Mike Hanson. A big seven-run second inning for Havre stunned Scobey, as Havre sent 11 men to the plate with hits and errors to chase Dick Puckett, who was relieved by Terry. Terry pitched seven innings of shutout ball after relieving Dick in the second inning, but his fine pitching was wasted as the damage in the second inning was too much for Scobey's bats to overcome. Mike Hanson scattered five hits for a complete game win, "handcuffing" Scobey with what the *Leader* referred to as a "screwball," and Havre won 7-2 over favored Scobey. The year before in Glendive, Scobey had shocked Havre 12-2 in the first game, with Dick and Terry throwing a combined two-hitter against them. A year later, Havre returned the favor, forcing Scobey to go through the "dirt route" (as the *Leader* put it) to win their first state tournament.[9]

Wolf Point was the third team still standing on Saturday, as they had won games over Glendive and Baker, who had eliminated Great Falls 8-4 in a 14-inning marathon. Scobey sent Craig Audet to the mound against Wolf Point, and Scobey—led again by Randy Legare, who smashed his second

Rocky Ware scores the go-ahead run against Havre in the top of the 10th inning of the first championship game. *Leader.*

home run of the tournament*—won big 17-2 over "fiery" Dick Wilson's Wolf Point team. Craig Audet got the win going five innings, and Danny Wang pitched four innings of relief. This set up the first championship game between Havre and Scobey on Saturday night, with Scobey needing to win to stay alive in the tournament and Havre needing a win to claim its second consecutive state championship.

The first championship game was scheduled for 7:30 p.m. on Saturday. The proud baseball tradition of Scobey and Daniels County and the passion for the sport was evident for the seventeen hundred fans in attendance that night: the new field, built in 1957, had been renovated with new lights, new concrete dugouts, and a well-manicured grass infield; the volunteers, too many to mention, had provided the very best of everything for the coaches, players, and umpires; Frank Reemsnyder, commander of American Legion Post 56 and head of the gate committee, ensured the record crowd got in on time to watch the first pitch.

Beginning with Scobey's first baseball team in 1914, it was obvious there was a passion for baseball in Scobey: from the businessmen who brought Swede Risberg and Happy Felsch of the Chicago White Sox to play in Scobey in 1925, to Scobey's first American Legion team in 1930, who played Billings to go to the state championship, to the Plainsmen state championship teams, to the fans, parents, and kids who played the game—the passion was there. Scobey had the infrastructure, the community support, and the fan base to generate revenue for games and tournaments hosted there. That passion and commitment are what led to the development of the Scobey Ball Park in 1957, the hosting of several NBC state tournaments, the Plainsmen state championships in 1958 and 1960, and the Plainsmen's seventh-place finish at Nationals in Wichita in 1960. It led to the insistence by the parents of the players that Doc Norman coach the talented 1967 team, the first Scobey American Legion team to qualify for the state tournament, and now it had led to Scobey hosting its first American Legion state tournament at Scobey Ball Park.

The scene was set for baseball brilliance and the defining moment in Scobey baseball history. But could Doc's team—a team that had been developing since 1965 when five of its star players started playing Legion baseball in the county—and defending champion Havre—with many returning starters from its previous-year championship—match the moment? Yes, they could—and they did. And the following day, too. Two one-run games with dramatic finishes. Looking back on it, it was meant to be.

Let's let Larry Bowler's wonderfully descriptive writing in the *Daniels County Leader* set the scene for us on Saturday evening, August 9, 1969:

```
Scobey Ball Park was bursting with fans that
evening. Clear, warm weather continued for the
tournament. That night the national colors in
the center field hung straight down; and the
playing field, thanks to Joe Anderson and his
ground crew, was in excellent shape and draw-
ing many laudatory comments from knowledgeable
fans for its excellent condition. MDU's presi-
```

Randy Legare approaches home after hitting his second home run of the tournament, a three-run blast against Wolf Point in Scobey's 17-2 win. Batboy Kelly Norman congratulates him as Rick Danelson (7) and on-deck hitter Craig Audet (9) wait to do the same. *Leader.*

---

* Randy Legare's second home run of the tournament, hit deep to left, hit a crossbar in fair territory on the foul line pole and bounced back onto the outfield. Had the ball hit the pole itself, it would have been ruled foul but being in fair territory and well above the high outfield wall, it was ruled a ground rule home run.

dent, Dave Heskett, had flown in from Bismarck to inspect that company's renovation of the field lighting and pay his compliments to the community. John Russell, the state baseball chairman, quoted the official rules of sportsmanship of the American Legion Baseball code. Jack McIntyre, a doughty catcher on Scobey's first baseball team in the year one (1914), was presented earlier and given a special seat. Scobey Color Guard ran the colors and the ball game was on.[10]

Doc started Jerry LaPierre—who had pitched the first four innings against Baker on Thursday and had eight innings of eligibility left—in the championship game. Havre countered with Kurt Grimm. Scobey was the visiting team. Havre jumped on LaPierre and Scobey for four runs in the bottom of the first, but Scobey scored a single run in the second and two in the third to crawl back to 4-3. Havre then scored two more in the fourth to take a 6-3 lead, but Scobey came back to tie it 6-6 with a three-run fifth, chasing Kurt Grimm, and Havre brought in Scott Kato. Havre got to LaPierre for another run in the bottom of the fifth to take a 7-6 lead, and that is where the score stood until the top of the ninth, as LaPierre and Kato pitched scoreless ball for the next three innings. Then came the dramatic ninth inning.

Scobey had hopes in the top of the ninth, as their top of the lineup was up against Kato, but Jack Higgins and Rick Danelson were both retired in order, bringing up shortstop Dick Puckett—who batted third in the lineup—with two outs and nobody on. Scobey, the tourney favorite hosting its first state tournament, was now down to its final out. I will hand the pen over to the *Daniels County Leader* to describe what happened next:

Probably the largest crowd ever out to Scobey Ball Park, predominantly Scobey team fans, waited patiently for the third out. But not really patiently nor without hope as Dick Puckett came up. The count went to two strikes and two balls. The next pitch from Scott Kato was met by Scobey's hardworking, most experienced player at the right time and right place. At the crack of the bat, the swelling cheers of the crowd mounted to a roaring crescendo as the ball soared over the left field wall to tie up the ball game. Dick Puckett of Peerless, Scobey's shortstop and pitcher, had his second and most crucial home run of the tournament.[11]

There was joy in Scobey, for mighty Dick had gone yard.

But the joy was that the team was still alive, and Jerry LaPierre, who was pitching well, had exhausted his 12-inning limit after the eighth inning, so Doc needed to bring a new pitcher for the bottom of the ninth to hold Havre and force extra innings. Who would that be? Doc brought in left-hander Jim Hansen—who had three innings of eligibility left after pitching a complete-game win against Great Falls on Thursday—and he held Havre in the bottom of the ninth. In the top of the tenth, Hansen contributed with his bat, as he drove in Rocky Ware from third base on a groundout to give Scobey a one-run lead. Hansen again held Havre scoreless in the bottom of the tenth, and Scobey jubilantly ran off the field with an 8-7 win, forcing an extra game on Sunday for the championship. Jim Hansen got the win in relief and drove in the winning run with his RBI groundout. And Scobey, down to its final strike in the top of the ninth, had somehow managed to stave off elimination and lived to fight another day.

But the drama was not over, as it would be another one-run game on Sunday that would decide the 1969 State American Legion Class A state championship. Let's everyone get a good night's sleep to prepare for that!

When the sun rose brightly Sunday morning in Peerless, Aunt Lauretta (Fouhy) Puckett, as she always did, had the Reese Puckett family sitting close to the front pew for Mass at Saint Ann's Catholic Church in Peerless. In 1969, Dick, Terry, and Don were still at home, so they joined Uncle Reese and Aunt Lauretta in the same pew. The three Puckett boys were dressed in their baseball uniforms—Dick and

Danny Wang scores a run in Scobey's 17-2 win over Wolf Point. *Leader.*

Terry with their Scobey Legion uniforms and Don with his batboy uniform. Baseball did not take a backseat to church for Aunt Lauretta, but as you will see, she did strike a compromise. The Tiny Puckett family, thanks to my Italian Roman Catholic mother, Faustine (Sparagno) Puckett, were all sitting on the same side of the church but several rows toward the back. Our family did not run on the same clock as Uncle Reese's, so we would sit toward the back, as sometimes we didn't make it to Mass on time for Father Ray Nyquist to yell "Play ball!" so to speak. My mother, God forgive her, adhered to Mediterranean—specifically Italian—time. It was better to sit toward the back so you could sneak quietly in and not have the walk of shame to the front of the church.

It was always difficult for an eight-year-old boy, who I was then, to pay attention to the priest on Sunday, but it was especially tough on this late Sunday morning. This was state championship day. And Dad was taking all of us—Bill, Dianne, Jon, and me—to the game in Scobey to see it. And there, sitting in front of me, were my three older cousins, standing and sitting to the methodical rhythm of the Catholic Mass, each with their baseball uniforms on, and I could not take my eyes off them. My eyes focused on Dick, who, up until the previous year, was the only Puckett boy in the front to have his uniform on in church. Then Terry started to play, so he was up there too. Now Don had his batboy uniform on. I have so many memories of Dick sitting in the front row with his baseball uniform on, then having to leave church early to drive to a road game, or sometimes, like today, leaving for Scobey to be there in time for the pregame talk with Doc and the team, batting practice, and warm-up for the 1:30 p.m. game.

I wondered when the time would come this morning for Dick, with Terry following closely behind (Don did not need to leave early), to walk reverently down the church aisle between the two columns of pews and leave for Scobey. Dick would always exit when the congregation was standing so that it was less noticeable, but how do you leave church from the front with a baseball uniform on and not have it be noticeable? I always noticed. After Dick exited the pew and genuflected, he would slowly approach the back of the church, hands clasped and hanging gently in front of him. I would always try to catch his eye. He would look for me, too. As he passed our pew, he would gently smile at me—the most beautiful smile—and wink. And I would smile back. Dick's smile and wink this morning were special. I knew where he was going, and I would be there to watch him play. In a structure built for people to worship God, I looked up to Dick in awe as a god, idolized him, and hoped that someday I could be half the athlete he was, especially a baseball player. I also dreamed that maybe someday I would wear the Scobey American Legion uniform to church and get to leave early, too, although I would be in the back so no one would notice.* As Dick and Terry passed our pew, I looked behind me and watched them slowly exit the church. I would somehow have to force myself to turn my head toward the altar, listen to Father Nyquist's sermon, and not think about the game that would shortly follow. The smile and wink from Dick at church that Sunday—I saw many of them—is an image I will forever have etched in my mind, and it is how I will always remember Dick. I see this image in my mind, and it inspires a feeling of God, love, family, and baseball—a combination too powerful ever to forget. And although the movie *The Rookie*[12] would not be made for another 33 years, Ann Lee's favorite line from that movie could have been whispered in my ear by Dick as he passed by me: "You know what we get to do today, Joey? We get to play baseball!"

Fifty-six years later, I wonder how Dick's confession to Father Nyquist might have gone earlier that morning before church. After Father Nyquist left Peerless in 1973, he came to watch the Peerless Panthers play at the state basketball tournament in Helena in 1979, so I think he liked sports. Maybe it went something like this:

"Bless me, Father, for I have sinned." Dick opened with his confession. "It has been one week since my last confession."

"And what sins do you have to confess this week, my son?" Father Nyquist asked.

"Well, Father, I've had thoughts of impurity—"

"Yeah, yeah, yeah, Dick, I know, I know. Tell me something I don't know."

"Father?"

"Tell me about the Havre game on Friday."

"Oh . . . well, Father . . . we lost 7-2. I started but didn't get out of the second inning when Havre scored all their seven runs. Terry came in and finished the second, then pitched seven innings of scoreless relief. But we beat them 8-7 last night. I hit a home run—"

"I asked you about the game on Friday. What are you going to do differently today? No doubt, Doc is going to hand you the ball. How are you going to last more than an inning-plus today and not put the pressure on your little 14-year-old brother to bail you out in the state championship game?"

---

* I never got to do that; something called Saturday Night Mass was invented.

"Father, I'm not going to try to throw my fastball by them every pitch, mix it up a little, move the ball around, change speeds. I can't get my fastball by them every pitch. I learned that Friday."

"Sounds good. Your home run last night was your penance for getting shelled on Friday, so you get a pass on that one. I know you need to leave the church early today, so I won't load you up with Hail Marys; plus, I got Terry coming in behind you and don't want to hold things up. For your penance, make a good Act of Contrition. Try to take communion before you leave, but God will forgive you in advance if you can't. If Lauretta lets you go early, God will turn the other way. What's good for Lauretta is good for God. Good luck today. A week from now, I expect to hear good news. Now go forth and sin no more."

"Thank you, Father. I am sorry for these and all the sins of my past life."

(Could have happened.)

After Dick arrived in Scobey that day, Doc did indeed hand him the ball to pitch. It's funny how things work out sometimes. Because Havre had chased Dick in the second inning on Friday, he had the most unused innings of any pitcher on the staff, including Terry. When Dick pitched, Scobey's defense was altered: Craig Audet would move from his regular position at catcher to short, and young Danny Wolfe would catch. This combination had worked every game that season except for one—the Havre game on Friday. Dick had an 8-1 record, and who you would want on the mound competing in the state championship game but Dick? So, all of these defensive decisions by Doc were completely expected.

But what was completely *unexpected* was Doc's decision after winning the coin toss. In an extraordinary move, Doc ceded the home team after winning the coin toss in favor of having the choice of dugouts. Doc said, "The boys said they wanted their west [third base] dugout where they had never lost, so we were willing to spot them last bats in turn for that."[13] The *Leader* referred to this decision as "a form of baseball insanity."[14] Many of us would agree with the *Leader* that this was "insanity," but Doc's decision would prove to be brilliant, his mad genius at work. Later, when I played for Doc, I often scratched my head at some of his decisions, but there was always a method to his madness.

Back to the expected. Havre sent out Barry Damschen, their ace, to the mound in this game. At the previous year's state tournament in Glendive, Damschen carried a no-hitter against Scobey with two outs in the eighth inning. In the 1969 tournament, he had only pitched five innings against Wolf Point on Thursday, so he was fresh and had all 12 of his innings back. Coach Tom Nielson had pitched Kurt Grimm and Scott Kato the day before, so he was obviously saving Damschen for this game, if needed. He was now needed.

Scobey's lineup that day was the typical lineup Doc used when Dick pitched:

- Higgins CF
- Danelson 3B
- Puckett P
- Legare LF
- Audet SS
- LaPierre RF
- Ware 1B
- Wang 2B
- Wolfe C

Validating Doc's bizarre decision to choose the third base dugout over the home team, Scobey jumped on Damschen and Havre for five runs in the top of the first inning to seize the lead, a lead they never relinquished in the game. Jack Higgins walked, then Rick Danelson and Dick Puckett each reached on errors to load the bases. Cleanup hitter Randy Legare followed with a bases-loaded single to drive in two runs, and Jerry LaPierre hit a double to drive home Dick and Randy. Rocky Ware then singled home LaPierre, and faster than anyone could order a Legion hamburger at the concession stand, Scobey had plated five runs in the inning, sprinting to a 5-0 lead before Havre even had its first at-bat. There really must have been something to that third-base dugout!

Havre countered with two runs of its own in the bottom half on singles by Damschen, Micky Williams, and Corky Morris, and it looked like the game was headed toward a slugfest after the first inning, which ended 5-2 Scobey. But both pitchers settled down after that and went the distance. Damschen yielded only two more runs in the next eight innings. Scobey picked up another run in the fifth when Legare

Dick Puckett hits a ground ball against Havre pitcher Barry Damschen in Scobey's five-run first inning in the state championship game. Dick reached on an error to load the bases, and Randy Legare followed with a two-run bases-loaded single to score Scobey's first two runs. *Leader.*

singled, and LaPierre brought him home with a big double. Havre had scored a single run in the fifth, then two more in the sixth on two singles and an error. So, after the dust had settled in the sixth, Scobey was barely clinging to a 6-5 lead after its five-run outburst in the first. In the top of the seventh, Jerry LaPierre walked, Rocky Ware and Danny Wang singled, then Scobey scored what proved to be the winning run on a bases-loaded RBI single by Danny Wolfe—his first hit of the tournament but a big one—to make it 7-5.

And there the score stood until the bottom of the eighth, when the nail-biting tension and drama of the final game reached a crescendo. The only memory I have of the 1969 state tournament on the field was in the bottom of the eighth inning, watching the game from the third base side, right next to the magical dugout. I was not acutely aware of the tension, but I could sense that this was a big moment because I had never before heard a baseball crowd that loud. I was caught up in the atmosphere even though I wasn't completely tapped into what was happening. In the bottom of the eighth, Havre got a walk and three hits, including a double by John Bryant and a single by Darryl Smith, and came dangerously close to tying the game and even taking the lead. But they only scored one run, thanks to a long throw from Randy Legare in deep left field to Danny Wolfe at home plate to peg a runner out. This is the memory I have: I remember Danny Wolfe jumping as high as I'd ever seen anyone jump at home plate. The distance between the bottom of his spikes and the ground was nothing like I'd ever seen. The throw from Legare was high but right on the plate. I also remember a runner from third base barreling toward Danny while he was high in the air. After jumping and catching the ball, he landed and snapped the tag in front of the plate. There was a cloud of dust as the runner slid, and the umpire called him out.

Then the crowd roared! The tying run had been cut down at the plate by Legare. In his interview, Danny Wolfe remembered the play this way: "There was a ball hit to left field, and it went, I think, close to the wall. I was catching, and Randy Legare picked that ball up in left field, and I had dropped one earlier in the year, so I was just shitting my pants that I was going to drop the ball and it was going to be close. Randy Legare picked that thing up and he heaved that goddamn thing and I kept thinking to myself, 'I hope it's so far over my head that I can't fuck this up.' I jumped up in the air and caught the ball; whoever it was came sliding under me, and down I went, and I don't really know if he was safe or out. I came down right on top of him, and the ball was in my glove, and they called him out.'"

Randy Legare's arm was so strong he "could throw strikes across the plate from the outfield,"[15] but according to Jack Higgins, it was not uncommon for Legare to throw high to the plate. Jack said, "Randy had one of the strongest arms I had seen in Legion ball. In the past, he had thrown over the backstop and overthrown the catcher several times, so it was always an adventure when a ball was hit to left field and a baserunner was trying to score." He also said that "any throw from Randy that the catcher caught was a perfect throw as many couldn't be caught!" First baseman Rocky Ware, when discussing Randy Legare's arm in his interview, said, "As a first baseman, you would take cutoffs from the outfield. Randy caught a fly ball at the fence in practice one night, and I was in perfect position to cut that thing off. It came so fast and so hard that I didn't have a chance to get my glove up, and it hit me right in the chest." From the fence!

Scobey's infield got the other two outs when they caught Hank Tweeten, who was on with a walk, at second, and John Bryant was thrown out at third. Three hits, one walk—four baserunners—but only one run, and Scobey escaped the eighth with a razor-thin 7-6 lead heading into the ninth.

Scobey went down in order in the top of the ninth, and Havre came to bat in the bottom half of the inning. Scobey needed three outs to win its first state championship, and Havre needed only one run to stay alive—two runs to walk off with its second consecutive state championship. Dick Puckett was on the mound to finish it. Dick was "now very tired [but] still working hard."[16] He struck Bruce Nelson out to get the critical first out, but an error at third put the tying run on first. However, the next two hitters popped up to the infield, and Scobey and Daniels County celebrated their first state championship on their home field. "The Scobey 'iron men' had brought home the first state title in American Legion Baseball for northeastern Montana. The crowd roared its approval of what will be a long-remembered great Legion ball club from Scobey."[17]

And it was the five-run top of the first inning that did it. The new third base dugout, built by the Scobey Jaycees earlier that season, proved to be the magical charm. Doc Norman's decision—"a form of baseball insanity"—was the gamechanger. Unbelievable.

TOURNAMENT SUMMARY

THERE HAVE BEEN MANY DRAMATIC GAMES IN SCOBEY American Legion Baseball history, but anyone would be hard-pressed to find a game to match the drama of that first championship game between Scobey and Havre in 1969, where Scobey was down to its last strike before staving off

Dick Puckett receives the state championship trophy and accepts congratulations from tournament co-director Jack Reiner as his teammates and Doc Norman (behind Dick) look on. Larry Bowler, Northeastern Legion District Commissioner, is on the right. *Leader.*

elimination with Dick's clutch home run.* My dad would often talk about this game—and the 1969 state tournament—for years to come. It was incredible.

The 1969 state tournament in Scobey was special—it was Scobey's first time hosting and its first state championship. I am so grateful I have a memory of it, a connection to it, because, like the first man walking on the moon earlier that summer, I always looked up to that 1969 state championship team. Not only my older cousins Dick and Terry, and Don who was batboy, but the entire team. It was the first state championship in Daniels County, and seven state Legion baseball championships would follow. Like Doc's first team in 1959, there was something special about being the first. As Danny Wolfe said, "There's something to be said about the first one in 1969; it kind of opens up like floodgates and shows everybody the thing can be done."

If I tried to list all the volunteers who made the 1969 state tournament happen, Rod Tande told me, "You would miss some." It really was the entire community. On the tournament's opening day on Thursday morning, when Scobey played Baker, "Scobey businessman, catching the spirit, closed en masse from 9:30 to 11:30 for Scobey's first tourney game" Perhaps the best way to recognize the volunteers would be to mention what the State American Legion Baseball Commissioner John Russell complimented Scobey on the tournament's planning and execution: "You folks sure know how to do it up here. I've never seen anything like it."[18] And maybe the best way to close the books on 1969, bookending Jack Reiner's comment in the *Leader* the day the tournament started that you're going to see a good tournament because "Scobey is baseball country,"

1969 Havre Legion Team, State A Runners-Up. Front row: Micky Williams, Curt Smith, Jim Chenoweth, Darryl Smith, Corky Morris, Bruce Nelson, John Bryant. Back row: Coach Tom Nielson, Scott Kato, Dan Cole, Bob Olson, Barry Damschen, Mike Hanson, Kurt Grimm, Hank Tweeten, Lynn Chenoweth. *Leader.*

1969 Scobey Legionnaires, State A Champions. Back row: Coach Doc Norman, Larry Grayson Craig Audet, Rocky Ware, Randy Legare, Dick Puckett, Rick Danelson, Jack Higgins, Danny Wang, Asst. Coach Gene Thompson. Second row: Jerry LaPierre, Jim Hansen, Dennis Miller, Terry Puckett, Danny Wolfe, Don Higgins, Jim Miller, Pete Dickson. Batboys: Danny Danelson, Pat Anderson, Kelly Norman, Don Puckett. *Leader.*

---

* Another state championship game where Scobey was down to its last strike was in 1976 in Cut Bank. With two strikes and two outs and Scobey trailing 5-4 in the bottom of the ninth, Greg Fjeld hit a liner down the right-field line to drive in Wade Tryan and then scampered around the bases himself to score for a 6-5 walk-off win against Wolf Point.

would be to quote what the *Leader* said about his comment in its tournament summary: "Scobey demonstrated that Daniels County is truly 'baseball country' as they turned out in large numbers for every game, whether or not Scobey was playing. Late but fine harvest prospects here, with fine weather for ripening grain as well as baseball brought a feeling that 1969 will be a year to be remembered."[19]

Yes, the year 1969 is indeed a year to be remembered. Perhaps I will be forgiven if I do mention one category of volunteers at the expense of omitting everyone else: the Scobey Jaycees who build the new concrete dugouts, especially the third base dugout—the dugout that Doc chose to be the winner, a visitor on his own home field. The magical dugout that is the reference point for the only memory I have of the 1969 state tournament.

Dan Danelson (Blues 1974–79), younger brother of Rick Danelson, was an eight-year-old batboy for the 1969 state tournament team. He remembers the players on that team, and what a tremendous influence they had on his career. In honor of the 1969 team and his early baseball memories, he shared this letter, which talks about those 1969 players:

After reading through all the Scobey baseball history, I can't help but reminisce on my time either as a batboy or player for Scobey baseball. I remember Cliff Hagfeldt telling stories about teams and players that had come before us and how talented they were. I heard what Cliff was saying but it didn't really sink in how deep the history was. I feel so fortunate to have been a part of some special teams and the memories and friendships that will last a lifetime.

My early love of baseball was the result of a friendship between my parents—Ben and Dolores (Roland) Danelson—and Doc and Marge. Dad and Doc were both military veterans (Dad-U.S. Army and Doc-USMC) who had a mutual respect for each other and enjoyed visiting about anything and everything.

Mom and Marge both ran their respective households and were the loving moms who made all the sacrifices behind the scenes so the boys of summer could have their fun. I'd like to have a head count for how many ballplayers Marge fed.

Kelly Norman and I were both the youngest in our families—only a year difference in age—so we played a lot together growing up. We hung out at the ballpark as batboys and idolized the ballplayers. We would be the first ones at practice, usually because Doc was our ride. We would go through the ball bag looking for the pearl of the group so that we could entice one of our idols to play catch with us before all the players assembled along the outfield third base line to begin throwing. I remember Dick Puckett for me as the guy I looked for. He was the man. From the eyes of a six- or seven-year-old, he was everything a baseball player was supposed to be. He was graceful in the field and was magic with the bat in his hands. He had a big smile and his competitiveness was second to none. When I played catch with him it was absolutely the best feeling of inclusion into the Scobey Legion family. I wanted to be like him. Then there was my cousin Danny Wang—my favorite person of all time. His laugh was contagious and his fun personality made me so happy when I was around him. I loved that guy. My brother Rick was a talented younger player with this group. He learned a lot on and off the field with these guys so I learned a lot from him. Rick could switch-hit and we would play wiffleball at the farm having to switch back and forth after every at-bat hitting left- and right-handed. I used to get so pissed off at how well he could do it and then talk shit. Makes me smile because I learned to hit both ways too because of his smack talk. Rick was instrumental in helping me to improve.

I was fortunate to have a great group of older Legion players who were nice enough to take the time to educate me and fill me in on the things Doc didn't teach me. Some good and some maybe not so good but it didn't matter because I had a group to try and emulate. I wanted to be a pitcher and wasn't very good at it but through years of being around the likes of Dick, Terry and Don Puckett, Jim Hansen, Danny Wang, Jay and Mike Hagfeldt, Duke and Dallas Trangsrud—to just name a few—I learned to compete. Terry Puckett was poetry in motion. He was smooth and so good. Doc made me into a pitcher by teaching the mechanics and the players I grew up watching from the dugout taught me what it took to be successful and to compete.

Scobey baseball was a breeding ground for young teenagers to join forces from around the area and compete against anybody and everybody. Scobey baseball was a collection of talented baseball players under the guidance of Doc who aspired to win championships. We expected to win. In reflecting back on things, the winning culture was probably our biggest advantage. We won games we probably shouldn't have because we competed to the end. My last couple of years playing with a pitching rotation that included Joe and Jon Puckett, Kelly Norman and me (and Ray Chapman and Randy Stolen when we needed them) we believed we would win every game. Some talent, yes, but a winning culture that was cultivated by those before us.

—Dan Danelson

And thus, the Doc Norman championship era had begun.

TOURNAMENT STATS

Hitting

RANDY LEGARE, WHO BATTED CLEANUP, LED SCOBEY IN hitting with a .448 average for the tournament. Of his thirteen hits, two were home runs—a grand slam against Baker and a three-run shot against Wolf Point—and he had several doubles. No doubt he led the team in RBIs. Randy was described as "the young farm boy from Flaxville" with the "Harmon Killebrew swing."[20] When asked about the best player he ever played with, Rocky Ware said, "When I saw one particular guy dragging his bat up to home plate to hit, it had to be Randy Legare. When he walked up to the plate, he didn't walk up there; he just kind of sauntered up there, dragging his bat behind him. He was built like a caveman, and oh my God, he could hit the ball. Of course, there were lots of other guys on the team who could hit the ball, but Randy Legare, he was awesome. He just hit the ball so hard; he was so strong." Jack Higgins, who grew up with Randy playing sports in Flaxville, said almost the same thing: "A Legare special was his walk up to home plate when it was his turn to bat. One of the Havre players once asked me, 'Who was that big guy who used to mosey up to home plate dragging his bat on the ground behind him when he was getting ready to bat?' Randy was a pretty intimidating guy when he came up to bat!" Second to Randy in batting average was right fielder/pitcher Jerry LaPierre, who had a great tournament on the mound and at the plate, with a .434 average. Leadoff hitter Jack Higgins followed at .345, then Dick at .333. Dick also hit two home runs in the tournament. The tournament was a record for home runs by all teams for any Montana Legion tournament, A or AA.[21] Rocky Ware led the team in one painful hitting category: he was hit by pitch three times in the tournament!

Pitching

To win five out of six games in four days, you must have a pitching staff, and Doc had one in 1969. He used six pitchers in the tournament—three left-handers and three right-handers. Dick, with a 2-1 record, figured in three decisions. Jim Hansen was 2-0 and Craig Audet 1-0. Here was the innings count by pitcher: Dick Puckett (13), Jerry LaPierre (12), Jim Hansen (11), Terry Puckett (9), Craig Audet (5), Danny Wang (5). Several players have told me that Gene Thompson helped with the pitchers that year, so he must be credited—total team effort.

Fielding

Scobey's outfield was solid throughout the entire tournament. The "stellar fielding performance" of Legare and LaPierre and their "throwing strikes from the outfield to catch runners at home"[22] was huge for Scobey. No doubt Legare's throw from deep left—and Wolfe's leaping catch and tag—to cut down the tying run at the plate in the eighth inning of the championship game was the most critical defensive play of the tournament. Speedy center fielder Jack Higgins's "tremendous performance"[23] in the championship game, chasing down several fly balls for outs to help pitcher Dick Puckett, provided additional defensive punch for Scobey. The *Leader* also mentioned the "very fine infields of Great Falls and Havre."[24] Baker employed a bizarre defensive set in their 14-inning win against Great Falls. Coach Mert Rustad sent their left fielder, Dan Stenglein, to come in and play a very short infield in a bunting situation in the twelfth inning, with the score tied at 4-4, which worked: they got the out.

PLAYOFF WITH GREAT FALLS

As with Havre the year before, Scobey had no time to celebrate their Sunday afternoon victory—the Great Falls Electrics one-game playoff to get into the state AA tournament was on Tuesday. Scobey was exhausted: "It would be an understatement to say that Scobey had a tired team."[25] There was so little time, the *Leader* article for the playoff game was in the same issue as the state tournament. Jim Hansen started for Scobey, and the Electrics got off to an early 6-1 lead, eventually winning 11-3. A four-run first and five-run seventh were the two big innings for Great Falls.

Scobey got its three runs on five hits and two Electrics errors. But sportswriter Mayo Ashley of the *Great Falls Tribune* recognized the class of the Scobey championship team. He wrote that "Scobey had nothing to be ashamed of" and that they were "one of the better Class A representatives to enter the playoff in recent years, and they almost pulled off a victory." He finished by writing, "With the exception of the first inning and that fateful five-run seventh, the Scobey club played the Electrics on even terms."[26] Imagine what they might have done with just a few days' rest.

EXTRA INNINGS

The 1969 state championship team honored Doc and Marge Norman and Assistant Coach Gene Thompson at a holiday social gathering at the N.C. Wolfe home in December 1969. The team presented Doc, Marge, and Gene with gifts. The party on a cold December winter night brought back the warmth of Scobey's first state championship won in the summer sun four months earlier.

Jack Higgins fondly recalls one member of the 1969 team, Danny Wang, who passed away in 2020. Jack said, "One of the special guys on the 1969 state championship team was Danny, aka 'Charlie,' Wang. Danny was the regular second

Gene Thompson, Marge and Doc Norman receive gifts from the 1969 state championship team at a holiday gathering at the N.C Wolfe home in December 1969. *Leader photo Babe Holyk.*

baseman but pitched on occasion. Danny always had a smile on his face and had an infectious laugh. Unfortunately, Danny said goodbye to us too early, but we will always remember him for the great guy he was.

"Back in the early days, we didn't have a travel bus and went to away games in private cars. Remember many road trips in my Impala SS with me and Dick Puckett up front and Danny Wang, Dan Wolfe, and Rick Danelson in the back. Those kids in the back seat always provided nonstop entertainment, and think Wang was the instigator with Wolfe and Danelson putting on the show.

"Charlie Wang was experimenting with his secret pitch, the forkball, and Doc began to use him in some of our games. When Charlie pitched, Dick Puckett was on short, and I was in center. Anytime the catcher signaled for the forkball, Dick would signal behind his back to me, and I would take a few steps back. That was because if Charlie's forkball didn't fork, it was going for a long ride if the batter connected. We had many laughs about the batters looking foolish when Charlie's forkball fluttered toward the plate and jumped around the bat for a strike!

"We still miss Danny Wang but remember what a great guy he was!!"

Terry Puckett remembers Dick's game-saving home run against Havre. "It was a line drive to straightaway left. I just remember being so excited and jumping up and down in the dugout. It was the first home run I remember seeing."

Dana Audet, who played for the Scobey Legion team from 1971 to 1974, also remembers Gene Thompson working with him and his cousin Danny Audet one night in Babe Ruth practice: "He was a really good coach and had both of us throwing harder than we ever did before. I learned a lot from him in that session."

Terry Puckett, who was only 14 in 1969, remembers some shenanigans on the road trips. "Back then, we didn't have a team bus, so some 'interesting' things would happen on road trips in our cars. The players would drive our own cars on road trips. Sometimes we would drive side by side on the road with the windows down and throw Vienna sausages with mustard on them into the car beside us in a sausage battle. One time, pitching coach Gene Thompson was passing cigarettes to a player from one car to driving side-by-side on the road. I'm pretty sure the cigarettes were for Danny Wolfe." Terry added another story about Wolfe. "In the Northern Hotel in Billings, when we were playing the Royals, Danny Wolfe (it was always Wolfe) got in trouble for throwing water balloons down on the street from our hotel room."

Terry shared a special memory of Doc and Marge he has of the game he pitched against the Royals on Cobb Field. He said, "Doc and Marge were kind of like our mom and dad in the summers, and they took care of all of us. They treated us like we were their own kids. In the 1969 game I pitched against the Royals at Cobb Field, Doc saw that my pitching-toe spike was worn, so he called Marge down to the dugout and told her to go out and buy me a new pair of spikes. She did and came back to the field with a new pair of spikes for me! Back then, we were playing with wooden bats, so a lot of them would break, and Doc would take care of all of it."

After two state tournaments, Havre and Scobey had played each other five times, with Scobey having the early edge with a 3-2 record. In the five games, big early innings were the determinant in three of them. In Glendive in 1968, Scobey jumped on Havre for eight runs in the first and went on to win 12-2. In the first game at Scobey in 1969, Havre had that seven-run second inning and won 7-2, then Scobey had the five-run first inning in the championship, winning 7-6.

Darryl and Curt Smith and Lynn Chenoweth, who all played for Havre in the 1969 tournament, had close ties to Scobey. Darryl and Curt were the younger brothers of Dan Smith, who had played for Scobey before their parents, Dale and Billie Lou Smith, moved to Havre in 1966. Their grandmother, Mrs. Frank Smith, remained in Scobey. Lynn, who played second base, was the son of Harland Chenoweth and the former Marie Larson, both from Scobey.

On July 4, 1969, 16-year-old Dave Fanning, pitching for the Klamath Falls, Oregon Hawks, won a 3-2 "mound feud" over pitcher Rolly Renfro of the Cheney Studs from Central Point, Oregon. Dave's parents would move to Havre in October 1969, and Scobey would run into this left-handed buzzsaw from Klamath Falls in the state tournament the next two seasons. Dave told me that Doc told him at a game in Havre in 1970 that if he had been the coach, he would have arranged for Dave to live with him. He said to him that the coach must have been crazy not to do something to keep him there.

In May 1969, Phil Audet, pitching for the Northern Montana Lights, faced brother Craig, an outfielder for the Eastern Montana Yellowjackets, in the second game of a doubleheader in Havre.* The result? Well, let's let Phil tell it: "I got him out! I don't know how many games Craig called and caught when I pitched over the years, but this time was a little different. He was trying to hit it instead of catch it! My first thought was, he really knows me. Most of the time, Craig threw the ball back to me harder than I had thrown it to him! So, I didn't want one of my blazing fastballs to hit the barrel of that Nellie Fox he held in his hands. He received all junk, fortunately grounded one of them to short for the out. We had a good chuckle and short visit before the Jackets hit the road."

In the bottom of the ninth inning of the state championship game, when Scobey needed three outs to win it, where were Doc's "girls of summer," Marge and Ann? They decided they wouldn't cook to watch the championship game that day, but the tension was too much when it got to the ninth inning. Ann said in her interview, "We couldn't watch, we just couldn't! We were holding hands and hugging each other behind the big green grandstand. We were listening, and when the crowd made this big roar, we knew we'd won. We just cried, and it was so exciting."

Gene Thompson worked with the pitchers that season, but his most significant contribution might have been helping center fielder and leadoff hitter Jack Higgins get back on the team after Doc booted him off. Jack stayed home to work on the family farm in Flaxville and missed the barnstorming road trip across Montana against the AA teams, so Doc kicked him off the team. Gene and Marge talked to Jack and said Doc wanted him back but wouldn't ask him. Gene told Jack to "just show up at the next practice," which he did, and everything was fine with Doc, who reinstated Jack before the state tournament began. But Jack said, "I don't think Doc ever forgave me for putting my farm job ahead of the road trip." He also said, "I think Marge loved me more than Doc!" Maybe Doc got back at Jack three years later when he ordered Terry Puckett to "hit that sonofabitch in the chest" with a pitch in an early-season Plainsmen game. Terry, as instructed, beaned Jack.

Ron Scott—Libby native who started at guard in basketball and shortstop in baseball for Montana State from 1962–66—was the head coach of the 1969 Libby baseball team. Dick Puckett pitched Scobey to a 4-2 win over Libby on their AA road trip. Coach Ron Scott led Libby to a 17-3 conference record (23-5 overall) and the Western AA title in 1969. Ron Scott had close ties to Scobey and their baseball players. He began his coaching career with the Scobey Spartans basketball team in 1967-68, where he coached Dick Puckett—who had transferred from Peerless—Craig Audet, Rocky Ware, Danny Wang, and Jim Hansen. Ron later became the head girls' and head boys' basketball coach at Peerless from 1973-1976 (I played for him in junior high and my freshman of high school). Libby lost 1-0 to Helena in 13 innings in their first game of the AA tournament, then were eliminated by the Royals. Libby's ace pitcher, Jim Stedman, was drafted in the second round of the MLB draft and played in the Cardinals organization for four years.

Left fielder Randy Legare had a cannon for an arm, but so did catcher/shortstop Craig Audet. Like Legare, occasionally a throw would get away from Craig, demonstrating the power of his arm. In the game at Libby, Terry Puckett recalls, "Someone hit a ground ball to Craig at short, and he uncorked a throw that sailed over the first baseman's head, over the fence behind first base, over the road next to the field, over the trees on the other side of the road, and then into a swimming pool on the other side of the trees! In that same game, Jim Hansen caught a fly ball in left and fell over the fence. It was a snow fence. He caught his pants on the fence as he went over!"

Terry Puckett and Phil Audet mentioned how hard Craig would throw the ball back to them when Craig was catching, that it would hurt their glove hands when they caught the ball. I have memories of Craig catching as I sat next to my dad in the grandstand. I could see that the ball was

---

* Phil Audet started his college career at Western Montana College but transferred to Northern. But if a certain letter had been opened on time, he might have attended the College of Great Falls, where he had been offered a scholarship to play basketball—but didn't know it. Phil recalls, "It was a couple of days before I was leaving for college at Western when my mom mentioned I had a letter on top of the refrigerator from College of Great Falls. It was from the basketball coach asking if I would be interested in playing for them. The letter had been received quite a while before she remembered to tell me. I started school at Western Montana College the next week. Looking back, it was maybe meant to be!"

going back to the pitcher faster than it was coming in, and I could hear the glove popping sound louder on the pitcher's end than when the ball hit Craig's glove. Sometimes, Craig would throw the ball back harder to the pitcher—you could see and hear it. Dad would start chuckling whenever this happened. I asked Dad, "Why is he throwing the ball back to the pitcher harder now?" Dad laughed and replied, "Because he's mad at the pitcher for not throwing what he wants him to throw. He's sending him a message. It's faster than going out to the mound to tell him." I honestly can't remember a throw coming to the plate faster than Craig threw it back to the pitcher when he caught. Kelly Norman remembers Craig's throw from catcher to second: "Craig had the shortest arm angle of all time, not sure if his hand made it high as his ear. He would throw from a crouch or on his knees on a line. A cannon!"

Fourteen-year-olds Rick Danelson and Terry Puckett started playing Legion ball as 13-year-olds the previous season in 1968. They both had the magical post-August first birthdays for an extra year of eligibility. They would play Legion ball together for six years (1968-73), the longest tandem in Scobey Legion history.

Since 1949, the two divisions in Montana American Legion Baseball had been Class A and B, but for one season only in 1969, Montana American Legion changed from Class A and B to Class AA and A, so Scobey's state championship patches for 1969 are in the A Division. The state reverted to Class A and B the following season in 1970. The seven other Scobey state championships were all in the B division. Montana State American Legion went to Class AA and A in 1987.

Dick Puckett started at second base for four years for the Jackrabbits and was team captain his senior year. *Sioux Falls Argus-Leader.*

In the spring of 1969, Dick Puckett started at second base as a freshman for South Dakota State's baseball Jackrabbits and helped them to a share of the North Central Conference title with North Dakota State. Dick was fifth on the team with a .284 average and banged out several home runs. Jack Higgins joined Dick at SDSU for one year in 1970 and started in center field, but transferred to Montana State after one season when, as Jack put it, "I figured out there wasn't any payday in my future playing baseball."

Brian Bechtold, who played for Baker against Scobey at the state tournament three times in 1969-70, had this to say about the Scobey teams: "Scobey teams were fundamentally sound; they didn't make a lot of mental errors. They were also very athletic and well-coached. If you were going to beat them, you had to play an almost perfect game."

1970

A Tough Act to Follow

> *Doc told me in later years that taking second place in 1970 could have been his best coaching job ever.*
>
> —**Danny Wolfe, Scobey Legionnaires (1968–71)**

1970 Scobey Legionnaires, State B Runners-Up. Batboys, L–R, Kelly Norman and Jeff Richardson, Kneeling: Don Higgins, Dan Wolfe, Brad Murray, Jim Darchuk, Gary Nieskens, Barry Higgins and Don Puckett. Standing: Dr. C. H. Norman, coach; Dan Wang, Rick Danelson, Jim Hansen, Pete Dickson, Terry Puckett, and Jerry LaPierre. Not in the picture is Daryl Fladager. *Leader.*

PRESEASON

FOLLOWING THE 1969 SEASON, THE ASCENDANCE OF Havre in the west and Scobey in the east as the two dominant teams in Montana Class B American Legion Baseball was now firmly established. The Montana Class B baseball map was now an ellipse with two focal points: a Northstar in the west and a Bluesy sky in the east, with Coach Tom Nielson and Coach Doc Norman the center of gravity for each focal point. However, the center of gravity in the east was a little heavier. (Doc in heaven will laugh with me and forgive me for saying so.)

Beginning in 1967, when Scobey and Havre played each other for the first time in the state tournament, each team had ended the other's season in the state tournament. In 1967, Scobey beat Havre 7-3; in 1968, Scobey beat Havre 12-2, but then Havre eliminated Scobey 12-0 and went on to win the state championship; in 1969, Havre beat Scobey 7-2, but then Scobey went on to win two one-run games, 8-7 and 7-6, to win the championship. The year 1970 would continue the rivalry and Legion baseball excellence in Post No. 11 and Post No. 56. This time, Havre would host its first state tournament, and the two teams would meet again in the final.

There were wholesale changes to Scobey's roster for the 1970 season. Since 1965, Dick Puckett, Jack Higgins, Randy Legare, Rocky Ware, and Craig Audet—all stars on the 1969 state championship team—had been playing Legion baseball, but they had now finally aged out and were gone. Gone, too, were Jim and Dennis Miller and Larry Grayson. Eight boys out. That's the bad news. But there was some good news, too. A lot of good, experienced players were returning who had played in state tournaments and against tough AA competition, including Danny Wang (P/2B/SS), Danny Wolfe (C), Rick Danelson (3B), Terry Puckett (P/1B), Jerry LaPierre (P/OF), Jim Hansen (P/OF), and Don Higgins (CF). And joining the team were talented newcomers Brad Murray, Gary Nieskens, Daryl Fladager, Jim Darchuk, Barry Higgins, and 14-year-old Don Puckett, who would end up starting at second base before the end of the season.

True to form, Doc was bringing players up Babe Ruth–age to get them Legion experience. Would you believe that switch-hitting Rick Danelson and Terry Puckett, now in their third year of Legion ball, were still only 15 years old and eligible to play Babe Ruth? Probably the most significant strength on Scobey's 1970 roster was their pitching depth: Terry Puckett, Jerry Lapierre, Jim Hansen (all left-handers), and fork-ball specialist Danny Wang could all pitch.

Would this all be enough for Scobey to repeat as state champions? Coach Tom Nielson and Havre had other ideas.

REGULAR SEASON

Rather than waiting to play each other in the state tournament, Tom Nielson and Doc Norman got on the phone and scheduled nonconference games with each other. Two, three-game series—a total of six games—were scheduled at Havre at the end of June and Scobey in mid-July. Havre won all six games, clearly demonstrating that they were the team to beat in 1970. Scobey's fielding was their Achilles' heel, as in Scobey, they committed 25 errors in three games. Their pitching was enough to keep them in the games, but the fielding hurt them. Their fielding improved at the end of the season, but cost them earlier in the season. Another thing: Doc did not pitch Terry in the three-game series in Scobey, and there is no record of him pitching in Havre, so he might have been deliberately not showing Terry to Havre until the state tournament.

Scobey also played the Williston Keybirds home-and-home during the regular season, another tough couple of losses, but the team was getting good competition. At Scobey, Williston scored two runs in the ninth to win a close game, 4-2.

Doc also got on the phone with his friend Ed Bayne and scheduled a game with the Royals at Cobb Field. This one was a dandy as Scobey almost came away with the win against another tough Royals team. Scobey scored two runs in the top of the seventh to tie it 3-3, as Terry Puckett tripled, followed by run-scoring singles by Danny Wang and Don Higgins. The score was tied 3-3 in the bottom of the eighth, but pinch-hitter Paul McClure blasted a three-run triple off Danny Wang to provide the winning runs for Billings. Scobey scored a single run in the top of the ninth, and the final score was 7-4 Billings.

While Scobey was "playing up" against the Royals, Coach Tom Nielson did the same in the west by scheduling a game against the Great Falls Electrics. Havre lost to the Electrics 13-5 in an early-season game but used four pitchers to gain valuable experience against the tough-hitting Electrics team.

The format for the regular and postseason in 1970 was the same as in 1969. There were three Divisions—northeast, southeast, and west—with the top two teams in each division qualifying for the state tournament. Scobey won the northeast with Plentywood second. In the Southeast, Glendive won with Baker second. In the west, Havre was first, and the Helena Representatives, newcomers to the state tournament, second. In 1970, the names of the Montana State American Legion divisions reverted to Class A and B from Class AA and Class A. One significant change in 1970, due to complaints from Havre and Scobey, was that the State B champion received an automatic bid to the State A Tournament. Commissioner John Russell, the state baseball chairman, decided the two previous years' fiascoes when Havre and Scobey were forced to travel to Great Falls to playoff the day following their state championships after playing five or six games in four days. The host of the state tournament was Havre, which began a pattern of alternate hosts between Scobey in the east and Havre in the west through 1975, after which Havre moved up to the Class A Division.

To prepare his team for State in Havre, Doc took the team on a road trip to play Minot in a doubleheader at Minot the weekend before the tournament. In the first game, Danny Wolfe started on the mound but got roughed up in the first inning as Minot scored eight runs. There were some errors, too. Doc brought Terry in to relieve Wolfe in the first inning, with Danny switching from pitcher to catcher. (Dallas Hagfeldt caught when Danny pitched.) Minot went on to win the game 9-2. Terry only allowed one hit in eight-plus innings of relief. Minot won the second game 4-2, but Jim Hansen pitched a dandy for Scobey, allowing only three hits in nine innings. Hansen's pitching kept Scobey in the game, and the score was tied 2-2 in the bottom of the seventh, but Minot scored two unearned runs to win it.

Terry remembers the Minot game where he came in to relieve Wolfe. "Doc started Danny at pitcher, and he was pitching horrible. [I told Danny Wolfe at our interview that Terry thought he was a horrible pitcher and he laughed.] We were all playing like shit and getting clobbered by Minot. Doc brought me in to pitch and moved Danny to catcher. As catcher, Wolfe picked up that the third base umpire, who was standing between third and short behind me pitching, was flashing the signs Wolfe was giving to me to the Williston hitters so they knew what pitch was coming. When Doc learned of it he came absolutely unglued in the dugout. A couple of times, Danny didn't throw the ball back to me as catcher, he rolled the ball back to me. I remember it because I thought it was funny. I don't know if it was because he was sulking because Doc took him out as pitcher or if it was to piss the umpire off, but I remember him rolling the ball back to me."

STATE TOURNAMENT

Havre was the clear favorite to win its second state tournament, this time on its home field. The opening day matchups pitted Scobey against Baker, Glendive against Helena, and Havre against Plentywood. Against Baker, Doc's strategy to save his ace Terry Puckett for Havre later in the tournament backfired, as the heavy-hitting Baker team erupted for 13 runs on 16 hits, scoring 10 runs in the first five innings to chase left-hander Jerry LaPierre, an excellent pitcher, now in his final season. Baker won the game 13-5, with Dennis Bechtold getting the win, relegating Scobey to the "dirt route" for the fourth consecutive year in the state tournament. If Scobey were to repeat as state champions, they would have a long, dusty three-day road ahead of them. In other first-round action, Glendive beat the Reps 10-1, and Havre smashed Plentywood 18-4, with Mike Hanson getting the win for Havre, pitching a no-hitter through six innings and finishing with a six-hitter.

In the second round, Baker's bats again boomed loudly as they plated 14 runs against Glendive to win another slugfest 14-9 and gain a berth in the semifinals. Baker scored 11 runs in the third inning to blow the game open. Glendive did not commit an error in the game, so all 14 Baker runs were earned, coming on 11 hits. Havre had a second-round bye, so they would face Baker in the semifinals. Scobey smashed out 20 hits and committed only one error to eliminate their old nemesis, Plentywood, 13-8 in the loser-out game, with Jim Hansen getting the win for Scobey. Jim also had a double in the game, as did Brad Murray. Grove pitched for Plentywood. The *Leader* described Grove as "a good sticker and fine ballplayer, very fast," and wrote that Danny Wolfe, Scobey's catcher, felt "proud as punch when his peg caught the speedster trying to steal second."[27] Not the only baserunner Wolfe threw out at second that season, to be sure.

Continuing along the dirt route, Scobey faced Helena in its third game. In my interview with Terry Puckett, he told me that he was frustrated not to get the ball handed to him earlier in this tournament—Doc was saving him for Havre—but Doc could not wait any longer and started Terry against Helena. Terry, perhaps unleashing some of his frustration, responded by carrying a no-hitter into the seventh inning, ending with a three-hitter, as Scobey won 11-6. Scobey had 13 hits, including a double by Jerry LaPierre, who was "coming out of a prolonged batting and pitching slump."[28] Danny Wang also had a triple for Scobey. Defensively, Don Higgins made a sensational running catch at the 380-foot marker in center field, and his shoulder hit the fence as he made the catch. Scobey played well defensively, committing only two errors, correcting the shoddy fielding problems they had demonstrated earlier in the season. Helena had a good team, winning over Havre in the season.

In the semifinal against Baker, Havre coach Tom Nielson, as he would do the following year in the semifinal against Scobey, handed the ball to Dave Fanning, the fire-balling southpaw from Klamath Falls, Oregon. Baker coach Dennis Moran responded with his ace, left-hander Dennis Bechtold, who had seven innings of eligibility remaining after pitching five innings in his opening day 13-5 win over Scobey. Bechtold had a good curve ball and was good at hitting the corners. The two left-handers treated the fans to a riveting pitcher's duel through seven-and-a-half innings. The game was 0-0 for five-and-a-half innings, then Havre got Curt Smith on third, and Darryl Smith lashed a single to left, scoring Smith, making the score 1-0 in favor of Havre in the bottom of the sixth. (Why did the Smiths ever have to move from Scobey? Doc should have kept them there. What's up, Doc?) The score stood until the bottom of the eighth, with Havre leading 1-0. However, Dennis Bechtold had exhausted his innings after pitching seven innings and had to come out of the game. The crafty left-hander from Baker was not overpowering but had good control, keeping Baker in the game and getting outs. Havre rallied to score five runs in the bottom of the eighth, the big blow coming on a bases-loaded triple by Dave Fanning to drive in three runs, and Havre took a 6-0 lead entering the final frame. Baker touched Fanning for a single run in the top of the ninth, then loaded the bases, but with two outs, Fanning struck out the final hitter to snuff the rally. The score ended 6-1, vaulting Havre to the championship game for the third consecutive year and putting them in the driver's seat to win its first state championship on its home field.

This set up a rematch with Scobey and Baker to gain a berth in the championship against Havre. As is the case historically in many state tournaments, the rematch is often won by the team that lost the first game, and this happened in the Scobey-Baker rematch, as Scobey overwhelmed Baker 19-2. Jerry LaPierre, who was chased with 10 runs in five innings in the first game, went the distance for Scobey and "gained his revenge"[29] by pitching a four-hitter. In his fifth and final season, Jerry LaPierre ended his career with a victory. The year prior, he had pitched eight strong innings against Havre in the first championship game, keeping Scobey in the game and allowing them to win in extra innings.

After losing their opening game to Baker, Scobey won three consecutive games to make it to the championship game. "Tournament fans were seeing how teams from 'Scobey Country' get their deserved reputation for being able to scramble back from the underside."[30] In the championship game, Kurt Grimm started for Havre, and Doc started fork-baller Danny Wang in what would be his last game wearing a Scobey Legion uniform. Wang pitched well, yielding only four runs through the first six innings to keep Scobey in the game and eventually going the distance, but it was not enough to corral the strong Havre team, as Kurt Grimm pitched a three-hitter to lead Havre to a 6-1 win. However, the game was closer than the final score indicated, as "Scobey threatened all the way" and "had the bases loaded on several occasions."[31] Brad Murray and Jim Hansen hit the ball hard for what would have been extra-base hits, but a couple of "desperate diving catches" by Havre fielders robbed Scobey of any run production. The exceptional fielding by Havre "kept Scobey from repeating its sensational performance against Havre here last year."[32]

TOURNAMENT SUMMARY

Havre had some excellent teams through the years, but this might have been the most dominant Havre team to win a state tournament, as they outscored their opponents 30-6 in three games. Havre had "an excellent ball club again this year, probably better than the fine club they had last year."[33] Their depth at pitching was remarkable. In their first game against Plentywood, Mike Hanson had a no-hitter for six innings, finishing with a six-hitter. Havre committed seven errors in the game, or he might have yielded less than the four runs he did. In the second game, Dave Fanning pitched a three-hitter against Baker, yielding only one run, and Kurt Grimm matched that in the final—another three-hitter with only one run allowed. According to the records, Scott Kato, who had pitched 10 innings in Scobey the previous year, yielding only two runs (albeit one of them being the home run by Dick Puckett to tie the championship game), did not deliver a single pitch in the tournament.

The "dirt route" had become the norm for all four state tournaments Scobey had played in since 1967, as they had never reached the state championship game without a loss yet. It wouldn't be until the year 1973 that this would happen. Doc told Danny Wolfe that this season might have been his best coaching job ever, as the Scobey team overachieved, making it to the state championship game. After losing the likes of Dick Puckett, Jack Higgins, Randy Legare, Craig Audet, and Rocky Ware from the previous season, a second-place finish was a fine showing indeed. Doc said, "I have never been prouder of our boys than in that [state] tournament. After getting off to a bad start in the first game, they got back on the stick and showed what a courageous bunch of kids can do."[34]

The *Leader* commented on the situation regarding byes in the state tournament. In its four state tournament appearances, Scobey had to play two games on the first day, while some of the other teams, even if they were not the top seed from their division, did not. It made the point that the previous season, when Havre was the number two seed from the west, tournament officials accorded Havre a bye as they were last year's state champion. It was expected that this "gentleman's agreement" would continue with tournament officials in 1970, with Scobey receiving a bye being the previous year's state champion, but that did not happen. The northeastern district commissioner stated, "This has now become a nonnegotiable item for the next meeting." This difficult situation of how to handle byes would be corrected the following season at the state tournament in Scobey, when the state switched to two divisions from three, with each division winner receiving a first-round bye.[35]

The *Leader* also mentioned that more baseball was being played in Montana by Class B teams than by Class A teams and that most of that baseball was being played in eastern Montana.[36]

1970 Havre Legion Team, State B Champions. Standing, L–R: Coach Tom Nielson, Scott Kato, Darryl Smith, Dave Fanning, Mike Hanson, Kurt Grimm, Lynn Chenoweth, Arlen Hanson, and Dan Cole. Kneeling: Micky Williams, Dick Clark, John Bryant, Mike Welch, Dave Cole, Jim Chenoweth, Curt Smith. *Havre Daily News.*

TOURNAMENT STATS

Hitting

Brad Murray led Scobey in hitting with a .528 average in the tournament, followed by Jim Hansen (.450), Danny Wolfe (.416), Terry Puckett (.400), Don Higgins (.389), Danny Wang (.380), and Jerry LaPierre (.363). Danny Wolfe hit a grand slam against Baker.

Pitching

Jerry LaPierre started and took the loss in the opening game to Baker but pitched a complete game in the second game against Baker, yielding only one run. Jim Hansen went the distance to get the win over Plentywood. Terry Puckett had a no-hitter into the seventh against Helena, ending with a three-hitter for the win. Danny Wang pitched the championship game against Havre, yielding 10 hits in the complete game.

Fielding

Scobey's fielding had been an issue earlier in the season, as in the series at Havre in June, they committed 25 errors in three games. In the state tournament, they committed four errors against Baker, one against Plentywood, two against Helena, four against Baker in the second game, and four in the championship against Havre. That's an average of three errors a game, a remarkable improvement from earlier in the season.

Don Higgins had a running catch against the 380-foot marker against Helena, his shoulder hitting the fence as he made the catch. The sportswriters in Havre unofficially declared Don Higgins, with "his great speed, a good hitter, and great talent in center field,"[37] the best center fielder in the tournament.

Scobey turned two infield double plays in the tournament: 5-4-3 (Danelson to Don Puckett to Terry Puckett) and 6-4-3 (Wang to Don Puckett to Terry Puckett). In his last season, Danny Wang had switched from second base to shortstop, making room for 14-year-old Don Puckett to start at second base.

STATE CLASS A PLAYOFF

After winning the state Class B championship, Havre received an automatic bid to the State A Tournament in Anaconda as the third-place seed in the east and did not have to play off against a Class A opponent to make the tournament. In their opening game, they faced western champion, Missoula, coached by MLB Hall of Famer Lloyd Waner. Notably, Ed Bayne, coach of the 47-7 Billing Royals, said that Havre "could be a dark horse" in the tournament.

Havre showed they belonged in the State A Tournament and represented the Class B division well. Dave Fanning started against Missoula, and Havre led 6-4 after seven innings, but Missoula scored two runs in the top of the eighth to tie the game 6-6. The game went into extra innings, with 16-year-old Arlen Hanson, the youngest of Tom Nielson's staff, relieving Fanning in the tenth for Havre. Missoula scored a single run in the top of the 12th inning on a home run by center fielder Jay Ryan to win the game over the "balky" and "win-hungry" Havre team 7-6.[38] Larry Eyer went all 12 innings for Missoula for the win. Havre again was plucky in their second game against Libby, scoring five runs in the ninth to close the gap to 12-10, but the rally fell short. Mike Hanson went five innings, and Scott Kato finished for Havre. Coach Ed Bayne and the Billings Royals won the tournament, their 16th in 17 seasons.

EXTRA INNINGS

During the latter part of the season and the first game of the state tournament, Brad Murray, a "natural hitter," avoided wearing his glasses, causing him to "miss at the plate and grossly misjudge fly balls in left field."[39] Brad put his glasses back on, and things improved greatly (and how!) as he led the team in hitting for the tournament with a .528 average. Imagine what it could have been had he worn his glasses in the first game against Baker. So the dilemma is this: Do you get more girls leading the tournament by hitting with your black-rimmed sports glasses on or by taking them off and looking better on the field? The answer to this dilemma was clear to my high school basketball coach, Clark Shaffer, who once said, "It doesn't matter if you win or lose, as long as you look good."

At this stage of his Legion career, Rick Danelson was a switch-hitter, but he would swing over to be a purely left-handed hitter later in his career.

Don Higgins's fine performance in center field at the state tournament in Havre prompted the *Leader* to write that Don "promises to be even a finer ball player than his brother."[40] We'll let the two of them sort that one out over a friendly beer.

In his interview, Danny Wolfe mentioned a funny story involving Danny Wang in the state tournament in Havre. Wolfe remembers it this way: "It was hot, like 90 degrees in the shade, only like it can get in Havre up on that hill. We weren't supposed to do anything in '70. We lost those five studs from the '69 team, but we made it to the championship game. We lost, of course. Anyway, I don't remember which game it was, I was catching, and Wang was playing shortstop, and as the pitcher was winding up to pitch, Wang just turned and ran right off the field and out the gate. The pitcher threw the pitch, and it was a ball. I called timeout, and the ump called time, and I watched Wang as he ran up over to where the cars were. Well, what had happened was somebody was lying on the ground there, and he thought it was his dad who had a heart attack—another one because he had a heart attack before. Anyway, he didn't do anything; he just took off right out the gate to where it was. Well, it turned out it was Ray LaPierre who was lying on the ground there. Those guys would sit up there and drink, and it was hotter than hell, and I think he just blacked out and fell onto the ground there. It was old Ben Danelson and Johnny Wang, all those guys, they would sit and drink their whisky during the game."

1970 was the only season Scobey ever finished in second place in a state tournament. Scobey made it to the championship nine times as one of the two final teams and won it eight times.

Baker had three pitchers—Dennis Bechtold, Larry Moser, and Jim Robinson—but Jim Robinson (from Wibaux) broke his ankle on a base-stealing attempt against Glendive, severely hurting Baker's chances to go deeper in the tournament, as they had no more depth at pitching. Jim Robinson had a good fastball but could be wild. Following his Legion career in 1971, Jim was drafted by the Kansas City Royals but could not follow through because of a knee injury. Larry Moser and Brian Bechtold went to Jamestown and played for the Jimmies the following year, 1971.

Brian Bechtold said about facing Dave Fanning: "I was left-handed, so Fanning was really tough. I managed one of the three hits he gave up: a cheap flare over the third baseman, blooping in front of the left fielder. He was the toughest left-handed pitcher I faced in Legion or college."

The Baker team wore white spikes like the Oakland Athletics at that time. It's hard to believe that, at that time, Oakland was a winning franchise in baseball. They won the AL West in 1971, losing to Baltimore in the AL championship series, but then they won three consecutive World Series from 1972-74.

Scobey finished their season with a 21-14 record, including the state tournament. Of their 14 losses, seven were to Havre, one to the Royals, and two were to the Williston Keybirds.

Don Higgins stole 29 bases during the 1970 season. What was it with speedy center fielders from Flaxville who batted leadoff for Scobey? Jack Higgins started the tradition in 1968-69, followed by Don (1970-71), Barry (1972), Jack Tryan (1973-74), and Wade Tryan (1976-79).

The *Leader* once again called out the former Scobey players who had moved to Havre, citing Lynn Chenoweth as "one of Havre's outstanding ballplayers who has an undramatic manner and again this season is one of Havre's most consistently stellar players."[41] Lynn Chenoweth was the son of former Daniels County natives Harland and Marie (Larsen) Chenoweth. Of course, Darryl and Curt Smith, formerly from Scobey, were starring for Havre as well. Shame on Doc for letting these players get away.

Yes, the year 1969 was a tough act to follow. After all, it's not every year you win a state championship for the first time *and* walk on the moon—I'm not sure which of those is more difficult. But the 1970 team played determined baseball the entire season. "It was the spunky spirit of Scobey's team this year, in trying to measure up, that provided for interesting action, and the boys certainly did that this season."[42]

Looking ahead to 1971: "If Danny Wolfe, Terry Puckett, Don Higgins, and Ricky Danelson continue to improve next year as they have this season, Scobey next year should again be a serious contender for the state title. They will be aided by Don Puckett, Barry Higgins, Gary Nieskens, plus some very likely talent upcoming from the Babe Ruthers."[43]

1971

Third Place is No Consolation for Scobey

> *It was just one of those years where everything went right. Just a dream season.*
>
> —**Dave Fanning, 1971 Havre pitcher**

1971 Scobey Legionnaires, State B third place. Standing, L–R: Coach Doc Norman, Barry Higgins, Larry Grayson, Jim Hansen, Terry Puckett, Rick Danelson, Dan Wolfe, Kurt Jackson. Kneeling: Don Higgins, Don Murray, Vic DeTienne, Dana Audet, Howard Dickinson, Doug Veis, Don Puckett. Batboy in front: Jeff Richardson. (Dallas Hagfeldt is not pictured.) *Leader photo, Milton Gunderson.*

PRESEASON

Following Scobey's overachieving second place finish at State to Havre in Havre in 1970, which Doc in later years told Danny Wolfe could have been his best coaching job ever, the *Leader* looked ahead to 1971 this way: "If Scobey continues to improve next year as they have this season, they should again be a serious contender for the state title."[44] And that was the expectation entering the 1971 season. Six-foot-three Jim Hansen, now in his fifth season, was 18 years old and a powerful left-handed pitcher. Eighteen-year-old catcher "with moxie"[45] Danny Wolfe—who set the unofficial standing high jump record for Scobey leaping to catch Randy Legare's high throw to home plate in the bottom of the eighth inning at the 1969 tournament—anchored Scobey's strong defense behind the plate. In his final season, Don Higgins would also bat leadoff and roam center field, chasing down fly balls as if they owed him money. Terry Puckett and Rick Danelson were still young at 16 but were physically maturing and were now in their fourth season. They were experienced, having already played in three state tournaments together. Speedy outfielder Barry Higgins and 15-year-old second baseman Don Puckett were also back, and Larry Grayson, who was on the 1969 team but had missed the 1970 season, and Howie Dickinson also joined the team.

The *Leader*'s positive outlook for 1971 also mentioned "some very likely talent upcoming from the Babe Ruthers." One of those talented newcomers was 15-year-old Dana Audet, who would replace Danny Wang at shortstop. But another talent not on the *Leader*'s scope was catcher Dallas Hagfeldt from Glasgow. How did Scobey, who historically seemed to be able to recruit talented baseball players—think Swede Risberg and Happy Felsch in the 1920s and Joe Anderson's late 1950s and early 1960s Plainsmen teams—land catcher Dallas Hagfeldt, from Glasgow? It's a long story, but since *The Blues of Summer* has no pitch clock, let's step through it. Dallas "Pete" Hagfeldt moved from Scobey to California around 1956, returning to Glasgow in 1969. Cliff and Pete had enlisted in the Army, and Cliff returned to Scobey, but Pete stayed in California. Dallas Hagfeldt, in his interview, explained that when the family moved back to northeastern Montana from California, they moved to Glasgow because Pete found work there. Glasgow didn't have a Legion team, and neither did Wolf Point, so Dallas could come to Scobey and play, and Jay and Mike followed him. Glasgow and Wolf Point would later form teams before the end of his career, but the rest, as they say, is history.

For pitching, Jim Hansen and Terry Puckett were two of the finest left-handed pitchers in the state. But more than two pitchers are required to win three or four games (or more) in a six-team state tournament. Gone were Jerry LaPierre and Danny Wang, who had provided the necessary pitching depth the year before to make it to the state championship. Who would step up in 1971? Doc's third pitcher was Danny Wolfe, and Larry Grayson was a possible fourth pitcher who could provide some innings if needed.

In the west, Havre had lost some excellent players like Micky Williams, the Smith brothers, and the Chenowith brothers, but 5-10 140-pound left-hander Dave Fanning from Klamath Falls, Oregon, the best pitcher in the state, was returning for his final season. Many key players were returning, like Kurt Grimm, Scott Kato, and Arlen Hanson, who were all on Tom Nielson's pitching staff the previous year. If Vegas put odds on another Havre-Scobey rematch in Scobey for the state championship, they wouldn't be high. Oddsmakers would also give Havre the edge to win it because of their pitching depth. We'll see how that plays out.

REGULAR SEASON

SCOBEY, CLEARLY THE CLASS OF NORTHEASTERN MONTANA Legion baseball, handily won its district again in 1971, finishing the regular season at 20-7. As he always did, Doc scheduled Class A competition to prepare for state. This time, he took the team to Minot, ND, to play two games, losing 4-2 and 9-2. The 9-2 game was actually when the funny incident occurred, where Danny Wolfe rolled the ball back to Terry Puckett several times on the mound. In the Minot games, Hansen and Puckett yielded only two earned runs in 17 2-3 innings, showing these two left-handers could compete at any level.

Jim Hansen led Scobey's pitching staff with a 10-1 record, with Terry Puckett close behind in wins. Scobey had a .340 team batting average, led by Danny Wolfe with a .422 average, Don Higgins at .398 (I wonder how many of those hits were credited to his legs), and Terry Puckett, who could now hit for power at .380. I always remember Terry as a power hitter—I saw him hit several home runs—but it wasn't until his fourth season, when he was 16 years old, that he emerged as such. One stat that doesn't show up is that Scobey had an excellent fielding team in 1971.

Havre also handily won their district in the west, and Coach Tom Nielson scheduled several games against class A opponents to sharpen his team. They had two wins over the Great Fall Electrics, who then went on a 32-game win streak. They also beat Missoula twice, Helena once, and Kalispell twice. The defending Class B champions were 38-11 for the season. Fanning was 14-0, including two no-hitters. He had struck out 150 hitters in 81 2-3 innings—almost two hitters per inning. But perhaps even more astounding was that he had walked only 11 hitters in those 81 innings—one walk per seven and a third innings—which is remarkable for a power pitcher. Philadelphia, Baltimore, and San Francisco scouts had been looking at him. On the other hand, Scobey would prefer not to look at him. They had seen him before.

DIVISIONAL TOURNAMENTS

THE 1971 POSTSEASON FORMAT CHANGED FOR THE BETTER. There were now only two divisions—west and east—instead of three, with a postseason tournament to determine the top three teams in each division to qualify for State. The top seeds from each division would receive a first-round bye in the six-team state tournament. This avoided the previous season's dilemma of which of the three division winners should receive a bye. It had never been Scobey.

Seven teams—Scobey, Poplar, Glendive, Miles City, Ekalaka, Plentywood, and Circle—competed in the eastern divisional hosted at Circle. Scobey, the top seed, received a first-round bye and won its first game 10-0 over Circle, who had beaten Plentywood 8-6 in 10 innings to earn the right to play Scobey. Terry Puckett pitched the shoutout, yielding six hits, striking out 12, and walking three. Scobey then won the championship over Ekalaka, 11-3, with Jim Hansen winning. Scobey banged out 14 hits, including a two-run home run by Terry Puckett. In the two games Scobey played, their defense only committed two errors, demonstrating a solid strength of the 1971 team. In what would prove to be a very significant game two weeks later, Plentywood, trailing Circle 6-2 in the ninth inning, shockingly scored five runs, *all with two outs*, to come from behind and win 7-6, earning the third seed in the east and a berth in the state tournament. Could Scobey's old archrival and nemesis thwart them at the state tournament two weeks later in Scobey?

The western divisional, hosted at Havre, was played a week after the eastern divisional, and it was double elimination. Eight teams participated: Fairfield, Conrad, Great Falls Sparkies, Helena Reps, Malta, Cut Bank, Toole County Can-Ams (Toole County Can-Ams?), and Havre.

Some bizarre things happened on the field at the western B divisional in Havre. In their first game, the Great Falls Sparkies turned a dropped third strike into a double play to eke a 6-5 win over Fairfield. With one out in the ninth inning, Fairfield had scored one run and had the tying run on third base. Scott Cornell struck out, but the catcher dropped the ball, so the catcher threw to first, nailing Cornell, then the first baseman threw to home for the final out. In another bizarre game, the Great Falls Sparkies scored 37 runs on 31 hits to win 37-20 over the Toole County Can-Ams, who used five pitchers in the game. This score made the 24-23 Wolf Point slugfest over Scobey in the 1975 eastern divisional championship game look like a pitcher's duel. Then, Havre's semifinal game against Cut Bank on Friday was suspended due to darkness—Havre's field did not have lights at the time—with the score tied 3-3. The Havre and Cut Bank players had to get up at six o'clock on Saturday morning to resume the game! Finally, not to be outdone by Plentywood, who had scored five runs with two outs in the ninth to beat Circle 7-6 and earn the third seed in the east, Fairfield matched the feat in the west. Trailing the Great Falls Sparkies 7-3 in the bottom of the eighth, Fairfield scored five runs *with two outs* to take the lead 8-7, then held Great Falls in the ninth to win it and earn the third seed in the west. They did one-up Plentywood, though—their two-out rally started with *no one on base*. Unbelievable. Plentywood had baserunners on before their second out was recorded. Only in Legion baseball. And only in the wild, wild west.

After winning their first game 21-0 over Malta, Havre went on to win the west, winning the suspended semifinal game 4-3 over Cut Bank, then Conrad 29-5 in the chipper on Saturday. Havre then met Conrad again in the championship on Sunday. In that game, Conrad's Bill Schlepp hit a two-run home run in the top of the eighth to tie it 4-4, but Havre went on to win another one-run game, 5-4. The championship win for Havre was significant because it earned them a first-round bye in the state tournament and did not require them to play another game on Monday against Conrad in the double-elimination tournament.

So, when all the dust settled in in the Wild West on Sunday—including dropped third strike game-ending double plays, 37-20 slugfests, six o'clock in the morning start times, five-run, two-out rallies, and 14 games—it was Havre, Conrad, and Fairfield headed to State in Scobey on Thursday.

STATE TOURNAMENT

THE EXCITEMENT IN DANIELS COUNTY WAS BUILDING FOR opening day on Thursday, August 12, 1971, as Scobey hosted its second state tournament. On the opening day of the tournament two years earlier in 1969, Havre left fielder Micky Williams recalls, "When we got to Scobey to check in the hotel, there was no one there, only a sign that read, WENT TO BASEBALL GAME, SIGN IN AND TAKE A KEY." No doubt the 1971 tournament was the same. In its opening day edition, the *Daniels County Leader* trumpeted the arrival of all the teams and again communicated the pride of Scobey's baseball tradition, saying, "The tournament will be played at the Scobey Ball Park, one of the finest diamonds in the state of Montana."[46] John Higgins, tournament director, commended the crews and committees, mentioning that MDU had the lighting system ready to go and that Nemont Telephone had provided telephones at the dugouts and official points.

KCGM radio, "Voice of the Prairies"—its first broadcast not two months earlier on June 21, 1971—was broadcasting the tournament live on the radio, with Cliff Hagfeldt calling the games. The 24-page tournament program, prepared by Charles Cassidy, was top-notch and included pictures of all the tournament teams, the 1925 Scobey baseball team, the 1960 Plainsmen, and the 1969 state championship team. It

Cliff Hagfeldt, with earphones and microphone in hand, announcing the ball games at the Legion baseball state tournament for Scobey's new radio station, KCGM. At his right, Jack Reiner, official scorekeeper; then, Don Murray, chairman of the grounds committee; and John Higgins, tournament director. *Leader photo, Milton Gunderson.*

had a fantastic article titled "AREA BASEBALL," which covered "Baseball Country" history from the homesteaders in the early 1900s through 1971.

Jack Reiner, tournament director two years earlier and now official scorekeeper, welcomed everyone by saying, "No matter how it goes, the fans will see interesting action. This is baseball country." The pride of the Scobey baseball tradition was on full display.

While everyone knew that Havre and Scobey were favored to meet again in the championship game, Tom Nielson and Doc Norman were generous in their pre-tournament assessments of the chances for the other teams in the field. In the *Great Falls Tribune*, Tom Nielson said, "Don't discount the rest of the field," and Doc said, "Don't discount the other teams in the eastern division. They can really hit the ball."[47] Havre had two one-run wins in their divisional, while Scobey had a much easier time in the east.

First-round play pitted Ekalaka against Fairfield and Plentywood against Conrad. Havre would play the winner of the Ekalaka-Fairfield game and Scobey, the winner of the Plentywood-Conrad game. In the first game, Ekalaka drubbed Fairfield 18-8. (What was it with those bats in Baker and Ekalaka? Doc had said the "eastern teams could hit the ball," and he was right.) And Conrad beat Plentywood 11-5, setting up the Havre-Ekalaka and Scobey-Conrad matchups in the evening.

In the first evening session game, Havre trounced Ekalaka 15-2, with Scott Kato going the distance, striking out seven. Havre collected 15 hits, with Dave Cole going 4-6 with four singles, driving in five runs. Kurt Grimm was 2-5, and John Bryant was 3-5. The *Gazette* wrote that Havre "gave every indication that it will repeat as champion."[48] Well, one blowout opening game win against a three-seed doesn't guarantee that. Scobey, meanwhile, won a close one over Conrad 2-1. Big Jim Hansen went the distance for Scobey, scattering eight hits, outdueling Rod Hauer from Conrad in the pitcher's duel. Scobey's two runs were the result of leadoff hitter Don Higgins. He led off the game with a triple and scored on Rick Danelson's single for Scobey's first run, then slammed "a towering 345-foot home run" in the third, which proved to be the winning run. Bill Schlepp produced the only run off of Hansen on a double in the third. There was no scoring after that. Scobey's defense again was strong, as they only made one error and allowed Hansen to yield only one run on eight hits.

The Havre and Scobey's expected opening-day wins set up the highly anticipated semifinal matchup. Tom Nielson would start his ace, Dave Fanning; Doc would start his ace, Terry Puckett. Havre vs. Scobey. Fanning vs. Puckett.

Ace left-hander vs. ace left-hander. State Legion semifinal. Scobey Ball Park. What more could you ask for? Could Scobey finally get over the hump and avoid another "dirt route" path to a championship? Facing undefeated Fanning was daunting, but Scobey had Terry Puckett on the mound and a good defense. They had a chance. If they could just manufacture a run—or two—off Fanning, maybe. Stranger things have happened. Maybe.

The game started at 5:30 p.m. on Friday. Dad had talked a lot about Fanning at home, and Uncle Reese told Dad that Terry was pitching for Scobey, so the dream matchup would happen. After Dad drove Jon and me to the game, I stood to the right of home plate as you faced the field, behind the backstop, under the crow's nest, just in front of the Legion Burgers stand. This was the best position to watch a game at Scobey Ball Park. You were close enough to home plate that you could see the hitters, and since most hitters were right-handed, you could see them facing you and their expressions as they were up to bat. You could also see the pitchers and hear the seams of their fastballs cut the air as they hissed toward home plate. The only thing you had to resist was the smell of the Legion burgers behind you wafting through the air. I reached my hands out in front of me, shoulder height, and clawed my fingers through the wires on the backstop—I was ready to watch this game. And, if Doc needed me, this ten-year-old boy from Peerless was ready to go in.

Weirdly, Scobey was in the first-base dugout. I watched them play many games, but never remembered them in the first-base dugout. When it was just a regular season game, they were always in the home third-base dugout, which I had been in sometimes during games. Two years earlier, in 1969, Doc won the coin flip for the championship game and chose the third base dugout *over the home team*. Scobey was the home team for this game, and they were in the first base dugout, so I wonder if Doc won the coin flip and chose the home team for this one, and Tom Nielson chose the third base dugout? Maybe Tom was superstitious, too.

Once the game started, it moved fast. Blink, and you will have missed it. Hitter after hitter, pitch after pitch, out after out, the pitcher's duel quickly unfolded. Modern Major League Baseball would have loved it—the game was skipping by. Fanning and Puckett had command of all their pitches—mostly fastballs—and were always getting ahead of hitters. Baserunners were a rare commodity. The only exception was one walk issued by each pitcher and two singles by Dave Fanning in each of his first two at-bats. There were no extra-base hits. Standing where I was under the crow's nest on the first-base side, I could see the

Scobey hitters walking back to the first-base dugout after a strikeout, shrugging their shoulders at the on-deck hitter, like "What can you do?" They would gently carry their bats with them. There was not a lot of action for the Scobey batboys in this one.

In every half-inning, the monotonic drone from Vern Veis's voice over the microphone in the crow's nest was "no runs, no hits, no errors, no one left on base." No errors. The superb fielding by both teams matched the excellent pitching. Balls were getting put into play—granted, not getting hit sharply—and fielded cleanly by both defenses. The final box score showed no errors by either team. There were strikeouts, of course—11 by each pitcher at the end of the game—but each team fielded 16 balls cleanly for outs. At Scobey Ball Park on August 13, 1971, no better baseball was being played on the planet. These were two well-coached, talented American Legion teams competing at an extremely high level of baseball. Goose egg after goose egg went in the scorebook, and the innings went by fast with virtually no traffic on the bases.

Then, with one gone in the bottom of the sixth, a breakthrough for Scobey. Speedy center fielder Don Higgins laid down a perfect bunt and beat it out for a single. Homering and tripling the day before to beat Conrad, Higgins now used his legs to get on base against Fanning. The fact that he had just broken up Fanning's no-no was not important—Scobey had a baserunner! And a speedy one at that.

When a baserunner gets on in a pitcher's duel in the later innings, the strategic baseball wheels start to churn. Somehow, Scobey had to get this baserunner to second base. I love pitcher's duels—strategy and tactical execution can win or lose the game, not a three-run home run. Doc had three options to get Higgins to second: sacrifice bunt, hit-and-run, or all-out steal. I learned these three options by playing Strat-O-Matic baseball with Kelly Norman and my friends in Peerless when the weather was too hot or cold to go outside and play. My favorite was the hit-and-run. What option would Doc choose? Answer: all-out steal by Higgins. Doc probably gave him the green light, but who knows?

Rick Danelson was the next hitter up, and he had converted from a switch-hitter to batting all left in 1971, so this was a left-on-left matchup. My eyes were riveted on the gazelle at first; as he slowly stepped his lead toward second, his eyes locked on Fanning. Fanning went into his stretch, raised his right leg high toward first, but looked at catcher Kurt Grimm, and Higgins broke for second. All-out steal! Fanning then quickly shot his eyes toward first and slung a sidearm fastball to the first baseman. Higgins was sprinting toward second. Knowing he didn't have any time, the first baseman delivered the ball quickly, but the throw was high. Havre's shortstop leaped high to make the catch, landed, and snapped the tag down. Higgins slid in a cloud of dust. Out or safe? Out! No! Almost as soon as Scobey had a baserunner, he was quickly removed from the board, and the "threat" (can we call it that?) was over. There was a groan from the crowd, and I was among them.

Don Higgins remembers the pickoff this way: "I had taken off for second base, and the Havre first baseman threw the ball high, and I was safe at second. That is how I remember it." Asked why Doc didn't bunt Rick to sacrifice him to second, Don said, "I can't remember Rick ever bunting. Stealing me was the way Doc always played it." He had stolen 29 bases in as many games the year before, so why not?

The irony in this game is that as close to perfect as Fanning was on the mound, he was closer to perfect at the plate. In his first two plate appearances against Terry, he singled. In his interview, Terry recalls, "It was a fast game, and there were not a lot of baserunners on either side. As well as I pitched, Dave was a little better. I think Dave either drove in the only run or scored the only run; I can't remember which." Well, it was the latter, Terry. Dave scored the only run.

In the top of the seventh, the next half-inning after Higgins's bunt single, Fanning, having singled twice off Terry, approached the plate for the third time. He singled again—another rare baserunner for Havre. The game being in the late innings, it was time for Tom Nielson to decide. He chose the sacrifice bunt, executed perfectly by Kurt Grimm, and Fanning made it safely to second. Fanning became the first—and only—baserunner in scoring position in the entire game.

Fixated on the game and resisting the urge to turn around to get a better whiff of the Legion burgers sizzling behind me, I remained standing under the crow's nest, fingers still clawed to the backstop, as I watched Terry deliver the fateful pitch to the next hitter, Arlen Hanson. He swung. It was a ground ball, not hit that sharply, but it was between third baseman Rick Danelson and shortstop Dana Audet. Because of where I was standing, I had a clear view of the ball's path. It was just past Rick's forehand reach at third, but maybe Dana could get to it with his backhand? Oh, so close, but no! The ball just evaded his outstretched backhand reach and rolled into left field. Hansen charged it and picked the ball up, but it was barely rolling to him when he got to it. With two outs, Fanning was running on contact. Tom Nielson was waving him home, and he scampered around third base, scoring easily. There was no play at the plate. Jim Hansen's throw came into second base. My memory of Fanning crossing home plate with his pitcher's jacket on was how he picked up Hanson's bat nonchalantly and carried it back to the dugout with him.

Beat by a single, a bunt, and another single. Small ball. It seemed like winning a game like this should be a bigger blow, but it wasn't. Havre took the lead 1-0, and Fanning was perfect the rest of the way. He had beaten Scobey with both his arm and his bat. The game lasted only 95 minutes. Not counting fouled pitches, Fanning threw only 80 pitches; Terry about 100.[49]

The two teams then shook hands. There was mutual respect between the coaches, players, and teams of those golden Havre-Scobey years in the late 1960s and 1970s. Dave Fanning said, "Every time we played Scobey, especially if I pitched, Doc was the first one to shake my hand and talk. Great man, coach, and fan." As the teams lined up to shake hands, Dallas Hagfeldt remembers a few Havre players saying, "See you in the championship." That is what everyone expected, but Plentywood had other ideas.

Dana Audet, who Arlen Hanson's RBI single had barely evaded at shortstop, said about the epic game: "It was one of the greatest games I was ever part of. Dave Fanning and Terry Puckett were pitching. The only hit against Dave was a bunt single by Donnie Higgins, whose time from home to first was impressive, to say the least. I still tell people that one of my baseball claims to fame is grounding out and flying out against Dave and only striking out once. Two of the best pitchers to ever play Legion ball in Montana, in my opinion." And Danny Wolfe said, "I remember the Havre game, Dave Fanning against Terry Puckett, and thinking to myself, these have got to be the two best pitchers in the state."

Once again, as they had done two years earlier, Havre had beaten Scobey in the semifinal and put themselves in the driver's seat to win the tournament. Could Scobey come back through the dirt route to set up their third consecutive state championship matchup against Havre? If that was going to happen, they had to get past Plentywood, their old rival, first. The *Gazette* referred to them as Scobey's "archfoe."[50] In his interview, Dana Audet mentioned the rivalry Scobey and Plentywood had, not just in baseball, but in football and basketball. Recall that two weeks earlier, Plentywood had scored five runs with two outs in the ninth against Circle at the eastern divisional in Circle just to qualify for the state tournament. This was a scrappy team. At the state tournament, Plentywood had traveled their dirt route. In their first game, they lost to Conrad 11-5 but then won successive games against Ekalaka (10-5) and Conrad (11-5) to earn the right to play Scobey. Scobey had handled them easily during the regular season, so that shouldn't be a problem, right? Baseball can be cruel.

Doc's two left-handers had pitched brilliantly in their two complete-game wins against Conrad and Havre. Jim Hansen and Terry Puckett had yielded only two earned runs in eighteen innings, an ERA of 1.00. And as well as they had pitched, their defense was even better, committing only one error against Conrad and no errors against Havre. What had been silent to this point was their bats.

Doc's third pitcher in 1971 was Danny Wolfe. He was expected to start against Plentywood to get to the championship game, but Doc did not always do the expected—he often did the unexpected. He handed the ball to Larry Grayson, who had pitched limited innings during the season but had started two games and had a 2-0 record. What was Doc's calculus here? Danny Wolfe said, "Doc thought we could beat Plentywood easy, and he would pitch Grayson and save me for the championship."

It's uncanny how Doc's head-scratching decisions almost always seem to work. Larry Grayson pitched brilliantly. He had a *shutout* going into the bottom of the seventh inning. Six goose eggs had gone on the board for Plentywood—a good-hitting team—and Scobey had mustered four runs against Terry Lee to take a 4-0 lead headed into the stretch. But what happened next was nothing anyone could have predicted.

To that point in the tournament, Scobey had committed only one error in 24 innings, fielding all but one chance cleanly. Their pitching had only allowed two runs in 24 innings, a 0.75 ERA. Then, the train went off the rails. The wheels came off. The floodgates opened. The walls

Dave Fanning, Havre pitcher 1970–1972. *Great Falls Tribune.*

Dave Fanning in 1971

collapsed. Pick your metaphor. Two errors in the bottom of the seventh led to an unearned Plentywood run, and Grayson's shutout was gone, but Scobey still led 4-1. But a small hole had been punctured in the dam, and water was trickling out. The contagion of the two errors in the seventh carried into the eighth when the dam broke for Scobey. A well-oiled fielding machine to that point, Scobey committed four errors, Hansen came in to relieve Grayson, and Plentywood plated five runs—four unearned—on just two hits. Shockingly, Plentywood, as they had done two weeks earlier against Circle, scored five runs to come from behind and carried a 6-4 lead into the ninth. Grayson had yielded only one earned run on six hits—two each by Russ Anderson and Lee Kitzenberg—in eight innings; he had done his job. The gloves were the culprit.

Gary Lee—pitching to his twin brother Terry—needed just three outs to complete the upset, but those three outs for Plentywood were not easy; Scobey rallied and went down with a fight. They came back in the top of the ninth and loaded the bases, but managed to send only one runner home, and Plentywood ran off the field with a 6-5 upset, spoiling the Scobey-Havre rematch for the state championship for the hometown fans. Baseball can be cruel.

Dallas Hagfeldt remembers the error contagion. In his interview, he said, "A ball popped out of my glove in right field." He felt bad about it; it was what he remembered about the game. However, in the photo of Danny Wolfe sliding home safely against Plentywood and Hansen running to third, that was on a hit to right field by Dallas, but that's not what he remembers. It's strange how, fifty years later, that is his main memory of the 1971 tournament. I am the same way, and other players I talk to, especially my teammates from the 1976-79 teams, remember the mistakes better than the good plays. Why is that? I think it is because the feeling of letting your teammates down is the most powerful memory an athlete can have, and it sticks with you. You want to go back and change it, but you can't. It haunts you. Dana Audet also recalls Plentywood as one of his main memories of the 1971 tournament, saying, "We never should have lost to Plentywood." But the scrappy Plentywood team has to be given a lot of credit for battling and seizing their opportunity.

Havre was in the state championship for the fourth consecutive year, this time facing Plentywood, who "seemed to get stronger each game in the tournament."[51] But they would have to get much stronger to beat Havre—twice. That was an almost impossible task, as "Plentywood was a tired team, playing its fifth game, and also running out of pitchers."[52] As he had done the two previous years, Coach Tom Nielson handed the ball to Kurt Grimm to start the championship game. Plentywood coach John Lagerquist started Terry Lee. Havre scored two runs in the bottom of the first, collected single runs in the third and fourth, two in the fifth and sixth, and a single run in the eighth

Dan Wolfe slides home safely with a run against Plentywood. Catcher **Terry Lee** has already received the long throw from the field and is making his move toward the runner. *Leader photo, Milton Gunderson.*

to win 9-2. Kurt Grimm went the distance, scattering six hits. He also helped his cause with two hits, including an RBI triple, and Havre celebrated its second consecutive state championship on Scobey's home field. As the sun set that evening in Scobey, the North Star rose in the west, twinkling a little brighter than usual. And as the sun rose the following day, the sky was not quite as Blue to the east.

Deprived of their second state championship on their home field by Havre in the west and foiled by their age-old nemesis and archrival in the east, Plentywood, Scobey's bronze medal in the 1971 state tournament was bitter to accept, especially for the players in their final season: Danny Wolfe, Jim Hansen, and Don Higgins. It had to be little consolation for these outstanding players that Scobey's future was bright, as Rick Danelson, Dana Audet, Don, and Terry Puckett—their entire starting infield—were all returning, as was new catcher Dallas Hagfeldt.

His younger brother Jay would follow him to Scobey from Glasgow the next year. Barry Higgins, another gazelle from the Higgins herd in Flaxville, would dart into center field to replace older brother Don. This was a young and talented team with a bright future. Expectations for the 1972 season would be high. Could Scobey break through and give Doc his second state championship in 1972? Or would Tom Nielson's Havre team, who had joined Plentywood as another thorn in Scobey's side, again thwart Doc's quest for his second state championship?

TOURNAMENT SUMMARY

As in 1969, the 1971 State B Tournament hosted by Scobey was another successful tournament. "There was exciting and dramatic action in every game."[53] Good crowds were present for most sessions, but the beginning of a fast harvest cut down some attendance.

So many volunteers were needed to host a successful state tournament. Dale Grove was the commander of Post

1971 Plentywood Legion Team, State Runners-up. Standing L-R: Coach John Lagerquist, Gary Lee, Jay Anderson, Rick Syme, Lee Kitzenberg, Terry Lee. Kneeling: Steve Johnson, Russ Anderson, Mike McLean, Dennis Mair, Tom Christensen and Ken Eckerdt. Donnie Holyk of Scobey is batboy. *Leader photo, Milton Gunderson.*

56. John Higgins was tournament chairman, with Reese Puckett and Ben Danelson helping him on the committee. After the tournament, John said it was a great experience, but he didn't know as he wanted to go through it again. The other major volunteers were Cliff Hanson (tickets), Don Murray (grounds), Jack Reiner and John Murphy (scoring); Vern Veis, John Murphy, Reid Grayson (public address); Joyce Wolfe, Marge Norman, Mazel Audet (housing); Else Daniels, American Legion Auxiliary (meals); Cliff Hagfeldt, Duane Holtan, Plentywood (radio); and Charlie Cassidy, "the dependable loose ends man" (tournament book preparation). The umpires, who "did an excellent job,"[54] were Ron Ewing, umpire-in-chief, Sidney; Jerry Butner, Sidney; Andy Stolen, Glentana; and Stuart Polk, Plentywood. These volunteers all "brought high praise" from State Legion Commissioner John Russell from Anaconda.

The *Leader* proudly summed up the Daniels County effort to host the tournament: "The conduct of the tournament, the conditions of the grounds, the officiating, and the

1971 Havre Legion Team, State B champions. Back row, L-R: Coach Tom Nielson, Jay Waterman, Steve Malmberg, Mike D'Hooge, Gary Sohm, Kurt Grimm, Arlen Hanson, Dave Fanning, Ass't Coach Hank Tweeten. Front row: Dean Elliot, John Bryant, Dave Cole, Scott Kato, Dick Clark, Mike Welch. *Leader photo, Milton Gunderson.*

Cliff Hanson (left) was tourney ticket chairman, and besides overseeing the job, helping with tournament preparations, and lining up sellers, he was at the gate at every session but one. To the right, with the apron on, is **Oscar Thompson,** one of the helpers. *Leader photo, Milton Gunderson.*

John Russell of Butte, State Legion ball chairman; **John Bryant** of Havre, State chairman of Class B; and **John Higgins** of Flaxville, Chairman of Post 56 baseball and tournament chairman. *Leader photo, Milton Gunderson.*

accommodations provided the visiting teams in housing and meals once again demonstrated that Scobey is baseball country. And for the second time in three years, Daniels County baseball enthusiasts have proven that it doesn't take a big town to host state tournaments."[55] Nobody could host a state baseball tournament like Scobey could back in the day.

The *Leader* added, as a coda to its meticulous coverage of the 1971 tournament, "Incidentally, perhaps it's about time the Legion team here is called the 'Daniels County Legionnaires,' or something like that, considering the major contribution in players being made by other communities in the county, especially Flaxville and Peerless."[56] This was an interesting comment about the team's name. Before 1977, when the Scobey American Legion team was first dubbed the "Blues," the *Leader* routinely referred to the team as the "Scobey Legionnaires." The first reference to the team as the "Legionnaires" was in a headline in 1949; in 1959, writer Printer Bowler routinely referred to the team as the Scobey Legionnaires in his articles. This moniker stuck, and the teams in the 1960s and 1970s were referred to as the Scobey Legionnaires by the paper up to 1977. Separately, the high school teams in the 1950s were sometimes called the "Scholars." The first reference to the town team as the "Plainsmen" was in 1948.

TOURNAMENT STATS

Hitting

DAVE FANNING, IN ADDITION TO PITCHING HIS ONE-HIT SHUTout against Scobey, was also the leading hitter in the tournament with a .545 average. He had three of the five hits off Terry in the 1-0 pitcher's duel and scored the game's lone run. Scobey had clutch hitting from Don Higgins, who had the bunt single in Fanning's one-hitter. Against Conrad, he tripled in the first inning and scored on Rick Danelson's single, then hit a 345-ft home run off Conrad's Hauer in the third inning, scoring both runs for Scobey's single-run victory to lead them to the semifinal against Havre.

Pitching

THERE WAS GREAT PITCHING IN THE 1971 TOURNAMENT. The Fanning-Puckett 1-0 pitcher's duel in the semifinal was a marvel to watch, but the Scobey-Conrad game was also a great pitcher's duel between Jim Hansen of Scobey and Ron Hauer of Conrad. Scobey won 2-1, with Hansen and Hauer both going the distance. In the tournament, Havre's pitchers—Kato, Fanning, and Grimm—only allowed four earned runs in three games (1.33 ERA). Scobey's pitching was even better, only allowing three earned runs in 26 innings (1.03 ERA), as five of the six runs off Grayson and Hansen were unearned. Until the eighth inning against Plentywood, Scobey pitchers had only allowed three total runs in 25 innings, but Plentywood's five-run eighth—with only two hits—doomed them. Scott Kato and Kurt Grimm were the other winners for Havre besides Fanning. Havre's fourth pitcher, Arlen Hanson, did not have to deliver a pitch in the tournament. Hansen, Puckett, and Grayson pitched for Scobey. If Terry was a hard-luck pitcher, Pat Whaley of Fairfield might have had it worse—he struck out 17 Conrad hitters but lost the game 13-5, as his team committed 10 errors behind him. Plentywood's winning pitchers in their three wins were Russ Anderson, Terry Lee, and Gary Lee. Rick Syme took the loss against Conrad.

Fielding

EXCEPT FOR SCOBEY'S FATEFUL SEVENTH AND EIGHTH-INNING implosion against Plentywood, Scobey's fielding was stellar, as they only committed one error in 25 innings. Tournament champion Havre's defense was as good as their pitching. They played errorless ball against Ekalaka and Scobey, then committed four errors against Plentywood in the championship, but it didn't matter. Plentywood's defense had to be good to win three games, and it was. After booting seven balls against Conrad in their opening-game loss, they settled down, averaging only two errors per game. Fifteen-year-old Plentywood shortstop Mike McLean, who went on to play baseball for Minot State from 1976-79, was steady at short the entire tournament. He said of the Fanning-Puckett duel, "It was the best game I ever saw up to that point in my life."

STATE A TOURNAMENT

STATE B CHAMPION HAVRE AGAIN AUTOMATICALLY QUALIFIED for the State A Tournament, this time as the number three seed in the west. As such, they were pitted against the Billings Royals, the number one seed in the east, at Cobb Field in Billings in the first game. On the day of the game, the *Leader* wrote that it would be "interesting" to watch Havre play the Royals.[57] "Interesting" would be one word for it—"incredible" would be better. Or how about sportswriter Norm Clark's word in the *Gazette*: "Fannnnntastic"?[58]

After his compelling duel against Terry Puckett in Scobey, Dave Fanning once again found himself engaged in a pitcher's duel, this time against another left-hander, Paul McClure, from Billings. Through seven innings, no runs were scored, and McClure had a no-hitter. Then, Billings scored a run in the top of the eighth on a single up the middle by Ed Yurick. Havre answered in the bottom half when ninth-place hitter, 6-foot-8 first baseman Gary Sohm tagged a 335-foot home run, breaking up McClure's no-hitter and tying the game 1-1. The score stood through 12 innings when both pitchers had to be removed from the game due to the Legion 12-inning rule. Fanning had struck out 25 Royals—a record—and McClure struck out 11 Northstars. Fanning yielded five hits and walked four; McClure gave up three hits, walking five.

In the top of the 13th, Tom Nielson brought in Arlen Hanson—who had not pitched in Scobey—and Billings relieved McClure with Jim Rogers. Catcher Charlie Yegen drove in a single run for Billings in the top of the 14th for a 2-1 Billings lead, but once again Havre countered in their half. Billings pitcher Jim Rogers walked in the tying run and was relieved by Scott Keller. The next hit was a ground ball to the infield. The throw to the plate was in time for the force-out, but the catcher dropped the ball to allow the winning run to score, and Havre jubilantly walked it off with a 3-2 win on Cobb Field in Billings. Clarke wrote that the game was "one of the most dramatic contests staged at Cobb Field."

Havre received a second-round bye and played Miles City—who had beaten the Electrics and Missoula—in the semifinal. Miles City came away with a close 8-6 win. Scott Kato started, and Arlen Hanson relieved for Havre. In their rematch against Billings, Kurt Grimm pitched for Havre and went the distance, striking out eight, but the Royals won 5-2, squelching a Havre rally in the ninth to advance. Billings beat Miles City twice—13-2 and 7-6—to win their 17th state championship in 18 years. Billings catcher Charlie Yegen, who committed the error to allow the winning run to score in their loss to Havre, drove in the tying and winning runs with a two-run single in the seventh to win the championship for Billings. It's nice to see that, especially after the *Gazette* had referred to him as the "goat" after their first game.[59]

It was an incredible year for Coach Tom Nielson and the Havre American Legion Post 11 Northstars, winning the State B Tournament in Scobey and finishing third at the State A in Billings. Havre finished the season with a 55-13 record. In his interview years later with Assistant Sports Editor Scott Mansch of the *Great Falls Tribune*, Dave said about the 1971 season: "It was just one of those years where everything went right. Just a dream season."[60]

EXTRA INNINGS

PLENTYWOOD HAD PREVIOUSLY TAKEN SECOND PLACE AT STATE to Sidney in 1966. They won state in 1954.

One of the no-hitters Fanning threw earlier in the season was in a seven-inning 16-0 win over the Billings Scarlets. He struck out 22 hitters in seven innings. How do you strike out 22 hitters in seven innings? Wouldn't that only be 21 hitters? One strikeout was a wild pitch, so on the dropped third strike rule, the hitter reached first base. One other hitter walked. No Scarlet *hit a fair ball* in the game. That's amazing, you think. Yes, but Dave McNally can top that. Against Livingston, he pitched a seven-inning no-hitter, striking out all 21 hitters, where *not even a foul ball* was struck! No hitter from Livingston even touched the ball.

Paul McClure, who pitched 12 innings against Havre in the first game, came back to pitch nine additional innings for a total of 21 innings in the tournament. He pitched seven innings in the 13-2 win against the first game against Miles City, then threw two shutout innings in the final for a save. Paul McClure went on to play college ball as an outfielder and first baseman for the University of Wyoming. The Boston Red Sox drafted him in the 8th round of the 1974 MLB June Amateur Draft from the University of Wyoming. He played three seasons of minor league A ball in Florida and North Carolina from 1974-76, finishing with a .271 minor league average as an outfielder and first baseman. In 1970, Paul McClure hit a three-run triple off Danny Wang to give Billings a 7-4 win over Scobey.

The Miles City Mavericks were referred to as "the dirty dozen," as several of their players were injured during the season, and they scrapped their way to the championship game against Billings with only 12 players. The crowds were big at Cobb Field as many fans came down from Miles City to watch the championship games against Billings. A crowd of 2,370 watched the 7-6 championship game.

Cobb Field's official scorekeeper, Bob Pasquarello, missed the Friday games because his wife was having a baby. At Thursday's tense Havre-Royals game, the Brooklyn native quipped, "This is more fun than having a baby."[61]

Cary Veis, whom I mostly talk to about basketball on the phone, was at the Havre-Billings game and remembers it as the best baseball game he ever saw.

Clark Shaffer was the starting shortstop for the Missoula Mavericks in the 1971 State A Tournament. Clark was my basketball coach at Peerless High School during the 1977 and 1978 seasons and led the Panthers to their first-ever state tournament berth in 1978. Jon, Ray, and I got to play with him on the Peerless baseball field when he came to play in a fast-pitch tournament in Peerless in August 1979, which we won. He pitched, I played short, Jon played third, and Ray played first. I remember him telling me once that Legion ball misses a lot of good athletes on the field because many of them work during the summer months.

Seven scouts saw Fanning pitch his 25-strikeout gem against the Royals, although he was being watched long before that. He signed a contract to play with the Phillies organization and won 29 games with a 2.97 ERA in his professional career, striking out 268 hitters. He pitched for Auburn in the A-New York-Pennsylvania League (1972), Spartanburg in the A Western Carolinas League (1973), and Rocky Mount in the Carolina League (1974).

Dave said he regretted signing the professional baseball contract and wished he had accepted a full-ride scholarship to play at Gonzaga, where his parents could have watched him play. "I had a full-ride offer to Gonzaga; they were in the Big Sky at the time. My parents were a different denomination, so they weren't thrilled about it. My dad really wanted me to sign with the Phils. When I signed it was supposed to be in Walla Walla, Washington, then it ended up in Auburn, New York. Thought my folks would get to see me; as it turned out, they didn't. I received a note from Doc after the A state tournament in Billings, congratulating me on my game, and he wished I would have gone to college instead of signing with the Phillies. I had a lot of respect for him and Tom Nielson. I wish now I would have talked to both of them more before I made my decision. Water under a lot bridges."

The *Gazette* recognized Fanning's brilliance, but knowledgeable sportswriter Norm Clarke also saw the brilliance in Coach Tom Nielson, writing that Fanning "has to share kudos with Coach Tom Nielson, who has molded a well-polished and heads-up crew."[62]

The 1971 tournament program was dedicated to N. C. Wolfe (1917-1971), who passed away on May 10, 1971. He was chairman of the Post 56 baseball committee at the time of his death.

Doc protected his players on and off the field, sometimes bailing them out—literally in this case—of unseemly situations. In the 1960s and early 1970s, "mooning" became a popular "sport," and the craze did not escape the Scobey Legion team. As Terry Puckett recalls in his first year with the team as a 13-year-old in 1968, "There was a lot of bad stuff the older players did. Some of it was pretty bad. Sticking body parts out the window, mooning people, getting stopped by cops for mooning, it goes on and on, and getting Kelly to do it when he was just so little. I don't know how Kelly grew up to be normal." I said to Terry, "Kelly's not normal." He replied, "He shouldn't be! Growing up with the old guys on the 1968-69 team kinda ruined all of us!" Danny Wolfe, in his interview, elegantly defined mooning as "hanging your ass out the window when passing a car on the road." Wolfe recalls an incident in May 1971 where things came to a head. Some of Doc's former players—Wolfe remembers Craig Audet, Jerry LaPierre, and Danny Wang, but there was one other, maybe Dick Puckett—were driving back from Billings to Scobey from his dad's funeral. They got behind a woman driving slowly and couldn't pass her. Once they could pass, a couple of the boys flipped their moons out the window. The driver took down the license plate number and contacted the sheriff's department in Scobey, who then contacted the county attorney. Wolfe tells it, "When those guys got to town, I don't know if you'd call it arrested, but there they were up in front of the county attorney, who was, I think, Mike Traynor at the time. I don't know if somebody called Doc, but Doc got wind of it. Anyway, he called down there and said, 'What the hell, Mike, what's going on? You got my boys down there.' Mike said, 'Well, apparently, they took their pants down and stuck their asses out the window; they call it mooning.' Then Doc said, 'Jesus Christ, Mike, you're not gonna get my boys for something like that; they're just kids.' Anyway, they got a scolding from the county attorney, and then they let them go. Mike Traynor was the county attorney, and of course, he and Doc played cards. They played bridge, and they played poker and all that stuff. I think maybe Craig or Wang or somebody called Doc."

Doc's needle saw plenty of action in the 1971 state tournament. As Terry Puckett recalls, "In the dugout at the state tournament, Doc was shooting me up with the needle in my pitching arm just before the game. Doc would sometimes give me painkillers before games and DMSO, and sometimes the needle. He normally did it at the hotel or some other place prior to coming to the field, but this time it was in the dugout. Ron Ewing [home plate umpire for the game and chief umpire for the tournament] walked by the dugout just as Doc was shooting the needle in my pitching arm and asked, 'Whatcha doin' there, Doc?' Doc quickly replied, "He's got a cold, Ron, he's sick." Danny Wolfe recalls the incident exactly as Terry tells it, adding that "Doc always had his black bag in the dugout."

One of the things I'm grateful for from the 1971 tournament is that I got to see my older cousin Terry pitch when he could still throw, even though, by this time, the wear and tear on his arm was already there. As Terry said about the needle incident, "My arm was already bad by 1971." In the spring and summer, Dad would always tell me that Uncle Reese would tell him that Terry had a sore arm. I would wince when I heard it—I wanted to hear that Terry's arm was strong, not weakened. Terry's arm would steadily decline after 1971. In 1972 and 1973, his arm would progressively worsen after all the innings he had pitched. His arm had already seen a lot of innings at this point. As a 13-year-old in 1968, he had pitched a combined two-hitter with Dick against Havre at the state tournament. As a 14-year-old in 1969, he pitched eight innings against the Royals, giving up only two runs, then pitched seven shutout innings against Havre in the 1969 tournament, relieving Dick. But when I think of Terry Puckett and the brilliant pitcher that he was, it will always be that game against Fanning at Scobey Ball Park on August 13, 1971. That was Terry Puckett at his best.

Danny Wolfe recalls Terry's needle-in-the-dugout incident with the chief umpire, but he also got his own needle from Doc in the 1971 tournament. Wolfe recalls, "My back went out before the state tournament, so Doc took me up to the office, got me on the table, and got this needle out. I was looking over there, and he said, 'You just don't be looking here.' He got this goddamn six-inch needle out and said, 'Now goddamn it, this is really serious business here, now goddamn it, you don't move.' He got up on the table and put his knee between my shoulders. He said, 'Now goddamn it don't move, and he starts sticking that needle in my back, and I flinched, and he said, 'Goddamn you, I told you not to move, now don't move anymore,' and I said, 'Well, it hurts,' and he says, 'Oh, buck up!'" and so anyway, he gave me the shot in my back and I went on to play."

I asked Terry what the best game he ever pitched was. Would you believe he did not say the 1-0 pitcher's duel with Fanning? He said, "I think the best game I ever pitched might have been against the Plainsmen in 1971 when I was 16. Doc wanted to kick their asses because a lot of the former Legion players from the 1969 and 1970 teams were back from college for the summer, and they were cocky. Danny Wang was playing. When Danny was running off the field in between innings, he asked me to tell him what my first three pitches would be when he came up next. I told him fastball, slider, curve, but I told him I didn't know what would come after that! I struck him out. In that same game, Doc told me to hit Jack Higgins with a fastball. He said, 'The next time that cocky sonofabitch comes up, you hit him in the chest!' I knew that Jack would know it was on purpose if I hit him." John Murphy remembers the game: "Terry threw a two-hit shutout against a pretty good Plainsmen team I put together when he was 16. Dick threw for the Plainsmen and took the 1-0 hard-luck loss."

The previous year, 1970, there was not an Audet on the Scobey Legion team roster for the first time since 1963 (Phil), but with Dana joining the team in 1971, an Audet would be on the roster through 1983 (Pat). Between 1963 and 1983, there was an Audet on the roster every year except 1970.

Three of the five hits off Terry in the 1-0 pitcher's duel were by Dave Fanning, who also scored the lone run. In Terry's interview, he said he was "pissed off" each time Dave got one of those hits. You would think the left-on-left matchup between Terry and Dave would have made it more difficult for Dave to get those three hits, but Dave batted right-handed. What was that? Dave tells it this way: "Dad said when I grabbed my first bat, I stepped up right-handed, and he tried to change me, but I always went to the right side. So he quit trying. He said he tried to get me to switch-hit, but I always went to the right side. I guess I was always stubborn. My wife would probably say I haven't changed. Ha!" Fanning's stubbornness might have cost Scobey the game. If Fanning batted left-handed, he might not have gotten that third hit, and they might still be playing. If they were, my fingers would still be clawed to the backstop watching the game, and I would be a skeleton, still not having eaten a Legion burger.

Who the hell were the Toole County Can-Ams? Recall they were on the losing end of a 37-20 slugfest in the western divisional against the Great Falls Sparkies. Still, they won a few games during the season, including over the Sparkies and Conrad, and one game in the tournament against Malta. In 1971, Shelby formed its first baseball team, calling them the "Toole County Can-Ams." The *Great Falls Tribune* wrote an article on the team, with the headline titled, "Goodwill via Baseball."⁶³ The Can-Ams were an international team consisting of players from northern Montana and southern Alberta, the only known team in Legion baseball at the time. Players came from Shelby, Milk River, Warner, Coutts, Sunburst, and Kevin. Lloyd Evers, a U.S. citizen, coached the team, but he was a school principal in Canada during the offseason. The Can-Ams were ahead of their time with the international Legion play, as Montana Legion baseball would eventually become Montana/Alberta Legion baseball. So, while they were only in existence for one year, the Toole County Can-Ams were trailblazers for future Montana/Alberta Legion baseball play. Get out, eh.

The notoriety of the Can-Ams' and Sparkies' 37-20 slugfest made international news, as there was a United Press International (UPI) article on the game titled, "What it was was baseball."⁶⁴ The Sparkies had 31 hits in the game, and the Can-Ams scored eight runs in one inning without a hit.

KCGM radio* officially went on the air on Monday, June 21, 1971. In the lead-up to the first broadcast, Larry Bowler was adamant that the station be locally owned and operated. In March 1969, when plans were developing, he said in the *Leader*, "It is essential that this station be owned and operated by people living in the area, to pursue intelligently the best interests of the area, in the public interest." In working with Larry's son, Burl, without whose help *The Blues of Summer* could not have happened, I am grateful that the paper is still locally owned and operated, with the community's interest at heart. I have learned that is not always the case with many other small-town newspapers in Montana.

I mentioned Terry Puckett emerging as a power hitter in 1971. Terry and Don Puckett became power hitters later in their Legion careers, but they didn't start that way. Notice in the team picture how small Don is. How did they get stronger? Terry told me a lot of it had to do with isometrics. Uncle Reese had a book on isometrics by Charles Atlas. I remember seeing the book and leafing through it a few times while visiting. I also remember seeing an ad for Charles Atlas's book in comic books, which showed a bully kicking sand in a skinny kid's face at the beach. Jon and I picked up on the isometrics and got stronger doing isometrics, mostly push-ups, but we never approached the physique or hitting power of Terry and Don.

When Don Higgins got on base against Dave Fanning, the hit-and-run was mentioned as an option. The best hit-and-run I ever saw executed (on TV) was by Tim Foli when he played shortstop for the Montreal Expos in the early 1970s. I used to love watching the Montreal Expos—part of the 1969 baseball expansion—play on Canadian TV. The Expos franchise moved to Washington, DC, in 2005 and became the Washington Nationals. Yet another reason the French Canadians hate us. In Foli's at-bat, the runner took off from first, and the pitcher knew the hit-and-run was on, so he threw the ball high and outside, almost a pitchout, but it wasn't. Foli, as he was swinging, released his bat in the direction of the ball on the same plane, kind of like swinging where the ball was, but he just let the bat slip out of his hands toward the ball. As he released the bat out of his hands, it struck the ball sharply, and it was a line drive between first and second base for a perfectly executed hit-and-run, ending with runners on first and third. He protected the runner. I never executed a hit-and-run quite like that in Strat-O-Matic! With modern-day analytics, you don't see the hit-and-run so much anymore. Hitters do not alter their swings to make contact, whether in a hit-and-run situation or with two strikes. "Protect the plate, choke up, just make contact" are not things you hear anymore, at least not at the major league level. Bat control has faded with every swing, the same in any count or situation.

There were two reasons I watched the complete Scobey-Havre game as a ten-year-old. One was because I loved watching baseball and my older cousin Terry pitch. Still, another reason was that I was lousy at chasing foul balls and retrieving them for a quarter at the Legion burger stand. I tried to compete when I was younger, but couldn't hang with the pros. Chasing foul balls at Scobey Ball Park was not something to be trifled with. I got close to a foul ball once but lost the battle to Alvie Baldry. This was way too competitive and subtle for me. I quickly realized that I was in over my head and that it was much safer to stay in the grandstand, watch the games with my dad, and learn things like why Craig Audet would throw the ball back harder to the pitcher when he was mad at them. There were strategies and analytics; kids knew where the players would hit the ball before they came up. There were coalitions, factions, and

---

* My first memory of KCGM radio was sitting around the kitchen table at night in December 1971, listening to Cliff Hagfeldt broadcast basketball scores from around northeastern Montana. Previously, we had to wait until the next day to read the scores in the *Billings Gazette* or the *Great Falls Tribune* that were brought to the Puckett Mercantile. You could hear the excitement in Cliff's voice announcing the scores over the radio for the first time. It was a Friday night, so I could stay up. Scores were being called into Cliff from various towns throughout northeastern Montana at halftime and even quarter breaks. Peerless was playing in Antelope that night. Percy Kegel made a shot against Antelope with eight seconds left, and Peerless won 60-59. How is that relevant to baseball? The game was won when Terry Puckett rocketed a full-court baseball pass to Percy Kegel for the game-winning layup. Kurt Ueland, Antelope's scorekeeper, unofficially clocked the basketball, traveling 90 miles per hour. It's nice how my first memory of KCGM is of Terry, basketball, and (somehow) baseball.

profit-sharing. By 1971, Gerry Veis had established himself as the alpha. As Dana Audet recalls, "He was always there. He was there so much, I think he knew the tendencies of every player and where they were going to foul it to. Maybe even some opposing players." Before Gerry's reign, John Murphy recalls that "oldsters would remember Pete Darchuk from the late fifties with terror in their hearts!" Sometimes Gerry Veis would nimbly climb up the backstop like Spiderman behind home plate to retrieve a ball when it would get stuck there, then climb down. He would wait between innings to do it, so he didn't interfere with the view of the fans sitting in the stands. Chasing foul balls was part of the Scobey baseball tradition. At the 1983 American Legion World Series in Fargo, North Dakota, Ron Meyer recalls, "Ken Meyer, Maury Audet, and I would chase foul balls for a quarter at the Blues games and were holding our own with the foul balls in Fargo."

I was 10 years old in 1971, playing for Dad in my fifth season for the Peerless Pirates. One of the memories I have of that season is actually at the Scobey Ball Park. I got to catch Jim Hansen warming up between innings in 1971 at a home game in Scobey. When Dad brought Jon and me in to watch the Legion team play home games in Scobey, Jon and I would wiggle our way into the dugout to hang out with batboys Danny, Kelly, and Kirby whenever we could. I loved being in that dugout with the older players, my older cousins Terry and Don, and Doc. My vocabulary expanded significantly in there, with words my mother didn't like me to say. Danny Wolfe must have made the last out of the inning, so someone needed to warm up Jim Hansen in the middle of the inning. I grabbed my glove and ran out to do it. When I got behind home plate, Jim Hansen looked down at me on the mound and couldn't believe it. He wouldn't pitch to me. He was afraid that I couldn't catch the ball and would hurt me if he pitched. He looked into the dugout at Doc, hunched his shoulders up, and held both of his hands out to the side with his palms up like he was pleading: "Doc, I'm not going to pitch to this kid." From the dugout came Doc's booming voice: "Pitch to him!" So he did. At first, he probably threw about 50%, but as each pitch came down, he realized I could catch the ball and he started to throw a little harder. I was beaming with confidence after each pitch came in a little faster. *I'm catching Jim Hansen!* I thought to myself. As each pitch was thrown harder, the most difficult thing about catching it wasn't the speed; it was how much his fastball tailed. It was a very live ball and moved a lot. He might have tapped out at 75 percent, but I can say, to this day, that I caught Jim Hansen.

1972

The North Star Rises in the West for the Third Consecutive Year

> *" I think this is the best chance a B team has had to take it all.*
>
> —**Doc Norman, Great Falls Tribune,** *August 9, 1972* "

1972 Scobey Legionnaires. Standing left to right: Terry Puckett, Rick Danelson, Coach Doc Norman, Dana Audet, Dallas Hagfeldt, Don Puckett. Kneeling left to right: Lee Cook, Mickey Wiley, Duke Trangsrud, Doug Hagfeldt, Jay Hagfeldt, Barry Higgins, Ass't Coach Phil Audet. Sitting: Batboys Kelly Norman, Dan Danelson, Kirby Halvorson. *Leader.*

PRESEASON

We will start the 1972 season with some dramatic time travel, returning to August 14, 1971, and placing ourselves in the Scobey Ball Park dugout with Doc and the team. Doc was addressing the team following Scobey's devastating 6-5 season-ending loss to archrival Plentywood at the 1971 State Tournament in Scobey. In his interview, Dana Audet revealed a shocking announcement from Doc: he would not be returning as coach the following season. What?! This had happened once before with Doc, following the end of the 1966 season, where Scobey had won a 4-2 playoff game against Plentywood to qualify for their first state tournament but was disqualified due to an ineligible player. Doc did not plan to return to coach in 1967. Fortunately, in both instances, Doc returned to the field the following season, as his love of the game and his players could not keep him away despite his demanding day job as a physician. Phew! Doc, those players felt terrible enough after losing to Plentywood and didn't need that drama!

After returning to the field to coach in 1967, something remarkable happened: Doc and ace pitcher Phil Audet led Scobey to its first-ever state tournament appearance. Upon his return in 1972, could Doc also accomplish something special by winning his second state championship? Scobey's roster favored that possibility, although there were huge losses from the 1971 team. Gone were big left-handed pitcher Jim Hansen, veteran catcher Danny Wolfe, speedy center fielder Don Higgins, and pitcher Larry Grayson, who had pitched well against Plentywood in the final game. But a solid nucleus of talented players was returning, including Rick Danelson, Terry Puckett, Dallas Hagfeldt, Don Puckett, Dana Audet, and Barry Higgins. In addition, Jay Hagfeldt, Doug Hagfeldt, Duke Trangsrud, Lee Cook, and

Mickey Wiley joined the team as rookies. The big question for Scobey in 1972 would be their pitching. Terry Puckett was back, but Jim Hansen, Dan Wolfe, and Larry Grayson were gone. Two 16-year-olds, Dana Audet and Jay Hagfeldt, would be the two additional pitchers who would start in the divisional and state tournaments for Doc in 1972.

Looking to the west, Havre lost their top three pitchers, Kurt Grimm, Dave Fanning, and Scott Kato, with only Arlen Hanson returning. They would certainly not be as strong as they had been, but would they still be good enough to win their third consecutive state championship on their home field in Havre?

Scobey had new uniforms in 1972. In his interview, Dana Audet mentioned that they were modeled after the Chicago Cubs. The black pinstripes were still there, but now, on the left front of the jersey was a large, white capital *S* on a red background enclosed in an outlined circle. The previous uniform from 1969-1971 had been "Scobey" in cursive letters on the front with black pinstripes. These uniforms were passed on to the Plainsmen.

REGULAR SEASON

A SIGNIFICANT HIGHLIGHT OF THE 1972 REGULAR SEASON WAS in early June when Doc's friend Ed Bayne brought his legendary Billings Royals team to Scobey Ball Park to play. Since 1950, the Royals had won 20 out of 22 State A championships, including *14 in a row*. Ed Bayne was coaching for Billings for all those 20 championships, as he was assistant coach from 1950-51 and became head coach in 1952. It would be hard to find a program this dominant in any sport, at any level, anywhere, anytime. Scobey had played the Royals before on Cobb Field in Billings, but this was the first—and only—time the storied Post 4 American Legion team from Billings would visit Scobey to play. And it was a close game for eight innings. Doc, as he had done three years earlier in Billings when Terry Puckett was only 14 years old, handed the ball to Terry. And he pitched well against the Royals again. Scobey and Terry were shutting out the Royals and were leading 1-0 in the top of the sixth when Billings picked up two runs on an error and three singles to take a 2-1 lead. The Royals got to Terry for three additional runs in the eighth and won 5-1. But it had to be special for Doc to stay on the field in a close game with the Royals and his friend Ed Bayne at Scobey Ball Park. No moral victories, but still . . . 20 out of 22 championships. Wow.

The following day, another Class A team with a solid program, the Helena Senators, played against Scobey in Scobey Ball Park. Helena was powerful in 1972, setting a team record with an incredible 43-6 season record, taking second to the Great Falls Electrics in the State A Tournament. The game was not so close this time, as Helena won 17-2. A couple of "interesting" things about this game: (1) Dallas Hagfeldt, in his interview, mentioned that Doc brought in Jim Hansen—not eligible to play but who was sitting in Scobey's dugout—to pitch in the later innings after Doc had exhausted his pitchers. Doc did not want to get pummeled by Helena. (2) The *Helena Independent Record*, in its article about the game, stated that Helena played a "Tri-County team" consisting of players from Scobey, Glasgow, Plentywood, and Wolf Point.[65] Hmm. What's up, Doc?

For the fourth consecutive year, Scobey won the district, followed by Wolf Point, Circle, and Poplar. Good to see Wolf Point back on the field again in 1972. Since Wolf Point had won the state championship in 1965, the program had gone through some tough times, as in two seasons—despite winning the district—the team was ruled ineligible to play in the postseason due to late roster submissions, and some years they did not field a team. They had taken third place in the 1969 state tournament in Scobey but had not been on the field since. But a solid Wolf Point team, loaded with talented all-around athletes, was building and would contest Scobey for the title in 1973.

DIVISIONAL TOURNAMENT

THE 1972 EASTERN DIVISIONAL TOURNAMENT WAS PLAYED AT Meissner Memorial Field in Glendive. It consisted of seven teams: Scobey, Wolf Point, Circle, Poplar, Glendive, Ekalaka, and the Billings Scarlets. Scobey was the number one overall seed and received a first-round bye.

In their first game against Glendive, Doc started Terry, who yielded only two runs and struck out nine in Scobey's 5-2 win. Rick Danelson and Dallas Hagfeldt each had two hits to lead Scobey's hitting. It was interesting that Doc started Terry in this game. He usually saved him for later in the tournament, but with the first-round bye, he needed only one win to qualify for State, so that was probably his calculus. A week later, at the state tournament in Havre, he would not start Terry in the first game, and it would backfire on him.

Scobey's second game in the semifinal against Wolf Point was a wild 30-hit slugfest, with Scobey winning 20-11. Terry Puckett hit a 480-foot grand slam home run in Scobey's 11-run third inning.[66] I remember hearing this on KCGM radio as Cliff Hagfeldt's voice boomed over the airwaves when Terry struck the ball. Cliff's voice was so powerful that when I listened to the loud crack of Terry's bat, there was no question the ball was gone. It was good to see in Terry's later Legion years that although his arm was progressively weakening, his bat was getting stronger. Terry had another hit besides his homer, and Jay Hagfeldt, Doug Hagfeldt, and Rick Danelson each had three hits to lead Scobey's 16-hit attack. Dana Audet went the distance and got the win for Scobey, striking out 11.

In the championship game, again against Glendive, Scobey came from behind to win. Trailing 4-2 in the sixth, Scobey tied the game with two runs. Then, trailing 5-4 in the eighth, Glendive committed three errors, and Lee Cook made them pay with a bases-clearing triple. Scobey plated an additional run to take an 8-5 lead. They added a run in the ninth to win 9-5. Lee Cook had two triples and four RBIs to lead Scobey's hitting, with Dana Audet adding three hits and Terry Puckett two. Jay Hagfeldt went the distance for Scobey, yielding only three hits and one run after the third inning when Glendive led 4-1. Advancing to State in Havre from the east were Scobey, Glendive, and Wolf Point. In the west, it was the Great Falls Sparkies, Havre, and Cut Bank. Havre beat Cut Bank 12-7 for the west championship, and the Great Falls Sparkies received an automatic number one seed as they won the regular season.

STATE B TOURNAMENT

HAVRE WAS HOSTING THEIR SECOND STATE TOURNAMENT, AS they had hosted in 1970 when they beat Scobey for the championship. In the pre-tourney preview in the *Great Falls Tribune*, the six coaches agreed that any of the six teams could win it, with no clear favorite. The article's title was "Scramble in the Offing for Best Legion B Team."[67] The coaches talked more about how the State B winner might have a chance to win the State A. Doc said, "I think this is the best chance a B team has had to take it all." This assertion was primarily because the Billings Royals, who had won 20 out of 22 state A championships, had their lowest regular-season mark in years. The article stated that Havre's roster, while losing Fanning, Grimm, and Kato, "features a solid nucleus of tournament-tested veterans," but the same could have been said about Scobey. Terry Puckett was labeled the "most feared hitter" in the tournament with six home runs, including a grand slam the week before against Wolf Point that Doc said traveled 500 feet. The *Leader* had it at *only* 480 feet. The article mentioned Carmen Birdsbill from Wolf Point as a strong pitcher, but that the rest of their pitching "thins out" from there. Tim Cody, a five-foot-one, 240-pound second baseman, led the heavy-hitting Wolf Point team—averaging seven and a half runs a game—in hitting. Havre was led by shortstop Bob Bronson, Dave Cole, and Tom Bandy, but Cole and Bandy were playing in the East-West Shrine football game and couldn't play in the tournament.

The top two seeds—Scobey in the west and the Great Falls Sparkies in the west—received first-round buys. Scobey played the winner of the Havre-Wolf Point game, which Havre won 10-3. Wolf Point's bats were quieted by Havre's 16-year-old pitcher, Dale Kuntz, who only allowed three runs.

Havre's win against Wolf Point set up another Havre-Scobey matchup in the state tournament. This was the sixth consecutive year—and the ninth time—that Havre and Scobey would play against each other in the state tournament, starting in 1967. At this point in the rivalry, the series was tied at four games apiece, with these scores, winning pitchers, and year:

- Scobey 7-3, Dick Puckett (1967)
- Scobey 12-2, Dick Puckett (1968)
- Havre 12-0, Barry Damschen (1968)
- Havre 7-2, Mike Hanson (1969)
- Scobey 8-7, Jim Hansen (1969)
- Scobey 7-6, Dick Puckett (1969)
- Havre 6-1, Kurt Grimm (1970)
- Havre 1-0, Dave Fanning (1971)

Doc handed the ball to 16-year-old Dana Audet to start the game against Havre. The game started auspiciously for Scobey, as Terry Puckett blasted a three-run homer—his seventh of the year—in the top of the first inning to stake Scobey to a 3-0 lead, but Havre tied in the bottom half with three runs of their own. Scobey scored again in the top of the second to lead 4-3, but from then on, it was all Havre, as they buried Scobey with 18 hits and two 6-run innings to win 20-5. According to the *Havre Daily News*, Barry Higgins was brought in to pitch in the seventh inning for Scobey.[68] Most likely, Doc was conserving Dana's innings for later in the tournament after the game was out of reach. Scobey committed four errors in the game. A significant blow to Scobey in this game was the injury of starting catcher Dallas Hagfeldt, whose severe ankle sprain sliding into second base would significantly hamper any chance Scobey had to come back through the dirt route and make the championship game, let alone win it. The outlook wasn't brilliant for the Scobey nine that day.

In their second game, Scobey eliminated Cut Bank 3-2, getting another strong pitching performance from Terry Puckett. Despite his perpetual arm troubles, the left-hander could still hurl a mean game at this point in his career. He went the distance for Scobey, pitching a three-hitter and striking out 10 to get the win. He also drove in two runs to help his cause. Roger Askelson pitched well for Cut Bank, holding Scobey scoreless after the third inning and striking out eight Scobey hitters. Scobey played well defensively, committing only one error.

After losing to Havre in their first game, Wolf Point beat Glendive 5-4. Carmen Birdsbill pitched a three-hitter and struck out 12 to get the win, and Dan Bartel hit a double and a triple to lead Wolf Point's hitting. Wolf Point's win set up a Scobey-Wolf Point matchup. Scobey and Wolf Point had last met in a state tournament in 1969 in Scobey, with Scobey winning 17-2. In this game, however, Wolf Point shut out Scobey 9-0, eliminating Scobey from the tournament.

Scobey's defense collapsed, as it had done the year before against Plentywood, committing five errors behind Jay Hagfeldt's pitching, who allowed only seven hits against the heavy-hitting Wolf Point team. Dave Johnson pitched the shutout, with Dave Madison relieving in the ninth. Scobey outhit Wolf Point 9 to 7, but Wolf Point turned two double plays to snuff out Scobey's rallies.

Havre won the semifinal game 7-3 over the Sparkies to earn another berth in the state championship game, with Arlen Hanson getting the win. Wolf Point eliminated the Sparkies 5-4 to complete their dirt-route path to the championship game. With the score tied 4-4 in the ninth, Wolf Point won the game on a walk, an error, and a sacrifice fly.

Havre beat Wolf Point 13-5 in the state championship game to win their third consecutive state championship and second on their home field. Wolf Point led 4-3 in the seventh inning, but Havre scored four runs and added six more in the eighth to salt the game away and capture their third consecutive state championship on their home field. Fourteen-year-old Kirk Stetson was the winning pitcher for Havre.

TOURNAMENT SUMMARY

SCOBEY'S SEASON-ENDING LOSS TO WOLF POINT WAS ANOTHER disappointing end to a season that showed promise of a possible state championship; however, the team was still one year away, especially with their young pitchers still developing. Although Terry's arm would continue to weaken in 1973—finally breaking in the end—the entire staff would strengthen, with right-handers Dana Audet and Jay Hagfeldt and left-handers Duke and Dallas Trangsrud continuing to develop, providing solid depth on the pitching staff—an essential ingredient to winning a state championship.

Scobey's season-ending loss to Wolf Point was a fitting prelude to the 1973 season, as Wolf Point's edge over Scobey would continue into the next season when they won the regular season series against Scobey before Scobey beat them in the divisional championship game in Miles City. The road to the state championship would not be easy for Scobey in 1973, and—with a down year for Havre—it would run through Wolf Point, ending dramatically with two incredible games at the Scobey Ball Park in August 1973.

STATE A TOURNAMENT

AS THE STATE B CHAMPION, HAVRE AGAIN RECEIVED AN automatic berth into the State A Tournament. They faced pre-tourney favorite Helena, who had a 43-6 record, in their first game. And Havre again represented the State B well, losing to Helena 3-2, getting an extremely well-pitched game from Dick Clark. Havre loaded the bases in the ninth with no outs but could not push a run across to tie the game. Havre eliminated the Glacier Twins 15-2 in their next game, with Dale Kuntz getting the twin. Jay Waterman and Dave Cole each had three hits for Havre to lead the barrage. In their final game, Havre was eliminated by Miles City 10-6, but it was another strong showing from Havre in the State A Tournament. The Great Falls Electrics won the state championship over Helena.

EXTRA INNINGS

DANA AUDET REMEMBERS A STORY ABOUT HOW IMPOSING DOC could be to umpires in a game against the Grenora Gophers that summer. "We were in Grenora, and Barry Higgins was leading off the first inning, and I was on deck. He promptly struck out on three pitches swinging. He then proceeded to turn and huck his bat towards the backstop. It came within about a foot of going over and into the parking lot. I'm sure it would have cleared the bleachers. As expected, the young umpire exclaimed, 'You're outta here.' Before I could move into the box, here comes Doc out of the dugout. That should have been expected as well, I guess. He moved extremely close to the umpire and stated, 'If you kick him out of the game, we are packing our bags and heading back to Scobey right now.' I was thinking, *Nooo Doc! We drove 80 miles to get here. We don't want to drive back without playing, especially a game that should add a W to the record.* The umpire paused for a few seconds and then said 'Okay, he can stay in, but no more of that shit.' We were all happy and did get the W. Doc could definitely be intimidating."

Terry has a few signed baseballs from the home runs he hit later in his Legion career, but he said, "After I started hitting home runs in Legion when I got older, Doc stopped giving me the ball, so I don't have too many signed baseballs!"

Phil Audet, who was helping Doc coach in 1972, recalls another funny story involving Doc's needle. "We were in

Doc's room getting ready for the game," Phil said, "and Doc had just given somebody a shot. I turned around, and all of a sudden I felt something go through the backside of my uniform, a jab. I turned around, and Rick Danelson had taken that syringe and shoved it into me. And he laughed like a son of a gun. Doc says, 'Goddam it, Rick, put that away before somebody gets hurt!' And I said, 'It's too late!' Back then, nobody thought too much about it, but if it'd been a few years down the road, you'd have had to watch that like crazy after he did that, you know."

Coach Tom Nielson stepped down from coaching the Havre Legion team in 1972, replaced by coaches Harvey Welch and Frank Schend. Coach Nielson had revived the Havre Post 11 American Legion Baseball program in 1966, led them to their first state tournament appearance in 1967, and won state B championships in 1968, 1970, and 1971. He was Doc's counterpart in the west.

The Havre Legion team used two teams in 1972: a B team of 16-year-olds and the regular A squad, or traveling team, which played all conference and non-conference games. In a touch of irony, the Havre 16-year-old team was called the Blues.

The Havre-Wolf Point matchup in the state championship game was the only time these two storied Legion programs faced each other in a state championship game. Scobey met Havre twice in the state championship game, in 1969 and 1970.

Kirk Stetson, Havre's 14-year-old pitcher, was the winning pitcher in the state championship game against Wolf Point. I played basketball with Havre pitcher Kirk Stetson for one year when I was a freshman at Carroll College in 1979-80. He was a senior predental student at the time. Kirk was an excellent student, athlete, and person.

In 1972, pitching for the Auburn Phillies in the New York-Pennsylvania League (A), Dave Fanning, former Havre pitcher in 1970-71, posted a 9-3 record, 1.71 ERA, and struck out 128 hitters in 95 innings.

Nineteen seventy-two was the fourth time Wolf Point was runners-up at the state tournament, losing to Sunburst in 1962, Cut Bank in 1963, and Glendive in 1964. In most cases, it was big, late innings from the opposing team that doomed Wolf Point when they ran out of pitching. That would again prove to be the case the following season in 1973 in the final game against Scobey.

1972 Scobey Plainsmen. Standing L-R: Danny Wolfe, Jack Higgins, Larry "Zip" Thompson, Jim Hansen, Danny Wang, Rocky Ware, Jerry LaPierre. Kneeling, left to right: Paris French, Rick Sampsen, Craig Audet, Phil Audet, Don Higgins, Brad Murray. Not pictured is Dick Puckett, who had been injured in a farm accident. *Leader.*

The Plainsmen, consisting of former American Legion players you would recognize and coached by John Murphy, were active in 1972, mostly playing in tournaments in Saskatchewan, but they would always play the Legionnaires. During their interviews, many players said that Doc "always wanted to beat the Plainsmen." The games were competitive. Terry Puckett said that the best game he ever pitched was a 1-0 shutout against the Plainsmen, with older brother Dick taking the hard-luck loss.

1973

Scobey Wins Its Second State Championship

> *Thus again the final confrontation between the two proven top teams of Class B American Legion Baseball in Montana, Wolf Point and Scobey.*
>
> —**Daniels County Leader, August 5, 1973**

PRESEASON

MANY REFERENCES HAVE BEEN MADE TO SEASONS where Scobey looked good to win a state championship but fell short in the end. However, no Scobey roster—except for the 1969 team—was returning stronger than the 1973 team. The only starter gone was Barry Higgins. Rick Danelson and Terry Puckett, who began playing together as 13-year-olds in 1968, were returning to the diamond to play in their sixth and final season together. Between the two of them, they had played in 10 state tournaments, winning it all in 1969 when they were only 14. Dallas Hagfeldt was returning for his third and final season as well. Rick, Terry, and Dallas had all graduated from high school in 1972 but had the post-August birthday, so they could all play another season. Experienced players Dana Audet, Don Puckett, Jay Hagfeldt, Doug Hagfeldt, Lee Cook, and Duke Trangsrud were all returning for another season, and Greg Fjeld, Dallas Trangsrud, Jack Tryan, Mike Gunderson, and Keith Zieske would join the team to round out a strong roster for a state champion. Phil Audet and Rod Tande assisted with Doc's coaching. If there was ever a year for Doc and the Scobey Legionnaires to win a second state championship—on Scobey's home field once again—1973 was it.

But another team returning a championship-caliber roster in 1973 was Wolf Point, who had beaten Scobey 9-0 to end Scobey's 1972 season, finishing second to Havre for the state championship. Wolf Point's edge over Scobey would carry over into the 1973 season, and their season destinies would find them meeting for the eastern divisional championship in Miles City and two state championship games in Scobey. Wolf Point's roster in 1973 included Carmen Birdsbill, Dave Stengel, Dan Bartel, Brian Jones, Tim Cody, Dave Johnson, Larry Monson, Ken and Keith Lee, Warren Crowe, Lenny Vine, Jeff Neubauer, Lane Pickthorn, Jon McMaster, and Mike Green. Ten of these players played against Havre in the 1972 state championship game. They could hit, field—and run. The pressure their speedy baserunners put on the defense was phenomenal. The question for Wolf Point, as it would be for Scobey, was their pitching. Carmen Birdsbill was their ace, but the *Great Falls Tribune* State B pre-tournament preview in 1972 stated that Wolf Point's pitching "thinned out"[69] from there. But sidearm-throwing Dave Johnson pitched a rare shutout against Scobey to beat them 9-0 in their final game. Dana Audet said, "It was a nightmare as a right-handed batter to bat against that sidearm delivery he had. We hated it."

There was no question that Scobey had the talent and experience at the plate and in the field to win it, but what about *their* pitching? To win a state championship, it always comes down to pitching. Terry Puckett, the seasoned left-hander from Peerless who might have logged more innings than Phil Audet, was returning for his sixth season, but the stress on his arm had begun to show years earlier. He had pitched in the state tournament against Havre in Glendive when he was only 13 years old in 1968, against the Royals as a 14-year-old in 1969, a three-hitter against Helena at State in 1970, a 1-0 pitcher's duel against Dick and the Plainsmen and a 1-0 pitcher's duel against Fanning in the state tournament in 1971, the Royals again in 1972, and on and on. Could his fraying labrum hold out for one more summer before it succumbed to the pressure and stress? Under the right conditions—a hot day, Doc's needle, a little DMSO, and Doc's other secret ingredient (which shall remain nameless)—Terry could still deliver a gem on the mound. He had proven that in his last two starts of the previous season, where he scattered seven hits to beat Glendive 5-2 at the eastern divisional and pitched a three-hitter against Cut Bank to win 3-2 at State, striking out 19 in the two games, with an ERA of 1.50. One more summer, Terry, that's all we need.

But it would be up to the rest of the staff, namely right-handers Dana Audet and Jay Hagfeldt and left-hander Duke Trangsrud, to win the state championship for Scobey in 1973, as Terry's arm would finally give out after pitching 12 innings against Wolf Point in the eastern divisional championship game in Miles City. Catcher Dallas Hagfeldt said, "Terry was pretty much done after that game."

REGULAR SEASON

It seems that each season, there is something unique about Scobey's schedule that sets it apart from all the others, something that happens for the first time and doesn't happen again. In 1960, for example, it was the barnstorming trip on the red bus through North Dakota, Minnesota, and Wisconsin, or the Billings Royals coming to Scobey to play in 1972. In 1973, it was a trip down south to play against Baker (coached by Brian Bechtold) and Ekalaka. In his interview, Dana Audet described catching Terry in his first full game as a catcher in the second game of a doubleheader against Baker. He said, "It was like a hundred degrees; I mean, it was really, really, hot, which was the only time Terry would even think about pitching." Terry pitched a seven-inning shutout. Dana said, "They weren't hittin' him; he was throwin' good." This was a good sign for Scobey early in the season—Terry could still bring it under the right conditions.

The unique road trip continued further south to Ekalaka. Dana described Ekalaka's field by saying, "Their field was on like an alkali-seep thing; there wasn't a blade of grass within two miles, and it was hot. We beat 'em like 20 to 1 and got the hell out of that godforsaken place." After careful consideration, the Ekalaka Chamber of Commerce reviewed Dana's comments and has decided not to include them in the 2024 Carter County Tourist Brochure.

But the most critical Scobey games in the 1973 regular season were not played against Baker and Ekalaka in Fallon and Carter Counties; they were played against Wolf Point in Daniels and Roosevelt Counties, where Wolf Point won 3 out of 4 games to win the northeastern district. Since they had beaten Scobey 9-0 to end the 1972 season, Wolf Point had gained an edge over Scobey—both in confidence and results—heading into the divisional tournament in Miles City. The stakes were high for Scobey and Wolf Point in the divisional tournament, where the outcome would have enormous implications for the state tournament in Scobey a few days later.

Scobey Legionnaires, 1973 Eastern Divisional Champions. Standing left to right: Mike Gunderson, Jay Hagfeldt, Lee Cook, Dallas Hagfeldt, Terry Puckett, Doug Hagfeldt, Don Puckett, Rick Danelson. Kneeling left to right: Coach Doc Norman, Duke Trangsrud, Dana Audet, Jack Tryan, Greg Fjeld, Keith Zieske, Dallas Trangsrud. Sitting left to right: batboys Kelly Norman, Danny Danelson, Kirby Halvorson. *Miles City Star.*

DIVISIONAL TOURNAMENT

The divisional tournament played at Denton Field in Miles City consisted of six teams: Wolf Point, Scobey, Circle, Baker, Ekalaka, and the Miles City Colts. The top three teams would advance to State in Scobey the following week. In its first game, Scobey trailed Baker 3-0 in the early innings before starting pitcher Jay Hagfeldt "settled down on the mound"[70] and struck out 20 Baker hitters—a divisional tournament record—to lead Scobey to a 12-3 win. KATL Radio, Miles City, described Jay's 20-strikeout performance against Baker as "spectacular pitching." Terry Puckett, whom the *Leader* described as coming out of an earlier season slump, hit his fifth home run of the season to lead Scobey's hitting.[71]

Wolf Point's first game was against the Colts, whom they beat handily. Carmen Birdsbill started for Wolf Point and struck out 13 Colts in five innings before being relieved by Brian Jones.

In Scobey's semifinal game against Circle, Scobey got another well-pitched game from Dana Audet, who pitched a complete-game shutout to lead Scobey to a 10-0 win. Terry Puckett hit his second home run of the tournament—and sixth of the season—to lead Scobey's hitting. This win set up the all-important divisional championship game between Scobey and Wolf Point, the two best B teams in the state in 1973. Due to its number-one seed, Wolf Point received a second-round bye to make it to the divisional championship game.

Doc handed the ball to Terry Puckett to start the championship game. Not knowing that he was pitching with a partially torn labrum hanging on by a thread, Terry still had enough left in his arm to pitch. But before the game started, he would have no idea how grueling it would be, as he would end up pitching 12 innings. He was matched against Carmen Birdsbill, Wolf Point's ace, who had seven innings of eligibility left after pitching five innings against Miles City, striking out 13 of 15 hitters. This game would be an incredible back-and-forth affair from start to finish. The *Miles City Star* described the game as "a thriller all the way through,"[72] and the *Leader* referred to it as "a thrilling contest of evenly matched teams."[73]

Scobey opened the scoring in the top of the first when Dallas Hagfeldt doubled, bringing home Jay Hagfeldt, who led off with a single and was advanced on a single by Rick Danelson. Wolf Point tied in the bottom half when Carmen Birdsbill singled home Dan Bartel, who had doubled. Then, Scobey scored three runs in the third on two home runs: a solo home run by Rick Danelson, followed by a two-run shot by Terry Puckett, driving in Dallas Hagfeldt, who had singled. Rick's homer was his first of the season; Terry's was his seventh and the third straight game he had homered in the tournament. Wolf Point touched Terry and Scobey for two runs in the fifth to make it 4-3 Scobey. Scobey added a run in the top of the eighth on two costly Wolf Point errors. Leading 5-3 in the bottom of the ninth, Scobey needed only three outs to win it, but Wolf Point scored two runs on a lone single and two Scobey errors to tie it 5-5. Terry recalls the fielding by Scobey in the game was so bad that "even Donnie made an error at short, and he didn't make many."

Mike Gunderson recalls, "His arm was just a rag after nine innings, but he kept going out there." Lee Cook added, "Terry pitched until his arm was about to fall off." Each team scored a run in the tenth, and the 11th was scoreless. Dallas Hagfeldt led off the top of the 12th with a double, then Wolf Point, not wanting to see Terry hit his fourth home run of the tournament, intentionally walked him. Dana Audet, Don Puckett, and the bottom of Scobey's order made them pay, driving in Dallas and Terry and scoring two additional runs to take a 10-6 lead. Terry set Wolf Point down in order in the bottom of the 12th, and Scobey won the divisional championship. Somehow, someway, Terry found a way to go the distance, striking out 16 hitters. But as good as Scobey's pitching was at divisional—Jay Hagfeldt striking out 20 Baker hitters, Dana Audet pitching a shutout against Circle, and Terry going 12 innings against Wolf Point—their hitting was even better. They pounded out 43 hits and scored 32 runs in the three games. Terry hit three home runs, and Rick Danelson added another. This 1973 Scobey team could hit. Their fielding was okay, but the two errors in the bottom of the ninth against Wolf Point forced three extra innings.

Although both teams had already qualified for State, the championship game was a critical win for Scobey. Wolf Point had won 4 out of 5 games against Scobey, dating back to the state tournament in 1972. Dallas Hagfeldt and Dana Audet mentioned in their interviews that the win gave them the confidence they needed to beat Wolf Point headed into the state tournament. But as the team celebrated their hard-fought 12-inning championship victory on Denton Field, some of them knew that it was likely they would need to win the state tournament without the left arm of Terry Puckett, whose arm, after recording the last three outs in the 12th, was now literally hanging on his shoulder. Terry would somehow appear on the mound in the state tournament but would be less than a shadow of his former self, his effectiveness gone. Perhaps just as important as the confidence they gained, the win over Wolf Point secured a first-round bye in the state tournament, saving a precious nine innings for a pitching staff that had just lost its wounded ace.

STATE B TOURNAMENT

SCOBEY WAS HOSTING ITS THIRD STATE TOURNAMENT—THE excitement of another State Legion baseball tournament in Scobey!—and like the previous two in 1969 and 1971, hopes and prospects were high for a state championship. Because the state tournament was the week following divisional, the *Daniels County Leader* had to balance its coverage of the dramatic divisional tourney with the state tournament preview, but "The Little Newspaper Doing a Big Job" was up to the task, running two major articles: "Scobey Wins Divisional Tournament at Miles City" and "State Legion Tourney On Here Today."[74] In the state tournament preview, the paper announced that the opening game on Thursday would feature Wolf Point against Cut Bank, followed by Circle against Helena, with Havre (champion in the west) and Scobey (champion in the east) receiving first-round byes. Helena had taken second in the west and Cut Bank third. The Associated Press article in the Kalispell *Daily Inter Lake* previewing the tournament stated, "Havre shoots for its fourth straight Class B American Legion Baseball title,"[75] but this tournament would prove to be a two-horse race between Scobey and Wolf Point.

Not starting your ace in the first tournament game can backfire, and that happened to Wolf Point against Cut Bank in their opening game. Scobey experienced it the year before in Havre when Doc chose to save Terry for later in the tournament, and Scobey got pummeled by Havre in their opener. Cut Bank, third seed from the west, scored six runs in the first two innings, shocking Wolf Point 8-5, forcing them through the dirt route for the remainder of the tournament. Dale Brekke pitched three innings of no-hit relief for Cut Bank to save it for Cut Bank. Dave Johnson and Brian Jones pitched for Wolf Point. Dan Bartel of Wolf Point hit the only home run of the tournament in the game.

The Helena Representatives beat Circle 6-3, setting up Scobey's first game of the tournament. Doc started Dana Audet, and he got the win, with Jay Hagfeldt earning the save. The game was close, with Scobey taking an early 3-0 lead after three innings, but Helena came back to tie it 3-3 with two runs in the fourth and a single run in the fifth. Scobey scored a single run in the seventh. Then, in the bottom of the eighth, with Scobey leading 4-3, Terry Puckett walked, Doc sacrificed him to second, and he scored on an error, which proved to be the winning run. In the top of the ninth, Helena rallied to score a run to make it 5-4 and had the potential tying run on the third and the winning run on first with two outs before Jay Hagfeldt retired the next hitter on a long fly ball to earn the save and give Scobey a hard-fought one-run win. Nothing comes easy in the state tournament.

As had been the case in the 1969 and 1971 tournaments, Scobey's opponent in the semifinal was expected to be the three-time defending champion and top seed in the west, Havre. However, third-seed Cut Bank, having already upset Wolf Point 8-5, shocked Havre with an identical 8-5 score to advance to the semifinal against Scobey. Havre led 3-0 in the third and 5-3 in the sixth, but Cut Bank got to Havre pitcher Kirk Stetson for five runs on four hits and two walks in the sixth to take an 8-5 lead. Cut Bank pitcher Dale Brekke allowed Havre no runs and only one hit after coming in with two out in the fifth to get the win. Cut Bank had beaten two good teams on Thursday to earn their berth against Scobey in the semifinal on Friday. Could they do it again with a third upset against top-seed Scobey?

Doc started Jay Hagfeldt against Cut Bank, and Cut Bank started Dale Brekke, who had yielded only one hit in seven and one-third innings of scoreless relief the previous day against Wolf Point and Havre. But Scobey quickly ended Brekke's scoreless-inning streak with a run in the first, then scored three more in the second to jump to a 4-0 lead. Dallas Hagfeldt broke the game wide open in the fifth with a bases-loaded double, then scored on two errors to make it 8-0 Scobey. Meanwhile, winning pitcher Jay Hagfeldt—who helped his cause by scoring three runs in the game—was pitching well and had a shutout into the sixth when Cut Bank scored a single run to make it 8-1. Duke Trangsrud came in to relieve Jay and pitched well, but Scobey, catching the error bug, committed five errors behind him. Cut Bank scored two runs in the seventh and added two more in the eighth, but Duke shut them down in the ninth to make the final score 8-5, Scobey, earning a berth in the championship game on Saturday. Interestingly, all three of Cut Bank's games had ended with identical 8-5 scores, but this time with a loss.

After losing their opener 8-5 to Cut Bank, Wolf Point had clawed their way through the dirt route to make it to the championship game, winning 9-3 over Helena, 8-6 over Circle, and 9-2 over Cut Bank. Coach Harvey Langager got good pitching from Lane Pickthorn, Dave Johnson, and Brian Jones and managed to preserve some innings for Carmen Birdsbill. Key hitters for Wolf Point along the dirt route were Brian Jones, Larry Munson, Carmen Birdsbill, Dave Stengel, and Jeff Neubauer, who drove in four runs in Wolf Point's win over Cut Bank. Wolf Point's three wins set up the rematch of the divisional championship game a week earlier in Miles City, but Wolf Point would have to beat Scobey twice to win the state championship. Wolf Point did not have to play Havre on their dirt route as Circle had eliminated them 3-1 on a well-pitched game from Wade Sukut, who had a no-hitter through five innings and struck out six, going the distance to get the win.

In the state championship game on Saturday, Dana Audet and Terry Puckett pitched for Scobey, but the *Leader* is unclear who started or what their innings were. Harvey Langager started his ace Carmen Birdsbill, but Scobey jumped all over him for six runs in the first inning, adding another run in the second to chase Birdsbill and take a 7-0 lead. What a start for Scobey! Seven runs after two innings, and Birdsbill was knocked out of the game. Scobey's outlook for a second state championship was flying high—but how quickly the tide changed for Scobey.

In the top of the third, Scobey's defense, which had committed five errors against Cut Bank to allow them back in the game, had another meltdown against Wolf Point, committing four errors, enabling Wolf Point to score five runs on just two hits to get back in the game, 7-5. Carmen Birdsbill drove in two unearned runs with a single in the inning. Meanwhile, Dave Johnson, who had pitched a shutout to eliminate Scobey from the state tournament the year before in Havre, came on in relief of Birdsbill to hurl two and two-thirds innings of hitless ball before Birdsbill returned to the mound with two outs in the fifth. After five complete innings, with Dana Audet still pitching for Scobey and Carmen Birdsbill back on the hill for Wolf Point, the score stood 7-5, Scobey.

In the top of the sixth, Wolf Point pushed another run across, closing to within 7-6, but they failed to score in the seventh and eighth innings, so Scobey clung to a one-run lead entering the top of the ninth. In the top of the ninth, Scobey got two outs, but Wolf Point had loaded the bases for Dan Bartel when he came to the plate for Wolf Point. Scobey only needed to retire Dan Bartel, and the state championship was theirs. In a touch of irony, four years earlier, Scobey trailed Havre by the same 7-6 score when Dick Puckett tied the state championship game with his dramatic two-out home run, sending the Scobey crowd into a frenzy. But this time, it was Wolf Point's turn for the dramatic two-out ninth-inning hit, as Dan Bartel laced a line-drive triple to left-center to clear the bases, then scored on a throwing error on the play to plate the fourth run and complete Wolf Point's shocking comeback from seven runs down. Carmen Birdsbill, who had reentered the game in the fifth after getting shelled for seven runs in the first two innings, slammed the door on Scobey in the bottom of the ninth, and Wolf Point ran off the field with a 10-7 victory, forcing a second game on Sunday.

What a devastating psychological blow for Scobey. Leading seven to nothing in the second inning after scoring a converted touchdown on Wolf Point's ace, they failed to score another run and went hitless the rest of the game, committed four errors in the third to let Wolf Point back in it, but still were one out away from winning it all in the ninth. A bitter pill to swallow. Dana Audet, in his interview, said, "Losing to Wolf Point on Saturday night under the lights, that was one of those games we shouldn't have lost. We were a little bit down after that loss, knowing we have to play them again tomorrow." In many ways, the loss recalled the horrible 6-5 loss to Plentywood at the state tournament in Scobey two years earlier. But this time, there was another game to play. The sun would rise the next day. Dana added, "You just gotta come back tomorrow and do the best you can do. You're not coming in tremendously confident, but we also know that we can play with these guys, and we also know that Carmen Birdsbill was going to run out of innings." As was the case four years earlier against Havre, a second game on Sunday was needed to determine the State American Legion champion. Get a good night's sleep, everyone.

Scobey lost the coin toss for the home team, which is why you see the team standing along the first baseline while the sportsman's oath was being administered before the start of the game. But had Doc won the toss, he might have chosen the lucky third base dugout over the home team, which he did four years earlier in the championship game against Havre. Let's let the *Leader*, whose coverage of the state tournament was again second to none, set the stage for this game: "A large turnout again assembled at the Scobey Ball Park Sunday afternoon for the final title game. Thus, again, the final confrontation between the two proven top teams of 1973 Class B American Legion Baseball in Montana."[76]

Dana Audet started for Scobey, and Carmen Birdsbill started for Wolf Point. Both pitchers had pitched in the game the previous day. In the top of the first, three hits by Rick Danelson, Dallas Hagfeldt, and Dana Audet, coupled with two Wolf Point errors, led to two Scobey runs. Wolf Point went scoreless, and Scobey led 2-0 after one inning. It was another excellent start for Scobey, but we've seen this movie before. In the bottom of the second, Wolf Point got

State Legion Baseball Commissioner Bob Shaw of Miles City administers the Legion oath to the players before the state championship game. *Leader.*

to Dana for four runs on four hits and one costly Scobey error to take the lead, 4-2.

And there the score stood until the top of the eighth. From the second inning through the seventh, Scobey had mustered four hits but no runs. Scobey left several baserunners on in the fourth and fifth innings. Meanwhile, Dana Audet had held the heavy-hitting Wolf Point team scoreless after the second inning, allowing them only three scattered hits. Several balls were hit sharply to the outfield, but 16-year-old left fielder Duke Trangsrud "handled six chances flawlessly," and center fielder Jay Hagfeldt recorded another three putouts. Dana had kept Scobey in the game. It was now up to the bats.

Trailing 4-2 in the top of the eighth, Scobey was now down to its final six outs. Every at-bat was critical. Cleanup hitter Terry Puckett led off the top of the eighth against Brian Jones, who was now pitching for Wolf Point. Terry singled but was forced out at second on a fielder's choice ground ball by Dana Audet. Don Puckett and Duke Trangsrud then singled to load the bases with one out, setting the stage for rookie 15-year-old second baseman Greg Fjeld, the eighth hitter in the lineup, to come up the plate. What a clutch situation for Greg to be in. He responded with a single, and "the rally was fully underway."[77] Jack Tryan, the ninth hitter in the lineup, got on base on an error by the shortstop. Leadoff hitter Jay Hagfeldt singled. Rick Danelson singled. Dallas Hagfeldt singled. The order returned to Terry Puckett, who had led off the inning with a single. He singled again! By the time the dust had settled on the basepaths, Scobey had scored seven runs on eight singles and one Wolf Point error. At the end of the inning, Wolf Point was using its fourth pitcher in the game, Dave Stengel. Going into the bottom of the eighth, Scobey led 9-4.

In its half of the eighth, Wolf Point threatened, getting two runners in scoring position with a hit and a Scobey error, but Dana struck out the last two batters to snuff out the rally and strand the runners.

Scobey's scoreless top of the ninth set up the dramatic finish, with Scobey needing three outs to win its second state championship. They would not come easy. This battle-tested Wolf Point team, who had come back through the dirt route to win four games, would not go down without a fight or swinging. The *Leader* wrote, "Wolf Point had proven just the night before that it could overcome a seven-run lead, and the well-balanced team had come from behind in a number of its other games."[78] From that perspective, Scobey's five-run lead did not seem much.

Jay Hagfeldt went to the mound "to see if he could hold the anxious Wolves in the bottom of the ninth."[79] In his interview, Dana Audet mentioned that Jay Hagfeldt told him at the Scobey 50-year reunion, "I came in and threw nothing but curve balls; I was not going to give those guys a fastball to hit. I knew if I threw nothing but curve balls and sliders, they were going to struggle to really get the bat on the ball and pound it." Tim Cody, the ninth man in the order, walked, and Jon McMaster was put in as a pinch runner for him. That brought up the dangerous top of the lineup for Wolf Point, Dan Bartel. He hit a ball to left field, but Duke Trangsrud got it. Brian Jones hit another one to left, but Duke got it again, his sixth putout

Rick Danelson, leading hitter of tourney, hits a single to left in the big eighth inning of the championship game. *Leader.*

of the game—one more out. Carmen Birdsbill got on base, moving McMaster to second. Jay then worked a two-strike count on Larry Monson, and now Wolf Point was down to its last strike, but Monson singled with two strikes to drive in McMaster, and Birdsbill went to third, who then scored to make it 9-6; Wolf Point got another baserunner, then Lane Pickthorn walked to load the bases, becoming the tying run on first base. The winning run was now at the plate in the form of Dave Stengel. "By now, the Wolf Point cheering section was a roaring crescendo."

The *Leader* wrote that Dave Stengel was "known as a clutch-hitter as well as the heady quarterback of a Wolf Point championship football team."[80] He was not the man you wanted to face in this situation, but Jay got him to pop up to short center. This ball was dangerous as it slowly ascended, as the three baserunners were running on contact with two outs. If it dropped, it would hit like an exploding bomb in the outfield, as at least two runs would score and possibly a third, Lane Pickthorn, who was the tying run on first. But rookie second baseman Greg Fjeld took charge, waving his arms in the air and yelling, "I got it! I got it!" to call off center fielder Dana Audet and shortstop Don Puckett. The *Leader* wrote he "jumped up in the air, taking it high over his head and squeezing it for the final out."[81] Scobey had the big pile up at the pitcher's mound and celebrated their second state championship on their home field.

Epitomizing the great team effort and togetherness of the Scobey team, Greg Fjeld, who had just made the game-winning catch in shallow center field, handed the ball to pitcher Jay Hagfeldt on the mound, who turned and gave the ball to winning pitcher Dana Audet, saying, "This ball is yours." Dana still has the signed ball with the final score of 9-6 written on it.

TOURNAMENT SUMMARY

THE 1973 STATE CHAMPIONSHIP FOR SCOBEY WAS A COMPLETE team effort. I remember watching several World Series where players I hadn't heard of or paid much attention to before would step up and make a great play or get the big hit to win the game and be a hero. Bernie Carbo's pinch-hit, game-tying, three-run home run in Game Six of the 1975 World Series for the Boston Red Sox against the Cincinnati Reds immediately pops to mind. (Of course it would; I am a Red Sox fan!) Every player on the roster is needed to win a championship. For Scobey in 1973, the big guns—18-year-olds Rick Danelson, Dallas Hagfeldt, and Terry Puckett, and 17-year-olds Jay Hagfeldt, Dana Audet, and Don Puckett—were all expected to play well and they did, but it was lesser-known players at the time, like 7-8-9 hitters Duke Trangsrud, Greg Fjeld, and Jack Tryan—who all had hits in Scobey's seven-run eighth inning against Wolf Point and batted over .300 for the tournament—whose names popped up in the *Leader* as key players who contributed to the championship.

It was fitting that young 15-year-old Greg Fjeld got the big game-tying hit to spark Scobey's seven-run rally in the eighth inning in the championship game and made the great catch in shallow center field to record the final out—it epitomized Doc's method of developing younger players by bringing them up to Legion while still Babe Ruth age and play them. Terry Puckett and Rick Danelson started playing Legion ball for Doc when they were only 13 years old in 1968. As a 13-year-old in 1968, Terry had relieved Dick against Havre in the state tournament in Glendive. At the state tournament in Scobey in 1969, Terry pitched seven innings of scoreless relief against Havre as a 14-year-old, rescuing Dick, who got knocked out in the second inning,

Trophy awards after final game are handed out by (right to left) Commissioner Shaw, Norm Brekke, representing Ford Motor Co. who gave the awards, and Scobey Post Legion Commander Gene Marley. *Leader.*

1973 Scobey Legionnaires, State B Champions. Standing, L–R: Jay Hagfeldt, Don Puckett, Doug Hagfeldt, Dana Audet, Lee Cook, Dallas Trangsrud, Mike Gunderson. Kneeling: Coach Doc Norman, Greg Fjeld, Duke Trangsrud, Jack Tryan, Keith Zieske, Ass't Coach Phil Audet. Kneeling in front: Dallas Hagfeldt, Rick Danelson, batboys Kelly Norman, Dan Danelson, Rick Lee, Kirby Halvorson, Terry Puckett. *Leader.*

and Rick Danelson started at third base that season and tournament. It's like Doc was winning championships with younger players while at the same time developing them to win future championships.

It was sad that Terry's arm was hanging by a thread and that he couldn't pitch effectively in his final state tournament at home. As a 14-year-old in 1969, he had pitched seven scoreless innings of relief against Havre, and in 1971 at the ripe old age of 16, he lost the epic pitcher's duel to Dave Fanning, 1-0—sixteen innings pitched with one earned run for an ERA of 0.56. Normally a power-hitter—he hit three home runs in three games the week before in Miles City and had 14 home runs in his final two seasons—he contributed to the championship with several clutch singles. Against Helena in the opening game, he hit a single in the eighth inning, was sacrificed to second, and then scored what proved to be the winning run. Against Wolf Point in the championship, he started the big seven-run inning in the eighth with a single, then hit a second single in the same inning to drive in two critical insurance runs after the team batted around. Terry's performance in the state tournament symbolized how each player contributed what they needed to help the team win.

This Wolf Point team was the fifth to finish second at State. Wolf Point won the state championship in 1965, but another hard-luck Wolf Point team came up a little short in the championship game, losing it in the eighth inning. The previous year, this same team was leading Havre 4-3 in the seventh inning of the state championship, but Havre came back to win it. With today's format, where the top two teams advance to the regional, all of these great Wolf Point teams could have gone on to play and do damage at the regional, but as it was, their season was over. Hats off again to Wolf Point: a tremendous collection of all-around athletes, well-coached by another superb all-around athlete, Harvey Langager. Future heart-breaking losses in state championship games (1976) led Mike Neubauer to say, after coaching Wolf Point to the State A championship on Cobb Field in 1987, "We got the monkey off our back. There have been a lot of second-place teams over the years."

Although Havre didn't play well at the 1973 state tournament—losing out in two games—this was a young team, and they would continue to grow. Havre would be back with stronger teams at the state tournament in Havre in 1974 and in Scobey in 1975, before the Montana State Legion Baseball Commission—based on having a Class AA high school and city population—moved them up to American Legion Class A in 1976.

And Scobey should thank Glasgow and Wolf Point for not fielding Legion teams in 1971, the first year Dallas Hagfeldt from Glasgow played American Legion ball. Legion rules stated the player could play in the closest town with a Legion team, Wolf Point, but Wolf Point also did not field a Legion team in 1971. So, the next nearest town was . . . Scobey. Jay followed Dallas, then Mike followed Jay, and the rest is history.

TOURNAMENT STATS

Hitting

RICK DANELSON WAS THE TOURNAMENT'S LEADING HITTER with a .470 average. Five other Scobey hitters batted over .300: Terry Puckett (.357), Duke Trangsrud (.353), Dallas Hagfeldt (.333), Jack Tryan (.333), and Dana Audet (.312). Three other Scobey hitters—Jay Hagfeldt (one of Scobey's leading hitters the entire season), Don Puckett, and Greg Fjeld—had clutch hits in Scobey's seven-run eighth inning in the championship game. Dan Bartel of Wolf Point had the lone home run of the tournament, a solo shot in the first game against Cut Bank. John Murphy kept stats for the tournament.

Pitching

DANA AUDET, JAY HAGFELDT, DUKE TRANGSRUD, AND TERRY Puckett—his labrum almost completely torn—pitched for Scobey in the tournament, with Dana and Jay bearing the brunt of the load. Dana started and got the 5-4 win over Helena, with Jay Hagfeldt earning the save in relief. Dana and Jay combined to pitch a five-hitter in the game. Jay Hagfeldt started and was the winning pitcher in the 8-5 win over Cut Bank, with Duke Trangsrud pitching in relief. Dana Audet and Terry Puckett pitched in the first

1973 Wolf Point Legion Team, State B Runners-Up. Front row, left to right: Ken Lee, Dan Bartel, Brian Jones, and Lane Pickthorn. Second row: Larry Monson, Tim Cody, Mike Green, Warren Crowe, and Keith Lee. Back row: Dave Johnson, Carmen Birdsbill, Dave Stengel, Jeff Neubauer, and Coach Harvey Langager. Not pictured are Jon McMaster and Lenny Vine. *Leader.*

championship game on Saturday. On Sunday, Dana Audet started and went eight innings for the win, with Jay Hagfeldt pitching the final inning in relief. Dana and Jay each appeared in 3 of 4 of Scobey's games.

With Terry's arm shot, someone had to pick up the slack, and it was Dana and Jay. Dana likely logged nearly 20 innings of work over four days. (Legion rules allowed 12 innings over three days at the time.) However, the number of innings took their toll on Dana. In the championship game on Sunday, Dana recalls, "By that time, you've just played so much baseball and thrown so many balls your arm just hurts. In that game, it was my elbow. I remember just saying to myself, in about the third or fourth inning, 'Well, I'm not coming out. So what are you gonna do?' In between innings, I just got the Ben-Gay (he didn't like the DMSO) and rubbed it on there. I wanted to finish the game and pitch the ninth inning."

Ironically, the painful end to Terry's progressively declining six-year Legion pitching career was not on a pitch to Dallas Hagfeldt but on a one-hop throw from right field to Rick Danelson at third base. In the ninth inning of the championship game on Sunday, Carmen Birdsbill went to third on Larry Monson's single, and Terry tried to throw him out. When I interviewed Terry, he said he knew exactly when he completely threw his arm out, and this was it. Although he didn't learn this until 30 years later in his fifties, his shoulder labrum—partially torn before the throw—completely tore, not allowing him to rotate his arm overhand. He said he would have had to come out if it had happened earlier in the game. A few days later, at the State A Tournament in Great Falls, he had to roll the ball underhanded to Duke in center field on a hit to him in right field because he could not throw the ball overhanded anymore, let alone pitch. It was also ironic that Terry's biggest win in a state tournament was at a divisional tournament—the 12-inning, 16-strikeout win over Wolf Point a week earlier in Miles City. As a result, the first-round bye Scobey received saved a precious nine innings for a depleted staff in the first round, and Wolf Point lost their opening game to Cut Bank. The divisional championship game was a critical part of the state championship for Scobey.

Mention has to be made of Wolf Point's pitching. The team played six games and 54 innings in four days, and overall, their pitching, except for a couple of bad innings, was good. Lane Pickthorn pitched a complete game win over Helena, yielding only three runs. Against Circle, Dave Stengel started, Dave Johnson got the win, and Carmen Birdsbill pitched three innings of scoreless, one-hit relief to earn the save, recording six strikeouts. Brian Jones pitched a complete-game win over Cut Bank to get Wolf Point to the championship game, allowing just two runs and avenging Wolf Point's opening-day loss to Cut Bank. After Scobey knocked Carmen Birdsbill out in the second inning of the first championship game, Wolf Point held Scobey hitless for the last seven innings, as sidearm-throwing Dave Johnson came in to pitch two and two-thirds innings of hitless ball, and Carmen Birdsbill returned in the fifth to pitch four scoreless innings. On Sunday, Carmen Birdsbill and Dave Johnson had seven innings of eligibility left between them, and they held Scobey to two runs until that fateful seven-run eighth inning for Wolf Point. There was no doubt that Carmen Birdsbill was Wolf Point's ace, but Dave Johnson always gave the Scobey hitters trouble, dating back to the 9-0 shutout he pitched against them a year earlier at Havre.

Wade Sukut of Circle must be recognized for his dominant game against Havre, pitching a five-hitter to beat Dale Kuntz, who also threw a five-hitter, 3-1.

Fielding

SCOBEY'S DEFENSE PLAYED WELL AGAINST HELENA, committing just two errors, but they booted five balls against Cut Bank, leading to unearned runs. Then, in the third inning on Saturday—an inning which recalled the horrible seventh and eighth innings against Plentywood 1971—they committed four errors to allow Wolf Point to score five runs and get back in the game. Against Wolf Point on Sunday, their defense committed three errors, but there is no mention of any of Wolf Point's six runs being unearned, so the defense held when it needed to.

The *Leader* specifically called out the exceptional play of Duke Trangsrud in left field in the championship game, as Wolf Point hit the ball sharply several times to the outfield "but saw young left fielder Duke Trangsrud in left handle six chances flawlessly." Then it added, "Trangsrud was playing one of the best games of the season."[82]

Dave Stengel's shallow fly ball to center, had it dropped between Greg Fjeld at second and Dana Audet in center, would have been disastrous for Scobey, as Wolf Point could have scored the tying run. Communication between the infield and outfield on balls hit to the shallow outfield is critical. Greg, Dana, and Scobey executed this perfectly to end the game and win the tournament.

STATE A TOURNAMENT

SCOBEY GAINED AN AUTOMATIC BERTH IN THE STATE A Tournament in Great Falls—Doc and Scobey's first. They were the number-three seed in the east with its State Class B championship and played the tournament's opening game against Libby. Terry recalls, "Doc was pissed that I couldn't pitch." He remembers getting the needle in the dugout before the game, but after he completely tore his labrum trying to get Carmen Birdsbill out at third in the state championship game, all the King's horses and all the King's men couldn't put Terry's arm together again. He played right field in the tournament, and the one chance he got on the ground, he rolled the ball underhanded to Duke in center field to make the throw back into the infield.

Dana Audet said that Scobey could have played much better in the State A Tournament. The competition is always better in the class up, and sometimes the psychological factor can cause a team to get a little jittery, especially in the field. I experienced this in my Legion career years later, but after playing against the Class A teams many times, our team learned we could stay on the field with them and win. Scobey committed three costly errors in their first game against Libby, leading to Libby's 7-3 win. Only one of Libby's runs was earned. Dean Smith, Libby's solid left-handed pitcher, went the distance, striking out 11. For their part, Libby didn't play well in the field either, committing six errors. Scobey scored one run and had the bases loaded with the tying run at the plate in the ninth, but couldn't push another run across to close the gap. Rick Danelson had a single to drive in two runs to lead Scobey's hitting. Dana Audet pitched seven innings, and Duke Trangsrud pitched one inning for Scobey.

The opening-game jitters were gone, and Scobey played much better in their second game against Kalispell. As the *Leader* wrote, "The Scobey club seemed to have a better feel of things."[83] Kalispell scored five runs in the bottom of the first, but Scobey clawed their way back to close the score to 6-5, rallying in the top of the seventh inning. In the rally, Scobey's big three guns gave it one last push for Scobey. Rick Danelson tripled, and Dallas Hagfeldt singled him home. Terry Puckett followed with a double to put the tying run on third and the winning run on second. But the *Leader* mentioned that Dana Audet was called out at first when he was "obviously safe," and that snuffed out Scobey's rally.

The *Leader* stated, "Scobey had the Kalispell team very worried" when they closed to within 6-5. But Kalispell scored three runs in the bottom of the eighth to make the final score 9-5. After the rough first inning, Jay Hagfeldt— who went the distance for Scobey on the mound—settled down and allowed Kalispell only one run until the eighth. The *Leader* mentioned again, however, that "Scobey errors were a bit costly." Terry Puckett led Scobey's hitting with three hits, including a double.

The State A Tournament was a disappointing footnote to a storybook season for Scobey, but the team fought hard to the end and went down swinging. Terry Puckett (.429) and Rick Danelson (.333), playing in their last games and tournament together, led Scobey's hitting, and Dallas Hagfeldt, "a tower of strength in the catching position," had hits in each game.[84] It was incredible that photographer Mike Drapak of Scobey captured the picture of Rick Danelson crossing home plate on a single by Dallas Hagfeldt, with cleanup hitter Terry Puckett standing at home plate to welcome Rick home. These were the last at-bats of their Legion careers in the seventh-inning rally against Kalispell, and they all got hits to try to bring Scobey back. The rest of the Scobey team stood on the shoulders of these three giants in 1973 to win the state championship. "In the lineup for next year, Terry Puckett, Rick Danelson, and Dallas Hagfeldt will leave big holes."[85] For sure. But the team would return six starters, including pitchers Jay Hagfeldt, Dana Audet, and Duke Trangsrud, so if everyone stayed healthy, Scobey would be competitive the following season. *If everyone stayed healthy.*

EXTRA INNINGS

DANA AUDET RECENTLY DISCUSSED THE 1973 STATE CHAMPIonship game with Dave Stengel of Wolf Point. He said, "I had an interesting conversation with Dave Stengel (a great athlete) about the '73 championship game in Scobey. The two of us stayed in touch, attending MSU and playing some intramural football together. As avid Cat fans, we were both at the big pep rally celebration in Frisco, Texas, for the 2022 FCS championship the night before the game and crossed paths.

"We replayed the highlights, especially when the Wolf Point pitcher, Carmen Birdsbill, reached his 12 innings over a 72-hour limit and had to come out. We were behind 4-2 at the time, and I felt pretty good about holding the explosive Wolf Point lineup to four runs through seven complete innings with an arm heavily doused in Bengay. Brian Jones came in to pitch for them, and we proceeded to scatter nine singles, resulting in seven runs to go up 9-4. He was throwing batting practice. Jay Hagfeldt relieved me in the ninth and we held on for a 9-6 win for the championship.

"Dave reminded me that Wolf Point had unparalleled speed, and I wholeheartedly agreed. If Dave or Dan Bartel or Lane Pickthorn, among others, got on base, they were virtually impossible to hold and guaranteed to successfully steal. Dave also made a point to mention that since we were aware of that speed, we had the field plowed into loose, deep dirt that nobody could run on, prior to State.

This is the point where I disagreed. As you all well know, that was the hardest chip gravel infield in the state. I recall Doc bringing in assorted plows to try and break it up with absolutely no success. It was hard. I kidded Dave that he had used that as the excuse for losing to us for all these years. Ha."

Jay remembers relieving Dana in the ninth. He said, "My arm was so sore I was sure the game was not going to end well. When Doc motioned me in from center field, I wanted to shake my head. The only pitch I could throw without a lot of pain was a slow curveball. Wolf Point were great fastball hitters but not so much with sliders and curves (except for Birdsbill; he could hit anything), so that worked to our advantage and we won the game. Jack Cassidy took me over to the high school afterwards, and we soaked my arm in a hot tub for a while and rubbed in horse liniment. Was always appreciative of that."

Jay commented on how strong Scobey was at the corners defensively in 1973. He said, "Rick was strong playing third. Doc also worked with Lee Cook at first. Lee took all the advice Doc gave him and was solid defensively. I also remember when Rick lost the tip of his little finger on his glove hand in a farming accident. Doc sewed it back on, and he was playing again in a day or two. When somebody told me about it at practice, I didn't believe him, so I asked Rick about it. He took off his glove and there it was, stitches still in place. I remember thinking that was some kind of tough."

Doc asked pitcher Ron Fjeld—former Scobey Legionnaire, Whitetail Oiler, and Scobey Plainsmen pitcher—to come to Legion practice at Scobey Ball Park and pitch to the 1973 team the week of the state tournament. Carmen Birdsbill from Wolf Point had a good curveball, and Doc wanted the team to get some good practice by hitting Ron's curveball. Ron said, "Doc called me up to pitch to the team. I was over 40 years old and hadn't pitched for a couple years. He wanted me to throw some junk at the kids to see if they could hit it." Ron had snapped off a few curveballs in his career, once pitching for 27 innings in one day for Whitetail in a tournament in Saskatchewan. He had a good fastball, too.

Ron said none of the Legionnaires could hit his drop curve that day.* He said, "I struck just about all the guys out, mainly with that drop curve." I asked Ron if one of the guys he struck out was his son Greg. He laughed, then said, "I don't remember." He continued laughing, then paused and added, "I think I struck him out. That's terrible to strike your own son out."

The Legionnaires, including his son Greg, didn't need to feel bad about not being able to hit Ron's drop curve that day. They weren't the only hitters who had trouble with it. Ron shared a story about a frustrated Williston hitter in a game in Williston while he was pitching for the Plainsmen. He said, "Their catcher was batting. I threw him a drop curve and it scared him. It was a ball. The second drop curve I threw him was a strike, but he didn't pay attention to it. He charged the mound after me, but I outmaneuvered him and I uppercut him and knocked him out." Thankfully no frustrated Scobey Legionnaires rushed the mound that day Ron pitched to the team, and nobody got hurt.

The 1960 team had the "red bus" for road trips, and the teams Dana Audet played on had the "green van." Dana Audet recalls one story riding with Doc in the green van. He said, "Doc had a reputation for being quite a multitasker. He could be watching TV, reading a book and carrying on a conversation with the people in the room. We were traveling somewhere back from a game, and he was driving the green baseball van and I was riding shotgun. He proceeded to reach down and grab a book and begin reading it. This is where the multitasking was taken a bit too far. I said, 'C'mon Doc, I can drive if you want to read.' Fortunately, he agreed and I took over. If I recall correctly, we actually made the switch without slowing down a bit. Standard procedure in those days." Kelly Norman, who would have been a batboy at the time, remembers the green van, too. He added, "He had a siren and light for the green van. One time we hid behind a building in Redstone and when Rick Danelson came speeding by in Mom's silver Pontiac and Dad hit the siren and Rick slowed down real quick and we went fast by him. Probably a few moons being shot as everyone was laughing. Never a dull moment!"

Dana Audet remembers Greg Fjeld's catch of the pop-up to end the championship game as his most vivid memory of Legion ball. At the Scobey 50-year class reunion in 2023, Dana asked Greg if he remembered the play. Greg's response: "Ah . . . yeah. I remember it like it was yesterday. All I wanted to do was make sure I didn't bobble it and drop it!"

---

* Ron described the grip for his drop curve this way: "On the narrow part of the seams, I placed my two fingers and the thumb under, this created a drop curve."

Rick Danelson spent his honeymoon playing in the State B Tournament in Scobey, as he was married to Wendy Tryan just before the tournament began.

Rick Danelson playing his final Legion ball game, scores in Kalispell game on a hit by **Dallas Hagfeldt**, during a rally. **Terry Puckett** at right. Dallas and Terry were also playing their last game. *Photo by Mike Drapak.*

In this *Leader* picture of Frankie Tymofichuk and Doc Norman, Frankie is handing Doc a check for $500. Frankie donated this $500 to the team after the State B Tournament to "help things along" before the Scobey American Legion Baseball team left for the State A Tournament in Great Falls. "Frankie, a prominent farmer-stockman north of Scobey and the son of early-day pioneers who helped settle the north Scobey area, said, 'Ukrainians have always been Scobey boosters, and I'm doing this personally to show we're still wanting to do our part in helping build the community by continuing opportunities for our young folks.'"[86] By the way, $500 in 1973 is the equivalent of about $3,500 today.

Frankie Tymofichuk hands Doc Norman a check for $500 to help things along, before the Scobey American Legion Baseball team heads out to Great Falls. *Leader.*

Another Ukrainian who was part of the 1973 American Legion season was Mike Drapak, who snapped pictures of the Scobey crowd and Rick Danelson crossing home plate at the State A Tournament in Great Falls and shared them with the *Leader*. Mike, who enjoyed photography, was the son of William Drapak, the priest for Saint Michael's Ukrainian Greek Orthodox parish and church north of Scobey for many years. The church was built in 1917 by donations from 16 Ukrainian families. Thank you, Mike, for taking the pictures and being part of the 1973 season.

Scobey crowd at the 1973 State A Tourney at Great Falls. The sessions were attended by many fans rooting for the Scobey team. *Photo by Mike Drapak.*

In this picture of the 1973 Scobey Plainsmen, taken before one of the classic early-season competitive games with the Scobey Legion team, players spanning 1959 (Rod Tande) through 1971 (Danny Wolfe) were on the team.

1973 Scobey Plainsmen. Standing, L–R: Rod Tande, Rick Sampsen, Jim Hansen, Jack Higgins, Dick Puckett. Kneeling: Rocky Ware, Danny Wolfe, Craig Audet, Phil Audet, John Murphy. *Leader.*

My lone memory of watching the 1973 state tournament in Scobey was Carmen Birdsbill slamming the door on Scobey in the bottom of the ninth inning of the first championship game. Trailing 7-0 in the second inning, the Wolf Point team—and fans—had come back to life in the top of the ninth, completing their seven-run comeback on Dan Bartel's two-out, three-run triple. I had watched a lot of baseball by then and had never seen a pitcher get shelled like Birdsbill had in the first two innings, then return and be dominant in the same game. I had seen it in consecutive starts, but not in the same game. It was odd. The memory mainly relates to how loud the Wolf Point fans were and how eerily quiet the Scobey fans were in the bottom of the ninth inning. There was no joy in Scobey that night.

In the State A Tournament in Great Falls, Don Puckett got sick in the Kalispell game, so Dana Audet needed to come in to play short, the position he started playing his first year in 1971.

Fifteen-year-old Greg Fjeld was the youngest player in the State A Tournament.

The Great Falls Electrics won the State A Tournament, defeating the Billings Royals, 4-0. The incredible Royals dynasty with Doc's friend Ed Bayne as coach, winning 20 of 22 state A championships from 1950-1971, had come to an end. Since 1971, the Royals have won nine state championships. The Billings Scarlets have won 14 during that same time.

Ted Anderson, Havre's head coach in 1973, played baseball at Western Montana College and Gonzaga University, being named the most valuable player each year at those schools. He also played semipro baseball in Spokane for three years and coached Legion ball there for seven years.

Doc's theory for what caused a sore arm and his prescribed remedy is rated NC-17 and must remain confidential to the Scobey dugout only. Doc had a great sense of humor and kept everyone loose in the dugout. It's important to remember Doc was an Marine veteran, not a choirboy.

Terry's torn labrum has been called "the career-ender," "baseball's toughest injury," and "a pitcher's death sentence." In 2004, Baseball Prospectus's injury expert Will Carroll wrote an article titled "Labrum: It Nearly Killed Him" in *Slate* magazine. In it, he labeled the torn labrum as "baseball's most fearsome injury." Of the 36 pitchers Carroll studied who had undergone labrum surgery, only one had returned to his previous level. Carroll wrote, "The leading minds in baseball medicine are flummoxed by the labrum. Doctors can't agree on how to detect a tear, don't know the best way to fix one, and aren't sure why, almost without fail, a torn labrum will destroy a pitcher's career. If pitchers with torn labrums were horses, they'd be destroyed." In 2012, Jay Jaffe wrote an article for baseballprospectus.com where he did his own survey to compare it to the results of Carroll's. He found that out of 67 players he surveyed, only nine returned to some level of success post-surgery. That's about a 14 percent chance of achieving success after tearing a labrum. By comparison, Tommy John surgery, which repairs a pitcher's elbow, has a return-to-play rate of 80% to 95%. Some notable MLB pitchers who had labrum surgery were Roger Clemens, Curt Schilling, Mark Mulder, and Mark Prior. In the NFL, Andrew Luck of the Indianapolis Colts had labrum surgery.

Kelly Norman completed his seventh year as a batboy in 1973, but the appearance of Rick Lee in the team picture foretells the transition to a new era, when Rick, Mike, and Josh Lee would, in turn, become batboys over the next 10 years. Danny Danelson and Kirby Halvorson were also batboys in 1973. Kirby's memories as a batboy: "I remember Kelly and I pitching sunflower seeds to each other trying to swing the big bats when our guys were in the field, a lot of trips to the concession stand, Doc getting on us for not paying attention and getting a real-life education from the players including multiple mooning episodes." Kids grew up fast in a Doc Norman dugout. Danny remembers, "Randy Legare had a size eight batting helmet. We used to put it on and spin around our head."

I got to catch Terry Puckett when he came back from Montana Tech in the spring of 1973 to play his last season in Scobey. I was 12 years old at the time. Like older brother Dick, Terry had that magical birthday after August 1st, so he got to play another season after his senior year, when he wouldn't turn 19 until after August the following year. Uncle Reese had built a pitcher's mound between Dad's house and his, next to a little driveway between our houses. Terry asked me, "Joey, would you catch me?" He needed to get in shape for the 1973 season after coming home from college. I said, "Sure!" I was nervous but excited. I had watched Terry pitch for Scobey for five years (he pitched for Scobey when he was only 13 in 1968). I knew he went eight innings against the Royals in 1969 when he was only 14 years old, and I had watched him duel Dave Fanning in the 1971 state tournament when he was 16. I idolized him.

As he started to warmup, my focus was intense because I wanted to show him I could handle his pitches. I wanted to be able to handle his fastball so I could see it. He ended up working out with me for probably 20-30 minutes. I don't know if I ever saw his fastest, but the ball hopped around it was so lively. It tailed too. It was very difficult to catch but I hung in there. I went the distance. And at the end of it, Terry thanked me. Never got another chance to catch him, but I will never forget that spring day in Peerless in 1973 when I got to catch my older cousin Terry Puckett.

1974

A Streaker Steals the Show at Divisional and the Scarlet Tide Rolls

> *Many of the Legion players look back at that time as a special time in their lives. I know I do. I wish my sons and grandsons had the same opportunity.*
>
> —Jay Hagfeldt, Scobey Legionnaires (1972–74)

1974 Scobey Legionnaires. Standing L–R: Coach Doc Norman, Don Puckett, Doug Hagfeldt, Dallas Trangsrud, Mike Gunderson, Lee Cook, Greg Fjeld, Duke Trangsrud, Jack Tryan, Rusty Shane. Kneeling: Pat Anderson, Don Hagfeldt, Craig Miller, Bill Bartole, Mike Hagfeldt, Jeff Richardson, Jim Chapman, Dana Audet, Ass't Coach Phil Audet. Sitting: Batboy Kelly Norman. Not pictured is Jay Hagfeldt, who had sustained his injury at this time. *Leader photo by Milton Gunderson.*

PRESEASON

When Doc addressed the team at the first practice in April 1974, three familiar faces—Terry Puckett, Rick Danelson, and Dallas Hagfeldt—were not looking back at him. The departed talented trio left big holes in the lineup. Rick and Terry had played for Doc for six seasons and Dallas for three. Tough to see them go. But plenty of familiar faces looked back at him, including six starters from 1973: Jay Hagfeldt, Dana Audet, Don Puckett, Duke Trangsrud, Greg Fjeld, and Jack Tryan. Four additional players who sometimes started or saw action in 1973 were also there: Lee Cook, Doug Hagfeldt, Dallas Trangsrud, and Mike Gunderson. Mike would replace Rick Danelson at third base after Rick had played the position for six years, going back to 1968.

Three faces were gone, and 10 familiars. What about the new faces? Perhaps the biggest rookie crop ever had assembled before Doc that day, and the bunch had plenty of talent. Joining the team in 1974 were Mike Hagfeldt, Craig Miller, Jeff Richardson, Bill Bartole, Don Hagfeldt, Tully Tryan, Pat Anderson, Rusty Shane, and Jim Chapman.

The nineteen-player roster included solid pitching, as Dana, Jay, and Duke returned from 1973. Don Puckett and Dallas Trangsrud could also pitch, as could 16-year-old left-handers Mike Hagfeldt and Craig Miller. This was probably the deepest pitching staff Doc ever had, with seven legitimate pitchers—three right-handers and four left-handers. Dana Audet, who played every position in his Legion career, would slide behind the plate to catch in his final season, following in older brother Craig's footsteps.

A significant fashion change for Scobey in 1974 was their new blue uniforms. Doc was so excited about the new uniforms when they arrived, he called Dana Audet, who was on a date at Richardson's Theater, to come to the Norman house and model the new uniform. Gone were the button-down jerseys, pinstripes, and belts around the waist, replaced by pullover jerseys and beltless pants made of synthetic stretch material. This style was following the lead of Major League Baseball at the time. It began when the Pittsburgh Pirates donned their new Pirate uniforms in this style on the day Three Rivers Stadium opened, July 16, 1970. By Opening Day of the 1973 season, all 24 MLB clubs had transitioned from the old uniforms to the new synthetic design. Wolf Point wore the uniform style in 1973, and Scobey followed "suit" in 1974. The new blue uniforms eventually led to the Scobey Legionnaires being dubbed the Scobey Blues in 1977.

Another significant change to baseball in 1974 was the NCAA's approval of the use of the aluminum bat. Little League Baseball had approved of the use of aluminum bats in 1971. I think I first used an aluminum bat in Little League in 1973. I am unsure what year American Legion approved using the aluminum bat. The principal driver for the decision was financial—wooden bats break and cost money to replace, but aluminum bats do not—so the coaches supported it.

Most coaches estimated that only eight bats would be needed for the season. One of the concerns was that the financial savings would be at the expense of injuries, as the ball comes off the aluminum bat faster. However, the transition to all aluminum bats in Scobey was not immediate. Some of my teammates—Wade Tryan, for example—used the wooden bat up to his final season in 1979, and all of us used them interchangeably with the aluminum bat at various times. I've included a picture of Doc in Sidney in 1977, which shows an extensive collection of wooden bats behind him.

REGULAR SEASON

Doc took the team on another epic barnstorming tour of Montana in June, traveling to Havre, Helena, Great Falls, back to Helena, and then Billings. In their first game, Scobey played Havre, who was hosting the State Class B tournament later that summer. Two familiar names to Scobey fans—Fanning (Ron) and Kato (Mark)—pitched for Havre, with Dana Audet and Jay Hagfeldt pitching for Scobey. Jeff Richardson hit a booming three-run double to left in the top of the seventh to give Scobey a temporary 6-5 lead, but Havre came back to tie in their half of the seventh, then scored the winning run in the bottom of the eighth to win 7-6—another classic one-run game between Scobey and Havre, this time in the regular season. Scobey then played the Class A Helena Senators tough, losing only 7-5. Doc took the team back to play the Great Falls Electrics, losing to the Class A team, 19-2. They then returned to Helena to play the Representatives and won 8-6. Their last game of the road trip against the Billings Scarlets on Cobb Field was the trip's highlight. The game went 11 innings, with Scobey scoring the winning run on a squeeze play to win it 4-3 in the 11th. Jay Hagfeldt pitched a gem for Scobey, yielding all three runs in the first inning, then mowing the Scarlets down for 10 shutout innings for the comeback win. The 1200-mile road trip was significant for Scobey, as the Helena Reps, Havre Northstars, and Billings Scarlets would all be in the state tournament in Havre. The Scarlets were playing their last year of Class B Legion, moving up to Class A the following year. They had a loaded lineup and were a powerful team, so Jay's pitching and Scobey's win was a huge indicator they could play with and beat the best. We will see the Scarlets again in Scobey at the eastern divisional tournament and the state tournament in Havre.

But then came the devastating injury to Jay Hagfeldt. It happened during a regular season game in Glasgow, of all places, where Jay went to high school. Doug Hagfeldt, Jay's cousin, was playing right field, and Jay was playing second, which was unusual, as this was normally Greg Fjeld's position. Jay normally pitched or played in the outfield. Dana Audet was pitching. Dana recalls that a shallow fly ball was hit to right field. Jay ran out to get it, but Doug Hagfeldt was coming in on the ball, and they collided. Doug got up, but Jay remained on the ground, holding the front side of his stomach and visibly in pain. Lee Cook, playing first base, said, "Jay dropped like he was shot in the head." It was apparent it was a serious injury, so he was taken to the hospital in Glasgow, where it was discovered he had ruptured his spleen, which had to be removed. This incident was awful to Jay and the team's state championship aspirations. Dana Audet recalls, "That was such a big loss, because Jay was such a great player." Many people I've interviewed put Jay up with the all-time greats to have played for the Scobey Legion team. He could hit, run, field, throw, and perhaps most importantly—pitch. He could do it all. And he was a tremendous all-around athlete. During his senior year at Glasgow High School, he won the State Class A javelin event at the state track and field meet, throwing it 199-9. But Jay would return in a limited capacity at the divisional in Scobey, pinch-hitting twice and even pitching a little at the state tournament in Havre. So he could be on the field with his teammates in the end.

There were six teams in the east that season. The Billings Scarlets (8-2), Wolf Point (7-3), and Scobey (6-4) finished 1-2-3. The other teams competing in the east that summer were Circle, Ekalaka, and Glasgow. After Scobey beat the Scarlets 4-3 in 11 innings, the Billings Scarlets won their last six conference games, outscoring their opponents 87-13. In their final regular season game at Scobey, right-hander Jim Knudtson of the Scarlets tossed a rare no-hitter against Scobey (the only one I know of), as the Scarlets won 6-0. Knudtson struck out 10 and didn't walk a batter. The Scarlets had previously beaten Wolf Point 4-1 on the road trip to win first place. Wolf Point was again strong in 1974, returning many starters from the previous season with some talented newcomers on the roster. The six teams would congregate in Scobey for the divisional tournament, with the top three teams advancing to the state tournament in Havre.

DIVISIONAL TOURNAMENT

BY 1974, SCOBEY HAD HOSTED THREE STATE TOURNAMENTS (1969, 1971, 1973) but hadn't hosted a divisional tournament since 1965. The *Leader*'s tournament coverage was every bit as robust as if it were a state tournament. If Scobey was hosting *any* tournament, it was a *big* deal.

Scobey opened the tournament against Circle and needed a two-run rally in the bottom of the 10th inning to win it 5-4. Circle had taken a 4-3 lead in the top of the 10th, but in the bottom half of the inning, Mike Hagfeldt and Don Puckett—who hit a two-run double in the sixth to tie it—singled to start the rally. Wade Sukut then walked Lee Cook and Mike Gunderson to force in the tying run. Joe Sukut relieved Wade but walked Greg Fjeld to force in the winning run. Craig Miller started for Scobey and pitched strong into the sixth inning. He was relieved by Don Puckett; then Dana Audet came on in the tenth to get the win in relief for Scobey. Bill Bartole caught for Scobey when Dana pitched.

This win set up Scobey's second game against the strong Billings Scarlets, who had received a first-round bye due to their number-one seed. The Scarlets won the game 11-1. Scobey had plenty of base runners and chances to score, as Billings pitcher John Martin walked 12 Scobey hitters, but they couldn't get the hits they needed to push any runs across. Dallas Trangsrud, Craig Miller, and Don Puckett pitched for Scobey.

Sixteen-year-old left-hander Mike Hagfeldt pitched a 5-0 shutout against Ekalaka, scattering six hits. Don Puckett and Duke Trangsrud each went 2-4, and each had a double to lead Scobey's hitting. Scobey beat Circle 18-6 for the second time to clinch a berth in the state tournament in

Mike Hagfeldt scores the first run of the 1974 Eastern Division Legion Tournament against Circle. Mike crossed the plate in the first inning. *Leader photo by Milton Gunderson.*

Havre the following weekend. Scobey had 13 hits, led by Don Puckett, who went 5-5, including a double. Dallas Trangsrud started for Scobey, relieved by younger brother Duke in the third inning.

Bill Neumiller of Wolf Point then tossed a two-hitter at Scobey to lead Wolf Point to a 13-0 win and eliminate Scobey from the tournament. Neumiller walked three and struck out six. Dana Audet pitched well for Scobey, allowing only six singles in six and one-third innings, but 11 Scobey errors doomed Scobey. Doc described Scobey's fielding as "shabby." Wolf Point also stole eight bases in the game.

The Scarlets made it to the championship game by beating Scobey 11-1 and then Wolf Point 7-3. Wolf Point had outclassed Glasgow 18-2 and Scobey 13-0 to get there. In the championship game, the Scarlets trailed Wolf Point 12-10 in the top of the ninth but scored six runs to take a 16-12 lead, then held Wolf Point to two runs in the bottom of the ninth for a 16-14 win in the slugfest. The two teams had 34 hits between them. So, at the end of four days of baseball in Scobey, the Scarlets, Wolf Point, and Scobey were headed to the state tournament in Havre.

Despite having major surgery less than a month earlier in Glasgow, Jay Hagfeldt pinch-hit twice in the tournament. Jay's injury "left a big hole in the local club."[87] A big hole indeed, but great to see Jay back on the field, if only as a pinch-hitter. He would get to see some more time on the field in Havre, but Dana Audet said, "Jay's injury was a huge loss for us because he was just such a great player, both

Wolf Point's Lane Pickthorn delivers a pitch to the Scarlets' Jim Yeager in the first inning of the championship game. Yeager doubled to deep center, driving home two runs to start the 16-14 slugfest victory for the Scarlets. *Leader photo by Milton Gunderson.*

1974 Billings Scarlets, State B champions. Standing L–R: Assistant Coach Loren Kovik, Chuck Ball, Jim Yeager, Dan Benjamin, Kit Kittelson, Bill Sebring, John Martin, Rick Popp, Perry Morrison, Kelly Varnes, Mike Krivee, Coach Peterson. Kneeling: Doug Luscombe, Jim Knudtson, Leininger, Greg Peterson, Jerry Vincent, Don Jacobson, Dan Fuchs, Dick Peterson, and Manager Del Jones. *Leader photo by Milton Gunderson.*

as a center fielder and a pitcher. We just really weren't the same team after that."

STATE B TOURNAMENT

HAVRE WAS HOSTING THE STATE TOURNAMENT FOR THE THIRD time, as they had hosted it in 1970 and 1972, winning it on their home field both times. After their down year in 1973, Havre was again the west champion with a 13-3 conference record, and they received a first-round bye along with the Billings Scarlets. Cut Bank and the Helena Reps were the other teams in the west. The Scarlets were identified as the team to beat in the tournament, as they were hot, riding a nine-game win streak into the state tournament, beating both Scobey and Wolf Point (twice) in the divisional tournament to win the east, and beating them both a week earlier to win the regular season. Wolf Point was the other team mentioned as a possible champion.

Scobey played the Helena Reps—the number-two seed in the west with a 15-7 record—in their first game, bright and early at eight o'clock on Thursday morning. Scobey had played the Reps on their early-season road trip, winning 8-6 in Helena. I remember listening to his game on KCGM radio in my house in Peerless and was disheartened to hear Cliff Hagfeldt's voice announce that Scobey fell behind 6-1 after four innings. Scobey was not playing well and had committed several errors, leading to the five-run deficit. But then, Cliff's voice boomed over the airwaves in the top of the fifth when, with one swing of the bat, Don Puckett brought Scobey back with a 350-foot grand-slam home run. There was nothing like hearing Cliff's voice when he got excited for a big play for the home team in a game! And just like that, Scobey was back in the game at 6-5. Then, in the top of the ninth, Scobey's four-year veteran starters, Don Puckett and Dana Audet, kept Scobey's hopes alive. With two outs, Don doubled, then Dana brought him home with a clutch single up the middle to tie the game 6-6, completing the five-run comeback. Don Puckett entered the game as a pitcher in the bottom of the fifth and had pitched four innings of shutout relief. But in the bottom of the ninth, Helena started the inning with a bloop single to right and followed with another single. Then, Don—always steady at shortstop—uncharacteristically mishandled a sacrifice bunt as the pitcher to load the bases with no outs. Helena then walked it off on a sacrifice fly by pitcher Tom Morgan, who had gone the distance for Helena. It was a devastating first-game loss for Scobey, dropping a heart-breaking one-run game after coming from five runs down to tie the score with two outs in the ninth. Dana Audet, Dallas Trangsrud, and Don pitched for Scobey. Mike Gunderson also doubled for Scobey in the game. Scobey's five errors in the field proved costly in the outcome. As I went outside to play after listening to the game on KCGM radio in Peerless that morning, the summer day was not as bright. I was a big fan of the Scobey Legion team that I would eventually play for, and of course, the Peerless boys—Don Puckett, Dallas and Duke Trangsrud, and Jim Chapman—who were on the team. I had watched Don and Dallas lead Peerless to its first divisional tournament basketball appearance earlier that year, an iconic moment for Peerless High School and the Peerless community.

Scobey then played Havre in a loser-out contest, as Havre had lost to Wolf Point 6-3 in their first game. Scobey had played Havre earlier in the season, with Havre winning 7-6. This game was the ninth time Scobey and Havre had faced each other in a state tournament, dating back to 1968 when they first played in Glendive. Although this game was in the loser's bracket, this Scobey-Havre game was a classic, well-played game between the two best Class B Legion programs in the state, as these two teams had won state six state championships between them dating back to 1968.

No other team besides Scobey or Havre had won the state tournament during that time. It would remain to be seen if that streak would be broken in this tournament.

Doc handed the ball to Jay Hagfeldt—back from major surgery a month earlier—to start, and Havre countered with Mark Kato. Jay, Scobey's ace during the season until his injury, had not pitched in a game since he ruptured his spleen in Glasgow. He pitched two scoreless innings to start, but got in trouble in the bottom of the third when Havre scored three runs on four hits and a walk. And who do you think trotted in from right field to relieve Jay? No other than his 16-year-old younger brother, Mike. Mike pitched three innings of scoreless relief before Duke Trangsrud came in to finish the game in the sixth inning.

Havre's 3-0 lead after three innings stood until Scobey came to bat in the top of the eighth. Mark Kato was pitching a shutout, and Mike Hagfeldt and Duke Trangsrud had held Helena scoreless after the third inning. Both teams were playing well in the field, as there were only three errors between the two teams in the game. But Kato "tired in the eighth," and Scobey got to him for two runs, closing to 3-2. And it was Scobey's veterans who brought them back once again. Jay Hagfeldt singled, and Don Puckett was hit by a pitch. Dana Audet then walked to load the bases. The three veterans, playing their last game and tournament, were now on base. Mike Gunderson brought Jay home on a fielder's choice, and then Duke Trangsrud walked with the bases loaded to drive in another run. But Kato struck out Greg Fjeld on a 3-2 count to end the rally—and Scobey's chances for a comeback. Havre scored an insurance run in the bottom of the eighth, and Kato slammed the door on Scobey in the ninth to end Scobey's season with their second tough loss of the tournament, 4-2.

Meanwhile, Wolf Point and the Scarlets met in the semifinal to see who would advance to the undefeated championship game. Wolf Point beat Cut Bank 10-3, Havre 6-3, and the Scarlets pummeled the Reps 21-0 to get there. Starting pitcher Dave Johnson, the hard-throwing sidearmed pitcher from Wolf Point who gave Scobey fits the previous year, kept Wolf Point in the game for six innings with solid pitching against the hard-hitting Scarlets team, who had lit up Helena pitching for 21 runs and 21 hits in their first game. However, with the score tied 3-3 in the seventh, Billings got to Johnson for two runs and then scored another run in the ninth to win 6-3, putting themselves in the driver's seat for their first state championship in their final year competing in the Class B division.

Wolf Point's semifinal loss set up a rematch against Havre to determine who would play the Scarlets in the championship game. Wolf Point scored three runs in the fifth to take a 5-2 lead. Bill Neumiller, Dave Johnson, and Dennis Loendorf—the three Wolf Point pitchers—had quieted Havre's bats, but with Dennis Loendorf sailing along with a 5-2 lead going into the ninth, Havre came from behind to score five runs on four singles and three walks to win it 7-5. This game would be another late-inning, heart-breaking loss to end a season for Wolf Point but a tremendous come-from-behind win for Havre on their home field.

The Scarlets proved they were the best team in Class B Legion baseball when they drubbed Havre 10-2 in the championship game for their 12th consecutive win. The Scarlets jumped on starting pitcher Mark Kato for six runs in the first two innings and never looked back. This young Scarlets team looked good enough to do some damage in the State A Tournament. And they did.

TOURNAMENT SUMMARY

SCOBEY'S TWO LOSSES—7-6 AND 4-2—WERE CLOSE, AND EACH game could have gone either way, but it would have been difficult for them to beat Wolf Point and the Scarlets and go deeper in the tournament had they won. It was amazing that Jay Hagfeldt was able to return to the lineup and play—and even pitch a little—after his serious injury earlier in the season, but he said, "I wasn't recovered enough to be of much help." However, although not his former self, he pitched into the third inning, got two hits off Mark Kato, started the rally in the eighth, and scored one of Scobey's two runs. Jay was so good that at 50%, or whatever he was, he could still help the team.

Jay, the quintessential team player, honored some of his former teammates by saying, "I feel privileged that I was able to play alongside so many good players. Terry was awesome to watch, both pitching and hitting. If I were to describe it in one word, it would be powerful. He could throw hard and hit with power. Rick Danelson was a great hitter too. He was consistent. Dana Audet was a great athlete. Felt confident that whatever position he played was well-covered. I also can't say enough about Don Puckett and Greg Fjeld. Both were solid infielders and could hit. Duke was great on the mound. Have to mention Lee Cook. He wasn't our best hitter, but I watched Doc work with him over the course of two years, and he became a good first baseman. Doc taught him, and Lee paid attention. He became proficient at first."

Jay then turned his attention to older brother Dallas, recalling his youthful baseball journey with him and the athlete that Dallas was: "We had a long history of baseball together. Most of the time we played on the same team, from Little League, Pony League (California), Senior Little

League, and finally American Legion. He was always one of the best players on whatever team he played on. He could hit, run, had a strong arm, and was a good catcher. I preferred that he caught when I pitched because he knew my strengths and weaknesses and I trusted him calling for the right pitches (most of the time). When we were young, he and I would play baseball wherever we could. During summers in California, we would get up early, and go down to the playground area at the nearby school and we would choose teams and play all day. We'd play 4 to 9 innings and then mix up the teams. It was rare that we didn't have enough kids to make up two teams. Dallas was always the first or second one chosen for a team. We would do this all summer long. He made the all-stars every year. Have to admit I was a little jealous sometimes. I think he was one of the anchors of the Scobey Legion team, at least when I played in 1972 and 1973. Always felt that when he was up to bat, he could make something happen. I remember that either Rod Tande or Phil Audet asked me who I thought was the fastest person to first on the team. I told him I thought it was either me or Jack Tryan. He corrected me and said it was Dallas. Dallas ran the mile relay in track and also threw the discus, and sometimes the javelin. I think our batting lineup had to be one of the strongest in the state, with Dana, Rick, Terry, and Dallas."

Many of the former players I have interviewed mention Jay as one of the greats ever to play American Legion Baseball for Scobey. He was undoubtedly one of the best I had ever seen play or played with. In listening to him describe his former teammates, never talking about himself, I think perhaps his greatest contribution—in addition to his all-around baseball skills and athleticism—was his humbleness and what a great team player he was. This was symbolized by his handing the game ball to Dana Audet on the mound following Scobey's state championship win in 1973.

The loss to Havre in the state tournament was the final game for Don Puckett, Jay Hagfeldt, Dana Audet, Dallas Trangsrud, Doug Hagfeldt, Lee Cook, and Jack Tryan, all of whom had played on the 1973 state championship team the year before. One of my memories of watching this team play was seeing Lee Cook scoop a lot of throws at first base and field a lot of ground balls. He was a good defensive first baseman. I asked Lee if he remembered Doc mentoring him at first base (he did) but he told me he began scooping balls at an early age on the farm in Flaxville. Lee recalls, "Out on the farm, there wasn't a lot of fun things to do, so I remember throwing a red rubber ball against a concrete wall and I would catch it, over and over. Later, I got a super-ball and did the same thing." Skipping forward a few years, Lee remembers how he became a better first baseman. "Joe Miller was a great Babe Ruth coach in Flaxville. When I got to Legion, Doc would have me stand by the old pitching machine at practice to protect it from the hitters. It was a short distance to home, and I would scoop up some hot shots coming off the bats during batting practice, which got me limber and helped my fielding at first. I was confident to try to scoop every ball that came to me at first, because I knew I was being backed up if I missed it. Whoever was playing right field would back up the throw, and when the ball was hit, catcher Dallas Hagfeldt (he was fast and ran the 440 in track) would sprint down to first, sometimes beating the hitter there, to back up the throw. We were so well-coached; we knew what to do with the ball before it was hit, where we were going with it. We had the best equipment because Doc spent his own money to get it. One of the advantages I had was a great Rawlings first baseman mitt that Doc bought in 1972. In 1974, the Rawlings needed new laces so Doc bought a new Wilson mitt, but we had the Rawlings repaired with new laces because it was so good. That Rawlings mitt is still being used by my grandson in Beulah, North Dakota. For hitting, I found a big-barreled Al Kaline that Doc bought. I always made sure the trademark was facing me when I hit. I loved that bat."

Lee added that Terry Puckett was the starting baseman, but Lee played there when Terry pitched, and Terry had to move to right field when his arm completely gave out in 1973. Lee said, "One of my jobs at first was to run out to right field and get the cutoff from Terry if a ball was hit out there. He would flip it to me, and I would relay it back into the infield." Lee also recalled what a good middle infield Scobey had when he played first. He said, "There was no better shortstop than Don Puckett. He turned a lot of double plays with Greg Fjeld and Pat Anderson at second"

The loss of seven starters on the 1974 team—combined with the loss of Terry Puckett, Rick Danelson, and Dallas Hagfeldt the year before—left little doubt that the younger players would need to step up for Scobey to be competitive in 1975. Scobey was returning three starting pitchers—Duke Trangsrud, Mike Hagfeldt, and Craig Miller—who were all left-handed. Although the season ended with two disappointing losses, the positive part of the 1974 season was that many of the 16-year-olds got to see plenty of action and gain valuable experience. The 1975 team would continue to grow and develop. The team came razor close to a deep run in the state tournament in Scobey in 1975 after losing another heart-breaking 1-0 pitcher's duel to

Havre in the semifinal. This young team would continue building up to the state championship team of 1976. While losing some of its key veteran players, Wolf Point would boast a strong roster in 1975, and Havre was returning a good team, including their two top pitchers, Mark Kato and Kirk Stetson.

STATE A TOURNAMENT

AFTER WATCHING THE SCARLETS BLAZE THROUGH THE EASTERN divisional tournament in Scobey and the state tournament in Havre to win their 12th consecutive game—beating Scobey twice, Wolf Point four times, and Havre once—many thought the Scarlets were good enough to compete with the rest of the teams in the State A Tournament. And they were—the Scarlets won two games and took third place. They lost their first game to Butte 5-4 when the Miners scored two runs in the bottom of the ninth to win it. They then beat the Helena Senators 5-3 and the Kalispell Lakers 10-4 before being eliminated by the Great Falls Chargers 7-0. The Royals eventually won the tournament against the Chargers, who were playing in their first season in Class A. The new Chargers team in Great Falls consisted of players mainly from CMR High School. This Scarlets team would move up to Class A the following season, beginning the era when both Great Falls and Billings had two Class A Legion teams. Havre would join the Class A ranks in 1976.

EXTRA INNINGS

DANA AUDET RECALLS ANOTHER FUNNY STORY ABOUT DOC AND the green van on the epic 1974 road trip. He said, "On the road trip, we played Havre, went to Great Falls and played the Sparkies, went to Helena and played the Representatives, back to Great Falls and played the Electrics, back to Helena to play the Senators, on to Billings to play the Scarlets and on to Miles City to play them. What a trip it was.

"At some point, we stopped to pick up sandwich stuff for lunch on the run as we had spent some serious time on the road. I was riding shotgun in the green van and Doc was driving. He looked back and said, 'Cookie you still got those fireworks?' Lee Cook always seemed to have firecrackers, cherry bombs, M-80's, etc. He said, 'I got some Zebra firecrackers' and Doc said, 'Let me see 'em.' We all knew he was up to something. He looked at me and said, "Let's make a sandwich bomb and get those guys in Margie's car behind us.' (I think Doc was getting bored with all of this road travel.) Anyway, I tied as many firecracker fuses together as I could—maybe 6 to 8 and grabbed the bag of buns. Doc's like, 'Get that mustard up here' and I proceeded to squirt as much in there as I could, but it wasn't holding together very well. Doc says, 'Get some tape outta my doctor bag and secure that thing,' so I lightly taped it up best I could. It was somewhat of a mess.

"At this point he's liking it and smiling. We're on a four lane and he rolls the window down and proceeds to wave up the guys in Marge's silver car. I think maybe Jay was driving. As was always the case, Doc has a cigarette in his mouth. He's driving with his right hand and has the sandwich bomb in his left and attempting to light it with his cigarette which is still in his mouth, all while we're cruising 80 on the freeway. The guys behind us are just a bit back and the fuses are lit—we are all very nervous at this point understandably, hoping we remain on the road. I recall yelling at Doc to throw it cause the fuses were burning down. He lets it fly and it goes off right in front of those guys. We were all just screaming at this point and we knew it was a direct hit when their wipers and washers came on. Oh my what fun. When we got to the next stop there was considerable mustard splattered and dried on the car."

Lee Cook remembers bringing his fireworks with him on the road trips. "I would put the firecrackers in Vienna sausages, and we'd launch them out the windows. Sometimes we'd get good direct hits on the other cars."

Jay Hagfeldt also remembers the crazy shenanigans on road trips. "Sometimes we'd throw grass at the cars from the barrow pits and turn the car lights off and on when we drove at night. One time, two cars sideswiped each other on the highway. Jack Tryan was one of the drivers. I also remember driving one of Doc's cars at 80 miles an hour in second gear with smoke billowing out the back. Surprised we never had an accident with some injuries."

However, as much fun as it was, the shenanigans by players traveling in separate cars on road trips came to an end in 1974. (Even playful Doc had his limits.) Mike Hagfeldt recalls the incident when Doc realized things had gone too far. "We were driving to Glasgow. Me and a couple of others were riding with Doc. (I think Doc had the rookies ride with him, probably to try to save us from shenanigans like that.) Jack Tryan was driving his car two cars behind us. I see Doc looking in his rearview mirror and he says, 'Goddammit!' in the way only Doc can say it. I look behind and I see a car passing another car on the right side—in the ditch. Well, it was Jack. That was the last time we took cars. After that, we started with the bus."

In addition to Jay's injury, another harrowing event happened in Glasgow that summer. Lee Cook, who was directly involved in the incident, said, "Everything bad always happened in Glasgow. They hated us like poison for stealing the

Hagfeldts from them." Mike Hagfeldt and Duke Trangsrud also remember what happened. Mike said, "The first base umpire, Barry Icenhower, was a classmate of mine, and he had made several bad calls at first. Nice guy. Terrible ump. I don't even think he played baseball. Doc goes out to argue after a particularly terrible call. He gets nowhere, of course." Duke added, "The umpire said to Doc, 'Get your fat ass back in the dugout,' and then Doc looked at Lee on first base and said, 'Cookie take him,' and Lee Cook went after that umpire." What happened next was hilarious. Mike said, "Lee took a couple steps toward him to go after him and my classmate started running in the outfield, looking over his shoulder. Damn that was funny." Lee said he was relieved the umpire moved away from him. "I would have probably been thrown out of the game for fighting with a Legion umpire and Doc would have got in trouble, too." As it was, Barry Icenhower made "the right call," and no one got hurt.

In the divisional game against Circle, Duke Trangsrud walked the first three hitters he faced—then struck out the next three to end the inning. Six hitters in the inning, and the ball was not put in play.

Manager Del Jones of the Billing Scarlets was a former Daniels County resident who attended Scobey public schools in the 1940s.

For their first appearance in the state tournament in Havre on Thursday, the Billings Scarlets arrived at the field in a grain truck. Scarlets coach Jim Peterson figured it would be easier, with less confusion, to keep the team together and transport them from their motel rooms to the field in the truck rather than several private vehicles. The *Havre Daily News* wrote, "The Billings Scarlets didn't come in a luxury limousine or even an air-conditioned bus, but they did come to play baseball."[88] Only in Montana.

The no-hitter Jim Knudtson of the Billings Scarlets pitched against Scobey in Scobey during the regular season is the only known no-hitter thrown at the Scobey Legion team, but Scobey had come close to getting no-hit before. Dick Puckett broke up Barry Damschen's no-hitter in the 1968 state tournament in Glendive on a single with two outs in the eighth inning after the previous hitter had reached first base on a dropped third strike. Damschen finished with a two-hit shutout. Donnie Higgins's bunt single in the sixth inning broke up Dave Fanning's no-hitter against Scobey at the state tournament in Scobey in 1971. Dave finished with a one-hitter, outdueling Terry Puckett in the epic 1-0 pitcher's duel.

For their first appearance at the state Legion tournament in Havre, the Billings Scarlets arrived in a grain truck loaned to them by G&B Motors. *Havre Daily News photo by Paul Kuka.*

All four umpires in the eastern division tournament were from Sidney. Umpire-in-chief Ron Ewing (second from left) was a tour de force as an umpire in those days, a formidable presence at all the big tournaments. The story about Doc telling him that Terry Puckett had a cold when Ron asked him what he was doing while shooting Terry's arm with a needle in the dugout has already been told, but Dan Wolfe shares another funny story about Ron Ewing, demonstrating his absolute control of the field. As Wolf tells it, "I was catching, and I think Terry was pitching, and he was a little off that night. I would move the glove back to the middle of the plate on balls. On one pitch that was called a ball, Doc said, 'Where was that at Wolfe?' I shrugged my shoulders and said, 'Right down the middle, Doc.' Pretty soon, I got a tap on my shoulder. I turned around, and there was Ewing standing behind me, and he said, 'Son, when you get to be able to catch as good as I ump, then you can pull that shit, but till then, you just do your job, or I'll throw your ass right out of this game.' So the next time Doc asked

Umpires for the divisional tournament in Scobey were Bob Plank, Ron Ewing, Jim Haugen, and Mike Gear, all of Sidney. At right is State Legion Baseball Commissioner **Bob Crawford** of Miles City. Jack Reiner, official tourney scorekeeper, was not present for the photo. Leader photo by Milton Gunderson.

me where a ball was, I said, 'Inside Doc. Inside.' He let me know in no uncertain terms he was boss."

Don't look, Marge! *The Streak*, written and sung by Ray Stevens, was all the craze in 1974, and streaking did not bypass Scobey's Eastern B Divisional Tournament. The *Daniels County Leader* photo by Burl Bowler caught one of the two perpetrators in the act and showed one of them at the end of the streak in the far corner of left field, the entry and exit point for the streak. Burl Bowler recalls that the plan to streak had been hatched earlier in the evening when a little drinking had emboldened the streakers. Right before the streak, a foul ball had been hit down the left field line, temporarily delaying their grand entrance on the field, as the rabid foul ball chasers were undeterred by the naked men and wanted to retrieve the foul ball for their money. A chain was harmlessly and mockingly swung at the kids by one of the streakers to ward off the foul ball chasers, but the feigned attempt at deterrence worked to no avail, as the ball was retrieved, and the entrance was delayed. When the white skin of two naked bodies broke on the scene under the lights of the night game, the left fielder attempted to chase one of them off the field.

A week later, the caption for the photo published in the *Leader* read, "Streakers at the recent tourney in Scobey took advantage of the balmy weather and gathered spectators to go into action. There were a couple of them. This *Leader* camera catches one of them."[89] The photographer, the *Leader*'s own Burl Bowler, was in on the scheme all along. He had been drinking with the streakers earlier in the evening and knew of the plan but didn't commit to participate—at least not on the field. Knowing it was going to happen, he ran home, grabbed the *Leader* camera, and snapped the photo, deliberately not making it high-resolution quality to protect the anonymity of the streaker. This was one photo of a divisional or state tournament that regular *Leader* photographer Milton Gunderson didn't take!

Burl didn't tell the streakers the photo would be in the *Leader*. When the paper was published, Patti Audet, reading the paper in her house, saw the photo and immediately recognized her son, as only a mother could. She yelled out, "Danny!" It turns out Burl's deliberately poor-quality photo was not bad enough to fool a mother. The streaker in the photo was Danny Audet. Mark Chabot, the second streaker, did not make the paper. Over fifty years later, the anonymity is broken. Dana Audet recalled the incident and added, "If Dan was endowed like Tom, we might have seen something in the pic."

Dana Audet tells a funny story about when the new uniforms arrived: "It was winter of 1974, and I was on a first date to watch a movie at Richardson's theater. Partway through the movie, the audio gets interrupted by, 'Dana Audet to the snack bar please?' I was thinking, *What the heck?* So I go back, and they tell me I got a phone call. 'Hello?' 'Yeah, Hoot, this is Doc. The new uniforms came in today. Get your butt over here after the movie and check 'em out.' So after the movie, rather than head somewhere in the hopes of trying to reach second base, we headed to Doc and Marge's place. He had my number 10 picked out and insisted I model it. It fit great, and they were the coolest uniforms. Stretchy blue and comfortable. The Toronto Blue Jays still wear similar outfits. I believe these uniforms may have been the beginning of the Scobey Legion team being called the Blues."

Dana Audet also shared a humorous story about Scobey's 4-3 win in 11 innings over the Billings Scarlets at Cobb

Streakers stole the show at the 1974 Eastern Divisional Tournament. *Leader photo by Burl Bowler.*

Field in Billings, a big win for Scobey against the eventual state champion on their early season road trip. "We had this plan, Jay Hagfeldt, Doug, and I, we were all 18. We were talking and said, 'You know, Billings has got this Studio-1, an X-rated film place, we should check that out. Now that we're 18, we can go in.' So we start checking movie times and found one at nine o'clock in the evening. The game was a night game and started at six. So we're playing and checking the time and looking at each other in the dugout, 'Are we going to be able to make the movie? Yeah this game is moving right along we'll be alright.' Some runs were scored early, but Jay was pitching, and I was catching, and he was just mowing them down; they weren't hitting him.' But the game went 11 innings, so we're like, 'Oh my God, we're not going to make the movie.' But we actually flew out of there, and after we won the game, we had a quick handshake, got in the car, and took off and we actually managed to get in there for like that last half hour. It was a little anticlimactic at that point. We were like, 'Well, it was a fun try anyway.' What was kind of funny about that was I still had my cup on in the theater."

While Burl's camera was pointed at the left field corner to capture the iconic photo of a streaker, *Leader* photographer Milton Gunderson's camera was pointed in a different direction to capture an iconic photo of a different sort: Pete Kurtz and Earl Randall. The *Leader*'s caption stated, "They were two regular fans at the tournament and also during the season's play. Earl also is an annual financial contributor to Legion ball in Daniels County. This shot was taken during action in the Scobey-Billings game as the two old-timers sat in the grandstand's top row. Another longtime east-county baseball fan who saw most of the tournament action was Jess Wiley, grandfather of Scobey's veteran first baseman Lee Cook. It would be a good bet that on any given summer

Pete Kurtz and Earl Randall in the grandstand watching the divisional tournament in Scobey. *Leader photo by Milton Gunderson.*

Sunday afternoon 60 years ago that at least one or two of the above-mentioned fellows were playing baseball somewhere around the county area!"[90] The faces of these two men watching baseball symbolize the baseball tradition in Daniels County, how the homesteaders brought the game to Scobey in the early 1900s, and why the book goes back that far. The sport preceded all of us who played Legion ball for generations, and the passion for the sport was passed down to us. We were simply part of something much bigger than all of us, and we were lucky. Jack Reiner captured the importance of baseball to Scobey when he proudly said, "This is Baseball Country," in the *Daniels County Leader* before the 1969 state tournament.

The *Leader* always carefully recognized the volunteers who made things happen at the tournaments. The team mothers ran the hamburger stand, as it had been all season long, with Marge Hagfeldt "always on the scene or nearby." Charles Cassidy kept it supplied and opened it before the sessions. A pop and candy stand was operated by the Legion Auxiliary with Patty Marley in charge. Gene Marley, chairman of the baseball committee, "was constantly on the job taking care of innumerable details." Cliff Hanson, committee treasurer, was in charge of tickets and "did anything else asked of him." Ticket, food, and refreshment sales grossed about $2,600 for the tournament. That is $16,000 in today's dollars—for a *divisional* tournament. The *Leader* also recognized MDU's volunteer work. MDU always revamped the lights, providing the labor for free before the tournaments, beginning with the 1969 state tournament, the first year Scobey hosted.[91]

The year 1974 marked the end of a Class A Legion baseball era in Montana. Ed Bayne, Doc's friend who had coached the Billings Royals to 20 state championships in 24 years, was not on the field coaching, retiring after the 1973 season. Sportswriter Bruce Bartley of the *Great Falls Tribune* wrote an article titled, "Royals aren't quite the same without Bayne."[92] One of the critical points in Bartley's article was the discussion about Bayne's key to his success in winning so many championships. His players said it was his attention to detail: Nothing was too small for Bayne's eye. He conducted practices for 50 or more players at a time and never was a single one of them idle for a moment." Bayne, of course, had coached Dave McNally from 1958 to 1960. Twenty of his former players signed professional contracts, but McNally was the only one to make it big. He was also connected to numerous college coaches. One year in the late 1960s, Bayne sent seven players to the University of

Wyoming, and they all became starters. The article also stated what an honor it was to play for and against him. Many former Scobey Legion players can say they played against the legendary Coach Ed Bayne of the Billings Royals.

This season also marked the end of an eight-year run for Kelly Norman as batboy for the Scobey Legion team. Kelly can probably boast he was the only batboy to get an at-bat in a Legion game, substituting for Duke Trangsrud against the Mon-Dak All-Stars as a 12-year-old.

I loved listening to games on KCGM. It opened a door for me to stay connected with sports in the county when I couldn't be at the games. My first memory of KCGM radio was sitting around the kitchen table at night in December 1971, listening to Cliff Hagfeldt broadcast basketball scores around northeastern Montana. Initially, KCGM did not broadcast games, just the scores from the studio. Before KCGM, we had to wait until the next day to read the scores in the *Billings Gazette* or the *Great Falls Tribune* that were brought to the Puckett Mercantile. You could hear the excitement in Cliff's voice announcing the scores over the radio for the first time. It was a Friday night, so I could stay up. Scores were being called into Cliff from various towns throughout northeastern Montana at halftime and even quarter breaks. Peerless was playing in Antelope that night. Percy Kegel made a shot against Antelope with eight seconds left, and Peerless won 60-59. How is that relevant to baseball? The game was won when Terry Puckett rocketed a full-court baseball pass to Percy Kegel for the game-winning layup. Antelope's scorekeeper, Kurt Ueland, unofficially clocked the basketball traveling 90 miles per hour.

Kudos to Percy for being able to handle the pass. It's nice how my first memory of KCGM is of Terry, basketball, and (somehow) baseball.

Dave Fanning, who had outdueled Terry Puckett 1-0 in the 1971 State B semifinal in Scobey and struck out 25 Royals a week later in the State A Tournament, finished his third and final season in the minor leagues with the Phillies organization in 1974. Pitching for the Rocky Mount Phillies in the Carolina League, Dave posted a 6-7 record with a 3.40 ERA. In his three-year career in the Phillies organization, he finished with a 29-18 record and a 2.97 ERA, striking out 268 hitters in 324 innings. Dave told me he regretted signing the professional baseball contract and wished he had accepted a full-ride scholarship to play at Gonzaga, where his parents could have watched him play.

1975

The North Star Shines Brightly in the West for the Fifth Time

> *It would appear that Scobey will continue to host state tournaments; this one again was well-run in so many of those ways, large and small, that continue to give Scobey an enviable state-wide reputation.*
>
> —Daniels County Leader, August 7, 1975

1975 Scobey Legionnaires. Standing, L–R: Coach Doc Norman, Mike Gunderson, Dale Barstad, Dan Danelson, Tully Tryan, Mike Hagfeldt, Don Hagfeldt, Craig Miller, Allan Audet, Bill Bartole, Duke Trangsrud, Greg Fjeld. Kneeling: Jeff Richardson, Kelly Norman, Wade Tryan, Pat Anderson, Ross Chapman. *Leader photo, Milt Gunderson.*

PRESEASON

NINETEEN SEVENTY-FIVE MARKED THE 50TH ANNIversary of American Legion Baseball, created in Milbank, South Dakota, on July 17, 1925. The organization was founded as "a program of service to the youth of America." Those words are inscribed on a Milbank, South Dakota, marble monument. I have mentioned how lucky we all were to have had the opportunity to play baseball all those summers ago, and we can thank The American Legion—and all the veteran volunteers of Scobey Post 56—for that. Since its beginning, more than 10 million young people have played American Legion Baseball.

1975 also marked the 50th anniversary of Swede Risberg and Happy Felsch of the Chicago White Sox—enticed with money from local Scobey businessmen—coming to play for the Scobey Outlaws in 1925. Risberg and Felsch had been banned for life from organized baseball after their involvement in the gambling scandal to throw the 1919 World Series against Cincinnati. They were hired to compete with Plentywood, who had formed a strong team that year. It's funny how the Scobey-Plentywood rivalry dates back then. Ironically, the anniversary of the American Legion program, founded to serve the youth of America, would coincide with two Chicago Black Sox players coming to play baseball in Scobey.

Fifty years later, we turn to the baseball field in Scobey on another cold April day as Doc assembled another team to compete for a state championship. After losing seven players from the previous season—including Jay Hagfeldt, Don Puckett, and Dana Audet—1975 looked to be a rebuilding year for Scobey. Only two 18-year-olds—Duke Trangsrud and Mike Gunderson—were returning. However, nine

17-year-olds formed the team's nucleus: Jeff Richardson, Bill Bartole, Don Hagfeldt, Greg Fjeld, Mike Hagfeldt, Craig Miller, Tully Tryan, Pat Anderson, and Dale Barstad, who was a rookie. Interestingly, Doc's pitching staff in 1975 was entirely left-handed: Duke Trangsrud, Mike Hagfeldt, and Craig Miller. Youngsters Ross Chapman (16), Allan Audet (15), Wade Tryan (14), Dan Danelson (14), and Kelly Norman (13) also joined the team. Allan, Wade, Dan, and Kelly would also play Babe Ruth that summer.

REGULAR SEASON

THE HIGHLIGHT DURING THE 1975 REGULAR SEASON WAS NOT one—but two—no-hitters thrown by Peerless left-hander Duke Trangsrud. Duke was indeed peerless in both games. The first no-hitter came in an 8-2 win over Plentywood, where Duke struck out 17 Athletics. The *Billings Gazette* wrote that Duke "combined a strong fastball with an occasional curve" and Plentywood "never figured out the combination."[93] Duke's second no-hitter was in the final game of the regular season against Frazer at Scobey Ball Park. "The Duke"—as the *Leader* referred to him—struck out 20 Bearcubs in the 15-0 no-hit shutout. Mike Hagfeldt led Scobey's 16-hit attack with a seventh-inning home run. Scobey only committed one error in the game, so Duke's game would have been close to perfect, depending on how many walks he issued.

But perhaps the most intriguing part about Duke's two no-hitters had more to do with the catcher than the pitcher. How many catchers do you know that can say the first game they ever caught was a no-hitter? Jeff Richardson can say that. What? Yes, Jeff Richardson caught Duke's no-hitter against Plentywood in his first game behind the plate. Jeff, in his first outing behind the plate, "did a fine job as catcher."[94] *It was the first game he ever caught.* How was that? Duke explained, "When you got catchers like Dallas Hagfeldt and Dana Audet, you got to come up through the ranks." I was surprised when Duke told me this, and I read it in the *Leader* because when I first watched Jeff catch in 1975 and pitched to him in 1976, I thought he might have started catching in the womb—he was a natural. He was a quarterback in football, and he was also a quarterback in baseball, commanding the game from behind the plate with his booming voice and his powerful arm. Duke said that Jeff threw the ball harder back to him than he did to the plate, which is pretty hard because Duke threw hard. Mike Hagfeldt—who also threw hard—said the same about Jeff's arm. Many pitchers said the same thing about Craig Audet.

When I asked Duke who taught him how to pitch, he responded, "I had two of the greatest teachers, Joe: Doc and Terry Puckett." Wow. Two great teachers indeed, Duke.

In addition to Plentywood and Frazer, Scobey's regular season schedule that summer included games against Glendive, Glasgow, Wolf Point, and Circle. They also played Tioga and Grenora, North Dakota. With a heavy-hitting team coached by Don Lekvold, Wolf Point was the best team in the east during the regular season, with Scobey finishing second. Wolf Point also finished ahead of Scobey in the regular season standings in 1973 and 1974. The divisional tournament would determine the top three teams in the east to make it to the state tournament, to be hosted for the fourth time in Scobey.

DIVISIONAL TOURNAMENT

NINETEEN SEVENTY-FIVE ALSO MARKED THE 45TH ANNIVERsary of Scobey's first American Legion team, fielded in 1930. Scobey and Wolf Point met for the northeastern district championship in 1930, with Scobey winning 9-8 in 11 innings to advance to play Billings for the eastern division championship. Forty-five years later, Scobey and Wolf Point again met for the divisional championship, with the game again being decided in extra innings. Boy, this divisional championship was one humdinger of a game. It became the mother of all slugfests—epic in proportion—and one of the most entertaining games I've ever experienced. Dad, Jon, and I listened to the game on KCGM radio in the comfort of our backyard in Peerless. Little did I know a year later that I would be the 15-year-old starting pitcher for Scobey against this same powerful Wolf Point team in the Divisional championship game, where I would be the losing pitcher in another epic slugfest between these two heavy-hitting teams.

Scobey had made it to the divisional championship game by drubbing Ekalaka 23-8 and then Glasgow 5-3 in a well-played semifinal contest, as Mike Hagfeldt pitched a complete game to beat his high school classmates from Glasgow. Wolf Point had won their semifinal game to set up the championship game between these two familiar foes.

As we listened to Cliff Hagfeldt call the game on KCGM radio in our backyard, as each inning passed, the score continued to creep up, sometimes with leads of several runs being eclipsed with a snap of the finger—or a crack (ping) of the bat. No lead was safe. The score quickly resembled that of a football game, and in the end, Dad said the only reason Scobey lost was because they failed to convert an extra point on one of the touchdowns they scored. Pitcher after pitcher attempted to hold the other team, but to no avail, as the two teams continued to pound each other mercilessly from the plate. Of course, playing in the divisional championship game meant the two teams had already qualified for state, so what were the two teams really playing for? A divisional championship, for one thing, and a first-round bye in the state tournament, for another.

After 10 innings on Saturday, the score stood at 20-20, but it was getting dark. Because the game was played in Wolf Point, there were no lights, so the game had to be suspended due to darkness. The teams would have to return the following day to determine the champion. The next morning's headline in the *Gazette* read, "20-20 Legion Tie," and the article stated, "Scobey and Wolf Point are hooked up in a classic American Legion Baseball game. The contest was suspended Saturday night because of darkness with the score tied at 20-20."[95] Dad, Jon, and I—and all of KCGM's listeners—would have to go to bed on Saturday night without knowing the outcome. Still, we were all three buzzing about the game, talking about how we hadn't seen the aging Ronnie Lancaster and the Saskatchewan Roughriders hang 20 points on a team the entire CFL season, but Scobey could score 20 runs in a baseball game.

1975 Wolf Point Legion Team, Eastern Division Champions. Front row, L-R: David Hopson, Rick McGeshick, Alan Hoversland, Fred Rhoads, Jerry Moran, Jim Stein, Mike Neubauer. Back row: Ken Lee, Jeff Neubauer, Bill Neumiller, Dennis Loendorf, Darrell Nefzger and Grant Boysun, Assistant Coach Don Lekvold. *The Herald-News.*

The game was decided in 12 innings on Sunday, as Wolf Point "finally shoved across the winning run"[96] on the game-winning hit by Jeff Neubauer in the bottom of the 12th inning to win it 24-23, mercifully ending the two-day marathon. Pitchers had trouble finding the plate, as over *30 walks* were issued in the game. Scobey had 21 hits, with Wolf Point probably as many. Thank God the pitchers had three days to rest before the state tournament began on Thursday in Scobey!

Plentywood beat Glasgow to qualify as the third seed from the east. Remember what happened the last time Plentywood qualified as the third seed from the east in 1971? Archrival Plentywood couldn't eliminate Scobey on its home field at a state tournament again, could they? Oh boy. Baseball can be cruel.

STATE B TOURNAMENT

THE FOURTH STATE TOURNAMENT WAS TO BE HOSTED IN SCObey! Scobey was ready to host: "The entire community has entered in, with good spirit, to again make Scobey an outstanding host for the state event."[97] The *Leader* also announced the teams' arrivals in its Thursday edition and printed the tournament bracket. Havre had won the west, with Cut Bank second and Livingston third. Fairfield had taken third place in the west but couldn't attend the tournament, so Livingston replaced them as the third seed. Of course, it was Wolf Point, Scobey, and Plentywood in the east. On Thursday, Scobey played Livingston, and Plentywood played Cut Bank, with the Scobey-Livingston winner facing Havre and the Cut Bank-Plentywood winner facing Havre. Havre, with its 29-6 record, was the clear favorite to win the tournament. All six losses were to Class A teams, and they had a perfect 18-0 conference record. They had also beat Kalispell, Helena, the Great Falls Chargers and Electrics, and the Glacier Twins. But Wolf Point and Scobey could go far in the tournament if they didn't lose early. Neither team could afford to lose and come back through the dirt route, as the pitching depth wasn't there. Cut Bank, the second seed from the west, also had a chance. The *Leader* commented that Scobey's regular season had not been great but had a chance: "The Scobey Legion team had a mediocre season but came on toward the end and showed some real strength at the district tournament last week. They are ready for state . . . and carry a winning tradition!"[98]

Greg Fjeld scores the first run of the state tournament in the first inning of the Scobey-Livingston game. Scobey went on to win 10-1 on a one-hitter by Craig Miller. *Leader photo, Milt Gunderson.*

Bad weather, in the form of rain, would force the tournament to be delayed for one day. This delay was good for Scobey and Wolf Point's pitchers, who could use the extra day of rest after the carnage of the slugfest on Sunday. And pitching—at least in their first two games—would be the strength for Scobey in the 1975 state tournament. Craig Miller ungraciously greeted Livingston with a one-hitter in the tournament's first game on Friday. Scobey won 10-1, taking advantage of every opportunity, turning only five hits into 10 runs. Scobey also played well in the field, committing only two errors. Cut Bank won their opener against Plentywood 14-5, setting up Scobey-Havre and Cut Bank-Wolf Point in the evening session Friday.

Scobey versus Havre. Again. At State. In Scobey. Each team without a loss. We had seen this movie before, the last time in 1971, when Dave Fanning outdueled Terry Puckett in the epic 1-0 semifinal. Could any Scobey-Havre matchup in a state tournament match that epic game's drama? And could the pitching ever even come close to the brilliance? The answer is, yes . . . it could . . . it could come close. Mike Hagfeldt of Scobey and Barry Kato of Havre each delivered gems for their respective teams, hanging goose egg after goose egg on Scobey's new electronic scoreboard, inning after inning, until another fateful seventh for Scobey. In 1971, Fanning had singled to open the seventh, advanced to second on a sacrifice, and scored the winning run on another single. In 1975, the seventh inning would again prove to be Scobey's undoing, this time on an error. Hagfeldt "did a masterful job, controlling the powerful Havre batters."[99] He had not been in trouble until the seventh when Havre placed runners on first and third with one out. A missed sign by Scobey on a coordinated pickoff play on a double steal by Havre led to an unearned run, as Mark Kato scampered home from third on the error. Scobey had played well in the field, with only one other error, but this one proved costly. Barry Kato finished Scobey off in the eighth and ninth, and Havre had won another 1-0 pitcher's duel in Scobey, advancing to the undefeated semifinal in the tournament.

The following day, the headline in the *Gazette* read, "Kato and Kato help Havre edge Scobey,"[100] as Barry had pitched a four-hitter, striking out nine Scobey hitters, and Mark had three singles, his third one leading off the seventh, scoring the winning run on the error. Mike Hagfeldt had three of Scobey's four hits, but the rest of the team could muster only one hit, and Scobey was shut out. Another tough 1-0 pitcher's duel loss to Havre on its home field in the state tournament for Scobey.

Meanwhile, another pitcher's duel unfolded in the second semifinal on Friday night between Cut Bank and Wolf Point. It was a night for good pitching in Scobey by the four teams. In the 1973 state tournament in Scobey, Wolf Point lost a tough game in its opener to Cut Bank 8-5, forcing them through the dirt route to the championship game. And once again—as Havre had done with Scobey—the Lobos thwarted Wolf Point in their first game, winning 2-1 in 10 innings. Hank Weaver of Cut Bank drove in the winning run on a single, which scored Mark Coryell, who had reached base on an error. Brent Goldrick went all the way on the mound for Cut Bank, hurling a five-hitter while striking out eight. Left-hander Jerry Moran took the tough loss for Wolf Point, scattering eight hits and striking out eight.

Scobey's tough loss in the semifinal against Havre led to another matchup against archrival Plentywood in the state tournament in Scobey. In 1971, Plentywood had shocked Scobey 6-5 when Scobey imploded with four errors in the eighth inning. Could lightning strike twice? As with the pitcher's duel with Havre, we had seen this movie before, and we would watch another repeat in this game, as Scobey—playing well in the field to that point—once again broke down, committing eight errors. Plentywood broke the game open with seven runs in the sixth inning and came back with six in the ninth to eliminate Scobey 17-9. The game as "error-filled," as Plentywood committed nine errors of their own. Scobey outhit Plentywood 13 to 10, but Plentywood took advantage of the eight Scobey errors and numerous walks issued by four Scobey pitchers in the sloppy game. Dan Danielson from Antelope went the distance for Plentywood to get the win. I can't imagine what his pitch count might have been. Harvey Lee—a superb all-around athlete from Antelope—led Plentywood's hitting with a triple and two singles. Greg Fjeld, Jeff Richardson, Duke Trangsrud, and Mike Hagfeldt got 12 of Scobey's 13 hits.

But the story of this tournament—for the teams that won anyway—was solid pitching and good defense. And the teams that won were Havre and Cut Bank. After receiving a well-pitched game from Mike Sherrill, who was relieved by Barry Kato, Havre beat Cut Bank 4-3 to make it to the finals undefeated. After losing their opener, Wolf Point came back to beat Livingston 6-4 on an eight-hitter by Bill Neumiller, then outslugged Plentywood 22-13 but lost to Cut Bank 8-6 for the second time to take third place.

Cut Bank's second win over Wolf Point set up an all-west final between Havre and Cut Bank for the state championship in Scobey. In the seven years of Scobey hosting the state tournament, this would be the only year an all-west final occurred. And what a final it turned out to be! Naturally disappointed by Scobey's elimination by Plentywood, the *Daniels County Leader* and Scobey baseball fans still appreciated good baseball. Havre and Cut Bank played excellent baseball on the state championship stage in Scobey. "Baseball buffs heralded the final game as one of the best ever at Scobey Ball Park."[101]

Havre coach Ted Anderson had reserved his ace, Mark Kato, for the championship game, so he had all 12 innings available to pitch. Barry Kato had pitched 11 innings—nine against Scobey and two against Cut Bank—so he had only one inning of eligibility remaining. Thirteen innings between them—and they would need every one of them. Cut Bank used four pitchers: Craig Cummings, Mark Slezak (6), Rick Dooley (11), and Mike Sheridan, who absorbed the loss.

Cut Bank scored its only run in the third, and Havre tied the game 1-1 in the fourth. And there the score stood 1-1 after 12 innings when Mark Kato ran out of eligibility to pitch. Cousin Barry, who had only one inning of eligibility remaining, came in to pitch for Havre in the top of the 13th and held Cut Bank scoreless again. In the bottom of the 13th, Dennis Lammerding doubled off the top of the right field wall, advanced to third on a sacrifice bunt by Laroy Borchert, then scored the winning run on a single by Kirk Stetson. Havre walked it off and celebrated their fifth state championship on Scobey's home field.

The pitching in this game was outstanding. In 12 innings pitched, Mark Kato scattered six hits and struck out 13. Cut Bank's four pitchers yielded 11 hits across the 13 innings. Most significantly, each team issued only one base on balls.

But it was not only the fine pitching by both teams that made this game special; there were also some "spectacular catches" in the outfield by Havre to preserve the 1-1 score. In the eighth inning, when Cut Bank had a runner on third, and only one out, Kirk Stetson fielded a fly to right and threw a strike to catcher Dana Roe to catch Dooley trying to score. In the ninth, left fielder Tim Casey and Stetson made diving one-handed catches to rob the Lobos of sure hits and the potential winning run.

As the Montana State American Legion Baseball Commission moved Havre up to Class A in 1976, this would be the last time we would see Havre in a state tournament in Scobey until 1985, as Havre had returned to Class B by then. Scobey hosted the state tournament in 1985 for the final time. Havre and Scobey would meet in the first game of this tournament in what could be considered the most exciting game ever played between these two storied Legion programs. But we have a lot of baseball ahead of us before we get to 1985.

TOURNAMENT SUMMARY

"Havre's sharp Legion baseball team"[102] came into the tournament with a 29-6 record—all six losses to Class A teams—and was clearly the favorite, but did not dominate, as they won each of their games by only one run: 1-0 over Scobey, 4-3 over Cut Bank, and 2-1 over Cut Bank in 13 innings. It was their pitching and defense that won the tournament for them.

It was uncanny how Scobey's pattern of two well-played, well-pitched games, including a 1-0 pitcher's duel loss to Havre—then breaking down in their third game against Plentywood—repeated itself in 1975. The same scenario had played out in 1971.

Four of the 10 tournament games were decided by one run, and two runs decided two games.

Mention must be made of the ground crew for this tournament, as they had their hands full getting the field playable. Official ground crew members were Pete Hagfeldt, Joe Anderson, Art Audet, Dan Wolfe, Phil Audet, and Danny Wang, and a lot of fans pitched in to help. After the field was deemed unplayable on Thursday, a burning mixture of straw and gasoline was attempted to dry the infield grass on Friday morning. I remember sitting in the grandstand watching this, and it was hard to see the infield grass get burned as it did. This tournament began the end of the grass infield at Scobey Ball Park, as the following season, in 1976, the infield would be converted to all dirt. I missed that grass infield, as I had always loved playing on it in Babe Ruth. The grass infield was initially put in for the first state tournament Scobey hosted in 1969.

The Scobey Legion Baseball Committee comprised Gene Marley (Chairman), Ron Fjeld, Cliff Hanson, Cliff Hagfeldt, Milt Gunderson, and "Tiny" Puckett.

Charles Cassidy and Frank Reemsnyder pressed some 1,100 burgers sold at the tournament food stand during the three days. Between the County Fair and the Legion baseball tournament that week, over 4,000 of the famous "Legionburgers" were sold. I had a couple myself.

The umpires were Don Bergenheier, Andy Stolen, Dick Puckett, Randy Smith, and Vern Veis. Notice they were mainly from the Scobey area. The Scobey Legion Baseball Committee normally hired umpires from out of the area, but the original crew from Sidney canceled, so the committee pulled this crew together at the last minute. Jack Reiner was the official scorekeeper, as he had been for the previous three state tournaments in Scobey.

The 1975 season was the last for 18-year-olds Duke Trangsrud from Peerless and Mike Gunderson from Flaxville. Mike, whose father, Milt Gunderson, recently passed away, honored his dad for sharing the game of baseball with him. "I vividly remember when he brought home my first 'real' leather baseball glove and him playing catch with me in the yard. He built a baseball backstop and diamond out in our pasture and hit fly balls to us for many hours."

While it was another disappointing end to Scobey's season at its state tournament, the team was only losing two starters. The future looked positive for Scobey in 1976, as solid nucleus of 17-year-olds were returning for their final season, plus some younger talent already on the roster, to be joined by some rookies who had played a lot of baseball. However, Coach Don Lekvold's Wolf Point team also returned almost their entire roster in 1976 and would have some younger talent join. These two heavy-hitting teams would again compete for the top two teams in the east and the state championship. The state tournament in Cut Bank the following year would be the most bizarre five days of baseball played by Scobey and Wolf Point with the unlikeliest outcomes. It was a doozy.

TOURNAMENT STATS

Hitting

Mike Hagfeldt led Scobey hitters in the tournament, as he had three of the four hits against Barry Kato and three hits against Plentywood's winning pitcher, Dan Danielson. He hit over .500 for the tournament. Only two home runs were hit in the tournament, both in the same game: Ken Lee of Wolf Point and Roger Keto from Livingston.

Pitching: In its first two games, left-handers Craig Miller and Mike Hagfeldt did not allow an earned run between them in 18 innings for a perfect 0.00 ERA. Even Scobey's pitching in the 1971 tournament was not that good for the first two games. However, against Plentywood, four Scobey pitchers allowed 17 runs on 10 hits and several walks, but Scobey's eight errors led to countless unearned runs. Havre's pitching overall was phenomenal, yielding only four earned runs in 31 innings. Kato and Kato were sublime: Barry pitched 12 innings, gave up no earned runs, got two wins, and saved the other game; Mark pitched 12 innings and gave up only one earned run. Between the two of them, they gave up only one earned run in 24 innings. Mike Sherrill, Havre's third pitcher, pitched seven innings against Cut Bank, yielded only three runs, and got the win. Kirk Stetson, Havre's winning pitcher in the state championship game against Wolf Point three years earlier as a 14-year-old, did not pitch in the tournament, but his throw from right field to home plate cut down the winning run in the eighth. Cut Bank's pitching was also good. Brent Goldrick tossed a five-hitter against Wolf Point, allowing only one earned run, and in the championship game, Craig Cummings and Mark Slezak allowed only one earned run in 11 innings. And Wolf Point got two well-pitched games from left-handers Jerry Moran and Bill Neumiller. In the 2-1, 10-inning loss to Cut Bank, Jerry Moran scattered eight hits and struck out eight. Bill Neumiller also scattered eight hits to beat Livingston 6-4.

Fielding

Scobey committed four errors in their first two games: two against Livingston and two against Havre. However, the second error against Havre was costly, allowing the winning run to score from third base in the seventh inning. Then came the horrific fielding debacle against Plentywood, where the team committed eight errors. Did Plentywood put a hex on Scobey's fielders in state tournament games? Havre's defense was not as good as their pitching, but was good enough to win the tournament. They committed six errors in three games.

STATE A PLAYOFF

The 1975 format for State Class B champions to qualify for the State A Tournament had reverted to a one-game playoff against the third-place Class A team. In 1975, this was Miles City in the east, so Havre played off against them in a one-game playoff at Kindrick Field in Helena, three days after the completion of the State B Tournament. It was yet another pitcher's duel for Havre, as Ron Miller of Miles City pitched a three-hit shutout against them, striking out 14 Northstars to lead the Mavericks to a 2-0 win. The Kato and Kato show for Havre was brilliant once again, as Mark went eight innings and gave up only six hits and two runs—both unearned—and Barry relieved in the ninth, giving up one hit but striking out the other three hitters. Although losing to Miles City, Havre had proven they could compete at the Class A level in 1975. They would move up to Class A in 1976.

EXTRA INNINGS

The first reference to the Havre Post 11 American Legion team as the Havre Northstars was the 1975 season. Cut Bank was also dubbed the Lobos that year. Scobey would not be called the Blues until the 1977 season, and Wolf Point became the Yellowjackets in 1978.

Milt Gunderson took a photo of the 2-1 Havre-Cut Bank score of the state championship game on the new electronic scoreboard. Havre was the "home" team and winner of the championship in the 13-inning defensive dual. Note the MDU sign directly below the scoreboard. Space for this sign was donated by the town of Scobey, and painting was arranged by The American Legion in appreciation of MDU's crews repairing lights at the ballpark before the tournament. As a public service, MDU repaired, replaced,

Final score in the state Class B Legion baseball tournament shows in 18-inch letters on the new scoreboard at Scobey Ball Park. Havre was the "home" team and winner of the championship in the 13-inning defensive dual. *Leader photo, Milt Gunderson.*

and sometimes adjusted the ballpark lights before every major tournament at the Scobey Ball Park since 1969, Scobey's first Legion state tourney.

Scobey was always trying to improve everyone's experience at the state tournament. In addition to the new electronic scoreboard, other new things at Scobey Ball Park in 1975 were live music over the speakers for the national anthem and between-inning entertainment. Loyal Brenden had his van and electric organ on the scene, and Nellie LaPierre aided him in the playing. Perry Wolfe helped in getting this arranged.

Barry Kato had ties to Scobey, as he was Gerry Veis's first cousin. His mom, Lois Pattison, was born in Froid and raised in Homestead and Plentywood. Patricia Pattison—Gerry's mom—was Lois Pattison's sister. After graduating from Plentywood High School, Lois moved to Havre and entered the Sacred Heart School of Nursing. She married Ray Kato of Havre, and they had eight children. Her older son Scott played in Scobey's state tournaments in 1969 and 1971. Scott was the pitcher in 1969 when Dick Puckett hit his dramatic two-strike, two-out home run to tie the championship game. Mark was Barry's cousin, the son of Mark and Johanna Kato.

Mike Hagfeldt shared a funny story about Duke's second no-hitter against Frazer: "The Frazer pitcher was struggling mightily. He had trouble throwing strikes, and when he did, he got pounded. Have you ever seen an opposing manager call time and go talk to the opposing pitcher? Well that is what happened. Doc calls time and walks out to the mound to talk to the Frazer pitcher. We were all wondering what the heck he was doing. He gets out there and starts talking to the kid, takes the ball from him and shows him how to grip it and gives him a few pointers on his mechanics. I wish I could remember who was batting next for us, but that kid from Frazer struck him out! You should have seen the smile on the Frazer kid's face. Priceless! Of course, our hitter heard plenty from us when he got back to the dugout. Classic Doc."

1967–1982
The Hellcats of Summer

> *Softball and baseball were national pastimes then. Many games had been played by young men during their service in WWII to pass the time, and I suspect Dad, Uncle Bob, and 'Uncle' Pat had all played softball or baseball while serving in their respective branches of the armed forces. These were the men who raised their daughters to play softball with the same enthusiasm as they had. There was so much more to playing softball than most of us realized at the time, and it was a time filled with experiences that helped shape us individually and collectively.*
>
> —Mary Kay Fouhy, Peerless Hellcats

No history of Daniels County baseball and softball would be complete without a chapter dedicated to the Peerless Hellcats teams of 1967 to 1982. Ed Puckett had previously coached the Peerless Wranglerettes, Pansies, and Belles fast-pitch softball teams from 1957 through 1965, which was his daughter Gerri Puckett's* (my cousin) last year in high school. I remember watching Gerri play after I got a little older. She was an excellent fielding shortstop, had a really strong arm, and could hit for power. Just a tremendous all-around softball player. Gerri remembers those early years with her dad and the fast-pitch teams. "I started playing when I was pretty young, maybe the start of junior high. At that time, I was playing with the older women, and we were playing fast-pitch. I don't remember exactly when it switched to slow pitch or when the name became Hellcats. I graduated in 1965 and that was my last year before I moved from Peerless. When I was married and living in Chinook, we had a softball team and there were times when about three of us from the Chinook team would go to tournaments with the Hellcats and play with them. It was a top-notch team and very competitive. We all had great times together. Dad was a great coach, and he pushed me hard to get better."

I remember Uncle Ed being a sports fanatic, but so was every other Puckett who lived in Peerless. I was too young to remember watching him play basketball with the Pirates, but I remember watching him coach girls' basketball and softball. In the section on "Edwin and Norma Puckett" written by Norma Puckett in *Daniels County History* book it reads, "Ed has always been active in sports, playing high school basketball and was one of the noted Peerless Pirates Independent Basketball team. He coached and managed the

1971 Peerless Pink Panthers: Peerless High School's first girls' basketball team, but not officially through the school yet. Back row, left to right: Coach Ed Puckett, Patti Dighans, Taunya Fouhy, Wanda Hames, Pamla Fouhy, Mary Lystad, Assistant Coach Shauanna Fouhy. Front row, left to right: Pixine Snare, Della Lystad, Kathleen Fladager, Donna Wasser, Donna Sletten. Pam Fouhy: "Our hot pink lace up tops and turquoise shorts were sewn by our mothers. Pretty in Pink. This is the year that Gerri Puckett gave her dad and our team the Pink Panther which we named Pilford. Our group always called him Pilford Geraldine Peydrock the Pink Panther." *Family photo.*

---

* Maiden names for the Hellcats are used throughout the chapter.

girls' softball teams, starting in 1957 until he retired from it in 1974. Ed began the first women's fast-pitch softball team in Peerless in 1957 with the Peerless Pansies. In 1967 he started a slow-pitch softball team known as the Peerless Hellcats; they went to tournaments all over the state and had a very impressive record of wins. During these years George Larson, Maynard Lystad and Pat Fouhy were assistant coaches. Ed also started the first girls' basketball team in Peerless in 1970 and continued until 1972 when the state legalized girls' basketball for a school sponsored program. Norma has been active in Auxiliary work over the years, being one of the first members, where in 1977 she was serving as president."[103] Although Aunt Norma's write-up in the history book states that "Ed retired from coaching in 1974," his absence from the field was temporary, as he came back to coach after that. You couldn't keep Uncle Ed away from the softball field.

I asked the players who came up with the name Hellcats. Pixine Snare replied, "I remember two names were suggested, Pumas and Hellcats. We went with Hellcats. I thought that was very exciting to use the word *hell*, our name had a swear word in it." Donna Fladager added, "I remember we wanted to be some kind of cat since we already had the Bobcats and Panthers. So we agreed on the Hellcats. It seems like our team then had thrown that around and made that decision.'"

After Ed started the team back up again in 1967, it is difficult to pinpoint what year the Hellcats actually became known by their edgy name. When asked what year she thought the Hellcats became the Hellcats, Shauanna Fouhy—one of the older players of the next generation of softball players in Peerless—said, "We became the 'Hellcats' when we were actually able to make enough money to get jerseys made. As for a women's softball team; that's harder. I started playing with the 'old women's' before I turned legal at 14. I remember playing summer softball all through high school. I remember playing first with Bonnie and Bitsy Fouhy."

Two themes in this book are the passion for baseball and softball in northeastern Montana and the connection between the sport and our nation's Armed Forces. A major baseball/softball family in Daniels County was the Fouhy family. I played Peewee, Little League and Babe Ruth baseball with Matt Fouhy, and all his older sisters and cousins all played softball. Pat Fouhy, Matt's dad, was Uncle Ed's assistant coach. Annabelle (Bingham) Fouhy, Lauretta (Fouhy) Puckett and Helen (Brenke) Fouhy played for the Peerless Pansies the first women's fast-pitch softball team in Peerless in 1957. Mary Kay Fouhy, who played for the Peerless Hellcats slow-pitch softball team in the early 1970s, remembers how passionate the Fouhy family was about baseball and softball. She said, "The interest in baseball/softball ran deep in at least the Fouhy clan. It was an Independence Day family get-to-gather at Fouhy Bros. that included Bob and Helen and family, Pat and Annabelle and family (and, well, whatever kids they had at that time as I was not very old when this took place), and some of Powell's as well as their mom was our aunt. Somebody suggested playing softball, but the only area big enough was in what we called the calving pasture, close to the house and barn, which was overgrown with big weeds that love cow manure (and drive a gardener crazy if the manure dumped on the garden isn't well aged). Some of the guys stomped down a ball diamond outline in the weed patch, and the adults commenced playing softball, men and women, husbands and wives, and older children. I recall them running through the weeds to get to a base or to find a dropped ball or a grounder. I don't recall who the ump was. Just recall, everyone had a great time making do with a weed-filled softball field out in the pasture; some folks had ball gloves, but many didn't. The softball was scruffy and beat up, but softball and baseball were national pastimes then. Many games had been played by young men during their service in WWII to pass the time, and I suspect Dad, Uncle Bob, and 'Uncle' Pat had all played softball or baseball while serving in their respective branches of the armed forces. These were the men who raised their daughters to play softball with the same enthusiasm as they had. There was so much more to playing softball than most of us realized at the time, and it was a time filled with experiences that helped shape us individually and collectively."

Mary Kay's memory of playing softball in the pasture on Independence Day (what's more American than that?!) and honoring her father and uncles who served in the Armed

Seaman Ed Puckett, United States Navy, 1945–1946. *Family photo.*

---

* The Hellcats were also known as the Peerless Bar Girls' Softball Team and in private as Ed's Bar Flys.

Private First Class Francis G. "Pat" Fouhy, United States Marine Corps, 1946–48. *Family photo.*

Forces touches on both themes of *The Blues of Summer*, so I will take this opportunity to honor coaches Ed Puckett and Pat Fouhy, both veterans. Ed Puckett served overseas in the United States Navy during WWII in 1945, and Pat served for two years in the United States Marine Corps in the immediate aftermath of the war, spending 18 months overseas in China. Thank you for your service, Uncle Ed and Pat. And thank you for coaching the Peerless Hellcats softball team.

Some of the players commented on their experience playing for Ed and Pat. Here are just a few of those comments:

- **Patsy Fouhy:** "Ed was such a good coach! Never yelled, never spoke much, but you could sure tell if you disappointed him. And you never wanted to disappoint him!"
- **Pixine Snare:** I began playing when I was in 7th grade for Ed Puckett and Pat Fouhy. A bar owner/farmer/mailman and a farmer/rancher who had the love of the game, and dedication to a bunch of goofy girls. In the beginning it seemed like all we did was practice.
- **Laura Fouhy:** "Ed and Pat were both amazing coaches with very little to say. I can still hear Pat chuckling and looking at the ground shaking his head! And Cowboy boots. They both wore cowboy boots. Coaches today would be mortified! But our coaches were absolutely the best!"
- **Donna Fladager:** "We certainly didn't want to disappoint Ed. I remember sliding into second base once, too aggressively since we were in the lead by many runs and he told me I could slow down—I could tell he thought I didn't need to be told that since we had the game well in hand. He never said anything bad, but you knew!"
- **Vicki Fouhy*:** "I remember Pat twisting his mustache and eyebrows—A LOT! I also can remember when so many of us were cousins and fought so much between us that I think that made us a tough team all around."

1967

REGARDLESS OF WHEN THE HELLCATS BRANDISHED THEIR NEW name, the team that would become known as the Peerless Hellcats was playing ball in 1967, although many of the future Hellcat players were not on the team yet. Donna Fladager remembers a sad day at a tournament in Glendive in August of 1967. "All our parents generally followed us which was terrific. This one tournament we were playing, the police came and it scared all of us because we were concerned about our parents who hadn't arrived yet. Ed did all he could to keep our heads in the game. I was up to bat and by then we were crying. I was trying to clear my eyes and I swung and blasted one down the right field line. I don't hit home runs and I normally don't place them down right but that is where this one went. Ed was the third base coach. Bases had been loaded and I was rounding third and kicked the third base out into the baseline towards the dugout. And ran on home. Ed cheering, etc. Then they called me out for missing third base. Ed said how in the world could that be when the third base was not where it should be and he had to move because it was heading towards him. I was still out but by then we had found out it was Bobby Machart who had been in the accident. Cessy [Bobby's wife] was on our team that year. That was so sad."

The tournament in Glendive in 1967 was just one of many tournaments the Hellcats barnstormed in the late 1960s, as in the early years of the Hellcats, there weren't many other softball teams competing in northeastern Montana. Consequently, Ed hauled the team across the state to play in tournaments. Pixie Snare, who started playing when she was only a 7th grader in 1968, recalls what it was like in the early years. "There were very few teams in our area. When we did play, we went to tournaments in Roundup, Chinook, Billings, Glendive, Miles City and Havre. Ed and Pat would load us up in a bunch of cars, and off we would go."

1970

THIS 1970 PHOTO OF THE TEAM IS THE FIRST PICTURE OF THE team Ed and Pat were coaching. Some of the girls on this team were only 14 years old at the time, only rising freshman in high school. Pixine remembers who was on this early team. "Most of the girls in the Peerless area played softball for Ed. The team I recall when I began was, Aquina Hersel, catching, Nola Fladager pitching, Shauanna Fouhy

---

* This comment from Vicki was made on Facebook in June 2009. Sadly, Vicki passed away in November 2016.

1970 Peerless Hellcats. Standing, left to right: Coach Ed Puckett, Garnet Jones, Donna Fladager, Shauanna Fouhy, Janet Chapman, Pamla Fouhy, Assistant Coach Maynard Lystad. Front, left to right: Aquina Hersel, Lorna Fladager, Karen Fladager, Nola Richardson, Wanda Hames and Mary Lystad. *Leader.*

on first, Garnet Jones on second, Karen Fladager on third, Donna Fladager on shortstop, I don't remember who were in the outfield, but Wanda Hames and Debbie Hames played, and Janet Chapman, Mary Kay Fouhy, Pam and Taunya Fouhy, Patsy and Jeannie Fouhy, and many I can't remember right now." Pam Fouhy Hendrickson added, "I remember this is the team I started with."

1971

The trophy the Hellcats are posing with in the first picture is the third-place trophy from the Roundup Invitational Tournament in July 1971. For the photo's caption, the *Leader* wrote, "PEERLESS HELLCATS girls softball team recently won third place trophy at an invitational tourney in Roundup." The second picture is of the Hellcats at the Roundup tournament. Pixine recalls the excitement of bringing this trophy home to Peerless. "It was a while before we actually brought home a trophy. I recall that we were in Roundup eating at a little cafe looking at the bracket. Someone realized that the least we would finish would be third place. They gave trophies for third place! This was a momentous occasion. Shauanna Fouhy and Donna Fladager decided that it should be marked with a gift to Ed for putting up with us. They bought him a gift, had it wrapped and handed it to him. He didn't open it for the longest time. I believe that he was nervous about the contents. Finally with a deep breath he ripped the wrapping off, to find a little plastic statue of a walnut. The writing below read, 'Head Nut.' That phrase said it all!"

Pixine added, "Ed bought us a trophy every year we won the district. For many years we were the only team in the district!"

1971 Peerless Hellcats (partial roster). Coach Ed Puckett in back. Standing, left to right: Patsy Fouhy, Pixine Snare, Pam Fouhy, Janet Chapman, Shauanna Fouhy. Kneeling, left to right: Wanda Hames, Mary Lystad, Mary Kay Fouhy, Sue Dixon. *Leader.*

1971 Peerless Hellcats, Third Place at Roundup Tournament. Front row, left to right: Pixine Snare, Patsy Fouhy, Pam Fouhy, Mary Kay Fouhy. Back row, left to right: Mary Lystad, Wanda Hames, Taunya Fouhy, Coach Ed Puckett, Susan Dickson, Janet Chapman, Shauanna Fouhy.

---

* This was the first reference in the *Leader* to the Peerless softball team as the "Hellcats." *Daniels County Leader*, August 5, 1971.

In addition to the Hellcats bringing home their first tournament trophy, the summer of 1971 was exciting for other reasons in Peerless—a new high school and gymnasium were being constructed. I remember walking from my house to the construction area (it wasn't a long walk) to monitor the progress daily, imagining what it would be like once it was finished, especially the new gymnasium. Not wanting to miss the opportunity to get his Hellcats some practice, Uncle Ed finagled the construction workers to come down to the Peerless ballfield and play some softball against his Hellcats. Pixine Snare recalls how that went. "The building of the new school added a whole new gang to softball practice. Ed being the con that we all loved, talked the construction crew into coming down and practicing with us after they had put in a full day of work. Visiting with Norma a few years ago she asked Pam and I how old we would have been then, we did some figuring, and admitted we were around 15. Norma just hooted. She said that the construction guys thought that they were going to waltz in there and soundly defeat 'those little girls.' But they came back to the bar the first night and told Norma they felt like they had been hit with a load of TNT. We gave as good as we got, never held back. And made some good friends in the bargain. The next tournament we played in Miles City the foreman of the crew let us stay at his house. We slept all over, including in his yard in tents."

1972

Two pictures of the 1972 Peerless tournament. Referring to the picture of the Peerless crowd, Gerri Puckett said, "The player accepting the trophy from my dad is Patti Conroy. She was the pitcher on the Chinook team I played on." Jeannie Fouhy is in the lower left corner. Myrna is in front of her. I love how this picture shows the crowd, the cars, and the opposing team. That is Bob Larson in the background with the mic. I remember him calling all the games on the microphone.

In 1972, the Hellcats, many who had started playing when they were 7th and 8th graders, were growing up, getting stronger, and better. Peerless won the invitational tournament they hosted each summer. Pam Fouhy wrote this comprehensive summary for the 1972 season:

1972 Peerless Hellcats, Peerless Tournament Champions. Back row, left to right: Coach Ed Puckett, Pixine Snare, Taunya Fouhy, Pam Fouhy, Mary Lystad, Shauanna Fouhy, Jan Traynor, Donna Fladager, Coach Pat Fouhy. Front row, left to right: Susan Drummond, Wanda Hames, Mary Kay Fouhy, Nancy Olson, Patsy Fouhy, Donna Wasser and Myrna Baldry. Missing from the picture are Patti Dighans (working in stands) and Susan Dickson who left for Girls' State last day. *Leader.*

In 1972, we added some Scobey players to the roster. Who played: Pixie Snare, Taunya Fouhy, Pamla Fouhy, Mary Lystad, Shauanna Fouhy, Jan Traynor, Donna Fladager, Susan Drummond, Wanda Hames, Mary Kay Fouhy, Nancy Olson, Patsy Fouhy, Donna Wasser, Myrna Baldry, Patti Dighans, and Susan Dickson.

There was also a Peerless Kids vs Plentywood Kids game in July where JoAnn (Mutt) Dickson, Jeannie Fouhy, Della Lystad and Win Hames played. They were probably too young to be on the regular roster.

Teams in the Peerless tournament were Hinsdale, Plentywood, Roundup, Avco (Glasgow Air Base) and Chinook.) Officials were Marvin Hash, Tiny Puckett, and Lalon Trang. Bob Larson announced the games. Teams were served a free supper Saturday evening by the mothers. Two weeks after winning the Peerless tournament, the Hellcats spent June 17 and 18th in Glendive kicking butt (and maybe jumping in the pool at the Derrick?). Lost our first game 4-14 to Penney's (Glendive) then came back to beat Miles City 21-2 that afternoon. Sunday, we won a close one 6-5 over Emco, then tromped MDU 23-5. Unfortunately, Charlie Brown beat us 10-8. Not sure where we placed but guessing maybe third or so.

July 7th and 8th found us in Chinook for their first invitational tourney. We beat Havre and Chinook and then lost two close games to High Crest Oil of Havre to take second place.

1972 Peerless Tournament. Peerless crowd following a big tournament in June 1972. *Leader.*

Circa 1972 or 1973 Peerless Hellcats in Roundup. Back row: Coach Ed Puckett, Myrna Baldry, Win Hames, Jeannie Fouhy, Laura Fouhy, Mary Kay Fouhy, Assistant Coach Pat Fouhy. Front row: Donna Fladager, Wanita Paulson, Pixine Snare, Patsy Fouhy, Pamla Fouhy, Shauanna Fouhy. *Family photo.*

Chinook took third with Jerry Girard as their coach and our Gerri Puckett Girard as tough competition.

The Roundup tournament was held July 14–16 and featured Roundup, Chinook, Peerless, Bid Lake, Miles City and three Billings teams—Jail House, First National Bank and First Citizens Bank. We started with a 12-2 win over Jailhouse, then an 18-6 win over First Citizens. Sunday we defeated Roundup 15-5 to meet Chinook for the championship which we won 31-7. Chinook had a great tournament losing their first game and then coming back through the losers bracket to challenge us for first.

We also played Plentywood and Westby a few times that summer, but our main focus was the tournaments we attended. Our final tourney of the year was the State Softball Tournament in Miles City, August 4th thru 6th. We lost two close games, 7-9 to Hysham and 2-3 to Anaconda. According to the article the Hysham game was filmed by KYUS television and broadcast at 10:30 Saturday night. I don't remember us being TV stars!

This picture of big Hellcats team in 1972 was taken when we were heading to Miles City to the State Tournament. We were Hellcats by then. As you can see there were several girls in this photo that only played for a summer or two.

In her summary, Pam mentioned the addition of the Scobey players to the team in 1972. Pixine Snare recalls the transition with the addition of the Scobey players. "I do remember when the Scobey girls joined the team, it was a little hard to take at the first, but when they were so much fun, and admittedly good players they became part of the team. Sue Dickson played a mean first; Myrna Baldry was all-state shortstop, and Kelly Veis was a good second baseman."

1973

I REMEMBER THE GREAT MATCHUPS BETWEEN THE HELLCATS and Chinook at the tournaments. It always seemed to be the Hellcats and Chinook FU (Farmer's Union) in the championship game, and 1973 was no different. The picture shows Chinook FU, champions of the 1973 Peerless tournament. One of the memories I have is how competitive the games were, but also the good sportsmanship between the two teams. It was intense but fun. It was difficult to see my cousin Gerri and Uncle Ed competing against each other (I could remember when I saw them on the field with Gerri playing for Ed), but at the same time, it was fun to watch. It was good softball. Remembering the Peerless-Chinook games, Gerri said, "Our teams got along great, but very competitive when we played each other."

In a hard-fought one-run game, Chinook FU beat Peerless 8-7 in the championship game to win the 1973 Peerless tournament. The *Daniels County Leader* provided an excellent summary of the tournament:

1973 Peerless Tournament. Chinook Gets First In 2-Day Series

```
Chinook FU gals copped first place in the two-
day tourney at Peerless last weekend. They edged
```

1972 Peerless Hellcats. Back row, left to right: Taunya Fouhy, Donna Fladager, Shauanna Fouhy, Sue Dixon, Pam Fouhy. Middle row, left to right: Mary Lystad, Pixine Snare, Patsy Fouhy, Myrna Baldry. Front row, left to right: Donna Wasser, Susan Drummond, Patti Dighans, Mary Kay Fouhy, Jan Traynor. **Leader.**

1973 Chinook FU, Peerless Tournament Champions. Gerri Puckett is kneeling second from the right. Leader.

the Peerless Hellcats, 8-7, in the final game of the double elimination tourney. Hellcat Coach Ed Puckett took some consolation in the fact that his daughter, Mrs. Jerry Girard, a former player with the Peerless Hellcats, was a member of the winning Chinook team. Saturday's games saw Peerless Hellcats roll over Rocky Boy, 45-3; Westby took the measure of Roundup Stripers, 27-5; Roundup Bears won from the Peerless Kittens, 21-7 and then Roundup Stripers from Rocky Boy 23-4. Peerless Hellcats won over Westby 10-6, and Chinook beat the Roundup Bears 18-14, Sunday games saw Roundup Bears beat the Stripers 15-13; Peerless Kittens* lost to Westby 22-10. Peerless Hellcats bowed to Chinook 31-11. Then the Bears beat Westby 24-22. Peerless Hellcats got into the finals, defeating Roundup Bears 13-11, and then dropping the final to Chinook 8-7 in a game that was tied up 3-3 and 6-6 durings its course. The Chinook infielder's performance in fielding and throws to the bases propelled the team to the win.[104]

1974

By 1974, Chinook and Peerless had played against each other in so many tournament championship games that the *Daniels County Leader* was referring to the two teams as "old rivals."[105] And in 1974, the Hellcats avenged their previous year's loss to Chinook in the championship game of the Peerless tournament by winning 11-5. To get to the championship game Peerless beat Westby 10-2 in the undefeated semifinal. Chinook, who had crawled back through the dirt route after losing earlier in the tournament, then shut out Westby 8-0 to challenge Peerless for the championship. (Shutting out a team in slow-pitch softball is indicative of a very strong defense.) Summing up the Hellcat's win, the *Leader* wrote, "The final game Sunday evening, just before supper, saw the Peerless Hellcats again meeting their old rival from Chinook. The Hellcats were able to turn back several rallies by the visitors to win 11-5 in the championship game."[106] Donna Fladager was selected tournament MVP, one of several she earned in her softball career, which spanned close to 15 years.

The 1974 season was the last for many of the Hellcats who had started playing for Ed and Pat since they were in junior high. Pixine Snare, who started playing in 1968 when she was a 7th grader, was one of them. In reflecting on her seven-year career with the Hellcats, Pixine said, "We had a lot of fun playing and a lot of fun traveling together. Those were the days!" Then she added, "Norma told us that the years Ed coached us were the happiest of his life. His bedroom was full of the trophies we had won. Right on his bedside table was that little plastic statute, Head Nut."

1975

In 1975, the Peerless Hellcats won all but one league game to win "the large" District 13 championship. They also played in several nonleague games and tournaments."[107] This picture shows the five Hellcats and coach Pat Fouhy who were selected for the District 13 All-Star Team to play in the state tournament in Great Falls. Noting the common last name of five of the people appearing in the photo, the *Leader* wrote, "It's kind of a family affair as four of these six players are cousins, plus the very interested coach, also a relative."[108]

1974 Peerless Hellcats. Back row, as heads appear: Coach Ed Puckett, Mary Kay Fouhy, Wanda Hames, Nancy Olson, Shauanna Fouhy, Laura Fouhy, Pam Fouhy, Assistant Coach Pat Fouhy. Kneeling, left to right: Donna Fladager, Patsy Fouhy, Myrna Baldry, Pixine Snare, Jeannie Fouhy, Win Hames. *Leader.*

Peerless Hellcats on the District 13 All-Star Team. Back row, left to right: Pam Fouhy, Mary Kay Fouhy, Patsy Fouhy, Mary Lystad, Coach Pat Fouhy. Front row, left to right: Win Hames and Myrna Baldry. *Leader.*

* The Peerless Kittens were comprised of younger Peerless girls who aspired to be Hellcats someday.

1975 District 13 All-Stars. Back row, Coach Ben Holt, Dawn Selvig, Sue Meyer, Kim Holt. Middle row, Myrna Baldry, Mary Lystad, Connie Ryals, Pam Fouhy, Carol Jensen, Lori Samuelson, Coach Pat Fouhy. Front row, Patsy Fouhy, Mary Kay Fouhy, Jeannie Fouhy, Kari Selvig, Mary Johnson. *Leader.*

This picture of the District 13 All-Stars was taken after the team took second place in the State Softball tournament in Great Falls, qualifying for the Northwest regionals in Seattle. Three District 13 players—Myrna Baldry, Connie Ryals, and Sue Nielsen—were selected to the all-state tournament team. Mary Kay Fouhy recalls the state tournament. "A few of us were out a bit late the night before the last day of the tournament thinking, what the heck, we won't make it past the morning game, as we were in the loser's bracket, so why not see a bit of the town as we will be headed home by noon the next day. Well, we dug in, applied that grit and determination us gals from northeastern Montana are well known for, and by golly if we didn't win the first game that morning, and went on to win enough games to place second at state and qualify to go to Seattle for the regionals. I am old enough now to realize all of our parents must have had mixed emotions about our great achievement—seriously take all those girls to Seattle to play softball during harvest and we didn't even have proper uniforms much less

Myrna Baldry, Connie Ryals, Sue Nielsen, District 13 first-team all-state tournament selections. *Leader.*

everything else that was needed to make the trip happen. But we were *so* proud and also *so* tired and sunburned."

Patsy Fouhy remembers the regional tournament. "We chartered a bus to Seattle. Connie Ryals was on our team. She was a heckuva shortstop. I remember practicing softball in a big city park in Seattle. Everything was so green. It rained the night we played Alaska. I remember slogging through the mud in the outfield. It was the first time we played under the lights, I think. We won one game and lost two. I remember Pat and Ed stopping somewhere and buying us all small, individual trophies! We wore white jerseys and light blue softball pants."

Pam Fouhy added, "The bus we chartered was out of Plentywood. I remember riding through the night, trying to sleep. I could be wrong but I think we drove straight through from Plentywood to Seattle. So maybe there were two drivers? Matthew and Ray Chapman were along as batboys and Mom as chaperone of course. I know I felt overwhelmed and definitely out of my league! I don't remember the teams we played but they were very good. We were kind of underdogs at the tournament and the crowd was supportive of us. We were so excited when we actually won a game! After the game Patsy mentioned, we were so muddy and I remember Mom had to collect all our uniforms and find a laundromat to wash them so we could wear them the next day. I remember they drove the bus down to a place where we could get out and put our feet in the ocean if we wanted to. That is my claim to 'seeing' the Pacific Ocean! We couldn't have been there very long and it seemed like it was cold and rainy so I for one didn't actually walk in the water!"

Mary Kay Fouhy also has memories of the regional tournament. "I remember getting to Seattle, trying to find the ballpark, getting stuck on a single-lane street where the bus had to back up, couldn't turn around—remember this was *way* before GPS or Google, just street maps. And it felt so cold—Annabelle took us somewhere so we could buy long-sleeve shirts to wear under our uniform tops to help with the cold. I remember standing in a deep puddle of muddy water at the base of the pitcher's mound, water pouring off the brim of my ballcap, looking up into the lights watching the water droplets fall through the light rays, and trying to find the batter's box—it was raining so hard. The game had already been delayed, had to be played or forfeited to keep to some kind of schedule as there were teams from all over the northwest gathered in Seattle to play the tourney. The team that beat us was a local team, and in a day and age when most of us had little acquittance with folks who weren't white, that black women's team that beat us and went on to take the tourney were amazing to watch play softball. We played two games, lost both, but came home proud to have been awarded the good sportsmanship award. Many of us had never been out of the state, some had not traveled out of northeastern Montana—it was one of those broadening your horizons, bonding experiences where memories just get better and better. God bless all the adults who in whatever way made that trip possible for us!"

1976–1982

Following the 1975 season, Judy Fouhy recalls, "The Hellcats continued to play for many years. I remember playing in red unis, then green, and finally gold. Coached by Ed, by Pat Fouhy, by Bob Fouhy and then I'm not sure. Likely whoever we could find to help so we could still play. I think the first year I played was 1975, at age 12, and I am certain we had a team every summer through 1981. After that, maybe, or we just played tourneys with some of us from different communities, including Opheim, Westby, and Scobey."

Carissa Brandt also remembers playing with those later Hellcat teams. "Mary Drummond and I played with the women's softball league in the early '80s as 14-year-olds. We were so sad when they decided to quit. Bob Fouhy and Roger Trang were coaches. Great memories."

⚾ ⚾ ⚾

One of the questions I asked the Hellcat players was, "When you think about playing softball in Peerless all those summers ago, what is it that you remember most?" Here are some of the responses I received:

Jeannie Fouhy: "Fouhy at bat, Fouhy on deck, Fouhy in the hole. And Fouhy's in the dugout and coached by Fouhys!"

1977 Peerless Hellcats. Back left to right: Lita Brackee, Coach Ed Puckett, Della Lystad, Donna Fladager, Marcae Nieskens, Laura Fouhy, Jeannette Nieskens. Front left to right: Vicki Fouhy, Judy Fouhy, Myrna Baldry, Jacky Drummond, Darla Drummond. *Family photo.*

Circa 1980 Peerless Hellcats. Back left to right: Lita Brackee, Coach Ed Puckett, Della Lystad, Donna Fladager, Marcae Nieskens, Laura Fouhy, Jeannette Nieskens. Front left to right: Vicki Fouhy, Judy Fouhy, Myrna Baldry, Jacky Drummond, Darla Drummond. *Family photo.*

Donna Fladager: "What I remember is the support we got from Peerless and the community. It did not matter whether they had relatives or family playing, people were there cheering us on. Someone might have been having a beer at the bar and hear honking and cheering; they would wander to the ballpark to see what was happening. It was amazing. No matter how old we were our parents still traveled to our games. I loved all my years playing and Peerless in general. It will always be home."

Patsy Fouhy: "I remember the other girls, most of whom I was related to. We were all friends, and I loved going to practice with them. For some odd reason, I remember the dugout. I remember being lined up with the others cheering out of our little dugout! And, I remember the field, where I spent much of my softball life. I swear I knew every dip and bump out there!" Patsy also remembers the tournaments Peerless hosted. "I remember all the cars lined up around the field with their horns honking!"

Laura Fouhy: "It was just so much fun!" She added, "I love the sound of the 'ping of spring' off a metal bat, the feel of a great catch in my glove, a great fly ball catch, a double play, being part of a team I loved, with coaches I loved! So much, and 50 years later, it still rings true!"

Win Hames: "Some of the best times of my youth! I couldn't wait to cross the tracks to get to the ballfield. Dad (Bill Hames) always drove his pickup to the ballfield to watch us. He never got out of the truck, but he always honked his horn when we had really good plays or scored a run." She added, "Softball was so much fun. I think I joined the team when I was 12 which would be in 1972. How lucky were we to have Ed as our coach."

Judy Fouhy: "When I think about playing softball every summer, I think about relief from doing chores on the farm. Painting fences, weeding, cleaning out grain bins, etc. All week long it was working but the one thing I had to look forward to was going to practice and better yet, to the games. Especially those at Westby, or Antelope and Dagmar because we got to stop working way earlier to travel longer distances, and got to stop at the DQ on the way home. Kids in town might have had more fun, but growing up out of town was quiet and productive (at least for our parents). Softball was an escape. Albeit a really fun one that fulfilled all of our competitive natures and solved social needs . . . at least for a time."

Pam Fouhy: "Time spent with friends, laughter, and hard work. The sound of the bat hitting the ball, the feel of the grounder I just snagged or the throw I just made. Great coaches who encouraged us. The joy of achievement and disappointment of loss. Underneath it all, the friendship, the teamwork, the community and sense of being part of a whole was almost a tangible feeling while playing. The smells and sounds and feel of summer. Softball was part of the framework of my life and I loved it. Memories that have lasted a lifetime."

Mary Kay Fouhy: "When I think about playing softball all those summers ago, what is it I remember most? That the team was sort of 'rag-tag' but hell on wheels for effort. We were a diverse group, and I don't recall tryouts were required to play on the team. Girls, ladies, gals, women—I am going to call us the Girls of Summer Peerless Hellcats—were farm/ranch gals, and town girls. Some of us were young, some were older and married. Some ran fast, threw hard, hit long and hard, stole bases on a dare, slid into bases risking road rashes or raspberries—those gals had skills and talent. Some of us, not so much—we ran slow, hit easy to catch pop-ups or infield grounders, were never sent to steal a base or slide-in as we had no talent for either skill, and could not throw any distance or with much accuracy. What I remember is how the coaches found a place for anyone who showed up to play with the Hellcats regardless of their skills, abilities, or talents. And how the team embraced everyone and each other who played for the Hellcats. There were sets of sisters that played, together or in succession, and cousins and friends—but when you played for the Girls of Summer Peerless Hellcats you were part of a big family. And takeaway lessons learned without realizing I was learning them: play nice with others, be fair and considerate, support and encourage others, be a good sport, practice hard so you know how to play hard, and be appreciative of what others do to make it possible to do what you do. I remember most about playing softball all those summers ago what a great and wonderful time it was. Quite possibly the best time of my life."

EXTRA INNINGS

DONNA FLADAGER HAD THE LONGEST CAREER PLAYING SOFTball for Ed, starting in 1964 or 1965 and playing through 1977. Recalling here many years with the Hellcats, Donna said, "We had so much fun for so many years. Thanks to Ed (and Norma)!" She added, "I remember early on when I first started—I was at second base then and Gerri at shortstop. We were at a tournament and going to play the Butte girls. We were these skinny little kids from Peerless, and they were stocky girls (very stocky) from Butte. We were paranoid to play them. Not sure how badly we were beaten but that was scary being a young girl."

Pixine Snare shared this memory of Donna. "I recall Donna Fladager hitting the ball into the far outfield, she had rounded second and was nearly to the shortstop when the base coach was yelling, 'Get back, get back!' Donna did a rapid about face, raced for second, deciding a little late to slide, her momentum took her past second base into right field, but she had grabbed on to the bag so tightly that she ripped it out of the ground, taking it with her! There she laid laughing, hugging second, turning bright red as only Donna could do."

Laura and Pam Fouhy remember the slush burgers at the concession stand for the home tournaments. Laura said, "I remember our moms running a concession stand at times. Slush burgers were on the menu, and I think, if I remember right, fried chicken and potato salad!" Pam added, "Definitely remember the slush burgers! And the rickety concession building. Health hazard nowadays but people were just glad to get something to eat." I remember the slush burgers, too. I wouldn't be at the field too long before I walked behind the backstop to the old concession building to order a slush burger. Scobey had Legion burgers, and Peerless had slush burgers.

There were some photos of the Hellcats through the years that the players weren't sure what year they were taken. To help place the year, an interesting tactic was employed. Mary Kay Fouhy, when pinpointing the year for one photo, said, "1971 seems right looking at the length of my hair. Guessing Joe is thinking, 'Length of her hair, what's that got to do with anything?' Well, we gals tend to recall hairdos as event and era markers in our lives."

Pam Fouhy remembers her first tournament as a Hellcat. "The first tournament I ever went to was in Glendive. I was too young to play officially but had been coming in to practice with Shauanna. They were going to be shorthanded for the tournament, so I went along and played as Karen Fladager. They had to keep reminding me when it was my turn to bat because they were calling for Karen!"

Several of the girls remember awful sunburns back in the day. Laura Fouhy recalls "horrible sunburns that blistered and peeled. Wet tea bags helped, but the pain was awful. Days before sunscreen!"

Pixine Snare shared a funny anecdote about Annabelle Fouhy—mother of Shauanna, Taunya, and Pam Fouhy. Pixine said, "Way back when you could buy breakfast for a couple of bucks. The Hellcats entrusted Annabelle Fouhy with handling the money raised to feed and pay hotel costs for the team. Annabelle was and still is a force to reckon with. With stunning red hair, standing almost six-feet tall she was hard to miss. One tournament we were in a motel with outside doors to each room. All the teams' rooms were right in a row, making Annabelle's morning duty of handing out two dollars per player an easy job. Bursting into each room without knocking, waving a fist full of money, shouting, 'Two dollars, two dollars, two dollars!' was her morning wake-up call for us. Only her count was off; she went one room too far, bursting in waving money, shouting, 'Two dollars, two dollars, two dollars!' From the bed, a very startled young couple leaped to their feet. Annabelle, as stunned as they were, mumbled an apology and bolted from the room, to come back into my room, threw herself on the bed, laughing hysterically, trying to explain what had just happened. She was a sight laying on the bed, money clenched in her hand, laughing until tears ran down her face!"

Shenanigans on road trips were the order of the day for the Hellcats. Pixine told this story: "Ed would get us in a lot of tournaments; we would travel to far flung places like Glendive. We stopped in Circle to eat. Sue [Dixon] locked her keys in the trunk of her car, at least twice on that trip. Shauanna forgot her glove and had to borrow one from the other team. We would stay in the cheapest motels possible. In Glendive we had rooms at the Derrick Motel, with a small pool behind a tall chain link fence. There were signs that warned NO RUNNING, and the pool closed at 10:00 p.m. Well, if there was ever a challenge that was one! A gal, I can't remember who, was running across the wet deck, fell and slid under the chain link fence. She raked her legs terribly bad, to the point she went to the ER, got patched up and a tetanus shot. Ed said, 'NO MORE SWIMMING.' And they locked the gate. Challenge two! By now it's late, Myrna Baldry climbs the fence and is running around the deck, slipped, slid under the fence raking up her legs. They sneak-hauled her to the ER to get her patched up and a tetanus shot, then snuck back into their rooms thinking Ed was no the wiser. The next day was over 100 degrees, Myrna wore long jeans, hid from Ed and Pat as much as possible. They never said a word; they knew."

Pixine recalls another funny story about Myrna Baldry. "We were playing in a tournament in Roundup, and it rained and rained and *rained*. They were determined to finish the games, so creative measures were taken. Trenches were dug off first and third bases, but there was a low spot near third that formed a puddle. So wood chips and shavings were hauled in. Games continued. Myrna hit a long fly ball and ran the bases with a full head of steam, rounding second headed for third, Ed is yelling for her to '*Slide!*' Myrna slid into the pile of wood chips. She was wearing shorts! Hundreds of slivers of wood became embedded in her leg and hip. The rest of the tournament Myrna's leg was very swollen and infected. But it didn't slow her down!"

1967–1975
Tiny's Champions and the Peerless Pirates

After spending some time with the mighty Peerless Hellcats, and before moving on to the 1976 Legion season, I'm going to hop in the Wayback Machine and travel back in time to my hometown of Peerless, in the year 1967, which was my rookie year in Peewee baseball playing for my dad. This book is about 95% history and 5% memoir; this is the part where the book becomes a memoir of my memories growing up playing baseball for my Dad, with my brother Jon, and all my childhood friends and teammates in Peerless in the late 1960s and early 1970s.

Opening Day in Peerless, April 1972. I was 11 years old. The baseball field is in the foreground, and the basketball gym is in the background. Patches of snow on the ground were often the case when we began practicing baseball in the early spring. Our house is in the middle to the left with the two tall poplar trees. This was my life growing up in Peerless—one big playground. *Family photo.*

I started playing baseball for Dad when I was six years old. As soon as the snow melted in Peerless in March or April until the last game of whatever season-ending tournament we played in was in August, we lived, breathed, ate, and slept baseball—baseball cards, Wiffle ball, Strat-o-Matic Baseball, pickup games at Roseland Park in Scobey the day of swimming lessons,* watching Scobey Legion practice and play, watching NBC's *Major League Baseball Game of the Week* on Saturdays (if we weren't playing), watching the Montreal Expos (they became my favorite team in the National League) play their game of the week on Canadian television, Jon and I pitching to each other in our backyard and swatting ground balls to each other—it was our life.

We could never get enough players to the Peerless field to have a full sandlot game because there were only two other boys who lived in town (Bernie and Rick Wasser), so we had to play baseball games that required less players. One of my favorite baseball games to play was workup. Workup was best played with 13 players, with nine players in the field and four batters, but we usually had to play with six or seven players. On a good day, maybe we'd have eight or nine. With seven players, we'd have two batters and five fielders, and the on deck batter would be the catcher. The fielders had to "work their way up" to bat. When the batter made an out, he grabbed his glove and ran out to the highest numbered position in the field and the pitcher would grab a bat and hit. Everybody else moved up one position until it was their turn to bat, and the cycle repeated. But if a batted ball was caught in the air, the fielder who caught it became the batter and the batter swapped with that position in the field. There was no score kept, but we used to track the number of runs each batter scored and the batter who scored the most runs was the winner. What was fun about this game was you got to play every position in the field, and there were a lot of pickles because with only two batters the first baserunner would have to try to score, running around all the bases. Sometimes we would play it where the batter who reached base could return to bat again, leaving a "ghost runner" on base. The ghost runner could advance the same number of bases as the batter and could be forced out. This game could go on forever. When I watched the movie *The Sandlot*, a quote from the narrator during the scene where they are playing in the sandlot transported me back to playing workup. "They never kept score, they never chose sides, they never even really stopped playing the game. It just went on forever. Every day they picked up where they left off the day before. It was like a dream game."[109]

---

* The day of swim lessons, Kelly Norman knew Jon and I were coming to town, so we'd always get a sandlot baseball game going outside the pool after swim lessons. A patch of dirt was permanently carved into park lawn where we stood to bat. I was a lousy swimmer, though. I failed my initial test to swim in the deep end because I couldn't swim two lengths of the pool, but Craig Audet, the lifeguard, passed me because he played with Dick and I was a Puckett. I was walking in the shallow end of the pool the last half quarter length.

Workup was perfect for 13 players, but if we ever had enough players to play baseball with two teams, we would usually only have two outfielders and the shortstop would cover both third and short, and the team hitting would provide the catcher. I remember how we determined who would be the home team. Two players would stand facing each other with one of them holding the barrel of the bat at the bottom. The other players would grab the bat just above where it was being held by the other player, and the hands would continue to crawl up the bat until the top of the bat was reached. If one of the players couldn't grab the knob of the bat with his fingers, the other team was home. There were some intense faceoffs with this game!

Another fun game we would play when we had only four or five players was 500. In 500, one batter would swat balls to the other players in the outfield. If a ball was caught in the air, it was 100 points; a one-hopper was 75; two hops was 50; and three hops or more was 25. If you made an error, you lost the same number of points you would have made. When you reached 500 points, you got to go in an hit and the batter went out to field. One thing about this game, it was negative training for calling for a fly ball—everybody went for the ball to get the points!

But my favorite game to play was getting caught in a pickle. There was something about escaping from a pickle and making back to the base safe—or better, home plate to score a run—that was exhilarating.

TINY'S CHAMPIONS PEEWEE TEAM: 1967–1969

When Jon and I were six years old in 1967, Dad organized our Peewee team. (He had previously organized the first Peerless Little League team in 1954.) The original team members were Rick and Bernie Wasser, Roger and Kelly Trang, Ross and Ray Chapman, Joe and Jon Puckett, Matt Fouhy, Tim Gilchrist, Tim Feltis, Bill Fladager, and Willard Fladager. The oldest player on the team was seven years old. Two members, Tim Gilchrist and Tim Feltis, later moved to Opheim and Glentana, and new members joined the team, including Randy and Greg Stolen of Glentana, whose dad Andy assisted Dad in later years, especially with the pitchers. Andy taught Jon and me how to throw our curveballs and Ray Chapman how to throw his knuckleball.

My first memory of playing baseball in 1967 is one of the most special memories I have in my life. There was a Little League game between Peerless and Flaxville at the Peerless field. Don Puckett (five years older than me) and the rest of the Peerless Little Leaguers at the time had just finished playing Flaxville in a game. When the game was over, Dad arranged for a group of us younger kids (Jon and me, but I can't remember who else) to play with the bigger kids in a game so that we could actually get on the field and play in a game situation. When Dad said, "Okay, Joey take the field," I remember I started shaking I was so excited—but nervous—at the same time. I scrambled to find my glove in the dugout and ran out to third base, the only time I remember playing third base in baseball. Don Puckett was playing first base. He threw me a grounder and I remember being so excited that my older cousin (who I idolized) was throwing me a grounder to field. Don't miss it! Don't make a bad throw! I fielded it clean and threw it right back to him. Wow! I did it! I was in the big leagues now!

Jon was pitching. It seemed like the Flaxville players were so big and they were so close to me because I was playing third base. As much as I wanted to play, I remember thinking to myself, Oh my God, don't hit it to me, you'll knock me over! Jon pitched great from 33 feet. I thought each time he threw the ball that the Flaxville players were going to smack it way out there, but he threw a lot of strikes right by them.

In my first official at-bat in baseball, I walked. I remember watching four balls sail way over my head and my bat didn't come close to coming off my shoulder. I was frozen stiff at the plate. I loosened up when I got to run to first base after the walk.

Then it got dark, and we couldn't play anymore. I remember thinking I just wanted that game to go on forever. After the game, I was addicted to baseball. I wanted to play a game every night after that. And maybe next time even swing the bat and pitch.

⚾ ⚾ ⚾

1968 Tiny's Champions, taken at Outlook. Standing, L-R: Ross Chapman, Bill Fladager, Willard Fladager, Bernie Wasser, Steve Feltis, Roger Trang, Tim Gilchrist, Coach Tiny Puckett. Sitting L-R: Joe Puckett, Matt Fouhy, Rick Wasser, Jon Puckett, Ray Chapman, John Machart, Joey Thode, Kelly Trang. *Family photo.*

Joe or Jon Puckett pitching for Tiny's Champions in Outlook, 1968. Family photo.

IN 1968 I PLAYED MY SECOND SEASON OF PEEWEE BASEBALL for Dad and Tiny's champions. We had blue T-shirts for jerseys* and wore the Minnesota Twins hats with TC (for Twin Cites) on them, but Dad told us the TC stood for "Tiny's Champions." Dad was extremely competitive and never knew how to coach a game without the objective of winning, regardless of age. To allow us to pitch at that age, he "invented" a pitching distance of 33 feet and called the league "Peewee." He would play us up against older teams because that would make us tougher (just like Doc did) plus none of the other towns had teams with boys seven and eight years old who formed a complete roster, most of them were 9-12 years old. On the first trip we took to Outlook in 1968, the game was delayed because Dad was arguing with Dick West and the umpire that the pitching distance was to be 33 feet. Outlook was not having it, and I remember there was a lot of controversy about moving up the pitching rubber up from the standard Little League distance of 46 feet. Dad was not going to put the team on the field until they moved the rubber up (only Jon and I could pitch) so it finally happened. The Outlook boys were older, and I remember them laughing in their dugout, saying things like, "Look, they've got to move the rubber up for their pitchers because they're so little!" I was uncomfortable with all that and just wanted to play baseball. In the end, Outlook won a slugfest 14-13 after a walk-off grand slam when our reserve left fielder, Joey Thode, got a bloody nose and ran to the dugout, just before an Outlook player laced a line drive to straightaway left field with the bases loaded. When the ball was hit, my head snapped to left field to see if the ball might be caught, but we didn't have a left fielder. Then, someone from the Outlook dugout yelled out, "Look, they don't have a left fielder!" Laughter on the Outlook bench ensued. The center fielder had to retrieve the ball off the left field fence, but all four runs scored before I got the ball at short on the cutoff throw to the infield. Tough loss.

⚾ ⚾ ⚾

I WAS EIGHT YEARS OLD IN 1969 AND PLAYED MY THIRD YEAR of Peewee ball. The highlight of the year was a big come-from-behind win in a game against Flaxville at Flaxville. Flaxville lead 11-3 in the top half of the final inning. Flaxville was bagging up their equipment in front of their dugout while their pitcher was warming up for the final three outs. Dad came over to our bench, knelt on one knee, and addressed the team: "Do you see that? They're bagging up their equipment. Is this game over? Or do we have three more outs?" We ended up rallying for 11 runs on several hits, walks, and errors to take the lead 14-11, and we held Flaxville scoreless in the bottom half to get the win. I have

1969 Tiny's Champions, taken at Opheim. Standing L-R: Coach Tiny Puckett, Ross Chapman, Willard Fladager, Roger Trang, Bernie Wasser, Joe Puckett. Kneeling L-R: Bill Fladager, Kelly Trang, Tim Gilchrist, Matt Fouhy, Ray Chapman, Jon Puckett. *Family photo.*

---

* I still have my Peewee jersey.

never seen Dad smile more than when he was watching Flaxville unbag their equipment for the bottom half of the inning after we had scored the tying run. Dad was coaching third base and we were on the first base side, so I could see his face clearly, and was watching him because I knew he would be smiling after that tying run scored.

PEERLESS PIRATES LITTLE LEAGUE: 1970-1972

It was more exciting than Christmas morning when the new Peerless Pirates uniforms arrived in spring, 1970. Jon and I had to "pose" with them. *Family photo.*

1970 Peerless Pirates Little League team. Standing L-R: Bill Fladager, Rick Wasser, Coach Tiny Puckett, Ross Chapman, Jack Snare, Roger Trang, Joe Puckett, John Machart. Sitting L-R: Matt Fouhy, Bernie Wasser, Jon Puckett, Ray Chapman, Kelly Trang. *Family photo.*

IN THE SPRING OF 1970 WHEN I WAS NINE YEARS OLD, DAD bought us new uniforms for our Little League team, including jackets with a pirate emblem on the front of them and our names on the back. I can't remember being more excited when they came in. This season was a big leap for Jon, me, and our team, because now that we were nine years old, we were playing Little League Baseball, moving up from Peewee. We were in the big leagues now. Because we were all so young—we might have had one 11-year-old on the team—we were always playing boys who were 2 to 3 years older than us. It had been the same when we were playing Peewee. I remember the first game we played against Frazer that summer, the Frazer Little League team was all 12-year-olds. When we ran onto the field to take infield in Frazer, their team was looking at us curiously (I could feel them watching us), and one of their players on the bench said, "They're *so* little." We *were* little, but as Dad often said, "We're going to get our noses a little bloody," and in the end we bloodied a lot of noses ourselves.

⚾ ⚾ ⚾

MANY BIZARRE EVENTS HAPPENED ON THE BASEBALL FIELD IN Peerless, known as the "Home of the Pirates," through the years. One curious incident happened at a Peewee game between Peerless and Flaxville on June 29, 1970. I have a vivid memory of this event, but the scorebook (thanks to my mom) has helped me fill in some of the details. In the bottom of the first inning, with left-hander Craig Miller pitching for Flaxville, Roger Trang was at the plate with the bases loaded. Flaxville had scored three runs in the top of the first to take a 3-0 lead. Roger cracked a rope to left center field—it was one of the hardest hit balls I ever saw in Little League—and left fielder Gord Tryan, who was only six years old, ran back to retrieve it to get it back to the infield as four Peerless Pirates scampered around the bases. But he couldn't find the ball!

He couldn't find the ball?

It seems that Joe and Esther Vandenburg—the de facto groundskeepers for the Peerless outfield—had not yet cut the grass with their horse-drawn swather in the deep outfield for their hay that year, and it was a particularly wet spring, so the grass was extremely long and green. Gord ran into the tall grass to retrieve the ball as the bases were clearing but couldn't find it. As Roger was rounding second base, Gord realized he couldn't find the ball, turned to the infield, raised his hands in the air to signal he couldn't find the ball, and pleaded for a "grass rule double," but the ump didn't hold up his arms, so Roger circled the bases for a grand slam home run.

Meanwhile, Flaxville's coach, Gordie's dad Don Tryan, was livid because Gordie couldn't find the ball and he came running out to argue the play with the home plate umpire that it should be a grass rule double. Well, guess who had the final say on this? Coach Tiny Puckett, coaching third base, argued that the ball was still in play even when it entered the tall grass because there was no fence, so the ball was still in fair territory. Result: a grand slam for Roger Trang, assisted by the tall grass in left field.

The Doc Norman Championship Era

Joe Puckett, pitcher, 1970. *Family photo.*

Joe Puckett, shortstop, 1970. You can see the two big poplar trees in our yard in the background. When I pitched, Jon played short, and vice versa. *Family photo.*

Jon Puckett, pitcher, 1970. *Family photo.*

Jon Puckett, shortstop, 1970. *Family photo.*

Ross Chapman, third baseman, 1970. *Family photo.*

Ray Chapman, first baseman, 1970. *Family photo.*

Bernie Wasser, outfielder and catcher, 1970. *Family photo.*

Matt Fouhy, outfielder, 1970. *Family photo.*

However, with Peerless leading 6-4 in the top of the fourth, Flaxville scored two runs (Wade and Tully Tryan), then scored the go-ahead run on a single by Shawn French. But it wasn't the winning run because the game was called due to darkness in the bottom of the fourth. The cars parked around the diamond kept the game going for as long as they could with their headlights shining on the field for Peerless to score the tying run, but the suspended game ended with Flaxville leading 7-6 after the third out in the top of the fourth. We'll have to complete the game someday. Ray Chapman, leadoff hitter, is leading off the bottom of the fourth for Peerless, followed by Jon and Joe. Fifty-five years later we could complete the suspended game—at Peerless, of course. It would set the record for the longest suspended game in baseball history.

And Roger's hit has become forever known in Peerless Pirate baseball lore as "the grass rule double that wasn't."

⚾ ⚾ ⚾

IN JUNE 1970, I READ A COMIC ABOUT GORILLAS PLAYING baseball that I was absolutely enthralled with. I read comics all the time at that age (nine), but rarely—if ever—did I come across a comic about baseball; however, an edition of the *Brave and the Bold: Strange Sports Stories* was about baseball. The original story was published in 1963 but was reprinted in a *DC Special: The Strangest Sports Stories Ever Told* in June 1970. That is the comic book I read in my dad's store in Peerless during the summer 1970 Little League baseball season. My daughter, Cosette, a lover of classic comic books herself, bought me the comic for Christmas in 2022.

The story goes like this: a scientist was experimenting with how to quickly evolve nine gorillas to the level of intelligence of humans. It was working, but all the gorillas wanted to do was play baseball! The gorillas, coached by the scientist, played a game against the American League and National League All-Stars at Incirlik Air Base, Turkey, then got a tour to go barnstorming against American League and National League teams in the United States the following season. They destroyed all the major league teams they played, including the Yankees and Dodgers.

After their tour, so the story goes, all nine gorilla hats were donated to the National Baseball Hall of Fame in Cooperstown.

DC Comics Special: "The Strangest Sports Stories Ever Told," June 1970.

DC Comics Special: "The Strangest Sports Stories Ever Told," June 1970.

But the gorilla nine never played the 1970 Scobey Legionnaires. Doc tried to get them scheduled in Scobey to prep the team for the state tournament in Havre. Had they come, their undefeated record might have ended at Scobey Ball Park. The game might have been a bigger draw than Swede Risberg and Happy Felsch in 1925. Havre would have had a chance to beat them too. Fanning would have started, I'm sure.

Maybe someday a game can be arranged with the gorillas on the Field of Dreams.

⚾ ⚾ ⚾

BUT SECOND TO THE GORILLAS ON THE DIAMOND, THE HIGHlight of the 1970 Little League season was a trip to Wolf Point. Dad called Ron Harcharik in Wolf Point to arrange a doubleheader between the Peerless Pirates and the Foodtown and Buttrey teams in Wolf Point. This was a very exciting trip for the Peerless nine heading down to Wolf Point. Up to that point, we had only played Opheim, Flaxville, Scobey, Plentywood, and Westby in competitive games, so we were anxious to see how we would do against the Wolf Point teams. Dad told us, "We got some competition, boys, we might get our noses a little bloody."

In the first game, Mike Neubauer pitched for Foodtown, and I pitched for Peerless. In the first game of the doubleheader, I was pitching, and after I had hit a two-run double in the top of the last inning, we were leading Foodtown 5-4. But in the bottom half, Mike Neubauer of Wolf Point hit a two-run walk-off single to win the first game 6-5 for Foodtown. I'll never forget Kip Harcharik rounding third base and coming around to score. Kip said he didn't know he was the winning run until after the game. It was the first walk-off game I had ever played in, so I didn't understand why we had to walk off the field while there weren't three outs yet. I wanted to keep pitching and get the next out, but Dad said, "The game's over, Joey." We were not used to losing. That game stung.

In that game, Jon and I had never seen a curveball before. Mike Neubauer threw one to Jon, he ducked out of the way, but the ball broke over the plate and umpire Ron Harcharik called a strike.

We won the second end of the double dip against Buttreys 6-4 to earn the split. A five-run second against Wolf Point pitcher Dana Buckles proved to be the difference. My mom and older sister Dianne kept score for these games.

⚾ ⚾ ⚾

FINALLY, I HAVE A MEMORY IN 1970 OF PLAYING AGAINST ONE of my future teammates at a home game in Peerless. We were playing Opheim and Randy Stolen was playing second base. I was a baserunner on first and ran to second when the ball got past the pitcher. Randy received a throw from the pitcher and caught the ball with his foot on the base but didn't tag me. The throw was well ahead of me, and I would have been dead out had he tagged me, but I slid in and was safe. He didn't know he needed to tag me. I thought, "Wow, who is this kid? He doesn't even know he needs to tag me when it's not a force out." Then I heard a voice come from the Opheim dugout on the first base side. "You have to tag him, Randy. You have to tag him." It was coach Andy Stolen. Randy looked into the dugout and nodded.

Little did I know at that time that Randy would become my friend and teammate, and his dad Andy would be my pitching coach, and that we would play in so many games and practices together through Peerless Little League and Babe Ruth then play together on three State championship teams for the Scobey Blues. Randy would become, safe to say, one of the best all-around baseball players in Scobey Blues history. He could hit with power and average, was fast and could steal bases, played a mean left field, had a canon for an arm, and when he pitched, although he had control problems, could throw the ball right by hitters.

I will be careful in my next lifetime not to judge a young player who doesn't know to tag me when it's not a force out—you never know who they might become.

⚾ ⚾ ⚾

IN 1971, MOST OF US ON THE LITTLE LEAGUE TEAM WERE NOW the ripe-old age of 10 years old. There were two big tournaments we played in that summer: one in Wolf Point, and the other in Glentworth, Saskatchewan, which was our first trip across the border to play in a tournament in Canada. There would be many others to follow, and the Canadians would come to play in our tournaments in Peerless, too.

In the Wolf Point tournament, after a disappointing 6-5 loss in our first game to Poplar, we came back to win three consecutive games to take third place by beating Circle 12-2, Scobey 7-1, then Poplar 14-11, avenging our earlier loss to them. Randy Stolen hit a big grand slam home run in the third inning and we scored seven runs in the last inning to pull the game out. Playing in our fourth game of the tournament, Jon and I had pitched a ton of innings, and it was a hot summer day, so our arms were hanging in the last game. Jon was pitching the last game, and Poplar loaded the bases in the bottom of the last inning. Dad brought in Ray

Chapman, who hadn't pitched much, to save the game, and he held on to the one-run lead by striking out Poplar's best hitter to get the final out. After the game, I remember Dad saying, "[Ron] Harcharik said he bent it," when referring to the last pitch Ray threw to get the strikeout. I didn't know what "bent" meant, because I was not throwing a curveball yet. But apparently pitching coach Andy Stolen had already taught Ray Chapman how to throw a curveball at 10 years old, and it got us out of there with a win.

At that tournament, I remember riding in the backseat of our car after we played our fourth game, and "Riders on the Storm" by The Doors came on the radio. I was hot and exhausted but feeling good because we came back to win that last game and take third. I often think of that special day in Wolf Point when I hear "Riders on the Storm."

Our first trip to Saskatchewan, Canada, to play in a tournament was exciting. One thing about playing in tournaments in Canada that was different than playing locally was that many players over the Little League age limit of 12 years old would play, but no could prove it because the teams didn't know each other, and birth certificates were not required. Dad brought Scott Dighans and Duke Trangsrud with us to play in Glentworth. Scott was 13 and Duke was 14 at the time. Duke caught Jon and me during the tournament. The Canadians had players who were as old or older.

We played Limerick, Saskatchewan, in our first game. (Yes, their uniforms were green.) Although we lost the game, 5-3, I have a unique memory of this game. I was caught off guard by how aggressively vocal the Limerick team was razzing us on the field. It was nonstop, loud, and obnoxious. I was pitching and got the brunt of it. I had never experienced anything like that before playing locally. Our team didn't do that; we would cheer each other on, but we never razzed an opponent on the field. Dad would not allow that, but I don't think any of us were wired that way anyway. But as the game progressed, I noticed that the Limerick players quieted down and stopped razzing us. They saw that we didn't do that, and they calmed down and just played baseball. Then, around the third inning, Limerick's Little League fast-pitch softball team showed up to the field to cheer their boys on, and whoa, did they ever start in with the heckling. They were standing behind the Limerick bench and all of them immediately began hurling insults at our players and razzing the pitcher, which was me. It was unbelievable. Try to imagine 12 Little League girls' fast-pitch softball players dressed in green shouting at the top of their lungs. But one of the Limerick boys players said to the girls, "Shh, stop, they don't do that." Then the girls stopped razzing us and just watched the game and cheered their boys on. It was cool. We lost the game, but I think we would have won the sportsmanship trophy it they had one.

⚾ ⚾ ⚾

ONE OF MY FAVORITE MEMORIES OF PLAYING LITTLE LEAGUE baseball in Peerless is of Snoopy, our plump little collie, who would bury his bones right behind the pitcher's rubber at the Peerless Ball Park. Whenever Jon or I pitched during a game, Snoopy would get nervous and come out behind the pitcher's mound and start to dig up his bones. It would always be right in the middle of a game, and he seemed to time it just right so that it would be tense moment and then he'd run out of the dugout to the pitcher's mound. "Snoopy! Snoopy!" Everyone would yell to get him to come off the field and the umpire would have to stop the game of course. Whenever I was pitching, I would always just smile and tell Snoopy he needed to get off the field. "Go on Snoopy now, gotta play ball here." You have no idea how comforting it was to have your dog come out to you on the mound in a tense moment in a game. If only Snoopy could have been with me in American Legion in Scobey my ERA might have been a little less. Snoopy was named after Charlie Brown's dog from the *Peanuts* gang. Snoopy played shortstop for the *Peanuts* nine, managed by Charlie Brown. I always enjoyed reading *Peanuts* and especially the baseball episodes.

Our dog **Snoopy** would bury his bones behind the pitcher's rubber. He was named after Snoopy from the Peanuts gang. Snoopy played shortstop for the Peanuts nine, managed by Charlie Brown, who was also the pitcher.

1972 Peerless Pirates, Fort Peck Invitational Champions.
Family photo.

⚾ ⚾ ⚾

When Jon and I were 11 years old in 1972, we were playing in our sixth year of "organized baseball" (Peewee and Little League) for Dad. It was nice to be getting close to the same size and age as the players on the other teams we were playing. The highlight of the 1972 season was winning the first-place trophy at a season-ending tournament in Fort Peck. We beat Nashua 17-5 in our first game and Frazer 15-4 in the championship. Jon and I pitched, and Ross Chapman and Bernie Wasser caught. After playing together for six years, and getting a little older and bigger, our team was getting pretty good. The *Leader* wrote, "All members of the Peerless Pirates contributed to the barrage of base hits and runs." We concluded the 1972 season with a 16-1 record.

I only wrote two poems when I was in grade school, one about basketball and the other about baseball, which I wrote when I was 11 years old in 1972. Whenever we had an assignment to write a poem, I would write about sports, which was my passion. My baseball poem was written on November 16, 1972, for an English assignment at Peerless Elementary. I got an A! (I made a few grammatical mistakes, but apparently, they got by the teacher, and it's the spirit that counts, right?) Here is the unedited poem:

Baseball, by Joey Puckett

Baseball is a sport,
But not of any sort,
It's an exciting game,
And if your good your never ashamed.
Its fun to stand at the plate,
And hope you don't make a mistake.
The white blur comes in,
You can see it spin,
You bring your bat around,
The ball hits the bat,
It's a base hit,
How about that!
Your standing at first base,
Hoping to keep up the pace.
The ball is hit to the shortstop,
It's a one hop,
He throws to second and I am too late.
He fires to first and he is out.
What a mistake.
What luck!
Well, I better get out on that mound and chuck.
The catcher gives the signal,
You take your wind-up,
Here's the pitch.
It's a pop-up!
Now there's one down,
You feel like a king with a crown on.
And when the second batter strikes out
Your just about ready to shout.
You lead by one run,
There's two down now.
You just about have it won!
But now the question is how?
It's the bottom of the ninth,
Bases are empty,
The clean-up hitter is up,
You just about want to throw-up.
Here's the pitch.
It's a hit to left field,
My fingers are crossed,
He robs him of a home run!
Oh my baseballs fun.

I also dabbled in some sketches and pictures; the subject matter also dominated by sports. Mom cared about preserving the record of my passion for sports, and she kept everything related to sports in one place, which is why I still have the pictures and the poem. The pictures were just done in my free time when I wasn't outside playing baseball in the summer. I made a few technical mistakes in the pictures, too: I got left field mixed up with right field; home plate is pointed the wrong direction (twice), and I misspelled Tandy's for Tande's on the outfield fence. Notice on the fictional scoreboard for the sketch Peerless

The Doc Norman Championship Era

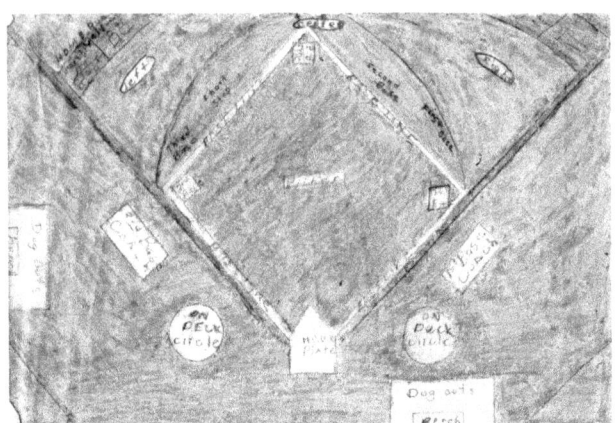

Joe Puckett sketch of ballfield, c. 1972.

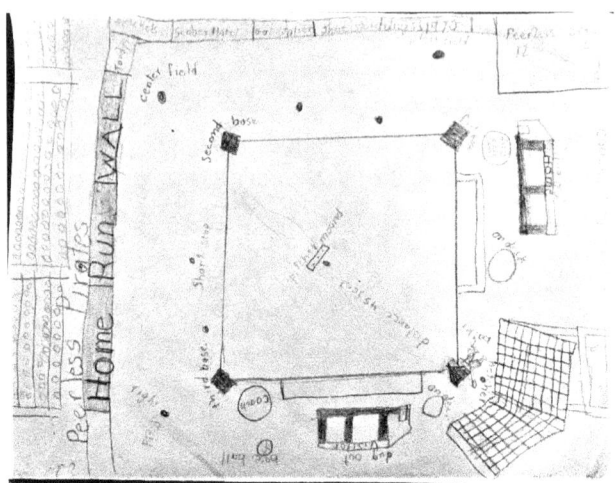

Joe Puckett sketch of Scobey Ball Park, c. 1972.

beat Scobey 12-6. The game would have had to have been in Scobey because we only had a snow fence in Peerless and couldn't paint sponsors on it.

⚾ ⚾ ⚾

My mom Faustine and sister Dianne always supported Jon and me as we grew up playing Peewee, Little League, and Babe Ruth baseball for Dad in Peerless. We have good records of all our games because Mom and Dianne would keep score, and Mom meticulously stored those records in a safe place to preserve the records all these years after.

In addition to supporting Dad, Jon, and me in sports, my mom was a talented artist, and she painted many beautiful oil paintings. Her artistic talent was passed down to my sister, Dianne, who now paints watercolors in Missoula, Montana. Her watercolor painting on the back cover of this book, which she painted from a memory, is of Jon and me walking home from the Peerless ball diamond after a game in Peerless when we were 11 years old in 1972. She painted it for our 60th birthday. She didn't remember our numbers, so she called me to ask what numbers Jon and I wore in Little League. Everything else is from her memory. What a beautiful painting and memory. Thank you, Dianne, for sharing your memory in a painting.

Dianne Beesley watercolor, painted from a memory, 1972.

1973: PEERLESS PIRATES LITTLE LEAGUE AND BORDER LEAGUE ALL-STARS

The coaching rivalry between Dad and Doc began in earnest in Little League in 1973, carrying into Babe Ruth the next two seasons. Dad and Doc only coached against each other competitively a handful of times, but every game was intense. The feeling was different. You knew the stakes were high if Doc was in the opposing dugout, and there was an extra charge of competitive electricity in the air when he was there. During the regular season, we played Scobey four times, and Doc was in the Scobey dugout for every game. Doc sniffed competition and wanted in. In the games at Scobey, Doc had his team prepared for Brad Pratt, our flame-throwing right-hander from Opheim Air Force Station, who had a hissing fastball. Doc cranked up his pitching machine for the Little League team the week before the games, and they pounded Pratt in the first game. Not only were they hitting him, but they were also pulling him. I remember Gerry Veis hitting a shot to left center that was one of the hardest-hit balls I saw in Little League. I also remember how difficult it was to hit Kelly Norman. He had a curve ball and slider and never threw anything you could hit—nothing was ever out over the plate. He would walk a lot of hitters, never giving in to them, never giving them anything good to hit. But he was an effective pitcher, carrying this style into Legion ball. Scobey won the first game 4-2 (Kelly Norman pitched) and the second game ended in a 4-4 tie after the game went into extra innings, and the game was called due to darkness after eight innings. (There were no cars parked around the Scobey Little League field so the game couldn't continue "under the lights.")

⚾ ⚾ ⚾

There were two pitches—one a straight changeup and the other a curveball—I threw in two separate tournaments in Saskatchewan in early June 1973 that shaped my pitching repertoire for the rest of my pitching career. The results of both pitches were radically different and shaped what was to come next.

The first pitch was a straight changeup thrown against host Glentworth in the championship game of their tournament. I was engaged in a 0-0 pitcher's duel with Glentworth's pitcher in the bottom of the fifth and their best hitter was up with two outs. I had two strikes on him, but he was fouling off my fastball. I never really had thrown a changeup before but for some reason, I decided to take a little off the next pitch. Big mistake! I just shaved a little off it by slowing my arm speed, it floated straight down the plate, and the hitter rocketed a line drive straight over Jon's head at shortstop. My heart sank. I thought, *This game's over*. There was no fence at Glentworth and the field was hard and sloped downhill so the ball was going to roll as far it could. The hitter was fast and was rounding second before Randy Stolen retrieved it deep in left center. Jon ran out to shallow left field for the cutoff and received a perfect throw from Randy, then pivoted on a dime and delivered a dart to catcher Bernie Wasser at home plate who put the tag down on the sliding Canadian. It was one of those plays where you didn't know what the umpire was going to call until the dust cleared. If he was safe the game was over; if he was out, we would get another at bat. He called him out! Phew! Third out! In the top of the sixth Bill Fladager hit a home run almost to the exact same spot and we ended up winning the game in six innings 1-0. I vowed, after that changeup, never to throw another changeup again in my life, and I never did.

The second pitch, the curveball, was delivered a week later in the championship game of the LaFleche, Saskatchewan Invitational. I had been working in the backyard that spring and early summer with Andy Stolen from Glentana, who was teaching Jon and me how to throw a curve ball. He taught me the grip and arm motion. I can't believe I had a pitching coach of that caliber at 12 years old! Andy had pitched for the legendary Scobey Plainsmen teams and played in the National Baseball Congress (NBC) tournament in Wichita, Kansas in 1960 for the Montana state champion Plainsmen.*

We had beaten Glentworth, Saskatchewan 2-1 in the first game of the tournament, as Bernie Wasser delivered a clutch two-run single in the top of the fifth to drive in Matt Fouhy and Bill Fladager for the winning runs. Brad Pratt, from Opheim Air Force Station, went the distance for Peerless.

We were playing host LaFleche in the championship. I was pitching and Kevin Baldry was catching. We scored five runs in the first and two in the second to take a 7-0 lead. I was pitching well, but Lafleche had a *huge* cleanup hitter, who played first base. There is no way he was Little League age. He had to be six feet, two inches tall if he was an inch. I think his wife and kids might have been in the stands cheering him on. The first time I faced him, he pulled a couple foul balls sharply, so he was on my fastball.

---

* Randy told me that Andy loved baseball so much that on some summer days that he would grab his glove and spikes and drive to Saskatchewan where he knew baseball was being played and ask if any of the teams needed an extra player so he could play.

I tried to throw a third fastball by him, thinking if I threw it harder, I might get it by him.

Big mistake.

He turned on it and hit a towering drive that landed in a lake somewhere in southern Saskatchewan. It had to be about over 300 feet. As I watched him round the bases, I felt like Charlie Brown on a bad day, smaller than my less-than-five-foot-tall stature. The hometown LaFleche crowd was cheering loudly as his teammates came out to greet him at home plate.

When Goliath came up to bat again, I had a one-hitter—his home run—and only one other batter had reached base, so I was cruising. I threw him two fastballs again, and he hit two rockets down the line that might have traveled farther than the home run he hit before but just twisted foul. With two strikes on him, a 7-1 lead, my arm tired, and this monster all over my fastball, I put the horrible memory of the changeup the week before out of mind. I decided it was time to unleash the "Andy Stolen curveball." I had been working with Andy on my curveball in the backyard and had a good break on it but never had "unleashed" it in a game as I was still trying to find the right moment.

This was the right moment.

So, I gripped the ball as Andy taught me, brought my elbow up, and snapped the shade down. He swung before the ball got halfway to the plate. I could feel the blast of air from the whiff on the rubber. He twisted up like a pretzel and was fooled so badly that he almost fell. Kevin didn't know I was going to throw the curve—we didn't have any signs—so he was fooled too, and the ball harmlessly rolled back to the backstop as we weren't playing the dropped-third-strike rule.

Strike three.

At that moment, I became addicted to junk. I had a slingshot and had slayed the giant. Don't try to throw the ball by hitters; make them think you are then fool them. It was counter to everything I had been taught in sports: run faster, jump higher, throw harder. On that day I became a pitcher and a junkie—the junkie from LaFleche, Saskatchewan. Dad didn't know it, but as we crossed the border back into Montana, he was smuggling contraband over the border.

I couldn't wait to get back in the backyard to work more with Dad and Andy, to master the pitch, control it, weaponize it, and start throwing it routinely in games. But when we got in our backyard and started practicing pitching again, Jon delivered the nastiest pitch I'd ever seen, which put the curveball I threw in LaFleche to shame. The pitch became known as the "sparrow curve": the latest-breaking, sharpest-breaking curve ball ever delivered by Jon Puckett.

On one late afternoon day in our backyard in Peerless Jon was pitching, and I was catching. The routine Jon and I had for practicing pitching was one of us would pitch, the other would catch, and Dad (and sometimes Andy) would coach. When we were younger, Dad would catch us, and Jon and I would exchange pitching to him, but as we got older, we could catch each other, and Dad would coach us from the rubber. To the right of the pitcher to the left of the catcher, about an eight-foot-high wire stretched across the backyard into our house. Several birds would often perch on the wire, watching the two of us pitch and catch, as there wasn't a lot else for birds to do in Peerless in the summer. I think they were grateful for the entertainment. Their beaks would move from left to right and back again like they were watching a tennis match, as the boys methodically threw back and forth to each other daily.

Jon was throwing particularly hard on this day, and his control was good. He was moving his fastball up and down and left and right, but he hadn't learned how to throw a curve ball yet, so it was just straight fastballs. No changeup either. But then, towards the end of his pitching session, something bizarre happened—a curve ball was thrown, the nastiest, dirtiest curve ball ever thrown in the town of Peerless. Unhittable. And, as it turned out, also uncatchable.

I didn't call for the curve, but it came just the same. Jon delivered the pitch. It was headed up and in, a little "chin music" if a right-handed hitter had been at the plate. I raised my glove to catch the ball, but just as I was about to catch it, a grayish, brownish streak of color appeared out of the left corner of my eye. The ball broke sharp and late and smashed me right in the left eye. I was sporting the fashionable black square-rimmed glasses of the day, and what scared me the most wasn't the searing pain of the impact of the ball directly on my face, but the sound of the ball hitting my glasses. Of course, I wasn't wearing a mask, so I felt the full force of the late-breaking pitch.

I fell straight back from the force of the impact. Immediately, Dad and Jon were on the scene. "Are you alright Joey?" Dad asked.

"Yeah, I'm okay. What the hell was that, Jony? I saw something out of the corner of my eye, right before the pitch hit the plate."

"I think it might have been a bird," Jon said. He wasn't sure; it all happened so fast.

After I assured Dad and my brother that I was okay, the next order of business was to find my glasses—which had flown off my face after the ball hit—and maybe find the bird, or whatever else it was that might have impacted the ball's trajectory, we weren't sure. We found my glasses close to home plate, but one of the lenses was missing. Oh no! We had a the all-star tournament in Glasgow upcoming, and I needed both lenses to see the ball, whether hitting, fielding, or pitching. A trip to Williamsport, Pennsylvania, to the Little League World Series was on the line. That was our dream. What was originally an amusing event had suddenly become a crisis. To get a lens replaced in 1973 took days, if not weeks, and we didn't have that much time before the district tournament started. All three of us began searching for the missing lens. We had thought that whatever had caused the breaking ball had gotten away scot-free, so we all felt good about that—except for perhaps Jon, who was insecure that his fastball might not be fast enough to put a dent in whatever it was it impacted. Minutes of searching revealed no sign of anything, not even a feather. We scoured every square inch of the grass around home plate but found no lens.

Resigned to the gloomy outcome of the fruitless search, we finally gave up and decided to go inside and take a break before my pitching session started. The anxiety was high, leaving the scene of the crime without my lens. Dad wanted to immediately get to work to find a replacement lens.

But before we went inside after a session, we always brought our gloves in. I dropped the catcher's glove right on top of home plate when the pitch hit me before I fell back. I stooped down to pick up the glove, grabbed it with my left hand, and pulled it up to me: there on home plate, staring straight up at me on its back, was a stiff sparrow, legs and feet pointed up, deader than Kelsey's nuts.

And there, lying next to the unlucky sparrow, was the missing lens.

Williamsport was still in play.

⚾ ⚾ ⚾

THE TOURNAMENT IN GLASGOW FOR THE DISTRICT CHAMPIONship was the first time I had played on an all-star team. The Border Little League that my dad formed and registered with Little League Baseball in 1973 consisted of Opheim, Peerless, Scobey, and Flaxville. We didn't have all-star uniforms, so we just wore our regular uniforms. We beat the Tri-City All-Stars 14-2 in our first game, then the Glasgow All-Stars 8-2 for the championship. I struck out 13, and I bet most of those strikeouts were on Andy Stolen curve balls. The curve wasn't breaking as sharply as the sparrow curve, but it was good enough. It became my out-pitch. And the high the junkie from LaFleche got after getting a hitter to chase a curveball never wore off his entire pitching career, and he never went into recovery.

1973 Border Little League All-Stars, District Champions, (at Glasgow). Back row, left to right: Head Coach Tiny Puckett, Assistant Coach Andy Stolen. Standing: Joe Puckett, Kenny Bies, Brad Pratt, Kevin Hatfield, Dan Danelson, Brad Henderson, Scott Fjeld. Kneeling: Ray Chapman, Wade Tryan, Kelly Norman, Jon Puckett, Greg Stolen, Randy Stolen, Craig Ross, Kirby Halvorson. Ten of these players played on 6 of 8 Scobey Legion state championship teams (1976-80 and 1982). *Glasgow Courier photo.*

After we won the district championship over Glasgow, we traveled to Billings to play in the eastern division tournament. We lost to the Billings Giants 8-5 in our first game. It was a devastating loss. I had watched the Little League World Series on television every year for as long as I can remember, and my dream was to win the state of Montana, the western regional in San Bernadino, California, then play in the international Little League World Series in Williamsport, Pennsylvania. There was something about my 12-year-old season that seemed like it was a one-time opportunity to do something special, and when I turned 13 the opportunity would be gone. I can think of no other sport where there is such a well-known international competition that gets TV coverage than the Little League World Series.

After we lost to the Western Giants, we played the Bozeman Nationals for third place in the eastern division. This game contains my first memory of Doc Norman, who had driven down to Billings from Miles City to watch his son Kelly and our team play after he led the Scobey Legion team to the eastern divisional championship the previous day. I was pitching in the game. It was just a little over a month earlier that Andy Stolen had taught me how to throw a curveball and I had thrown my first one in LaFleche, Saskatchewan, but after several games since then I had mastered it and was throwing it a lot. It had become my best pitch. Kirby Halvorson was catching—it was just one for fastball and two for curve that was it. Doc was sitting behind the home plate backstop watching the game, just over the right shoulder of the umpire as he faced the pitcher. As the game progressed, I started to notice out of the corner of my eye, that Doc was flashing me signs from where he was sitting behind home plate. It was distracting. I don't think he could watch the game and not be involved as he was such a coach and I think he liked the junk I was throwing. When Doc would give me the sign, he would do it very deliberately. When I was looking in to get the sign from Kirby, he would raise his right hand straight up and then down so I could see it, but he would keep it above the lower part of the backstop. It was always two fingers. He called for the curveball every time! I was confused and didn't know what to do. Kirby was giving me one set of signs and then Doc another. If I shook Doc off would Kirby think I was shaking him off? Of course he would! How would he know Doc was flashing me signs? What I did was just go with Kirby's sign. But this was the legendary Doc Norman, my future coach, so I couldn't shake *him* off! It made me a little nervous and was a little distracting, but I smile when I think about it now.

The game was tied at 3 after six innings and ended up going into extra innings. We went a full nine innings (three extra innings after six inning normal game in Little League). Kelly led off the bottom of the ninth with a bunt single, advanced on Ray Chapman's single, and scored when Randy Stolen hit one over the center fielder's head for a 4-3 win. I went the distance and had 18 strikeouts, the most I ever had in any game at any level. And Doc Norman called the game.

A week later in Scobey, Doc's 1973 team won the state championship against Wolf Point, handing him his second state championship. Doc didn't know it at the time, but eight of the nine players on the field that day in Billings would go on to play for him on five state championship teams, and Greg Stolen, our batboy, would play on a sixth. The only thing that changed for me when I pitched in Legion, however, is Doc would flash the signs to Kirby from the dugout and not from behind the grandstand as a spectator. And there was only one set of signs.

After playing in Billings, Dad continued to schedule games for us for our last year in Little League. There was something special about that 12-year-old year. Dad scheduled a tournament in Peerless which he titled "The Tournament of Little League Champions," with Glentworth, Saskatchewan, the southwest Saskatchewan champions; Wolf Point Little League champions; and Zoonie McLean's Sheridan County Plentywood Little League champions. We beat Plentywood 10-2 and Glentworth 33-1 to win the tournament.

The last games we played were in a highly competitive tournament in Minot AFB, North Dakota. We beat the Regina Barkers twice in the tournament, 7-1 and 3-1, but lost to the Regina Royals and host Minot AFB. A funny incident (for me, anyway) happened in the second Regina Barkers game. I pitched both those games, and the Barkers were having a hard time hitting my curveball. I also hit a home run in each game. After I hit the home run in the second game, the Barkers decided they were going to hit me by a pitch the next time I came up to bat. Except Jon batted second and I batted third in the lineup, so they thought he was me, and beaned him with a pitch! Then I came to the plate as the next hitter, and they realized they hit the wrong twin! The pitcher smiled and looked over at Jon on first base and asked him if he was okay, and Jon smiled back and nodded his head. I smiled too. I got to hit!

There were three moments in my baseball career I recall being the most emotional, and after we lost our last game to Minot AFB in Minot when I was 12 years old was one of them. The other two were my last game in Babe Ruth when I was 15 and last game in Legion when I was 18. The realization that my life of playing baseball with my twin brother Jon and my childhood friends in Peerless for Dad was going to change affected me deeply. I was only 12, but something in me knew this was all temporary, that time was moving on, and there was nothing I could do to stop it. My sister's watercolor painting captured this sentiment perfectly. I was also disappointed we didn't make it to the western regional in San Bernadino. That was a real goal for me, and at that moment, I couldn't think of anything else other than that it was over. I had a lot of baseball in front of me, but I couldn't think of that then. The quote from the movie *Moneyball* is especially poignant here: "We're all told at some point in time that we can no longer play the children's game, we just don't . . . don't know when that's gonna be. Some of us are told at eighteen, some of us are told at forty, but we're all told."[110] I could take comfort in that I wasn't told at age 12, but something in me knew my time was coming.

1974: PEERLESS PIRATES BABE RUTH

I THINK I HAD A HARDER TIME TRANSITIONING FROM LITTLE League to Babe Ruth than transitioning from childhood to adolescence. When I stood on the mound for the first time and looked at home plate, I felt like I needed binoculars to see the catcher. Sixty feet, six inches, was a long way away from the 46 feet I had pitched in Little League. Every baseball player goes through this, of course, but that didn't make it any easier for me. Then the bases increased from 60 feet to 90 feet. I felt like I needed to pace myself to get from home to first.

One of the nice things about playing Babe Ruth was that I got to rejoin some of my former Peewee and Little League teammates on the field who were not eligible go play Little League anymore, like Ross Chapman, Roger Trang, and Bill and Willard Fladager. Dad also recruited some good Opheim athletes to play for us, including Mark Stevens, Eric Tokerud, and Jeff Larsen. Most of us on the team were 13 years old (Randy Stolen was 12), but after getting our noses bloodied early in the season to the older teams from Froid and Plentywood, Dad still led us to the Mon-Dak district championship our first year in Babe Ruth.

I have a special memory of winning the district championship tournament at Fjeseth Field in Froid that summer. Dianne was home, and of course, Mom was there too. I was pitching in the championship game against Froid and Rick "Fireball" Hansen from Bainville. He had a live fastball. It was rumored he struck out 21 hitters in a seven-inning game once. He did throw hard. Most of the players from Froid were 15 years old, including Rick Hansen, Brent Leibach from Medicine Lake, and Jeff Ryder from Froid.

Rick and I engaged in a pitcher's duel for the championship, as each of us pitched a two-hitter. We ended up winning the game 3-1 when I somehow got around on his fastball enough to line a two-run single to right field late in the game. During the game, my curveball was breaking well, and I was getting a lot of Froid hitters to chase it, but most of the outs I was getting were coming on lazy fly balls to the outfield. The special memory I have is when I was pitching late in the game, Jeff Ryder was on deck and after I snapped off one of my curveballs for a strike, he glared at me from the on-deck circle and derisively said, "You junkie." It was the greatest compliment anyone ever paid me. After the victory, Dianne said, "You guys looked like a bunch of farmers out there, beating a team with flashy uniforms. (We didn't have any uniforms in 1974, so we looked a little ragged on the field.)

The Mon-Dak all-star team was formed after we won the district championship. To help prepare us for the Eastern Divisional All-Star Tournament in Glendive, Dad scheduled two practice games with the Scobey Legion team at the Scobey Ball Park. After watching the Scobey Legion team play for so many summers, I got to play against the team I hoped to play for someday. The games were at night, so I got to play under the lights for the first time, if you don't count the cars turning their lights on late at night around the Peerless Ball Field as "playing under the lights." I was nervous before the games. My older cousin Don, who I idolized, brought the lineups to home plate for each game. He was in uniform but had his sandals on, so obviously, he wasn't going to play. I remember looking up at him, thinking, "Darn, I wanted to play against him," but Doc didn't play him. I have the scorebooks for the games. Doc pitched Mike Hagfeldt in the first game and Craig Miller in the second. I remember each of them had fastballs that tailed like I had never seen before, and they were both difficult to hit. Mike threw harder, but Craig's ball moved more, both his curve and fastball. I didn't know it then, but they would be my teammates two years later on the 1976 state championship team, along with Don Hagfeldt, Jeff Richardson, Bill Bartole, and Greg Fjeld, who were also on the field for both games that night. Jeff Richardson was not yet catching, as Bill Bartole and Jim Chapman caught the two games. Dan Danelson was my teammate at first base on the Mon-Dak All-Stars, as was my brother Jon. Doc played some of his starters in the first game, and Duke hit a massive three-run triple to left-center off Brad Pratt. Brad walked eight hitters, and the game was a blowout 17-1. Doc substituted Kelly Norman—only 12 years old, a batboy, and not on the roster—for Duke later in the game. Kelly was playing Little League that summer. My highlight was pitching in the second game, giving up three runs, one hit, and striking out five in the five-inning game. After the first game, I was very nervous that I would get shelled and embarrassed in front of Doc, the team, and my older cousin Don, but that didn't happen. The score ended 3-1. The one hit was a double by Bill Bartole. Damn you, Bill!

Some of the older players who played that night were Duke and Dallas Trangsrud, Lee Cook, and Mike Gunderson. I will never forget that experience. It was a special moment for me to be on that field, playing under the lights against the team and the legendary coach I aspired to play for someday. It gave me confidence that I could play at the next level. Although I wish I could say I played against my older cousin.

From the perspective gained after over 50 years, pitching against the Scobey Legion team as a 13-year-old gives me a greater appreciation for the two 13-year-old Scobey pitchers who not only pitched for the Scobey Legion team as 13-year-olds but also pitched *in the State Legion Tournament*. Those two players were Terry Puckett (1968) and Greg Stolen (1979).

I was excited to play in my first Eastern Divisional Babe Ruth Tournament at Whipkey Park in Glendive, a beautiful little ballpark made especially for Babe Ruth baseball. But I didn't get to play. Taking infield before our first game, Dad hit a pop up behind shortstop, I backup on it, but my cleat hit the rim of the outfield grass where it meets the infield and I fell back and landed on my right wrist, breaking it. In the hospital, they put the baseball game on the radio for me so I could listen to it. The announcer was top-notch. He sounded like an announcer I listened to that called the Minnesota Twins games. I later learned it was "Dapper Dan" Frenzel,[*] and right before I was put under to set the

---

[*] Dapper Dan Frenzel worked at Glendive Broadcasting for 39 years until he died in 2003. For many years, he was the voice of Dawson County Red Devil and Dawson Community College Buccaneer basketball and announced baseball games from Little League to American Legion.

The Doc Norman Championship Era

1975 Peerless Pirates Babe Ruth Team, Mon-Dak League champions. Standing left to right: Bernie Wasser, Jon Puckett, Randy Stolen, Bill Fladager, Jeff Larsen, Roger Trang, Coach Tiny Puckett. Kneeling left to right: Matt Fouhy, Greg Stolen, Jay Beck, Ray Chapman, Todd Deer, Joe Puckett. *Leader photo, Burl Bowler.*

Jon Puckett, 1975 Peerless Pirates. Family photo. c. 1972.

Joe Puckett, 1975 Peerless Pirates. *Family photo.*

Joe or Jon Puckett pitching at Plentywood, 1975. *Family photo.*

arm, I heard Dapper Dan say, "Jon Puckett squares around to bunt, and it's popped up!" And I thought, *Why is Jon bunting? We never bunt.* That was the last thing I remember before going under.

1975: PEERLESS PIRATES BABE RUTH

I HAVE TO BUST MY TEAMMATE DAN DANELSON'S BALLS WITH this story. At a regular season Babe Ruth game in Peerless in 1975, Dan Danelson, playing for Scobey, laced a single to center field in the top of the first inning. I was playing shortstop and ran out to center field to get the cutoff from center fielder Roger Trang. After he fielded the ball, I saw Roger's eyes open wider and wider. I mean, they were *huge*. He was not looking to throw the ball to second base. He had either locked on to a meteoroid in the southern sky plummeting toward the Peerless Ball Field or had spied Dan Danelson loafing into his single trot to first base. It was the latter. Roger whipped the ball to first baseman Ray Chapman on a line and nailed my future Legion teammate Dano by a half step. Score that 8-3.

Doc was coaching Scobey in that game. It was another classic matchup between coaches Tiny Puckett and Doc Norman, who respected each other, but wanted to beat the other badly. Dad always fielded a tough team, and Doc sniffed the competition and wanted in, especially when Kelly was playing. In addition to Kelly and Dano, Doc brought Legion players Wade Tryan and Allan Audet to Peerless for the game, as he did later in the season in the championship game of the Mon-Dak League.

The game was a back-and-forth affair. Kevin Baldry scored a run in the top of the seventh to give Scobey a 5-4 lead. In the bottom of the seventh, with Scobey leading 5-4, Kirby Halvorson was pitching for Scobey, and I was leading off the inning for Peerless. Kirby struck me out on a nasty curve ball, but the ball got past catcher Wade Tryan, so I got to first base on the dropped third strike. Kirby then walked Jon, and I got to third base on two passed balls during the at-bat. Jon then stole second, so Jon was the winning run on second and I was tying run on third with no outs. But Kirby then struck out the next two hitters and got ahead of the next hitter 0-1. He was sailing along, so I figured we could only tie the game if I stole home. I nodded to Dad as I took my lead at third, and Dad nodded back, confirming that I had the green light to steal, but the hitter didn't know I was stealing. (We didn't have a steal home sign.) Kirby was not pitching from the stretch because he thought he could strike the hitter out, so I broke for home when he went into his windup. As I approached the plate, I had no idea if the hitter would swing or where the pitch would be. The pitch was a little low and outside, so there was no swing. Wade went to snatch it to tag me out as I went into my slide, but he snapped his glove back too quickly, and the ball skipped past him to the backstop. I had stolen home—the only time I stole home in my career!—to tie the game. Kirby struck the hitter out—his fourth strikeout of the inning—to strand Jon at third. The game went into extra innings but was called due to darkness after nine innings, ending in a 5-5 tie. I will never forget that classic Babe Ruth game in Peerless between Doc and Dad. It was fitting this game should end in a tie.

Later that same season in 1975, Doc came out after an American Legion game in Scobey to coach Scobey Babe Ruth against Peerless in the Mon-Dak district championship game in Peerless. We won that game 13-3, after a rough first inning, in which Kevin Baldry and Allan Audet homered. I didn't watch Allan's home run because it was hit so hard to left center it landed in my mom's flower garden in our yard behind the field, probably about 350 feet from home plate. I'm not sure we ever found the ball. I hung a slider belt-high over the plate and he smashed it. I did strike him out his next at-bat though. It was a lot easier to play with Allan and company than it was against them. Rod Tande and KCGM came out to Peerless to broadcast the game that day, a first for us. We felt special in Peerless that day.

The previous day in the same tournament, there was plenty of drama in the semifinal contest between Scobey and Plentywood. Peerless Schools Superintendent Marvin Hash, home plate umpire for the game, tossed Zoonie

1975 Scobey Babe Ruth Team. Standing left to right: Bill Webster, Scott Fjeld, Jesse Cook, Don Holyk. Kneeling left to right: Mark Barstad, Kelly Norman, Kevin Baldry, Wade Tryan, Brad Henderson. Jimmy Lighthizer is batboy. Not pictured are Dan Danelson, Allan Audet, and Kirby Halvorson. Doc Norman is Babe Ruth coach. Leader photo, Burl Bowler.

1975: Zoonie McLean cartoon from 1950 when he played for the Minot Mallards in the ManDak League. *Courtesy of https://attheplate/wcbl.com.*

McLean* out for arguing balls and strikes—well, sort of. Plentywood was batting in their half of the second inning, and Marv called a ball in the dirt a strike. Then he did it again. (Marv liked to call t`he low strike—as did Andy Stolen by the way.) Zoonie came unglued in the third base coaching box. He started quickly pacing back and forth in the box, then turned to home plate and started yelling directly at Marv. His voice boomed across the diamond and the entire town of Peerless: *"You call that a strike? That ball barely cleared the plate! Boy what is this I've seen everything this is one for the books!"* He continued booming and Marv finally gave him the hook: "You're out of the game!" So Zoonie, still fuming, walked behind the third base dugout, and sat down right on the first row of a bleacher right behind home plate . . . and continued to argue with Marv and coach his team. There was no security at the game; there was nothing Marv could really do but continue to look straight ahead and call the game as Zoonie coached the team from behind him. Zoonie finally eased his attack on Marv but continued to coach his team. In the next half inning, right after Marv had thrown him out, he made a big move on the field coaching from the bleachers: "Cory [Benson], take the equipment off and move to pitcher." He made some other big moves as well. His team just did what they were told with him coaching from the bleachers. There was nothing Marv could do and Zoonie continued to coach the game through to the end.

But the story doesn't end there. I asked Marv about the incident, and he did. Marv added, "Now for the irony. I had a lot of respect for Zoonie as did your dad. Your dad was my school board president and, like, my best friend there and as we talked later about this and that, I asked him what his feelings were about having Zoonie as the guest speaker at our athletic banquet a couple years later. I invited Zoonie and he came. Zoonie opened his remarks by asking me (I was sitting with my wife in the gym bleachers) if I'd let him deliver his speech before I threw him out! Very funny!!"

We repeated as Mon-Dak district champions but were eliminated in two games at the eastern divisional tournament at Denton Field in Miles City. I couldn't pitch because I slid off the back of a pickup truck while it was slowly moving and badly bruised my tailbone days before the tournament. It was another disappointing end to the season for us. I had now missed the first divisional Babe Ruth tournament with an injury, then couldn't pitch or play shortstop in the second one. Jon and I had only one more year playing for Dad in Babe Ruth before we donned uniforms for the Scobey Legion team, as Dick, Terry, and Don had done before us. In 1976 when we were 15 years old, we would play Babe Ruth for Dad and Legion for Doc, then play for the Scobey Legion team in 1977—at least that was the plan. But Dad would have other ideas about that, as we shall see.

EXTRA INNINGS

IN THE FALL CLASSIC IN OCTOBER 1975, THE LONG-SUFFERING Boston Red Sox fans—which the Tiny Puckett family in Peerless could be counted among—had their hearts broken again, as the Red Sox lost to the Cincinnati Reds in seven games. This was the third World Series loss (1946, 1967, and 1975) Dad had experienced as a Red Sox fan, and the second for my older brother Bill. For Jon and me, it was the first Series I remember watching, although I was six years old in 1967 when the Red Sox lost to the Cardinals in seven games. I asked my older brother, Bill, if he remembered the seventh game of the 1967 World Series. (Red Sox fans have good memories when it comes to bad moments.) He said, "Yes. I remember it well. Jim Lonborg pitched for the

---

*   Zoonie McLean was a great baseball player. Prior to his high school coaching career at Plentywood, he played semiprofessional baseball for the Minot Merchants, Minot Mallards, and the Williston Oilers in the ManDak League in North Dakota from 1947 to 1959. He won the batting title one year and played on four league championship teams for the Mallards. His son Mike was also a great baseball player. (He played shortstop for Plentywood and then college at UND-Williston and Minot State.) Mike coached basketball in Peerless for a couple years. So like father like son. At a Peerless independent game in Lustre, Mike was frustrated at a call and yelled out, "Jesus Christ!" (Not the best choice of words on the court at Lustre Bible Academy.) The ref gave Mike the hook, but Mike didn't leave the court. He sat on the bench, and calmly asked the ref, "How do you know I wasn't talking to him?"

Red Sox. They pitched him on two days' rest, and he got hit hard. Ironically, the Red Sox also lost the 1946 World Series to the Cardinals. The following year, Lonborg tore up his knee skiing and never returned to his old form. I also remember the 1975 World Series. Denny Doyle (second baseman) booted a ground ball in what should have been a double play, ending the inning. Cincinnati went on to score several runs, and Boston lost the game. Bill Lee was pitching. I believe that was the second game of the series. The Red Sox would have been up two games to none if they had won that second game. I saw Bill Lee shut out the Royals in 1975."

In October 1975, Dad, Jon, and I were glued to the television set every game, except for one of the games in Cincinnati, which was the night Jon and I were confirmed in the Catholic Church on confirmation night in Glentana. At some point during the confirmation service in Glentana, it must have been a break or something, I remember being outside standing next to our car, and Dad had the game on the radio. We were all huddled around the car listening to the game but we had to get back in the church for confirmation. Bob Fouhy was with us listening to the game on the radio. The entire series was a classic, but Game Six was unforgettable when Bernie Carbo hit a clutch, pinch-hit three-run home run in the bottom of the eighth inning to tie the game 6-6, then Carlton Fisk hit his dramatic solo home run in the bottom of the 12th inning to walk it off for Boston, 7-6, forcing a game seven.

Unbelievably—perhaps she sensed the gravity of the moment—Mom captured Dad, Jon, and me watching Game Six on TV with this sketch. Included in the sketch is our cat Bianca, who was also a big Red Sox fan and was watching the game with us. Mom was an extremely talented artist but was just learning how to sketch at the time. I'm glad her subject matter turned to sports to hone her skills that night.

Dad never got to see the Red Sox win a World Series in his lifetime. In 1978, we watched light-hitting New York Yankee shortstop Bucky Dent hit a three-run home run over the left field wall at Fenway to give the Yankees a 3–2 lead in the American League East tie-breaker game, and the Yankees went on to win. Then, in Game Six of the 1986 World Series, I remember watching Red Sox first baseman Bill Buckner let the ball roll between his legs for an error in the bottom of the ninth inning, and the winning run scored to force game seven, which the Mets won. Bill remembers that game, too. "Who can forget Bill Buckner booting a ground ball at first base in 1986 in what should have been a game-ending out. The Red Sox would've won the series in six games. Ironically, Johnny Pesky, the Boston shortstop, booted a grounder in game seven that cost Boston the 1946 series. Dad often talked about it."

Dad was long gone in 2004 when the Red Sox finally swept the Cardinals in four games to win their first World Series since 1918. Dad was born in 1920. I wish he could have seen it. But the American League Championship Series against the Yankees to get the Red Sox to the World Series was the most incredible comeback in a series I've ever seen in sports. Down three games to none, the Red Sox came back to sweep four straight games to win it. I remember watching the deciding-game seven on TV. I was standing up holding my five-month-old daughter, Emma, against my shoulder, and she was sleeping. Johnny Damon was batting in the top of the second inning with the bases loaded and he jacked a grand slam homerun into the right field seats at Yankee Stadium to vault Boston to a 6-0 lead. When I saw the ball bounce off Damon's bat, I yelled, "Get outta here!" forgetting that I was holding a sleeping baby in my arms. The baby was not sleeping after that.

Faustine Puckett sketch of Dad, Jon, Bianca, and me watching Game Six of the 1975 World Series.

Emma pooh-poohing the Yankees in New York City in 2015.
Family photo.

Emma and her older sister Cosette didn't have a choice becoming Red Sox fans. We were living in New Hampshire when the Red Sox won the World Series in 2004 and got to experience firsthand the passion the local New England fans had for their beloved Red Sox. One thing I learned: they hated the Yankees as much or more than they loved the Red Sox. After Boston came back from three games down to win the 2004 ALCS against the Yankees, I don't think many of the Boston fans cared what happened next—they had beaten the Yankees. At the 2005 Super Bowl parade four months later when the entire city of Boston and New England were celebrating the Patriot's third Super Bowl championship in four years, the entire crowd of one million people, to cheer the Patriot's championship, began chanting, "Yankees suck, Yankees suck."

Emma grew up hating the Yankees, too. (She doesn't actually hate them, but she appreciates the rivalry.) When our family traveled to New York City to visit the Big Apple in 2015, 11-year-old Emma sported her Red Sox jersey and boldly walked into a Yankees merchandise store, stuck her tongue out, made a snarky face, and pointed with her thumb at the Yankee uniforms hanging on display. Later that day, my wife struck up a conversation with a friendly, native New Yorker, who was a Yankees fan, of course. After they had been talking a while, he noticed Emma's Red Sox jersey, and he said to my wife, "Ma'am, may I cuss?" My wife said, "Yes." He jokingly said, "Your daughter's got a lot of nerve wearing that damn Red Sox jersey in New York City like that. I like that. She's got spunk." Then he turned to Emma and said, "Don't ever let anyone push you around." At 11 years old, Emma had earned the respect of a Yankees fan in New York City wearing her Red Sox jersey. I raised my baby well.

1976

The Wild, Wild West: The Madness That Was Cut Bank

> *The 1976 Scobey Legion baseball team will go down here in history as the 'Iron Men.' They won Scobey's third title and amply demonstrated they had the spirit, talent, and gutty stamina in the best tradition.*
>
> —**Daniels County Leader, August 19, 1976**

PRESEASON

On a chilly day in Scobey in April, the first sign of spring was not the sound of a western meadowlark piercing the cool air with its beautiful song; it was Doc Norman assembling a bunch of hopeful young boys at Scobey Ball Park for another Legion baseball season. This rite of spring in Scobey had begun 18 years earlier, in 1959, when Doc first moved his family to Scobey to practice medicine. However, for Doc, practicing medicine was just a lifeline to do what he loved the most: coach baseball. You can ask Hazel Smith or Veronica "Ronk" Cromwell—two of Doc's assistants through the years—about that. How many times did they have to yell at Doc not to keep his patients waiting when he was talking baseball with one of his boys who had come to visit him at his office? Try to tear Doc away from one of his boys when he was talking baseball.

The winter that had just passed was a season to remember on the basketball court for Scobey and Flaxville, as both teams qualified for the state tournament. Flaxville took things a step further and won it. Many of the baseball players shivering on the field that day had been hot in warm gymnasiums earlier that winter, leading their teams to big wins in tournaments. They were familiar with winning for their respective high schools, but Doc had to mold a team into a winner with an odd mix of players across Daniels County. It was an odd mix partly because the players were from Scobey, Peerless, and Flaxville, but mostly because it was effectively a Legion team and Babe Ruth team combined. The team was composed of seven 18-year-olds: Jeff

Richardson, Bill Bartole, Don Hagfeldt, Greg Fjeld, Mike Hagfeldt, Craig Miller, and Dale Barstad, one 16-year-old (Allan Audet), four 15-year-olds (Wade Tryan, Dan Danelson, Joe Puckett, and Jon Puckett), and two 14-year-olds (Kelly Norman and Kirby Halvorson). Six of the 14 players on the roster were Babe Ruth age. All 14 players would be needed on the field to win the state championship later that summer in Cut Bank.

For me, a 15-year-old wide-eyed boy from Peerless, there with my twin brother Jon, my first practice was an odd experience. I had never played baseball for anyone but Dad before, not even when I played for the Mon-Dak Babe Ruth or Border Little League All-Stars because Dad's teams always won the conference, so he coached the All-Stars, too. Dad started coaching Jon and me in Peewee in 1967 when we were six. But Doc made the transition easy because he was so funny and laid-back. He was one of the boys. One of my favorite things about playing for Doc was his sense of humor. He could be stern when he needed to; usually, when guys were goofing around, he would yell, "Stop the grab ass!" or "All right, you peckerheads, pull your head out of your ass and start shootin' some baseball." But most of the time, to me, he was funny. At the end of one practice later that summer, we were in the dugout, and he was talking to us about the divisional tournament where we would be playing a night game and needed to prepare for it. He said our next practice would be later in the evening to prepare for the game. I blurted out, "You mean under the lights, Doc?" He replied, "Well, sure, Joe, what are we gonna do, use the fuckin' moon?" Everyone laughed. I remember he was wearing a *Wizard of Id* T-shirt with "The King is a Fink" written on it and had bloody surgeon pants on. That was Doc. (I always wondered if Doc saw himself as the king in the *Wizard of Id*.)

But the melding of the old and young was easy, not just because of Doc's coaching, but because the older players on the team were—as my Millennial daughter, Cosette, would say—"chill." They were cool. Easy going. And they were winners. At that first practice, I was warming up with Jon, but Don "Hairy" Hagfeldt—one of the funniest guys I've ever known—tapped Jon on the shoulder, like someone cutting in at a dance, and asked me to throw the ball to him. He held his glove above his left shoulder as a target and said, "Hit the glove, rookie." I aimed but missed badly with the throw. Oh shit. His glove didn't flinch to catch it; he just let it go past him to the backstop and said, shaking his head and smiling at me, "You'll never make the bigs, rookie." I was relaxed from that moment on. Hairy was right, too: I never did make the bigs.

At the end of the practice, Doc called us all in to address the team. I was having difficulty concentrating on what he said because Peerless's prom had been the night before. As a freshman, I took the cutest girl ever from Peerless, Darla Drummond, whom I had liked from first grade. At the end of the night, I asked her to go steady with me, but she said no, so I was smarting a little bit. Nevertheless, some of what Doc was saying did come through: "We have a lot of older guys who have played a lot of baseball. . . but some younger guys with talent who have played a lot of baseball too . . . if we come together as a team . . . we can win it all and go to Washington." (The Western Legion regional was in Yakima, Washington, that year.) Doc wasn't just telling us we could win State B; he was telling us we could win *State A*. That was always his goal. To win it all. Wow. I was in the show now. After Doc's talk, I felt two inches taller and 20 pounds heavier than my five-foot-six, 135-pound frame, and later that summer, Darla agreed to go steady with me, which made me feel like Captain America.

But Dad's goal in 1976 was to win it all, too—in Babe Ruth. Jon and I were 15 years old and playing in our last year of Babe Ruth for the Peerless Pirates. Dad agreed with Doc that Jon and I could play Legion, but Peerless Babe Ruth and Mon-Dak All-Stars had priority. Dad had groomed our team for this season, our last in Babe Ruth, and everything would take a back seat to that. His boys were his boys, and he had designs on fielding a Peerless Legion team for Post 107, the "Elwood Lien" Post, the following year. Peerless had previously fielded Legion teams from

Doc wore a T-shirt with the *Wizard of Id's*, "The King is a Fink," on it. I wonder if Doc ever thought of himself as the King? The Wizard of Id was created by Brant Parker and Johnny Hart. I read it every day in the newspaper.

1955-1960. Doc and Dad deconflicted the schedules to avoid games on the same day, but sometimes there was a conflict. Doc needed to coordinate with Dad if he planned to pitch Jon or me, but Dad needed to approve it. Kelly and Kirby also came to Peerless to play with our Babe Ruth team. Randy Stolen, Ray Chapman, Bernie Wasser, Brad Henderson, and Dave Selvig played All-Stars with us. We were loaded but would have been more so if Wade and Danny had played. So, you had two coaches who wanted to win it all, sharing some of the same players.

The State Babe Ruth championship and the State Class B Legion championship were on the same weekend, so there was the possibility that things could come to a head later in the season. Would they?

REGULAR SEASON

AS WAS THE CASE ALMOST EVERY YEAR IN THE NORTHEASTERN district in the 1970s, Wolf Point and Scobey were at the top, and they would be the top two teams in the eastern division again as well—and the state. In Wolf Point, Coach Don Lekvold took over as head coach from Harvey Langager and had a powerful team. Like Scobey in 1976, Wolf Point had a cluster of experienced, talented players returning from the previous year, where they had taken third at State. Wolf Point's roster included Dennis Loendorf, Al Hoversland, Fred Rhoads, David Hopson, Grant Boysun, Bill Neumiller, Jerry Moran, Mike Neubauer, Bill Zimmer, Rick McGeshick, Terry Thompson, Dave Sorenson, and 15-year-old Kip Harcharik, a talented rookie who was also playing Babe Ruth for Wolf Point and the Hi-Line All-Stars.

In comparing the two teams, there was no question that both Wolf Point and Scobey could hit. Both teams could pound the ball and light up the scoreboard like a pinball machine. The 24-23 track meet in the divisional championship game the year before had proven that. For Scobey's pitching, 18-year-old left-handers Mike Hagfeldt and Craig Miller anchored the staff, but after that it was up to the 15-year-old arms of Dan Danelson, Joe and Jon Puckett, and 14-year-olds Kelly Norman and Kirby Halvorson, and Kirby was the backup catcher to Jeff. Danelson had not yet come into his own as a pitcher in 1976. In 1976, he was still developing. Wolf Point's ace was right-hander Dennis Loendorf, followed by left-handers Jerry Moran and Bill Neumiller, and right-handers Grant Boysun, Mike Neubauer, and 15-year-old Kip Harcharik.

The *Leader* never pulled any punches regarding its assessment of the Scobey Legion team's performance. It never singled out individuals but would refer to the team's performance. In 1975, the *Leader* had referred to Scobey's regular season as "mediocre"; in 1976, it described it as "so-so."[111] It was partly because Wolf Point, as they did in Scobey's state championship 1973 season, had the upper hand against Scobey during the regular season, winning the northeastern district. We also lost to Glasgow 3-2, but Wolf Point also lost to Glasgow 5-1 during the regular season, when Glasgow pitchers Al Hopstad and Norm Braaten almost pitched a combined shutout against Wolf Point. We finished third in the northeastern district behind Wolf Point and Glasgow.

Glasgow had a good team in 1976, the best they had had in years. They finished with the best record in the regular season district standings. Several good athletes like Kent Schindler, Norm Braaten, Don Ressmeyer, Tony Erickson, and Al Hopstad were on the team. They were also well-coached by Mark Yoakam. Undoubtedly, if Mike Hagfeldt's arm and bat had been in their lineup, things might have ended differently for Glasgow that year. In a regular season game, Doc started me on the mound against Glasgow in Scobey. I got in trouble in the first inning, gave up a couple of runs, but then settled down and went the distance, giving up three runs in the 3-2 loss, throwing curveball after curveball. After the game, Doc addressed the team in the dugout and said, "And you can thank this 15-year-old pitcher for keeping you in the game." Greg Fjeld looked at me and nodded. Although we lost, I felt great. I now felt part of the team and that I could contribute something. Doc, I think, knew that was important for the younger players and was part of his method of melding the team together. The nod from Greg Fjeld confirmed that the players were getting it, too.

DIVISIONAL BABE RUTH TOURNAMENT

OUR PEERLESS BABE RUTH TEAM WON THE MON-DAK district championship for the third consecutive year by beating Outlook, 4-1, in the championship. I pitched a two-hitter, and Dick Puckett, who umpired behind the plate, came up to me after game and said, "Joey, If you pitch like that in the tournament, you're not going to get beat." That was special coming from my older cousin, who I idolized and he knew baseball better than anyone.

After winning the district championship, our all-star team traveled to play in the eastern division Babe Ruth tournament at Moose Memorial Park in Sidney. Dad thought he had the team that could go all the way in Babe Ruth and win the state championship. So did we. If we finished just second in the east, we would advance to the state Babe Ruth tournament in Havre, to be played the same weekend as the State B Legion tournament in Cut Bank. If that happened, four players on the Legion and Babe Ruth roster—Joe and

Jon Puckett, Kirby Halvorson, and Kelly Norman—could not be in two places at the same time and would have to play in one or the other tournament. We know where Dad would have had Jon and me. It would have been interesting to see how that would have played out with Doc, Kirby, and Kelly.

We played the Hi-Line All-Stars in our first game. Ron Harcharik was coaching, and they had a good team. Jon pitched a one-hitter against Hi-Line to win our first game, 3-0, outdueling Kip Harcharik, who pitched a three-hitter. Terry Baldry from got the only hit for Wolf Point. Jon recalls Terry's hit. "Little Buck roped a single to left center. My arm was actually tired that day. I pitched a legion game three days before. A lot of innings in the legion game too."

I was excited to pitch the second game. Due to injuries the previous two years, I had yet to deliver a single pitch in the divisional tournament. Perhaps making up for lost time, I pitched a no-hitter (I always had to outdo Jon), and we beat Miles City 1-0. After our first two games of the tournament, the conflicted schedules seemed inevitable, as we now just needed one more win to advance to State. But we lost 6-3 to Sidney in the undefeated semifinal and were eliminated by Glendive in a heart-breaking 3-2 loss, which went nine-innings. I pitched all nine innings. I'm unsure about Babe Ruth pitching rules, but I pitched 16 innings in three days. I remember crying in the dugout with Kirby after the loss. It was a devastating loss for Jon, Kirby, Kelly, me, and the rest of the team, as we had planned to go to the state tournament and do some serious damage for Dad. Little did we know that two weeks later, we would be on the diamond in Cut Bank playing against Hi-Line All-Star Kip Harcharik for the state Class B Legion championship.

The loss against Glendive at Moose Memorial Park was a tough one for Dad, Jon, and me. Dad started coaching us in Peewee baseball when we were six years old, and we had spent every waking minute of every summer playing baseball together since then. We had always won but could never get over the hump in all-stars and make it to State. Dad did not want this to be the end, and we didn't either. There was a chance Dad might field a Peerless Legion team the following season. We will have to see about that.

DIVISIONAL LEGION TOURNAMENT

Doc's pitching rotation for the divisional and state tournament was to start me in the first game, see how far I could go, then bring Craig Miller in to finish. The longer I could go, the more innings I could save for Craig later in the tournament. Our first game was against Glendive, who started Doug Frenzel. Doug Frenzel was 16 years old in 1976. He was a great pitcher—and an excellent all-around baseball player. I had watched him in a 1-0 pitcher's duel with Jeff Lebsock from Fairview (who played for Sidney) in the previous year's Eastern Divisional Babe Ruth Tournament. After pitching 16 innings in the Babe Ruth Tournament that had finished just three days earlier, my arm was a little tired, but I got my curveball going and went seven innings—saving Craig some precious innings—and we won 4-2. Craig and I scattered eight hits between us. Doc started Mike Hagfeldt in our second game against Glasgow. Mike treated his former classmates and teammates from the Glasgow Scotties rudely, pitching a two-hitter and striking out 17 Reds, leading Scobey to an 8-1 win and the undefeated semifinal against Wolf Point, who had beaten Ekalaka-Baker in its first game but was almost upset by southeastern champion Sidney in their second game.

Sixteen-year-old Jeff Lebsock from Sidney pitched a gem against the heavy-hitting Wolf Point team. Sidney was leading 2-1 in the top of the ninth inning and needed just three outs to force Wolf Point through the dirt route for the remainder of the tournament. But two untimely errors in the ninth by Sidney enabled Wolf Point to score two runs to win 3-2. Lebsock finished with a four-hitter and struck out nine.

In the semifinal, Wolf Point beat Scobey, winning 16-4 and advancing to the championship game undefeated, as "all the bad things piled up in one game for the Scobey boys" in that game.[112]

Craig Miller pitched Scobey to a 12-11 win over Glasgow to get to the championship game. Scobey's bats boomed with 18 hits, and Craig went the distance, giving up seven hits and striking out 14, but issued several walks, which led to most of Glasgow's runs.

That set up the Scobey-Wolf Point matchup for the eastern divisional championship, a rematch of the 24-23 slugfest the year before. I hoped this one wouldn't turn into a slugfest because Doc handed me the ball to start against Wolf Point while Don Lekvold started Jerry Moran. I was tired as I had pitched 23 innings in six days—16 innings in the Babe Ruth tournament the week before and seven against Glendive two days earlier in this tournament.

The game did turn out to be a slugfest. That hot summer day in Glendive would be the worst outing of my pitching career. I ran out of gas—my curveball wasn't snapping, and I couldn't get my fastball by them. Hit after hit was pounded to the outfield by Wolf Point. Bill Bartole was playing shortstop, and after one of the hits, he said, "Come on, Doc, give the kid a break." Doc finally gave me a break in the third inning after Bill Neumiller hit a home run—about three feet foul. Doc strolled out to the mound to take me out of the game in the middle of a count. I wish Doc could have walked a little faster because the longer I stood on that mound, the more humiliated I felt. I had given up six runs in two and two-thirds innings but still didn't get the loss because we were shelling Jerry Moran. Our bats were sizzling under the hot Glendive sun, too, as we had scored six runs in just the first two innings against Moran. When Doc replaced me with 14-year-old Kirby Halvorson on the mound after two and two-thirds innings pitched, the score was tied 6-6. I had given up six runs on eight hits. Good luck, Kirby.

The previous year, Dad, Jon, and I sat in our backyard, listening to the 24-23 slugfest between Scobey and Wolf Point, laughing about the lack of pitching. A year later, standing like Charlie Brown on the mound on a bad day, I wasn't laughing. When I got to the dugout, I started crying. I now know that "there's no crying in baseball," but no one knew that because *A League of Their Own* wouldn't come out until 1992. I had never been hit like that before and been pulled out of a game so early. A week earlier, I had pitched a no-hitter and pitched seven strong innings against Glendive two days ago, but now I was shell-shocked. Then, Craig Miller consoled me in the dugout in a gesture I will never forget. I don't remember his exact words, but he told me that I was young, that Wolf Point could hit everyone, including him, and that I had a lot of baseball left to pitch. Many athletes remember coaches or players who influenced them early in their careers. This is one of the memories I have that influenced me. At my lowest point, an older teammate picked me up.

We got to Moran for two more runs in the bottom of the third to take an 8-6 lead, and another classic slugfest between Scobey and Wolf Point was on. Wolf Point scored one run in the fourth and another in the fifth on a solo home run by Moran to tie it 8-8. We again got to Moran for two more runs in the bottom of the fifth to take the lead 10-8, but Wolf Point countered with three runs in the top of the sixth to vault ahead 11-10. Don Lekvold replaced Moran on the mound with Kip Harcharik in the bottom of the sixth and then brought in Grant Boysun. Doc used four pitchers in the game: me, Kirby, Jon, and Craig Miller. Wolf Point extended their lead to 16-10 with a big five-run seventh.

But in a classic Scobey-Wolf Point slugfest, no lead was safe, and Wolf Point's six-run lead was not safe. Our bats boomed again in the bottom of the ninth, and we closed to 16-14. We had the tying run on base, but Boysun got the last out, and Wolf Point won another close slugfest for the eastern division championship, 16-14. I felt a lot better as I watched the two teams slug it out, and I understood that these two teams could hit like no other I had ever seen. As I look back on it now, as far as Scobey-Wolf Point slugfests go, I might have kept our team in the game, pitching as poorly as I did. Jerry Moran got the win, giving up 10 runs in five innings pitched, but Wolf Point was leading 11-10. Kirby Halvorson took the loss. I wasn't the only Scobey pitcher who was shell-shocked—Kirby remembers Wolf Point hitting him hard too. He said, "I held them at bay for a while. Don't remember how long I lasted but I do remember 'KABOOSH'—that's the sound the ball made when they started banging balls off that metal fence in Glendive. I can't totally reproduce the sound here of course, but it seemed really loud and almost echoed. The stuff nightmares are made of. Anyway, so I gave up a dinger to Moran."

Wolf Point outhit Scobey 19-12. Jerry Moran had three hits, including a solo home run. Kip Harcharik also had a single and a triple for Wolf Point. Greg Fjeld had three singles and Dan Danelson had two singles to lead Scobey's hitting.

At the end of four days in Glendive, the top four teams—Wolf Point, Scobey, Glasgow, and Sidney—were headed to the state tournament in Cut Bank, which began in four days. I know none of us wore seatbelts back then, but it might be a good idea to fasten them for what would happen next.

STATE B TOURNAMENT

THE STATE CLASS B TOURNAMENT HAD SWITCHED TO AN eight-team format in 1976. The top four teams in each division advanced, so there was no longer a first-round bye for the top seed from each division. In the west, the top four teams were the Cut Bank Lobos, the Butte Muckers, the Great Falls Sparkies, and the Browning Indians, coached by Don Paulson of Scobey. It is strange how all four teams in the west had a team name, but none of the teams in the east did.

In our first game against the Great Falls Sparkies, Doc handed me the ball to start, as he had done at the eastern divisional the week before. Before the first pitch, as I was throwing my warmup pitches to catcher Jeff Richardson with my experienced teammates on the field behind me, I felt confident because they were all so good. I also felt confident because of the successful Scobey baseball tradition I was now part of. I had memories of all four state tournaments played in Scobey—including the two state championships in 1969 and 1973. Plenty of people were in the stands, too, as this was the tournament's first day, so all eight teams were there.

Eyes were on us as we warmed up and they saw that we had a team that could win. I was also humbled that Doc was confident to pitch me in the opener. I wanted to meet the moment and go as far as I could—maybe even the distance—before Doc would bring in Craig Miller. I had pitched seven innings in Glendive a week earlier. I felt strong early in the game, as I remember snapping a good curve ball off to a Sparkies hitter. He bailed out of the batter's box and hit the dirt on a curveball called strike. My target for my curveball was always at the hitter's head, not Jeff's glove, and when my curveball was working, it broke sharp, late, and down into the glove. I liked pitching to hitters who hadn't seen my curveball before—always the case with the western teams—because they were usually on their heels when the first one came. In this case, the hitter ducked, bailed out of the box, and hit the dirt—on a called strike! As the hitter got back up and dusted himself off and took a few practice swings like nothing happened, I caught his eye and smiled at him. I was feeling good early on the big stage.

It looked like I was going to pitch deep into the game, as we led 3-1 in the top of the fifth. But I got into a bases-loaded jam with one out, and Doc brought in Craig to get us out of it. I was frustrated about handing Doc the ball because I wanted to continue to pitch and thought I could get us off the field, but Doc was taking no chances. I felt like I could get them out and finish the inning and he gave me the hook too early. As willing as I was to hand Doc the ball four days earlier when getting shelled by Wolf Point in Glendive, I was as unwilling to hand him the ball here. But Craig got us out of the inning with minor damage, and in the bottom of the fifth, the score was tied 3-3. We scored a single run in the bottom of the fifth to take a 4-3 lead, then our bats came alive in the bottom of the sixth, as we plated five runs to take a 9-3 lead. We added two runs in the seventh and led 11-4. To save Craig some additional innings and get his young pitchers some experience pitching in the state tournament, Doc brought in Kelly to pitch the seventh and eighth, and Jon Puckett pitched a scoreless ninth inning. Greg Fjeld and Bill Bartole led our hitting. Greg was 4-for-5 with two doubles and a homer, and Bill Bartole was 3-for-4 with a homer and three runs batted in. Don Hagfeldt tripled, and Dale Barstad doubled for Scobey's other extra-base hits. The final score was 11-4 Scobey.

The east won all four games in the first round: Glasgow defeated Butte 13-5 behind Al Hopstad's six-hitter and 13 strikeouts; Wolf Point got past Don Paulson's scrappy Browning team 7-2; and Sidney came from behind to beat Cut Bank 5-3 when Chris Dana hit a two-run home run in the seventh to give Sidney the lead. Dana also had a single and a double in the game. Rick Dooley of Cut Bank hit his first home run of the season in the Sidney game. Tom Paladichuk pitched a three-hitter for Sidney and struck out 10 Lobos. This set up our second-round game against Sidney, who had a good team in 1976, winning the southeastern district.

The story of our second game against Sidney was not our bats but our pitching, as Mike Hagfeldt pitched a two-hit shutout, striking out 17 Sidney hitters and leading Scobey to a 5-0 win. This was Mike's second consecutive two-hitter, as he had beaten Glasgow 8-1 a week earlier in Glendive, where he also struck out 17 hitters. He also collected one of Scobey's eight hits in the game. This pushed us into the undefeated semifinal game against Wolf Point.

Wolf Point narrowly averted an upset by Glasgow in their second game, which would have forced Wolf Point down the dirt route path for the remainder of the tournament. I mentioned earlier that Glasgow had a good team in 1976. They had beaten Scobey and Wolf Point during the regular season and finished second behind Wolf Point in the northeastern district. And they almost upset Wolf Point in the other winner's bracket matchup. This game was a pitcher's duel between Mike Neubauer of Wolf Point and Norm Braaten of Glasgow. With the score tied 1-1 in the ninth, Grant Boysun hit a dramatic two-run home run to win it for Wolf Point 3-1. Mike Neubauer pitched a three-hitter for Wolf Point to get the win. In this game, Tony Erickson and Al Hopstad—two of Glasgow's best players—didn't play for disciplinary reasons, as Coach Mark Yoakam had benched them for missing curfew the night before. Wolf Point advanced as the second undefeated team in the tournament on Saturday.

I've written extensively about slugfests between the 1975 and 1976 Scobey and Wolf Point teams. Would it be possible for a pitcher's duel to occur between the two teams? Yes, it would. In the undefeated semifinal, Dennis Loendorf of Wolf Point and Craig Miller silenced the opposing team's bats in a well-pitched game from both teams. Stealing a page from Mike Hagfeldt's book, Dennis Loendorf hurled a complete game two-hitter, striking out 17 Scobey hitters to lead Wolf Point to a 4-1 win. Craig Miller pitched a fantastic game and kept the heavy-hitting Wolf Point team at bay by hurling a three-hitter and striking out 12. But costly walks and errors led to Wolf Point's four runs. Loendorf's gem vaulted Don Lekvold's Wolf Point team into the championship game as the only undefeated team in the tournament, and it forced Scobey into a game on Sunday to earn a berth in the championship game against Cut Bank.

Cut Bank, the number-one seed from the west, had snaked their way back through the dirt route to earn the

Trailing 4-3 in the bottom of the ninth, Cut Bank scores the tying and winning runs on an overthrew to third on a bunt. *Pioneer Press.*

right to play Scobey on Sunday. After their first-round 5-3 loss to Sidney, Cut Bank had beaten the Great Falls Sparkies 5-2 and Glasgow 9-8, setting up their rematch against Sidney, who had beaten the Butte Muckers 6-4 to stay alive. This game ended horribly for Sidney and would be the first of two gut-wrenching season-ending losses for Sidney at State in Cut Bank, the second one coming two years later against rival Glendive. With Sidney leading the Lobos 4-3 in the last of the ninth, the first two Cut Bank hitters walked to put runners on first and second. Then, Lobos' Brian Ledbetter bunted along the third baseline to move the runners up. The third baseman for Sidney charged the ball and threw to the shortstop, covering at third as a Cut Bank man headed from second base. However, the ball went through the shortstop and into left field, scoring the runner from second on the error. But Mark Lewis, who was on first base at the time of the bunt, also sped around the bases and slid home with the winning run on the throwing error. So Cut Bank walked it off without a hit to win it 5-4. The Sidney loss was a horrible end to an excellent season for them when they had found their way back onto the Legion field after not fielding a team for several seasons. Sidney and Glendive would field outstanding teams in the following years as well.

When talking on the phone to my girlfriend Darla Saturday night at my Cut Bank host's house, I told her that although we lost to Wolf Point that day, we just needed to win one more game against Cut Bank, and we would be in the championship game against Wolf Point, but that we would have to beat them twice to win it. After I hung up the phone, I went right to sleep. Let's everyone get a good night's sleep for the big games on Sunday.

But not everyone would get a good night's sleep on Saturday night.

I didn't know if I would return when I was leaving my host family's house on Sunday morning for the game. To stay alive in the tournament, we needed to beat Cut Bank, the number-one seed from the west, on their home field,

then beat Wolf Point, who had owned us during the regular season and the eastern divisional tournament. If we could win both those games, we would play Wolf Point again on Monday for the championship.

Doc started Dan Danelson against Cut Bank. Dan hadn't pitched much that season, as he was still physically and mechanically developing as a pitcher when he was only 15. He grew from a little over six feet to six feet five between his freshman and sophomore year in high school. Dan said, "I didn't pitch a lot in 1976 because I hadn't figured out the location aspect of being an effective pitcher." Well, he figured it out in this game, as he hurled a four-hitter at Cut Bank, giving up only two runs and leading us to a 9-2 win. However, to summarize the game, the Cut Bank *Pioneer Press* focused on Scobey's hitting: "The Cut Bank baseballers were just 'out hit.' Scobey got 12 hits to Cut Bank's four."[113] Bill Bartole, who hit well throughout the tournament, led Scobey's hitting, going a perfect 5-5. The only aspect of the game Scobey did not play well in was fielding, as we committed six errors.

That set up the first championship game against Wolf Point on Sunday. I was sitting next to Mike Hagfeldt in the third base dugout before the game as the Wolf Point players arrived to the field and filtered into the first base dugout. I liked to sit next to Mike because he was funny, and we would always talk baseball during the game. The funniest thing he ever said about me was to Jon, which Jon told me about later. Against Glendive at the eastern divisional, I got my second hit off pitcher Doug Frenzel. Mike said to Jon in the dugout, "Look at that. I'm struggling to get a hit, and that goddamn kid dinks another flare to right. What do I gotta do to get a fucking hit?"

As Mike and I were sitting in our dugout, I looked across to the Wolf Point dugout and saw something shocking: Jerry Moran was sitting there with his left arm in a cast in a sling. Whoa! What? We expected that Gerry would be pitching against us that day, but he was obviously not going to pitch—or play—that day. I said, "Mike, do you see that? Jerry Moran's pitching arm is in a cast." "Yeah," he said sheepishly, his eyes looking straight ahead and not at me, "I see it." Then he sighed. I looked at him and frowned. I can't explain it, but I felt like there was something he wasn't telling me like he knew something about why his arm was in a cast but was being evasive. It turns out he knew something about it.

The night before, all hell had broken loose in a bar in Cut Bank, with the older players from Scobey and Wolf Point involved. As Mike Neubauer recalls, "Z [Bill Zimmer] and I were at the back bar, Fred [Rhoads] come and said, 'We gotta go there's trouble brewing.' Hell we got outside and trouble was there. Supposedly, Cut Bank's toughest—they called him 8-ball—was coming at Gerry. Gerry was backing up saying 'I don't want to fight.' The guy took two swings, Gerry ducked them both and absolutely unloaded his left and knocked him cold and broke Gerry's hand. Another guy tried to step in and Rick [McGeshick] laid him out with a forearm-elbow. The greasers were filing out of the bar as we were leaving, our car being bombarded with beer bottles, cops with sirens on. We made it home. Gerry was hurting so I took him to Doc's room at about 2:30 a.m. Doc sent us to ER."

Allan Audet said, "Yeah I was there standing right above him as he pounded the hippie guy. Was quite a night. Do remember running the hell out of there." Greg Fjeld remembers running out of there, too. He said, "Scobey and Wolf Point were being ganged up on, and the two teams had to get out of there together." Tom Paladichuk from Sidney remembers high-tailing it out of there as well. Who *wasn't* there that night?

Kip Harcharik added, "Had the hippie group and the Mexicans that wanted to rumble and who stepped up, Rick McGeshick and Jerry Moran. Probably the calmest I've ever seen them but got pushed too far and put about six of them in the hospital. Kenny Lee and Kevin Woods fly up in pickups and cart us away. Can't remember who picked up the Blues players, but we could of all been in jail!"

Kip can't remember who picked up the Blues players in the getaway car, but Mike Hagfeldt can. It was the man himself, Doc Norman. Mike said, "I remember the brawl flowing out to the sidewalk, and either Rick or Gerry was pounding the crap out of some guy on the ground. Doc pulls up at that moment, leans over and opens the door and says, in an almost resigned tone (I can still hear it in my head), 'Get in, knuckleheads.' Four or five of us climb into the car, and we just drive away before the cops get there."

Back to the Scobey dugout with Mike. Yes, there was something he wasn't telling me. That was the madness off the field. Now to the madness *on* the field, where the 1976 State Class B championship was ultimately decided. Almost fifty years later, Mike said, "It took not one, but two miracles for us to pull it off. We had no pitching left, but Doc somehow squeezed some innings out of 'the kids.'"

After beating Cut Bank 9-2 earlier in the day, we needed to win the first championship game against Wolf Point on Sunday to stay alive in the tournament and force a second game on Monday. The drama from the night before followed the teams to the field. Allan Audet recalls, "Doc told us all to grab a bat when the gang of thugs showed up behind center field the next day," Kip Harcharik re-

Jeff Richardson catching against Wolf Point in the first championship game. Jon and I both learned not to shake him off the next day. *Edgar Richardson photo.*

members, "We couldn't even leave our houses, and they blocked the only road into the field. We were only 15, and I was freaked out."

The first championship game against Wolf Point on Sunday was probably the most dramatic finish in a state tournament game for Scobey, maybe even more dramatic than Dick Puckett's two-out, two-strike solo home run to tie the first championship game against Havre in 1969 and send it into extra innings, which Scobey won to force a second game. If not, it is a close second.

The game was a back-and-forth affair between the two teams, with the score tied or a one-run lead as each inning passed, and there was never much daylight between the two teams. This game would go "right down to the wire,"[114] and by "wire," that would mean the last strike. Wolf Point led 5-4 in the bottom of the ninth, and we were down to our final three outs. Grant Boysun, who had hit the dramatic two-run home run in the ninth to beat Glasgow 3-1 earlier in the tournament, was pitching for Wolf Point. He got the first two outs, so we were down to our last out with no one on base, with our ninth-place hitter, Wade Tryan, coming to the plate. Mike Hagfeldt recalls, "I remember thinking it was probably over, but held on to hope. Two outs, nobody on, number nine hitter up . . . looked pretty bleak." But Wade coaxed a two-out walk from Boysun to become the tying run on first. Wade could run. With two outs, there was still hope.

This brought up leadoff hitter Greg Fjeld. No one could have predicted what would happen next. Greg got two strikes on him, so we were now down to our last strike, as Scobey was in the 1969 state tournament against Havre when Dick Puckett hit his dramatic two-out, two-strike solo home run to tie the game and send it into extra innings. Could Greg do something special here? As I sat in the dugout, I knew the next pitch could be it, and our season would be over. To add to the drama, Greg fouled off a couple of pitches with two strikes to stay alive. Then, on the next pitch, Greg hit a line drive to right field, which tailed towards the foul line as it struck fair, forcing the right fielder to chase the ball and field it in foul territory before getting it back in. With two outs, Wade was running on contact, and he could run! The right fielder bobbled the ball when trying to pick it up. Wade was barreling toward third, and I could already see Doc waving him home to tie the game. Was there going to be a play at the plate? The throw came home, but there was no play at the plate as the catcher took the throw and then rifled a throw to second to try to get Greg, who had never stopped running as he rounded first after he saw the throw coming home. The throw to second was wild. Greg, in stride, continued rounding second towards third as the ball sailed into the outfield. Then, the ball went through the outfielder's legs. Doc was waving Greg home with the winning run! Greg, who seemed to be accelerating with each stride, was rounding third and heading for home as the team raced out of the dugout to mob him at home plate. A two-out, two-strike single, followed by three errors, and Wade and Greg scored to walk it off 6-5 for Scobey. Greg said, "I was rounding first, and Doc was waving for me to keep going, so I just kept going. I was tired as hell when I crossed home plate, and everyone dogpiled me. Best moment of my life, well, one of them anyway!" Just moments before, it looked like we were done; now, moments later, we lived to fight another day.

Mike Hagfeldt, who had three innings of eligibility left, was the winning pitcher in relief. Grant Boysun took the loss for Wolf Point.

That set up the second championship game between Scobey and Wolf Point on Monday. Tensions were still high in the town following the brawl on Saturday night, and at the end of the day on Monday, the Scobey and Wolf Point teams had to be escorted out of town by the police. But the drama off the field could still not match the drama that was to happen on the field that day in Cut Bank, as the two teams would once again square off for the final time—for the state championship—in 1976. The *Leader*, ever mindful and proud of the baseball tradition of Scobey and Wolf Point, wrote, "This was the final, and something had to give, as these two teams from northeastern Montana had disposed of all others around in the state tourney, demonstrating, as so often in the past, that this is where baseball country is in rural Montana."[115]

The *Leader* was also mindful that this deep into a tournament pitching would be a challenge: "Both teams were running out of eligible pitchers."[116] We were playing our sixth game, and Wolf Point was playing its fifth game. For Scobey, Craig Miller's innings were gone. Mike Hagfeldt had innings, but his arm was hanging off him, as he had pitched 12 innings already in the tournament. That left it up to the 15-year-olds, or so all of us thought. But Doc, true to form, surprised everyone and decided to start catcher Jeff Richardson, who no one remembers pitching at all that season. He had a cannon of an arm going from home plate to the pitcher's mound and down to second, but we weren't sure what would happen when the ball traveled in the opposite direction. Fourteen-year-old Kirby Halvorson would start at catcher for Scobey with Jeff pitching. For Wolf Point, Bill Neumiller and Grant Boysun's innings were gone, and Jerry Moran—from the brawl—and Dennis Loendorf—who had three innings of eligibility left—could not pitch due to a back injury, so it would be up to 16-year-old Mike Neubauer and 15-year-old Kip Harcharik. Little did Kip, Jon, and I know that when we pitched against each other in the Babe Ruth tournament three weeks earlier as Mon-Dak and Hi-Line All-Stars in Sidney, with our dads coaching us, we would be pitching against each other in the state championship at the Legion level.

Wolf Point won the toss for the home team and opened the scoring with an unearned run in the bottom of the first to take a 1-0 lead. Mike Hagfeldt hit a "booming" two-run home run in the second to give us a 2-1 lead. Jeff Richardson was pitching well and didn't give up any runs in the second and the third innings but got into trouble in the fourth on some walks and Scobey errors. As the rally for Wolf Point began to build early in the inning, Doc said to me, "Joe, go warm up." I was excited to pitch and be a part of this game. With one run already across for Wolf Point, the bases loaded, and a 3-0 count on Mike Neubauer, Doc

The Scobey dugout poured out onto the field to mob Greg Fjeld after he circled the bases on his two-out, two-strike hit in the bottom of the ninth inning to walk it off for Scobey. *Edgar Richardson photo.*

slowly walked to the mound to remove Jeff as pitcher and move him to catcher, replacing Kirby, and motioned for me to come to the mound. As I ran in for my warm-up, I was excited to be in this situation. I wanted to pitch us out of it. I don't remember being any more nervous than in other situations, but it was unusual for me to be coming in as a relief pitcher, as I usually started, and I was always a pitch-to-contact pitcher. I could get a strikeout, but most of my outs were balls put in play. I hated to give up walks.

I inherited three baserunners, and there was a 3-0 count on Neubauer. Jeff called for a curveball for a strike, then another for strike two, and the count was full. Jeff then signaled for another curveball, but I thought I could sneak a fastball past Mike after two curveballs (he had swung and missed badly on one of them), so I shook him off—big mistake. On the full count, Mike jerked a flyball to the gap in left center. The ball was hit high; it wasn't a line drive. My head snapped toward the left field to see if left fielder Mike Hagfeldt could get to it, and it looked like he might as I watched him close on the ball, but the ball dropped just out of reach of his glove, bouncing past him as he overran the ball toward center field. This started the merry-go-round on the bases, and when all the dust had settled, Mike Neubauer was standing on third base with a three-run triple, vaulting Wolf Point to a 5-2 lead.

Sonofabitch.

Doc was not happy with the pitch or the result. He wanted the curveball on the full count and yelled from the dugout, "What was that, Jeff?" Jeff yelled back at him, "Well, he wanted it!" That was the last time I ever shook Jeff Richardson off. And, as we shall see later, brother Jon would not shake him off either.

But I got out of the inning without further damage, as Mike was stranded at third. We scored a run in the top of the fifth to close to 5-3, and I pitched a scoreless fifth, getting us to the top of the sixth inning down two runs. We went scoreless in the top of the sixth.

In the bottom of the sixth, two Wolf Point batters got on with one out, so Doc decided to bring Mike Hagfeldt in from left field. I ran out to left field, swapping with Mike. I had never played left field before—Dad had always played me at shortstop when I didn't pitch. I was more nervous playing there than pitching. What if someone hit the ball to me?

Someone did hit the ball to me. The next hitter lined a single right at me in left. Holy shit. With runners at first and second and us already trailing by two runs, I knew the throw needed to go home, so I charged it and fired the ball on a one-hop to Jeff Richardson at the plate. The runner at third held. I'll never forget Jeff bellowing out, "Nice throw!" He was also yelling orders to the infield about the situation—a force at every base—and pumping his fist for them to buckle down and get out of the inning. A quarterback behind the plate was Jeff.

But Jeff's command of the field could not prevent what happened next. Big Bill Neumiller was stepping up to the plate for Wolf Point with the bases loaded. Part of the reason Doc had brought Mike in when he did was to get this left-on-left matchup, but Mike's arm was done. I could see that from left field. His velocity was not there, as he had already pitched 12 innings in the tournament, getting a complete-game two-hitter win over Sidney on Friday and three innings in relief to get the win over Wolf Point the day before. Mike said, "My arm was hanging. I had nothing left. It was all I could do to get it over the plate." On the next pitch, Mike said he "laid a nothing ball over the middle of the plate," and Neumiller blasted it over the right field fence for a grand slam home run. With Neumiller's powerful swing of the bat, Wolf Point now led 9-3.

Meanwhile, 15-year-old pitcher Kip Harcharik was pitching brilliantly for Wolf Point and silencing Scobey's powerful bats throughout the game. The only hard-hit ball had been the two-run home run by Mike Hagfeldt in the second inning. Kip again held Scobey scoreless in the top of the seventh to keep Wolf Point's lead at 9-3.

Mike's arm was done, so Doc brought 14-year-old son Kelly to pitch in the bottom of the seventh. Kelly told me, "The only time Dad pitched me in 1976 was when we were behind." Well, we were behind, and Wolf Point scored two runs in the inning to extend their lead to 11-3. But Kelly got three big outs against Wolf Point's toughest hitters (not that they had any weak spots) to get us off the field and in the dugout to hit. During the inning, Doc was barking pitching instructions to Kelly from the dugout, and Kelly was jawing back at him from the mound. It was like father and son working together in their backyard, except this was on the state championship stage. I had observed this exchange between Doc and Kelly before and was familiar with it with my Dad. I was also observing first-hand how Doc developed younger players while using them to win games. This was his model in action. As I watched helplessly as the game slipped further out of reach, I didn't realize there was always a method to Doc's madness, putting a 14-year-old pitcher in the game. I had forgotten that Doc had one more arrow left in his quiver—Jon Puckett. But sitting in the dugout and watching a game that seemed out of hand get further out of reach was difficult. I was not alone in that sentiment. The *Leader* perfectly captured our

The outlook was not bright for the Scobey nine in the bottom of the seventh inning. Faces were tense and heads were hanging. But then the 10-run rally came. *Edgar Richardson photo.*

mood: "The Scobey dugout was a bit subdued. There was little to indicate the explosion about to follow."[117]

Bill Bartole, who would be the ninth man to bat for Scobey in the inning, remembers when the rally started. He was not subdued: "I remember being so fed up with losing to Wolf Point, looking out through the dugout fence, yelling and shaking the fence, rooting for my teammates, who also got into it, not wanting to be the next out, scoring all those runs."

The "explosion" in the top of the eighth started benignly enough when third-place hitter Jeff Richardson drew a walk. "Fans watched something they had never before seen in their baseball lives; a team trailing 11-3 in the top of the eighth inning turning it around."[118] Dan Danelson singled, driving in two runs. Dale Barstad singled, Don Hagfeldt singled, Kelly Norman singled, Wade Tryan singled, Greg Fjeld singled, and Bill Bartole doubled. Richardson's leadoff walk and three costly Wolf Point errors contributed to the deluge of runs.

When the score got to 11-11, Doc turned down to the end of the bench and said, "Jon, go warm up." Holy shit, Jon. (Being a twin makes you a little nervous when the other one's on stage.) By the end of the inning, we had scored 10 runs on eight hits and three Wolf Point errors to take a 13-11 lead. The only extra-base hit was a double by Bill Bartole. Every player in the lineup scored at least once. During the inning, Kip Harcharik—who had pitched a fantastic game until that point—was replaced on the mound by Mike Neubauer for Wolf Point. At the end of the inning, our subdued dugout had transformed into a fired-up team that now carried a two-run lead and momentum into the bottom of the eighth, needing only six outs to win Doc's third state championship with a second miracle in as many days.

But getting six outs against Wolf Point was not easy, and it was up to 15-year-old Jon Puckett to get it done. "Wolf Point had proven it could have big innings too, and it needed more against Scobey."[119] Jon had pitched against Wolf Point at the eastern divisional championship game in Wolf Point a week earlier, so he knew their hitters.

But catcher Jeff Richardson knew them better. In the eighth inning, Jon allowed one hit when Mike Neubauer roped a double to left—his third hit of the game—but Jon stranded him at second after striking out Al Hoversland to end the inning. Jon remembers the Hoversland at-bat: "Richardson called for a curveball, and I shook him off. It was a 2-2 count, and I didn't want it to go to 3-2. I've never seen a catcher flash the same sign as fast as he did. I did not shake him off the second time, and he chased my wrinky low-outside curve." Strike three and out of the inning. Jeff was not about to allow another Puckett to shake him off after I shook him off in the fourth inning, and Jon struck Hoversland out to end the inning.

We got another rally going in the top of the ninth when Dale Barstad singled, Wade Tryan walked, and Bill Bartole drew a two-out walk to load the bases. Jeff Richardson then drove a ball to the outfield, but Bill Zimmer got under it to make a fine catch and end the inning.

Bottom of the ninth. Three outs to go for an improbable state championship comeback victory for Scobey and another heartbreaking, gut-wrenching, late-inning loss for Wolf Point in a state championship. The *Leader*—as it was always able to do—met the moment with its descriptive writing and set the stage for the game's dramatic conclusion: "Spectators at the game and around the state listening to it over the radio, were wild with excitement as Wolf Point came up for its share of the inning."[120] And the *Leader* was again spot on with its assessment of the inning, as after Scobey's 10-run eighth, the game had transformed into a slugfest: "A two-run lead wasn't much in this kind of game, and the Scobey team was playing its sixth game in five days with a lineup liberally sprinkled with Babe Ruthers from the current season, and all a bit tired."[121]

Jon seized the moment and got the last three outs we needed. It happened fast. Kip Harcharik grounded out to Jon on a comebacker for the first out. Wade Tryan then fielded a hot grounder at third and made a good throw to first for

1976 Scobey Legionnaires, State Class B Champions, Cut Bank, Montana. Standing, left to right: Bill Bartole, Dale Barstad, Greg Fjeld, Dan Danelson, Don Hagfeldt, Allan Audet, Craig Miller, Mike Hagfeldt. Kneeling, left to right: Doc Norman, Kirby Halvorson, Jeff Richardson, Jon Puckett, Kelly Norman, Joe Puckett, Wade Tryan, Dick Atwood.

Doc celebrating with Greg Fjeld, Dan Danelson, Jeff Richardson, and Don Hagfeldt following the championship game. Notice Doc holding the victory cigarette. That reminds me of a funny story Dad told me about Doc and Helen Trangsrud. Helen had gone to see Doc about some health problems she was having. She told Doc about her issues, and Doc told her she had to quit a lot of stuff she was doing to get healthier. Helen got defensive and said to Doc, "What about you? Look at you! You smoke, you're fat, you don't exercise . . . what about you?" Doc calmly replied to Helen's outburst: "I'm not the one complaining." *Family photo.*

the second out, and he did it again at third for the final out. The five of us in the dugout—who had all seen action in the game—rushed out onto the field to join our teammates in celebration on the mound, mobbing Jon, who, as a 15-year-old, had just earned a two-inning save to secure Scobey's third state championship, with 14-year-old Kelly Norman getting the win. The madness that was Cut Bank. Unbelievable.

Bill Bartole, who doubled in Scobey's 10-run eighth inning, summed it up best for Scobey, "It was a magical summer day."

TOURNAMENT SUMMARY

To say that the 1976 state championship was the most improbable of all of Doc's eight state championships would be a massive understatement. Some things happened off the field that were bizarre, unpredictable, and unfortunate—especially for Wolf Point. But at the end of the day on Monday, August 2, 1976, after Wolf Point and Scobey had played each other three times in three days, the bizarre and unpredictable things that happened *on* the field decided the outcome. All 14 of Scobey's players—the 14 players that Doc told they could win it all on the first practice in April—were part of it. Doc had melded the team together and made the young and the old champions.

Coach Don Lekvold and the 1976 Wolf Point Legion team could quite possibly be considered the best Legion team to not win a state championship. Kip Harcharik, referring to the impact of the barroom brawl, said, "I played a lot of sports in my life but had never been on a better team than the 1976 Legion team. Two heartbreaking losses to Scobey. Worst losses of my life knowing we had the better team." This is a sentiment that is likely shared by Coach Lekvold and every member of that team, I'm sure. But one thing that struck me about observing the older players from Wolf Point and Scobey that year was that they were friends, on and off the field. Even though they had battled for two seasons—including epic slugfests and pitcher's duels—there was no bad blood between them. It was the opposite: they talked to each other on and off the field, joked and laughed with each other. Mike Hagfeldt said about Wolf Point, "I have to say that I had the greatest respect for them. Not only good ball players but a nice group of guys. At least, that is how I saw them. I never had a bad word to say about any of them. Well, except when I gave up that grand slam to Bill Neumiller. I had a few words for him under my breath then." Mike Neubauer responded, "I can say the same about all the Scobey players; there have been great relationships throughout the years, and it all stems from Legion baseball. I believe Doc was the kingpin of it all. What a great man!"

1976 Wolf Point Legion Team, State Runners-Up. Front row, left to right: Dennis Loendorf, Terry Thompson, Mike Neubauer, Alan Hoversland, Kip Harcharik, Jerry Moran. Back row, left to right: Assistant Coach Ken Lee, Head Coach Don Lekvold, Fred Rhoads, David Hopson, Grant Boysun, Bill Neumiller, Bill Zimmer, Rick McGeshick.

Maybe it's best to end the 1976 tournament summary with an attempt at some levity. Things might have been different had the movie *Bull Durham* come out before the 1976 tournament. In the film, catcher Crash Davis from the Durham Bulls meets his right-handed pitcher Ebby Calvin "Nuke" LaLoosh for the first time at a bar. Crash goaded Nuke into a fight to teach him a lesson, and Nuke threw a punch and hit Crash in the face. Crash says, "Did you hit me with your right hand, or did you hit me with your left?" Nuke replies, "My left," to which Crash replies, "Good! That's good; when you get in a fight with a drunk, you don't hit him with your pitching hand."[122] Had Jerry Moran swung with his glove hand, he maybe could have pitched the next day. We'll never know.

TOURNAMENT STATS

Hitting

SCOBEY'S HITTING AND RUN PRODUCTION IN THE TOURNAMENT was good, averaging 7.5 runs per game over the six games. But the big story was the clutch hitting: Greg Fjeld's clutch two-out, two-strike hit against Wolf Point in the first championship game, then the entire batting order in the 10-run eighth inning—with each player scoring a run—in the second championship game. For individual game highlights, Greg Fjeld went 4-for-5 with two doubles and a home run against the Sparkies, and Bill Bartole was 3-for-4 with three runs batted in. Bartole was also 5-for-5 against Cut Bank. Mike Hagfeldt hit a two-run home run against Wolf Point in the championship game.

Wolf Point's hitting was also good, as they averaged six runs per game in the tournament. Grant Boysun's dramatic two-run home run in the ninth to beat Glasgow 3-1 stands out for individual highlights. In the second championship game, Bill Neumiller hit a grand-slam home run, and Mike Neubauer was 3-for-4 with a triple, double, and single, and three runs batted in. Wolf Point scored seven runs with two swings of the bat in that game.

Pitching

SCOBEY'S PITCHING IN THE TOURNAMENT WAS GOOD. IN THE 11-4 win over the Sparkies, Joe Puckett gave up two earned runs in four and one-third innings. Craig Miller got the win, pitching one and two-thirds innings of scoreless relief. Kelly Norman pitched two innings, and Jon pitched one. Mike Hagfeldt pitched a two-hit shutout against Sidney, striking out 17. Craig Miller kept Wolf Point's bats at bay on Saturday, striking out 12 and allowing four runs. Dan Danelson's four-hitter against Cut Bank led Scobey to a 9-2 win. Mike Hagfeldt got the win in relief in the first championship game. In the second championship game, Kelly Norman got the win in one inning of relief, and Jon Puckett pitched two scoreless innings of relief to earn the save. Of Scobey's 54 innings pitched, 30 innings were pitched by 15-year-olds and 14-year-olds.

Wolf Point's pitching was good, too. Bill Neumiller pitched Wolf Point to their 7-2 win over Browning. Mike Neubauer pitched a three-hitter to beat Glasgow 3-1. Dennis Loendorf pitched a two-hitter and struck out 17 against Scobey in their first game. Grant Boysun held Scobey to four runs in eight and two-thirds innings of the first state championship game until Greg Fjeld's two-out heroics and the errors. Fifteen-year-old Kip Harcharik appeared in three games for Wolf Point and kept Scobey in check until the eighth inning of the second championship game, allowing only three runs in seven innings pitched to that point.

There was some fine pitching by other teams in the tournament, too. Glasgow's Al Hopstad pitched a six-hitter and struck out 13 Butte Muckers, and Norm Braaten silenced Wolf Point's bats over eight innings, allowing only one run until Grant Boysun's two-run home run in the ninth. Sidney's Tom Paladichuk hurled a three-hitter and had 10 strikeouts in Sidney's 5-3 win over Cut Bank. Wayne Slezak pitched a three-hitter for Cut Bank to eliminate the Sparkies 5-2.

Fielding

THE GREATEST STRENGTH OF THE 1976 SCOBEY AND WOLF Point teams was not their fielding, but as former Saint Louis Cardinal catcher and baseball broadcaster Joe Garagiola once said, "It's pitching, hitting, and defense that wins. Any two can win. All three make you unbeatable." Scobey and Wolf Point's pitching and hitting were good enough to win, but their defense did not make either team unbeatable. Several Scobey errors led to unearned runs in Scobey's 4-1 loss to Wolf Point. Then, in the first championship game, three Wolf Point errors on one play led to the winning run being scored after Greg's single. In the eighth inning of the second championship game, Wolf Point committed three errors, leading to several unearned runs in Scobey's game-deciding 10-run inning. Giving either Scobey or Wolf Point more than three outs in any one inning could prove costly in 1976, and it did.

Baserunning

JOE GARAGIOLA LEFT OUT A CRITICAL INGREDIENT OF BASEBALL proficiency to win: baserunning. When talking about the 1973 Wolf Point team, Dana Audet mentioned the tremendous pressure their speedy base runners like Dave Stengel and Brian Jones put on the defense once they got on base. In Scobey's

6-5 walkoff win in the first championship game, both Wade Tryan and Greg Fjeld could run. They were the speediest runners on our team. Their speed put pressure on the outfielders to try to nip the tying run—Wade—and the winning run—Greg—at the plate. As Mike Hagfeldt recalls, when Wade got on first with two outs, "Hey, he can run." Kirby Halvorson added, "I was thinking we were very fortunate that probably our two fastest guys were involved . . . as they say, speed kills."

STATE CLASS A PLAYOFF

Try to keep up with the odyssey Scobey went on to western Montana following their return to Scobey early Tuesday morning following the state championship in Cut Bank. Scobey traveled to a hotel in Kalispell on Friday night, waiting to play fourth-seed Kalispell in a best-of-three series, with a doubleheader on Saturday and a possible third game on Sunday. But the Lakers still had games to play to determine the standings, so the doubleheader on Saturday was postponed to Sunday. Kalispell beat Libby Friday night, then beat the Glacier Twins Saturday night to move into a tie with the Great Falls Electrics for third place, so a coin flip was necessary to determine third and fourth place. The Lakers lost the coin flip, so they had to play Scobey as planned. Had they won the coin flip, Scobey would have had to travel to Great Falls to play the Electrics.

However, on early Sunday morning, as preparations were being made on the Griffin Field for the doubleheader, Jack Whelan, Montana State Class A Legion baseball chairman, ruled the number-one-seed Missoula Mavericks ineligible due to issues with several players on its roster. With the ruling, Missoula was required to forfeit all its conference games, and with them out of the standings, each team advanced one notch, so Kalispell moved up to third place, the Electrics to second, and the Chargers to first. As of Sunday morning, Scobey knew they would not be playing Kalispell that day. At this point, Bruce Sayler of the *Missoulian* wrote, "Scobey is getting an extended, scenic tour of northwestern Montana with hopes of landing in the right ballpark and in the right town,"[123] and George Geise of *The Daily Inter Lake* wrote that Scobey was "waiting to play somebody. Anybody."[124]

Libby, who had finished fifth in the standings, then moved up to the fourth-place slot. Whelan ruled that Scobey and Libby should play a doubleheader on Sunday in either Kalispell, Whitefish, or Libby. However, Libby Coach Tony Smith could find only four players in the allotted time, so it was ruled that Scobey and Libby would play the first game of the doubleheader on Monday at four o'clock in the afternoon in Libby.

Libby Logger Steve Lee slid around Scobey second baseman Greg Fjeld's tag to steal second base in game three, then advanced to third. But Mike Hagfeldt struck out the next three Libby batters, standing Lee on third. *The Western News.*

Once the teams finally got on the field in Libby on Monday, Scobey won the best-of-three series by splitting the doubleheader on Monday—clobbering Libby 21-3 in seven innings in the opener and losing the nightcap 14-9—then winning the rubber match on Tuesday night 7-5. The series win earned Scobey a berth as the fourth seed from the west in the State A Tournament in Miles City, which started on Saturday. Scobey's bats boomed in the series, scoring 37 runs in three games. Mike Hagfeldt started the first game and was relieved by Dan Danelson after Scobey got the big lead. Craig Miller started the second game and was relieved in the eighth inning by Mike Hagfeldt. In the rubber match, Mike Hagfeldt got the win for Scobey.

The *Leader* did not pull any punches when discussing the fiasco of Scobey's long road trip, writing that while Scobey won despite being "a sorely tried and very weary team" as the "upper powers of Legion baseball in Montana argued about how many angels can dance on the point of a needle without regard to the several values going down the drain."[125]

Jon and I missed all the fun on the road trip as we were on an extended vacation of our own. Following the State Babe Ruth tournament, which Dad had thought we would be playing in, he had planned a summer vacation to Kansas City to see our older brother Bill and Denver to see our sister Dianne. He hadn't considered that Scobey could win the state Legion championship. Jon and I felt like we were abandoning our teammates by going on vacation, and we wanted to stay with the team for the playoff series and the State A Tournament, but that was not a choice for Jon and me to make. However, the trip included baseball, of course.

While in Kansas City, we saw a three-game series between the Kansas City Royals and the New York Yankees, the two best teams in the American League that year.

STATE CLASS A TOURNAMENT

SCOBEY OPENED THE STATE A TOURNAMENT AGAINST THE number-one seed from the east, the Billings Scarlets, who were now in their second year of Class A competition. Mike Hagfeldt, whose arm had to be hanging off his shoulder by that point, had pitched over 12 innings in the State B Tournament and almost that many innings against Libby earlier in the week—started for Scobey. He pitched well against the tough Scarlets team, surrendering eight hits—six singles—in eight innings of work. Scobey was staying on the field with the Scarlets and trailed only 5-2 in the seventh, but the Scarlets broke it open with a three-run rally to go ahead 8-2, which was the final score. Scobey got five hits off Scarlets' starter Lance Leininger, including RBI doubles by Mike Hagfeldt and Jeff Richardson. Scobey played well defensively, committing only two errors.

The Royals eliminated Scobey the next day 6-1 in a game the Helena *Independent Record* described as a "masterpiece of fielding"[126] by both teams. The Royals "reeled off three double plays and a lightning-quick triple play,"[127] and Scobey "added two flashy double plays of its own."[128] The triple play happened in the first inning. After Greg Fjeld and Bill Bartole both singled, Jeff Richardson smashed a "low, sizzling line drive"[129] to the right side of the infield that was snared by the Royals first baseman, who tagged Bartole and fired to second to double off Greg Fjeld. Scobey put eight runners on base but left only men on due to the double and triple plays. Royals pitcher Wes Rogers held Scobey to three hits.

Scobey's performance in the State A Tournament was respectable, especially considering how travel-weary the team was. The pitching was good, and they played well enough in the field but couldn't muster much in the way of hitting against tough pitching from the Scarlets and Royals. The Royals and Scarlets did not take Scobey lightly. In the context of Doc's speech to the team on the first day of practice in April—"If we come together as a team, we can win it all and go to Yakima, Washington"—the team went as far as it could. The older and younger players did come together, and we played to our potential to get as far as we did. In the end, that is all a coach can ask for, and I am sure Doc was proud of the team for getting as far as we did.

A big story of the Royals game for Scobey, looking ahead to the future, was the solid pitching performance delivered by 15-year-old Dan Danelson. He pitched a complete game, scattering eight hits and issuing only two walks. Scobey committed four errors, so only some of the six runs were unearned. Although not used much during the regular season, Dan came on strong in the end, pitching Scobey to a 9-2 win over Cut Bank, relieving Mike Hagfeldt in the 21-3 win over Libby in the playoff, and then pitching well against the Royals at the State A Tournament. Strangely, Dad taking Jon and me on vacation might have opened the door for Doc to lean on Dan more as a pitcher in the Libby series and against the Royals. During the regular season, I was the third man in Doc's rotation, starting the first game in Glendive and Cut Bank. The day before the Royals game, Dad got a call from Doc that he wanted to fly Jon and me to Billings so we could pitch in the State A and that Jon would start against the Royals. The momentum of Dan's improvement would carry over into the beginning of the next season, where Doc would continue to work with Dan, and he would become the powerful pitcher we all remember him to be.

The loss to the Royals ended a remarkable postseason run by Scobey, winning the State B championship with two dramatic late-inning comeback wins over Wolf Point and beating Libby in a best-of-three series to qualify for the State Class A tournament while sightseeing in western Montana in the process. While the *Leader* rightly described Scobey's regular season as "so-so"—taking third behind Wolf Point and Glasgow in the northeastern district—the postseason was anything but.

Although a loss to end a season is never positive, the solid pitching performance delivered by 15-year-old Dan Danelson against the Royals symbolized the bright future for the Scobey Legion team, as seven players who had been on the field in the final game of the State B championship game would be returning the following year: Allan Audet (16), Dan Danelson (15), Wade Tryan (15), Joe Puckett (15), Jon Puckett (15), Kirby Halvorson (14), and Kelly Norman (14). Three players Dad had developed in Peerless Little League and Babe Ruth—Ray Chapman (15), Randy Stolen (14), and Bernie Wasser (14)—would also join the team, along with former Babe Ruthers Brad Henderson (15), Don Holyk (15), Mike Abar (15), and Don Boos (15) from Scobey. Doc's model of simultaneously developing younger players while using them to win state championships would reap huge dividends in the coming years, as 1976 would mark the first of five consecutive state Class B championships for Scobey, a record that stands today.

EXTRA INNINGS

MIKE HAGFELDT REMEMBERS THE UMPIRE IN THE PHOTO OF the third game of the Libby series. Mike said, "He warned me about licking my fingers when I was pitching. I told him I wiped them off on my jersey every time. I'd never had an issue in my entire career until then. I can't remember exactly what he said but it pissed me off. Something like I needed to be off the mound when I did that. Later in the game I stared him the face, licked my fingers and swiped them hard across my chest." Then he added, "I remember Doc trying to teach me how to throw a greaseball."

The *Leader* labeled the 1976 Scobey Legion team the "Iron Men" because, during the postseason, the team traveled over 2,500 miles and played 16 games in a little over 18 days. Scobey traveled to Glendive for the eastern divisional tournament and played five games, then back to Scobey, to Cut Bank, where we played six games (the boxing on the way to Cut Bank adding to the fatigue), back to Scobey, to Kalispell and Libby, where they waited two days to play Libby three games, back to Scobey, to Miles City where they played two games, and finally back to Scobey. In the 16 postseason games, the Iron Men posted a 10-6 record.

The *Leader* issued a harsh rebuke to the Montana American Legion Baseball program. Referring to the best-of-three playoff to get into the State A Tournament, the paper wrote, "The Class B champions can be very capable competitors when not beat down and worn out by unfairly arranged playoff games on a 'poor relative' basis." The *Leader* always referred to the Class B teams as "poor relatives" compared to how the Montana American Legion Baseball program treated the Class A teams.[130]

There was no question Jerry Moran's loss was huge for Wolf Point, both his arm and bat. As Mike Neubauer recalls, "Gerry beat the Scarlets that year 3-2 and led us in hitting at .476. He was a big loss, especially with Denny [Loendorf] being hurt."

Wolf Point wasn't the only team affected by the loss of players in Cut Bank. In the Glasgow-Wolf Point game, Al Hopstad and Tony Erickson were benched by Coach Mark Yoakam for missing curfew. Mike Neubauer, who pitched a three-hitter against Glasgow, said, "Tony absolutely owned me, and Hoppy (Al Hopstad) wasn't a slouch by any means. So I'm not so sure we deserved to win that game. Glasgow was a damn good team."

The following year, 1977, Coach Don Lekvold married JoAnn Loendorf from Wolf Point, and the couple made their home in Scobey. Don became Doc's assistant coach from 1977-1982, then head coach from 1983-1991. Don was the assistant coach for five state championships (1977-80, 1982) and led Scobey to two third-place finishes at State (1985 and 1990) during his tenure as head coach. The Loendorfs were a huge baseball family in Wolf Point. Coach Lenny Loendorf led Wolf Point to its first state championship in 1965.

Head coach Mark Yoakam of Glasgow, who disciplined two of his best players for missing curfew in Cut Bank, was inducted into the National High School Athletic Coaches Association (NHSACA) Hall of Fame in July 2020. During his 45-year career to that point, Mark was an integral part of 60 state trophies, as either head or assistant coach, including 28 state championships. He was in Glasgow for 26 years, where the girls' cross-country teams set a national record, winning eight straight titles, with Mark heading the program for the final five. During his tenure, the Scotties collected eight state titles, six in girls CC and one each in boys' and girls' track. Mike Hagfeldt, in describing Mark Yoakam, said, "He was very much a disciplinarian. You don't win eight consecutive state cross-country titles without that!" Yoakam also helped organize the Girls' Softball Association and served as president and was also president of Regional Soccer, American Legion Baseball, and Babe Ruth Baseball.

In describing Al Hopstad as a pitcher, Mike Hagfeldt ssaid, "Al Hopstad owned me. I couldn't touch him. He made me look bad. He had that nasty sidearm curveball. I would just flail at it. That's when I decided to learn that pitch myself. The first time I threw it in a game was against him I believe. Struck him out with it, and he gave me a tip of his cap on the way back to the dugout. Always thought that was pretty classy of him."

Scobey left-hander Mike Hagfeldt from Glasgow and Wolf Point right-hander Dennis Loendorf finished 1-2 in the javelin at the State Class A Track Meet in May 1976. Mike threw it 197-2 to win; Dennis 191-6 for second. Mike also took second in the discus. Jay Hagfeldt has bragging rights over Mike, however. Jay won the State Class A javelin event in 1973 at 199-9.

Joe Garagiola's baseball announcing annoyed me. Whenever a big-league pitcher served up a hanging curveball, and it got tagged, he would refer to it as an "American Legion curveball." I would have liked to have thrown my American Legion curveball just once to Joe to see if he could hit it. Joe was a catcher for the St. Louis Cardinals prior to broadcasting baseball.

My mom was a Yogi Berra fan. Yogi was an assistant coach to manager Billy Martin for the 1976 Yankees. When we got to Royals Stadium for the first game, my mom's first question to Dad, while looking on the field, was, "Where's Yogi?" Dad got a picture of Yogi, of course.

The one-hitter by Jon against Hi-Line in the Eastern Divisional Babe Ruth Tournament, followed by my no-hitter later that day, was not enough for Dad. The *Leader* had Jon's one-hitter upgraded to a no-hitter, and my no-hitter upgraded to a perfect game the following week. Dad would have called that in. Most sports stories take longer than a week to become exaggerated, but Dad moved fast. Or maybe he just thought that was what happened?

Our family saw some great players on the field in the Yankees-Royals series in Kansas City. Yankees catcher Thurman Munson and Royals' third baseman George Brett were two of them. But the coolest thing about the series was seeing Royals outfielder Ruppert Jones play. He had been brought up from the minor leagues to play late in the season. Jon and I had seen him play for the Billings Mustangs at Cobb Field in 1973, and now he was in the bigs. The Billings Mustangs were the farm club for the Kansas City Royals at the time.

History repeated itself in 1976, as Scobey also came back to beat Wolf Point in the 1973 state tournament in Scobey in the top of the eighth inning. Scobey trailed Wolf Point 4-2 in the top of the eighth inning but rallied with eight singles and one Wolf Point error to score seven runs, turning the 4-2 deficit into a 9-4 lead, eventually winning 9-6. In 1976, Scobey also got eight hits in the top of the eighth inning, with three Wolf Point errors, scoring 10 runs to win 13-11.

Almost fifty years later, Mike Hagfeldt added a little perspective on the bar incident in Cut Bank: "As far as the brawl goes, you have to remember the drinking age was 18, so underage drinking was common. Maybe not at a state tournament, but still, it happened." Montana raised the drinking age to 19 in 1979.

In their second year competing in Class A, the Billings Scarlets swept all four games to win the state championship, beating the Chargers 7-0 in the championship game. The Scarlets won the state Class B championship in their last year in 1974.

While Kelly Norman was the winning pitcher in the state B championship game as a 14-year-old, once again, Havre beat us to the punch—Kirk Stetson, at 14 years old, was the winning pitcher for Havre against Wolf Point in the 1972 state B championship game in Havre.

The *Leader* stated that baseball fans had never seen a team trailing 11-3 come back to turn it around . . . but I actually had—and thought about it during the championship game. When I was playing Peewee baseball for Dad as an eight-year-old in 1969, we trailed Flaxville by an identical 11-3 score in the top of the last inning. Flaxville was bagging their equipment in front of their dugout while their pitcher was warming up for the final three outs. Dad came over to the bench, knelt on one knee, and said: "Do you see that?" pointing to their dugout. "They're bagging up their equipment. Is this game over? Or do we have three more outs?" We rallied for 11 runs on several hits, walks, and errors, then got three outs in the bottom half to win 14-11. I have never seen Dad smile wider than when he had the satisfaction of watching Flaxville unbag their equipment for the bottom half of the inning after we had come back.

The older boys weren't the only ones to get in trouble in Cut Bank. After the first game against Wolf Point on Saturday, we had some free time, so Kelly talked Doc into taking Jon, Kirby, Kelly, and me to the Cut Bank Golf and Country Club to play nine holes of golf. Kelly got a little wild driving the golf cart and crashed it, resulting in a reprimand from the groundskeeper and seizure of the golf cart. Undaunted, Kelly teed off on several golf balls, driving them over the edge of the golf course into the Cut Bank Gorge and Creek below the golf course.

Jon and I pitched for Scobey and Kip Harcharik, and Mike Neubauer pitched for Wolf Point in the state championship game. Our "rivalry" went back to 1970 when Jon, Kip, and I were nine, and Mike was 10. We played a doubleheader in Wolf Point. Mike had the game-winning hit to drive in two runs, with Kip Harcharik sliding across home plate with the winning run to walk it off for Wolf Point, 6-5. I threw a fastball to Mike in 1970, and I threw one again in 1976. Both had the same result—an extra-base hit with multiple RBIs. The only difference was that I didn't have a curveball in 1970.

In a game earlier in the season, Doc started me against Plentywood. I went jogging four miles earlier in the day. What was I thinking? I learned how much you use your legs for pitching that day. I walked the first two hitters in the top of the first, then mishandled a bunt to load the bases. My legs felt like jelly. Doc took me out before I recorded an out—shortest outing of my career. Here's a tip for all you youngsters: don't go jogging four miles on the day you pitch.

In the dugout in Cut Bank, the older players were debating whether the 1976 Scobey Spartans or the 1976 Flaxville Cardinals had the better basketball team at the end of the season. Scobey and Flaxville had played each other in the first game of the year at the Flaxville Invitational Tournament, and Flaxville had won 46-44, but they never played each other after that. Craig Miller of Flaxville was holding his own against the Scobey players, but he was outmanned. The conversation amused me, but suddenly, Jon and I got dragged into it. Craig said, "Hey, let's ask the Pucketts. They played us both. Let's see what they have to say." Oh shit. I didn't want to piss any of the older players off by taking a side, so I gave a very political answer, something like, "Well, both teams were so much better at the end of the year in the state tournaments than they were that first game . . . so it's really hard to say." But after almost fifty years, I'll respond, with the safety of the virtual world as my buffer: "I think Flaxville was the better team at the end of the season. They bulldozed through the district, divisional, and state tournaments and seemed to improve as each minute of each game went by." (Mind you, that is my archrival I'm talking about.) For the record, we lost to Scobey 52-47 at that same Flaxville tournament but then beat Scobey on their home court in February, 62-51, leading 37-20 at halftime. We lost to Flaxville 61-54 at Flaxville and 59-46 at Peerless.

Scobey's last appearance at the state basketball tournament was 22 years earlier, in 1954, when Cliff Hagfeldt led Scobey to the state tournament with an upset win over Fairview in a challenge game. Scobey had finished sixth in the conference in 1954. In 1976, Scobey upset top-ranked Broadus in a challenge game to make it to State. 1976 was Flaxville's first trip to the state tournament.

In the category of "What were they thinking?" Jon and I brought two pairs of boxing gloves on the bus for the long Cut Bank trip. What were the chances that something could go wrong with that? Everyone wanted to see the Puckett twins fight, so Jon and I squared off against each other, the bus aisle being the ring. I'm not sure who won or if there was any money wagered. Jon said, "I remember not liking it because we went against each other." One mismatch in a weight category occurred when heavyweight Jeff Richardson was somehow matched with lightweight Jon Puckett. I think the boxing ring on the bus was closed by Doc after that.

Jon and I both remember driving home to Peerless in the early morning hours after the bus arrived to Scobey from Cut Bank. We were listening to Seals and Crofts' 8-track tape album, *Summer Breeze*, and the song "Summer Breeze" came on, which contains the lyric, "Sweet days of summer."[131] Sweet days of summer, indeed. The sweetest days.

So incredible was Scobey's comeback win over Wolf Point in the final that the sportswriter for the Cut Bank *Pioneer Press* reported Wolf Point as the winner. In the tournament summary edition of the newspaper, this is what was written: "Wolf Point then went on to defeat Scobey for the Class 'B' championship, 13-11, although the losers put a scare into the Wolf Point team in the eighth inning as the Scobey boys got eight hits and Wolf Point made three errors to give Scobey 10 runs. Wolf Point now plays the fourth-place Class 'A' team in a best-of-three series. If it wins in this series, Wolf Point will go on to the State Class 'A' tournament."[132]

After we got home to Peerless, later in the week, I took a letter to mail to the post office, which was in the front of Uncle Reese Puckett and Aunt Lauretta's house. When I got to the window, Aunt Lauretta said, "Congratulations on winning the championship, Joey, but oh, Reese and I thought that was such an awful situation Doc put you in against Wolf Point with the bases loaded when you're so young." (It was commonplace in Peerless to critique Doc's coaching, especially after Terry's arm troubles.) I nodded and thanked Uncle Reese and Aunt Lauretta for their concern, but I did not agree that Doc put me in a bad situation. I embraced the challenge and was glad Doc had the confidence to hand me the ball in that situation, not that he had a lot of choices. I executed the pitches I always did and felt good. I wish the outcome of that inning would have been different. But the game's result was the only thing that mattered—we had won.

Greg Fjeld played his fourth year at second base in 1976, starting at second base on the 1973 state championship team as a 15-year-old. He had the quickest relay from second to first I saw for a Scobey Legion player. Greg got the final out against Wolf Point in 1973 by catching a pop fly behind second base with the bases loaded. He foiled Wolf Point again in 1976, but this time with his bat. When things got quiet, and Doc needed to fire the team up, he always called from the dugout, "Let's hear it, Birdseed!" Greg would whistle his high-pitched whistle at second base.

1977

Tiny Puckett's Decision

> *Both teams would be good, but I don't think either team could win it all. Together, though, we could win it.*
>
> —Dan Danelson to Joe Puckett, discussing the possibility of Tiny Puckett forming a Peerless Legion team in 1977

BEFORE DELVING INTO THE 1977 SEASON, I'D LIKE TO briefly discuss how razor-thin close Dad came to organizing a Peerless Legion baseball team in 1977. We had been playing for Dad on his baseball teams from 1967 to 1976, and Dad intended to keep the winning team he had developed to stay and play for him in Peerless. He had molded a winning team every season with players from the time they were six years old. We had won baseball tournaments in Saskatchewan and North Dakota and major tournaments in Eastern Montana. After Dad started the Border Little League, he won it twice, and in Babe Ruth he won the Mon-Dak League in 1974, 1975, and 1976. Dad had won league championships every year there was a league. His teams from 1967-76 had an overall record of 124 wins and 21 losses, an 86% winning percentage.*

It was difficult for Dad to let go of the team he had developed for 10 years. All those players who had played for him, like Ross Chapman, Roger Trang, Bill Fladager, Matt Fouhy, Willard Fladager, Bernie and Rick Wasser, and others, would have played Legion ball for him in Peerless in 1977 and beyond. All the good athletes from Opheim he coached would have come to play, too, as well as Randy and Greg Stolen from Glentana.

Dad was very serious about doing this, but in the end, decided not to. I am not sure why he decided against it. I talked with him about it, but I don't remember when he decided not to field a team. I do, however, remember having a conversation with Dan Danelson about it. Doc had caught wind of Dad's intentions, probably through Jon and I talking to Kelly. It felt like Dan had been sent

Coach George "Tiny" Puckett surveys his Mon-Dak All-Star team on the field before the first pitch against Miles City at the 1976 Eastern Divisional Babe Ruth Tournament at Moose Memorial Park in Sidney. *Family photo.*

---

* George and Faustine Puckett, Peerless, *Daniels County History*, 614, "Peerless Peewee, Little League, and Babe Ruth Baseball, 1967-1975." Dad's record from 1967–1975 was 104-20. Our last year in Babe Ruth in 1976 we were 21-1, so Dad ended with an overall record of 124-21.

as a baseball ambassador by Doc to talk to sense into the Pucketts about the situation. As Dan and I talked, I was flattered because we were being courted like recruits to play in Scobey. Dan remembers the possibility of Peerless going solo or joining Scobey. He said, "Doc did talk to me about it and my feelings were I've idolized many ball players during my adolescence, many being Pucketts, and no fucking way was I not going to be heard regarding the potential we had together. We had played together just enough to know how good it could be."

In discussing the possibility of separate Scobey and Peerless teams back in early spring 1977, Dan told me, "Both teams would be good, but I don't think either team could win it all. Together, though, we could win it." I also remember thinking how right Dan was, that each team would be good but probably couldn't win the state championship.

I relayed what Dan said to me to Dad. I'm not sure if that was why he decided not to field a team, but it might have heavily influenced his decision. It made sense. In the end, Dad was able to let go of his team and retired from coaching, and on the first day of practice in Scobey in April 1977, Joe and Jon Puckett, Ray Chapman, Randy Stolen, and Bernie Wasser—five of Dad's boys—were on the field, playing for Doc in Scobey. The rest, as they say, is history.

Mom was like Marge was to Doc. She was the Peerless Pirates chief of staff and number-one fan and cared for everything else, enabling Dad to coach us. She kept score for all our games or made sure someone did and saved all the scorebooks. She captured and saved all the articles of our games. She also took pictures of our teams and individual players. You can't find her in any of the pictures because she took all of them, symbolizing her quiet, behind-the-scenes support. Mom always took a backseat to Dad but was behind it all, quietly supporting him and us. She saw that sports were our number one priority and made it her priority, enabling the three of us to do what we loved most. There aren't words to describe how my mom and dad gave me the best childhood a boy could ask for. Mom's dedication to teaching me fundamental values and Dad's dedication to an old-school coaching style molded me into a better person and player.

Having two World War II veterans—Dad, a soldier, and Doc, a marine—coach me from when I was six to 18 . . . I can't say how lucky I was. Kelly told me that Doc always said, "If they're keeping score, we're playing to win." The same was true for Dad. Every game I ever played for Dad, we kept score. We always played to win, and he established a winning culture for Jon, me, and all our teams. The 43-6 record for the team he organized and coached from 1954 to 1958 and 124-21 record and five league championships from 1967 to 1976 speak for themselves.

⚾ ⚾ ⚾

Skipping forward in time to June 1998 now. On June 19, 1998, just 19 days after my dad's death on May 31, 1998, a special dedication was held on Peerless Ball Field in honor of the three Puckett brothers—Reese, Ed, and Tiny—before the start of a Bambino baseball tournament. Had he been alive to see it, Dad would have been deeply moved by the ceremony. Uncle Reese had already passed away in 1987, so it was just Uncle Ed who could be there. Mary Machart captured a wonderful photo of Uncle Ed standing in front of the sign and wrote a touching article commemorating the event. You can see the two poplar trees in our backyard in the background, but, due to declining health, my parents had moved to Helena, so they were no longer living in Peerless. Here is Mary's article printed in its entirety.

Ed Puckett stands in front of the newly christened "Puckett Field" in Peerless. The field was named for the Puckett family, who played a very large role in bringing baseball to the community. Blue Rock Beverages of Glasgow installed the new scoreboard, donated by Pepsi, just prior to the tournament. On hand to receive the scoreboard the day it was installed were the coaches for the Peerless Pirates, Ross Chapman, Bill Fladager, and Ray Belling. *Mary Machart photo and caption.*

Peerless Ball Field Dedicated[133]

```
The teams have all gone home and the dust
has settled, but there is something new that
remains in Peerless after the Bambino baseball
tournament June 19-21. Many preparations were
made for the event including improvements on
the field, a new score board, a fence was start-
ed in the outfield, made of boards from local
businesses, donations and brand boards, with
brands from local ranchers painted on them.
    Amidst all of the new and wonderful improve-
ments, there is a bit of nostalgia that was
```

unveiled on the Friday night of the opening ceremony, above the score board there is a sign now that reads, "Puckett Field."

For those familiar with the history of Peerless, a large smile appears on their faces with this news.

In 1954, the late George "Tiny" Puckett who passed away in June of '98, organized the first Little League baseball team in Peerless. This league was active for four years and earned a record of 43 wins and 6 losses. In 1967, Tiny put together a boys' baseball team which started out as a Pee Wee Team, that grew to be "Peerless Little Leaguers" and then on to "Peerless Babe Ruthers."

Two of the members of the original Pee Wee Team, Bill Fladager and Ross Chapman, are now coaches of the Peerless Pirates. Tiny coached these teams and took them to tournaments in Canada, North Dakota, and major tournaments in Eastern Montana.

His brother, Ed Puckett was also very active in sports. Ed coached and managed the girls' softball teams in Peerless, from 1957 until 1974. Ed enjoyed the sport so much, he began the first women's fast-pitch softball team in Peerless in 1957 which called themselves the Peerless Pansies and a slow-pitch softball team in 1967 called the Peerless Hellcats. The Hellcats went to tournaments all over the state of Montana.

At one time, all three Puckett brothers, Tiny, Ed and Reese, coached a variety of successful sporting teams, from baseball to basketball.

As folks reminisced about the dedication of the field, comments were made that it was the Pucketts that brought sports to the Peerless community. Over the years, it wasn't uncommon to spot them at a sporting event in town.

Bill Fladager (pictured here as a 10-year-old playing second base for Dad on the Peerless Pirates Little League team in 1970) was one of Dad's original players on the 1967 Peewee team and played through Babe Ruth in 1975. He was our steady second baseman. Bill passed away in 2021. *Family photo.*

Forgey Reese (F. Reese) Puckett (right), Principal of Peerless High School, 1932–1942, with his three sons (from left) Ed, George "Tiny", and Reese. My favorite memories of my dad and uncles together are of when I got to go on deer hunting trips with them in the fall when I was little boy. At the end of the hunting day, when we were in the camper together, the conversation would inevitably shift to sports, and I just loved to listen to them talk about it. *Family photo.*

The passion for sports they shared came from their father, F.R. Puckett, who came to Peerless as superintendent, teacher, coach and band director. Also assisting in the building of the little league and softball in Peerless was George Larson.

Known for being more of a quiet man, behind the scenes, Ed Puckett along with his wife Norma, were on hand to take in the excitement of the 1998 Bambino Border League baseball tournament, watching from their vehicle on the sidelines.

For those who didn't know the history of this small-town field, after hearing just a portion of it, find that it is appropriately named, "Puckett Field."

The final verse in the Sportsmanship Code of Babe Ruth Baseball seems to sum up what the Puckett brothers did with their time and dedication to the baseball programs in Peerless, "Develop into real, true CITIZENS."

⚾ ⚾ ⚾

REFLECTING ON THE INFLUENCE DAD HAD ON HIS LIFE, BERNIE Wasser, my former basketball and baseball teammate and one of Dad's former players, said, "I played Peewee, Little League, and Babe Ruth for Tiny back in the day. Some of the best days of my life. Was also my basketball coach during my younger years. He was my coach, father figure, and one of the most inspiring men I ever knew. He was a big part of why I became a coach.* He was a major reason for the success of Peerless sports."

---

* Bernie Wasser coached the Malta Mustangs to two State Class B basketball championships in 1996 and 1998.

1977

The Young Blues Repeat as State Champions

> " *The Blues were not picked to win it, but they put it all together for the tournament with solid defense behind outstanding pitching.*
>
> —Daniels County Leader, August 4, 1977 "

PRESEASON

After Dano and I had our heart-to-heart talk about the perils of Scobey and Peerless fielding two separate Legion teams, and after I relayed that to Dad, Dad decided not to field a Legion team in Peerless. It didn't hit me at the time, but when the first day in April came when Dad, Jon, and I would normally walk down to the Peerless ball field from our house for the first spring practice . . . the day never came. That was hard. In *The Dream*, I wrote about my feelings after our last home basketball game in Peerless, my senior year in 1979. Rather than try to write something similar here, I'll reprint that text in *The Dream* because the feelings are the same: "My heart was heavy the night we played our last home game in Peerless. Part of the reason I was so sad was because I knew it was the end of an era for Dad, Jon, and me. Our lives and relationships with each other were so intertwined with basketball that it was impossible at that point to imagine our lives without it. And this game would be the last time we would go up to that venerable gym and play a game on our home court, the last time we would come back home after the game to talk about it."[134] All that's needed is to substitute the word "baseball" for "basketball" and "baseball field" for "gym" and "court," and it works. And so it was in the spring of 1977 with Dad, Jon, and me and the Peerless baseball field. After 10 seasons of walking to the field to practice, there wouldn't be another one. We were Scobey Blues now, and Doc was our coach.

There were some significant changes for the Scobey Legion team in 1977. First, the Blues became the Blues. Before 1977, the *Leader* referred to the team as the "Scobey Legion Team" or the "Legionnaires." Second, the Scobey Blues had two new batgirls—DeeAnn Lekvold and Jacki Tade—which became a unique part of the Scobey Blues baseball tradition for the next several years. DeeAnn and Jacki joined Mike Roland and Ricky Lee as batboys to form a unique ensemble supporting the team. Third, Coach Don Lekvold and his new bride JoAnn Loendorf had moved to Scobey from Wolf Point, and Don became Doc's assistant coach from 1977-1982, taking over as head coach from 1983-91. Bus driver Dick Atwood was an integral part of the team, too, and was issued a uniform to show it.

Now to the young roster, which—with an average age of 15 years and nine months—could best be described as Babe Ruth-plus. Missing on the field at Doc's first practice in April 1977 were seven 18-year-old starters from the 1976 state championship team: Mike Hagfeldt, Jeff Richardson, Greg Fjeld, Bill Bartole, Don Hagfeldt, Dale Barstad, and Craig Miller. The roster was gutted—not even the powerful 1969 team lost that many starters. That's the bad news. The good news is that seven players—the other half of the 1976 roster—were returning who had been on the field in the final game of the State B championship game in Cut Bank: Allan Audet (17), Dan Danelson (16), Wade Tryan (16), Joe Puckett (16), Jon Puckett (16), Kirby Halvorson (15), and Kelly Norman (15). Three players Dad had developed in Peerless Little League and Babe Ruth—Ray Chapman (16), Randy Stolen (15), and Bernie Wasser (15)—would also join the team, along with former Scobey Babe Ruthers Brad Henderson (16), Don Holyk (16), Mike Abar (16), and Don Boos (16). There was not an 18-year-old on the roster. The entire team would return the following year, and only one (Allan Audet) would be gone the year after.

The lineup that Doc would form would become the lineup for the next three years, except for Allan Audet, whom Greg Stolen replaced after he aged out in 1979. This was the lineup in 1977-78:

- Wade Tryan CF
- Kelly Norman 2B/P
- Joe Puckett SS/P
- Dan Danelson 3B/P
- Allan Audet RF/C
- Kirby Halvorson C/RF/P
- Randy Stolen LF/P
- Jon Puckett 3B/SS/2B/P
- Ray Chapman 1B/P

Kelly mentioned changing this lineup to Doc once, and Doc told him, "You wanna make the lineup get your own team." Kelly never mentioned the lineup to Doc again, but eventually got to coach his own team. One thing to notice on the 1977 roster is that seven players could pitch, and all seven pitchers would either win or save a game in a state tournament over the next four years. This depth at pitching was one of the strengths of this team, as someone who knew how to pitch and get outs could be brought in deep into tournaments.

One of those seven pitchers was Danny Dale Danelson. On the first day of practice in April, my eyes popped wide-open at shortstop as Doc worked on the mound with Dan. Because Dad had taken Jon and me with him on his previously planned summer vacation following the 1976 state championship—a championship Dad never thought Scobey could win (he was not alone)—I missed seeing Dan's fine pitching performances in the playoff series against Libby and the nine innings he had pitched against the Billings Royals in the State Class A tournament. He came on strong in the postseason in 1976, including his 9-2 win over Cut Bank in the state tournament, but I had not seen Dan pitch much in Little League, Babe Ruth, or Legion.

In practice, Doc was teaching Dan to be slow and deliberate in his windup, then, in the end, uncoil and explode toward the plate with his six-foot-six frame. After Dan would slowly wind up, Doc would yell, "Go, Dano!" Then Dan would unwind his long, spindly frame towards the plate. The ball just zipped. Wow. I had noticed in my career that some pitchers would be dominant in Little League and Babe Ruth but become average pitchers in Legion, but Dan was the opposite. He was a late bloomer. Dan would perfect two additional pitches—a sidearm fastball and a knuckle curve—during the 1977 season. Dan had good control and did not walk many hitters.

The next two pitchers Doc could go to were Joe and Jon Puckett. The twins were not overpowering pitchers but mixed our fastballs in with curveballs and sliders to keep hitters off balance, so our fastballs seemed faster than they were, and we could sneak them by hitters. Perhaps most importantly, we had good control and could throw our breaking balls for strikes when we were behind in the count. Because we had good fielders behind us, balls put in play usually resulted in outs, and we did not issue many walks. This reduction in walks and errors, even with fewer strikeouts, allowed Jon and I to generally avoid big innings, as there was less traffic on the bases when hits were allowed. Andy Stolen from Glentana taught Jon and me how to throw our breaking balls.

Kelly Norman was the fourth pitcher in the rotation. His strength was that he would never give in to a hitter. I knew this first-hand as I had batted against him in Little League and Babe Ruth. Nothing was left out over the plate, and no ball that didn't have some form of movement on it came toward the plate. He would never give hitters anything good to hit. Because he never gave in to hitters, he would walk many hitters, but he didn't allow a lot of extra-base hits, so often those baserunners would get left on base. With any count, he mostly threw curveballs and sliders, constantly keeping hitters off balance. Kelly's most significant contribution to the team on the mound was his performance in big games when he was at his best. Kelly was the winning pitcher in three state championship games and pitched a big win against Kalispell in the 1979 State Class A tournament.

Ray Chapman, the only left-hander on the Doc's staff, was a knuckleballer taught by Andy Stolen. When Ray got his knuckleball going, he was tough to hit. Ray also kept hitters off-balance with a curveball. He rarely threw his fastball for a strike but tried to get hitters to chase it because their eyes would light up if they saw anything traveling toward the plate that wasn't hopping around. Ray was a very effective pitcher when he established his knuckleball. Ray was throwing a knuckleball when Andy Stolen taught him how to perfect it. Ray recalls, "Growing up, I'd been a huge fan of Wilbur Wood, who at that time pitched for the Chicago White Sox. I found it amazing that he could make a baseball do such things on that 60' 6" journey to home plate: it fluttered and floated, it dropped, it went sideways and back again. I wanted to make a baseball do that. So I began throwing knuckleballs every time I threw the ball, always. I must have already thrown it thousands of times by the time Andy saw me attempting the pitch. Little did I know that Andy had made his name in the semipro and independent leagues years before as an incredible knuckleball pitcher. Our exchange went something like this:

"What are you doing there, Ray?"

"I'm throwing a knuckleball."

"With your knuckles?"

"Well, yeah, that's the name of the pitch, right?"

"You ever try throwing it with just your index and middle fingers, pushing the ball off with those two fingernails at once?"

"Uh . . . no."

"Try it . . ."

Randy Stolen, who had a cannon for an arm in left field, would be the first to tell you that he could pitch, but he wasn't a pitcher. But if he could get his fastball over the plate, I don't remember many hitters catching up with it. Because his delivery was straight over the top, he would miss either high or low if he missed. Mostly high. There were many swings and misses on high fastballs. He could be overpowering. Like Kelly, though, he would walk many hitters. Like Ray, if he could establish his out pitch, he would be a very effective pitcher.

Kirby Halvorson could pitch, too. Like Randy, he had a strong arm. He also had a good curveball. I don't remember Kirby or Randy pitching much in 1977-79, but they would come in and get outs when called on. In 1980, after Dan, Joe, Jon, and Ray left the team, Randy and Kirby would have to step up on the mound to round out Doc's staff, and they did. But in 1977-79, our team was strongest with Randy in left field and Kirby or Allan behind the plate, with someone else on the mound.

Our defense might have been the greatest strength of the 1977-79 teams. The team was solid at every position. With several pitch-to-contact pitchers, most outs would come from balls put in play. The steady play of Scobey's fielders resulted in wins in big games, as strikeouts were not needed to get outs. There was depth at catcher, as Kirby Halvorson and Allan Audet had powerful arms and good gloves behind the plate. Wade Tryan, who had played third base in 1976, was moved to center field when the three infielders from Peerless arrived. This was a better position for him because his speed was exploited there. Although his arm wasn't the strongest, Wade was fast and would chase down many balls for outs in center field. Randy in left field and Allan in right field were also fast and had cannons for arms. Those outfielders got many outs on assists to the infield and home plate.

Middle infielders Joe and Jon Puckett and Ray Chapman (first base) had ball after ball swatted at them by Tiny Puckett in Peerless since they were six years old. Ray prided himself on his defense. In addition to scooping up every grounder that came his way, Ray saved many errors by scooping ground balls in the dirt on throws, although several balls would get over his head due to his five-foot-nine height. Since Ray was now our first baseman, Dan Danelson moved to third base, following in his older brother Rick's footsteps. Dan would play first when Ray pitched.

Somehow, Jon became the utility fielder when everyone else pitched. He would play short when I pitched, third when Dan pitched, second when Kelly pitched, left field when Randy pitched, and sometimes catch when Kirby pitched. In one state tournament, Jon played six different positions. Finally, the steady, make-every-routine-play second baseman was Kelly Norman. Born to play second base was Kelly.

For hitting, everyone in the lineup could hit for average, but wall-banging, over-the-fence power came only from deeper in the lineup, from Allan Audet, Kirby Halvorson, and Randy Stolen, in the five, six, and seven slots. Other hitters in the lineup got stronger after 15 and 16 years old, but none were power hitters. This power deeper in the lineup made it difficult for opposing pitchers, as they couldn't let up. Run production could come at any part of the lineup.

The toughest out in the lineup might have been Ray Chapman in the number-nine slot. Pitchers would labor to get him out. Although stats were not kept, Ray likely had the team's highest on-base percentage (OBP). Ray would take many pitches—often two strikes without swinging—and then would foul pitches off because he had good bat control, often extending at-bats to six pitches, full counts, and walks. Sitting in the dugout, I would watch the opposing pitchers struggle, and, as a pitcher myself, would feel sorry for them when Ray somehow, someway, after several pitches, would get on base. The lineup would wrap back to the top with Wade Tryan and the pitcher was exhausted from battling the ninth-place hitter in the lineup.

Kelly had good bat control, too, and was a good bunter, which made him perfect for the number two position in the lineup, with speedy Wade Tryan at leadoff. Doc would often hit-and-run with Kelly hitting in the two spot. With Wade on first, Kelly would square to bunt, see who was covering second on Wade's steal, pull back the bat, and slap the ball to the side of the infield vacated by the shortstop or second baseman covering second for the throw. Often, Wade would end up at third and Kelly on first. Doc would also have Kelly bunt and run. Wade would steal, and Kelly would bunt. If the throw went to first, Wade would continue to third and often end up there with a two-base sacrifice by Kelly. I miss the hit-and-run in baseball. You don't see it much anymore.

For baserunning, most everyone in the lineup could steal a base when needed, but only Wade Tryan and Randy Stolen possessed exceptional, lightning-fast speed. Our three outfielders, Randy, Wade, and Allan (also catcher) were fast, as it should be. Doc was extremely aggressive on the bases with this team, and runners were constantly moving.

So that was basically the team for the next three years. After Doc trained us in April and May, the young team was ready for the regular season and to learn some lessons along the way.

REGULAR SEASON

GLASGOW HAD A GOOD TEAM AGAIN IN 1977 AND REPEATED as champions in the northeastern district with a 14-2 record. The last time Glasgow had won the district title was in 1952 under coaches Bunky and Sully Sullivan, when they won three consecutive district titles. Several players on Glasgow's 1976 team, including 18-year-old left-handed pitcher and power hitter Al Hopstad, had returned for another season. But their pitching fell off a cliff after Al Hopstad, so they weren't a threat to win a tournament. The 1977 team was again well-coached by Mark Yoakam.

We finished 11-5 in the conference for second place in the northeastern district. As the season progressed, we continued to improve as a team and play better baseball. Good teams, like good relationships, take time to grow. When the team picture was taken in June, the *Leader* wrote, "The team this year has about the lowest age ever, but the kids are coming along well."[135] At that point, our conference record was 4-1.

Since the theme here is how the young team was learning and growing, I will talk a little bit more about the losses rather than the wins, as we had much more to learn from losses than wins. In the regular season, we had 8-5 and 2-0 nonconference losses to Sidney—an excellent team from the southern district. In the 2-0 loss at home to Sidney, Kelly Norman pitched a four-hitter and went the distance, but he was outpitched by Sidney's Jeff Nesper, who pitched a two-hit shutout. We committed only one error in the game. In the 8-5 loss in Sidney, I hit a three-run home run to pull us to within 6-5, but Sidney scored two runs late to salt it away.

Like Scobey, Wolf Point's roster was decimated in 1977, losing several key players from the powerful 1976 team. However, several strong players had returned, including Jerry Moran and Rick McGeshick (two players involved in the 1976 barroom brawl in Cut Bank), Grant Boysun, Mike Neubauer, Kip Harcharik, and Bill Zimmer. We lost 3-2 to Wolf Point in 12 innings at Wolf Point. I pitched well and went all 12 innings (you'd be surprised how many pitchers can say that back then), but Wolf Point pushed the winning run across in the bottom of the 12th inning to walk it off. This was an extremely well-played game by both teams in Wolf Point, as each team committed only one error in 12 innings.

We also lost to Wolf Point in Scobey when Rick McGeshick hit a game-winning home run for Wolf Point in the later innings. We later beat Wolf Point 5-4 at Wolf Point, as Jon Puckett went the distance, scattering eight hits. Two other conference losses were 9-5 and 3-2 to Glasgow. In the 3-2 loss to Glasgow, Dan Danelson pitched a four-hitter but took the loss against strong left-hander Al Hopstad, who pitched a five-hitter. We played errorless ball in the game. Our fifth conference loss was to Plentywood at home. Plentywood had a good team in 1977, with players like Brent Leibach from Medicine Lake and Randy Wangerin from Outlook, and other good athletes from across Sheridan County on the team, like Mike Anderson, Larry Berland, and Cory Benson.

If there was a silver lining in Scobey's close regular season losses, it would be that the young pitching arms and gloves were doing well. During the regular season, six different Scobey starting pitchers posted wins, including a one-hit shutout by Jon Puckett in an 18-0 win against Poplar. Doc was developing and using all his pitchers to prep for the tournaments. In the field, the box scores would often show only one or no errors. The *Leader* was aware of how important good defense was to winning and would always mention the errors in the game recaps. And the young bats started to come alive too, as in the final week of the regular season, Scobey exploded for 17 runs on 15 hits against Glasgow to hand them their first loss of the season, 17-6.

A highlight of the 1977 regular season was a doubleheader against Browning on the Fourth of July in Scobey. Don Paulson had led Browning to its first-ever state tournament appearance in 1976, and Browning came to Scobey to play on the Fourth of July in 1977. What is more American than a doubleheader on the Fourth of July? I remember how special it was playing that day. We swept the doubleheader in two well-played games, but Browning had a good team. We expected to see the scrappy Browning Indians team back at Scobey for the state tournament later that month, and we did, as they again qualified for the state tournament.

Finally, no recap of the 1977 regular season would be complete without mentioning a towering home surrendered by Kirby Halvorson in Scobey's 6-3 win over Poplar in Poplar. If you ever get the opportunity, ask Kirby about it sometime. No player has received more grief through the years from his teammates than Kirby giving up that home run. Jon Puckett was catching, so maybe he should receive part of the blame for calling the pitch?

Heading into the eastern divisional tournament at Moose Memorial Park in Sidney, the top four teams in the northern district were Glasgow (14-2), Scobey (11-5), Plentywood

(9-5), and Wolf Point (6-10). The top four teams (in order of finish) from the southern district were Sidney, Glendive, Baker-Ekalaka, and Circle. Sidney and Glendive were the top two teams in the south again.

DIVISIONAL TOURNAMENT

OUR FIRST GAME OF THE EASTERN DIVISIONAL TOURNAMENT in Sidney was against Baker-Ekalaka. Doc handed me the ball to pitch, as he had done a year earlier at the eastern divisional in Glendive.

Warming up before the first pitch, I oddly felt like an experienced veteran, even though I was only 16 years old. The experience I had the previous year as a 15-year-old calmed my nerves, as I had pitched in the Eastern Divisional Legion Tournament before, getting the 4-2 win over Glendive. I had also pitched two games—including a no-hitter—and 16 innings in the Eastern Divisional Babe Ruth Tournament on this same field the year before in 1976, so I was familiar with the mound and the field. I liked playing in Moose Memorial Park. It had a nice grass infield, a quaint grandstand for fans to watch the games, and lights for night games. Fans came to watch the games, too. Sidney was a great baseball town. And Sidney had a good team in 1977.

We beat Baker-Ekalaka 8-3. I pitched eight innings to get the win, and Doc brought Jon in the ninth inning to close it out. Dan Danelson had a triple to lead our hitting. Our next game was against Sidney, the champion from the south, who had beaten us twice in nonconference games earlier in the season. Sidney had beaten Wolf Point 10-7 in their first game to advance. I remember our team being emotionally up for this game, playing a good Sidney on their home field, knowing that if we won, we would advance

Joe Puckett pitching and Jon Puckett playing shortstop against Baker-Ekalaka, 1977 Eastern Divisional Tournament, Sidney. *Family photo.*

to the undefeated semifinal. Doc pitched Dano in the big game. We jumped out strong in the top of the first inning, as Wade led us off with a single, Kelly sacrificed him to second, and I drove him home with a single to left. We followed with another run that inning. In the second inning, we scored five runs to take a 7-1 lead. Then, in the fifth, Allan Audet clubbed a solo home run to expand our lead to 10-2, and we never looked back, winning 11-4. Sidney committed four errors in the game, which led to several unearned runs. Our defense was good again, as we committed only one error in the game. In addition to Audet's home run, Wade Tryan was 3 for 4 at the plate, including a double. Dan pitched well, recording 10 strikeouts and walking only three in nine innings to get the complete-game win. Sidney did get nine hits, but our defense and Dan's strikeouts kept their runs in check.

Dedicated Scobey fans at the 1977 Eastern Divisional Tournament.

That put us in the undefeated semifinal against Glendive, who had beaten Plentywood 11-4 and Glasgow 8-5 to advance. Glendive withstood 13 strikeouts from Al Hopstad and scored three runs in the eighth inning to beat Glasgow, the number-one seed from the north. Glendive had a good team in 1977, as they had finished second behind Sidney in the south.

Prior to our undefeated semifinal game against Glendive on Saturday, Baker-Ekalaka had eliminated a good Glasgow team 9-8, and Sidney had eliminated a good Plentywood team by the identical score of 9-8, which secured state tournament berths for Baker-Ekalaka and Sidney. With Wolf Point, Glasgow, and Plentywood eliminated, that meant Scobey was the only team from the north to qualify for the state tournament, which was extremely rare. But there was much more to the story in Sidney's 9-8 win over Plentywood.

As Dick Atwood was parking our bus after we arrived at Moose Memorial Park for the Glendive game, I noticed the Plentywood team filtering out of the park, but they were animated. It was not a peaceful exodus. They were hot. I mean, raging, maniacal, steaming-hot mad. As we got off the bus and walked toward the grandstand, several of the Plentywood players were screaming and yelling back at the stadium, or just into the hot summer air, or to anyone who would listen. I heard several expletives, followed by "umpires." Randy Wangerin was the hottest of them all. He came up to me and explained, trying to control himself through his heaving chest and heavy breathing. I had never seen him this upset before. What had happened was this: He had smacked a home run to left center, but as he was rounding the bases—or maybe even after he had rounded them—the third base umpire negated the home run and all the runs that scored because he had called timeout prior to the pitch being delivered, as a ball had landed on the field from the bullpen. The home run—and the runs—were wiped off the board, and Wangerin had to return to the plate to hit, where he went out, and Plentywood lost the game. I now understood why they were so hot. They felt they had been homered on Sidney's home field. Had Plentywood won that game, Sidney, the number-one seed from the south, would have been eliminated, and Plentywood would have qualified for state the following week. That's a helluva way to end a season. Normally, flags get thrown on football fields, and plays get called back, but not so much in baseball. Wangerin's home run for Plentywood would have been their third in the game, as Brent Leibach and Cory Benson had already homered in the game.

Doc started Kelly against Glendive, and he was pitching okay (keep in mind, he was 15 years old) against the strong Glendive team, but we had a letdown in this game defensively—making five errors—not typical for us. Glendive seized on the errors and several extra-base hits, including a home run by Mike Jones, a triple by Terry Hood, and a double by Doug Frenzel, to score several runs early and win going away, 17-7, embarrassing us with the 10-run mercy rule in the seventh inning. Doc conceded the game after we got behind 13-2 in the fifth, knowing we had at least one more game to play the next day. After pitching eight innings against Baker-Ekalaka on the first day of the tournament, then playing shortstop the next day, my arm was a little sore, but Doc put me in to relieve Kelly midway in the game, saving Jon for the next day, as Jon had only pitched one inning in the tournament and was fresh. Our team had never been humiliated like that before, let alone in a big game. "Everything seemed to go wrong for the Blues in this game."[136] We did hit well, as we had 11 hits, including doubles by Wade Tryan, Joe Puckett, and Randy Stolen, and Kirby Halvorson was 3 for 4, but it wasn't nearly enough, as Glendive took it to us. But that's baseball. It was just one game, and the sun would rise again the next day.

Our embarrassing loss to Glendive on Saturday pushed us to the championship play-in game with Sidney on Sunday. Sidney had come back through the loser's bracket after we beat them and had beaten Plentywood 9-8 and Baker-Ekalaka 17-7.

Doc started Jon against Sidney, and he pitched extremely well. I was playing shortstop, and I noticed that Jon's confidence in his breaking ball and the velocity of his fastball were better than I had ever seen before. Pitching has everything to do with confidence—knowing your pitch is going to be effective *before* you throw it—and Jon had it, finishing with 12 strikeouts. He was getting ahead of hitters, and his control was close to perfect, as he wasn't walking any hitters. Jon's confident, efficient, and effective pitching would carry over to the state tournament, which started four days later in Scobey.

We were leading 2-0 in the sixth, but Sidney rallied for five runs—including a double by Jay Nesper—to break up Jon's shutout and take a 5-2 lead. Jay's double was Sidney's only extra-base hit of the game. In the seventh, Allan Audet blasted his second home run of the tournament, a two-run shot to deep left center, pulling us to within 5-4. Our defense was back to form in this game, as we committed only one error, and Jon pitched three more shutout innings in the seventh, eighth, and ninth to keep us close, so we entered the bottom of the ninth trailing 5-4. Sidney got Wade and Kelly on two quick outs, and our dugout was silent when I came up. But I managed to hit a single

Doc Norman at the 1977 Eastern Divisional Tournament, Sidney. *George Puckett photo.*

between third and short to become the tying run on first base and keep us alive.

That brought Allan Audet to the plate. Our dugout had come back to life now as Allan was swinging a hot bat—a bat that had power. But with two outs, Doc wanted to get the tying run to second, so after I got on first base, I immediately picked him up in the third base coaching box, and sure enough, the steal sign came. Skin-on-skin indicator, washing his hands, followed by his hand to hat, chin, chest—down to second for the steal. I was going. With two outs, Allan was not taking a pitch, so he could be swinging on the first pitch if he liked it, which meant I might be able to score on a long single to tie the game.

Tom Paladichuk was pitching for Sidney as he relieved starting pitcher Jeff Lebsock in the fifth. Allan hit his two-run home run off him in the seventh. Closely eyeing Paladichuk, I quickly shuffled off the base, then slowly extended my lead. Tom knew I could run and did not want to allow the tying run to get on second base in this situation. He quickly snapped a throw to first, but I dove back in safely, got up, dusted myself off, and we did it again. I got back easily, so this time, after he came set, I extended my lead a little more. Then, after coming to the set position, Tom became completely still on the mound. He froze. And for a moment in time, I froze, too. The field seemed to fall into complete silence as I became mesmerized by the pause. I thought Allan would step out and call time, but he didn't. I started to lean toward second, anticipating the pitch, and just as I did, Tom spun and fired a fastball strike to first base. I was leaning and couldn't get back in time—I knew I was dead before I even dove back to the base. Picked off. Third out. Game over. Go home. I had taken the bat out of our hottest hitter's hands. There was no joy in Scobey, for Mighty Casey had . . . not even got a chance to bat.

As we gathered our stuff, left the dugout, and got on the bus for the long, quiet, somber ride to Scobey, no one said anything to me—no one had to. I could see the disappointment in their eyes, but no one was more disappointed than I was. I knew better than to get picked off in that situation. There is no greater feeling in sports than to make a great play that leads to a victory, with all your teammates celebrating your contribution—and there is no worse feeling than making a bonehead play and causing the team to lose. Their silence spoke louder than any words could have cut. I almost wished someone would have said, "Goddammit, Joe, what were you thinking?" but no one did. They didn't have to. So, almost fifty years later, I'll say to myself, "Goddammit, Joe, what were you thinking?"

The bus ride home on Sunday afternoon after the Sidney game was unusually quiet. After winning our first two games, we faltered against Glendive and Sidney, finishing third in the tournament. As Dick Atwood navigated the bus home, I sat in my seat and watched the beautiful prairie of eastern Montana roll past my window like a scenic movie.

I started to reflect. When the pain of the loss began to wear off, and as I started the process of forgiving myself for the unforgivable mistake, my thoughts pivoted to the future rather than the past. We were headed home to Scobey, to "Baseball Country." And in four days, I would play in my first state tournament on our home field. People from all over Daniels County would come to watch us play. I had vivid memories of the four previous state tournaments in Scobey: Danny Wolfe's game-saving catch at home plate in the state championship game against Havre in 1969; Terry Puckett and Dave Fanning's 1-0 pitcher's duel in 1971; Wolf Point's Carmen Birdsbill slamming the door on Scobey in the ninth inning of the first state championship game in 1973; and Mike Hagfeldt and Barry Kato's 1-0 pitcher's duel in 1975. I had memories of watching my three older cousins, Dick, Terry, and Don Puckett, playing in those games, and each of them winning a state championship. Now, I would be making my own memories playing on that field. I got goosebumps thinking about it. By the time we got to Scobey, I was ready to put on my uniform and play the first game of the state tournament. What loss against Sidney? What pickoff play? What third-place finish? What mercy-rule loss to Glendive?

The sun would rise the next day. And in four days, it would rise on the state tournament in Scobey, where a young but talented team would try to repeat as state champions and hand Doc his fourth state championship in front of our hometown fans. Could it be done?

STATE B TOURNAMENT

THE STATE TOURNAMENT IN SCOBEY BEGAN ON THURSDAY, four days after our last game against Sidney at Moose Memorial Park on Sunday. Those practices in Scobey on Monday, Tuesday, and Wednesday leading up to our first game on Thursday were special. There is a different feel to practice in the postseason. The focus is there, of course, but there is also more excitement and fun. You know the next game you play isn't some regular season game that might not mean much—it's the state tournament. The repetitive grind of taking infield and batting practice isn't so repetitive. Playing in any state tournament is an incredible experience, but hosting one, playing in front of your fans in

Daniels County—referred to as "Baseball Country" by Jack Reiner in the *Leader* on the first day of the state tournament in 1969—makes it even more special. I had seen the previous four state tournaments in Scobey in 1969, 1971, 1973, and 1975 and remembered how loud the crowd could get. That's what I was looking forward to the most.

One of my favorite things about practice was shagging balls in the outfield during batting practice. Players would form separate clusters and discuss things teenage boys would discuss, including music. Many sports memories I have are associated with music. For example, after we clinched Peerless's first conference basketball championship in 1979, I was listening to Toto's "Hold the Line" on the bus. Whenever I hear that song, I have that wonderful memory. In one of the outfield clusters at practice that week, I brought up Fleetwood Mac's new *Rumours* album, but Wade Tryan quickly switched the conversation to girls—specifically Stevie Nicks. I learned that night that Wade *really* had a crush on Stevie Nicks but didn't care so much for her music. In his own words, Wade professed his undying love for Stevie Nicks that night, and try as I may, it's hard for me to shake Wade's words—and the image they form in my mind—when I listen to *Rumours*, my favorite album. Thank you for that, Wade. Not sure it ever would have worked out with Wade and Stevie—he didn't like her music. It seemed . . . more physical for him.

The 1977 state tournament was the fifth for Scobey as host. On the first day of the tournament on Thursday, the *Daniels County Leader*, as it always did, welcomed the eight teams to "Baseball Country," trumpeted their arrival, and previewed the tournament. The *Leader* stated that Scobey first hosted the state tournament in 1969 and that "because of the fine attendance and all-around tournament then, has been the host alternate years since."[137]

The *Leader* announced that, in order of finish in the western divisional, the four teams were the Great Falls Vigilantes, Cut Bank Lobos, Great Falls Sparkies, and Browning Indians. From the east, it was the Glendive Blue Devils, Sidney (Richland County) Patriots, Scobey Blues, and Baker-Ekalaka Legion team. Baker-Ekalaka was making its first state tournament appearance since 1971 in Scobey. Glendive trounced Sidney 14-1 to win the east, as Sidney ran out of pitching. Doug Frenzel pitched a four-hitter and struck out 15 Patriots. What was notable about the four teams from the east was who *wasn't* there: Glasgow, Wolf Point, and Plentywood—three good teams—were all eliminated at the divisional in Sidney by the teams from the south.

There was no clear favorite in the tournament, but Glendive, who had mercy-ruled Scobey (17-7) and Sidney (14-1) in the eastern divisional, would have to be considered. Also, Sidney, as they had won the southern district regular season for the second consecutive year and had beaten Scobey 3 out of 4 times that season. In the west, the Vigilantes went undefeated in the tournament and beat Cut Bank 4-3 in the championship to earn the number-one seed.

Browning was once again a surprise, as they upset Missoula and Butte to reach their second state tournament berth in as many years after never before qualifying.

The first-round matchups on Thursday were Sidney vs. Sparkies, Vigilantes vs. Baker-Ekalaka, Glendive vs. Browning, and Scobey vs. Cut Bank. I remember driving into Scobey with Jon in our 1972 light-blue Ford Pinto station wagon—nicknamed "The Shark"—listening to Boston's "More than a Feeling," "Long Time," and "Peace of Mind" on the 8-track tape. We often listened to Boston, driving to and from Scobey that summer. I was nervous and excited to play in my first state tournament game, a night game under the lights. We had a pregame meeting with the team at Doc's house before going to the field for the Cut Bank game. Wonder what Doc would say to us?

Doc, as he addressed the team, was calm but firm. His voice commanded attention, and all fourteen players hung on to his every word; I know I did. He said, "You're young but talented, and you've played more baseball than any of these other boys. Play to your potential, and you will win this tournament." His speech went on but had the same theme: he told us to forget how young we were and focus on how much baseball we had played, how good we were, and that we were better than the other teams. It wasn't, "You're young, nobody expects you to win, just do your best, etc."; it was, "You're good, you're experienced, you've played more ball, play like you can, shoot Scobey baseball and go take it." I remember leaving the house feeling confident but still nervous about the game and the tournament.

As we arrived at the field, the first thing that struck me was the crowd. The grandstand was packed, as were bleachers on both sides of the field. Cars lined both sides, too. People came to see baseball in Scobey. This was the tournament's first night, so all eight teams were there. Another thing I noticed was former Legion players, like Rod Tande, Phil Audet, Danny Wolfe, Rocky Ware, Danny Wang, Dana Audet, and others, were there. Dick Puckett was umpiring. Rod Tande had played on Doc's first Scobey team in 1959; Phil Audet led Scobey to its first state tournament appearance in 1967. Rod and Phil assisted

Doc in coaching many of the teams after their Legion playing days were over. Danny Wolfe, Danny Wang, Rocky Ware, and Dana Audet had played on previous state championship teams. There were many other former Legion players there as well. Although many of these men were small in stature, I was walking in the shadow of giants. I noticed—and felt—their presence.

So did Ray Chapman. Ray recalls the presence of these former Legion players this way: "I was *very* aware of the former Legion players being all around us, supporting us, helping us, cheering us on, encouraging us to do better, to do our best. I remember Rocky Ware, Danny Wang, Danny Wolfe, and so many others there, near the dugout, in the stands, of course, Cliff up in the announcer's booth, too, all of them everywhere. Along with all the other fans, they were all there with us and carrying us. We didn't win that thing alone. The entire community carried us and lifted us and moved us to be better, to be the best, and we responded in kind by giving everything we had and then some. Our team was not just the players on the field or coaches in the dugout; it was not simply a team trying to win a baseball tournament, it was a community working together, encouraging each other, making each other better, collectively helping a group of kids to grow into young men and, in turn, both then and now I hope we reflected to the world the incredible community from which we came. I also hope we did them proud and met their measure."

Doc started Jon against Cut Bank. He was pitching with confidence, with good velocity on his fastball, a sharp-breaking curveball, and excellent control. In his last outing against Sidney three days earlier, he had struck out 12 Patriots and had only one bad inning. Cut Bank countered with Wayne Slezak, their ace, who had pitched a three-hitter in the 1976 state tournament in Cut Bank.

This game turned into a tense pitcher's duel. Cut Bank got to Jon for one run—their only run of the game—in the top of the first. Miles Lewis led off with a single, Doug Ray was safe on an error, and Chuck Olmstead singled to load the bases. It was not a great start, as the first three hitters reached base. Mark Lewis hit a sacrifice fly to score Ray, but Jon got out of the inning without further damage. After that, inning by inning, the score remained 1-0 as Jon Puckett and Wayne Slezak hung goose egg after goose egg on the scoreboard. It wasn't easy playing from behind the entire game, even though it was only one run.

Jon's pitching—and two huge defensive plays—kept us in the game. With two outs and a baserunner on, Randy Stolen chased down a long drive to the left-field corner. The ball was hit so hard the Cut Bank third base coach was yelling for the ball to "get out of here!" I was running out to left field to receive what I thought would be a cutoff throw from Randy to try to cut the runner down at the plate. I saw the ball arching toward the left-field corner. Randy was on a dead spring to get it, but it didn't look like he had a chance. Then, at the very end, already at a full sprint, he seemed to accelerate, closed on the ball, reached out with his glove fully extended, and speared the ball with his backhand on a dead run, his momentum almost carrying him into the fence. The ball was hit so deep I was way out in left field for the cutoff, so I had a front-row seat to see Randy's catch. Even as his teammate, I marveled at his athleticism, his speed—out three. No runs. Game-saving catch. The crowd's roar was electrifying as I ran back into the dugout to hit.

There was also a close play at the plate in the later innings, where a Cut Bank runner was called out on a throw from the infield and tagged out by Kirby Halvorson, who was blocking the plate. The crowd erupted as Kirby's tag kept the score 1-0. Jon's fine pitching and two stellar defensive plays kept us in the game, but we needed to get a run to tie it.

That run came in the eighth inning. Wayne Slezak had scattered four hits over the first seven innings to hold the one-run lead scored by Doug Ray in the first inning. Jerry Chadwich relieved Slezak in the eighth, as Slezak's back hurt throughout the game, and he could not continue. We rallied for the tying run in the bottom of the eighth to tie the score 1-1, scoring on a base on balls and a bad hop grounder that bounced over Brian Ledbetter's head—the only error of the game for Cut Bank. Jon shut down Cut Bank again with three quick outs in the top of the ninth—his eighth consecutive shutout inning after the single run Cut Bank scored in the first. So, we entered the bottom of the ninth with a chance to walk it off on our home field, in front of our home fans, and advance in the tournament.

With one out, I came up to bat and quickly got behind 0-2, but on the third pitch, I managed to get my bat on a good pitch on the outside of the plate to loft a fly ball down the right-field line. I rarely hit the ball to the right side—I was mainly a pull hitter—but with two strikes, I was protecting the plate. I could see the ball was arching to the right down the line, but it was going to land fair, so I was on a dead sprint out of the box, knowing that if I could make it a double, I would become the tying run on second with one out. I decided I was going to second before I rounded first base; I'm not sure if first-base coach Don Lekvold was waving me on. I made it into second safely on a head-first slide and popped up, ready for what would come next.

Dano was up next but was retired, which brought Allan Audet to the plate with two outs. Allan was our Mighty Casey at the bat. This was who we wanted up to the plate in this situation. He was our oldest player at 17 years old and our fiery leader. Still, on second base with two outs, I advanced to third on a wild pitch, which brought me 90 feet closer to the winning run. Come on, Albert! Their infield was back with two outs, so Allan needed to punch a ball to the outfield to get me home. On the next pitch, Allan laced a sharp line-drive single to left field. I knew I would score as soon as he hit it, so I hopped and galloped home with the winning run, racing to beat my teammates to home plate, who were all pouring out of the dugout to greet me there. The crowd erupted as my teammates swarmed me at home plate. What a moment! Allan had come through again in the clutch. We walked it off. Blues win! Blues win! Never in my wildest dreams did I think my first game in the state tournament at Scobey would end like that.

Jon's magnificent four-hitter, two huge defensive plays by Randy and Kirby, and Allan's clutch, two-out RBI single to walk it off in the bottom of the ninth had advanced us with the 2-1 win. Wow. What a start to the state tournament. Could we keep it going the next night?

In other opening-day action, the Sparkies edged Sidney 2-1, forcing Sidney through the dirt route for the remainder of the tournament. The Sparkies scored their two runs in the third inning off three consecutive singles. Sidney scored a run in the sixth but was unable to threaten after that. Fred Peres got the win for Great Falls, while Jeff Nesper and Jeff Lebsock pitched for Sidney, with Nesper taking the loss. The Vigilantes capitalized on five Baker-Ekalaka errors to win 10-6. The Vigilantes took a 7-1 lead after four innings, putting the game out of reach.

Glendive scored three unearned runs in the seventh inning to break up a 2-2 pitcher's duel to beat Browning 5-2. Doug Frenzel pitched a four-hitter for Glendive.

Glendive's win against Browing set up our next game with them on Friday night. The team met again at Doc's house, and his message was the same: relax and play baseball as you know how. Doc handed the ball to Dan Danelson to pitch while Glendive countered with Craig Ballantine, their second-best pitcher after Doug Frenzel, who had pitched the opener against Browing. One odd thing about this game was that we were in the first base dugout, which felt strange. It was the only time we were in the first base dugout in the state tournaments I played in.

There was an electric buzz at the ballpark before the game, a low hum, and I could feel it. We were also hyper-focused and emotionally up as a team. The team we were playing, Glendive, had mercy-ruled us a few days earlier in Sidney. At his house at the pregame meeting, Doc told us to forget about that and play this game, but we didn't forget about it.

As happened the night before against Cut Bank, we found ourselves behind early, as Glendive got to Dano for single runs in the second inning and fifth innings to take a 2-0 lead. We were playing well in the field—we committed only one error in the game—and he was pitching brilliantly, stepping up big in the big game as he always did. But we were struggling again at the plate, as Craig Ballantine, who had a good fastball, was also pitching well for Glendive. After five innings, we trailed 2-0. We had yet to score a run before the eighth inning in the tournament.

But Dano's steady pitching and our solid defense were keeping us in the game.

Then, in the top of the sixth, we broke through for the first time in the tournament. We got baserunners on, and then the big blow came on a bases-loaded, two-out, two-run hit to left by Jon Puckett. Sitting in the first base dugout, I saw the hit clearly: a sinking line drive to left center. The Glendive left fielder got to the ball, got his glove on it, and slipped to the ground. I couldn't see if he caught it, but I saw the ball dribble away from him on the ground to his left. It was a hit and then an error. When I saw the ball hit the ground, I knew two runs would score.

And the crowd knew, too. Waiting for something to cheer about the entire game, they suddenly came alive, and a roar rocked the field. It was the loudest I had ever heard the crowd at a state tournament game I played in. When all the dust settled, we had rallied for four runs in the inning to take a 4-2 lead and sprinted back onto the field for the bottom of the sixth inning to play defense. After playing from behind the entire tournament, we were finally playing with the lead, which made a huge difference psychologically.

Dano's solid pitching continued, and our defense kept getting outs, putting zeroes on the board for Glendive in the sixth, seventh, and eighth innings. Meanwhile, we scored a single run in the eighth, then a precious insurance run—this would be huge—in the ninth to take a 6-2 lead into the bottom of the ninth. Three more outs, and we would be moving on to the undefeated semifinal against the Vigilantes. With Dano in cruise control on the mound, we were confident we could get three quick outs and get off the field with a win.

But the ninth inning turned out to be the tensest ending to a game I ever played in. Glendive got a couple of baserunners on and, with two outs, scored a run to close to 6-3. But Dano was still in control and looked confident on the mound. Then, with two outs and two on, the tying run came to the plate. He hit a lazy pop-up toward right field behind second base. I breathed a sigh of relief at shortstop when I saw the soft hit because it was hit high and looked like Kelly could get under it for the third out. Allan was running in from right field, but it looked like it was Kelly's ball to catch. Then, at the last moment, Kelly heard Allan yell, "Kelly!" Kelly peeled off from the pop-up, and the ball plopped on the ground between him and Allan. I was seduced by the laziness of the pop-up, which seemed so harmless when hit and hanging in the air but was deadly when it landed, exploding like a bomb. I was mad at Kelly because it looked like he quit on the ball, but I didn't know Allan had called him off. Kelly recalls, "I took a lot of heat for that play, but we were taught if you hear the outfielder, peel off, so I did." Part of that heat came from me. It looked like Kelly quit on the ball, but I didn't know Allan called him off.

Two runs scored on the bloop single, making the score 6-5, and now the tying run was at first, and the winning run was coming to the plate. What would have been the third out—and the end of the game—ended up being a two-run single. The game's tenor instantly switched from cruise control to a rollercoaster ride.

But the heat Kelly got from me was nothing like the heat he got from Dano's "death stare." Dan was visibly upset about the play. In complete control up to that point—a machine delivering a menu of pitches to Kirby with precision—the machine broke down. The next pitch delivered was wild. He was not the same pitcher. He had lost control, both his temper and his pitches. Oh no.

The next two hitters walked, loading the bases, with the tying run at third and the winning at second. The next two pitches were balls, and the count was quickly 2-0. We were two more balls away from blowing a four-run lead. Then Doc slowly walked out to the mound to make the change in the middle of the count. He had done that the year before in Cut Bank when he brought me in on a 3-0 count to Mike Neubauer in the state championship game. Doc would bring in Jon and me in those situations because he knew we were control pitchers and could deliver strikes, and the last thing we wanted was the tying run to walk home from third. Which Puckett would Doc call in? I was standing at short, thinking it would be me because Jon had pitched nine innings the day before against Cut Bank. I stepped toward the mound, fully expecting Doc to wave me in. But he summoned Jon at third. Doc's instincts were always right. Jon was pitching the best I'd ever seen him pitch—before or since—and Doc saw it, too. Jon seemed eager to take the ball from Doc, and Dano—still fuming from the drastic turn of events—exchanged places with Jon at third.

The Glendive hitter stepped in. It was so tense because if even one pitch delivered by Jon were off the plate, the count would go to three balls, with no margin for error on the next pitch, as a base on balls would walk in the tying run. Jon remembers the sequence: "Doc brought me in on a 2-0 count. My arm never felt more alive. I threw a fastball for a strike, then a crossfire, and got even 2-2. He took both pitches. The third pitch was a curve low and away, and he dribbled it to Dano at third."

To Dano at third.

Playing shortstop, I had a front-row seat to what happened next. Dano used two hands to field the ball and never removed his throwing hand from the ball as he fielded it cleanly and brought it up to his chest. Jon remembers, "Dano kind of grunted, and a little spit came out the side of his mouth when he fielded it. I could tell he was still pissed." With a force at third, he was clearly not going to throw the ball or step on third base for the force out. He was going for the tag on the runner. He cradled the ball in his glove through the tag. Dano recalls, "I still remember both hands did not leave my glove." I saw Dano's eyes widen as the runner ran toward him. Then came the tag on the baserunner's chest. It was so forceful that the Glendive runner was knocked on his back to the ground, and then he brought his arm back high above him and spiked the ball just to the side of the runner as he was lying on the ground. When he pulled his arm back, I was genuinely concerned that he might spike it on the runner. The ball bounced back up higher than a spike by Gronk at a Super Bowl touchdown. Kelly recalls, "And he sneered at him! With the look only Dano can give." Jon added, "Dano may have hiked his pants up a bit, as he was prone to do in tense situations." Dano's reaction to getting that last out was partly because of frustration for the miscommunication between Allan and Kelly, partly because of what happened on the mound next, and partly because he wanted to make sure he didn't drop the ball on the tag. But mostly, it was because, as Dano said to me when I approached him to celebrate the win, "*Why the fuck did he have to hit it to me?*"

Dano remembers the groundball and tag this way: "I was frazzled after losing control on the mound. I still can remember thinking, *You can't fuck this up* when the grounder came to me. I squeezed that ball in the mitt so hard. I looked up, and the runner was coming at me, so I decided to tag him a little harder than normal, but honestly, both hands were squeezing the glove and ball, and I knew it wasn't coming out. I don't think I did anything that bad.

If there is any intent to knock the ball loose, it's my job to make sure he doesn't try again." Then Dano added slyly, "He did lower his shoulder." In the end, I think it was poetic justice that the ball was hit to Dano to make the last putout unassisted because he had pitched such a brilliant game up to that point.

So, we had escaped, and after two dramatic one-run wins under the lights, each coming down to the last out in the ninth inning, the young Scobey Blues were advancing to play the Great Falls Vigilantes in the undefeated semifinal the next day.

After two days, the rhythm of the tournament had become the rhythm of my life: drive to Scobey with Jon; go to Doc's house for the pregame meeting; go to the field to play the game; play the game; drive home with Jon; talk to Dad about it. Get up the next day and do it all over again.

Superstition had become part of my rhythm, too. I'm not sure why baseball lends itself to superstition, but it does. Before the first game against Cut Bank, something happened where I had to wear a pair of unwashed socks to the game, and we won. My Mom asked me after the game to give her my dirty socks so she could wash them, but I told her they were fine and didn't need washing. As long as we kept winning, I would not give her my dirty socks to wash, and I never did. I wish I could have picked a cleaner superstition, but the dirty socks kept us undefeated, so you can't argue.

At the pregame meeting at Doc and Marge's house before the Vigilantes game, Doc announced that I would be the starting pitcher. I don't remember what else he said, but it was like, "Keep playing baseball the way you're playing, and you're going to keep winning." It was similar to what he told us before the first game against Cut Bank. Just play baseball the way you know how, and you'll win. So far, it was working.

I was excited to pitch in my first state tournament game in Scobey. It was cool, damp, and windy that Saturday. The wind was blowing straight out to center field, in my face as the pitcher. I normally liked to pitch when it was hot, but the dampness allowed me to get a better grip on my curveball. Whenever the wind blew straight out at Scobey (it normally blew from the west, right to left as you face the hitter at the Scobey Ball Park), my curveball seemed to break better. I established it early in the game and probably threw more curveballs than in any other game I pitched. They weren't hitting hit, so Kirby kept calling it, and I kept throwing it.

Unlike the previous two games, we jumped on pitcher Mickey Monahan and the Vigilantes for two runs in the top of the first to take the lead 2-0. That gave us confidence early. But the Vigilantes got solo runs in the first and third, and after three innings, the score was knotted 2-2. Then we scored a single run in the top of the fifth and added three more in the top of the sixth to take a 6-2 lead. I got in trouble in the bottom of the sixth. The bases were loaded, but there were two outs. The hitter grounded a ball to Jon at shortstop. The runners were moving because there were two outs, so Jon couldn't go the short route to Kelly at second base; he had to throw it to Ray at first. Jon bobbled it, and being unable to throw to Kelly for the force at second, he got out of his throwing rhythm. His throw to Ray was a little low, and Ray couldn't scoop it—probably the only ball he couldn't dig the entire tournament. The ball skipped up Ray's arm and past him to the fence in right, and the merry-go-round on the bases swung into full motion. One run across, two runs across, and the runner from first came all the way home to score, too. Three unearned runs scored on the two-base throwing error by Jon, and the hitter ended up at second base. Suddenly, the score was 6-5, with the tying run at second. Damn, Jon—but this was not the time for "the stare." Jon hung his head and said, "Sorry, Joe."

I thought not to focus on Jon's error but on what I could control—my pitches to the next hitter—and preserve our one-run lead in the game. I had made plenty of errors behind Jon at short when he pitched, so I couldn't cast stones. Plus, I could needle him about it later on the ride home—if we won, that is. When asking Jon about the play, he said jokingly (I think), "I only remember being a hero or when someone else fucked up." Jon was the hero a lot in that tournament, but not on that ground ball to short with two outs and the bases loaded. But we got the last out, and despite the three-run error, we got off the field with the 6-5 lead preserved.

A one-run game again. Back to normal now. But we scored two runs in the top of the seventh to extend our lead to 8-5, then broke it open with a big seven-run inning in the top of the eighth to take a 15-5 lead. With the big lead, we started to relax just a little bit and have some fun; not that we weren't having fun before that, but every game had been so intense, with games either tied or a one-run difference. But now we had a big lead, were finally hitting (we had 18 hits in the game), and knew we were in control. In the big rally in the eighth, Kelly Norman—who went 5-5 that night and was our leading hitter in the tournament—had two singles in the inning. Kelly recalls, "Using my Johnny Bench 32-inch bat, one of my hits was about 3 to 4 feet to the left side of second base and not on the first base side, one of my few hits to the left side. The dugout stood up, clapped, and cheered! I'm sure it was because of my pure power." At 15 years old, Kelly did not have much power and usually hit the ball to the right side of the infield. He developed power as he got older and hit the ball to the left side, including over the fence at Scobey.

Running out to the mound in the bottom of the eighth, I knew if I got three outs and didn't allow a run, we could ten-run rule them and advance to the state championship game. The juices were flowing—and the curveball was breaking. We got the three quick outs and danced on the field, celebrating our third straight win in the tournament and advancing to the state championship game undefeated the next day.

Who would we play in the state championship game? Sidney. After their disappointing opening-day 2-1 loss to the Great Falls Sparkies, the Patriots had clawed their way back through the dirt route to win four straight games. They rapped out 20 hits to eliminate Baker-Ekalaka in seven innings, 20-7. Tim Thogerson had two doubles and a triple, Ken Barnhart had a home run, a double, and a single, and Jeff Lebsock also homered for Sidney. Tom Paladichuk pitched a five-hitter for the seven-inning win. Sidney then outslugged Glendive 14-10. Sidney scored all 14 of its runs in the first six innings, including a home run by Tom Paladichuk, to take a 14-5 lead, then held on for the win. Jeff Lebsock got the win with Bryce Larsen in relief.

Sidney avenged their loss to the Sparkies by beating them 9-2. Sidney scored six runs on three singles, two walks, and two errors in the top of the fourth inning to take a commanding 7-0 lead. Tom Paladichuk struck out 15 Sparkies to get his second tournament win. Then, in the game before the state championship game on Sunday, Sidney won a close game, 5-3, over the Vigilantes to earn their berth in the state championship game. With the score tied 3-3 in the top of the ninth, Jeff Lebsock led off with a double and scored on an error (which put Jay Nesper on base) to make the score 4-3. Ken Barnhart, hitting .500 in the tournament at that point, knocked in Nesper with a single to give Sidney the 5-3 lead. Jeff Lebsock, who relieved Bryce Larsen in the eighth, held the Vigilantes scoreless in the ninth to gain his second tournament win. Larsen and Lebsock combined for a four-hitter in the game. The *Leader* summed up Sidney's four-day journey on the dirt route: "It was a tired bunch of Sidney boys in the championship game."[138]

Sidney had beaten us 3 out of 4 times that season, including 5-4 a week earlier in Sidney to eliminate us from the eastern divisional. Jon had gone the distance in that game, striking out 12 Patriots. Who would Doc hand the ball to for the state championship game? Jon again. Jon was pitching the best I'd ever seen him pitch. He had pitched a complete game four-hitter against Cut Bank in the opener for the 2-1 win, then came in with two outs in the ninth to get the ground ball to Dano at third to earn the save against Glendive. When I asked Jon why he thought he was pitching so well at the end of the 1977 season, he said, "Toward the end of that season, my arm felt stronger. I felt like I could get anyone out."

Coach Craig Price countered with Jeff Nesper, who had pitched a two-hit shutout against us earlier in the season, but we had scored 10 runs against him a week earlier in the second game of the tournament in Sidney. But Sidney committed four errors in that game, so not all those runs were earned.

One special thing about playing in the state championship game was that each player on each team was introduced and got to run out of the dugout to stand on the baseline. Standing on the baseline, I couldn't resist peeking at the packed grandstand, the full bleachers, and the rows of cars down the left- and right-field lines. This was the crowd I had seen at the 1969, 1971, 1973, and 1975 state tournaments. People from

Opening ceremonies at the state B Legion championship game included the Scobey Color Guard's flag-raising in center field. Sidney and Scobey teams are lined up on the first and third base lines as they and the crowds prepare to stand at attention during the national anthem. *Leader photo, Milt Gunderson*

Daniels County came to watch baseball. It was special. Then, the Scobey Color Guard held a flag-raising ceremony in center field before playing the national anthem. State Chairman of Class B Legion Baseball, Gene Marley, read the Legion Code of Sportsmanship. Of course, Dano, as he always did, kept us loose while we recited the Legion Code of Sportsmanship. He wouldn't get the words quite right. He would substitute his word for the word "keep." Dano's version was, "I will . . . break the rules, lose faith in my teammates, lose my temper, . . ." He did it every time, and it would make me giggle and loosen me up before a big game. I did, however, recite the words correctly myself. Dano said, "All my fucking around was my way of not letting nerves take over." It helped us, too.

In the top of the first, we didn't get off to a good start in the field. I couldn't reach a sharply hit ground ball to my left at short, and the ball skipped off my glove for an error into center field. If I got to it, it likely would have resulted in a double play. Kelly said, "Ah, Joe, that was two." Things got worse from there. The inning had a second error, and two unearned runs were scored. Sidney loaded the bases with one out and was threatening to score more. But we got a groundball force-out to Kirby—who stretched like Ray Chapman—at home to get the second out, and Jon got the third out to escape further damage, so only two runs scored, both unearned.

Allan Audet approaches home plate on Randy Stolen's big 3-run blast over the right field wall during the deciding 10-run third inning. *Leader photo, Milt Gunderson.*

In the fourth, we added two runs off Lebsock to take a 13-2 lead. With the 13-2 lead, Jon took over on the mound, getting stronger and stronger as each inning passed. His control was impeccable, as he didn't walk a batter in the game. Our defense strengthened, and the outs started quickly clicking off as we ticked closer and closer to the ninth inning—no ten-run rule in the championship game. Sidney got to Jon for another run—the third unearned run of the game—in the sixth, but that was it. Entering the top of the ninth with a 13-3 lead, we needed three more outs to repeat as state champions on our home field.

After we finished our at-bat in the bottom of the eighth, I couldn't wait to sprint out to shortstop for the final three

Kirby Halvorson takes a throw (the ball is in mitt) which forces out Sidney's Lonnie Herman for a big bases-loaded out in the first inning of the championship game. *Leader photo, Milt Gunderson.*

We countered with a run in the bottom half to close to 2-1; then, the floodgates opened in the bottom of the third. Our bats exploded, and we hung 10 runs on the scoreboard with eight hits, the big blow coming on a three-run home run by Randy Stolen. I had a double and a single in the inning, chasing Jeff Nesper, who was relieved by Jeff Lebsock after my second hit. Jeff Nesper was staying at Doc's house during the tournament, and Doc said to him, as he moved to third base after the rally, "Sorry about that, Jeff."

Kelly Norman crosses the plate as he watches the action during the Blue's 10-run third inning during the Sidney game. Kelly was Scobey's leading percentage hitter at .526 during the tourney. He was runner-up for the tournament batting title. *Leader photo, Milt Gunderson.*

outs and celebrate with my teammates on the field. But Doc said, "Donnie [Holyk], you go in for Joe at short, and Bernie [Wasser], you go in for Kelly at second." I was deflated. The year before, I sat next to Doc in the dugout in Cut Bank when we beat Wolf Point for the state championship after I had pitched earlier in the game and ran out of the dugout to swarm Jon on the mound, who finished the game for us. I looked forward to celebrating on the field with my teammates this year.

So, Kelly was sitting on the top step of the dugout, and I was sitting next to Doc on the bench, watching Jon pitch the last inning from the dugout. Sidney got a baserunner. Oh-oh. Could this be the start of a big inning for them? Big innings can happen in Legion, especially in later innings in games late in the tournament. But Jon's fastball was hopping, and he was in complete control. As Jon released the ball, Doc would yell, "Go, Jon!" Ziiiiip! It was the same thing as the year before, except Jon's fastball was not the same as it was a year earlier against Wolf Point. He relied on his curveball to get Wolf Point out, but his fastball was live against Sidney.

The next hitter hit a ground ball to Donnie Holyk at short. He fielded it cleanly and snapped a sidearm throw to Bernie Wasser at second, who quickly relayed the throw to Ray at first for a 6-4-3 double play: Holyk to Wasser to Chapman. Kelly and I just looked at each other, smiled, and shook our heads. The next hitter hit a pop fly to Bernie at second, who calmly squeezed the ball for the third out, and Kelly, I, and our other teammates in the dugout ran onto the field to mob Jon and Kirby on the mound. The young Blues had repeated as state champions.

Dan Danelson Scobey's third baseman and pitcher accepts the coveted state championship trophy for the jubilant Blues. State chairman of Class B Legion ball Gene Marley and Post 56 Commander Don Oaks made the presentation. *Leader photo, Milt Gunderson*

TOURNAMENT SUMMARY

THE HEADLINE IN THE *LEADER* READ, "BLUES WIN FOUR Straight Games; Keep State Legion Title Home," and it summed up Scobey's unexpected championship this way: "The Blues were not picked to win it . . . but they put it all together for the tournament and solid defense behind outstanding pitching held opposing teams to an average of 3.5 runs per game while Scobey averaged nine runs."[139]

Until the 1977 state tournament, the season was considered a rebuilding year, as Scobey had lost the core of the team that won the 1976 championship. But seven of us had also played on that state championship team. During the regular season, expectations of us weren't high; we felt no pressure because we were all so young. Taking second to Glasgow in the district didn't bother us so much. However, when we took third place at the divisional in Sidney, it was disappointing because—regardless of what everyone else expected of us—*we* expected to win; that had always been *our* goal. Everyone on the team was extremely competitive, and every time we took the field, our goal was to win.

Doc's expectations for us at the state tournament were high, too—he told us we could win it if we played to our potential. In his four pregame meetings, Doc instilled confidence in us by emphasizing that we were talented and had played a lot of baseball. The key was to coalesce as a team. Ray Chapman, as only he can, articulated the transformation this way: "The state tournament felt completely different from the entire season up to that point. I don't know how to describe it exactly, but the 1977 state tourney was where our whole team moved to that proverbial 'next level.' And the great thing was, it wasn't in the way that phrase is often talked about, on an individual level; the entire team began working and playing together as one, and the game of baseball took on a whole new meaning.

1977 Scobey Blues, State Class B Champions. Standing, left to right: Doc Norman, bus driver Dick Atwood, Brad Henderson, Kirby Halvorson, Don Boos, Dan Danelson, Allan Audet, Kelly Norman, Mike Abar, Ass't Coach Don Lekvold. Kneeling, left to right: Ray Chapman, Jon Puckett, Joe Puckett, Randy Stolen, Wade Tryan, Don Holyk, Bernie Wasser. Sitting, left to right: Jacki Tade, Rick Lee, Mike Roland, DeeAnn Lekvold. *Leader photo, Milt Gunderson.*

It wasn't just a game we were playing anymore: the State Legion Tournament of 1977 was where we transformed from a group of individuals into a team that was a far greater thing than the sum of our parts."

The *Leader* also saw what Ray recognized as a player: "It would be difficult to pick an MVP from Scobey's championship team as its strength came from not having any weak spots. All positions were filled by good, steady ballplayers."[140] The *Leader* also credited the coaching of head coach Doc Norman and the "able assistance of Don Lekvold, former Wolf Point Legion coach and grandson of long-time baseball fans the B.J. Lekvolds of the Silver Star community. These two coaches are given a lot of credit for bringing the young Blues along so well this year."[141]

Without a doubt, the team that entered Doc's house for the pregame meeting on Thursday before the Cut Bank game was not the same team that exited the field as champions on Sunday. In four days, the young Blues had grown up.

All nine starters would return the following year, and eight starters (except for Allan Audet) the year after. If expectations were not high for the 1977 season, they would be for the following two years—and beyond. Could the Blues rise to the challenge and three-peat in 1978?

TOURNAMENT STATS

Hitting

TIM THOGERSON OF SIDNEY WON THE BATTING TITLE WITH A .600 average, including five doubles and a triple. Kelly Norman was the tournament's second-leading hitter with a .526 average. Joe Puckett was Scobey's second-leading hitter, batting .444. Allan Audet's clutch, two-out, ninth-inning, game-winning RBI single against Cut Bank to walk it off was *the* clutch hit for Scobey in the tournament. Randy

Tim Thogerson batting against Jon Puckett in the 1977 State B Championship game in Scobey. Tim led the tournament in hitting with a .600 average (15-25), including three doubles and a triple. Note the shift to the right of the Scobey Players—Joe Puckett at short, Wade Tryan in center, and Kelly Norman at second. This was before analytics, but Doc (and we) had seen enough of Tim to know he was a pull hitter.

Stolen's three-run home run in the championship game broke the game open for Scobey and was the big blow in the big 10-run third inning.

The tournament had seven home runs—"goobs," as the Sidney players called them. Three Sidney players hit goobs: Ken Barnhart, Jeff Lebsock, and Tom Paladichuk. Also homering in the tournament were Rick Thomas and Scott Campbell (a grand slam) from the Sparkies, Mike Lewis of Cut Bank, and Randy Stolen of Scobey in the state championship game.

Pitching

Jon Puckett batting in the state tournament. His biggest contribution was from the mound, as he pitched 18 and one-third innings and gave up only one earned run in the tournament. *Leader photo, Milt Gunderson.*

THE *LEADER* TAGGED JON PUCKETT AS THE MOST VALUABLE pitcher in the tournament. He pitched 18 and one-third innings, allowing one earned run for a 0.49 ERA. He was credited with two wins (2-1 over Cut Bank and 13-3 over Sidney) and one save in the tournament, getting the final out against Glendive. He gave up three walks against Cut Bank and none in the final. Dan Danelson, 6-5 over Glendive, and Joe Puckett, 15-5 over the Vigilantes, got the other two wins for Scobey.

Some other notable pitching performances: Fred Peres pitched a six-hitter in the Sparkies' 2-1 win over Sidney, while Jeff Nesper and Jeff Lebsock combined to limit the Sparkies to six hits and two runs. Doug Frenzel of Glendive pitched a four-hitter against Browning to win 5-2.

Wayne Slezak of Cut Bank held Scobey to one run in eight innings. Tom Paladichuk—who during the regular season threw two one-hitters during the same week and a three-hitter against Glendive—got two wins in the tournament: a five-hitter against Baker-Ekalaka and another five-hitter with 15 strikeouts in Sidney's 9-2 win over the Sparkies. Jeff Lebsock also won two games for Sidney, one over Glendive and one in relief of Bryce Larsen against the Vigilantes.

Ray Chapman's big stretch became a familiar sight at first base during the state tournament as he earned "most valuable defensive player" honors. That's Sidney's Bryce Larsen, who missed a base hit by inches in the eighth inning of the final game. *Leader photo, Milt Gunderson.*

Fielding

Ray Chapman was named the most valuable defensive player of the tournament by the KCGM broadcast team. The *Leader* also identified Ray for his "outstanding defensive play at first base, with his big stretch, agility, and ability to 'dig them out of the dirt' he kept a number of runners off the base paths, while playing near errorless ball."[142] He also hit over .300 for the tournament.

The *Leader* also identified Kirby Halvorson for his "fine job behind the plate." The *Leader* stated that Kirby "made the toughest job in baseball look so easy."[143] Kirby was catching well as a 15-year-old. The *Leader* also recognized him for his catching at the eastern divisional in Sidney, where he "was repeatedly praised for his defensive play by the radio announcer in Sidney."[144]

Randy Stolen's game-saving catch in left field against Cut Bank, robbing the hitter of extra bases and preventing two runs from scoring, was the most outstanding defensive play of the tournament. As Allan Audet's clutch hit in that game, Randy's catch preserved Jon's fine pitching performance and allowed us to win.

The Blues outfield, Randy Stolen, Wade Tryan, and Allan Audet, committed only two errors in the tournament, and the "refused to be 'shook' by the normal amount of errors and bad breaks and came up with the big play when needed."[145]

Sidney pulled off a triple play against the Sparkies. After two Sparkies walks, Sidney shortstop Tim Thogerson caught a looping fly ball to short center field, fired to second for the second out, and the relay to first was also in time as both runners thought the ball would drop for a hit.

STATE CLASS A PLAYOFF

After our fourth tournament win, when we got home to Peerless, I allowed Mom to wash my socks before the best-of-three-game series against the Helena Senators the following weekend. It might have been a mistake. We played like shit.

The best-of-three series to qualify for the State Class A tournament was against the Helena Senators, who had finished in fourth place in the Class A eastern division. The games were played at Kindrick Legion Field in Helena. Doc started Dan Danelson, who pitched well. The Senators got to him for 10 hits and nine runs (seven earned), but the "rangy, hard-throwing right-hander"[146]—as the *Helena Independent Record* described him—struck out 11 Senators. Carter McKnight pitched a five-hitter for Helena and gave up only one earned run in eight innings to lead Helena to a 9-2 win.

Jon also pitched well in the second game, but our ordinarily solid defense let us down, committing six errors behind him in the first four innings, leading to six unearned runs. Despite our poor defensive play, we were still in the game in the eighth inning after a three-run double by Wade Tryan that was lost in the lights by the Helena left fielder, pulled us to within one run, 7-6. But Helena scored an insurance run in the bottom of the eighth, and relief pitcher Bob Chilton shut us down in the ninth for an 8-6 Helena win. In the box score, we had eight hits, and Helena had 10, but the two-run difference in the game was revealed when looking at the errors in the box score: Scobey had six, and Helena had one. Of Jon's eight runs allowed, only two were earned. The Helena playoff series was another disappointing footnote to a sparkling Scobey state Class B championship.

As there was learning in the regular season losses, the playoff losses to Helena also taught the young team something—there was no margin for "error" against Class A competition. You had to play well in the field to win, giving them three outs. Our pitching was good in both games, and we had eight hits and six runs in the second game—enough to win had we played well defensively. Two years later, when we returned to play the Senators in another playoff when most of us were 18, we would remember this embarrassing defensive performance at Kindrick Field, and the result would be different. The key to beating Class A competition was to play well defensively; it took us a while to figure that out—and get it right. Thank goodness we had more than one chance to get it right.

The 1977 Scobey Blues finished with a season record of 28-10.

EXTRA INNINGS

Thanks to all the volunteers, Scobey's fifth state tournament as host was another success, and the *Leader* was always careful to recognize the many people who made it happen. Tournament Chairman Cliff Hanson reported that the tournament was "financially sound." Cliff was a pillar of the Scobey community, not just with his contribution to American Legion baseball. In the *Daniels County History* book, Cliff wrote, "My outside work is devoted to my church and veterans organizations, The American Legion and the Veterans of Foreign Wars. I am treasurer of the local Legion Baseball Committee. I think Daniels County and Scobey is the only place on earth and plan on spending the remaining years 'here.'"[147]

Cliff, aided by State Class B Legion Chairman Gene Marley, oversaw arranging ticket sellers and most other tournament arrangements, including supplying the Legion burger stand. He and his wife, Bernice, made 300 pounds of hamburger into patties (over 1,650). Patty Marley was in charge of the pop stand.

Umpires for the tournament were Umpire-in-Chief Ron Ewing, Dick Puckett, Jerry Marshall, Don Pertuit, and Don Higgins.

Art Audet was the grounds-keeping chairman, with Dan Wolfe, Dana and Phil Audet, and others assisting.

Music was provided over the public address between innings from Loyal Brenden's van with Loyal, Bev Plante, and Beverly Lund at the keyboard. Perry Wolfe was music chairman.

Marge Norman and Mazel Audet were responsible for getting workers for the hamburger stand. Marge, Mazel, Pearl Lee, and Esther Narveson also arranged to feed the teams. Delores Danelson joined Marge, Mazel, and Pearl on the housing committee as visiting teams stayed at various homes in Scobey.

Charles Cassidy was in charge of the program booklet, dedicated to Miles City Legionnaire and youth worker Glenn Denton. The book was also in special memory of David Casey (son of Dennis), a member of the Wolf Point Legion team who had been recently killed in an auto accident.

Jack Reiner was the official scorer and on the protest committee with Ron Ewing and Gene Marley.

The *Leader* finished the list of volunteers by writing, "There were many others who worked on (and/or donated to) this community effort to make Scobey a real 'tournament town' for fans and players alike."[148]

The 1977 team was Scobey's only state championship team to take third at divisional. The 1976 team took second. All six other state championship teams won the eastern divisional tournament.

If the 1976 state championship was the most improbable of Doc's eight state championships, 1977 might be the runner-up in that category, but we'll have to reserve judgment until we get to 1982. With an average age of 15 years and nine months and a third-place finish at the divisional, the 1977 championship was also a step above expected. But not for the players.

Doc's 1960 team, with an average age of 15 years and three months, was younger than the 1977 team, but the max age for Junior Legion was 17 years old then. The Legion age increased to 18 years old in 1962.

Bernie Wasser still has the ball he caught at second base for the last out of the 1977 state tournament against Sidney.

Sidney's loss in the first game, forcing them through the "dirt route"—as the *Leader* so aptly described that difficult path—resulted in their playing in six of the 14 games in the tournament. Winning a tournament through the dirt route is difficult—you have to win five games to do it—but not impossible. Two of Scobey's eight state championships came through the dirt route: Scobey's first state championship team in 1969 won five games, and the 1976 team did the same in Cut Bank.

I asked Allan Audet if he remembered the fly ball in right in the ninth inning against Glendive, which led to the bloop single. Specifically, I asked him if he remembered Kelly calling him off. Allan responded, "Sure, Kelly would say that, ha." Was it a popup behind second base, or was it a shallow fly to right field? Like most things, the truth lies somewhere in between—where the ball landed.

As we were the same age as the Great Falls Vigilantes and Great Falls Sparkies in 1977, we would see many of these players again in State A competition the following two years. Pitcher Mickey Monahan, who started for the Vigilantes against us, pitched the first game as a Charger against us in the playoffs a year later. Rick Thomas from the Sparkies, who hit a home run in the tournament, was the leadoff hitter for the Electrics, who we played in the first game of the 1979 State A Tournament two years later.

In the state championship game against Sidney, I noticed Jeff Richardson sitting behind the first base fence on a car as I threw the ball to Ray on a warmup toss between innings. I caught his eye. We were leading Sidney by 11 runs at that point. It was in the later innings, and we were in control of the game, so I was playing very relaxed. I smiled when I remembered playing with him the previous year. What a great catcher he was. If I ever pitched to him again, I would not shake him off when he called for a curveball as I did when Mike Neubauer hit a three-run triple off me in Cut Bank in the state championship game. I probably should have snapped a curveball to Ray at first to prove it to him.

One big inning was the difference in all four of Scobey's state championships: in 1969—after Doc won the coin flip and chose to be the visiting team—Scobey jumped on Barry Damschen of Havre for five runs in the top of the first inning and never relinquished the lead, winning 7-6; in 1973, Scobey scored seven runs on eight hits in the eighth inning to beat Wolf Point 9-6; in 1976, Scobey scored 10 runs on eight hits in the bottom of the seventh inning to beat Wolf Point 13-11; and in 1977, Scobey scored 10 runs on eight hits in the third inning to beat Sidney 13-3.

Tim Thogerson, the leading hitter in the tournament at .600, was an incredible all-around good baseball player. Kirby Halvorson recalls, "Timmy Thogerson was not only a good hitter, but he was lightning quick. I remember in a night game vs Sidney, he hit a gapper, and I was watching him run between first and second with white cleats on . . . they were just a blur, almost cartoonish, as I think, back on it. I thought to myself, *that sonofabitch is FAST!!*"

Star Wars has the "Death Star," and the Scobey Legion team has the "death stare." Kelly Norman's reference to the "death stare" he got from Dan Danelson after the popup dropped behind him in the Glendive game was also something Phil Audet talked about in his interview. When Phil played shortstop for the 1963 Scobey Legion team as a 14-year-old, he spoke of the "stare" he would get from 18-year-old pitchers Baldy Sell, Bill Thompson, and Charlie Mueller when he would make an error at short. "If I made an error, I got the stare." He asked me in the interview if I got the stare at shortstop, too. The answer is yes, Phil. The death stare is the genesis of this book. Almost two years ago now, Dano was discussing old times with Jon about the Scobey Blues, and he told Jon he remembered me staring at him at third after he made an error, which was my retaliation for him staring at me at short after I made an error. Dano said to Jon, "I got the point," and never stared me down again after that error he made. After that discussion, Jon suggested I write a book about the Scobey Blues, the same as I did for the Peerless Panthers, so I am writing the book to capture all the stories from all the players and teams. It is ironic how it all started with the death stare story. There are so many funny stories, but getting the death stare was never fun, especially from Dano. Laser eyes. Also, not casting a death stare after an error is a very Christian thing to do. As Jesus said, "He that is without error among you, let him first cast a stare." I think that's close. My knowledge of scripture is not good.

If Sidney might have caught a break at the eastern divisional when 10-year-old Mitch Melby tossed a ball on the field just before Plentywood shortstop Randy Wangerin whacked a home run (which was not allowed because time had been called), we caught a break at the state tournament in Scobey against Glendive. Except this time, the break didn't come from a 10-year-old kid; it came from Umpire-in-Chief Ron Ewing, and it wasn't the right call; it was the wrong call. With runners on first and second, Dan Danelson was batting for Scobey. He struck out, but the ball got past the catcher. Dano ran to first, and the two other runners moved up on the passed ball to load the bases. With less than two outs, this was a dropped third strike, and Dano should have been called out, but he ended up on first to load the bases. The Glendive coach did not catch it in time to file a protest before Craig Ballantine delivered the next pitch. (This did not occur in the four-run sixth inning.) The day after the call, Ewing admitted, "We blew it," but the *Leader*, ever forgiving, had this to say about the umpires: "The umps, of course, felt bad about this. However, it should be noted that they are human too and are subject to errors just as the ball players are."[149]

Umpire-in-Chief Ron Ewing from Sidney had complete control of the field. In the Browning-Glendive game, he tossed a Browning player out for arguing balls and strikes at the plate. From first base, he pointed his finger at him and yelled, "You're out of this game!" When we were playing Cut Bank the next game, the same player was in the stands and yelled, "Don't say anything to the first base umpire, or he'll throw you out of the game." I held my breath at what might happen next, but since the player was off the field, Ewing didn't do anything.

Jeff Lebsock, who won two games for Sidney pitching and hit a home run in the state tournament, was a tremendous all-around athlete from Fairview. Recognizing Lebsock's all-American athleticism, the Sidney players would say, "Baseball, hot dogs, apple pie, and Lebby." Not sure if he drove a Chevrolet.

Ron Ewing from Sidney headed up the fine umpiring staff at the State B Legion Tournament. Ron was "giving the word" to the official scorer when this photo was snapped. *Leader photo, Milt Gunderson.*

Allan Audet's two-out, walk-off hit to beat Cut Bank 2-1 was the first walk-off win for Scobey at a state tournament hosted in Scobey. The year before in Cut Bank, we had walked it off 6-5 against Wolf Point in Cut Bank on Greg Fjeld's two-out, two-strike hit.

As we were warming up along the right-field line before our regular season game in Sidney that year, a kid was watching us warm up and asked, "Where you guys from?" I thought, *He doesn't know where we're from?* We were the defending state champions and had won four state championships. We all ignored the question, and no one responded. Finally, Kelly, who I was playing catch with, replied, looking straight ahead at me as he threw the ball, "Scobey. As in State Champions."

During the regular season, we played Poplar twice, winning 18-0 early in the season in Scobey on Jon's one-hit shutout and then 6-3 later in the season in Poplar. Following the 6-3 win in Poplar, the *Leader* mentioned that the Scobey coaches noticed a big improvement in the Poplar team from earlier in the season. However, the Scobey coaches—Doc Norman and Don Lekvold—did not know that several Scobey players were massively hungover from Jay Crandell's annual summer blowout party the night before, where many players saw daylight. (I was not one of them.) This might have partially explained the improvement. That, and Kirby Halvorson's meatball to previously unheralded Dorn Steele for the moonshot home run. Catcher Jon Puckett, who signaled for the notorious pitch, thinks the ball might have landed in the Missouri River.

In a regular season game against the Grenora Gophers at Grenora in 1977, Doc requested Jon Puckett to do his Mickey Rivers impersonation at the plate after the game was well in hand. Mickey Rivers was the speedy left-handed center fielder for the Yankees (1976-79), and Jon and I had seen the dynamo play at Royals Stadium in Kansas City in 1976. He was exciting to watch, and he caught Jon's eye for sure. When Mickey Rivers would come to the plate, he was very animated. He would step out of the box, alternately tap his bat on both cleats as he kicked his feet up, take a couple of quick practice swings, step back into the box, crouch, and vigorously wiggle his bat on his shoulder, waiting for the pitch. Jon had the impersonation down to a T, and Doc had seen it in practice, so he wanted to see it in a game. Jon came up to bat; Doc said, "Let's see Mickey, Jon," so Jon did his Mickey Rivers impersonation perfectly. He stepped into the box and, batting left-handed, slapped a single between third and short to left field. Doc and the entire dugout were howling. However, the home plate umpire was not so amused, and he told Jon it was "bush league" when he recognized what was happening. Undaunted, Jon, with his Mickey Rivers speed, stole second base. Not sure if he did his Mickey Rivers slide.

In the week leading up to the eastern divisional tournament in Sidney, we were prepping to play Baker-Ekalaka, whom our team had never played before, but Jon, Ray, and I had played against many of the players on their team on the State Line All-Stars in the eastern divisional Babe Ruth tournaments in 1974 and 1975. We had seen some good pitching from Aaron Olsen and Mitch Anderson in those tournaments, which had been brought up in practice—more than once. Jon recalls, "We were sitting around in our dugout, probably a few days before the tournament. Dano had heard 'Mitch and Aaron' one too many times, and Chapman chiming in may have been the straw that broke the camel's back." Dano's Mitch and Aaron–meter was pegged, and he said, in his diplomatic way, "Fuck Mitch and Aaron; we're gonna kick their ass!" "Mitch and Aaron" were never mentioned again, and we did kick their ass, 8-3. Mitch did pitch a decent game though.

On Friday night before the regular season game against Sidney at Sidney, I found myself at Doc's house at about midnight getting stitches in my head after I got involved in a scuffle outside the Ponderosa Bar in Scobey. I had been drinking a little, let's just say, and Doc recognized I didn't need a local anesthetic for the stitches. As he shaved my hair—got a nice little punk rock haircut I hadn't counted on—and gently stitched the cut, he said, "You know, Guiseppe"—what Doc called me—"you should probably just stick to baseball." Good advice, Doc. At the game at Sidney the next day, I hit a three-run home run. As I rounded first base, I missed it as I admired my first Legion home run leaving Moose Park. I am not sure who was playing first base for Sidney, but whoever it was, I would like to thank them for also watching the ball leave the park and not looking to see if I touched first base.

One of my favorite things to do was to discuss baseball with Aunt Lauretta (Fouhy) Puckett at the Peerless Post Office on mornings after baseball games. I was hauling mail for Dad, and in the mornings, I would stop in the Peerless Post Office to pick up the mail to take down the line to Richland, Glentana, and Opheim. Following the Fourth of July doubleheader against Browning, Aunt Lauretta complimented me on playing shortstop. I considered that high praise coming from her, considering her two sons, Dick and Don, were two of the best shortstops to ever play for Scobey.

At 17 years old, Allan Audet was the oldest player on the team and the team's leader and alpha. He had found his place. But his baseball journey through Little League, Babe Ruth, and Legion was difficult. Allan said, "What I remember always bugging me was that I was the only kid my age. Think there was a year or two that I didn't have a team to play on due to everyone being younger or older. Most were in Little League while I sat idle. 1976 was my worst year; just felt out there by myself. Almost quit, glad I didn't, though. When I was 15 on Legion, Duke Trangsrud and Mike Gunderson kind of took me under their wings. In practice one night, I was in left and Beak [Mike Gunderson] was on third. He was having a bad night, so Doc said, 'Get out in left with Albert.' They hit him a high fly; he ran in a little and missed the ball as it bounced off his head and over the fence. He dropped like a brick, and so did I, laughing at him."

Allan would often needle the younger players in practice, especially from Peerless and Opheim. In one of the outfield clusters during batting practice—as I attempted to blow a bubble gum bubble but couldn't—he announced to everyone: "Puckett's face is totally retarded: he can't blow a bubble, he can't wink, he can't roll his tongue, and he can't whistle." (All true at the time, but I'm a hell of a whistler now.) On a separate occasion, Randy Stolen told the group about a confrontation earlier that day with another boy in school in Opheim. Randy told us he would fight the boy the next day. He said, "I got a fight. I got a fight tomorrow after school." Allan puffed up and said, "You Opheim people are weird! You gotta fight when you're mad. You can't schedule a fight for the next day."

Kirby Halvorson echoed Ray Chapman's comment about the team coming together: "We were a *team*, the whole stronger than the independent parts. We all had our roles, and all served those roles well offensively and defensively. Collectively, I think we all understood, appreciated, and accepted that. I also believe that's why we were successful and won . . . that *and* we were all bulldogs in our own way . . . *hated* and *refused* to lose."

Dano added two deadly pitches to his repertoire in 1977: a sidearm fastball and a knuckle curve. Dano's inspiration for the sidearm fastball was Dennis Eckersley, who pitched for the Cleveland Indians then. To help Dano master the pitch, Doc would have us stand at the plate, then shake his head and say "nasty" when Dan fired a good one. The source of inspiration for the knuckle curve, however, was different. Dan recalls the day it was born: "So the knuckle curve was conceived at one of our intense practices. After smoking a couple of bowls of Booger's homegrown ragweed, I came to practice with clarity that I had never experienced before. I knew this practice would be different than all others that I had fucked around at. I laced the cleats and grabbed my glove. Wade was my throwing partner as he usually was more stoned than I was, and I knew if my experimental grip did anything, Wade would go ballistic. I slid my bent index and fuck fingers behind the ball, reared back, and let it go releasing those two fingers at my target. I could see the ball, almost like in slow motion, drop off the table as Wade stuck his mitt out in nonchalant fashion, snared it, and replied, 'What the fuck was that?'"

1978

The Blues Rise to the Challenge of the Three-Peat

> *Solid defense behind good pitching and an offensive attack bolstered by seven home runs combined to give the Scobey Blues their third consecutive State Class B baseball title.*
>
> —*Daniels County Leader, August 3, 1978*

PRESEASON

The players in Daniels County competed against each other in basketball earlier in the winter of 1978. All three Daniels County high school basketball teams competed in challenge games to qualify for the state tournament. Peerless beat Flaxville 61-52 in a challenge game at Wolf Point to qualify for the first state tournament in the school's history and finished third at State. Scobey lost to Circle 70-60 in their challenge game. But back on the baseball field in April, the challenge for the boys from Peerless, Scobey, and Flaxville—and Glentana—was to come together and three-peat as State Class B Legion baseball champions.

A new set of uniforms arrived that spring, the first to display "BLUES" on the front of the jersey. The uniforms were white with blue trim. The original all-blue uniforms from 1974 were still an option, as were the mesh jerseys with "SCOBEY" on the front. One of my favorite things about having the three uniform sets was when Kelly would call the team and let us know the combination for that day's game: "White jerseys with blue pants today."

All nine starters from 1977 were returning and were one year older, but, with an average age of 16 years and eight months, were still young by Legion standards. Allan Audet was the only 18-year-old on the roster. Players still eligible to play—but missing on the field at Doc's first practice in April—were Bernie Wasser, Don Holyk, Brad Henderson, Mike Abar, and Don Boos. They were all excellent baseball players—the double play Don Holyk and Bernie Wasser turned in the ninth inning of the state championship game demonstrated the depth of talent on this team. Had Dad fielded a Legion team in Peerless, this would have made room for these talented players on separate Peerless and Scobey rosters, but as it was, Doc "had his nine." These five players were as much a part of the 1977 championship team as any other player on the team. We had good chemistry in the dugout. Peerless would have had a good Legion team in Peerless, and Scobey would have had a good Legion team in Scobey. But would each team have been good enough to win a state championship? Dan Danelson recognized the greatness that could be if we combined when we discussed Dad going solo with a Legion team in Peerless. Dano said, "Doc did talk to me about it, and my feelings were I'd idolized many ball players during my adolescence, many being Pucketts, and no fucking way was I not going to be heard regarding the potential we had together. We had played together just enough to know how good it could be. Our run of championships was exactly what we talked about that day."

The nine players forming the starting lineup from 1977 were all returning in 1978:

- Wade Tryan (17) CF
- Kelly Norman (16) 2B/P
- Joe Puckett (17) SS/P
- Dan Danelson (17) 3B/P
- Allan Audet (18) RF/C
- Kirby Halvorson (16) C/RF/P
- Randy Stolen (16) LF/P
- Jon Puckett (17) 3B/SS/2B/P
- Ray Chapman (17) 1B/P

Joining the team as rookies in 1978 were David Corey (17) from Scobey and Ron Higgins (15) from Flaxville, who was following in his three older brother's footsteps—John "Jack," Don, and Barry. Jack and Don played on the 1969 state championship team, and Don and Barry played on the 1970 second-place and 1971 third-place teams. Barry's last year was 1972. Jacki Tade and DeeAnn Lekvold were back as batgirls, and Mike Roland and Rick and Mike Lee were batboys. Don Lekvold was the assistant coach again, and Dick Atwood continued to drive the bus and helped manage things on the field.

Doc was feeling good about the upcoming season: "Coach Norman—now with a new hip—as usual, is optimistic about his club's chances this season. 'They're the greatest,' he said."[150]

REGULAR SEASON

Doc had arranged an ambitious schedule for the 1978 team with 16 conference games and 18 non-conference games, including a doubleheader against the Royals and Scarlets to open the season in mid-May. Other non-conference games were against Sidney, Glendive, Grenora, and the Williston Keybirds. Conference teams in 1978 were Scobey, Wolf Point, Plentywood, and Poplar. The divisional tournament was scheduled for Scobey, and the state tournament was back in Cut Bank, where we had won the state championship in 1976.

I was excited to hear we would open the season with a doubleheader against the Royals and the Scarlets in Billings in May. I had never played either team and had never played on Cobb Field before. I watched several Billings Mustangs games on Cobb Field and always hoped I could play on that field someday. Previous Scobey teams had played there, the first in 1966 when Phil Audet and Dan Smith led Scobey to a 4-3 win over the Scarlets. The 1969 Scobey Legion team played there, too, losing to the Royals 4-1. The 1974 team, on a solid pitching performance by Jay Hagfeldt, also beat the Scarlets 4-3 on Cobb Field.

But because it was so early in the season, Cobb Field was not ready for baseball, so the games were moved to Rocky Mountain's Klindt Field. I was very disappointed that I could not play on Cobb Field. I still hoped that someday I would get to do that. I had one last chance in 1979.

In the first game, we lost to the Royals 2-1. Dan Danelson pitched an exceptional game, giving up five hits and striking out 14 Royals. We played well in the field, but the one error we made in the outfield led to the winning run for Billings. To stay in games with Class A competition, you have to play well in the field, and we did that. Mike Day had two hits and drove in one run for the Royals. We remembered Mike Day from the Billings Western Giants Little League team. He hit a two-run home run off us in the first inning when we lost to the Western Giants 8-5 in Border League All-Stars when we were 12 years old, spoiling our run to win the western divisional tournament. He now batted leadoff for the Royals, was a good shortstop, and was fast. He symbolized the Royals' supremacy over Scobey, and we wanted to beat him and the Royals, whom Doc had a 0 and 4 lifetime record against. We hoped to get another chance to beat Mike Day and the Royals. That chance would come in 1979, and we would make the most of it.

The second game against the Scarlets had more of a practice-game feel. Doc started Ray Chapman against the Scarlets. His knuckler wasn't working that day, and they jumped on him for four runs in the first inning. Jon had come in by the end of the second inning, but the Scarlets had scored nine runs in the first two innings and put the game out of reach, eventually winning 14-2. But we played some good competition in the first two games in May and were ready to take on the Class B competition in the regular season.

We opened our conference season on Memorial Day at Scobey Ball Park against Plentywood. This was a special day at Scobey Ball Park, as the Post 56 American Legion, comprised of military personnel who had served in the United States Armed Forces, were honored that day, and those service members who had made the ultimate sacrifice were remembered. Playing on the Fourth of July against Browning the previous year was special, as was on Memorial Day in 1978. It doesn't get any more American than playing baseball on Memorial Day and the Fourth of July.

The game was a back-and-forth affair, and Plentywood took the lead 10-9 in the top of the ninth. Randy Wangerin from Outlook was brought in from shortstop to pitch for Brad Partyka to save the game for Plentywood in the bottom of the ninth. But with two out, I hit a single between third and short to drive home the tying run, and we went on to walk it off, 11-10, winning our home opener. As I stood on first base after the game-tying hit, Randy looked over at me, shook his head, and smiled, and I smiled back at him. He said, "Goddamn it, Puckett." We had faced each other on the baseball field dating to our first game as Peewee players in Outlook 10 years earlier in 1968, with me pitching for Peerless and Randy pitching for Outlook. We were two old Class C rivals who guarded each other in basketball for 10 years. Outlook had won the state championship in 1978, but we beat them in the conference and district tournament. But today, we faced each other in baseball, playing for Scobey and Plentywood, two old Class B rivals. There was mutual respect between us, which allowed us to smile. On some days over those 10 years, Randy had gotten the best of me, and some days, I had gotten the best of him, but today was my day. What I wouldn't give for another day on the court or on the field, where Randy might have the opportunity to get the best of me.

Our opening-day walk-off win over Plentywood on Memorial Day was not the only walk-off win for Scobey during the regular season. Trailing Wolf Point 6-5 entering the ninth inning, Ray Chapman's RBI single drove in the winning run to win it 7-6. Those were the only two close calls we had during the regular season.

In other games against Class A teams, we split a home-and-home series against the Williston Keybirds, who had won the North Dakota State AA championship in 1976. In the game in Scobey, Dan Danelson pitched a six-hit shutout, and we beat them 2-0. In the game in Williston, Doc started Ray, and his knuckleball was working that day. He pitched six strong innings, relieved by Dano in the seventh. Allan Audet caught, as Kirby was injured during the season, so Allan caught most of 1978 with Kirby in right field. The game was a back-and-forth affair.

Williston opened the scoring in the third inning with a single run, then widened its margin to 3-0 after a two-run fifth. We led off with four consecutive singles in the sixth frame to knot the score at three, and each team added two runs in the seventh to up the score to 5-5. Kelly McNary from Williston then singled with the bases loaded in the ninth inning to give the Keybirds a 6-5 win and end the see-saw battle. I remember the umpire saying to me as we left the field, "You can't win them all," as he knew we were undefeated against Class B teams in Montana that season.

Regarding progression for the 1978 team, with one more year of physical maturity, more extra-base hits were being hit. Power on the team had always come from Randy, Kirby, and Allan, but now extra-base hits started to come from other positions in the lineup, making the run production significantly more potent. Kelly Norman, now 16 years old, was routinely hitting doubles. After flashing a little power at the 1977 state tournament, Cliff Hagfeldt nicknamed Kelly "King Kong Kelly Norman." Kelly was growing into the title. Our defense and pitching were getting better, too, but if there was one aspect of the game where there was marked improvement from 1977, it was in hitting, especially power. The *Leader* saw the team increasing its power at the season's midpoint when it wrote, "The Blues have been coming up with more extra-base hits in recent games, led by Danelson, Norman, Halvorson, Stolen, and Tryan." The *Leader* also recognized that the team was strong in all three aspects of the game when it wrote that the Blues had a "solid pitching staff, good fielding, and some big bats."[151]

A significant highlight of the 1978 regular season was a no-hitter—the fifth in Scobey Legion history—pitched by Ray Chapman against Poplar in Poplar, with Kirby Halvorson calling the signals. Ray said, "Yes, I definitely remember that one and, especially, [Randy] Stolen's no-hitter saving catch. He pretty much laid out to catch it. The knuckleball was working that day; I remember distinctly the wind was blowing in my face, which, of course, was perfect for the knuckleball to flutter." Yes, it was. I was watching it dance around the plate at shortstop all day. He struck out nine Poplar batters and walked four, leading us to the 11-0 win. His only close call came in the fourth inning when center fielder Randy Stolen made a diving catch to preserve the pitching gem. Scobey scored two runs in the first and two in the fifth off Fred Steele, then exploded for seven runs on eight hits in the seventh, including doubles by Kelly Norman and Dan Danelson.

In addition to Ray's no-hitter, there some other regular season highlights: Dan Danelson struck out 19 Reds in a 14-5 win over Glasgow; Kelly Norman pitched Scobey to a 6-3 win over Doug Frenzel and Glendive; in a stretch of 12 consecutive games, the team committed only one error or played errorless ball; Jon Puckett had consecutive 11-strikeout complete-game wins over Circle and Wolf Point; in addition to his no-hitter, Ray Chapman had two three-hitters; in a doubleheader against Poplar and Wolf Point on the same day, Joe Puckett went 7-10 with five doubles; Kelly Norman pitched a four-hitter and struck out 11 in a 7-1 over Plentywood; Allan Audet led the team in extra-base hits—mostly doubles—during the regular season.

One thing to note in the regular season highlights was that Doc was getting plenty of innings on the mound for Kelly and Ray. The pitching rotation was five deep; he would need this depth in the divisional and state tournaments. Doc had won the state tournament the year before with just three pitchers—Dan Danelson, Jon and Joe Puckett—but that was a one-off. Jon pitched out of his mind in that tournament with two complete-game wins and a save in 18 and one-third innings pitched, appearing in three of the four games. You normally need four—sometimes five—pitchers to win an eight-team tournament. Kelly and Ray would be ready to go if we needed them, and we would.

The Blues steamrolled through the conference undefeated with a 16-0 record and carried a 25-3 overall mark entering the eastern divisional tournament in Scobey, winning all 25 games against Class B competition. The only three regular-season losses were to the Royals, Scarlets, and Keybirds. Returning to the previous season, where we won four straight games to win the State Class B state tournament, the winning streak against Class B competition was 29 games. Our last loss was to Sidney, 5-4, in the eastern divisional in Sidney in 1977.

We were ready and excited to play on our home field in the eastern divisional tournament, with the top four teams advancing to the state tournament in Cut Bank.

DIVISIONAL TOURNAMENT

IF PLAYING IN THE STATE TOURNAMENT IN SCOBEY WAS EXCITing, playing in the eastern divisional tournament was no less so. Seven teams traveled to Scobey for the tournament. The *Daniels County Leader*, American Legion Post 56, all the volunteers, and the fans treated this tournament like any other Scobey hosted, as Scobey was "Baseball Country." The *Leader* wrote, "Since the most successful state tournament ever in 1969, area baseball fans and players prove year after year that this is top baseball country."[152]

As always, Cliff Hanson and state Class B Legion baseball commissioner Gene Marley spearheaded arrangements with committees made up of Post 56 members, fans, and parents of players. The Legion concession stand, with the famous Legion Burgers, was open all three days. A kickoff breakfast was hosted on Friday morning for the tournament officials, coaches, and various committee members.

The *Leader* identified Scobey, with its 16-0 conference and 25-3 overall record, as the pre-tourney favorite but also called out Sidney as the southern champion with its 8-4 conference record. This was the third consecutive year Sidney had won the southern district. The bracket printed in the *Leader* showed the opening-day matchups: Baker-Ekalaka vs. Wolf Point, Glendive vs. Glasgow, Sidney vs. Plentywood, and Scobey vs. Circle.

Allan Audet is surrounded by happy Scobey teammates as he crosses the plate after a mighty line drive home run over the left-center field fence in the Circle game. *Leader photo, Milt Gunderson.*

Doc started me in our opening game against Circle. Allan was catching as he had been for most of the regular season with Kirby's injury. There was a fine crowd on hand for this night game, as there were for all games in the tournament. It felt no different than playing in the state championship game the year before. Allan Audet hit a booming home run to left center in the third inning for our first run, and we added another run in the fourth to take a 2-0 lead.

I was pitching well with my good defense behind me, yielding only one run in the fourth inning, but Jeff Sukut, with Kevin Sukut catching, kept Circle in the game. This was a pitcher's duel until the bottom of the seventh when we rallied for four runs off Sukut to take a 6-1 lead. Circle rallied for three runs off me in the eighth to close to 6-4, but I shut them down in the ninth, and we won 6-4 to advance. Circle was the fourth seed from the south but had a good baseball team. No team in this tournament was a slouch, and each game was a battle. The *Leader* called it an "evenly matched eight-team tournament."[153]

Wade Tryan is out attempting to score from third in the third inning of the Circle game. Circle catcher Kevin Sukut made the tag. *Leader photo, Milt Gunderson.*

In other opening-round results, pitchers played critical roles in Glendive, Wolf Point, and Sidney's victories. A pair of two-hitters earned Wolf Point and Glendive their wins as Glendive's Doug Frenzel tossed a two-hit shutout, 12-0, at Glasgow, and Wolf Point's Mike Neubauer pitched a two-hitter and fanned 13 Baker-Ekalaka batters en route to a 4-2 win. Frenzel and Neubauer also helped their causes at the plate. Frenzel cracked a three-run homer in the fifth to pad Glendive's lead; Neubauer hit a three-run triple in the eighth, then scored himself to key Wolf Point's winning four-run rally. Until Neubauer's triple, pitcher Mitch Anderson from Baker-Ekalaka had shut out Wolf Point. In Sidney's 13-3 win over Plentywood, Tom Paladichuk pitched a three-hitter, and Sidney racked up nine hits, including a three-run home run by Jeff Lebsock in the fourth inning to put Sidney ahead, 5-3.

Glendive's win over Glasgow set up our semifinal against them. Recall the dramatic 6-5 victory over Glendive the previous year under the lights in the state tournament. Glendive returned many players from its 1977 team, and we were the same team. Doc started Dan Danelson, and Glendive countered with Craig Ballantine, the two starting pitchers from the previous year. This game was again under the lights.

We scored two runs in the top of the third to take a 2-0 lead, but in the bottom half, Glendive scored four runs on three walks and two singles to take a 4-2 lead. Dano, who finished with a six-hitter, settled down after that, and our defense did not allow a run in the last six innings. Several miscues by Glendive—they committed seven errors in the game—helped us to score enough runs to come back and win. We scored a single run in the fourth to close to 4-3. The tying and go-ahead runs came in the sixth when Allan Audet singled and scored on a fielder's choice. Randy Stolen reached base on another fielder's choice and came home on an error to make it 5-4 Scobey. We added an insurance run in the seventh. Dano's pitching after the rough fourth inning, our defense, and some timely hitting allowed us to come from behind and win 6-4. Bob Clump had a pair of hits for Glendive in the loss. Dan Danelson tripled, and Kelly Norman singled and doubled to lead Scobey's hitting.

Allan Audet bats against Glendive's Craig Ballantine in Scobey's come-from-behind 6-4 win over Glendive in Saturday night's semifinal game in the Eastern Divisional. *Photo by Mazel Audet.*

In the other semifinal, Sidney beat Wolf Point 5-1. Wolf Point tallied its sole run in the top of the fourth to end a scoreless game. But a triple, double, and single in its half of the inning gave Sidney a one-run margin and the lead for good. Tom Paladichuk opened with a triple and scored on a double by Jeff Nesper, who crossed the plate on a Craig Smith single. Sidney added another run in the fifth and two more in the eighth to cushion its lead. Jeff Lebsock gave up five hits and fanned seven en route to the win, while Wolf Point's Dan Jensen yielded nine hits for the loss.

Sidney's semifinal win over Wolf Point set up the divisional championship game between Scobey and Sidney, which also recalled the previous year's state championship game between these two teams on this same field. And like the year before, Doc handed the ball to Jon Puckett in the championship game. Coach Craig Price of Sidney countered with Tom Paladichuk as his starter for the championship game.

There's nothing like playing a championship game on your home field in front of your home fans. Scobey Ball Park was packed for the championship game on a beautiful summer day in northeastern Montana. I felt tingly when the crowd cheered our team as I ran out to take my usual position at shortstop to start the game, and Jon was warming up on the mound. I was aware of our 27-game winning streak, but you don't want to think about that or talk about it; that's a jinx.

This game was treated like any other on the streak: play solid for 27 outs and come out on top. Sidney had a good team in 1978, as they had the previous two years. We didn't have any fantasies about blowing anyone out, just being the better team. Our two wins in the tournament had been by identical two-run scores of 6-4 and 6-4. In both wins, different players stepped up to make key plays defensively, and Dano and I came through with big pitches when needed and bats popped when it mattered most.

Sidney took a 1-0 lead in the first inning when they scored an unearned run on the only two errors we committed in the game. We tied it in the bottom of the third when Wade Tryan singled, and Kelly Norman drove him home with a double. Sidney strung together four consecutive singles off Jon in the top of the fourth but only scored one run, enough to give it the edge again, 2-1. We came back to tie it 2-2 in the bottom of the inning when Randy Stolen clubbed his first of two doubles in the game and crossed the plate on a single by Jon Puckett.

In the top of the fifth inning, with the score tied 2-2, Jon Puckett uncharacteristically ran into control problems, and Sidney loaded the bases with no one out. It was time for Doc to dial 911-DANO. Recall a year earlier in the game against Glendive when Dano got into trouble with control problems and walked the bases loaded, and Doc brought Jon in to squelch the fire; now it was the opposite. Dano "threw smoke"[154] and struck out the next three Sidney hitters to get us off the field without any runs allowed, and

Kirby Halvorson is batting, and Randy Stolen is on deck in the Eastern Divisional championship game against Sidney. *Family photo.*

we sprinted into the dugout to grab our bats and try to get the go-ahead run off Tom Paladichuk, who was pitching well for Sidney.

Dano, who had three innings of eligibility left after pitching nine innings against Glendive the night before, also held Sidney scoreless in the sixth and seventh. We took the lead for the first time in the bottom of the seventh inning off Jeff Lebsock—who had relieved Tom Paladichuk in the sixth—when Jon Puckett singled, went to third on a fielder's choice, and came home on an error for what proved to be the winning run. Jon hit his third single of the game in the eighth to drive in the final two runs, his second and third RBIs of the game. We threatened further in that inning, but with me batting with a full count and the bases loaded, catcher Jeff Nesper called for a curveball from Jeff Lebsock, and he got me to chase it off the plate for strike three. After facing each other as many times as we had in 1977 and 1978, the Sidney pitchers and catchers knew how to pitch us. I was looking for a fastball on the full count and got fooled.

Doc brought in Kelly to preserve the 5-2 lead for Scobey in the eighth and ninth innings. Kelly always pitched well in critical situations, and he held Sidney scoreless for the final two innings to save the game and win our first divisional championship as a team. The crowd cheered us as we swarmed Kelly and Allan Audet—who caught every game in the tournament—on the mound. Catching the divisional championship game, winning the tournament—and hitting a home run earlier in the tournament against Circle—was a storybook ending for 18-year-old Allan Audet, playing in his last three games on Scobey's home field.

Dan Danelson earned his second tournament win in three innings of relief, relieving Jon Puckett in the fifth, striking out the side after Sidney loaded the bases. Jeff Lebsock, who relieved Tom Paladichuk in the sixth, took the loss for Sidney. Jon Puckett, who started the game as a pitcher, ironically won the game for Scobey with this bat: he had three singles, drove in three runs, and scored a run, factoring in four of Scobey's five runs. Jon's three singles and three RBIs as the eighth-place hitter in the lineup symbolized how any player on this team could step and produce in any game to key the team's victory. It also showed how, in the same game, one player could contribute to the team in multiple ways, as a pitcher, hitter, and fielder.

The next day's headline in the *Gazette* read, "28th straight win gives Scobey title."[155] Going back to the four-game sweep of the 1977 state tournament in Scobey, the streak was now 32 games.

The other two teams to advance to State were Glendive and Wolf Point. Kip Harcharik hurled a three-hitter against Plentywood and allowed only one run in the eighth as Wolf Point won 8-1. Terry Baldry provided the offensive punch for Wolf Point, belting a two-run double in the fourth and blasting a solo homer in the eighth to account for two of his team's seven hits.

Glendive, meanwhile, took full advantage of eight Circle errors for a 15-7 triumph. Glendive totaled 12 hits in its game, but numerous Circle miscues proved more crucial. Circle jumped on a 4-2 lead after one inning, only to see Glendive knot the score in the second on a two-run homer by Doug Frenzel. The two clubs played evenly until the seventh inning when, with the score locked at 7-7, Glendive posted four runs on two hits and two errors. Another four-run explosion in the eighth allowed Glendive to add more than enough padding to its lead. Frenzel relieved starter Mike Jones and pitched five innings for the win. Teammate Bob Clump gathered three hits, all doubles, while Circle's Jere Murphy and Kevin Sukut both had three hits.

Wolf Point and Glendive met in the consolation game Sunday evening to finalize the third and fourth seeds in the tournament. Wolf Point won the slugfest 15-11 to earn the third seed.

So, we were headed west on the Bluesmobile ("not of Blues Brothers fame," as Ray Chapman says) to the state tournament in Cut Bank, with Dick Atwood at the wheel. We were riding high with a 28-3 overall record and a 32-game winning streak against Class B teams, with the eastern divisional championship getting further behind us in the rearview mirror. We were playing good baseball with tempered confidence and were heavily favored to win the state tournament. However, sitting on the bus, watching the beautiful state of Montana pass by as the bus rolled westward, I thought about the bizarre events of the 1976 state tournament in Cut Bank two years earlier when I was 15. I wondered if Cut Bank could again be the scene of madness, on and off the field. Could anything match the drama and unpredictability of that 1976 tournament in Cut Bank and the improbable state championship win over Wolf Point?

One thought that haunted me was what the umpire in Williston said to me after Williston walked it off against us in the bottom of the ninth inning to win 6-5. He said, "You can't win them all." It's one thing to go undefeated in basketball, but it's quite another in baseball. Could we sweep the tournament again in four games to win it and stay undefeated?

DIVISIONAL TOURNAMENT SUMMARY

THE 1978 EASTERN DIVISIONAL TOURNAMENT WAS ANOTHER successful tournament hosted by Scobey and a well-played tournament by all eight teams. "Fine baseball weather prevailed, and fans flocked in to support their teams."[156] As it always was careful to do, the *Leader* recognized all the volunteers who made the tournament a success, including the groundskeepers, scorekeepers, announcers, people who provided room and board for the visiting players, ticket sellers, Post 56 baseball committee, and the concession stand crew. These volunteers "all joined together to prove once again that unpaid labor is the best there is."[157] It also recognized Head Coach Doc Norman and Assistant Don Lekvold as volunteers, mentioning that they "received the same pay as those mentioned above."[158] Umpires for the tournament were Don Pertuit, Duke Trangsrud, Dick Puckett, Rocky Ware, and Jeff Richardson.

The eight teams were "evenly matched"[159] and of the 12 games played, 10 were cross-conference, with the southern and northern conferences splitting those games. Each conference sent two teams to State: Scobey and Wolf Point from the north and Sidney and Glendive from the south.

Five home runs were hit in the tournament, including two by Doug Frenzel of Glendive and one by Allan Audet, Jeff Lebsock, and Terry Baldry from Wolf Point. Sidney won the team batting trophy with a .285 average. Two two-hitters were thrown in the opening-day games: Doug Frenzel and Mike Neubauer. Scobey's winning pitchers were Joe Puckett against Circle and Dan Danelson against Glendive and Sidney, with Kelly Norman earning the save against Sidney.

One significant positive change to the 1978 Eastern Divisional Tournament format was removing the double-elimination requirement, reducing the tournament to 12 games and from four days to three. There were no back-to-back games scheduled. The consolation game was played after the championship game but was only for seeding for the state tournament. In the previous format, Wolf Point would have played Sidney, with the winner of that game playing Scobey for the championship. If Scobey had lost that game, an additional game would have been played for the championship. This reduced format saved pitching arms. Good call.

1978 Scobey Blues, Eastern Division Champions. Standing, left to right: Coach Doc Norman, Allan Audet, Kelly Norman, Dan Danelson, David Corey, Kirby Halvorson, Randy Stolen, Ass't Coach Don Lekvold. Kneeling, left to right: Manager Dick Atwood, Jon Puckett, Ray Chapman, Wade Tryan, Joe Puckett, Ron Higgins. Sitting, left to right: Rick Lee, DeeAnn Lekvold, Jacki Tade, Mike Roland. The photo was taken minutes after the championship win over Sidney. *Leader, caption and photo by Milt Gunderson.*

1978 Richland County Patriots were the southern conference champions and won the second-place divisional trophy. Standing, left to right: Coach Craig Price, Ken Barnhart, Steve Heit, Todd Morasko, Tim Thogerson, Craig Smith. Kneeling, left to right: batboy Troy Butner, Jeff Lebsock, Tom Paladichuk, Scott Kemmiss, Jeff Nesper, Bryon Johnson, and batboy Matt Price. *Leader photo, Milt Gunderson.*

EXTRA INNINGS

ALLAN AUDET REMEMBERS AN INCIDENT DURING THE EASTERN divisional tournament that was scary then but is funny now: "We dodged a bullet in 1978. There was a dance in Flaxville. All the teams were there. Dan was in the backseat of my car as we were slowly passing the barn, and he yelled, 'Let me out.' Just as I was slowing down, he opened the door and stuck his long-ass leg out. Being that we had those baggy pants back then, my tire grabbed his pant and he shot out like a rocket and I literally ran over his leg. I thought, *Oh shit*, and jumped out to see him lying there. He stood up and had a big ol' hunk of skin missing on his ankle. He was scheduled to pitch the next day. He said, 'Don't tell Doc.' We wrapped it up, and he pitched. The next day, I remember going to the mound to see blood soaking through. Can't believe I felt the bump as I rolled over Dan's leg."

All the teams were there at the dance that night in Flaxville. I remember Mike Neubauer from Wolf Point looking at Danny Elfring from Glasgow and saying, "Elfring, you sorry sonofabitch." If Scobey and Plentywood were rivals in Class B, Glasgow and Wolf Point were rivals in Class A.

At the season-opening doubleheader against the Royals and Scarlets in Billings in May, the band Rush—with Uriah Heep as the opening act—performed live at Billings Metra on the Saturday night before the doubleheader, and several Blues players went. For many, it was the first concert they saw. I was not among them as I wanted to prepare for the Royals and Scarlets the next day. (Boring, I know.) Kirby said he couldn't hear for three days after the concert. The price for a concert ticket was $6 in advance and $7 the day of the show. Can you imagine seeing a concert for $6 today? The first concert I saw was Manifest Destiny at the Scobey Saddle Club. That counts, right? I also saw some killer concerts at the Catholic Center. But the best concerts and dances in Daniels County were always in Flaxville. Just be careful getting out of cars while they're still moving on the main street.

Rocky Ware, who played first base for Scobey's first state championship team in 1969, started a disco for kids in the front room of the Ponderosa Bar in 1978. It was fantastic to have something like that for teenagers and tournament players. I remember dancing in there to rock and roll music with the lights flashing. I wouldn't say I liked most of the disco music of the 1970s—except *Saturday Night Fever*—but I loved rock and roll music with the disco lights. My one specific memory in the disco was dancing with Chris Handy from Flaxville to the song "Carry On Wayward Son" by Kansas. We danced all night together; it was fun, and I remember it well.

I'm glad the *Leader* wrote that our 1978 team was "holding up the Scobey Country baseball tradition, which dates back to teams before 1920."[160] *The Blues of Summer* started with the first Scobey baseball town team in 1914, discussed the 1925 team with former Chicago White Sox players Swede Risberg and Happy Felsch, Scobey's first Legion team (district champions) in 1930, and the famous Plainsmen teams in the 1950s and 1960s. Our Legion team was carrying on the Scobey baseball tradition, which had preceded us by generations. The baseball story in Scobey goes back that far, and not starting there would have made this story incomplete.

In 1976, I referenced former Saint Louis Cardinal catcher and baseball broadcaster Joe Garagiola's quote, "It's pitching, hitting, and defense that wins. Any two can win. All three make you unbeatable." The context of that quote was that the Achille's heel of the 1976 Scobey and Wolf Point teams was their fielding, but each team's pitching and hitting could carry them to wins in any game. Heading into the state tournament in Cut Bank, the Blues were firing on all three baseball cylinders—pitching, hitting, and fielding—leading to 32 consecutive wins against Class B competition, validating Garagiola's comment that all three make you unbeatable.

In the regular season game against Circle in Scobey, Jon Puckett pitched a six-hitter and struck out 11 Zephyrs, leading Scobey to a 9-4 win and running his pitching record to 3-0. However, one Circle hitter did not strike out and had one of the six hits was Darrel Kleppelid, who smashed a booming home run over the left field fence. Jon remembers the home run: "I think it bounced off the curling rink. I even changed the lyrics to the song, 'Mr. Custer,' because of him. The lyric is, 'Please Mr. Custer, I don't want to go.' I changed it to, 'Please Mr. Kleppelid, I don't want to throw.'"

Dan Danelson remembers a tobacco-chewing story while pitching during the 1978 regular season. Dano recalls, "A liner was hit up the middle and close enough to my head that I flinched and swallowed leaf tobacco. The only thing that saved me was I wrapped it in bubble gum, so it didn't have the full disgusting taste going down, and I probably kept it down, too. I called Kelly in to buy some time. I didn't think it would be too cool to barf all over the mound. And when he got to the mound, he said, 'Just stand here.'

I swallowed my chew, and so we chatted and laughed." Kelly recalls a similar incident when they were batboys. "We did get into Beech-Nut, and we puked." Almost every Legion player I've interviewed has a funny story about chewing tobacco. Terry Puckett shared his with me: "One time before a game Doc gave me some Beech-Nut leafy tobacco to chew. I didn't know I was supposed to spit it out, so I got sick!"

On the bus ride to Cut Bank, Albert was teasing me again about my retarded face. This time, it was in the 4B's Restaurant in Havre, where we stopped to eat on the way to Cut Bank. I ordered a salad ahead of my main course, but before I took my first bite, Allan announced to the team sitting at the table, "Hey, wanna see something funny? Watch Puckett eat." Goddamn it, Albert.

Sidney pitcher Tom Paladichuk threw a one-hitter and struck out 15 Yellowjackets in a 5-0 shutout over Wolf Point during the 1978 regular season. Kip Harcharik (who else) broke up the no-hitter with a double in the eighth inning. Tom said, "I always tease Kip when I stop and see him in Billings. It was a bloop double over second." But Kip might remember it differently? Maybe a line shot to right?

Tom Paladichuk, when remembering his playing days with Sidney, recalls playing the Blues: "We had to be at our best when we played you guys. I love the game of baseball. And I loved playing against good competition, and you guys were definitely all of that. I loved getting up to play you guys and the Williston Keybirds, two of my favorite teams to play against, because you both played good fundamental baseball and were the best." Sidney, coached by Craig Price, had excellent baseball teams during those years. With our win streak against Class B teams at 32 games before the state tournament, the Patriots were the last team to beat us, 5-4, in the 1977 Eastern Divisional Tournament in Sidney. We got up to play you, too, Tom.

At a game in Sidney, the Sidney players demonstrated the "tea kettle" sign for the steal (and/or for a called third strike?) that colorful umpire Jerry Callen from Sidney used in the 1970s. It was funny to see. When Tom Paladichuk remembered it, he said it made him smile. Thirty-five years later, in 2013, I used the tea kettle steal sign for my U10 recreational girls' fast-pitch softball team in Germany. They loved it and thought it was funny, too. I also used the sign for the parents in the parent-daughter game. If a parent got on first base, they wanted me to flash them the "tea kettle" steal sign. I passed on the love of baseball from Sidney to Germany, and everyone was smiling. Please pass it on.

David Corey was on the roster for the 1978 season and for part of the 1979 season. I remember him as a friendly kid who wanted to learn to play baseball. He was part of the team, and I enjoyed talking with him in the dugout. I wondered how it came to be that he was on the team. Kelly told me he and his family were neighbors, and David wanted to play baseball. Kelly said, "Doc always let anybody do it; he thought he could help them." Doc had a nickname for everyone on the team, including the batboys and batgirls, and David did not escape a nickname for himself. Typically, Doc tagged you with your nickname (mine was Guiseppe), but Dano tagged David with his. Dano recalls, "I came up with 'the Buzzard' while waiting with Doc on the bus for David. David was tall and long, and when he walked, he covered some ground. I envisioned him swooping like a buzzard to get his prey. I told Doc that, and he said to give him a call as he was walking over from next door. Every time he would walk to the bus, Doc would say, 'Dano, give him the buzzard call,' so I would call, 'Cacaw, cacaw!' He was usually next to the last group of players there. We know the final group [the Pucketts]. It was fun to watch the Shark pull up and entertain for five minutes rummaging around looking for pieces of clothing to complete their uniform."

One name noticeably missing from the list of big hits for Scobey in the regular season and tournament was Kirby Halvorson. Kirby was injured in 1978 but was still able to play right field. He had two injuries that were hampering him—his knee and his hip. He injured his knee while playing football in his freshman year and again in his sophomore year. He had knee surgery in October of 1977, but he kept having issues with soreness and swelling and the knee giving out. He only made it through a couple of weeks of basketball. The knee improved but would swell some, and the patella would subluxate. Then, early in the 1978 baseball season, he badly pulled his right hip flexor. So, he couldn't squat repeatedly due to both those issues. Kirby thought that not catching might have been affecting his hitting. He said, "I went through a 2 for 23 stretch leading up to and through the divisional tourney. I struck out about half of those outs. I felt like I wasn't tracking the ball. So, I talked Doc into letting me catch during batting practice off the machine." We'll have to wait until the state tournament in "Part 2" to see if catching batting practice off the machine might awaken Kirby from his hitting slumber.

After Kirby's hip injury early in the 1978 season, Allan Audet took over all the catching duties. We were lucky to have depth at that position, as Albert was an excellent catcher and knew how to handle our pitching staff, from left-handed knuckleballer Ray Chapman to right-handed flamethrower Dan Danelson and everything in between. Thank God we had Albert as a catcher with Kirby's injury.

STATE B TOURNAMENT

As Dick Atwood rolled the bus into Cut Bank, my memories of the bizarre 1976 tournament flooded back to me. Wow. What an experience that was. Now, two years later, it was a different feeling. We were favored to win, and everyone knew we were the team to beat. Two years earlier, the Scobey baseball program was respected, but we weren't expected to win it. Before the start of that tournament, Doc had won two state championships. Now he had four—two in a row—and we were going for a third consecutive and fifth overall.

It was a contrasting experience as a two-sport athlete playing basketball and baseball that year. At the state basketball tournament in Helena five months earlier, no one—except Outlook—knew who the Peerless Panthers were, and no one expected anything from us. We were the underdog of underdogs. But we exited that tournament with three wins and a third-place trophy, which we considered a resounding success. Entering Cut Bank, when the people saw "Scobey Blues" on the side of the bus, everyone knew who we were. We wouldn't sneak up on anyone with two consecutive state championships and a 28-game winning streak. Anything short of winning the tournament would be considered an abject failure, but I felt no pressure. I enjoyed the feeling of being the favorite. During my senior year in basketball, though, I did not enjoy it—there was too much expectation and pressure.

The four teams from the west, who would join the Scobey Blues, Richland County Patriots, Wolf Point Yellowjackets, and Glendive Blue Devils from the east, were—in order of finish—the Butte Muckers, Cut Bank Lobos, Great Falls Vigilantes, and the Laurel Dodgers. The Muckers, led by pitcher Todd Moriarity, who struck out 15 Lobos, had beaten Cut Bank 5-3 for the western title, and the Vigilantes beat the Dodgers 5-4 for third place.

Our first game of the tournament was against Laurel, the fourth seed from the west. Although they historically had a successful Legion baseball program, Laurel had disappeared from the American Legion Baseball scene for several years. Twenty years earlier, in 1959, Doc's first Scobey team, led by pitcher Kevin Sell, lost to Laurel in a best-of-three series in Laurel for the eastern division championship, but that was the only time the two programs had met. Laurel won state Class B championships in 1950, 1956, and 1960-61, so they had four state championships, as many as Scobey did then. Had any of us known that, it would have given us an extra incentive to beat them and win the tournament, but as it was, we didn't need any incentive. Laurel was just another game on the path to the championship.

We had a solid following at the tournament. "Every parent of the Scobey ballplayers was in attendance to watch their boys win. They were joined by a number of other fans from the area, plus numerous former county residents who converged on Cut Bank for the tournament."[161] As the other fans, players, and coaches from the opposing teams watched us warming up, they knew that if their team was going to win this tournament, they would need to beat us—maybe twice—to do it. We were confident.

Loyal Scobey fans at the state tournament in Cut Bank. Family photo.

Doc Norman handed the ball to the crafty left-handed knuckleballer, Ray Chapman, to start the game. We jumped on Laurel early, as Kirby Halvorson, mired in a 2 for 23 slump at the end of the regular season and through the divisional tournament, smashed a line shot home run over the left field fence in the second inning to stake us to a 1-0 lead. Seeing Kirby break out of his slump was inspiring because I knew we needed his bat to win the tournament. His request to Doc to catch batting practice off the pitching machine had worked. Kirby told me that getting out of his catching rhythm, his usual position, might have thrown him off his hitting rhythm. Whether or not that was true didn't matter. If he *thought* it was affecting his hitting, it was. That's baseball.

We were in complete control of this game; after Kirby's home run, we scored five runs in the third to take a 6-1 lead, then added a solo run in the fourth, two in the fifth, three in the sixth, and three more in the seventh to take a 15-2 lead. Ray pitched a one-hitter through six innings to get the win, and Jon came in the seventh to finish the combined one-hitter off. Doc knew he needed to get Ray some mound time and experience pitching in a state tournament, as we might need him later in the tournament, and we did.

In other first-round games, the *Billings Gazette* headline read, "Sweep by East in Legion."[162] The power was in the east in baseball those years, as in basketball. A familiar cheer ringing through fieldhouses at state tournaments from cheerleaders and fans from eastern Montana in the late 1970s was, "Powers in the East, powers in the East!" It was no different in baseball. Jeff Lebsock pitched a one-hitter as Sidney blanked the Great Falls Vigilantes 6-0. Glendive stopped Butte 4-3 as Doug Frenzel struck out 16 Muckers in a five-hitter. In the day's final game, Wolf Point beat Cut Bank 8-7 in 10 innings when Wolf Point coach Clifford Page called a squeeze play with the bases loaded in the tenth inning to win it for Wolf Point.

Wolf Point's dramatic extra-inning win over Cut Bank set up our second-round game with Wolf Point on Friday. Oh boy. Many players on both teams were on the field two years earlier for what ended up being a best-of-three series between the two teams for the 1976 state championship on Saturday, Sunday, and Monday. Three players from Wolf Point—Mike Neubauer, Bill Zimmer, and Kip Harcharik—played on that team, and they all played in the final championship game. Seven players from Scobey—Dan Danelson, Kelly Norman, Allan Audet, Kirby Halvorson, Wade Tryan, and Joe and Jon Puckett—had all played in that game for Scobey. Of course, Don Lekvold had coached the 1976 Wolf Point team but now was in the other dugout for Scobey as Doc's assistant. I remembered those games against Wolf Point from two years ago, and I'm sure the other players and coaches did as well. Two old, friendly rivals from northeastern Montana were again on stage in Cut Bank for this crucial second-round game.

Forget about our 29-game winning streak. This was Wolf Point. They had come close to handing us our only loss earlier in the season, as we came back from a 6-5 deficit in the bottom of the ninth inning in Scobey to walk it off on a single by Ray Chapman. As far as I was concerned, we were both 1-0 in the tournament, which was the only record that mattered. Doc started Jon Puckett in this game, and Coach Page from Wolf Point countered with Mike Neubauer. While not a slugfest, this game had plenty of scoring and power hitting, characteristic of Scobey-Wolf Point games from years past. If there was one thing Wolf Point could always do, it was hit.

Wolf Point jumped to a 2-0 lead in the top of the first, but we countered in the bottom of the second to tie it 2-2. Wolf Point again got to Jon for two runs in the top of the third to take the lead back at 4-2, but we had a big five-run rally in the bottom of the third to go ahead 7-4. Wolf Point added a single run in the top of the sixth, but we again countered in the bottom half, scoring two runs to take a 9-5 lead. In the top of the eighth, Doc brought me in to relieve Jon. I was able to limit Wolf Point to one run in the final two innings to preserve the 9-6 win.

Jon Puckett was the winning pitcher for Scobey, going seven innings. We committed some errors behind Jon, so not all those runs were earned, but Wolf Point hit him. Mike Neubauer took the loss for Wolf Point, going the distance. Now safely out of his slump, Kirby Halvorson banged his second tournament home run and had a double for Scobey. Allan Audet and Randy Stolen also homered. Most of our nine runs came off these three home runs. Wolf Point also flexed their muscles at the plate as Craig Lewis homered and Kip Harcharik doubled. The *Leader* called this game a "tough 9-6 win over Wolf Point," and it was. Wolf Point was never easy. But after the win, we were moving to the undefeated semifinal and looked good, as Doc had yet to use Dan Danelson for a single pitch in the tournament. No doubt he would be the starter for the third game.

Who would our opponent be in the third game? It would be either Sidney or Glendive, who had both won their openers on solid pitching performances by Doug Frenzel and Jeff Lebsock. This game would pit Craig Ballantine from Glendive against Tom Paladichuk from Sidney, and it would be another good game between the two best teams from the southeastern district in Montana. Glendive scored two runs in the first and four in the second to jump to a 6-2 lead after two innings. Paladichuk shut Glendive out for the remaining seven innings. However, the 6-2 deficit was too much for Sidney to overcome, as Glendive won 6-5—their second one-run win of the tournament—forcing Sidney through the dirt route again. The long ball proved critical in this game, too, as Doug Frenzel and Brent Oakland went yard for Glendive, and Tim Thogerson hit a goob for Sidney.

Warming up before the Glendive game on Saturday, we were one win away from the championship game. We were confident but not cocky we could get the job done. As expected, Doc started Dan Danelson, and Mike Jones started for Glendive, with Bob Clump relieving in the third and Dwight Robbins in the seventh. We put all three aspects of the game together in this game with strong pitching, power-hitting, and solid defense to push through the championship game with our third win in the tournament and 31st straight win, 9-0 over Glendive. Dano threw seven innings of two-hit ball—the only two hits were a broken-bat single and a popup misjudged in the outfield—and Kelly Norman pitched two innings of hitless relief to preserve the two-hit shutout. Offensively, Joe Puckett homered and doubled, and Wade Tryan homered for Scobey's sixth home run by five players in three games. Defensively, we committed only one error behind Dano and Kelly. A great win all around. One more win on Sunday, and the three-peat was done. But it wouldn't be easy. We would be playing another tough team from the east, and they were all good. Which one would it be?

Following our win over Glendive, Wolf Point played Sidney to determine who would play Glendive the next day; the winner of that game would play us in the championship. The four teams remaining in the tournament were all from the east. The *Leader* was aware of this when it wrote, "The eastern division teams proved where the baseball power is by copping the top four tourney spots. In the six tourney meetings between east and west, eastern teams won them all."[163] I loved how the *Leader* was always quick to trumpet the pride of the Scobey baseball tradition and, in this case, expanding it to all of eastern Montana.

How about a good old-fashioned slugfest—Wolf Point style—between Wolf Point and Sidney on Saturday night? Wow. Wolf Point trailed Sidney 12-4 in the bottom of the sixth but scored six runs to close to 12-10. In the top of the eighth, Sidney plated three more runs to make it 15-10, only to see Wolf Point score five runs in their half of the inning to tie the game 15-15 after trailing by eight runs in the sixth. Sidney then scored three runs in the top of the ninth, and Jeff Lebsock held Wolf Point scoreless in the bottom of the ninth for a wild 18-15 Sidney win. The bats were booming in this one. Kip Harcharik was one single away from hitting for the cycle, as he had a double, a triple, and a home run. Terry Baldry also homered for Wolf Point. Tim Thogerson hit a grand slam goob for Sidney, and Jeff Lebsock went yard, too. In all, 23 hits were banged out by both teams. So, when the sun set in the wild wild west Saturday night, Sidney, Glendive, and Scobey were still alive in the tournament. Sidney and Glendive would square off Sunday morning, the winner taking on Scobey for the championship. Get a good night's sleep, everyone (no barroom brawls); Sunday would be wild.

The Sidney-Glendive game would be another classic matchup between the two best teams from the southeastern district. Frenzel was starting for Glendive and Lebsock for Sidney, and the two battle-hardened teams were playing for the right to challenge Scobey in the state Class B Legion championship.

Two years earlier, in Cut Bank, Sidney lost a heart-breaking walk-off game to Cut Bank in this same game. With Sidney leading the Lobos 4-3 in the last of the ninth, the first two Cut Bank hitters walked to put runners on first and second. Then, Lobos' Brian Ledbetter bunted along the third baseline to move the runners up. The third baseman for Sidney charged the ball and threw to the shortstop covering at third, but the ball went through the shortstop and into left field, scoring the runner from second, and the runner from first base came all the way around to score the winning run on the throwing error. So Cut Bank walked it off 5-4 in the bottom of the ninth without a hit. Although it was a clear, sunny, windy day in Cut Bank two years later, could lightning strike twice for Sidney?

Unfortunately for the Richland County Patriots, the answer was yes. With Glendive leading 3-2 and Sidney batting in the bottom of the eighth, Sidney scored three runs to take a 5-3 lead into the top of the ninth. Lebsock got two outs in the ninth, but with two outs and a baserunner on, a comebacker to the mound was tossed underhanded to first, and the ball got through the first baseman's legs, leaving two runners on the base after what should have been the third out.

Doug Frenzel, who had already homered and doubled in the game, came to the plate and smashed a two-out, three-run home run over the left field fence to shock Sidney and vault Glendive to a 6-5 lead. Frenzel shut Sidney down in the bottom of the ninth and Glendive ran off the field with the 6-5 win, their second win by that score against Sidney in the tournament.

When the bus arrived at the field for the championship game, the two teams were shaking hands. Looking at the players on the field, I sensed something dramatic had just happened. I walked up into the stands and asked Dad who won. Dad said, "It was the damnedest thing I ever saw, Joey. Frenzel hit a three-run home run with two outs to win it. Sidney just needed to get the third out on a comebacker right before that. You're playing Glendive for the state championship."

In the write-up in the *Sidney Herald*, Coach Craig Price labeled the game "Heartbreak Hotel"[164] for the Patriots. It was a heartbreaking loss for Sidney, preventing a rematch between Sidney and Scobey for the state championship in the next game.

Doc handed me the ball to start the championship game. I had not pitched much in tournament, and my arm was a little sore; I had been plagued by a sore arm all year. Frenzel, who had three innings of eligibility left after pitching nine innings in the previous game against Sidney, started for Glendive. He had now pitched 18 innings in the tournament in four days.

Glendive got to me for two runs in the first and two more in the third, and Doug Frenzel pitched three scoreless innings. After three, it was Glendive 4-0. But Frenzel had exhausted his innings, and we scored three runs in the top of the fourth off relief pitcher Dwight Robbins to close to 4-3. I pitched a scoreless fourth, but Doc brought Dano in the fifth, as he had five innings of eligibility left and had two-hit Glendive the day before. Both Robbins and Danelson pitched scoreless ball until the bottom of the seventh when Doug Frenzel dealt a severe blow, a two-run blast over the left field fence on a hanging curveball by Dano. My feet didn't move at shortstop. They were stuck in concrete, and I looked only at Dano's frustrated face—who had turned his head to follow the ball—because I knew it was gone as soon as he hit it. I didn't want to watch it leave the park. The wind was blowing out that hot, windy day in Cut Bank, and Frenzel got it up, and it just carried, staking Glendive to a 6-3 lead after seven. Dwight Robbins pitched a scoreless eighth and ninth, and Glendive snapped our 31-game winning streak. Robbins had kept us off balance all day. As Kelly Norman recalls, "He had a slow curve ball and slow fastball, and we were out front and really frustrated as hitters." But more importantly, Glendive had forced a second championship game on Monday. The umpire from Williston was right: "You can't win them all." Both teams were now 1-1 in the tournament. That was the only record that mattered. The headline the next day in the *Great Falls Tribune* read, "Glendive upsets Scobey in Legion B,"[165] and went on to write, "The upset broke Scobey's 31-game winning streak,"[166] but there was still one game left to play, winner take all.

Frenzel was a "one-man wrecking crew"[167] that day for Glendive. He hit three home runs in the two games, scored six runs, drove in eight, and collected six hits in nine at-bats. His two-out, three-run homer in the ninth inning of the first game gave Glendive a come-from-behind win over Sidney. He was the winning pitcher in the game, giving up five runs and six hits in nine innings. He struck out nine Sidney hitters. He started the game against us but had to leave after hurling three scoreless innings because of the 12-inning tournament rule. But baseball is a team sport, and credit must be given to relief pitcher Dwight Robbins, who, after yielding three runs in the top of the fourth, pitched five scoreless innings against us to get the win.

Mike Jones also had a key double off me to drive in two of Glendive's six runs. Glendive had a good team. They were the fourth seed from the east but had now forced a second championship game against us.

When I went to bed that night, I wondered who Doc would start in the fifth game of the tournament. Dano had pitched 12 innings, and Jon had pitched seven, each with a win in the tournament. Ray and Kelly had made appearances earlier in the tournament. Who would it be? It would be my roommate Kelly Norman, who was staying with me at our host family in Cut Bank.

"The sun always rises the next day." That is true—unless you lose two games in a tournament, then it doesn't rise the next day. It sets on your season and doesn't rise again; it only rises for the next season—if you're lucky enough to have one. When the hot Cut Bank sun rose in the blue eastern sky on Monday, the shadows it cast included a 31-game winning streak that was over and a 3-0 record in the tournament that was now blemished with a loss. But we only cared about scoring more runs than Glendive and getting 27 outs to win our third consecutive state championship and Doc's fifth overall. No amount of shade could darken that goal.

Warming up before the game on Monday, there was only a smattering of fans at the ballpark. All the other teams had gone home, Cut Bank had long since been eliminated, Scobey was 372 miles from home, and Glendive was 433 miles from home. The Glacier Hutterite Colony—18 miles north-northeast from Cut Bank, who had shown up earlier in the tournament to watch some baseball—had gone home. When the Hutterites arrived, they doubled the attendance at the ballpark, occupying an entire stand. But I did see all the parents of the Scobey players there, and of course, my mom and dad. If I saw them in the stands, the stadium was packed, as far as I was concerned. And all the other parents, too.

I have written previously that Kelly Norman always stepped up big in the big games, and today would be no exception. His performances on the mound could be unpredictable. Allan Audet, who caught the entire staff, said that Kelly could be "wild," and Dano added that Kelly "was like a box of chocolates, didn't know what you were going to get, but more times than not, it was dark chocolate with a nut center." However, Kelly's performance in a big game was not unpredictable. You knew he was going to show up. A fierce competitor who knew how to win, he was pitching for his dad, his teammates, the parents, the town of Scobey, and on this day, for Scobey's third consecutive state championship. On Monday, July 31, 1978, we needed Kelly's pitching performance to be dark chocolate with a nut center (if you like that). He had pitched seven and two-thirds innings of four-hit ball to beat Glendive and Doug Frenzel 6-3 in Scobey in June, with me pitching one and one-third innings to save it. We would need that kind of performance from Kelly again to win the state championship.

Getting the lead early in a big game like this was essential, and we did. We got to Glendive starter Mike Jones for a run in the bottom of the second, then two more in the bottom of the third to jump to a 3-0 lead. But Glendive got to Kelly for their only three runs against him with a single run in the fourth and two in the fifth to tie the game 3-3. We scored two runs in the bottom of the sixth to take the lead back, 5-3—a lead we never relinquished.

Meanwhile, Kelly held Glendive scoreless in the sixth but tired in the top of the seventh, and Doc recognized it. With two outs and baserunners on for Glendive, Doc slowly walked to the mound to make a change. Much like the night before, I wondered who Doc would beckon to the mound. I was standing at short, thinking it would be Jon at second, but Doc's finger summoned left-handed knuckleballer Ray Chapman at first. Another puzzling decision by Doc that proved to be brilliant. In the four-player switch, Jon moved to third, Dano moved to first, Kelly moved to second, and Ray grabbed the ball for the most important save opportunity of his Legion career. The crafty left-hander got the last out of the inning to strand the Glendive baserunners, and we got off the field with the precious two-run lead preserved. The book on Kelly closed at six and two-thirds innings pitched, three hits, three walks, three runs—two earned—and 10 strikeouts—another clutch performance from Kelly.

But we needed some breathing room, as the 5-3 lead was tenuous, with Glendive having two more at-bats. We had stranded a lot of baserunners—12 in the game—and we needed a big hit to break it open. That big hit came from our leader, 18-year-old catcher Allan Audet, in the bottom of the seventh. With a runner on, Allan blasted his second home run of the tournament deep over the left-field fence to give us a 7-3 lead. There was no question it was gone when it hit the bat. Albert recalls the hit: "It was really windy, and Doc stood in front of the dugout and said to all of us, 'Would you stop swinging for the damn fence and go for singles.' Right after that, I hit one out over left, and as I was rounding third, I said to Doc, 'Thought we couldn't hit it out.' He said, 'Only you, Albert.'" We added another run in the inning on an RBI single by Jon—his third hit and third RBI of the game—to take an 8-3 lead after seven.

Ray's knuckler was dancing with abandon in that Cut Bank wind. Allan Audet said, "I remember Chappy coming

Allan Audet is greeted at home plate after hitting a booming home run in the seventh inning in the state championship game in Cut Bank. *Family photo.*

in late in the game. His knuckleball was going crazy, the best ever. No one could hit it. I remember going to the mound and saying to him, 'I don't know what you're doing, but keep doing it.'" Ray kept doing it. Despite walking some hitters—his knuckler was hard to control in that wind—he kept the Glendive hitters off balance and held Glendive scoreless in the top of the eighth. Mike Jones pitched a scoreless bottom half for Glendive, so we needed three more outs for the state championship.

But as was the case a year earlier against Glendive in the state tournament in Scobey, where we entered the ninth with a four-run lead, those three outs would not come easily. It never seemed to be easy to close a game with Glendive. Once again, Glendive rallied in the top of the ninth. Sprinkled between two outs and an error, Ray walked some hitters—the wind was making it difficult to control his knuckler—and Glendive mustered two singles—one a soft infield hit to me at short—to score three runs and close to within 8-6. Allan's two-run home run in the seventh now loomed large, providing the precious two-run margin. There was a lot of traffic on the bases, but no solid contact was being made by any of the hitters. But this was Ray's game to save, as Doc never budged from the dugout. With two outs and a runner on second, the tying run came to the plate. The hitter hit a high pop-up behind me at shortstop. Oh no. Flashback to the 1977 state tournament in Scobey, when the bloop single to right dropped for a single in the ninth, and two runs scored for Glendive. I started back on the ball to make the catch, but it was hit really high, and my eye caught Randy Stolen running in from left. It was hit so high that I could have got under the ball to make the catch, but Randy waved his arms and called me off, and I stopped giving chase. Randy was camped under the ball when it finally dropped down, and I watched him calmly squeeze it in his glove for the third out. Randy and I then quickly ran to join the mob on the mound with Ray, Allan, and the rest of our teammates, celebrating the state championship. We had done it! Three-peat. Final score, 8-6 Scobey.

1978 Scobey Blues, State Class B champions. Standing, left to right: Doc Norman, Ray Chapman, Allan Audet, Kelly Norman, Dan Danelson, David Corey, Kirby Halvorson, Randy Stolen, Ass't Coach Don Lekvold. Kneeling, left to right: Wade Tryan, Ron Higgins, Jacki Tade, Rick Lee, DeeAnn Lekvold, Jon Puckett, Joe Puckett.

TOURNAMENT SUMMARY

THE NEXT DAY, TWO DIFFERENT HEADLINES ANNOUNCED TO the state of Montana that Scobey had won its third consecutive state B Legion championship. The *Great Falls Tribune* read, "Audet's homer gives Scobey Class B title."[168] The *Billings Gazette* had it, "Norman, Audet lead Scobey to B crown."[169] Undoubtedly, these two Blues—Audet and Norman—were the key to the win. Kelly had pitched a three-hitter and struck out 10 through six and two-thirds, and Allan's two-run home run in the seventh proved the margin of victory. It was a storybook ending for Allan's Class B Legion career that he came through like that, especially after Doc told us not to swing for the fence: "Only you, Albert."

But Allan and Kelly would be the first to tell you that the championship was a team effort, and everyone contributed to the win. The *Tribune* wrote, "The hard-hitting Scobey team, with players from Flaxville and Peerless [and Glentana] on the roster, banged out 15 safeties. Jon Puckett had a double and two singles, stole two bases, and knocked in three runs."[170] Despite a rough ninth, Ray Chapman earned the save, getting the third out in the seventh with no runs allowed to preserve the two-run lead. He also had a hit, an RBI, stole a base, and scored a run. It was a testament to the depth of this team that Jon Puckett—hitting in the eighth position—and Ray Chapman—in the ninth—would combine for four hits, two runs, and four RBIs. Jon also stole two bases in the game. Production came from anywhere in this lineup.

Perhaps the biggest story of the tournament, though, was how the team handled the adversity of the first loss to Glendive in the championship game. The papers made a big deal of our 31-game win streak being snapped, but we were trying to win the tournament. Dano said, "I don't remember any panic. I remember we talked and were more pissed at our performance than anything." Jon added, "I wasn't all that disappointed or worried. I figured we'd just win the next game." Kirby was more direct: "I don't recall any stress or panic either. We knew who the alphas were and then proved it."

I wish I could say I felt the same confidence as my teammates, but I was wired differently. I was rattled about my four-inning start, forcing Doc to go to Dano in the fifth. I felt like I had let my teammates down in the big game. Dating to the 1976 eastern divisional game in Glendive against Glendive when I was 15 years old, Doc had handed me the ball to start in five postseason games, and we had won all five of those games up until that sixth start against Glendive. Three days earlier, I had confidently stared down a Laurel hitter and smiled at him after he hit the deck on a curveball strike; now, I was the losing pitcher in the state championship game. I was a bit of a perfectionist. The four-inning start shook me up a little, and I wanted to do something the next day to make up for it, so I pressed. Pressing as I did, I went hitless at the plate—the only hitter in the lineup not to get a hit—and made two errors at short. Thankfully, the errors did not lead to any runs. Confidence is everything in sports, but sometimes doubt seeps in. When it does, it is hard to exorcise it. I use the word *exorcise* because, to an athlete, doubt is a demon. Sometimes, you have to play your way out of it. My confidence was not high in myself that day, affecting my play. But on winning teams, teammates pick you up, and my teammates picked me up that day. I was just one of nine players.

One of the benefits of interviewing former players is learning the similarities across different teams and tour-

Allan Audet, the team captain and only 18-year-old on the team, receives the state championship trophy. *Family photo.*

naments. The 1973 team was the only other Scobey team to play in the undefeated state championship game and lose. Scobey blew a seven-run lead against Wolf Point in that game and was forced into a second game. The circumstances were different in that Scobey had a big lead and lost it. Dana Audet recalls, "You just gotta come back tomorrow and do the best you can do. You're not coming in tremendously confident." I felt more like Dana than my teammates after the loss to Glendive. But the sun did rise the next day, and we won.

The four teams from the east swept all games against the western opponents and finished in the top four spots: Wolf Point fourth, Sidney third, Glendive second, and Scobey first. The Glendive team, led by pitcher Doug Frenzel and catcher Mike Jones were good. Steve King was a solid shortstop and leadoff hitter, and Craig Ballantine was a great second pitcher to Frenzel. Dwight Robbins pitched six innings the day before and held us to three runs to get the win for Glendive. The rest of the team battled every inning of the tournament. The fourth seed from the east won four games—including two close 6-5 wins over Sidney—beat us 6-3 in the first game and almost pulled off a five-run comeback in the ninth in the second game. My dad recognized grittiness when he saw it. He saw that the scrappy Glendive had played their hearts out over six games in the hot and windy Cut Bank weather and insisted on taking a picture of the team after the state championship game. There were not too many smiles, but it captured a team that gave it everything they had but came up a little short.

Now that Doc had won his fifth state championship in nine years, and Scobey had won its third in a row, the word "dynasty" could safely be applied to Doc's American Legion Baseball program in Scobey. If there was any doubt before the state tournament, there was no doubt following it. When Dick Atwood rolled the bus toward Scobey in the darkness shortly before midnight Monday, the winners were met by a caravan of fans south of Scobey and "were led triumphantly into town by a police escort."[171] Although Jon and I didn't listen to Seals and Crofts' song "Summer Breeze" on the way home as we did two years earlier returning home from Cut Bank with the 1976 state championship team, the lyrics of that song had never resonated more: "Sweet days of summer." Sweet days of summer, indeed. The sweetest days.

When the sun rose six hours later on Tuesday morning, the sky in the east had never been so Scobey blue. The sun was rising on an American Legion Baseball dynasty in Scobey. And while the sky was blue and the sun shone brightly that morning, it would flaunt a deeper blue and shine even brighter in summer mornings to follow. Ten Blues—eight starters—would return to play another year of Legion baseball the following season when Scobey would host the state tournament for the sixth time. In the state tournament summary, the Cut Bank *Pioneer Press* touted Scobey as a powerhouse in Class B baseball. "Scobey, which has only one 18-year-old player on the roster and is thus one of the youngest teams in the state, finished the season with a remarkable 32-4 record, making it the powerhouse of the 'B' division."[172] The blue wave that had started as a small ripple in 1959 when Doc arrived in Scobey and led Scobey to its first district championship in 12 years, had built up steadily in the 1960s when Phil Audet led Scobey to its first state tournament appearance in 1967, and rose further with the first all-Daniels County team in 1968. It increased with Scobey's first state championship at home in Scobey in 1969 and ascended higher and higher with four state championships to follow. The town of Scobey and Daniels County had been riding this steadily rising blue wave for 20 years, and it was not even close to cresting yet.

TOURNAMENT STATS

Hitting

Bats had never boomed louder—aluminum pings and wooden cracks—than they did for Scobey in the 1978 state tournament. The Blues scored 44 runs on 56 hits in five games for an average of nine runs and 11 hits a game. Scobey hitters banged out seven home runs, as Kirby Halvorson and Allan Audet each had two, and Randy Stolen, Wade Tryan, and Joe Puckett each hit one. The team also had several extra-base hits. In addition to Allan Audet's

1978 Glendive Blue Devils, State Runners-Up. Standing, left to right: Dave Seeberger, Dale Raisl, Doug Frenzel, Craig Ballantine, Mark Scheuffele, Clint Lohman, Coach Wayne Emter. Front row, left to right: Kevin Miller, Dwight Robbins, Robbie Johnston, Bob Clump, Steve King. Not pictured are Mike Jones and Brent Oakland, who left for the East-West Shrine game following the game.

Doc Norman, with his always dependable chief of staff, Marge, and able Assistant Coach Don Lekvold, display the 1978 Class B American Legion Baseball state title. *Leader photo, Milt Gunderson.*

two-run home run in the championship game, Jon Puckett had two singles and a double with three runs batted in and scored a run Scobey's offense. As potent as Scobey's offense was, Sidney's was one run better—they scored 45 runs in five games.

Power was the name of the game in Cut Bank, as 18 balls left the park. Sidney's Tim Thogerson had two home runs, including a grand slam against Wolf Point. Thogerson also had two doubles and a triple, hit .523, and scored 12 runs. Jeff Lebsock also hit a goob for Sidney and hit four doubles. Wolf Point's Kip Harcharik, Craig Lewis, and Terry Baldry each homered. Harcharik was a single away from hitting for the cycle against Butte, as he had a double, triple, and home run. Glendive's Doug Frenzel hit four home runs—including three in one day on Sunday. Brent Oakland also homered for Glendive. However, of the 18 home runs, the two most important were Doug Frenzel's two-run shot against Scobey on Sunday and Allan Audet's two-run blast against Glendive on Monday.

Bruce Milbrandt of Cut Bank won the Denton Award as the tournament's leading hitter with a .571 average.

Pitching

Ray Chapman got the win in Scobey's seven-inning, 15-2 victory over Laurel, pitching a one-hitter. Jon Puckett pitched in relief. Jon Puckett got the 9-6 win against Wolf Point, going seven innings with Joe Puckett pitching two innings of relief. Dan Danelson got the win over Glendive, pitching a two-hitter over seven innings, with Kelly Norman pitching two innings of hitless relief. Joe Puckett took the loss against Glendive on Sunday, pitching four innings and yielding four runs. Dan Danelson pitched four innings of relief and gave up two runs, the two-run homer to Doug Frenzel in the seventh.

Doc needed to go deeper in his staff than the typical Puckett-Puckett-Danelson rotation to win this state tournament. The year before, all 36 innings had been pitched by the Puckett twins and Danelson, but the fifth game in 1978 forced Doc to go to his fourth and fifth pitchers, Kelly Norman and Ray Chapman. Kelly Norman pitched six and two-thirds innings of three-hit ball against Glendive on Monday, yielding three runs—two earned—and striking out 10 in his second state championship game win. Ray Chapman entered the game with the tying runs on base in the seventh and got the last out to retire the side. He pitched two and one-third innings and gave up three runs, earning the biggest save of his Legion career.

Other pitchers delivered solid performances in the tournament. Doug Frenzel struck out 16 Muckers and pitched a five-hitter to beat Butte 4-3. Butte pitcher Mike Pelly pitched a three-hitter in the game and struck out nine, but five Mucker errors led to four unearned runs, and he took the tough loss. Jeff Lebsock pitched a one-hit shutout against the Vigilantes, leading Sidney to the 6-0 win. Wolf Point's Dan Jensen held the Muckers to one run and struck out 10 to lead Wolf Point to a 4-1 win. Both Sidney-Glendive games were 6-5 battles, and the pitching was good. In the first game, Tom Paladichuk went all nine innings for Sidney. Craig Ballantine pitched a complete-game win for Glendive with a six-hitter. In the second game, Jeff Lebsock pitched all nine for Sidney, giving up six hits and only three earned runs, as the last three runs were unearned, coming with the error with two outs in the ninth. Doug Frenzel got the win for Glendive, pitching all nine innings and yielding five runs on seven hits.

Fielding: Scobey committed only eight errors in the five games, for an average of only one and a half errors per game. The *Leader* summed up Scobey's tournament: "The boys from Daniels County outscored opponents 44-20 and committed only eight errors as they won four of five games for the state title."[173] Our offense and defense carried us in the tournament, and the pitching was good enough to win. The five pitchers on the staff were all needed to finish the job, especially with the loss to Glendive on Sunday. Allan Audet handled the staff as catcher for all five games.

STATE CLASS A PLAYOFF

Our opponent in the best-of-three series to play into the State A Tournament was the Great Falls Chargers. The Chargers were the defending State Class A champions, having advanced to the Northwest Regionals in Oregon a year earlier, and most of their players had returned, including some from college, as shortstop Gary Brastrup started for the North Idaho College earlier that spring. We were scheduled to play the number-four seed from the western division, but the Chargers had actually tied for second place. The fourth-place team, the Electrics, were exempt from playoffs since they were automatically seeded into the state meet as tournament hosts. Missoula, who was tied for the Chargers for the second-best record in the west at 14-6, beat the Chargers three out of four times, putting them into second in the state seedings. So, we were playing the number-two seed from the west, the defending state champions, to get into the State A Tournament as the fourth seed from the west.

We carried a 32-4 record into the series, with our only losses to the Class A Royals, Scarlets, Keybirds, and Class B Glendive at State. But as good as our record was, the Chargers were almost as good, as their season record was 35-7 against Montana Class A clubs. Chargers coach Ken Kelly was not taking us lightly. He said in the *Great Falls Tribune*, "No way are we underestimating Scobey. Some of our kids have played against them in B competition the past few years, and we know they can play baseball. Scobey has always had an outstanding baseball program, and you can't take a thing away from them."[174] Coach Kelly's reference to "some our kids have played against them" was to the Vigilantes team we had beaten 15-5 a year earlier in Scobey. Many of these players were now Chargers, including the starting pitcher in the first game, Mickey Monahan, who we had beaten in that 15-5 game in Scobey.

So, our opponent was good. So were we—if we played well in the field. Doc said before the game, "These kids have won three state championships in a row, and we've still only got one 18-year-old on the team. I think we can play with the Class A teams this year if we don't kick the ball around."

If we don't kick the ball around.

It is difficult to write about this series because, as was the case a year earlier in the best-of-three series against the Helena Senators, we did not play well defensively, and it cost us again against Class A competition. Doc's comment before the series that we could play with Class A teams "if we don't kick the ball around" would prove prophetic.

Doc started Dano in the first game, and he pitched well enough to win the game—scattering nine hits, issuing no walks, and yielding only three earned runs—but six costly errors led to three unearned runs and a 6-5 Chargers win. Six players committed the six errors, so a bad joke would be that we had a well-balanced collapse defensively. We hit

Dan Danelson delivers a pitch in the bottom of the third inning in the first game of the best-of-three playoff series against the Great Falls Chargers. *Family photo.*

Monahan hard with 10 hits, including doubles by Norman, Halvorson, and Stolen and a triple by Danelson. Coach Kelly from the Chargers said, "They hit him [Monahan] pretty good." The *Tribune* wrote, "The inability to convert opportunities into runs hurt the northeast Montana team," as we left eight baserunners on, one too many to overcome our "shaky fielding" in the one-run game.[175]

Following Kelly's excellent pitching in the state tournament in Cut Bank, Doc shuffled the rotation and started Kelly—still only 16 years old—in the second game. The Chargers were a heavy-hitting team—they had nine hits off Dano in the first game. Against Kelly, they got eight hits and eight runs—but only six earned—in five innings. However, another four errors—again by four players—cost us again, leading to two unearned runs, and we lost 9-7, the two unearned runs being the difference. Jon pitched four innings of relief and kept us in the game, yielding one run. We had eight hits off Great Falls ace right-hander John Leister, who won his 14th game, but he struck out 12 Blues, and many of his strikeouts squelched key rallies. We left nine baserunners, including two in our final push to tie the game in the ninth. We did not go down without a fight. Leister entered the ninth inning with a seemingly safe 9-3 lead. But four walks, a sacrifice fly, and singles by Kirby Halvorson and Randy Stolen whittled the Chargers' lead to 9-7, with the potential winning run at the plate.

Allan Audet scores on a double by Randy Stolen during the first game of the best-of-three playoffs with the Great Falls Chargers. At right is umpire Andy Anderson and Chargers catcher Dave Scanson. Jon Puckett welcomes Allan home, and Mike Lee is the batboy. *Great Falls Tribune photo by Bert Lindler.*

But Leister's 12th strikeout was the final nail in the coffin, ending our season with another disappointing loss in the best-of-three State A playoffs.

The *Great Falls Tribune* summarized the series the next day by writing, "The Great Falls Chargers overcame some scary moments in the ninth inning of both games to sweep the series."[176] We were in both games in the ninth, but so what? The *Tribune* also wrote, "Scobey contributed heavily to its own demise as the Blues committed 10 errors in the twin-bill, three of them in the fourth inning of Sunday's second game when the Chargers broke a 2-2 tie with three gift runs, which put Great Falls ahead to stay."[177] Doc summarized the series by complaining in the *Great Falls Tribune*, "Too many guys kicking the ball. We usually play better baseball than that."[178] Nothing more needs to be said.

What would it take to get it right against the Class A teams? As good as we were, we still weren't good enough to beat them. We could stay on the field with them, yes, but we wanted to do more than that. Three of our losses to Class A teams in 1978 were by one run—2-1 to the Royals, 6-5 to the Keybirds, and 6-5 to the Chargers—and our fourth loss was by two runs, 9-7 to the Chargers. One run to break even. Another run to win. We needed to get better by two runs.

I have written about the strength of our defense on the 1977-78 teams. The *Leader* credited our "solid defense" with our state championship, as we committed only eight errors in five games in the state tournament. We also made only one error or less in 12 consecutive games during the regular season. But against the Chargers, we had 10 errors in 2 games. What gives? I think we became tentative defensively when playing against tougher competition. An extreme example of this was the 1946 Scobey Legion team, who won the district championship and played off against Miles City in the eastern division playoffs. They committed 13 errors in the game and lost 10-2. The *Billings Gazette* referred to the team as "frightened"[179] but scrappy. The week before, the team could not have committed that many errors to beat Wolf Point, Malta, and Glasgow and win the district championship. Nerves were the only possible explanation. It's the same ground ball, the same fly ball, the same throw, just under different conditions—the opponent was stronger.

In this context, it's time to bring the "death stare" back into the discussion, not as a joke, but as the remedy to the problem. Referring to the stare, Dano said Doc's message to him was, "Keep them in the game, Dano! The stare. Buckle-down time. Are you in the game? Let's not make another error. Don't let the mind wander. Or don't fuck up again! However it was interpreted, it [the death stare] was my way to relay Doc's message, 'Stay in the game!'"

If a pitcher needs to be confident in making a good pitch before the ball is thrown, a fielder needs to be confident to make a solid play before the ball is hit. That was it. Our fielding needed to become proactive—make the play before the ball was hit.

So, it was no secret what we needed to do. Doc knew it. We knew it. The *Daniels County Leader* knew it. Even my girlfriend, Audrey Tryan, knew it. I brought up the losses from the series when we returned home to Scobey. Before I could explain why we lost, she said, "I guess you guys made too many errors?" Jesus Christ. *Everybody* knew it. Doc's comment that we could play with the Class A teams if we didn't "kick the ball around" was it. But we wanted to do more than play with them—we wanted to win. We were already playing with them, even with all our errors. We needed to sharpen our focus on the field for 27 outs. Reduce the errors and unearned runs. Our pitching and hitting were fine—good enough to win.

We finished the season with a 32-6 record, with five losses to Class A teams. It was a consolation for eight starters that we would play another year of Legion baseball in 1979, but it was Allan Audet's last Legion game. When looking ahead to 1979, the *Leader* recognized the big spikes that would need to be filled with Allan's loss: "Next year looks bright for 3-time state champion Blues as only one man (the very capable Allan Audet) is lost to the age limit." Very capable indeed—our leader who had caught all five games in the State B Tournament and hit the game-winning two-run home run in the championship game. Albert would be missed.

The eight starters returning in 1979 were lucky because we had a third chance to get it right against the Class A teams. In his interview in the *Great Falls Tribune* before the Chargers series, Doc said, "Next year should be the best team we've ever had."[180] We would work hard to sharpen our defensive focus in 1979. It would take a lot of hard work to correct the weakness, a lot of repetitions, and a lot of staying late after regular practice under the lights at the Scobey Ball Park so that we could finally, after three tries, get it right against the Class A teams. They say the third time's a charm.

EXTRA INNINGS

AFTER BEATING US IN THE BEST-OF-THREE SERIES, THE DEFENDing champion Chargers went on to take second place in the State A Tournament. They won four games but lost twice to Kalispell, including 6-5 in the championship game, in which John Leister struck out 17 Lakers.

It's a small baseball world. Mike Hagfeldt (Scobey Blues, 1974-76) was Charger shortstop Gary Brastrup's teammate at North Idaho College (NIC) in 1978. Mike played for the Cardinals from 1977-78. Mike said of Gary, "I remember Gary. In my opinion, he was our best hitter. Man could he hit. In my opinion, he was our best stick. Nice guy, too." However, Scobey's pitching—Dano, Kelly, and Jon—limited cleanup hitter Brastrup to one single in the series in eight at-bats.

Not pictured in the Glendive team picture following the championship game on Monday were Mike Jones and Brent Oakland, who left after the last out to drive to Great Falls to begin two-a-day workouts on Tuesday in prep for the 32nd East-West Shrine football game. Jones, a defensive back, and Oakland, a linebacker, played on Glendive's state championship football team that school year and were selected as all-stars for the game. Doug Frenzel, Bob Clump, and Clint Lohman also played on that state championship team. Glendive—defending state Class A basketball champions and ranked number one—lost to Butte Central in the state championship. Jones, Lohman, and Frenzel played on that team, which finished 22-2. Todd McGovern was a two-time state championship singles tennis player. This was a talented group of all-around athletes on that 1978 Glendive team.

When I congratulated Todd McGovern on his two tennis championships, he said, "Easier to hit a ball with a racket than a bat." That's funny, but I'm not so sure it's true. It's hard to hit a tennis ball right.

I was reminded of the term "goob" for a home run by Jeff Nesper and the Sidney players when watching the movie *Meet the Robinsons* (2007). In the film, 12-year-old right fielder Michael "Goob" Yagoobian misses the winning catch in a big game, and later in life, his fury becomes uncontrollable as he is always in such a bad mood because he is so fixated on the error that he believes everyone hates him for it. After my home run against Glendive, I was introduced to the term goob when Jeff Nesper said to me as we cleared the dugout before their game with Wolf Point, "So, I hear you hit a goob."

I asked Ray Chapman and Randy Stolen to share any memories of Cut Bank in 1978. Neither had any specific memories, but Ray responded with a letter to the *Daniels County Leader* editor from the host family he and Randy stayed with in Cut Bank. It was printed in the *Leader* a week following the tournament. Ray remembers the letter: "After the tournament, I remember Mom coming to me in the library at school. I was in study hall, and she asked if I'd seen the paper and this letter to the editor. I was such a teenager. I was embarrassed that Mom would make such a big deal about this. I mean, it wasn't about baseball! But it was the most emotion I'd ever seen Mom exhibit in our lives together. She was so, so proud of me. I wish I could go back in time and let her know how much I appreciated her pride in me and her love for me. Ah, life." Here is the letter:

Larry Bowler, Editor, Daniels County Leader, Scobey, MT 59263

Dear Sir:

During the Class B American Legion tournament held in Cut Bank recently, two young men from Scobey—Ray Chapman and Randy Stolen—stayed with my family in our home. Quite frankly my wife and I were very impressed with these gentlemen; they were well-mannered, considerate and a credit to their parents, team, coaches and community.

The fact that we heard some real horror stories from families who had taken members from teams from other towns into their homes, only made us more appreciative of Ray and Randy.

Too often young people only get into the newspapers in connection with criminal or other such activities. We feel that when praise is deserved, it should be given, and in this instance we feel that your community has two young men it can be proud of.

Sincerely,
JIM NELSON, Cut Bank

Although Randy Stolen didn't have any specific memories of Cut Bank, he said, "I remember the feelings of being a part of such a special group of athletes—I remember feeling so grateful to be a part of all of it. I felt like such a small part of the Blues—nothing special. I was always in the background—the players out front were Joe and Jon,

Dano, Kirb, Audet, Tryan, Norman, Chappy . . . I felt like we all felt—unselfish. The Blues were all that mattered. God Joe—just thinking of those days and how it shaped all of our lives as Blues champions and how it led all of us into successful adults and husbands and fathers!!"

The Laurel Dodgers, whom the 1959 team played for the eastern divisional championship, are now the only team to have more state championships—nine—than Scobey. The Bitterroot Red Sox are tied with Scobey with eight. The following season, a much-improved Laurel team and Scobey would clash for the state championship in Scobey.

At the 1976 state tournament in Cut Bank, Doc had to pull up the getaway car to extract 16-year-old Allan Audet and other Blues from the barroom brawl before the cops got there. But Albert's beer drinking in 1978 was in sharp contrast to that. Albert, now 18, said, "I probably hold a record for being the only player in Scobey baseball history to legally have a pitcher of beer with Doc and Don after the 1978 championship." This was the last year that could happen. Concerns about teenage drinking, particularly among high school students, led to a Montana voter initiative in 1978 to raise the legal drinking age to 19, a law that went into effect on Jan. 1, 1979.

When discussing calling signals for the pitching staff, Allan Audet said, "One thing that we took for granted was calling most of the pitches between me and the pitchers. Occasionally, Doc would yell, 'Hey Albert,' and give me a signal. My son played for the Scarlets, and coaches call most of the pitches, which, in my opinion, takes the players out of the game and puts undue stress on pitchers."

In reflecting on the pitchers he caught during his Legion career, Allan added, "When Joe and Jon Puckett pitched, it was my favorite time to catch as they had such good control. Dan was just awesome with the heat he had and his sinker. Kelly was just wild as hell—never knew where his pitch was going."

Great Falls Tribune sports editor George Geise wrote a great article on Doc before the Chargers series titled, "Just call him a Goliath among a whole lot of Davids."[181] It is reprinted here in its entirety:

Call him a Goliath among the Davids.
Call him a messiah from the east. Or just call him Doc.

Call Dr. C.H. Norman "Goliath," because he's a squat 300-pounder who stands out starkly among a group of skinny, young baseball players.

Call him a messiah, because he's led dozens of Scobey Blues American Legion Baseball teams out of remote northeast Montana and into the limelight of baseball tournaments in this state.

Call him Doc, because that's precisely what he is, a physician and surgeon serving Scobey and surrounding communities in extreme northeast Montana when he's not coaching Legion baseball.

His latest Scobey Blues' ballclub entered Sunday afternoon's playoff series against the Great Falls Chargers with a gleaming 34-4 record. "Yeah, but we lost three of those games to Class A ballclubs, the Scarlets, Royals (both of Billings) and Williston (N.D.)," Doc pointed out. There was also a 31-game winning streak, all against Class B Legion opponents, before Glendive broke the string.

For the past 20 years, Doc Norman has been coach, manager, and foster father to the baseball program in Scobey. And he still is. "The only thing I don't do now is hit ground balls to the infield before the game," said the large fellow, who sets an imposing shadow as he fills the third base coach's box.

Doc's latest edition of the Scobey Blues may well be his best ever. "These kids have won three state championships (Class B) in a row, and we've still only got one 18-year-old on the team," Norman said. "I think we can play with the Class A teams this year if we don't kick the ball around," he added. "But next year should be the best team we've ever had."

As you might expect, baseball players don't come hand-delivered in Scobey, a town of about 1,000 people located in Daniels County.

"We've got three kids from Peerless, two from Flaxville, one from Opheim and the rest from Scobey," Doc announced. "When we get 'em, they don't know too much about baseball. We have to teach 'em everything," he said.

One advantage Norman does have is that he doesn't wait until the players are 15 or 16 before he teaches them baseball, Scobey-style. "There's no law that says a kid has to be 15 years old to play in this league," Doc barked. "I've got a kid with me who's only 12 years old, and he can make that throw from third base to first as well as the kid for the Chargers. He's not on our roster this year, but you can bet he'll be playing next year," Doc said.

Dan Danelson, a 6-foot-7 right-hander who hurled Sunday's first game in the best-of-3 playoff series, may already own a distinction among Montana American Legion players. "He's started for me since he was 13 years old," Norman said of Danelson, a superb all-around athlete who will be a senior this fall at Scobey High School.

Two of Norman's other standouts, infielders Joe and Jon Puckett, are top athletes in their own right, having led Peerless into the State Class C basketball tourney last winter.

And Doc's own son Kelly, one of the club's top hitters and its second-best pitcher, will only be a junior in high school this fall.

Clearly, the Scobey Blues will be a baseball team to respect in the coming years. And you can bet that the guy with the right prescription for success will be one Dr. C.H. Norman M.D.

Rick and Dan Danelson experienced Doc's successful model of developing players at a young age, as they both started playing Legion when they were only 13. They discussed it, and Dano related this: "My brother and I were visiting about coming into the Blues program at a young age, and it was interesting how similar our feelings were. Playing alongside older players immediately makes you pay attention to detail. You don't want to fuck up too often and be the reason for a defeat. You want to contribute and make the plays. We also agreed that playing in pressure games you felt the nerves but being around the older players who were so dialed-in that you couldn't help but learn from them and play in the moment pitch by pitch. You grew more comfortable playing in big games. Mentally and physically you played all 27 outs. You do your best and hope it's enough."

1979

Taking It to the Next Level

> *The Scobey Blues made a very creditable showing in the Class A tournament, one that will be long remembered as the finest showing by the Scobey Blues in their American Legion Baseball history. Fans believe that except for Dan Danelson's injured pitching arm in the earlier Helena playoffs, they might have gone all the way.*
>
> —**Daniels County Leader, August 16, 1979**

PRESEASON

THE 1979 SEASON MARKED THE ANNIVERSARY OF TWO milestone dates in Scobey American Legion Baseball history. It was the 20th anniversary of the first team Doc coached in Scobey, when the 1959 team won the northeastern district for the first time in 12 years and played off with Laurel in a best-of-three series for the eastern division championship. It was also the 10th anniversary of the first year Scobey hosted—and won—the state tournament.

In late March and early April 1979, when the first meadowlark pierced the cold sunshine with its beautiful song, announcing spring had arrived, it had no idea the excitement it had missed earlier that winter on the hardwood. In an unprecedented championship run by Daniels County teams, Scobey beat Plentywood for the State Class B championship, and Flaxville beat Peerless for the State Class C championship. All five of Peerless's losses that winter were to Scobey and Flaxville; five of Flaxville's seven losses were to Scobey and Peerless. Scobey's only loss during the regular season was to Class A Sidney. But on the baseball field in April, the same athletes who had competed against each other on the hardwood floor would play together on the baseball field to win Doc's fourth consecutive state championship and sixth overall—and take it to the next level against the Class A teams.

1969–1982

1979 Scobey Blues, State Class B Champions. Standing, left to right: Assistant Coach Don Lekvold, Randy Stolen, Allan Audet, Kelly Norman, Dan Danelson, David Corey, Kirby Halvorson, Coach Doc Norman. Kneeling, left to right: Manager Dick Atwood, Jon Puckett, Joe Puckett, Wade Tryan, Ray Chapman, Ron Higgins, Mike Lapke. Sitting, left to right: Jacki Tade, Rick Lee, Mike Lee, DeeAnn Lekvold. Head batboy Mike Roland is not pictured. *Leader photo by Milt Gunderson.*

Never had expectations for a Scobey Legion team to win it all been higher. Eight two-year starters—Wade Tryan, Kelly Norman, Joe and Jon Puckett, Dan Danelson, Kirby Halvorson, Randy Stolen, and Ray Chapman—were returning from the 1977 and 1978 championship teams, and six starters had played on the 1976 championship team. Ron Higgins and David Corey also returned in 1979, and five talented rookies joined the team: 17-year-old Jesse Cook; 14-year-olds Pat Audet, Jim Lekvold, and Gord Tryan; and 13-year-old Greg Stolen.

The big question for Scobey's roster was who would replace Allan Audet in the lineup. Doc gave some indication of who it might be when he was interviewed by George Geise of the *Great Falls Tribune* before the Chargers playoff series in 1978. In discussing his method of developing younger players early with Geise, Doc said, "There's no law that says a kid has to be 15 years old to play in this league. I've got a kid with me who's only 12 years old, and he can make that throw from third base to first as well as the kid for the Chargers. He's not on our roster this year, but you can bet he'll be playing next year."[182]

The "12-year-old kid" Doc was referring to was Greg Stolen—now 13—who, during the regular season, competed against several other talented young players—including Ron Higgins, Pat Audet, and Jim Lekvold—to win the starting position in right field and become the ninth-place hitter in the lineup. Dad had coached Greg in Little League in Peerless. Greg—nicknamed "Super Flake" by Dad and "Greggie" by his teammates—began playing for Dad with us as a seven-year-old in Little League in Peerless.

Jacki Tade and DeeAnn Lekvold were back as batgirls, and Mike Roland, Rick, and Mike Lee returned as batboys. Don Lekvold was the assistant coach, and Dick Atwood was team manager.

In an article titled, "What's Uniquely Different About This Ball Club?" the *Leader* identified an unusual aspect of this team in the early season team photo: "EVERY player on the squad—except for two—is the youngest in his family; and that exception is fence-busting Randy Stolen, whose youngest brother is Greg, also a member of the squad, and Gordy Tryan. The *Leader* believes that the Scobey Blues team this year, which again plans to go all the way, provides one statistic unequaled in all of American Legion Baseball, past or present, with its youngest-in-the-family roster."[183] Technically, the *Leader* could have identified me as an exception, too—I am, after all, seven minutes older than Jon. He is my little brother.

The lineup remained the same as in 1977 and 1978, except everyone who batted after Dano moved up one spot to replace Allan Audet, who had batted fifth. Kelly said, "Dad did not like changing the order at all." However, at the IGA Tournament in Billings in July, Doc did change the lineup, moving Jon to the second slot, Kelly to cleanup, and Dano to fifth. Following that tournament, Doc settled the lineup by moving Dano to the second spot and Kelly to cleanup. The nine players forming the starting lineup for 1979 from July onward:

- Wade Tryan (18) CF
- Dan Danelson (18) 3B/P
- Joe Puckett (18) SS/P
- Kelly Norman (17) 2B/P
- Kirby Halvorson (17) C

- Randy Stolen (17) LF/P
- Jon Puckett (18) 3B/SS/2B/LF/RF/P
- Ray Chapman (18) 1B/P
- Greg Stolen (13) RF/P

Seven of the nine starters pitched during the regular season, as did Pat Audet, who would also see some innings. That gave Doc his deepest staff ever, with eight pitchers earning a win as a starting pitcher during the regular season. Kirby Halvorson could pitch but was dedicated to catching full time in 1979.

This being my final season in Legion, I made some changes that spring to focus exclusively on baseball. I decided not to participate in track and field, where I ran the mile and two-mile. I also vowed to take care of my arm better to avoid another sore arm that plagued me during the 1978 season. No more throws from deep short while taking infield the day after pitching. I would field the ball but not throw it; I wouldn't even warm up. I would rest it for at least two days, sometimes three, before throwing again. If we had a game, I would take balls at short during infield but not throw to first base unless it was a live ball during the game. As a result, my arm was strong at the end of the year—the strongest it had ever been. Finally, knowing that our weakness against the Class A teams had been our fielding, as our losses in the previous two playoff series had proven, I put extra effort into improving my fielding that summer, taking as many extra ground balls during practice as possible. After taking infield, I would ask the on-deck hitter in batting practice to hit me ground balls at shortstop in between pitches on the pitching machine. Then, less than midway into the season, Kelly, Jon, and I—all middle infielders—would stay late after practice, turn the lights on, and hit ground balls to each other, repeatedly, working on our double-play combination, picking ground balls, repetition after repetition, late into the summer nights. I also studied Walter Alston's *The Complete Baseball Handbook*,[184] which contained a section on how to play every position, including shortstop. As I had been fortunate in grade school and high school in Peerless to "have the keys to the gym" and be able to practice basketball whenever I wanted, I had the same fortune in baseball. This extra work would pay off, and our fielding would improve dramatically. If we were to get beat by Class A competition, we would not beat ourselves in the middle infield. Not this year.

REGULAR SEASON

I WAS EXCITED TO SEE OUR SCHEDULE INCLUDED SIX GAMES—three doubleheaders—against the Class AA Williston Keybirds; however, I was disappointed that the Billings Royals and Scarlets were not on the schedule. Now that Doc's friend Ed Bayne had retired as Royals head coach, it was not as easy for him to schedule games with Billings. I knew we needed to play the tougher Class A competition to get ready for them in the playoffs and, hopefully, the State A Tournament; plus, I always wanted to play on Cobb Field. In 1978, we got to play the Royals and Scarlets, but not at Cobb Field. Many previous Scobey Legion teams had played on Cobb Field, including the 1966, 1969, and 1974 teams. I had seen the Billings Mustangs play Pioneer League games there with Mom, Dad, and Jon, and I hoped I could someday play there.

That summer, Scobey, Glasgow, Plentywood, and Wolf Point competed in the northeastern district. In the southeastern district, there was Glendive, Sidney, Circle, and the Miles City Colts.

True to form, Doc was developing the younger players—the "Baby Blues"—on the team for future state championships, and there would be more after 1979. Against Sidney in a nonconference game at Sidney, Doc started 13-year-old Greg Stolen, who pitched seven shutout innings, allowing only five hits. However, leading 5-0 in the bottom of the eighth, several Blues pitchers couldn't save it for little Greggie, and Sidney scored eight runs in the bottom of the eighth to win 8-5. The younger players on this team were talented and showed it whenever they could. In a game against the Grenora Gophers in Scobey, Pat Audet and Greg Stolen combined to pitch a shutout, and the Blues won 19-0, with all the younger players starting.

However, the highlights during the regular season were the eleven games we played against Class A competition, which toughened us up for the Class A playoffs and State A Tournament and prepared us to take our game to the next level. Six of those games were against the Williston Keybirds. The Williston Keybirds had a good program and finished second in the Western AA Division of the North Dakota State Legion that season. We split the six games against them, winning 10-7 and 6-4 and losing 9-8 and 9-3 in a doubleheader at Scobey. The two other games were shortened due to the weather. We were leading 6-1 in one of them, and Williston was leading 9-6 in the other. Kirby Halvorson and Randy Stolen hit back-to-back home runs in the 9-6 weather-shortened game at Ardean Aafedt Stadium in Williston. Kirby's home run to left center at Ardean Aafedt Stadium was the longest home run I ever saw hit in my Legion career. With many Minnesota Twins fans in North Dakota, it was called a "Harmon Killebrew" home run in the paper in Williston. Kirby and Randy would also go back-to-back at the State A Tournament in Butte later in the season.

In our 10-7 win over Williston at Ardean Aafedt Stadium in Williston, *Williston Herald* sports photographer Kurt Clemmensen captured a great sequence of photos on a close play at the plate. On the play, left fielder Randy Stolen caught a fly ball and then gunned a throw home to catcher Kirby Halvorson. Kirby jumped high in the air to snag the throw, then quickly leaped back to the plate to double off Keybird Jody Munson, who was tagging from third on the play. It was an incredibly athletic play by Kirby to complete the double play. I was pitching, so I was backing up the plate and passionately agreed with umpire Larry Grondahl's call. There is no better friend to a pitcher than a double play, especially with a runner at third! Randy threw two Keybirds out at the plate that day.

Christmas came early in 1979, at least to me as a baseball player. In a surprising last-minute turn of events, we were a late replacement as the sixth team in the Billings IGA Tournament, July 2-3-4, at Cobb Field. Scottsbluff, Nebraska, had to cancel due to the gas shortage, so Billings invited Doc and the Blues to fill in. Doc said yes, of course, and our schedule needed to be reshuffled because we had games scheduled with Williston, Miles City, and Glasgow on those dates. I was so excited when Kelly called to let Jon and me know. We would get to play five games against tough competition—on Cobb Field! Let's get packed and get ready to go to Billings!

Because the call came so late, I didn't have time to appreciate the level of competition we would be facing. Aurora, Colorado, was the defending State Class A champion in Colorado, and the players in that Legion post had all played on the Colorado State 3-A state championship high school team earlier that spring. The team from Colorado Springs took third in the Colorado state high school championships. The Casper Oilers won the Wyoming State Class A Legion championship later than summer, finishing with a 39-15 record. Then there were the Royals and the Scarlets. The Royals were leading the Class A eastern division and were riding a 10-game winning streak, and the Scarlets were in second place. The Scarlets would win the State Class A state championship later that summer, eliminating us from the tournament. So, the Legion state champions from Colorado, Wyoming, and Montana—Class A and Class B—were in the tournament, along with the eastern division champion Royals. The 1979 IGA Tournament could have been called the Tournament of Champions.

The competition was stiff—all the better. "'The bigger they are, the harder they fall,' is the motto of the Scobey Legion team as they prepare to meet the big towns in a six-team tournament in Billings."[185] This tournament was our chance to prove that we could compete with the best. But we had to win some games, not just stay on the field with them. We had stayed on the field with them before, only to walk off the field with close losses. The most important thing was not to beat ourselves by making mistakes in the field, which was our major weakness against these teams. I can't describe how exciting this opportunity was; it came out of nowhere.

Doc knew how important this tournament was for us and was optimistic about our chances. The *Leader* stated that Doc "feels this is a big chance to improve by competing against some of the West's stronger American Legion ballclubs. We will give them plenty of trouble down there and win a few games."[186]

Dano relished playing against the tougher competition. He said, "When we played better opponents the juices got flowing a little faster. I know when we played the A schools, I always had a chip on my shoulder. Don't try to intimidate us with your arrogant bullshit cause we'll bring it. We were battle-tested. A lot of confidence in each other to do our jobs."

Our first game was against the Billings Royals. The 1979 Blues had a backstory with this 1979 Royals team. We had lost to the Royals the previous season 2-1, and Doc was 0-4 lifetime against them, including when his boyhood friend Eddie Bayne coached them. The backstory dates to 1973, our Border Little League team. Eight of the 1979 Blues started on that team, and Greg Stolen would have, but he was seven years old and was our batboy instead. We lost 8-5 to the Billings Western Giants in the eastern divisional tournament, ending our dream to play in the Western Regional in San Bernadino, California.

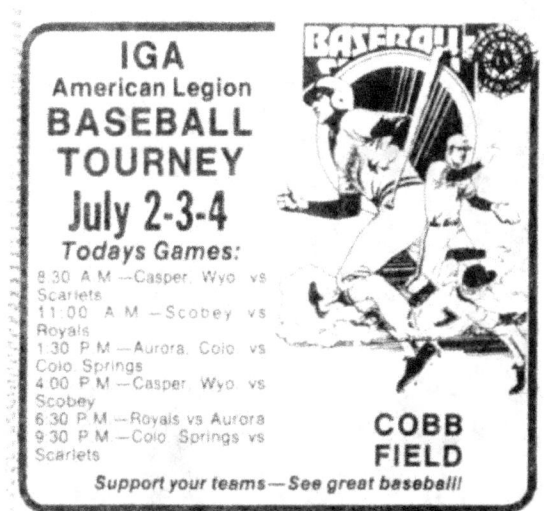

One of the most memorable experiences of my Legion Baseball career was playing on Cobb Field. Billings IGA Tournament flyer, *Billings Gazette*.

The Doc Norman Championship Era

Williston Herald photo by Kurt Clemmensen.

Williston Herald photo by Kurt Clemmensen.

Williston Herald photo by Kurt Clemmensen.

The umpire called the runner out; I emphatically agreed with his call. *Williston Herald photo by Kurt Clemmensen.*

The Western Giants went on to win the Montana state championship and played in San Bernadino. Six starters from that Western Giants team were starting for the 1979 Royals, including shortstop Mike Day, who had hit a two-run home run off us in the first inning of that 1973 game. He also hit an RBI double, had a walk and a stolen base, drove in three runs, and scored three. He made an unassisted double play at shortstop on a line drive by Dano to kill a rally we had going in the first inning with two runners on and one out. In the top of the sixth, we were trailing 8-1, and the Billings coach substituted liberally, thinking the game was over. Don't think we didn't notice. We came back to score four runs to make the score 8-5 and had two base runners on with two outs and Kirby at the plate. One of the substitutes in center field made an unbelievable sliding game-saving catch on what would have been a two-run line-drive double to right center by Kirby Halvorson. Fifty years later, Kirby thought it was Mike Day who made that catch because . . . who else would it be? He had done everything else to us. As a 15-year-old in 1976, in the State A Tournament against Scobey, Mike Day turned a triple play at shortstop in the fourth inning, ending the only real threat Scobey had in the game, and the Royals eliminated Scobey 6-1. In 1978, Mike Day was again our nemesis, as he had two hits and drove in the winning run in the Royals' 2-1 win. We had seen him get on base and steal bases against us. He was the face of the Royals'—and Class A—dominance over us. So, we had a chip on our shoulder against the Royals and Mike Day and were fired up to win this game. Never had we been more emotional before a game. I mentioned before how competitive the players on this team were. This game demonstrated that like no other.

How much of a chip? How badly did we want to beat this team? The intensity started with Dano's first pitch in the bottom of the first inning. Kirby and Dano had planned to hit leadoff hitter Mike Day with the first pitch and then throw him out stealing, which we all knew he would try to do. Dano remembers, "We were going to hit leadoff hitter Mike Day to send a message, and then Kirby was going to throw that fucker out trying to steal. Everyone on our team knew that I was going inside to Day on the first pitch; 90% chance I was hitting him. We were sending the message we would pitch inside. The error in this instance would be to possibly hit him and not leave the ball over the plate. I hit him first pitch high butt lower back but was aiming for the ribs, high and tight. Kirby knew the plan for the next hitter: we were throwing high fastballs, and when he tried to steal, Kirby would throw a strike to second and show off his arm. On the second or third pitch, Day went. Kirb moved targets around on all the pitches, but the fastball he went on was up and away, so Kirb, coming out of his crouch, had the ball out of his mitt so fast and made the perfect throw that it wasn't even close."

Yeah, it wasn't even close. Playing shortstop, I covered second base on the steal and had the ball in my glove before Day started into his slide. That is not an exaggeration. I waited for him to get to second base and slapped the tag hard on him when he finally got there. Then the trash-talking started from our second baseman, Kelly Norman, who said to Day, among other things, "Why even bother?" It was the strangest thing that everyone on the team knew he would be stealing and that Kirby would throw it. When we executed the play, the entire dugout and team on the field erupted, and we were charged to take things further.

That's a lot of ink for a regular-season game's first pitch and leadoff hitter, but it's an integral part of the story of the 1979 Blues. That hit-by-pitch and successful execution of the throw-out at second on the steal attempt set the tone for how we would play against tougher competition and showed the Royals and the Class A teams that we meant business in 1979 and would compete. Dano summed up the successful strategy: "I showed that I'd throw inside, and Kirby showed the cannon. Try to steal at your own risk."

The game was not without further "incident." Dano was a fierce competitor, but so was his counterpart, Royals pitcher Toby Lindsey. As the two pitchers were dueling in the middle innings with us leading 1-0, the feud spilled over into a heated exchange between the two, which mirrored the intensity of the game. After Lindsey hit a feeble comebacker to Dano and Dano threw him out easily at first, Lindsey was slowly trotting back across the diamond to return to the Royals' third-base dugout. Watching from shortstop, I could see Dano staring at him like he was looking for trouble. Dano remembers what happened next: "As I looked at his smiling face jogging slow as fuck between home and the pitcher's mound back to his third base dugout. I complimented him with, 'Nice fucking bunt.' He started talking smack, so I said, 'Nice fucking bunt, asshole.' He got a little hotter and said something about us hayseeds or something to that effect. He kept jawing at me, so I started hurling more obscenities at him and spewing more vomit from my mouth." Jon Puckett, who was playing third base, remembers what Dano said, but it is not printable here. Jon said, "I remember it vividly. For whatever reason, it seemed to me that it was totally appropriate for Dano to tell him that, and I applauded his retort. I also remember (and I don't think I'm embellishing the story) that Dano may have hiked his pants up as he said it. And, quite possibly, a droplet or two of saliva may have spewed from his mouth."

We scored a run in the top of the second to take a 1-0 lead, which gave us confidence. We played clean in the field and gained confidence as each inning went by, with Danelson hanging goose egg after goose egg on the Cobb Field scoreboard through five complete innings. We had six hits off Lindsey but had managed only one run. Then, in the bottom of the sixth, the Royals got to Dano for their first hit and first run and tied it 1-1. Both pitchers hurled scoreless seventh innings. In the top of the eighth, Kelly Norman lashed a line-drive single to right field to drive Jon Puckett home from third with what proved to be the game-winning run, as we held the Royals in the bottom of the eighth to win 2-1 and celebrated on Cobb Field. We got Doc's first win over the Royals, ended their 10-game winning streak, and snapped our five-game losing streak against them—counting the Western Giants, which we all remembered. To the Royals, we were just another game on their 60-game schedule. To us, it was the seventh game of the World Series. It would be hard to imagine another game that was more emotional or meant more to us than this game. The monkey was finally off our back.

The headline the next day in the *Billings Gazette* read, "Scobey's Danelson one-hits Royals, 2-1,"[187] and stated, "Dan Danelson did what few others have done—shut down the Billings Royals bats."[188] Dano finished with six strikeouts and five walks. His counterpart, Toby Lindsey, who also pitched well, struck out 10 and yielded eight hits and two walks. Most importantly, we played well defensively and made only two errors, neither costly. Kirby summed up the Day hit-by-pitch and the win over the Royals this way: "Maybe it was subconscious payback from the Western Giant loss in Little League. I know I felt vindicated beating the Royals. Day came out of nowhere to rob me of a bases-loaded double to right center when we played them in 1973."

What a great start to the tournament. Our next game was against Wyoming state-champion Casper Oilers. Playing as well as we did against the Royals, including defensively, we had confidence playing against Casper. We were just like any other team in the tournament. In the first inning, Wade Tryan got on base and stole second, and I drove him home with a single to take a 1-0 lead. However, we couldn't hold it, and the Oilers went on to win 3-2. Casper pitcher Mike Devereaux pitched a five-hitter against us, but we left two runners on base in the sixth and seventh innings and couldn't push home the tying run.

I have two vivid memories of the Casper game, both concerning umpires. In the first inning, with Kelly pitching, the Oilers had a runner on third with two outs. The batter hit a scooting ground ball to my left at short. I got to it, squared to first, and made a good throw to Ray to get the speedy runner by a half-step, and we got off the field with no runs allowed. The second base umpire nodded and said, "Nice play." I remember it because it validated the hard work I had been putting in at short in practice, and as a team, we were playing better defensively—as well as any team in the tournament. Later in the tournament, another umpire told me, "Your team is doing well because you don't make mistakes."

My second memory of that Oilers game had to do with my pitching. Doc had never pitched me against a Class A Montana Legion team before. I had pitched against the Williston Keybirds but never a Class A Montana Legion team. I had missed the opportunity to pitch in the 1976 best-of-three series against Libby and the State A Tournament as a 15-year-old because Dad took Jon and me on his previously planned family vacation to Kansas City after the 1976 state championship in Cut Bank. I would have surely pitched against Libby. In 1977, Doc pitched Dano and Jon in the best-of-three playoffs against the Helena Senators, and in 1978, Dano, Kelly, and Jon pitched in the series against the Great Falls Chargers. Against the Royals and Scarlets in May 1978, Doc pitched Dano, Ray, and Jon.

So, when Doc called me in from short to relieve Kelly against the Oilers, I was nervous but excited to have my opportunity. I pitched well, but as good as the second base umpire had made me feel about my fielding at short, the home plate umpire pissed me off. One of my pitches was a three-quarter-arm curve, more like a "slurve"—a combined slider and curve. It broke more horizontally right to left, rather than vertically down and left like my curveball. But in this game, I was throwing the slurve because it was easier to control, as I had come in relief from short, so I didn't have time to warm up and establish the curve. I was not used to pitching in relief—Doc normally started me—so this was new for me.

As I was warming up between innings, the home plate umpire walked to the mound and started coaching me on how to throw a curveball, like I didn't know how to throw a curveball—Andy Stolen taught me how to throw it! I felt like he was treating me like some hayseed kid from northeastern Montana who didn't have any coaching, and he, the umpire, was going to step in and teach me how to pitch. I had the best coaching any Legion player in the state could have with my Dad, Andy Stolen, Doc Norman, and

Don Lekvold. I turned my back on him and walked away when he was talking to me. I wanted to say, "Just call the balls and strikes—I know how to pitch," but I knew better. I sure thought it, however. I was getting outs with the pitch, so I didn't understand why he was even talking to me.

After that game against the Oilers, I gained confidence that I could get outs against these tougher hitters, and as the tournament progressed, Doc handed me the ball twice more, and my confidence grew. Unexpectedly, I had entered the tournament hoping I would exit it with more confidence in my fielding—which I did—but I left it with even more confidence in my pitching. This would pay huge dividends for our team later in the season when a serious injury to our best pitcher would put pressure on the rest of the staff to step up and deliver. More on that later.

After the Casper game, we watched the Billings Royals play Aurora, Colorado, in the last game of the day under the lights at Cobb Field. I was sitting by Kelly. Knowing we had beaten the Royals and didn't beat ourselves against Casper was a good feeling. We had played well and could relax now and watch the other teams play baseball. In the Royals game, I studied how Mike Day played at shortstop because he was the best I'd ever seen in Legion baseball. He made an error at short. Kelly said, "See, Joe, even Mike Day can make an error." Why would Kelly say that? He knew I scoured the newspaper daily for MLB box scores to see if the shortstops made any errors. As I perused the box scores, I noticed that shortstops committed the most errors because shortstop is the most difficult position to play in baseball. You have to field the ball cleanly *and* make a good throw to the out, whereas at third, second, and first, you can sometimes knock the ball down or bobble it slightly but still have time to get the runner at first. That is not the case at shortstop. Kelly's comment made me feel better, knowing that all good shortstops make errors and that playing the position perfectly was impossible, although that was my goal. Kelly knew that, and his comment picked me up.

Our next game the following morning was against Aurora, the defending Colorado state Class A American Legion champion and high school state Class 3-A champion. They had beaten the Royals 7-3 on Monday evening. This team was smooth. You could tell they had played a lot of baseball together and had seen it all. Doc started Ray Chapman against them. We scored first, but Aurora got Ray for some runs off some walks and key hits with baserunners on in the early innings to go ahead 3-2, so Doc called me in to pitch from shortstop again. I again gained more confidence pitching, getting outs against the tough Aurora lineup, with my defense playing so well behind me.

Aurora added another run to make it 4-2, where the score stood until the seventh.

We came back in the top of the seventh. Wade Tryan and Jon Puckett both got hits and got on base. I came to the plate with no outs and a chance to tie it, but I got duped by the crafty left-handed Aurora pitcher. I had singled and doubled off him previously in the game, so he was pitching carefully to me in this situation. On the double I hit earlier, he had thrown me a knuckler that didn't knuckle and smiled at me as I stood on second base, knowing it was a bad pitch and that he gave me one. He got ahead of me on the count in this at-bat, but I fouled a couple of pitches off, took some balls, and pushed the count full. On his next pitch, he went into his stretch, then just held the ball, looking at home plate. No pitcher had ever done that to me before. I should have called time and stepped out, but I had never been in that situation before and froze. After the long pause, he finally delivered a fastball straight down the middle, and I just stared at it, frozen, for strike three. Our dugout was on fire at the prospect of a big hit from me, but getting caught looking was deflating. Not used to seeing me get called out on strikes in that situation, someone in the dugout said, "That was straight down the middle." I didn't bother explaining what happened and just took my seat, hoping someone else could do what I couldn't.

Kelly Norman, who was hitting the cover off the ball in the tournament, then picked us up with a big hit that drove Wade home to make it 4-3, and Jon made it to third base as the tying run with one out. As he had done with me, the left-hander got Dano in a two-strike hole, so Doc decided to call a suicide squeeze with Jon at third. Jon broke, Dano squared but missed the bunt for strike three, and Jon was caught in a rundown. Jon recalls, "The third baseman bobbled throw in the run-down but I slipped changing directions and took out the catcher best I could at the plate." So that ended the game, 4-3. Disappointed at missing the bunt, Dano said, "It was one of the most pissed-off moments at myself ever. A feeble fucking bunt attempt. Anyone should be able to foul it off. Tight game, emotions running high and I do that! I wanted to fucking strangle myself." It was a tough loss, as we had the tying run on with no outs, but Dano and I couldn't come through with the key hit we needed to tie it. Kelly came through with a big hit, but it wasn't enough. One small consolation was that we played well defensively and didn't beat ourselves that way.

Later that day, we played the Billings Scarlets, where we banged out 17 hits and won a slugfest, 16-9. This was our fourth game in two days, so Doc used three pitchers, and the Scarlets got 11 hits. Jon got the win, and I again came in relief in the later innings. Appearing in my third game of the tournament, my arm was hanging off me, and I was having control problems late, but somehow, I was able to push a strike across the plate and get the last out with the bases loaded on a 3-1 count on a popup to Jon. Seeing that ball pop up to get that final out was a relief! We were now 2-2 in the tournament and had beaten the Royals and Scarlets. By now, our confidence against the tougher competition was firmly established. We belonged in this tournament with these teams.

The next day was special. We were playing baseball on Cobb Field on the Fourth of July. It was an incredible moment for me and our team. Before we took the field, we watched some good baseball, with Casper and Aurora—the Colorado and Wyoming state champions—playing stellar baseball. Not only did I get to see great baseball on the Fourth of July, but I also got to play. Our fifth game of the tournament was against Colorado Springs. Dan Danelson and Randy Stolen combined to pitch a five-hitter against Colorado Springs, but Colorado Springs's pitching also allowed only five hits. Randy Stolen was pitching with Colorado Springs leading 3-2 in the top of the seventh. The Colorado Springs hitters were not catching up with his lively fastball. If Randy missed with his fastball, it was usually high, and the hitters would sometimes chase the high fastball for swinging strikes. With runners on second and third and two outs, their speedy leadoff hitter hit a high hopper to deep short. I fielded the high hop, but after pitching three games and playing shortstop, I couldn't muster enough on the throw to get him at first. It was a tie, and he was safe. Colorado Springs then scored another run to make the final score 5-2. This ended the remarkable IGA Tournament for the Scobey Blues.

The *Leader* summed up our performance in the IGA Tournament: "The Blues showed fine form against these Class A clubs from the bigger towns, outscoring them 25-22."[189] The opportunity we had to play in the IGA Tournament can safely be credited with our success later in the season against Class A competition in the best-of-three playoffs and in the State A Tournament. We were given a chance and made the best of it. As with the 1977 state tournament in Scobey when most of us were 16 years old, we were not the same team that exited the IGA Tournament that had entered it. We had confidence that we could beat the Class A teams now. As Ed West from the *Gazette* wrote in his article, "No Class A team is relishing a possible matchup with Scobey in the elimination playoff this year."[190] Thank you for the gas shortage, and to the Scottsbluff, Nebraska, Legion team for not coming to Billings to play. As far as I was concerned, Santa Claus was from Nebraska, and he came in July of that year, bringing me the greatest gift ever. It made our season. I got to play on Cobb Field on the Fourth of July—memories to last a lifetime.

The weekend following the IGA Tournament, we played Williston in our third doubleheader, then traveled to Wolf Point for a conference game. Against Williston, we won the first game 6-4 and were leading in the second game 6-1 in the fourth inning, but it was called due to weather. That Sunday, Wolf Point brought us back down to earth when we lost our first conference game in two years, 6-4. Naturally, it would be Wolf Point—our friendly rival in northeastern Montana who always played good baseball—who would beat us. After the Wolf Point loss, we won our remaining conference games. We headed into the divisional at Sidney with an 11-1 conference record and were 24-7 overall, with five losses to Class A competition. Our record against Class B competition was 20-2, and we were 4-5 against Class A teams. Our regular season—especially the games against Williston and the teams in the IGA Tournament—had prepared us well for the postseason tournaments. We were confident and ready to take it to the next level.

EXTRA INNINGS

THE SIGN DOC HAD FOR THE SUICIDE SQUEEZE FOR DANO'S bunt against Aurora was he would bend over and place both hands on his knees. For Doc's other signs, the indicator was skin-on-skin—either hand-on-hand, hand-on-arm, or hand-on-face—then the bunt sign was chest-chin-hat—direction up—and the steal sign was hat-chin-chest—direction down. This was easy to remember because I was "up" to bat and would run "down" to second to steal. I was surprised to learn that these same signs carried over to Doc's successors in the third base coaching box, namely Don Lekvold, Ken Meyer, and Mike Lee. When I coached fast-pitch softball in Germany over thirty years later, I used Doc's signs, and it always made me remember the times I played for him at Scobey. It took me home. The Germans also understood the "up to bat" and "down to second" connection. A not-so-subtle "sign" Doc had for instructing a pitcher to throw at an opposing hitter was to yell, "Stick it in his ear!" from the dugout.

Later in the summer, Aurora was 32-8 heading into the Colorado state tournament. They were the defending state Legion and high school champions. However, they were unable to repeat as champions as they lost to the Pueblo

Elks for the state championship. The Casper Oilers were 39-15, won the Wyoming state championship, and played in the Northwest Regional. The Scarlets won the Montana State A Tournament and played in the Northwest Regional with Casper. The Billings Royals won the State A eastern division but were eliminated by the Scarlets at State.

I had seen Dano get angry a few times in Legion ball, but I never saw him erupt more intensely than in the dugout at IGA Tournament. Dano jokingly said, "Looking back on it. I may have had an anger problem." I think it was more of a "competitor" problem if you can call it that. He just wanted to win and became very frustrated when his performance did not meet his expectations. Regarding the failed suicide squeeze bunt attempt against Aurora, Dano said, "Like all of us, the intensity level when we played good teams rose. The IGA Tournament was that. This was the last year for many of us to get a crack at beating the top competition, to show we not only belonged on the same field but that we were just as good, if not better. I definitely had a chip on my shoulder, wanting to prove we could beat the best we faced. For me, the intensity moved to a level that, I guess, in retrospect, I had a hard time controlling at times. Doc had enough confidence in me to lay down a suicide squeeze with two strikes against Aurora. I felt like I should be able to do that 9 out of 10 times. I failed in a critical part of the game, and emotions blew a top. I went back to the dugout looking for something to hit, kick, throw. It didn't matter. I decided to kick the garbage can or water container and missed that, too! Fuck! My cleats slipped out from under me, and I landed on my back. Bottom line, I get the bunt down we tie the game." The dugout incident was not funny at the time—everyone was too afraid to laugh with Dano lying on the dugout floor—but we can safely laugh about it now.

Athletes always remember the bad because the memory of letting their coach and teammates down never goes away. Dano and I both struck out that last inning against Aurora and remember it well. Dallas Hagfeldt remembers the fly ball that popped out of his glove in right field in the 1971 state tournament against Plentywood, which opened the floodgates for five more errors, six unearned runs, and a shocking 6-5 upset loss to Plentywood.

The intensity of Dano's angry outburst in the dugout was impressive because it matched that of my dad's. I had not been around anger of that magnitude since we blew a 7-1 lead in the fifth inning to Froid in a Babe Ruth game at Fjeseth Field in Froid in 1974. Froid came back, and we lost the game 8-7 in extra innings. I was pitching. As he pulled out of the Fjeseth Field parking lot, driving the van home with several players inside, Dad yelled, "No one says a goddamn word the entire way home!" We didn't stop for dinner, either. That was the longest van ride home because my cousin Eddie Puckett—the funniest guy I've ever known—was with us, and he kept making faces to try to get us to laugh and get us in more trouble.

It should be noted that Mike Day was not cocky; he was just good. It was nothing personal; he symbolized the Royals' dominance over us and had been the focal point of our losses, from Little League in 1973 through Legion in 1979. He started as a middle infielder for the Royals in 1975 when he was only 14 years old—unheard of for a Class A team—and played shortstop for the Royals from 1975-79. He went on to play baseball for Gonzaga in college. He was elected to the Billings American Legion Hall of Fame—The Ed Bayne Award—in 2016.

The six players on the 1973 Montana State championship Billings Western Giants Little League team were never able to win a Legion title as the Royals. In 1979, they were beaten by the same two teams that beat us in the State A Tournament—the Great Falls Electrics and Billings Scarlets.

Our fielding woes against tougher competition started in 1973—we made six errors in that game against the Western Giants—but not in 1979. Our defense was solid throughout the IGA Tournament, the best-of-three series against the Helena Senators, and the State A Tournament.

I might have been more disappointed at age 12 for not making it to the Little League Western Regional in San Bernadino than I was at age 18 for not making it to the Legion Northwestern Regional in Yakima, Washington. The Little League World Series in Williamsport, Pennsylvania, was very visible. I remember watching it on TV as a little boy. Little League baseball has always had the allure of the media.

Later in life, Dan Danelson and Toby Lindsey laughed about their exchange on the pitcher's mound that day. Dano said, "Toby and I talked over the years and chuckled about it. Toby was a competitor just like we were."

The only tag I slapped down harder on Mike Day was on Bobby Damm of the Glasgow All-Stars in the northeastern district Little League championship game in 1973. We were leading 5-2 in the fifth inning, and leadoff hitter Bobby

Damm got on base; then Steven Miller hit a double to left center, which should have put runners on second and third with no outs. Dad always taught me to back up bases as a pitcher, so I ran to the back of third base in line where the throw might come from left center in case of a play at third. There was no play, but Bobby rounded third and was taunting us, dancing on the baseline between third and home, thinking there was no one covering third behind him because third baseman Kelly Norman went out to cut off the throw from Randy Stolen. I quickly moved up to third base and yelled, "Kelly!" Kelly quickly snapped a throw to third base, and Bobby was deader than Mike Day at second. I slapped the tag down hard on the lip of his helmet before he got to the base, and it dropped down and covered his face. Just like that, we had one out with only a runner at second instead of no outs and runners at second and third. Standing on second base, Steven Miller yelled, "Ah, Bobby, how could you?" Had he not taunted us, I might not have slapped the tag down so hard on him. We got out of the inning with no runs scored and went on to win the game 8-2. Those are the two tags I remember most in my career.

Regarding the Mike Day hit-by-pitch by Dano, it was not unusual for Doc to order a pitcher to hit a hitter—he was old school—but he did not order it in this case—it was all Dano and Kirb. Several former pitchers, including Phil Audet, Terry Puckett, and Dana Audet, had told me that Doc would yell, "Stick it in his ear!" when he wanted them to throw at a hitter. The most extreme case was when Doc ordered Terry Puckett to bean former Legion player Jack Higgins with a pitch in a Legion-Plainsmen game in 1971. Terry said, "Doc told me to hit Jack Higgins with a fastball. He said, 'The next time that cocky sonofabitch comes up, you hit him in the chest!' I knew that if I hit him, John would know that it was on purpose."

Dano said, "I have definitely hit people on purpose before. Sometimes by my choice sometimes it came from the coach. I got nervous if the coach called one because if you didn't make it good and hit the batter squarely you knew there would be hell to pay. I was taught to establish the inside corner of the plate, especially letter high. Inside high strike! My best games were usually when I could locate there. Opens every other part of the plate to use. I usually also hit a batter or two."

We had a chip on our shoulder against the Class A baseball teams, but no one had a greater chip on his shoulder than Gerry Veis with the Class A—in this case, Class AA—basketball teams. I was playing at the Grizzlies basketball camp in Missoula in 1978, and Gerry Veis was there. Greg Palmer, who was the starting guard for Great Falls Russell in 1979 and later the Bobcats, was there. It was an elite camp. While Palmer was playing in the championship game, Veis was all over him. He said, "You're double-A bullshit, Palmer." Palmer was getting upset and said, "You wanna step outside?" Veis replied, "No, you're just double-A bullshit, Palmer."

In our 5-3 nonconference win over Sidney in Scobey, Kelly Norman hit the first home run of his Legion career, but Ray Chapman, who was pitching, remembers another home run that game, one he surrendered to Tim Thogerson. Ray said, "It was a knuckle that didn't knuckle. Knew it as soon as it left my hand. I'd get away with those once in a while, but no way that would happen against Thogerson. He was too good. Like Voyager 1, it was launched into space in the 1970s and, also like Voyager 1, is still traveling somewhere in the constellation of Ophiuchus. Literally and metaphorically, it was more than a moonshot. Again, very similar to Voyager 1.

"Future generations of scientists will be studying that tiny white orb as it progresses through the universe."

Kirby became the idol of a little boy at the Billings IGA Tournament. Kirby recalls, "During one of the IGA games, DeeAnn [Lekvold] called me out of the dugout. She said a little boy wanted my autograph—I thought she was joking. So I went out, and sure enough, there was a little dude outside the fence (probably 10 or 11), and he wanted me to sign his hat. He told me he was a catcher, too. My first—and only—autograph."

Williston, like Billings, is a baseball town. It has hosted the Babe Ruth World Series at Ardean Aafedt Stadium five times, the last in 2022. Aafedt Stadium was built in the early 1950s and is named after the founder of Williston baseball, Ardean Aafedt. The stadium originally housed the Oilers, a semipro baseball team in the 1950s, but is now home to Williston's two American Legion teams: the Keybirds and Oilers. Zoonie McLean from Plentywood played in the North Dakota semipro league for the Minot Merchants and Monarchs from 1947-57 and the Williston Oilers from 1958-59.

Larry Grondahl, the umpire in the series of pictures of Kirby Halvorson's play at the plate in Williston, was the host president of the 2022 Babe Ruth World Series in Williston. He oversaw 35 committees under six divisions in the planning, preparation, and execution of the tournament.

This was the fourth Babe Ruth World Series in which he acted as host president.

If there was ever a time for the death stare, it was from me to my brother against Glendive in a nonconference game at Glendive. With two outs and the bases loaded, the Glendive hitter hit a sky-high popup to short, and Jon lost it in the lights. The baserunners were running with two outs, so all three runners scored. Worse, losing a ball lost in the lights is ruled a hit—at the time—so all three runs were earned. We won the game 17-7. Jon said, "Sorry, Joe." I just smiled. We were winning big; it didn't matter.

My dad nicknamed Greg Stolen "Super Flake" at a Little League game in Peerless in 1973. Jon and I were 12, and Greg was seven. Greg would practice with us when Andy brought Randy but hadn't appeared in a game yet. We needed a player in one game, so Dad put Greg in. With the bases loaded in a key situation, the pitcher got a 3-0 count on Greg, so Dad yelled from the third base coaching box, "Take it, Greggie, take it Greggie!" Greg thought "take" meant swing, so he swung on the 3-0 count and laced a single up the middle, scoring two runs. I don't think Dad ever gave the Super Flake the take sign after that.

Playing at Denton Field in Miles City against the Colts in a regular season game in 1979, someone on the team offered me some Red Man chewing tobacco before the game. Many of our players chewed, so I thought I'd join the crowd and see what all the fuss was about. I took some and crammed it into my mouth, then got sick as hell. After we jogged to the center field fence for warmup—a long jog because Denton Field is 438 feet to center—I puked on the outfield grass. It was the first—and last—time I ever "chewed" tobacco, not counting the time in college when I picked up a can of Mountain Dew and took a swig with Jon's chew in it. Kelly and Dano remember a time when they were batboys when they got into Beech-Nut and puked. Dano said, "We weren't ready yet. Had to be at least 13 years old to handle that stuff." Apparently, I needed to be older than 18.

The first Scobey team to play on Denton Field was the 1946 American Legion team, which Ron Fjeld played on. The 1973 Scobey Legion team won the eastern divisional tournament there. I played there in the 1975 Eastern Divisional Babe Ruth Tournament. I remember a ball got past our center fielder, and I thought the ball would never stop rolling, as it is 438 feet to straightaway center at Denton Field.

The article "Scobey's friendly doctor is a lot like Eddie Bayne," by Ed West of *The Gazette* Staff, appeared in the *Gazette* on the first day of the IGA Tournament.[191] Doc and Eddie Bayne date back to the 1930s when they were friends in Billings. The IGA Tournament article is reprinted here in its entirety:

C.H. "Doc" Norman has been coaching American Legion Baseball for 29 seasons, the last 20 at Scobey. And just like a boyhood friend of his, Norman has built a dynasty.

The friend? None other than Billings' Ed Bayne, the architect of the greatest Legion dynasty in Montana history.

Norman and Bayne grew up together in Billings in the 1930s and they'll have a chance to talk over old times this week as Norman brings his 1979 edition to Billings for the IGA Tournament which starts Monday at Cobb Field.

Beginning in 1950, Bayne established a matchless tradition for the Billings American Legion programs with a flock of state championships and national tournament appearances.

With less notoriety Norman has constructed a legitimate dynasty of his own in northeastern Montana. During his tenure, which began in 1959, Scobey has won five state B championships, including the last three in a row.

And with a deep pitching staff and robust hitting there's a good chance Scobey might make it four in a row.

Scobey takes a 14-3 overall record into weekend games with Wolf Point and Williston, N.D. and they lead the Eastern B race with a 6-0 mark.

The pitching staff is headed by Dan Danelson who has good speed and control. Danelson, who was a starting forward in the recent Montana-Wyoming All-Star basketball series, has a 4-0 record.

"He's got a lot of talent," Norman said of his 6-6 right-hander. "He's a big kid. He's intelligent and very cooperative."

Among the other starters in Norman's five-man rotation are son Kelly (2-0), Joe Puckett (3-0), Jon Puckett (1-2) and Ray Chapman (3-1). Randy and Greg Stolen and Pat Audet have also seen action, giving Scobey plenty of pitching depth.

All of the pitchers also take turns manning infield positions and some draw outfield assignments. Among the regular outfielders are Wade Tryan, David Corey and Ron Higgins.

Another mainstay is catcher Kirby Halvorson, who is a seasoned veteran at handling the pitching staff.

There's usually plenty of runs for the pitchers to work with since "most were hitting over .400," according to Norman.

Even though Scobey hasn't been able to win the Class A state tournament, they haven't been embarrassed against A teams.

Scobey was beaten by the Great Falls Chargers 6-5 and 9-7 in a playoff for a state tourney berth last year and lost 9-2 and 8-6 decisions to Helena in the 1977 playoff.

In 1976 the Class B champion received an automatic bid into the A state meet. [Scobey actually beat Libby in a best-of-three series to qualify for the State A Tournament.] Scobey lost 8-2 to the Scarlets and 6-1 to the Royals in the State A Tournament.

With those performances in mind, no Class A team is relishing a possible matchup with Scobey in the elimination playoff this year.

The Class B champion will meet an eastern division team this year, and since Butte has an automatic bid as host team, it appears that it will be the third-place team. At present, Helena and Anaconda are battling for third place.

The winner of the playoff advances to the state tourney where it will be seeded against the winner of the western division.

Scobey is a late replacement for Scottsbluff, Nebraska, in the IGA tourney. Scottsbluff decided to bow out because of the gas shortage.

But that just gives Norman a chance to get back on his old stomping grounds.

DIVISIONAL TOURNAMENT

The final northeastern district standings were Scobey 11-1, Wolf Point 7-5, Glasgow 5-7, and Plentywood 0-12. Glendive won the southeastern district with a 13-3 conference record, followed by Sidney 12-4, Miles City Colts 9-7, and Circle 7-9.

The 1979 Eastern Divisional Tournament was played at Moose Memorial Park in Sidney. Our first game was against Circle, the fourth seed from the south. Doc handed the ball to Jon Puckett for the opener. Led by Dan Danelson's hitting and Jon Puckett's pitching—and errorless fielding—we beat Circle 12-1 in seven innings. Jon struck out nine and walked two, and Dano led our 15-hit attack with three hits, including a home run, an RBI triple, and an RBI single, driving in three runs. Randy Stolen also homered, belting a two-run blast in the third. Kelly Norman had a double and two singles, and Jon Puckett and Ray Chapman each doubled and singled.

Our second game was against host Sidney. Doc started me, and I felt the strongest pitching I'd ever had. Taking care of my arm by not throwing following days that I'd pitched helped keep its strength. I carried the confidence that I'd gained getting good hitters out in the games at the IGA Tournament against Casper, Aurora, and the Billings Scarlets. As it was with Jon two years earlier, in 1977, it was the same for me. Jon said then, "Toward the end of that season, my arm felt stronger. I felt like I could get anyone out." I couldn't say it any better myself. I struck out the first two hitters on three pitches each, and then Tim Thogerson came to the plate. I got two quick swinging strikes on him as he was not catching up with my fastball. I didn't know it then, but I was one pitch away from what baseball refers to as an "immaculate inning"—when a pitcher strikes out the side on nine pitches, three up and three down. I knew that all eight pitches I'd thrown had been for strikes, and I'd struck the first two hitters out, so I felt confident I could get a strike past Thogerson for the third out. The next best pitch should have been a high fastball out of the strike zone, and Kirby called it, but I shook it off and thought I could fool him with a curveball. Having thrown eight consecutive strikes, I was confident I could get him with the curveball for strike three. I threw it for a perfect strike, which I never should have done. It didn't fool him, and he hit an opposite-field home run that just cleared the fence in the left-field corner. It was quite a blow when I saw the ball leave the park and was disgusted with myself for making the pitch. Lesson learned: if someone is not catching up with your fastball, don't throw an off-speed pitch, at least not in the strike zone. And so much for the immaculate inning.

Thogerson's two-strike, two-out home run in the first would be the only run Sidney scored. Jeff Nesper was pitching well for Sidney, as we were only leading 4-1 in the top of the fifth when we erupted for eight runs to take a 12-1 lead, ending the game in seven innings by that score. I remember pitching in the seventh and Coach Jerry Callen saying in the third base coaching box, "He's just rearing back and firing now." The *Billings Gazette* stated that Scobey earned the title-game berth on "near-perfect" pitching: "Joe Puckett struck out 14, walked none, and gave up just four hits."[192] What *was* perfect that game—for the second game in a row—was our fielding; as the *Gazette* stated, the "near-perfect" pitching was supported by Scobey's "errorless fielding." Two games without an error in the field. Dan Danelson, swinging a hot bat, led us at the plate, homering for the second consecutive game, and Randy Stolen was 3 for 4 with a double and two RBIs.

That set up our berth in the championship game on Sunday against Wolf Point, who, behind Bob Moran's five-hitter and 12 strikeouts, beat the Miles City Colts 5-2 in their first game. Terry Baldry doubled, and Jim O'Tremba tripled for Wolf Point. Wolf Point pounded Plentywood 15-0 on 20 hits in the semifinal. In Wolf Point's 20-hit barrage, Dan Jensen drove in five runs with four hits, winning pitcher Jim O'Tremba knocked in three runs with a three-for-five performance, and Kip Harcharik had four hits in five trips, including a triple.

But we would have to wait until Monday to play Wolf Point in the championship game, as a severe thunderstorm Sunday evening forced the postponement of the Sunday evening game to Monday evening.

This game was another classic matchup between Scobey and Wolf Point for the eastern divisional championship game, except this time, instead of a slugfest, which had been the case in many previous eastern divisional championship games, this one featured strong pitching. Kip Harcharik started for Wolf Point; naturally, Dan Danelson was the starting pitcher for Scobey. Dano pitched a three-hitter, striking out eight and walking only one to lead us to the 4-1 championship victory. Playing shortstop, I marveled at the fluidity of Dano's windup and delivery, and the control of all his pitches. It was a beautiful thing to watch; he "kept complete control of Wolf Point during the championship game."[193] We had 10 hits, but Kip Harcharik scattered them as he "worked his way out of a jam in nearly every inning."[194] We were leading 4-0 with two outs in the bottom of the ninth, but Dano lost his shutout when an unearned run scored, coming on the only error we committed in the tournament. There was understandably and justifiably a death stare following the error, although I had seen much worse, considering a pitcher had just lost a shutout with two outs in the ninth. As I would say to Mom when I got in trouble as a little boy, "It wasn't me." It was the other twin at third. Following the error, the next hitter hit a groundball to me at short. It was hit sharply, so after fielding it, I had time to shuffle my feet to first base and get the momentum moving horizontally and directly toward the bag to help keep the throw straight and level, plus make the throw shorter. I had watched several good shortstops do this. To be extra sure of the throw, I quickly shuffled my feet again—I was not going to airmail the throw to Ray. Mom also used to say, "If it isn't one of you, it's the other." I didn't want *both* twins to screw up. I made a good throw to Ray for the third out. After we met on the mound to celebrate the 4-1 championship win, Kirby Halvorson said, "I was wondering if you were ever going to throw it." I replied, "Just making sure, Kirb."

This was the best our team had ever played in all three aspects of the game—pitching, fielding, and hitting—over an entire tournament: "Blues defense allowed only one run in each game and committed only one error in the tournament, to back up excellent pitching. Meanwhile, the big bats averaged 12 hits per game."[195] We outscored our opponents 28-3 in the three games. Winning pitchers Jon and Joe Puckett and Dan Danelson issued only three walks and gave up two earned runs in 23 innings pitched. Dan Danelson hit two home runs—let's call them "goobs" since we're playing in Sidney—and Randy Stolen had another.

Circle beat Sidney 8-7 in 12 innings to take third, leaving Scobey, Wolf Point, Circle, and Sidney as the top four teams to advance to State. Glendive, the champion of the southeastern conference with a 13-3 record, was upset 3-1 by Plentywood—who had finished 0-12 in the northeastern conference—in their first game. Cory Germann of Plentywood pitched a three-hitter, striking out six and walking only one batter. Glendive was then eliminated by the Miles City Colts 2-1.

Riding home on the bus to Scobey after the Monday game championship gave me time to reflect. Two years earlier, in 1977, I had been riding home on this same bus from Sidney after the eastern divisional tournament, except then, I was thinking about playing in my first state tournament in Scobey. Now I was thinking about my last. My American Legion Baseball career was winding down. I was excited to play in my final tournament in Scobey, but it was bittersweet, as the games I would play would be my last at Scobey Ball Park.

What a ride it had been. My memories trailed to the beginning 12 years earlier, in 1967, when Dad taught Jon and me how to pitch in our backyard and play baseball on the ballfield in Peerless, and my mom kept score for all the games and always supported us. I remembered watching all the state tournaments in Scobey—1969, 1971, 1973, 1975—and the one I played in 1977. I had been at the 1967 Eastern Divisional Tournament in Plentywood when Scobey, led by Phil Audet's pitching, qualified for the state tournament for the first time. Baseball during the summer had been my life growing up, playing Peewee and Little League baseball with Jon and my friends from Peerless and then All-Stars with players from Scobey, Peerless, Flaxville, Glentana, and Opheim. Dad and Andy Stolen coached us in Babe Ruth for three years, and then Jon and I started to play for Doc and the Blues when we were 15 years old in 1976. I had been blessed to play with other committed and talented athletes my entire career, and they were all sitting around me on the bus. All the precious memories. My life in summer. Soon, it would all be over.

One more time in Scobey. Four more games to win our fourth consecutive championship. I wasn't looking past the state championship or even our next game, whoever we would play three days later on Thursday. Could we make it four in a row for Scobey and Doc's sixth overall?

EXTRA INNINGS

PLENTYWOOD'S LOSING PITCHER IN THE 15-0 LOSS TO WOLF Point at divisional was 15-year-old Randy Pederson. Randy would figure prominently in Scobey's eighth state championship in 1982. When Plentywood did not field a Legion team in 1982, Randy could play for Scobey, à la Dallas, Jay, and Mike Hagfeldt from Glasgow.

When the championship game was moved from Sunday evening to Monday evening because of the storm, some housing problems for players and fans arose, as our motel reservations did not include the extra day. We had to check out by 11 a.m. Monday. We wondered where we would spend the afternoon to stay out of the heat. Sidney's assistant coach, Delmar Nesper, realized the problem and offered his home to us. Mr. Nesper said, "'Both Mrs. Nesper and I work all day, so the house is empty. Come on over and rest up for the game.'" So the entire Blues team enjoyed the air-conditioned comfort of the Nesper home in Sidney Monday afternoon."[196]

While at the Nesper home on Monday—or maybe Jon and I went to the Ackerman home, I can't remember—I talked to Todd Ackerman, who was 16 years old and played for Sidney. His dad, Ted Ackerman, was from Glentana and graduated from Peerless High School, and he played with Dad on the legendary Peerless Pirates basketball team. My dad often spoke of Ted Ackerman, a great athlete and coach. He coached and taught for over 25 years, including at Hardin, Belt, Great Falls, and Billings. When I discussed the tournament with Todd, he said, "You guys don't make any mistakes." My ears pricked up when he said that because we had been working hard to improve our fielding. It was gratifying to hear someone acknowledge the hard work. He asked me, "Why do you and Jon play on the outfield grass at shortstop?" My answer was that the outfield grass at Moose Memorial Park cut too close to the infield, so playing normal depth at short was a couple of steps back on the outfield grass. As a result, Jon and I fielded many balls at shortstop in Sidney on the outfield grass.

With some time on our hands on Sunday night following the storm and postponement of the championship game to Monday, some of us decided to see a movie at the Centre Theater in Sidney. The movie was *Halloween*. We also saw some Wolf Point players there, like Jim O'Tremba. It was a nice theater. I'll never forget seeing Jamie Lee Curtis, one of my favorite actresses, in her first role on the big screen. *Halloween* is still my favorite horror film. The Centre Theater in Sidney was an excellent movie house. Of course, the R-rated *Halloween* couldn't compare to *Love Amazon Style*, the XXX-rated movie that 18-year-olds Dana Audet, Jay, and Doug Hagfeldt saw at adult movie theater Studio-1 in Billings after they played the Scarlets in 1974, but it did have its moments.

Thorgerson's home run on my two-strike curveball was the only home run I surrendered in Legion to that point. I wish I could have that pitch back, but at least it's not in orbit like Ray Chapman's knuckler to Thorgy that didn't knuckle in Scobey earlier that season. Based on those two pitches resulting in home runs, it might have been best to stay away from breaking balls in the strike zone to Tim Thogerson. Or maybe not pitch to him at all.

The immaculate inning (three strikeouts on nine pitches) used to be rare in the major leagues, but not anymore. Due to modern-day analytics—with hitters no longer focused on making contact with two strikes—immaculate innings have become much more common. There were none from 1929-52, but they started to tick up in the 1990s. In the 2010s, there were 37. There were seven alone in 2022, and so far in the 2020s, there have been 15 immaculate innings, and we're only 40% through the decade. The term "immaculate inning" was coined by Boston Red Sox pitcher Lefty Grove in 1922. He used it to describe his performance, where he struck out three batters using nine pitches in one inning against the Cleveland Indians. While other pitchers previously achieved this feat, Grove was the first to use the term "immaculate inning" to describe it.

STATE B TOURNAMENT

THE *LEADER*, CONSTANTLY AWARE OF THE SCOBEY BASEBALL tradition, recognized the historical significance of the 1979 state tournament in Scobey: "It marked the tenth anniversary of two things: the first time, in 1969, when Scobey hosted a State Legion Tournament—and the first state title achieved here in what was one of the most thrilling tournaments ever held in the history of American Legion Baseball in Montana."[197] After that incredible first state tournament in 1969, Scobey hosted it in alternate years, so the 1979 State Class B Tournament was Scobey's sixth. "Interestingly enough, this year, there are four team members from families whose sons figured largely in the first state tournament won here—the Pucketts, the Danelsons, the Audets, and the Higgins."[198] Kelly Norman was the batboy for the 1969 team. Nineteen seventy-nine was also the twentieth anniversary of the first year Doc coached in Scobey in 1959.

Because the eastern divisional had been delayed a day by rain, there wasn't much build-up to the state tournament once we arrived home from Sidney late Monday evening. We had two practices on Tuesday and Wednesday, and the tournament started on Thursday. The *Daniels County Leader* printed the bracket for the first day's games:

- Wolf Point (2E) vs. Laurel (3W)
- Great Falls Sparkies (1W) vs. Sidney (4E)
- Circle (3E) vs. Great Falls Vigilantes (2W)
- Scobey (1E) vs. Fairfield (4W)

The *Great Falls Tribune*, in its tournament preview, stated that Scobey was "heavily favored" and that the "main competition" for Scobey would be the Great Falls Vigilantes, the Sparkies, and Wolf Point.[199] In discussing Wolf Point's chances, the *Tribune* mentioned Scobey beat both the Royals and Scarlets, and immediately following those games, "Wolf Point handed Scobey its only league loss."[200] Wolf Point had also played us close in the eastern divisional championship game, losing 4-1. Wolf Point was always a threat, no matter what team they put on the field.

But the *Tribune* failed to mention the Laurel Dodgers. Laurel entered the tournament with a 23-10 record. They played in the T.V. Appliance Memorial Day Tournament at Cobb Field earlier in the season and beat the Scarlets 7-5. They won the western division with an 11-3 record but faltered in their first game of the western division tournament against Fairfield. With Laurel leading 5-3 with two outs in the ninth and no one on base, Fairfield got three hits, Laurel had an error, and Fairfield pulled off a three-run comeback to win 6-5. Laurel then won their next three games of the western divisional tournament to take third place. Laurel was the best team in the west but entered the state tournament as the number-three seed with that loss to Fairfield.

The first game of the day—Wolf Point against Laurel—was at nine o'clock in the morning. I usually did not drive in from Peerless to watch the earlier games because I stayed home to rest and prepare for the night game, as the host team was always scheduled for the last game of the day. But Mom needed me to bring some food to the Legion burger stand, so I arrived at the field mid-game. The atmosphere and intensity level of the state tournament were incredible. It was exciting to be at this game. After delivering the food to the Legion stand, I turned to watch. Wolf Point and Laurel were battling in a close game. I stood in the same spot under the crow's nest that I had stood in 1971 when I watched Terry Puckett and Dave Fanning engage in their epic 1-0 pitcher's duel. Here I was eight years later. This time, Kip Harcharik from Wolf Point was dueling Tim Byrne from Laurel. I got there with the score tied 1-1 in the sixth inning. I had to tear myself away from the field to go back home to rest and prepare for the night game, but I missed a helluva finish when I did. The downside of playing is you miss some great games. Laurel scored a run in the bottom of the seventh to take a 2-1 lead, but Terry Baldry from Wolf Point drove in Larry Rowe in the top of the ninth to tie the game 2-2 and force extra innings. In the bottom of the eleventh, in another horrific ending for Wolf Point in a state tournament game, Laurel walked it off on two errors on a pickoff play by Wolf Point. Wolf Point had not committed an error the entire game until the two errors on the same play brought Nick Markovich home with the winning run from second base in Laurel's 3-2 walk-off win.

In other first-round games, Sidney beat the Sparkies 2-1, and Circle beat the Great Falls Vigilantes 4-2. Tim Thogerson tripled and scored both of Sidney's runs to provide enough run support for Steve Heit—who pitched a four-hitter—to beat the Sparkies. Circle's Mel Zuroff had a single and two doubles, and Kevin Sukut pitched a six-hitter to beat the Vigilantes. Laurel's 11-inning win over Wolf Point spoiled another clean sweep by the east, as had been the case in 1978 in Cut Bank.

Taking the field against the Fairfield Blue Hawks for the final game of the day on Thursday was special. The crowd was there, of course, but it was more of a sentimental feeling of playing in my last state tournament in Scobey. Four more games—one at a time—to win it again and hopefully take it to the next level against the Class A teams. Doc, who Kelly said "did not like changing the batting order," also did not like altering his pitching rotation, but he did in this game. After seven consecutive opening post-season tournament games—dating to Joe Puckett's start against Glendive in the 1976 Eastern Divisional Tournament in Glendive—Doc did not hand the ball to Joe or Jon Puckett to start the tournament's first game. Kelly Norman got the start in the opening game.

After playing near-perfect ball in the field in the eastern divisional tournament, committing only one error in three games, we played sloppy in our opening game against the Athletics, committing five errors. The *Leader* described the game as a "bit ragged in spots."[201] The errors all came early, and the good news is we got it out of our system as we returned to form the rest of the tournament, but it was a rocky start. Kelly Norman pitched three shutout innings to start the game, and we led 5-0 in the bottom of the fourth when Doc brought in Jon Puckett. Fairfield got their lone earned run of the game in the inning, but two unearned runs scored on an error in the outfield, and Fairfield plated three runs in the inning.

Then, with us leading 6-3 in the bottom of the sixth, Fairfield scored two more unearned runs to close to 6-5. Fairfield had runners on second and third after a walk, a wild pitch, a single, and a stolen base. The next hitter bunted. It was a safety squeeze, so Jon had a chance to get the runner at the plate but rushed the throw and threw wild to Kirby. The ball bounded back to the backstop, two runs scored, and the bunter advanced to second. On the next play, with the runner at second, the hitter hit a grounder to me at short. The runner from second, who should have been holding because there was only one out, ran to third, and his unexpected baserunning decision got me out of my rhythm. I short-armed the ball to Dano to third, and the runner was safe on our fifth error of the game. After that error, our vocal center fielder Wade Tryan—who had made an error himself earlier in the game—yelled, "Get your shit together in there!" Had we been playing at Yankee Stadium, there might have been a smattering of boos, but I did hear some disappointed gasps. Our fans expected more from us, and we expected more from ourselves. The *Leader* was very generous when it described the game as "a bit ragged in spots." I could say we were playing down to our competition, but that would be a disservice to Fairfield, who was battling to pull off a major upset. We had no one to blame but ourselves.

After my error at short, Jon had had enough and decided that getting *his* shit together meant striking out the next two hitters—the leadoff and number-two hitters—to strand the tying run at third. He got us off the field with no more runs scored but coming to bat in the top of the seventh, we unexpectedly found ourselves in a tight game with Fairfield, leading only 6-5.

We broke it open with seven runs in the seventh—partially on some shoddy fielding by Fairfield—to take a 13-5 lead. Our fielding stabilized, Jon retired the side in order in their last three at-bats, striking out six, and we advanced with an ugly 13-5 opening-game win. But I'd rather win ugly than lose pretty, and we got the shoddy fielding out of our system for the remainder of the postseason. Kelly pitched three shutout innings, and Jon Puckett pitched six innings of relief to get the win, striking out 13 Athletics and giving up only one earned run. Joe Puckett had three hits to lead Scobey's 12-hit attack. Jon summed up the game perfectly: "I remembered having good stuff that night, but somehow didn't feel good about the outing. Might have been that error that plated two runs." However, Jon was not alone in the error department. Dano had an error at third, Wade in center, Ray at first, and then my error at short in the sixth capped off the five-error fest. Thankfully, we got the errors out of our system and played well defensively for the remainder of the tournament—and postseason. Let's put the Fairfield game in our rearview mirror and move on.

Our second game was against Circle, who played well in their opening game, a 4-2 win over the Vigilantes. Doc, again shaking up his pitching rotation, started Randy Stolen. We had easily handled Circle the week before in Sidney 12-1, and we would again cruise, as we were pounding them 13-1 after five innings. In the top of the sixth, Doc relieved Randy Stolen with younger brother Greg, who was 13 years old, to get him experience pitching in the state tournament. Doc had pitched Greg during the regular season, including seven scoreless innings against Sidney. Greggie pitched a scoreless sixth. We scored three more runs in the bottom half of the inning to take a 16-1 lead into the top of the seventh. Doc then substituted freely, inserting Pat Audet, Ron Higgins, Jim Lekvold, Jesse Cook, and Gord Tryan into the game. This was Doc's method on full display: in the process of winning his sixth state championship, he was preparing his younger players for future state championships, giving them valuable experience in a state tournament, including Greg as pitcher. All the substitutes in that sixth inning would start for Scobey the following year when Scobey would win its fifth consecutive state championship.

However, Greg got into trouble in the seventh, and Circle—who could hit—scored five runs on five singles and a Scobey error to close the game to 16-6. In a bizarre ending, Doc brought in Dan Danelson from third base with two outs to get the final out and preserve the 10-run

Randy Stolen moments before driving in two Scobey runs with a single in the first inning of the opener against Fairfield. *Leader* photo, Milt Gunderson.

rule. Dano got the last out, striking out leadoff hitter Jaron Schillinger—the 11th Zephyr to bat in the inning—and we advanced to the undefeated semifinal with a 16-6 seven-inning win over Circle. Randy Stolen pitched five innings, giving up one and striking out seven, to get the win. Kirby Halvorson clubbed a two-run home run to lead Scobey's 13-hit attack. Wade Tryan tripled, Kelly Norman had two doubles, and Joe and Jon Puckett doubled for Scobey's other extra-base hits. We committed only one error in the field.

That set up our undefeated semifinal matchup with Sidney, who beat Laurel 10-0 in seven innings in their second game. With Craig Smith of Sidney and Todd Watkins engaged in a 0-0 pitcher's duel after five innings, Sidney broke it open with five runs in the sixth and five more in the seventh to win by the 10-run rule. The Dodgers, who had played errorless ball through five, had six miscues in the last two innings—including four in the decisive seventh frame—to provide Sidney with some gift runs. Russ Barnhardt had two hits, including a double, and Tim Thogerson had a triple for the Patriots. Craig Smith carried a no-hitter into the seventh inning, but it was broken up on a single by Brad Dantic.

Doc started Dan Danelson in the undefeated semifinal against Sidney on Saturday. We jumped on Sidney starter Scott Johnson for four runs in the first inning, the big blow coming on a two-run double by Kirby Halvorson, and these would be all the runs Dano would need. He was masterful once again, pitching a five-hitter, walking only one, and striking out 12 Patriots to lead us to a 9-1 win. Scobey's other two extra-base hits came in the eighth inning. Jon Puckett led off with a triple and scored on Ray Chapman's single. Danelson then doubled home Chapman, icing the victory. Todd Ackerman doubled for the only extra-base hit in Sidney's five hits. Again, we played well in the field, committing just two errors.

That put us in the championship game against the Laurel Dodgers, who, after losing 10-0 to Sidney in their second game, came through the dirt route by beating the Vigilantes 7-4, Wolf Point (for the second time) 12-6, and avenged their loss to Sidney by beating them 5-3 to get to the championship game. Laurel had to be good to win four games in the tournament, including two over Wolf Point and one over Sidney. But no matter who we were playing, we would play all out.

As he had done the previous year in Cut Bank in this same game, Doc handed me the ball to pitch the championship game. I had never been so prepared—and so excited—to pitch a game. I was fortunate to have this opportunity. I have written about how I had carefully taken care of my arm that summer; it was strong, and I had confidence. That was not the case the year before, but it was in this, my final season. I had taken my loss the previous year against Glendive hard, forcing the extra game, and I had not forgotten that feeling. A year later, because of how the pitching rotation had played out in the tournament, the stars had aligned for me to have a second chance to win a state championship game, the first in my Legion career. It was a gift.

In the last inning of the Sidney-Laurel game, I walked over to the Little League field across the way to start my

Jon Puckett slides into third after hitting a lead-off triple in the eighth inning against Sidney. He scored on the next pitch. Jon Puckett played six different defensive positions for the Blues during the tournament. *Leader photo, Milt Gunderson.*

warmup with Kirby, who, along with Allan Audet, had been my catcher for six years. It was always the same. I would start close, a few feet away, with easy tosses, then gradually back up, increasing the velocity, finally stepping off as close to sixty feet six inches as I could, as there was no mound on Little League field. Kirby and I talked about the signs and the pitch sequences but not about the hitters because we didn't know who we would be playing yet. We knew the Sidney hitters but not Laurel. With Sidney, of course, it was essential to be careful with Torgy (Tim Thogerson). I had settled into a four-pitch repertoire that summer. After watching Dano master his sidearm fastball and slider for two years, I added both pitches. I now had four pitches: fastball (1), curve (2), sidearm fastball (3), and sidearm slider (4). I started to throw each pitch to Kirby in the warmup. My confidence was high that I could throw each of them for a strike. A week earlier in Sidney, I was aggressive, constantly attacking the strike zone, getting ahead of hitters, wasting very few pitches, and being very efficient. Kirby and I were in synch on the sequence, and I rarely shook him off, except for Torgy's home run in Sidney. In the state championship game in Scobey, I don't remember shaking Kirby off once.

As I was warming up with Kirby and the game wound down, I glanced around to the sky in the north and west. There had been showers earlier in the day, and one of the games was delayed, and the night sky looked threatening. I hoped the rain would hold off. I felt strong, warmed up, and ready to go. The crowd was there. It was state championship night. Please, let's play ball tonight.

As we warmed up on the Little League field and the ninth inning of the Sidney-Laurel game wound down, my mind had time to consider the moment. This was the championship game, but—if we won—it would also be my last game at Scobey Ball Park. Comparing Senior Night in basketball to "Senior Night" in baseball was quite a contrast. In basketball, you play your last home game in a regular season game on your home court. The game is often meaningless and does not count in the standings. But it is special to be playing your last home game for a state championship. This, combined with the fact that we were warming up on a Little League field, stimulated my memory of playing baseball as a little boy in Peerless. I was almost overcome by emotion, but I held it in check because there was a game to play. There would be time for emotion later. For the time being, it was surreal for me to be warming on a Little League field to play in an American Legion game. My 12-year baseball career, playing in Peerless from 1967 to Scobey in 1979, was symbolized by both fields—my summertime life. There was a hint of fall in the air that late-July night and autumn was closing in on this Blue of Summer.

We were the visiting team against Laurel. Tim Byrne, who gave up only one run in eight innings in Laurel's 3-2 11-inning win over Wolf Point, started for the Dodgers. He held us scoreless in the top of the first. Then, it was our turn to take the field. When I trotted out to the pitcher's mound to begin my warmup with Kirby, I noticed the packed crowd in the grandstand and the bleachers crammed with people to the left and right. But one face stood out among them—my dad. He had crawled out of the crow's nest where he had been announcing the tournament to watch me pitch in the state championship game. He was sitting behind the home plate backstop, just to the right of the umpire and catcher. I had never noticed him sitting *there* before. He was watching every pitch I delivered in warmup. His intensity and focus—the man who taught Jon me how to pitch in our backyard when I was six—might have been greater than mine. Then, sitting next to Dad on his right, I saw my cousin Terry Puckett. During the game, I saw them talking to each other about what my next pitch might be. Seeing them sitting together behind home plate was an incredible adrenaline shot. I had watched Terry pitch, including in the 1971 state tournament against Dave Fanning from Havre, and he was the best pitcher I had ever seen pitch for Scobey in American Legion. Now, here he was, sitting next to my dad, watching me pitch in the state championship game. Every pitch I delivered, my dad and Terry were in the background. Can you imagine?

I felt the best I'd ever felt pitching on the mound and had command of all my pitches early, aggressively attacking the plate and getting ahead of hitters. Kirby and I were totally in synch. He would flash the sign, and I would take my windup almost simultaneously because we knew the sequence. We scored two runs in the top of the second and third to take a 4-0 lead. We scored a single run in the top of the sixth

Kirby Halvorson scores the first run of the championship game against Laurel. Kirby had the only homer for the Blues (against Circle). *Leader photo, Milt Gunderson.*

and added two runs in the top of the seventh to take a 7-0 lead. We scored two more runs in the eighth to make it 9-0, chasing Tim Byrne, whom Todd Watkins replaced.

I carried a one-hitter—a single to Greg Mogen in the first—into the bottom of the eighth and had only walked one hitter. I had breezed through the first seven innings, working fast with Kirby and me entirely in synch. I quickly got the first two outs in the eighth but then faltered, walking the next hitter on a full count, then got behind the next hitter 2-0 and gave up my second hit, leaving runners on first and second. Dano, playing third, sensed I needed a little talking to and said calmly but firmly, "Okay, that's enough now." That helped settle me down and get me refocused. I had been working fast to that point, wanting to take the sign from Kirby as soon as I got the ball back from him, but now it was time to step off the mound, take a deep breath, and refocus. Dano's comment helped slow me down. We picked each other up like that—get it back together and finish this. I came and struck out the next hitter on four pitches—my 14th of the game—to get out of the inning with the shutout intact, leaving baserunners stranded at first and second.

We added two more runs in the ninth to carry an 11-0 lead into the bottom of the ninth, needing three more outs for Scobey's fourth straight championship. As he always did, Kirby yelled out the hitters to me when I trotted out to the mound: "Three-four-five, Joe!" The first hitter, Tim Byrne, reached on an error in the infield—our only error of the game—and then stole second base. (We weren't worried about him with an 11 run lead.) Cleanup hitter Todd Watkins then hit a dribbler down the first base line, and I tagged him out, but the runner on second advanced to third with one out. Laurel coach Brad Krause then had Monte Hoppel try a safety squeeze to break up the shutout. The bunt came back to me in front of the mound, and there was time to make a good throw home. I made a good throw, and Kirb tagged the runner out at the plate for the second out, preserving the shutout. Buoyed by recording the second out at home to preserve the shutout, I struck the last hitter out on four pitches and sprinted toward the plate to meet Kirb halfway, jumping in his arms to hug him (it wouldn't have worked the other way). We were immediately swarmed by the rest of our teammates, celebrating Scobey's fourth consecutive state championship and Doc's sixth overall on our home field.

The *Billings Gazette* summed up the game: "Scobey easily claimed its fourth straight State Class B American Legion Baseball championship with an 11-0 thumping of Laurel. Joe Puckett hurled a two-hitter at the Dodgers, fanning 15 batters while walking only two. The Blues played consistently throughout the game, scoring in all but three innings. The team racked up eight hits, including a double by Puckett and a triple by Wade Tryan."[202] We also played well defensively, committing only one error in the last inning. It was a storybook ending for the five 18-year-olds—Jon and Joe Puckett, Dan Danelson, Ray Chapman, and Wade Tryan—in our last home game at Scobey Ball Park.

All that remained was the presentation of the trophies, the picture-taking, the recognition of the "seniors" playing their final home game, and departing Scobey Ball Park for the last time following the game. My dad quickly got out on the field and took pictures of the team and trophy presentations. Although the quality of the photos is not good, what he tried to capture was evident. He captured the three Peerless boys in two pictures—Ray Chapman, Jon, and me. He had coached us since 1967, almost started a Legion team with us, and had just finished watching us play our final home game at Scobey. He also took two pictures of the five "seniors" receiving the trophy and being recognized for playing their final home game.

When the lights went down at Scobey Ball Park that night, no one knew this would be the last state championship Scobey would win on its home field and the last state tournament Doc would see there. Scobey would host the state tournament one final time in 1985.

TOURNAMENT SUMMARY

FOLLOWING THE "RAGGED IN SPOTS" GAME AGAINST FAIRFIELD, we played well in the state tournament, outscoring our opponents 49-12 over the four games, with an average margin of victory of over nine runs per game. Underneath the headline, "Blues Breeze to Championship; 4th in a Row for 'Doc's Boys,'" the *Leader* summed up the dominance: "Scobey Blues were tops in every category as they won their

1979 Scobey Blues, State Class B Champions, moments after the state championship game against Laurel. Standing, left to right: Coach Doc Norman, Joe Puckett, Pat Audet, Kirby Halvorson, Dan Danelson, Kelly Norman, Jesse Cook, Randy Stolen, Ass't Coach Don Lekvold. Kneeling, left to right: Greg Stolen, Ron Higgins, Gord Tryan, Wade Tryan, Jim Lekvold, Ray Chapman, Jon Puckett. Sitting, left to right: Mike Roland, Josh Lee, Rick Lee, Mike Lee.

The Doc Norman Championship Era

1979 Laurel Dodgers, moments after being defeated by Scobey in the State Class B American Legion Baseball championship game. Standing: Coach G. Smith, Nick Markovich, Brian Miller, Todd Watkins, Darren Schmutzler, Brad Dantic, Scott Melcher, Matt Dantic, Coach Brad Krause. Front Randy Cellmer, Jeff Wojick, Bill Caldwell, Greg Mogen, Tim Byrne, Monte Hoppel. *Leader photo, Milt Gunderson.*

fourth consecutive state championship. The local boys led opponents in hitting, stole more bases, made fewer errors and Blues pitchers had more strikeouts and fewer walks."[203]

The *Leader* recognized the many volunteers who contributed to the tournament's success. Committee heads for the tournament included Ernie Halvorson and Art Audet, ballpark and groundskeeping; Marge Norman and Cliff Hanson, lunch stand; Marge Norman, Alice Halvorson, Delores Danelson, housing and feeding of players; Cliff Hanson, tickets; Tiny Puckett, announcing; and Charles Cassidy, tourney booklets. The 1979 state tournament booklet was dedicated to Bob Tande. The program includes a photo of him in his baseball uniform and a write-up of his over thirty years of contribution to Scobey youth baseball. This is what was written in the program:

> *BOB TANDE began coaching kid's baseball in Scobey soon after graduating from the American Legion program. He continued his close involvement, including Little League, Babe Ruth and Legion programs for over 30 years. He also coached and played on adult "town team" for several years during this period. Bob's many other community activities included being the PA announcer or emcee for just about every event in the area: rodeos, races, parades and ball games. His work with area baseball was rivaled in time and effort only by his loyalty to the Scobey Saddle Club, of which he served as secretary for over 30 years. Bob had a hand in authoring, organizing, directing or emceeing many community variety shows over the years, several of which were benefits for the building of Scobey Ball Park in the early '50s. Although health problems have curtailed his activities in recent years, Bob Tande still keeps up a sharp interest and knowledge of area baseball and community affairs.*[204]

Gene Marley of Scobey was the state Class B Legion baseball chairman and headed up the protest committee with official scorer Jack Reiner and umpire-in-chief Jerry Mooney of Wolf Point. Other umps included Duke Trangsrud, Phil Audet, Mike Neubauer, and Rocky Ware. The lunch stand reported selling 2,280 Legion hamburgers. I had at least one of them. Attendance was very good again, perhaps setting a record for gate receipts. It was rivaled only by the 1969 state tournament for numbers in attendance.[205]

Doc's method of developing younger players while winning state championships must be acknowledged. Ron Higgins, Pat Audet, Gord Tryan, Jim Lekvold, and Jesse Cook—inserted into the game in the seventh inning against Circle—would all start for Scobey the following year, replacing the five 18-year-olds who would leave the team in 1979. Greg Stolen would return as a 14-year-old "seasoned veteran," and Kelly Norman, Randy Stolen, and Kirby Halvorson would return as 18-year-olds to play their final season. Although losing five starters—and four pitchers—the Blues would be strong again in 1980, where the Blues would shoot for their fifth consecutive state championship and Doc's seventh overall.

Now that the 1979 State Class B Tournament championship was in the books, we could turn our attention to the next step and our season's goal: winning the best-of-three series against a Class A opponent and doing some damage in the State Class A Tournament. We had been frustrated the two previous seasons with painful sweeps—albeit close games—against the Helena Senators and Great Falls Chargers to end our season. Who would we play off against this year? The night of the State Class B championship, it was known that it would be either the Helena Senators or the Anaconda Athletics.

TOURNAMENT STATS

Hitting

WOLF POINT'S MIKE EGGEBRECHT WAS THE TOURNAMENT'S leading hitter with a .533 average. Ray Chapman hit well throughout the tournament and was a close second at .461. Ray would probably have won in *Moneyball*'s key statistic of on-base percentage (OBP), as in addition to his six hits, he walked five times for an OBP of .611. Ray likely led our team in OBP throughout his three-year Legion career. The Blues edged Wolf Point for the team batting title with a .310 average.

The tournament had 56 extra-base hits, including 37 doubles, 15 triples, and four home runs. Dan Jensen of Wolf Point had two homers in the same game in Wolf Point's 12-6 loss to Laurel. Kirby Halvorson hit the only home run for Scobey. Kirby remembers his two-run home run in the fifth inning against Circle: "I hit it off my shoe tops to almost dead center. I was thinking double because it was a line drive, but it did that thing where some liners rise and then rise again. I think it only cleared the wall by a foot or so." Chuck Mayers of the Great Falls Sparkies had the other home run, a 355-foot solo blast to left center field off Wolf Point's Bob Moran.

Pitching

OUR PITCHING IN THE STATE TOURNAMENT WAS EXCELLENT. Kelly Norman pitched three shutout innings against Fairfield, with Jon pitching six innings of relief to get the win, yielding only one earned run and striking out 13 Athletics. Randy Stolen pitched five solid innings against Circle to get the win, yielding only one earned run and striking out seven. Dan Danelson pitched a five-hitter against Sidney, striking out 12 Patriots and walking only one. He lost his shutout in the eighth when Todd Ackerman doubled, then scored on two ground ball outs to second. Joe Puckett pitched a two-hit shutout against Laurel, striking out 15 Dodgers and walking two. Scobey's pitching struck out 51 hitters in four games, with an average of almost 12.75 hitters per game.

Some other pitching performances in the tournament were notable. Laurel pitcher Tim Byrne quieted the Wolf Point bats in the first game, yielding only one run in eight innings. Kip Harcharik went all 11 innings and struck out 13 Dodgers in Wolf Point's 3-2 loss to Laurel. Steve Heit of Sidney pitched a five-hitter in a 2-1 win over the Sparkies, while Rusty Strickland was strong for the Sparkies, giving up only one run in seven innings. Kevin Sukut yielded only six hits in Circle's 4-2 win over the Vigilantes. With Jeff Nesper calling the signals behind the plate, Craig Smith of Sidney narrowly missed a no-hitter against Laurel in Sidney's 10-0 seven-inning win. Brad Dantic broke up Smith's no-hitter in the seventh with a single. Laurel's Bill Caldwell and Monte Hoppel combined on a five-hitter to beat Sidney 5-3.

Fielding

FOLLOWING THE OPENING-GAME FIVE-RING CIRCUS AGAINST Fairfield, in which we committed five errors, we settled down in the field, committing just one error against Circle and Laurel and two against Sidney. Our defense throughout the postseason was good, except for that Fairfield game. In the tournament, Jon Puckett played six positions—second base, pitcher, left field, right field, third base, and shortstop—for Scobey, rotating to the position in the field vacated by a pitcher when they pitched. Jon's versatility in the field was a key to our success. I only played shortstop,

Wade Tryan steals second in the first inning of the Sidney game. "The Blues' lead-off batter was one of the real speedsters in the tourney." Scobey stole a total of 15 bases in the four games. *Leader photo, Milt Gunderson.*

so I could focus on mastering that position, likewise with the other players.

Baserunning

SCOBEY STOLE 15 BASES TO LEAD ALL TEAMS. MILT GUNDERson captured a picture of Wade Tryan stealing one of them against Sidney. Batting leadoff and playing center field, Wade was our fastest runner and leading base stealer. And the other teams didn't run on Kirby: "Opposing runners had heard too much about Blues' catcher Kirby Halvorson's arm to challenge him often."[206]

EXTRA INNINGS

FOLLOWING THE STATE CHAMPIONSHIP GAME, I DROVE MY CAR up and down Scobey Main Street to take a "victory lap" and savor the moment. Some Laurel players walking on the sidewalk recognized me and motioned for me to pull over to talk. We talked a little bit about the game. Laurel was much improved over the previous year when we beat them in Cut Bank and won four games in the tournament to get to the championship game. The conversation included their budget for baseball. They noticed how many bats we had—including wooden bats—outside our dugout. "Wow, you guys have all those bats." They said they had only two or three aluminum bats for the entire team to share. Part of Scobey American Legion Baseball's success was the personal financial resources Doc shared with the team. As Larry Bowler used to say, "Doc was running a champagne program on a beer budget." Doc paid for the champagne.

Laurel finished the season with a 27-12 record, with four losses coming to Class A teams. They had some good athletes on their team, including center fielder Brad Dantic and pitcher/catcher Nick Markovich. Dantic led Laurel to back-to-back State Track and Field titles in 1978 and 1979, winning the 100-yard dash in 1979 in 10.2 seconds. He later walked on with the Grizzlies and became a four-year starter at wide receiver, becoming the sixth leading wide receiver in

Grizzly history with 689 total yards after his senior year in 1983. Markovich was an all-state defensive back selected to play at that position in the East-West Shrine game a week after the tournament. He also set the single-season record for assists on the Locomotives basketball team. He had college prospects in football. However, he twisted his knee in the batter's box against us, tearing cartilage, and had to leave the game. Kirby said, "I heard a crack when he went down." He couldn't play in the East-West Shrine game after the injury and "struggled after that," according to Matt Dantic, who said that to Kirby when they were at UM together.

Following the Laurel-Wolf Point game, Kirby remembers being in the cafeteria at the school, sitting with his cousin, Terry Baldry. Kirby said, "A group of Laurel kids came in all cocky and talking smack. Terry said something like, 'Enjoy it while it lasts fuckers because Scobey will kick your ass.'" Didn't know Terry Baldry was a prophet.

To my recollection, Dano coming in to "save" the game with Scobey leading 16-6 Circle with two outs in the seventh was the only time Doc brought Dano in to finish a game. In this case, to preserve the 10-run rule and avoid playing into the eighth and ninth innings against Circle.

Jon Puckett played six different positions in the state tournament. He also caught some in 1977 but never played center field or first base. However, Dana Audet played all nine positions—and every inning of every game—in his four-year Legion career spanning 1971-1974, perhaps the only Scobey American Legion player to do that.

According to the records, Wolf Point's Dan Jensen is the only hitter to hit two home runs in the same game in a state tournament in Scobey. Many players have hit more than one home run in the state tournament, like Dick Puckett and Randy Legare in 1969, but not two in the same game.

Wade's profane outburst from center field to the infield in the Fairfield game was unusual, as his eruptions were normally reserved for the umpires—through Kelly Norman at second. Standing at short, I would often hear Wade yell from center field, "Hey Kelly, ask the ump, where the fuck was that? Hey Kelly, tell the umpire to pull his fucking head out of his ass!"

The 11-0 shutout in the state championship game was the only shutout in Scobey's eight state championships, although the three runs Jon Puckett yielded in Scobey's 13-3 win over Sidney in Scobey in 1977 were all unearned. Our fielding had improved in two years, and I was the beneficiary of that as a pitcher. Here are the scores for Scobey's eight state championships:

- Scobey 7 Havre 6 (1969)
- Scobey 9 Wolf Point 6 (1973)
- Scobey 13 Wolf Point 11 (1976)
- Scobey 13 Sidney 3 (1977)
- Scobey 8 Glendive 6 (1978)
- Scobey 11 Laurel 0 (1979)
- Scobey 18 Missoula Reds 3 (1980)
- Scobey 15 Sidney 8 (1982)

Tim Thogerson was a great hitter and a good shortstop. Because of his speed, he would have been a better center fielder, but coaches Craig Price (1976-78) and Jerry Callen (1979) used him best at shortstop. In our 9-1 win over Sidney, I hit a scooting ground ball to his left that barely got under his glove for a single. It was a "ground ball with eyes." When I got to second base, he said, "I gave you one." Following the game, Torgy asked Jon and me if he could come to Peerless to spend the night. He thought he might get in trouble with his host family in Scobey, but he didn't care. He said, "I gotta see how the Pucketts live in Peerless." Honestly, I was hesitant to say yes. Whatever illusion he had of how the Pucketts lived in Peerless, I didn't want it to be shattered. There's not a lot to do in Peerless. But he and another Sidney player staying at his host family's house came home with us, and they ate some of Mom's leftovers. Torgy thought the whole Puckett-living experience thing in Peerless was "awesome." I think Mom's food might have had a lot to do with why he felt it was awesome. We had to drive him and the other player to Scobey the following morning because they had a game at one o'clock against Laurel, the play-in game for the state championship. I don't know what he told his host family.

In the picture of the "Welcome to Scobey, Home of the Scobey Blues" sign, three additional State Class B baseball championships—1979, 1980, and 1982—would be added. Since it also contained the 1979 State Class B basketball championship, getting the sign current would be a challenge. Four state boys' basketball championships (1996, 2011, 2020, and 2021), three state football championships (1995, 1996, and 2002), and two state boys' track and field championships (1996 and 2019) for Scobey would need to be added. If you look at the sign, you'll notice that the first state championship came in 1969. As Danny Wolfe said,

"There's something to be said about the first one in 1969; it kind of opens up like floodgates and shows everybody the thing can be done."

Greg Stolen was the second 13-year-old pitcher from Scobey to pitch in a State Class B Legion Tournament. Thirteen-year-old Terry Puckett pitched against Havre in 1968 in Glendive. In Scobey's 12-2 rout of Havre in the opening game, Dick and Terry Puckett combined to hurl a two-hitter at Havre. Doc put Terry on the mound in the later innings to get him some state tournament experience and save Dick some innings. Although Greg's seventh inning against Circle was rough, he gained valuable experience pitching in the state tournament as a 13-year-old. As a 14-year-old the following year, he was the winning pitcher against Cut Bank in the state tournament, and, at the ripe old age of 16 in 1982, he won the undefeated semifinal against Sidney in the state tournament.

I noticed my mom Faustine Sparagno Puckett's signature on my tournament program. Her "signature" is on everything I write. I have her to thank for preserving all the precious memorabilia from when Jon and I played. Going through all my stuff from almost fifty years ago has been special because it brings back all the wonderful memories I have of her and how much she cherished the moment by preserving it with all the memorabilia.

Scobey Commercial Club had this and two other signs like it painted and put up before the 1979 State B Baseball Tourney in Scobey. They put one at each entrance to Scobey. Members pictured are Dave Billehus, Jim Heaton, Jim Vachal, and Perry Wolfe. John and Dale Barstad helped with their post-hole digger and tractor. *Leader photo by Burl Bowler.*

STATE A PLAYOFFS

THE BEST-OF-THREE SERIES THE WEEKEND FOLLOWING THE State B Tournament would be against the Helena Senators, who finished third place behind the Billings Royals and the Billings Scarlets in the Class A eastern division. The Butte Miners, who finished fifth, were the host team in the State A Tournament, so they had an automatic berth. The Senators had edged out the Anaconda Athletics for the third seed, so if we won the series, we would qualify for the State Class A tournament as the third seed from the east.

It was a poignant moment for me to be returning to Helena to play in this best-of-three series in 1979. I say "returning" because two years earlier, in 1977, when most of us were 16 years old, we had played the Senators in this same series, had not played well defensively, and got eliminated in two games, 9-2 and 8-6. Since the 1977 series, Jon, Ray, and I had played in the 1978 and 1979 State Class C basketball tournaments in Helena. Finally, three weeks after the series, I would return to Helena to enroll at Carroll College for my first semester, playing for Coach Jim Trudnowski, who had recruited me to play basketball for the Carroll College Fighting Saints. It was three weeks away, but it seemed like three years away. The only thing on my mind was beating the Senators to get into the State A Tournament.

Could the third time be a charm for our team to win a best-of-three series? We were determined not to repeat the defensive mistakes of the past. We had learned from our 10 errors in two games against the Great Falls Chargers a year earlier, losing 6-5 and 8-6. To beat Helena, we knew we had to excel in all three phases of the game: pitching, hitting, *and* defense. If we lost a best-of-three series again, I would not have considered my Legion career successful, even though I had played on four state Class B championship teams. The 1976 team did win the best-of-three series against Libby, but Dad took Jon and me on his preplanned summer vacation after we won the State Class B tournament. He didn't plan on Scobey winning that tournament—the odds were high—so Jon and I didn't get to be on the field for that series or the State A Tournament.

In this series, we needed to take it to the next level and play our way into the State Class A tournament. We played the first game on Saturday at 10:30 a.m. on Kindrick Legion Field, with the second game following 30 minutes after the first game. Doc's pitching rotation had Dan Danelson starting the first game, me starting the second game, and Jon scheduled for the third game on Sunday, if needed.

Game One

WE NEEDED TO GET OFF TO A GOOD START AND TAKE THE LEAD, which we did. We scored three runs in the second on three hits and twice in the third on three more hits to take a 5-0 lead off big left-hander Dan Marshall. And it was the bottom of the lineup that came through, as 13-year-old Greg Stolen, batting ninth in the lineup, drove in three of the five runs with two singles. In the second, Kirby led off the inning with a single. It was a rocket off the left field fence that was hit so hard that it bounced right back to the left fielder, and he held Kirby to a single. Randy walked, and Jon singled to drive in the first run. Ray Chapman hit a sac fly to drive in another run, and Greg Stolen drove in the third run with a single. Greg drove in two more runs—his third RBI of the game—in the third with a huge two-out single, scoring Kirby and Jon, who had both singled for the second time. However, the five runs we scored in the second and third would be the only runs we would score, as Dan Marshall settled down and yielded only one hit—a ninth-inning single to Randy Stolen—in the final six innings.

Meanwhile, Dan Danelson was in control. Helena got a run in the fourth when Andy Bryan's triple to right knocked in Jim DeMars, who had singled, but through four and two-thirds innings, he had only allowed one run and three hits. Then, pitching with two outs in the bottom of the fifth, with Scobey leading 5-1, the unthinkable happened. After delivering his third pitch to leadoff hitter Alan Riecker, Dano said, "I immediately felt a twinge in the inner elbow that sent a burning sensation down to my fingertips. I knew I was hurt then." Dano threw one more pitch. With two strikes on Riecker, he threw a fastball for strike three and the third out of the inning. I heard his elbow pop from shortstop. Randy Stolen heard it pop from left field. Dano said, "I felt a pop. Pain radiating down to my fingers. I couldn't grip the ball. I knew I was hurt pretty good. Pain like I had never experienced before." He immediately grabbed his right arm and was in obvious pain as the Scobey nine ran into the dugout to hit.

It was unsettling in the dugout. None of us, including Doc, knew the extent of Dano's injury when we got in there. It was like the Titanic had hit the iceberg, but it wasn't until later that anyone knew the extent of the damage. And like the Titanic, the ship continued to move after the blow. Dano was the on-deck hitter in the inning and had to get ready to hit. Doc immediately got out his black bag and loaded a needle, but Dano wanted none of it. He darted across the dugout away from Doc, holding his right arm up with his left arm, and said, "Nope, no needles, Doc. No goddamn needles!" Dano had seen plenty of Blues—including Terry Puckett—get the needle in this combined batboy-player Legion career. But he knew no needle would remedy what had just happened to him. Dano alone felt the severity of his injury. He said, "When Doc offered the needle, I already knew my answer subconsciously was no. Doc didn't know the severity of my injury and was offering relief for my pain, but I knew this was different. This was not a sore arm."

Dano had delivered his last pitch in American Legion Baseball. The Titanic had been hit. But unlike the Titanic, the ship didn't sink.

Psychologically, this was a massive blow to the team. Our best pitcher was wounded and couldn't really throw. There were so many questions. Who would Doc bring in to pitch? Where would Dano play in the field? Could he hit? Could he even play? Dano said, "There was no way I was coming out." He took his at-bat in the top of the sixth and flied out to left field. We did not score and entered the bottom of the sixth, leading 5-1.

It was now time for the team to step up and pick up Dano. Dano said, "The depth and talent of our pitching staff rose to the occasion. We would not be denied. Just goes to show the makeup of our team." Kirby Halvorson added, "Dano was still a presence and had been for so long. We would not have been whole without him. I think we implicitly understood we would all have to pick it up somehow."

Doc altered the rotation and brought in Jon Puckett, who was scheduled to start game three, and Dano went to third. He could barely get his arm up sideways to throw but could kind of half-arm it to first. Second-place hitter Jim DeMars greeted Jon with a single, then Phil Hauck followed with a single to center, but the ball got through Wade Tryan's legs for a two-base error and an unearned run, and DeMars scored. Jon then retired the next three hitters, and we moved to the seventh with a 5-2 lead, where the score stood until the dramatic bottom of the ninth.

In the ninth, the Senators loaded the bases with no outs on consecutive singles, followed by a walk. The tying run was on first with no one out. Doc then went to the mound and made a pitching change, signaling me to come in from short to relieve Jon.

I had been in this situation once before. When I was 15, I was brought in to relieve Jeff Richardson to pitch against Wolf Point with the bases loaded and no one out in the state championship game. But that was in the bottom of the fourth—this was in the bottom of the ninth. Mentally, as I trotted in from shortstop, I was preparing to get the three biggest outs of my Legion career as I started warming up with Kirby.

My mental approach and strategy to pitch was no different than if I was a starting pitcher—attack hitters, get ahead in the count, and make them hit the pitch I wanted them to hit. But there was a physical adjustment—I had to bring gas on the first pitch and continue to bring it. I normally "paced myself" as a starting pitcher, knowing I was in it for the long haul. I normally got stronger in the later innings, but I had to come out strong on the first pitch in this one.

I was facing the ninth-place hitter in the lineup, pitcher Dan Marshall. He promptly greeted me with a run-scoring single on a 1-0 pitch, making the score 5-3. The tying run was on second, and the winning run was on first, with the top of the lineup coming up. I did not change my approach. I went after hitters and trusted my fielders behind me. Leadoff hitter Alan Riecker lofted a high fly to shallow left field that Randy caught for the first out. Jim DeMars hit a pop-up behind first base, which Ray Chapman caught for the second out. Then I got left-handed hitter Phil Hauck, a dangerous hitter, to hit a low inside slider to Kelly Norman at second, who fielded it cleanly and threw to Ray at first for the third out. I had retired the side on eight pitches, and we had won the all-important first game of the series. I glove-tapped Kelly for fielding the third out as we ran off the field. He said calmly, "Routine, Joe, routine."

Dano got the win, somehow getting the third out on a strikeout in the fifth after injuring his arm on the previous pitch, to finish the 1979 Legion season with a perfect 9-0 record. Jon Puckett pitched three innings of relief and gave up only one earned run for the hold, and I got the biggest save of my Legion career, allowing only one inherited runner to score in the ninth. This was the only time in four years that both Pucketts and Danelson pitched in the same game. Doc was pulling out all the stops and had now used the three pitchers he had planned to start each game of the three-game series in one game. He was doing what he had to do to hang on and win game one. And it was a total team effort. Our ninth-place hitter, 13-year-old Greg Stolen, had driven in three runs, and we had won the all-important first game of the series. We played well defensively—only one error led to one unearned run. One more win and we were headed to the State A Tournament in Butte. It would not be easy.

Game Two

I was the game two starting pitcher following the one-inning save in game one. One more win was needed to achieve our goal of getting to the State A Tournament in Butte, and the ball was in my hands to do it. I started and went all nine innings. After playing nine innings at short and then pitching an inning, I did not have my best stuff that day but managed to keep us in the game, even though I gave up nine hits and walked five batters. One thing that affected me on that mound that day was the base umpire calling three balks on me. I had not had a balk called on me the entire year, and then I got three in one game.

Each team took different routes scoring in this game. Helena spaced theirs out, scoring single runs in the first, third, fourth, eighth, and ninth innings, while we scored all our runs in the sixth when we bunched half of our 10 hits to score four times to take the lead 4-3. Randy Stolen opened with a double, and Jon Puckett, Greg Stolen, and Wade Tryan followed with singles, chasing Helena starter Kelly Spawn, who was relieved by Randy Redpath out of the bullpen.

Redpath gave up a walk and Kelly Norman's run-scoring single before retiring the side.

Pitching with the lead for the first time in the seventh, I felt good about getting the next nine outs down the stretch to get us to Butte. I skipped off the mound after the top of the seventh, getting three outs on three fly balls. I remember Jacki Tade laughing at me as I skipped off the mound into the dugout—six outs to go. But the skipping didn't last long, as in the top of the eighth, Mike Bartsch hit the first pitch over the left field fence for a home run to tie the game 4-

4. I went after him with a fastball to get ahead, but I was fading after bringing a lot of energy to get the last three outs of game one and playing 17 innings in the hot sun. We went down in order in the bottom of the eighth, so the game entered the ninth tied 4-4.

As in the first game, the ninth had plenty of drama—this time, both halves of the inning. In the top half, I walked the first hitter, Jim DeMars, who moved to second base on my third balk of the game. Cleanup hitter Andy Bryan then hit a double to left to knock in the go-ahead run with one out. He moved to third on a wild pitch, but I struck out the next two batters to end the inning. So, we came to bat in the bottom of the ninth trailing 5-4, needing one run to tie it and two to walk it off and get to Butte.

We battled back in the bottom half of the inning. Kelly led off with a walk, and after Kirby flied out to center, Randy Stolen was safe on an error to leave runners at first and second. Jon Puckett lined a single to center—his fourth hit of the series—and Doc waved Kelly home with one out. However, center fielder Andy Bryan, who had seen plenty of action in the series, made a good throw to the plate to cut down Kelly at the plate. Home plate umpire Bob Chilton called Kelly out, but we all thought he was safe. Helena *Independent Record* sportswriter Roy Pace wrote, "Scobey thought [it] was the tying run."[207] Catcher Alan Riecker of Helena blocked the plate and forced Kelly to take a round-about route in his attempt to score. What happened, Kelly? Were you out or safe? "I was so safe, but the catcher went back and tagged me like I missed the plate. Smart play by him. I slid to the outside because the throw was to the inside of the plate. Both arms went across the plate. When I was two to three feet past the plate, the catcher [Alan came back and tagged me, and 'You're out.' My best guess is because the catcher hurried up and came back and tagged me, the ump thought oh, he's out. Then I remember yelling and jumping around, and Dano was there saying what he thought, and Dad too."

Later, Wade Tryan would weigh in on the call as well, but Kelly was only the second out of the inning, and we still had a chance to tie the game—even win it. Ray Chapman walked to load the bases with two outs, and it brought Coach Mike Foster out of the Helena dugout to make another change. He brought Jim DeMars in from third base to take over as pitcher to get the last out, with Greg Stolen coming up to bat. Greg had singled three times in the two games and driven in three runs, so weirdly, I was happy our 13-year-old ninth-place hitter was at the plate. DeMars threw what would have been a wild pitch except for a good stop by Alan Riecker before he finally struck out Greg on a 2-2 pitch to end the game and even the playoff at one game apiece. We were so close but couldn't finish it in the second game, losing 5-4.

Then, chaos. The controversial call at the plate did not end after the game. That's when the fireworks really began. Wade Tryan—whose temper was the hottest on the team—did his Billy Martin impersonation. Unleashing a stream of profanity, he picked up a pile of bats and slung them toward home plate. Batboy Mike "Karch" Lee dutifully picked them up but recalls that after he did so, Wade threw them out a second time, cussing all the way. So Karch had to go pick them up again. Kelly recalls that earlier in the game, Wade had shown indications of dissatisfaction with the home plate umpire. Kelly said, "What's crazy is the same Wade said, 'Hey, Kelly tell that ump to pull his head out of his fucking ass.' His son, the base ump, was standing 15 feet from me. Also, Wade would say, 'Ask him where the fuck that pitch was at?'"

Everyone—me included—was visibly angry at that call at the plate by the home plate umpire, but I was internally seething at the base umpire about the three balks; the last one moved the winning run into scoring position, and he scored. He said I was not coming set when I went into my stretch before I delivered the pitch to the plate. The balks cost us two runs, as the runners scored after advancing to scoring position at second base on the balks. One of them might have cost us a double play. No one had called a balk on me the entire year until that game, and the base umpire called three on me. I yelled "balk" out the bus window to the base umpire as Dick Atwood was driving us out of the parking lot. Following Wade's outburst from the dugout to the home plate umpire and mine to the base umpire, we would not have won the sportsmanship trophy in that series as we did a week later in Butte. And it was not just Wade and me. The entire team—Doc and Don Lekvold included—was unhappy with the officiating.

But there was still another game to play the following day, and no amount of bitching or complaining would change the outcome of game two. We were frustrated but needed to refocus and come back strong the next day to get game three. On Sunday, the winner was headed to Butte, and the loser was going home. I did not want that to be us. I wanted to keep playing ball and achieve our goal of getting into the State A Tournament.

Game Three

WE WON THE TOSS AND WERE THE HOME TEAM. DOC STARTED Randy Stolen, while Helena countered with Mike Hinman. Defensively, we had a different look. Doc moved Dano from third base to first base due to his injury. Ray Chapman was moved to left. Doc would have normally moved Jon to left when Randy pitched, but he played third.

Warming up at short, I noticed a lot of people were in the stands to watch game three. The *Independent Record* described it as a "good-sized crowd."[208] Some of the fans from Helena were rooting for Scobey because Jon and

Alan Riecker of Helena blocks the plate and forces Scobey's Kelly Norman to take a round-about route in his attempt to score from second base on a single to center. Umpire Bob Chilton prepares to call Norman out in a key play in the second playoff game. *Helena Independent Record photo by Roy Pace.*

I had picked up some local fans after playing as massive underdogs in the 1978 state basketball tournament and as favorites to win it when we returned in 1979. Some of them approached us after the game to congratulate us. But our most vocal and loyal fans were from Scobey, and there were many of them. Cliff Hagfeldt and Tiny Puckett called the game on KCGM radio.

Again, it was important that we get the lead early and play ahead, and we did. Randy had a good first inning, issuing only one walk before retiring the side on two fly balls and an infield popup. We jumped on Hinman for two runs in the bottom of the first to take a 2-0 lead, thanks to some key baserunning. Wade grounded a single to left, stole second, and went to third when Alan Riecker's throw went into center field. Then, Wade scored on a passed ball. Dano followed with a walk. I hit a sharp ground ball to shortstop Joe McMahon, and he tossed to second baseman Kevin Farry for the force, but Farry threw wildly to first while being taken out hard by Dano. I ended up at second and went to third on an infield out, then scored when McMahon dropped a bouncer by Kirb. Dano aggressively took the second baseman out on the force out, which allowed us to score the second run—old school. And Dano was injured, too.

Meanwhile, although "troubled by wildness,"[209] Randy was not giving up many hits. There was a lot of traffic on the bases and a lot of deep counts on hitters—a lot of walks—but he came through with big pitches when needed, and our defense was making plays to strand baserunners. Helena left 15 baserunners on in the game. Helena punched through with their first run in the fourth when Bartsch led off with a walk and stole second. He scored when Hinman single to right-center for the Senators' first hit. It was 2-1 Scobey after four innings.

Kirby made a big play in the fifth to preserve our one-run lead. On a play at the plate, he took a huge hit from Phil Hauck, an all-state running back for Helena Capital who had been selected to play in the East-West Shrine game. Hauck was trying to score from first on an error Ray made in left, but Ray got the relay to me at short, and I threw a strike to Kirby at home to nail Hauck. Kirby recalls the play, "Not only did he run me over, but he stuck his forearm/elbow up and caught me on the bridge of the nose. It made me see stars. But I held on to the ball." Nowadays, a runner would be thrown out and suspended for the next game, but that was not the case in 1979.

After five innings, it was 2-1 Blues. Randy got into trouble in the top of the sixth and Helena tied it. Bartsch led off with a double to the gap in left-center, and Kelly O'Connor walked. It was Randy's seventh walk of the game, but he had only given two hits and allowed only one run. It was a typical Randy outing—a lot of traffic on the bases, but no big hits with the runners on. He had done his job and left the game with us in the lead. Doc then brought left-handed knuckleballer Ray Chapman, and Randy exchanged places with a Ray in left. Ray had not pitched in the postseason that year. His last appearance in a game was against Aurora in the IGA Tournament in Billings a month earlier. Kevin Farry hit a sac fly to right that drove in Bartsch to tie it. Ray walked Hinman, and leadoff hitter Riecker hit a bloop single to load the bases with one out.

Never had a game been so dense with big decisions for Doc. Dano's injury had forced Doc to shift his decision-making into hyperdrive. With the score tied 2-2, the bases loaded, and only one out, "Doc went into another one of his shuffling acts."[210] He brought Jon in to pitch from third base, moved Chappy to right field, and switched Greg Stolen to third base. Ray had never played right field the entire year, and Greg had never played third base, but Doc had to do what he had to do. The move worked. Jon struck out DeMars on a tense full count and got Hauck to pop up to first to get us out of the bases-loaded jam. He did not allow a run, and we sprinted off the field to hit, relieved to be still tied 2-2.

The bottom half of the sixth inning sent us to Butte. Kirby drew a leadoff walk, advanced to second on an infield out, and went to third on a single to center by Jon. Starting pitcher Hinman was relieved by Jim DeMars, who moved in from third base. He gave up a walk to Ray Chapman to load the bases. Then, ninth-place hitter Greg Stolen did it again. He hit a ground single to left past Helena's drawn-in infield

Helena catcher **Alan Riecker** awaits the collision with Scobey catcher **Kirby Halvorson**, who was trying to score from third base on a double steal. Halvorson was out at the plate, but the Blues won the game 6-3. *Helena Independent Record photo, Gene Fischer.*

to score Kirb. It was Greg's fourth hit and fourth RBI of the series, and none had been more significant. Wade Tryan followed with another single to left to bring in Jon. Dano lined out to third for the second out, but DeMars walked me to force in another run and make it 5-2. Second baseman Kevin Farry prevented further damage when he dove for a hard-hit ball by Kelly and flipped it to first for the final out while still on the ground.

Jon pitched a hitless/scoreless seventh, and we added an insurance run in the bottom half of the inning. Kirb led off with a booming triple over Mike Bartsch in the right. With one out, Jon walked, and Doc tried a double steal, with Jon stealing second and Kirb trying for home on the throw. Helena's shortstop executed the cutoff perfectly and nailed Kirb at the plate Kirb said, "I guess I shoulda tried to bowl him over like their dude [Hauck] tried on me." But Chappy promptly singled to right field to drive in Jon for our sixth run. Again, the bottom of the lineup was coming up big in the series.

Jon pitched a hitless/scoreless eighth, and we entered the top of the ninth inning leading 6-2. Three more outs, and we were headed to Butte as the third seed in the east. Three more outs.

But as in the previous two games of this hard-fought series, there would be more drama in the ninth. Why couldn't the ninth ever be easy? The ninth reminded me of the Glendive game at the state tournament in Scobey in 1977, when we entered the ninth with an identical 6-2 lead. This half-inning was the most intense I ever remember playing in baseball, but it was even more so for Jon, who was pitching. Jon said, "My soul tells me it was by far and away the most intense 30 minutes of any game I played, in any sport." *Any* sport. That would include basketball.

Why was it so tense? Psychologically, when you have a four-run lead, you're not cocky, but you're thinking just three outs, and you're done. Then, suddenly, the lead is threatened, you're in danger of losing, and the pressure intensifies. Of the seven hitters Jon faced that inning, five had three-ball counts, and three were full counts with the bases loaded, where the next pitch—if it was a ball—would have led to a run. But somehow, Jon managed to get through it. The home plate umpire's strike zone seemed to narrow, and the inning seemed to drag on forever, pitch after pitch. Not counting foul balls, Jon delivered 36 pitches in the inning. It had to last over 30 minutes in the hot, 90-degree Helena sun.

So what happened in the wild inning? Phil Hauck walked on four pitches to lead off the inning and advanced to second on a balk. (Yeah, another balk, this time on Jon. Apparently, the base ump made no distinction between the twins coming to a complete stop in their stretch. Or, he thought it was me pitching again.) Andy Bryan followed with a single to left on a 3-0 count to put runners on first and third. Joe McMahon drove a single to left to score Hauck, and, on a full count, Bartsch singled to left to load the bases. Suddenly, the four-run lead had become 6-3, the bases were loaded, and there were no outs. The first four hitters had reached base on a walk and three singles, the tying run was on first, and Jon looked like he was done. Jon recalls, "I got in trouble in the ninth. And there was a meeting on the mound. It's actually kind of a blur in my mind, but it seemed like there were a lot of guys on the mound during that meeting. I think Doc was asking me if I could get through it. Somehow, I still wound up with the ball."

It's funny that Jon doesn't remember how he "somehow wound up with the ball," but I do. Doc strolled to the mound to make arguably the biggest decision of his Legion coaching career. A trip to the State A Tournament hung in the balance. The entire infield came in for the conference. What happened next was incredible. Doc wasn't sure what to do. I had never seen that before. He was looking at us to help him. He looked at me, asking with his eyes if I was ready. I shook my head from side to side. I had pitched 10 innings the day before and had expended a lot of energy in the one-inning save. As much of a competitor as I was, I didn't think I was the man for the job. I was tired, playing 17 innings at short, and had thrown over 150 pitches the previous day. Had Doc taken the ball from Jon and handed it to me, I would have given it everything I had to get those last three outs, but he left the choice up to me. If I wanted the ball, I could have nodded and taken it, but I didn't. He looked around at the rest of us, again asking with his eyes. Dano was off the playing board with his injury. Kelly hadn't pitched in the series, but wouldn't be the best to bring in because a pitcher with excellent control was needed with the bases loaded. As precocious as he was, Greg Stolen was not the solution at 13 years old. That brought the spotlight back full circle to Jon. Finally, after what seemed like an eternity, Jon assertively grabbed the ball from Doc, put it in his glove, and said, "Fuck it. I'll get 'em out." The ball wound up in Jon's hands because he wanted the ball. Doc told the infielders to play even with the bag on the corners and double-play depth in the middle. The corners were instructed to go home with the ball if they could get the force out at home. We all ran back to our positions, knowing that what happened next would determine the game's outcome—and our season. Would it be the third consecutive disappointing loss in the State A playoffs? Or a berth in the State A Tournament?

After the conference, Jon continued to labor in the hot summer sun, falling behind 3-0 on the next hitter. Jon said, "The plate umpire wouldn't call a strike. I threw three fastballs, I swear, inside the black on the outside corner." The tension mounted as one more ball in the next three pitches, and it would be 6-4 with the tying run in scoring position. Jon was fighting the umpire mentally, as was I at short. That only exacerbated the problem, but it was unavoidable. The strike zone became narrower, and Jon had to throw it right down the heart of the plate to get a strike. At that point, he had to throw himself at the mercy of the hitter and the umpire. Forget a strikeout; get the ball over the plate. Then, on the next pitch, Jon said, "Same spot, and he gave it to me." He then got another called strike to run the count full. On the full count, Kelly O'Connor hit a ground ball to Greg at third, who calmly fielded it and fired a strike to Kirby at home to get the all-important first out of the inning. Phew! On the next hitter, Kevin Farry, the count *again* ran full—the third consecutive full count of the inning—but he popped up to Jon for the second out. One more out! Then, on a 2-2 count, the next hitter popped up to me at short. I had never been so relieved to see that last pop-up sky-high in the infield. I called for it and squeezed it for the third out. For the second time in the game, Jon had pitched us out of a bases-loaded jam without allowing a run. The celebration began on the mound. We had finally taken it to the next level. The Scobey Blues were headed to the Mining City for the State A Tournament!

PLAYOFF SUMMARY

ALTHOUGH WE WON THE SERIES, DOC WAS APOLOGETIC ABOUT our performance. He told the *Independent Record*, "We were real tired. We didn't hit real well. This was our third tournament in three weeks, and the other two were eight-team tournaments. That can take a lot out of you. Besides that, it was really hot out there today."[211] Doc always stood up for his boys. He said we beat Helena even though we could have played much better.

The series win was a total team effort—as wins by our team always were—but with Dano's injury, this one was special. It was extraordinary how Dano contributed after his injury and how the rest of the team stepped up.

Hitting-wise, the bottom of the lineup—the 7-8-9 hitters—produced the most runs in the series. Of our 11 earned runs, eight of them were driven in by Jon (1), Ray (2), and Greg (5). Greg also had four hits. Jon scored five runs to lead the team and had four hits. Ray Chapman walked *eight times* in the series and led the team in OBP at .692 (9 for 13). We did not hit for much power in the series—Randy Stolen had a double, and Kirby Halvorson had a triple for our only extra-base hits—but the singles we got were timely. Of Dano's gutsy three-hit performance in game two, Roy Pace of the Helena *Independent Record* wrote, "Danelson's elbow injury even made him wince when he was batting, and the throw from third to first was painful. But he managed to get three hits in the second game after he was injured."[212]

For pitching, Dano went five innings in game one to get the win, getting a strikeout on the last pitch he delivered in Legion baseball. Jon pitched three-plus innings to get the hold, and I got the save in the ninth, retiring three hitters with the bases loaded. In game two, I took the loss, going the distance, giving up the tying run in the eighth on a home run and the winning run in the ninth after a leadoff walk and a balk put the winning run in scoring position. Finally, in game three, Randy Stolen, although he issued a lot of walks, went five-plus innings, allowed only two hits and two earned runs, and left the game with us in the lead. He did his job. Ray retired a hitter in the sixth, getting a big out, and Jon got the win with his gutsy final three and two-thirds innings, twice pitching us out of bases-loaded jams without allowing a run. Our team ERA for the series was 3.33, and good enough to win.

Finally, the fielding. I've written a lot about how the previous two exits in the playoff series were marred by shoddy fielding. We were not perfect in this series, but our defense was stronger. We committed only one error in game one, leading to one unearned run, the only unearned run we allowed in the three-game series. We committed three errors in game two, but none led to an unearned run. Again, we committed three errors in game three, but no unearned runs resulted. In the three-game series, we average a little over two errors per game, much better than the previous year against the Chargers, where we committed 10 in two games, and the year before that against Helena, where we committed six errors in the second game, leading to six unearned runs and a loss. Although imperfect, we finally got it right against Helena in 1979. 1. Most importantly, we played better than our opponent defensively, as Helena committed 11 errors, which led to four unearned runs.

Wade's baserunning also has to be mentioned. His speed got us to the 1-0 lead in game three. After singling in the bottom of the first, he stole second and took third when the throw went into center field. He then scored on a passed ball. Wade's speed on the bases was a huge part of our team's success.

But the balks. I had three, and Jon had one. Balks are not technically scored as errors, but two led to runs that otherwise would not have been scored in game two as the runners advanced into scoring position. Kelly said I was "quick to the plate" on my release, but Doc would have corrected it if he saw a problem earlier in my career. The three balks called on me in Helena were the only three that were called on me the entire season.

Decision-wise, Doc made all the right calls to adjust to Dano's injury. In game one, he brought in Jon for three innings to get the hold and brought me in with the bases loaded and no outs in the ninth to save it. Ironically, Doc's decision to defer to the pitchers to decide at the mound visit in the ninth inning of game three might have been the best decision he ever made. Jon got the next three outs, and Greg, who he had moved to third base defensively, got one of them on a force play at home.

Following the game-three win, we carried a 33-8 overall mark into the State Class A Tournament, with six losses to Class A teams. Mining City, here we come.

EXTRA INNINGS

The only other balk I remember in my career was called by home plate umpire Mike McLean at a Babe Ruth game in Plentywood in 1975. Well, his dad, third-base coach Zoonie McLean, called it first. I was pitching from the stretch with a runner on third, and as I kicked my leg up coming out of the stretch, I faked to third but went home with the ball. It was clearly a balk. I didn't know you couldn't do that then because I had never pitched out of the stretch with a runner on third before. Zoonie immediately yelled, "That's a balk!" After the catcher caught the ball, Mike took his mask off and walked around the catcher. Clearly irritated, he said to his father, "I'll call it," and pointed for the runner on third to come home on the balk.

Scobey's 1973 state championship is another excellent example of a player and a team that stepped it up after their ace pitcher was injured. Following Terry Puckett's 12-inning win over Wolf Point for the eastern division championship a week earlier, his arm was done for the state tournament. But he contributed with his hitting, as Dano did after his injury in Helena. Against Wolf Point in the championship, Terry started the big seven-run winning rally in the eighth with a single, then hit a second single in the same inning to drive in two critical insurance runs after the team batted around. Terry's performance in the state tournament symbolized how each player contributed what they needed to help the team win. Dana Audet, Jay Hagfeldt, and Duke Trangsrud stepped up as the pitchers, and the 7-8-9 hitters came up big. Duke Trangsrud, Greg Fjeld, and Jack Tryan—who all had hits in Scobey's seven-run eighth inning against Wolf Point and batted over .300 for the tournament—were key players who contributed to the championship. It was very similar in Helena.

On Kirby's single in game one, which rocketed off the left field fence because it was hit so hard, Kirby said, "Don [Lekvold] gave me the hold sign as I was getting to first. I'm thinking, WTF, because I thought I had a double." As we returned to take the field following our at-bat and Kirby was warming up Dano, the home plate ump asked Kirby who hit the ball that ricocheted off the wall. Kirby told him it was him. The ump said it was the hardest hit ball he'd seen hit at Kindrick Field, including minor league players in the Pioneer League.

Recalling his triple to right field in game three, Kirby jokingly said, "I stretched a lot of triples into doubles." Not this one. Kirby was a pull-hitter, so his triple to right was rare.

Catcher Kirby Halvorson agrees it was the right choice when Jon grabbed the ball to close out game three. Remembering the Glendive game in the 1977 state tournament, Kirby said, "I recall Jon coming in and throwing strikes and closing the door. In fact, I seem to recall other instances of him coming in relief and not only shutting but *slamming* the door on hitters. He was definitely a gamer with ice in his veins. Not to say any of the other pitchers weren't, but he was a stone-cold killer." I believe that Jon's prowess at closing games came from the confidence he gained following his two-inning save against Wolf Point in the 1976 state tournament in Cut Bank when he was only 15 years old. Doc's method of playing and developing young players paid off for him further downstream.

Following the State Class A Tournament in Butte, Dano was diagnosed with an ulnar collateral ligament (UCL) tear and hurt the ulnar nerve. Although Doc didn't know it then, Dano said he "had a pretty good idea and knew I couldn't hurt it much more." He taped it heavily so he could hit. Amazingly, Dano got three hits in game two following the injury and had four hits in the series. Doc did not know the severity of Dano's injury. Following the game three win, Marty Mouat in the *Independent Record* wrote, "Norman thinks he will be able to pitch in Butte. 'It is a muscle injury in the elbow,' Norman said, 'but it should be resolved with rest, hot packs, and the whirlpool.'"[213] But Roy Pace, *Independent Record* sportswriter, was more pessimistic. "Dan

Danelson is probably through pitching this season."²¹⁴ Roy Pace was right. The final pitch Dano delivered in the fifth inning of game one to get the strikeout—and the win—was the last pitch he delivered in his Legion baseball career.

The good-sized crowd that was there for game three included our loyal fan base from Scobey, of course, but there were a lot of Helenans in the stands cheering for Scobey. Why was that? The State Class C State Basketball Tournament was always held in Helena in those days. The Peerless Panthers played in the 1978 and 1979 state tournaments, and each year, the Helena fans picked a team to be their favorite and cheered heavily for that team. The team they would like would usually be an underdog, with a fast-paced style of play, guard-oriented with good outside shooters. We fit all those criteria in 1978 and hugely became that favorite. Many of those same fans who had watched us play in the state basketball tournaments were there to watch the Panthers from Peerless play baseball. Some of them came up to congratulate us on the win after the game. Richard and Jane Joy and their daughter Sharon were three of them. They came up to Jon and me after the game to congratulate us. Richard said, "One of them pitches it, and the other one catches it. Fantastic!"

As if winning the series wasn't special enough, meeting some of the fans who had cheered for us in the state tournaments and recalling those wonderful memories—except the state championship game against Flaxville in 1979—made the series win even more special. Richard Hoy said of the Peerless Panthers state tournament appearances in Helena, "Go Panthers!

When Alan Nielsen led Westby to the championship in 1975, beating Antelope, I first realized the power of district 1-C. I was part of the noisy crowd that cheered for the Cinderella Peerless team in 1978 and 1979. At our Rotary Club, Howard Retz and I talked excitedly about those amazing Puckett twins. Cato 'the Cat' Butler invited me to assist him in hosting breakfasts for selected coaches and fans each tournament day for several years. Roy Pace and I agreed that the state Class C tournament would never be the same not being played in the Carroll College PE Center."

Following the game, I chose to ride home with Mom and Dad instead of riding the bus with the team. Why was that? This was a special moment for my Dad and me. He had called the series with Cliff Hagfeldt on KCGM radio and had watched five of the boys on the field, Joe and Jon Puckett, Ray Chapman, and Randy and Greg Stolen—who he had coached in Peewee, Little League, and Babe Ruth in Peerless for 10 years—emerge victorious. Dad was always my first coach, and Mom was always my first support. I sensed they wanted to share the big win with one of the twins after the game when I talked to them on the field, and I said I would ride home with him and Mom. We talked about the series and shared the victory. Dad was such a big part of it, developing those five players like he did. He had come close to starting a Legion team in Peerless to continue coaching us. I know it was hard for him to let go of coaching, even though he knew it was right. There were some benefits to riding home with him, too. He had some cold beer in the car. As I was sitting in the back seat when he was driving between Helena and Great Falls, I got to drink one of those cold beers to celebrate with him. To this day, it is the best, coldest beer I have ever drank. Nothing has come close. Sharing a huge victory beer with my Dad, knowing that I would be traveling in the opposite direction in a few days to play in the State A Tournament in Butte. I bet the guys on the bus didn't get that cold beer like I did. Or the second one, either.

As I drank the beers, I self-assessed my performance in the series. When he critiqued himself, Dano said, "I was my own worst critic. Internal death stares are the worst." I was the same way. The thing I felt the best about was that I had played clean at shortstop the entire series—no errors. I was proud of that. The hard work under the lights had paid off. Also in the plus column, I had gotten the save in the first game, getting the last three outs with the bases loaded while allowing one inherited run to score. That was the biggest save of my Legion career. In the minus column was my game two pitching performance. I got tired in the eighth and ninth and gave up that game-tying home run in the eighth, then the leadoff walk, followed by the double in the ninth. But it was my third goddamn balk that allowed him to score. I would not miss that base umpire. Finally, in the minus column, my hitting. I had gone hitless in the series and left a lot of runners on base. I had made good contact sometimes, but nothing fell on the grass. But in the sixth inning of game three, I had coaxed a walk with the bases loaded to drive in the third run of the inning, and that run proved to be huge insurance in the ninth. Ultimately, I felt the product I had put on the field contributed to the team's win. There is no greater feeling than that—and no worse feeling than the opposite.

Jon recalls the Helena ninth inning of game three as the most intense 30 minutes of *any* sport, but I would rate overtime in the semifinal game against Opheim in the 1979 Eastern Divisional Basketball Tournament higher. We won that game 54-51 in overtime, barely avoiding an upset and not returning to Helena for the state tournament our senior year in 1979.

Dano preferred playing first base, where he played in the third game. He said, "I was a first baseman playing third base. I was much more comfortable at first, but our lineup didn't fit as well with me there." Dad played Dano at first and moved Ray to left field on the 1973 Border League All-Stars, but Doc always played Ray at his natural position of first base.

Game one was the only time that starting pitchers Joe and Jon Puckett, as well as Dan Danelson, pitched in the same game in four years of Legion baseball. Doc had to pull out all the stops to win it.

Kelly and I would say "routine" to each other after we made a play in the middle infield. It was born out of the late summer nights we worked together with Jon to improve our fielding and became part of our "routine" to say it in games. Kelly said it to me after he made the 4-3 play at the end of the first game when we were running off the field together. It was a routine ground ball. That was a tense moment with the tying run on second and Hauck up. It was the best "routine" play Kelly ever made.

Phil Hauck, an all-state running back for Capital High on their 1978 Class AA state championship team for quarterback Bobby Petrino, chose baseball over football to play in the series. He had been picked for the East-West Shrine game in Great Falls and had gone to practice early in the week, but when the Senators placed third in the east and were in the playoff, he decided to stay with baseball for the rest of the season and gave up his spot on the West Team for the football game.

Kindrick Legion Field is another excellent ballpark in Montana. It is the current home of three Legion teams: the Helena Senators, Representatives, and Independents, and was previously the home of the Helena Brewers Minor League Baseball team, which left after the 2018 season. The stadium was built in 1932 and holds 2,100 people. Formerly called Legion Park and later Memorial Park Field, the ballpark's name was changed in the mid-1970s to Kindrick Legion Field in honor of longtime American Legion supporter Ace Kindrick.

Kindrick Legion Field has strong connections to the Scobey through Keith Sell, who pitched for Scobey High School, Scobey Legion, and the Scobey Plainsmen teams in the early 1950s. His younger brothers Kevin and Baldy played on Doc's first Scobey Legion team in 1959, winning the district championship for the first time in 12 years. In 1953, a Legion team wasn't fielded in Scobey, so as a 15-year-old, Keith Sell won several games as a pitcher for the Plainsmen, including a one-hitter. The Annual Keith Sell Tournament is held each summer at Kindrick Legion Field, and this summer will be the 29th year. The tournament is in honor of Keith, who was the longtime general manager of the Helena American Legion Program. He was involved with Senators baseball in various capacities off and on for more than 40 years. Beginning in the mid-1960s, he has served as an assistant coach, head coach, and general manager. A former Copper League pitcher, Sell was ambidextrous and would throw batting practice for the Senators with either hand "with something on it," according to a former player. Keith's son, Mike Sell, played for the Senators from 1984 to 1988. Mike played second base and was the lead-off hitter all five years. The New York Mets drafted him in the 1988 Major League Baseball draft. He went on to play college baseball at Taft College his freshman year and Yakama Community College his sophomore year before returning to Montana. Mike's son Caden Sell (Keith's grandson) played for the Independents, Reps, and Senators between 2017-2021. The field tarp used to cover the infield at Kindrick Legion Field has been coined the "Keith Sell Tarp," as the proceeds from the first Keith Sell Tournament were used to purchase the tarp. Kindrick Legion Field was the field the Blues played on in their last state tournament appearance in 1997.

STATE A TOURNAMENT

AFTER WINNING THE BEST-OF-THREE SERIES AGAINST HELENA on Sunday, we had some time to rest, as the State A Tournament did not start until Saturday. It was the most time off we had since before the IGA Tournament in Billings over the Fourth of July weekend, and we needed it. Unfortunately, however, no amount of rest or treatment would heal Dano's arm in time for the state tournament. Dano recalls, "I did take a needle before the last practice in Scobey. Doc and I talked about it, and he said it was up to me. It didn't work out too well. I was trying to play catch with Wade and the ball kept coming out five feet in front of me. Pain wasn't as bad when releasing, but I had no idea where it was going. When it wore off, we were back to square one. I couldn't throw. But the needle was one of a few things we tried to see how I would react. I knew what pain I had, so the needle only dulled the pain. I didn't continue to throw like some had after the injection. Painkillers made me sick. Ibuprofen was the best option back then for me." So, Doc, Dano, and the team had to accept that we would have to play the best without our ace on the mound. But he could play on the field and at the plate. His fierce competitive spirit and willingness to play in pain inspired the team to take our game to the next level. And if we were going to win against the best American Legion teams in Montana without our ace pitcher, we would all need to step it up.

The 1979 State A Legion Tournament was played in Butte at Alumni Coliseum on the campus of Montana Tech. The tournament field, with their seeds, consisted of the following:

- Great Falls Electrics (2W) vs. Scobey Blues (3E, state B champion)
- Billings Royals (1E) vs. Missoula Mavericks (4W)
- Billings Scarlets (2E) vs. Great Falls Chargers (3W)
- Kalispell Lakers (1W) vs. Butte Miners (4E, Host)

There was no clear favorite in the tournament. However, Kalispell, the defending State A champion and three-time defending Western A Division champion, was mentioned in a lot of articles. The Billings Scarlets were also mentioned, as they had come on strong late in the year and tied with the Royals for the best record in the east. Jack Whelan, Class A Legion Chairman and Tournament Director, in the *Great Falls Tribune*, said the tournament teams were "probably most evenly talented baseball teams I've seen in Montana for the last 12 years. It's really up for grabs."[215] Ed West of the *Gazette* added, "They've all had their moments, but there isn't a solid favorite among them."[216] While there was no clear favorite, West identified the "hottest teams" and wrote that Scobey could be included among them, but "the Blues received a severe blow when ace pitcher Dan Danelson suffered an arm injury in the playoff against Helena."[217]

Great Falls Electrics: Game One

AS THE THIRD SEED FROM THE EAST, OUR FIRST GAME WAS against Great Falls Electrics, the second seed from the west. Doc started me in the first game. I was ready, rested, and felt good. The game was delayed for 35 minutes because the mound was not covered when they watered the infield the night before. After Great Falls pitcher Skip French set us down in order in the top of the first and I began my warmup on the mound, I requested a lot of dirt be brought out to the mound, because my foot was slipping on my delivery. It was frustrating that at the State A Tournament, the mound was in this condition, but I was not going to deliver a single pitch until it felt right. Once it felt right, I had a good first inning, striking out leadoff hitter Rick Thomas on a 2-2 sidearm slider to get the first out. Getting that first out was huge. It set the tone for us in the tournament. We played with poise and confidence and belonged on the field with every team in the tournament.

With the score tied 0-0, I got in trouble in the third when I plunked Tom Bushly to start the inning. Scott Tollefson then sacrificed, but it was a good bunt, and I couldn't get him at first. Then I hit leadoff hitter Rick Thomas to load the bases with no outs. I don't remember hitting too many hitters in my career, and now I had hit two in the same inning. But we almost got out of it with no damage. I got ahead of the next hitter, Dave Rowe, and Great Fall's third base coach, Jim Wilkinson, called a suicide squeeze. Dano, playing third that game, yelled, "Going!" but I also saw Bushly break from third out of the corner of my eye as I delivered the ball to the plate because he broke too early. Dano was following him home step-for-step as he knew the squeeze was on. My dad and Doc always taught us to throw at the hitter's head on a suicide squeeze, so I did precisely that. It tied Dave Rowe up in knots, and he tried to avoid getting hit by the pitch while still trying to get his bat on the ball to protect the runner. He missed the ball badly, and Kirby immediately popped his arm up with the ball in it, showing it to Jon Puckett, who had come in behind Dano to cover third. Kirby began running Bushly back to third, where he threw to Jon to tag him out for the first out, 2-6. Phil Smith of the *Great Falls Tribune* saw the play this way: "Bushly left third base too early, and Scobey picked up

Blues before taking the field in their first against the Great Falls Electrics. *Family photo.*

the play. Puckett threw the pitch high, and Rowe had no chance to bunt."[218] The other two runners had advanced on the steal so there were now runners at second and third with one out. Rowe then popped up to Kelly on the next pitch, and suddenly, we had two outs in the inning with on runs in, and it looked like we might get off the field with no damage.

But I got behind 3-1 on third-place hitter Todd Stubbs, who was left-handed. Looking back on it, I maybe should have pitched around him to load the bases and bring the right-handed hitter up, but I had already hit two batters in the inning, so I didn't want to load the bases again. I threw him a fastball, and he hit a ground ball to short, but Jon was shifted toward second, playing him to pull, so he couldn't get to the ball before it bounced into the left field for a single, and two runs came scampering home. The ball was not hit hard, but it had eyes. Phil Smith, the *Tribune* sportswriter, mistakenly wrote that the ball was "hit past a drawn-in infield,"[219] but it wasn't—there were two outs. It would have been a routine ground ball, but it got through because of the shift. Stubbs just went with the outside pitch and drove it to left for the hit. Kirby got Stubbs out trying to take second on the throw to the plate so that ended the inning. As we were running off the field, Jon said, "Sorry, Joe," but I would have been shifted for a left-handed hitter, too, especially one we didn't know. Jon had him played correctly. The third was the only real trouble I was in the rest of the game, but Great Falls got the big two-out hit they needed with the runners in scoring position to maximize their opportunity.

In the sixth inning, my one bad pitch resulted in the game's only extra-base hit. I hung a curveball on a 2-2 count to cleanup hitter Wade Brogdon, who hit a double deep to left center. He smiled at me as he stood on second base, knowing I had made the mistake. I did not smile back. The ball was hit deep, but Randy almost got to it; it barely escaped his reach. He said, "Sorry, Joe," to me as we were running off the field, but Alumni Coliseum had deep dimensions, and the ball probably would have been out of most parks we played in. As it was, it hit the warning track and bounced over the wall for a ground rule double.

The Electrics added their third run (unearned) in the eighth when Tim Mills reached on an error with two outs, stole second, and scored on a single by Skip French, a line shot to Jon at short that was a short hop and too hot to handle, making the final score 3-0. Again, Jon said, "Sorry, Joe." As all of us in the infield were pitchers, we were sensitive to how our play affected the pitcher. But there was no death stare here. We were past that. That was a solid hit and was scored as such. Jon did not commit an error in the entire tournament at any position.

"The difference in this game was that the Electrics took advantage of one of their few scoring opportunities while Scobey missed out on two of its own."[220] Our first opportunity came in the top of the third when Jon led off with a single, Ray walked, and Greg sacrificed them to second and third. But French retired the next two hitters to get out of it. In the top of the fifth, Greg reached on an error, and Wade got hit by a pitch, but French again got the third out to escape with no runs.

I pitched well that game (two earned runs), and our defense played well too (two errors), but unfortunately, Great Falls was a little better, as we ran into a buzzsaw in pitcher Skip French (no earned runs) and a solid Electrics defense (one error) to shut us out, 3-0. Skip French limited us to four singles, walked only two, and had eight strikeouts. He had a sharp-breaking curve ball and kept us off balance all morning. I had two hits to break out of my slump from the Helena series, but no baserunners were on when I hit them. It was a tight game the entire way. "The Scobey Blues did just about everything they had to do to win. Scobey pitcher Joe Puckett gave up only six hits, only one of those for extra bases. The Blues committed only two errors and gave up only three runs. But, bad luck for Scobey, the Electrics did everything a little bit better."[221] It was a well-played game by both teams. Bruce Sayler of the *Montana Standard* wrote, "The country boys from northeastern Montana showed that their pre-tourney record of 33-8, including wins over the Billings Royals and Scarlets, was no fluke in giving a very tough Electrics team an intense battle in what was probably one of the best Legion baseball games ever played in the state."[222] I felt good that we had played well and didn't beat ourselves, but I was disappointed that we lost.

Missoula Mavericks: Game Two

WE FACED ELIMINATION IN OUR NEXT GAME AGAINST MISSOUla, who lost to the Royals 6-1. They had a good team with a 33-15 record and led the western division up to the season's final week. We couldn't go two-and-out in the State A Tournament. We had a lot of pride and wanted to get a win. One of the things I noticed in the State A Tournament was that teams would watch us closely as we warmed up. There was a tremendous amount of hype surrounding our team with our 33-8 record, beating the Royals and Scarlets during the regular season, then Helena in the playoffs, and we had a 13-year-old who was starting for us. Bruce Sayler of the *Montana Standard* wrote that Greg Stolen "charmed the crowd with his poise and promise." As we were taking infield before the Missoula game, the Missoula players were watching us from their dugout. I was fielding ground balls at short but not throwing them to first. I mentioned earlier that I was careful to care for my arm that season. Following a day that I pitched, I would field the ball at short, and then backup shortstop Ron Higgins would throw it to first. I had pitched eight innings and thrown 119 pitches the previous day and thought I might be needed later in this game, which I was. Not throwing infield is what enabled me to pitch three strong innings later. I saw some quizzical looks from the Missoula players when I would field a ground ball but not throw it to first. I'm not sure they knew the reason why. We all did.

Doc started Randy Stolen against Missoula, while Missoula countered with their ace, Brian Peck. Defensively, Doc switched Dano to first base, Ray Chapman moved to left, and Jon to third because Electrics' Coach Wilkinson had repeatedly bunted on us to exploit that Dano's arm was hurt, and it was difficult for him to make strong throws to first.

Missoula scored an unearned run in the top of the first. Leadoff hitter Jeff Pollack singled, and then Troy Biering followed with a second single to start the inning. They advanced to second and third on a wild pitch. Doc was known to make puzzling decisions, but what he did next made me scratch my head. He pulled the infield in with the bases loaded and one out and instructed us to go home with the ball. Scott Anderson then popped up to first for the first out. Then, Willie Reed hit a ground ball to me at short, and I fielded it and made a snap throw to Kirby to nail the runner at the plate, who was trying to score from third. We then moved back to normal depth with runners at the corners. Joel Fish then hit a hard, high-bouncing ball to me at short. It ate me up. I couldn't field it cleanly, and it bounced off my chest. The runner on third scored, and when the dust had settled, runners were again on the corners. E-6. I heard the derisive shout "Eeeeeeeee" from the Missoula dugout, and it echoed in my head. It was a tough chance, but it cost us an unearned run. It bothered me mentally because I knew how important it was to play clean at short for us to win. I did not make another error for the rest of the tournament. Kirby then caught Joel Fish trying to steal second for the third out.

We countered by scoring two unearned runs in the bottom of the first on two walks and two errors. Wade and Dano both drew walks and then I hit into a fielder's choice to put runners on the corners. Then Doc manufactured two unearned runs for us. He gave me the steal sign, and Missoula catcher Greg Miller threw the ball into center field. I was credited with a stolen base and took third on the throwing error. Then the center fielder misplayed the overthrow, so Doc waived me all the way home, and I never stopped running rounding third base. Two gift runs on one play to give us a 2-1 lead. Peck struck out the next two hitters, so Doc created those two runs with his aggressive baserunning.

Randy got in trouble in the top of the second, walking the first two hitters. Doc brought Jon in to pitch and moved Greg to third base from right field, Randy to left, and Ray to right. Jon gave up a couple of singles, and the inherited runners scored. Missoula took the lead 3-2, but Jon got us out of the inning without further damage.

We had a big four-run rally on three hits in our half of the second to take a 6-3 lead. Randy led off with a triple. Wade had an RBI single, and the big blow came on a clutch two-out, two-run single with the bases loaded by Kelly Norman, our leading hitter with a .420 season average.

But after the second inning, Brian Peck and Jon Puckett silenced the bats until the seventh. Jon was pitching well and gave up only two hits in four innings, but he got into trouble in the top of the seventh when Missoula loaded the bases with nobody out on two walks and a single. Doc then called me in to pitch from short. I felt strong and wanted the ball in this situation. The ball was in my hands to get us our first win in a State A Tournament. With the three-run lead, Doc had our defense play at double-play depth. I got Joel Fish to ground into a fielder's choice from Kelly to Jon, but a run scored. Greg Miller then slapped a single to right to score another run, but I got the last two outs when Greg stepped on third for a force out and got the third out on a fly ball to Ray in right. We got off the field, still holding a 6-5 lead.

But Missoula tied it with an unearned run in the top of the eighth. With two outs, I walked Troy Biering, and then Scott Anderson hit a single to center. Wade Tryan slipped trying to field the ball, and it got past him, so the runner scored from first on the two-base fielding error. That tied the score 6-6.

Coming to bat in the bottom of the eighth, we needed one run to regain the lead. Ray Chapman beat out an infield single to get on first, then Greg sacrificed him to second. Among all the things Greg could do, he was also a good bunter. Wade Tryan walked, then Greg and Wade advanced to second and third on a wild pitch by Peck. Dano just missed a sac fly, as he got under the ball a little too much and popped out to third for the second out, so I came to the plate with two outs and runners at second and third, needing to get a hit to bring the winning run home.

This was the biggest of all the at-bats I had ever had in my baseball career. If I could get Ray home from third, we would need three more outs to get our first win in a State A Tournament. Brian Peck threw hard, and with a 2-2 count, I got a piece of a fastball to stay alive. Peck was working fast, so I called time and stepped out of the box. I had to get this hit. Since we had scored six runs in the first two innings, he had shut us out for six innings, and we might never get his opportunity again. I looked down at Doc at third, and he did what he always did: clapped his hands together, skipped his right hand over his left hand, and pointed toward the outfield, signaling me to swing level and hit a line drive. I turned back toward the batter's box, leaned over my bat, put my head down, and said a short prayer. I don't remember doing that in any other at-bat in my career, but I did it here. I did not pray for a hit but for strength to do my best. Being raised Catholic, the prayer for strength was to Mother Mary. It helped calm me, and when I stepped back into the box, I was focused and ready. On the next pitch, I laced a one-hopper down the line at third, and the ball skipped off the third baseman into foul territory for a hit. I hit it hard, so I saw it glance off him before I started running to first, and I knew it had gone far enough away from him that Ray would score, and I would make it to first. What a feeling! I sprinted to first base and hoped we could get another run, but Peck got the last out of the inning, stranding Wade at third and me at first.

We had the lead 7-6 in the top of the ninth. Three more outs and we had our first win in the State A Tournament, and we would still be alive. I had more energy pitching than I ever had. This was my eleventh inning in two days, but it didn't matter—I was pitching on pure adrenaline to get our first win.

But it's never easy. Joel Fish led off with a single. Anticipating a bunt by Greg Miller, Doc moved Greg up at third. I had never thrown harder than I was throwing; I knew that. I was not going to my breaking ball much and was mainly throwing fastballs, which was abnormal for me, but it felt right. After I delivered the first fastball to Greg Miller, I heard Greg Stolen at third say, "Jeez." He had never seen me throw that hard, either. Miller laid down a perfect sacrifice bunt to Greg at third, who made an excellent play to get the out at first. I needed to get the next two outs with a runner in scoring position. On a 1-1 count, I got Steve Denning to pop to Dano at first for the second out—one more out. Then, on a 1-0 count, Pat Dryden hit a little pop-up to the left of me on the mound, and I quickly called for it and squeezed it for the third out. I never jumped so high! We had won a game in the State A Tournament and were celebrating as if we had won the World Series. It was an incredible feeling. The best part of the win was that I knew I would get to play at least one more baseball game with this amazing team.

Kalispell Lakers: Game Three

AFTER THE HARD-FOUGHT ONE-RUN WIN AGAINST MISSOULA, our next game would be against the Kalispell Lakers, the defending state champions and three-time defending Class A western division champions. Although the tournament field was even, Kalispell was identified as "an early favorite" in one of the pre-tournament reviews.[223] The Lakers had won their first game against Butte but then lost to the Chargers to face us in this elimination game. We knew they were good, but we were ready for whatever came next after getting our first win against Missoula. We wanted to stay alive and go deeper in the tournament. We were not satisfied.

Because of rain, our game was delayed, and then tournament officials moved it to Washoe Park in Anaconda as Alumni Coliseum was not playable. Earlier in the day in Butte, Dad was hoping for a rainout. I remember him saying that if the game got postponed to the next day, I would get eight innings of eligibility back and could pitch. That's my dad for you. The Royals and Scarlets played the game before us in Anaconda. One of these Billings teams was going to send the other home. This was another one of those situations where I just enjoyed watching good baseball. Playing in this State A Tournament was special; I savored every moment. And this was a special game, as these two cross-town rivals were going at it. The Scarlets won 4-3 in 11 innings, so if we beat Kalispell, we would play the Scarlets.

The big question before the Kalispell game was who would pitch. Jon had pitched five strong innings the previous day, and Randy had thrown one-plus. After pitching 11 innings in two days, I had one inning left, but my arm needed rest. Ray had pitched a third of an inning against Helena in his only postseason appearance. He hadn't pitched since the IGA Tournament in Billings, and I don't think Doc had planned on using him much in the postseason. In situations like this, Doc had previously called on his son, Kelly, who had come through with a big win in the 1978 State B Tournament against Glendive. Kelly had only pitched three innings in the postseason, pitching three scoreless innings against Fairfield in the State B Tournament in Scobey. With Dano hurt, someone had to step up. We needed someone to do that now. And Doc again handed the ball to Kelly to get the job done and keep us alive in the tournament.

Defensively, Doc moved Dano back to third and Ray to first.

The game didn't start until ten at night, but it didn't matter; we were ready to play. There weren't many fans in the stands, but this made it easier to hear the Scobey fans, including Marge Norman. I remember hearing her voice often late that night in the stands, cheering us on. It made me feel like I was back in Scobey. So did the dirt infield in Anaconda. That felt familiar, too.

Kelly felt good warming up before the game. He told me his slider "felt good." He said, "The most I remember about pitching was warming up. I think I tried gripping my slider (or curve) differently. I was throwing it hard, and it had a sharp break at the end. The only game I ever had that pitch! With my breaking pitch and being a little wild helped most of the time."

There was an air of cockiness about the defending champion Lakers that was noticeable. Kelly said, "They all were pretty arrogant before the game. Stoick and company. But they were fairly quiet when we were kicking their ass. I'm sure they liked our smiling faces walking through the handshake line."

Kelly pitched two scoreless innings to start the game, and then our two power hitters, Kirby Halvorson and Randy Stolen, shocked Kalispell pitcher Dave Stoick with back-to-back home runs leading off the bottom of the second. Kirby's shot was over the 320-foot marker in left, and Randy's was deep to right-center. Jon, who batted seventh in the lineup after Randy, recalls, "When I came to the plate after Kirb and Randy went back-to-back. I remember the catcher [Mike Rauthe] saying, 'Now if you do that, I'm really gonna be pissed.' I remember that clear as day. They were shell-shocked." The back-to-back home runs set the tone for our bats as they came alive the entire game. We scored two more runs in the third when Kirby and Randy each hit RBI singles to vault us to a 4-0 lead. We added a single run in the fourth to make it 5-0 when I drove in Greg Stolen with an RBI single.

Meanwhile, Kelly was pitching brilliantly. He was walking some hitters, and there was a lot of traffic on the bases. He hit two batters in a row, and when pitcher Rick Eckelberry came to the plate, he said to Kirby, "You better not hit me." But with the walks and hits batsmen, Kelly wasn't giving the Kalispell hitters anything good to hit. His slider was virtually unhittable. Kirby said, "Kelly's slider that night was breaking late, and a lot of the pitches were right around the corners. They couldn't barrel anything up." Kelly added, "I had a lot of three-ball counts. I've told people I had more confidence throwing a breaking pitch than a fastball with a three-ball count." That was one of the keys to Kelly's pitching success. His wildness served him. Jon commented, "From my view at second, he had them fooled the whole game. I remember seeing a lot of knees buckle and a number of lazy swings chasing low outside curves. Eckelberry saying 'don't hit me' reminds me of that Bull Durham movie when that pitcher started finding some control. Kevin Costner [Crash Davis] called time out and went to the mound. He told him to 'throw it at the mascot' so the other team would think he was still wild. I think Kelly hit enough mascots during that game to get them thinking. I wouldn't have wanted to hit against Kelly in that game." With a lot of three-ball counts, Kelly would throw breaking balls, and if he walked the hitter, he walked them, so be it, but he never gave in to a hitter. The key was that he couldn't give up a big hit with baserunners on, and in this game, he didn't—Kalispell stranded 13 baserunners.

In the top of the fifth, we had an inspiring inning-ending double play—our only double play of the tournament. At the end of it, Jon fired a laser across the diamond to Dano at third, who snapped the tag down for the double play and the third out of the inning. The first out was scored 3-2, Ray to Kirby at home, which was also a tag out. The second out was scored 1-4-5. It was very emotional for us because we went from one out and two base runners to no runs allowed and three outs and got off the field, leading 5-0. We were fired up like we'd never been before and sprinted into the dugout to add our five-run lead.

Which we did. We broke it open in the bottom of the fifth on four consecutive singles by Kelly, Kirby, Randy, and Jon, with Jon's single bringing home two runs. Kalispell then brought in ace pitcher Rick Eckelberry in relief, whom Ray Chapman greeted with another single to bring home two more runs. Eckelberry, clearly rattled, balked Ray to second, then uncorked a wild pitch to send him to third. Ray then scored when Greg Stolen hit a line drive past his head. After Greg's hit, we returned fire from the dugout, yelling, "How does it feel to get ripped by a 13-year-old?" Dan Danelson doubled Greg home to score the sixth run of the inning, and we took an 11-0 lead after five innings against the "shell-shocked Lakers"[224]

Kelly, still cruising, set the Lakers down in order in the sixth and carried a two-hit shutout into the seventh. But the Lakers broke up Kelly's shutout with three unearned runs on two singles, an error, a wild pitch, and a passed ball. Ironically, Kelly, who had been pitching so well and who played so well at second base throughout the tournament, made the error that cost him the unearned runs and his shutout, as he threw the ball into center field on a comebacker with runners on first and second. Kelly regrets the throw: "I remember how pissed and bummed I was when I threw the ball to Wade instead of Joe. I hurried and reshuffled and threw it in to center. Easy double play blown. And the shutout was gone!" I was playing well at short. During the inning, I had saved a run by diving to save a ground ball hit in the hole between third and short from going into left field. I remember the third base umpire saying, "Nice play," as I slid on the outfield grass toward him. The next hitter looped a soft liner to short center field that I caught on a dead run going out toward center field, then pivoted to make a throw to Kelly to prevent the runner from third scoring on a sac fly. Following that play, the PA announcer in Anaconda said over the loudspeaker, "That is Joe Puckett playing shortstop for Scobey." I will never forget that. The hard work I had put in that summer paid off; I was playing at a State A-level at shortstop.

After our six-run explosion in the fifth, we only got one baserunner in the next three innings, so we entered the top of the ninth inning leading 11-3, needing just three more outs to eliminate the Kalispell and move deeper into the tournament to face the Scarlets. All three of our previous wins in the post-season—two over Helena and one over Missoula—had come down to the last out in the ninth. The tying and/or winning runs were on base in all three games. In two games, the bases were loaded. We did not expect the same drama in this game unless something went terribly wrong. But something did go terribly wrong, and we ended up with that drama. Why could the ninth never be easy? It's like we didn't know what to do unless the game came down to the last out.

Kelly, who had pitched brilliantly, tired in the ninth and walked the first three hitters. It was now time for Doc to do what he always did in this situation with this team—bring in Jon Puckett to close out the game. But Mike Rauthe greeted Jon with a two-run double to make the score 11-5. The next hitter walked, loading the bases, but then Jon settled down and got two quick outs on easy popups to me at short. The next batter, Tim Nielsen, then hit a flyball to center field, and it looked like the game was over, but Wade, who I'd never seen drop the ball before, fumbled and dropped the ball—perhaps losing the ball in the lights?—and two unearned runs scored. Suddenly, the score was 11-7, and the Lakers were threatening. What was a blowout had become a tense game.

More drama to follow. The next hitter singled in another unearned run to make it 11-8, then Jon issued his second walk of the inning to load the bases again with two outs. The tying run was on first, and the go-ahead run was at the plate. Thinking we had a blowout to start the inning, we were now hanging on to win the game. Although Jon was struggling, he should have been out of the inning two batters earlier, but for the error. It was Jon's game to win or lose. Doc did not budge from the dugout. There was no one else he would rather have on the mound in this situation but Jon.

So here we were again as a team, and here Jon was again as a pitcher in a tight game. Bases loaded. Two outs. Ninth inning. Tying run at first. Winning run at the plate. Got 'em just where we want 'em. Left-handed hitter Dave Stoick was up. I had noticed he had pulled the ball in his previous plate appearances, hitting the ball to the right side and grounding out to Jon at second base twice. In his book, *The Complete Baseball Handbook*, which I had read that summer, Walt Alston wrote that if you don't know a left-handed hitter, the shortstop should take one step in because left-handed hitters get to first base faster. You should also take one step toward second base because, absent any other info, most hitters are pull-hitters. Knowing this hitter was a pull-hitter and remembering what Alston wrote, I took things a half-step further (literally): I took one giant step in and one giant step and a half toward second base. It would have looked like I was playing close to a shift position from behind the plate. I did think about Stubbs, the left-handed hitter from the Electrics, who got the two-run single off me, hitting the ball directly to shortstop with Jon shifted toward second. But I saw Stoick hit both balls to second in this game, so I played the percentages. The same shift that had cost us two runs against the Electrics would save us two runs—and possibly the game—against the Lakers.

Stoick lined a one-hopper right at me at short. It was sharply hit and skipped to me quickly, but I had positioned him perfectly and stayed down on it to snatch the one-hopper. Had I been playing in a normal position at short, the ball would have easily skipped past me into center field for a base hit, scoring two more runs. As it was, the ball was hit so hard that I had to wait for Kelly to get to second base, who was also playing him to pull and was not playing double-play depth because there were two outs. I didn't want to go to first base with the ball to risk a longer throw. I also didn't want to get in a foot race with the baserunner to second base, who was moving on contact with two outs, so I flipped the ball sidearm to Kelly as he was approaching the bag, and he caught the ball in stride and stepped on second base for the third out. "Routine, Kelly, Routine," I said as I glove-tapped him as we ran off the field winners. It was gratifying to see the frustration on Stoick's face as he ran past first base, grabbing his helmet with both hands in disbelief, thinking he had a single, but I had him played perfectly to take it away from him. Game over.

Phew! We had survived. Kelly had pitched brilliantly for eight innings to get the biggest win of his Legion career,

Kirby and Randy had gone back-to-back to get our bats going, Dano had a big RBI double, Jon and Ray had two-run singles, and Jon had done it again on the mound, getting us off the field as winners in a bases-loaded situation. I don't remember a huge celebration; it was more of a sigh of relief that we had hung on to win. And . . . we were a little tired. The game had lasted over three hours, and it was past one o'clock in the morning. Wade, of course, felt awful about the error, but we all picked him up. All of us have made mistakes like that. That's what teammates do—pick each other up when they are down. And we won. No harm, no foul.

Kelly described playing at Washoe Park Anaconda as "surreal." He said, "The lights were a little yellow, the locker rooms were old and run down and smelled damp, musty, and mildewy, just like below Scobey's grandstand. The old stadium, grandstand, and covered bleachers, starting at 930ish, made it feel surreal. That was out of a movie." Jon added, "That field was fun to play on. Something about the lighting made it kind of seem like a dream when I think back on it." It was dreamlike. I remember the yellow lights, too, and how late in the evening it was (early in the morning at the end). It was dark, quiet, damp. You could hear voices from the grandstand but couldn't see any faces. And what a late "surreal" and "dreamlike" evening and early morning it was for us.

Kirby described the win this way: "Of all the wins we had I rate this in my top three. It was so gratifying beating the defending A champs. We beat Stoic, who was 9-1. Actually, we didn't just beat him, we pounded him. Everyone in the lineup contributed something. Kelly pitched the best game he ever had until that point—just what the doctor ordered. His slider was breaking late and they couldn't square up on it. It had drama. Wade dropping that fly ball was just unbelievable, and others had errors, but we persevered. Of course, I'll never forget the back-to-back home runs. Watching that ball disappear into the darkness was one of my best memories in all the sports I've ever been involved in. And maybe I'm an asshole for thinking this, but my favorite memory was Eckleberry's exclamation of 'I'm sick of this Class B bullshit' I can see and hear it in my mind like it was yesterday. Hmm, this Class B bullshit just kicked your ass, and it could've been worse."

Reflecting on his pitching performance, Kelly said, "I never pitched that good before or after that game." Dano agrees: "Without a doubt, Kelly's best pitching performance ever. Clutch. I remember Eckelberry and a few others yapping. And then Kelly would hit someone."

So, the gutsy Scobey Blues—without their ace pitcher—had just won their second game of the State A Tournament and eliminated the defending champions. The headline the next day in the *Great Falls Tribune* read, "Scobey Upsets Kalispell,"[225] but if you ask any of us, we didn't think it was an upset. We belonged. We were still alive, wanting to go deeper in the tournament and looking forward to playing the Billings Scarlets later that day. (Yeah, it was after midnight.)

At this stage in the tournament, we felt good about how far we'd gone, but we weren't satisfied. No one was deluded that the road would be easy without Dano pitching, but until a team drove a stake through our collective hearts, we would keep coming at them. And that is precisely what we did the last game against the Scarlets—we kept coming at them and didn't quit.

Doc handed the ball to Randy Stolen for the second time in the tournament to start the game. Randy was being called on to pitch in big games and doing his best against the best hitters in the state, even though he hadn't pitched many innings that season. Doc hadn't planned on needing to go this deep in his staff in the postseason before Dano got hurt. Doc started Dano at first and Ray in left, as he did against Missoula.

The Scarlets had a big five-run second inning to take a 5-0 lead, scoring five runs on four hits and four walks. Doc brought Jon in to relieve Randy in the inning and moved Randy to left, Ray to first, and Dano to third. Jon got the last three outs, then pitched scoreless ball the next three innings. We scored a single run in the top of the fourth on an RBI single by Ray Chapman and trailed 5-1. Then, because of more rain in Butte, the game moved to Anaconda. After the bus got to Anaconda, I remember playing pepper before we took the field in the bottom of the fourth. It was just fun. The score and weather didn't matter; we were playing baseball in the State A Tournament and savoring every moment. I recall seeing a few Scarlets looking over at us from their dugout. They were impressed at how much fun we were having playing the game, considering how bad the weather was, how late it was, and us being behind.

Playing on our favorite field, we got back in the game with three runs in the top of the fifth. Wade led off with a single, then Dano smashed a towering home run to left. It was the hardest ball I'd ever seen Dano hit. On the homer, Dano said, "I was guessing fastball, and he delivered belt high. Lucky the bat was there too." I followed with a single, stole second, and went to third on a ground ball by Kelly. As I stood on third base, the third base umpire said, "Boy, you guys sure like playing here, don't you?" He was referring to the fact that we had scored 11 runs against Kalispell there, and now we were getting back in the game against the Scarlets. (I think playing on the dirt infield in Anaconda and being a smaller ballpark made it feel more like home, which may be why we played better there. However, we were used to having more fans in Scobey than we saw in the State A Tournament in Butte.) I scored on a sacrifice fly to shallow right field by Kirby. It was a close play at the plate, but I slid past the tag to score our fourth run. I remember Kelly came out of the dugout to shake my hand, knowing I had gone all out to steal second and the sac fly to score that run. Kelly had moved me to third on a ground ball to second. We were back in the game at 5-4 and had chased starting pitcher Jeff Benjamin with eight hits and four runs in four innings.

But just as we had gotten back in the game in the top of the fifth, the Scarlets had another big five-run inning in the bottom of the sixth. The stress on our pitching staff started to show as our arms were tiring. Jon, who had pitched the long ninth inning to get three outs against Kalispell earlier after midnight and had gone five-plus innings against Missoula the day before, was now pitching into his fifth inning against the Scarlets and 12th inning in the tournament. When we batted in the inning's top half, Jon recalls, "My arm was so tired and sore. I was sitting on the top step of the dugout with my jacket on. Dano was sitting next to me. He looked at me and asked, 'How's your arm?' I said, 'It's fine.' He looked back at me and said, 'Yeah, right,' maybe with a little smirk. I kind of gave him the same look back. I think in that moment, we reconciled that we had given it our best shot as a team. The odds were stacked against us at that point. But we finished strong, and I think every team in that tournament had our respect."

The Scarlets loaded the bases on Jon with two singles and a walk. With one out, Doc then brought me in to pitch. I had pitched 11 innings in the tournament but got eight innings of eligibility back after two days. When warming up, I knew I had no gas left in the tank. I might have gotten eight innings of eligibility back, but my arm and body didn't know that. I was tired. I walked the first two hitters I faced, allowing two inherited runners to score, then cleanup hitter Jerry Welk, who batted left, hit a two-run double to right center to bring two more runs home. I then plunked the next hitter, followed by another run-scoring single, the Scarlets' fifth run of the inning, and the second charged to me.

I had now faced five hitters and had not recorded an out. All three inherited runners scored, and I allowed two of my own. The bases were loaded with only one out, and I felt empty and powerless. Against one of the right-handed hitters, I had thrown a sidearm fastball inside him that bounced to the backstop. I was so embarrassed I buried my face in my glove—I usually didn't throw wild pitches. It was bleak.

But I didn't want our fantastic season and my Legion career in Scobey to end this way. I stepped off the mound and turned around to look out at all my teammates. They all looked back at me, seeing nothing there, knowing I was tired. But nothing was looking back at me either.

There was no one else. Kelly, playing second base, turned this back, looked down, and said, "Come on, Joe, suck it up." He was encouraging me, himself, and all of us. He didn't want it to end this way, either. No one did. I was too tired to say a prayer for strength. In the end, pride won out. Doc had handed me the ball to get us through to the end of this game, and there was no way I was going to let my teammates down and for us to get blown out by the Scarlets in our last game together. I wanted to finish strong for Mom and Dad, too, who were sitting in the grandstand watching their son play what would be his final Legion game.

I stepped back on the rubber, looked down at Kirby, took the sign, and delivered my next pitch as if it would be the last I'd ever throw in my Legion career. It was a strike. Each successive pitch after that I treated the same way. I was determined to close it out. With the bases loaded, I struck out the next hitter, then got the last out on a ground ball to Jon at shortstop, who picked it cleanly and fired a strike to Ray at first. My two teammates picked me up, got the last out, and we got off the field, trailing 10-4 but still within striking distance of the Scarlets if we could get something going.

And we did get something going. In the top of the seventh, Dano led off with a walk. I followed with a single for my third hit of the game, and then Kelly singled to drive Dano home with our fifth run. But relief pitcher Brent Bolin got the next three outs to snuff out the rally, and we ran back on the field in the bottom of the seventh, trailing 10-5 but still in the game.

I felt renewed, starting the inning fresh, and was determined to finish strong. I retired the side in order, getting Brent Bolin to pop up to first, then struck out the next two hitters—Doug Lewis and Tim Hahn—at the top of the lineup. My curveball was breaking sharply. While pitching to Doug Lewis, my curveball snapped in for a called strike, and he rolled on his heels. I remember seeing the second base umpire shaking his head after the pitch. After the strikeout, the ball whipped around the infield—we were finishing strong.

We went scoreless in the top of the eighth; then we ran back on the field for the bottom of the eighth, which might be the last time this team did that and the last time I would pitch in Legion. It didn't matter about the score or the game's outcome—I wanted to finish it. As he always did, Kirby yelled out the order one last time to me as he took his place behind the plate to warm me up: "Three-four-five, Joe." Third baseman Jeff McNally, Dave McNally's 16-year-old son, who was named tournament MVP, batted third for the Scarlets and led off the inning. We were all aware of who he was, of course, and wanted to get him out. I worked a full count on him, and then Kirby called a sidearm slider on the full count. I got him to chase it low and outside for my fourth strikeout of the game. Even though we were trailing by five runs, Kirby started the ball around the infield as if we were leading by five runs. The next hitter, cleanup hitter Jerry Welk, had hit a two-run double off me in the sixth, and I wanted to get him out, too. I got him to ground out to Ray at first on a low inside slider. Knowing I felt bad about the two-run double earlier, Kelly said, as he was snapping the ball around the infield, "See, you got him, Joe." He wanted to pick me up. I got the last out on a flyball to Wade in center field, which, looking back on it, was fitting. He got the last putout of his Legion career after the error against Kalispell earlier that morning. After allowing the first five hitters to reach base in my last Legion appearance, I retired the next eight Scarlets in order, striking out four, and we finished strong as a team.

There was one last at-bat for us, and we went down swinging. It went quickly. Kelly and I grounded out to short, then Kirby came to the plate as our last hope. In that situation, with two outs and trailing by five runs, getting on base would be the objective, but Doc wanted to go out with a bang. Kirby remembers, "I'm getting ready to hit. Getting in the box, Doc calls me down the line from the third base coach box. I'm expecting some instructions, but Doc simply says: 'Go for the fucking boards, Snirb.'" That was so Doc. Kirb came close—he hit a fly ball to deep right that pushed the right fielder back to the warning track, but it fell a few feet short as he caught the ball to make the last out, and thus our dream to make it to the Northwest Regionals also fell short. The final score was 10-5 Scarlets. I remember seeing the eventual state champions celebrate the win as I sat in the dugout, but we had given them a game and were in it till the end. It was time to shake hands and wish them well for the rest of the tournament.

When asked to reflect on the tournament and the last game we played together, Dano said, "I don't think I had ever thought truly about our baseball together ending. I always thought we would find ways to get the W. Joe and Jon pitched until the end, just like they had since we were introduced on the playing field as little leaguers. You both showed everyone at the tournament that the Puckett Twins were the real deal. Put my name in the pitcher's box, and I guarantee they don't get five early runs, period. The 'what if' for all of us! I believed then, and still believe to this day, that we were the best team there. Still hard to swallow." He added, "We grew up together. First competing against and then together winning a lot of games and championships along the way. We accepted each other for who we were and managed to get the best out of each other. Every one of you motivated me to win each and every time we stepped on the field. You were all competitive and loved the taste of winning like I did. More importantly, you were my brothers. We might not agree all the time, but we had each other's back. It was that togetherness and success that just kept growing and growing. We also had the talent. No matter who pitched, we could put a solid team out there. Like we have all agreed to before, it would have been so helpful to have played against the better competition more. We would have lost a few more games, but we would have been driven to kick the shit out of them even more. We were a group of young boys growing up together, playing baseball in the summer and winning championships. We were never satisfied. Doc was never satisfied. We all heard the optimism in Doc's interview before Helena: Regionals or bust. We were never intimidated by anyone. We believed in each other. We were a team in every sense of the word. The bond that we have is special!"

Randy Stolen remembers the Blues teams he played on as selfless. He said, "I remember the feelings of being a part of such a special group of athletes, feeling so grateful to be a part of all of it. I felt like such a small part of the Blues—nothing special. I was always in the background. I felt like we all felt—unselfish—the Blues were all that mattered.

On Dano's injury and our performance in the State A Tournament, Kirby said, "Injuries happen even under the best of circumstances. I'd like to believe we understood this, as evidenced by the fact that we could have folded, but we didn't. We battled and came up short. But I'm certain we earned respect. How could we not have?"

As I have read sports articles through the decades, I often see quotes from coaches or players that catch my eye. I latch onto them and apply them to my own experience playing sports. One quote I read from University of Tennessee Lady Vols basketball coach Pat Summitt, who won eight NCAA national championships, applies to the Scobey Blues' performance in the 1979 State A Tournament, especially the last four innings against the Scarlets. Pat Summitt said, "Winning is fun . . . sure. But winning is not the point. Wanting to win is the point. Not giving up is the point. Never letting up is the point. Never being satisfied with what you've done is the point."

Sitting on the bus following the game, we were all devastated that our run in the tournament was over and that this team—the eight of us who had played together since Border League All-Stars in Little League in 1973 and Greg was the batboy—would never play another game together. But I was too tired to cry. I remember Wade Tryan, the toughest, grittiest, most fiery player on the team, came up to me in my seat. He was crying, hugged me, and said, "It was fun playing ball with you, man." I hugged him back and said, "Same with you, Wade." There were a lot of tears, but for me personally, I knew we had taken it as far as we could in the postseason without Dano. We left nothing on the field. We had finished strong as a team against the Scarlets, and I knew personally that I could never play better as a pitcher, a shortstop, or a hitter. I had reached my ceiling in the State A Tournament. What more can you do but do your best? I was sad but also at peace. No regrets. No feeling that there was something more I could have done to help us win. No feeling that I could have worked harder during the season to take it higher. That was a good feeling then, and it's a good feeling now.

Kelly Norman and Dan Danelson also remember how emotional they were on the bus. Kelly said, "I was sobbing. I knew I wouldn't get to play with the seniors ever again, and I knew it was our only chance to win the State A tourney." Dano added, "The Scarlets game was the most emotional I was after a loss. That one was sad knowing our run was over."

Ray Chapman—who recalls very little details about the games but recalls the important things—remembers the scene on the bus after the Scarlets game. He said, "I was crying, the end of a hell of a run for several of us, when I suddenly realized I wasn't alone. The sobs and tears from a number of us got so bad, Kirby started going around to everybody with a box of Kleenex, which, as it happened, turned out to be the perfect antidote to all our crying. We all started laughing, not big guffaws or anything, just laughter at maybe realizing we didn't need to be crying *that* much. It was funny and it snapped us right back to what we needed to remember: that we'd all contributed to one of the greatest runs—still not finished at that time—in American Legion Baseball. More importantly, the tears and laughter we shared were good because they reminded us of what really mattered in that moment: we all got to play the amazing game of baseball together while making lifelong friends and starting our journeys of life in the world outside our blessed northeastern Montana. Of course, we didn't realize consciously that's what we'd all just gone through but, in retrospect, nothing could be more true. We were friends who had a helluva lot of fun together and that part of our lives was over. It brought sadness, but we knew we were lucky to be part of something far greater than each one of us individually. We were a team, each one of us made better as individuals because of our bond of brotherhood, a bond which lasts forever."

After the Scarlets game, Doc and Marge took the team to dinner to celebrate our run in the State A Tournament. Like Ray, DeeAnn Lekvold doesn't remember many details of the games but remembers the important things. She recalls, "We dined on steak and lobster (for the first time in my life) at Lydia's in Butte. The dining area we sat in had high-backed, cushioned chairs that made me feel like we were royalty! I'm not sure who paid for the expensive meal that night but I'm guessing it was Doc and Marge—another example of how generous they were in giving to the Scobey Blues." Pat Audet also remembers the dinner: "I felt the same way! I remember not being able to eat my main course due to the onslaught of many appetizers they had served beforehand. I've been there a few times through the years after. They had not changed a thing including the plenitude of appetizers."

After dinner that night, we all got together in one of the hotel rooms and shared some laughs. It was a special moment because we all knew we had taken it as far as we could, and winning two games in the tournament was a good showing, considering Dano was injured. Jon was impersonating some alligator from a cartoon, and I don't remember my teammates and me laughing harder. He is definitely the funny twin. I remember talking about music with DeeAnn Lekvold, who was there. She and Jacki Tade had been with us as batgirls since 1977, and they were my friends. I went to the Scobey prom with DeeAnn in 1976 and the Peerless prom with Jacki in 1977. They were as much a part of this team as any player, having been with us in games and tournaments from Williston, North Dakota, to Cut Bank, Montana, and everything in between. The Scarlets game was the last for DeeAnn and Jacki, as it was for 18-year-olds Ray Chapman, Wade Tryan, Dan Danelson, and Joe and Jon Puckett. DeeAnn, recalling her days as a batgirl, said, "One heartwarming memory that comes to mind would be the nicknames Doc gave us—Jackson and DeeDee. Another is learning to keep the book for the Scobey Blues! It ended up being useful in my adult years! Summer of '90 or '91, now living in Malta and Bernie Wasser is coaching the baseball team! Yep, I kept the book for his team that summer. Fast forward to summer 2020, the adult co-ed softball league in

Malta needed a bookkeeper—again, I'll do it! I've changed over the years, but that book is still the same!"

In addition to DeeAnn and Jacki, batboys Mike Roland, Rick, and Mike Lee, bus driver Dick Atwood, Assistant Coach Don Lekvold, and the talented younger players—Ron Higgins, Pat Audet, Jim Lekvold, Jesse Cook, and Gord Tryan—were all an integral part of the 1979 Scobey Blues. The younger players' time to shine would come the following season when they would all be starters on Scobey's fifth consecutive state championship team, and many of them would also play on the 1982 state championship team. All the parents, volunteers, the community, American Legion Post 56, the *Daniels County Leader*, KCGM radio, and of course, at the center of it all, were Doc and Marge Norman.

TOURNAMENT SUMMARY

WE FINISHED FOURTH OUT OF EIGHT TEAMS IN THE TOURNAMENT, going 2-2. After beating us 10-5, the Billings Scarlets won their next three games—4-2 over the Chargers and 2-1 and 17-7 over the undefeated Electrics—to win the tournament. Phil Smith of the *Great Falls Tribune* covered the tournament end-to-end. In his entertaining article, "Predictably, the Legion tournament was unpredictable,"[226] he has many things to say about the Scobey Blues team and players. He captured the tournament's spirit best, so I'll let him write the summary. His article is reprinted here in its entirety:

Predictably, the Legion tournament was unpredictable

BUTTE —In American Legion Baseball in Montana, the bizarre is often commonplace. And, not surprisingly, the 1979 state tournament, which concluded at 12:30 Thursday morning, was one collection of weird occurrences after another. Fans who managed to sit through approximately 40 hours of baseball in five days in two cities were treated to the following sights and sounds:

Tournament officials pouring gasoline on the pitcher's mound and torching it while attempting to dry out the mound before the first game. It seems the Alumni Coliseum field had been watered overnight, but the mound had not been covered.

The Missoula Mavericks, considered one of the top teams in the state prior to the season, losing ignominiously in their first two games.

The Kalispell Lakers, the defending state champions and one of the tournament favorites, falling behind 11-0 to Class B Scobey, before finally losing 11-8 and being eliminated from the tournament.

The following comments from a Kalispell player during the Scobey game: "Show 'em what Class A ball is like." Kalispell was losing 9-0 at the time.

A switch in sites in the middle of a game between the Billings Scarlets and Scobey Blues. It resumed raining in Butte and the game was moved lock, stock and baseball bat to Anaconda's Washoe Park.

Four games lasting past midnight with the grand champion being the Scarlet-Great Falls Chargers game, which didn't end until 1:20 Wednesday morning. The king of the post midnight games? The Scarlets, who were 2-0. And the big losers? The Kalispell Lakers, who were 0-2 in games that finished on different days than when they started.

The general manager of the Butte Copper Kings, Bruce Manno, blasting Legion officials in the paper one day, for deciding to play on a field he considered unplayable and dangerous, then apologizing the next day when officials took offense to his statements, and explaining it was simply a difference of opinion.

A triple play that wasn't a triple play. Kalispell pulled off a triple play in the fifth inning of its game against Butte. Third baseman Doug Ingram tagged out a sliding Glenn McLaughlin for the third out of the play, to the accompaniment of thunderous applause from the Kalispell fans. Only trouble was, there was one out before the play ever started. Everybody had forgotten that.

Three different shortstops committing four errors in one game.

A 2-1 game that lasted 3 hours 15 minutes and a 17-7 verdict that lasted 2:45 -on the same night with the same teams playing, the Scarlets and the Great Falls Electrics. Seven games that lasted longer than 3 hours.

A grand total of two games that started at their scheduled time.

Great Falls Charger pitcher Bob McGregor, in failing to last more than 1/3 innings in three appearances, then going the route in striking out 13 in a 4-2 loss to the Scarlets.

THERE WERE, of course, the highlights also: Scarlet pitcher Tim Leininger winning three games; Scobey shortstop Joe Puckett hitting .500 to win the tournament batting title; Rick Thomas of the Electrics stealing seven bases; Sam Fudge of the Chargers hitting a shot to left field at Alumni Coliseum that would have been a home run in any ballpark.

And there was the entire Scobey Blues team, which defeated Kalispell and Missoula and pushed both the Electrics and the Scarlets to the limit.

Scobey was awarded the Sportsmanship trophy and could conceivably have gone home with a bigger trophy had pitcher Dan Danelson been available.

Danelson, 9-0 for the season, pulled a muscle in his right elbow while the Blues were defeating Helena to advance to the Class A tournament. He started the tournament at third base, but it quickly became apparent he could barely get the ball from third to first, much less pitch. When Missoula began bunting on him, he was quickly moved to first place and spent most of the tournament there. Joe Puckett, easily the tournament's best shortstop, is a certain All-tournament selection, and outfielder Randy Stolen, who counted a home run and two triples among his hits, is another possibility. Stolen's 13-year-old brother Greg, was the youngest player in the tournament.

Phil Smith of the *Tribune* was correct in his all-tournament predictions for Scobey, as the next day, the all-tournament team was announced in the *Montana Standard*, and it included three Scobey Blues. The *Standard* wrote, "Joe Puckett, who was a cog in Class B champion Scobey's run at the Class A flag, won the hitting award for batting .500. Puckett was also named to two positions of all-tourney first team—pitcher and shortstop. The fourth-place Scobey Blues were given the team sportsmanship award."[227] I was hitless in the best-of-three series in Helena a week earlier; now, I am the leading hitter in the State A Tournament—that's baseball for you. Randy Stolen, who hit two triples and a home run, was also selected as a first-team outfielder. It was fitting that Randy was selected to the first team at his native position in left field because he was called on to pitch in the tournament and had a couple of rough outings on the mound. Kelly Norman, because of his incredible pitching performance against Kalispell, was selected as a second-team pitcher. The complete all-tournament first, second, and third teams, as voted on by the coaches, were as follows:

- **First Team:** First base – Tim Hahn, Billings Scarlets. Second base – Dan Arredondo, Billings Royals. Third base – Jeff McNally, Billings Scarlets (MVP). Shortstop – Joe Puckett, Scobey Blues. Outfielders – Sam Fudge, Great Falls Chargers; Tom Klunder, Billings Scarlets; Randy Stolen, Scobey Blues. Catcher – Jim Krivec, Billings Scarlets. Pitchers – Joe Puckett, Scobey Blues; Tim Leininger; Billings Scarlets; Mike Monahan, Great Falls Chargers; Skip French, Great Falls Electrics.
- **Second Team:** First base – Scott Fiechtner, Great Falls Chargers. Second base – Tim Mills, Great Falls Electrics. Third base – Doug Ingram, Kalispell Lakers. Shortstop – Larry DeBolt, Great Falls Chargers. Outfielders – Rick Thomas, Great Falls Electrics; Ted Benn, Great Falls Chargers; Dave Rowe, Great Falls Electrics. Catcher – Todd Stubbs, Great Falls Electrics. Pitchers – Fred Peres, Great Falls Electrics; Brian Peck, Missoula Mavericks; Rick Eckelberry, Kalispell Lakers; Kelly Norman, Scobey Blues.
- **Third Team:** First base – Warren Hillukka, Great Falls Electrics. Second base – Warren Helmer, Billings Scarlets. Third base – Wade Brogdon, Great Falls Electrics. Shortstop – Doug Lewis, Billings Scarlets. Outfielders – Bill Osborne, Butte Miners; Jerry Welk, Billings Scarlets; Mike Powell, Billings Scarlets. Catcher – John Kangas, Billings Royals. Pitchers – Mike Powell, Billings Scarlets; Wes Secord, Great Falls Electrics; Jeff Ballard, Billings Scarlets; Bob Bush, Butte Miners.

I'll submit that if there had been a category for utility infielders, Jon Puckett would have been selected number one. He played errorless ball the entire tournament at three different infield positions: third base, shortstop, and second base. His versatility in playing multiple positions well was a key to our success. The rest of us were fortunate to have gotten to concentrate on one position.

The 1979 Scobey Blues finished the season at 35-10, with eight losses to Class A teams and two Class B losses to Sidney and Wolf Point in the regular season.

TOURNAMENT STATS

Hitting

SEVERAL SCOBEY HITTERS HAD BIG HITS IN THE TOURNAMENT. The Blues hit three home runs, the most by any team in the tournament. Kirby and Randy hit back-to-back solo home runs against Kalispell, and Dan Danelson hit a two-run home run against the Scarlets. Other extra-base hits were Randy Stolen's two triples and Dan Danelson's double.

For RBIs, Kelly Norman had a big two-run single against Missoula, and Joe Puckett had the game-winning RBI on a single in the eighth. Against Kalispell, Kirby and Randy each had two RBIs, and Jon and Ray each had two-run singles. Dan Danelson led us with two RBIs against the Scarlets with his two-run home run. Joe Puckett led the team (and tournament) in average at .500 and walked five times for an OBP of .632. Finally, Greg Stolen had three sacrifice bunts in the tournament, moving runners up to scoring position each time. Bunting doesn't appear big in the box score, but is important to a team's offense. Bunting was just one of Greg's baseball skills.

Pitching

THE PITCHING STAFF WAS STRESSED WITHOUT DANO'S ARM IN the rotation, but somehow, Doc managed to muster two wins with the depleted staff. Of the 34 innings logged by Scobey pitchers, Joe Puckett (13 and two-thirds innings) and Jon (10 and one-third innings), pitched 24 of them, each appearing in three of the four games. Joe was the losing pitcher against the Electrics, going eight innings and yielding two earned runs. Randy Stolen pitched one inning plus against Missoula and was relieved by Jon, who pitched five-plus innings and allowed two earned runs. Joe Puckett was the winning pitcher, yielding no earned runs in three innings of relief. Kelly Norman pitched eight-plus innings against Kalispell, giving up three earned runs and getting the win. Jon again worked a tumultuous ninth to get three outs and get us off the field against Kalispell, but it was not a save opportunity. Randy started against the Scarlets and went one inning plus, then was relieved by Jon, who pitched four and one-third innings, allowing three earned runs. Joe then closed the game with the Scarlets, pitching two and two-thirds innings and giving up two earned runs. Joe Puckett (ERA 2.63) was selected as a first-team all-tournament pitcher, and Kelly (ERA 3.38) was selected to the second team.

Fielding

EXCEPT FOR THE KALISPELL GAME, OUR FIELDING WAS GOOD. We allowed some unearned runs, but most came against Kalispell. We allowed only one unearned run against the Electrics, two against the Mavericks, but five against the Lakers. Thankfully, the game against the Lakers was a slugfest, and we had plenty of run support to overcome the errors. Our team committed nine errors in the tournament for an average of 2.25 per game, which isn't bad. A good way to measure our fielding was that it was on par with the teams we played against, as our four opponents also committed nine errors against us. Most importantly, our middle infield—the core of the defense—committed only two errors in the tournament. Kelly and I had one, and Jon played errorless ball at both short and second (and third). Joe Puckett was selected first-team all-tournament shortstop, and Randy Stolen was selected first-team outfielder.

Dano's injury obviously affected our pitching, but it also stressed the defense. It was evident that Dano was playing in pain, and making the throw from third to first was difficult. Opposing coaches saw that, and both the Electrics and Mavericks started bunting on us to exploit that. As a result, Doc was forced to move Ray to left field when Randy pitched, and Dano played first base a lot during the tournament, sometimes rotating from third to first in the same game.

We had one big double play in the tournament. With one out in the fifth inning against Kalispell and runners on the corners, Ray threw to Kirby to nab the runner at third, trying to score at the plate (score that 3-2). The ball then went back to Kelly, the pitcher, who saw the runner at second was too far off the base. He threw to second to Jon, who threw across the diamond to Dano at third to nail the runner trying to take third base (score that 1-4-5). The double play got us off the field in the fifth, leading Kalispell 5-0.

Baserunning

WITH OUR OPPONENTS' STRONGER ARMS PITCHING AND CATCHing, Doc was not nearly as aggressive as he normally was on the bases, but he did create two critical runs in the first inning against Missoula. With Wade on third and me on first, he had me steal. The throw from the catcher went into center field. Wade scored from third base, and I took third on the overthrow and then scored when the ball got past the center fielder. For the tournament, Wade Tryan and Joe Puckett stole two bases each. No one was caught stealing.

EXTRA INNINGS

I'M SURE NONE OF US WERE THINKING THIS AT THE TIME, BUT six of us on the field knew that the 11-3 lead we had over Kalispell in the ninth inning was not insurmountable. This was the game's score in 1976 when we came back to win the state championship game against Wolf Point, scoring 10 runs in the bottom of the seventh inning to win 13-11.

On his barnstorming tour of western Montana with his first Scobey Legion team in 1959, Doc took the team to play the Butte Miners in Butte. To my knowledge, this was the only other time the Scobey Legion team played in Butte, twenty years later.

After winning the State A championship, the Billings Scarlets went on to finish third place in the Northwest Regional in Yakima, Washington.

The 3-0 shutout loss to the Electrics was the only second time the 1977-79 team was shut out. Jeff Nesper combined with Tom Paladichuk to pitch a 2-0 shutout against us in a regular season game in Scobey in 1977. When I played in 1976, Dennis Loendorf from Wolf Point shut the Blues out 4-0 at the state tournament in Cut Bank.

Doc's first win in the State A Tournament as head coach of the Blues came against the Missoula Mavericks, a team he formerly coached. He was an assistant coach to Gene Thompson in Missoula in 1958 and head coach in 1961, where he led Missoula to a second-place finish in the Western A Division. Doc coached against Dave McNally of the Royals in the 1958 State A championship game when McNally shut out Missoula 5-0 and struck out 19 Mavericks. Doc then coached against Dave's son, Jeff McNally, of the Billings Scarlets in 1979.

The 1979 Scobey Blues finished fourth with a 2-2 record in the eight-team State A Tournament. The two wins tied with the 1974 Billings Scarlets for the most in a State A Tournament for a Class B team in Montana American Legion Baseball history. (The 1974 Scarlets were Class B, moving to Class A in 1975.) The Havre Northstars won one game in two different State A Tournaments. In 1971, Havre beat the Billings Royals 3-2 in 14 innings, in which Dave Fanning of Havre struck out 25 Royals in 12 innings. Havre then received a second-round bye and then lost to Miles City and the Royals, finishing third in the six-team tournament with a 1-2 record. Havre again won against the Glacier Twins in the 1972 State A Tournament. Besides the 1971-72 Northstars and the 1979 Blues, no other Class B team won a game in the state A Tournament. Class B teams stopped competing against Class A teams in the playoffs and State A Tournament in 1984 and began competing in regional B tournaments in 1985.

The 1979 Scobey Blues had eight starters from the 1973 Border Little League All-Stars on the 1979 team, and Greg Stolen was a batboy for the 1973 team. Greg probably would have started, but he was only seven years old. In 1973, the Billings Western Giants beat Missoula West Side Little League 12-11 to win the Montana state Little League championship. The 1979 Missoula Mavericks and Billings Royals each had six starters from those 1973 Little League teams. As 11-and 12-year-olds, it was a huge goal for us to win the state of Montana Little League championship and go to San Bernadino to play in the Western Regional, as it was in 1979 to make it to the Northwest Legion regionals in Yakima, Washington. But in 1979, the Blues beat the Mavericks (7-6) and the Royals (2-1), finishing higher than both in the State A Tournament, so we got closer to regionals than they did and got the last laugh.

I closely watched the games we didn't play in, as the baseball was so good. Whenever the Royals played, I studied shortstop Mike Day to see if I could learn something from him, as he was the best Legion shortstop I ever saw play. Against the Electrics in their second game, Royals pitcher Joe Aldridge uncorked a wild pitch to bring the winning run home for the Electrics in the ninth, forcing the Royals through the dirt route for the remainder of the tournament. My attention to Day didn't stop with his play on the field. I watched him run off the field, where he angrily threw his glove into the dugout before going to shake hands with the Electrics. The Scarlets eliminated the Royals in the next game.

Jeff Ballard of the Scarlets, selected as a third-team all-tournament pitcher as a 15-year-old, later played college baseball for Stanford University and was inducted into the Stanford Athletic Hall of Fame as one of Stanford's top pitchers. He held Stanford's all-time record in wins, strikeouts, and innings pitched for more than 20 years, earning First Team All-Pac-10 twice. He was drafted by the Baltimore Orioles in the seventh round of the 1985 MLB June Amateur Draft from Stanford University and played in the majors from 1987 to 1994 for the Baltimore Orioles and Pittsburgh Pirates. In 1989, he finished in a tie with Dennis Eckersley and Gregg Olson for sixth place in American League Cy Young Award voting. In 1995, Ballard's car collided with a semi-truck on a highway in Idaho, breaking his neck and several ribs. The accident ended his career.

The Great Falls Chargers' third-place finish in the 1979 State A Tournament was the first time in the team's five-year history that they did not play in the state championship game.

In addition to the Kalispell game, Kirby and Randy had also hit back-to-back home runs earlier that season in Williston. In the 1973 eastern divisional championship game against Wolf Point at Denton Field in Miles City, Rick Danelson and Terry Puckett hit back-to-back home runs. Kirby and Randy would do it again in 1980, but we won't get ahead of ourselves.

Butte in 1979 was not the only time Doc and Scobey had to play in the State A Tournament without their ace pitcher. In 1973 in Great Falls, Terry Puckett had a partial tear in his labrum in the State B Tournament, then completely tore it making a throw from right field to third base. He could only play right field in the two games in Great Falls and had to roll the ball to Duke Trangsrud in center field to make any throws he needed. Like Dano, Terry was able to hit but not pitch. Doc and Scobey had hard luck when it came to State A Tournaments and their aces pitching.

Having five days rest between the State Class B tournament and best-of-three series with Helena, and another five days rest between the best-of-three series and the State A Tournament, was not a luxury previous State B champions had. Through the years, the powers that be had stopped treating the State Class B champion as a second-class citizen and planned it so there was time to rest between tournaments. In 1968, after Havre played its sixth game in four days on a Monday to win the State B championship, they had to travel from Glendive to Helena to play the Senators *the next night*. After winning its first state championship in 1969, Scobey experienced the same thing. Following their sixth game on Sunday, Scobey had no time to celebrate the championship—the Great Falls Electrics one-game playoff to get into the state A tournament was on Tuesday. Scobey's pitching arms were dead, and the team was exhausted. The 1976 team had it a little better, with three days' rest between the Libby playoff and the State A Tournament. However, the *Leader* pulled no punches in rebuking the "rigged" system. Referring to the best-of-three playoff in Libby in 1976 to get into the State A Tournament, the *Leader* wrote, "The Class B champions can be very capable competitors when not beat down and worn out by unfairly arranged playoff games on a 'poor relative' basis."[228] The *Leader* always referred to the Class B teams as "poor relatives" compared to how the Montana American Legion Baseball program treated the Class A teams. Ace pitcher Mike Hagfeldt, who pitched heavily in the best-of-three series in Libby, had only three days' rest before pitching against the Royals.

The lucky "nanu nanu" handshake between Ron Higgins and me before the game against Missoula was from *Mork & Mindy*, a popular sitcom (1978–82) starring Robin Williams. What I love about this picture is how it shows the camaraderie between the players. That is what I miss the most. Playing the game was fun, but the best part was playing it with my friends and all those memories I have of them. I can't believe my mom or dad captured this picture.

Nanu Nanu. The lucky Nanu Nanu handshake (from Mork & Mindy) between Ron Higgins and Joe Puckett just before the State A Tournament Legion game against Missoula in Butte in August 1979. *Photo by Tiny Puckett.*

Alumni Coliseum in Butte, now officially called Bob Green Field at Alumni Coliseum and used for football only, was built in 1962. It was the former home of the Butte Copper Kings (now Grand Junction Jackalopes) Pioneer League baseball franchise. The Copper Kings shared the stadium with Montana Tech until their demise and the Butte Miners American Legion Baseball team until a new field was built for that purpose. The grandstands that were used for baseball have been removed and replaced with expansions to the Montana Tech campus. Alumni's dimensions were huge: 350' to left, 410' to center, and 360' to right.

Washoe Park baseball field in Anaconda, where we played two games, was originally home to Anaconda's town baseball team. It is now home to the Anaconda Athletics, who compete in Class A American Legion. The Anaconda Copper Company had the diamond and grandstand built in 1949, and the city's different fraternal lodges organized the first teams to play. The grandstand has a classic look, and nearby is the refreshment/ recreation center, a building in the Rustic style, an architectural type associated with parks of all sorts in the first half of the 20th century.

Later at Montana Tech, Jon and I were friends with Greg Miller ("Mills"), the catcher for the 1979 Missoula Mavericks. When we discussed eliminating them from the tournament, he would jokingly say, "Yeah, we got the Scobey Blues." He played football at Tech and started at quarterback for the Montana Tech Orediggers his senior year in 1983.

Phil Smith's tournament summary article in the *Great Falls Tribune* wrote that a Kalispell player said, "Show 'em what

Class A ball is like"[229] when Kalispell was losing 9-0. That player was Rick Eckelberry, who was drafted in the second round of the regular phase of the 1980 winter draft by the world-champion Pittsburgh Pirates and pitched for South Idaho Junior College earlier that spring.

Eckelberry wasn't the only player to chirp at the Blues in the tournament. Kelly Norman recalls, "I was sitting near Phil Hauck [Helena Senators] at Butte at a game. He knew I was there. He kept saying, 'I can't believe we lost to Scobey,' then shook his head. He thought it was a fluke. Happy he got to see us play at the State A tourney." First baseman Tim Hahn of the Scarlets also ripped us. After the Scarlets beat the Royals ahead of our game against the Lakers, he yelled to the entire Kalispell team, "Get this Class B bullshit of the tournament." We were all standing right there. Yeah, we weren't welcome in the State A Tournament. The press and fans liked us as underdogs—the players did not. Good thing we weren't mic'd up in the dugout against Kalispell, or we might have lost the sportsmanship trophy. Also, no specific names will be put in the book, but in this private group, we are among friends.

Following the 1979 season, three Scobey Blues—Joe, Jon Puckett, and Dan Danelson—went on to play collegiate athletics. Jon was offered a scholarship to play basketball for the Montana Tech Orediggers, and I was offered a scholarship to play basketball for the Carroll College Fighting Saints in the Frontier Conference. Jon and I had an interesting collegiate experience. We played against each other on the court in the first game of the season in 1979—Jon as an Oredigger and me as a Fighting Saint. In my sophomore year, I transferred to Minot State to play baseball, but I transferred to Montana Tech my junior year for academic reasons, as I wanted to study computer science at Tech. I joined Jon on the court at Tech our junior year, where we played together as Orediggers for Head Coach Kelvin Sampson, appearing on the court at the same time in many games. Following Jon's junior year, he transferred to Carroll College for academic reasons, and he became a Fighting Saint at Carroll, playing for Coach Jon Driscoll. We each had a redshirt year, so we ended up playing against each other on the court our last two seasons in 1983 and 1984, but this time, I was an Oredigger, and Jon was a Fighting Saint. Did you follow that?

Dan Danelson's collegiate experience was much simpler. He wanted to play both baseball and basketball in college, but not many offers came in other than junior college to do both. Lewis-Clark State College (LC State, Lewiston, Idaho) recruiters saw the Montana-Wyoming all-star basketball game, and they offered him a basketball scholarship. He sent a letter to Ed Cheff, head baseball coach, and said he wanted to play baseball there and if they had any interest in someone who wanted to try two sports. Dano said, "Thankfully, Cheff said yes. Doc talked to Cheff when we were trying to bring the swelling down after Helena. Trying to set up appointments when I got to Lewiston for doctors. I spent two days in Doc's office in Scobey with treatment. It worked in bringing the swelling down." Dano played basketball his freshman year but took one year of physical therapy to strengthen the rotator cuff muscles for baseball, which took the strain off his elbow. He redshirted in baseball the first year while rehabbing. In his second year at Lewis & Clark State College, Dano played both basketball and baseball but stopped playing basketball in his junior year to focus solely on baseball in his last two years, hoping to get drafted.

While Dano played both basketball and baseball at L-C State, said, "Baseball was my true love of sports." Dano pitched for Lewis & Clark State College in three NAIA World Series, winning the national championship in 1984 and finishing second in 1982-83. He threw in the 1982 NAIA College World Series in Lubbock, Texas. Dano said,

Dan Danelson pitching for the Lewis-Clark State Warriors, Lewiston, Idaho. *Family photo.*

"That was probably the hardest I threw. My arm got really strong again. I was throwing hard again during my sophomore and junior years, but in my senior year, it started aching." His decision to focus on baseball did work out, as following the NAIA championship in 1984, Dano was drafted by the Texas Rangers in the 33rd round of the 1984 MLB June Amateur Draft. He pitched for the Tri-Cities Triplets (Richland, WA) in A ball in the Northwest League. He appeared in 18 games and pitched 36 and two-thirds innings. His record was 2-1, with an ERA of 2.45, striking out 33 hitters with a WHIP of 1.200. Good stats, but Dano said, "That was it. Arm had had enough. Rangers released me. I needed surgery, and the Giants said I could rehab with them if I wanted to give it a shot. I was done. Had a blast." One of Dano's professional career highlights was pitching against the 1984 USA Olympic Team, facing the likes of Will Clark, Oddibe McDowell, Mark McGuire, and Barry Larkin. McDowell was 0-3 against him, and Mark McGuire "hit a pop-up to the moon." Bobby Witt pitched for the Olympic Team, and Dano said he threw "the first fastball where I heard the seams. Our hitters were shitting."

Jon and I appeared on the court against and with each other, but we also played against Dano in basketball when he played at LC State. I played against him when Carroll traveled to Lewiston during our freshman year. In Jon's sophomore year at Tech, at a game in Lewiston, Dano said, "Jon and I got in a shoving match. We had a play in the key. We went face to face and smiled at each other. The refs came over in a hurry and then saw we had no intent but love. It was funny." Jon added, "We talked before the game and said, 'Let's stage a shoving match,' and we did."

Kirby also faced Dano in college while playing baseball at Pacific Lutheran University. Kirby said, "He [Dano] came in to relieve and I was called on to pinch hit. Dano threw a fastball right down the cock, and I watched it. I looked at the mound, and there was no death stare, just a huge grin. I don't know if he said anything, or else I just picked it up that I wasn't getting any more of those. So, I worked the count to either 2-2 or full, and he kept pounding the outside corner. I fouled a couple off to stay alive. I then ripped one between first and second . . . or maybe it was a medium hard grounder that the second baseman would have fielded with a couple of steps to the left. I like the former. Anyway, the ball hit the runner going to second. Dead ball. Runner is out. I'm allowed first base. And back then, it was scored a hit [still is]. So yeah, I singled off my boy Dano!!" Of the hit, Dano said, "It was hit hard. I'm thinking double-play ball, but then again, I'm biased. It made me smile, and it still does today. The same goes for facing off with Jon. I always thought it was special to go against a brother."

Following the State A Tournament, my last memory of playing ball in northeastern Montana before I left for Carroll College was in a fast-pitch softball tournament in Peerless. Clark Shaffer, from Missoula, who had coached basketball in Peerless from 1976-1978, was our pitcher. I played short, Jon played third, and Ray played first on a pickup team thrown together at the last minute. There were a few Canadian teams there, and we won the tournament. Audrey came out to Peerless to watch the games, and in between games, we walked up to our house, where Dad taught Audrey how to pitch baseball in our backyard. The same things Dad taught Jon and me, he was teaching her. "Just rock and fire, rock and fire," he would say. I caught her as I caught Jon when he pitched, and Dad coached him. It was like old times. As I watched Dad, I also realized that although I was a pitcher, I didn't know how to teach anyone how to pitch. Dad did. I later learned how to teach the game when I coached my daughters in fast-pitch softball, passing the game I loved on to the girls I love.

So, my baseball career in northeastern Montana ended where it began—in our backyard and on the Peerless ball field, where Dad taught Jon and me how to pitch and play baseball 12 years earlier. From my first memory of playing baseball on the Peerless ball field when I was six years old—with Don Puckett throwing a ground ball from first base to me at third base in a Little League game against Flaxville—it was always fun. And the people I loved—my Mom and Dad, my brother, my cousins, and all my friends—were associated with it. All those summer days, baseball was a part of every day, including when Dick Puckett started playing for the Scobey Legion team in 1965, and we would go to the Scobey Ball Park to watch him play.

After my freshman year at Carroll in 1979, I transferred to Minot State College to play baseball, where I was offered a scholarship, but it wasn't the same. Sure, I loved to play baseball, but at Minot, I learned that my love of baseball was deeper than just the game. I loved to play baseball with my brother and the boys I grew up with in northeastern Montana, playing for my dad and Doc, with my Mom at the games, keeping score. The social aspect of baseball was missing in Minot for me. My love of the game was fueled by my love for my teammates, coaches, parents, and community. I played okay at Minot but lasted only one baseball season there before transferring to Montana Tech, where I finished my collegiate career playing basketball for Kelvin

Sampson. For me, there was something about baseball that was like it was for the homesteaders who brought the game to northeastern Montana in the early 1900s—Sunday picnics and town teams playing baseball. The game was stitched into the fabric of summer life for communities and families. All the memories I have of watching the awesome Peerless Hellcats softball team play in the big tournaments they would host in Peerless. I knew all the girls, and my Uncle Ed Puckett coached them.

I have a memory of my mom playing second base in a softball game on a beautiful summer day in Peerless, holding her right hand over her eyes to shade them from the sun because she didn't have a hat and couldn't see . . . my sister driving us to baseball games and cheering for us . . . my older brother playing in a fast-pitch softball tournament for the Plainsmen in Peerless . . .

And it was summertime,
Sweet summertime, summertime.

The last celebration for the 1979 Scobey Blues was a party at Don and JoAnn Lekvold's house in Four Buttes. DeeAnn Lekvold recalls the party: "It was a celebration at Don and JoAnn's when they lived in the country near Four Buttes. It was a big gathering with the team and families with lots of food and a keg (maybe two!). Us 'kids' partied and camped out there, sleeping in the back of pickups, in cars, and maybe there was a tent or two. What I remember most is waking up the next morning, and Jacki's bottom lip and chin were swelled up hugely! Doc checked her out and said it was from a spider bite!" Rookie Pat Audet remembers the party, too: "I was only 14 and blasted out of my mind!"

Regarding the gathering, JoAnn Lekvold recalls, "I am actually surprised, now that I think about it, that we didn't get turned in because of the keg. Life was sure different back then. My memory of that night was Kirby Halvorson and I think Ray Chapman singing Barbara Ann. They were so entertaining and sounded so good!" (Not to worry about the keg, JoAnn. Dad was justice of the peace and probably would have cut the Blues some slack.)

However, the celebration was bittersweet for me. I was at the party briefly but couldn't stay long, as this was my last night at home before I left for the fall semester at college. I also had a date with Audrey to say goodbye to her. That night, I was not only saying goodbye to my girlfriend but to 12 summers of playing baseball for the Peerless Pirates and the Scobey Blues. Driving home that night to Peerless, as the sun set in the west, it also set on all those summers in northeastern Montana.

Ain't it funny how the night moves,
 When you just don't seem to have as much to lose. Strange how the night moves,
 With autumn closing in.[230]

But the sun never set on my memories of those golden years on the ball fields. When it rose the following day, those memories were still with me, as they are to this day. The baseball summers of my youth on the dusty ballfields of northeastern Montana still burn in my soul—memories to last a lifetime.

In reflecting on my baseball career and growing up in Peerless in the 1960s and 1970s, I didn't really have a reference point to appreciate just how lucky I was to have a twin brother who was an instant playmate whenever I got the bug to play baseball, which was constant. Now that I'm older, I realize that without Jon I wouldn't have had that opportunity. I have a lot of gratitude for the hand I was dealt in life, growing up in a small town in Montana with a twin brother.

It was a good hand.

In the spring, summer, and into the fall, Jon and I would practice pitching/catching (with Dad coaching and later Andy Stolen as pitching coach), bat ground balls and fly balls to each other, throw batting practice, or sometimes just play catch with each other.

But that was practice.

The most fun we had was the competitive games we played against each other. We each made fictional line-ups—some hitters batted left, some right, some speedy, some power hitters—and would play nine-inning games. We made a ball made from Kleenex and wrapped freezer tape tight around it and used a cut pipe for a bat. These were our "hand-held devices." Our "field" was in our front yard, where a gravel street ran between our front yard and our neighbor (everyone was a neighbor in Peerless) Art and Virginia (Puckett) Machart's fence. If an occasional car or truck would pass by we would have to pause the game. For singles, doubles, triples, and home runs (the fence), we would place items out a certain distance. If the "ball" was hit past the markers, it would be a single, double, or triple. If the ball didn't reach the single marker, it was an out.

The game this picture captures (Mom of course took the picture) was actually at Prairie Dog Field at Nelson Reservoir, Saco, Montana, and was played well after our Blues careers (circa the late 1980s), but we still played the games whenever we could. As you can see, it was just a tad bit cold to swim in the lake that day, so we fired up a game with the back of the cabin as the backstop. Jon and I never left home without our "toys." In the picture, this is me pitching to "Jarvis"—Jon's fictional third-place hitter in his lineup who batted left and hit for both power and average and could also run. Now that I look back on it, Jarvis might have batted out of turn a lot, as he always seemed to come up in key situations with runners on base, and he always seemed to deliver. Jarvis was the toughest out I ever faced as a pitcher, and that includes Doug Frenzel and Mike Jones from Glendive, Alan Hopstad from Glasgow, Bill Neumiller and Mike Neubauer from Wolf Point, and Jeff Lebsock and Tim Thogerson from Sidney.

I watched a lot of good Legion baseball players compete against Scobey at Scobey Ball Park when I was a boy and played against a lot of good ones when I got older. At the end of my Legion career, I'd like to recognize some of those opposing players who I remember being something special on the ballfield, whether I was a spectator or a player.

Dave Fanning, Havre (1970-71): The best pitching duel I've ever seen on any level was Dave dueling with Terry Puckett at the State B Tournament in Scobey in 1971. Dave pitched a one-hitter and Havre won 1-0. Will never forget that game. Never even broke off to get a Legion burger. I watched both pitchers warm up before they pitched in each inning. After Havre won State B in Scobey that year, Dave went on to strikeout 25 Billings Royals in 12 innings at the State A.

Carmen Birdsbill, Wolf Point (1971-1973): I was lucky to get to see him play in the 1973 State B Tournament in Scobey. He was a tremendous all-around athlete—as many of those Wolf Point players were—who had a commanding presence on the field. Great pitcher, hitter, all of it. The Wolf Point team that year was powerful and took second only to Scobey in the State championship. Coming through the loser's bracket, Wolf Point forced a second championship game by beating Scobey on a bases-loaded triple by Dave Stengel in the top of the ninth inning, and Carmen Birdsbill slammed the door in the bottom of the ninth with three outs. Lee Cook remembers Carmen Birdsbill robbing him of a home run in center field in the eastern divisional tournament. Lee said, "Carmen could do it all; he could pitch, hit, run, everything."

Al Hopstad, Glasgow (1975-77): Great left-handed pitcher and power hitter. Until my fastball got stronger in Legion, I was not as effective pitching to left-handed hitters because my curve ball broke into them. Al was a tough out. He was also a good pitcher. Because I batted right-handed, his nasty sidearm curve broke into me so I could get the bat on the ball, but he gave left-handers fits with that pitch. Mike Hagfeldt recalls, "Hopstad owned me. I couldn't touch him. He made me look bad. He had that nasty side arm curve ball. I would just flail at it. That's when I decided to learn that pitch myself. The first time I threw it in a game was against him I believe. Struck him out with it, and he gave me a tip of his cap on the way back to the dugout. Always thought that was pretty classy of him."

Bill Neumiller, Wolf Point (1974-76): There was not a weak spot in the 1976 Wolf Point team's lineup, but Bill was a tough left-handed power hitter and would usually damage us. Hit a grand slam against us in the State B championship game in 1976 in Cut Bank.

Dennis Loendorf, Wolf Point, 1974-76: Threw aspirin tablets. The hard-throwing right-hander struck 17 Blues in a two-hitter against Scobey at State in Cut Bank 1976 in the undefeated game. The 1976 Blues team was a heavy-hitting team and I never saw a pitcher silence our bats more than Dennis did in that game.

Jerry Moran, Wolf Point, 1975-1977: Tough left-handed hitter and pitcher. Could hit for power and we always had trouble hitting him.

Mike Neubauer, Wolf Point, 1975-1978: Golden glove catcher, could hit for power and average. Owned me at the plate from the first game I faced him against Foodtown as a nine-year-old in Little League in 1970 through the time he hit a three-run triple off me in the State championship game in Cut Bank in 1976.

Joe Puckett pitching to left-hand-hitting Jarvis on Prairie Dog Field at Nelson Reservoir, Saco, Montana, in the late 1980s. Jarvis had lost a step or two at this stage but could still hit. *Photo by Faustine Puckett.*

Kip Harcharik, Wolf Point, 1976-1979: Fierce competitor and was always a tough out. One of those hitters that could lace a single on any pitch and had a good eye, so counts were always deep. Pitchers always had to labor to get him out.

Jeff Lebsock, Sidney (from Fairview), 1976-1978: Tremendous all-sport athlete who could do it all on the field: hit, pitch, field, throw, and run. Sidney players used to say, "Baseball, apple pie, hot dogs, and Lebbie."

Tim Thogerson, Sidney, 1977-1979: I saw him play for the first time in Babe Ruth All Stars in Glendive in 1974 where he batted leadoff. He was one of the fastest baserunners I ever saw and hit for a high average. When he got on first base it was a triple because he was going to steal second and third. Tim was like that kid in the baseball lyric of the 1978 Meat Loaf song, "Paradise by the Dashboard Light." I love the baseball part of that song, narrated by New York Yankees radio announcer Phil Rizzuto. When I hear that part of the song, Tim Thogerson is who I think of. That was Tim—that kid really made things happen.

OK, here we go, we got a real pressure cooker going here. Two down, nobody on, no score, bottom of the ninth. There's the windup and there it is, a line shot up the middle. Look at him go, this boy can really fly! He's rounding first and really turning it on now. He's not letting up at all, he's gonna try for second.

The ball is bobbled out in center. And here comes the throw, and what a throw. He's gonna slide in head-first. Here he comes—he's out. No, wait, safe, safe at second base! This kid really makes things happen out there. Batter steps up to the plate. Here's the pitch and he's going, and what a jump he's got. He's trying for third. Here's the throw—it's in the dirt, safe at third. Holy cow, stolen base!

He's taking a pretty big lead out there, almost daring them to try and pick him off. The pitcher glances over, winds up and it's bunted. Bunted down the third-base line. The suicide squeeze is on. Here he comes, squeeze play, it's gonna be close. Here's the throw, here's the play at the plate. Holy cow, I think he's gonna make it!

Doug Frenzel, Glendive, 1976-1978: The best all-around baseball player I played against in American Legion. The ace of the Glendive staff for three years, he had a tough, late-breaking curve ball and his fastball hopped. Hit for average and power and drove in a lot of runs. At State B in Cut Bank in 1978, he did this on one day: hit three home runs in two games, scored six runs, drove in eight, and collected six hits in nine at bats; hit a three-run home run against Sidney with two outs in the ninth inning in the first game to give Glendive a 6-5 come-from-behind win over Sidney and end Jeff Lebsock's career; was the winning pitcher in that game, going all nine innings and striking out nine Sidney batters; pitched three scoreless innings against us in the championship game but had to be removed due to the 12-inning rule; hit a two-run home run off Danelson in the seventh inning to seal a 6-3 win for Glendive against us to end our 31-game winning streak and force an extra game on Monday. Not a bad day's work, but that day epitomized his career.

Mike Jones, Glendive, 1976-78: Great catcher who called the signals for Doug Frenzel and who batted cleanup in their lineup behind Doug Frenzel. It takes great catchers to catch great pitchers and Mike fit that category. You couldn't really pitch around Doug with Mike behind him, as he was a tough out and could hit for power and drive in runs. Mike shared a great memory with me he had of Billings native Dave McNally, who pitched for the Baltimore Orioles. He remembers attending the 1970 American League Championship Series between the Twins and the Orioles. He said, "There were a lot of Hall of Fame players in that series. After one of the games my mom and dad took me to the parking lot to see if we could get Dave McNally's autograph. In those days the players rode in yellow school buses just like us. We located the Orioles team bus and nervously approached. Elrod Hendricks was sitting on our side with the window open. I said we were from Montana and asked if we could get McNally's autograph. He leaned over the aisle and repeated the request to Dave. Dave's answer was, 'Ask them where from in Montana.' After answering Glendive, I got an autographed baseball that I still have. I've always wondered what would have happened if we had said Billings, likely the only city anyone not from the area was familiar with."

I can think of no better way to end the story of my last year of Legion Baseball in 1979 than by sharing my childhood friend and teammate Ray Chapman's poignant letter, *My Reflections of the Scobey Blues*. Ray's letter is open, honest, and—despite some of its more somber themes—humorous. It is ironic that this thespian from Peerless who found a creative outlet with his acting career to exorcise some of his demons, might have been saved by his competitive and social outlet in sports. The letter, while addressed to me and speaking to me directly, is shared here in its entirety with Ray's permission and blessing. It is addressed to all of us.

The following are just a few of my thoughts on one of greatest experiences of my life: playing American Legion Baseball for the Scobey Blues. If you'll bear with me for a bit, the Blues story for me begins with your Dad and the Peerless Pirates Little League and Babe Ruth teams.

Playing the game of baseball (and basketball) was only part of the equation in the formation of all our young hearts and minds: the other, and more important, part was the guidance and attention all of us kids received from the adults throughout our journeys through Little League, Babe Ruth, and American Legion Baseball. I can't emphasize enough how important several different adults were to this father-less child during those important growing years, George "Tiny" Puckett being first among them. Only with the perspective of many years have I come to realize just how vital all these people were to me and my survival and ability to live a life out in the world.

I don't think I've kept a secret from you, Joe, regarding my deep, deep insecurities and unhappiness growing up. There were many externals of course that contributed to this, but I also think I was simply and fundamentally a deeply sensitive kid who, like all of us at one time or another, had been hurt by certain circumstances of life. I didn't know it at the time, but I was filled with suicidal ideation growing up and later, while in college, nearly took my own life.

I mention the childhood troubles I had because they put into great relief just how important and vital the baseball (and basketball) teams I played on growing up were; and, just as importantly, the vital role the adults heading up those teams played in my survival and my ability to thrive in adulthood. Tiny was the first. And, like all of the adults involved in this upbringing, Tiny had faults. They all did, as we all do, we're all human.

But the fact that he cared enough about his own children and, let's be honest, all of us kids who weren't his own but were treated as such, well, that says it all to me. He spent endless hours being coach, grounds crew, batting practice pitcher, chauffeur, hamburger buyer and cooker and, yes, occasional ass-chewer, and the perspective of the decades now tells me that that was love, freely given to all of us kids.

I have one particular memory of Tiny I must relate because it ties in with something I told you years ago which wasn't quite true. I said then that Tiny was great with us kids who weren't his own because, unlike with you and Jon, he never really got angry at us. Fortunately for us, he saved most of his ass-chewing for you two. But there was one time I now remember that he really let me have it. It's a memory that sticks, of course, because I don't ever remember his getting mad at me like that, before or after. I remember at practice one day, Tiny was hitting grounders to the infield and I let one go right between my legs and out into the outfield. Big mistake. Tiny yelled at me and spent the next few minutes drilling grounders at me that had a bit of spice on them. Scorcher after scorcher came my way and the only thing I could do was either glove them or, at the very least, knock them down with my chest. It was either that or face Tiny's wrath. I chose the former. I mention this episode because I'm not one who normally responds well to anger being directed at me like that. But, even at the time, I knew I could get through this test because I knew deep down, on some sort of fundamental, visceral, and unconscious level, that Tiny loved me and that I could do what he was asking of me. And I did it. And, years later, the skills that Tiny taught me stood me in extremely good stead during my Scobey Blues playing days.

Andy Stolen was another of the adults in the sporting arena who was so important to me growing up. He was, of course, Tiny's right-hand man for a long time, teaching and loving and driving and supporting all of us right along with Tiny through the years. He also brought along a couple of extremely talented sons to our Daniels County baseball party. My deep gratitude to Andy is a bit more specific and specialized than for all the other folks mentioned in this space: Andy taught me how to throw a real knuckleball, a pitch that on good days (NOT on those Tim Thogerson moonshot days) served me quite ably during my time on the mound for the Scobey Blues.

Growing up, I'd been a huge fan of Wilbur Wood, who at that time pitched for the Chicago White Sox. I found it amazing that he could make a baseball do such things on that 60' 6" journey to home plate: it fluttered and floated, it dropped, it went sideways and back again. I wanted to make a baseball do that. So I began throwing knuckleballs every time I threw the ball, always. I must have already thrown it thousands of times by the time Andy saw me attempting the pitch. Little did I know that Andy had made his name in the semi-pro and independent leagues years before as an incredible knuckleball pitcher. Good fortune was once again mine in our encounter. Our exchange went something like this:

"What are you doing there, Ray?"

"I'm throwing a knuckleball."

"With your knuckles?"

"Well, yeah, that's the name of the pitch, right?"

"You ever try throwing it with just your index and middle fingers, pushing the ball off with those two fingernails at once?"

"Uh . . . no."

"Try it."

Andy, a knuckleballer through and through, took the time to teach me his best and most difficult pitch. To a young boy who loved baseball and never had a father, could there possibly be a greater act of love and devotion?

Which brings me to the Scobey Blues American Legion Baseball team, a team full of love and devotion. I'd be remiss here,

Joe, if I didn't mention the absolute importance of your and Jon's friendship during this time of transition for me. You two had already played on Scobey's third Legion state championship the year before in 1976. You were already well-established and respected on the Legion team in 1977. I was brand new to the whole deal and, frankly, Scobey terrified me both as individuals and as a town. The girls were too damn pretty and the boys scared the living hell out of me just because. Honestly, Scobey was the big town in the county and, as a country kid who grew up in the 60s and 70s around here, it was a town of 1500 that to me felt like a metropolis of a million or so. All this is a long way of saying that I was terrified when I first came to play for the Blues in 1977. Rightly or wrongly, the one thing I felt I had going for me was I was friends with you and Jon. You two were already liked and respected in sports circles around the area, and rightly so. I could tell that Scobey folk in particular knew talent when they saw it and viewed you and Jon as winners, through and through. The fact I was friends with you guys eased my apprehension somewhat at this new thing I was facing.

Oddly, the person who intimidated me the most as we started the 1977 Legion baseball campaign was the man himself, Doc Norman. Doc never showed me anything but kindness and patience throughout my three years with the Blues but, as with so many adults growing up, he scared me. Kind of a common theme for me I know, this being afraid of other people, but it was what it was. Doc could be a bit gruff at times, but it seemed like he had to work at it. There was a very evident heart of gold that belied his attempts at sternness.

The reason I mention Doc intimidating me is that it highlights the importance to me of assistant coach Don Lekvold's presence on the Scobey Blues teams during our years 1977-1979. Don had coached a very good Wolf Point legion team in the years immediately preceding the Blues 1977-79 run and was an outstanding coach in his own right. He also made me laugh a lot which was enormously helpful for obvious reasons. It's hard to be scared and intimidated by others while you're laughing. And if you're more relaxed from laughing you're certainly going to play better baseball. Don did that for me. Of course, Don's real gift wasn't just being able to keep players like myself loose and ready to play, it was the fact that he combined that "find the fun" nature with a deadly serious competitive streak. "Fiercely competitive," there was no more apt phrase to describe Don Lekvold, and, judging by his kids and grandkids, I'd say that quality is highly genetic. His joy of the game and making it fun for us, combined with his "take-no-prisoners" attitude made Don one of the best possible coaches for us young men.

The other coach, of course, was Doc, and I don't think I can talk about Doc without talking about his dear Marge, which I believe is exactly how Doc would prefer it. Simply put, they were mother and father to all us boys. I have a feeling the amount of things they did for us that we know about is only exceeded by the amount of things they did for us that we don't know about. And many of these things have nothing or very little to do with baseball, and some of these moments are with me still. They may seem silly to some but they meant the world to me as a boy and I'm sure many others.

In 1979, shortly after we'd beaten the Helena Senators two games to one in games to advance to the Montana Class "A" Legion baseball tournament, we stopped to eat supper in Great Falls on the way home. I was thinking we'd stop at a drive-in for some burgers and fries; how very wrong I was. Doc directed our bus driver non-pareil, Dick Atwood, to one of the finer dining establishments in "The Electric City". Whereupon we were directed to order any dish on the menu that we desired, and that Doc and Marge were buying. Have I mentioned that it's one of the unwritten laws of physics that the words "free food" makes a teenage boy even hungrier? Since the first guy ordering wanted steak and lobster, naturally the rest of us were soon of the same mind and we had a massive supper planned including many, many, many orders of steak and lobster. For some of us, it was the first lobster we'd ever tasted. Granted, this was over 40 years ago and prices were a lot lower then but, still, a couple or 3-dozen orders of steak and lobster adds up to a pretty penny in any day and age. Doc and Marge paid the bill gladly and with hearts full of love. These are the kinds of acts a boy soon forgets but, many years later, a man remembers in his bones.

As I mentioned earlier, Dick Atwood was the man who drove the original Bluesmobile (not the one of Blues Brothers fame), our team bus. Dick, Doc, Marge, and Don all indulged us boys on the team bus by letting us play darn near any kind of music we wanted on the sound system. I think I remember Doc muttering a few times here and there about the loud music but, still, he let the music play. And it led to some incredible memories. In particular, I'm thinking of a time on the way home from a night game, it was dark, it was late, and for the most part, most of us were quiet or talking sotto voce. All was quiet save for the deep and soulful tones of Kirby Halvorson singing along in full voice to Supertramp's "Take the Long Way Home." There's nothing quite like hearing your big stalwart catcher sing along to Supertramp, a guy you were used to seeing behind the plate nailing would-be base stealers or, as a hitter, smashing the ball like it owed him money, a guy now transformed into a soulful crooner in the dark and quiet of the night. Money can buy a lot of things but it can't buy that. And we experienced things like that on the Scobey Blues because of who we all were and because people like Doc and Marge loved us and let us be the best parts of ourselves while helping us improve the parts that needed work.

I wrote earlier that I spent much of my childhood and early adulthood wanting to be out of the pain I was in and to have the courage to leave this earth, to kill myself. My close lifelong friend Matt helped keep me alive just by being who he was: quite simply, he was a friend to me when I most needed one. The same can be said of all the sports teams I've ever played on and especially, in light of your asking us to write about our experiences with this particular team, the Scobey Blues. It was the being part of something greater than myself, part of a group that helped me grow and laugh and cry and laugh a whole lot more and, most especially, the having of a helluva lot of fun and, perhaps most importantly, learning to win and lose with grace and humility that saved me. To be honest, I feel like we sometimes didn't succeed at that last one: teenage boys can sometimes be a bit too prideful in our accomplishments and too ashamed of our failures. Like many of us, we sometimes forgot what was most important about life in general and sports in particular: the people we meet and the friends we make along the way. There is nothing more important to me than the connections between all of us as human beings, and I know I sometimes forget that fact. And team sports, in this case the Scobey Blues of Doc and Marge Norman, were and are a constant exercise and reminder to me of the interconnectedness of us all. That when a group of people comes together, for instance a high school baseball team full of talented and, ultimately, good-hearted kids, led by some incredible and giving adults, then we can be a part of something that is greater than any one person, that is part of the very essence of the best of life. And to me that is a love which saves, that allows us to live to be what we were meant to be and to pass on those gifts and that love to others. And so the world goes.

Love, Ray

1979 Scobey Blues are presented with their 1979 trophies at the Legion Post No. 56. Trophies shown are for the State B Championship, Eastern Division Championship, State A Batting Championship (Joe Puckett), and State A Sportsmanship. Pictured are Greg Stolen, Doc Norman, Pat Audet, Jon Puckett, Randy Stolen, Jim Lekvold, Kirby Halvorson, Ron Higgins, Kelly Norman, Joe Puckett, Wade Tryan, Jesse Cook and Gord Tryan. Ray Chapman and Dan Danelson are not pictured; they had already left for college. *Leader photo, Burl Bowler.*

1980

Scobey Playing in a League of Their Own

> *The Scobey Blues swept four straight games to demonstrate by a wide margin it is clearly the most outstanding Class B American Legion Baseball team in Montana this year—as it has been for the fifth straight year in a row.*
>
> —Daniels County Leader, July 31, 1980

PRESEASON

When Doc assembled the 1980 version of his team on the field in April, plenty of familiar faces were gone, but there were plenty of new faces, too. Five multi-year starters—Dan Danelson, Wade Tryan, Ray Chapman, Joe, and Jon Puckett—were no longer with the team. Objectively, those were some big cleats to fill, as Scobey's top three pitchers and infielders, speedy center fielder, and defensive first baseman—who also had a no-hitter and state championship save to his credit as a pitcher—were gone. Dan, Wade, Joe, and Jon had played on four consecutive state championships (1976-79) and Ray on three (1977-79). The biggest hole to fill would be in the pitching, as in 34 postseason games between 1977-79, Dan Danelson, Joe and Jon Puckett had pitched in 32 of them and were the winning pitcher in all but five of those games.

Although Scobey lost five starters, four came back, as Kelly Norman, Kirby Halvorson, and Randy Stolen returned to play in their last season. Kelly and Kirby had been playing since 1976, and Randy had been playing since 1977. Dan Danelson, an assistant coach in 1980, said of this trio, "It was men amongst boys with the core group, the best players on the field. Kelly, Kirby, and Randy just dominated." The other returning starter from 1979 was 14-year-old Greg Stolen, who oddly seemed a seasoned veteran in his second year. These four players formed the team's core and would become the top four pitchers.

Kelly was the only one who had pitched consistently, as the depth of the staff in the previous years didn't require Randy, Kirby, and Greg to pitch much. However, for the 1980 team to be successful, these three would need to step up as pitchers, and they did. Randy and Kirby had powerful arms and needed some reps on the mound to gain confidence and control and develop a breaking ball. Randy always said, "I could pitch, but I wasn't a pitcher." But in 1980, Randy—and Kirby—became good Legion pitchers, as did Greg Stolen. Kirby described Randy's pitching in 1980: "I would have liked to transport 1980 Stoley to 1979 to pitch. He was much more mature and confident, less wild, and his curve was damn near unhittable." Randy and Kirby often overpowered hitters in 1980, resulting in high strikeout counts in games.

Five talented players were returning from the previous season—Ron Higgins (17), Pat Audet (15), Jim Lekvold (15), Jesse Cook (18), and Gord Tryan (16)—and they would step up to fill the other gaps. Those five players all saw action during the 1979 regular season and against Circle in the blowout game at the state tournament. Doc, when asked by Cliff Hagfeldt on KCGM radio about these players, said, "They look pretty good. Don't forget, next year they'll be a year stronger and bigger." Doc specifically called out Jimmy Lekvold at second base, who had turned three double plays in 1979, one unassisted. Doc's dominant 1980 team would prove that his program—the Scobey Blues—was bigger than any individual player or team.

Pat Audet could also pitch, and he would see plenty of mound action in 1980 as well. A talented all-around athlete from Opheim, Andy Eliason (17), joined the team and was also a pitcher, giving Doc six pitchers for a solid staff. Andy, a first cousin of Randy and Greg—nicknamed "Lil' Andy" by the family—was also a strong position player in the infield, started some games, and became a key player for the Blues that season. Finally, Mike Tryan (Gord's younger brother), Steve Schaefer, Jeff Mann, and Tony Vigliotti joined the team as rookies, and would figure prominently in Scobey's future.

Doc and Don Lekvold experimented with several different lineups—referred to by the *Leader* as "blooding the feather merchants, trying out various combinations, and generally striving to find the best combination"[231]—during the regular season. Kelly started the season at short but, like Dana Audet in his second year, struggled a bit at that position and asked Doc to move him to his seasoned position at second, with Greg Stolen moving to short. Kelly would still play short when Greg pitched. Kelly also moved behind the plate to catch in 1980. He returned to his usual position in the lineup of hitting second. By the time the eastern divisional tournament came around, Doc and Don had settled on the following lineup:

- Pat Audet, CF/C/P
- Kelly Norman, 2B/SS/C/P
- Kirby Halvorson, C/1B/P
- Randy Stolen, LF/CF/P
- Greg Stolen, SS/P
- Jim Lekvold, 2B/LF
- Gord Tryan, 3B
- Jesse Cook, 1B (sometimes Andy Eliason, P/3B)
- Ron Higgins, RF

In addition to the missing players, some familiar faces, such as batgirls and batboys, were also gone. Jacki Tade and DeeAnn Lekvold, who had been batgirls from 1977-79, had left, replaced by Allison Marlenee and Michelle Audet. Mike Roland and Rick Lee, who had been batboys for several years, had moved on, and Mike Lee emerged as chief batboy for the 1980 Blues. Assistant Coach Don Lekvold returned for his fourth season, and Dan Danelson, back for the summer from his freshman year at Lewis-Clark State, helped the team as an assistant coach.

One notable thing when looking at the 1980 Scobey roster was that for the first time in 15 years—since Dick Puckett started playing for Scobey in 1965—there was not a player from Peerless on it. There had also been a Puckett on the roster every year except 1975 during that same period. The first all-county team was formed in 1968 when Randy Legare and Jack Higgins joined the team from Flaxville.

REGULAR SEASON

SCOBEY'S DOMINANCE BEGAN IN ITS SEASON-OPENING 13-4 win over Glasgow in May and never let up through the season. Kelly Norman and Randy Stolen combined for a one-hitter, striking out 15 Reds. Kelly struck out six hitters in three innings and yielded only one hit, walking five.

Randy Stolen pitched six innings of no-hit ball, striking out nine and walking four. This game showed how Randy was a similar pitcher to Kelly: he would walk hitters but yielded few hits—in this case, none—and was a very effective pitcher.

Here are some other highlights of the 1980 Scobey Blues conference and regular season:

- In the second end of a doubleheader (games scheduled for seven innings) against the Miles City Colts in Scobey, five Scobey pitchers—Kirby Halvorson, Ron Higgins, Grant Hughes, Gord Tryan, and Jeff Mann—pitched a combined no-hitter in five innings in the 18-3 win. Kirby Halvorson started and struck out four in two hitless innings, then was relieved by the four other pitchers, who also did not allow a hit. Gord Tryan and Ron Higgins were self-deprecating when I asked them if they recalled the no-hitter. Gord said, "I assume I allowed the three runs." Ron said, "While my main pitching role was as a 'live' batting practice guy, I did pitch a time or two in the 1980 season and then a number of times in the 1981 season. Doc would call pitches for me—relied upon a quasi-knuckleball and a sidearm 'changeup' to contrast against my over-the-top 'fastball.' Let's just say that my defense always needed to be in ready position anytime I took the mound." Andy Eliason pitched a one-hitter in the first game, also shortened to five innings, with Scobey winning 11-1.
- In the first inning of the first game of a doubleheader against the Colts at Denton Field in Miles City, Kirby Halvorson and Randy Stolen hit back-to-back home runs for the third time in their career. They had previously done it against Williston and Kalispell in 1979.
- In the fifth inning of the game, the Blues turned a rare triple play. With runners at first and second, Kirby Halvorson started the triple play by snaring a line drive at first base, stepping on first for the second out, and then throwing to Andy Eliason for the third out at second. Fifteen-year-old Pat Audet got the win on the mound, and the Blues won the game 12-5.
- In the second game of the doubleheader in Miles City, 14-year-old Greg Stolen pitched a one-hit shutout—the first shutout of his career and first for Scobey that season—in a 10-0 win, striking out 17 Colts. Older brother Randy hit his seventh home run of the year and added a triple to provide the only offensive punch Greg would need.
- Randy Stolen homered and had a pair of singles off losing pitcher Terry Baldry to lead Scobey to an 18-8 win over the Yellowjackets in Wolf Point. Greg Stolen got the win for the Blues.
- Boosted by doubles from Pat Audet and Jesse Cook, Scobey overtook the Richland County Patriots with 15

runs in the final five innings as the Blues won 18-14 at Moose Memorial Park in Sidney. Sidney scored all 14 runs in the first four innings, including eight in the fourth. This game could be the largest comeback win in Scobey American Legion Baseball history, as the Blues were trailing 14-3 after four innings but then exploded for 15 runs in the final five innings—including seven runs in the eighth—to complete the comeback. Randy Stolen got the win, pitching five scoreless innings of relief. The Blues trailed Wolf Point 11-3 in the seventh inning in the 1976 state championship game, which might be the second biggest comeback win, but certainly the first in importance!

- In a 13-3 win over Plentywood, three Scobey pitchers—Pat Audet, Andy Eliason, and Kirby Halvorson—struck out 16 hitters and pitched a combined four-hitter, with all four hits coming from Doug Selvig from Outlook. It could be said it was a four-hitter against Selvig and a no-hitter against Plentywood. Scobey had 15 hits, including a home run by Randy Stolen.
- Kirby Halvorson struck out 14 Reds in a 14-3 win over Glasgow.
- Pat Audet hit a two-run double in the 12th inning to beat Wolf Point 7-5. Audet's double scored Gord Tryan and Andy Eliason, who had singled. Randy Stolen got the win in four and two-thirds innings of relief, striking out 12. James O'Tremba pitched all 12 innings for Wolf Point.
- Kelly Norman hit a walk-off single up the middle to score Jesse Cook in the bottom of the ninth inning to beat Plentywood 12-11 in Scobey.
- Randy Stolen struck out 18 Yellowjackets and combined with his teammates to bang out 20 hits in a 16-2 win over Wolf Point.
- Greg Stolen and Kirby Halvorson combined to strike out 20 Blue Devils in a 16-10 win over Glendive.
- Scobey's only conference loss—and only loss to a Class B team—was to Glasgow, 11-7, at a doubleheader in Glasgow. Four starters were missing for the game, including Kelly Norman. Kelly said, "Glasgow was crazy. I forgot my cleats, and things weren't going well. I had no traction at all on the dirt, hitting or on the grass, changed positions, and went to left field, whined, and bitched. Dad then benched me, and I sat on the yellow bus for a game in half. It was hot. Bad dream! I used to have dreams occasionally about forgetting cleats or hoop shoes and not being able to play." Except this one wasn't a dream, huh Kelly? Scobey avenged their sole loss of the season to Glasgow by beating them in Scobey a week later by an identical 11-7 score.
- In the final game of the regular season at Scobey Ball Park, Kelly Norman and Randy Stolen homered in their last at-bats in a six-run seventh inning to lead Scobey to a 14-4 romp over Glendive. Kirby went the distance on the mound, pitching a six-hitter to get the win, and Kelly caught him. It's funny how Kirby had always caught Kelly since Little League, but the battery was flipped in their final home game at Scobey. How's that for a storybook ending for Randy, Kelly, and Kirby in their final home game at Scobey Ball Park? Homering in their final at-bats of their careers at home. It's tough to top that. The only way would have been if Kirb had homered, too. Back-to-back—to back. Jeez, Kirb, way to blow it. Jesse Cook also finished fine in his last game, going 2-for-4.

Kirby Halvorson, Jesse Cook, Kelly Norman, and Randy Stolen went out with a bang their last home game in Scobey. *Family photo.*

Scobey blazed through the conference with a 15-1 record, losing only to Glasgow 11-7 and finishing the regular season with a 25-4 record. Their three other losses were to the Class AA Williston Keybirds, one in Scobey and two in Williston. The Blues would enter the eastern divisional tournament—and the state tournament—as prohibitive favorites.

DIVISIONAL TOURNAMENT

THE 1980 EASTERN DIVISIONAL TOURNAMENT WAS PLAYED at Circle. Scobey's first game was against the fourth seed from the southeastern district, the Miles City Colts, whom Scobey had handled easily in all four of their meetings. This game would prove no different, as Scobey demolished the Colts 12-1 in seven innings. Greg Stolen pitched five shutout innings, and Andy Eliason pitched two innings of relief in a combined four-hitter. Randy Stolen doubled, and Kelly Norman tripled to lead Scobey's hitting.

The tournament had to be moved to Moose Memorial Park in Sidney after the first day due to heavy rain, making the Circle field unplayable. In Scobey's second game against Glendive, Randy Stolen struck out an incredible 21 out of 24 Blue Devils to lead Scobey to an 11-2 win, putting Scobey in the championship game against Circle.

Scobey easily won the championship game over Circle 17-3 in seven innings. Kelly Norman started and had a no-hitter through four innings but got in trouble in the fifth, yielding three hits and two runs. Kirby and Kelly switched places as pitcher and catcher, and Kirby pitched two and two-thirds innings of scoreless relief—striking out 5 of 7 hitters—to get the win. In the fifth inning, Kirby Halvorson hit a towering two-run home run, and Randy Stolen followed with a shot that nearly resulted in back-to-back home runs for the power-hitting duo again; however, Randy's shot hit the top rail of the fence, bounced high, and landed back in the outfield, so he had to settle for his second triple of the game, to go along with a double. Kirby also had a double in the game. That's 14 total bases between them in five at-bats, by the way.

Randy Stolen was selected as the MVP of the tournament. "Randy Stolen demonstrated in the tourney, as he has most of the season, that he is the outstanding American Legion Baseball player in eastern Montana this season, hitting, fielding, and pitching."[232] Kirby Halvorson also had a great tournament. "Seldom has there been an athlete who has had the power, energy, and versatility as Kirby Halvorson. He plays any position."[233] The three veterans—Randy, Kirby, and Kelly—led a team with a lot of younger players on it to another eastern divisional championship for Scobey.

Scobey completely dominated the tournament, outscoring their opponents 40-6 in three games, with two wins shortened to seven innings. The *Leader* wrote, "Doc Norman's boys are doing it again. After winning the state title last year and, in the process, also losing several key players, it was thought the 1980 season would have a much-weakened team. It hasn't happened that way. This 'weak' team in regular season and divisional play has carried off the wins by a wider margin of victory than ever before."[234]

Greg Stolen won the first game, Randy the second, and Kirby the third, with Kelly Norman pitching four innings of no-hit ball. As the Blues freight train barreled down the tracks, nothing seemingly could stop the momentum of a fifth consecutive state Class B championship. "The Scobey Blues easily won the tourney and again travel the well-worn path to State Class B American Legion Baseball competition in Cut Bank."[235] Now 28-4 headed into the state tournament, with only one loss to a Class B team, the supremacy of Scobey Blues baseball in Class B American Legion was unquestioned. The dynasty had never been more powerful.

STATE B TOURNAMENT

THIS WAS THE THIRD TIME IN SIX YEARS THAT CUT BANK HOSTed the state tournament, as they had hosted in 1976 and 1978, where Scobey won both tournaments. In the preview to the tournament, the Cut Bank *Pioneer Press* wrote, "Scobey, the defending state champion for the last four years, is the favorite going into the tourney."[236] That was an understatement.

The Laurel Dodgers, who Scobey beat for the state championship the previous year, had lost some good players from that team but dominated the western division in 1980 with an 11-1 conference record and were 19-7 heading into the western divisional tournament in Deer Lodge. However, they were upset by Fairfield in their first game and then were eliminated by the Great Falls Vigilantes in their second game, so they did not make the state tournament. They might have been Scobey's best competition. The first day's matchups were as follows:

- Circle (2E) vs. Butte Muckers (3W)
- Missoula Reds (1W) vs. Glasgow Reds (4E)
- Fairfield (2W) vs. Glendive (3E)
- Scobey (1E) vs. Cut Bank (4W)

Doc started 14-year-old Greg Stolen in the first game against host Cut Bank, and Greg and Scobey were rude to their host. Scobey jumped out to a 9-0 lead after three innings and scored six more in the fifth to make it 15-0. Greg lost his shutout in the fifth, as Cut Bank scored two runs to make it 15-2. Andy Eliason pitched a scoreless sixth but got in trouble in the seventh when Doc brought in Kirby Halvorson to preserve the 10-run rule, as the final score was 17-7 in seven innings. Kirby Halvorson went 3-for-5—including a double—and Randy Stolen was 4-for-4 to lead the 16-hit barrage for the Blues. Gord Tryan also had a double for Scobey. Greg Stolen was the winning pitcher, yielding two runs in five innings to get the win.

Scobey faced Glendive in their second game, and Doc handed the ball to Kirby Halvorson to pitch. It was another blowout, as Scobey led 9-0 after two innings. Then, in the fifth, Scobey scored another run to make it 10-0, at which point the game was called due to darkness. Kirby Halvorson pitched a two-hitter and struck out 11 Blue Devils in five innings to get the win. Randy and Greg Stolen each had a double for Scobey's extra-base hits. Scobey played well defensively, making only one error.

This put Scobey in the undefeated semifinal against the western division champion, Missoula Reds, the B team for the Missoula Mavericks. The Reds had made it this far by pounding Glasgow 11-1 in eight innings in their first game, then won 9-8 in 13 innings over the Butte Muckers. The Reds were 21-5 on the season entering this game, with three losses coming to Laurel. Doc handed the ball to ace Randy Stolen, and he was again dominant, matching Kirby's previous game by pitching another two-hitter and striking out 17 Reds to lead Scobey to the 7-2 win. However, this was a close game and the only actual test for Scobey in the tournament. The young boys from Missoula County—although Scobey had players younger, like starters Greg Stolen (14), Pat Audet (15), and Jim Lekvold (15)—showed why they were the best team in the west, staying on the field with the powerful Scobey team the entire game. In the *Missoulian*, Missoula coach George Weier said, "We played a really good game. We just played a heck of a good club."[237] The *Leader* wrote that this game was Scobey's "sternest test of the tournament."[238] Leading 5-0 in the eighth, Randy lost his shutout when Brian Fortmann—who had both hits for the Reds—drove in two runs with a single to make it 5-2. But Stoley got out of the jam, leaving the bases loaded, and Scobey scored two runs in the top of the ninth to make it 7-2. Stoley then held Missoula in the bottom half to preserve the 7-2 win, vaulting Scobey to its fifth consecutive state championship game.

The Missoula Reds then had to win *another* extra-inning game—this time 5-4 in 12 innings over the Fairfield Blue Hawks—to make it to the championship game. This made two extra-inning games for the Reds in the tournament—a 13-inning affair against the Muckers and now a 12-inning affair against the Athletics—which did not bode well for the Reds' young pitching arms, playing their fifth game against Scobey for the championship and back-to-back after the 12-inning game against Fairfield.

What a moment for Doc Norman, Don Lekvold, and the three veterans—Kelly Norman, Kirby Halvorson, and Randy Stolen—as they prepared to take the field for the state championship game against the Missoula Reds. There were so many baseball memories on this Cut Bank field. Four years earlier, Scobey and Wolf Point had squared off in two epic championship games, with Scobey coming from behind in both games to win 6-5 and 13-11 to win the championship. Don Lekvold was coaching Wolf Point then, but joined Doc as assistant coach in 1977. In the 1976 state championship game against Wolf Point, Kirby Halvorson started as a catcher at 14 because Jeff Richardson started that game as a pitcher. Kelly Norman got the win as a 14-year-old pitcher, getting three outs in the seventh inning before Scobey erupted for 10 runs in the bottom half to take the lead 13-11. Two years later, in 1978, Doc again handed the ball to Kelly—then 16 years old—in the state championship game against Glendive, and Kelly pitched six and two-thirds innings of three-hit ball to get his second win in the state championship game, striking out 10, as Scobey beat Glendive 8-6, with Randy Stolen catching a shallow fly ball in left field for the final out of the game. Two years later, in 1980, Doc again handed the ball to his 18-year-old son to pitch in his third and final state championship game in Cut Bank, with Kirby catching him. This classic battery had been on baseball diamonds in northeastern Montana since the two boys were in Little League. In 1976, Jeff Richardson caught Kelly; in 1978, it was Allan Audet, so this was the first time Kirby caught Kelly in a state championship game. The stage was set for a storybook ending in the 1980 State Class B championship in Cut Bank. Could Kelly deliver again in a big game and get his third win?

The answer was yes. He went the distance, had a one-hitter through seven, and had given up only one run. He finished with a four-hitter, yielding a hit in the eighth and two more runs on two hits and two walks in the ninth. Kelly was "in his best form all season."[239] Meanwhile, Scobey's bats boomed, banging out 20 hits on the Reds and plating 18 runs. The Reds committed eight errors, which did not help. Scobey jumped out to a 3-0 lead in the bottom of the first. Missoula got a lone run in the third to make it 3-1, but Scobey broke the game open in the fifth with another big 10-run inning in a state championship game—the third time that had happened. Scobey's 10 runs came on seven hits, two walks, and a couple of Missoula errors, but the big blow in the fifth came off the bat of Randy Stolen in the form of a three-run home run. The Blues exited the inning with a commanding 13-1 lead and never looked back.

Then, leading 14-1 in the bottom of the eighth, the ultimate symbol of Scobey's dominance in Class B American Legion Baseball in 1980 occurred. Kirby Halvorson came to the plate in his final at-bat in a State B Tournament. A right-handed hitter, he switched to batting left-handed. How did this come about? Kirby recalls, "I joked with Dano I could hit it out lefty." Kirby had a single earlier in the tournament, batting left in the blowout win over Glendive when he got disgusted that the pitcher was "throwing junk at less than batting practice," so he went to the other box. And earlier that year, he hit one in Scobey over the right field fence against Miles City that hooked a foot foul. Kirby said, "So I knew I had the pop from that side."

Kirby recalls the at-bat: "I missed the first offering by a foot! Then, I connected on the next one over the right field wall. Then I remember a big smile down to the third-base coach, a certain Mr. Dano. He refused to shake my hand."

Dano recalls, "The way I remember it, Kirby told me he was going to jack it. He might have been joking, but amazingly, he did. It was disbelief! I thought, *I'm going to be hearing about this for the rest of my life*. I thought I gave him the old fake handshake."

Kirby's left-handed home run added to Scobey's already insurmountable lead, and it came "in a manner of great style."[240] Great style, indeed, and it punctuated the dominance, as Scobey scored four runs in the inning and entered the ninth leading 18-1 when Missoula scored two runs to make the final score 18-3 Scobey. Dano was more specific about the form of the punctuation, saying Kirby's home run was "quite the way to put an exclamation point on things." The *Leader* recognized the 18-year-olds who had played their final Class B games as Blues going out in great style too: "For four of the boys, Randy Stolen, Kirby Halvorson, Kelly Norman, and Jesse Cook, playing their last game in Class B baseball meant ending up in great style."[241]

Many readers might construe Kirby batting left-handed in the state championship game as bad sportsmanship, but I think the result of the at-bat negates that, and he didn't "jazz it up" in the box. He wasn't taunting the opposition or showing them up. It was an inside affair between him and Dano, not between him and the Missoula Reds. However, the radio announcer in Cut Bank *did* think it was bad sportsmanship. Kirby recalls, "My sister was listening to the game on KCGM. It was a Cut Bank announcer. She said the announcer indicated that I was making a mockery out of the game. She then said he was pretty much speechless after I jacked it."

Scobey's 20-hit barrage was led by Randy Stolen and Kirby Halvorson, who each went 3-for-6 with a home run (not back-to-back this time), with Kirby adding a double to his home run. Greg Stolen also doubled. Pat Audet had four hits in his leadoff position, and Kelly Norman, in addition to pitching the four-hitter, had three hits. It was Kelly's third game as the winning pitcher in a state championship game—all three in Cut Bank—as he got the win in 1976 over Wolf Point, in 1978 over Glendive, and now in 1980 over the Reds.

When the Bluesmobile pulled out of Cut Bank early that evening, it was leaving behind a legacy of baseball greatness in its rearview mirror as the sun set in the western Montana sky behind it. Three state tournaments and three state championships in Cut Bank. This was the third and final time Cut Bank hosted the state tournament. A shift was coming in western Montana Class B baseball, with more teams and different state tournament hosts. Deer Lodge hosted the western divisional for the first time in 1980 and would host the state tournament in 1982.

Havre would rejoin Class B baseball in 1981. Teams from Alberta would also join the fray. This was a sign of things to come, as Class B American Legion Baseball would grow in western Montana and Canada in the early 1980s.

The 18-3 final over Missoula was Scobey's largest margin of victory in a state championship game. A year earlier, at the state tournament in Scobey, following Scobey's 11-0 win over Laurel for the state championship, Rod Tande, speaking of Scobey's dominance after sweeping the tournament in four games, said on KCGM radio that "there was Scobey and seven other teams in the tournament." Rod would likely have said the same thing if he were in Cut Bank in 1980. After winning their fifth consecutive state championship and seventh overall, the Blues were playing in a league of their own.

TOURNAMENT SUMMARY

An MVP and an all-tournament team were selected for the first time in the State B Tournament. Randy Stolen, who won the battle title with a .555 average (10 for 18) and had 17 strikeouts in the 7-2 win over the Reds, was selected

1980 Scobey Blues, State B Champions. Standing, left to right: Coach Doc Norman, Greg Stolen, Pat Audet, Kirby Halvorson, Jesse Cook, Kelly Norman, Randy Stolen, Assistant Coach Don Lekvold. Kneeling, left to right: Tony Vigliotti, Jim Lekvold, Andy Eliason, Ron Higgins, Mike Tryan, Steve Schaefer, Gord Tryan. Sitting, left to right: Allison Marlenee, Mike Lee, Michelle Audet. Not pictured is Jeff Mann. *Leader photo.*

MVP. Randy, brother Greg, and Kirby Halvorson, who hit .474, were also chosen for the all-tournament team. Other members were Hugh Maxwell and Jim Stolte of Fairfield, Kevin Miller of Glasgow, Jeff Hickethier and Bruce Madsen of Missoula, and Pat Kissel of Butte.

But the entire Blues team was the story of the tournament. The Blues outhit, outpitched, outran, outfielded, outcoached, outbatgirled, outbatboyed, outbusdrivered, outdrank (Dano was there)—outeverythinged—their opponents, outscoring them 52-12 for an average margin of victory of 10 runs per game in sweeping the four games. In its tourney preview, the Cut Bank *Pioneer Press* predicted that Scobey would win it, and then, in the tournament summary wrote, "Things went pretty much as predicted. The Scobey Blues won the Class B Legion state championship for the fifth consecutive year."[242] Ho hum, Blues win again. I could have just started—and ended—with that.

However, beyond the Blues' dominance, the tournament was a rollercoaster of dramatic moments and games, a testament to the unpredictability of Class B baseball in Montana. In what could be a State B Legion tournament record, there were five one-run walk-off wins, two of them in extra innings:

- On the tournament's opening day, Glendive delivered a stunning walk-off win against the Fairfield Blue Hawks. With two outs in the bottom of the ninth, Steve Poleski for the Blue Devils blasted a double, then scored the game-winning run on an error, sealing a 5-4 victory.
- In the Circle-Glasgow elimination game, Glasgow was down 6-5 in the bottom of the ninth but scored two runs to pull out a 7-6 win to eliminate Circle.
- In the Muckers-Reds 13-inning game, the score was an 8-8 slugfest after six innings, then the two teams played seven innings of scoreless baseball before Missoula scored a run in the bottom of the 13th to walk it off 9-8.
- In the Athletics-Muckers elimination game, the Muckers scored four runs in the top of the ninth inning to take an 8-4 lead, only to see the Athletics score five runs—all with two outs—in the bottom half to walk off with a 9-8 win. It was the tournament's second consecutive 9-8 walk-off loss for the Muckers.
- In the 12-inning game between Fairfield and Missoula, the Reds scored a run to walk it off 5-4 in the bottom of the 12th for its second extra-inning walk-off win in the tournament. Hugh Maxwell for Fairfield pitched 11 innings of four-hit ball but lost his eligibility in the 12th inning. Maxwell also hit .500 for the tournament, 10 for 20. Bruce Madsen from Missoula pitched all 12 innings for the Reds to get the win. The walk-off game was Fairfield's third of the tournament, winning one and losing two.

Gotta love State Class B American Legion Baseball in Montana—predictably unpredictable.

TOURNAMENT STATS

Hitting: Scobey banged out 54 hits and scored 52 runs in four games for an average of over 13 hits and 13 runs per game, but two of the games were shorted to seven innings and five innings, so it could have been a lot worse. Randy Stolen led the Blues hit parade—and the tournament—with an average of .555, including a home run and a double. Kirby Halvorson hit .474 and had a triple and a double, along with his opposite-hand home run. There were four other extra-base hits: Greg Stolen had two doubles, as did third baseman Gord Tryan. Pat Audet had a great game in the finale, going 4-for-6 at the plate.

Pitching: Scobey's pitching was dominant, with finesse pitchers Greg Stolen and Kelly Norman getting two wins, while Randy Stolen and Kirby Halvorson overpowered hitters in their two-hitter wins. Greg Stolen went five innings and allowed only two runs in the opener; Kelly Norman pitched a four-hitter and gave up three runs in the nine-inning final. He had a one-hitter through seven, then gave up a hit in the eighth and two hits, two runs, and two walks in the ninth. Kirby struck out 11 hitters in five innings in his two-hit shutout against Glendive.

Randy Stolen struck out 17 in his two-hitter against the Reds. Kirby and Randy struck out 28 hitters in 14 innings pitched, an average of two strikeouts an inning. That's Dave Fanning–like numbers. That's ridiculous.

Fielding: With their dominant pitching and hitting, Scobey's fielding did not need to be outstanding to win, but it was plenty good enough. Scobey committed three errors against Cut Bank, only one against Glendive, but four and five in their two games against the Reds, for a total of 13 in four games, an average of 3.25 per game. But the Blues' opponents committed a whopping 23 errors in four games, for an average of 5.75 errors per game. So, Scobey decidedly out fielded their opponents, which is a good yardstick by which to measure fielding—the opposition had almost twice as many errors.

STATE A PLAYOFFS

Scobey was headed to a best-of-three series for the fifth consecutive year to play their way into the State A

Tournament. Scobey had split the previous four series, winning two and losing two. Their two wins came against Libby in 1976 and the Helena Senators in 1979; the two losses were to the Helena Senators in 1977 and the Great Falls Chargers in 1978. The 1969 team lost in a one-game playoff to the Electrics a day after the State B Tournament, and the 1973 team automatically qualified for the State A Tournament, as there was no playoff that year.

Scobey's opponent in the 1980 best-of-three series was the Great Falls Electrics, who finished fourth in the west with a 29-19 record. The Blues were entering the series with an amazing 32-4 record. The games would be played at Optimist Field—rather than Legion Park—as the Great Falls Giants were playing a weekend series against Butte there. The Electrics did not relish playing Scobey to get into the tournament. Phil Smith wrote in the *Great Falls Tribune*, "The Electrics must face a Scobey team that blitzed the opposition in last weekend's State Class B Tourney at Cut Bank."[243]

Doc, as he always did, touted his powerful Blues team prior to the series. Phil Smith wrote, "Doc Norman says this team is as good as or better than last year's outfit. 'We hit the ball harder and farther than last year,' he said. 'And I think we've got a little better pitching depth.'"[244] Phil Smith's tournament preview also looked at some of Scobey's players: "The Blues best player may be Randy Stolen, who will be the starting pitcher and also is the team's cleanup hitter. He's hitting .486 and has seven home runs. But he's only one of seven regulars over .300. Kirby Halvorson, whom Norman considers the best catcher in the state, is hitting .458 and also has seven homers." Other starters hitting over .300 were Kelly Norman (.400), Pat Audet (.394), Greg Stolen (.390), Gord Tryan (.304), and Jim Lekvold (.300). In the article, Doc, describing his 1980 team, was characteristically confident: "We hit the ball farther and harder than last year. And I think we've got a little better pitching depth."[245]

Defensively, Doc had to shuffle the defense as regular first baseman Jesse Cook could not make the playoffs. Gord Tryan moved to left field, and Andy Eliason played third base.

The two games played at Optimist Field on Saturday, August 2, 1980, would result in two heart-breaking, gut-wrenching ninth-inning losses for the Blues, a horrific ending for the three 18-year-olds—Randy Stolen, Kelly Norman, and Kirby Halvorson—playing their last games for the Scobey Blues. The storybook ending for Scobey in the Class B Tournament in Cut Bank a week earlier, waltzing through the tournament with ease, would prove to be the opposite at Optimist Field in Great Falls, as the Electrics rallied for two runs in the bottom of the ninth to walk-off the opener 5-4, then scored five in the top of the ninth to come from behind again and take a 12-9 decision in the second game. Without question, these were two of the most brutal losses in postseason history for Scobey. I've said it before: baseball can be cruel.

So how did it happen?

Scobey was the visiting team in the first game, and things started auspiciously—or so it seemed—in the top of the first, when Kirby Halvorson scored Scobey's first run, staking Scobey to an early 1-0 lead. However, the run proved costly as Kirby partially dislocated his knee running the bases. Scobey sustained a devastating injury early in game one for the second consecutive year in the postseason playoffs. The year before, it was Dan Danelson pitching in the fifth; now, it was Kirby Halvorson running the bases in the first. Kirby recalls the injury: "I was on second base, and Stoley singled, and I was rounding third hauling ass because I thought it was going to be close, and that's when I subluxed my knee, hitting an uneven spot. I kept going and made it safely, literally limping across the plate. You want irony? There was no throw." Kirby did try to catch in the bottom half of the inning and gutted it out behind the plate for as long as he could, but Kelly Norman had to come in from short to catch early in the game. Kirby moved first, and Greg Stolen moved short.

Jim Lekvold waits to tag out Dan Rausch after Rausch got caught in a rundown in the first game of the best-of-three series. Scobey shortstop Greg Stolen backs up the play. *Tribune photo, Randy Vance.*

Randy Stolen pitched brilliantly in the first game, keeping the Electrics hitters off balance the entire game, mixing his lively fastball with his over-the-top curveball—the *Tribune* referred to it as an "effective change-of-pace pitch"[246]—striking out 14 Electrics. He was dueling Rusty Strickland, who was keeping the heavy-hitting Scobey nine at bay as well. Both teams were playing well defensively, as each team only committed one error in the game, and no runs were unearned. Through four innings, the score was level at 1-1, then Scobey scored two runs in the top of the sixth to take a 3-1 lead.

But Great Falls tied the game on a fluke play in the bottom of the fifth on a "two-run homer to the fence in left."[247] How do you hit a home run *to* the fence in left? Shouldn't it be *over* the fence? There was a special ground rule at Optimist Field. The *Leader* described the home run as a "peculiar episode," explaining that "an Electric got a sharp hit to the left that got stuck in the fence. The ball under the fence under a special ground rule would have been limited to a double if left fielder Gordy Tryan had not tried to dig the ball out, but being as he did try to do so and after great difficulty, the runner was allowed an inside-the-park home run."[248]

Gord Tryan recalls the play: "It was my fault. It wasn't the nice field in Great Falls. We were playing on another field [Optimist], and the outfield fence was chain-link. The bottom of the fence was curled up. It was my first and only time as an outfielder. The umps in the pre-game said to raise your hands if the ball hit stuck under the fence. So, I raised my hands to signal that it was stuck under the fence. What I didn't know was that you were supposed to leave it there for an ump to come out and see it. So, I dug it out of the fence. Which was a no-no, and the batter was awarded an inside-the-park home run. Still, get an icky feeling whenever I relive it in my mind." Then he added, "As stupid as I felt that day, there wasn't one person on the team that blamed me or put me down. Doc, being Doc, protected me from it all. But that is what it meant to be on the Blues."

Big right fielder Chuck Mayers, who had hit the two-run inside-the-park homer, then doubled home the go-ahead run in the bottom of the eighth to give Great Falls a 4-3 lead entering the top of the ninth.

It looked grim for Scobey in the top half as Strickland retired the first two hitters, but the fight was not over. Strickland walked the bases loaded as Pat Audet, Kelly Norman, and Kirby Halvorson drew two-out walks. That brought Randy Stolen to the plate. Who else but Randy would Scobey want in the batter's box in this situation? Randy came through with a big two-run single just past the outstretched glove of second baseman Pete Tucker, and Scobey had regained the lead at 5-4 entering the bottom of the ninth. Three more outs and game one was Scobey's.

But then, the first bad ending. Dirk Sandefur opened the ninth with a triple to right, then John Wilkinson singled up the middle to tie the game 5-5. After Dan Rausch forced out Wilkinson at second, Rausch stole second, putting the winning run in scoring position with one out. Stoley struck out shortstop Pete Tollefson for the second out, but pinch-hitter Mike Fought hit a two-out single to left, driving Rausch home with the winning run, standing-up to walk it off 6-5 for the Electrics.

It was a brutal ending to a tough game, but Scobey had to come back strong to get game two. Doc started Kirby on the mound, although Kirby had been injured and playing hurt since the top of the first inning of the first game. Kirby again gutted it out on the mound for as long as he could, and Kelly caught game two as well.

Scobey did come back strong in game two, jumping on the Electrics left-handed starting pitcher Mike Fought— who had pitched a two-hitter against the Havre Northstars a week earlier—for five runs in the bottom of the first to lead 5-0. Kelly Norman and Jim Lekvold had RBI triples, and Greg Stolen had a two-run single to right. Scobey then added a run in the second to go back ahead five runs, 6-1, and through five complete innings, Scobey had its third five-run lead at 7-2.

Pitching in the second game, Kirby said, "I ignored the pain on my landing leg. Also, my medial elbow (same as Dano) had been sore since the two-hitter I threw against Glendive." But playing in and through pain, Kirby was turning in a gutsy performance for Scobey. Through seven complete innings, he had yielded only three runs and struck out eight Electrics, and Scobey led 7-3. But after injuring himself early in the first game, catching some, and then pitching seven strong innings in the second game, Kirby was tired coming back out to pitch the eighth. Kirby said, "I felt I had no more to give." But he came back out to pitch anyway. Charles Gardner, the *Tribune* sportswriter, saw how tired Kirby was. He wrote, "The Blues' Halvorson quickly began to tire."[249] The Electrics started the inning with three consecutive singles, scoring a run and chasing Kirby. Doc brought in Randy Stolen to try to squelch the rally. But Bob Scott singled to drive in two more runs, then the tying run scored from third on a double play grounder—Scobey's second double play.

But as in the first game, Scobey battled back to regain the lead. Leadoff hitter Pat Audet, who went 4-for-5 in the game and scored three runs, led off the bottom of the eighth with a double down the left-field line. Kelly Norman drove Pat home with the go-ahead run on a clutch single to right and later scored on a single to left by Greg Stolen. Scobey again entered the ninth with a lead, this time 9-7.

But this was not Scobey's day in the ninth. Randy Stolen, who was now pitching his 11th inning of the hot summer day, was tiring too. The Electrics opened the ninth with three walks, a hit batsman, and a bunt single, and just like that, the score was tied 9-9. Doc then brought 14-year-old Greg Stolen in with the bases loaded and nobody out to put the fire out.

Bring in a 14-year-old in a tie game with the bases loaded in the ninth inning against the Great Falls Electrics?

This is the point in the story where we must pause and recognize the young players on this team and Doc's method. Bringing a 14-year-old in this situation in a "normal" conversation would be insane. But Doc's method was not "normal," and we have become desensitized. This is partly because of how talented Greg was. He was selected to the State Class B all-tournament team at *14 years old*. That's incredible. But playing younger players—the best players—to win games had always been Doc's method while also developing them to gain confidence and play at a higher level as they matured. Doc's method started on his first team in 1959 when fourteen-year-olds Bill Thompson and Rod Tande—among other 14-year-olds—started. Phil Audet started on the 1963 team at shortstop and became a strong pitcher on the staff as a 14-year-old a year later, eventually leading Scobey to its first state tournament appearance in 1967. In 1965, Dick Puckett, Rocky Ware, and Craig Audet all started playing as 14-year-olds, later becoming state champions in 1969, along with Randy Legare and Jack Higgins, who had started playing as 14-year-olds on Flaxville's Legion teams. Terry Puckett and Rick Danelson started playing for Doc as 13-year-olds in 1968. Doc pitched Terry Puckett against Havre as a 13-year-old in the 1968 state tournament in Glendive, then started Terry Puckett at Cobb Field against the Billings Royals as a 14-year-old in 1969, where Terry pitched into the eighth inning and allowed only two earned runs. A week later, Terry pitched seven shutout innings against the defending champion Havre Northstars at the 1969 state tournament in Scobey. Fourteen-year-old Rick Danelson was the starting third baseman for the 1969 state championship team. Fifteen-year-old Dana Audet started at shortstop as a 15-year-old on the 1971 team and later played for the 1973 state championship team. Fifteen-year-old Greg Fjeld was the starting second baseman on the 1973 state championship team and later played for the 1976 state championship team. On the field against Wolf Point in the state championship game in 1976 were four 15-year-olds and two 14-year-olds. The list goes on.

The point of the pause is that we must remember how young these players were and how well they were competing against Class A competition. In the top of the ninth, 15-year-old Pat Audet had doubled for this fourth hit and scored the go-ahead run, his third run; Greg then singled for his third hit, driving in Kelly for his third run. Jim Lekvold had tripled to drive in a run, scored in the first, and was part of two double plays at second. Starter Gord Tryan, seemingly "old" by comparison at 16, was also young, had two hits, and drove in a run. These four players would all later play on Doc's 1982 state championship team. Such was Doc's method.

I asked two of the "Baby Blues," Pat Audet and Jim Lekvold, to comment on their experience playing as 15-year-olds in 1980. Pat said, "One thing I would definitively pay forward is the 1979 season laid the groundwork of winning ways to carry on to 1980. My experience as a rookie in 1979 gave me many observations of what it takes to win in attitude, discipline, and fundamentals of playing the game. You play to win . . . as much as many of us dicked around in our summer-mode lives around the diamond and even sometimes during practices . . . when it was game time, the focus was on we all meant business. I think every one of us playing for Doc developed a high IQ of how to play the game, play our positions, and, mainly, how to win. I'd add that watching the vets in 1979 added to each of those factors. For me, and I think Jim would agree, that 1979 team and how far the Blues had gone that season was the solid basis of the 1980 team, and we youngsters continuing the flow of winning due to learning and knowing how to win."

Jim Lekvold added, "Ditto on what Pat said. We were able to play quite a bit in 1979 because the veterans would get big enough leads, so we were able to see a lot of playing time. That really helped to get our feet wet. Just like Doc said in that conversation with Cliff and Rod on KCGM radio, we would be a year older and stronger going into 1980. We believed in winning, and when it came crunch time, we stepped it up. I think growing up in Scobey and Daniels County it was kinda bred into us. Baseball was the thing. Doc really had a lot of faith and confidence in us younger players and he gave us the opportunity to show what we were capable of doing. He didn't seem to 'bat' an eye when it came time to put us out there. There was probably a lot of criticism, but it definitely was constructive criticism. The veterans would also take the time to work with us. I remember Kelly showing me a ton of things at second. So, for me going into 1980, I really felt comfortable stepping in."

But now, back to the game, and the 14-year-old trying to put the fire out. Unfortunately, there was no storybook ending—for the young or the old—that day at Optimist Field for the Blues. There was no joy in Scobey. The Electrics scored the go-ahead run on a wild pitch. Greg got the next two outs, and it appeared like he might escape without further damage, but Mike Fought again delivered a clutch two-out single to drive in two insurance runs. Greg got the third out on a strikeout, but not before Electrics had plated five runs—all charged to Randy—and took a 12-9 lead entering the bottom of the ninth. The Blues needed three runs to tie the game, but Fought retired the side in order, and Scobey's amazing 32-6 season was over. The headline in the *Great Falls Tribune* the following day summed it up: "Scobey blue as Electrics rally twice for victories."[250]

The loss of two leads in the ninth inning that day at Optimist Field was a bitter pill to swallow for all the Blues, but it was especially hard for 18-year-olds Kelly Norman, Randy Stolen, and Kirby Halvorson. Kelly reflected on the losses, saying, "It's just one of those things for a few games that I've played and coached that just eat at you. Because we had a chance, but we didn't get it done. And unfortunately, those thoughts don't really go away. It's just that it would have been so badass to get there [State A Tournament] one more time." Kirby added, "It's depressing to think about. Now I know how Joe, Jon, and Dano felt finishing up 1979. I didn't have my best stuff that day. I think both my velo and control were affected by the left knee issue." It was also an emotional day for Doc and Marge, as their son Kelly had played his last game as a Blue.

But the two tough ninth-inning losses in Great Falls that day did not define Kelly's, Kirby's, and Randy's careers. It was a much broader body of work than that. Kirby and Kelly had played on five consecutive state Class B championship teams—1976-1980—the only two players in Scobey American Legion Baseball history to do that. Randy Stolen had played on four, as he did not begin playing Legion baseball until 1977. When I asked the talented trio what they remembered most about their Legion careers, it wasn't the series in Great Falls. Kirby said succinctly, "That's easy. Building friendships that have lasted a lifetime." Kelly expounded on what Kirby said: "Playing with my best friends who are still my best friends and brothers is at the top, and that starts from Little League, Babe Ruth till the end. Even with the tough losses to the Electrics, it was a big success; five in a row with Kirby and Dad kinda speaks for itself." Randy added, "Those days and our group of guys were so amazing. I still carry all the success because of those days and the team we had. It shaped me and put me on the path I live out. I believe it helped shape all of us! What a fantastic start to life! The fact that Tiny and Faustine [Puckett] invited me to be a Pirate and all the success I started with—was the only reason I was able to follow Joe, Jon, and Ray to move on to the Blues! Love it—always will!

I will die a Scobey Blue!! Means more to me than anything I have done athletically!"

Let's let the *Leader* tie a bow on the fabulous 1980 season for the Blues: "For Doc Norman, who has coached American Legion Baseball for the past 21 years in Scobey, the addition of another state title adds luster to his legendary figure in Montana American Legion Baseball. His two hip operations the past year, the last one during the start of this season, he considered only minor obstacles to getting the club into championship shape; aided in a less visible but no less effective manner by his capable adjutant and chief errand runner, wife Marge, assistant coaches Don Lekvold and Dan Danelson, those steady people at the concession stand in the home park, and the baseball committee headed by Cliff Hanson, plus many other enthusiastic supporters."[251]

Looking to the future, as bluesy a day it was for the Blues in Great Falls, the sun would rise the next day in the east in the blue sky over Scobey, and it would rise on a dynasty that now claimed five consecutive state Class B championships and seven overall. It would also rise on another promising season for Scobey, where state championship aspirations had become the norm. No less than six starters on the field that day in Great Falls—Ron Higgins, Pat Audet, Greg Stolen, Jim Lekvold, Gord Tryan, Andy Eliason—were returning for Scobey the following year, and four of those starters would be back the year after that. Certainly, Doc, Don, and the boys were not done yet. Could the Blues make it six straight in 1981? Who could stop the streaking Blues machine? What new faces would join the team?

EXTRA INNINGS

This picture of Allison Marlenee and Michelle Audet was taken at the doubleheader at Denton Field in Miles City. I love how the photo captures the intensity of their faces and shows how focused they are on the game. In this image, Photographer Jim Anderson of the *Miles City Star* preserved their contribution to the team. In his caption, he wrote, "Much of Scobey's success on the diamond in recent years has been the result of Coach Doc Norman's use of game statistics. Kept accurately, they tell the percentages he wants to know about each Blue player. From the left are Allison Marlenee and Michelle Audet who do an excellent job of scoring the game."[252] I think it's wonderful that this picture captures Allison's and Michelle's contributions and represents DeeAnn Lekvold's and Jacki Tade's contributions before them from 1977-79. What a unique and special part of the Scobey baseball tradition it was. I don't think most of the boys on the team could be captured on film with this amount of focus on the game. Allison and Michelle obviously took their jobs very seriously, and the program was stronger for it. Wolf Point's Mike Neubauer offered a different perspective on the batgirls' contribution to the Blues' success, saying, "They were definitely beautiful 'distractions' to the opponent."

During her years as batgirl, Allison Marlenee said, "Ah, these were the good old days for sure! Michelle and I were batgirls from 1980-83, I believe. Doc's names for us were Alli and Shellie. I know for a fact we sure felt special, and what a job to have! It was so much fun. One thing is that Doc made sure we were respected by the boys and probably expected us to be respectable as well. Or maybe he just didn't give a s***! What an honor—thanks for that, guys!"

It was ironic that Randy, the son of Andy Stolen—a crafty left-handed pitcher who was a two-time all-district pitcher who led the Opheim Legion team to the District 4 Legion championship in 1949, then pitched for the championship Scobey Plainsmen teams of the late 1950s and early 1960s—did not develop as a pitcher earlier in his career. When Andy brought Randy to Peerless to play for Dad when Randy was nine years old in 1971, Dad already had three pitchers—Joe, Jon, and Ray—and that's a pretty good staff in Little League. Andy became the pitching coach for Peerless when he came, but Randy was not one of the pitchers. Andy taught Jon and me how to throw our curveballs and Ray how to throw his knuckleball. When Brad Pratt joined the rotation in 1973, that was four pitchers, pushing Randy lower down the pitching food chain in Little League and later Babe Ruth.

Kirby was on a similar track in Scobey, although his limited pitching before 1980 had more to do with his being the stalwart catcher who could catch anyone who tried to pitch rather than a slew of pitchers in front of him in Scobey. Kirby had the catcher's gear on at a young age, and that followed him. However, he did pitch a little in Babe Ruth because I remember him striking me out on a nasty curveball when he was 13 years old.

Although Randy and Kirby emerged as Scobey's top two pitchers in 1980, I will always remember Randy as the gold-glove left fielder who could hit for both power and average, could run, and had a cannon for an arm. And when I think of Kirby, I will always remember him as a gold-glove, power-hitting catcher with a rifle arm to second base. Despite Kirby's two-hit, 11-strikeout shutout against Glendive in the state tournament, his pitching legacy—at least with his cronies—will always be surrendering a moonshot home run to Dorn Steele home run in Poplar in 1977. He will never live that one down.

After beating Circle 13-8 in a regular season game in July—Greg Stolen was the winning pitcher and had a double and a triple to lead Scobey's hitting—Kelly, Randy, and Kirby drove to Mandan, North Dakota, for a Cincinnati Reds tryout camp. Mike Hagfeldt (Blues 1974-76) was also at the tryout. The Blues at the tryout were not impressed by the level of talent of the rest of the players there. Mike said, "I had one at-bat against a kid that would have been a mediocre Babe Ruth pitcher. I was waiting for a decent pitch to hit and never got one. I was just expecting better." Kirby agreed: "I hit against some kid from Bismarck who was supposed to be a stud. He had a slider he kept hanging by my chin, and the ump called them strikes. So, I had no choice but to swing. I hit one pretty hard to short but right to him. Defensively, I had the strongest arm by far. They wanted 1.90–1.95 pop to pop at second. I threw 1.98–2.10, but every pitch was way inside, so it took longer to transfer. I asked the guy running it if I could try it again with a pitcher who could find the strike zone, and he said, 'No.'" No Blue was picked up by the Reds that day, but the Blues there did carry on the proud tradition of Scobey Legion players mooning cars, which had started with Dick Puckett and Craig Audet in the 1960s. Kirby's principal memory of the camp? "I remember we mooned some family on the interstate."

From left are Allison Marlenee and Michelle Audet who are intently keeping stats and scoring the game for the Blues against the Miles City Colts at historic Denton Field in Miles City. *Miles City Star photo, Jim Anderson.*

Steve Schaefer, son of Larry Schaefer, was a rookie in 1980 and was the grandnephew of Bob Schaefer, who pitched on Scobey's first American Legion team in 1930, leading them to the district championship in their first year and a playoff against Billings. It was rumored that Bob Schaefer could pitch with either hand. Pat Audet was also Bob Schaefer's grandnephew, as he and Steve were first cousins. Pat's mom, Patti, was the first of five kids of Howard and Berniece Schaefer.

You can see Doc's crutches next to him in the team photo. He had two hip operations within a year of the start of the season, the second one coming right at the beginning of this season. But Doc considered the two operations "only minor obstacles to getting the club into championship shape."[253]

Randy Stolen was overpowering in the postseason. He had 21 strikeouts against Glendive at the eastern divisional, 17 against the Missoula Reds at State, and 14 against the Electrics in the playoffs—52 strikeouts in 26 innings pitched, an average of two per inning. That's just stupid. That's Dave Fanning–like strikeout counts without the precision control.

Pat Audet caught the last three innings of the state championship game, and Kirby moved to play in the field, talking Doc into letting him play shortstop for an inning. Pat had caught several games during the season.

Speaking of Pat Audet catching, Jesse Cook played first base that year, following in his older brother Lee's footsteps to play at that position. Both Lee and Jesse were excellent defensive first baseman. It was a law in Daniels County that if you were an Audet, you must be a catcher, and if you were a Cook, you must play first base. Craig, Dana, Allan, and Pat Audet all caught, and Lee and Jesse were first baseman.

In the first inning of an eight-in-the-morning game against the Colts at the eastern divisional in Circle, Kelly, playing shortstop, almost committed an "error" that would have led to several "runs" that would have been difficult for him to overcome the rest of the game. Kelly recalls, "I actually called timeout in the middle of the game and ran off the field to the restroom. I had diarrhea and had to go. Then I went back out. They stopped the whole game. All I know is I barely made it."

Commenting on hitting his home run left-handed, Kirby said, "I'm right-eye dominant and didn't learn until about 1993 that I had tracking issues in my left eye. So, I actually saw the ball better hitting left." Ironically, Randy Stolen, who batted left in Legion, was originally a switch-hitter but switched to all left for the same reason. Randy said, "Yes, originally, I was a switch hitter—just not a good one. My lazy eye (left) made it virtually impossible to see the ball batting right. Dad realized that in my young years and flipped me over to the left side, which was brilliant on his part. Funny how that makes a difference in trying to swing at an object coming at you when you can actually see it! But I did switch-hit when I found it hard to stay in the box against a good left-handed pitcher, like Al Hopstad from Glasgow." Rick Danelson was also originally a switch-hitter but moved to bat all-left later in his career. Jeff Jones, who played for the Blues from 1985 to 1988, was a true switch-hitter who hit from both sides of the plate, including home runs.

The "towering home run"[254] Kirby hit in the divisional championship game against Circle had the Sidney locals saying it was the farthest they'd ever seen hit out of Moose Memorial Park. It was hit in the power alley to left-center (356 feet) and was still rising as it passed about two-thirds up the light tower. It went over the houses, and the current Sidney mayor found the ball on the opposite side of the street. Del Nesper—Jay and Jeff's dad—said he had never seen a ball go over the house before or since. Fred Barkley was the home plate umpire. He saw Kirby in the hospital one day a few years ago and asked him if NASA was still tracking that ball. The furthest ball I saw Kirby hit was when Kirby and Randy hit back-to-back home runs at Williston in 1979. The Williston paper called it a "Harmon Killebrew" home run.

Randy Stolen and Kirby Halvorson each hit seven home runs in their final season. Kirby hit one more home run in Glasgow earlier that season toward his favored left-center alley, but it was ruled a ground rule double. But Kirby said, "It went out by quite a ways." Glasgow had a chain-link fence, and the ball was seen to bounce on the other side of it clearly. However, the left fielder put his hands up and sold it to the umps as a ground rule double. Kirby was later told the ball was way gone by 30-plus feet.

Kirby finished his Legion career with 14 home runs, and Randy had 15. I asked each of them to provide their favorite home run. Kirb said, "Probably the epic shot in Sidney in divisional, with Kalispell (because it got us jump-started) and the lefty one (because it was cool!) ones a close second. Randy said, "The home run I hit in the 1977 state tourney against Sidney is my favorite, and listening to the audio recording of that was amazing! I think I have probably eight or nine of the signed balls still . . . unfortunately, the ink has faded." Terry Puckett told me that after hitting as many home runs as he did, Doc stopped him from getting any more signed balls.

I never had the experience of being in the Blues dugout after I played my last year of Legion ball, so I asked Dano about his experience as an assistant coach. He said, "It was a blast coaching because I could talk to the team as I always had since we were youngsters. Nothing changed except I wasn't playing." Kirby said, "We loved having Dano around. He always kept it real, too, even though we had a lot of fun, and that always helped. I think having him there also helped the younger kids."

A scout from the San Francisco Giants attended the Blues-Electrics playoff series to watch Kirby catch; however, Kirby was injured in the top of the first inning, so he didn't get to see what Kirby could do behind the plate. Kelly had to come in to catch early in the first game, and then Kirby pitched the second game.

The talented trio of Kelly Norman, Kirby Halvorson, and Randy Stolen played college baseball. Kelly played his freshman year at Southern Oregon University, then transferred to Colorado State, where he made the team as a catcher, red-shirted, then played one year there, joining his old Blues teammate Randy Stolen on the field with the Rams. The irony of Kelly making the CSU team as a catcher was

Kelly Norman and Kirby Halvorson as Little Leaguers wearing Scobey Legion uniforms, 1972 or 1973. *Family photo.*

Kirby's injury in the state A playoffs against the Electrics helped him develop as a catcher, and he was able to make the team at that position rather than an infielder. And at the end of their Legion careers, in their final game, Kelly caught Kirby.

Kirby played for three years at Pacific Lutheran University (PLU), where he injured his knee during a drill his freshman year. It was the same partial dislocation of the knee that happened at Great Falls, and it had happened to him 10 or so times in high school. He had his second surgery on the

Kelly Norman catching for the Colorado State University Rams during the 1983 season. *Family photo.*

Kelly Norman practicing his swing as a little boy in Scobey. *Family photo.*

Randy Stolen batting for CNCC in 1980. That is Doug Frenzel in the foreground. Mike Neubauer was also Randy's teammate at Colorado. *Family photo.*

Randy Stolen played at Colorado College Community in 1980 and 1981. *Family photo.*

knee a month later, so he was done his freshman year. In his sophomore year, he played some varsity and some JV, and he played some varsity his junior year, mainly DH. The injury bug bit him again in his junior year when he injured his shoulder and had surgery after the school year. He gave up college baseball after that.

Randy had an August birthday and graduated from high school in 1979. Like Bill Thompson, Dick Puckett, Craig Audet, and other Scobey Blues players who had that birthday, Randy played college ball in the spring and then Legion ball later in the summer. His collegiate career started in January 1980 because he almost lost two fingers in a farm incident with a grain auger in the 1980 harvest and needed time to heal. Mike Neubauer from Wolf Point and Doug Frenzel from Glendive—who Stoley had played against in Legion—were playing at Colorado Northwestern Community College (CNCC) in Rangely, Colorado, and convinced him to walk on in the spring of 1980. He played at CNCC for two years and had good success. He was all-conference and almost won the conference batting title. Because of his success at CNCC, he got a scholarship to play for the Rams at Colorado State University in Fort Collins, where he played for two years, playing with Kelly for one season. His junior year at CSU in 1982, he was the Rams' second leading hitter with a .398 average and led the team in home runs (nine) and on base percentage (.692), and made only three errors in the outfield. The CSU baseball program wrote that Randy "has the potential to be drafted." He played against some tough teams—including BYU, Air Force, Wyoming, and Utah—in the former Western Athletic Conference (WAC). He was nominated for WAC Player of the Week in the same week as Wally Joyner and Cory Snyder of Brigham Young, who both had very successful careers in Major League Baseball.

Randy actually came in to pitch against Wally Joyner and Cory Snyder at a conference game against BYU in Provo, Utah. Stoley shared a funny story about that game he pitched, and Kelly was the catcher. The story's context was that Randy never saw himself as a pitcher; he was very self-deprecating. He said, "I am a retired outfielder and a hitter. Pitching really wasn't my thing. I only pitched my last year in Legion. I was wilder than a March hare—I was effective, though, at times. Now my brother Greg, he was a pitcher!"

Facing Wally Joyner and Cory Snyder from BYU, Stoley said, "I hadn't pitched for years, and it definitely showed." Here is Stoley's funny story:

"Kelly came to Fort Collins and made the team as a catcher. We were in Provo, Utah, playing BYU in a doubleheader. We lost the first game—they were unbeatable. Loaded with guys like Cory Snyder and Wally Joyner—both ended up playing in the majors. Anyway, it was the second game, and I was as ornery as ever in center field, complaining that our pitchers couldn't throw a strike! Coach Ran Railey told me to clam up in the dugout. I told him I could throw strikes . . . put me in coach!! He ignored me for a couple of innings, and then in the middle of the second game, we were in the field, and the pitcher (Valdez, I believe) walked two runners on. Railey came to the mound and waved me from center field. I couldn't believe it—I didn't move. He waived me again and said, "Stolen, get your ass in here"! I trotted to the mound with a smile, looked at Kelly Clyde Norman, whose eyes were as big as watermelons, and said, "Let's show them some Bluesball Kelly!" Kelly shook his head and said, "Just play catch, Stoley. You don't have to throw as hard as you can. Throw to the mitt!" I looked at him and said, "Get back to the plate—I got this." Yeah, sure I did. I was shaking in my cleats! I looked to the first hitter, and it was Cory Snyder, and on deck behind him was Wally Joyner. I hadn't even thrown a warm-up yet, and I was sweating the eye-black down my face, and my uniform was drenched in dirt from the head-first slides from earlier in the game. Anyway... back to the first warm-up throw: Kelly beat his glove, I took my stretch to honestly just throw a medium fastball... looked over at Cory and Wally watching to see what I was going to do... and at the top of my wind-up, I decided, here it comes—everything I got! The ball left my hand at a fiery pace and headed straight for the plate... only hitting the front edge of the plate and going straight up into Kelly's neck! *Oh shit*, I thought, *I just killed my roommate and lifelong Blues Buddy!* Kelly dropped like someone had shot him! Both trainers came out from both teams. Kelly rolled and tossed on the ground as the BYU fans *booed* me. All I could do was pace around Kelly and tell him to get up... let's go. After 10 to 15 minutes, Kelly got up. Fans applauded him—I just wanted to redeem myself and get back to work. I know... kind of a jerk, right? I think so too! Anyway, we are ready now for the second warmup pitch. Kelly is at the mound with me, tears rolling down his face. He tosses me the ball and says to me, "Come on Stoley! Just play catch, don't overdo it, and try to throw too hard." I agreed. So I went back into my stretch, and at the top of my stretch, I happened to glance over at a smiling Cory Snyder and Wally Joyner in the on-deck circle... and I bore down again and let what I thought was most definitely a 100-mph fastball that was going to scare everyone on the BYU team. I let go... and as God is my witness—and I know Kelly will admit the same—the pitch I threw went *exactly* 59 feet, hitting the front edge of the plate, and came straight up *again* and hit my poor old Scobey Blue Buddie in the *exact* same place in the throat!! OMG... this time, Kelly went down even harder and rolled all over the place. I thought the crowd was going to climb the fence and charge the mound and kill me!! I think Kelly was down for another 15-20 minutes. Worst experience of my life, but even more important was how I almost killed my Buddie! Kelly—I know I have apologized many times after that event—just know I meant it!!"

I asked Randy how he had done after the rough warm-up. "It wasn't pretty—I think I ended up walking Cory, and if memory serves me, Wally hit a bomb over left center. I don't think I lasted much longer than an inning. Ended up going back into center field with a bit of humble pie!"

Kelly's response to Randy's story: "Wow! Stoley was wilder than me. And he threw harder... dangerous!" Terry Baldry from Wolf Point, joking about Randy's wildness said, "Randy Stolen was one of the hardest throwing pitchers I faced. I think I had 16 plate appearances against him and was 0-for-1."

Although it is dangerous to compare players across eras, it is safe to posit that Randy Stolen must be considered one of the best all-around players to don a Scobey Legion uniform. But Randy would be very embarrassed by this discussion because he only saw himself as a role player, just one cog in the Blues machine. He said, "I was a role player in the middle of the Pucketts, Danelson, Tryan, Audets. I was only in awe of being a part of that dynasty!"

Nevertheless, Randy, we're going to embarrass you. Mike Hagfeldt said, "I loved playing with Randy on the Plainsmen teams. I recall playing a Canadian team. They had a runner try to score on a hit into the gap in left center. Randy was playing left. The runner thought he would easily score. Randy unleashed a rocket and threw the guy out by 10 feet. It was pretty funny actually. After he was tagged out (didn't even slide) the guy turned around and looked to see who just threw that ball. Later in the game there was a similar play. The Canadian runner rounded third, got about 15 feet down the line and obviously thinking about Randy's throw earlier in the game, hit the skids and hustled back to third. I just laughed. Playing with Randy was an honor and a great pleasure. I'd have to say he was one of the top three players I ever played with or against at any level."

Jon Puckett added, "Saying that Randy 'had a cannon' is hugely understated. The defense he played in the outfield would have earned him many gold gloves if there was such an award in Legion. He used to track down balls with his speed, then effortlessly glide to them, nonchalantly one-handing them for the out. I remember he tracked one down in 1977 against Cut Bank; I pitched that game. Cut Bank kid hit one deep into the left field corner late in a 1-1 game. Their third base coach was yelling for it to get out. My heart sank. It was a night game, and our outfield lights weren't so good. I didn't even see him catch it. But I did see him get to the corner. Then he turned and started jogging back in with that familiar, confident trot, ball in glove. I was so relieved. We all played multiple sports. I always felt like I might have been a basketball player playing baseball. Randy was a baseball player playing baseball. We went on to win that game 2-1 in 10 innings. Great memory of Randy from me."

Danny Wolfe—who saw them all—said Jack Higgins and Randy Stolen were the two best all-around Scobey American Legion players he ever saw play. Danny said, "Well, in my mind, the two best, at least the two best outfielders and maybe the two best players all-around that I watched play baseball were Randy Stolen and Jack Higgins. They were the cream of the crop for me. I watched Randy play, and of course, I played with Jack. Jack was one fine athlete; he was a baseball player, pure and simple. They both hit for power. They both hit for average. They both ran the outfield like nothing. It was just effortless, and they had speed, power, and good arms. That was my personal opinion of it. Those two stuck out my mind as far as all-around players." Baseball refers to this category of all-around player today as a "five-tool" player—speed, arm strength, fielding ability, hit for average, and hit for power. These are the five skills Danny mentioned. In my interviews and chats with former players, Jay Hagfeldt's name has also been mentioned several times in this five-tool player category.

Although Jon described Randy as "a baseball player playing baseball," Randy's favorite sport in high school was basketball. Randy said, "I loved all sports growing up. My favorite in high school was basketball, but it was a sport that did not come easy to me. I had to work so hard at it. I was lucky to have had Coach Loren Baker—such a great influence on my life in high school. Baseball was what I was best at, though—it came to me so naturally."

Randy, looking back on his baseball career, said, "One of the best decisions ever was when Dad, knowing Opheim would never have a chance at doing anything with any baseball seekers, moved me over to Peerless to play with the Pirates . . . guys like you and Jon, Ross, Ray, Billy, Bernie, Joel, and Willard . . . and of course, Tiny and Faustine! It was the start of my baseball life for certain as we moved on to Babe Ruth, then the experiences of a lifetime with the Scobey Blues!"

My brother Jon's fledgling slow-pitch softball career began in the summer of 1980. There was no Plainsmen team, so he played softball. When I returned home from summer school in August 1980, I heard Pat Anderson, one of his softball teammates, call him "Whiff" in a bar. I wondered what that was all about, but never asked Jon anything.

Forty-five years later, while writing this book, I asked Jon Puckett about the nickname "Whiff." It turns out he has been haunted by a bad slow-pitch softball memory for almost 50 years. To this day, he is not a big fan of the game. At my coaxing, Jon has been courageous enough to share the "Epic Story of Whiff":

It all started at the Four Buttes Bar the night before I was to play in a slow-pitch softball tournament in Wolf Point. I had a great time drinking and catching up with some old friends, but the problem was that I stayed up until the wee hours of the morning and headed to Wolf Point without sleep.

Early in the tournament, I was feeling especially good about myself. I thought I could make it through the day playing this hit-and-giggle game, get a good sleep, and regroup the next day. We were doing okay in the tourney, maybe a couple of wins. Ron Scott was playing second base, and I got some kudos from him.

I'm guessing it was around mid-July—the big tournament in Wolf Point with tons of teams. I remember in the first game, I was playing shortstop and caught a sharp liner shoelace, then quickly pivoted to first to double off some unsuspecting dweeb who probably never played a game of baseball in his life. It was a great play. Cliff Hagfeldt was pitching and told me, "You can stay out all night every night if you can make plays like that."

But we got into a close game with a good team. I think we were down one run, last inning. Bases loaded, two out.

Then came the at-bat. I strode to the plate.

Earlier in our at-bat, I remember Dano lacing a double to left center off the wall. I remember it because gobs of spit came from his mouth when he swung, and his calves flexed.

We were in a big rally. On the first pitch, the pitcher (a good slow-pitch pitcher) lobbed a sky-high pitch that landed just behind the plate. I took it for strike one. Ron Scott was in the on-deck circle, rekindling the fire in me of what it meant to be a Peerless Panther. "Come on, you ol' Peerless Panther, rip it, and let's get out of here."

I feared and respected Ron Scott as a teacher and a coach.

The pitcher gave me a decent pitch, and I pulled it hard foul down the left field line. Now it was 0-2, fucking hell.

I stepped out to gather myself.

Let's do this. Stand in. The pitcher threw it sky-high, just like the first pitch. I thought, "I can't get called out looking in fucking slow-pitch." That would be game over. Legacy tainted. Four-time Blues champion disgraced.

But I was indecisive. The ball was almost as high as the sun. I thought, how do you make contact with it? Seeds of doubt entered my mind. But I'm not taking the pitch. Big swing ensued, and I caught nothing but air. The ball bounced unceremoniously right behind the plate.

So yes, I did strike out in slow-pitch softball. On a good pitch but an indecisive swing that probably looked like an unfolding lawn chair. Or possibly an octopus falling out of a tree.

I don't remember much after that. I'm pretty sure it was Wang that started calling me Whiff. Then it caught on.

The End.

How the mighty have fallen.

Finally, let's close 1980 with a funny story about a "whacky game" played on the 25th anniversary of the first baseball game between Peerless and Four Buttes in 1955. Team captains for the whacky game were Tony LaMotte of Four Buttes and George "Tiny" Puckett of Peerless. The article, "Players will pay to play in whacky game," written by Addison Bragg of the *Billings Gazette*,[255] captures the zaniness of the event, but it also underscores the tradition of baseball in Daniels County, brought to the area by the homesteaders in the early 1900s. Baseball—and softball—were fun and brought small communities together in the summer. The Plainsmen and Blues state championships and the success of both programs were a wonderful part of that tradition, but the joy of playing the game and the togetherness the sport fostered in the small towns is what made the tradition special and still does to this day.

"Players will pay to play in whacky game," Addison Bragg, *Billings Gazette*, July 30, 1980

An upcoming ball game between Peerless and Four Buttes stands well to make the Mad Tea Party from "Alice in Wonderland" look like a study in decorum and order.

Once you know the game starts at 2 p.m., Sunday, Aug. 23, at Peerless, you've drained about all the sanity there is to be found in it.

That, at least, is the impression drawn from talking with Tony LaMotte, captain of the Four Buttes nine.

To begin, said LaMotte, the game will mark the 25th anniversary of the first such contest between the two communities.

Nobody remembers who won back then. But, added LaMotte brightly, nobody cares. "It just seemed like a good idea to play again."

It will cost each player $1 to bat. If he gets a hit, another 50 cents is added to his tab. It'll also cost him 50 cents if he strikes out.

Pitchers will find themselves out of pocket $1 for every home run. Errors will find the offending player shelling out 75 cents.

And every time a player comes up on the batting order throughout the game it's another buck for the kitty.

LaMotte said the money will be donated to "some good cause."

And, should the first game fail to reach the goal, Four Buttes and Peerless planners are ready. "We'll play 'er again," said LaMotte.

Tiny Puckett, who'll captain the Peerless team, estimates an initial outlay of $1.50 will ensure a player at least one time at the plate—one dollar to bat, fifty cents to buy the umpire off.

No one under 40 will be permitted to play—and, planners of the Peerless-Four Buttes silver anniversary spectacular assure those considering a spot on the lineup, there'll be oxygen available at first base.

1981

The Streak Ends: "A Bitter Bill to Swallow"

> *Unfortunately, we fell short of the goal of bringing another State championship for the Blues. I remember the great disappointment, if not embarrassment, of falling short of the championship. However, I distinctly remember Doc and Don giving us encouragement to keep our heads up, saying that we had done our best with the crew that we had assembled and that the Blues would be back better than ever in 1982.*
>
> —Ron Higgins, Scobey Blues (1978–1981)

1981 Scobey Blues. Coaches in the back: Doc Norman and Don Lekvold. Kneeling, left to right: Steve Schaefer, Greg Stolen, Pat Audet, Len Floyd, Brian Gilbert, Jeff Mann, Gord Tryan, Jim Lekvold. Sitting, left to right: Joey Girard, Rick Lee, Larry Trangsrud, Andy Eliason, Ron Higgins, Mike Tryan, Tony Vigliotti. Sitting in front: batboys Mike and Josh Lee, batgirl Michelle Audet. (Not pictured is Allison Marlenee.)

PRESEASON

BEFORE THE 1981 BASEBALL SEASON, A SIGNIFICANT change occurred in Daniels County and the Norman family. After 23 years of dedicated service as a physician in Scobey, Doc was forced to retire due to health issues related to his heart. However, the heart ailment could not affect Doc's love for coaching his beloved Blues, and with the approval of his doctors, he continued to guide the team, albeit with certain restrictions. A poignant article, "Scobey loses a doctor but keeps a coach," by Dennis Gaub of the *Billings Gazette*, documented this transition and provided a comprehensive overview of Doc's life as a player and baseball coach. It is reprinted here in its entirety:

```
Scobey loses a doctor but keeps a coach[256]

   Scobey recently lost the services of a long-
time family doctor.
   But the Northeastern Montana community re-
tained the services of its longtime American
Legion Baseball coach.
   Dr. C.H. Norman is ending his practice for
medical reasons relating to his heart. As he
```

explained in a recent letter to the editor appearing in the Daniels County Leader: "I have been ordered by my physicians to immediately cease the practice of medicine, having been told that I have cerebellar ataxia and an aortic aneurysm; also, that due to the seriousness of these things, I must retire."

But the Scobey Blues, a perennial power in Montana's Class B Legion ranks, have the same coach this year that they've had for the past 23 years: Dr. C.H. Norman.

And Norman, who turns 61 this summer, got his doctor's OK to pilot the Blues—with conditions.

"It appears at this time that I will be able to continue my various hobbies, within reasonable limits," Norman said in the letter.

In a telephone interview last week, he explained the "reasonable limits" of coaching baseball. He was told, "I could sit in the dugout and run the ballclub."

Norman is no Billy Martin firebrand. "We don't get too excited. It's going to be fun. I can sit in the dugout and run things without any trouble, like Connie Mack when he got old."

The famed Philadelphia Athletics manager wore street clothes while running his club and retired when he was 88, giving him a record for longevity few can match.

But Norman's managerial career, albeit shorter, is studded with noteworthy accomplishments. He has guided the Blues to seven state titles, starting with the 1969 championship. The second came in 1973. And when the Blues won in 1976, that began a string of five titles, including last year.

"We've had some remarkable talent around here for such a little town," he said, noting that the Blues also draw players from Peerless and Flaxville. "Altogether, it wouldn't be a very big town. . . . It wouldn't break 2,500 altogether."

Norman, a Billings native, briefly attended the University of Montana, then was recruited to play football by Northwestern University. After a stint with the First Marine Division in World War II, he finished his medical education at the Big Ten school.

While in Chicago, Norman played semipro baseball. Upon returning to Montana in 1951, he began his practice in Columbus and discovered "the kids didn't have anything to do" in the summer. But Norman gave them something to do.

He established a Legion program with the assistance of Gene Brown, a highway patrolman who died this year.

"We ran it together. He was a former second baseman for Portland's AAA club. He was a wonderful fellow," Norman recalled.

That partnership lasted four years, until Norman moved to Missoula in 1954. He came to Scobey in 1958 and began coaching the Blues [in 1959], starting a coaching tenure that's now approaching a quarter-century.

"There had always been a Legion team here. They were a bunch of very talented young people," Norman recalled of those early years.

The "big man" of one early team [1959] was a 17-year-old who weighed 130 pounds; remaining players were 14-year-olds. That team played Laurel—"I remember a bunch of great big kids chewing tobacco"—for Eastern Montana championship honors and lost two out of three games.

Happier occasions followed. In 1969, Scobey and Havre played for the state B crown, as they often did. "We were behind by one run going into the ninth. With two outs, a guy tried to throw a fastball by Dick Puckett. He hit one over the left-center field fence about a country mile. That tied up the ball game and we won it in the 10th," Norman recalled.

A year later, it was a Scobey-Havre finale again. The Blues had Terry Puckett, "a very fine left-handed pitcher who could throw hard," Norman said. But that wasn't quite enough. "We ended up getting beat 1-0 by a boy named (Dave) Fanning. That was a hairy one, too."

If there's a secret to Scobey's success, it's that the Blues have had top-notch batteries over the years, Norman said. "I think that's the single most important thing, the catching and pitching, that's kept us in business."

The Blues' roster is modest in numbers—16 players this year, compared to an average of 14-15 with an occasional peak of 18 or so. "We don't have any way of making 'em play. The kids who play really want to play," Norman said.

And this year's squad is "very young. Oh, they're babies," he said, noting that the outfield for a recent game included a 13-year-old and a pair of 14-year-olds. But Norman quickly added: "They were getting the job done, catching the ball and throwing 'em out."

The Babe Ruth program makes a pool of 13-year-olds available. "We just borrow 'em a little bit, which means kids can play Legion ball for 5-6 years. By the time they're 17 or 18, they're pretty good. The only trouble is we can't have a team of all 17- or 18-year-olds," Norman said.

Several ex-Blues players are currently playing college ball. Dan Danelson is at Lewis and Clark College, Kirby Halvorson is at Pacific Lutheran, Joe Puckett is at Minot State, Kelly Norman (the coach's younger son) is at Southern Oregon, and Randy Stolen has just finished a sterling season (.470), eight home runs, team most valuable player) at Colorado Northwestern Community College. Stolen will be transferring to Colorado State this fall.

Asked how much longer he plans to coach, Norman didn't answer directly.

"Oh, gosh, I don't know. I have grandchildren, three of them. One is working out as a catcher. There's a long ways to go. The youngest is only six," he said.

Another significant event before the start of the 1981 season was that Doc was nominated for the Montana Coach of the Year Award. His nomination was based on his 1980 state championship and overall career achievements—seven state championships, including five in a row. The winner was announced at the Montana Sports Banquet in April. The Coach of the Year was chosen by a committee of sports writers and sportscasters from north-central Montana. Doc didn't win the award, but was always our Coach of the Year in Scobey. And each of his teams was always *his* team of the year, which makes a good segue into the composition of the 1981 team.

Four starters—Randy Stolen, Kelly Norman, Kirby Halvorson, and Jesse Cook—had aged out for the 1981 season. The loss included Scobey's top three hitters—including seven home runs apiece the previous season from Randy and Kirby—their top three pitchers and top two catchers. That was the bad news, and it was very bad news indeed. Randy, Kirby, and Kelly had all gone on to play college baseball. These were some huge cleats to fill, to be sure.

But there was some good news, too. Six starters—Ron Higgins (18), Andy Eliason (18), Gord Tryan (17), Pat Audet (16), Jim Lekvold (16), and Greg Stolen (15)—were returning. These starters were experienced and had played on several state championships: Ron Higgins played on three; Gord, Pat, Jim, and Greg had played on two. For pitching, Andy, Pat, Ron, and Greg could pitch. Jim Lekvold and little 15-year-old left-hander Tony Vigliotti would also see some innings on the mound for Scobey. Pat had caught a lot in 1980, so he would share catching duties with Jim Lekvold, who caught Pat when he pitched. Jim would later become the number-one catcher for Scobey, and Pat would play center field. Greg would be the go-to pitcher. Also returning from the 1980 season were second-year players Mike Tryan (15), Tony Vigliotti (15), Steve Schaefer (16), and Jeff Mann (16).

Rookies Joey Girard (15), Rick Lee (13), Larry Trangsrud (13), Len Floyd (17), and Brian Gilbert (16) were the new Blues.

It's good to see another Peerless boy, Larry Trangsrud, back on the field for the Blues after a one-year absence of Peerless players in 1980. Larry recalls, "Doc called me when I was 12, wanting me to play the next year. That was a pretty incredible call. I pretty much was in Babe Ruth my 13 and 14 years. I did dress out when we didn't have Babe Ruth games. Not sure I ever saw the field." But the experience was good: he would become Scobey's starting catcher for Coach Don Lekvold as he matured and developed in the years to follow.

Joey Girard recalls his first practice for the Blues. "Like many of us, I was sent out to second base and took a few grounders, which I booted at least half of them. After that debacle, Doc called me into his corner of the dugout. 'Let me see your glove [little old rag]. Joey, unzip my bag over there and grab my glove,' which I did. 'How's it fit?' I nodded. 'That's your glove now.' I never forgot that. A few years back, Kirby Halvorson and I were discussing those types of things we learned from Doc that we have carried into our adult lives and coaching days, especially generosity.

Dr. C.H. Norman is shown with mementos of his successful coaching career. *Billings Gazette photo*

Not sure any of this was possible without the generosity of Doc and Marge. Pretty sure a lot of personal checks were written for the Blues by them."

This was Scobey's youngest team since 1977, when no 18-year-old was on the roster, and five 16-year-olds and three 15-year-olds started. When Dennis Gaub asked Doc about his 1981 team, he said, "They're young. Oh, they're babies."[257] But as with the 1977 team, the 81ers knew how to play baseball. Would 1981 finally be a rebuilding year for the Blues? Or would they have enough experience and enough firepower to land a sixth consecutive state title? This was always the expectation in Scobey at the time: a state championship. And that was the goal of Doc and his young team.

REGULAR SEASON

THE 1981 SEASON STARTED AUSPICIOUSLY FOR THE YOUNG BLUES team. In their season-opening game against Glasgow in Scobey, Gord Tryan smashed a three-run home run to lead Scobey to a 14-8 win. Scobey also took advantage of *20 walks issued by Glasgow pitching.* Wow, that's a lot of walks. As he would do the entire season, Greg Stolen led the team in hitting with a 3-for-5 day, including a triple. Greg Stolen and Andy Eliason pitched, with Andy getting the win in relief.

Greg and Andy also had control problems, issuing 10 walks between them. In addition to the six returning starters, Len Floyd, Jeff Mann, Mike Tryan, Joey Girard, Steve Schaefer, Rod Rust, and Tony Vigliotti all saw action that day—an excellent start for Scobey.

Here are some other regular-season highlights for Scobey in 1981:

- Gord Tryan hit a three-run triple, and Pat Audet added a two-run triple to account for five Scobey runs in a 9-7 win over Plentywood. Tony Vigliotti and Andy Eliason combined to strike out 12 Athletics, with Andy Eliason pitching six innings of relief to get the win. Randy Pederson pitched all nine innings for Plentywood and struck out 10 Blues.
- Doug Selvig, returning for the summer after playing his freshman year of basketball for the University of Montana Grizzlies, pitched eight innings to get the win in Plentywood's 13-11 win over Scobey. Randy Pederson pitched the ninth to earn the save for Plentywood. Pat Audet started and took the loss, with Andy Eliason and Greg Stolen pitching in relief. Steve Schaefer doubled, and Jeff Mann and Jim Lekvold tripled, leading Scobey's hitting.
- Trailing Sidney 8-2 in the bottom of the seventh inning, the Blues scored seven runs in their last two at-bats to come from behind and win 9-8. Greg Stolen went the distance, striking out nine Patriots and walking only two to get the win. Jim Lekvold tripled and went 2-for-3 to lead Scobey's hitting. Scobey had lost badly to Sidney 19-5 earlier in the season in Scobey. Todd Ackerman, Sidney's left fielder, recalls, "I remember going over to shake Doc's hand after the game, and he made the comment which was so true that this game was a lot more fun than the last game. And I remember answering, 'Yes, it was.' It really was a lot more enjoyable game to play in."
- The Class A Helena Senators traveled to Scobey on a road trip, and the young Blues played them well. The Blues were leading 5-3 after five innings, but Helena scored seven runs in the final four frames to win 10-8. Scobey scored their eight runs on 13 hits.
- Led by a three-run triple by Greg Stolen and a two-run single by Gord Tryan, Scobey erupted for nine runs in the first inning to jump all over Circle and held on to win 12-5. Jeff Mann doubled for Scobey's other extra-base hit. Andy Eliason went the distance for Scobey to get the win.
- Greg Stolen pitched seven innings of shutout relief and struck out 11 Athletics to lead Scobey to a 5-2 over Plentywood. Jim Lekvold started for Scobey, and Greg relieved him in the third. Randy Pederson went the distance for Plentywood and took the loss. Pat Audet and Greg Stolen doubled for Scobey.
- Scobey scored single runs in the fifth and sixth innings to erase a 5-4 deficit and came from behind for the second consecutive game to beat Sidney 6-5. Greg Stolen got the win, relieving Pat Audet in the fifth.
- In Scobey's 3-2 win over Glasgow in 10 innings, Greg Stolen reached second base on a two-base error with two outs in the top of the tenth, went to third on a passed ball, then scored on another passed ball to walk it off for Scobey. Greg Stolen pitched all 10 innings, striking out 12 Reds and issuing only one walk.
- The Blues scored four runs in the seventh to come from behind and beat Glasgow 11-8. Four singles and a two-run triple by Pat Audet sparked the rally. Ron Higgins, Scobey's third pitcher, picked up the win in relief. Scobey upped its record to 10-8 with the win.
- Greg Stolen went 2-for-4 and drove in four runs to lead Scobey to a 6-4 win over Wolf Point. Greg hit a three-run triple in the first after the first three hitters singled. He also went the distance on the mound, striking out 10 Yellowjackets and improving his record to 7-1.

As he had done the previous year, Doc experimented with several lineups with his young team during the regular season, but by the time of the Divisional tournament, the following lineup was mainly employed:

- Pat Audet, C/P/CF
- Ron Higgins, OF/P
- Jim Lekvold, 2B/C
- Greg Stolen, SS/P
- Gord Tryan, 3B
- Jeff Mann, OF
- Andy Eliason, SS/P/OF
- Tony Vigliotti, 1B/P/OF
- Mike Tryan, OF

Steve Schaefer and Len Floyd also saw plenty of action in the tournaments.

After a slow start to the regular season (2-7), including losses to each team in the district, the young Scobey Blues finished the second half of the regular season strong and took second in the conference behind Wolf Point. They headed into the Divisional tournament in Glasgow with a solid chance to be the best in the east again. With Glendive hosting the State B Tournament, Scobey needed to place in the top three at Divisional to advance to State, as Glendive received an automatic bid as host.

DIVISIONAL TOURNAMENT

The 1981 Eastern B Divisional Tournament was played in Glasgow. Scobey, the number-two seed from the northeastern district, faced Circle in their first game. Greg Stolen, relieving Pat Audet in the second inning, pitched seven shutout innings of relief to lead Scobey to an 8-4 win. Scobey trailed 4-0 in the bottom of the second but scored two runs in that end, then had a big five-run fifth to take a 7-4 lead, adding a single run in the eighth to score the last eight runs of the game.

The Blues faced Plentywood—who had beaten Glendive 7-1—in the semifinal. Doc started Andy Eliason, while Plentywood countered with their ace Randy Pederson. Plentywood jumped on Scobey for three runs in the bottom of the first to take a 3-0 lead, but Scobey countered with a three-run second to chase Randy Pederson, who was relieved by Doug Selvig for the final seven innings. Plentywood had pitched ace Randy Pederson six innings and Doug Selvig three in their first game, so they might have been a little tired. This game was decided in the late innings as Scobey, leading 8-6 after six, erupted for nine runs in the last three innings to win 17-9. Andy Eliason pitched eight innings to get the win, relieved by Ron Higgins in the ninth. Greg Stolen had an incredible day at the plate, going 6-for-6 with a double, home run, and four singles, driving in four runs and scoring four more. A one-man wrecking crew at the plate, he missed hitting for the cycle by a triple. Jeff Mann and Andy Eliason also doubled for the Blues. Scobey did not play well in the field, committing seven errors, but their hitting and pitching were enough to overcome that liability.

The semifinal win guaranteed Scobey a berth in the State B Tournament and placed them in their familiar position of playing for the eastern divisional championship. They would play against a familiar opponent—district champion Wolf Point. Wolf Point had gotten to the championship game by beating Forsyth-Colstrip 9-2 and Sidney 14-5. This would be another classic matchup between the two friendly old rivals in the eastern divisional championship game. The *Leader* described it as "a very tense and exciting game" between "the two best teams in the tournament."[258]

Doc handed the ball to Ron Higgins to start the game while Wolf Point countered with Mark Page, Wolf Point coach Cliff "Satch" Page's son, who went the distance for Wolf Point in an "excellent pitching performance."[259] Ron also pitched well, pitching into the sixth inning when Greg Stolen relieved him for the rest of the game. Scobey again committed seven errors in this game, but unlike against Plentywood, the errors proved costly, as Wolf Point scored some unearned runs. Ron and Greg only gave up one walk but the errors were their undoing. With the score tied 5-5 in the seventh, Wolf Point scored two runs to take the lead 7-5 and went on to win by that same score.

Sidney scored three converted touchdowns and a field goal to beat Glasgow 24-10 to take third place, rounding out the top three teams from the east. Glendive, as host, got the automatic bid, so Glasgow did not advance.

Wolf Point's third baseman, James O'Tremba, was voted MVP of the tournament. He hit 3-for-5 in the championship game and played well defensively at third base. For the tournament, he hit .533 with two doubles and five RBIs. But if Scobey had won, Greg Stolen "would have gotten it going away, with his sensationally consistent hitting. He was 6-for-6 against Plentywood with a home run and four RBIs, and in the final game, he had three hits and got on base all five times at bat. He also started the sequence in a triple play—shortstop to second to first—in the championship game."[260] Greg was the top hitter in the tourney with a .647 average. Other all-stars included catchers Ed Sifuentes of Sidney and Scott Jakanowski of Glasgow; infielders Greg Stolen of Scobey; J.R. Rasmussen, Glasgow; Mark Price, Sidney and Scott O'Tremba, Wolf Point. Outfielders were Russ Barnhart, Sidney; James McGeshick, Wolf Point;

Craig Lee, Plentywood; Tony Barnes, Wolf Point; and Bob Connors, Glasgow. Pitchers named to the team were Scott Johnson, Sidney, and Mike Stuber, Glasgow.

However, individual accomplishments aside, the most important outcome of the eastern divisional tournament in Glasgow was Scobey advancing to the State B Tournament in Glendive as the second seed in the east. The Blues would take the field to defend their title for the fifth consecutive year. During the regular season, they had beaten the other two teams in the east, Sidney and Wolf Point. They had a legitimate chance to win the state championship again despite losing several regular season games and having a young roster.

STATE B TOURNAMENT

FOR THE FIRST TIME SINCE 1969, AFTER SIX CONSECUTIVE alternating years hosting the state tournament—1969, 1971, 1973, 1975, 1977, and 1979—there was a new host in the east: Glendive. Scobey also hosted the eastern divisional tournament in 1974 and 1978 during that same period. The last time Glendive had hosted the state tournament was in 1968, when Havre won its first state championship.

There was no clear favorite to win the State B Tournament, but Scobey was undoubtedly not a dark horse. In the western divisional tournament, the Great Falls Vigilantes beat Havre—who had returned to the Class B ranks in 1981—14-3 for the championship, while Fairfield had beaten the Butte Muckers 15-14 to take third. The Great Falls Vigilantes had the best record going into the four-day tournament at 25-8. Havre also had to be considered with its 20-12 record. Rita Balock, *Havre Daily News* sports editor, wrote that Havre, after returning to Class B, was "a definite contender in the 1981 state tournament."[261] By default, the champions of the west and east—the Great Falls Vigilantes and Wolf Point Yellowjackets—had to be considered, but no team in the east or west had dominated during the regular season. The field was wide open. Northstar coach Jim Berna mentioned Scobey, saying, "Scobey is very young. At one point this season, they were 2-8, but evidently, they've been on a tear the second half of the season." Coach Berna liked how his team was playing, saying, "Including Divisionals, we've won 10 or our last 12 games, and in general, we've been playing well." In discussing his first-round opponent, Sidney, Berna said, "Sidney, I understand, is fairly mature; they have six 18-year-old starters. They've scored 14, 13, and 24 runs in some of the scores I've seen, so they must have some sticks."

These were the opening-day pairings at Meissner Memorial Field in Glendive:

- Wolf Point (1E) vs. Butte (4W)
- Scobey (2E) vs. Fairfield (3W)
- Havre (2W) vs. Sidney (3E)
- Great Falls Vigilantes (1W) vs. Glendive (4E)

In Scobey's first game against the Fairfield Blue Hawks, the game was a nail-biter until the top of the seventh inning, with Fairfield leading 4-3. But the Blue Hawks scored three runs in the seventh and added four more in the eighth to break it open, winning 11-5 and forcing Scobey through the dirt route for the remainder of the tournament. It was a tough opening-day tournament loss for Scobey, but Scobey had come back to win state tournaments through the dirt route before, so it was not over.

The other games on opening day made Scobey and Fairfield's 11-5 game look like a pitcher's duel by comparison, as Butte outslugged Wolf Point 16-14 and Sidney outslugged Havre by an identical score. Coach Berna of Havre said Sidney "had some sticks" before the tournament, and he was right. The Vigilantes beat Glendive 20-12 in the day's final game. That is some serious run-production by all teams.

In their loser-out game against host Glendive, the Blues had four-run rallies in the fourth and seventh innings to eliminate the host 10-5. Greg Stolen got the win for Scobey. The other second-round elimination game saw Wolf Point beat Havre 7-6. Butte beat Sidney 10-7 in the winner's bracket, and Fairfield beat the Vigilantes 7-6.

Scobey's next game was against Sidney on Saturday. Facing elimination every game, the Blues lost to Sidney 12-1, as Mark Price fired a four-hitter, and Todd Ackerman was a perfect 4-for-4 at the plate to lead Sidney's 13-hit attack. Thus, Scobey's run of five consecutive state championships ended on Meissner Memorial Field in Glendive.

It was fitting that the team that ended Scobey's run was Sidney, as they slogged (slugged) their way through the dirt route and remarkably won the tournament after finishing third in the eastern divisional. Their second game on Saturday was postponed due to rain and wind to Sunday, so they had to win two games on Sunday and two on Monday to come back and win it, and they did. On Sunday, they eliminated Wolf Point 13-7 and the Butte Muckers 18-7. On Monday, needing to beat the undefeated Fairfield Athletics twice, Sidney won the first game 7-3 on a four-hitter by 16-year-old Tom Barnhart, then won the second 19-10 in a slugfest, claiming Sidney's second state championship. Scott Johnson was named tournament MVP.

TOURNAMENT SUMMARY

1981 Richland County Patriots, State Class B American Legion champions. Top row, left to right: Assistant Coach Jack Walker, Alan Herbert, Charles Ritter, Rob Gratz, Scott Johnson, Head Coach Jim Baldwin. Second row, left to right: Tom Barnhart, Eddie Sifuentes, Russ, Barnhart, Mickey Mulholland, Jeff, Hansen, Mark Price, Todd Ackerman. Front row, left to right: Terry Heit, Lance Butner, Mike Jensen, Steve Johnson, Lee Harris, Greg Hansen.

SCOBEY'S 12-1 SEASON-ENDING LOSS TO SIDNEY SEEMED AN abrupt and anticlimactic ending to the Blues' season and consecutive state championship run. After starting the season slowly with a 2-8 record, the Blues came on strong in the second half, took second in the divisional tournament, and had legitimate hopes to win State. But we must remember that the ace pitcher and leading hitter Greg Stolen was 15 years old, and Jim Lekvold and Pat Audet were only 16. The average age of the starting lineup was just a little over 16 years old. The fact that there was any expectation Scobey could win was a testament to how talented these young players were. Although the quick exit was not what everyone expected, the team gained valuable experience, and Doc and Don smartly developed the younger players through the season. And "younger" meant many players less than 16 years old—that's how young the 1981 Blues were. Scobey finally had a rebuilding year. It had to happen. It wasn't Doc's or the team's goal (Doc didn't dump his best players before the Legion trade deadline and tank the season), but, in hindsight, "rebuilding" is the best way to characterize 1981.

Pat Audet summed up the 1981 season this way: "I believe we suffered from a bit of a hangover trying to compensate for losing the last of the big guns—Kirby, Kelly, and Randy—that were instrumental in the 1979 season and carrying into the 1980 season. A 'rebuilding' year is fair to say in explaining some of the woes and results of 1981. The team chemistry waned a bit, and we felt it. As disappointing as the state tournament was, we did have a legit chance to go deep and even win it, as the confidence was building going into it. With that said, the heartache of losing, coupled with the final results of the 1981 state tourney, made it much, much more of an emotional impact, knowing we failed in conquering the state chippers—the streak ended with us." But looking forward to the following season, Pat added, "As bitter a pill as that was to swallow, it didn't take long to rebuild, reload, and enter 1982 with lessons learned and a return to the winning ways!"

Scobey's two losses in the tournament were to the first- and second-place teams, Sidney and Fairfield. Sidney's dirt-route championship was the second for the town with a fine baseball tradition, as the Sidney Majestics had won the state tournament in 1966, the same year Scobey was disqualified from playing in State for having an ineligible player after beating Plentywood 4-2. The tournament was dominated by hitting, as there were several slugfests throughout, but the heaViest-hitting team in the tournament was state champion Sidney. Sidney, coached by Jim Baldwin and Jack Walker, scored an incredible 93 runs in seven games, an average of over 13 runs per game.

The 1981 state tournament was the last for 18-year-olds Ron Higgins and Andy Eliason. Ron had played on Scobey's state championship teams of 1978-1980, and Andy had played on the 1980 team. Ron's last game also marked the end of an era for the Higgins family from Flaxville playing for the Blues, as Ron was the last of the line behind Jack, Don, and Barry. Reflecting on his years playing for the Scobey Blues, Ron provided the following thoughts and memories:

My last year of Legion baseball was interesting. There was an expectation that this crew would continue the Blues tradition of state championships (five straight at this point) while we were also cognizant of the huge holes left over from the last two years of so many great athletes aging out—specifically from the last year for us—Kirby, Kelly, and Randy from the 1980 championship squad. We knew there were big shoes to fill, and we had a lot of great "young" guys to step in to fill in the gaps to try and continue the tradition, but we knew it would be challenging.

As has been noted in previous "Blues of Summer" posts, I was the youngest of five boys of John and Iris Higgins, three of which played significant roles in the Scobey Legion baseball program. Jack was part of the very first Scobey championship in 1969, and then Donnie and Barry played in the early 70s as the program continued to establish itself further in the state. I don't know that I felt pressure to live up to my sibling predecessors, partly because I don't think I fully understood just how good they were—Jack has been described by a few as possibly being the best all-around hitting center fielder (with the best first step off of fly balls, as well as amazing bat speed) that the program has produced. Donnie was likely the fastest base stealer in the program, followed closely by Barry. I, by contrast, had average skills in running and fielding, with middling hitting skills, even as a Little Leaguer and Babe Ruth player. Thus, at 5'3" and 125 lbs. as I joined the 1978 squad, I was quick to realize that I was definitely a "boy" surrounded by a bunch of "men" (i.e., Albert and Wade, in particular). I pretty quickly realized that, while I was a decent Little League and Babe Ruth baseball player, I may not ever rise to the level of my brothers. They were truly legit baseball players, while I was, well, a great teammate and someone who could rally the troops, but not necessarily someone who was likely to hit an extra-base hit in a bottom-of-the-ninth clutch situation. However, I looked up to so many prior Blues mentors (Kirby, Randy, Joe and Jon, Kelly, Dano, Ray, and so many others), to provide inspiration for seeking a sixth straight state title. It was actually a big expectation for us as the season progressed, particularly as we started to sense that Doc may be nearing the end of his coaching tenure. He spent many practices coaching us from his little car (a Ford Fiesta, I believe), parked near home plate, and we began to focus on peaking at the right time.

Unfortunately, we fell short of the goal of bringing another state championship for the Blues. I remember the great disappointment, if not embarrassment, of falling short of the championship. However, I distinctly remember Doc and Don giving us encouragement to keep our heads up, saying that we had done our best with the crew that we had assembled and that the Blues would be back better than ever in 1982 (which turned out to be true, as they collected another title the following season). I definitely still carry a feeling of responsibility for us not bringing home the title to this day—maybe I should have taken a few more rounds in the cage during practice that season.

Interestingly, as I've read through so many of "The Blues of Summer" posts, I'm amazed at the recollection and clarity that some former Scobey ball players possess—many seem to remember the exact count in a particular at-bat, who was pitching, where they hit the ball, how many runs scored, etc. I, on the other hand, seem to have a brain that remembers memories and experiences much more than specific baseball at-bats. I do, however, have three distinct baseball memories:

(1) Albert's emotional response in the dugout when our 1978 squad lost out in the State A playoff game in Great Falls to the Chargers. I remember thinking, "This game and this team means A LOT to this guy." (2) As I mentioned, I was a pretty little guy in 1978, and we were playing Poplar, I believe, in a blowout game, and Doc had me go in and bat left-handed (it would be one step closer to first base) and he gave me the "ear" indicator first, followed by the belt-chest-cheek bunt signal. I successfully executed a successful drag bunt for my first (and only) hit of the season, and you would have thought that I had hit one over the left field fence based upon the reaction of my Blues teammates in the dugout. A seriously proud moment for this guy—thanks to all of you for your encouragement that day. (3) My last at-bat in the 1980 season was during our State A playoff game in Great Falls against the Electrics. I came up in the ninth inning with two out and needing a successful at bat for our season to continue and for us to get back to the top of the lineup (I was batting 9th). I wasn't a particularly good hitter, to be honest, and I had many, many strikeouts during the season, but I went up to the plate with a degree of confidence that I could at least make contact and make the defense make a play on me. I don't remember the score or if we had runners on base. I just didn't want to make the last out of the season. As luck would have it, I worked the at-bat to a full count, as I recall, and I was determined NOT to be caught looking at strike three to end this run; however, with that approach, I went down swinging at what may have been ball four. I have wondered what might have happened had I taken that pitch and we would have turned the lineup over back to the top of the order.

While I may not have vivid details of many of my baseball stats and game situations, I do have many fond memories of my years with the Blues. As others have noted, I remember Doc's signs, and I even used his steal and bunt signals as I coached my own son's Little League team to a city championship in our hometown. I remember singing with Kirby, Jesse, and many others on many bus rides as well as at the Lee's house west of town at our end-of-season barbeque. I remember rooming with Kirby in 1978 for the state tournament in Cut Bank and staying with a host family who had a cute daughter near my age. I'm sure she would have preferred Kirby, but I think he and Missy were already a couple, so I made my way in to become friendly with her. We returned to Cut Bank two years later, and at the Street Dance one evening, I tried to reconnect with her, and it turned out she had a girlfriend herself! I remember getting shit about that for a long time.

I recall long bus rides with lots of poker, stories (and a few drinks), and lots of camaraderie. I remember pitching batting practice night after night with my weak knuckleball and slurve. I remember steak and lobster dinner at Lydia's in Butte. I remember being reminded to be a good model and mentor to the younger players (Steve, Mike, Tony, and others) when I was in my last year . . . just as so many had been to me during my early years. I remember playing catch with Randy in the outfield in between innings, throwing knuckle balls and fork balls back and forth to one another as I complained, "How in the hell do I strike out three times in a row?" and Randy just laughing and relaxing me, saying that next at-bat, I'd have a clean slate and a new opportunity.

Being a part of the Blues program taught me so many things: how to prepare and be ready for anything, how to enjoy and celebrate the joys of victory, and how to handle the agony of defeat. Over the years, I've been thankful and appreciative of the connections that were made during Scobey Blues baseball. Thanks, Joe, for putting all of this together.

Thank you, Ron, for reflecting on your time as a Scobey Blue and the 1981 season. It is a heartfelt letter that contains humor and captures the goal of the 1981 team—and the disappointment for not achieving it—but then Doc and Don putting it in perspective. I have noticed consistently across letters, interviews, and inputs that most players remember when they feel they let the team down more than any other memory. I am in that category, too. It says a lot about how all the Blues were team players, and no one wanted to let their teammates down.

Andy Eliason from Opheim, reflecting on his Blues experience, said, "I had an awesome time with the Blues and met a lot of good people in the process. I am glad my cousins (Randy and Greg Stolen) got me to play for the Blues. I had a good two years with them and learned a lot."

I asked him if he had a favorite memory of playing for Doc. He said, "The best memory I have is when Doc started me at third base in the playoff game in Great Falls. I'd never played there, but I was really happy he played me there."

Andy then went further back in time and reflected on his baseball journey. "I played baseball since I was old enough to hold a baseball, and then when got older, kids used to come to my house because I had a big backyard. We had a baseball game in my backyard. "We had a Babe Ruth team in Opheim, and we played all the Glasgow teams. My dad, Glenn Eliason, was the coach. I got chosen to play in the all-stars for the Glasgow league. We won the tournament for our region, and then we had a playoff series game in Missoula to see if we got to go to regionals. We got to play two games just like the Blues to see if they could go to the State A Tournament. In the one I played for Glasgow all-stars, we lost the first game by one run, and in the second game, in the bottom of the seventh, with the bases loaded, I was up, and the count went 2 – 2. I got a good pitch to hit, and I got hold of one and hit it deep to right field, but the guy climbed the fence to rob me from a grand slam, so no regional. It was fun, just like when I played for the Blues."

Andy was cousins with Randy and Greg Stolen because his mother, Gertrude Stolen, was Andy's sister. I asked Andy who taught him how to pitch. "My uncle Andy taught me how to throw a really good curveball; he was the best." Yes, he was. Andy taught me how to throw my curveball too.

Scobey would have seven starters returning for 1982, but they would still be young by Legion standards, as Gord Tryan would be the only 18-year-old among them. But as Doc said in his interview on KCGM about his younger players on the 1979 team, "Don't forget, next year they'll be a year stronger and bigger." The future was bright for this talented young team. Could an eighth state championship be possible in 1982?

EXTRA INNINGS

SIDNEY TOOK THIRD IN THE EASTERN DIVISIONAL THEN WON the state tournament. The only other team to do that was Scobey in 1977, when Scobey was eliminated by Sidney in the eastern divisional tournament then beat them in the state championship game a week later.

A devastating thunderstorm accompanied by tornado-like winds on Saturday night postponed the game between Wolf Point and Sidney. The storm leveled the bleachers, a large portion of the fence surrounding the field, and ripped off the roof of the Rustic Inn Motel across the street. Several Sidney players and fans narrowly escaped injury as they bailed out of a van on the ground just as it was upset by the high winds. The Ackerman's camper was totaled. Todd's mom and dad—Ted and Doris (Nieskens)—and Jerry Butner and his wife were staying in the camper. Ted and Jerry were still inside when it rolled over but were okay. Butte Muckers Coach Jim "Sly" Sullivan, whose team was playing Fairfield when the storm hit, said, "It was quite an experience. We might be lucky to be alive. I don't know where the scorebook is. I'm real anxious to get back to Butte."

Sidney played the Butte Miners at Alumni Coliseum in Butte in a best-of-three series to qualify for the State A Tournament. They lost in two games, 17-3 and 18-14, but by scoring 14 runs in the second game, they demonstrated the heavy hitting that had won them the State B championship that year.

Scobey's run of five consecutive State Class B championships (1976-80) is still a record. Several Class B (now Class A) Legion teams have won three state championships in a row, but no other team has won four or five. In Class A, the Billings Legion team won an incredible 14 consecutive state championships from 1954-67, the record for all-class Montana State American Legion Baseball. Like Class B, several Class A (now AA) teams have won three in a row, but none have won four or five. In Major League Baseball, the New York Yankees (1949-53) are the only team to win five consecutive World Series. The Yankees also won four consecutive World Series (1936-39). Two teams—the New York Yankees (1998-2000) and Oakland Athletics (1972-

74)—have won three consecutive World Series. So, does the fact that the New York Yankees are the only MLB team to win five in a row make the Scobey Blues the New York Yankees of Montana Class A/B American Legion Baseball? As a Red Sox fan, I don't care for the comparison.

I worked as a seismographer in eastern Montana (mostly near Glendive) that summer, so I did not get to see the Blues play, but I did get to listen to a state tournament game on the radio. "Dapper Dan" Frenzel called the 1981 state tournament on KXGN radio in Glendive. Before the start of the game, as the Blues were taking infield, Dapper Dan commented on how "sharp" the team looked with their blue uniforms and their infield routine. He also remarked on Scobey's excellent baseball tradition and said that this team was defending the state title for the fifth time. I got goosebumps listening to him describe the team and the tradition; it reminded me of the four state tournaments I played in.

Welcome back to Class B baseball, Havre Northstars! Due to population, the Montana State American Legion Commission moved Havre from western division Class B to the Western Class A Division in 1976, where they played for five seasons through 1980. Unfortunately, Havre did not fare well in its five years competing in Class A, as the best the Northstars did was finish fifth place in the western division in 1978. The worst it got for Havre was their final season in Class A in 1980, when they finished 1-17 in conference play. In their first year in 1976, they finished sixth in the west with a 10-18 record. In his article, "Profound apologies are due to some dedicated kids," *Havre Daily News* sports editor Les Rickey lamented the lack of fan support for the team, writing that there were no more than "25 or 30 fans at any single game."[262] Coach Doug Sheppard said, "We can compete in Class A, there's no doubt about it. They [the kids] have the desire, and if they get the support they deserve, they'll really get it together. But that's if we get the support."[263] But things did not get any better in the next four years. In the same article, Rickey contrasted the success of the Havre Legion team in Class B with their first year in Class A: "While in Class B, Havre became so much a fixture of the state tournament as that division's champion that it's going to make people who know the game call motels around town to see why they haven't shown up yet. Havre has made the state tournament through thick and thin—mostly thin. It's been that long road of Class B tournament, challenge game, and then right into the fray with little sleep and lots of guts. But this year [1976], they didn't have the backing."[264]

But there were some high points to Havre's five years in Class A. In 1977, brothers Jeff and Barry Kato pitched back-to-back shutouts against the Great Falls Electrics. That same year right fielder Greg Peterson was selected to the western division all-star team.

It was good to see the Havre Northstars back in Class B. Before they left for Class A in 1976, Havre won five State Class B state championships, including three in a row from 1970-1972. Coach Tom Nielson had raised the Havre Legion program from the ashes in 1966 and developed it into a perennial state champion, their first coming in 1968. Although they were eliminated in two games at State in 1981 and Scobey and Havre did not play each other, there would be some future games between these two storied Legion programs that would recall the classic matchups of the late 1960s and early-to-mid 1970s.

In Dennis Gaub's interview with Doc in the *Billings Gazette*, the 17-year-old "big man"[265] who was referred to from the 1959 team and weighed 130 pounds was pitcher Kevin Sell. He was the only 17-year-old on that young team, Doc's first Scobey team. Rod Tande, Baldy Sell, Mike Norman, and Bill Thompson were just four of the 14-year-old starters on that team. The Junior Legion was younger then—18-year-olds couldn't play—but this was still a group of babies playing Junior Legion. Doc started with the young ones right out of the gate.

Like Doc, Dennis Gaub graduated from Northwestern University. He was born and raised in Montana and worked for the *Gazette* for 20 years after earning his journalism degree from Northwestern. An avid baseball fan (and Northwestern Wildcats), he is writing his fifth book, *Never Give an Inch: How Dave McNally Sparked a Revolution in Major-League Baseball and Professional Sports*.

Doc was in good company for the 1981 Montana State Coach of the Year award. Or should we say the other nine nominees were in good company with Doc? Eight of the nominees had coached state championships the previous year, but Doc had won seven and five in a row. The nominees included Jack Johnson, CMR football coach; Bill Ryan, Billings West basketball coach; Dave Edington, Ronan wrestling coach; Bill Hogan, Columbus football coach; Dick Kloppel, Great Falls High girls' basketball coach; Bob Petrino, Carroll College football coach; Jim Street, Butte High School wrestling coach; Bob Raeth, Whitefish football coach, and Mark Yoakam, Glasgow girls' cross-country coach. Mark Yoakam had also coached the Glasgow Reds in baseball. The award winner was CMR football coach Jack Johnson, but I would have voted for Doc. Not to take anything away from the other esteemed nominees, but seven state championships, including five in a row, was a strong resume for coach of the year.

Before a regular-season game against the Williston Keybirds at Ardean Aafedt Stadium earlier that summer, Doc called the Williston coach and told him his team was a bit young that year and asked him if he could bring Kirby Halvorson, Randy Stolen, and Kelly—all three back from college—with him to play. Williston's coach and players were good with it, so the trio joined the team on the trip and on the field for the game, but Doc and Kelly were tossed out of that game. Kelly called the incident "fucking nuts."

So what happened?

In his typical pitch-my-youngest-against-the-best fashion, Doc trotted out little left-hander Tony Vigliotti, 15 years old, to pitch against the formidable Keybirds. Tony recalls, "I would have just finished my freshman year, was not very big, and probably could not have broken a pane of glass with my fastball." Kelly, who was catching, thinks Tony might have "broken 55-60 mph" with his fastball. Kelly admits, "I was back from college and thought I knew a thing or two." He said the umpire's strike zone was narrow, and Tony was struggling as a result. Tony said, "I remember that Kelly was not happy with the umpire's strike zone." Kirby, who was also playing, was a little more direct in his assessment: "Big Vig was pitching his 15-year-old ass off, and the fucking ump was squeezing the zone on him." After catching each pitch called a ball that he considered a strike, Kelly started to hold the ball over the plate in his glove for a few seconds before throwing it back to Tony, sending the message that the ball was, in fact, a strike. After Kelly held the ball for one of the pitches, the ump's tolerance meter was pegged and said, "Throw the ball back."

Uh-oh.

That triggered Kelly and set him off. Kirby said, "'The Storm' had finally had enough." Kelly yelled back at the ump, "You've got a 15-year-old kid out there, and you're just screwing his ass!" The ump tossed Kelly out of the game for arguing balls and strikes.

Then, the fun really began. While in the dugout, taking his catcher's gear off, with an audience of both teams on the field and in the dugout and the fans in Ardean Aafedt Stadium watching, Kelly let loose with a string of f-bombs directed at the ump as he flung his shin guards off and threw them. The ump then proceeded to throw Kelly off the field, and he was directed to leave the dugout.

Furious, Kelly—once he got all his catching gear off and thrown in the dugout—stormed out onto the field past the on-deck circle toward home plate and continued his profane outburst. While Kelly was yelling at the home-plate umpire in Billy Martin–fashion, Doc, on crutches, moved as quickly as he could out of the dugout to back up Kelly—and his 15-year-old pitcher. Doc joined Kelly's verbal assault, and the ump threw him out of the game and the dugout, too. Both Normans were tossed.

Sitting on the bus with Doc after they departed the stadium, Kelly recognized the irony in the incident. A year earlier in Glasgow, Doc had made Kelly leave the field and sit on the bus for a game and a half because he forgot his spikes and was "bitching and moaning" that he couldn't get any traction on the field. Now, here he was, sitting on the bus with his dad a year later after both getting tossed off the field. What did they talk about? Kelly said, "We bullshitted about baseball."

But even more ironic was what Dennis Gaub wrote—and what Doc said—in his article in the *Gazette* earlier that summer. Gaub wrote, "Norman is no Billy Martin firebrand," and Doc said, "We don't get too excited. It's going to be fun. I can sit in the dugout and run things without any trouble, like Connie Mack when he got old."[266] But there was no sitting in the dugout like Connie Mack when he got old with his son Kelly around. Is it any wonder Kelly had the nickname "Stormin' Norman"?

And little Tony's assessment of the show? "Being fairly new to the town and the program, I do remember feeling that I was accepted as a Scobey Blue that day." Kelly had Tony's back; Doc had Kelly's back. That's how it went down—message sent and received.

The Williston game was the only time an umpire tossed Doc out of a game, but Doc tossed an umpire out of a game. What? How did that happen? This old Cliff Hagfeldt story occurred in the late 1960s or early 1970s and was told many times, including to Kelly Norman and Dan Danelson. Danny Wolfe says it's a "true story." How it happened was Cubby Richardson was drinking with his pals in Ginger's Bar the night before a Legion game. He would be calling balls and strikes for the game the next day. He was shooting his mouth off, saying to Cliff and whomever else would listen to him, "If Doc says one word to me, I'm gonna throw his ass out." But the next day, when Doc started jawing at Cubby, Cubby got mouthy back. Cubby took it too far, and Doc kicked *him* out of the game. Kelly said, "He was fresh out of umpiring school, and that was part of his spiel. It embarrassed Cubby but was funny to a lot of other people. He poked Papa Bear." Yep. Doc owned the field. However, the same scenario would not have happened with Umpire-In-Chief Ron Ewing of Sidney. *He* was king of the field.

For the first time in several years, the Scobey Plainsmen, described as "liberally sprinkled with stars of former championship Legion teams,"[267] formed a team and played some games in the summer of 1981. The Plainsmen hosted a season-ending round-robin tournament in Scobey with Weyburn and Kindersley from the Saskatchewan Major League and Circle. A $1,000 prize was awarded to the winner, Weyburn, Saskatchewan, who won all three of their games with good pitching and hitting. Back from his second year at Colorado Northwestern Community College, Randy Stolen, where he hit .470, had eight home runs, and was the team's most valuable player, hit three home runs—two grand slams—to lead Scobey's hitting. Randy and Kelly were headed to Colorado State after the tournament to play for the Rams. Randy said, "Maybe Kelly and I can show 'em some ball there."[268]

I played baseball at Minot State in the spring of 1981. I was recruited to play shortstop, but the team ran out of pitching in a mid-season tournament in Dickinson, so I told the coach I could pitch. I hadn't pitched since the Scarlets at the State A Tournament in 1979. I pitched against Dickinson and went the distance to get the win, mainly relying on my fastball, as after that amount of time, I didn't have any command of my breaking ball. My Beaver teammates (and Coach Ken Becker) didn't know I could pitch—I hadn't thrown a ball all season—so they were surprised. Mike Hagfeldt was there watching the game, and we talked following the game. He said, "I remember you as a curveball pitcher, Joe. I don't remember you throwing that many fastballs." I replied, "That was when I was 15 years old, Mike!" Seeing a former Scobey Blue on the road in North Dakota was good. Made me feel at home.

In my first baseball game as shortstop for the Minot State Beavers in early April, I played against Mike Neubauer from Wolf Point, who was catching for Black Hills State in Spearfish, South Dakota. We were on our first road trip

RANDY STOLEN picked up some birthday presents in advance last weekend when he hit three home runs—two of them grand slams—for the Scobey Plainsmen in the baseball round-robin at Scobey Ball Park. He will be 20 on Aug. 29. A native of the Glentana community, Randy and Kelly Norman, (former Scobey Blues stars on state championship teams) both of whom have starred in college baseball at different places, this fall will go together to Fort Collins, Colorado, to finish their college studies. Randy (son of Andy and Carol of rural Glentana) told the Leader, "Maybe Kelly and I can show 'em some ball there." In college Randy has been a star right fielder and hitter, and Kelly has been showing lots of stuff catching and at the plate. *Leader caption and photo*

"south." I guess Spearfish, South Dakota, is considered "south" compared to Minot, North Dakota. It was spitting snow in the second game of the doubleheader, barely above freezing. After the games, Mike and I went out and had a beer. It was good to see him. We talked about the good ol' Legion days playing baseball for the Blues and Yellowjackets—those golden summer days in northeastern Montana.

1982

Doc Norman and Scobey Win Their Eighth State Championship

> *Overcoming a 5-1 deficit for more than four innings, the Scobey Blues against Sidney made one of their typically classical breakouts in the fifth inning when Pat Audet hit a two-run homer to get Scobey back in the game again for the American Legion Class B state championship.*
>
> **Daniels County Leader, August 5, 1982**

1982 Scobey Blues, regular season photo. Standing, left to right: Coach Doc Norman, Jim Lekvold, Larry Trangsrud, Len Floyd, Greg Stolen, Armand Fladager, Brian Gilbert, Pat Audet, Steve Schaefer, asst. coaches Kelly Norman and Don Lekvold. Kneeling, left to right: Mike Tryan, Joe Girard, Gordy Tryan, Randy Pederson, Tony Vigliotti, Marty Davis, Tom Trang, Bob Tryan, and Michelle Audet (in front). Assistant coaches Kirby Halvorson, Randy Stolen, batgirl Allison Marlenee, and batboys Mike and Josh Lee are not pictured. *Leader photo.*

PRESEASON

THE MONTANA AMERICAN LEGION BASEBALL COMmission made some changes in 1982 to Class B American Legion Baseball. Two teams from Alberta—the Vauxhall Spurs and the Lethbridge Miners—joined the Class B western division. Get out, eh? The international baseball partnership would eventually become the Montana/Alberta American Legion Baseball (MAALB) program. The Lethbridge Elks had joined the Class A western division the previous year—and won the State A Tournament their first year in the league. The new format formed a new northwestern Class B district, adding a second district in the west. A second change instituted was the addition of a Class B All-Star Game at the end of the season for the best 18-year-olds in the state. Another format change, although not officially in the Legion rule book yet, was seven-inning games during the regular season when teams traveled to play each other instead of a single nine-inning game. All the games were seven innings in the western division Class B tournament. In addition, Montana Class B baseball was growing; there were 27 Class B Legion teams in 1982, and many of the new teams were from the west. There would be more changes to Montana American Legion Baseball in the following years.

But bigger changes than additional teams and seven-inning games were coming to American Legion Baseball in Scobey. In the previous season in 1981, in Doc's interview with Dennis Gaub of the *Billings Gazette*, "Scobey loses a doctor but keeps a coach,"²⁶⁹ Doc did not divulge to Dennis—nor many in his inner circle, including Kelly—the severity of his chronic illness. It turned out his health problems were much more severe than what he was letting on. Doc had central pontine myelinolysis (CPM), a neurological disorder that affects the brain. "Pontine" refers to the pons, a part of the brain stem. "Myelinolysis" means that the myelin—the covering that protects nerve cells, including the pontine nerve cells—was being destroyed. It affects the central nervous system and voluntary and involuntary muscles. As Doc's disease progressed, his crutches in 1981 gave way to a walker in 1982, then to a wheelchair and three-wheeled cart in 1983. Kelly said his problems began at the end of 1980. Doc knew it but kept it to himself. "I did not know it at the time either, but he had the disease of the pons. It starts the deterioration of voluntary muscles and then involuntary muscles. I'm sure he just told people he had a heart problem. Towards the end of 1980, Dad quit doing surgery because of his deteriorating fine motor skills before he fully retired in 1981." Because of his declining health, the 1982 season would be the last for Doc as head coach of the Scobey Blues, the team he had coached since 1959. It sure would be nice if the boys of '82 could send him out as a winner.

Doc, aided by Assistant Coach Don Lekvold, assembled his team again at Scobey Ball Park in April 1982. Although two-year starters Ron Higgins and Andy Eliason had aged out for the 1982 season, Scobey the outlook for Scobey was promising in 1982, as many of the younger players who started as babies as 13-and 14-year-olds were growing up, and several starters were returning from 1981. Gord Tryan (18), Pat Audet (17), and Jim Lekvold (17) were returning as two-year starters and had been with the team for four years. Greg Stolen, 16, was finally Legion age and had started on the team since he was 13. All four players had played in two state championships. They were experienced and physically maturing. That's a solid core right there.

Mike Tryan (16), Steve Schaefer (17), Len Floyd (18), Joey Girard (16), Tony Vigliotti (16), and Brian Gilbert(17)—some who started and all who saw action in 1981—returned. Larry Trangsrud (14) also returned for his second season. New faces in 1982 were Armand Fladager, Marty Davis, Tom Trang, and Bob Tryan.

Scobey generally looked good going into 1982. Many experienced players were returning, and the team was not so young anymore. However, Pat and Greg were the only mature pitchers, and a state championship couldn't be won with two pitchers. Scobey needed a third pitcher.

Enter Randy Pederson from Plentywood. From Plentywood? Yep. Once again, Scobey was the beneficiary of a neighboring town that did not field a Legion team, which allowed players from that town to play for the nearest Legion post, in this case, Scobey. When Plentywood's Legion team folded early in the season—they had even played Scobey one game—Pederson could come to Scobey and play. This had been the case with Dallas Hagfeldt in Glasgow in 1971 when Glasgow didn't field a team, and he was followed by younger brothers Jay and Mike. Dallas and Jay played on the 1973 state championship team, and Mike played on the 1976 championship team. The *Leader* described Pederson as the "Scobey Blues' import from Plentywood; a blond, sturdy, and demonstrably rugged lad."²⁷⁰

Randy remembers how Plentywood's season ended and how he was able to come to play for Scobey. Doc was all over Randy when he heard about Plentywood folding. Randy said, "We played a doubleheader with Sidney on the road on Sunday. We only had nine players. Our outfield was all Babe Ruth age, 15, 14, and 13. We were outscored 39 to 1. Monday night, there was a meeting, and the team disbanded. Then the phone started ringing. I got a call from my coach that the season had ended. Within 45 minutes, Doc called me. You know, like the shot heard around the world, like from Massachusetts. It was kind of comforting talking to him. He invited me and asked if I had any teammates that might be interested. I said I needed to run it by my folks and asked if it was okay if I called tomorrow night. He said, 'Yeah, sure, no problem.'"

Randy talked it over with his parents, and they had numerous reasons why he shouldn't play for Scobey, including saving money for college, the wear and tear on his car driving back and forth to Scobey for two months, a player from Scobey needing to sit on the bench if he played, etc. Randy continued, "So that next evening, I called up Doc, which kind of made me apprehensive: How do I politely decline the offer I received from Doc? He was very patient. He let me get through all the reasons my mother gave for not playing. And at the end of that, he goes, 'Well Fuck it, come anyway. We practice at six tomorrow.' I never bothered to tell my mom that he swore because that wouldn't go so well with my mother." So, Randy went to practice the next night. He just told his mom he might go after work, and he did—in his blue jeans. And that is the story of how Randy became a Blue. Doc would not take no for an answer.

Randy had been pitching for Plentywood since he was 15 in 1979. The previous year, he had pitched against Scobey four times, striking out 10 Blues in one game and earning a save for Doug Selvig in another. He was now 18 years old, experienced, and ready to help Scobey win another state championship. He could also catch, as did Pat and Jim, so Scobey had three solid pitchers and three solid catchers, but Jim caught most of the innings. He played shortstop when Greg pitched, and he could hit—becoming the clean-up hitter. Tony Vigliotti and Brian Gilbert also got some innings during the regular season, but in the postseason, it was Audet, Stolen, and Pederson on the mound.

Pat Audet recalls how easily Pederson assimilated with the Blues. "We all loved Petey; just an all-around great dude. Always friendly despite being highly competitive; great talent and got along with everyone."

Doc continued to call the shots from the dugout, with Assistant Coach Don Lekvold assuming more and more of the daily responsibilities of managing the team as Doc's health continued to decline. Kelly Norman, Kirby Halvorson, and Randy Stolen were also assistant coaches in 1982.

Batgirls Michelle Audet and Allison Marlenee returned for their third season, and Mike and Josh Lee returned as batboys. Dick Lannon drove the Bluesmobile for most of the bus trips, with Russ Malone driving occasionally.

REGULAR SEASON

Scobey's 1982 regular season—mirroring the 1981 season—started slowly but finished strong. Scobey's record at their season's lowest point was 3-7; however, their schedule was front-loaded with challenging games, as most of those losses were to Williston and defending state champion Sidney. Randy Pederson had also not yet joined the team for some of those losses.

They finished the regular season by winning 10 consecutive games to close out the regular season at 18-10 and finish second to Sidney in the conference. Here are some highlights of the Blues' regular season:

- Pat Audet had two doubles, and Randy Pederson tripled to lead Scobey to a 10-7 win over Wolf Point. Todd Baldry hit a three-run triple in the eighth to give Wolf Point a 6-5 lead, but Scobey scored five runs in their half to win it. Greg Stolen went the distance to get the win for Scobey.
- Scobey split a doubleheader with the Willison Keybirds at Scobey Ball Park. The Blues won the opener 14-4. Brian Gilbert pitched six innings, and Randy Pederson relieved in the seventh, holding Willison to four runs. Gord Tryan led a 13-hit attack for Scobey by smashing a three-run home run, Scobey's first of the season. Gord remembers the home run: "It was over the left field fence, the longest ball I ever hit. The first bounce was off the Peerless Highway." Williston won the second game 17-9.
- Scobey lost the first game of a doubleheader 13-11 to Glasgow, committing nine errors. Greg Stolen had four hits, but his hits and Scobey's 11 runs were not enough to offset the nine errors. But in the second game, Brian Gilbert pitched a four-hitter, and Greg Stolen had three hits as Scobey won 8-2. The loss put Scobey's record at 3-7. This was the lowest point of Scobey's season, but they turned it around from there.
- In a classic pitcher's duel between Pat Audet and Mark Page of Wolf Point, Pat Audet helped his cause by tripling home a run in the first and scoring the winning run in the sixth as Scobey squeaked out a 2-1 win over Wolf Point. Each pitcher hurled a four-hitter.
- Len Floyd knocked in Greg Stolen with the winning run in the bottom of the seventh inning to give Scobey a 10-9 walk-off win over Glendive and a sweep of a doubleheader in Scobey. Pat Audet, the winning pitcher in relief of Brian Gilbert, had a home run, a double, and four RBIs to lead Scobey's hitting. Scobey had an eight-run third to win the opener 10-8. Greg Stolen homered for Scobey.
- Getting big four-run innings in each game, Scobey swept a doubleheader from Circle. Trailing 3-0 in the bottom of the sixth in the first game, the Blues scored four runs and went on to win 4-3. Gord Tryan had three RBIs to lead Scobey. In the second game, Scobey's four-run third inning—the big blow coming on a two-run double by Randy Pederson—was the difference, as the Blues won 7-3. Randy Pederson won the opener, and Pat Audet won the second game, with Tony Vigliotti earning the save. Scobey had 10 doubles in the two games, coming from Gord Tryan, Jim Lekvold (2), Randy Pederson, Len Floyd, Greg Stolen, Randy Pederson (2), Mike Tryan, and Joey Girard.
- Greg Stolen pitched a three-hitter, struck out 11 Reds, and homered and doubled to lead Scobey to a 10-2 win over Glasgow. Gord Tryan smacked a two-run homer with two singles, and Randy Pederson had a double and three singles for the Blues.
- Randy Pederson pitched a four-hitter, and Mike Tryan and Greg Stolen doubled to lead Scobey to a 3-1 win over Glasgow.
- In their final two regular season games, the Blues swept a doubleheader from Circle. In the 11-9 win for Scobey in the opener, Len Floyd barely missed hitting for the cycle as he homered, tripled, and singled in his 3-for-4 performance to lead Scobey's 18-hit barrage. He only

needed a double to complete the cycle. Jim Lekvold doubled, and Randy Pederson was 4-for-5 with a triple and three singles. Mike Tryan also tripled for Scobey. Tony Vigliotti got the win in relief. Scobey won the first game with its bats but the second game with pitching, as Pat Audet spun a four-hitter to lead Scobey to a 10-3 win. The win was Scobey's 10th in a row.

Doc and Don, as they had done the year previous, experimented with several different starting lineups during the regular season but had settled on the following lineup for the postseason:

- Jim Lekvold, C/2B
- Pat Audet, CF/C/P
- Greg Stolen, SS/P
- Randy Pederson, P/SS/C/CF
- Tony Vigliotti, LF/1B/P
- Gord Tryan, 3B
- Len Floyd, 1B
- Joey Girard 2B
- Mike Tryan/Steve Schaefer/Marty Davis, RF

Scobey's 10-game win streak to close out the regular season demonstrated they were again a divisional and state title contender. Scobey finished the regular season at 18-10 with its doubleheader sweep over Circle. However, Sidney, the defending state champion, had a strong team in 1982 and owned Scobey during the regular season. They were managed by Craig Price and coached by Jeff Lebsock, former Fairview High School prep star and Patriot (1976-78). The *Leader* wrote, "The Richland County Patriots had demonstrated all season they were one of the strongest in all of Montana."[271] Sidney had ended Scobey's season a year earlier in the state tournament, eliminating them with a humiliating 12-1 mercy-rule win, then proceeded to win the state championship, ending Scobey's streak at five. Wouldn't it be a great story if Scobey and Sidney met for the eastern divisional and state championships? What a script that would be if Scobey avenged the team that eliminated them from the state tournament the previous season, stopped their state championship win streak at five, and held the upper hand during the regular season. If only sports could play out like it does in Hollywood movie scripts.

DIVISIONAL TOURNAMENT

The 1982 Eastern Divisional Tournament was played at Thompson Park in Laurel. No one knew it then, but this would be Doc's last eastern divisional tournament.

Twenty-four years earlier, after leading Scobey to its first district championship in 12 years, Doc and his young 1959 Scobey team had traveled to Thompson Park to play a best-of-three series for the eastern divisional championship, where they lost in two games to the experienced Laurel team. Although Doc's team was eliminated in two games, the *Laurel Outlook* recognized the team's potential: "Scobey is the team to watch. Young and inexperienced, Scobey showed promise of turning into a fine ball club as soon as they gain a little size and experience."[272] That was this team now. They had gained "a little size and experience" and were poised to make a serious run in the postseason. The Blues had not played in Laurel since 1959. Wouldn't it be nice if Doc could win the eastern division on the same field where the postseason started and ended for him 23 years earlier?

The day one matchups were as follows:

- Scobey Blues vs. Lewistown Redbirds
- Billings Cardinals vs. Glasgow Reds
- Wolf Point Yellowjackets vs. Billings Blue Jays
- Laurel Dodgers vs. Richland County Patriots

Lewistown, a team the storied Scobey Legion program had never played before, proved no match for the Blues in the first game, as the Blues won 9-3, although the game was close after six innings, with Scobey leading 6-3. Scobey got a well-pitched complete game from Pat Audet, who hurled a four-hitter. Greg Stolen smacked two doubles to lead Scobey's 10-hit attack.

Scobey overwhelmed the Billings Cardinals 23-9 in the semifinal when Scobey's bats boomed. The *Leader* recognized Greg Stolen in the win: "That tremendously talented Greg Stolen did his substantial bit both on the mound and at bat."[273]

Sidney made their way to the championship game on the opposite side of the bracket by beating Laurel 13-6 in their first game and Wolf Point in the semifinal. That set up the showdown between the two top teams in the east, with Sidney dominating during the regular season. After pitching Pat Audet and Greg Stolen in the first two games, Doc handed the ball to Randy Pederson to pitch the championship game. Sidney countered with Terry Heit.

This would be an epic pitcher's duel for the eastern divisional championship.

Heit and Pederson each pitched three scoreless innings to open the game, but in the top of the fourth, Sidney touched Pederson for the only run he gave up to take a 1-0 lead. Scobey answered with the tying run in the bottom of the fifth when Gord Tryan scored from third on a bases-loaded walk. Tom Barnhart had come in to relieve Heit in the fifth, and from the fifth inning on, Pederson and Barnhart alternated putting goose eggs on the Thompson Park scoreboard, inning after inning—until the bottom of the 11th.

Barnhart got in trouble in the bottom of the 11th when Scobey loaded the bases on two walks and a single. With two outs, he looked to escape the inning when a routine ground ball was hit to the infield, but the throw was wild, and Tony Vigliotti scored the winning run from third.

It was a walk-off 2-1 win for Scobey in the bottom of the 11th inning—an instant classic.

Jim Lekvold, who caught all 11 innings, recalls Petey's performance. "The thing that stands out the most is the longer the game went on, the stronger he got. Pitching that many innings puts a toll on a person, but not him. And as the game went on, I didn't seem to wear out either. Even in seven- or nine-inning games, a catcher can get pretty tired. Petey wasn't all over the place, so I didn't have to dig a lot of balls out of the dirt because he wasn't wild. There may have been a few, but I don't recall a whole lot. He seemed to get stronger and had excellent control. Maybe adrenaline kicked in for both of us. I think Doc, Don, and Kelly asked numerous times if he was OK or said he could be replaced. If that was the case, Petey talked them out of it. Glad he stayed in. I don't recall all the stats for the game as to who had hits or extra-base hits, but Petey's pitching performance outweighed them."

Pat Audet remembers the classic game this way: "There were lots of men left on base on both sides that day, and bats were not on fire when needed, but what a defensive showing and nail-biter going extra innings. Jimmy, 'Sneed' had the hops to get Petey through the entire game catching! My whole family was there at the time and remember how excited they were after watching a great game with Scobey winning the chipper over a very formidable foe in the Sidney Pats."

For Randy Pederson, two things about pitching that game dominate his memory. "One thing that sticks out was the first batter—I walked him on four pitches. I did just one of them behind-the-mound things, talking to myself for a little bit. You know, *don't mess this up*. I struck the next three guys out, and then things seemed to level out. I just kind of got mad at myself.

Another thing that sticks out was, starting in the ninth, Doc wanted to take me out, so I kind of had to fight to stay in. Anyway, it all worked out. What an awesome memory."

It was a shame that such a well-played game had to end on an error, but that's baseball. It was only Sidney's second error of the game, but it was costly. Although they committed three errors, Scobey made some outstanding plays in the field to back up Pederson in a "great defensive effort" by Scobey. "Vigliotti made some great catches in left field, any one of which could have given Sidney a substantial margin, and Mike Tryan in right field made one spectacular play on his back in right field. Pat Audet was strong in the outfield. That boy plays any position well. Gordy Tryan at third rifled his catches with accuracy over to first. Jim Lekvold [catching] and Greg Stolen [shortstop] did stellar duty."[274]

But the player of the game for Scobey was "Iron Man" Randy Pederson, so dubbed by the *Leader*, who raved about his performance at divisional: "Baseball buffs may find some statistics somewhere, in any league, if they can to equal the 11-inning pitching performance of 'Iron Man' Randy Pederson, whose excellent pitching, and a good defensive infield and outfield, took Scobey Blues to the eastern divisional championship in Class B American Legion Baseball. This blond, sturdy, and demonstrably rugged lad pitched 11 straight innings and did that arduous chore marvelously well. In reviewing the baseball annals at any level, in any league, when a pitcher goes for 11 straight innings and does it as well as Randy Pederson did, well, it is indeed something very special, in any league, at any game, in any year at any place."[275]

Sidney's Tom Barnhart, Pederson's worthy counterpart, also pitched well. "The Blues' bats were not at all noisy when Barnhart came in at the fifth inning from center field."[276] The "noise" of the bats by each team was limited: six hits apiece for Scobey and Sidney over 11 innings.

The picture of the jubilant Blues taken just after the trophy presentation at the eastern divisional championship was not choreographed, but it could have been because it is near perfect and rich with symbolism.

Near the center of the photo is the man himself, Doc Norman. His walker might be holding him up, but the excitement of the championship, surrounded by his beloved Blues holding up their index fingers signaling number one, appears to be what is lifting him. The number-one signal is not just for the 1982 team; it symbolizes the number-one Class B American Legion program in Montana, a dynasty—eight state championships in 14 years—and the culmination of 24 years of coaching in Scobey. Doc also symbolizes The American Legion, as he was a United States Marine Corps WW II veteran and a Scobey American Legion Post 56 member. Scobey American Legion Post 56 sponsored Scobey baseball, with tireless veterans like Charles Cassidy, Gene Marley, and Cliff Hanson providing undying support to the program through the years. Doc and these veterans

1982 Scobey Blues, Eastern Division champions. Left to right: Larry Trangsrud, Kelly Norman, Jim Lekvold, Kirby Halvorson (behind Jim), Josh Lee, Gord Tryan, Len Floyd, Randy Pederson, Pat Audet, Randy Stolen, Tony Vigliotti, Greg Stolen, Bob Tryan, Brian Gilbert, Joey Girard, Marty Davis (behind Doc), Steve Schaefer, Mike Tryan, Don Lekvold. At Thompson Park, Laurel. *Family photo.*

served their country, but also served their communities when they returned from overseas. This was Doc's last divisional tournament—within spitting distance of his hometown of Billings—and state tournament, and this team sent him out as a winner in both tournaments.

In the background is the dugout at Thompson Park in Laurel. Thompson Park was where Doc's first postseason began in 1959 when Scobey played off against Laurel in a best-of-three series for the eastern division championship. No one could have imagined—not even Doc himself—the program and the team he would bring back 24 years later. Thompson Park symbolizes time—building a successful team and program takes time. Doc had a young team in 1959, and his program was in its first year. Dennis Gaub in the *Gazette* wrote in his 1981 article, "The 'big man' of the 1959 team was a 17-year-old who weighed 130 pounds; remaining players were 14-year-olds. That team played Laurel. Doc said, 'I remember a bunch of great big kids chewing tobacco.'"[277] Laurel won the series in two games, but year after year, he was building teams and a program that would become a dynasty. Success took time; Doc won his first state championship in 1969. In 1979, Scobey beat Laurel 11-0 for the state championship in Scobey. And it all started with the 1959 team at Thompson Park in Laurel. Doc returned to the same field and won the eastern divisional championship 24 years later, in 1982, the last year of the dynasty. It was fitting that Doc's postseason

legacy in Eastern Montana ended where it began: Laurel is a great baseball town, and the Dodgers have a great Legion program—Laurel is the only town to have more state championships (nine) than Scobey (eight). The eastern division championship in Laurel was Doc's tenth in his coaching career.

Success—defined in Scobey as winning state championships—also required combining the boys' talent across Daniels County. (And Valley County and Sheridan County in 1982, too.) In addition to all the talented boys from Scobey, boys from Opheim (Len Floyd), Glentana (Greg Stolen), Peerless (Larry Trangsrud), Flaxville (Mike, Gord, and Bob Tryan), and Plentywood (Randy Pederson) are in the photo. These boys symbolize that for Scobey to compete against the larger Montana towns for state championships, the talents of the boys in Daniels County—and Valley and Sheridan counties in 1982—needed to combine. The first all–Daniels County team was formed in 1968, and Scobey's first state championship followed a year later in 1969.

At the right of the photo is Don Lekvold, who symbolizes continuity. Don Lekvold was Doc's right-hand man for six years. He had the same competitive spirit, passion for the game, and baseball knowledge as Doc. He had been with the Blues since 1977 and had been the assistant coach for four state championships, as the four patches on his jacket show. Where would the fifth patch go, Don? It doesn't look like there is any more room. Don would take the reins of the Blues program the following season, beginning the Don Lekvold era, which would run for nine years, from 1983 to 1991.

Just behind and to Randy Pederson's left is Pat Audet; the second from the left is Jim Lekvold. Pat and Jim symbolize leadership. They started playing Legion ball in 1979, my last season when they were 14. They were part of our state championship run as young boys in 1979; now, they were 17 years old, Legion age, and leaders on the team. All of Scobey's successful Legion teams had good leaders. Randy Pederson was also a leader on the 1982 team. When talent, a strong work ethic, a positive attitude, and a propensity to lead combine, that is a recipe for success. The others will follow.

Doc faces batboy Josh Lee, his grandson, the son of Ken and Ann (Norman) Lee, who would later become a starter for the Scobey Blues. Josh symbolizes the passing of baseball down to the next generation. Josh's last season playing Legion ball was 1993, and his older brother Mike would play on Don Lekvold's best team in 1990, taking third at State and narrowly missing a trip to regionals. Rick played on the 1981 team. All three of the Lee boys—Rick, Mike, and Josh—had been batboys for the Blues for several years. Ken Lee helped coach for some years, and Mike Lee coached the last Scobey Blues team to make it to the state tournament in 1997. Mike Norman started the generational play of the Norman family in 1959 when he started at first base as a 14-year-old on Doc's first team in Scobey.

Behind Randy Pederson is Assistant Coach Randy Stolen, barely visible, but the mustache gives him away. Randy symbolizes the excellence of the Blues. He had just finished his first season playing center field for Colorado State University, where he was the Rams' second-leading hitter with a .398 average and led the team with nine home runs. His coach felt he should have been selected to the All-Western Athletic Conference team. As Doc said in his interview with Dennis Gaub, "We've had some remarkable talent around here for such a little town."

Then there are the Blues themselves, who had just won their 13th consecutive game and the eastern divisional championship over Sidney. Holding the trophy is Randy Pederson, "the import from Plentywood," who would help the Blues win their eighth state championship the following weekend. Randy symbolizes opportunity—the opportunity to play American Legion Baseball. When Plentywood was not able to field a team after the start of the season, Randy was able to come to play for Scobey. The same happened for the Hagfeldt boys in Glasgow when, in 1971, Dallas Hagfeldt could come to Scobey to play because Glasgow did not field a team. Think of all the boys who lived in towns with no Legion baseball program and never had an opportunity to play baseball in the summer when they got older. Remember Doc's interview with Dennis Gaub from the *Billings Gazette* in 1981? Doc started his medical practice in Columbus in 1951 and helped start an American Legion Baseball program there. Doc said, "The kids didn't have anything to do" in the summer, but Doc gave them something to do. That was Doc. He loved baseball, but he also loved giving. And all the Blues who ever played for him can thank him for the opportunity to play baseball in the summer.

Tony Vigliotti is helping Randy hold the trophy—although the "sturdy and demonstrably rugged lad" from Plentywood needed no help. Tony symbolizes the youth of Doc's program, how he "drafted" players at a young age, indoctrinating them into his program and teaching them how to play Blues baseball when they were Babe Ruth–age. Tony had started playing for the Blues as a 14-year-old in 1980, played in 1981, and now was the starting left fielder on a state championship team in 1982. Standing to the far left with the glasses and jacket is Larry Trangsrud, whom Doc called when he was only 12 to recruit him to play for the Blues as a 13-year-old. Now 14, Larry would become the starting catcher for Don Lekvold in the following years, catching on Don Lekvold's third-place 1985 team, playing in the last state tournament Scobey hosted. Larry was the last of Doc's "recruited" players to play when he finished his Legion career in 1986.

Symbolically, Marge Norman is not in the picture because she was always the woman behind the scenes, the quiet force that underpinned the entire operation; without her contribution, none of it could have ever happened. Marge was aptly described in the August 3, 1978, *Leader* as the "always dependable chief of staff" of the Scobey Blues American Legion Baseball Program. In an article in the August 18, 2016, *Leader* titled "Blues Cruise To 8 State Titles in 14 Seasons to Spawn a Dynasty," the *Leader* wrote, "She was involved in all eight as her husband, Dr. Clyde H. 'Doc' Norman, was the head coach of all eight. She washed uniforms, set up where the team would eat and sleep while on the road, plus a myriad of other things it takes to make a baseball program run smoothly, including 'keeping them out of mischief,' she said. 'I was the gopher, and I loved it.'"

Behind Larry Trangsrud is Kelly Norman, who symbolizes the contribution of the entire Norman family to Scobey baseball. Besides Marge and Doc, the only other person involved in all eight state championships was their son, Kelly, who was a batboy (1969, 1973), player (1976-80), and assistant coach (1982).

Finally, who took the photo? It was Patti Audet, Pat Audet's mom, who symbolizes the love and support that the Blues got from our parents, the community, and the countless volunteers who made it possible for all of us to play American Legion Baseball in the summer.

If "a picture says a thousand words," I used 1,023 to describe it, so I guess that's close. The picture of the 1982 Scobey Blues symbolizes the end of an era but the beginning of a new one. The Scobey Blues were the best team in the state of Montana in 1982, and they were the last state championship for Scobey, but Don Lekvold would ensure the boys would have the opportunity to play American Legion Baseball the following season, and the storied baseball tradition of Scobey—"Baseball Country," as Jack Reiner always used to say—would continue. A lot of American Legion Baseball was left to play in Scobey, Montana. And many teams and boys would shine in the northeastern Montana summers.

Randy Pederson embraces Steve Johnson of Sidney following the Eastern Divisional championship game. Doc Norman is to the right, and assistant coach Randy Stolen is to the left. *Family photo.*

The Billings Cardinals beat Glasgow 3-2 to finish third in the East Division, so the four teams advancing to State from the east were Scobey, Sidney, the Billings Cardinals, and Glasgow.

Following the championship game on Sunday night, Doc made a decision—very popular with the players—to proceed directly to Deer Lodge from Laurel on Monday rather than return to Scobey and then have to turn right around on Wednesday and head for the state tournament in Deer Lodge, which began on Thursday. Pat Audet recalls the special experience: "In what other program could you actually go on a two-week, postseason road trip kicking ass while having a great time as a *team* and, more importantly, as friends? After winning the 1982 divisional tourney in Laurel, Doc said, 'Boys, we are not going back to Scobey; we are heading straight to the state tourney in Deer Lodge.' Priceless."

As the Bluesmobile rolled into Deer Lodge on Monday, not only were the Blues riding into Deer Lodge as the champions of the eastern division, but they were also riding a 13-game winning streak. They had just defeated the team that had dominated them during the regular season. Scobey was not a team or a program you wanted to face with momentum and confidence heading into a state tournament, and the Blues had both as they entered the "Prison City."

And the Blues would take no prisoners in the Prison City over the next few days.

STATE B TOURNAMENT

THE STATE CLASS B AMERICAN LEGION TOURNAMENT WAS played on Roy Chapman Memorial Field in Deer Lodge. The western divisional, as it had been the year before, was also played on Roy Chapman Memorial Field in Deer Lodge. Both number-one seeds during the regular season—the Missoula Reds in the southwestern district and the Havre Northstars in the northwestern district—were upset at the western divisional. The four teams that survived were Lethbridge, Fairfield, Deer Lodge, and Vauxhall, joining Scobey, Sidney, Billings, and Glasgow from the east.

Lethbridge and Vauxhall? From Alberta? Get out, eh? Yes, 1982 was a significant change for American Legion Baseball in Montana, as the Lethbridge Elks joined the Class A ranks, and the Lethbridge Miners and Vauxhall Spurs joined the Class B ranks, all of them qualifying for the state tournaments. I had played baseball against a lot of teams from Saskatchewan growing up in Peerless, but never from Alberta. However, whether from Saskatchewan or Alberta, any American who had played against the Canadian teams would know they knew how to play baseball, and stiff competition was to be expected from north of the border.

The opening-day matchups on Chapman Field were as follows:

- Billings Cardinals (3E) vs. Fairfield Blue Jays (2W)
- Scobey Blues (1E) vs. Vauxhall Spurs (4W)
- Sidney Patriots (2E) vs. Deer Lodge Wranglers (3W)
- Lethbridge Miners (1W) vs. Glasgow Reds (4E)

Doc started Pat Audet in the first game against the Spurs. The game was historically significant, marking the first time a Montana team had played a Canadian team in the state tournament.

Scobey started strong against the Spurs, scoring two runs in the first and then adding two more in the third on a two-run home run by starting pitcher Pat Audet. The Blues scored three more in the fourth on a bases-loaded triple by Greg Stolen to jump to a 7-1 lead. Vauxhall countered with three runs in the top of the fifth, then added a run in the seventh to pull to within 7-5.

Scobey scored an insurance run in the top of the ninth to close out the scoring and win the 8-5 opener over Vauxhall. Greg Stolen came in to pitch in the seventh and pitched the final three innings for Scobey to earn the save and preserve Pat's win. Many of Vauxhall's five runs were unearned, as the Blues committed seven errors in the game. Pat Audet's two-run homer and Greg Stolen's three-run triple—Scobey's only extra-base hits—proved to be the difference, as those two swings accounted for five of Scobey's eight runs.

Scobey faced the Billings Cardinals in their second game, who had beaten Fairfield 10-9 in 10 innings to advance. Scobey had pummeled the Cardinals 23-9 a week earlier in the eastern divisional semifinals, but this game would be different. It was a very tense game.

Doc handed the ball to "Iron Man" Randy Pederson in this game, who had pitched all 11 innings in the eastern divisional championship game a week earlier, giving up only one run to win 2-1. Scobey jumped on Billings for two runs in the top of the first and never trailed in the game, but the stubborn young Billings hung around and wouldn't go away. Scobey scored three runs in the top of the fifth to make it 5-1, but the Cardinals countered with three runs in their half to close to 5-4. Single runs by each team in the seventh left the score 6-5, with Scobey coming to bat in the top of the eighth. This was way too close for comfort, and Scobey needed a rally to put some distance between them and the Cardinals.

And the rally came—in the form of a grand slam home run by Jim Lekvold. Well, an *apparent* grand slam. Joey Girard missed home plate, so one of the runs was taken away, but when the three runs were counted, Scobey had that space they needed and led 9-5. Randy Pederson shut down the Cardinals in the bottom of the eighth, and Greg Stolen came on in relief again to close out the game in the ninth, and the Blues advanced with a 9-5 win on the strength of Lekvold's home run. Pat Audet had three hits in four trips to the plate, with a double and a triple. Greg Stolen also doubled for Scobey. Randy Pederson pitched eight strong innings to get the win, and Greg pitched a scoreless ninth to preserve it.

That put Scobey in the undefeated semifinal against defending state champion Sidney, who had made its way to the semifinal by overpowering host Deer Lodge 17-4 in five innings in the opener, then beating the Lethbridge Miners 7-3 in their second game on the strength of Mark Price's four-hitter.

So, the two best teams in the state were pitted against each other in the critical semifinal, and everyone at State knew it. "It had become apparent to state tournament fans and officials early on that the two best teams in action were Scobey Blues and the Richland County Patriots from Sidney. They've been going head and head at each other all season, but at the recent divisional, Scobey edged them for that title 2-1 at Laurel."[278] The winner of this game would be in the driver's seat to win it all. The Scobey Blues versus the Richland County Patriots. Scobey, winners of seven state championships and five in a row until the Richland County Patriots ended their season—and the streak—a year ago in Glendive. Scobey was playing to take the state championship back; Sidney to defend it. Two teams from the east were playing on the western stage, so far from home, reminiscent of Cut Bank, where Scobey played for the state championship against Wolf Point in 1976 and against Glendive in 1978. The stage was set for some eastern-style baseball in the undefeated semifinal on Roy Chapman Memorial Field in the Prison City. And everyone there would be treated to what would be considered the most well-played game in the tournament.

Doc handed the ball to the "strong and talented"[279] Greg Stolen to pitch the all-important semifinal while Sidney countered with Ted Ritter. Greg had pitched in relief in the first two games but still had nine innings of eligibility left. He started the damage against Sidney with his bat, smacking out his first of three hits in the first inning, driving in two runs and staking Scobey to a 2-0 lead. Scobey had a three-run rally in the fifth to take a 5-1 lead, but Sidney got to Greg for two runs in the bottom half to close to 5-3. Scobey scored their final run in the top of the eighth, and Sidney scored their final run in the bottom of the ninth to make the final score 6-4. After his first-inning two-run single, Greg got two more hits for a 3-for-4 day at the plate, but he mostly hurt Sidney with his arm as he held the heavy-hitting Sidney team at bay, striking out nine Patriots, scattering six hits and walking only one. Scobey committed three errors, but the Blues "kept the bad stuff scattered,"[280] minimizing the damage.

So, at the end of the day on Saturday, the Scobey Blues found themselves in a familiar situation: 3-0 in the tournament and needing one more win to claim the state championship.

The following day, Sidney won their play-in game to the championship 7-3 over Lethbridge, setting up the championship game between the two best teams in the tournament and a rematch of the eastern divisional championship. The

Scobey-Sidney game on Saturday was an "exciting dress rehearsal"[281] for the game on Sunday. The two teams had gone head-to-head all season; now it was time to determine the best team. It would take only one win for Scobey but two for Sidney.

Pat Audet started for Scobey in the state championship game, while Tom Barnhart—who had pitched the 2-1 duel in Laurel—started for Sidney. Tom Barnhart picked right up where he left off in Laurel, holding Scobey scoreless in the first three frames, while Sidney got to Scobey for three runs in the third to take a 3-0 lead. Scobey countered with a run in the top of the fourth, but Sidney came right back with two in their half to take a 5-1 lead after four innings.

Trailing 5-1 after four against a strong Sidney team was not a good place to be in the state championship game. The Scobey bats needed to get going. A breakout inning was needed, and the Blues got it in the fifth, as they plated four runs to tie the game 5-5. The big blow for Scobey was a two-run home run by Pat Audet, his first of two dingers in the game.

Doc made a pitching change in the fifth, as Randy Pederson, who had been catching, took his catcher's gear off and swapped places with Pat, who put the catcher's gear on.

The game seesawed back and forth at that point, with Sidney regaining the lead in the bottom of the fifth by scoring a single run to make it 6-5, but Scobey came right back in the top of the sixth to take their first lead—a lead they never relinquished—at 7-6. Scobey added another run in the top of the seventh to make it 8-6. In the bottom of the seventh, Doc brought in his third pitcher of the game, Greg Stolen, to close out the game for Scobey. Sidney got a single run in their frame to close to 8-7. This was a nail-biter of a championship game. Scobey did not want to lose and go to a Monday game, as Doc was exhausting the innings of his top three pitchers in this game, going all out to win it. "Doc Norman and his talented staff decided to go all out in this game and close the books."[282] Even with a one-game cushion, Scobey was playing this game as if there was no tomorrow.

Then, as had been the case in many of Scobey's previous state championship victories, one big inning was the deciding factor. That inning in this game for Scobey came in the top of the eighth when the Blues broke it open, exploding for six runs, with the brunt of the barrage coming on Pat Audet's second two-run home run of the game. By this time, Sidney was using its fifth pitcher, and Scobey ran back on the field in the bottom of the eighth with a commanding 14-7 lead, needing only six more outs to claim their eighth state championship. When Greg pitched a scoreless eighth, Scobey's championship out-count was down to three.

Pat Audet is congratulated after hitting his second home run of the State championship game against Sidney. That is assistant coach Randy Stolen with the double high five. *Family photo.*

But Scobey was not done at the plate, as they scored one more run in the top of the ninth to make it 15-7. Sidney got to Greg for a run in the bottom of the ninth, making the final score 15-8 Scobey, and the Blues celebrated their eighth state championship on Roy Chapman Memorial Field in Deer Lodge. For the game, tournament-MVP Pat Audet was 3 for 5, had a double and two home runs for the only extra-base hits, drove in four runs, and scored four times to lead Scobey to the win.

Doc and his staff had indeed managed this game as if there were no tomorrow. In the championship game, he threw his top three pitchers at Sidney, exhausting their 12-inning limits, as all three pitchers had pitched previously in the tournament. Randy Pederson, who relieved Pat in the fifth, was the winning pitcher, getting his second win of the tournament, and Greg Stolen earned his second save of the tournament to go along with his win over Sidney the previous day. Greg had pitched in all four of Scobey's games. Pat Audet was the winning pitcher in the first game against Vauxhall. The arms were done. Sidney out-hit Scobey 12 to 10, and Scobey committed a whopping eight errors, which is not good, but Sidney's four errors were more costly, and Pat Audet's two two-run home runs, plus an RBI double, were too much for Sidney to overcome. Scobey had wrestled the state championship from the team that ended the streak a year earlier.

TOURNAMENT SUMMARY

Scobey's eighth and final state championship in Deer Lodge was unique and historically significant for several reasons: it was the swan song for Doc, and he went out a winner; it was Scobey's last state championship; they beat the team (Sidney) that had dethroned them the previous

Scobey Blues, 1982 State Class B Champions. Back row left to right: Doc Norman, Randy Stolen, Jimmy "Sneed" Lekvold, Larry Trangsrud, Greg Stolen, Brian Gilbert, Pat "10er" Audet, Steve "Red" Schaefer, Don Lekvold, Kelly Norman. Front row left to right: Mike Tryan, Joey Girard, Randy "Iron Man" Peterson, Len Floyd, Gordy Tryan, Tony Vigliotti, Marty Davis, Bob Tryan. Roy Chapman Memorial Field, Deer Lodge. *Family photo.*

Scobey Blues during the trophy presentation. Left to right: Jim Lekvold (or Tony Vigliotti), Brian Gilbert, Steve Schaefer, Pat Audet (triumphantly signaling state champions), Larry Trangsrud, Joey Girard. *Family photo.*

year; they played their first Canadian team in a state tournament; the team started 3-7 and won their 17th straight game in the state championship game; Pat Audet hit two home runs in the state championship game, the only Blue to do that.

Their trail was steady through the tournament. They won 8-5 over Vauxhall, 9-5 over Billings, 6-4 over Sidney, then finished with a flourish, winning 15-8 over Sidney in the championship game.

Assistant Coach Kelly Norman provided his perspective on the success of the 1982 Scobey Blues: "The main players—Pat Audet, Jim Lekvold, and Greg Stolen—had been around since 1979. Add Randy Pederson and a bunch of kids who scrapped and competed hard. Len Floyd from Opheim was a decent player. Mike Tryan was quick and stole a lot of bases. Pat and Petey were vocal leaders, while Greg . . . was Greg—he was so talented. Jim Lekvold was solid all the way around and was a leader, too. He knew and loved baseball and the Blues. He was always around the teams and our house when younger and batboy, too. He was our biggest fan growing up. Most of the kids grew up wanting to be a Scobey Blue. For lack of another word, the Blues' mystique and history helped them and probably affected the other teams. 'Scobey Blues just win!'"

The *Leader* summarized the Blues player's postseason performances: "The batting order in both divisional and at State proved to be effective: Jim Lekvold (usually catching), Pat Audet (plays anywhere as well, but most center field or catching), Greg Stolen (usually at shortstop, but also a very strong pitcher), Randy Pederson (pitching, catching, short), Tony Vigliotti (generally in left field; he gets on base more different ways), Gordy Tryan (sturdy 3rd baseman, strong arm and often a key hitter), Len Floyd (first base, very steady with the glove at first; in the final game he struck out, got three walks and a hit); Joe Girard (usually at second base, still a bit green but he's got moxie handling that tough spot; Joe got five walks in the two Sidney games). Mike Tryan (good defensive right fielder, often gets on base at key times); and Steve Schaefer and Marty Davis alternating in right field."[283]

The 1982 state championship was the third for Pat Audet, Jim Lekvold, Greg Stolen, and Gord Tryan and the second for Tony Vigliotti, Mike Tryan, and Steve Schaefer.

1982 Richland County Patriots, State Class B Runners-Up. Standing, left to right: Head Coach Jeff Lebsock, Todd Schlenker, Mike Jensen, Chuck Ritter, Jim Miller, Tom Barnhart, Tim Mulholland, Mark Price, Assistant Coach Bryon Johnson. Kneeling, left to right: Terry Heit, Steve Johnson, Chris Volk, Brian Paladichuk, Lance Butner, Ron Melin, Mitch Melby. Travis Frandsen, Robby Gratz, Bob Thilmony, and Robert Lovegren are not pictured.

TOURNAMENT STATS

Hitting

SCOBEY'S RUN PRODUCTION AT THE STATE TOURNAMENT WAS good, as the Blues averaged 9.5 runs per game, with most of the output and power coming from the top three hitters in the lineup, as they had the highest averages and all 11 of Scobey's extra-base hits. Leadoff hitter Jim Lekvold was 6 for 13 (.462) with a homer and two doubles for a slugging percentage of .846; Pat Audet, who batted second, was 9 for 19 (.474) with two doubles, a triple, and three home runs for an incredible slugging percentage of 1.158; third-place hitter Greg Stolen was also 9 for 19 (.474) with a double and a triple. Scobey's run-scoring and hitting were opportunistic, as the Blues only hit .254 as a team. But as Assistant Coach Kelly Norman said, "Yes, our lineup was very top heavy, but those others got on base, had some speed, would occasionally hit, and could bunt. They were good defensively, and each found ways to help offensively at different times." Jim Lekvold's grand slam home run was an excellent example of that. He batted leadoff, so the bases would have been loaded with Blues from the bottom of the lineup when he hit his grand salami. A team doesn't average 9.5 runs a game, with only the top four hitters getting on base. Gord Tryan, who batted sixth, could also hit for power.

Pat Audet was named the tournament's MVP. He hit 9 for 19 (.474) with two doubles, a triple, and three home runs, was the winning pitcher in game one, and started the championship game. He also played center field and caught in two games. *Family photo.*

Pat Audet was named the tournament's MVP, and his unbelievable hitting performance was a big part of why. He was also the winning pitcher in game one and started the championship game, played center field, and caught in two games. Pat said, "Had a good tournament. After struggling a bit at the plate during divisional, bat got hot at the right time."

Pitching

DOC AND HIS STAFF USED ONLY HIS TOP THREE PITCHERS IN the tournament, deftly managing their innings across the four games and 36 innings to win it. Greg Stolen was the workhorse, pitching 14 innings. He appeared in all four games on the mound and was the winning pitcher against Sidney in the semifinal, scattering six hits and striking out nine Patriots. He earned two saves, one against Vauxhall and the other against Sidney in the championship game. Pat Audet pitched 11 innings. He started against Vauxhall and pitched into the seventh inning to get the win, giving up five runs, then started and pitched into the fifth inning of the championship game, giving up five runs, but many were unearned due to "butterfingered action"[284] as Scobey committed eight errors in the game. Randy Pederson also pitched 11 innings. He got the win against the Cardinals, going eight solid innings and giving up five runs, and Greg Stolen pitched a scoreless ninth to close out the game. Randy relieved Pat in the fifth inning of the championship game and pitched into the seventh inning to get the win. Greg Stolen was brought in the seventh in a save opportunity with Scobey leading 8-6 and earned his second save of the tournament in two-plus innings of relief. Jim Lekvold did most of the catching, but Pat Audet and Randy Pederson would also get some innings behind the plate.

Fielding

SCOBEY'S FIELDING WAS NOT WHAT WON THEM THE STATE championship, but as Joe Garagiola once said, "It's pitching, hitting, and defense that wins. Any two can win. All three make you unbeatable." Scobey's superiority in pitching and opportunistic hitting was enough to win the state championship. Scobey's error count across the four games was seven errors against Vauxhall, three against the Cardinals, five against Sidney in the undefeated semifinal, and eight in the final, averaging 5.75 per game. But the Blues made the plays they needed to win, and that is all that matters. They only averaged one more error a game than their opponents, and their bats and pitching won them the tournament.

STATE A PLAYOFFS

THE BLUES, AS THEY HAD DONE TWO YEARS EARLIER IN 1980, would play off in a best-of-three series against the Great Falls Electrics, the third-place finisher in the Western Class A Conference with a 13-11 record, for the right to qualify for the State Class A tournament. Scobey needed to play the third seed because Anaconda was in last place in the standings and was hosting the State Class A Tournament later that week.

This time, the series would be played at the finer Legion Park instead of Optimist Field, where the series between Scobey and the Electrics was played two years earlier. And

Gord Tryan would get to play his normal position at third base instead of left field and not worry about funky ground rule double rules at Optimist's curled-up chain-linked outfield fence.

Unfortunately for Scobey, it might not have mattered where this series was played or what position Gord played because the Blues ran into a buzzsaw in the form of a 17-year-old, five-foot-nine, 160-pound left-handed flame-thrower named Bill Wilkinson. One player does not win a two-game series, but . . . maybe.

In the first game, Wilkinson pitched eight innings, gave up one hit, and struck out 20 Blues to lead Great Falls to a 10-3 win. Great Falls scored five runs in the first two innings to take a 5-0 lead, which was way more run production than Wilkinson needed. With Great Falls leading 10-1 in the eighth, Electrics Manager Joe Campagna took Wilkinson out to save his innings in case he needed him in the second game, and he did. For Scobey's pitching, Pat Audet started and went five innings and was relieved by Tony Vigliotti, who finished the game. Scobey needed to play well defensively to stay in the game, and their six miscues didn't help. Pat Audet, Greg Stolen, and Steve Schaefer got Scobey's three hits, but only one off Wilkinson.

The second game was different, and Scobey had a chance to win it. Greg Stolen started, went the distance, and pitched a fine game against the Electrics, keeping Scobey in the game. Scobey was leading 3-1 in the bottom of the sixth when the Electrics picked up one run to make it 3-2. Then, with two outs in the bottom of the seventh, Les Mills hit a two-out, two-run single to give the Electrics a 4-3 lead.

You can guess what happened next.

Bill Wilkinson was brought in to close it for Great Falls as he relieved starter Ken McKnight in the eighth. And when Wilkinson entered the game with the one-run lead, *Tribune* sportswriter Tim Roby said all that needed to be said: "The contest was history."[285] Wilkinson surrendered a hit, but he pitched two scoreless innings of relief to earn the save, striking out five of the seven Blues he faced, including striking out the side for the fifth time on the day. In 10 innings pitched, Wilkinson struck out 25 Blues, gave up two hits and no earned runs, getting the win in the first game and the save in the second.

Joey Girard said, "That Great Falls series was humbling." Pat Audet agreed: "It sure was my friend. It sure was. I just remember nobody could get a bat on this guy. Came with the heat." Of the 30 outs Wilkinson recorded in the two games that day, 25 came via strikeout, so only five Blues put the ball in play off him. One Blue who did get the bat on the ball and put the ball in play was Steve Schaefer, who got the only hit off Wilkinson in the first game, breaking up his no-hitter. Steve said, "I remember getting a swinging bunt off of him and reaching first base." Pat Audet got the second hit of the day off Wilkinson in the second game. Randy Pederson said of Wilkinson, "Like he was only 17, and the word on the street was he pitched 93 miles an hour. Well, I don't know if it was 93, but it had to be 12 miles an hour faster than I'd seen a pitch that year. I don't really know if I struck out three times, but I did improve over seeing him more. I think the first baseman was getting me out by the last two times I batted off him."

Although the Blues lost both games, *Tribune* sportswriter Roby recognized their solid play: "The Electrics needed a seventh-inning rally to stop a tough Scobey club that won the State B title."[286] Scobey had nothing to be ashamed of, especially running into the likes of Bill Wilkinson. Don Lekvold was naturally disappointed in the two losses and reflected on the games, saying, "We didn't play as well as we're capable of, we had too many errors, and we quit hitting when we needed the bats the most." But he then reflected on the successful year the Blues had. "We were 3-7 at one time, and we finished 25-12, so we've had a good year. But it's tough to win here (Legion Park), when you're playing the Electrics, especially with a pitcher like Wilkinson."

It was indeed a successful year for Scobey, winning the state championship after a 3-7 start, and this wasn't the first time a season had ended with a disappointing footnote in the Class A playoffs. The following year, 1983, would be the last year the State Class B champion would play off against a Class A team to get into the State A Tournament, and more changes were coming for Class B Legion baseball in Montana after that, with a regional tournament at the Class B level.

The 1982 state title would be Scobey's last and the end of the Doc Norman era. But not the end of American Legion Baseball in Scobey, as Don Lekvold would ensure the continuity of the fine tradition would continue. And the Daniels County boys can be grateful to Don for providing them with the opportunity to continue to play Legion baseball in the summer, as Doc Norman had been doing since he started the Legion baseball program in Columbus in 1951, continued coaching Babe Ruth and Legion in Missoula from 1955 to 1958, then Legion in Scobey beginning in 1959.

For Len Floyd, Gord Tryan, and Randy Pederson, the games against the Electrics were their last in a Scobey Blues uniform, but all three of them would return to Great Falls and finish their Legion careers playing in the first Class B American Legion All-Star game later in August at this same park.

Randy Pederson remembers his magical summer with the Blues well. He spent a lot of time in Doc and Marge's house as he was away from Plentywood all summer. Randy said, "Being a guest in Doc and Marge's house . . . I kind of get choked up about it. Doc kind of felt like another dad, I guess you could say. I never had that amount of mentoring—five coaches (Doc, Don, Kelly, Randy, and Kirby) at practice and the games. I'm just used to one. That's got a powerful effect when you have people helping you, you know. Don Lekvold was always there. I never got so much help pitching. I improved in two months an extreme amount. It was the greatest summer I ever had." And he added what an amazing program Scobey had. "Scobey had as many uniforms as the Oakland A's. They don't have one batboy; they have two batboys. They don't have one batgirl; they have two batgirls. It was just a top-notch organization."

Gord Tryan developed as a baseball player through the Flaxville farm club, playing for his dad, Don Tryan, as had his older brother, Dan Tryan, before him, and his younger brother Mike. Flaxville had fielded a Legion program through 1967, Dan Tryan's last year. Randy Legare and Jack Higgins joined the Scobey Legion team in 1968, and three more Flaxville players joined in 1969, the first year Scobey won the state tournament. I asked Dan and Gord to share their baseball stories, and they each wrote a letter telling their respective tales. Dan's letter is in 1967, and here is Gord's:

Growing up on our farm south of Flaxville, baseball was always a topic at the dining table. My older brother Dan was playing baseball when I came around, so I was always tagging along to be with him to the fields. My dad always helped coach, so it was easy for me to be there. I cannot remember a time when I did not have a glove, ball, or bat.

Papa, my grandfather George Tryan, listened to every Minnesota Twins game on the radio. (He never missed a game.) So, I grew up listening to the exploits of Harmon Killebrew, Tony Olivia, and Rod Carew (my favorite). All three are in the Hall of Fame.

Little League was always the highlight of my summers. I started playing at the age of six, and with an August 2nd birthday, I was still playing Little League when I was turning thirteen. Growing up in a rural area of Montana, we had long drives to play ball. We would travel as far as sixty miles just to get a game in. When we traveled, we always played doubleheaders. So, the moms always had slush burgers, chips, and drinks after every game. There was no fast food to stop and get on the way home.

Growing up, the rodeo scene was very popular in Flaxville. So, there were not a lot of kids playing ball. I would find any way I could to hit a ball. One of the baseball memories from growing up that always puts a smile on my face is playing home run derby with Cory Tryan. We had a home plate, and the barn and pig fence were the home run. We would toss it up ourselves to hit it over the fence. If you did not hit a home run, it was an out. We would play until dark as often as we could.

I played Babe Ruth for Plentywood. I remember one of the first practices; our farm was 47 miles from Plentywood, and I was nervous since I did not know anyone very well. When it was my turn at batting practice, I could not hit the ball to save my life. Zoonie McLean was the coach. He was doing his best to help me, but I continued to struggle. Finally, he grabbed the bat and showed me how to hit. He never missed a pitch. What made it even worse, he turned the bat around, held the barrel, and hit it with the handle. He still did not miss a pitch.

1982 was my last year of Legion, and we had a team that got along extremely well. We were a team of really good players from top to bottom. I even got to play with my younger brother, Mike. We added Petey (Randy Pederson) from Plentywood to our team that year, and he was the missing cog that allowed us to climb back to the top of the Class B ranks. I do not remember how many innings he pitched, but his arm never got tired.

Behind the backstop at home plate was the scores booth. In front of that, in the shade, was a bench that all the old-timers sat on. Papa, my grandfather George Tryan, was one of those who never missed a game on that bench. I think the pressure to perform for those guys was just as intense as performing for Doc. There was a lot of Blues history and knowledge sitting on that bench.

Divisionals that year were in Billings, and we won the tournament, beating Sidney in the championship game. When it was over, Doc decided we would not drive back to Scobey, so we turned around and drove to Deer Lodge for state. So, we stayed in Laurel and worked our way to Deer Lodge, including a stop at the Big Timber water slides. That was over a two-week road trip. (I do not know who funded all that, but I have an idea.) That culminated in us winning the state championship again.

My favorite Doc story has nothing to do with baseball. This story exemplifies how Doc felt about those of us who were fortunate enough to play baseball for him.

It was the fall of 1978, and I had to go to Doc for my school physical so I could participate in high school sports for Flaxville. It was my first physical, and I did not know what to expect. So, I walked into his office; there was no exam room or anything like that, just Doc sitting behind his desk. He had me walk around to him at his desk, listened to my heart, and asked how I felt. I said fine. He had me sit down, and the rest of the appointment was talking about baseball.

My last thought. Who still has the red Webster's Dictionary that they got from Doc and Marge for high school graduation? I do!

PLAINSMEN

THE SCOBEY PLAINSMEN, MANAGED BY DAN WOLFE, WERE active again in the summer of 1982. This was the last year the Scobey Plainsmen fielded a team, ending the town team baseball tradition that had started when Scobey fielded its first baseball team, managed by Lou Boyd, in 1914. When I returned from summer school at Montana Tech, I remember playing with the team for a few games. I am proud to be able to say I got to play on the Scobey Plainsmen town team, a team with so much history and tradition I was amazed by how much my former teammates had improved now that several of them had been playing college baseball, and they were older, physically stronger, and more mature. (Not mentally more mature; that never happened.) Dan Danelson was playing at Lewis and Clark State, Kirby Halvorson at Pacific Lutheran, Randy Stolen and Kelly Norman at Colorado State, and Mike Hagfeldt had played at North Idaho College for two years, then transferred to Dickinson State and played two more years there, making the first team All-Conference both years and throwing discus and javelin at the same time. What was extraordinary about the 1982 Plainsmen team was that players from seven state championship teams—1969, 1973, 1976-1980—and players who had played Legion ball from 1968 to 1981 were on the same field. This was similar to the 1973 Scobey Plainsmen team, which had players from Doc's first team in 1959 (Rod Tande) to 1971 (Jim Hansen) on the team.

Danny Wolfe planned a rambler schedule for the Plainsmen that summer against teams from Saskatchewan, as there were no town teams left in northeastern Montana. While the Blues played Vauxhall, Alberta, at the state tournament in Deer Lodge, the Plainsmen played teams from Saskatchewan in Canada and Scobey.

There were some intriguing games for the Plainsmen that summer. Although several of us hadn't played competitive baseball for a few years, others were still actively playing college baseball and in peak condition. In a game against the Moose Jaw Astros, Dan Danelson, with Kelly Norman catching, pitched five innings of one-hit ball and struck out 10 to lead Scobey to an 8-6 win. Danelson pitched into the seventh inning when I relieved him, then Mike Hagfeldt came in to finish it off. (Never thought I'd ever be a middle-inning reliever.) Mike Hagfeldt got the save. We jumped on the Astros with a four-run first inning. After two walks, Randy Stolen singled, then Wade Tryan and Kirby Halvorson followed with back-to-back doubles. In this game, Billy Bartels came in to pitch for Moose Jaw in the fifth inning and pitched three innings. Kirby remembers him. "My first job out of college was as the Head Athletic Trainer for the Great Falls Dodgers in the Pioneer League. Bartels pitched collegiately at Cal State, Fresno, was drafted by the Dodgers, and pitched in Great Falls when I was there. He was a good pitcher—smart, crafty. Couldn't and didn't overpower anybody but had good off-speed stuff. We were having a chat one day, and he asked me where I was from. I told him Scobey, a little town in northeastern Montana. He said, 'You're kidding—I remember we went there when I was playing summer ball in Moose Jaw. That rag-tag bunch could play.'" Billy Bartels pitched for three years in the minors, two in the Dodgers organization and one with the Red Sox.

Plentywood formed a town team for a few games that summer. Kirby Halvorson slammed a two-run homer to lead the Plainsmen to a 10-4 win. Halvorson also had two singles and drove in four runs. Doug Selvig was 2 for 4 for Plentywood, and Mike McLean had a double. Mark Johnson and I each had two hits for Scobey, and Don Hagfeldt tripled. This game was historically significant, as it was the last town team played between old baseball rivals Scobey and Plentywood. The baseball rivalry dates back to 1914 when Scobey and Plentywood split the season series two games apiece. However, the "rivalry" in 1982 was not even a shadow of what it once was, as we probably all went out to have a beer together after the game. Or at least went to the same bar.

In another game against the Moose Jaw Astros, Randy Stolen hit a three-run homer, and Mike Hagfeldt added a solo shot as the Plainsmen outslugged the Moose Jaw Astros 10-9. Mike Hagfeldt remembers his home run. "It was almost to dead center which was around 400 feet. There were some Lombardi poplars behind the fence, and it went over those. I never had that much power and I remember wishing we had aluminum bats like those back when I played." This was the second win of the season for the Plainsmen over the Moose Jaw Astros, champions of the Saskatchewan Major Baseball League in 1982.

In the first game of a doubleheader against the Weyburn Merchants, Dan Danelson pitched a one-hitter to lead Scobey to a 10-0 win. Mike Hagfeldt banged a two-run homer to lead the hitting. In the second game, Terry Puckett clubbed a three-run home run, and Kelly Norman added a two-run blast to lead Scobey to an 11-1 win and the sweep.

In a tournament played on the Fourth of July weekend in Scobey, the Plainsmen swept all three games to win the second annual round-robin tournament championship. The Plainsmen defeated the Saskatoon Patrick Liners, 13-7, Rouleau, Saskatchewan, 11-10 in 10 innings, and Circle 21-3. In the win over Rouleau, Jon Puckett went 3 for 5 with a home run and a double, and Dan Danelson and Kelly Norman also homered for Scobey. Dan Danelson got the win for Scobey pitching. What was unique about this game was that brothers Dan and Rick Danelson played in the same game together, with Dano pitching and Rick playing third. Dano remembers the special experience: "Funny how we all just picked right up where we left off. Winning a few games. That was a blast playing with Terry and Rick. Two people I grew up admiring and then having the steady influence of Mike again."

In the 21-3 win over Circle, Terry Puckett and Jon Puckett pitched a combined four-hitter. Terry Puckett got the win, pitching five innings, and Jon pitched the final four innings. Terry, who was pitching with a torn labrum from Legion and had torn his ACL playing flag football in college in 1976, recalls, "I couldn't rotate my arm over my head. I couldn't throw like normal, straight overhead. It had to be slightly sidearm. I had no ACL in my right leg after the '76 championship intramural flag football game at Butte. I turned to catch a pass behind me, and it blew. But we won! They carried me off the field and laid me in the stands till the game was over! Then to the hospital. Had surgery three times. Didn't work. So, I always wore a brace to stop further damage when playing sports. It made it so I couldn't play after Legion. No left arm and no right knee kind of handicap you! Replaced the knee in 2000." When I reminded him he got the five-inning win over Circle, Terry said, "They must have been in worse shape than me!" Wade Tryan went 4 for 5, Kelly Norman and Randy Stolen doubled, Jon Puckett tripled, and Kelly Norman hit a home run. About his torn labrum, Terry added, "After I completely tore my arm apart in 1973, I couldn't rotate my arm after that. I couldn't swim because the rotation of the arm swimming was the same as pitching. When I got in my fifties, I got a job that had good insurance. I was doing water therapy for it and learned that I had a torn shoulder labrum [a thick piece of tissue attached to the rim of the shoulder socket that helps keep the ball of the joint in place.] My arm would have to go out of socket in order to rotate. The doctor put anchors in there and it is much better now."

In the 13-7 win over Saskatoon, Kelly Norman hit two home runs, one a grand slam. That gave "King Kong" Kelly Norman four home runs in the tournament. Five years earlier, flashing a little power at the 1977 state tournament when he was only 15 years old, Cliff Hagfeldt nicknamed him "King Kong" Kelly Norman. In that tournament, Kelly recalls, "Using my Johnny Bench 32-inch bat, one of my hits was about 3 to 4 feet to the left side of second base and not on the first base side, one of my few hits to the left side. The dugout stood up, clapped, and cheered! I'm sure it was because of my pure power." Five years later, Kelly had grown into the nickname Cliff gave him and did have "pure power." The tournament was remarkable: Dan Wolfe managed; Rick and Dan Danelson played together; Terry and Jon Puckett pitched a combined four-hitter; Kelly hit four home runs; Hairy and Mike Hagfeldt played together again. Imagine that lineup with four left-handed sticks: Rick Danelson, Terry Puckett, Randy Stolen, and Mike Hagfeldt. Dano said, "That would be a tough lineup for a righty." Yes, it would.

Jon Puckett impersonated his second MLB baseball player—this time unintentionally—playing for the Plainsmen that summer. Jon recalls, "In one of the Plainsmen games, I started on the mound. Kelly was catching. He came to visit me on the mound before I faced my first hitter to get our signs straight. Before he could get a word out, he started snickering because the uniform I was wearing was an old Plainsmen uniform with some baggy pants. He said I looked like Mickey Lolich." Thus, Jon's baseball career concluded with the impersonation of two Mickeys: speedy leadoff hitter Mickey Rivers batting and chunky left-hander Mickey Lolich pitching. Quite the range there, Jon.

Plainsmen Manager Dan Wolfe arranged some road trips to Canada that summer. Dan recalls, "We went to Canada, and Terry Puckett wanted to pitch one more time. I remember Terry started the game, and I think he went maybe one or two innings before his arm gave out." Terry remembers the game, "I told Wolfe I'd try pitching one more time. I think it was Moose Jaw. I pitched one inning, went back out for the second, and couldn't even get the ball to the plate. I remember trying to pitch overhead in that inning in Canada because they were very good [champions of Saskatchewan]. The arm was really painful, and the knee was really bad. Not replaced yet, though. They put me on first 'cause we only had nine guys!"

That game against the Moose Jaw Astros took a nasty turn. Terry Puckett recalls, "I got my pitching index finger cut bad sliding into second. The whole team had to wait in the hospital for me to get stitches. A guy on their team was taken out by someone sliding into second. He was at the hospital, too, with a knee injury!" Mike Hagfeldt recalls the incident. "Hairy [Don Hagfeldt] took the kid out at second.

He was a stud hockey player who had recovered from a knee injury. They weren't happy. It was after that when they brought in their ace lefty. Next time up, sure enough, Hairy got plunked. The poetic justice in the whole thing is that he ended up coming around to score the winning run. Terry was bleeding like a stuck pig from his finger. Talk about guts! He stuck it out because we only had nine players. We went to the hospital after the game, and he needed stitches. It was a bit uncomfortable there because that shortstop was there at the same time. I remember Hairy saying he wasn't watching the shortstop and was concentrating on getting to the bag. The shortstop caught the ball and stayed on the bag. It was the third out."

Another game in Moose Jaw was the Plainsmen's only loss of the season. Kirby recalls, "They threw a big lefty that had pitched for the Canadian National Team. I think I had a couple of doubles off him." The "big lefty" that pitched was Rod Heisler, selected as a pitcher for the Canadian National Team and as a first-team All-Star for the Saskatchewan Major Baseball League, along with three other Astros.

On one of the road trips to Canada, Danny Wolfe recalls, "I remember calling Dave Fanning to see if he wanted to go up with us also, but he couldn't come." Fanning remembers the call. "I couldn't get off work. I was working for Burlington Northern at the time. I was pissed I couldn't go. Sounds like it would have been fun." Imagine Terry Puckett and Dave Fanning on the same pitching staff—in their prime. I told Dan, "You probably could have won a few games managing with those two pitchers on your staff." He replied, "When they were in their prime, for sure, I wouldn't have done much managing, though, just watched them pitch." But Dan did see the two left-handers pitch in 1971 with the best seat in the house—he caught Terry Puckett and batted off Dave Fanning in their epic 1-0 pitcher's duel at the state tournament in Scobey.

Kirby Halvorson remembers playing a game on the road trip to Unity, Saskatchewan, six and a half hours from Scobey. "Mike Neubauer caught. Kelly at short. Me at third. Had a lot of ground balls to third, and the infield was rough and ruts everywhere. I couldn't fucking stop anything. Some dude in the crowd yelled out, 'Hey, third baseman, why don't you just put your legs together like a goalie, eh?' We had to stop the game because Kelly was lying on the ground laughing." Mike Hagfeldt recalls how far north the Unity trip was. "I swear it was above the Arctic Circle! Looonnggg trip."

Dano remembers that one of the teams they beat in Saskatchewan that summer was loaded with three quality Americans from the University of Washington and Oregon State and three or four Canadians playing in the states. Dano said, "One of the guys I played with at LCSC made the comment to me after we got back together at college, 'You guys play a little baseball where you come from.' Duh."

And, of course, former Scobey Blues traveling on a road trip to Saskatchewan playing for the Plainsmen would have to be involved in some shenanigans. It wouldn't be the Scobey Blues without that. Kirby remembers, "For various reasons, we were running late driving to the Unity Cardinals game. I was driving my Firebird and got through Port of Scobey and was whipping along listening to the Big Timber State basketball game on cassette tape (got screwed and lost). Kelly flipped a double-bird at the radio just when a Canadian biker gang was coming the other way. I hit the jets . . . the yellow bird got up to 110 mph at least. We didn't make Unity until the third inning." Kelly said, "I told Kirby to drive fast as a motherfucker baby! I was so scared that those bikers were going to come back and kick this little white boy's ass." Coming back on the same trip, Kirby remembers, "Kelly, Stoley, and I stopped in Swift Current or Saskatoon and met teammates at a Pizza Place. It was getting late, so the Opheim and Scobey ports were closed. We didn't want to drive all the way to the Port of Raymond, so we drove south of Coronach and Rockglen on some gravel road that turned into a section road and ended up by Carney's farm to Peerless turnoff. We stopped on the side of the road, and Kelly pulled it out and pissed on the side of the road without even standing up. We're getting ready to head out, and the Mounties pull up behind us. One goes to the driver's side, and the other inspects Kelly's puddle. He says, 'What's this?' and Kelly says something like, 'I just couldn't hold it, man.' Meanwhile, the other RCMP is talking to Stoley. 'Where are you boys from? Don't you know we have an open container law in Saskatchewan?' 'No, officer, we didn't know.' 'Don't they have open container laws in Montana, in Scobey?' 'Well, no, officer, we are not aware of any open container laws in the States.' Anyway, they made us dump our existing open beers, told Stoley to drive carefully, and 'have a nice day, eh?'"

Kelly wishes the Plainsmen could have played more games that summer. "Too bad we didn't play a 25-game schedule and be in that league. With these players, we could have played every day and been good! Versatile bunch of players and loaded pitching." But the town-team era was over long ago.

EXTRA INNINGS

IN HIS LETTER, GORD TRYAN REMEMBERED HIS GRANDPA George Tryan sitting behind the backstop watching the games and wondered who some of the old-timers were who sat there. Three of them—all amputees wounded in World War II—were Ernie Halvorson, Ben Danelson, and Cliff Hanson. Pete Kurtz, Earl Randall, and Jess Wiley would also be at many games but usually sat in the grandstand. There were others. There is a great story about Josh Lee and those old-timers who sat behind the backstop. As Kelly tells it, "When Josh was little, one of the amputees showed him his leg. He was wide-eyed. Then another showed him—and another. They asked him why he didn't have one."

Since we're talking about the old-timers sitting behind the backstop, Dan Danelson shared a funny story about his dad, Ben Danelson. "Dad [Ben] was in the bar after one of our championships, not in Scobey. He was sitting on a bar stool and whoever was with him helped concoct a plan to have Dad loosen his belt that held his artificial leg on. He would pretend to have a cramp and have the barhop come over and ask her to please pull on his foot to help get rid of the cramp. Sure enough, she obliged and fell on her butt when pulling. Ended up on the floor with a leg in her hand, screaming or laughing or both."

Mitch Melby was playing his final season for Sidney in 1982. Growing up in Sidney, he lived just outside the left-field fence at Moose Memorial Park and was involved in the infamous "timeout-gate" incident. In the ninth inning of an elimination game between Plentywood and Sidney in the 1977 Eastern Divisional Tournament at Sidney, Mitch threw a ball over the fence into left field just before Randy Wangerin of Plentywood clubbed what would have been a game-winning home run over the left field fence. However, the home run was called back because time had been called by the third base umpire due to the ball on the field. Sidney went on to win the game. Wangerin and the Plentywood team were naturally upset (to put it mildly), but Jeff Nesper recalls, "The third-base ump *did* call 'time,' but the home plate ump and pitcher did not hear it, and the hitter [Wangerin] did launch it over the fence. I think Mitch got that one as well." Sidney went on to finish second at Divisional—and second at State a week later in Scobey—but would have been eliminated had they lost that game to Plentywood. This time, Mitch was helping his team win games on the field rather than throwing balls onto the field just before game-winning home runs were hit. Mitched played in the East-West All-Star game.

Scobey's last state championship in 1982 marked the end of the Scobey dynasty but also the end of the Havre-Scobey dynasty. Between 1968 and 1982, Havre and Scobey won 13 of 15 state Class B championships. The two teams that spoiled the Northstars and Blues party were the Billings Scarlets in 1974 and the Richland County Patriots in 1981.

Scobey's six-run eighth inning against Sidney in the state championship was the sixth time in eight state championships that Scobey used one big inning to win a state championship. In 1969, Scobey had a big five-run first inning and went on to beat Havre 7-6; in 1973, Scobey used a seven-run eighth to beat Wolf Point 9-6; in 1976, it was a 10-run seventh against Wolf Point to come from behind an 11-3 deficit to win 13-11; in 1977, Scobey scored 10 runs in the third inning against Sidney, going on to win 13-3; in 1980 Scobey had a big 10-run fifth to blow open the game against the Missoula Reds, going on to win 18-3. In these six state championships, Scobey scored an average of eight runs in one inning.

Not since 1971, when Dave Fanning of the Havre Northstars outdueled Terry Puckett 1-0 in the semifinal at the state tournament in Scobey, had the Blues seen the likes of a left-handed flamethrower like Bill Wilkinson. Fanning struck out 11 Blues that day in Scobey. In comparing the two left-handers, it is uncanny how similar Dave Fanning and Bill Wilkinson were. Both were small in stature, especially considering they were pitchers and how hard they threw.

Wilkinson was 5'10" and 160 pounds; Fanning was 5'11" and 155 pounds. (They were probably smaller than that in Legion; those numbers are when they were pitching professionally.) Both pitchers hurled one-hitters at the Blues. In 1971, leadoff hitter Don Higgins beat out a bunt to spoil Fanning's no-no; in 1982, Steve Schaefer broke up Wilkinson's no-no with a "swinging bunt." (How Steve Schaefer refers to his hit.) Both pitchers effectively ended Scobey's seasons and were drafted. Wilkinson's 25-strikeout performance against Scobey in 10 innings in two games recalls Fanning's performance against the Billings Royals in the 1971 State A Tournament when he struck out 25 Royals in 12 innings. To steal a quote (and modify it slightly) from catcher Crash Davis in *Bull Durham*, "They had a gift. When they were babies, the gods reached down and turned their left arms into thunderbolts."

Scobey and Sidney had a history of dethroning each other as state champions in baseball, and it ran in the family. In 1958, the Scobey Plainsmen won the Montana National Baseball Congress (NBC) state championship but were knocked off in 1959 by the Sidney Gems. Then Scobey won the 1960 NBC state championship, taking the title back from Sidney. Craig

Price played for the 1958-60 Sidney Gems; his son Mark played for the 1980-82 Patriots. Andy Stolen and Kenny Lekvold played for the 1958-1960 Plainsmen; their sons, Greg and Jim, played for the 1980–82 Blues.

Although it seemed unusual when Legion posts like Scobey and Plentywood combined to form a Legion team in 1982, that happened every year in Babe Ruth with the Mondak All-Stars. I always played with kids from Plentywood—Opheim, Glentana, Scobey, Flaxville, Outlook, Froid, and Culbertson—on Mondak All-Stars. Phil Audet played with Randy Pederson's older brother, Gary, on the Mondak All-Stars in 1963, along with Dan Tryan from Flaxville. Then, in 1966, Phil and Gary pitched against each other in Legion in a one-game playoff between Scobey and Plentywood to go to State at Cobb Field, with Phil winning the pitcher's duel 4-2. Gary pitched for runner-up Plentywood at the state tournament at Cobb Field in 1966 and collegiately at Rocky Mountain College. In 1969, he pitched for Rocky against Phil Audet at Northern and Craig Audet at Eastern. Gary passed away in 2015.

Joey Girard was not the only Scobey Legion or town team player to miss a base on a home run. In the 1930 Eastern Montana championship between Scobey and Billings, Smith missed second base on his extra-base hit with two outs and the bases loaded, and as a result, three runs, and possibly a fourth—his own—were voided on the appeal. "Scobey had the ball game won, except for the late Smitty, whom they claimed did not touch second base when he drove in what would have been the winning run and was on his way to score."[287] Another costly base running incident happened in the deciding game of a three-game series between Scobey and Fairview in 1914. "Scobey pitcher Cliff Rule stepped up and knocked a ball clean out of the park, with two men on base. Rule jogged around. The umpire said he didn't touch second base and called him out. Scobey lost that game, 3 to 2."[288] So please don't feel bad, Joey, it happens! And Joey's miss of home plate on Jim Lekvold's home run against the Cardinals was harmless, as it only cost Scobey one run because there were less than two outs, so three runs scored, and Scobey won the game 9-5. For the record, I missed first base on a three-run home run I hit at Moose Memorial Park in Sidney in 1977, but the umpire did not see it, and Sidney did not appeal, so all three runs counted.

In Major League Baseball, Fred Merkle of the New York Giants made the worst baserunning mistake in a game against the Chicago Cubs on September 23, 1908. It became known as "Merkle's Boner." Merkle failed to advance to second base on what should have been the game-winning hit, leading instead to a force play at second and a tied game. The Cubs later won the makeup game, which proved decisive as they beat the Giants by one game to win the National League pennant for 1908. Now, that's a costly baserunning mistake. The pennant!

Pat Audet commented on how much Randy Pederson meant to the team in 1982. "Acquiring Petey (we called him 'Pete' or 'Petey,' never Randy) early in the season when Plentywood folded was probably one of the more important pieces that put us over the top from not just being a good team but a championship team. He was a tough player and had the grit needed to get the job done anywhere on the field, but especially on the mound and offensively at the plate. His going the distance in the divisional chipper was no surprise to anyone; he was that tough and had the endurance. I like how the *Leader* referred to him as 'Iron Man' heading the game article. I think we'd all agree that he was also the secret sauce that got us over the hump in finally tapping Sidney when it counted, not only at divisional but two more times at State. (He wasn't with us yet when we lost to Sidney earlier in the season)."

Assistant Coach Kirby Halvorson also commented on Randy Pederson's contribution to the team. "Petey was a good kid. He was very appreciative of having the opportunity to play for a good program. He was very competitive and a real bulldog on the mound. He threw pretty hard but learned to mix it up a bit that year, which I believe made him more effective. He had a little Jon [Puckett] in him—start, relieve, and come in whenever needed."

Pat Audet has fond memories of playing poker on the Blues bus trips. "The bittersweet feeling you got when someone lost their ass at poker. . . especially on a huge pot of acey-deucey. And the hot, flushed, dismal feeling when it happened to you. Yep, felt it a time or two."

Jim Lekvold recalls the 500-mile trip home to Scobey after winning the state championship: "It was lots of fun! Longest bus trip I've ever been on (especially after a night of sitting in rooms, watching TV, and drinking pop—*not*.) Deer Lodge to Scobey, with stops in every damn town to give updates on where we were. I will never forget it, though. Fun bunch of guys to hang out with: 'Blues Brothers.'" The trip back to Scobey from Deer Lodge for the 1982 team terminated an 11-day, 1100-mile road trip for the Blues, bringing back two pieces of hardware in their triumphant return to Scobey.

In the category of *not* drinking pop, the 1980 and 1982 state championship teams had it good, celebrating their state championship wins. They were the beneficiaries of assistant coaches who provided the beer. In 1980, in Cut Bank, it was Assistant Coach Dan Danelson. Pat Audet recalls, "Dano bought the beer, and Dick Lannon even had a beer while driving. Not so sure we stopped along the way to get more booze." In 1982, in Deer Lodge, it was Assistant Coach Kelly Norman. The championship teams I played on that won on the road didn't have it so good—we drove back to Scobey after winning the 1976 and 1978 state tournaments in Cut Bank, arriving in the early morning hours. However, Allan Audet shared a pitcher of beer (legally) with Doc and Don Lekvold following the 1978 state championship in Cut Bank. The rest of us were not so fortunate; none of us was 18.

The Electrics won two games in the State A Tournament and took fourth place. Bill Wilkinson went seven and two-thirds innings in the first game and gave up only two singles to Helena, but took the loss when he ran into control problems in the eighth. He walked five hitters, was relieved, and Helena scored five runs to win 8-6. Wilkinson saved the next two games, but his arm gave out in his fourth appearance, and he took his second loss of the tournament. The Electrics heavily depended on his arm, as he pitched 20 of the 34 innings in the tournament.

Bill Wilkinson's family moved to the Denver, Colorado, area in the fall of 1982 for his senior year in high school. In the spring of 1983, Wilkinson was 12-0 with a 0.17 earned-run average and 115 strikeouts in 56 innings for state-champion Cherry Creek High School. He didn't allow an earned run until the final game of the regular season. He then pitched for Cherry Creek Legion and was 5-0 before being taken in the fourth round of the 1983 MLB June Amateur Draft by the Seattle Mariners in June. He chose to sign a contract to play professional baseball rather than finish his Legion career and play baseball for the University of Nebraska. He made his major league debut for the Mariners in 1985 and pitched for the Mariners in 1987-1988. In his three years in the majors, he had a win-loss record of 5-8 with 12 saves and an ERA of 4.13, logging 113 innings and striking out 103 hitters. He pitched eight seasons in the minors, mostly AAA, and had a record of 33-34 with a 4.17 ERA, striking out 509 hitters in 593 innings pitched.

Normally, a long foul ball wouldn't be discussed, but Gord Tryan's booming hit that arched just foul down the left field line in Deer Lodge made such an impression on his teammates that, through the years, some remembered it as a mammoth home run. Gord Tryan recalls the plate appearance: "It was on a 3-0 count in our last at-bat against Sidney. There were huge trees over the left-field fence. I hit it over the top of them just foul. I ended up with a single." Jim Lekvold recalls, "Kelly would say, a 2-0, 3-0 pitch will be cock high. Let her rip!" So Gord let it rip on the 3-0 cock-high fastball and barely missed a home run. The Doc Norman Hitting School had additional hitting instructions with consistent messaging. Kirby Halvorson recalls how Doc taught him to hit a curveball: "Wait on it till it gets right in front of your dick."

A Class B All-Star game for 18-year-olds was played for the first time. The Class B East-West All-Star game—played before the Class A All-Star game at Legion Park in Great Falls—pitted the best 18-year-olds from the western division against the eastern division. Len Floyd, Gord Tryan, and Randy Pederson made the team from Scobey, and they all played. Randy Pederson pitched four and one-third innings of relief and got the win for the East. Chuck Ritter from Sidney was named MVP, and the East won the game 11-8 over the West.

Randy Pederson was the only pitcher for the Blues besides Dick Puckett in 1969 to be the winning pitcher in both the eastern divisional championship game and the State championship game. Let's throw in the East-West All-Star game, too—the trifecta.

Great Falls was not the friendliest of places for the Scobey Legion program—5 of 8 seasons ended on Legion Park or Optimist Field in Great Falls. In 1969, Scobey lost to the Great Falls Electrics at Legion Park in a one-game playoff. In 1973, Scobey was eliminated from the state tournament in two games at Legion Park. In 1978, the Blues lost to the Chargers at Legion Park in two games. In 1980, the Blues lost to the Electrics in two games at Optimist Field; in 1982, the Blues lost in two games to the Electrics at Legion Park. But Gord, Len, and Randy got to play in the East-West All-Star game at Legion Park, and the East won, so we'll call that a win.

It's hard to resist comparing the 1982 season to the 1973 team. In each season, another team had eliminated Scobey from the state tournament the previous year and dominated Scobey during the regular season to win the conference, but Scobey won the Divisional championship in extra innings and then won the State championship over the same team. In 1972, Wolf Point eliminated Scobey 9-0 in the state tournament, then dominated Scobey during the 1973 regular season, winning 3 out of 4 games to win the district. But Scobey, led by Terry Puckett's 16-strikeout performance pitching all 12 innings with a partially torn labrum, beat Wolf Point 10-6 in the 12-inning Divisional championship game, then beat Wolf Point twice the following week to win the state championship. Likewise, for the 1982 team, Sidney had eliminated Scobey from the 1981 state tournament 12-1, then dominated Scobey during the regular season, winning the conference. Randy Pederson pitched all 11 innings in the 2-1 win in the Divisional championship, and Scobey beat Sidney twice the following week to win the State championship.

Second baseman Joey Girard shared a story about Doc at practice in 1982. "We were playing the Great Falls Electrics in a series to get into the A state tourney. They had a kid named Wilkerson who threw gas (mid-90s). In order to give us a chance, we had that old pitching machine cranked beyond 90. It was wild and horrifying, and most of us were pussing out pretty hard in the cage. Doc had had about enough of us whiffing. For the record, Donnie Lekvold was feeding the machine and protesting pretty hard about Doc being in the cage! As I remember it, he laid down a couple of legit bunts before dropping down one off the butt end of the bat. In retrospect, it was awesome and scary. Doc had again made his point."

Jim Lekvold remembers Doc coaching from his Ford Fiesta during practice. "The Fiesta was an orange two-door hatchback. He would drive that car right onto the field and park close to home plate. I remember when we would be taking batting practice, if you lay down or sat down in center field, Doc couldn't see us while he sat in the car. The ground in center field was lower than home plate, and the mound also obstructed the view."

Pat Audet remembers Bill Wilkinson. "He could bring it—mid-nineties was maybe average, but he topped three digits every now and then. I remember eyeing up ole Bill on the mound, not realizing it was him. Here's this kid on the mound, not very big, uniform two sizes too big for him, and glasses that turned dark in the sun—a real pile of nerd warming up. As we started the game, Jim Lekvold was leadoff, and I was on deck. Bill threw his first smoke show down the tube. Jimmy looked over at me with eyes wide and mouthed, 'I didn't even fucking see it.' From there, I was good with intimidation and got sat in three pitches."

Pat reflected on his three home runs in the state tournament this way: "I attribute the crisp mountain air to the dingers at Deer Lodge. I had one in the opener against Vauxhall and two (almost three) in the chipper with Sidney. The two-bagger went off the wall, which could have been a three-bagger, but I left the batter's box in a home run trot." Had Pat not broken into his home run trot on the double, he might have tripled and joined Jack Higgins as the only Scobey player to hit for the cycle in the state tournament—the shame the MVP must bear.

Rob Fladager is the only Blue besides Pat Audet to hit two home runs in the same game. In the 1992 eastern divisional championship game at Sportsman Park in Plentywood, Rob hit two home runs in his first two plate appearances against Sidney, leading Scobey to a 15-9 win. He also had five RBIs in the game. Rob is the only player to do this in my research and collection of players' memories. Please let me know if anyone remembers another Blue who hit two home runs in one game.

Jim "Sneed" Lekvold recalls his grand slam (three-run) home run against the Cardinals in the state tournament. "I went opposite field. (Of all my home runs, most of them were to the opposite field.) There is no better feeling than hitting a home run, but a 'Grand Poobah' in a state tournament was overwhelming. There were tennis courts down the right-field line. Part of the chain-link fence came out to the playing field. That distance was, I'm guessing, 275' or maybe a little further. The fence came out to the playing field and then did a 90-degree turn to meet up with the rest of the playing field fence. That distance probably was 315' or further. Not really sure of the fence dimensions of that field. According to some people, that home run would have cleared the fence if it was a normal outfield fence. I get harassed about it only going that 275 feet or so. That's OK. A home run is a home run. Supposedly, Joey went back to home plate and touched it. Other players saw he did miss it and yelled for him to go back. Ump must not have seen that. I was so damn excited that I really had to slow up so I wouldn't pass the other runners. I never really did the home run trot. I was probably at second by the time it went over the fence. Then I guess I did finally slow up rounding third."

While Sneed could hit home runs in the leadoff position, his teammates, Joey Girard and Pat Audet, recall his ability to get on base and speed. Joey said, "Sneed just always found a way on base." Pat described Jim as "the perfect leadoff man. Smart and could read the pitch well, off the release." Joey added, "Dude could fly as well. Can't imagine how many runs he scored."

Doc rarely called anyone by their first name; he had a nickname for everyone. Sometimes, he would make one up if someone didn't have a nickname. (For example, Doc made up the nickname "Guiseppe" for me, but no one else called me Guiseppe but Doc.) In other cases, the players—batgirl, batboy (it didn't matter)—came with a prepackaged nickname, and Doc would use that. Jimmy "Sneed" Lekvold's nickname had an interesting "etymology," and Doc was part of its development. Sneed recalls, "When a bunch of us neighbor kids would do something cool, someone would say, 'But *steeba* or *steema*.' Why that word was said, I have no idea. So, in 1979, while we were taking infield practice, when someone did something so-called 'cool,' I would say, 'But *sneed*.' Come to find out, I was saying it wrong. So, when I would do something 'cool,' Doc would say, "But *sneed*' and then others would say that too as time went on. It stuck. Something funny. When I was living in Billings, people would call me 'Jimmy Sneed.' Some people thought that was my last name. So, 45 years later, there are lots and lots of people who still call me that. They may have even forgotten my real name." The neighborhood kids who said, "steeba or steema" when Sneed was younger were Steve and Brad Metts, Keith Becker, Mike Lapke, and Paul Fugere.

Right fielder Mike Tryan remembers a funny story about Doc, where Doc wore his two hats as a physician and a baseball coach on the field. "I was feeding the pitching machine at baseball practice, and I think it was Len Floyd who hit a line drive, and I took it right on the chin. It knocked me out for just a second. Everyone came running up. I came to right away and I remember Doc yelling, 'Bring him to me.' I got help, they walked me up to Doc, and I yelled, 'I can't see! I can't see!' Then Doc replied, 'Open up your eyes.' I did, and I could see. I remember asking him if I should go see a doctor. He replied, 'You just did that will be fifty dollars.' My mom told me that he called her three times that night just to see how I was doing. He was such a great man."

There were some off-the-field shenanigans in Deer Lodge. It wouldn't be the Blues without that. This tale is known as the "leave a dump" story to the 1982 Blues. Pat Audet recalls, "I think it was our first night in Deer Lodge, and these girls came over to the hotel to check out the team, I guess. I'm not sure who invited them, but they were in our room visiting with us and whatnot. One went into the bathroom; needless to say, she didn't flush, leaving a present for all to see. I noticed my Bengals hat was gone either that night or the next morning. Somebody had their names; then, I think we looked up the last names in the phone book or something, eventually arriving at where one lived. Kelly, Randy, me, and maybe one or two others jumped in the car and went to her place. Think her mom was there; anyway, she gave up the hat, and low and behold, it was the girl who isolated herself in our bathroom—now with the moniker "leave a dump."

Mike Tryan recalls more shenanigans at the state tournament in Deer Lodge. "We were staying at a motel, and the night before the championship game, Pat Audet and I snuck out of our room and went out walking with some girls. Somehow, Pat and I got separated, but I kept walking with this girl to a party. It got late and I was there alone and didn't know what to do, so I sat outside the door on the porch, and all of a sudden, Coach Lekvold and Kelly Norman drove up. I was so glad to see them. I asked them if Doc was mad, but they said it's your dad that was mad. The next day, right before the game started, I remember Coach Lekvold and Doc were talking about what they should do. We were home team, so we went out in the field first. Well, I was benched for what I did. Doc did not want to do this because he said we are here to win this damn game. But it happened. Someone else started in right field, and I was benched. When we were in the first inning, I remember I was sitting in the dugout with my head hung low, and the player who was playing for me went up to get ready to hit. All of a sudden, Doc yelled, 'Tryan pinch hit!' I remember Doc and Don arguing about me hitting, but all I remember is Doc saying, 'We came here to win this damn game, and we're gonna win it, Tryan pinch hit.' And the rest was history. We did win the game. State champs once again."

Scobey wasn't the only team at the tournament with batgirls. Pat Audet remembers the walk that resulted in Mike getting benched at the start of the championship game. "I was walking with the bat girl from Deer Lodge, Lisa Greany. Lisa and Stephanie Gray were the bat girls for Deer Lodge; Stephanie was the daughter of Deer Lodge coach Mike Gray, I believe. They signed my three home run balls for the tourney and the team." Great sportsmanship, eh? (Since Canadian teams were at State, let's use that.) But none of the Deer Lodge Wranglers signed the home run balls, so maybe there was more to the story. Pat still has the signed home run balls, along with his Blues teammates' signatures.

In the summer of 1982, I would drive my dad's mail route west to Opheim. On the days I would layover in Opheim at midday to deliver the mail on the rural route, I played Greg Stolen in tennis in Opheim. Yes, Opheim had a tennis court—and a three-hole golf course. It was a veritable resort town. In the tennis matches I played Greg, I was amazed at what a remarkably talented athlete he was. I don't think I ever beat him (not that I was Jimmy Connors or John McEnroe). The balls would come back at me with a helluva lot more mustard on them than I was hitting the other way. No matter what sport Greg played, he was good at it—just a natural athlete.

Another memory from the summer of 1982 is visiting Kelly at Doc and Marge's house and watching baseball on TV with Doc. Since he was retired, he was at home during the day. If they were playing at home at Wrigley Field, the Chicago Cubs would play afternoon games because Wrigley Field did not have lights—they were not installed until 1988. I was watching the Cubs on WGN-TV with Doc and Kelly. Harry Caray was calling the game in his first year broadcasting for the Cubs. Doc was in heaven watching the games. He would analyze the game, always anticipating the manager's next move, and comment on the plays being made. Dana Audet said the Scobey Legion uniforms in 1972 were modeled after the Chicago Cubs. On the left front of the jersey was a large, white capital *S* on a red background enclosed in an outlined circle

The summer of 1982 was a good one for baseball in Scobey. The Scobey Blues won the eastern divisional tournament and Scobey's eighth state championship; the Scobey Plainsmen went 10-1, winning their round-robin tournament and beating the Saskatchewan Major Baseball League champions twice. But 1982 also marked the end of three baseball eras in Scobey: it was Scobey's last American Legion state championship, the end of the Doc Norman era, and the last year the Plainsmen fielded a team. The folding of the Plainsmen ended the town-team baseball tradition that had started when Scobey fielded its first baseball team in 1914. The Plainsmen, managed by Joe Anderson, won two National Baseball Congress Montana state championships in 1958 and 1960 and were runners-up in 1959. The Scobey Plainsmen also won several Northeastern Montana League championships. Peerless, Opheim, Four Buttes, Whitetail, and Flaxville also used to have town teams. Looking back on Daniels County baseball history, the town teams were the hottest ticket in town before the baby boomers got to be American Legion age in the early-to-mid 1960s, and then it became American Legion Baseball. Raising the Junior Legion age to 18 in 1961 also contributed to the rise of Legion ball. Before that, the 18-year-olds would have to play with the town teams. For example, in 1982, based on the Legion age before 1961, Randy Pederson, Gord Tryan, and Len Floyd would have all had to play on a town team if they wanted to play baseball. While Scobey's first town baseball team was in 1914, the first year the team was dubbed the Plainsmen was in 1948. Thus, the Scobey town team years were 1914-1982.

But the sun would rise on a new era of Scobey American Legion Baseball the following season. Plenty of Legion baseball was left to be played in Scobey. Coach Don Lekvold would ensure the Scobey Blues American Legion Baseball tradition would continue, with many talented players, teams, and memorable state tournament moments to follow.

1969–1982

SECTION NOTES

1. "Local Legion Drops Scorcher to Scobey," *Missoulian*, June 15, 1969.
2. "Schuster Fans 15; Tops Scobey," *Billings Gazette*, July 30, 1969.
3. Ibid.
4. Ibid.
5. "Scobey: Legion Team to Beat," *Billings Gazette*, August 6, 1969.
6. "Scobey Ready for State Tourney Here," *Daniels County Leader*, August 7, 1969.
7. "Team to Beat," *Gazette*.
8. Ibid.
9. "Scobey Wins Area's First Baseball Title," *Daniels County Leader*, August 14, 1969.
10. Ibid.
11. Ibid.
12. *The Rookie*, directed by John Lee Hancock, Walt Disney Pictures, 2002.
13. "Scobey Wins Title," *Leader*.
14. Ibid.
15. Ibid.
16. Ibid.
17. Ibid.
18. Ibid.
19. Ibid.
20. Ibid.
21. Ibid.
22. Ibid.
23. Ibid.
24. Ibid.
25. "Tired Scobey Club Loses to Great Falls," *Daniels County Leader*, August 14, 1969.
26. "Electrics Blast Their Way into State Tourney," *Great Falls Tribune*, August 13, 1969.
27. "Scobey Wins Second, State Legion Tournament," *Daniels County Leader*, August 20, 1970.
28. Ibid.
29. Ibid.
30. Ibid.
31. Ibid.
32. Ibid.
33. Ibid.
34. Ibid.
35. Ibid.
36. Ibid.
37. Ibid.
38. "Havre Out of Tourney," *Montana Standard*, August 22, 1970.
39. "Scobey Wins Second," *Leader*.
40. Ibid.
41. Ibid.
42. Ibid.
43. Ibid.
44. "Scobey Wins Second," *Leader*, August 20, 1970.
45. Ibid.
46. "Scobey Hosts State Tourney . . . Starts Today," *Daniels County Leader*, August 12, 1971.
47. "Havre Eyes 2nd Title," *Great Falls Tribune*, August 12, 1971.
48. "Havre Wins Opener," *Billings Gazette*, August 13, 1971.
49. "Fanning's 1-hit win puts Havre in finals," *Billings Gazette*, August 14, 1971.
50. "BULLETIN," *Billings Gazette*, August 14, 1971.
51. "Havre Wins State Class B Tourney Here," *Daniels County Leader*, August 19, 1971.
52. Ibid.
53. Ibid.
54. Ibid.
55. Ibid.
56. Ibid.
57. Ibid.
58. "Havre Beat Royals in 14th," *Billings Gazette*, July 11, 2010.
59. Ibid.
60. "Recalling When Havre Hurler Fanned Foes with Regularity," *Great Falls Tribune*, Scott Mansch, July 11, 2010.
61. "Impossible dream ends in nightmare," *Billings Gazette*, Norm Clarke, August 21, 1971.
62. Ibid.
63. "Goodwill via baseball," *Great Falls Tribune*, July 4, 1971.
64. "What it was was baseball," *Billings Gazette*, August 8, 1971.
65. "Senators Win, 17-2," *Helena Independent Record*, June 6, 1972.
66. "Scobey Wins Eastern Division," *Daniels County Leader*, August 10, 1972.
67. "Scramble in the Offing for Best Legion B Team," *Great Falls Tribune*, August 9, 1972.
68. "State Class B Tourney Off to Colorful Start," *Havre Daily News*, August 11, 1972.
69. "Scramble in Offing for Best Legion B Team," *Great Falls Tribune*, August 2, 1972.
70. "Scobey Wins Divisional at Miles City," *Daniels County Leader*, August 2, 1973.
71. Ibid.
72. "Scobey Takes Eastern District 'B,'" *Miles City Star*, July 30, 1973.
73. "Scobey Wins," *Leader*.
74. "State Tourney on Here Today," *Daniels County Leader*, August 2, 1973.
75. "Havre Shooting for Fourth Legion B Title," *The Daily Inter Lake*, August 1, 1973.
76. "Scobey Wins State Title in Thriller," *Daniels County Leader*, August 9, 1973.
77. Ibid.
78. Ibid.
79. Ibid.
80. Ibid.
81. Ibid.
82. Ibid.
83. "Legion Club Takes In State Series," *Daniels County Leader*, August 16, 1973.
84. Ibid.
85. Ibid.
86. "Scobey Wins Thriller," *Leader*.
87. *Daniels County Leader*, "Scobey Hosts Eastern Divisional Tournament," July 18, 1974.
88. "Team Transportation," *Havre Daily News*, July 26, 1974.
89. "Billings, Wolf Point, and Scobey Head to State," *Daniels County Leader*, July 25, 1974.
90. Ibid.
91. "Billings, Wolf Point, and Scobey Head to State," *Daniels County Leader*, July 25, 1974.
92. Bruce Bartley, "Royals Aren't Quite the Same without Bayne," *Great Falls Tribune*, July 3, 1974.
93. "Trangsrud hurls Legion no-hitter," *Billings Gazette*, June 9, 1975.
94. "Duke No-Hits Plentywood," *Daniels County Leader*, June 12, 1975.
95. "20-20 Legion Tie," *Billings Gazette*, July 27, 1975.
96. "Wolf Point Outlasts Scobey 24-23 for District Title," *Herald-News*, July 31, 1975.
97. "State American Legion Class B Tourney Opens Here Today," *Daniels County Leader*, July 31, 1975.
98. Ibid.

The Doc Norman Championship Era

99 "Havre Champs in State Legion Tourney Here," *Daniels County Leader*, August 7, 1975.
100 "Kato and Kato help Havre edge Scobey," *Billings Gazette*, August 2, 1975.
101 Ibid.
102 Ibid.
103 "Edwin and Norma Puckett," *Daniels County History*, 1977.
104 "1973 Peerless Tournament. Chinook Gets First In 2-Day Series," *Daniels County Leader*, June 14, 1973.
105 *Daniels County Leader*, June 27, 1974.
106 Ibid.
107 *Daniels County Leader*, August 7, 1975.
108 Ibid.
109 *The Sandlot*, directed by David Mickey Evans, Island World, 1993.
110 *Moneyball*, directed by Bennett Miller, Columbia Pictures, 2011, based on *Moneyball: The Art of Winning an Unfair Game* by Michael Lewis.
111 "Amazing Comeback by Scobey Wins Marathon State Tourney," *Daniels County Leader*, August 5, 1976.
112 "Scobey Legion Wins Div. 2nd; On to State," *Daniels County Leader*, July 29, 1976.
113 "Cut Bank Legion takes third in state baseball," *Pioneer Press*, August 4, 1976.
114 "Amazing Comeback," *Leader*.
115 Ibid.
116 Ibid.
117 Ibid.
118 Ibid.
119 Ibid.
120 Ibid.
121 Ibid.
122 *Bull Durham*, directed by Ron Shelton, Orion Pictures, 1988.
123 Bruce Sayler, "Mavericks declared ineligible for state," *Missoulian*, August 9, 1976.
124 George Geise, "Mavs out, Lakers advance," *Daily Inter Lake*, August 9, 1976.
125 "Legion Kids Win Rubber at Libby," *Daniels County Leader*, August 12, 1976.
126 Associated Press, "Electrics, Scarlets battle in game of undefeateds," *Helena Independent Record*, August 16, 1976.
127 Ibid.
128 Ibid.
129 Ibid.
130 "Legion Ball 'Iron Men' End Season," *Daniels County Leader*, August 19, 1976.
131 Seals and Crofts, "Summer Breeze," *Summer Breeze*, Warner Bros. Records, 1972.
132 "Cut Bank takes third," *Pioneer Press*.
133 Mary Machart, "Peerless Ball Field Dedicated," Daniels County Leader, July 2, 1998.
134 Puckett, *The Dream*, p. 150.
135 "Scobey Has Young Team," *Daniels County Leader*, June 16, 1977.
136 "Blues Take 3rd in East Tourney," *Daniels County Leader*, July 28, 1977.
137 "State Legion B-B Tourney Starts Here Today," *Daniels County Leader*, July 28, 1977.
138 "Blues Win Four Straight Games; Keep State Legion Title Here," *Daniels County Leader*, August 4, 1977.
139 Ibid.
140 Ibid.
141 Ibid.
142 Ibid.
143 Ibid.
144 "Blues 3rd in East," *Leader*.
145 "Blues Win Four Straight," *Leader*.
146 "Senators sweep Scobey, head for state tourney in Great Falls," *Helena Independent Record*, August 7, 1977.
147 "Clifford Hanson," Scobey, *Daniels County History*, 197, 1977.
148 "Blues Win Four Straight," *Leader*.
149 Ibid.
150 "Blues Look to Three-Repeat," *Daniels County Leader*, April 20, 1978.
151 "4 Wins, 1 Loss for Blues in Past Week," *Daniels County Leader*, July 13, 1978.
152 "East Divisional Legion Tourney Here," *Daniels County Leader*, 20-23, July 20, 1978.
153 Ibid.
154 Ibid.
155 "28th straight win gives Scobey title," *Billings Gazette*, July 24, 1978.
156 Ibid.
157 Ibid.
158 Ibid.
159 Ibid.
160 Ibid.
161 "Scobey Blues are State Champs Once Again," *Daniels County Leader*, August 3, 1978.
162 "Sweep by East in Legion," *Billings Gazette*, July 28, 1978.
163 "Blues Champs Again," *Leader*.
164 Craig Price, "Patriots left out in the cold, after outstanding tourney performance," *Sidney Herald*, August 3, 1978.
165 "Glendive Upsets Scobey," *Great Falls Tribune*, July 31, 1978.
166 Ibid.
167 "Glendive Upsets Scobey," *Montana Standard*, July 31, 1978.
168 "Audet's homer gives Scobey Class B title," *Great Falls Tribune*, August 1, 1978.
169 "Norman, Audet lead Scobey to B crown," *Billings Gazette*, August 1, 1978.
170 "Audet's homer," *Tribune*.
171 "Blues Champs Again," *Leader*.
172 Cut Bank *Pioneer Press*, August 3, 1978.
173 "Blues Champs Again," *Leader*.
174 George Geise, "Chargers-Scobey Clash: no Championship today," *Great Falls Tribune*, August 6, 1978.
175 George Geise, "Chargers sweep Scobey, make tourney," *Great Falls Tribune*, August 7, 1978.
176 Ibid.
177 Ibid.
178 Ibid.
179 "Miles City Eliminates Scobey; To Meet Billings in Semifinal," *Billings Gazette*, July 22, 1946.
180 Geise, "Chargers sweep."
181 George Geise, "Just call him a Goliath among a whole lot of Davids," *Great Falls Tribune*, August 8, 1978.
182 Ibid.
183 "What's Uniquely Different About This Ball Club?" *Daniels County Leader*, June 14, 1979.
184 Donald Weiskopf and Walter Alston, *The Complete Baseball Handbook*, 1972.
185 "Blues in Big Holiday Tourney," *Daniels County Leader*, June 28, 1979.
186 Ibid.
187 "Scobey's Danelson one-hits Royals, 2-1" *Billings Gazette*, July 3, 1979.
188 Ibid.
189 "Blues Suffer First Conference Loss to Wolf Point," *Daniels County Leader*, July 12, 1979.
190 Ed West, "Scobey's Doctor is a lot like Eddie Bayne," *Billings Gazette*, July 1, 1979.
191 West, "Scobey's friendly doctor."
192 "Scobey, Wolf Point win," *Billings Gazette*, July 22, 1979.

193 "Blues Repeat Divisional Champs," *Daniels County Leader*, July 26, 1979.
194 Ibid.
195 Ibid.
196 Ibid.
197 "Scobey Again Hosts State Legion Ball," *Daniels County Leader*, July 26, 1979.
198 Ibid.
199 "Scobey Blues seek fourth straight title," *Great Falls Tribune*, July 26, 1979.
200 Ibid.
201 "Blues Breeze to Championship; 4th in a Row for 'Doc's Boys,'" *Daniels County Leader*, August 2, 1979.
202 "Scobey blanks Laurel for State B Legion title," *Billings Gazette*, July 31, 1979.
203 Ibid.
204 *1979 State Class B Legion Baseball Tournament Program*, July 1979.
205 "Scobey blanks Laurel," *Leader*.
206 Ibid.
207 Roy Pace, "Blues, Senators split; deciding game today," *Independent Record*, August 5, 1979.
208 Marty Mouat, "Blues oust Senators," *Independent Record*, August 6, 1979.
209 Ibid.
210 Ibid.
211 Ibid.
212 Roy Pace, "Blues, Senators split; deciding game today," *Independent Record*, August 5, 1979.
213 Mouat, "Blues oust Senators."
214 Pace, "Blues, Senators split."
215 "Legion tourney looks 'close as a clone,'" *Great Falls Tribune*, August 11, 1979.
216 Ed West, "Legion tournament has no favorites," *Billings Gazette*, August 11, 1979.
217 Ibid.
218 Phil Smith, "French, Electrics blank Scobey," *Great Falls Tribune*, August 12, 1979.
219 Ibid.
220 Ibid.
221 Ibid.
222 Bruce Sayler, "Electrics, Royals win in first round," *Montana Standard*, August 12, 1979.
223 Phil Smith, "Scobey upsets Kalispell in state Legion tourney," *Great Falls Tribune*, August 15, 1979.
224 Ibid.
225 Ibid.
226 Phil Smith, "Predictably, the Legion tournament was unpredictable," *Great Falls Tribune*, August 17, 1979.
227 "McNally voted MVP," *Montana Standard*, August 18, 1979.
228 "Blues Make Good Showing in 'A' Tourney," *Daniels County Leader*, August 16, 1979.
229 Smith, "Predictably unpredictable."
230 Bob Seger, "Night Moves," *Night Moves*, Capitol, 1976.
231 "Blues Keep Rolling On," *Daniels County Leader*, June 26, 1980.
232 "Blues Easily Win Tourney; MVP Stolen," *Daniels County Leader*, July 24, 1980.
233 Ibid.
234 Ibid.
235 Ibid.
236 "Big weekend ahead for sports buffs," *Pioneer Press*, July 23, 1980.
237 "Scobey topples Reds, 7-2," *Missoulian*, July 27, 1980.
238 "Blues Sweep State Tourney; 5th Straight," *Daniels County Leader*, July 31, 1980.
239 Ibid.
240 Ibid.
241 Ibid.
242 "Scobey—as predicted—is Class B Legion champ," *Pioneer Press*, July 30, 1980.
243 "Electrics, Scobey play this weekend at Optimist," *Great Falls Tribune*, July 31, 1980.
244 Phil Smith, "Electrics host powerful Blues," *Great Falls Tribune*, August 2, 1980.
245 Ibid.
246 Charles Gardner, "Scobey blue as Elects rally twice for victories," *Great Falls Tribune*, August 3, 1980.
247 Ibid.
248 "Blues Hitting Good; Defense Bad at Class A," *Daniels County Leader*, August 7, 1980.
249 Gardner, "Scobey blue."
250 Ibid.
251 Ibid.
252 Jim Anderson, "Scobey scoring twins," *Miles City Star*, June 27, 1980.
253 "Blues Keep Rolling On," *Daniels County Leader*, June 26, 1980.
254 "Blues Easily Win Tourney; MVP Stolen," *Daniels County Leader*, July 24, 1980.
255 Addison Bragg, "Players will pay to play in whacky game," *Billings Gazette*, July 30, 1980.
256 Dennis Gaub, "Scobey loses a doctor but keeps a coach," *Billings Gazette*, June 10, 1981.
257 Ibid.
258 "Blues Runner-Up at Divisional; to Glendive," *Daniels County Leader*, July 30, 1981.
259 Ibid.
260 Ibid.
261 Rita Balock, "Title possible for Havre," *Havre Daily News*, July 30, 1981.
262 Les Rickey, "Profound apologies are due to some dedicated kids," *Havre Daily News*, July 29, 1976.
263 Ibid.
264 Ibid.
265 Gaub, "Scobey loses a doctor."
266 Ibid.
267 "Baseball Not Over Here Yet," *Daniels County Leader*, August 6, 1980.
268 "Randy Stolen," *Daniels County Leader*, August 13, 1980.
269 Gaub, "Scobey loses a doctor."
270 "Blues Win; 'Iron Man' Pederson," *Daniels County Leader*, July 29, 1982.
271 Ibid.
272 "Division champs to host Legion B," *Laurel Outlook*, August 5, 1959.
273 "Iron Man Pederson," *Leader*.
274 Ibid.
275 Ibid.
276 Ibid.
277 Gaub, "Scobey loses a doctor."
278 "Scobey Blues Do It Again; 8th State Title," *Daniels County Leader*, August 5, 1982.
279 Ibid.
280 Ibid.
281 Ibid.
282 Ibid.
283 Ibid.
284 Ibid.
285 Tim Roby, "Electrics oust Scobey," *Great Falls Tribune*, August 10, 1982.
286 Ibid.
287 "Scobey Loses to Billings 8-4," *Daniels County Leader*, July 31, 1930.
288 "Former Pitching Star Revisits Scobey Scene," *Daniels County Leader*, Aug 04, 1949.

The Don Lek
1983 – 1991

1900 – 1924
The Homesteaders
and Early Town Teams

1930 – 1945
The Sons of
the Pioneers

1957 – 1968
The Baseball
Renaissance

*The Scobey
Giants*
1925 – 1929

*Baseball is Back
in Daniels County*
1946 – 1956

*The D
Cham*
1969

old Era

	1998 – 2003 *The Last Years*	*2016 – 2019* *The Revival*	
...rman ...hip Era	The Ken Meyer/Mike Lee Era 1992 – 1997	The Long Winter 2004 – 2015	The Froid Bulls 2020 – 2024

1983

The Passing of Doc Norman and the End of an Era

> *Doc's passing marks the end of an era—but the legacy he left for youth should continue to be an inspiration to all who find themselves fighting from the bottom side.*
>
> —**Daniels County Leader, November 24, 1983**

PRESEASON

On April 30, 1983, at the third annual Montana Sports Banquet in Great Falls, Doc was named Montana Sportsman of the Year for "his many years of service to the Scobey Blues American Legion Baseball program." Doc could not attend because of his declining health, so Ann Lee accepted the award. The *Great Falls Tribune* wrote the following about Doc and his award:

```
In honoring Norman, the Optimists recognized
a man who has spent nearly 30 years in service
to the youth of northeastern Montana. Norman
graduated from high school in Billings and
attended Northwestern University in Evanston,
Illinois, where he also played football. He
received his medical degree in obstetrics and
gynecology from Northwestern and returned to
Montana in 1951, first settling in Columbus.
He moved to Missoula and coached from 1954
until he went to Scobey in 1958, where he
began an unbroken association with the Scobey
Blues American Legion Baseball club. Under
his direction, the Blues won eight state
Class B championships, including five in a row
in the 1970s. More than winning titles, Nor-
man's volunteer services were credited with
keeping Legion baseball alive in that region
of the state.[1]
```

That last sentence, Doc "keeping Legion baseball alive in that region of the state," is probably the most important of the award because Doc was not only the reason baseball thrived in Scobey but also in other towns. When I interviewed Coach Craig Price of Sidney, who coached the Sidney teams in the late 1970s and whose son Mark played in the early 1980s, he told me that Scobey's competitive program inspired the other towns to field competitive teams to compete with Scobey. When Scobey's program went away in the early 2000s, he said that made it difficult for their programs to keep going. The competitive fire was gone.

Another thing Craig told me about Doc was how he helped his son play college baseball. Doc not only helped the Blues, but his generosity included the other players. Craig said, "My son Mark graduated high school in 1982. He was a very fine baseball player—both my boys were. But Mark was the oldest and he couldn't decide about going to college; he couldn't make a decision. Here it is, August 1, 1982, and he can't decide. He said, 'I don't know. I wanna play baseball and go to college.' And I said, 'Okay, I'm gonna call Doc Norman, see if he can help us find a place to go.' If he would go, then that's where I want him to go and get him out of the oil field, you know. So I called Doc. He made a call to Southern Idaho College in Twin Falls. There was a coach named Walker there, and Walker said, 'Yeah, Doc, I'll take him as a walk-on on your recommendation.' And so Mark went over there and made that team. But it was because of Doc Norman getting that door open for us. And I assume he did that for several young men and especially your guys, when your team, you had so many college-capable kids playing on your team." Yes, he did, Craig.

Doc's ill health prevented him from traveling to Great Falls to receive his award. As his chronic neurological disease continued to progress and ravage his body, the devices that helped him move around were "progressing" too. The crutches in 1981 had given way to a walker in 1982—and the Ford Fiesta at practice. Early in 1983, Doc was confined to a wheelchair with a three-wheeled cart—"an electric bubby"[2]—to get him around at practice. Kelly recalls the first time he saw his dad in a wheelchair in the spring of 1983. It was quite an emotional experience for him but also a special day. "When I was playing baseball at Colorado State, Mom and Dad were down at Lake Havasu in the winter and early spring of 1983. Dad didn't need care then. We were playing UTEP in El Paso. They had the old, old stadium and bleachers. I remember seeing my dad in a wheelchair. I saw my mom walking behind the backstop, pushing him in the wheelchair. I went 2-3 with a single, a double off the right-field fence, and an RBI. It was kinda cool that he came that day. I can vividly remember seeing my mom wheeling him. I had always seen Dad as a big, strong Marine; now it was near the end."

Kelly recounted how the progression of Doc's disease adversely affected his coaching. "He retired in 1981 and coached in 1982. He coached out of the Ford Fiesta in 1982. He didn't coach third. He was in a wheelchair by 1983. It was more of a presence than any actual coaching in 1983." Don Lekvold was now responsible for "the brunt of the work with the team" but Doc kept "in daily touch with his beloved Scobey Blues despite his serious handicaps."[3] Doc made it for a photo opportunity with pictures of him with Kelly and his grandsons Mike and Josh—and one final picture of him with the team.

Although losing starters Gord Tryan, Len Floyd, and Randy Pederson from the 1982 state championship team, the Blues looked promising for a chance to repeat as state champions in 1983. This was an older team now, with most players having several years of Legion experience and multiple state championships. Jim Lekvold (18), Pat Audet (18), and Greg Stolen (17), their top three hitters in the lineup—and two solid pitchers and their top catcher—would be back playing in their fifth season. They had all played on three state championship teams. Also returning were starters Tony Vigliotti (17), Joey Girard (17), and Mike Tryan (17): six returning starters from the state championship team, and all 17 and 18 years old. Steve Schaefer (17) and Marty Davis (17) also saw action at the Divisional and state tournaments in 1982. Jeff Mann (18)—who had been on the field at the state tournament in 1980 in Cut Bank when he was only 15—rejoined the team. Also returning were Bob Tryan (18), Brian Gilbert (18), and Larry Trangsrud (15). Rookies joining the team in 1983 were Jim LeProwse (16), Mike Heaton (16), and Ivan Domenech (16).

But when Coach Don Lekvold assembled the team for the first day of practice in April 1983, there was one player—four-year starter Greg Stolen—who wasn't there. This was troubling. Greg was one of the main reasons Scobey looked strong, but mental health problems prevented him from playing with the team. He could only make it to a couple of games and could not routinely practice or play with the team. Everyone on the team—and Doc and Don—sincerely hoped Greg would get better and join the team, but, tragically, for both Greg and the team, it was not meant to be. Pat Audet said, "Greg tried to come back and play in the beginning, but he couldn't." Jim Lekvold

1983 Scobey Blues. Sitting at left, Doc Norman. Standing, left to right: Coach Kelly Norman, Jim Lekvold, Bob Tryan, Steve Schaefer, Brian Gilbert, Pat Audet, Larry Trangsrud, Jeff Mann and Coach Don Lekvold. Kneeling, left to right: Mike Heaton, Joe Girard, Jim LeProwse, Ivan Domenech, Mike Tryan, Marty Davis, Tony Vigliotti. Sitting, left to right: batboys Mike and Josh Lee. Not pictured is Greg Stolen. *Family photo.*

Doc Norman with his grandsons Mike and Josh Lee and son Kelly. *Family photo.*

added, "Greg would show up occasionally for games, but we never knew when."

The psychological adjustment the 1983 Blues had to make to not having Doc as their head coach and the unexpected loss of Greg would be too much for the Blues to overcome that season. Greg was only 17—with two years of Legion eligibility remaining—when his amazing four-year career was abruptly curtailed. In his four years with the Blues, Greg had started and played on three state championship teams. As a 13-year-old in 1979, he was a starter, pitched in the State B Tournament, and led Scobey in hitting in the best-of-three series against the Helena Senators to help get Scobey into the State A Tournament. In 1980, he had been selected to the State all-tournament team in Cut Bank *as a 14-year-old*; in 1982, he was a workhorse and pitched 14 innings in four games of the state tournament, getting a win and earning two saves. He hurled a complete-game six-hitter against Sidney in the semifinal and got the save against Sidney in the championship game. He led the team in hitting with Pat Audet. Had Pat not had such an incredible state tournament at the plate, Greg would have undoubtedly been named MVP. Greg was among the most talented baseball players to don a Blues uniform. He could hit, field, throw, and pitch. Next to his older brother Randy, Greg was the best all-around baseball player I ever played with. The only component Greg didn't have in his game that Randy did was speed, and he didn't hit for as much power—but his career effectively ended at 16 years old, and he homered in his first game back as a 17-year-old, so the power would have come. He was now six feet, three inches tall. Pat Audet, commenting on what could have been with Greg, said, "To this day, I would have considered him one the best put-together athletes to ever come out of our corner of the state."

Batgirls Michelle Audet and Allison Marlenee were back, marking 1977 to 1983 as the seven seasons Scobey had the unique tradition of batgirls on the team. Mike and Josh Lee returned as batboys.

REGULAR SEASON

Scobey opened the 1983 season in an *extremely* competitive six-team round-robin Memorial Day Tournament at Cobb Field in Billings. The five other teams were Cody, Wyoming, Miles City Mavericks, Billings Royals, Billings Scarlets, and Cherry Creek, Colorado. Pitcher Bill Wilkinson, who had ended the Blues season the year before in the best-of-three series against the Great Falls Electrics, was pitching for Cherry Creek. Was he stalking the Blues like a bad dream? He had transferred to Cherry Creek with his family for the 1983 season. The Legion games at Cobb Field would be his last in a Cherry Creek uniform, as he would get drafted the following week and sign a contract to play professional baseball for the Seattle Mariners. Pat Audet recalls him pitching in the Memorial Day Tournament. "We watched their game at IGA in Billings. He threw a rocket into a kid's head and knocked his ass out cold."

What a special experience for this team to play on Cobb Field. I will never forget the opportunity to play on Cobb Field in my last year in 1979. I savored every moment of playing there—and watching the other games. And so did the 1983 Blues. Joey Girard recalls, "That tournament was awesome! Cobb field was the best in the state, in my opinion." Pat Audet agreed. "It was a lot of freakin' fun playing there. It definitely felt big time!"

Not unexpectedly, Cherry Creek swept all five of their games to win the tournament. Although the Blues didn't win a game, they were competitive. In their final against the Royals, Pat Audet found himself engaged in a pitcher's duel with Jason Adkins. Jay Bauer from Opheim, who caught 4 of the 5 games in the tournament, was Pat's catcher. This was another classic Blues-Royals game on Cobb Field that recalled 14-year-old Terry Puckett's amazing eight-inning performance against Jerry Schuster and the Royals in 1969 when Terry gave up only two runs in Scobey's 4-1 loss and Dan Danelson's one-hitter to outduel Toby Lindsey and beat the Royals 2-1 at the IGA Tournament in 1979. Behind Pat Audet's one-hitter, Scobey was leading the Royals 2-1 in the top of the seventh when the Royals plated two runs on two hits to take a 3-2 lead. The game-winning hit came from P.J. Malloney, who drove in the two runs. The Royals held on in the bottom of the seventh to escape with a 3-2 win. Pat finished with a three-hitter, and his performance added to the Scobey Blue's lore of classic pitcher's duels against the Royals. The 1983 Memorial Day Tournament marked the last time Scobey played against the Billings Royals or the Billings Scarlets.

Sixteen-year-old rookie Jim LeProwse, who would become Scobey's ace pitcher the next two seasons, was Scobey's workhorse on the mound in the tournament, pitching 18 innings and appearing in 3 of the 5 games. Pat Audet logged 12 innings, and Tony Vigliotti and Brian Gilbert pitched the other innings in Scobey's five games. Pat Audet and Jay Bauer each had doubles for Scobey's only extra-base hits in the tourney. The five games in the Memorial Day Tournament were the only ones for Jay Bauer that season, as he could not continue playing for the team afterward.

Following the Memorial Day Tournament in Billings, Scobey's aggressive early-season schedule continued as they traveled to Great Falls to play the Electrics and Chargers, losing both games. Scobey's front-loaded schedule with seven games against Class A teams was "fast company for the Blues so early in the season, as they generally are slow starters."[4] What the *Leader* was referring to by "slow starters" was that the previous two years, the Blues had started 2-8 and 3-7, only to turn the season around at the midpoint and finish strong both years.

But the Blues would not finish strong in 1983. Following a doubleheader sweep of last-place Circle at the end of June, the Blues stood 4-5 in conference play, but they couldn't rally with a string of wins afterward. Toward the end of the season, the *Leader* described Scobey's season as one of "mixed fortunes" but that the "boys were coming along."[5]

Coaches and players recall Greg's attempt to rejoin the team. Joey Girard remembers, "Greg, who was a huge part of our 1982 state championship team, had not gone out for baseball the year after. About halfway through the next year, the Blues were struggling a little and headed to play Glasgow. I believe Doc had talked Greg into joining us. He had not touched a baseball in 10 months but managed to be the winning pitcher and go 5 for 5 at the plate. Greg was an extremely talented ball player, but I loved his quirky sense of humor. After that game, of course, we went to Connors' Dairy Queen for treats. I had the green mint grasshopper milkshake and offered to share it with Greg. To this, he replied, 'I don't like grasshopper shakes cuz, well, I don't really like grasshoppers!'" I remember Greg's sense of humor, too. I played with him in Little League and Babe Ruth in Peerless, then my final year of Legion. What I remember most was his facial expressions. He wouldn't say anything but would make me laugh by the way he just looked at me. He was hilarious. Assistant Coach Kelly Norman recalls Greg's first game back. "His first game was at Circle. He had not even practiced at that point. I threw him batting practice before the game. So, almost 11 months without swinging a bat, Greg was 3 for 3, doubled, and I think homered [he did]. He was so talented."

As the season wound down, Doc's health was steadily weakening, and so were Scobey's chances of playing in the postseason. It was almost as if Doc's decline was mirrored by the Blues' troubles on the field. In 1983, the eastern division was split into two districts—six teams in the north and seven in the south—with only the top four teams in each district advancing to the divisional tournament. Scobey, Glasgow, Wolf Point, Sidney, Glendive, and Circle competed in the northern division. Headed into the last game of the season at Scobey Ball Park against Wolf Point—a makeup game of a rainout—the Blues needed a win to place in the top four to qualify for Divisional, but they lost the game, unceremoniously ending their season without a chance to defend their state title by playing in the Divisional tournament. Pat Audet recalls, "I have a faint memory of losing that final game and feeling totally deflated walking off the field." It is much more challenging to cope with defeat once you've tasted victory, and the 1983 Blues had experienced the sweet smell of success aplenty. It was a callous way to end the five-year Legion careers for 18-year-olds Pat Audet and Jim Lekvold, who had each played on three state championship teams. The season-ending loss also snapped Scobey's 16-year run of State B Tournament appearances, which had begun when Phil Audet led Scobey to its first state tournament berth in 1967.

In trying to make sense of the season, Pat Audet said, "I still don't really know to this day what happened. We never made it out of the district and did not advance, although we basically had a similar team to 1982. Greg tried to come back and play in the beginning, but his mental health issue took its toll on him. Don Lekvold was at the helm, and he was a good coach, but it was a difficult adjustment for him and us. He had *huge* shoes to fill in, taking over for Doc. We, especially us older players, were missing Doc immensely. There was a lot that Don and all of us faced that season that seemed a bit out of our control. But the bottom line is that we did not play well down the stretch and did not hold up the Blue's traditional post-season dominance in any way, shape, or form. Our team dynamic faltered, and again, I'm not sure why; the fire just wasn't there, especially after losing our best in Greg. The story of 1983 leaves one numb and thinking about what could have been if we had just stepped up through the thick and thin of it all. I know we suffered on the mound with not enough good pitching. Jimmy and I went on to play in the All-Star game in Great Falls in the finality of '83. I still think about Greg Stolen a lot, and it breaks my heart to think about what happened to him."

When I asked him what he thought happened in 1983, Jim Lekvold replied, "That is the million-dollar question! We had a handful of experienced players. The key missing piece was Greg Stolen. I guess we never really hit on all cylinders. In the 1982 year, we were loaded top to bottom. Randy Pederson really helped. He could throw forever. We really gelled that year." But Jim added, reminding us all that, in the end, baseball is just a game, "Since we didn't play in any post-season tournaments, I was able to water ski quite a bit that year with Tangi [Hellickson]."

Pat's comment that "we suffered on the mound" and Jim's comment that Randy Pederson "could throw forever" pinpointed the gaping hole in pitching with the loss of Randy Pederson *and* Greg Stolen in 1983. Removing Randy's and Greg's arms from the pitching rotation was too much to overcome. In the 1982 Divisional and state tournaments, Randy and Greg pitched 46 innings and had five wins and two saves.

In addition to Pat and Jim, Jeff Mann, Bob Tryan, and Brian Gilbert played in their last season in 1983. With the loss of these five older players, the lineup in 1984 would be depleted, and Don Lekvold would face a tough challenge as head coach in his second season at the helm. Could Scobey regain their form and make it back to the state tournament?

EXTRA INNINGS

THE HEARTBREAKING, SEASON-ENDING LOSS TO WOLF POINT ended Scobey's streak of 16 consecutive state tournaments from 1967 to 1982, which began when Phil Audet led Scobey to its first state tournament in 1967. An Audet had played in every one of Scobey's state championships: Craig (1969), Dana (1973), Allan (1976-78), and Pat (1979-80, 1982). The five Audets who played for Scobey are in the attached picture. Between 1963 and 1983, an Audet was on a Scobey Legion team every year except 1970.

Tony Vigliotti recalls a funny story (which also revealed how resilient Doc was) about Doc at practice in 1983. "Doc would show up to practice on his three-wheeled cart with the orange flag on the back. We were in the cage doing some bunting—or not doing some bunting. Doc told us to 'get the fuck out of the way' and he would show us how it's done. He bunted three in a row off the very end of his bat sitting on his cart."

Rookie Jim LeProwse remembers his first day of practice with the Blues. "Doc was there in his wheelchair, and he called me over to him. I had white spikes on, and when I got close to Doc, Doc spit on my shoes with a stream of chewing tobacco and said, 'Welcome to the Blues, son.'"

Kelly Norman assisted Head Coach John Ray of Glasgow for the East-West Legion B Game. Jim Lekvold started at second, and Pat Audet started at catcher for the East. Jim Lekvold scored the tying run from second in the third inning to knot the score at 3-3, but the West won the game 4-3. Mark Page of Wolf Point was selected MVP, pitching three innings and going 3-4 at the plate, including a triple and two RBIs. Mark Page, an all-State quarterback at Wolf Point his senior year, had turned down a full-ride football scholarship to play for Montana State and chose instead a

Jim Lekvold and Pat Audet at East-West Legion B Game at Legion Park, Great Falls. *Family photo.*

baseball scholarship to play baseball at Lewis-Clark State, where he would join Dan Danelson for his senior year.

The Whitehall Renegades won the State B Tournament—their only state championship—then lost in a best-of-three series with the Bozeman Bucks to advance to the State A Tournament. This was the last year the State B champion played off against a State A team to advance to the State A Tournament, as the Montana American Legion B champion would begin playing in a Northwestern B regional with several other states in 1984. Thus, the 1979 Scobey Blues were the last Class B team to play in a State A Tournament.

The Bitterroot Bucs American Legion Baseball team was formed by manager Bob Farmer and Coach Vestor Wilson in 1983. The Bucs were a combination of the Stevensville, Ravalli, and Corvallis Legion posts. This was the first Legion team in Bitterroot Valley since the Great Depression.[6] *Since the Great Depression.* Coach Wilson and the Bucs won the regular season title, the western divisional title, then finished third at State *in their first year of existence.* The valley noticed the Bucs and their instant success. In his end-of-year sports summary article, "1983 – The Year of the Bucs," Jack Tanner of the *Ravalli Republic* wrote that the Bucs "were born winning, catching the valley by surprise and the imagination of nearly all who encountered it. They took their first game, 14-8 over the Missoula Reds, and were off and running, hitting, throwing, and fielding for one of the most remarkable first seasons any baseball team has ever experienced. From a group of undisciplined and generally green athletes and dedicated coaches grew a winner in short order."[7] That sounds familiar, doesn't it? A dedicated coach taking "a group of generally green athletes and growing a winner in short order." That was

Doc Norman in 1959 with the Scobey Legion team, who he lead to Scobey's first district championship in 12 years with Kevin Sell and a roster full of Babe Ruthers.

Jeff Mann's teammates remember several funny stories involving him. Pat Audet shared this story about Jeff, who played his last year in 1983. "In 1980, while traveling to the state tournament in Cut Bank, we were at 4Bs in Havre, and he ordered a French Dip. When he received it, he said, 'Cool! This comes with free soup'—it was au jus." Kirby recalls it slightly differently: "At the 4Bs in Havre, Jeff Mann ordered a French Dip, and of course, au jus came with it. He looked at me dead serious and said, 'I didn't order any soup.'" Tony Vigliotti added, "To this day, every time I see a French Dip, I think of that." Pat Audet added another funny story about Jeff. "He had some goodies as he also extended the hard-hit baseball saying 'hit me a dot' to 'hit me a dot on the cowboy river!'" Joey Girard added, "I think it was Jeff who requested that new song from 'Lost Shepherd' (Def Leppard)."

Dan Danelson pitched his junior year for Lewis-Clark State College in 1983. He won the regional championship game 10-2 over Azusa-Pacific to run his record to 7-1. With the win, the Warriors advanced to the National NAIA Tournament, where they made the championship game but lost two games to Lubbock Christian to finish second. Their two losses to Lubbock Christian were the Warriors' only two losses to an NAIA team of the year. They finished the season with an incredible 69-11 overall record and 49-2 against NAIA opponents.

1983 was the last year of collegiate baseball for Kirby Halvorson (Pacific Lutheran), Randy Stolen, and Kelly Norman, both at Colorado State. Kirby and Kelly then transferred to the University of Montana. After he graduated, Kirby's first job was as the Head Athletic Trainer for the Great Falls Dodgers in the Pioneer League. He recalls, "Three of the pitchers on that '86 rookie team made major league rosters: John Wetteland, Yankees closer; Mike Munoz, Rockies starter; Kevin Campbell As. The only position player that I recall making the show was their number-two pick Dave Hansen (or Hanson). He was an infielder/utility man for the Dodgers for many seasons. Kevin Kennedy was the manager in Great Falls. He was the Red Sox skipper later on. So I was around some good baseball dudes. Learned a lot." And perhaps the best part of the job—Kirby got two signed baseballs from Sandy Koufax, one for himself and one for his friend Kelly Norman."

The Plainsmen played a game against a Canadian team on the weekend of Doc Norman's celebration, but the only opportunity I had to play ball in the summer of 1983 was slow-pitch softball, so I did. I played for Peerless Bar with former Blues Danny Wang, Dallas Trangsrud, Kelly Norman, Randy Stolen, and Brad Henderson. I never thought I would play slow-pitch, but what will you do when it's the only game in town, and you like to play ball? Actually, I had a blast. We had a good team with Bucky Henderson, Howie Dickinson, Bruce Fladager, Jeff Mattson, Wally Hames, and Chris Kasuske on the team. We won the district and took second at State in Kalispell, qualifying for the regional tournament in Oregon, which I couldn't attend because I had to get back to college, so Jon played in my place. One memory I have of that summer was how much fun it was to play with Danny Wang. He always had a smile on his face and made me laugh—and he was a good ballplayer. I was also amazed by what good ballplayers Bucky Henderson and Howie Dickinson were. I knew they were good athletes, but I didn't remember them playing Legion baseball. Rejoining my teammates Randy Stolen, Kelly Norman, and Brad Henderson (whom I played Babe Ruth with and Legion in 1977) was special, too.

Danny Wang embarrassed me—in a funny way, of course—sitting around the campfire at the State softball tournament in Kalispell. Being half Italian (my mom's parents were immigrants from southern Italy), I would tan in the summer. I played softball in shorts all summer, so my legs got tanned. Following the games on Saturday, the team showered together in the campground community shower facilities. Later, as we were sitting around the campfire with all the players and wives, Danny fired up, "You know, I noticed something about Joe in the shower earlier. He's got a white ass! He looks like he's dark, but he's got a white ass!" Everyone laughed, and I joined them.

Pat Audet and Jim Lekvold, who played together for the Blues from 1979 to 1983, rejoined each other on the baseball field for one season in college in 1985, playing together for the Dickinson State Blue Hawks. Pat was a two-sport athlete in college, finishing his career playing football and baseball for the Minot State Beavers. After college, Jim Lekvold became an umpire and went on to umpire six State AA tournaments.

The Meyer family from Scobey traveled to see the 1983 American Legion World Series, held in Fargo, North Dakota. The boys got a photo op with Roger Maris. Ron Meyer

Jim Lekvold umpiring at the State AA Tournament in Helena, 1992 or 1993. *Helena Independent Record photo.*

From left, Ken Meyer, Maury Audet, and Ron Meyer with baseball great Roger Maris at the 1983 American Legion World Series in Fargo, North Dakota. *Family photo.*

remembers the trip. "Gary and Bonnie Meyer (aka) Herbie and the Barracuda decided to take in the tournament. This is the same time these young bucks, Ron and Ken Meyer, and Maury Audet were chasing foul balls for a quarter at the Blues games (and were holding their own with the foul balls in Fargo). As it turns out we had a brush with greatness, none of us knew it at the time, but here it is. I was a little hesitant to share the picture, because of the buck tooth four eyed look, but being 52 years young and sporting the Blues cap I had to do it. Jeremy Ward (Wardo) was there I believe but missed the photo op."

The June 30, 1983, edition of the *Leader* announced, "The city of Scobey has officially declared Sunday, July 3rd, 1983, as 'Doc Norman Day,' honoring Dr. Clyde Harrington Norman for some 35 years of coaching American Legion Baseball—about a quarter-century of that time in Scobey."[8] The celebration was planned to begin on Saturday, July 2, with a players' reunion for all former and current Scobey ballplayers and a ceremony honoring Doc at the Saddle Club, followed by a public Cabaret-style dance. On Sunday at the Scobey Ball Park, an old-timer's game and a home run derby were planned, and the concession stand was to be open with the famous Legion burgers on the grill.

The response to the two-day celebration—planned by Danny Wolfe—was overwhelming, as was the outpouring of praise for Doc and Marge. Players from all the years Doc coached, including Kevin and Dwain "Baldy" Sell from the 1959 team, were there. The *Leader* provided a summary of the two-day celebration in the following week's edition:

```
"Normans honored by former players,"
    Daniels County Leader, July 7, 1983
```

```
Dr. C.H. "Doc" Norman and Marge were recipients
of plaques, certificates, and much-deserved praise
at a reunion banquet of former members of the
American Legion Baseball teams, which he coached
here since 1959. Congressman Ron Marlenee delivered
a letter and autographed picture from President
Ronald Reagan to Doc as the climax of the evening.
```

Former players, batgirls, and batboys assembled for the evening's proceedings, honoring Doc Norman, a legendary character in Montana American Legion Baseball. *Leader photo, Milton Gunderson.*

Cliff Hanson, longtime tireless worker in the baseball program, presented awards from Post 56 and the State American Legion to Doc and a special award to Marge Norman. Kevin Sell (on Doc's first team here in 1959) presented a plaque from all the players over the years.

Dwain Sell presented a special award to Marge who was a "mother" to all the players as well as being trainer, organizer, errand-runner and head cheerleader. He said he always felt he was "special" to Marge and it was later he learned that all the players felt that way.

Lee Cook, representing the Flaxville Jaycees, 750 Club and Whitetail Legion Post 121, gave Doc Norman a plaque, which included a handsome clock, for all he had done for young athletes from the east-county area. Scobey Mayor Perry Wolfe presented the Normans with a framed copy of the Proclamation, which created "Doc Norman Day" in Scobey.

There was not a dry eye in the Saddle Club as these former baseball players talked about Doc and Marge Norman's contribution to the community and their individual lives.

Gary Meyer, under the alias "Herbie Swartz," did a great job as banquet speaker with plenty of baseball humor and a serious message.

One of the more knowledgeable sportsmen in the area, Cliff Hagfeldt, used his knowledge as program emcee.

Dan Wolfe was chairman of the event, including activities at the ballpark on Sunday, but when it came to the meal, he turned it over to the mothers of former players, and they came through as always. Marge Hagfeldt, Iris Higgins, Delores Danelson, and Mazel Audet were among the banquet committee heads.

Doc's plaque—in the shape of the state of Montana with a baseball on it—was presented by Kevin Sell and had the following inscription:

Dear Doc,
We were truly the "Boys of Summer." We lost and we won,
Best of all we had fun.
If winning wasn't everything Then playing for you was!
Thanks for putting us on the map.
With every best wish
From
Your boys

Mike Hagfeldt, who won the home run derby, remembers some details about the old-timer's game and the home run derby on Sunday. "I remember Jerry LaPierre going down in a heap between second and third with a blown Achilles in the old-timer's game. In the home run derby, Randy and I were tied after the first round, so we both got five more pitches. I hit one more. Randy went last, and on his last swing, he just ripped a laser. The ball never got more than 20 feet off the ground and hit two-thirds of the way up the fence. I truly thought it would go *through* the fence. Man, could he crush it. He just attacked the ball." Other Blues to go yard during the derby were Jack Higgins, Kelly Norman, and Terry Puckett.

Doc Norman receives from Congressman Ron Marlenee special congratulations in writing from President Reagan, honoring Montana's dean of American Legion Baseball coaches, in connection with the City of Scobey's official "Doc Norman Day" proclamation. Wife Marge, his ever-faithful chief of staff, is at his side, and daughter Ann to the right. *Leader photo, Milton Gunderson.*

Mike Hagfeldt, with this swing, won the home run derby for his dad, Pete, who had purchased Mike at the Calcutta auction. A strong wind to right field favored left-handers Sunday, but lefty Mike put his first two homers over the deep center field wall. After the regulation 10 swings, Mike was tied with Randy Stolen with two homers each. Mike got one more with five more swings. Jack Higgins, Kelly Norman, and Terry Puckett were other former Blues players to put one over the fence in the competition. Calcutta money was split between the winner and the Legion baseball fund. *Leader photo, Milton Gunderson.*

"Herbie Swartz" took over Doc Norman's reunion banquet speaking chores at the last minute after the committee failed to get either of the first choices, **Lefty Grove or Dave McNally.** He did a tremendous job. He said that, like many youngsters, he used to dream about being a big-league baseball player. "But never, in my wildest dreams, did I ever think I would pinch hit for Lefty Grove or relieve Dave McNally." "Herbie" is Gary Meyer of Scobey. *Leader photo, Milton Gunderson.*

Celebration organizers had tried to get Lefty Grove or Dave McNally as the banquet speaker, but neither could make it. So, Gary Meyer, who played "Herbie Swartz," was a last-minute replacement. He had some great lines. Like many boys, he said he dreamed about being a big-league baseball player. "But never, in my wildest dreams, did I ever think I would pinch hit for Lefty Grove or relieve Dave McNally."[9]

My last memory of Doc is from the summer of 1983, which involves baseball. I remember sitting in his house watching the Cubs play an afternoon game on WGN-TV, with Harry Caray calling the game. He was actively engaged in the game, commenting on the plays and the strategy. Since Doc graduated from Northwestern and trained at Cook County Hospital and Saint Joseph's in the Chicago area, I asked Kelly if he was a Cubs fan. Kelly said, "No, he liked the Big Red Machine. He liked the Reds a lot, Bench, Perez, those guys." I asked him why he changed our name to the Blues. He said, "He liked George Brett and the baby-blue color of the Royals uniforms. But there was the Billings Royals, so he couldn't call us the Scobey Royals. That was already taken by Billings. So, the Blues was the next best thing."

Following "Doc Norman Day" and the end of the 1983 baseball season, Doc's chronic illness continued to ravage his body and finally took his life in November. Kelly recalls the deathly progression of Doc's disease from 1980 to 1983. "Dad came to Southern Oregon in 1981 and told me he had retired from his practice. He knew years before what he had. I was always on him about his smoking and his weight. He gave up surgeries at the end of 1980. The pons, the drive in the computer, or whatever got him. His voluntary muscles started to deteriorate. He would shake a little bit. That last year, in 1980, he referred his patients out to Billings for surgery. Then, he just continued being a doctor without surgeries. He didn't tell anyone but Marge about losing his fine motor skills. He didn't tell people until he got really sick. He wanted to tell everyone it was his heart. I think that was why he probably did that. His fine motor skills went first, then big muscles, speech, and then involuntary muscles (the heart being a major organ) along with the others, and his body finally just 'quit.'"

Kelly continued. "The plaque, 'The Boys of Summer,' was presented to him at the celebration in July. Cliff [Hagfeldt] was there, and Dad died four months later. He had full-time care. Myrna Baldry came over every day and helped Mom with Dad. She helped for quite a long time. He was in a wheelchair. We built a ramp out in front of our house. All the way to the left so he could get in and out. When I left in the summer of 1983, I knew I wasn't going to see him again. It wasn't a bad moment; it was kind of special in a way. His speech would get worse and worse. I knew he was sick. His speech was bad. But his speech was better when he talked to me."

Doc died on Tuesday, November 15, 1983. He was 63 years old. Kelly remembers the last days. "I talked to Dad on Saturday. His mom died a week before he did in Flathead, and he couldn't make it to her funeral. What kind of a man is so sick he can't make it to his mom's funeral? On Sunday, I got a call to come home from Flathead. I made it home on Tuesday. He could mumble, and he could hear me. I shaved him. As soon as I left, he slipped into a coma. He almost died the Friday before, but he waited until I got there on Tuesday. Doctor Fitz put the sheet over him, and that was it." Doc died shortly after ten o'clock in the evening.

Doc's funeral was three days later, on Friday, November 18. "The services were attended by the largest assembly of people at a funeral in the history of Daniels County."[10] Included in the assemblage were the six pallbearers, Don Lekvold, Frank "Butch" Goddard, Danny Wolfe, Phil Audet, Kevin Sell, and Rocky Ware. The selection of the six pallbearers was deeply symbolic of Doc's coaching and life. Four were former players who were all "firsts" for Doc in his coaching career in Scobey. Kevin Sell played on Doc's first Scobey American Legion team in 1959 and led Doc to his first district championship, the first for Scobey in 12 years; Phil Audet led Doc's first team to make it to the state tournament in 1967; Danny Wolfe and Rocky Ware played on Doc's first State championship team in 1969. Don Lekvold had been Doc's "sturdy assistant" since 1977 and had taken the reins as head coach earlier in the summer of 1983 when Doc's health no longer allowed him to do so. Don had been assuming more and more responsibility for the day-to-day management of the team since 1980, and now it was his turn to take the baton and keep the program alive, which he would do through 1991. Butch Goddard symbolized Doc's generosity off the baseball field. "Over the years, Doc and his chief of staff, Marge, affectionately housed and fed a number of 'stray dog' youths, who were at loose ends. One of those fellows, 'Butch' Goddard, came from Ashland, Oregon, to be one of the pallbearers at the services."[11]

As I write this, over 40 years after Doc's passing, I feel infinite gratitude for his and Marge's dedication to youth sports and development. As an athlete, I feel humbled that he had the confidence in me to put me in situations at a very young age to help the team win, and I am proud when I reflect on my performance that I did everything I could to prove to him that I was worthy of that confidence. Doc was a winner and brought out the best in all his players to be winners, too. His eight state championships speak for themselves. Doc once said, "As long as the score is what they go by, then I want the best score." You had the best score, Doc, on and off the field. If someday on the Field of Dreams, we have a chance to be on the field together once again, I will be eager to accept the ball from you to pitch a big game or maybe flash some leather at shortstop, the only two positions you ever played me. Until then, rest in peace, my mentor, coach, and hero. I will always be Giuseppe to you.

In honor of Doc, his obituary that appeared in the November 24, 1983, issue of the *Leader* is reprinted here in its entirety.[12] What an amazing life he lived.

The End of an Era
Clyde H. Norman
1920–1983

Born on August 26, 1920, in Rogers, Arkansas (near Fayetteville) to Clyde and Myrtle Norman, the namesake son came with his parents to Billings at an early age, and there received his grade and high school education. His parents operated a grocery store.

Clyde Harrington Norman passed on at the hospital in Scobey, Nov. 15th after being there only a couple of days. The onset of his increasingly debilitating illness (aneurysm and complications) began about two years ago when he had to totally suspend his very active family medical and surgical practice.

Even then, from his motorized wheelchair, he continued to guide the Scobey Blues Legion Baseball team, substantiated by Assistant Coach Don Lekvold and help from former stars of his championship teams, virtually until last season's team.

A brilliant student, young Clyde also excelled in football and baseball. His talented enthusiasm for many things was noted early by his teachers and he had a wide range of interests.

As a consequence of his brilliance and versatility, he graduated from Billings High School at the age of 14 and spent one term at UM, Missoula, where he was recruited—both for his athletic ability and scholarship—by Aldo Forte, for Northwestern University at Evanston, Illinois, a suburban city of the Chicago area.

Built like a brick outhouse, he lettered as a guard on Northwestern's Big Ten football team during some of its vintage years, while also impressing some of his professors with his scholastic capabilities.

One professor, who was an author of several books, however, made things plain to him when young Clyde came to class, proudly wearing his new letterman's sweater. A real status symbol in those days.

The professor, in class (college professors can be real dictators) mentioned, incidentally, "and I don't like athletes." In recollection, Clyde once told the *Leader*, I felt he was looking right at me. I got the message, and never again wore my letterman's sweater to his classes."

The young athlete-scholar received his bachelor of science degree at the age of 19, and enrolled as a student in medical school. During that period Pearl Harbor occurred on December 7, 1941. Young Clyde enlisted December 16, 1941, in the U.S. Marine Corps.

As a buck private in the famed Carlson's Raiders in America's first aggressive WWII action on Makin Island against Japanese invaders, he won corporal's stripes. Soon he was part of the 1st Marine Division on Guadalcanal.

The Don Lekvold Era

About five feet nine and 210 pounds, he continued to amaze his colleagues with his enthusiastic macho, sturdy action and spirit. He received a battlefield commission, and in 1943, was returned to the U.S. after Makin Island, Guadalcanal and Midway, to Quantico, Virginia, for officer's training and completed that in time to take part in the Iwo Jima campaign—which took more lives there than any other action in the South Pacific.

"After that," Doc Norman once told the *Leader*, I've been living on velvet (a gambler's term for being ahead of the game).

During his temporary return to the U.S. in 1943, he married a cute, spunky Montana gal, Marge Sampson, in Los Angeles. After his discharge from the Marine Corps he returned to Northwestern University Medical School, later getting back to Montana.

An awkward sequence of circumstances kept him from totally completing his residency in obstetrics and gynecology, so he set up practice in Columbus, Montana. He learned later Scobey needed one more doctor so moved his family here in 1958.

In the course of this, he used his spare hours to promote American Legion baseball. Over the years, he and his chief of staff, Marge, along the way affectionately housed and fed a number of "stray dog" youths, who were at loose ends. One of those fellows, "Butch" Goddard, came from Ashland, Oregon, to be one of the pallbearers at the services.

The services here last Friday were attended by the largest assembly of people at a funeral in the history of Daniels County.

During his twenty-five years in Scobey as American Legion baseball coach, aided by enthusiastic assistants, he won eight state championships, and at one point, just a few years ago won five straight—over cities from two to fifteen times larger population of this county area.

July 3rd this year, Scobey had a "Doc Norman Day," the first ever accorded any citizen in this county area. Earlier this year, at Great Falls, he was awarded the outstanding amateur coach in Montana.

Doc Norman never received a nickel for his coaching services; instead, he spent from two to five thousand dollars a year giving to the team. This was the "edge" that no other cities the size could compete with.

(Baseball committees all over the state, each season beforehand, wring their hands in regard to budgets and getting the right person to handle the Legion ball club.) For twenty-five years Scobey had that part ready-made, due to Doc Norman's enthusiasm, skill, indomitable spirit, and beneficence.

Meanwhile, with one of the most extensive general practices in northeastern Montana, Doc's energies and talents were devoted to his boys, but his infectious enthusiasm often did not impress the hard noses, when each year he would say, "We're going to have the finest team ever," as observers could see a very ragged beginning.

But so many times, he got the kids up, to go on and win state titles, that cynics were in confusion.

On the other side, as a general practitioner, he worked diligently every day—seven days a week, to look after his patients, including house calls, which nowadays no longer exist, except in the exceptions.

Along the way, Doc Norman would have been crippled without the chief of staff, his wife, Marge, a lady of great energy, patience and her unrelenting love for a guy whom she never knew what he would do next.

Besides his skill as a general practitioner, Doc Norman, the dean of Montana's American Legion baseball coaches, there were other sides to him, which should not be overlooked.

He studied Arabic, Greek, and also for a couple years engaged fervently in astronomy. He built a device and ground a 10-inch telescopic set of lenses, using the Foucault system of grinding them. (Check the Encyclopedia Brittanica on this.) In his study he had a large circular thing in the ceiling which when properly moved could tell one which stars would be visible in the night sky at that time.

Moreover, he was probably the most accomplished gourmet chef in northeastern Montana.

In addition, Doc Norman was an accomplished artist in oils and watercolors, in portraiture as well as scenery. He was, indeed, as Shakespeare once wrote, "a man of parts."

As a member of both veterans organizations, the Masons and other pertinent organizations, Doc Norman probably needs to be considered as the most prominent "Renaissance Man" of northeastern Montana.

His passing, Nov. 15, marks the end of an era—but the legacy he left for youth should continue to be an inspiration to all who find themselves fighting from the bottom side.

He never gave up, even when the "big casino" finally got to him. Doc Norman went down swinging, which any other way the would have deplored.

As a fellow who never paid much attention to economic necessities, Doc Norman, aided by his wife's devoted efforts, paid no attention whatsoever to financial problems. During his quarter century practice here, he was both skilled and very compassionate.

But he was a hard-nosed guy when it came to winning. He once said, "As long ass the score is what they go by, then I want the best score."

Once described by the *Leader* in appearance as a cross between a kewpie doll and the Buddha, he maintained "all we need is to give these kids a chance to excel; we got the talent."

Over the past quarter century, the mothers of those kids could see this, and they were his greatest supporters. "The gals are really the only ones who know where it is," Doc said.

Doc Norman is survived by his wife, Marge, of Scobey. A daughter, Ann (Mrs. Ken) Lee of Scobey; Mike a specialist in anesthesia in Alaska and owner of a successful commercial fishing boat, an adopted son, Kelly, in college and a fine baseball player and former Legion star here; and Doc's sister, Grace Rosich of Polson.

Pallbearers at the services here last Friday were Don Lekvold (sturdy assistant in baseball), Frank "Butch" Goddard of Ashland, Ore., Danny Wolfe, Phil Audet, Kevin Sell of Great Falls and Rocky Ware.

As Lutheran Pastor Dick Widerholdt stated at the impressive services, "He has passed on, but he last left a legacy and established goals for our youth, the measure of which we do nothing which can do nothing less than try to measure up."

Waller Funeral Home did an excellent job of handling by far the largest assemblage of funeral goers in the history of our county.

1984

The Blues Return to State and the North Star Rises in the West One More Time

> *The success of this young team bodes well for next season when the state tournament will come back to Scobey for the first time since 1979.*
>
> —Daniels County Leader, August 9, 1984

1984 Scobey Blues. Back row, left to right: Steve Lapke, Rod Hudyma, Ivan Domenech, Mike Heaton, Tony Vigliotti, Mike Tryan, Coach Don Lekvold. Front row, left to right: Mike Roland, Tommy Fugere, Joey Girard, Steve Schaefer, Jim LeProwse. Not pictured, Larry Trangsrud. *Leader photo.*

PRESEASON

AFTER MISSING THE STATE TOURNAMENT FOR THE FIRST time in 16 years in 1983, Coach Don Lekvold faced an enormous challenge getting Scobey back to the state tournament in 1984. Five-year veteran ballers Pat Audet and Jim Lekvold—who had each played on three state championship teams—had aged out, and Greg Stolen—who had also played on three state championships and was still age-eligible in 1984—could not play due to his debilitating mental illness. Those three big guns would leave gaping holes on the field and the mound. Jeff Mann, Bob Tryan, and Brian Gilbert had also aged out. However, age and experience were returning in starters Tony Vigliotti (18), Joey Girard (18), Mike Tryan (18), Steve Schaefer (18), Jim LeProwse (17), and Ivan Domenech (17). Mike Heaton was returning for his second year, and Larry Trangsrud (16) was returning for his third season. Talented rookie Mike Roland (15)—Dan Danelson's first cousin and also a pitcher—joined the team, along with Steve Lapke and Tom Fugere. In 1984, Tony Vigliotti, Jim LeProwse, Ivan Domenech, and Mike Roland shared pitching duties for the Blues. Larry Trangsrud would slide behind the plate, becoming Scobey's number one catcher for the next three years.

REGULAR SEASON

FOR THE FIRST TIME SINCE 1959, DOC NORMAN WAS NOT ON THE field at Scobey Ball Park in 1984, but the first Doc Norman Memorial Invitational Tournament was held in Scobey to honor his memory and legacy. The Doc Norman tournament would become an annual event in Scobey for many years.

During the regular season, Larry Trangsrud remembers the first home run he hit in his Legion career. He said, "The first home run I hit was July 4th, 1984, in Sidney. July 4th, easy to remember. I thought I flied out to left. Moose is

304 down the line; it didn't clear by much!" That's a special memory to hit your first home run on the 4th of July! The first home run I hit was at Moose Memorial Park in Sidney in 1977, also down the left-field line. So Larry and I have that in common. Later in the season in Williston, Larry hit two runs in one game at Williston.

Scobey played decently during the regular season, finishing with a respectable 17-9 record and qualified for the divisional tournament at Thompson Park in Laurel.

DIVISIONAL TOURNAMENT

SCOBEY'S DEVASTATING SEASON-ENDING LOSS TO WOLF POINT in 1983 had eliminated them from qualifying for the divisional tournament, so getting back there was a huge relief in 1984. The goal for the team in 1984 was to win two games, finish as one of the top four teams, and qualify for the state tournament, which, for the first time, would be played in Alberta. The opening day matchups at Thompson Park in Laurel were as follows:

- Richland County Patriots vs. Billings Cardinals
- Scobey Blues vs. Billings Blue Jays
- Lewistown Redbirds vs. Glendive Blue Devils
- Laurel Dodgers vs. Glasgow Reds

Scobey pounded the Blue Jays 18-5 in their first game. Winning pitcher Jim LeProwse shut out Billings in every inning except the second when the Blue Jays got to him for five runs. Coach Lekvold inserted Tom Fugere after Scobey's big lead to save Jim some innings for the tournament. Mike Tryan and Steve Lapke doubled for Scobey to lead the Blues' hitting.

Scobey lost to the Billing Cardinals 12-1 in the semifinal, but the Blues came back strong on a one-hit shutout by 15-year-old Mike Roland to beat Glasgow 18-0 and clinch a berth in the state tournament. Mike Tryan, Tony Vigliotti, Larry Trangsrud, and Joey Girard each doubled, and Jim LeProwse had two triples to lead Scobey's 17-hit attack. The win proved costly for Scobey, however, as Mike Roland pulled several shoulder muscles on the last pitch of the game and would not be able to pitch in the state tournament.

In the game for third and fourth place, Scobey led Glendive 4-1 in the top of the sixth inning, but Glendive erupted for three home runs in the bottom of the sixth, scoring six runs and taking a 7-4 lead. Glendive added another homer—their fourth in the game—and won 8-4, but the most crucial thing was Scobey was back in the state tournament after a one-year hiatus.

STATE B TOURNAMENT

THE STATE B TOURNAMENT WAS PLAYED AT HENDERSON Field in Lethbridge, Alberta. Lethbridge sounds like a long way from Scobey—and it is (450 miles)—but it is 50 miles closer to Scobey than Deer Lodge, Montana, where Scobey played its last state tournament in 1982. Joining the Billings Cardinals, Laurel Dodgers, Glendive Blue Devils, and Scobey Blues from the east were the four teams from the west: Whitehall Renegades, Vauxhall Spurs, Havre Northstars, and host Lethbridge Miners. Whitehall had won the western division championship, played at Hamilton Athletic Field, hosted there by the Bitterroot Bucs.

Whitehall, the defending state champion, with a record of 26-7, was the pre-tournament favorite. Havre Northstars Coach Tom Nielson—who had raised the Havre Post 11 American Legion Baseball program from the ashes in 1966, led them to their first state tournament appearance in 1967 and won three state B championships (1968, 1970, and 1971)—was back as head coach of the Northstars. The Northstars had won the northwestern district title during the regular season and had a 28-8 record but were upset in the divisional semifinal by Vauxhall. They were also considered one of the favorites to win it. First-day matchups were as follows:

- Whitehall Renegades (1W) vs. Scobey Blues (4E)
- Havre Northstars (3W) vs. Laurel Dodgers (2E)
- Vauxhall Spurs (2W) vs. Glendive Blue Devils (3E)
- Billings Cardinals (1E) vs. Lethbridge Miners (4W)

Coach Don Lekvold started ace Jim LeProwse in the first game, while Whitehall coach Ted Miller countered with his ace, left-hander Barry Griffin. Griffin led the Renegades to the 1983 State B championship and was named MVP of the tournament. In 1984, he sported a 14-4 season record and pitched a no-hitter—and nearly a perfect game—in the western division championship game against Vauxhall, allowing only one walk and one baserunner to reach on an error, striking out 13 Spurs. He was headed to North Idaho Junior College on a baseball scholarship. Griffin was true to form, as he and reliever Scott Lusty combined on a four-hitter, and Whitehall beat Scobey 9-3. Scobey pitching allowed only seven Renegade hits, but seven costly errors in the field led to several unearned runs. LeProwse pitched well but had to be relieved by Ivan Domenech in the fifth after being hit by a line drive in his pitching arm. With Mike Roland already sidelined by armed troubles, Scobey's chances to crawl back through the dirt route in the tournament were not good. Tony Vigliotti had two of Scobey's four hits. Scobey left a lot of runners on base, as Whitehall pitching walked 13 Blues.

Scobey then eliminated Laurel 9-7 in the loser-out game. Tony Vigliotti went the distance on the mound and earned the win. Scobey banged out 12 hits, with each player getting at least one hit. Jim LeProwse and Larry Trangsrud each doubled for Scobey's two extra-base hits.

That pitted Scobey against the Billings Cardinals in their third game of the tournament. Bodean Derheim of Billings pitched a complete game to lead the Cardinals to an 8-5 win, eliminating Scobey from the tournament and ending their season. Ivan Domenech started the game, went five innings, and was relieved by Jim LeProwse, who was able to return to the mound after being injured in the first game. The Blues again left a lot of runners on base. The *Leader* stated that Scobey "had several chances to win this one but failed to get the key hits with men on base." Jim LeProwse and Ivan Domenech doubled for Scobey's only extra-base hits.

TOURNAMENT SUMMARY

Under Coach Tom Nielson, Havre won the State B Tournament for the first time since 1975. In the *Havre Daily News*, Rita Balock-Hamilton wrote, "The Havre American Legion Baseball team did what no local team has done in nine years—win a state championship. With only four returning players in 14, that is a remarkable accomplishment."[13] The Northstars swept the tournament in four games, winning 6-5 over Laurel, 8-5 over Whitehall, 23-8 over Vauxhall, and 16-5 over Vauxhall in the championship. His son, Tim Nielson (shortstop and pitcher), went 4-6 with a double and pitched two innings of relief to lead Havre to the championship win. Havre closed the year with a 36-8 overall record, including a regular-season Northwest B conference championship, third-place divisional finish, and state title, respectively. It was Havre's sixth state title.

In summing up the 1984 season, the *Leader* stated that Coach Don Lekvold "was pleased with the team's 20-13 showing" and indicated that it "was the result of hard work and discipline." After losing three big guns from the previous season and with many younger players on the roster, the 1984 Blues took it as far as they could, especially after losing Mike Roland and Jim LeProwse as pitchers in the state tournament. The team looked promising to be a strong host of the State B Tournament the following season when the state tournament would return to Scobey for the first time since 1979.

The 1984 season was the last for 18-year-olds Joey Girard, Steve Schaefer, Mike Tryan, and Tony Vigliotti.

TOURNAMENT STATS

Hitting

Tony Vigliotti had two of Scobey's four hits off Barry Griffin of Whitehall in the first game. For the tournament, the Blues had 20 hits in 3 games, averaging almost six runs a game. For extra-base hits, Jim LeProwse had two doubles, and Larry Trangsrud and Ivan Domenech each had a double.

Pitching

Jim LeProwse logged eight innings in the tournament despite being injured in the first game. He suffered both losses. Ivan Domenech pitched nine innings in two games. Tony Vigliotti went all nine innings for Scobey against Laurel, picking up the win. Mike Roland could not pitch due to the injury to his arm on the last pitch he delivered in his one-hit shutout against Glasgow in the divisional tournament. Unquestionably, the injuries to Jim LeProwse and Mike Roland severely diminished Scobey's chances of going deep in the tournament.

Fielding

Scobey committed 16 errors in the three games.

EXTRA INNINGS

The 1984 season was the last year a Tryan would be on the roster for the Scobey Blues. Mike Tryan, son of Don and Phyllis Tryan from Flaxville, was selected to the 1984 East All-Star Team and was the starting right fielder for the 1982 Scobey Blues state championship team, the last state championship for Scobey. His older brother, Gordon, was the starting third baseman for the 1982 team, and he also started at third for the 1980 state championship team and was on the 1979 state championship team. Gord was also selected as an East All-Star in his last year in 1982. Cousin Jack started on the 1973 state championship team, and cousin Wade started on the 1976-79 state championship teams. That meant a Tryan started for Scobey in every state championship except their first one in 1969.

As I have undertaken this project, I have learned that baseball tends to "run in the family." I knew that beforehand, of course, but through the interviews and letters, it jumped out at me even more. One thing I didn't know, however, was how entrenched baseball was in Flaxville. I remember playing Peewee and Little League baseball against Flaxville in the late 1960s and early 1970s, and Don Tryan was always the coach of Flaxville. Flaxville had good

Peewee, Little League, and Babe Ruth teams, but I didn't realize that they had fielded good American Legion teams going back to the 1950s. In 1958, the Flaxville American Legion team won the northeastern district and played off against Roundup in Scobey to advance to the state play-offs, losing the best-of-three series in three games. Flaxville fielded good Legion teams through 1967, Danny Tryan's last season.

Danny Tryan, older brother of Gord and Mike, was a good ballplayer, too. He played on Flaxville's last American Legion team in 1967. The following year, in 1968, Jack Higgins and Randy Legare started in the outfield for the Scobey American Legion team, and the year after that, Don Higgins, Jim Miller, and Dennis Miller joined the team. Dick Puckett from Peerless was already with the team, playing since 1965. The all–Daniels County team was the first to win a state championship for Scobey in 1969, and Doc, who had been desperately trying to recruit Flaxville players to play in Scobey since he arrived in 1959, had his first state championship.

It was hard for the small towns to let go of their Legion baseball teams. This is why Don Tryan and Flaxville resisted Doc's requests to combine until 1968. It wasn't just Flaxville that resisted. Bob Tande had also tried to recruit Reese Puckett, Jr., from Peerless to pitch for Scobey in the early 1960s. My brother Bill told me that Bob asked Reese, "Would you like to come and give the ball a whirl?" but Reese said no. My dad seriously considered fielding a Legion team in Peerless in 1977 with the strong team he had built through Peewee, Little League, and Babe Ruth since 1967. Ultimately, he thought his boys would have a better chance to win a state championship if they combined with Scobey (he was right!), but it was difficult for him to let go of his team.

Peerless (Post 107) fielded its last American Legion Baseball team in 1960. Outlook (Post 72) fielded its last American Legion team in 1965, followed by Flaxville (Whitetail Post 121) in 1967. This was all the inevitable effect of the declining population in northeastern Montana, which accelerated and eventually wiped out the high schools, too, as Outlook High School closed in 2005, Flaxville in 2006, and Peerless in 2009. The Flaxville Cardinals and Outlook Blue Jays combined to form the Flaxville-Outlook Knights in the 1995-1996 season so the kids could continue competing in prep sports before the schools closed. Somehow, Opheim High School has managed to stay open.

Watching your baseball program and high school die is not a lot of fun. All these high schools went through that. This is why one of the major themes of *The Blues of Summer* is nostalgia—as it was with the basketball book *The Dream*, which looked back on the heyday of the Peerless Panthers before Peerless High School closed in 2009. *The Blues of Summer* takes a nostalgic look at the Scobey American Legion Baseball program in its heyday before it—like the Class C high schools—could no longer sustain itself and be competitive, shutting down after an 0-29 season in 2003, renewing in 2016-19. The program could not survive partly because the "farm clubs"—Peerless, Flaxville, Opheim, and later Outlook—could no longer produce ballplayers through their Peewee, Little League, and Babe Ruth programs. The pipeline dried up. Jeff Welsch wrote in 406 Montana Sports that the small-town teams went "the way of the dodo."

As he was "the last Tryan" to play for Scobey, I asked Mike to write about his baseball experience, and he shared this letter:

Growing up in a baseball family was the best and most amazing experience I had in my whole life. Having a big brother three years older than me (Gordon Tryan) was perfect. I remember he would always take me everywhere, even to his practices.

My experience as a baseball player was the best thing ever to happen to me. I was fortunate enough to have two of the best parents, Don and Phyllis Tryan. My dad was a ball player in his early days, and my mom was the backbone. I remember my dad being my Little League coach when I was playing for Flaxville. We had talented athletes in Flaxville, but as we got older, my Flaxville friends had to work and did not move on beyond Little League. I remember playing a little bit of Babe Ruth.

I became good friends with Scobey kids on the Blues, like Pat Audet, Tony Vigliotti, Steve Schaefer, and a lot more. Growing up watching my brother play for Doc and the Blues, it was my dream to play for the Blues as well. I got to watch Dan Danelson and my idols, the Puckett twins. So, I really wanted to be on the team.

My dream became a reality, and I started to play for Doc Norman and the Scobey Blues when I was 13 years old. I played shortstop, but second base was my favorite position. I remember Doc and his son, Kelly, teaching me how to throw a quick throw to first base from shortstop. They also taught me how to slide and even slide to catch a low fly ball in the outfield. I was fortunate enough to get to play with great ball players like Randy Stolen, Kirby Halvorson, and Kelly Norman.

In my early days with the Blues, I remember when I got my uniform. It was number 8, and if I am right, that was Joe Puckett's old uniform. (Close, Mike, it was Jon's number!) I was not a home run hitter, but I did get on base most of the time. I was usually the leadoff hitter, and I remember coach Don

Lekvold telling me that because of my speed, I could do whatever I wanted—bunt or hit away—just get on base.

I still remember the signs Doc would give: Swipe the chest, then swipe the face, then the hat was a bunt. And hat, face, and chest, and I was off to the races, which meant steal. I hope I remember that correctly.

I will say, though, that my biggest joy as a baseball player I ever got to play with was to be able to play with my brother, Gordon Tryan. He was a great hitter and third baseman. I remember he hit a ball in practice once that went so far, I think it went all the way to Canada. It was at least 40 feet above the score clock in left field, past the fence.

Playing baseball for Doc Norman, I would say, was an honor. Then, in my last year of Legion, I played for Don Lekvold and Kelly Norman.

—*Mike Tryan*

In 1984, for the third year, Montana Class A and Class B East and West All-Star teams consisting of 18-year-olds were selected and played a single game in each class at Legion Park in Great Falls. The West All-Stars won the game 13-7. Barry Griffin of Whitehall was named MVP. Three Scobey Blues—Tony Vigliotti, Mike Tryan, and Joey Girard—were selected to the Class B East All-Stars.

Here was the roster for the 1984 Class B East All-Stars, coached by Gene Hansen, Glendive Blue Devils and Mark Schultz, Billings Cardinals: Travis Frandsen, Richland Patriots; Chris Volk, Richland Patriots; Rodney Siring, Livingston Outlaws; Michael Hodges, Laurel Dodgers; Trent Gardiner, Laurel Dodgers; Beaumont Bradley, Laurel Dodgers; Richard Fisher, Glendive Blue Devils; Michael Zimmer, Glendive Blue Devils; Shane Bakken, Glendive Blue Devils; Russell McCarvel, Glendive Blue Devils; Warren Quick, Circle Stars; Peter Helland, Glasgow Reds; Robert Reyes, Glasgow Reds; Mark Heidinger, Wolf Point Yellowjackets; Tony Vigliotti, Scobey Blues; Mike Tryan, Scobey Blues; Joey Girard, Scobey Blues; Mark Rapkoch, Lewistown Hawks.

And the roster for the West All-Stars, coached by Tom Nielson, Havre Northstars: John Shennum, Havre Northstars; Tim Nielson, Havre Northstars; Cub Shuland, Havre Northstars; Barry Griffin, Whitehall Renegades; Andy Hustava, Whitehall Renegades; Ted Miller, Whitehall Renegades; Dan Brozovich, Whitehall Renegades; Rob Jones, Deer Lodge Wranglers; Dan McGuire, Deer Lodge Wranglers; James Oikawa, Lethbridge Miners; Morey Terry, Lethbridge Miners; Lindsay Bell, Lethbridge Lakers; Jesse Wilson, Bitterroot Bucs; Brent Morrison, Vauxhall Spurs; Jay Turnquist, Vauxhall Spurs; Joe Hirst, Fairfield Blue Hawks; Stephen Gjerde, Fairfield Blue Hawks; Harvey Lake, Dillon Cubs

The 1984 season was the first year the State Class B champion did not play a best-of-three series against the fourth seed from the Class A eastern or western division to qualify for the State A Tournament. Instead, a regional tournament with State B champions from Montana, Washington, Idaho, and Oregon was planned. However, the Northstars didn't get to play in the tournament when Oregon, the tournament's host, fought the admission of Montana. Class B American Legion commissar Jim Rowe of Poplar said, "It is too bad for the Northstars the proposed regional challenge tournament never got off the ground, but I feel positive it will be a reality next year." (It was. State B champion Glendive played in the Northwest Regional in Yakima, Washington.)

1984 East All-Stars. Tony Vigliotti, Mike Tryan, and Joey Girard are on the bottom row on the right. *Family photo.*

Barry Griffin, the 6-foot-3, 185-pound left-hander who pitched a combined four-hitter against Scobey in the first game of the state tournament, won 39 games and lost 12 in three years with the Whitehall Renegades. While pitching for North Idaho Junior College, he was drafted in the seventh round by the Pittsburgh Pirates in the regular phase of the January 1985 annual winter free-agent draft but didn't sign a contract. In June 1985, the Baltimore Orioles drafted him in the fifth round of the amateur baseball draft's secondary phase. He pitched two years in the minor leagues (1987-88) for the Butte Copper Kings and Boise Hawks, finishing his minor league career with a 7-11 record and 4.79 ERA. Griffin was the third power-pitching left-hander who was drafted to end Scobey's postseason, following Dave Fanning (1971) and Bill Wilkinson (1982).

Speaking of players getting drafted, 1984 was the year Dan Danelson (Blues 1974-79) was drafted. With his wedding planned the day after the NAIA national championship game, Kelly had to "pinch hit" for Dano at the rehearsal because Dano was playing in the championship game that evening. The Warriors won the national championship that night, and Dano got married the next day. Then, as Coach Ed Cheff walked through the line after the wedding, he told Dano he had been drafted in the 33rd round of the 1984 MLB June Amateur Draft. Dano said, "I was surprised, to say the least. I had a free agent contract with the Giants, so I knew I was playing, but Texas had seen me in Lubbock, Texas, as a sophomore. In my opinion, that was the best I had ever thrown, so maybe they thought they might get that version." That's quite a 24 hours: win the national championship, get married, get drafted. Dano summed it up this way: "Good and bad things happen in threes many times." In his one-year minor league career in 1984, Dano pitched for the Tri-Cities Triplets (Richland, Washington) in A ball in the Northwest League. He appeared in 18 games and pitched 36 and two-thirds innings. His record was 2-1, with an ERA of 2.45, striking out 33 hitters with a WHIP of 1.200.

Tony Vigliotti, Mike Tryan, and Joey Girard were selected to the East All-Star Team and played in the East-West All-Star Game in Great Falls. They played for Glendive Coach Gene Hansen, and Tom Nielson of Havre coached the West. Barry Griffin from the Whitehall Renegades, who pitched against Scobey in the state tournament, was named the game's MVP. He pitched three innings of two-hit ball, struck out six, and hit a bases-loaded double to lead the West to a 13-7 win.

East All-Star Tony Vigliotti of the Blues comes from a baseball family. I remember watching his dad, Pat, umpire behind the plate in Scobey after the Vigliottis moved to Scobey in 1979. His dad was the real deal as an umpire, like a professional. I thought it was cool that someone with that much passion for the sport would move to Scobey because nowhere else in northeastern Montana was there more enthusiasm for baseball than in Scobey. It was a good match. Intrigued by Tony and his family's baseball story, I asked him to tell it, and he shared this letter:

I am not really sure where to start, so I guess I'll start at what I think is the beginning. You should know that my dad, Pat, was born, raised, and graduated high school (1960) in Central Valley, New York. It's about 52 miles from downtown Manhattan. (Thus, no choice but to be a Yankees fan.) He met my mom, (Patty Eichhorn) who is originally from Scobey in the Navy. They got married, and according to my dad, she only said yes because he promised they would not have to live in New York. They moved to Havre in 1964. (My grandmother and my mom's brother George Eichhorn and his wife Betty were here at that time.) I was born in November 1965. My dad was always a lover of baseball, a very good high school player, and always wanted to try to stay involved in the game. His umpire journey started in 1970 when he applied to the Major League umpire development program and was accepted. He finished the program, which included working spring training games, and then was assigned to work Single 'A' ball on the East Coast. My mom and I stayed in Havre that year. (1970) The powers that be liked what they saw, and in 1971, he was invited back to spring training and was then assigned to work double "A" ball in Florida. My mom and I moved to Central Valley that year and lived with my grandparents (Margaret and Anthony Vigliotti) for a bit, but we headed to Sarasota, Florida, in the spring to be closer to my dad. After that 1971 season is when things took a turn. Later that year, my grandfather had a work accident at the tire shop where he worked. A tire he was repairing blew off the rim, striking him in the head. He was in a coma for a bit and passed away. I believe he was 53 years old. In 1972, my dad was going to be assigned to a league in Texas, so my mom and I moved to Oklahoma so that we would be closer to him. However, the loss of his father changed his thinking, and he decided not to sign his contract. The head of the Major League umpire development program tried to talk him out of it, telling him that the American League was looking at him hard and he would have a shot to be in the big leagues if he chose to continue. He stayed with his decision and did not sign the contract. He told me through the years that he did regret that decision a bit as he was sure he was good enough to be a major league umpire. So, continuing the story, we moved back to Havre in 1972 and stayed here until our move to Scobey in 1979. My mom and dad purchased the Four Buttes Supper Club that year and off to Northeast Montana we went. My dad stayed involved in baseball and umpired American Legion Baseball in Scobey and across the state. He worked in approximately 15 state tournaments and was selected to work the 1990 American Legion World Series.

As you can see, baseball was a part of my life from the beginning; if I wanted to be near my dad, I was at the baseball field. The move to Scobey for me was not an easy one. I was in 8th grade and had been in Havre for most of my life. So, I was leaving my childhood friends and everything I knew behind. I was scared to death and, I'm sure, mad at my folks for a while, but it did turn out to be a great move. I didn't know it at the time, but I was fortunate to go from one Legion baseball hotbed to another. I was able to be a part of the Scobey Blues from 1980 to 1984. Didn't play much on the '80 and '81 teams but had a bigger role in '82, '83, and '84. I played with and admired so many of them. You and your brother were done by that time, but you were around some. I had mentors and looked up to guys like Kelly Norman, Kirby Halvorson, and Randy Stolen, and I played with a bunch of great guys. Jim Lekvold, Pat Audet, Gordy and Mike Tryan, Len Floyd, Greg Stolen, Jim LeProwse, and Randy Pederson, just to name a few. Scobey no doubt fueled my love of the game.

My last season in 1984 was a tough one. We did make it to the state tournament that year in Lethbridge and were beaten out of the tournament. The Havre Northstars won it that year, and those guys were my childhood friends in Havre, as well as the guys that I spent a lot of time with on the diamond. The best memories of being a Scobey Blue were, of course, Doc and Marge. They were everybody's surrogate parents and would do anything for any of us. The teammates I played with are some of the best. I regret not being able to help carry on the dominance but feel very fortunate to be a little part of the storied history of Scobey Blues Baseball.

I, of course, have stayed involved in some way since my playing days ended in 1984. My wife (Kathie Tade) and I moved to Havre in 1987, and I started umpiring and worked Legion and some junior college baseball. My umpire career included working in approximately 15 district, divisional, and state legion tournaments. I worked my last game in the 2010 State "AA" Legion Tournament in Medicine Hat, Alberta. I even worked a couple of state tournaments with my good friend, to this day, Jim Lekvold. The highlight of my umpiring career was umpiring a Legion game in Havre with my dad and my brother Tim Vigliotti (As I am writing this, Tim is currently working the State "AA Legion Tournament in Helena)

After that 2010 season, I took a couple of years away from the baseball field but jumped back in and was an assistant coach for the Havre Northstars for a few years. Stepped away again but couldn't stay away from the ballpark very long. I applied for and was hired as the head coach for the Havre High School Blue Ponies Fast-pitch softball team in 2018. I finished season 7 this spring. I have a Granddaughter who will be part of the High School program in the spring of 2025, so I guess I passed on the love of the game to her.

On a side note, I was involved in coaching my son (Scott) through the youth baseball leagues in Havre until he got to the Legion level. I was umpiring when he played for the Northstars and was on the field many times with him as a player and me as an umpire. A very hard dynamic but we made it work.

I could go on forever with stories about bus trips, practices, and games. The memories and friendships I have made through the game over the years are something I cherish. Baseball/Softball is part of who I am. It started with my dad and continued by being a part of two great Montana programs: the Scobey Blues and the Havre Northstars.

—Tony Vigliotti

I also asked All-Star Joey Girard, who started on the 1982 state championship team and had been with the Blues since 1981, to share his baseball story with me, and he provided this letter:

My baseball story started with a dad who was always willing to drop everything if his son wanted to play a little catch. We had pick-up games in the city park and anyone's back yard. We would grab any kids we could and just go. We had duct taped wiffleball bats and mini hoops balls or whatever we could round up to make do. I joined LL early when our field was actually at the Elementary school. Sometime in the late 70s the official field was moved over by the roping barn and Fairgrounds. Then we had 3 Scobey teams: Red Sox, A's, and my team the White sox. If I'm not mistaken our district also included Flaxville, Peerless, and Outlook. Many future Blues came up through those teams. We did have a 12 year all-star team that played in Wolf Point. I believe we lost out in 2. Memories of Babe Ruth years are really foggy. I don't think we played many games or practiced much. Some of us hung around and sometimes Doc would have us work in with the Blues. I do remember some of us catchers working in when the Blues would throw bullpens. It was pretty intimidating catching Danny D. or the Puckett boys when you were used to 13-year-olds who really didn't even throw curveballs yet! This would have been around '79 or '80. In '81 Doc called this year's rookies up and we were off. The learning curve was steep for some of us. I think Donnie referred to me in the Leader as "green" Lol! Eventually through Doc and Donnie's guidance our baseball savvy grew. Just like most years past, young boys were turned into real ball players. I was lucky enough to bond with friends through baseball and the other sports we played. Most of us still have lifelong friendships that started on that baseball field. In Doc's last years, I often was his go-between him and Donnie during games. Doc would say from his spot in the corner of the dugout, "Joe Joe, go tell Donnie. . ." It was frustrating to Doc to be stuck in the dugout and sometimes those conversations were heated, Lol! After Legion ball, we played club baseball at EMC. We brought together players from all corners of the state. When marriage and family eventually happed, I coached my boys through Little league and Juniors baseball. My oldest boy, Ty, played with The Billings Scarlets organization for 5 years and won a State championship in 2011. My youngest son, Jett, played in and won state championships in Juniors and Seniors basesball. Jett played travel-ball for Billings Upper Deck and traveled around the states playing baseball until it was time to go to college. Over the years, my boys played games against the sons of Blues players. (Tony Vig. Jim LeProwse, Dan Danelson.) They were in games where the umpire was an ex-Blues player. (Larry Trangsrud, Tony Vig.) As a sports photographer, I also was able to shoot games that had NE MT legion or Scobey ties. Like they say: "Everyone knows or is related to everyone." Sports brings us all together. Joe, thank you for starting and guiding these conversations! I look forward to seeing you this summer!

P.S. It is extremely uncomfortable talking about yourself, so writing this story with limited information is quite a gift. Thanks again for taking this on!

Blues Brother,
Joey

1985

Scobey Hosts Its Final State Tournament and a Northstars-Blues Game for the Ages

> *The American Legion State Class B State Tournament had it all: a stunning upset, a record marathon game, a Cinderella team, and a new champion.*
>
> —*Billings Gazette, July 29, 1985*

> *The Northstars held a 41-3 record going into the contest, but the hometown Blues outlasted them to advance in the winner's bracket.*
>
> — *Billings Gazette, July 27, 1985*

PRESEASON

WHEN COACH DON LEKVOLD ASSEMBLED THE BLUES for the opening-day practice in April, the buzz on the field was that the Blues were hosting the state tournament for the first time since 1979. This would be the seventh and final time Scobey hosted the state tournament. Could the Blues' final state tournament at Scobey Ball Park match the excitement and drama of previous state tournaments? One could only hope.

What kind of team would host Scobey have? They would be young, for sure. Four experienced players had aged out and would be missed. Left-handed pitcher Tony Vigliotti, Steve Schaefer, Joey Girard, and Mike Tryan—all starters and former state champions—were gone. Tony, Joey, and Mike had been selected to the East All-Star Team, and Steve Schaefer had broken up Bill Wilkinson's no-hitter in the 1982 playoffs. But of the five returning starters, four were from key positions. The 1985 Blues had only two 18-year-olds on the roster: ace pitcher Jim LeProwse, returning for this third season, and Mike Heaton. Ivan "Taco" Domenech (17) and Mike Roland (16) were returning, and both could pitch. Mike Roland had pitched a one-hitter in the divisional tournament as a 15-year-old the previous season. Starting catcher Larry Trangsrud (16) was back, so Scobey had three pitchers and an experienced catcher—an excellent nucleus to build a team around. Steve Lapke and Tom Fugere—who also could pitch—were back, too. Randy Pearce, Paul Shaffer, Jeff Jones, Danny Stephenson, Brad Gilbert, Rod Hudyma, and Mark Huwe joined the team as rookies.

REGULAR SEASON

SCOBEY'S REGULAR SEASON FEATURED SOME SPARKLING highlights:

- Mike Roland tossed a six-hitter to lead Scobey to a 12-1 victory over Wolf Point. He struck out nine and walked only one. The Blues scored nine runs in the second inning, highlighted by Ivan Domenech's two-run double.
- Ivan Domenech pitched a complete nine-inning game, and Steve Lapke and Mike Roland tripled to lead Scobey to a 10-3 conference win over Wolf Point.
- Mike Roland scattered six hits and yielded only three runs as Scobey beat Glendive 6-3 to earn a split in their doubleheader in Scobey. Steve Lapke doubled to lead Scobey's 8-hit attack. The win pushed Scobey's Northeast B record to 4-3 and overall record to 5-4.
- Ivan Domenech fired a one-hit shutout to lead the Blues to a 2-0 win over Ray, North Dakota, and a doubleheader sweep. He struck out five and walked only two batters, running his record to 4-1. The Blues scored both runs in the fifth inning when Jim LeProwse singled and scored on two errors; then Larry Trangsrud scored on Randy Pearce's double. The Blues won the first game 10-5. Domenech and winning pitcher Tom Fugere had

run-scoring singles, and two runs scored on walks. The two wins ran Scobey's record to 8-5.

- The Blues swept a doubleheader from Williston in Scobey. In the first game, Scobey broke a 5-5 tie in the sixth when Tom Fugere scored on a sac fly by Larry Trangsrud for the 6-5 victory. Jim LeProwse got the win in relief. Ivan Domenech pitched his second consecutive one-hit shutout to lead the Blues to the 8-0 win and the sweep. LeProwse went 3-4 with a double and a triple to lead Scobey's hitting. With the sweep, the Blues upped their record to 10-5.

Scobey finished its regular season with a 16-10 record, going 6-5 in its last 11 games. Along with Glendive, Sidney, and Glasgow, they advanced to the divisional tournament from the northeastern district. Glendive was the dominant team during conference play.

DIVISIONAL TOURNAMENT

THE 1985 EASTERN DIVISIONAL TOURNAMENT WAS PLAYED at Moose Memorial Park in Sidney. As host of the state tournament, Scobey had an automatic bid into the state tournament, but they were playing for pride and a higher seed. Here were the opening-day matchups:

- Billings Cardinals vs. Glasgow Reds
- Laurel Dodgers vs. Scobey Blues
- Glendive Blue Devils vs. Livingston Outlaws
- Richland County Patriots vs. Billings Blue Jays

In Scobey's first game against Laurel, Dodger ace Greg Fink pitched a two-hit shutout, striking out 14 Blues and leading Laurel to an 11-0 win in eight innings. At the plate, Laurel banged out 18 hits, including two home runs, to completely dominate Scobey offensively and defensively. It was a devastating opening-day loss for Scobey.

Pushed into the loser's bracket, Scobey lost their second game 4-2 to Glasgow and was eliminated from the tournament. They were sent packing for an early return home to Scobey to prepare for the state tournament, where they would be the number-four seed in the east with the automatic bid.

Glendive, the number-one seed from the northeastern district, won the tournament with an 8-5 win over the Billings Cardinals in 12 innings. Glasgow qualified as the third seed, winning the consolation game 6-5 over Sidney in 11 innings. However, Sidney could not play in the state tournament, as only the top three teams advanced.

STATE B TOURNAMENT

SCOBEY WAS HOSTING THE STATE B TOURNAMENT AGAIN! IT hadn't been since 1979, when Scobey won its sixth state championship, 11-0 over Laurel, that the little town referred to by Jack Reiner as "Baseball Country" had hosted. The *Leader*, as it always did, proudly welcomed the seven traveling teams to Scobey in its leadup edition, printed the bracket, and noted that the tournament was historically significant in that Scobey was hosting not one—but two—Canadian teams in the tournament for the first time, the two teams being the Lethbridge Lakers and the Vauxhall Spurs.[14] Here were the opening-day matchups:

- Lethbridge Lakers (2W) vs. Glasgow Reds (3E)
- Glendive Blue Devils (1E) vs. Vauxhall Spurs (3W)
- Missoula Reds (3W) vs. Billings Cardinals (2E)
- Havre Northstars (1W) vs. Scobey Blues (4E)

The Havre Northstars were returning to the state tournament in Scobey for the first time in 10 years. The last year the Northstars traveled to Scobey was 1975, after which Havre left to play in the Class A ranks from 1976–1980. In the 1975 tournament, another epic pitcher's duel (following Dave Fanning and Terry Puckett in 1971) manifested when Barry Kato outdueled Mike Hagfeldt for a 1-0 win, and Havre went on to win the championship in a 13-inning affair 2-1 over Cut Bank. It was Havre's fifth state championship.

Havre Coach Tom Nielson, who had coached in the state tournament in Scobey in 1969 and 1971, was returning as Havre's head coach. His assistant was Micky Williams, Havre's starting left fielder in 1969, when Scobey won its first state championship. So, there was a lot of history between these two storied and dominant Legion programs. The first year Tom Nielson coached Havre to a state tournament championship in 1968 was Don Lekvold's final year playing Legion ball. Since that year—between 1968 and 1984—Scobey and Havre had won 14 of 17 state championships. All pre-tournament bets were that Havre would make it 15 out of 18 in 1985.

The Northstars and Blues would face each other in the last game on the tournament's first day. Havre was the defending state champion, winning the State B championship in 1984 with a 36-8 record. In 1985, they completely dominated the west, losing only three games in the regular season. They bulldozed through the western division tournament in Havre, winning 9-1 over the Great Falls Electric Bs, 8-2 over Conrad, and 14-2 over Lethbridge in the championship, outscoring their opponents 31-5. They entered the state tournament in Scobey with a near-perfect 41-3 record and the overwhelming favorite to repeat as State champions. They were 77-11 (88% winning percentage) over the past two seasons. Even the powerful Havre teams of the late 1960s and early 1970s did not post records that were that win-heavy. Only Glendive, the eastern division champion, was given a chance to possibly challenge Havre for the title.

Meanwhile, Scobey was only in the tournament as the fourth seed from the east because they were the host team. The Blues were a "dark horse" and not given a chance. They had a 16-10 during the regular season—finishing their last 11 games just above .500—and had been embarrassingly eliminated from the eastern divisional tournament in Sidney in two games. The Blues were the Cinderella team of the tournament, and Havre was the prohibitive favorite. There was never a wider disparity between the two teams entering a state tournament, and it was unfamiliar territory for Scobey to wear the glass slipper. When I asked catcher Larry Trangsrud about his mindset going into the game, he said, "Expectations were not high."

How would Scobey do, wearing the glass slipper? Could they stay on the field with Havre, let alone win? Could the magical moments of the previous state tournaments Scobey hosted, including the dramatic two-out, two-strike ninth-inning home run over the left field fence by Dick Puckett to tie the 1969 state championship game and force extra innings against Havre, propel Scobey to play above their level and compete? The answer was yes.

Don Lekvold handed the ball to ace pitcher Jim LeProwse to start the game. Referring to Jim LeProwse, Don said, "Jimmy was one of those kids; it didn't matter how his arm was feeling, he'd go out and give you his best."

Knowing that Scobey was a heavy underdog, I asked Jim LeProwse about his mental approach to the game. "I was confident and relaxed. I knew that they were really good, but I also knew how good the teams in our conference were, and I had faced them on the mound all year long. I knew what our team could do when we were playing well. I have never been the person to let any kind of stress take me over. I try to see the positive in every situation. I just knew that if I did my job, my team would do their job, and we had a chance. I remember thinking that I needed to pitch well enough to keep it close, and we would definitely have a chance."

And Jim LeProwse did give it his best—and kept it close—for 12 innings. Coach Tom Nielson countered with Dude Evans, who sported a dazzling 12-1 record on the season. A year later, Dude Evans, when reflecting on what became the biggest upset in Havre-Scobey baseball history, said his team made a mistake in their mental approach to Scobey and the state tournament, saying we thought, "Look at our record; no one can beat us."

In every upset I've played, one key was not getting behind early. This was important because as the game progressed, the longer the underdog stayed on the field (or court) with the favorite, the more confidence was gained, and the more the underdog started to believe they could win the game. This was the case with underdog Scobey against the heavily favored Northstars. The *Havre Daily News* wrote, "Scobey forced Havre to play catch-up the entire game."[15] Tom Nielson said, "We never could get quite out ahead."[16] Scobey got to Dude Evans for a run early, then added another couple of runs, and was leading 3-0 after five and a half innings. Dude Evans pitched the first four innings for Havre, then was relieved by Tom's son, John (9-1 on the season), who pitched the next nine.

Through five innings, Jim LeProwse calmly hung goose eggs on the scoreboard. Hitter after hitter for the Northstars walked back to the Havre dugout carrying their bats with them, as LeProwse was striking out hitters at a rate of almost two per inning. Jim said his effectiveness was based on two pitches. "I was throwing a two-seam fastball, and my curve was more of a slurve—broke about 2 to 8. My two-seamer would run in on a right-handed hitter. I could throw my curve on any count. I was completely comfortable throwing it on a 3-2 bases-loaded two-out count. It didn't matter."

As each inning went by, Scobey's confidence increased. Then, in the bottom of the sixth, Havre finally broke through against LeProwse and put three runs on the scoreboard to tie the game 3-3. That score would stay on the scoreboard for the next five innings as LeProwse and Nielson held the other team scoreless.

Then came the wild 12th.

In the most bizarre play in the history of Scobey state tournaments, Scobey took the lead 4-3 in the top of the 12th on what the *Havre Daily News* called a "freak play." The *Havre Daily News* added that Scobey "ambushed the Northstars in a game which featured one of the most bizarre plays with which Coach Tom Nielson has been associated." Assistant Coach Micky Williams called it a "fiasco." Left fielder Alan Evans said, "A bomb exploded in our face." The play became notoriously known in Havre as the "Scobey foul line ball."[17]

Scobey just considered it a chalky miracle. So, what happened?

With Scobey batting and a runner at first base in the top of the 12th, a ball was hit down the right-field line. Havre right fielder Jason Innocenti barely missed a shoestring catch as the ball then rested and blended into the white foul line, camouflaged by its whiteness. How does a ball stick on the chalk line and not move after it hits the ground? A heavy rainstorm had hit the night before the tournament started, making the field damp and a little soggy in spots in the outfield. Assistant Coach Micky Williams saw the ball resting on the foul line and tried to get Innocenti's attention: "I was yelling at our right fielder [Innocenti] and pointing at the ball that was stuck in the wet white chalk line!" But by the time Innocenti had located the ball, the Scobey baserunner had circled the bases and scored the tie-breaking run.

Call it fate, luck, or "chalkgate"—call it what you want—Scobey scored the go-ahead run and carried a one-run lead into the bottom of the 12th, and starting pitcher Jimmy LeProwse—who had only allowed three runs in 11 innings—needed just three outs for Scobey to pull off a stunning upset.

Then, in the bottom of the 12th, Havre produced a run of its own "in more conventional means." It looked like LeProwse would get the 12-inning win, but with two outs and Gary LaChance on first, Dude Evans lined a clutch two-out double, scoring LaChance to tie the score at 4-4. LeProwse stranded Evans at second, and the game was headed to the 13th.

LeProwse's innings were done. He had exhausted his three-day limit of 12 innings in one game, striking out 21 Northstars in 12 innings, yielding only four runs. But there was still more baseball to play. Who would pitch for Scobey now that their ace was done? Coach Don Lekvold had another strong pitcher to bring in, that being 16-year-old Mike Roland. On the Havre side, Coach Tom Nielson stayed with John Nielson in the top of the 13th but replaced him with his third pitcher of the game, Bucky Lindstrand (10-1 on the season), in the 14th.

There was a scoreless 13th, a scoreless 14th, and a scoreless 15th. As each scoreless inning went by, the game grew deeper into the night, and the clock approached midnight. And we all know that Cinderella needed to get home by midnight, or the fairytale was over.

To the 16th we go.

Lindstrand, who had pitched two innings of scoreless relief after relieving Nielson in the 13th, appeared to be headed for another scoreless inning for Havre after he set down the first two Blues down in order. But with two outs, Scobey catcher Larry Trangsrud—who amazingly caught all 16 innings—smacked a double down the left-field line. (The ball didn't get stuck on the chalk line this time.) Then, as the clock approached midnight, Dan Stephenson hit a sharp grounder to Havre shortstop John Nielson, who made a difficult pickup but overthrew first base for an error. Not known for his speed (Doc had nicknamed him "Snail"), Larry scampered around third base to score the go-ahead run, putting Scobey back on top, 5-4. Referring to the play, Coach Nielson said, "The real important thing was getting the first runner on. That meant any good play by them or a mistake by us would score." In the end, Havre made a mistake that allowed the go-ahead run to score.

Now, Scobey was in the same position it was in in the 12th—a one-run lead needing just three outs to close the deal. And close the deal Mike Roland did, retiring the Northstars in order in the bottom of the 16th, preserving the most incredible upset in Scobey Blues baseball history. The exhausted Blues danced in celebration on their home field while the Havre nine sat in stunned disbelief in their dugout, watching the show. It was a devastating loss for the Northstars, an upset for the ages for the Blues. Scobey had 12 hits and two errors in the game, while Havre collected 10 hits and had four errors, the last one being the costliest. The game was a pitcher's duel—there were 42 strikeouts in the game. LeProwse fanned 21; Nielson struck out 14. Roland got the win, and Lindstrand took the tough loss on the unearned run with two outs.

In the legendary annals of state tournament matchups between Havre and Scobey—including the two one-run state championship games of 1969, the 1-0 Fanning-Puckett pitcher's duel of 1971, and the 1-0 Cato-Hagfeldt pitcher's duel of 1975—the opening-day 16-inning marathon of the 1985 state tournament stands alone in history, mainly due to the magnitude of the Scobey's upset and the bizarre play in the 12th. Coach Don Lekvold said, "That was one of the three or four best Blues games that I had ever been involved in coaching or even watching.

Havre's lineup, one through nine, was like our 1977-82 teams; I mean, they didn't have a weak spot in the lineup. They could all hit, they were all quick, they were all good fielders, and they had good pitching." The Northstars were talented but had a young roster, as they had only two 18-year-olds on the team. Don Lekvold then talked about the key to winning the game. "Jimmy LeProwse was just incredible. He pitched fantastic and the defense was good. And then Mike [Roland] got in there. Mike was just 16 at that time, but he was really coming on, and he pitched four innings and finished 'er up." Jim LeProwse, when asked to reflect on his pitching performance, recognized his catcher. "I think Larry Trangsrud caught all 16 innings. That is as impressive as anything that happened that day." Larry also doubled and scored the winning run.

The Cinderella Blues won the game just before midnight but got home after midnight, so their mode of transportation riding home was different than it was to the game. However, the Blues got safely home and advanced to play the Billings Cardinals the next night. Get a good night's sleep, everyone. The 1985 Blues' storied run in the final state tournament Scobey hosted was not over!

Oh, there were other opening-day games. Glasgow beat the Lethbridge Lakers 8-5, Glendive mercy-ruled Vauxhall 17-0, and, in a tightly contested contest, the Billings Cardinals—champions of the southeastern district—won 3-1 over the Missoula Reds. Billings's win set up the second-day matchup between the Blues and the Cardinals.

Meanwhile, the Northstars' woes continued in their loser-out game on Friday. Although the electrical storm that had hit Scobey occurred the night before the tournament started, the Northstars discovered that lightning could strike twice in the same tournament. In their loser-out game against the Missoula Reds—a team they had easily handled several times during the regular season—the Reds shocked them when Bill Stark doubled home John Olson with the winning run in the bottom of the ninth inning for the walk-off 8-7 win. It was Havre's second heartbreaking one-run loss in the tournament, sending them packing two days earlier than they ever thought possible.

Assistant Coach Micky Williams, reflecting on the shocking two losses to end the season, said, "That weekend was just unreal after the season we had. The field was so wet when we got to Scobey. The foul lines were kind of roto-tilled and soft and muddy. I'll never forget when that ball hit the chalk line and stuck, and our right fielder couldn't find it; I was yelling and pointing to it, but to no avail; it was a crazy game! Then, we lost in the bottom of the ninth inning against Missoula the next day. Wow! Two and a BBQ. After that loss, Tom Nielson was trying to console the team. He came up with the phrase—and I did not understand it myself but have used it many times since with some of my teams—he says, 'Well, it is hard losing, and it seems like the world just ended, but there are billions of people in China that it just doesn't matter.' What it means, I still don't really know, probably that everyone will get over it. Still sucks to lose!" Head Coach Tom Nielson, in the *Havre Daily News*, summed up Havre's performance in the state tournament as "disappointing."[18] He said, "We played two close games, and we didn't generate or get one of the breaks we've been getting all season, and it went the other way both times."[19] The Northstars finished the season 41-5, perhaps the best record in history for a team that didn't win a state championship.

There was a downside to Scobey's 16-inning win over Havre: Jim LeProwse's innings were burned up, and Mike Roland had pitched four innings of relief, leaving him only eight innings of eligibility left. Could the 16-year-old come back the next night and pitch strong? Don Lekvold recalls the Billings Cardinals' coach bringing the issue up with him after the Havre game the night before. Don said, "After the game, the Billings Cardinals' coach—who had been sitting behind our bench and was always talking to me a

Steve Lapke jogs toward home plate and the acclaim of his Scobey Blues teammates after he hit a bases-loaded, two-out grand slam homer in the third inning of the Scobey-Billings game. His stellar playing a-field and at-bat helped Scobey Blues win third place. Not a big lad, Steve got everything behind that big swing as the right-handed batter hit it over the right field fence. This has to be the thrill of a lifetime for any young athlete. An unprecedented two grand slammers were hit in this state B Legion tourney. Darren Popson of Lethbridge also got one against Vauxhall in the fifth game. *Leader photo, Milt Gunderson.*

little bit—said to me, 'Jeez, you had to use all your pitching. Who you gonna have left for tomorrow?' I said, 'Well, I guess we'll see.' And so the next day comes, and I threw Mike Roland again, and he picked up just right where he had left off the night before."

Yes, he did. Mike Roland chucked a three-hitter against the Billings Cardinals, and the "lowly Blues"[20] mercy-ruled the Cardinals 13-1 in seven innings for their second tournament win. Sixteen-year-old second baseman Steve Lapke, not known for his power, provided the big punch in Scobey's 13-hit attack when he smashed a two-out grand slam home run over the right field fence in the third inning, vaulting Scobey to an early big lead for Mike Roland, who had all the run support he needed with just one swing from Steve. Steve recalls the hit. "The grand slam was the most electrifying hit of my Blues' career. It was very special to hit it in front of our hometown fans and my family during the state tournament, but most importantly, it helped secure the win against the Cardinals. I was happy that I could contribute to a great team effort." Don Lekvold also remembers Steve's hit. "That little Steve Lapke. I remember him in the second or third inning. He comes up with the bases loaded, and he hits a grand slam over the right-field fence." Larry Trangsrud also banged out three doubles—all off the fence—as Scobey's bats came alive with 13 hits. LT remembers his doubles: "I went 3 for 4 that game with all three doubles off the left center field fence. Warning track power!"

After stunning Havre in 16 innings and mercy-ruling the Cardinals in seven, the amazing Blues were in the undefeated semifinal against Glendive. After going two and a barbecue at Divisionals—including an opening-day 11-0 loss to Laurel—and only qualifying for the state tournament as host, the Blues found themselves within one win from the championship game and a berth in the Northwest Regional in Yakima, Washington. Unbelievable.

The Blues had beaten Glendive 6-3 at a conference game in Scobey earlier in the season, with Mike Roland scattering six hits to get the win, so the Blues knew they could beat Glendive. But as is always the case with Cinderella teams, the clock eventually strikes midnight. In the undefeated semifinal against Glendive—who had pummeled Glasgow 23-11 to get there—both Jim LeProwse and Mike Roland had exhausted their innings, so Don Lekvold's options for pitching were limited. Ivan Domenech pitched well during the regular season—winning five games and pitching two consecutive one-hitters—so he gave the ball to Ivan. The heavy-hitting Glendive team, however, rolled to a 12-1 win, outhitting the Blues 12 to 4. Brian Dougherty pitched a four-hitter for the win. The Blues played better in the field than the Blue Devils, as they committed only three errors to Glendive's six, but Glendive's 12 runs and 12 hits were too much to overcome.

The loss to Glendive forced Scobey into the championship play-in game, which they lost to Lethbridge 14-4. Jim LeProwse, after two days' rest after pitching 12 innings against the Northstars on Thursday, tried to come back and pitch again but had been injured and didn't have his best stuff. Jim said, "Against the Cardinals, Donnie Lekvold told me to get down going into third, and I slid a little late and hooked the bag, and it wiped out my right ankle. It swelled up like a balloon, but I was able to finish that game. I remember going to the doctor the next morning and him recommending that I not play and me thinking there is no way that I am not finishing this out. We played Glendive that day in the undefeated game. I couldn't hardly walk and had to play first base. I normally played shortstop when I wasn't pitching. For two days I iced and elevated trying to get the swelling down and it worked somewhat. I tried with everything I had to pitch against Lethbridge the next day, but I couldn't push off the rubber like I normally did and they shelled me. It was really disheartening because I think we could have beaten them if I could have pitched like normal." The gritty kid from Butte gutted it out and played hurt, but the undermanned Blues could not take it any further than third place.

After losing their first game against Glasgow, Lethbridge came back through the dirt route to win four games, but they were no match for Glendive in the championship, as Glendive again won in a mercy rule, 20-8, earning the Blue Devils their second state championship.

TOURNAMENT SUMMARY

The *Leader* summarized the 1985 state tournament: "The Montana Class B American Legion Baseball tourney

1985 Scobey Blues, third place at State. Kneeling, left to right: Brad Gilbert, Mark Huwe, Jim LeProwse, Larry Trangsrud, Mike Roland, Tom Fugere, and Danny Stephenson. Standing, left to right: Paul Shaffer, Jeff Jones, Steve Lapke, Mike Heaton, Ivan Domenech, Rod Hudyma, and Coach Don Lekvold. John Richardson and Randy Pearce are not pictured. *Leader photo, Burl Bowler*

here last week was favored by the weather, enthusiastic fans, and energetic young players who ran the gamut from ridiculous to sublime."²¹

In using the term "ridiculous," the *Leader* was likely referring to the wild play down the right field line in the 12th inning between Havre and Scobey when Jason Innocenti lost the ball in the chalk line, and Scobey's runner came around to score. The other word the *Leader* used was "sublime," and Scobey's performance in the 1985 state tournament—the last time Scobey hosted—was indeed sublime, at least for the first two games. It was a nice finish for the host to perform as they did, upholding the proud Scobey baseball tradition. Coach Don Lekvold said, "We got up for that tournament; we wanted to make a good showing at home, and the kids really, really played well. Third place was a great showing, especially when considering the automatic bid." The Blues rose to the occasion, winning two games but running out of gas—pitching—before they could make it to the championship game. Considering they had only made it into the tournament as host after losing their first two games in the Divisional tournament, their performance was phenomenal. Following the Lethbridge game, the Blues "were glad to settle for third place."²² No doubt Coach Lekvold and the Blues' players wanted to do better and not "settle," but third place was good. Scobey finished their season with an 18-14 record.

Glendive completely dominated the tournament, winning every game they played by at least 10 runs. Their offensive production was staggering, as they scored 17, 23, 12, and 20 runs in the four games for an average of 18 runs per game. The Blue Devils were "clearly and by far the best team in the tournament."²³ Of course, Havre's two losses early in the tournament thwarted a matchup between the top team from the east and the top team from the west, but so goes the way of the upset.

The Blues-Northstars game was not the only extra-inning marathon in the tournament. The Lethbridge Lakers–Missoula Reds game went 15 innings, with the Lakers winning 10-8.

Scobey's final state tournament was successful due to the hard work of the volunteers. "Tremendous planning and work were aided by good luck in making the tourney a success: a rainstorm hit the night before the action started, then beautiful baseball weather all four days; both extra-inning (16 and 15) games came in the nightcaps, so they didn't foul up the schedule, although they challenged the stamina of KCGM announcers, players, and the many fans in attendance."²⁴

The all-tournament team selected by coaches, umpires, and news media consisted of Dave Kleppelid of Glendive, who batted .625 in the tournament, and teammates Tom Ryan, Anthony Campbell, Brian Dougherty, Brent Diegel, and Todd Glasser; Jim LeProwse, Mike Heaton, and Steve Lapke of Scobey; and Darren Popson and Scott Crowe of Lethbridge. Kleppelid was also unanimously selected as the tournament's most valuable player. "Jim LeProwse of Scobey set some kind of a record in state B Legion baseball play by pitching 12 innings and getting 21 strikeouts in perhaps the longest state tourney game ever played in Montana . . . 16 innings."²⁵ Mother Nature was granted honorable mention for her contribution—the rainstorm on Wednesday night—to what became infamously known in Havre as the "Scobey foul-line ball" incident.

The Lethbridge game was the last for 18-year-olds Jim LeProwse and Mike Heaton. Jim LeProwse was selected to play in the East-West All-Star game, which was played in Lethbridge, Alberta, that year. I asked Jim to share his experience of playing with the Scobey Blues from 1983 to 1985. It is an interesting story of how Jim, from Butte, got to play baseball in Scobey.

Glendive Blue Devils, State Class B Champions. Front left to right: Dennis Towberman, Jim Zimmer, Tom Ryan, Keith Polesky, Travis McRae, Hunter Fuqua. Second row, left to right: Kahle Campbell, Dave Kleppelid, Darrin Dobie, Tawn Frenzel, Mike Davis. Back row, left to right: Head coach Jerry Polesky, Greg Maher, Brian Dougherty, Todd Glasser, Anthony Campbell, Brent Diegel, Assistant Coach John Hawthorne. *Leader photo, Milt Gunderson.*

I remember my Dad telling me that we were moving to Scobey in the summer of '82. I was shocked and heartbroken when I got the news. He was a mechanic at the mine, and the mine closed down operations, which forced a lot of people to move. I had the choice of moving to Scobey at the beginning of the summer of '82 or staying in Butte and playing my last year of baseball with my friends. I chose to stay. In hindsight, this was a big mistake. I would most likely have been on the '82 Blues state championship team.

I had no idea what to expect when I got the opportunity to be a member of the Scobey Blues. It was the greatest baseball experience of my life. I absolutely loved every second of it. To move to a place with such a storied baseball history was an amazing experience. I did not get to meet Doc when he was in his prime. He was in a wheelchair when I moved there, but he always made me feel welcome and part of the team. He would call us players over and always be giving us pointers to help us be more successful. I had Donnie Lekvold for a head coach the next two years and loved playing for him. He had great knowledge and passion for baseball and was a great coach. I met some amazing people through Scobey baseball and have memories that will last a lifetime.

—*Jim LeProwse*

TOURNAMENT STATS

Hitting

SCOBEY'S HITTING IN THE TOURNAMENT WAS MORE ABOUT quality than quantity, as players came through with key hits in critical situations. The Blues had 12 hits in the 16-inning marathon against Havre, but none more critical than Larry Trangsrud's two-out double in the 16th inning, as he came around to score the winning run on Dan Stephenson's sharp ground ball to shortstop, which resulted in an overthrow error to first. Against the Cardinals, the Blues had 13 hits, the most important of which was Steve Lapke's two-out grand slam in the third inning that propelled Scobey to an early lead they never relinquished. Steve Lapke's grand slam was only the second in Blues history in a state tournament, as Don Puckett hit a grand slam against the Helena Reps in Havre in 1974. Larry Trangsrud also banged out three doubles against the Cardinals.

Steve's grand slam wasn't the only one in the tournament—Darren Popson of Lethbridge also had a grand slam against Vauxhall. The Blues ran into tough pitching against Brad Dougherty of Glendive, who pitched a four-hitter against them. They had nine hits against Lethbridge but missed the timely hit in that game, as they could only score four runs. Dave Kleppelid of Glendive batted .625 to lead all hitters in the tournament. Offensively, Glendive was impressive. In four games, they banged out 54 hits and scored 72 runs for an average of 18 runs per game. That's insane.

Pitching

THE "STURDY AND TALENTED"[26] JIM LEPROWSE WAS CLEARLY the MVP pitcher of the tournament based on his 12-inning, 21-strikeout performance against Havre. But Mike Roland was every bit as good. He pitched four scoreless innings and got the win against Havre, keeping the heavy-hitting Havre team at bay and enabling Scobey to win. Then, against the Cardinals, he pitched a three-hitter and allowed only one run in seven innings to get his second tournament win. In Scobey's first two games, LeProwse and Roland had only allowed five runs in 19 innings pitched for a team ERA of 2.37, and that was assuming every run was earned. Mike Roland was even more impressive: he allowed only one run in 11 innings pitched for an ERA of 0.82.

In addition to LeProwse and Roland, pitching dominated only a couple of games in the tournament: Glendive's Tony Campbell pitched a three-hit shutout against Vauxhall, and Glendive's Brian Dougherty pitched a four-hitter against Scobey, allowing only one run.

Fielding

SCOBEY'S DEFENSE AGAINST HAVRE WAS GOOD, COMMITTING only two errors to Havre's four. Of course, Havre's error in the 16th was costly, as it allowed the winning run to score. Against the Cardinals, the Blues' defense was good again, committing only two errors. They had three errors against Glendive, who they outplayed defensively, as the Blue Devils committed six errors in the game. Scobey's defense broke down in their final game against Lethbridge, as the team committed six errors. But overall, Scobey's defense in the tournament was good—they had fewer average errors per game than any other team—and it did not cost them any games. Larry Trangsrud, who caught all 16 innings against Havre, has to be mentioned for his endurance and stamina.

NORTHWEST REGIONAL

THE 1985 STATE B TOURNAMENT WAS HISTORICALLY SIGNIFIcant, as Glendive and Lethbridge were the first Montana (and Alberta) teams to play in the Class B Northwest Regional in Yakima, Washington. Glendive won one game and lost two games in the tournament. They lost 4-3 to the host Yakima Blues in the opening round, then beat Eugene, Ore., 16-5 before being eliminated 11-6 by Kennewick, Wash., who beat the Yakima Blues for the championship. I can't resist writing that the Blue Devils beat the Blues in Scobey, but the Blues beat them in regionals.

EXTRA INNINGS

STATE CLASS B COMMISSIONER JIM ROWE WAS PRESENT FOR THE tournament, and the opening ceremonies included introducing three local residents who were members of Scobey's first Legion Baseball team in 1930. The three players at the game were Larry Bowler, Larry Fjeld, and Raymond "Whitey" Waller of Whitetail. Blues' Terry Farver recalls Larry Fjeld. "I remember skating with Larry Fjeld when I was a kid. Great teacher."

Art Mueller, in his restored 1914 Model T Ford touring car, gives a ride to two 1914 and one 1916 models at State Legion baseball tournament opening ceremonies. Whitey Waller of Whitetail (upfront) and Larry Fjeld, and Larry Bowler of Scobey played on Scobey's first American Legion Baseball team in 1930. All hands aboard agreed the old Model T was running as good or better than they were. Scobey's first town-team baseball team was fielded in 1914. *Leader photo.*

The recognition of the three players from 1930 was historically significant, as in Scobey's last state tournament as host, the organizers had the sense of the moment to remember—and honor—the players on the 1930 team where the tradition began. That team suffered only one defeat that year, 8-4 in the state playoffs to Billings, the eventual state champions. The 1930 Scobey Legion baseball team was district champion and eastern division runners-up to Billings. The 1930 team was coached by Preston McLoughlin and managed by Irving Davis (who had played on Lou Boyd's first Scobey baseball team in 1914).

The 1985 season was the second time Scobey prevented Coach Tom Nielson and Havre from repeating as State champions. The first was in 1969 when Scobey came back through the dirt route after they lost to Havre and beat them twice in the championship games. Havre did repeat as State champions on Scobey's home field in 1971.

Scobey had also upset Havre 12 to 2 in the opening game of the 1968 tournament, but Coach Nielson and Havre came back through the dirt route, beating Scobey 12-0 on their way to their first State championship.

Jim LeProwse was selected to play for the East All-Stars in the East-West Class B American Legion All-Star game, played in Alberta for the first time.

Brent Diegel of Glendive was the head coach of the Dawson Community College Buccaneers baseball team for 12 years, from 1999 to 2011. He led the Buccaneers to three Mon-Dak Conference titles and a trip to the NJCAA Division III World Series in 2001. After Brent resigned as head baseball coach, he called Jim LeProwse to recruit him as head coach of the Buccaneers fast-pitch softball team, and Jim accepted. LeProwse coached the Dawson CC Bucs softball team for 11 seasons (2011-21), compiling a 263-143 record. His teams won eight Mon-Dak Athletic Conference championships and six Region XIII titles, and Jim was selected as the Mon-Dak Conference coach of the year eight times and NJCAA Region XIII coach of the year six times.

While in Glendive, Jim also assisted Coach Diegel on the Glendive Blue Devils' American Legion team. Following his coaching career at Dawson, Jim moved back home to Butte, where he took the reins of the Butte Miners American Legion Post 10 baseball program, leading the Miners to their first state championship in 69 years in 2022, also winning the Northwest Regional championship. Jim continues as head coach of the Miners today.

Jim Lekvold (Blues 1979-83) umpired in his first state tournament in Scobey in 1985 at the beginning of his umpiring career. He would go on to umpire several Class A/B and AA tournaments.

The 1985 State championship was Glendive's second in history. Their previous state championship was in 1964 when they beat Wolf Point 15-13 at Thompson Park in Laurel.

Dave Kleppelid, tournament MVP from Glendive, went on to star for the UND-Williston Tetons baseball team in 1986 and 1987. He was selected to the All–North Dakota Junior College baseball team in 1987 and was later elected to the Teton Baseball Hall of Fame for the 1980s.

Dixie Halverson was not happy with the *Billings Gazette*'s coverage of the 1985 State Class B Tournament, and she wrote a letter to the editor expressing that unhappiness. What I love about Dixie's letter is that it reflects the pride of the Scobey community in hosting a state tournament, the pride of Scobey's baseball tradition, and Dixie's championing of all the young American Legion ballplayers who played in the tournament. Here is the letter in its entirety:

Slighted by Class B coverage[27]

As a sports enthusiast and supporter of youth, I looked forward to the July 26, 27, and 28 editions of The Gazette with great anticipation as I knew they would have coverage of the Montana State Class B American Legion Tournament held in Scobey. I was disappointed to see no mention of it at all, other than a few line scores in Saturday's paper.

Teams came from Billings, Missoula, Glendive, Havre, Glasgow, and Scobey, as well as Lethbridge and Vauxhall, Alberta—and yet our leading state paper did not feel that this was a sporting event worth covering.

People may think to themselves that Scobey was negligent on its part as a host town by not reporting this event. But I know this is not true because I am the person who took the time to phone in all scores as well as additional information about the tournament teams and details as to how a town as small as Scobey happens to have a ballpark, built totally with donated funds and volunteer labor, that is second to none in the state.

I realize that we are not in a large metropolitan area and that you probably do not sell as many papers here as in Oslo, Norway, or Cooperstown, N.Y. (Re: Sunday, July 28 sports section). However, I would like to remind you that we are a part of Montana, and I feel that, as a state paper, you owe the youth in Montana some acknowledgment for activities other than crime.

These American Legion ballplayers are the "cream of the crop," and Scobey certainly was proud to host such a fine group of young men. I only wish you were as proud of Montana youth as we are.

—Dixie Halverson, Manager, KCGM Radio and President, Daniels County Chamber of Commerce and Agriculture, Scobey

As mentioned, the 1985 state tournament was the last that Scobey hosted. Micky Williams played left field for Havre in the first one in 1969 and was the assistant coach in the last one in 1985. First as a player and then as a coach, he was involved in two iconic moments in the history of Scobey Ball Park: Dick Puckett's dramatic home run in the 1969 state championship game and "chalkgate" in 1985. At the 1985 state tournament, he remembers sitting in the crow's nest looking at the scorebook from 1969, and it brought back memories of that tournament. He warmly recalls playing and coaching against the Scobey Blues, saying, "I have always enjoyed the experience of competing against Scobey. (Well, maybe not the 1969 state championship games when I saw a home run go over my head in left field for the tying run to force another game, or the 16-inning fiasco in 1985 when the ball got lost in the wet white chalk line. The home run was hit over my head in left field. I will never forget that, as I have forgotten so much over the years!) We had so many battles when I played against the Blues from 1968 to 1970 and again coached from 1978 to 2004. Scobey had such a great run through the 1990s." Mickey was selected as Coach of the Year in 1999 and coached the last Northstars team to face Scobey in a state tournament in 1996. Scobey won that game 12-10, coming from behind in the eighth inning to score five runs, then holding off a fierce Havre rally in the top of the ninth, with the game ending on a play at the plate—more on that in 1996.

Mickey says the fluke fly ball down the right field line that led to a Scobey run in the top of the 12th inning in the 1985 state tournament "still haunts me every time we are in any kind of tournament." It is fitting that Mickey should use the word "haunt" because, to this day, Scobey Ball Park is haunted by two ghosts every summer—one down the left field line and one down the right field line. In both cases, Mickey was at Scobey Ball Park the night the apparitions were born. On August 9, 1969, Dick Puckett hit a two-out, two-strike line drive home run over the left field fence in the ninth inning of the championship game, and Havre left fielder Micky Williams helplessly cried out "noooooooo" as the ball screamed over his head and disappeared into the northeastern Montana night sky to tie the game. Sixteen years later, on July 25, 1985, he was the assistant coach in the first base dugout when he desperately yelled to right fielder Jason Innocenti, "The ball's on the chalk line!" but couldn't get Jason's attention. Two desperate cries in the late night to stop the inevitable, but it couldn't be stopped—it was always meant to be.

Every summer on the late evenings of July 25th and August 9th, the two ghosts appear in opposite corners of the Scobey Ball Park outfield, still hoping to haunt visiting teams who might come to Scobey to play in another state tournament, thwarting them in the late innings to secure a Scobey win. And on those nights in Scobey, if you listen carefully, you can hear Mickey's desperate cries echoing across decades of time, pleading in vain with the baseball gods to stop what was always fated to happen. The cry in left field carries over the fence and trails off into the northern Canadian night sky. (And it's rumored that later in the evening, if you peer closely up at the northern sky, you can see the North Star dim slightly as it is eclipsed by the streaking shadow of Dick Puckett's home run.) On the other side of the outfield, the cry in right field sinks back into the ground as the white chalk line the ghost forms from is swallowed by the same white line from which it ascends. As it disappears, the apparition searches for a ball on the line to camouflage with its chalky whiteness. Both cries are followed by the roar of the Scobey crowd and the honking of horns.

The two baseball ghosts—each with a slight blueish hue—still appear on those nights, clinging in vain to the desperate hope that young Legion baseball players will run out on the field again and hear their lonely cries for help and the crowd's roar in another state tournament in Scobey.

If the Scobey outfield wall could talk . . . .

1986

A Down Year for the Blues

1986 Scobey Blues. Kneeling, left to right: Ivan Domenech, Mike Lee, Jerry Danelson, Arlin Kaul, Rod Hudyma, Jeff Jones, Paul Shaffer, and Ken Meyer. Standing, left to right: Pete Dighans, Tom Aldrich, Justin Garberg, Brad Gilbert, Tom Fugere, Mike Roland, Larry Trangsrud, David Nees, Steve Lapke, Randy Pearce, and Assistant Coach Jim LeProwse. Not pictured is Head Coach Don Lekvold. *Leader photo, Burl Bowler.*

PRESEASON

THE ASTONISHING THIRD-PLACE FINISH IN THE 1985 State Tournament at Scobey the previous year would be a tough act to follow in 1986, especially with the loss of starting pitcher Jim LeProwse. Mike Heaton—named to the 1985 State all-tournament team along with Jim LeProwse and Steve Lapke—had also aged out. That left 18-year-old Ivan Domenech and 17-year-old Mike Roland as the only returning starting pitchers. Tom Fugere and Brad Gilbert were back and also pitched in 1985. Pete Dighans from Peerless, who joined the team as a rookie, was a pitcher, and 16-year-old Jeff Jones could pitch, although he didn't see much action that year. Larry Trangsrud, who had been playing for five years and was the starting catcher in 1985, would anchor the staff behind the plate, returning from his first year at Eastern Montana College. Of the staff, Larry said, "Mike Roland was arguably the best I ever caught. Jim LeProwse was up there, too, but Mike was nasty." Other players returning from the 1985 third-place team included Randy Pearce, Rod Hudyma, Steve Lapke, and Paul Shaffer. The rookies joining the team were Mike "Karch" Lee, Ken Meyer, Jerry Danelson, Arlin Kaul, Tom Aldrich, Justin Garberg, and David Nees. Many of these players, including 14-year-olds Mike Lee and Ken Meyer, were dual-rostered on the Babe Ruth team and played on the district champion Babe Ruth All-Star team, which won two games at State. There were some talented young players up and coming for Scobey.

Jim LeProwse (Blues 1983-1985) assisted Don Lekvold as coach.

REGULAR SEASON

THE MONTANA CLASS B AMERICAN LEGION COMMITTEE changed the Class B 1986 season format. The committee formed five Class B conferences. Havre and four Alberta teams, who typically competed in the northwestern district, were formed into a "swing" conference (referred to as the "South Alberta Conference"), which would alternate competing in the western and eastern divisions. The rotation started in the east, so Havre and the Alberta teams would compete in the eastern divisional at Cobb Field in Billings.

For another reason, it was a historically significant year for American Legion Baseball in Montana/Alberta. This would be the last season that the two classifications would be designated Class A and Class B, switching to Class A and AA the following year in 1987. However, the change was in name only, as the same teams competing in Class B would compete in Class A, and the Class A teams would compete in Class AA. Montana American Legion had initially gone to the two-tiered classification system—Class A and B—in 1949. Strangely, in 1969, Montana changed to

Class A and AA—for one season only—so Scobey's first state championship in 1969 was in the Class A Division. The league reverted to Class A and B in 1970.

Based on its regular-season record in the northeastern district, Scobey did not qualify for the eastern divisional tournament and was eliminated from postseason play. It was a tough, down year for the Blues, but there were some highlights during the regular season:

- Scobey hosted the Third Annual Doc Norman Memorial Tournament with six teams participating: Westby, Circle, Laurel, Wolf Point, Glasgow, and Scobey. Laurel and Wolf Point tied for the best records at 4-1 each, but Wolf Point was awarded the trophy based on their head-to-head win over Laurel. Wolf Point's only loss was to Scobey, 6-5, when Larry Trangsrud hit a grand slam home run off Dirk Kuntz from Wolf Point. Larry remembers the homer going over the scoreboard. Scobey went 3-2 in the tournament.
- In a rematch of Scobey's epic 16-inning 5-4 win over Havre in the 1985 State Tournament, the Blues and Northstars played home-and-home doubleheaders. Havre was favored to win the State championship in 1986 because they only lost two players from the 1985 team, which finished 41-5 after their shocking two-game exit from the state tournament. In the doubleheader in Scobey, the Northstars dominated, winning 10-0 and 11-1. Coach Tom Nielson talked about how Havre was looking forward to the games. "They were important games to us because so many of the kids have memories of the finish of last year, and of course, Scobey played a big role. There was kind of perhaps a pride thing with them, but no revenge motive. We knew we could play better than we did then (in a 5-4 state tournament loss to Scobey in a record 16 innings last July). In a tournament, you don't get a chance to do better."
- Returning to Havre, the Blues competed better but lost both games. Larry Trangsrud, a freshman at Eastern Montana College in 1986, drove to Malta and caught the team bus there. The two games were very well played, with good pitching. In the first game, Havre won 3-0. Mike Roland pitched all seven innings and gave up only three runs on four hits—all coming in the first inning. Roland struck out seven and walked only one. Bucky Lindstrand pitched a three-hit shutout, striking out eight and walking three. Havre won the second game 3-2 on a walk-off double by Joe Koski in the bottom of the seventh inning. Scobey again got a well-pitched game, this time from Brad Gilbert, who gave up only one earned run on five hits, striking out seven and walking three. Dude Evans won the second game for Havre, yielding no earned runs. Havre's two winning pitchers that day had both pitched in the epic 16-inning marathon in Scobey the year before—Dude Evans started and went four innings; Bucky Lindstrand pitched the last three innings and took the loss.
- Scobey traveled to Thompson Park in Laurel to play in the 4th of July Invitational Tournament. Scobey lost a tough game to the Fort Macleod, Alberta Royals in their first game. The Blues jumped out to a 4-0 lead after two innings but were shut out the rest of the way, and the Royals came back to score six unanswered runs to win 6-4. Scobey had another tough loss in their second game, losing to the Billings Cardinals 7-6.

Glendive (the defending state champion), Glasgow, and Wolf Point advanced to the eastern divisional tournament as the top three teams from the northeastern district.

It was the final season for Larry Trangsrud, Randy Pearce, Ivan Domenech, and Tom Fugere.

EASTERN DIVISIONAL

COACH TOM NIELSON AND THE HAVRE NORTHSTARS HAD another solid regular season, going 30-9 and winning the South Alberta Conference with a 13-3 record, but defending champion Glendive and the Billings Cardinals were also considered contenders. The Northstars cruised to the eastern division championship game but were shut out 4-0 on a three-hitter by Jeff Schaff of the Billings Blue Jays in the championship game. The Blue Jays, Northstars, Lethbridge Miners, and Glendive Blue Devils advanced to State.

STATE TOURNAMENT

THE STATE TOURNAMENT WAS PLAYED AT VIGILANTE PARK IN Dillon, where the Havre Northstars had another bitter experience and were thwarted in their quest to capture a seventh state championship. It seems the Northstars were snakebit—again. At Scobey in 1985, Havre lost their first two games. In 1986, after winning their first two games, then pounding the Lethbridge Miners 11-3 in the undefeated semifinal, the Northstars lost their last two games—20-5 and 8-7—to the Miners, who had come back to challenge them. The Miners were the first Canadian team to win the State Class B championship.

More than 40 home runs were hit in the state tournament at Vigilante Park. *More than 40 home runs?* Coach Tom Nielson of Havre was not enthused about the dimensions of Vigilante Park. He said the home run that decided the one-run championship game was "a routine fly ball to center field. In that park, the ball escaped over the fence. Bucky (Lindstrand) was right there beside it; had it been in our park, it would have been an easy catch." The short field measured 330 feet to straightaway center. Tom Nielson continued his lament. "The worst part was simply fieldwise, they [Dillon] don't have the quality of field that should allow them to have a state tournament. That's not what people play with during the season. A routine fly ball shouldn't be a home run." But then he added, "Obviously, the fence is the same distance for both teams. It means luck becomes more of a factor than it is otherwise." That is true. Sometimes, a little luck is needed to win a state tournament, and in 1985 in Scobey and 1986 in Dillon, Havre had no luck. Whether it was a white ball camouflaged on a wet, white chalk line that right fielder Jason Innocenti couldn't find or a fly ball to center that Bucky Lindstrand helplessly watched drop for a home run, Havre couldn't catch a break. To add insult to injury, the Northwest Regional Tournament was hosted by the Hamilton Buccaneers at Vigilante Park in Hamilton, and the Bucs were automatically in as hosts. That meant only the State champion, the Lethbridge Miners, would advance to play. Usually, the top two teams in the state would advance to play in the regional. Havre finished the season 35-11, and their three-year record from 1984 to 1986 was an incredible 112-22.

Of the over 40 home runs hit at Vigilante Park, tournament MVP Todd Glasser, shortstop-pitcher from Glendive, had *five* of them. He batted an incredible .733 in the tournament.

NORTHWEST REGIONAL CLASS B TOURNAMENT

IT WAS ANOTHER HISTORICALLY SIGNIFICANT YEAR FOR American Legion Class B baseball in Montana, as the Bitterroot Bucs hosted the first Northwest Regional Class B American Legion Tournament to be held in Montana at Hamilton Athletic Field in Hamilton. The top two teams from the states of Washington, Idaho, Oregon, and Montana (the Lethbridge Miners and host Bitterroot) were in the double-elimination tournament. The Montana/Alberta teams did well, as the Bucs took fourth and Lethbridge took third. What I liked about the Class B Northwest Regional format then was that the top two teams from each state advanced. In the two State Class C basketball tournaments I played in 1978 and 1979, we (Peerless) were the second-place team at the divisional tournament. Forgiveness with tournament losses is nice, like a wildcard in MLB. The switch from the State Class B champion playing off against State A competition to playing in the Class B Northwest Regional was good for the kids to stay at their level of competition. Still, I wouldn't trade the experience of playing off against the Helena Senators and playing in the State A Tournament in 1979 for anything. However, many of Scobey's eight state championships had disappointing footnotes playing off against Class A competition, often just a day or two following playing four to six games in the State B Tournament.

EAST-WEST ALL-STAR CLASSIC

THE FIRST EAST-WEST ALL-STAR CLASSIC FOR 18-YEAR-OLDS was proudly hosted by American Legion Post 56 in Scobey at the Scobey Ball Park. It was a three-game series rather than a single game. Two Scobey Blues—Larry Trangsrud and Randy Pearce—made the East Team. Scobey was selected as the site for the classic because of its baseball tradition. The *Leader* wrote, "Although the Scobey Blues this season did not figure in the top competition, the illustrious record of the Blues during the 25-year tenure of the late Doc Norman when they won eight state Class B titles—including five in a row—and the outstanding reputation over the years gained by supporting fans here in hosting state tournaments, plus excellent field-playing facilities, officiating, and other arrangements, accounts for the first staging of this annual event in Scobey."[28] Thirty-six players—18 from the West and 18 from the East—and four coaches converged on Scobey for the weekend event, along with their families and fans. Players came from Dillon, Medicine Hat, Conrad, Havre, Hamilton, Fort Macleod, Vauxhall, Glasgow, Laurel, Wolf Point, Sidney, and Glendive. Gail Whitworth and Ted Miller from Dillon coached the West; Jerry Polesky from Glendive and Don Lekvold coached the East.

Scobey knew how to host a baseball event and make their guests feel welcome. On Friday night, a banquet for the 40 players and coaches was held at the Scobey Saddle Club, where 141 plates were served. Lettered caps and jackets were issued to the players and coaches to "help them remember their visit to Scobey country."[29] Judy LeProwse and Donna Roland, along with several "stalwart assistants," oversaw the concessions, housing, and meals.

On the field, the West All-Stars won the first two games, 13-5 and 12-6, but the East All-Stars came back to win game three, 10-4. In game three of the series, Larry Trangsrud hit a two-run home run off the left-field light pole and had a big hit in the eighth inning to drive in insurance runs for the East. Randy Pearce of Scobey, who hit .500 and got on base 8 of 11 times, was named MVP for the East All-Stars. He also made "some of the most spectacular defensive plays at his position in center field."[30] Randy said his experience playing in the classic was "a lot of fun." Kip Curtis, outstanding defensive shortstop for the Bitterroot Bucs, was named MVP of the West. Coach Gail Whitworth of Dillon said, "It was a great experience. I got to coach my ballplayers one more time, and I got to meet and coach some terrific other ballplayers."[31] Scobey would host the Classic again in 1987.

EXTRA INNINGS

LARRY TRANGSRUD WAS THE LAST "DOC RECRUIT" TO PLAY FOR Scobey. Larry remembers how it happened. "Doc called me when I was 12 (1980), wanting me to play the next year. That was a pretty incredible call." Following his six-year Legion career from 1981 to 1986, Larry Trangsrud stayed with baseball until he was 48. He umpired eight or nine State Legion tournaments and three Legion regional tournaments, then umpired five years of NCAA D-II baseball. Larry said, "Baseball is the greatest game ever!" Yes, it is, Larry.

Regarding Doc's phone call to Larry, Lee Cook (Legionnaires 1972–74) mentioned what an honor it was for parents to receive a call from Doc back in those days, courting their son to play baseball for him. "It was the height of status for the parents of an athlete in Daniels County to get that call. It was something special if Doc called and wanted you to play."

Ken Meyer, a rookie in 1986, remembers a funny story about pinch-running for Tommy Fugere. "I think it was during the Doc Norman Tournament. I was 13 at the time. Don Lekvold put me in to pinch run for 18-year-old Tommy Fugere on first base. Not sure who was up to bat, but I think it was Ivan Domenech. He hits a hard line drive to right field. I take off for second base, and the right fielder makes a nice catch and casually throws me out at first base for a double play. I get back to the dugout, and Tommy says, 'Jesus Christ—I could have fuckin' done that!' I obviously wasn't going to say anything back, but I was thinking to myself, 'Yep, you could have certainly done that!' Great times!"

Mike Lee remembers another Tommy Fugere story. "Tommy was playing third base, and a pop-up was going out of bounds toward the fence, and Donnie Lekvold kept saying, 'You've got room, you've got room, you've got room,' and all of a sudden, Tommy Fugere crashes straight into the fence. He picks himself up, looks at Donnie, said, 'I fucking thought you told me I had room!!'"

Five Northstars from their 1984-86 teams played collegiate baseball. Eric Hanson played at Waldorf College in Iowa. Tim and John Nielson were all-conference players at Carleton College in Minnesota. Bucky Lindstrand pitched at North Idaho College, and Dude Evans pitched for Pacific University in Oregon. Tim and John Nielson, Dude Evans, and Bucky Lindstrand were all members of the 1984 state championship Northstar team.

When commenting about Havre playing in the eastern divisional tournament for the first time in 1986, Havre coach Tom Nielson said the east was "traditionally stronger. Glendive won it last year. Scobey won it several years and Sidney—those teams always have been pretty tough." And don't forget Wolf Point. Tom was right about the power in Class B American Legion Baseball residing "traditionally" in the east. Before 1983—when the Whitehall Renegades won the State B Tournament for the first and only time—the last team from the west (besides Havre) to win the state tournament was Cut Bank in 1963 and 1967. After that, for over 20 years, every other state championship team was from Havre or the east. In the 1970s, a familiar refrain from cheerleaders and basketball fans in state tournaments was, "Power's in the East." The same held for baseball during that period.

But that was about to change. A significant shift in the demographic of Class B American Legion Baseball was coming, with the power moving to the west. The Bitterroot Bucs hosting the 1986 Northwest Regional in Hamilton was a leading indicator of that change.

1987

The Blues Stumble at Divisional, and the Yellowjackets Win the State Championship

> *We got the monkey off our back. There have been a lot of second-place teams over the years.*
>
> —Wolf Point Coach Mike Neubauer, *Billings Gazette*, August 3, 1987

1987 Scobey Blues. Standing, left to right: Mike Lee, Jerry Danelson, Steve Lapke, Paul Shaffer, Jeff Jones, Coach Don Lekvold. Kneeling, left to right: Shannon Albert, Tom Aldrich, Pete Dighans, Mike Roland, Brad Gilbert, Rod Hudyma. Sitting, left to right: Ken Meyer, Scott Fladager, Greg Larson, Arlin Kaul, and Ron Meyer. *Leader photo, Milt Gunderson.*

PRESEASON

FOUR PLAYERS FROM THE 1986 TEAM—LARRY TRANGSrud, Randy Pearce, Ivan Domenech, and Tom Fugere—had aged out, but Coach Don Lekvold had a deep 16-man roster in 1987, as lots of boys were out for baseball. Playing in their final seasons were 18-year-olds Mike Roland, Steve Lapke, and Pete Dighans. Five 17-year-olds—Paul "Peppy" Shaffer, Brad Gilbert, Rod Hudyma, Jeff Jones, and Ron Meyer—were returning. Back for their second year were Mike Lee, Ken Meyer, Jerry Danelson, Arlin Kaul, and Tom Aldrich, while Scott Fladager, Shannon Albert, and Greg Larson joined the team as rookies.

Mike "Fozzie" Roland, playing in his fourth season, would anchor Scobey's pitching staff as the ace. Jeff Jones said of his Mike, "He was an excellent pitcher with good stuff. He could hit his spots at a pretty elite level. We generally had a good chance of winning whenever he pitched." Don Lekvold put a lot of pitchers on the mound that season, but in addition to Mike, most innings went to Jeff Jones, Brad Gilbert, Paul Shaffer, and Pete "Oil Can" Dighans. Other players to see action on the mound during the regular season were Tom Aldrich, Jerry Danelson, Arlin Kaul, and Scott Fladager. Jerry Danelson, Tom Aldrich, Shannon Albert, and Mike "Karch" Lee would share catching duties.

Another change—although really in name only—came for Montana/Alberta Legion baseball in 1987. The American Legion Baseball Commission changed Montana Legion Baseball's two classifications from Class A and B to Class AA and A. This would be the first year the teams would compete under those designations.

The Don Lekvold Era

REGULAR SEASON

The most intriguing highlights during the regular season were the head-to-head matchups between Scobey and the eventual State champion, Wolf Point. As was the case during many years when Scobey won their eight State championships, Wolf Point would be one of the few teams to beat Scobey during the regular season. In 1973, Wolf Point dominated Scobey during the regular season, winning 3 of 4 games. In 1987, this was flipped, as Scobey beat Wolf Point twice during the regular season. Here are a few highlights of the 1987 regular season:

- In the season-opener against Plentywood, Jeff Jones and Paul Shaffer combined to strike out 20 Athletics in Scobey's 13-2 win. Jeff Jones and Mike Roland each had three hits to lead Scobey's 17-hit attack.
- The Blues banged out 31 hits in a doubleheader sweep of Malta. Jeff Jones and Steve Lapke each had three of Scobey's 17 hits in the opener, as Scobey won 17-1. Brad Gilbert pitched a four-hitter. In the second game, Pete Dighans had three of Scobey's 14 hits to lead Scobey to the 12-11 win.
- Jeff Jones recalls, "One of my favorite times of the season was hosting the Doc Norman Memorial Tournament because it seemed we had good teams come to that. I won the batting title at that tournament one year, maybe two." Jeff's memory was right: good teams did come to the Doc Norman tourney, as in the defending State Class A (now AA) champion Glacier Twins from Whitefish, who came in 1987. They swept the tournament in four games, but Scobey played them tough in the tournament. The Scobey-Glacier game in the tournament has an interesting backstory. Mike Lee and Ken Meyer were 15 years old in 1987 and played both Babe Ruth and Legion. Being dual-rostered, sometimes the schedule would conflict, and they couldn't be in two places at once. However, Mike remembers one day when they were able to play both Babe Ruth and Legion. "Ken and I had to play a doubleheader in Wolf Point against the Wolf Point Blue Jays on a Saturday morning. We had to win both games to secure the number-one seed in the district Babe Ruth tournament the following week. We were successful. After the doubleheader, we had to race back to Scobey because we played the Glacier Twins in the Doc Norman Memorial Tournament. Ken started at shortstop, and I started at third base. It was pretty cool when Gene Marley announced that Ken and I already played two games that day and now were playing in The Doc Norman tourney. I'm pretty sure Mike Roland pitched the game against Whitefish that night in the Doc Norman when we played. It was a close game, but we did take the loss."
- Rod Hudyma drove in two runs with his second base hit to key a four-run seventh inning, propelling Scobey to a 7-4 come-from-behind win over Plentywood. Scott Fladager got the win in relief for Scobey.
- In their second doubleheader sweep of Malta, Pete Dighans pitched a five-hitter in the first game to lead Scobey to a 12-2 win. Scobey won the second game 13-10 in a slugfest, with Paul Shaffer getting the win and Jeff Jones the save. Switch-hitting Jeff Jones hit a three-run home run from the left side of the plate for Scobey.
- In a classic pitcher's duel, Mike Roland of Scobey and Brian Stinglien of Glasgow dueled to a 0-0 draw until the bottom of the ninth inning, when Rod Hudyma of Scobey drove in the winning run with a double to lift Scobey to a 1-0 walk-off win. Mike Roland finished with a three-hitter, striking out 16 while only walking three. Brian Stinglien of Glasgow was almost as good, finishing with 14 strikeouts and only allowing four hits in a losing effort. Remembering Mike Roland, Jeff Jones said, "Mike was an excellent pitcher with good stuff. He could hit his spots at an elite level. We generally had a good chance of winning whenever he pitched. His nickname was Fozzie . . . after Fozzie Bear. I think that was because he sounded like Fozzie Bear?"
- The red-hot Blues extended their winning streak to 12 games with a doubleheader sweep of Circle. Scobey used 29 hits—including six doubles—to win 12-2 and 11-6. Brad Gilbert pitched a two-hitter in the opener, striking out 11 and walking three. Steve Lapke led Scobey's 16-hit attack in the second game with singles and drove in four runs. Banging out Scobey's six doubles in the two games were Jerry Danelson (2), Brad Gilbert, Rod Hudyma, Shannon Albert, and Tommy Aldrich. After the doubleheader sweep, the Blues were 12-1 on the season.
- In a classic regular season matchup with Wolf Point, Jeff Jones pitched a five-hitter and struck out 15 Yellowjackets to lead Scobey to an 8-4 win. Jeff walked only three and went 3 for 5 at the plate with a double. Steve Lapke hit a two-run homer for Scobey in the bottom of the fifth to give Scobey a commanding 7-2 lead. Scobey's record improved to 16-5 in conference and 16-8 overall with the win. Jeff Jones recalls the game. "They were loaded, but I was feeling it. It was an evening game, and the old curveball was dropping off the table. But

looking back, it was really a slider. My grip, movement, arm motion, etc.—was a slider. A swooping side-to-side movement more than dropping. Back then, though, we never thought about sliders. It was just a curve ball if it bent in any way."

- Jeff Jones hit a dramatic two-out walk-off grand slam home run in the bottom of the seventh inning to hand Scobey an 11-7 win over Glendive in the first game of a doubleheader in Scobey. Not only was this home run a game-winner, but the slam came from the right side of the plate, giving the switch-hitter a home run from each side during the season, a rare feat. Paul "Peppy" Shaffer went 5-5 with a double, and Mike Roland got the win in relief of Brad Gilbert. Steve Lapke's two-run double in the bottom of the fourth led Scobey to a 10-2 win in the rain-shortened second game. Jeff Jones got the win in relief of Mike Roland. With the win, Scobey was building momentum leading up to the divisional tournament, which would be hosted at Scobey.
- In their final games leading up to the divisional tournament, Scobey split a doubleheader with Wolf Point, handing the Yellowjackets only their third conference loss and fifth of the season. Scobey trailed 3-1 in the first game, but a four-run rally in the top of the seventh gave Scobey a 5-3 lead, which they held on to win 5-4. Brad Gilbert pitched a five-hitter for the win. Wolf Point came back to win the second game 11-7.

Scobey concluded an excellent regular season with an 18-6 conference record, good enough for second place behind Wolf Point, who was 21-3. With their two wins over Wolf Point and solid pitching from Mike Roland, Jeff Jones, Paul Shaffer, Brad Gilbert, and Pete Dighans, Scobey's chances looked good to advance to the State as one of the top two teams in the Divisional.

DIVISIONAL TOURNAMENT

THE 1987 EASTERN DIVISIONAL TOURNAMENT WAS HOSTED at Scobey for the fifth time. Scobey had previously hosted in 1958, 1965, 1974, and 1978. The Blues looked strong heading into the tournament, and hopes were high to finish in the top two—even win it—and advance to State. Although Scobey had beaten Wolf Point twice during the regular season, Wolf Point was favored to win the tournament. Opening-day matchups pitted the following teams (with seeds) against each other:

- Glendive Blue Devils (4) vs. Glasgow Reds (5)
- Wolf Point Yellowjackets (1) vs. Malta Mustangs (8)
- Sidney Patriots (3) vs. Circle Zephyrs (6)
- Scobey Blues (2) vs. Plentywood Athletics (7)

Scobey started strong, beating Plentywood 7-1 in the opener, as Paul Shaffer pitched a five-hitter and struck out 10 Athletics. He lost his shutout when Plentywood scored in the ninth inning. But against Sidney in their second game, Scobey's defense imploded, as the Blues committed seven errors—including a game-deciding three-run error in the eighth—leading to a 9-6 defeat. Mike Roland started, and Jeff Jones came on in relief. Each team had eight hits—one of Scobey's hits was a two-run homer by Steve Lapke—but Scobey's defense cost them the game, forcing them through the dirt route for the remainder of the tournament.

However, the dirt route was short-lived, as the Glasgow Reds ended the Blues' season with a 14-7 win. The score was tied 7-7 in the fifth, but things began to fall apart for the Blues, and the defense was again the culprit, as the Blues committed five errors. Brad Gilbert took the loss, with Scott Fladager and Paul Shaffer pitching in relief. Scobey outhit the Reds 12 to 10—and Glasgow had nine errors—but the Blues stranded 15 runners on base and couldn't get the big hit when needed. Jeff Jones remembers the disappointment of being eliminated early in the tournament. "We were very excited to be hosting. There was a lot of excitement and expectations were high to do well in the tournament. I remember we played like an entirely different team in that tournament. I remember sitting in the dugout after our second loss and being totally pissed off. I think we all knew that team was our best chance to make some noise at State, and we choked."

It was a disappointing end to a fine season for Scobey, who finished with a 23-16 record. The 1987 season was the last for Steve Lapke, Mike Roland, and Pete Dighans.

Meanwhile, first-year coach Mike Neubauer and the Wolf Point Yellowjackets bulldozed through the tournament to win the championship. After their opening-day 9-6 win over Malta, Wolf Point swamped Glendive 21-5, blasted Sidney 16-4, then completed their dominance with a 17-2 rout over Sidney in the championship. Wolf Point outscored their opponents 63-17 in the tournament. Seven of Wolf Point's 15 hits were doubles in the championship game. The *Leader* wrote that Wolf Point "seemed to get stronger as the tourney progressed" and that sportscasters covering the event "were impressed with the way the Wolf Point boys hit the ball and noted that they had good depth in the pitching staff."[32] The *Leader* concluded its coverage of the 1987 Eastern Divisional Tournament by stating that Wolf Point "should do well at the state tournament in Billings."[33]

1987 Wolf Point Yellowjackets, State Class A Champions. Front row, left to right: Kendal Mayer, Chris Antonson, Dirk Kuntz, Jon Kolstad, Troy Ault, Joel Sandau, John Whitmus. Back row, left to right: Head coach Mike Neubauer, Dave Parsley, Brett Gilman, Shane Peterson, Troy Cody, Dave Rensvold, Jim Redekopp, Kenny Azure, Austin Barr, Troy Halverson, Assistant Coach Jeff Neubauer. *The Herald-News photo.*

STATE TOURNAMENT

THE LEADER WAS RIGHT. THE YELLOWJACKETS PICKED RIGHT up where they left off in Scobey, sweeping the state tournament at Cobb Field in Billings in four games to complete a perfect 8-0 postseason run. In their first game, they beat the Great Falls Sparkies 13-6, as Troy Cody slammed a two-run home run and gained the pitching victory in relief. The Jackets then got a well-pitched game by Shane Peterson, who tossed a three-hitter to beat the Anaconda Athletics 3-1. Ken Azure, Brett Gilman, and Dave Parsley each knocked in a run for Wolf Point. In the undefeated semifinal, Wolf Point scored six runs on five hits in the sixth inning, leading to their 8-4 win over the Lewistown Redbirds. The big blow came on Jon Kolstad's two-run triple. Wolf Point's Austin Barr scattered eight hits to get the win. He had a shutout going into the bottom of the sixth. Wolf Point beat Lewistown again in the championship game, 9-5. Although Wolf Point's defense committed six errors, they made some big plays to overcome them, twice gunning down runners at the plate and picking one runner off base on a throw from the outfield. Kenny Azure went the distance to get the win for Wolf Point. The Jackets were 31-5 and, along with the Lewistown Redbirds (47-10), would travel to Idaho Falls, Idaho, to compete in the Class A Northwest Regional.

First-year Coach Mike Neubauer, who played Legion for Wolf Point (1975-78), was ecstatic after the win. "We got the money off our back. There have been a lot of second-place teams over the years."[34] Two of those second-place teams were in 1973 and 1976, with both losses coming on big eighth-inning rallies by Scobey in the State championship game. In 1973, Scobey trailed Wolf Point 4-2 in the top of the eighth but rallied with eight singles and one Wolf Point error to score seven runs, turning the 4-2 deficit into a 9-4 lead, eventually winning 9-6. In 1976,

Scobey trailed 11-3 in the top of the eighth but, on eight hits and three Wolf Point errors, scored 10 runs to shock Wolf Point 13-11. And that was the game after Greg Fjeld hit a two-out, two-strike, two-run inside-the-park-homer (there were some errors) to walk it off for Scobey 6-5 to keep Scobey alive to play a second game.

Coach Neubauer was also happy his team won the sportsmanship trophy, which is extremely rare for a championship team. His team's poise and discipline must have impressed the tournament organizers. Mike said, "That was our goal. To win the state championship and the sportsmanship trophy. I've never seen it done before. This is the best bunch of players I've ever coached." Not surprisingly, Mike Neubauer was named Class A Coach of the Year, leading the Yellowjackets to a 31-5 record and their first state championship since 1965 in his first year coaching Legion baseball. The 1987 State championship was Wolf Point's last.

Havre had another dazzling regular season and divisional tournament, as the Northstars won the northern division tournament and entered the state tournament with a 33-6 record. However, having been burned at the state tournament in 1985 and 1986, Havre coaches Tom Nielson and Micky Williams "were hesitant to make any predictions about the Class B state tournament. 'It's strange,' Nielson said. 'It's like a totally new season. You haven't seen the teams or the place you play. You do things you haven't done before.' Call it a prophesy. Call it snakebitten. Call it Murphy's Law. Call it 'deja vu.' For the second time in three years, the Northstars opened the Class B state tournament with a stunning loss, as the Anaconda A's humbled Havre, 11-4 in their first game." Havre then beat Laurel but was eliminated by the Bitterroot Bucs. It was another disappointing state tournament for Havre.

NORTHWEST REGIONAL CLASS B TOURNAMENT

WOLF POINT COMPLETED ITS FANTASTIC SEASON BY WINNING two games and losing two games to finish third in the Northwest Regional, the highest finish for a Montana team to date. The Yellowjackets beat Roseburg, Oregon, 5-3, with a three-run rally in the ninth, then beat Idaho Falls 15-6. They lost to Kirkland, Washington, 9-6, then were eliminated by the Yakima Blues, 12-10. Again, I can't resist writing that even though the Yellowjackets got the best of the Blues in Montana, they were bettered by the Blues in Idaho. You can't escape the Blues. The Yellowjackets placed three players on the All-Region Team: Troy Cody,

Dirk Kuntz, and Shane Peterson. Jim Wier of Lewistown was also named to the All-Region Team.

The Wolf Point Yellowjackets and first-year Coach Mike Neubauer finished the season with a spectacular 33-7 record.

EAST-WEST ALL-STAR CLASSIC

SCOBEY AGAIN PROUDLY HOSTED THE SECOND EAST-WEST All-Star Classic for 18-year-olds at the Scobey Ball Park, and Don Lekvold was again the coach of the East All-Stars. Mike Roland and Steve Lapke made the East All-Star Team, and both played well in the three-game series. The two teams split the Saturday games. The East won the first game, 14-4, with Brian Dougherty of Glendive pitching a six-hitter to get the win. Shane Park of Livingston homered for the East, and Steve Lapke was 2-3 with a triple. The West scored two runs in the bottom of the ninth to walk it off in the second game, 9-8. The East won the rubber game 11-7 on Sunday, with Scobey pitcher Mike Roland getting the win. Shane Park hit a two-run home run in the sixth to lead the East's hitting, and Steve Lapke was 2-5 with another triple. Shane Park was named MVP of the East, and Stacy Hagan of Vauxhall, Alberta, was named MVP of the West. East All-Star Coach Lekvold said errors were the difference in the games, noting the players only had two days to practice with each other, which had a lot to do with it. Regarding the errors, Don jokingly said, "We saw some outstanding plays made, and some that were not so outstanding."

EXTRA INNINGS

THE 1987 TEAM HAD A LOT OF COLORFUL NICKNAMES, INCLUDing "Oil Can," "Fozzie," and "Karch." How did they come to be? Mike Lee remembers how Pete Dighans was nicknamed "Oil Can Pete": "He used real motor oil (10W-30) to oil his glove! His left knee on all his game pants was covered with black oil." Ken Meyer added, "Yep, the saying was 'Motor Oil is Motor Pete!' I think it was from a Johnny Bench commercial back in the day!" Mike Roland's nickname was "Fozzie" because he laughed like Fozzie Bear on *The Muppet Show*. Waka waka! Mike "Karch" Lee remembers how he got his nickname: "The Fall of 1986, during 'Teacher Convention' weekend, I went and spent the weekend with Uncle Kelly in Billings. He took me to see the USA men's Olympic volleyball team play Japan at the Metra. Karch Kiraly was on the American team. Well, the next week back in Scobey, we happened to be playing volleyball in PE. I served either 7 or 11 points in a row to win a game, and the PE student assistant, Steve Lapke (who also was at the Metra watching volleyball), said, 'Hey, there is Karch Kiraly.' I laughed because I knew who he was talking about, but most people at school laughed because the name was foreign to them and sounded funny. After that, the seniors called me Karch off and on for a few days, and the whole school picked up on it, and I was labeled for life. I hated it at first but eventually got used to it." Interestingly, "Karch" is also the nickname for the volleyball player, whose real name is Charles Frederick Kiraly. *Karch* comes from the Hungarian word *Karcsi*, a shortened version of the name *Karoly*, the Hungarian equivalent of Charles.

The 1987 Glacier Twins, who were the defending State A champions and won the Doc Norman Memorial Tournament, were coached by Julio Delgado. He had been the head coach of the Twins for 10 years, compiling a 329-193 record (a .630 winning percentage). In the article "Delgado: Family outshines diamonds," by Mark Hogan of The *Daily Inter Lake*, Julio recognized his assistant coaches who had contributed to his success.[35] One name he mentioned was "former long-time assistant Craig Audet," who played for Scobey Legion from 1965-1969 and played on Scobey's first state championship team in 1969. The 1987 Twins built a record of 44-13 during the regular season, finishing second in the western division to Lethbridge, Alberta. That followed the most successful campaign in the team's history during its 1986 season, when the Twins went 46-14 in winning its first state title and placing third in the Northwest Regionals in Roseburg, Oregon. The Twins finished fourth in the 1987 state tournament, which they hosted in Whitefish. The Glacier Twins now compete in Class A Legion and have since won State A titles in 2014 and 2018. Julio Delgado was named State AA Coach of the Year in 1996. He learned the game from his father in Havana, Cuba, where he was born. "Baseball has been in my life ever since I can remember," he said. "My father taught me when I was very young how to play and compete." Delgado's father played professionally in Cuba and was a member of that country's Pan-American teams. He was good enough to be offered a contract by the St. Louis Cardinals.

Ken Meyer remembers the 1987 Wolf Point state championship team and their coach, Mike Neubauer. "They were damn good, but we held our own against them. Neubauer was a hell of a coach and got everything out of them. Great Guy." Mike Lee added, "Neubauer was my 13-year-old Babe Ruth All-Star Coach. He always stayed with Grampa and Grandma for state tournaments, so I knew him as a batboy."

In the postseason, fifteen-year-olds Mike Lee and Ken Meyer had to make a tough decision about which team to play on—Scobey Legion or Hi-Line Babe Ruth All-Stars. Their Hi-Line All-Star team won the District Babe Ruth Tournament, but unfortunately, the State Babe Ruth Tournament in Whitefish was the same weekend as the Eastern Divisional Legion Tournament in Scobey. Mike said, "Ken and I felt we should play with our age group for All-Stars instead of playing in the Legion divisional tournament. If we had stayed and played Legion, we would have started at shortstop and third, where Ken and I played." The Hi-Line All-Stars went 2-2 in Whitefish. Another future Blues star, 15-year-old Kevin Nelson, would likely have been the number three pitcher in Legion that year, but his parents only let him play Babe Ruth in 1987. Terry Farver, also 15 years old, played Babe Ruth in 1987. The following season, he would join Kevin Nelson on the Blues as a rookie. Together with Mike, Ken, and Kevin, the four would form the nucleus of a team that would compete for the state championship in 1990, Don Lekvold's best team.

The 1987 Eastern Divisional Tournament was the 12th time Scobey hosted a State or Divisional tournament, and the *Leader* recognized the experience of Scobey's hosting. "Years of experience by volunteer workers in the grounds crew, long hours in concession stands at the gate, and general organization kept everything progressing in good order, as has come to be expected at Scobey ballparks by those 'dependables in the trenches, so important to hosting.'"[36] Always so much pride came through the pages of the *Leader* when it wrote about Scobey's baseball tradition and community involvement.

At the eastern divisional in Scobey, Jim Lekvold of Scobey was the head umpire of the crew that included Larry Trangsrud and Pat Vigliotti of the county area, Jerry Butner and Tom Barnhart of Sidney, and John Harris of Miles City. Jim played for the Blues from 1979-83 and Larry from 1981-86.

I asked Jeff Jones how he came to be a switch-hitter. "I batted both playing Wiffle ball for years and always felt better left, but I didn't have the balls to try it until Legion. During practice one night in my first year with the Blues, Larry Trangsrud was pitching batting practice. He asked me to bat left, and I just laughed. Donnie Lekvold asked if I batted left. I said I did but never tried in 'real baseball.' Donnie told me to step into the box on the left side. On the second pitch, I hit a line drive off the wall in right-center. Donnie gave me the green light from then on out. Probably hit for a better average right, but more home runs left."

Jeff remembers the two home runs he hit from the opposite side of the plate. "The first one was against Malta, a three-run homer batting left. It bounced in front of a small car driving on the main road behind right field. That person retrieved the ball and brought it to the concessions stand, and then someone brought it to our dugout and shared the story with me that it bounced in front of this car on the main street. The grand slam was right-handed in the bottom of the last inning of our doubleheader with Glendive. I hit that over the left field fence."

The Bitterroot Red Sox broke onto the scene in 1987—but as a Senior Babe Ruth team. In an article titled, "Red Sox: the new kids on the block" by Brett French of the *Ravalli Republic*,[37] the Red Sox were introduced to the state of Montana. The team started as a Senior Babe Ruth team composed of 16-to 18-year-olds, mainly from Hamilton, but with players from Corvallis and Darby. Red Sox Manager Jim Kazebier explained why Hamilton started a Senior Babe Ruth team. "Last year (1986), we had six Babe Ruth teams with a maximum of five 15-year-olds on each team, 30 kids. Twenty-five to 30 kids graduate from Babe Ruth, and the [Bitterroot] Bucs only carry about 15 players. We decided to give them another team to play on."[38] The Bitterroot Red Sox competed as a Senior Babe Ruth team for seven years, moving to State Class A Legion in 1994. The Red Sox have since won eight state championships, the same number as Scobey. The Bitterroot Bucs, who started their American Legion program in 1983, are mainly from Florence-Carlton and have won four state championships.

1988

Third Place at Divisional is No Consolation for Scobey

> *That loss to Sidney [at Divisional] hurt because Wolf Point was on deck, and lightning doesn't strike twice in the same spot. No one said anything, but we all knew there was no way we were beating Wolf Point again.*
>
> —Mike Lee, Scobey Blues (1987–1990)

1988 Scobey Blues. Standing, left to right: Coach Don Lekvold, Paul Shaffer, Jeff Jones, Ron Meyer, Mike Lee, Greg Larson, Ken Meyer, Assistant Coach Gary Meyer. Kneeling, left to right: Terry Farver, Rod Hudyma, Brad Gilbert, Arlin Kaul, Scott Kanning, Kevin Nelson. Not pictured are Greg Olson and Ryan Linder. *Borderland photo.*

PRESEASON

MIKE ROLAND, STEVE LAPKE, AND PETE DIGHANS were not at Don Lekvold's first practice in April 1988, as they had aged out. The 1988ers would sorely miss ace pitcher Mike Roland, who had been a mainstay on the staff for four years since he started playing in 1984. Steve Lapke—who in his later years for the Blues could hit for both power and average—had been the starting second baseman for three years, and Pete Dighans had added depth to the pitching staff. Mike and Steve were selected for the East All-Star team in 1987. They would all be missed.

But Coach Don Lekvold and Assistant Coach Gary "Herbie" Meyer were returning five experienced 18-year-olds—Paul "Pepi" Shaffer, Brad Gilbert, Rod Hudyma, Jeff Jones, and Ron Meyer, so Scobey would be putting a veteran-laden team on the field in 1988, including its top three pitchers (Jeff, Paul, and Brad). Kevin Nelson, a talented 16-year-old all-around athlete from Opheim, would join the team as a rookie and strengthen the pitching staff. Sixteen-year-old Mike Lee, now in his third Legion season, would also start seeing some innings on the mound for Scobey. He would also become Scobey's full-time catcher that season—and for the next three years—as Jerry Danelson did not go out for baseball in 1988, so Mike moved from third base to catcher. Ken Meyer, who had seen plenty of action as a 15-year-old in 1987, was back too as the starting shortstop, as were Shannon Albert, Greg Larson, and Arlin Kaul. Joining Kevin Nelson on the team as rookies were Terry Farver, Scott Kanning, Ryan Linder, and Greg Olson.

Could this be the year the Blues broke through and qualified for State? The Blues had not qualified outright since 1984 when they placed fourth at Divisionals. But that was when the top four teams qualified. State Class A now had five Divisions, and only the top two teams from each division qualified for the 10-team state tournament in Great Falls. The road to State was tougher.

REGULAR SEASON

THE BLUES TRAVELED TO LEWISTOWN TO PLAY IN THE SECOND annual Redbird 4th of July Tournament. Lewistown, led by pitcher-outfielder Jim Wier—who would later play for the College of Southern Idaho—had taken second at State to Wolf Point the previous season and had a strong baseball program. The Scobey Blues, Havre Northstars, Wolf Point Yellowjackets, Bitterroot Bucs, and the host Lewistown Redbirds participated. Scobey went 1-3 in the round-robin tournament—losing to Lewistown, Havre, and Bitterroot and beating Wolf Point 4-3—but got some good experience against tough competition, which prepared them for the divisional tournament in Sidney two weeks later. The Bitterroot Bucs won all four of their games to win the tournament and looked to be the team to beat at State, as they exited the tournament with a 28-1 record.

Scobey's win over Wolf Point in Lewistown proved once again they compete against the best in the east, as Wolf Point, with eight 18-year-olds on their roster, repeated as league champions. Scobey again held their own against Wolf Point during the regular season, winning three games and losing four against the Yellowjackets. But the Blues' overall regular season was not spectacular—they finished fourth in the standings. They needed to win three games in Divisionals to advance to State, a daunting—but not impossible—task.

DIVISIONAL TOURNAMENT

THE 1988 EASTERN DIVISIONAL TOURNAMENT WAS HOSTED by the Richland County Patriots at Moose Memorial Park in Sidney. Due to Scobey's fourth-place seed, they were on the same side of the bracket as top-seeded Wolf Point, so the road to State—three wins—traveled through Wolf Point. Scobey's first game pitted them against the Glasgow Reds, the fifth seed. Here were the complete opening-day matchups:

- Scobey Blues (4) vs. Glasgow Reds (5)
- Wolf Point (1) Bye
- Sidney Patriots (2) vs. Plentywood Athletics (7)
- Glendive Blue Devils (3) vs. Circle Zephyrs (6)

Scobey and Glasgow opened the tournament with the first game on Thursday morning. The winner would play later that night against league-champion—and defending state champion—Wolf Point. Things looked rough for the Blues early against Glasgow, as the Reds were leading 8-5 after four complete innings, but Scobey rallied to score seven runs in the fifth, sixth, and seventh innings—the big blow in the seventh coming on a home run by Ken Meyer—to come from behind and get the all-important win 12-8. Jeff Jones started, and Brad Gilbert came on in relief in the fifth—pitching five innings of scoreless no-hit ball, striking out seven—to get the win. Ken Meyer homered for Scobey to lead the Blues' ferocious 18-hit attack. Ken remembers the home run. "Although it wasn't my first, it has to be my most memorable only because of how it happened and who it was against. The Glasgow pitcher was John 'Beaver' Fischer, who would later be a roommate of mine and a very close friend. Beaver was one of the top three pitchers in the league that year and would go on to play college baseball out in Oregon. Anyway, the pitch count was 2-0, and I was sitting dead red. I knew he was going to throw a fastball, so I loaded up. Connected for an opposite-field home run. I was jacked at the time because it was still a close game (I believe the home run came in the seventh inning), but it was memorable because it still gets traction 35-some-odd years later! It was the only home run Beaver ever gave up, so when us guys get together and reminisce about the 'old' days, it always comes up, and I will always have that one on him! I will go to my grave remembering that one."

Wolf Point was up next later that night. The Blues were playing their second game of the day, but they had beaten Wolf Point 4-3 at the Lewistown 4th of July Tournament two weeks earlier, so they knew they could beat them. Don Lekvold handed the ball to 16-year-old Kevin Nelson from Opheim to start against the Yellowjackets, and Paul Shaffer, also from Opheim, pitched in relief. Wolf Point took an early lead, but the Blues came from behind again to shock the Yellowjackets in a 13-11 slugfest and advance to play the undefeated semifinal against Sidney. Scobey's bats were hot—they pounded out 17 hits in the win after getting 18 hits against Glasgow. Thirty-five hits in two games. That's a lot.

What a first day of the tournament for Scobey! Coming from behind to win both games and knocking off the conference champion and defending state champion Yellowjackets. The *Leader* wrote, "The Blues started off with a bang."[39] Boy, did they. The Blues were now just one win away from qualifying outright for their first state tournament since 1984.

And the Blues came oh-so-close to getting it done, but it was not meant to be. With the score tied 5-5 and host Sidney batting in the bottom of the eighth, Patriots' John Peel hit a fly ball to right field with two outs and a baserunner on. Catcher Mike Lee thought it was a routine fly ball for the final out, but it was misjudged and became trouble.

Mike said, "When the ball was hit, I thought easy out. Then I saw our outfielder running back towards the fence, so now I'm thinking, WTF. We had regained momentum late in the game until that error. I felt like we were going to win up to that point." The ball fell for a double and drove in the go-ahead run. Then Sidney Pitcher Chris DiFonzo—who went the distance for Sidney—got the Blues out in the top of the ninth to secure Sidney's 6-5 win, but not before Scobey threatened to tie the game. With two outs and the tying run on base, Rod Hudyma hit a long fly ball which looked like it was trouble, but a fine defensive play at the wall preserved Sidney's win.

It was a heartbreaking loss for the cardiac Blues, who, for the third consecutive game, had come from behind—this time from a 5-2 deficit in the third inning—to knot the score 5-5 in the seventh, only to see Sidney plate the go-ahead run in the bottom of the eighth. Kevin Nelson started, and Paul Shaffer relieved, which was a carbon copy of the Wolf Point game. Scobey's bats were alive again, banging out nine hits, but it wasn't enough to overcome Sidney's 11 hits and six runs. With the win, Sidney advanced to the Divisional championship game and—more importantly—a berth in the state tournament. With the loss, Scobey was pushed into an elimination game with defending champion Wolf Point. Mike Lee was devasted after the loss. "That loss hurt because Wolf Point was on deck, and lightning doesn't strike twice in the same spot. No one said anything, but we all knew there was no way we were beating Wolf Point again."

Needing a win against Wolf Point—who had stormed back through the loser's bracket—for a berth in the Divisional championship game and the state tournament, the Blues could not find the same magic they did in their first game, and the Yellowjackets won 12-5. This deep into the tournament, Scobey's pitching was being stretched thin, and several pitchers saw action for Scobey. Wolf Point had more depth at this position, which was the difference in the game. Scobey banged out another 11 hits—totaling an incredible 55 hits in four games—but the heavy-hitting Yellowjackets had 16 and outslugged the Blues. It was a devastating loss for the Blues after coming razor-close to get to the promised land. However, the Blues did not implode in the field as they had the previous year against Sidney and Glasgow when they committed seven and five errors to beat themselves. This year, Wolf Point was just better.

The experienced, battle-tested, and veteran-laden Wolf Point Yellowjackets, with eight 18-year-olds on their roster, then beat Sidney 14-1 and 6-3 to repeat as eastern division champions. Austin Barr of Wolf Point was named tournament MVP. He hit a home run in both Sidney games—giving him four in the tournament—and pitched a complete game one-hitter in the first game, yielding only one run. Kenny Azure and Kirk Kuntz combined on a two-hitter in the second game. Dave Parsley, Wolf Point's stalwart catcher, called the signals for Wolf Point throughout the tournament and in both Sidney games. The Yellowjacket's Jim Redekopp was named the leading hitter in the tournament, going 9 for 17 for a .529 average. Wolf Point, along with Sidney, headed to State in Great Falls, where second-year Coach Mike Neubauer and the Yellowjackets hoped to repeat as state champions, a feat that had not been accomplished since the Scobey Blues won five state championships between 1976 and 1980.

The five 18-year-olds for Scobey all played well in the tournament. Paul Shaffer was third in the MVP balloting, hitting .450. Jeff Jones hit .500 and, along with Paul Shaffer, logged a lot of innings in the tournament. Brad Gilbert had strong innings pitched in relief on the mound, including five innings of scoreless no-hit ball against Glasgow, where he recorded seven strikeouts. Rod Hudyma also hit over .400 for the tournament and nearly tied the game against Sidney with a long fly ball to the wall. Ron Meyer was sidelined with a serious back injury and saw only limited action as a pinch-hitter.

While the season ended disappointingly after a promising 2-0 start in the Divisional tournament, Scobey's quest to recapture some of the glory of the Doc Norman years was gathering momentum—a Blue wave was building. Many of Coach Don Lekvold's talented younger players—like 16-year-olds Mike Lee, Ken Meyer, Terry Farver, and Kevin Nelson—had now gotten a taste of tournament intensity and had the state tournament horizon in full view, coming up a little short in the end. As the quest was building, so was the hunger. Scobey baseball was alive and well in 1988, and the future looked bright for Coach Lekvold and the Blues. The *Leader* captured it best in the last printed text of the 1988 season: "With some good young players coming up, Coach Don Lekvold is looking forward to another good season next year."[40]

STATE TOURNAMENT

WOLF POINT COULD NOT CONJURE THE MAGIC OF 1987 AND repeat as state champions, as a new kid on the block, the Bitterroot Bucs—the "Power in the West"—captured their first state tournament. The championship came five years after Bitterroot started their American Legion Baseball program in 1983. The Bucs marched through the tournament undefeated, walking it off in the bottom of the tenth inning to beat the Medicine Hat Monarchs 11-10 in the state championship game. After winning the state championship, Bitterroot's record was a staggering 44-3, with all three of their losses coming earlier in the season to Anaconda, who eliminated Wolf Point from the tournament. The Bucs and Monarchs advanced to the Northwest Regional in Roseburg, Oregon. Wolf Point won its first game 11-8 over the Great Falls Sparkies but then lost its next two games and was eliminated from the tournament, losing to Vauxhall and Anaconda. Sidney also went 1-2 in the tournament.

It is tough to repeat as state champions. Although they had eight 18-year-olds on their roster, the Yellowjackets missed their leader, Troy Cody, from the 1987 state championship team, ace pitcher Shane Peterson, and third baseman Brett Gilman. Troy Cody and Shane Peterson had been named to the All-Region Team in 1987. Then, starting catcher Dave Parsley injured his knee shagging fly balls at Wolf Point's last practice the day before the team left for Great Falls and couldn't play in the tournament. But the 1988 team did bring more hardware back to Wolf Point, as for the second consecutive year, Coach Neubauer and the Wolf Point Yellowjackets were awarded the Sportsmanship Trophy. Repeating as the best sportsmen might be more important than winning a second state championship.

NORTHWEST REGIONAL CLASS A TOURNAMENT

THE BITTERROOT BUCS REPRESENTED MONTANA WELL AT THE Northwest Regional in Eugene, Oregon, finishing in third place, as the Wolf Point Yellowjackets had done the previous season. The Bucs clobbered host Eugene 19-5, defeated Roseburg 4-3, then lost a tight 2-1 ballgame against Pocatello, Idaho, and fell 15-4 to Roseburg, Oregon, in the consolation. The Bucs finished the season with an amazing 46-5 overall record. Their championship marked the beginning of Western Montana's dominance in Class A American Legion Baseball, wresting the power from the east, where it had resided for over two decades.

SCOBEY OLD-TIMERS GAME

THE TOWN OF SCOBEY (EST. 1913) CELEBRATED ITS 75TH diamond jubilee anniversary in 1988, so there were many events that summer, including an old-timer's game at Scobey Ball Park. The team picture includes some notable faces who "years ago were energetically active on various teams in the Daniels County area" Of these old-timers, the *Leader* wrote, "It was a wearying but fun day for the players and much nostalgia for fans at the Scobey Ball Park in the old-timers Diamond Jubilee baseball game. For the players on the Scobey squad, muscle tone and coordination obviously weren't what they once were, but the spirit was still there."

"The spirit was still there" is what *The Blues of Summer* is all about.

The Scobey team—the "Diamond Jubilee Old-Timers"—played a team from Plentywood, put together by "that inveterate and enthusiastic sports fan and promoter," Aubrey Ferguson. Aubrey's team was "quite a bit younger—and the score in their favor, 22-1, was about the same spread in runs as the two teams were apart in years."

Scobey Old-Timers. Left to right: Bob Willard, Manager Joe Anderson, Andy Stolen, Ben Lien, George Larson, Bud Jensen, Ken Hansen, Jack Reiner, Fred Walker, Howard Farver, and Dallas Gaines. Grandfathers predominated on the Scobey Old-Timers Jubilee baseball team at an afternoon game at Scobey Ball Park. The team was composed of fellows over the years who have played on various teams in the county area. They gathered from all around northeastern Montana to form up this enthusiastic team, old in years, but young in spirit. *Leader caption and photo, Burl Bowler.*

Jack Reiner, a member of the original Scobey Plainsmen, presents Keith Whipple with a new baseball, which was autographed by the Scobey old-timer's squad. Whipple, who was then in his mid-80s, was the oldest surviving member of the rambling semipro Scobey team of the mid-20s, which starred two members, Swede Risberg and Happy Felsch of the scandal-ridden World Series champion Chicago White Sox of 1919, many of whose team members were banned forever from organized, professional baseball, including Risberg and Felsch. *Leader caption and photo, Burl Bowler.*

Ray Conger made a special trip to Scobey to umpire the old-timer's game. He was a behind-the-plate ump in 1958 when the Scobey Plainsmen won their first state Baseball Congress title.

EXTRA INNINGS

THE 13-11 SCORE THAT SCOBEY BEAT WOLF POINT BY IN THEIR first game at divisional was the same as the 1976 state championship game between Scobey and Wolf Point at the state tournament in Cut Bank in 1976 when Scobey scored 10 runs in the top of the eighth inning to erase an 11-3 deficit and win the state championship. Coach Don Lekvold was the head coach of Wolf Point at the time, and Mike Neubauer pitched for Wolf Point in the game. I wonder if Blues' Coach Don Lekvold and Wolf Point's Mike Neubauer gave any thought to that final score?

Mike Lee remembers an unusual event before the second Wolf Point game. "When we did play Wolf Point the second time for a berth in the state tournament, the game was delayed maybe an hour due to the Mayfly hatch. It literally looked like it was snowing in July. One of the most bizarre things I remember as a kid. They were using brooms to sweep off the infield."

Unfortunately for the Blues, the LeProwse family departed Scobey after the 1987 season, so Jim's younger brother Jeff—a fine all-around athlete—was unable to contribute to Scobey's success. Mike Lee recalls, "Jeff LeProwse moving to Butte in 1987 after Babe Ruth All-Stars was a huge

Jordan and Kayli Baker, in the stands at the old-timer's game, held up this sign that read, "Out of the park! Grandpa!" when their grandpa, Jack Reiner, came to bat. *Leader photo, Burl Bowler.*

setback for us. Jeff played AA for Butte and was a hell of a player. He would have been our utility player and pitched. He would have batted somewhere in the top five. Jeff might have been the difference-maker in us winning at least one state championship in 1989–90, whether it was baseball, basketball, or football. He was that good of an athlete and the missing piece, especially for baseball."

Mike Lee caught 80-90% of the games in 1988, with Kevin Nelson catching the others. Mike remembers how tough it was catching both ends of a doubleheader. "Nothing like catching both games of a doubleheader at Glendive in July with the temp over 100. Coach 'Herbie' Gary Meyer always had cold, wet towels to put on the back of my neck when we were up to bat."

Of course, no Blues team is without stories of riding the bus and the attendant shenanigans. Mike Lee recalls a couple of tales about the trip to Lewistown. "On our way to Lewistown, we stopped at the Home Cafe in Nashua and ate like kings. While we were waiting for our food, me and

The Don Lekvold Era

Dallas Gaines, Jack and Loyal Brenden showed up the Scobey Ball Park for a Blues home game a year later, but it's best to place the photo of these Flaxville baseball giants here, alongside the other great old-timers who played our nation's pastime in northeastern Montana. *Leader photo.*

a few other guys started playing poker machines. I hit a queen-high straight flush, which would pay out $300–$400. I was underage, so Paul Shaffer (who was 18) was going to cash out my ticket. He said, 'Watch this.' (I was totally jacked and had to stand up). Well, we hit the wrong button, and it dealt me a whole new hand. Talk about a high to a low!!! On that same trip on the road somewhere by Jordan, MT (it's over 100 degrees in a yellow school bus), someone in the back seat cracked open a warm PBR. Within seconds, Terry Farver (who always sat behind Donnie) was doing his usual bus trip routine 'reading the articles' in *Playboy*, popped his head up and said, 'What's that smell?' The fine aroma of a freshly opened warm can of PBR filled the bus. The bus got pulled over, and the PBR was poured out. The bus smelled like a bar for a good 50 miles." Ken Meyer knew who the "someone" was who opened the beer. "The beer opener was my brother, Ron," Ken said. "I don't think he poured it out."

Although Jeff Jones from Peerless was denied a trip to State at the divisional tournament at Sidney, he was not denied a trip earlier that year—in basketball. On a Monday night in Glasgow in early March, the senior guard scored 26 points to lead the Peerless Panthers to a 58-54 win over Saco in the Eastern C Challenge Game, qualifying Peerless for its fourth state Class C basketball tournament. Jeff later played two seasons of basketball for the UND-Williston Tetons, then basketball at Rocky. Jeff played in Peerless for Dick Puckett in Little League and Bucky Henderson in Babe Ruth, so he had some great coaching coming up. I asked Jeff to tell me his baseball story, and here is his letter:

My first memory of playing baseball was Wiffle ball during the summers. This is when I first tried batting left, just for the fun of it. I found that my swing left-handed felt very smooth and natural. Right-handed, I tended to swing pretty level at the ball, but batting left, I naturally had a slight uppercut, allowing me to drive the ball further left-handed than right. I never had the guts to try and bat left-handed in a game until I got to my first year of playing with the Blues. My cousin Larry Trangsrud was in his last year. He told our coach, Don Lekvold, that I could switch-hit . . . and Don just kind of laughed. Larry told me to get in the box left-handed, and he would pitch to me. Don and the rest of the team were watching . . . I had never batted left-handed before in front of any of them. LT threw me a couple of pitches pretty hard, I remember, and I watched them go by. His third pitch came inside just a bit and again had some heat behind it. I turned it on pretty well, and it one-hopped the fence in the right-center. Next thing I knew, I started batting left from time to time when there was a right-handed pitcher. The older I got through the years, I hit right-handed about 60% of the time and left-handed 40% of the time. It kind of depended on the type of pitcher I was facing. I had a quicker bat right-handed, so if the pitcher threw really hard, I would almost always bat right. If the guy was throwing beach balls, then I would usually bat left and try to drive it.

Some of my first and best memories with the Blues involved playing at night. It was pretty cool for a kid from Peerless to play under the lights with a big crowd on hand. I loved pitching at night, too, because it seemed like you could get the ball to move more. Also, it was always fun to have the older guys sitting on the bench in front of the grandstands, behind home plate. It is funny because my memories are all pretty foggy, but I can see George Larson clear as day watching from that bench behind home plate.

In my first couple of years with the Blues, I mostly played in the outfield, then occasionally second base, and shortstop from time to time. In my last couple of years, I played mostly shortstop, second base, and pitcher. Paul Shaffer (from Opheim) played shortstop when I pitched. We had a pick-off move to second base that worked 90% of the time. If I was on the mound and I could see the runner on second base was too far off or just looked like he might have a lot on his mind, I would make eye contact with Paul as I walked around the mound to head toward the rubber. I would take my hat off and put it back on. That meant to Paul, playing shortstop, that I was going to throw to him at second base to pick off the runner. I would take the rubber and look in for the sign from the catcher. I would not even look back at second base. Then I would lift my left leg like I was beginning my wind up but just keep swinging my left leg all the way back toward second base, all the while still looking at the plate (so kind of spinning on the ball of my right foot). When

I had spun around and was ready to throw it to Paul at second, the runner was usually stuck in cement and we would pick him off by several steps. Lots of times, they would just stand there and get tagged because Paul had the ball before they could react.

Another fun memory I had was being in the dugout with the entire team when we were on offense. We got pretty creative and loud with our yelling for our guy up to bat. One of my favorites was the "Press Your Luck" yell. Imagine the opposing team's pitcher stepping onto the rubber and our guy stepping into the box to hit. Then you have 15 guys in our dugout yelling and clapping at the top of our lungs "COME ON NO WAMMIES, NO WAMMIES, BIG MONEY BIG MONEYYYYYYY!!!!!" Then the pitcher would pitch the ball, and right when the ball would hit the catcher's mitt, everyone in the dugout would yell in unison, again loud enough to hear for several blocks, "STOP!!!!" The best was when the ump would call a ball, and then all of us would ERUPT in the dugout in cheers. Five seconds later, we were repeating it all over again for the next pitch. I can still see us doing that like it was yesterday. It makes me laugh to this day.

Another memory I have is when we played in Havre. I think it might have been my second-to-last year. We had a pretty good team, but Havre was way better than we were that year. It was a long bus ride there, and we played like crap. It almost felt like we mailed it in, and we were all very frustrated with our effort after the game. Don was not one to yell, really. He just pointed out the obvious that we sucked it up, and it was time to get back on the bus and put that one behind us. We all piled on the bus, and Don started to pull away from the ball bark. The bus was completely silent. On our way out of the parking lot, we passed three or four Havre players walking along the fence line. They waved at our bus in a nice way, and I remember watching Don as he drove our bus. Don waved back at them and said in a fairly quiet voice, "See you later. Thanks for the game fuckers." The way he said it was so matter-of-fact that the entire busload of players just busted out laughing. Probably one of those things that you need to be there, but it was pretty funny.

Some of my best memories playing for the Blues were getting to be teammates with kids from other towns. We competed hard against each other during the basketball seasons but then got to be on the same team playing baseball. At first, that seemed weird. But then, as the years went by, it became the thing that meant the most to me. I developed friendships with guys from Scobey and Opheim playing for the Blues. I also got to know guys from Wolf Point, Glasgow, etc., and got to be pretty good friends with those guys, too. To me, the friendships playing a sport I loved was my favorite part. My only regret—I wish we could have played more than just from May–August. I would have loved to have worked on my game year-round just to see what could have happened. I did end up playing college basketball and baseball at UND-Williston. I pitched and played center field in college. We played against some really good players from Canada. I mostly froze my ass off standing in center field. Then went on and played basketball at Rocky.

Jeff Jones remembers his teammate, Paul "Pepi" Shaffer from Opheim. Jeff said, "Pepi hit leadoff and batted left—one of the few kids at that age who could lay a drag bunt down with great accuracy. Being left-handed and fast as hell, if he laid it down, he was two steps from first before the ball was fielded. Common that there was no throw at all." Paul also remembers slap-hitting for base hits. "I batted left and would do a lot of those slap shots; just try to outrun it from the third baseman typically." A lightning-quick point guard in basketball who could dish, Pepi is ranked 10th all-time for career assists in MHSA basketball history.

I asked Paul how he got his nickname, "Pepi." I knew he was lightning fast, so I thought that was probably why, but that's not it. Paul said, "Well, believe it or not, my mom is from Mexico, and my dad's name is also Paul. So, when I was little, she started calling me *Pepi*, which is Spanish, meaning awe-inspiring. So, she really started calling me that to be different from my father. It kind of stuck with others when they heard my mom, dad, or sisters call me it. I hated it because I thought it was after Pepé Le Pew, the cartoon character from *Looney Tunes*. But I think others thought it was more about my speed and quickness in sports. And I was fairly sports-smart, given I was not very tall. So, I played point guard in basketball, quarterback in football, and played center field, pitched, or middle infield in baseball." I asked Pepi to tell his baseball story, and he provided me with this letter:

I remember first playing baseball when I was five years old, living in a small town in Southern California. My friends and I would have these epic Wiffleball games where you had different lines, and you got points for hitting it to certain spots if no one caught it. It was just one of those things we did as kids where everyone would gather in someone's driveway or cul-de-sac and you played until dark. I was a big San Diego Padres fan and remember going to games at the old Jack Murphy stadium to watch Gaylord Perry, Rolly Fingers, Ozzie Smith, and Dave Winfield.

My dad was a Customs Inspector on the US-Mexico border, and when I was seven years old, we moved to Opheim, Montana, in October of 1977 so he could be the Port of Opheim director.

The Don Lekvold Era

You can imagine the culture shock of moving from Southern California to Northeast Montana in October. I had never really seen snow before moving there, and our first winter was a bit of an experience!

I started playing little league baseball that spring, and funny enough, both of my sisters played that year as well. My oldest sister Vita was 12 at the time, and my other sister Tish was 10, so it was a family affair. I always batted left-handed but threw right-handed. I don't really know why, but it did help because I liked to slap, hit, or bunt to the opposite field and try and beat out the throws. I was always pretty fast. My nickname was Pepi. My mom, who was from Mexico, had called me that ever since I can remember. I think it was because my dad's name was Paul as well. I think my friends thought it was because I was fast, but I hated the nickname, lol! My mom and my sisters still call me that today, and whenever I see my friends from the Hi-Line, they still call me Pep or Pepi. One of my best memories was when we made it to the State Little League finals when I was 12. We went to Billings and won our first game and then played another team from Billings. If we won, we would move on to the West Regionals in San Bernadino, California. We lost 3 to 1, but it was a great time, and it is how I got to know so many people from Peerless, Scobey, Flaxville, and Outlook.

For Babe Ruth, I remember two of the basketball coaches getting the team going for Peerless and Opheim. I believe it was Larry Henderson and Steve Keller. It is crazy to think that Coach Keller is still coaching hoops!!! I remember playing on a beaten-up baseball field in Peerless for our games. Jeff Jones, John Ray Richardson and Travis and Scotty Fladager were the Peerless guys I got to know best. Jeff and I became good friends playing Little League, Babe Ruth, and Legion baseball together. We would often ride to games together and when we started playing Legion baseball, we hung out a lot every summer.

Our last year of Babe Ruth, we made it to State for all-stars. It was the summer of 1984, and I was supposed to go to the Olympics with my family, which was being held in Los Angeles. Jeff's parents convinced my family to let me stay behind so I could play, and then Jeff and I flew to LA to meet my family. We drove down to San Diego to watch the Padres play and got there pretty early. We actually met Steve Garvey as he was walking into the stadium and got his autograph. If you ask Jeff, he will probably mention that on our drive back to Montana, we were all crammed into the GMC Eagle, and our little dog Tuna was on the floor staring at him the entire trip!

When it was time to play Legion baseball, I knew I had a choice to make to either play for the Glasgow Reds or the Scobey Blues. It was a pretty easy choice for me since I played Babe Ruth with all the Peerless guys and then all-stars with the other guys from Scobey, Flaxville, and Outlook. Jeff and I would often carpool together, and a lot of times, I would just crash at his house. Back then, there was a 7-mile stretch from Opheim to Peerless that was all gravel road, and I had a little red Nissan Sentra that would get beaten up.

I was typically the leadoff hitter for our teams back then and would play second base or center field as well as pitch. One of my best friends, even today, is a guy named John Fischer, who played for Glasgow. We still see each other probably three or four times a year, and I still give him grief that I batted .750 against him. He said I was one of the only guys he could not get out and that Kenny Meyer was one of only two people who ever hit a home run off him.

Those summers playing with the Blues were the best. I remember Steve Lapke, Mike Roland, Howie Robinson, Arlin Kaul, Jerry Danelson, Greg Larson, Duane Hons, Kenny Meyer, Mike Lee, Tommy Aldrich, Rod Hudyma, Randy Pierce. That was my Scobey crew!! One of the things I remember fondly was sneaking into the drive-through movie in the back trunk of one of our friend's cars to save $5!! That seemed to be the meeting spot on the weekends, unless we were cruising Main Street. When we were 15, I remember Jeff and I getting in a car with some junior girls. We thought we were pretty cool back then, hanging out with juniors lol!!! And I will always remember the hamburgers with grilled onions. Damn, those were good!!

Donnie Lekvold was our coach back then. He was a good guy and pretty easygoing. The overnight trips were always a lot of fun. I remember when we drove to Whitefish in one of those yellow buses to play in a tournament. I had not been to Northwest Montana before then, and it was a haul from Northeast Montana. We always had a good rivalry with Wolf Point back then. Jeff and I would ride the team bus over there and then have a couple of friends pick us up after with an ice chest full of cold Miller High Life's.

Playing for the Blues made for the best summers. There wasn't exactly a lot to do living on the border, so hanging out with all the guys after practice and games will always have a fond place in my heart.

The year 1988 was also Ron Meyer's last season as a Blue. Knowing Ron is from a baseball family, I asked Ron to share his baseball story, and he provided this letter titled *The Blues of Summer*.

Before you can be a Blue, you have to go through a learning curve. My learning curve started in the backyard, where Steve Lapke, Clark Fjeld, and my brother Ken spent hours and hours playing all kinds of sports, but Wiffle ball was a summer pastime. It was normally two-on-two, with the Harmon fence as our home run fence. The base paths were well-worn, and the bases were evident.

As time passed, and we could hit the ball further, the field needed to change. We moved from plastic bats and balls to baseball bats and baseballs, so we moved to the empty lot behind Lapkes and Fjelds. As we got bigger, we needed more room, and we had to recruit my mom, Bonnie, to be the all-time pitcher. As it turns out, the empty lot was not enough room, and the day Steve Lapke hit it so far and through the garage door window of the house across the road was pretty much the last time we played there.

From there, we moved to the city park and recruited all the neighbor kids who could play to play pretty much every day. The new home run fence was the swimming pool. Not very often did we hit it into the pool, but it was decided that when we started doing it more frequently, we should probably have to stop playing at the park before some poor swimmer got taken out.

By this time, we were all in Little League, so our neighborhood pickup games came to an end. So, all the kids got split up when we went on to play Little League. The teams consisted of the White Sox, which Ken and I played on, the A's, which is where Steve Lapke ended up, and the Red Sox, where Clark Fjeld played. It's funny if you ask someone today which Little League team so-and-so played on, and they can remember; it was that important of a milestone, I guess.

As a White Sox, we were loaded and won a lot of tournaments; we had the likes of Mike Roland, Brad Gilbert, Rod Hudyma, Mike Lee, Ken, and myself. Our coaches were Ed Hinton and my dad, Gary Meyer. A couple of things I look back on from the Little League days were the amount of fans that always showed up to the games, it seemed like it was always a packed house. The other thing is the amount of volunteer hours given up by the people who took care of the field and the concession stands. My parents spent a ton of hours at the field, which was the original field by the roping barn.

We moved up to Babe Ruth baseball, and of course, each step you take moving up, you lose kids along the way who decided that they didn't want to play anymore or there were other things during the summer that their family had going. Looking back, I think we only had one Babe Ruth team at first, but I do know for a couple of years, there were two teams, and I believe the names were the Pirates and the Express. The two teams were okay, but if you could have had one team, we would have been better.

One thing was for sure when a Legion baseball game was going on when we weren't old enough to play: We had a group of guys who would chase foul balls so we could collect quarters. During one of the many Blues games we went to, if I remember correctly, Randy Stolen hit a ball over the right-field fence, and all I remember was I could have sworn the ball was still going up when it cleared the fence.

I passed up my first year of Legion ball because I went to my grandparents' farm for the summer. Ken was still playing Babe Ruth and would also move up to play Legion for some games.

When I started playing Legion the following year, we had some great players. Of course, Daniels County and Opheim had great athletes all around. As an example, you take players like Steve Lapke, Mike Roland, Jeff Jones, Paul Shaffer, Kevin Nelson, and my brother Ken just to name a few. These guys would also be the best players in other sports like football and basketball. If the three schools Flaxville, Peerless, and Scobey had been annexed around 1986 and the Opheim kids could have played football in Scobey there would have been more state championships won in football and basketball. Of course, it seemed like there were more kids back then, so maybe we would have still been class B.

With the amount of talent on the Blues when I started playing, I didn't get a lot of playing time, but it was such an awesome time. All the kids I played with and against growing up were now all my teammates.

I can't recollect every pitch and out in every game we played like some of the guys, but what I do know is Don Lekvold was such a good coach and was really good with the players. He made the different personalities and talents fit together. The amount of time he spent volunteering, coaching, and being on the road with us when he had a couple of young boys at home was unreal, and I appreciate everything he did for us. My dad helped out a ton as well and the amount of hours he put in was also crazy.

One of my favorite memories was when we were playing a doubleheader in Circle. Karch hit a home run and did his regular slow home run trot around the bases, but he was called out because he missed second base.

One night game we played at the divisional tournament in Sidney, the field had so many Mayflies flying around that it looked like it was snowing. That was a strange game.

I always liked to travel to tournaments like Lewiston because it was nice to play against good teams to see where we stood.

I mainly played some outfield, pitched, and caught. I didn't catch until I started playing Legion. Our three main catchers were Karch, Terry Farver, and myself. It was fun to catch, and we definitely had some different style pitchers. Mike Roland was a pinpoint strike-thrower; Brad Gilbert was similar; he could throw with decent velocity, and he had a pretty good curve ball. Arlin Kaul had some kind of crazy curve or sinker ball that made it hard to catch. Pete Dighans was a strike thrower with good velocity. Paul Shaffer was a good strike-thrower. Another good, solid stud pitcher was John Richardson. The best pitcher I ever caught was Kevin Nelson; he was a big, strong guy who could throw hard and just plain overpower other teams. He did have a decent curve, but his fastball was probably the first I saw that the ball had movement on it, which made it tough to hit.

The Don Lekvold Era

Playing so many games against Wolf Point from Babe Ruth on really made you respect their team. The team that won the state championship and went on to Idaho was the best team we ever faced, in my opinion. There were some real studs on that team. Troy Cody, Kenny Azure, and Austin Barr were some good pitchers we faced, and they just plain had some real athletes on that team. I always respected Mike Neubauer; he was such a great coach and the players he had played at an extra level that I don't know they would have if he wasn't coaching them.

It seemed like Glasgow always had some good teams, just not the studs that Wolf Point had. John Fischer from Glasgow had a great arm and could throw really hard, so when we faced him, we knew we were going to have our hands full.

I don't think my brother Ken pitched that much in Legion, but one game I do remember is when we went to Williston to play a doubleheader against the Keybirds. They had a field that resembled Fenway Park and the Green Monster. I was catching, and I'm pretty sure Ken came in in relief. Ken threw a fastball, and the Keybird smacked that ball well over the green monster. I grabbed my mask and turned around, shaking my head and kind of giggling over how far that guy hit it. The reason I know my reaction is because the Williston NBC news was there, and that is the highlight they showed on the news that night.

There are so many good memories from playing baseball. Scobey was a baseball town because of the players and the success before I played. It was an honor to wear the Scobey Blues jacket; that really meant something back then. As with all things in life, we move on, but some of the great memories I have revolve around the Wiffle ball games, the pickup games at the park, and all the games we played growing up. I have lifelong friends that I either was teammates with or played baseball against. It seems if I run into someone, a common topic of conversation is baseball from the Blues of Summer.

I know there weren't a lot of baseball stories, but thank you for the opportunity to give you a few. I'm sure I will think of more as I read your posts. Thanks for putting this book together; it is awesome the history of the other ball teams from other communities you have included. A lot of those names spark memories. I hope to see you next year at the Blues get-together over the all-class reunion.

Mike Lee remembers the day he missed second base on his home run in Circle. "I actually tripped and bit the dust before I reached second base. But the one-armed umpire still gave me a milkshake."

Ken Meyer remembers the soaring home run he surrendered in Williston. "There was a rec center behind the outfield fence that they played hockey in. The ball landed on top of it. I know I met the guy who hit it because I played college baseball there. I'll admit it was a bomb! One of my college teammates did the same thing in a game."

1989

An Upset by Plentywood at Divisionals Leaves the Blues Wanting to "Shout at the Devil"

> *Even if we pitched a 16-year-old against Plentywood, we should have won 10 out of 10 games against them. I'm still not sure how we lost—just a miserable day!*
>
> —Ken Meyer, Scobey Blues (1987–1990)

PRESEASON

1989 Scobey Blues. In front, left to right: Kevin Nelson, Tom Aldrich, John Ray Richardson, Scott Kanning, Terry Farver. Middle row left to right: Todd Sayler, Bart Conger, Arlin Kaul, Justin Fossum, Greg Olson. Standing, left to right: Assistant Coach Mike Roland, Ryan Linder, Assistant Coach Gary Meyer, Mike Lee, Ken Meyer, Coach Don Lekvold. *Borderland photo.*

Coach Don Lekvold was missing five experienced veterans—Paul Shaffer, Brad Gilbert, Rod Hudyma, Jeff Jones, and Ron Meyer—when he assembled his team in 1989. Scobey would return two players in their final year, Tom Aldrich and Arlin Kaul. Joining the team from Peerless that year was 18-year-old John Ray Richardson, who would provide much-needed help on the mound as a pitcher. The team that Don Lekvold continued to develop year-over-year now included a seasoned crop of veteran 17-year-olds: Mike Lee, Ken Meyer, Terry Farver, and Kevin Nelson. Ryan Linder and Greg Olson were also returning. Todd Sayler, Bart Conger, Scott Kanning, and Justin Fossum joined the team as rookies. Although the team had many returning players, the overall experience level was low. Ken Meyer, Arlin Kaul, Kevin Nelson, Terry Farver, and Mike Lee were the only five to see significant playing time in 1988 before the 1989 season. Coach Lekvold and his two assistants—Gary Meyer and Mike Roland (Blues 1984–87)—would have their work cut out, molding a team to get to the state tournament in 1989.

Kevin Nelson would anchor the pitching staff, with Ryan Linder, Mike Lee, Greg Olson, John Richardson, Arlin Kaul, and Ken Meyer all seeing action. Mike Lee handled the staff behind the plate, with Tom Aldrich and Kevin Nelson also sharing catching duties.

REGULAR SEASON

A highlight of the 1989 regular season was when Kevin Nelson pitched the seventh—and last—no-hitter in Scobey American Legion Baseball history. It happened in the first game of a doubleheader against Circle in early June. Scobey won the game by the ten-run rule in the fifth inning. Don Lekvold remembers, "Most of the outs were strikeouts." What was unique about Kevin's no-hitter was that he also pitched the second game of the doubleheader. Mike Lee remembers, "The Circle guys were pissed he threw both games!" Why did Kevin pitch the second game? Kevin said, "I was going to Boys State in Dillon, so I was going to be gone for a week." Apparently, Don Lekvold thought he needed the work. Good for Scobey; bad for Circle.

One of the highlights of every regular season for the Blues was playing in the annual Doc Norman Memorial Tournament, which Scobey hosted for the fifth time in 1989. Good teams would come to play in Scobey, which was tough competition for the Blues. In 1989, Williston, Lewistown, Laurel, and Wolf Point joined Scobey in the round-robin tournament. Here are the highlights of the tournament:

- R. C. Page of Wolf Point hit the very first pitch of the tournament over the fence to get the tourney off to a dramatic start. He hit .545 in the tourney and claimed the offensive MVP title. Scobey's first baseman, Justin Fossum, earned the defensive trophy. The *Leader* stated he won the trophy "by turning a number of potential errors into outs and coming up with other outstanding plays in the field."[41]
- Scobey went 2-2 in the tourney, losing to Williston and Laurel but beating Lewistown and Wolf Point. The Laurel Dodgers claimed the title trophy with a 3-1 record. Williston also ended up 3-1, but their loss to Laurel was the tiebreaker.
- John Richardson of the Blues gave a close chase for the tournament batting title with a .533 average. Three other Blues—Ken Meyer, Mike Lee, and Terry Farver—hit at an even .500 pace.

With several inexperienced players on the roster, the Blues' regular season started slow, and the Blues were below the middle of the seven-team conference standings in midseason, but a pivotal point of the season came when the Blues traveled over the 4th of July weekend to play in the Redbird Invitational at Symmes Park. The defending state champion Bitterroot Bucs, the Havre Northstars, the Glendive Blue Devils, and host Lewistown were there. Playing tougher competition makes you better, and that is precisely what happened at Symmes Park.

The Blues lost some games in Lewistown but improved. Mike Lee recalls the game against the defending champion Bucs. "We lost the game, but I still think it was a really close game—a low-scoring pitcher's duel. Bitterroot was the team to beat in '88, '89, and '90. I just remember feeling good after the game, and the rest of July, we played a lot better—until the divisional tournament."

After the Redbird Invitational, Scobey had an overall record of 13-17, but then got hot and turned it around. The Blues began to climb the ladder in the conference standings. Mike Lee recalls the change: "We did get hot in the second half of the season. Tom Aldrich had sat out the season before, and John Ray Richardson came home from college and decided he wanted to play Legion baseball for the first time. The two of them were a little rusty to start the year, but they turned it on in the second half. Then, the other three starters had never played Legion until that year, so up until about the first or second week in July, sixth through ninth in the batting order struggled, but then after the 4th of July Tournament in Lewistown we started playing better."

On the season's final weekend, the Blues beat Wolf Point 10-9, as Kevin Nelson and Ryan Linder each went 3 for 5, and Kevin Nelson and Terry Farver hit home runs to lead Scobey's 16-hit attack. Kevin Nelson and Mike Lee pitched. The Blues then swept Sidney in a doubleheader in Scobey, winning 11-1 and 10-7. Ryan Linder threw a three-hitter in the opener, Nelson went 4 for 4 and Farver 2 for 3, and the defense committed no errors. Greg Olson and John Richardson pitched in the second game, and Mike Lee got hot at the plate, going 4 for 4 with a homer. In his four trips, Ken Meyer added a double, a triple, and two walks.

With the three wins, the Blues ended their regular season winning 9 of their last 10 games, finishing with a 22-18 overall record and a 15-9 conference record, good enough for third place. Final conference standings were Glendive 18-6, Sidney 16-8, Scobey 15-9, Wolf Point 14-10, Glasgow 12-12, Plentywood 5-19, and Circle 4-20. Coach Don Lekvold said, "The boys have been hitting well the past few weeks, and the pitching staff is steady, with good depth." Four regulars ended the regular season with batting averages above .300, led by Ken Meyer's .374. Tom Aldrich, Mike Lee, and Terry Farver were the other leaders. The team batting average was a respectable .287.

The Blues had picked a good time to get hot; Scobey was firing on all cylinders heading into divisional. Momentum was important heading into the postseason. The *Leader* wrote, "The Blues have come on strong and are feeling optimistic going into the divisional tournament. With their strong finish, they feel they should be one of the two teams to advance to the State Legion tourney."[42]

Coach Don Lekvold and the Blues were hopeful they could finish among the top two teams in the division and "make some noise at State," but their old nemesis and rival, Plentywood, would have other ideas.

DIVISIONAL TOURNAMENT

THE GLENDIVE BLUE DEVILS HOSTED THE 1989 EASTERN Divisional Tournament at Meissner Memorial Field in Glendive. Scobey, the three-seed, played Plentywood, the six-seed, in their first game. Here were the opening-day matchups.

- Scobey (3) vs. Plentywood (6)
- Sidney (2) vs. Circle (7)
- Wolf Point (4) vs. Glasgow (5)
- Glendive (1) Bye

The Blues were hot, but as anyone who has played sports knows, the postseason can be completely different from the regular season. Sometimes, a team can limp into the postseason and get hot; other times, it can be hot and crater in the postseason. Ask the 1985 Havre Northstars about that. Unfortunately for Scobey, the Blues' run at the end of the season did not carry over into the postseason.

Part of the problem was some off-the-field drama the week of the divisional tournament. Two starters decided to go to the Mötley Crüe concert in Billings on the Tuesday of divisional week. They missed three practices, so Coach Lekvold benched them in the first game against Plentywood. Coach Lekvold told them they would not start or play the first game if they went to the concert. They went—and didn't start.

Sixth-seeded Plentywood shocked Scobey 5-4 in the tournament opener, relegating the Blues to the dirt route before they were barely unpacked. Mike Lee and Ken Meyer accounted for all the Blues' runs and RBIs, but four runs were not enough to win. Losing to Plentywood left Mike Lee and Ken Meyer wanting to "shout at the devil." Mike Lee said, "I was not upset with the coach's decision, and I was not upset with my two buddies going to Crüe. But I was beyond frustrated we lost to fucking Plentywood!" Ken Meyer added, "I'm not sure about the actual game stats, but even if we pitched a 16-year-old against them, we should have won 10 out of 10 games against them. I'm still not sure how we lost—just a miserable day!"

Scobey was not the only victim of an upset on opening day, as seventh-seeded Circle stunned second-seeded Sidney 6-5. Plentywood and Circle had a combined record of 9-39 in conference play. Call it July Madness. (Or maybe Sidney had some players at the Mötley Crüe concert, too?)

With the two players back from their one-game suspension, Scobey recovered in its second game, handily beating second-seeded Sidney 11-3. Had the first-round games gone according to the seedings, the two teams would have been playing in the winner's bracket, but with the two upsets, the second- and third-seeded teams were now facing elimination. Kevin Nelson started and got the win, with John Ray Richardson coming on in relief. Kevin Nelson, Mike Lee, and Ken Meyer each had two hits to lead Scobey's hitting.

But the Blues couldn't get anything going in their next game against Jack Sprague of Wolf Point, as the Yellowjackets won 12-2 in seven innings. Sprague pitched a complete game, while Torrence Clark had a two-run homer for the Jackets. Wolf Point went on to make it to the championship game, losing to top-seeded Glendive, 10-7. Both teams advanced to State.

Although Wolf Point failed to three-peat as Divisional champions, they qualified for State for the third consecutive year.

And that was all she wrote for Scobey in 1989. It was another disappointing season-ending that showed promise for a run at State, especially after the Blues closed the regular season by winning 9 of 10 games and finished third in the conference. Ken Meyer reflected on the 1989 season: "1989 was a weird year. We lost a lot of talent off of the '88 team. Our dedication just didn't seem to be there. We were coming off a berth into the semifinals for the first time ever in football and knew we were going to have a solid team coming up for our senior year. We were actually doing some summer training, lifting weights, etc., to get ready for it, which had never happened before when baseball season was going on. In a nutshell, our talent, top to bottom, was just not there. Throw in the lack of dedication to the game itself, and it is easy to be mediocre. We lost our first game of the divisional tournament to Plentywood, which should never have happened."

But the *Leader*, as always, was optimistic about the next season: "Scobey fielded a young team this year (only three players—Arlin Kaul, John Richardson, and Tom Aldrich—were aging out), and with several new boys expected from the Babe Ruth program, the Blues are planning to be a top contender next year."[43] Indeed, four strong veterans were returning, as Mike Lee, Ken Meyer, Kevin Nelson, and Terry Farver would be playing in their final season. Could 1990 be the year the Blues return to their winning ways, qualify for state, and make some noise at State? It had been a long time for the Blues . . . too long.

STATE TOURNAMENT

THE STATE A TOURNAMENT WAS HOSTED ON GRIFFIN FIELD in Kalispell for the first time. Glendive and Wolf Point represented the east. Both programs were solid year-over-year in the late 1980s, as Glendive had won the state tournament in Scobey in 1985 and Wolf Point in 1987. Under third-year Coach Mike Neubauer, the Yellowjackets were making their third consecutive state tournament appearance and had overachieved, considering they had lost eight starters from the previous season. After losing their first game to the Missoula Reds, 10-8, Wolf Point came back to win their three straight games—17-7 over Havre, 12-7 over Lewistown, and 13-11 over Missoula—before being eliminated by Vauxhall 13-3. Vauxhall's 16-year-old left-handed pitcher Troy Cleland—who would shut out the Blues in the undefeated state semifinal at State the following year in 1990—pitched a three-hitter for Vauxhall to end Wolf Point's season. Wolf Point took fourth at State and finished with a 26-18 record. The East's top seed, the Glendive Blue Devils, were eliminated in two games.

The Bitterroot Bucs, led by first-year coach Bubba Townsend—who had played on the Bucs' state championship team the year before—repeated as State champions, shelling Laurel in the state championship game, 17-2. Bitterroot's repeat state championship in 1988 was the first since Scobey's five consecutive state championships from 1976 to 1980. Bucs shortstop and pitcher Jason Goligoski, the second-leading hitter in the tournament at .571, was named MVP.

NORTHWEST REGIONAL

THE BUCS WERE ELIMINATED IN TWO GAMES AT THE NORTHwest Regional in Yakima, but Bitterroot's repeat state championship—the first since Scobey repeated from 1976–80—was a sign that the power in Class A American Legion Baseball had indeed shifted to the west and portended future western dominance.

EXTRA INNINGS

REFLECTING ON HIS 34-YEAR COACHING CAREER, COACH NEUbauer thought 1989 might have been his best year ever. "We lost eight starters from the 1988 team and took second to Glendive at divisional; they were tough. The state was in Kalispell. I think we lost our first game and then came back through the dirt to take fourth, and that was the last of the sportsmanship awards. When I look back, I think that might have been my most successful season. I coached a total of 34 years, from Tee-ball to Legion, and 10 years of girls' fast-pitch." Sportswriter Steve Stiffarm of the *Wotanin Wowapi* recognized the stellar year Coach Neubauer and the Yellowjackets had: "With their fine showing and displays of outstanding sportsmanship (as was indicated by many tournament-goers), the Yellowjackets deserve a pat on the back for a job well done not only in Kalispell but all year long."[44] The three-peat as the best sportsmanship trophy at the State A Tournament might be unprecedented and might never have been repeated since.

A lot of the Scobey Blues had played for Coach Neubauer for the Hi-Line All-Stars in Babe Ruth when they were younger, so they were familiar with his hard-nosed coaching style. Mike Lee recalls a story when he was playing Coach Neubauer when he was 13 years old: "Coach got so pissed at our catcher during the semifinal game he yelled out, 'Has anybody else on this team ever fucking caught before?' I sheepishly raised my hand, and he replied, 'Get the gear on.' So Mike proceeded to throw me dirt balls the next three innings in the bullpen while we were batting. I caught the rest of that game and every one after that. He beat the shit out of me, teaching me how to block balls." When I interviewed Mike, I asked him if he remembered that. He said, "Yes, I remember that, probably only because he reminds me every time we get together. Hi-line All-Stars, you have like one week of practice with kids you don't even know. True story—he was my catcher for the rest of the tournament."

Kevin Nelson's no-hitter in the first game of the doubleheader against Circle was the last in Scobey Blues history. Here are the nine Scobey Blues no-hitters:

- Bob Schaefer vs. Poplar, 1931 (Scobey 10-0. Bob struck out 20)
- Gary Davies vs. Flaxville-Whitetail, 1956 (Scobey 6-1)
- Kevin Sell vs. Flaxville-Whitetail, district championship, 1959 (Scobey 7-0)
- Bill "Oscar" Thompson vs. Sidney, 1963 (Scobey 4-3)
- Duke Trangsrud vs. Plentywood, 1975 (Scobey 8-2)
- Duke Trangsrud vs. Frazer, 1975 (Scobey 15-0)
- Ray Chapman vs. Poplar, 1978 (Scobey 11-0), seven innings
- Kirby Halvorson, Ron Higgins, Grant Hughes, Gord Tryan, and Jeff Mann (combined no-hitter) vs. Miles City Colts, 1980 (Scobey 18-3), five innings
- Kevin Nelson vs. Circle, 1989 (Scobey 10-0), five innings

For the Plainsmen no-hitters, in 1954, Vern Veis pitched a no-hit shutout and struck out 18 in a 10-0 win over Mineral Bench. Jack Reiner recalled catching three no-hitters for Vern in his Plainsmen career.

Ken Meyer remembers a bizarre event in the Scobey-Bitterroot game at the Redbird Invitational at Symmes Park in Lewistown. "Kevin Nelson was pitching, and he gave up a home run. However, a balk was called, and the home run was waived off. The very next pitch, the batter hit another home run—back-to-back pitches. I've never seen or heard of that ever happening before or after. I believe it was the only home run Kevin gave up in Legion ball." Kevin Nelson thought the home runs were given up against Lewistown. "I used to think I remembered everything, but apparently, this event is foggy. It's something you want to forget." Mike Lee added, "I believe Jason Goligoski hit those two home runs. He went on to play in the minor leagues." The homer-balk-homer sequence in the same at-bat might be the only time in baseball history!

Mike Lee remembers a funny story that happened at the Scobey Ball Park that season. "We decided to gut out and clean up the old 'Clubhouse' below the grandstand. We were juniors that year, so after prom, we took all of the black, heavy plastic and stapled/nailed it to the roof to stop the rainwater from coming. Well, through the course of the year, *dirty, filthy* rainwater started to accumulate in the plastic roof, creating huge bulges. Before a game, we were all down there getting dressed in our white tops, and

Bart Conger was all dressed, sitting in one of the recliners right below one of the bulges. All of a sudden, we hear this whoosh, and Bart got about 10 to 15 gallons of that dirty water dumped on him!!! Absolutely priceless the look on his face and everyone bursting out in laughter. We also had an old 8-track player and speakers for music. We must have listened to KISS's *God of Thunder* 50-plus times that summer.

The *Leader* was always aware of how well Scobey could host a tournament. Following the 1989 Doc Norman Memorial Tournament, it stated, "The annual round-robin at Scobey Ball Park was well attended, and the concession stands were busy. Favorable comments were forthcoming from a number of visitors on the ballpark, concessions, officiating, and the general handling of the tournament."[45]

Micky Williams again took over as head coach of the Northstars in 1989. He led the Northstars to the state tournament but was eliminated by Wolf Point. Mick would be the head coach of the Northstars from 1989 through 2006. He had coached the Northstars previously and would assume the reins again after 2006, but this was his longest tenure (18 years) as head coach of Havre.

Arlin Kaul's last season was the 1989 season. I have a special baseball memory of Buddy, Arlin's dad, a highway patrolman. Some of the pitchers on our 1978 team wanted to know how fast we could throw, but we'd never had a gun on us before. Guns on pitchers weren't really a thing back then, so Dad (or Doc) arranged for Buddy to bring his radar gun to the ballfield one night at practice. He stood behind the backstop and pointed his gun at the pitcher's mound, and several of us pitchers—me, Kelly Norman, Dan Danelson, Jon Puckett, Kirby Halvorson, Ray Chapman, Randy Stolen—started to uncork fastballs toward the gun, hoping to be the next Nolan Ryan. We were all disappointed at what the gun was registering—I remember thinking after the session that if I made the bigs, it would have to be as a shortstop and not a pitcher. But Kelly Norman thinks the guns are faster now. "The guns now are about three miles an hour faster than they were back then. Nolan Ryan would have been clocked at a hundred and seven at times."

Dr. Kirby Halvorson, always technical, weighed in on the speed-gun topic: "Both police and baseball radar guns work on a Doppler radar concept. Thus, the mass of the object one is measuring may have an impact. Technology nowadays is much better, so modern-day guns are likely more sensitive. Another important concept is that in the past, the velocity was formerly measured as the ball crossed the plate, whereas currently, values are determined as the ball leaves the pitcher's hand. So, we would expect some velocity decay by the time the pitch nears the plate. This may explain some of the discrepancies between the past and present. Another more cynical explanation is that the current guns are hyped to give higher values because our society is conditioned to believe more is better."

I will go with Kelly and Kirby and think my fastball would have been recorded at least three miles per hour faster today than it was on Buddy Kaul's radar gun in 1978. Still not good enough to make the bigs, though. I do, however, remember watching the Boston Red Sox play the Baltimore Orioles at Oriole Park at Camden Yards in September 2002, and pitcher John Burkett, at the tail end of his 15-year major league career, started for the Red Sox. Burkett threw eight shutout innings against the Orioles that day and got the win—his fastball topped out at 83 mph on the electronic scoreboard. I was watching it every pitch. He kept the Orioles' hitters off-balance with his curveball, changeup, and good control. I remember rooting for him every pitch he delivered—the guy with the 83-mph fastball got it done. I doubt we'll ever see another pitcher like John Burkett in the majors again with modern-day analytics. When he was in his prime, his fastball barely scratched 90. As Justin Verlander of the Houston Astros said, "Starting pitchers are being told to throw as hard as they can for as long as they can."

Crafty pitchers who get outs with off-speed pitches—like John Burkett and knuckleball pitchers—have been a dying breed in baseball. There is only one knuckleballer left in the game today, Matt Waldron of the San Diego Padres. Why is that? In an article titled "Why There's No Market in MLB for the Knuckleball," sportswriter Kevin Maney wrote, "It comes down to market perception. The market has been conditioned to dismiss the knuckleballer in favor of flame-throwing fastballers."

In the article, Maney interviewed former knuckleballer Tom "Candy" Candiotti and asked him why he thought the knuckleballers were dying. Tom said, "Most baseball people seem to think the knuckleball's disadvantages outweigh the advantages, so there's a negative spiral at work. The major leagues send the message that they only want hard throwers, so only kids who throw hard tend to become pitchers. No prospect is going to waste time practicing the knuckleball, so it becomes more scarce. Fewer coaches get comfortable with it, so the anti-knuckleball message gets stronger."

I miss the knuckleballers—and all the crafty pitchers who threw less than 90 and were successful and got outs, like John Burkett that day in Baltimore.

1990

The Blues Take Third at State

> *When the billboard went up behind the right field fence, showing all the years that the Blues won a State championship, it was a dream of mine/ours to someday have a year that represented when we played. Karch and I had discussed this. 1990 was a year that we had that chance. When we didn't capture the title in baseball, it hurt, but I can honestly say we put it all on the line. No regrets about how we played.*
>
> —Ken Meyer, Scobey Blues (1987–1990)

PRESEASON

Could 1990 be the year Coach Don Lekvold and the Blues broke through in the east? Scobey's last eastern divisional championship was in 1982, and their last outright qualification for the state tournament was in 1984 when they took fourth at divisional. In 1985, the Blues—who took third at State in Scobey—had only qualified as host. Scobey's hopes in 1990 hinged on the leadership and play of four returning three-year starters—Ken Meyer, Mike "Karch" Lee, Kevin Nelson, and Terry Farver—who had won a lot of games during the regular seasons but had experienced heartache and disappointment in the divisional tournaments in 1987-89.

Also returning were starters Ryan Linder and Justin Fossum. Justin would sustain an early-season knee injury, tearing his ACL, and would miss most of the season until Divisionals, when he was able to return to the starting lineup with a special brace on his knee.

For Scobey to win, the leadership and play of the four 18-year-olds were key, as were the contributions of second-year players Linder and Fossum. But it takes nine players to win—not six.

Enter a talented rookie crop for the Blues. In its final edition of 1989, the *Leader* mentioned that "several new boys from the Babe Ruth program" were expected to join the team in 1990. Who were these boys? Talented 16-year-old rookies Derek Solberg, Steve Stephenson, Mick Mueller, Rob Fladager, Brent Tarum, Ryan Oie, Scott Nelson, Lee Hackman, and Ben Hoversland. This baseball-savvy group now had joined the Blues to help them win a State championship in 1990. Yes, we are talking about the possibility of a state championship in 1990. The 1990 team was a composite mix of battle-tested veterans—frustrated in the postseason for three years and hungry to win—and a talented crop of young rookies looking to help contribute. In describing his team, Don Lekvold said, "We are a little young, but all our kids are good ballplayers. We know that our young players will come in and do a good job for us right away."

And they did.

Kevin Nelson would be the ace for the all-important pitching, and Mike Lee would become Don Lekvold's second go-to pitcher, followed by Ryan Linder. Steve Stephenson, Ryan Oie, and Brent Tarum would also see plenty of action as the season progressed and into the postseason. Don Lekvold had more depth at pitching than he had had for years. For the third year, Mike Lee would catch everything behind the plate.

Mike Roland again assisted Coach Lekvold in 1990.

Mike Lee remembers the start of the baseball 1990 season was different from previous years. "There was a different mindset to the start of the season," Mike said. "I think some of it carried over from the success we had in football, basketball, and track. Also, Kevin, Ken, and I were heading off to college in the fall to continue playing sports. But I think the biggest reason is we knew by far we had the best team coming back. One other factor was that Glendive was the host team for State so only one team out of the other seven was going to go to State. Wolf Point was the only team capable that year of keeping us from advancing. They had one of the best coaches in the state (Mike Neubauer) and a pretty deep pitching staff."

Ken Meyer agreed about a different feeling when starting the season. "We knew it was our last chance to win a state title, so our focus/dedication was definitely ratcheted up a notch from the previous year. Karch, Kevin, Terry, and I all had plenty of experience playing Legion. However, once Greg Olson entered into the National Guard, that left us pretty short-handed as far as any experience. Ryan Linder and Justin Fossum were the only two 17-year-olds, I believe, and the rest of the roster was all 16-year-olds."

Kevin Nelson echoed Mike and Ken's sentiments. "I also feel that there was excitement going into the year partly because of the talent we did have coming in in the 16-year-olds, which was from my memory, Ryan Oie, Derek Solberg, Robin Fladager, Brent Tarum, Ben Hoversland, Mick Mueller, and my brother Scott Nelson. We actually got some very good pitching from Brent and Steve Stephenson that year, also. Our lineup usually consisted of 2 to 3 of them playing consistently. Also, the leadership of this group was a little bit different than in years past, and the young ones had a lot of respect for the 17-and 18-year-olds. There still was a lot of dick-off, but we all knew what we were there to accomplish, and when things needed to be serious, they were serious."

Let the season begin—for the old and the new.

REGULAR SEASON

COACH DON LEKVOLD PLANNED AN AGGRESSIVE 38-GAME regular-season schedule in just 42 days to prepare the team to win the Division and be a state championship contender. The schedule opened with a doubleheader against Glasgow in Scobey, and the Blues sprinted out of the gate looking good, as Kevin Nelson pitched a two-hitter and Ryan Linder fired a four-hitter to lead Scobey to two impressive wins, 13-1 and 15-0. Nelson recorded nine strikeouts and drove in four runs in the opener, and he and Terry Farver each had two hits. In the second game, Ken Meyer led the hitting, driving in four runs with a double and a triple. Derek Solberg was 2-2, and Steve Stephenson was 1-2 with two runs scored. Linder fanned nine in his shutout in the second game. This opening-day sweep of Glasgow was a promising start for the Blues, as the veteran players and younger players both needed to play well for this team to be successful.

Here are some other highlights of the 38-game schedule:

- Mike Lee remembers an unfortunate early-season injury to Lee (Hackman) Malone. "He was starting in left field for us in May and June. He was batting ninth and was the perfect number nine batter. Then, sometime in June, he went to throw the ball into short from left field. When he reached down to grab the ball that was against the fence, his thumb got caught in the chicken wire, and he tore the ligaments in his thumb, and he was done for the season. He was the biggest surprise up to that point into the season, and in my opinion, left us scrambling to replace him both defensively and in the number nine spot. The kid was playing above his talent level and anyone's expectations. I felt bad for him when it happened. Up to that point in his sports career, he really wasn't that noticeable. Nice kid average player. So, getting a chance to start for the Blues as a 16-year-old was huge for Lee (Hacker, Rat, Russ). Kid had a few nicknames."

- Coach Lekvold took the Blues to the Maybelle Arthur Tournament in Dillon in early June. The five teams participating were the Idaho Falls Reds, Wolf Point Yellowjackets, Laurel Dodgers, Scobey, and the host Dillon Cubs—all good teams. Scobey won their opener over Idaho Falls 11-10, as they rallied for four runs in the top of the seventh to overcome a 10-7 deficit. Rob Fladager had an RBI double, and Ryan Linder hit a two-run double to bring Scobey back. Kevin Nelson and Ken Meyer smacked back-to-back homers for Scobey earlier in the game. Before their last games, Ken Meyer and Mike Lee had to leave for a week of practice to prepare for the annual Treasure State Class C All-Star Football game in Butte. Scobey then lost to Dillon and Wolf Point before the tournament was rained out on the last day. After Ken and Mike left, Coach Lekvold was able to experiment with different lineups and pitchers during the tournament, and the entire roster saw action in the three games. His goal in the tournament was to develop his team, not to win it.

- A week later, Wolf Point beat Scobey 21-4 in the championship game of the Sixth Annual Doc Norman Memorial Tournament in Scobey, but the Blues were short-handed, as Ken Meyer and Mike Lee played in the seventh annual Treasure State Class C All-Star Football game in Butte that weekend. The Yellowjackets dominated the tournament, taking home every trophy. Ryan Miller was voted the best defensive player of the tournament. He pitched eight innings and allowed only one hit. Mark Worley won the batting title, hitting .642. This was the second tournament in a row the Jackets had won, as Wolf Point also won the Maybelle Arthur Tournament in Dillon. Although the Blues were shorthanded without Mike and Ken, Kevin Nelson thought that, as a result, the younger players were able to develop. "As I look back, I believe our young kids grew up a lot that weekend with a lot of experience in a lot of different ways."

- The Blues then won an all-important conference game 9-6 over the Wolf Point Yellowjackets, who they knew they would have to beat to win the eastern conference and the eastern division. It was good to see the 1970s Scobey-Wolf Point best-in-the-East friendly rivalry back in northeastern Montana. Coach Mike Neubauer, now in his fourth season as head coach of the Yellowjackets, had lost only two starters—neither of them pitchers—from the 1989 team, which finished 26-18 and won three games at State, finishing fourth. In his four years at Wolf Point, Coach Neubauer had developed an elite program with talented players. The Yellowjackets won the state championship in 1987, the Division championship in 1987 and 1988, and they had played at State all three years. In its preview of Wolf Point at the Maybelle Arthur Tournament, the *Dillon Tribune* wrote that the Yellowjackets were "always one of the toughest teams in the east."[47] Mike Neubauer said of his 1990 version, "This is the most intelligent team I have ever coached. You tell them how to do something and they do it right the first time. They really work well together." This conference win for Scobey was huge, proving to themselves they could beat the best in the east.

- In other conference matchups between Wolf Point and Scobey, the Yellowjackets topped Scobey 12-6 and 11-6, with pitcher Jack Sprague getting both wins for Wolf Point. Wolf Point was trailing 6-2 in the second game but scored seven runs in the top of the eighth and added two more in the ninth to win 11-6. Scobey then beat Wolf Point by an identical score of 11-6, with Scott Nelson and Derek Solberg each having three hits, and Mick Mueller added a two-run homer. In the final conference game between the two rivals, Scobey won 6-5, beating Wolf Point pitcher Darin Miller, who was undefeated up to that point. Terry Farver hit a line-drive two-run homer which proved to be the game-winner in his final regular season game at Scobey. Ryan Oie and Steve Stephenson pitched. Of the Wolf Point games, Kevin Nelson said, "The Wolf Point games always carried a little more emphasis as they were guys we played with in Hi-Line All-Stars, and their team was coming off of three great years, and they were kind of who was standing between us and a trip to State because Glendive had the automatic bid as host."

- As they had done the previous three seasons, Scobey finished the regular season strong, winning 7 of their last 8 games. In their end-of-season run, the Blues swept Circle in two close games, 5-4 and 12-10. Mike Lee went the distance in the first game and hit a homer. In the second game, the Blues won the slugfest as Ryan Linder, Kevin Nelson, and Terry Farver each had two hits. The Blues then swept Glendive to clinch a tie for second place in the conference, winning 10-9 and 12-3. Ryan Linder and Brent Tarum pitched the opener, and Ken Meyer and Ryan Oie led the team with two hits each. Steve Stephenson went the distance in the second game and Scobey had six hitters with two hits each. Scobey then split a doubleheader with Plentywood, losing the opener 10-6 but winning the second end 12-9. Brent Tarum, Ryan Oie, and Kevin Nelson pitched in the first game, and Kevin Nelson, Scott Nelson, and Ken Meyer each had two hits. In the second game, Ben Hoversland went the distance, and Terry Farver had three hits in four at-bats to lead the Blues' hitting.

Scobey finished the regular season 18-6 in the conference and 27-11 overall, but despite their 18 conference wins and two wins over Wolf Point, they were not enough, as the Yellowjackets finished 19-5 in the conference—one game better than Scobey—winning the title for the third time in four years. Wolf Point was also one game better than Scobey overall, as they had a 28-10 record. As a result, the Yellowjackets earned the top seed and a first-round bye in the eastern divisional tournament. Final conference standings had Wolf Point in first, followed closely by Scobey, the Glendive, Circle, Plentywood, Malta, and Glasgow. Richland County did not field a team in 1990.

Regarding Scobey's end-of-season 7-1 run, *Leader* wrote, "The Blues look in peak form for the divisional tournament."[48] The conference wins over Wolf Point and end-of-season run were nice, but we had seen this movie before—Scobey had beaten Wolf Point during the regular season the previous three years and finished strong, only to falter in the postseason. Would 1990 be different? Could Scobey end their seven-year drought and win a Divisional championship?

The 1990 season "felt" different. This was the end of the road for three-year starters Mike Lee, Ken Meyer, Kevin Nelson, and Terry Farver. It was now or never. The Blues were playing at home, had momentum, had beaten the best in the east twice, and Don Lekvold had played a 38-game schedule preparing them for this moment.

It was time to step up to the plate and get it done.

DIVISIONAL TOURNAMENT

The eastern divisional tournament was held at Scobey for the sixth time. The *Leader* welcomed the seven teams to Scobey in its leadup edition, with Banjo's 109 sponsoring the tournament bracket, which looked like this:

- Circle (4) vs. Plentywood (5)
- Wolf Point (1) Bye
- Glendive (3) vs. Malta (6)
- Scobey (2) vs. Glasgow (7)

Normally, the top two teams in the east advanced to the state tournament, but since Glendive was hosting, Scobey (or Wolf Point or any other team) had to win the Divisional tournament to advance. The only exception would have been if Glendive made it to the championship game. So Scobey had to win it to advance—lose, and it was over.

The Blues got off to a great start in their first game, mercy-ruling Glasgow 12-2 in seven innings. Ryan Oie went the distance, striking out 12 Reds and issuing only two walks. Ken Meyer was 3 for 4 at the plate. Scobey committed only two errors in the game, which represented the team's season play. The 1990 team had a solid defense, one of the keys to their success.

Scobey then beat Glendive 10-4, with Ryan Linder, Kevin Nelson, and Mike Lee each pitching three innings, combining for 13 strikeouts. Justin Fossum, back from his injury, went 4 for 5, went 4 for 5, and Terry Farver 3 for 5 to lead Scobey's hitting. The Blues again played well defensively, committing only one error.

Scobey then faced top-seeded Wolf Point in the undefeated semifinal. Coach Lekvold handed the ball to his ace, Kevin Nelson, to pitch Scobey to the championship game, and he was brilliant, striking out 13 Yellowjackets in six innings of work, leading Scobey to a 16-4 mercy-rule win in seven innings. Steve Stephenson came in to pitch the last inning. Ken Meyer had three hits—including a two-run home run—and Kevin Nelson and Terry Farver each had three hits to lead Scobey's 16-hit mauling of Wolf Point pitching. But after three convincing wins, the Blues weren't done. They couldn't be. Wolf Point had come back through the loser's bracket, and Glendive had been eliminated, so the Blues needed to win the Divisional championship at home to advance to State.

In the championship game, the Blues jumped on Wolf Point for 12 runs in the second inning and continued the onslaught, drubbing Wolf Point 24-7 in nine innings (there was no ten-run rule in the championship game). Brent Tarum pitched the first two innings and Steve Stephenson the final seven to get the win. Ken Meyer led Scobey's hit barrage, going a perfect 5 for 5 with a two-run homer, his second of the tournament. Ryan Linder was also perfect at the plate, going 4 for 4. Kevin Nelson added three hits. With the large margin of victory against the team they knew they needed to beat to make it to State, the championship game was anticlimactic, but I am sure Coach Lekvold and the players didn't mind blowout, as this team had seen enough drama in previous postseason tournaments.

Ken Meyer remembers a great gesture of sportsmanship in the blowout Divisional championship game against Wolf Point in Scobey. "We were destroying Wolf Point. We didn't want to rub it in because we knew all those guys really well. I got a hit and was on first base. I told Marc Wholery, their first baseman, to have the pitcher throw it over to him to pick me off. I did dive back into the base but was out by a mile. I just got up and ran back to the dugout. We respected those guys and Coach Neubauer. It sucked that they didn't get to participate in the state tourney. They would have made some noise."

Coach Neubauer said this about not being able to go to State. "It was very disappointing because we hadn't peaked yet. Scobey was tougher than hell. Kevin Nelson was a fierce competitor and a great pitcher. Ken Meyer, Mike Lee (Doc's grandson), Ryan Oie, just to name a few of the studs they had."

Scobey completely dominated the tournament, winning 2 of their 4 games by the ten-run rule (the championship game would have been too, but the rule was off), outscoring their opponents 64-17, and thumping top-seed Wolf Point twice. The *Leader* summed up Scobey's convincing eastern divisional championship this way: "The Scobey Blues left little doubt who was the best team as they breezed through the Class A Eastern Divisional Tournament at Scobey Ball Park with four straight wins, two of them over league champion Wolf Point, all by wide margins."[49]

Perhaps the Blues were venting some pent-up frustration at previous postseason heartaches. But this was a well-oiled machine, firing on all cylinders. Scobey had finished the season winning 7 of 8 and had carried that momentum into the postseason. Not only did Scobey's bats come alive in the tournament, but their pitching and defense were also good.

The four 18-year-olds—Ken Meyer, Terry Farver, Mike Lee, and Kevin Nelson—ended their Legion careers at

Kevin Nelson (10) and Mike Lee (20) sit in Scobey's dugout following the divisional championship game in Scobey. Mike Roland is in the background between them. In the far-right background might be Mick Mueller. *Lee family photo.*

home in Scobey with a bang. It had to be a special moment for all the 18-year-olds to win the eastern divisional championship and go out winners on their home field, but especially Mike "Karch" Lee, son of Ken and Ann (Norman) Lee, grandson of Doc and Marge Norman, and Ken Meyer, son of Gary and Bonnie Meyer. Both had grown up living and breathing baseball. Like Kelly, Karch had grown up on the ballfield, having been a batboy for six years and four Scobey State championships—1978-80 and 1982. I remember when I played, Ann would often bring Mike to the field late, as he would be coming from a Peewee game, and then he would be batboy for our game, and Ken would sometimes join him in the dugout. They were always on the ballfield. It was a special feeling after getting to the state

Josh and Mike Lee following the divisional championship game. Josh was just added to the roster before the deadline. Mike said, "We only had 12-13 guys, so after he had Babe Ruth All-Stars, he joined the team." Josh was 15 years old in this picture. *Family photo.*

tournament as players. Mike said, "I really believe Ken and I were the last of the 'Old Guard' of Doc Norman baseball. We lived and breathed baseball since before first grade. Ken lived a block down from Grandpa and Grandma, so he was always there with me, or I was down at his house. We did not look forward to being a Spartan football or basketball player. We longed for the day that we could be a Blue!! Just like Kevin growing up wanting to be a Viking. It was part of our DNA."

Ken Meyer reflected on Scobey's brilliant performance in the tournament. "Going into this tournament, there were a couple of things that helped. Obviously, playing on our home field was an advantage (the crowds were great). Then, not making it to State the past couple of years was extra motivation, and we knew going in, only one team was going to get to go on because Glendive was hosting the state tournament. We just got on a roll, and everybody was hitting and pitching well." Mike Lee added, "I think the older guys felt it was ours to lose. Wolf Point had some good players, but they were not a better team than the Blues that year. Ryan Oie held down first base probably 85% of the season for us until Justin Fossum returned from his injury at Divisionals. He also pitched pretty well. The 16-year-olds came through for us all year."

The old and the new got it done.

Now it was time to show the state of Montana what Scobey Blues baseball was all about and make some noise at Meissner Memorial Field in Glendive.

And the Blues would make some noise—a lot of noise—at State.

STATE TOURNAMENT

Scobey, sporting a sterling 31-11 record, was back at State, and they had a legitimate shot to win the tournament. There was no clear favorite, as most coaches gave several teams in the ten-team field a chance to win it. However, the Bitterroot Bucs might have disagreed with that. The title of Ed West's article previewing the tournament in the *Billings Gazette* read, "Bitterroot gunning for 3rd title."[50] In just seven years of existence, The Bucs' meteoric rise had established themselves as a tour de force in Class A Legion baseball, winning the State championship the previous two years, and they were gunning for a three-peat, as they had won the western division again and carried a 29-12 record into the tournament. In Ed West's preview, some coaches were surprised that Coach Neubauer and Wolf Point were not there and wondered about Scobey, the team that had beaten them. Laurel Coach Fred Feuerbacher—whose team finished second to Bitterroot in 1989 and won the southern division—mentioned Vauxhall, Bitterroot, and Dillon and said, "One surprise is Scobey. They beat a veteran Wolf Point team."[51] Billings Cardinals coach Grant Grayson, who also gave several teams a chance to win it, added, "Scobey has a lot of tradition."[52]

And the 1990 Blues would carry on the tradition at the state tournament. First-round games pitted the following teams against each other:

- Bitterroot (1W) vs. Fort Macleod, Alberta (2N)
- Vauxhall, Alberta (1N) Missoula Reds (2W)
- Scobey (1E) Butte Muckers (2C)
- Glendive (2E), Billings Cardinals (2S)
- Byes Laurel (1S), Dillon (1C)

Although 10 teams were in the tournament, all games in the 1990 state tournament would be nine innings. This meant a path through the dirt route would be deadly, as pitching would wear thin. Winning early was always important, but even more so in this format.

Scobey opened against the Butte Muckers. Don Lekvold handed the ball to veteran Mike Lee to start the first game in the tournament, with Kevin Nelson catching. Scobey started strong, jumping on Butte starting pitcher Ryan Maloney for three runs in the top of the first as Mike Lee smacked a two-run double. The Muckers answered with one run in the bottom half, but the game then became a pitcher's duel until the top of the seventh. With the score still 3-1, Ryan Linder hit a clutch two-run single to give Scobey a 5-1 lead. Then, in the top of the ninth, Terry Farver hit a two-run homer, and Scobey scored three runs to take an 8-1 lead. Terry recalls the home run. "I remember a fat fastball coming down the pipe, and I made contact. Didn't realize it was a home run until I saw the second base ump giving the home run signal. I think it went over the right-center field wall. I got a personal pan pizza voucher from Pizza Hut." I asked Terry what kind of pizza he ordered. He said, "I got all meat." You get the joke, I'm sure.

Mike Lee pitched his eighth consecutive scoreless inning in the bottom of the ninth, finishing with a five-hitter, and Scobey won the all-important first game 8-1. Catcher Kevin Nelson had three hits, including a double, and Lee, Farver, Linder, and Ken Meyer each had two hits for Scobey. The Blues played errorless baseball defensively. Pitching, hitting, and fielding—all three were excellent. The outstanding play of Scobey's veterans in their first game was a positive sign of things to come.

Scobey got a nice second-round bye in the tournament, then faced the Laurel Dodgers, who had a first-round bye, then beat the two-time defending State champion Bitterroot Bucs, 4-2, as Bill Laurel pitcher Bernhart shut the Bucs down with a one-hitter.

Coach Lekvold handed the ball to ace Kevin Nelson to pitch Scobey into the undefeated semifinal. Laurel Coach Feuerbacher countered with Neal Peaton, and the two would engage in a pitcher's duel that lasted for eleven innings. *Glendive Ranger-Review* sportswriter Dooley Pauley wrote, "The Scobey Blues and Laurel Dodgers played a real classic. It was a shame that either team had to lose."[53] C.O. Wester of the *Laurel Outlook* wrote that the Scobey-Laurel game "went down to the wire."[54]

According to Pauley, who was interviewed by C.O. Wester of the *Laurel Outlook*, pitchers Kevin Nelson and Neal Peaton "provided one of the most exciting games ever played in the Class A State Tournament."[55]

There were some runs scored—but not many. Scobey scored a run in the first inning when Ken Meyer doubled home lead-off man Kevin Nelson. Ken remembers the hit. "It was a deep fly ball to left center. I thought it was out, but I think it hit the base of the wall. I ended up on third as they missed the cutoff man as I rounded second base."

Laurel scored their only two unearned runs in the third when Bill Bernhart and Travis Moran scored. Pitcher Kevin Nelson remembers how the two runs were scored. "They singled and then tried to bunt the runner over. The bunt was down the third-base line, and I airmailed it over the first base, which then, I think, on the throw back in it was either bobbled or overthrew the cutoff man, allowing the runner to score. I gave up another hit to score the next run. In true Karch fashion, when the play ended, he threw the ball back to me on the pitcher's mound, and it proceeded to come 90 miles an hour at my head, which was just a sign of saying get your shit together."

And Kevin did get his shit together after the third, pitching eight consecutive shutout innings. In the fifth, Scobey tied the game 2-2 on two hits and a Dodger error.

Mike Lee remembers a pivotal double play that helped Scobey get out of a jam in the middle innings and gave them a spark. "Runners were on first and third with one out, and the batter had two strikes. Kevin threw a nasty slider that broke perfectly, getting me out of my stance in the perfect throwing position. The batter whiffed at the pitch for strike three for the second out while the runner on first base tried to steal second. Meyer tagged him for the third out. I was pretty pumped after that."

Both pitchers were striking out a lot of hitters, and a lot of outs were being recorded without the ball being put in play. After Scobey tied it 2-2 in the fifth, each pitcher settled into a groove and held the other team scoreless for the next six innings. Scobey did threaten in the later innings after a double by Kevin Nelson, who then stole third with two outs. Kevin remembers how close he came to scoring. "My double was to right-center. I ended up stealing third and getting stranded there. There was a passed ball that I made about halfway up the line and came back; the ball bounced hard off the backstop and came right back to the catcher. I don't remember the exact inning, but I believe it was later, like seventh or eighth, because I remember wanting to steal that base so I could score on a passed ball, and I believe there were two outs because I can remember thinking, *you better not make the third out stealing third* and it was a very close play. The older guys all had the green light to steal. I do remember a few 'what the fuck were you doing' moments amongst us guys over the years over this."

With the score tied 2-2 after nine, the game went into extra innings. After a scoreless tenth, the game moved into the eleventh. In the top of the eleventh, Kevin Nelson was stronger than ever, striking out the side—his 17th, 18th, and 19th strikeouts of the game—and Scobey came to bat in the bottom of the 11th, needing one run to walk it off.

Ken Meyer, who batted third in the lineup, led off the bottom of the 11th with a walk and advanced to second on a passed ball. With no outs and Ken Meyer representing the winning run on second, cleanup hitter Mike Lee was up next in the order. Coach Don Lekvold now had a decision: Should he take a shot at a base hit with Mike or sacrifice his cleanup hitter and move Meyer to third with only one out, opening up other opportunities besides a base hit for fifth-place hitter Terry Farver—who could hit for power and could drive a ball deep to the outfield—to score him on a sacrifice fly? Don chose to bunt his cleanup hitter, and Mike laid down a perfect sacrifice bunt, moving Meyer to third with one out. Mike's sacrifice symbolized how important fundamentals were in baseball, and the lifelong baller got it done, giving himself up and doing what his coach asked him to do in that situation. The bat was now in Terry Farver's hands—literally—and Don Lekvold's strategy paid off, as Terry clubbed a fly ball to deep center field, and Ken Meyer easily came home to score the winning run.

Without a hit, Scobey had manufactured the winning run on a walk, a passed ball, a sacrifice bunt, and a sacrifice fly. Coach Don Lekvold had made the perfect call, sacrificing his cleanup hitter, Mike Lee. Ken Meyer recalls how the winning rally in the ninth unfolded. "I walked, and I believe the call from Don was hit and run. I was stealing second, and Karch was going to make contact. The pitcher threw the ball in the dirt (passed ball). So now I'm on second, and on the very next pitch, Don had Karch sac bunt me over to third. I'm not sure what the count was on Terry when he hit the fly ball to center, but it was far enough for me to tag up and score the winning run. I slid into home plate but probably didn't need to. It was a pretty wild ending! Farver putting the ball in play was clutch because I felt like I was going to score on anything that was on the ground or a decent fly ball."

Mike Lee recalls his critical sacrifice bunt to advance Ken to third. "I recall only bunting twice that year. The first was a suicide squeeze on a 3-2 count with Meyer at third against Wolf Point with Darin Miller pitching. I didn't question Don either time; I just did my job and didn't think twice about it. I was ready for that first pitch to hit on the hit and run, but it was an outside wild pitch, and I started yelling for Ken to go before the pitch got to the plate. And I had confidence in Terry Farver. He was hitting the ball very well all year."

Terry recalls his at-bat to drive home the winning run. "Don just told me to find a good pitch and make contact, maybe an opposite-field hit. I don't remember the count, but he threw a fastball that I was able to make good contact with. It was a pretty deep fly ball to left center, deep enough for Kenny to tag up from third and get home. I think that's the fastest I ever saw Kenny run."

So, after 11 long innings, in which two pitchers traded strikeout after strikeout—35 between them—Scobey ran off the field with a dramatic, hard-fought 3-2 win, advancing to the undefeated semifinal. Both pitchers went the distance in the epic duel. Kevin Nelson struck out 19 Dodgers in 11 innings, and Neal Peaton struck out 16 Blues. Don Lekvold was not surprised by Nelson's gutty performance, saying, "Kevin was the toughest kid I ever coached . . . both physically and mentally!"

Kevin Nelson recalls his epic pitching performance. "I threw fastballs and sliders. After the third inning, I remember telling myself there is no way I'm giving up another run. I truly remember feeling completely in control. I don't think they ever even threatened us after the third. I think I may have struck out the last five batters. I got stronger as the game went on, which was a thing for me all throughout my playing days."

Third base umpire Larry Trangsrud summed up Kevin's performance very simply by saying, "Dude was bringing it."

Shortstop Ken Meyer remembers Kevin's performance. "Kevin was throwing upper 80s low 90s in the latter innings. I'm not sure when the game ended, but it had to be eleven or so." Catcher Mike Lee remembers calling the entire game for Kevin. "He was clocked consistently in the

Kevin Nelson delivers a pitch during the early innings of his 19-strikeout performance in Scobey's 3-2 win over Laurel in 11 innings. *Ranger-Review photo, Ginny Archdale.*

90s from the sixth inning on. (A Houston Astros scout at the game was clocking both pitchers.) We were all friends with the Page family from Wolf Point. Greg was behind the plate that game.

Greg and I would talk between innings while Kevin was warming up. I told him I was having trouble tracking the ball right before it got completely dark sometime early in the game. After that, Greg would tell me each inning what Kevin was being clocked at. Kevin is right about him getting stronger as the game went on. Early in the game, it was 86-89, and then, probably around the seventh inning, it hit 90. And during the tenth inning, he hit 92. He was money hitting the inside corner that game. So much so that some of the batters started moving to the outside of the box because he was jamming them. They had zero chance of hitting his slider after they did that. Easiest game I ever called because whatever pitch and location I asked for, Kevin would deliver it with ease after they scored their two runs. Uncle Kelly taught me how to call a game and what to look for when the batter lined up in the box. He also told me to play to the strength of the pitcher, not the batter, in most cases. I was always very conscientious when a runner got to first and called the pitch the pitcher would like while maintaining getting a good pitch to throw that fucker out at second. Some pitches I could not see coming in, but they went right to where I had my glove framed up. It was truly amazing catching someone that good at night at the state tournament. It was everything I hoped for and dreamed of the last three years we played. Finally, it felt like we were

the Scobey Blues, the best team in the state that repeatedly won state championships. It was a feeling I wanted so badly because I had experienced it so much as a kid growing up. I got the best hug from my Grandma Marge after the game! She represented everything Scobey Blues to me."

The Scobey players knew they had played in an epic game. Mike Lee said, "It was the best baseball game I ever played in," and Ken Meyer agreed, saying, "It was by far the best game I was a part of whether it was a player or coach." Terry Farver added, "We all went nuts after Kenny got home, just beat a very tough team."

And Scobey was moving on. The Blues, now 33-11, faced northern division champion Vauxhall in the undefeated semifinal. Many coaches had picked Vauxhall as one of the teams to beat in the tournament. Champions of the northern division with a 25-7 record, the Spurs had two good pitchers—ace right-hander Alan Holt (who threw 85 miles per hour) and 17-year-old left-hander Troy Cleland. Both pitchers had already seen action in the tournament in Vauxhall's two wins. In the opening game, Cleland had pitched a combined two-hitter to lead Vauxhall to a 14-1 win over Missoula, and Holt went the distance in their second game, striking out 14 Dillon Cubs in Vauxhall's 6-5 victory. Spurs coach Greg Kuntz handed the ball to left-hander Cleland to start for Vauxhall against Scobey.

Don Lekvold, getting two outstanding pitching performances from Mike Lee and Kevin Nelson in Scobey's first two wins—they had only allowed one earned run in 20 innings pitched—needed another well-pitched game to beat Troy Cleland and Vauxhall. Don handed the ball to 16-year-old Steve Stephenson to start the undefeated semifinal.

The game got off to a horrible start for Scobey. In the bottom of the first, with two baserunners on, a routine flyball was hit to right field, but the ball was misplayed for a two-run error to hoist Vauxhall to a 2-0 early lead. With the crafty left-hander Troy Cleland on the mound for Vauxhall, Scobey had dug themselves a two-run hole early, a hole they could never recover from.

Steve pitched the first two innings and didn't allow an earned run, and Coach Lekvold brought in Ryan Linder to pitch in the third inning. He kept Scobey in the game—allowing only one run in six innings—but it wasn't enough to beat Troy Cleland, who pitched a five-hit shutout and struck out nine Blues to lead Vauxhall to a 3-0 win. Stephenson and Linder did their job, nearly outpitching Cleland. The two Scobey pitchers hurled a combined four-hitter, allowing only one earned run. Mike Lee remembers how good Scobey's pitching was in that game, saying, "Steve was a good pitcher, and Ryan shut them down; he pitched a hell of a game." Another advantage for Scobey when Ryan Linder pitched was that they had their best defense on the field when he did. Mike Lee said, "With me catching, Kevin at third, Meyer at short, Terry in center, and Ryan on the mound, was our best defensive lineup if Kevin was not pitching." The error in right in the first inning was the only error Scobey made in that game. But Troy Cleland, the "stylish, smooth-working left-hander,"[56] as sportswriter Hudson Willse of the *Montana Standard* referred to him, fired a rare shutout against the Blues, and Scobey's pitching would have had to allow no runs—earned or not—to match his performance. Ken Meyer remembers how the Vauxhall left-hander frustrated the Scobey bats. "That lefty didn't throw extremely hard but had a damn good changeup and had pinpoint accuracy. 30-some-odd years later, and it still bugs me to this day!"

Ken Meyer remembers a critical point in the Vauxhall game that snuffed out a Scobey rally. "They pulled the 'Oh Shit' play on us. It was a huge turning point in the game. It finally felt like we had a little momentum going for us, and then, 'Bam, what in the hell just happened!' I was up to bat, and we had a runner on second and maybe first base, too. The pitcher from Vauxhall was a lefty (Troy Cleland). He whirled around to pick off the runner at second. The shortstop (Alan Holt) jumped in the air. The second baseman started running to center field, yelling, 'Oh Shit.' The center fielder was on a dead sprint into the infield. The baserunner got up after diving back into the base. Don Lekvold was yelling, 'Let's go! Let's go!' waving his arm in a circular motion. The runner took off for third base, and the pitcher casually threw the ball to the third baseman for an easy tag out at third. It was by far the most well-executed fake decoy pickoff move I have ever witnessed! Every one of their players played it to perfection. That took any bit of momentum we had and swung it right back to them. Such a crushing blow in a critical part of the game! Ugh—that sucked!"

Scobey also had a runner picked off at first base to squelch another rally. As if that wasn't enough, late in the game, the Vauxhall left fielder robbed Ken Meyer of a home run that would have tied the game. Sometimes, you need a break to win, and Scobey couldn't get a break in this game. A two-run error in right field to start things off, two baserunners getting picked off, and a game-tying home run that was robbed—snakebit.

Scobey had some bad breaks, but they were also beaten by an excellent team. Ken Meyer, who was robbed of a game-tying home run, recalls the poise of the Vauxhall team. "They were so fundamentally sound. Just seemed like they never made any mistakes and played at a high level all the time. I know their head coaches were usually hired out of Arizona. That is how I eventually ended up going to Arizona and helping coach at a junior college." Terry Farver remembers a fine defensive play shortstop Alan Holt made to rob him of a base hit. "I hit a pretty good ground ball up the middle, but the shortstop fielded it behind second base and threw me out. I knew that team was good; we found out later that they started practicing in March in an indoor facility."

With the loss, the Blues were forced into a playoff against the Bitterroot Bucs, the winner advancing to the championship game against Vauxhall. Bitterroot, the western division champion and two-time defending State champion, was looking to three-peat in 1990, but they would have to get past the Blues first and then beat Vauxhall twice to do it. After their second-round 4-2 loss to Laurel, the Bucs had won three games—four in the tournament—but due to the ten-team format, they needed to win three more games—seven total—to win the tournament. Talk about a dirt route!

Don Lekvold started Mike Lee—who had his innings back after pitching his five-hitter over Butte—against Bitterroot. This would be another tough game for the Blues. Scobey jumped on Bitterroot for two runs in the top of the first—a great start—but Bitterroot rallied for five runs in the bottom of the second to take a 5-2 lead. Scobey countered with a four-run rally in the top of the fifth to take a 6-5 lead, but Bitterroot tied it in the sixth. Bitterroot's Brad Tadvick then hit a two-run homer in the bottom of the seventh to break the tie. Mike Lee recalls pitching the game. "By that game, I was basically throwing batting practice. Catching and pitching 30-plus innings in five days had the arm hanging a bit. Had so much Icy Hot on that it was stinging my eyes when I had the face mask on catching. I remember the feeling of getting gut-punched in the seventh when I gave up the two-run home run."

Scobey threatened to score in the ninth but came up short. Kevin Nelson said, "We had one runner on and down two. I took a first-pitch strike. I sat on a curveball on the next pitch, and all I could think was *hit this ball out*. I just missed it and sent a deep flyball to left field. Ask me about many other at-bats, and I don't remember, but I do remember that one."

And Bitterroot walked off the field with a hard-fought 8-6 win, ending Scobey's run in the state tournament and a fantastic season. For Scobey, Justin Fossum went 3 for 3, Terry Farver had two hits and two RBIs, and Kevin Nelson had two hits. For Bitterroot, winning pitcher Jay Brockett had two hits and two RBIs.

1990 Scobey Blues, Third Place at State. Back row: Asst. Coach Mike Roland, Ken Meyer, Derek Solberg, Ryan Linder, Mike Lee, Steve Stephenson, Mick Mueller, Coach Don Lekvold. Front row: Robin Fladager, Brent Tarum, Ryan Oie, Scott Nelson, Ben Hoversland, Terry Farver, and Kevin Nelson. Not pictured are Justin Fossum and Lee Hackman. *Leader photo, Burl Bowler.*

Vauxhall won the State championship 4-0 over Bitterroot, as Spurs right-hander Alan Holt scattered seven hits and struck out seven Bucs for Vauxhall's second consecutive shutout.

TOURNAMENT SUMMARY

Scobey played well at the state tournament, but their postseason run was ended by two outstanding teams, as Vauxhall and Bitterroot went on to finish 1-2 at the Northwest Regional in Anaconda, the best finish ever for Montana/Alberta Class A Legion. Getting good pitching from Mike Lee—who pitched a five-hitter and 17 total innings in two complete games—and Kevin Nelson—who struck out 19 Dodgers in 11 innings in the epic pitcher's duel against Peaton from Laurel—was key to Scobey's deep run in the tournament. The Blues also got an extremely well-pitched game from Steve Stephenson and Ryan Linder against Vauxhall to keep them close, but it just wasn't enough to offset the shutout by Troy Cleland. The two-run homer by Bitterroot in the bottom of the seventh off Mike Lee, tired after he was pitching his 16th inning of the tournament and had caught 20 innings, was the nail in the coffin for Scobey.

For Mike Lee, Ken Meyer, Terry Farver, and Kevin Nelson, the 1990 state tournament games were their last as Scobey Blues. They all needed to play at a high level for Scobey to win at State, and they had done just that. Mike Lee pitched a five-hitter and eight consecutive scoreless innings against Butte, and Terry Farver hit a two-run homer. Kevin Nelson pitched the game of his life against Laurel, and in the bottom of the 11th inning, Ken Meyer, Mike Lee, and Terry Farver—who batted 3-4-5 in the lineup—all contributed to the single run Scobey needed to win. Ken Meyer led off the inning with a walk, Mike Lee sacrificed him to third, and Terry Farver drove Meyer home with the winning run on a deep fly to center. Coach Don Lekvold had brought the team together with a mix of seasoned veterans and talented rookies to win the eastern division, a fantastic third-place finish as State, and a 33-13 season record.

The state tournament recognized the Blues' excellence, honoring Kevin Nelson with the Doc Norman Memorial MVP trophy and Coach Don Lekvold with the Montana/Alberta American Legion Coach of the Year trophy. Both were tremendous honors, and both were well-deserved. Coach Lekvold said, "The 1990 team was the best team I ever coached." The 1990 Scobey Blues carried on the legacy of the Scobey American Legion Baseball tradition.

Ken Meyer reflected on the 1990 season. "Growing up in Scobey as a youngster during the late 70s and early 80s, watching all the previous success of the Blues teams was something that was instilled in you. Being at the ballpark pretty much all summer year after year was part of life. Whether it was playing, preparing the fields for games, or helping with concessions. My dad and mom were very instrumental in the Blues program, so it was a family affair. The players were our idols growing up, and I'm sure they didn't know it at the time. I don't think I ever missed a home game the Blues played when we were in town. Chased a lot of foul balls for a quarter a piece. I was lucky enough to be a batboy from time to time with Karch. When the billboard went up behind the right field fence, showing all the years that the Blues won a State championship, it was a dream of mine/ours to someday have a year that represented when we played. Karch and I had discussed this. 1990 was a year that we had that chance. We were runners-up at State in football, and to be honest, second-place sucks! When we didn't capture the title in baseball, it hurt, but I can honestly say we put it all on the line. No regrets about how we played. You can woulda/coulda all day long! Trust me, over the years we have, but our last year was never in question as far as effort. We just came up short!"

Karch Lee was also disappointed about not winning state in baseball and had this to say. "I didn't know the saying at the time, but now, looking back to sum everything up for us in 1990, we were 'Riding for the Brand' for Blues Baseball!! We were lucky enough to start the 'Blues winning tradition' with Scobey eight-man football. There was not much tradition in Scobey with football and basketball at the time. (A few great seasons but not a lasting tradition.) We changed that for football and really wanted to bring the chipper back home for baseball to be part of the legacy. To this day, whenever I drive by Glendive, the first thing I think of is losing that last game."

When reflecting on the 1990 season, Kevin Nelson said, "I think about my wife's and my decision of taking our children to Scobey after it was getting hard to field teams in Opheim. When the time came to decide where to take the kids, there never was even a second thought of where to go, and that all stems from my time over there playing for the Blues and the friendships I developed within the Scobey community. I'm not a born and raised Scobey boy, but that community always treated me as one of their own. To this day, I still feel as the Lees and Meyers are my family, as I spent many nights and weeks at their homes. Brothers for life. I feel that many of the players in past Blues teams have the same feeling. Baseball seems to have this effect. Great sport."

Mike Lee added, "It truly was the Blues of Summer. Girls, parties, road trips, Legion hamburgers, the smell of icy hot, games, and most of all, friendships that turned into brotherhood that lasted a lifetime."

TOURNAMENT STATS

Hitting

KEVIN NELSON, WHO WAS SELECTED MVP FOR HIS OVERALL play, hit .476 in the tournament. In their first game against Butte, Kevin Nelson had three hits, including a double, and Mike Lee, Terry Farver, Ryan Linder, and Ken Meyer each had two hits for Scobey. Mike Lee had a double, and Farver homered for Scobey's other extra-base hits. But Scobey's bats were silenced against Neal Peaton of Laurel and Troy Cleland of Vauxhall. Against Bitterroot, their bats came back to life, as Justin Fossum went 3 for 3, Terry Farver had two hits and two RBIs, and Kevin Nelson had two hits.

Pitching

SCOBEY'S PITCHING WAS OUTSTANDING. MIKE LEE PITCHED A five-hitter and allowed only one run in the opener against Butte, pitching eight consecutive scoreless innings after yielding a run in the first. Kevin Nelson's performance against Laurel was epic. He threw a four-hitter, struck out 19 Dodgers, and allowed only two unearned runs in 11 innings. He finished strong, striking out the side in the 11th. And there was no let-up in game three against Vauxhall, as Steve Stephenson and Ryan Linder pitched a combined four-hitter and allowed only one earned run in the 3-0 loss. Don Lekvold could not have asked for a finer performance from his third and fourth pitchers, but Troy Cleland was just too much for the Blues. Mike Lee was a workhorse in the final game, as he went the distance again—logging 17 innings in the tournament—in the tough 8-6 to loss Bitterroot.

Fielding

SCOBEY'S DEFENSE WAS ALSO OUTSTANDING—AS IT HAD BEEN ALL season—and was one of the main reasons for their success. They played errorless ball against the Muckers and committed only one error against Laurel. Against Vauxhall, the Blues were again stellar in the field, committing only one error, but it was costly, leading to two unearned runs. However, it didn't cost them the game—the Blues could not produce a run off Troy Cleland of Vauxhall. In the final game against the Bitterroot Bucs, the Blues had a bit of a letdown defensively, committing three errors, but overall, the defensive performance of the Blues in the 1990 state tournament was excellent. They only committed five errors in four games for an average of just over one error (1.25) per game. That is good. The *Leader* cited Kevin Nelson as making some "outstanding defensive plays."[57] Kevin's overall outstanding performance on the mound, at the plate, and in the field led to his selection as MVP.

NORTHWEST REGIONAL

VAUXHALL AND BITTERROOT, THE TWO TEAMS SCOBEY LOST close games to at State, made history at the Northwest Regional in Anaconda, finishing 1-2 at the tournament. The Lethbridge Miners' second-place regional finish in 1986 at Hamilton was the highest previous regional finish. Wolf Point (1987) and Bitterroot (1988) previously owned the best Class A finishes by teams located in Montana, both finishing third. This was the first time in the tournament's six-year history that a Montana-affiliated team won it.

Vauxhall scored 12 runs in the final three innings in the championship game to beat Bitterroot 20-8. Troy Cleland picked up his third tournament win for Vauxhall in the championship game. The Spurs, behind two wins by Troy Cleland and a two-hitter by Alan Holt, had gone undefeated through the tournament until Bitterroot beat them 9-7 to force a second championship game. A near-brawl marred the championship game as both benches emptied after a collision at second base. A player from Bitterroot was ejected. Bitterroot was seeking revenge after losing to Vauxhall at State, frustrating their goal of a three-peat. Ironically, the only reason Bitterroot was able to participate in the eight-team tournament was that the second-place team from Oregon did not come, so three Montana/Alberta teams—Bitterroot, Vauxhall, and host Anaconda—were allowed in the tournament.

Bitterroot's ascent to Montana Class A baseball eminence was swift. Although they only became a team in 1983, they finished third in the 1986 regionals (as host), third in the 1988 regionals, and won the 1988 and 1989 state championships before being upended by Vauxhall in 1990.

EXTRA INNINGS

THE HISTORY OF DANIELS COUNTY BASEBALL WOULD NOT BE complete if a picture was not provided of where the famous Legion burgers were made. Thanks to Milt Gunderson of the *Leader* for capturing this photo at the divisional tournament, memorializing the little hut that kicked out such a big taste.

Before the start of the season, Mike Lee mentioned that "the success we [Scobey] had in football, basketball, and track" led to confidence that that same success could carry

Bruce Fladager and Vicki Mueller working at the popular ballpark Legion burger stand. Most of the time fans were lined up for the tasty Legion burgers, some as a treat and for some as a main meal, as they stayed at the park for continued games. *Leader photo, Milt Gunderson.*

over to the baseball field. What was that success? In the fall of 1989, Scobey had its best finish ever in football, making it to the state Class C 8-man football championship game against Absarokee before losing 44-6. Their basketball team made it to the State Class C Tournament, taking second at Divisional, losing to a tough Lambert team. Their track and field team won the district and eastern divisional championships, with Mike Lee breaking a 15-year-old Divisional meet record, chucking the javelin 190 feet, 10 inches. Terry Farver won the 100-, 200-meter dashes and the 110 hurdles. The two of them led Scobey to the eastern division championship. Mike then won the javelin at State, throwing it 197 feet, six inches, and Terry Farver took fifth in the 110 hurdles, running the event in 15.99.

Kevin Nelson's 19-strikeout performance against Laurel prompted me to search for the most strikeouts for Scobey Blues pitchers in a game. Going back through the archives, this is what I was able to find:

- Jim LeProwse (23) vs. Havre, 1985 State Tournament (12 innings)
- Randy Stolen (21) vs. Glendive, 1980 Divisional Tournament (8 innings)
- Jay Hagfeldt (20) vs. Baker, 1973 Divisional Tournament (9 innings)
- Greg Stolen and Kirby Halvorson (20), Glendive, 1980 (9 innings)
- Dan Danelson (19) vs. Glasgow, 1978 (9 innings)
- Kevin Nelson (19) vs. Laurel, 1990 State Tournament (11 innings)
- Randy Stolen (18) vs. Wolf Point, 1980 (9 innings)
- Mike Hagfeldt (17) vs. Glasgow, 1976 Divisional Tournament (9 innings)
- Mike Hagfeldt (17) vs. Sidney, 1976 State Tournament (9 innings)
- Randy Stolen (17) vs. Missoula Reds, 1980 State Tournament (9 innings)
- Dave Anderson (17) vs. Glasgow, 1995 Divisional Tournament (9 innings)
- Terry Puckett (16) vs. Wolf Point, 1973 Divisional championship (12 innings)
- Mike Roland (16) vs. Glasgow, 1986 (9 innings)
- Joe Puckett (15) vs. Laurel, 1979 State championship (9 innings)
- Several other pitchers with 15 strikeouts in a game

Kevin Nelson and Ken Meyer remember some of the players from Laurel. "Their pitcher, Neal Peaton, threw fairly hard and had a pretty decent curveball. He ended up pitching for Valley City over in North Dakota for college." Ken Meyer played with Bill Bernhart at North Idaho and said, "Travis Moran is a good dude, and I see him often."

Karch Lee had some humorous anecdotes to share about State in Glendive:

- "Don had these new hats made that were just ugly (dark navy). We all said no way."
- "We were booked to stay in a 1940s-style motel on the river with mosquitoes the size of sparrows. We said no way and made Don get us rooms at a newer hotel by the field."
- "All our parents thought that wearing dryer sheets in their hair and on hats would keep the gnats away. Our crowd looked funny in the stands."
- "In our downtime at the hotel, it seemed like we watched four days of a Madonna marathon on MTV while playing cards and taking it easy. Every time I hear a Madonna song I think of State in 1990."

Speaking of Madonna and baseball, wasn't she great as center fielder "All the Way" Mae Mordabito in *A League of Their Own*? Ray Chapman was in that film as a scalper at the movie's end.

Karch Lee remembers some humorous off-the-field stories about the 16-year-olds. "Our 16-year-olds in 1990 were quite the characters. One of them was driving home from a party (maybe two miles of road to get home), and he just didn't get one flat tire—he got four. A few of the 16-year-olds would drive down to Poplar to buy beer. They would take 'old man farmer costumes' with them. They would use wigs, canes, glasses, and other accessories. They would dress up and walk and talk like they were 80. The funny thing was that after a while, the owner knew what they were doing, but he was so impressed with the effort he would just laugh and sell them the beer anyway. They would usually go to the grocery store in Poplar, I think."

The back-to-back home runs Kevin Nelson and Ken Meyer hit against Idaho Falls in the Maybelle Arthur Tournament in Dillon was the fifth time in Blues history that happened. Rick Danelson and Terry Puckett did it in the 1973 eastern divisional championship game against Wolf Point at Denton Field in Miles City. Kirby Halvorson and Randy Stolen did it three times, including against the Kalispell Lakers at the 1979 State A Tournament.

Kevin Nelson remembers the only game he lost as a pitcher that year. "I believe the game was against Moose Jaw. Sixteen-year-old Brent Tarum had pitched a gem of a game, and I believe we were leading three to one in the seventh inning. It was the week before the divisional tournament, and Don wasn't going to pitch me, but Brent got into trouble in the seventh, so Don brought me in to close the game out, and they lit me up like a Christmas tree and scored three runs or so. And I blew the best game Brent pitched all year." It's funny how athletes always remember that bad stuff—that was the only game Kevin lost that year. Kevin added, "It seems like we can always remember the mistakes we made and poor plays that cost the team."

Mike Lee also remembers the bad. "The final memory that troubles me still when thinking of playing for the Blues is striking out looking on a full count on my last at-bat as an 18-year-old. Greg Page from Wolf Point was behind the dish. Meyer was at second with one out, and we were only down two against Bitterroot. I totally failed the team and five years of Legion ball, it felt like, and never goes away. I have told that story to a couple of kids who I have coached to help make the point of finishing and not hoping for someone to bail you out."

I asked Mike Lee how he got his nickname "Karch." Mike said, "In the fall of 1986, during 'Teacher Convention' weekend, I went and spent the weekend with Uncle Kelly in Billings. He took me to see the USA men's Olympic volleyball team play Japan at the Metra. Karch Kiraly was on the American team. Well, the next week back in Scobey, we happened to be playing volleyball in PE. I served either 7 or 11 points in a row to win a game, and the PE student assistant Steve Lapke (who also was at the Metra watching volleyball) said, 'Hey, there is Karch Kiraly.' I laughed because I knew who he was talking about, but most people at school laughed because the name was foreign to them and sounded funny. After that, the seniors called me Karch off and on for a few days, and the whole school picked up on it, and I was labeled for life. I hated it at first but eventually got used to it."

Karch remembers his batboy days and some good advice he got from his grandpa, Doc Norman. "I repeated everything you guys said except at home. Grandpa Doc would always tell me, 'What happens at baseball stays at baseball. If you say things to your mom that you hear at baseball, she won't let you come with us.' I was tight-lipped at home."

Three players from the 1990 Bitterroot team went on to play college baseball, and one was drafted. Brad Tadvick, who hit the two-run home run against Scobey to win the game 8-6, hit 18 home runs on the season, a Class A Legion record. He later played at Big Bend Community College in Washington. As a freshman, Jason Goligoski, Bitterroot's shortstop, started at Washington State and was named second-team All-PAC 10. He left WSU after two seasons when the program was put on two-year probation for recruiting violations. The Chicago White Sox then drafted him in the 8th round of the 1993 MLB June Amateur Draft. He played in the minor leagues for six years, making it to the AA level and finishing his career in 1998 with the Tulsa Drillers in the Texas League. Russ Frickey, Bitterroot's catcher, played for two seasons at Diablo Valley College in the Bay Area of California. He later played in the Bitterroot Baseball League (BBL), an amateur baseball league with five teams: the Missoula RedStixx, Hamilton Cobras, Stevensville River Bandits, Tri-City Mud Hens, and the Missoula Warthogs.

Slick left-hander Troy Cleland from Vauxhall was the fourth left-hander to stymie Scobey in the postseason, following Dave Fanning of Havre (1971), Bill Wilkinson of Great Falls (1982), and Barry Griffin of Whitehall (1984). Following his Legion career at Vauxhall, Troy Cleland pitched for two years at Community College of Spokane—where he was all-region—and two years at Gonzaga. He also pitched for the Alberta All-Star Team at the Canadian National Tournament for two years, then pitched seven years for the Calgary Longhorns in the Alberta Premier Baseball League.

Kevin Nelson was the second Scobey Blue to be named MVP of a state tournament after the honor began to be awarded in 1980. Pat Audet was named MVP of the 1982 state tournament in Deer Lodge. Kevin, a superb all-around athlete from Opheim, played basketball and baseball for the UND-Williston Tetons. He then finished his collegiate career at Dickinson State, where he was also a dual-sport athlete. At Dickinson State, he was named All-North Dakota College Athletic Conference (NDCAC) first team in baseball. He was inducted into the UND-Williston Baseball Hall of Fame in 2012 and his Hall of Fame writeup reads, "Kevin Nelson was one of the most outstanding pitchers to ever throw for the Tetons. He helped lead the 1991 team to the regional championship game, going 6-1 during that season, including five complete games.

Nelson was an All-State and All-Region selection before starring at Dickinson State." Following his collegiate career, Kevin pitched for the Minot Mallards of the Prairie League and the Ohio Valley Redcoats in the Frontier League.

Ken Meyer played baseball for one year in North Idaho, then joined Kevin with the Tetons, where he was also named to the North Dakota junior college all-state baseball team in his second year.

Mike Lee was a tri-sport athlete for the Jamestown Jimmies football, track and field, and baseball his freshman year, then transferred to Montana State for javelin his sophomore year. Karch joined Jay and Mike Hagfeldt as Scobey Blues who won the state championship in the javelin: Jay won state for Glasgow with a throw of 199-9 in 1973; Mike threw it 197-2 for Glasgow to win in 1976; Karch threw it 197-6 to win in 1990. Karch now coaches javelin at Laurel High School.

Head Coach Greg Kuntz of Vauxhall was the assistant baseball Coach at Azusa Pacific in California in 1990. He remarked on how much he enjoyed coaching the Canadian boys rather than the Californians, saying, "They [the Canadians] are just much more willing to play the game the right way. I don't have a bunch of kids who think they know the game inside and out, like the 12-year-olds back in California who think they know the game, and their fathers, too." Ouch. Coach Kuntz took Alan Holt, Vauxhall's shortstop and pitcher, back to Azusa Pacific with him.

At the 1990 Eastern Divisional Tournament in Scobey, Jim Lekvold was the head umpire, and Pat Vigliotti, Jerry Danelson, Jeff Jones, and Greg Page were part of the crew. The *Leader* wrote, "This crew drew praise for the consistent job."[58] Mike Lee remembers the professional umpires as one of the most significant aspects of Scobey's baseball tradition. "Always having Jim Lekvold and Pat Vig (Vigliotti) umpiring all of our home games made us better players (especially pitchers). Away games, we would get whoever showed up to watch the game sometimes and be asked to umpire behind the plate in jeans. We sometimes got homered on the road, but no one got a home job in Scobey. In a sense, the professionalism of the umpire crew in Scobey added to the mystique of the program in Scobey." The *Leader* identified other volunteers, naming Gary Meyer (official scorer and stat man), who "along with his wife Bonnie, did a lot of pre-tourney planning and work during the action."[59]

In 1990, the Montana/Alberta American Legion had 31 Class A teams—four from Alberta—in five Divisions. Scobey played in the eastern division, which had seven teams.

1991

Scobey Repeats as Eastern Division Champions and the End of the Don Lekvold Era

> *When I was playing, Scobey Blues baseball was the king. I mean, I remember the grandstands packed, and you could hardly park to watch a night game. And the winning—I don't think I ever played on a bad Blues team.*
>
> —*Ryan Linder, Scobey Blues (1988–91)*

PRESEASON

Repeating as Eastern Division champions and making a deep run in the state tournament—as the Blues had done in 1990—would be a tough act for Coach Don Lekvold and Scobey to follow in 1991, especially because the Blues lost their four big guns: Ken Meyer, Mike Lee, Kevin Nelson, Terry Farver. And their fifth big fun—Justin Fossum—was lost for his 18-year-old season due to his second knee surgery. The five players batted 1 through 5 in the lineup, and Kevin Nelson and Mike Lee were the top two pitchers and catchers. Justin Fossum's injury left Ryan Linder, a talented all-around ballplayer from Flaxville, as the only 18-year-old on the roster in 1991.

But the talented young group that had joined the team as 16-year-olds in 1990—Derek Solberg, Steve Stephenson, Robin Fladager, Brent Tarum, Ryan Oie, Scott Nelson, Ben Hoversland, and Lee Hackman—would be back for their second season, and they would a force to be reckoned with in the eastern division. Josh Lee, Todd Fuhrman, Zach Bowler, and Tyler Bucklin joined the team as rookies.

Ryan Linder, Steve Stephenson, Ryan Oie, and Brent Tarum were all experienced pitchers and would provide Don Lekvold with good depth at pitching. Steve Stephenson and Ryan Linder had pitched a combined four-hitter in the undefeated semifinal against Vauxhall at State in 1990, and Ryan Oie and Brent Tarum had also seen plenty of action during the 1990 regular season and both pitched in the divisional tournament. Although young, this was an experienced staff. Kevin's younger brother, Scott Nelson, would be the primary catcher, backed up by Josh Lee. It was likely not a coincidence that the Lee boys were catchers, as their grandfather, Doc Norman, was a catcher when he played. Kelly also ended his career behind the plate and was a catcher in college. Bart Gregerson would support Coach Lekvold as an assistant coach, and Jason Hackman and Morgan Lekvold were batboys.

REGULAR SEASON

To develop his young team, Coach Lekvold took the Blues to the second annual Maybelle Arthur American Legion Tournament in Dillon with some of the best teams in the state. The seven teams in the tournament were the Wolf Point Yellowjackets, Minia-Cassia, Idaho, Butte Muckers, Laurel Dodgers, Bitterroot Bucs, and host Dillon Cubs. Each team got four games.

The Blues got roughed up, losing all four games, but Don Lekvold was developing his team for another run at the eastern divisional championship, not winning the early-season tournament. Three of the four teams the Blues lost to would become Division champions later in the season—the Dillon Cubs won the Central, the Bitterroot Bucs won the west, and the Laurel Dodgers won the south. Derek Solberg thought the good pitching the Blues faced in the tournament helped them win the divisional tournament later in the season. "I think because we faced those good teams early on, we were confident against the top pitchers in our division, especially at the divisional tournament." Josh Lee remembers the pitching, too, and his first experience of being a Blue. "It was definitely an adventure. It was my 16-year-old year, so I was doing a lot of bench time. I do remember watching a couple of pitchers who threw hard. It was my first big bus trip, and

I was just loving finally getting to be a 'Blue.'" Two good pitchers the Blues faced were Jay Brockett of Bitterroot and Chris Bowker of Dillon.

Rob Fladager and Derek Solberg remember a 15-inning, five-hour marathon against Wolf Point as the "most memorable" game of the 1991 conference season. Unfortunately, the Blues lost the game, but it was memorable just the same. Here were some highlights of that game:

- Ryan Oie pitched the first 11 innings.
- Brent Tarum had a six-hit game.
- Rob Fladager, Ryan Oie, and Derek Solberg had five-hit games.

If you're doing the math, that's 21 hits for four Scobey hitters alone. Josh Lee remembers the marathon. "That game was a lot of fun! Baseballs were flying all over the place. Arms were definitely sore that next day. Ryan [Oie] threw a helluva game. He got a cortisone shot a couple of days after that game."

The eastern division consisted of eight teams in 1991. During the regular season, Scobey's record hovered in the middle of the pack, splitting most of their doubleheaders, and they finished fourth place in the conference behind Circle, Glendive, and Wolf Point. The final conference standings looked like this:

1. Circle
2. Glendive
3. Wolf Point
4. Scobey
5. Sidney
6. Malta
7. Glasgow
8. Plentywood

It was rare for the Circle Zephyrs to win the east, but they pulled it off in 1991, narrowly edging out Glendive and Wolf Point to win it. Headed into the divisional tournament at Plentywood, the Blues would need to win at least three games—and beat some higher seeds—to finish as one of the top two teams and return to the state tournament. However, as previous seasons had shown, the postseason was a completely different ballgame than the regular season. Scobey had seen multiple years of hot winning streaks at the end of the regular season, only to see the momentum fade in the divisional tournament. Maybe it would be the opposite in 1991.

And it was.

DIVISIONAL TOURNAMENT

THE EASTERN DIVISIONAL TOURNAMENT WAS HELD AT Sportsman Park in Plentywood. If it was rare for the Circle Zephyrs to win the east, it was also rare for Plentywood to host an eastern divisional tournament—the last time Plentywood had hosted was 1967, the first year Scobey qualified for the state tournament. Could the unlikely combination of Circle as top-seed and Plentywood as host be a fortunate odd mix for Scobey, resulting in another state tournament berth? Opening-day matchups looked like this:

- Circle (1) vs. Plentywood (8)
- Scobey (4) vs. Sidney (5)
- Glendive (2) vs. Glasgow (7)
- Wolf Point (3) vs. Malta (6)

In their first game against Sidney, Rob Fladager hit home runs in his first two plate appearances and drove in five runs to lead Scobey to a 15-9 win. Rob remembers the two home runs. "The first home run was on an 0-2 count. I was expecting the pitcher to make me chase a pitch out of the zone, but he threw a fastball right down the middle. The second home run went to straightaway center field." Scott Nelson added four hits, and Ryan Linder and Josh Lee three to join Rob in leading Scobey's vicious 18-hit attack. Steve Stephenson went the distance to get the win. Scobey played stellar defense, committing only one error in the game. Rob also remembers how important that first win in the tournament was. "That win over Sidney was the start to a great tournament for the team. Everyone really 'upped their game!'"

The eighth seed and host Plentywood shocked top-seeded Circle in their opening game, so Scobey faced their old rival in their second game on Plentywood's home field. Would Plentywood be a rude host and spoil Scobey's push for a repeat? This one would be a nailbiter and go down to the wire, with Scobey winning another slugfest, this time 10-9. Brent Tarum started on the mound, and Ryan Oie finished to get the win. Derek Solberg led Scobey's hitting, going 3 for 5, and the fourth-seeded Blues advanced to the undefeated semifinal against Glendive. Scobey committed five errors in the game, which they couldn't continue if they wanted to go deeper into the tournament.

The push for a repeat stalled against second-seeded Glendive as the Blue Devils thumped Scobey 17-7. Ryan Linder and Brent Tarum pitched. Ryan Linder and Derek Solberg homered, and Steve Stephenson had two hits in the losing cause. Scobey's defense again hurt them, as the Blues committed seven errors in the game; the defense would need to shore up if they wanted to return to State. Adding injury to insult, starting catcher Josh Lee was injured while scoring on a close play at the plate. Josh humorously remembers what happened—"I did my best Pete Rose impression at home plate and won a contusion on my left hip flexor." It wasn't funny then, however, as it reduced Scobey's roster to 10 players for the remainder of the tournament, which was now the dirt route.

The Blues' loss to Glendive pitted them against top-seeded Circle. Rob Fladager remembers how good Circle was. "Circle won the conference that season and was the one seed going in." If the Blues won, they would advance to the championship game against Glendive and clinch a berth in the state tournament; a loss would send them back to Scobey. The Blues put the sloppy fielding behind them as they played errorless ball, topping Circle 5-2 for the right to play for the championship and a berth in the state tournament. Steve Stephenson went the distance, scattering seven hits, and was backed up by tight defense. It was Stephenson's second complete-game win of the tournament. Ryan Oie got three hits, and Stephenson helped his cause at the plate, getting two hits. This was a well-played game by both teams, as Circle only committed two errors in the field, but Scobey sent the top-seeded Zehpyrs packing to Circle.

The championship game against Glendive followed the Circle game. Josh Lee remembers a meeting at home plate between Coach Diegel and Coach Lekvold before the game. "We needed to beat the Blue Devils twice to win the title. I don't know what was said at home plate, but Don and [Brent] Diegel agreed to just play one." Ryan Oie said there wouldn't be a second game because of what *wasn't* said at home plate: "Glendive thought they would win the first game easily." The game would be a winner-take-all championship, and the result would determine which team was the top seed or the second seed from the east in the state tournament. Down to 10 players after Josh Lee's injury and running short on pitching after four games, the task was difficult for the Scobey nine. But this was a scrappy young bunch of Blues who had played a lot of baseball together, and they were tough.

The Glendive game was one of the most dramatic finishes for Scobey in an eastern divisional championship—the game would go down to the last out. Don Lekvold used four different pitchers. Ryan Oie started and pitched five shutout innings, and Stephenson and Tarum followed. Scobey took a 7-3 lead into the ninth inning, but walks helped Glendive put on a rally, and the Blue Devils scored three runs to close to within one run, 7-6, and they had the bases loaded. Coach Lekvold brought in Ryan Linder with bases loaded and no outs, and he finally ended the game before the tying run could score to earn the pressure-packed save.

1991 Scobey Blues, Eastern Division Champions. Front row, left to right: Rob Fladager, Steve Stephenson, Derek Solberg, Brent Tarum, Lee Hackman, Ty Bucklin, Ryan Linder. Back row left to right: Scott Nelson, Ryan Oie, Head Coach Don Lekvold, Assistant Coach Bart Gregerson, Josh Lee, Ben Hoversland. *Leader photo.*

The Blues had repeated as eastern division champions! Four Blues had two hits each in a balanced 11-hit, but Scobey's pitching—the four pitchers scattered only five Glendive hits—and the defense—only two errors—won the game for them. The *Leader* recognized how critical Scobey's defense was to their success: "The Blues had a great defensive day Monday, committing only two errors in 18 innings and pulling off some outstanding plays in upsetting conference champion Circle and then winning the championship over Glendive in a close one."[60] The *Leader* added that the Blues "pulled off upsets, hung on to win a couple of one-run ball games, and came thru the back door to win their second consecutive divisional title."[61]

Rob Fladager summed up the championship repeat: "We were lucky to get the win over Plentywood with five errors. I remember Derek's home run against Glendive. I think it was off their best pitcher, Erickson. Huge win against Circle—took all the pressure off us since we punched our ticket to State again. I know we surprised a lot of teams in the tournament because this was a rebuilding year; maybe they overlooked us a bit. Tarum, Linder, Oie, and Stephenson were amazing on the hill. They never overpowered hitters, but they consistently threw strikes, not many walks. There were a handful of awesome defensive plays by the infield and outfield that really halted any momentum for Circle and Glendive in those final two games."

Although Don Lekvold was awarded Coach of the Year in 1990, coaching this young team to the divisional championship with only one 18-year-old on the roster might have been his best year ever. It was a gritty effort by the shorthanded Blues to win it. No tournament MVP was chosen, but Coach Lekvold called out Steve Stephenson, who pitched 21 innings and got two wins, played four different positions (including catcher after Lee was injured), hit well, and had an overall great tournament. Steve Stephenson was very humble when I asked him about his performance in the tournament. "I do remember the 21 innings I pitched. It was probably my favorite tournament. I did get tired, but I would never want to let anyone down." Steve's teammates agreed with Coach Lekvold's assessment of Steve as MVP. Rob Fladager said, "Steve had a phenomenal tournament and, in my opinion, deserved the MVP." Derek Solberg added, "Typical Steve, playing good defense at multiple positions and pitching tons of innings."

The players remember Don Lekvold being emotional before and after the tournament, knowing it was his last year. Josh Lee said, "He gave a speech on the bus before that tournament apologizing about his missed time through the season because of his business. He told us that although we didn't have a good regular season, it's tournament time and everyone is 0-0 so let's forget about the season and have a good tournament. We played loose with nothing to lose. We beat them and brought home the title. Don got on the bus and was pretty proud of us." Rob Fladager added, "We were the fourth or fifth-seeded team at divisional and were supposed to be in a rebuilding year coming off the third-place finish at State the year before. We came out of nowhere to win it. Don got on the bus after the championship game and was a little emotional talking to us; maybe that's when I figured he was done coaching Legion."

And the scrappy Blues were again advancing to State as the number-one seed from the east.

STATE TOURNAMENT

The 1991 state tournament was hosted at historic Denton Field in Miles City. As the number-one seed from the east, the Blues received a first-round bye and faced the winner of Bitterroot and the Miles City Colts. It turned about the early-season Arthur Maybelle Tournament was a leading indicator of the teams who would play at the state tournament, as four teams won their respective divisions—Laurel, Bitterroot, Dillon, and Scobey—and two of them—Bitterroot and Dillon—were favored in the tournament. Laurel Coach Fred Feuerbacher liked his team's chances, saying, "We feel we can win it. We believe it's our year." The Dodgers were 48-20 on the season, while Dillon had dominated the Central division, winning all 23 games, and they were 36-5 overall. Now in his tenth season, Coach Gail Whitworth of Dillon had built a solid program, as the Cubs were perennial state tournament participants.

But it was Bitterroot once again that looked tough to beat. The Bucs had gone 32-9 and won the western division for the fifth consecutive year.

- Bitterroot Bucs (1W) vs. Miles City (2S)
- Glendive (2E) vs. Laurel (1S)
- Libby (2W) vs. Great Falls (2C)
- Dillon (1C) vs. Havre (2N)
- Byes Fort Macleod (1N), Scobey (1E)

Josh Lee could not recover from his injury at Divisional, so Nelson assumed the catching duties at State. With the first-round bye, the Blues faced the winner of the Bitterroot-Miles City game, which the Bucs won convincingly 13-1. Scobey had played Bitterroot earlier in the season at the Arthur Maybelle Tournament in Dillon, losing 9-4. The Blues hoped their late-season run in the Divisional tournament would carry over to State, but it was not to be, as Bitterroot shut out Scobey, 14-0, with Glen Modler and Benji Bicha combining on a two-hitter. The Bucs got 12 hits, including a perfect 3-for-3 performance by John Fox and a triple from Bicha. Rookie Zach Bowler recalls getting in the game for the last out of the game. "I remember Tony Vigliotti as part of the umpire crew that tourney. I rarely struck out, but I did that night when I subbed for the last out of the game against Bitterroot. Fouled a few off, then struck out looking. Tony Vig was behind the plate." Tony Vig rung the hometown Scobey boy up.

Scobey then faced the Great Falls Sparkies in a loser-out game. Brent Tarum started for Scobey. The Blues were flying high after Ben Hoversland hit a grand slam home run in the top of the fifth inning to give Scobey a 5-0 lead. Brent Tarum pitched brilliantly until the sixth inning, but with the Blues leading 5-1, the wheels came off, as the Sparkies scored seven runs in the inning to take an 8-5 lead. Don Lekvold relieved Tarum with Ryan Oie, and then 15-year-old Tyler Bucklin (dual-rostered on the Hi-Line Babe Ruth team) came in. In the top of the seventh, Scobey jumped right back on top, scoring four runs to lead 9-8, but Great Falls had another big inning in the bottom half, plating five more runs to take a 13-9 lead. Ryan Linder appeared on the mound as Scobey's fourth pitcher. Scobey tried to come back again but pulled up a little short as the Sparkies went on to win the slugfest, 13-12. Rob Fladager, Scott Nelson, and Ryan Linder added doubles to Hoversland's grand slam to lead Scobey's hitting. Scobey outhit the Sparkies 10 to 5, but numerous walks and four costly errors led to Great Falls's 13 runs. When I asked the 91ers to comment on the Great Falls game, Derek Solberg said, "I think 13 runs and five hits pretty much sums it up."

It was a tough one-run loss for Scobey to end the season, who had played magnificently in the divisional tournament to win the east. The games in the state tournament were the last for 18-year-old Ryan Linder of Flaxville, who had been a three-year starter for the Blues. I asked Ryan to share his baseball story with me. Ryan said, "I started playing baseball in Little League in Flaxville. I remember it because we won the conference championship, and it was a big deal because Flaxville hadn't won it before. Reese Puckett, one of your many relatives, was our coach. I started playing Legion when I was 15 years old (1988). I remember the first guys I was playing with were Jeff Jones and Paul Shaffer. You used to get stripped down in the outfield, and they took your clothes to the gas station. You'd have to run downtown naked to get your clothes back. But Paul and Jeff took care of me, so I never had to do that. They were the old guys on the team at the time."

My conversation with Ryan continued, and I asked him if he remembered some details of the big games, like the stellar game he pitched in the 1990 tournament against Vauxhall. Like many players, he didn't remember the game specifics, but he remembered what mattered most. I asked him if he could talk a little bit about playing baseball with all those kids from the different towns in the summer and what the experience was like for him being a Scobey Blue.

Ryan said, "All the towns were separate, but us baseball players were all buddies. It didn't matter where we were from. We wanted to beat each other in basketball. I remember playing basketball against Kenny and Mike, and Rob Fladager in Peerless. We'd get done with a basketball game in the middle of the winter, and we'd sit and talk about baseball after the game. Win or lose, it didn't matter . . . I hate to say it, but baseball was my favorite sport because we were competitive. It was kind of like an All-Star team, the best athletes from every town played baseball. Kevin Nelson and me, I mean, he's from Opheim; I'm from Flaxville. They were in a totally different conference in basketball but we're lifelong friends because of baseball. And that's the biggest thing I remember. The Flaxville kids never liked to go to Scobey because there was a rivalry there, but I was friends with them because I played baseball with them all summer, 60 or 70 games. I remember taking bus rides to Dillon, Montana, and staying in the Civic Center in Lewistown; I mean, we'd spend every day together as a team all summer. I'm still friends with all those guys to this day. If it wasn't for baseball, I probably wouldn't know any of them kids."

Well said, Ryan. That was my experience, too—and every other Blue. I told Ryan, "You say you don't remember much, but you remember everything. What matters most."

The 1991 state tournament was also the last for Coach Don Lekvold. Rob Fladager remembers Don's reason for stepping aside. "His reason was that his boys, Jedd and Morgan, were becoming Little League age, and Don wanted to spend more time with them. Takes a 'hell of a guy!' to spend that much time away from his family/business to coach a bunch of kids that I'm sure stressed him out at times."

Don had joined Doc Norman and the Blues as an assistant coach in 1977 after coaching Wolf Point to divisional championships in 1975 and 1976 and a second-place finish at State in 1976 when Scobey defeated Wolf Point 13-11 in the championship game in Cut Bank. He assisted Doc on five State championships (1977-80 and 1982) and, as head coach, led Scobey to two division championships (1990 and 1991) and two third-place finishes at State (1985 and 1990). He was honored as Montana/Alberta American Legion Coach of the Year in 1990. He finished his coaching career with five golds, one silver, and two bronze medals at the state tournament. Don's passion for baseball and knowledge of the game were critical to the success of Scobey American Legion Baseball for 15 years. Since 1959, when Doc first came to Scobey, American Legion Post 56 had seen continuity in the head coaching position, which brought stability and success to the program. Don's coaching was part of that stability and success.

TOURNAMENT SUMMARY

THE BITTERROOT BUCS WON THEIR THIRD STATE CHAMPIONSHIP in four years, beating Laurel 5-3 in the championship game. It was the Bucs' fifth straight win in the 10-team tournament. Jay Brockett hit a home run, and Roger Shutz had three hits to lead the Bucs' hitting. Brockett was named MVP, and Shutz was the leading hitter in the tournament, batting .588.

Glendive, whom Scobey had beaten for the Division championship, fared well in the tournament. They upset runner-up Laurel on opening day and finished in third place, losing only to champion Bitterroot in the undefeated semifinal and runner-up Laurel in their rematch.

It was a tough two-and-a-BBQ tournament for Scobey. The Blues faced eventual state champion Bitterroot in their first game, then two rough innings against Great Falls, where the Sparkies plated 12 runs, did the Blues in. But the young team had punched above their weight in 1991 and had over-achieved: winning the eastern divisional championship over Glendive after coming back through the dirt route with a depleted roster might have been Coach Don Lekvold's crowning achievement as a coach, especially considering Glendive finished third at State.

The *Leader* summed up the 1991 season this way: "Last year's Blues placed a strong third at State, but this was a rebuilding season, and they had to pull off some upsets to win their division. The Blues will lose only one regular (Ryan Linder) due to the age limit for next year, and some exceptional talent is expected to move up from the Babe Ruth ranks. The boys and fans are already looking forward to next season."[62]

Mike Lee and Ken Meyer, who had led Scobey to a third-place finish at State in 1990, coached that "exceptional talent" in Babe Ruth in 1991. They were the coaches of the Hi-Line All Stars, who took second at Divisional and earned a berth in the state tournament.

Scobey would return eight starters in 1992, including many talented players who had been with the Blues for three years. With all but one starter coming back—and several 18-year-olds who had played in two state tournaments and won two eastern division championships—the Blues would be likely be favored to three-peat as eastern division champions and perhaps make some noise at State in 1992.

Who would step up to coach this talented and experienced team now that Don Lekvold had stepped aside? Could the Blues three-peat and make a run in the state tournament?

TOURNAMENT STATS

Hitting

The Blues were shut out on a two-hitter in their first game against Bitterroot, so Ben Hoversland's grand slam home run in the fifth inning against the Sparkies was the highlight of Scobey's hitting. Hoversland's grand slam was the third in history for the Blues in a state tournament, following Don Puckett in Havre in 1974 and Steve Lapke in Scobey in 1985.

Pitching

Scobey's pitching gave up 12 hits and 14 runs to Bitterroot, but against Great Falls, four pitchers only allowed five hits, which was good. The Sparkies scored their 13 runs on walks and costly errors.

Fielding

The four errors against Great Falls proved costly, as many Sparkie runs were unearned. Scobey's defense had been up and down in the Divisional tournament, but on the final day, they only committed two errors in 18 innings to win it. Errors can be contagious, however, and the slick fielding of the last day of the divisional tournament did not carry over to State.

NORTHWEST REGIONAL

The 1991 Northwest Regional American Legion Tournament was played in Coeur d'Alene, Idaho. Bitterroot lost to both Oregon teams and finished 1-2 in the tournament. The Bucs finished their season 38-11. Laurel also won one game in the tournament and finished the season 54-24. Mt. Vernon, Washington, won the tournament.

EXTRA INNINGS

Ryan Oie got tossed out of the 15-inning game against Wolf Point. He missed first base on a double, Wolf Point coach Neubauer appealed, and he was called out. Ryan argued and home plate umpire Jim Lekvold gave him the hook.

The 15-inning marathon between Scobey and Wolf Point was another in a long line of extra-inning games between the two friendly rivals. Scobey and Wolf Point had a history of playing extra-inning games against each other, dating back to 1930, when two towns first fielded Legion teams. In the 1930 district championship game, Scobey beat Wolf Point 9-8 in 11 innings, with Bob Schaefer going the distance and getting the win for Scobey. Here are the known extra-inning games between Scobey and Wolf Point:

- 1930: Scobey 9, Wolf Point 8 (11 innings). Bob Schaefer (W) went the distance in the district championship.
- 1973: Scobey 10, Wolf Point 6 (12 innings). Terry Puckett (W) went the distance in the divisional championship game.
- 1975: Wolf Point 24, Scobey 23 (12 innings). Duke Trangsrud and Craig Miller (L) each pitched six innings for Scobey.
- 1977: Wolf Point 3, Scobey 2 (12 innings). Joe Puckett (L) went the distance for Scobey.
- 1991: Wolf Point over Scobey (15 innings). Ryan Oie pitched the first 11 innings for Scobey.

The 15-inning game was the second-longest game in Blues history. The longest game was Scobey's 5-4 upset of Havre in 16 innings at the 1985 State Tournament in Scobey.

Mike Lee and Ken Meyer coached the Hi-Line All-Stars to second place at the divisional tournament and a berth in the state tournament that summer. The Legion and Babe Ruth divisional tournaments were played the same weekend, so Scobey's roster was even smaller at the Legion Divisional in Plentywood—Zach Bowler and Ty Bucklin were dual-rostered as Babe Ruth players. Mike Lee called coaching Babe Ruth a "dress rehearsal for the next summer when Ken and

I took over coaching Legion." Ty Bucklin and Zach Bowler were the two Scobey kids on the Hi-Line All-Stars. Josh Lee said, "Ty Bucklin (from Outlook) was Burl and Roz Bowler's third son every summer Babe Ruth through Legion."

Josh Lee remembers Ben Hoversland's grand slam against Great Falls at State. "After Hoze hit his home run, we all cheered, but he tripped and fell flat on his face rounding first. All you saw was a pile of dust. Then up from the dust cloud he came and proceeded to finish his trot. He came into the dugout and made the comment, 'It was a handle shot.' The entire dugout busted out laughing, and I remember the first base umpire looking towards our dugout like we were all idiots."

Hoversland's grand slam against Great Falls at State was the third in history for Scobey at a state tournament. Don Puckett hit a grand salami against the Helena Representatives in 1974 in Havre, and Steve Lapke hit a big bases-loaded four-bagger against the Billings Cardinals in Scobey in 1985.

Rob Fladager's two home runs in consecutive at-bats against Sidney at Divisional was the only time a Scobey Blue had hit two home runs in the same game in Blues history—to that point. Rob's record of two home runs in one game would stand until the eastern divisional in Glasgow in 1997 when Jay Hoversland hit three home runs in his first three at-bats against the Homestead Pioneers.

Ryan Linder had a job in Medicine Lake in the summer of 1991, so he couldn't make it to Scobey for all the practices. Don Lekvold allowed him to play, and of course, the team was okay with it because Ryan had been a vital part of the Blues since 1988. Before 1991, Ryan told me he worked as a garbage man in Scobey through high school in the summer. Art Holum was the city manager. Ryan said, "All the city workers had to work till whenever, but I would get off early. I shouldn't say this, but Art would always let me off work early to go get in the batting cage. That was kind of the nice part. All the city employees had to work till whenever, but he'd let me skate out of there at three thirty and go get some cuts in the batting cage." As Ryan said, Blues baseball was the king.

Josh Lee remembers a funny incident in the game before they played Circle. "Circle was good that year. I remember sitting in the bleachers watching the game before ours. Back when you had to 'stake your claim' to a dugout before your game to get the one you wanted. The Blues wanted the first base dugout which was occupied by Circle. We're all sitting there, and [Derek] Gackle was in the on-deck circle. Oie hollered at him, 'Call your shot!' Gackle smiled and pointed deep. I'll be damned; he took one out at his at-bat."

Justin Fossum, who was injured all year during 1990 but was able to return for the divisional and state tournaments, was also injured in 1991 and couldn't play, but he was cleared to play in the state tournament and got in the game against Great Falls. Josh Lee remembers the effect injuries had on a short roster in 1991. "I didn't play in the state tournament. In fact, most of my catching duties that year were because Scott's back gave him fits all summer. When you compete with a team of 11, it puts a lot of emphasis on injuries, whether it was arms, backs, ankles, or a stupid ass head-first slide into home."

SECTION NOTES

1. George Geise, "Dick Kloppel Named Coach of the Year," *Great Falls Tribune*, May 1, 1983.
2. "'Doc' Norman Day," *Daniels County Leader*, June 30, 1983.
3. Ibid.
4. "Blues Start Season," *Daniels County Leader*, May 26, 1983.
5. "Blues play dbh, Glendive tonight," *Daniels County Leader*, July 14, 1983.
6. "Legion ball opens today," *Ravalli Republic*, May 25, 1983.
7. Jack Tanner, "1983—The year of the Bucs," *Ravalli Republic*, December 30, 1983.
8. "'Doc' Norman Day," *Daniels County Leader*, June 30, 1983.
9. "Norman Honored by Former Players," *Daniels County Leader*, July 7, 1983.
10. "The End of an Era; Clyde H. Norman, 1920–1983," *Daniels County Leader*, November 24, 1983.
11. Ibid.
12. Ibid.
13. Rita Balock-Hamilton, "Time-Out with Rita," *Havre Daily News*, August 8, 1984.
14. "Scobey Hosts 7th State B Legion Tourney," *Daniels County Leader*, July 25, 1985.
15. "Scobey leaves Northstars singing 'blues,'" *Havre Daily News*, July 26, 1985.
16. Ibid.
17. "Havre loses opener," *Havre Daily News*, July 31, 1987.
18. "Singing 'blues,'" *Havre Daily News*.
19. Ibid.
20. "Glendive Takes State Title Going Away," *Daniels County Leader*, August 1, 1985.
21. Ibid.
22. Ibid.
23. Ibid.
24. Ibid.
25. Ibid.
26. Ibid.
27. Dixie Halverson, "Slighted by Class B coverage," *Billings Gazette*, August 4, 1985.
28. "Busy Sports Weekend Starts Friday," *Daniels County Leader*, August 14, 1986.
29. Ibid.
30. Ibid.
31. Ibid.
32. "Wolf Point Division Champs Over Sidney," *Daniels County Leader*, July 30, 1987.
33. Ibid.
34. Ed West, "Wolf Point Wearing Its First Legion Crown," *Billings Gazette*, August 3, 1987.
35. Mark Hogan, "Delgado: Family outshines diamonds," *The Daily Inter Lake*, August 16, 1987.
36. Ibid.
37. Brett French, "Red Sox: the new kids on the block," *Ravalli Republic*, May 22, 1987.
38. Ibid.
39. "Blues Action at Sidney," *Daniels County Leader*, July 28, 1988.
40. Ibid.
41. "Doc Norman Classic Sees Laurel Win," *Daniels County Leader*, June 22, 1989.
42. "Blues Sharp; Postseason Begins," *Daniels County Leader*, July 20, 1989.
43. Ibid.
44. Steve Stiffarm, "Yellowjackets win three of five at State A," *Wotanin Wowapi*, August 3, 1989.
45. "Doc Norman Classic Sees Laurel Win," *Daniels County Leader*, June 22, 1989.
46. "Blues Sharp; Postseason Begins," *Daniels County Leader*, July 20, 1989.
47. Kevin Whitworth, "Legion teams converge on Dillon," *Dillon Tribune*, June 6, 1990.
48. "7-1 Blues Run at Season End," *Daniels County Leader*, July 19, 1990.
49. "Blues Sweep Divisional in Four Games," *Daniels County Leader*, July 26, 1990.
50. Ed West, "Bitterroot gunning for 3rd title," *Billings Gazette*, July 28, 1990.
51. Ibid.
52. Ibid.
53. Dooley Pauley, "Vauxhall wins berth in state championship game," *Glendive Ranger-Review*, August 1, 1990.
54. C.O. Wester, "Dodgers play in state tournament," *Laurel Outlook*, August 1, 1990.
55. Ibid.
56. Hudson Willse, "Vauxhall, Bitterroot clash for Legion title," *Montana Standard*, August 15, 1990.
57. "Strong Third at State for Blues," *Daniels County Leader*, August 9, 1990.
58. *Daniels County Leader*, "Blues Sweep Divisional in Four Games," July 26, 1990.
59. Ibid.
60. "Blues Repeat as Division Champions," *Daniels County Leader*, July 25, 1991.
61. Ibid.
62. "Blues Play at State Tourney," *Daniels County Leader*, August 1, 1991.

The Ken Meye[r]

1992 – 1997

1900 – 1924
The Homesteaders
and Early Town Teams

1930 – 1945
The Sons of
the Pioneers

1957 – 1968
The Baseball
Renaissance

*The Scobey
Giants*
1925 – 1929

*Baseball is Back
in Daniels County*
1946 – 1956

*The D[...]
Cham[...]*
1969 –

r/Mike Lee Era

1983 – 1991
The Don Lekvold Era

1998 – 2003
The Last Years

2016 – 2019
The Revival

orman hip Era

The Long Winter
2004 – 2015

The Froid Bulls
2020 – 2024

1992

The Blues Win the Conference and Three-Peat as Eastern Division Champions

> *I remember playing very confident in '92. We went into every game expecting to win. I think winning the '91 divisional tournament helped our confidence going into '92.*
>
> —Derek Solberg, Scobey Blues center fielder (1990-92)

PRESEASON

With eight returning starters from the 1991 team, which repeated as eastern divisional champions, Scobey looked strong in 1992. Eighteen-year-olds Derek Solberg, Steve Stephenson, Robin Fladager, Brent Tarum, Ryan Oie, Ben Hoversland, and Lee Hackman were all back, as were 17-year-old Josh Lee and 16-year-olds Zach Bowler and Tyler Bucklin, who were dual-rostered as 15-year-old Babe Ruthers in 1991. Jon Hersel, Dave Anderson, Morgan Oie, Tyler Tarum, Casey Danelson, and Chad Falcon joined the team as rookies to complete Scobey's solid 16-man roster.

The question was, who would coach this promising team? After two seasons with Wolf Point in 1975 and 1976 and 15 seasons with the Blues—six as assistant coach and nine as head coach—Don Lekvold retired from Legion coaching in 1991. Ken Meyer and Mike Lee, who played for the Blues from 1986-90, would run the practices and coach the games, with their dads, Gary Meyer and Ken Lee, providing managerial assistance on the bench.

Three experienced pitchers, Steve Stephenson, Ryan Oie, and Brent Tarum—who all pitched in the 1991 divisional and state tournaments—would be back. Steve was the winning pitcher in the 1990 divisional championship game, and Ryan was the winning pitcher in the 1991 championship game. These three would lead the staff, with 16-year-old Tyler Bucklin—who saw action in the state tournament as a 15-year-old—providing solid depth on the mound.

Back from his season-ending injury the year before at the Divisional tournament, Josh Lee would anchor the staff behind the plate.

There was not a lot to poke holes at in this team. They were strong offensively and defensively, experienced, with good hitters, pitchers, fielders, speed (Derek Solberg stole over 40 bases a year in 1991 and 1992), and depth. This was a team poised to win Scobey's first regular season conference championship since 1980 and make a serious run in the postseason.

REGULAR SEASON

Some regular season highlights included:

- The Blues tied for first in the ninth annual Doc Norman Memorial Tournament. Rob Fladager said, "We played great competition." The Blues played two good teams: Regina, Saskatchewan, and the Lewistown Redbirds. The Blues walked it off against Lewistown 2-1 early in the tourney when Rob Fladager drove in Derek Solberg with the winning run on a sacrifice fly. Rob remembers his walk-off winner. "Our last at-bat in the bottom of the seventh with the score tied 1-1, with one out Brent was on second and Derek on third. I lifted a fly ball to deep center field, and Derek tagged up for the win. I was proud of this win against Lewistown because they were loaded and going to be at the state tournament. Great pitching on both sides."

- The Blues traveled to Saskatchewan to play against Canadian teams like Moose Jaw. Ryan Oie remembers hitting his only Legion home run on the trip. Rob Fladager said, "Staying in Regina will always be on my list [as a highlight] because of the off-field fun we had." We won't go there, though. An entire book could be written about Blues shenanigans off the field, but some things are better left alone. What happens in Regina stays in Regina.

- At the end of the season, the Blues beat the second-place Glendive Blue Devils in the first game of a doubleheader at Meissner Field to clinch the conference title, Scobey's first outright league title since 1980. With Scobey clinching first place with the win and Glendive having already won second place, Glendive forfeited the second game because it didn't matter in seeding and to save pitching for the divisional tournament a few days later.

The eastern division consisted of seven teams in 1992, and Scobey and Glendive looked to compete for the conference title. Scobey had an excellent regular season, playing up to their potential, and won the conference title for the first time in 11 years (1980), finishing with an overall record of 25-10. The final conference standings looked like this:

1. Scobey
2. Glendive
3. Glasgow
4. Circle
5. Sidney
6. Wolf Point
7. Plentywood

Headed into the divisional tournament as the top seed, the Blues were looking to three-peat as division champs and earn their third consecutive berth in the state tournament. Scobey was the king of the hill in 1992. Could anyone knock them off?

DIVISIONAL TOURNAMENT

FOR THE FIRST TIME SINCE 1975, THE EASTERN DIVISIONAL tournament was held at Burke Field in Wolf Point. Burke Field had been upgraded with new lights in 1991, which enabled Wolf Point to host postseason tournaments. With their first-place conference finish, Scobey received a first-round bye. Opening-day matchups looked like this:

- Scobey (Bye)
- Circle (4) vs. Sidney (5)
- Glendive (2) vs. Plentywood (7)
- Glasgow (3) vs. Wolf Point (6)

In their first game, Scobey faced Circle, who beat Sidney 6-1. The Blues started strong in the tournament, beating Circle 10-2. Brent Tarum pitched the first seven innings to get the win, and Josh Lee came in to finish the last two innings. Derek Solberg, Ryan Oie, and Zach Bowler each had doubles to lead Scobey's nine-hit attack.

With the bye and the win, Scobey quickly found themselves in the undefeated semifinal against second-seeded Glendive. Ryan Oie pitched a four-hitter to lead Scobey to an 8-1 win, a berth in the championship game, and a third consecutive berth in the state tournament. The Blues were rolling in the Divisional.

Glendive came back through the backdoor to challenge Scobey for the championship. The Blue Devils would need to win two games to prevent the Blues from a three-peat, and they took the first step, beating Scobey 10-3 in the first championship game. Glendive jumped on Scobey for five runs in the first inning to take a 5-2 lead, and they never looked back. The Blue Devils "took full advantage of many Blue's errors"[1] to force the second game. Scobey had been playing good defensive ball late in the season, but it all fell apart as the Blues committed eight errors, leading to several unearned runs. Scobey outhit Glendive 8 to 5 but still took a big loss. Tyler Bucklin took the tough loss for Scobey, with his defense collapsing behind him. Craig Berube struck out 10 Blues in eight innings to get the win for Glendive.

Rob Fladager remembers an incident in the Glendive game. "It was towards the end of the game. I hit a ball to left field that I figured was gone. I stood at home plate admiring the ball like I was 'Jose Canseco,' but it hit the top of the wall and stayed in the park. I trotted to first for a stand-up single. I remember Karch (first base coach) giggling and calling me an 'idiot.' Ken, on the other hand, was pissed! Benched me the rest of the game!" Josh Lee remembers the long single, too. "I remember H watching his single. Didn't dare laugh; we were losing. Fear of running."

But the sun always rises the next day in baseball, and the Blues looked to put the defensive lapse behind them and claim their third consecutive Eastern divisional championship. Rob Fladager, back off the bench and determined not to admire would-be home runs anymore, remembers the feeling going into the championship game against Glendive. "I know Glendive had to beat us twice for the championship, so I wasn't worried about the next game. I knew we would win. I was trying to keep an eye on the rest of the divisional tournaments in the state to see what Dillon, Laurel, and Bitterroot were doing. I was playing the 'which side of the bracket game do we want to be on.'"

Rob's confidence was warranted. The Blues jumped all over Glendive, taking an 11-0 lead after four innings, and the championship game looked like a blowout—but not so fast.

Glendive scored eight unanswered runs and trailed only 11-8 after seven innings. Scobey settled down after that, and each team scored one additional run to make the final 12-9

1992 Scobey Blues, Eastern Division Champions. Back row: Manager Ken Lee, Coach Mike Lee, Jon Hersel, Dave Anderson, Morgan Oie, Tyler Tarum, Coach Ken Meyer. Middle row: Lee Hackman, Tyler Bucklin, Josh Lee, Zach Bowler, Casey Danelson, Chad Falcon. Front row: Steve Stephenson, Ben Hoversland, Derek Solberg, Brent Tarum, Ryan Oie, Rob Fladager. *Family photo.*

Rob Fladager holds the trophy high over his head after the Blues won their third consecutive eastern division championship. *Family photo.*

Scobey and a three-peat. Starting pitcher Steve Stephenson got the win, and Tyler Bucklin and Brent Tarum pitched, with Tarum picking up the save. Scobey had 13 hits, led by Rob Fladager and Josh Lee, each getting three. Ryan Oie had Scobey's only extra-base hit, a double.

Scobey advanced to the state tournament for the third consecutive year with an eastern divisional championship. Glendive would accompany Scobey to State again. Rob credited some of the younger players on the roster with stepping up to help the team win. He said, "I was very impressed with rookies Zach, Casey, and Tyler. They played like seasoned veterans all year. They were very instrumental in helping Josh and us 18-year-olds win that season."

STATE TOURNAMENT

THE MISSOULA REDS HOSTED THE 1992 STATE TOURNAMENT at Lindborg-Cregg Field in Missoula. Pre-tourney reviews by coaches indicated that there was no clearcut favorite, and the tournament was wide open. The title of Ed West's pre-tourney review in the *Billings Gazette* said it all: "Dog fight expected at State A Legion showdown."[2] Ed West began the article by writing, "You could pick Lewistown to win it. Or Laurel, Scobey, or Libby. How about Anaconda or Dillon?"[3] Laurel coach Fred Feuerbacher liked Laurel's chances, stating, "I think we have a good shot at it. A lot depends on pitching, which it does in any game."[4]

For Scobey, Coach Ken Meyer was hopeful, saying, "We're going there with the feeling we have a chance."[5] The article said, "Meyer believes the Blues have a quality pitching staff with four starters—Brent Tarum, Ryan Oie, Steve Stephenson, and Ty Bucklin."[6] Scobey carried a 28-11 record into the tournament. Individually, Rob Fladager was the Blues' leading hitter, with a 400-plus average, and Brent Tarum led the pitching staff with a 10-1 record.

The opening-day matchups looked like this:

- Laurel (2S) vs. Anaconda (2W)
- Glendive (2E) vs. Okotoks (2N)
- Scobey (1E) vs. Dillon (2C)
- Vauxhall (1N) vs. Missoula Reds (2W)
- Byes Lewistown (1S) and Libby (1W)

In Scobey's first game against Dillon, Cub's starting pitcher Chris Bowker stymied the Blues, pitching a complete-game four-hit shutout, striking out 16 Blues to lead Dillon to a 7-0 win. Brent Tarum went the distance for Scobey, giving up nine hits. Scobey's defense was sound, as they only committed two errors, but they just couldn't get anything going against Bowker, who was simply overpowering.

In the loser-out game against Okotoks, it was another dramatic ninth-inning finish for the cardiac Blues. Coach Meyer handed the ball to Steve Stephenson to keep Scobey alive in the tournament. The Blues' bats came alive, and they jumped on Okotoks starting pitcher Geoffe Nickerson for six runs in the top of the third inning to take a 6-0 lead, but Okotoks responded with four runs in the bottom half to make it 6-4. Scobey added two runs in the top of the seventh to take an 8-5 lead, but things got tense in the bottom of the ninth. Okotoks plated two runs to make it 8-7 and had the tying and winning runs on base before Steve Stephenson, who went the distance, choked off the rally, preserving a nail-biting 8-7 win for Scobey, and the Blues lived to fight another day.

Stephenson struck out four and walked six in his nine-inning complete game win. Scobey's 13-hit attack was led by Brent Tarum, who had three hits, including a double. Rob Fladager and Zach Bowler each had two RBIs, and Ty Bucklin had a triple. Scobey played errorless ball in the field. In two games at State, the Blues were playing well defensively, as they had only committed two errors in 18 innings.

Due to "poor bracketing by tournament staff,"[7] the Blues would face the Dillon Cubs a second time, and the Cubs would get the better of Scobey again, this time by a score of 8-4. After a solo inside-the-park home run by Zach Bowler, the Blues led 2-1 after three innings, but Dillon erupted for four runs in the top of the fourth inning on a walk and three hits, and that was all the runs they would need. The Blues had to play from behind the rest of the way as the Cubs padded their lead with three runs in the seventh to lead 8-2. Scobey mustered a rally to score two runs in their half of the seventh, but Chris Bowker—who shut out the Blues with a four-hitter in the first game—came on in relief to pitch two scoreless innings and frustrate Scobey a second time. Ryan Oie remembers starting the game on the mound but getting injured and having to come out of the game as a pitcher. "I started that game, but I dove and cut my hand open pretty good. I was having a tough time pitching, but I pitched like four good innings, but they started to get to me, so I was removed then." Ryan was relieved by Steve Stephenson in the fourth, and Ty Bucklin came in in the seventh. Scobey outhit the Cubs 13 to 12 but left several runners on base and couldn't get the big hit when they needed it. They did have two big hits from Zach Bowler, who, in addition to his home run, also stroked a triple on a 3 for 5 day. Scobey had two errors in the seventh, which led to two unearned runs for Dillon. With the second loss to Dillon, Scobey was eliminated from the tournament but finished a successful season with a 30-13 record.

TOURNAMENT SUMMARY

The Laurel Dodgers went through the tournament undefeated, beating the Missoula Reds 20-17 to win the championship. Dan Bublitz of Laurel was named tournament MVP, and Justin Daniels of Missoula won the hitting award. The Lewistown Redbirds won the sportsmanship trophy.

For Scobey, who had hoped to make a deep run in the tournament, winning one game and losing two was disappointing, but Dillon ace Chris Bowker (11-1) frustrated the Blues with a four-hit shutout in the first game, and the Cubs continued their mastery of Scobey in the second game, running their record to 4-0 lifetime over Scobey. Rob Fladager reflected on the tournament and his Legion career. "I was sad after it was over; we were good enough to win it. I look back now and honestly thought we had similar traits/talent as the 1990 team that took third at State. We had 18-year-olds that were good players and battle tested. One 17-year-old in Josh and a group of really good rookies. I thought it would come down to Dillon, Laurel, Lewistown, and Scobey. We just needed to get hot at the right time and Lady Luck to help us a little. Sucked we dropped two to a very good Dillon team. I don't remember the four errors against Dillon in the second game, but I think if we played it clean, we would have beaten them. I guess the only satisfaction I get is that Dillon had to use their best pitcher (Bowker) in the tournament to beat us twice."

The 1992 state tournament was the final hurrah for seven veteran 18-year-olds—Rob Fladager, Brent Tarum, Ben Hoversland, Ryan Oie, Steve Stephenson, Derek Solberg, and Lee Hackman—who had played for the Blues in three state tournaments and on three Divisional championship teams. These seven ballers represented Scobey well and can be proud of their accomplishments in the three years they played together. In losing these seven players—including their top three pitchers—it would be challenging to fill the holes vacated in Scobey's lineup in 1993.

I asked Ryan Oie, who had played with the Blues since 1989, to reflect on his years with the Blues, and he said this: "Baseball's just been a part of me. Legion was just fun, some of the best times of my life, playing with players that you consider some of your best friends, like Derek and Brent and Rob. I could just count on my teammates. Most of us were 18 and we had good chemistry; we'd been playing together since we were 16. We kind of just clicked when we were 16 and kept it going till we were 18."

Rob Fladager reflected on his three-year Legion career with Scobey. "The Blues offered me a lesson on what it means to play baseball. I was able to make new friends on and off the field, be a part of a baseball family, and experience failure and success. Maybe along the way, the Blues helped me gain an identity, develop values, and establish goals by working hard and giving maximum effort. I know I gained 'life lessons' from those three summers, especially on how to perform in tough situations and coming up clutch in key situations. I loved playing for the Blues. I am so thankful to have had the Blues baseball team as a part of my life. There was something about turning a double play or hitting an RBI double that brings a thrill like no other sport can give me. I miss those glory days."

I miss them too, Rob.

Derek Solberg, who like Rob played on three consecutive divisional championship teams, remembered how special it was playing Legion Baseball with the same kids he did in Little League and Babe Ruth. "The best part of being a Scobey Blue was the brotherhood with all the guys. Getting guys from 4 to 5 towns to make one team was very special and I think we were better for it. Our 1991 team had players from Opheim, Peerless, Scobey, Flaxville, and Outlook; the exact same towns that made up our northern Border Little League. The Little League All-Stars and 13-year-old Babe Ruth All-Stars were essentially the minor leagues for the Scobey Blues. If you look at pictures from all those teams, there are tons of future Scobey Blues on those rosters. Melting the five towns into one team was easy because we had already played together for 4 to 5 years. Playing for the Blues was definitely the highlight of my high school sports career. I liked the other sports, but baseball was always my first love, and being a Blue was an honor, and I will never forget those memories."

TOURNAMENT STATS

Hitting

AFTER GETTING SHUT OUT ON A FOUR-HITTER BY CHRIS BOWKER of Dillon in their first game, Scobey's hitting was good, as they had 13 hits against Okotoks and 12 hits against Dillon in the second game. Rob Fladager, Scobey's leading hitter during the regular season hitting over .400, had five hits, and Zach Bowler had five hits to lead Scobey's hitting. Zach led the team in extra-base hits with a double, triple, and home run.

Pitching

SCOBEY'S PITCHING WAS GOOD ENOUGH TO KEEP THEM IN GAMES, and Ken Meyer used all four pitchers on his staff. Brent Tarum took the loss in the first game, going the distance and giving up nine hits. Against Okotoks, Steve Stephenson also pitched a complete game, holding off Okotoks in the ninth inning to preserve Scobey's one-run win. He gave up eight hits and walked six, striking out four to get the win. Coach Meyer used three pitchers in the second game against Dillon. Ryan Oie started and pitched three innings-plus, was relieved by Steve Stephenson in the fourth, then Ty Bucklin relieved in the seventh. Ryan Oie took the loss.

Fielding

WITH THE EXCEPTION OF THE SEVENTH INNING IN THE SECOND game against Dillon, when the Blues committed two errors, allowing two unearned runs, Scobey's defense was solid. They committed only two errors against Dillon in the first game and played perfectly in the field against Okotoks, committing no errors. They had four errors in the second game against Dillon, leading to two unearned runs. Compared to the other teams in the tournament, Scobey was one of the better fielding teams, if not the best. For example, the Missoula Reds committed 10 errors in the championship game against Laurel.

NORTHWEST REGIONAL

THE 1992 NORTHWEST REGIONAL WAS PLAYED IN PENDLETON, Oregon, with state champion Laurel and runner-up Missoula representing Montana. Laurel was eliminated in two games, but the Missoula Reds made an incredible run in the tournament, winning four games and taking second place. They lost the championship game to Burlington, Washington, 4-1. The Reds finished their successful season 53-18, while the Dodgers ended up 46-26, winning their fifth state championship.

EXTRA INNINGS

SCOBEY'S LEAGUE AND DIVISIONAL CHAMPIONSHIPS IN 1992 were the last in the storied history of the Blues program. Scobey would qualify for State three more times (1995-97) but not as Divisional champion.

The error in the bracketing in the state tournament in Missoula—where Scobey played Dillon in its first and third games—never would have happened in a tournament hosted at Scobey. The larger cities in Montana were not accustomed to hosting State A Tournaments like the smaller towns were. Josh Lee said, "I remember the big stink about the bracket. Playing Dillon twice was bullshit." Derek Solberg added, "That's the only tournament I've played in my life that I've seen anything that stupid."

Pitcher Ryan Oie remembers a funny incident that happened with Coach Karch Lee. "I remember one game, you know, Karch would call the pitches for me from the dugout. He would flash the sign to Josh and he would give me the sign. I shook Josh off and Karch yelled, "You little bastard, you shook me off! Don't, don't shake me off, you little bastard!"

Derek Solberg has a memory of the divisional tournament that was funny for every player except Brent Tarum. I would imagine the coaches were not laughing either. Derek recalls, "One of my only memories is Brent Tarum flying into the left field wall. The coaches moved Brent to the outfield for games late in the year. There was a ball hit deep, and he didn't know our outfield lingo about getting close to the warning track and ran thru my warning and straight into the fence he was pissed but the rest of us laughed our asses off."

In four previous postseasons, Scobey's run in the tournament was ended by a strong left-handed pitcher: Dave Fanning from Havre (1971); Bill Wilkinson from the

Great Falls Electrics (1982); Barry Griffin from Whitehall (1984); Troy Cleland from Vauxhall (1990). In 1992, the Blues' postseason run was end by a strong right-hander, Chris Bowker from Dillon, who shut Scobey out with a four-hitter in the first game of the state tournament, then pitched two innings of scoreless relief in the second game to preserve Dillon's win. The following year, Bowker was drafted by the Houston Astros in the 47th round of the 1993 MLB June Amateur Draft.

Bowker was the second powerful right-hander to end Scobey's postseason run. In 1978, our season was ended by another strong right-hander, John Leister of the Great Falls Chargers. We did get to him for eight hits and seven runs (all earned) but lost the game 9-7. Leister was drafted by the New York Mets in the 20th round of the 1979 MLB June Amateur Draft from the Chargers, the Oakland Athletics in the 6th round of the 1983 MLB June Amateur Draft from Michigan State University, and the Boston Red Sox in the 3rd round of the 1984 MLB January Draft-Secondary Phase, again from Michigan State. He pitched for two seasons with the Boston Red Sox (1987 and 1990), appearing in 10 games and saving seven.

Pitcher Steve Stephenson, who threw a knuckle curve, was called "rubber arm" by his teammates. Derek Solberg said, "His arm was always good enough to throw. It made my arm sore just watching Steve pitch all those innings." (Steve pitched 21 innings in the 1991 Divisional Tournament.) When asked if he ever had a sore arm, Steve said, "Not that I can remember. I just couldn't throw as hard as everyone else." He pitched in three Divisional championship games—winning two of them—and was the winning pitcher in Scobey's game at State in 1992.

But Steve's pitching career did not begin as well as it ended. His path to success on the hill was marked by resilience. When he was a Babe Ruther at 15 years old, he had two fingers cut off on his pitching hand by a chain and sprocket on an auger. Steve recalls, "The very first time I ever pitched in Babe Ruth I lost 44-11 against Wolf Point. Don't know why I even wanted to pitch after that. But I was glad I did. It always gave me something to look forward to." After the Babe Ruth game in Wolf Point (his ERA in Babe Ruth was never able to recover), Steve stuck with it, and could pitcher forever, developing a knuckle curve that gave hitters fits. Amazingly, Steve said the accident *helped* his knuckle curve. He said, "It helped me throw a knuckle curve a lot better." Josh recalls the pitch. "It [the accident] definitely gave new meaning to the term 'knuckle curve.' I'd call it, he'd smile and then dig in his glove for a good couple of seconds and then throw. It wasn't any secret to opposing batters what was coming. They would swing and miss not knowing what the fuck it was. I always just remember that when we ever needed two or three innings out of someone, it was usually Steve that took the hill. Steve was a helluva player and teammate. He got us a bunch of Ws and even more saves. The utility man . . ."

It was special for the town of Wolf Point to be able to host the divisional tournament again in 1992. Wolf Point had not hosted a postseason tournament since 1975. That year, the Divisional championship game between Scobey and Wolf Point was called due to darkness because Burke Field in Wolf Point didn't have lights. Wolf Point scored five runs in the bottom of the ninth to tie the game 20-20 innings, but the completion of the game had to be postponed until the next day. The game ended up 24-23 Wolf Point in 12 innings in a game that spanned two days, like a cricket match. But after a year-long effort to install new light standards at Burkie Field, which concluded in May 1991, Wolf Point was able to host postseason tournaments again. The *Wotanin Wowapi* reported that a day-long event titled, "Light Up Burke Field,"[8] was held to celebrate the community-wide effort on May 18, 1991. Activities during the "Light Up Burkie Field" celebration included a Babe Ruth game between the Red Hawks and the Blue Jays (both of the Wolf Point); an alumni contest of former Yellowjackets with the even-numbered years' alumni squaring off against those of the odd-numbered years; a home run derby; a free community barbeque; and was highlighted by a ballgame between the 1991 Yellowjackets against the Wolf Point Legion alumni team as the first game under the lights. The 1992 Eastern Divisional Tournament was the first time Wolf Point hosted a postseason tournament since that slugfest in 1975. The celebration recalls the community-wide effort in Scobey to install new lights at the new Scobey Ball Park in 1957, which enabled Scobey to host all those tournaments for the Plainsmen and the Blues for decades.

Playing for Doc my entire Legion career, I took for granted continuity at the coaching position. I'm sure many of us who played for him did. As Ken Meyer and Mike Lee were former teammates of the 18-year-olds on the team, I wondered what that experience was like playing for them, so I asked the players. Rob Fladager said, "No problem at all! We all looked up to Ken and Mike as teammates in the 1990 season, so I was real happy to have them as coaches my last year." Steve Stephenson agreed: "Couldn't have picked two better coaches than Ken and Karch." Ryan Oie said, "Karch and Ken were probably the best coaches I ever played for." Derek Solberg added, "I agree with all this. However, I did have one funny beef with Karch. I used a 34-inch bat most of the '91 season. About two weeks into the '92 season Karch noticed I was swinging a 34 and said nobody should use it. I told him, 'I hit three home runs with it last year.' He said 'bullshit' and then I threw in 'how the fuck would you know, you weren't here.' He won the argument, and the bat stayed in the shed for the rest of the year. No home runs in '92."

How did it come to be that two 20-year-olds who were former teammates with each other and former teammates of the 18-year-olds on the current team became co-head coaches for the Blues? Mike Lee remembers, "When they approached us, I was not expecting it or even thinking about it. I think Dan Wolfe and a few others came up with the idea when Don didn't want to do it after 1991. As far as the two dads being there, I know there was some concern with some of the baseball board members that we were too young and not removed long enough from the 18-year-olds we played with two years prior. So having Gary [Meyer] and my dad [Ken Lee] there put a few minds more at ease to the idea. I don't remember Dad or Gary being at practice, just games."

Josh Lee weighed in on the adult supervision. "I don't believe they trusted Mike and Ken with all of us, so they got 'Herbie' Meyer to be our bench coach/chaperone."

While in Missoula, Josh Lee tried to expand his cultural horizons in the big city. He said, "We walked into a porn shop by our hotel in Missoula. A group of us walked in and Oie asked the worker behind the counter (from the door so it was loud), 'Where's your Swedish sure-grip suck machine?' He immediately threw us all out. I was disappointed; I'd never been in a smut shop before. I was hoping to learn a few things. Had to settle for the 'ol gas station porn again."

Karch enjoyed his rookie season as coach. "We had a lot of familiarity with the players our rookie season as head Blues coaches. We played with the 18-year-olds in 1990 when they were only 16. Brent Tarum and Rob Fladager were instrumental in helping create a successful transition from Don to us. Practice was completely different. Ken [Meyer] and I came back from college with new drills, ideas and overall baseball knowledge having played in different programs at college." He added, "I really miss the bus trips from that year. Meyer and I took a lot of cash from those characters playing pitch! They couldn't wait to get on the bus and beat us. Some people may look at that as no good and bad influences gambling with the guys; however, the bus trips really helped build a different bond from player-to-player to player-and-coach. We were in charge, but we were still the same guys they played with a few years prior. It was a fun summer."

Josh Lee remembers some good players in the eastern division in 1991. "I think Glendive's Kevin Hess was the only catcher to throw Derek out. Guy threw from his knees. Brett 'Bubba' McKenzie from Glasgow threw pretty hard. He was a lefty. Pat Free from Sidney threw pretty hard."

Josh remembers how he would keep his own pitchers loose on the mound. "I would get our pitchers to bust out laughing when they were pitching. After I would visit them on the mound, I'd trot back to home plate imitating how the opposing catcher would do his trot."

We typically didn't have a rivalry with Glasgow when I played, and I don't remember other Scobey teams rivaled with Glasgow either, but the 1992 team did not like Glasgow, who finished third in the conference standings and the divisional tournament. Rob Fladager said, "I didn't care for their team; I would have rather chopped my balls off than lose to those idiots." Josh Lee added, "Glasgow was okay. They just had a chip on their shoulder and thought they were better than us. [Jerret] Hopstad was a kid that I knew and was nice. Met him during track. We both pole-vaulted. I didn't appreciate G-Town either." Derek Solberg weighed in on the 1992 Reds. "Glasgow was good, but I hated them. Bubba McKenzie was cool. They beat us once in Scobey when Bubba pitched. They had two guys go on to play college ball; Chad Maczka was one of them. One game Glasgow had to come into the clubhouse during a rainout. Not a lot of conversation. We just stared at each other and listen to Kiss *Destroyer*." Good to hear the Blues were still listening the great rock band Kiss in the 1990s.

I was superstitious when I played baseball—as were several of my teammates—but Rob "H" Fladager of the 1990-92 Blues took superstition to a whole new—voodoo—level. When I first heard about Rob's antics, I told the 92ers I as superstitious when I played too, that that was part of baseball. Not stepping on chalk lines, that type of stuff. But I didn't realize the depth of Rob and the 92ers involvement. When I told Josh Lee about my superstitions, he said, "Superstitions? Child stuff, Joe. Rob prayed to the baseball gods on a daily basis. He was a certified baseball shaman. His pregame prayers were fantastic. It was hard to stay quiet and not busy out laughing. Wishing broken arms and legs on the opponents. He'd pray for many Ks for our starting pitcher and summon bombs for our hitters. Then we'd steal their babes like pirates. We went full voodoo!" Rob recalls some of his rituals. "There were lots of sacrifices and witch doctoring. I think we had a deer skull in the dugout for a while. We dropped a doubleheader and had to smash it to break the losing curse. I think we even had Josh's dad, scorekeeper Ken Lee, believing in the spirts!" Derek Solberg's favorite shamanic tactic was when Rob planted a sagebrush in front of the dugout. Inspired by the character Pedro Cerrano—a Cuban who defected to the United States to practice his voodoo religion—of the movie *Major League* (1989), Rob and his teammates practiced their own brand of baseball voodoo in northeastern Montana with sagebrush and deer skulls. It is not known if Rob made sacrifices to Jobu or not. But unlike Pedro Cerrano, Rob could hit a curveball. "Are you saying Jesus Christ can't hit a curveball?" Maybe he couldn't hit Phil Audet's. "I'm pissed off now, Jobu . . . I go to you. I stick up for you. And you no help me now . . . I say FUCK YOU, Jobu. I do it myself."

Derek Solberg went on to play baseball for the Jamestown Jimmies and Rob Fladager played two years at UND-Williston (one with Ken Meyer) and two years for the Beavers at Minot State. Ryan Oie would have joined Rob and Ken at UND-Williston, but an accident cut short his athletic career. Brent Tarum also played two years at Jamestown with Derek.

Rob said, "I really enjoyed playing in college. It was fun to play against Derek." Derek recalls their last two postseason tournaments in college in 1996 and 1997. "In the '96 NDCAC tournament, the Jimmies and I ended Rob's season; in the '97 NDCAC tournament, Rob and the Beavers returned the favor. Derek and Rob finished strong in their last tournament: Derek had nine hits in four games—including one game where he hit a homer, a double, two singles and scored four runs—and Rob hit three home runs in his last game as a Beaver. Rob said, "Wish we would have won that game when I hit three."

Rob versus Derek was not the only former Blue versus Blue matchup in the NDCAC. Rob has bragging rights over Kevin Nelson—at least in one at-bat. In a regular season matchup between the Beavers and the Blue Hawks, Rob hit a home run off of Kevin Nelson, who pitched

Rob Fladager and Derek Solberg faced each other many times while playing for the Minot State Beavers and Jamestown College Jimmies in the North Dakota College Athletic Conference. *Family photo.*

for Dickinson State. Derek said, "I think Kevin thought it was a double off the wall. I remember one time Kevin and H were arguing about it." Rob said, "Kevin still gives me shit about that home run." (Wouldn't that be the other way around Rob?)

Derek and Rob also played a couple seasons in the Canadian Dunning League for the Rockglen Rats in the summers to keep their skills sharp for college. Rob said, "We were free agents and went straight to Rockglen. The team set us up with PO boxes to make us eligible. That experience was a book in itself!" I bet it was, Rob, I bet it was. Derek remembers the experience too. "I wish the men's town teams like the Plainsmen would have kept going. We were on first name basis with all the border guards, Canada and US."

The 1993 Blues would miss Rob, his teammates—and his voodoo—in 1993. Losing a baseball diamond full of talented 18-year-olds (including three pitchers), who had played together since Babe Ruth, three-peated as eastern division champions, and won Scobey's first league title since 1980 would be a challenge for second-year coach Ken Meyer to overcome. It had been a long time since Scobey lost so many studs in one season. But talented players were returning—and coming up. The pipeline was still flowing with plenty of good baseball players in the early 1990s.

1993

The Blues Rebuild and Finish Strong at Divisional

> *We had a lot of lack of experience in '93. There wasn't a bunch of 'I can do this' and 'we can compete' kind of attitude. It took us a while that summer to come together and put some wins together.*
>
> —Josh Lee, Scobey Blues catcher (1991-93)

PRESEASON

The 1993 season would be challenging for co-head coaches Ken Meyer and Kevin Nelson. It was hard to remember the last time Scobey lost seven 18-year-olds in one season—if they ever did. Derek Solberg, Steve Stephenson, Robin Fladager, Brent Tarum, Ryan Oie, Ben Hoversland, and Lee Hackman were all gone. The only 18-year-old on the roster in 1993 was starting catcher Josh Lee, who described himself as "the lone wolf." Three experienced players who started in 1992 were also back: Ty Bucklin, Zach Bowler, and Casey Danelson, as were second-year players Tyler Tarum, Jon Hersel, Morgan Oie, and Dave Anderson. Joining the team as rookies in 1993 were Eric Linder, Jim Goltz, Tim Vigliotti, Ryan Nelson, Cody Jacobson, Joey Boos, K.C. Holum, Wayne Linder, Levi Bowler, and Marshal Fladager. The 18-man roster included players from Opheim, Peerless, Scobey, Flaxville, and Outlook, which was typical in the 1990s. It was a tri-county team from Valley, Daniels, and Sheridan counties.

Ty Bucklin, now 17 years old—who had seen action in the previous two state tournaments—would be the lone starting pitcher returning. Dave Anderson, Tim Vigliotti, Morgan Oie, and Wayne Linder would round out the starting pitching staff. Josh Lee again anchored the staff behind the plate.

Managers Ken Lee and Gary Meyer again joined head coaches Ken and Kevin on the coaching staff. This staff had their work cut out for them, rebuilding a young team that had won three consecutive Eastern division championships, made three state tournament appearances, and won the league title, all for the first time since 1980. A stretch goal would be finishing in the top two at Divisional and returning to State.

It was incredible how close this young team would come to doing just that.

REGULAR SEASON

For the 10th consecutive year, Scobey hosted the Doc Norman Memorial Tournament. This one was special, not only because it was the 10th annual, but because Doc's grandsons Mike and Josh were participating in the tournament, albeit on opposing teams, and one as a player and one as a coach. This was Josh's last season with the Blues, Ken Lee was assistant coach, and Mike brought his team, the Bozeman Spikes, to play in the tournament. Naturally, Marge and Ann were at the game too. It was a family affair at the Doc Norman that year.

Would you believe the Spikes and Blues played for the championship in the round-robin Doc Norman Memorial? Tyler Bucklin remembers the game. "We beat Bozeman in the night game. Karch had coached us the year before and was coaching Bozeman, so we definitely wanted to beat them. I threw a one-hitter that game."

Josh Lee remembers catching left-hander Tyler Bucklin from Outlook, Scobey's ace pitcher in 1993 and 1994. "I always loved catching Bucky. He was a lefty and threw a ball that would 'move.' He always peeked between his glove and the brim of his beloved B hat to where you could barely see his eyes. Fun to catch."

Karch remembers the Blues-Spikes game, too. "I had a kid get real upset. Cody Schrader was his name (he later played linebacker for the Cats), and he was my 14-year-old catcher. For some reason, he thought we two coaches gave up during the Scobey game because I missed giving him signs for what pitch to call. I had to walk with him behind

1993 Scobey Blues, Doc Norman Memorial Tournament Champions. Back row, left to right: Coach Kevin Nelson, Ryan Nelson, Wayne Linder, Zach Bowler, Josh Lee, Casey Danelson, Dave Anderson, Eric Linder, Morgan Oie, Coach Ken Meyer, Manager Ken Lee. Front row: Marge Norman, Tyler Tarum, Cody Jacobson, K.C. Holum, Jon Hersel, Marshal Fladager, Ty Bucklin. *Leader photo, Burl Bowler.*

Marge Norman Shiell was presented the first place trophy as a token of appreciation of her efforts and support of "Doc's Boys of Summer". This is the first time the Blues have won the Doc Norman Memorial. Giving her the award were Coach Kevin Nelson, Josh Lee (her grandson and team captain), Coach Ken Meyer, and son-in-law Ken Lee. Josh was also the winner of the first Doc Norman Memorial Scholarship Award. Doc was not only a sports enthusiast but was an advocate of academics. Josh was selected for the award because of academics, leadership, and citizenship by the baseball committee. *Leader caption and photo, Burl Bowler.*

[Left] Tyler Bucklin was named defensive MVP for his outstanding fielding and pitching. [Above] Zach Bowler won the offensive award for batting .636, 4 stolen bases and 4 RBIs. They were given their plaques by Doc's son-in-law and assistant coach Ken Lee. *Leader caption and photo, Burl Bowler. Leader caption and photo, Burl Bowler.*

the dugout over by the elevators to calm him down during the game because he kept yelling. Art Holum was laughing about it after the game and said, 'Shit, Karch would strike out his own Grandma if it meant winning a game; he's got no quit.' I'll never forget Cody flipping out and being embarrassed in front of the hometown but feeling a lot better after Art expressed his opinion." (Would you really have struck Grandma Marge if it came down to it, Karch? Especially at the Doc Norman Memorial Tournament?)

The eastern division again consisted of seven teams in 1993. Glendive had a lot of returning players from its runner-up roster in 1992, so they would be the favorite. During its rebuilding year, Scobey had a so-so regular season, finishing 10-12 in the conference, good enough for fourth place, a half-game better than Plentywood. Josh Lee, the only 18-year-old on the roster, remembers the challenging 1993 season. "We had a lot of lack of experience in '93. There wasn't a bunch of 'I can do this' attitude. I believe we lacked a sense of we can compete kind of attitude. It took us a while that summer to come together and put some wins together. We struggled a lot with unforced errors. They came in waves that summer. Put together some great innings, then fall apart for one and cost us games." Tyler Bucklin added, "1993 was definitely a year where we were looking for our identity. We had lost some pretty big personalities from the year before, and Josh was the sole 18-year-old." Zach Bowler weighed in, too. "After losing so many 18-year-olds the year before, I would say we didn't have enough developed pitching. It was enough to get through most games, but not when it came to the stacked Glendive and Sidney teams. Josh was the lone 18-year-old and also the entertainer. We still seemed to be having fun that summer."

The final conference standings (with records) looked like this:

1. Glendive (21-3)
2. Glasgow (18-6)
3. Richland County (13-8)
4. Scobey (10-12)
5. Plentywood (10-13)
6. Wolf Point (6-19)
7. Circle (3-19)

DIVISIONAL TOURNAMENT

THE EASTERN DIVISIONAL TOURNAMENT WAS HELD AT MOOSE Memorial Park in Sidney. With their first-place conference finish, Glendive received a first-round bye. Scobey, the fourth seed, faced fifth-seeded Plentywood in its first game. Opening-day matchups looked like this:

- Glendive (Bye)
- Scobey (4) vs. Plentywood (5)
- Glasgow (2) vs. Circle (7)
- Richland County (3) vs. Wolf Point (6)

Coaches Meyer and Nelson handed the ball to 15-year-old Tim Vigliotti to start the first game against Plentywood, and the kid delivered, pitching a complete-game six-hitter to lead Scobey to a 6-4 win. Tim gave up only three earned runs, struck out nine Athletics, and issued no walks. Providing the offensive support to back up Tim's clutch performance on the mound was Casey Danelson, who went 3 for 4 with a double, driving in three of Scobey's six runs. Josh Lee and Zach Bowler each chipped in with two hits.

Scobey's win set up their next game against top-seeded Glendive, who had dominated the conference with a 21-3 record. But this was the postseason, and anything could happen—and it almost did.

Call it "July Madness."

This was a wild one from start to finish. Scobey jumped on Glendive for four runs in the top of the first inning and led 6-1 after three innings. But Glendive started to chip away at the lead, scoring a single run in the fourth and two in the fifth and sixth to tie the game at 6-6. Then Glendive scored three runs in the seventh to take a 9-6 lead. Scobey, down to their final at-bat, came up with a big three-run rally in the top of the ninth to knot the score at 9-9, only to see Glendive walk it off in the bottom half on a bloop single by Raleigh Strobel. Scobey came close to pulling off the upset, but seven errors were their undoing, as only 2 of Glendive's 10 runs were earned. Ty Bucklin started for Scobey and went six innings and was relieved by Dave Anderson, who pitched the last three. Each pitcher gave up only one earned run. In six innings of work, Ty Bucklin struck out six and walked four; Dave Anderson gave up only one earned run in his three innings. Dave remembers the tense game and Raleigh Strobel's at-bat that won the game for Glendive. "Tyler threw an amazing first six innings; he was on fire. Then they swapped us in center field and I went to the mound. It was just a grind out game and it came down to Glendive's last at-bat. Raleigh Strobel was up to bat with the bases loaded. Mike or Kevin came out to the mound to talk to me, and they said, 'How you gonna handle this batter?' and I said, 'I'm gonna throw him two heaters on the outside corner and then throw a slider in on his hands.' Surprisingly enough, I actually executed that but he hit a little blooper over second base and Tyler, Zach, and Levi were all within 10 feet of catching that thing, but it dropped right in between 'em all and they scored and won the game. That was a tough one for me to take." Josh Lee, Zach, and Levi Bowler led Scobey's hitting with two hits each, and Dave Anderson had a double. Scobey's pitching and hitting were good enough to win the game, but the third all-important aspect of baseball—fielding—was not what it needed to be to win.

Josh Lee remembers a trio of consecutive suicide squeezes in the late innings of the Glendive game. "Glendive squeezed me three times in Sidney. One of the baserunners, Chad Mahar, was a linebacker on their state championship football team. When he hit me, it hurt, but I hung on to the ball. Got all three of the fuckers out. After the third squeeze (Mahar), I got the wind knocked outta me, but I forced myself up and showed the ball to the ump. After the three squeezes were all done, as I trotted to the dugout, not getting any air, instead of rolling the ball to the mound, I rolled the ball towards their third-base coach a gave him a good stare. Only 'Big Dick' move I ever tried with an adult up to that point in my life. Whoever it was, I think they might have had a past beef with Ken. I'm not going to wear my tinfoil hat, but I'm pretty sure it wasn't because of me."

The tough, one-run walk-off loss to Glendive relegated Scobey to the dirt route, but the Blues steadily clawed their way back and went deep into the tournament. Scobey played Wolf Point in their next game, and this game was another wild one. This time, it was Scobey's turn to walk it off, as Dave Anderson doubled home two runs in the bottom of the 10th inning to give Scobey a dramatic 6-5 come-from-behind extra-inning win to stay alive in the tournament. Scobey had led Wolf Point throughout, but Wolf Point scored two runs in the top of the ninth to tie the game 4-4, setting up the dramatic tenth. Morgan Oie pitched a great game, going eight and one-third innings, but was relieved in the top of the ninth by Tim Vigliotti when Wolf Point rallied for their two runs to tie it. Morgan gave up four earned runs and had three strikeouts and three walks. Tim Vigliotti finished the ninth; then Ty Bucklin pitched a scoreless 10th to get the win in relief. Every Blue had at least one hit in Scobey's 10-hit attack.

The dramatic walk-off win against Wolf Point set up Scobey's next game against Glasgow, who the Blues had not beaten during the regular season. But the postseason is different, and the time was ripe for an upset, as the Blues knocked off the second-seeded Reds 10-4. The Blues "came to play"[9] in this one. Morgan Oie, who had three hits and two RBIs, led the hitting charge. Ty Bucklin also had two hits and drove in three runs, and 15-year-old Levi Bowler—who had a great tournament—chipped in his two hits. Dave Anderson went the distance on the mound for Scobey to get the win, giving up four earned runs and striking out seven with four walks.

Richland County had upset Glendive 7-0 in the undefeated semifinal, so Scobey's dirt-route path to the championship game—and back to the state tournament for the fourth consecutive year—now depended on upsetting top-seeded Glendive, a team they had almost beaten earlier in the tournament but lost 10-9 in a walk-off. Could the Blues work some magic and somehow knock the top seed off? It would be hard to do with a depleted pitching staff. And with the staff tired, the Blue Devils' bats feasted, blowing out Scobey 20-5 in seven innings, ending Scobey's season—and their deep run in the Divisional tournament. Glendive had 12 hits, but Scobey's bats were not silent, as Dave Anderson banged a two-run home run, and Zach Bowler and Ty Bucklin each had two hits in the losing cause. Tim Vigliotti started on the mound—his second start of the tournament and third appearance—and went four innings, with Ty Bucklin, Levi Bowler, and Cody Jacobson each pitching one inning of relief.

Scobey had beaten Glendive for the Divisional championship in 1991 and 1992, but not this year. Levi Bowler, only 15, remembers Glendive's dominance over Scobey in the years he played. "Glendive seemed to always have our number. Even going back to Little League All-Stars, they were the ones always standing in our way." Regarding the 10-9 loss to Glendive, Levi added, "They always seemed to be on the right end of the deal in the tight game." Older brother Zach agreed but mentioned Sidney, too. "Glendive and Sidney had a solid few years where they were tough to beat."

Sidney then beat Glendive 3-2 to win the Eastern division on their home field, and both teams advanced to State in Anaconda.

The Blues' third-place finish at Divisional was an excellent way to end a so-so season. Tyler Bucklin remembers the tournament. "I really think we came together at divisional tournament time and played a good tourney. I remember the squeeze play with Glendive, Bill (David Anderson) bending the left field fence in half when he ran into it, and Wayne Linder doing those crazy cheers in the dugout."

Zach Bowler reflected on Scobey's 1993 season, focusing on the pitching, which ran out in the second Glendive game. "Ty was our ace pitcher in '93 and '94, but you could obviously only pitch him so much. Vig [Tim Vigliotti] could pitch but was coming up from Babe Ruth that year. David

Anderson pitched well. Wayne Linder and Morgan Oie pitched some as well that year. My arm was toast, so my years of pitching were over."

Levi Bowler and Tim Vigliotti, two 15-year-olds, had finished their Babe Ruth season and saw plenty of action at Divisional, as did Joey Boos. Levi recalls, "I was young and remember being scared. Like Josh said, we lacked in experience that year. I believe it was Tim, Joey, and I who came up from Babe Ruth after our tournament and were cast into the rotation right away. I was 15 at the time and caught a lot of hell from the older crew as a young renegade. My only memory from that tournament was a triple I hit against Glasgow . . . that should probably only have been a double—I ran right through the signal to stop. I do remember catching an earful from Coach Kevin [Nelson]."

Tim Vigliotti added, "I remember pitching against Plentywood in that first game of the tournament. I hung a curveball to one of their 18-year-olds [Wade Gilbertson], and he took me deep. I started a couple of games and also threw relief. That was my welcome to American Legion. Ever since I could remember, I wanted to be a Blue!"

And you were now a Blue, Tim.

Scobey's third-place finish at Divisional demonstrated that this young team would be serious contenders in 1994, with several 15-year-olds on the roster who had played well returning, including Tim Vigliotti, Levi Bowler, and Joey Boos. Zach Bowler, Tyler Bucklin, and Casey Danelson would return for their final season, and Tyler Tarum, Dave Anderson, Morgan Oie, and Wayne Linder would join them. Coach Ken Meyer and his staff were building a state championship contender team. Could the Blues add one more championship trophy to their case in the years to come?

Josh Lee—Doc and Marge's youngest grandson, son of Ken and Ann (Norman) Lee, and younger brother of Rick and Mike—was the only 18-year-old on the 1993 team. Like his brothers, he grew up on the ballfield as a batboy, then later played three seasons for the Blues. Josh remembers one thing that Doc talked about a lot. Josh said, "I always remember Grandpa Doc telling stories about how good a pitcher Phil Audet was. Probably one of his favorites. Complete control and could throw any of his pitches for a strike or get an opposing batter to chase one."

STATE TOURNAMENT

Cubs win, Cubs win, Cubs win!

The Anaconda Athletics hosted the 1991 state tournament at Washoe Park in Anaconda. The Dillon Cubs, led by ace pitcher Chris Bowker—who had stymied Scobey with a four-hit shutout in the first game of the 1992 tournament and then pitched two innings of scoreless relief against them to save the second game—beat Fort Macleod 16-5 to win the championship. Bowker won his second complete game of the tournament and struck out 12 Royals. The championship was the first for Coach Gail Whitworth in Dillon, a reward for 12 years of dedicated coaching of the Cubs. Justin Alderson of Dillon was named MVP of the tournament. Dillon was an incredible 43-4 on the season.

Glendive did well in the tournament, winning two games and finishing third.

Dillon and Fort Macleod advanced to the Northwest Regional in Yakima, Washington.

NORTHWEST REGIONAL

The 1992 Northwest Regional was played in Yakima, Washington, with state champion Dillon and runner-up For Macleod representing Montana/Alberta. Dillon lost two one-run games and were eliminated early, ending their dream season with two tough losses. The Cubs finished their State championship season—their only one in history—with a 43-6 record. While frustrated with the results in the regional tournament (and the bracketing), Coach Gail Whitworth reflected on his team's success. "This has been our finest hour. It's been by far our most outstanding season. We did go out and make some memories; it's been an incredible ride."

Well said, Coach Whitworth. That's what we all did playing baseball; we went out and made some memories. And what wonderful memories they are.

While Dillon experienced frustration in the regional, Fort Macleod, Alberta, won the tournament, sweeping it in four games. This was the second time the Montana/Alberta team had won the tournament, following Vauxhall's championship in 1990.

EXTRA INNINGS

Chris Bowker, who pitched Dillon to the 1993 State championship and ended Scobey's 1992 season with an opening-day shutout win and a two-inning save in the second game, received the first annual Doc Norman Achievement Award, which included a $500 scholarship. It was not only the Doc Norman Memorial Tournament in Scobey that was keeping the memory of Doc's legacy alive. In an article titled "Bowker receives scholarship," the *Dillon Tribune* reported,

```
Dillon's Chris Bowker will receive the first
annual Doc Norman Achievement Award during the
American Legion Youth Luncheon Friday in Living-
```

ston. Bowker topped a field of nominees from the class A American Legion Baseball teams in Montana.

According to American Legion Commissioner Wayne Davis, Bowker was awarded the $500 scholarship because of his baseball skills, integrity, mental attitude, cooperation, citizenship, and conduct on the baseball field.

The award honors Doc Norman, a longtime legionnaire from the Scobey area. Norman dedicated financial support and time to the Scobey Blues, who, under his leadership, continually challenged for the state title.[10]

Mike Lee remembers the team he coached in Bozeman. "They were a bunch of 14-and 15-year-old kids, mostly from Bozeman and Belgrade. There was only one program in the Gallatin Valley at that time. The A team in Bozeman was called the Spikes. We were the first team in Spikes history to win a game at Divisionals. We went 2-2." The Bozeman area now has two baseball teams: the Bozeman Bucks compete in State AA, and the Gallatin Valley Outlaws compete in Class A.

During the Doc Norman Tournament, Josh Lee recalls hosting some of the Bozeman Spikes at the Lee farm. "A few players stayed out at the house. I still see one of them—Shawn Harrison—around town. See him and usually visit for a bit whenever we run into each other."

Josh's favorite off-the-field memory of the 1993 season was Marshal Fladager's car. "He had a $500 Buick Regal that had no reverse. He had a rock for a parking brake and no reverse. He always had to park sideways and downhill."

Josh Lee has fond memories of playing baseball. "I miss those summers entirely! Not a care in the world except for chasing girls and playing ball. I think H [Rob Fladager] and I came up with the 3-Bs slogan:

1. Baseball
2. Beer
3. Babes

In that order."

The regional tournament always seemed to have its own drama, usually associated with its organization. Whether it was Mike Neubauer arguing about the seven-inning games and pitching rules in 1987 or the near-brawl between Bitterroot and Vauxhall in 1990, it was always something. This time, it was the bracket for the Northwest Regional. In an article by J. P. Plutt in the *Dillon Tribune* titled, "Cubs take dream to Yakima, no further,"[11] Coach Gail Whitworth of the Cubs vented his frustration:

The Dillon Cubs dream season came to an end a little earlier than planned at the American Legion Class A Northwest Regional baseball tournament in Yakima, Wash. The Cubs lost two one-run games in their first exposure to regional play.

Dillon and the two teams they played entered the tournament with the shiniest records in the 8-team field. Dillon (43-4), Redmond, Ore., (35-5) and Mountain Home, Idaho, (40-9) were joined in the tourney by host Yakima, Wash., (23-20-2), Torrington, Wyo., (27-13), Fort Macleod, Alberta, (35-20), Everett Post, Wash., (31-5), and Tualatin, Ore., (32-25).

"I tell you, the way they set it up was a joke," said Dillon Coach Gail Whitworth. "When the number one team from Montana plays the number one team from Oregon (in the first game), there's something rotten in Denmark. To be truthful, the way they set it up just stunk."

The bracketing came under scrutiny at the beginning of the tourney, and Dillon's first game, originally scheduled for 5:00 pm Friday, was changed to 2:00 pm and then finally 7:00 pm.

The controversy started before the first pitch in the loser-out game on Saturday.

"I deliberately held my players out of the sun as long as possible," said Whitworth. "We went to the field a half hour before the game, and the Washington commissioner had awarded our opponent the home team advantage. Normally, you decide that with a coin flip. I kinda lost it after that, and so did some of my players."

"I thought that both ball games could have gone either way," said Whitworth. "Maybe with a break here or there . . . , but we didn't make our own breaks," Whitworth continued. These guys more than paid their dues. They worked hard, and they played hard."

"This has been our finest hour," said Whitworth of the team's success. "It's been by far our most outstanding season. We did go out and make some memories; it's been an incredible ride."

The 12-year wait for Coach Whitworth's first state championship was indicative that it takes time to build a championship-caliber program and how important it is to have continuity with a head coach. After beginning his Legion coaching career in Scobey in 1959, it took Coach Doc Norman eight years to qualify for his first state tournament (1967) and 10 years before he won his first state championship (1969)—seven more state championships followed. Good athletes are drawn to good coaches. Winning coaches attract winning players.

1994

The Blues Are Foiled by Plentywood at Divisionals—Again

> " *The goal was always to get to the state tournament. We never should have lost to Plentywood. I remember that we just couldn't get anything going at the plate. It was a tough loss to end on for sure.*
>
> —Tyler Bucklin, Scobey Blues (1991–94) "

1994 Scobey Blues. Back row: Coach Mike Lee, David Anderson, Jamie Veis, Ryan Nelson, Tim Vigliotti, Brent Veis, Kevin Holum, Gordy Leibrand, Coach Ken Meyer. Middle row: Tyler Bucklin, Wayne Linder, Zach Bowler, Casey Danelson, Morgan Oie, Levi Bowler Front row: Neil Hersel, Tyler Tarum, Joey Boos, batboy Cory Cromwell, Joel Smith, Cody Jacobson, Jon Hersel. *Leader photo, Burl Bowler.*

PRESEASON

After rebuilding in 1993, the Blues would be older, stronger—and better—in 1994. Scobey would miss Josh Lee, who had been their starting catcher for three years but was the only Blue not returning from the 1993 team. Tyler "Bucky" Bucklin from Outlook would return for his final season, as would 18-year-olds Casey "Fred" Danelson, Zach Bowler, and Wayne Linder. Jamie Veis joined the team as an 18-year-old in 1994. The Blues had plenty of other experienced players returning, as back for their third season were Morgan Oie, Dave Anderson, Tyler Tarum, and Jon Hersel. Back for their second year were Tim Vigliotti, Levi Bowler, Joey Boos, K.C. Holum, Ryan Nelson, and Cody Jacobson. Rookies joining the team were Brent Veis, Gordy Leibrand, Neil Hersel, and Joel Smith. Cory Cromwell was the batboy.

This was a loaded 19-player roster for the Blues—the largest in history.

Left-hander Tyler Bucklin would be the ace on the pitching staff, with Dave Anderson, Wayne Linder, Morgan Oie, Brent Veis, Zach Bowler, and Tim Vigliotti also getting innings on the mound for third-year coaches Ken Meyer and Mike Lee. Tim Vigliotti, who had pitched in three games in the 1993 Divisional Tournament as a 15-year-old, was moved behind the plate to replace Josh Lee at catcher, so Tim's innings on the mound were limited in 1994.

While this roster had experienced players and some promising younger talent, Coaches Meyer and Lee had their work cut out for them to return the Blues to State after getting them there their first year as head coaches in 1992, the Blues' third consecutive appearance. The two coaches planned an aggressive 53-game schedule to develop the team, including several tournaments. The 53 games were the most the Blues had played in one season in the team's history.

Zach Bowler said the 1994 Blues were solid. "We came back with several of the same players with more experience under our belt. We were a fairly solid team that year." Tim Vigliotti added, "We were loaded in 1994."

In addition to moving Tim Vigliotti from the pitcher's mound to behind the plate, Coaches Meyer and Lee had to do some other position-shuffling in 1994. Levi Bowler became a utility player and recalled his difficulty adjusting to different positions. "The 1994 season was another year of change for me. In '93, I had been catching mostly and a little bit of center field in Babe Ruth. When I moved up to Legion for the tournament, they put me in an unfamiliar position at second base. Going into the '94 season, I was at second base again, but sometime during the year, they swapped Zach and me, so I had to go to short. I think they were trying to get Zach's reps at second, thinking that's where he would play in college. I can't remember how long that lasted, but I remember playing positions I wasn't familiar with for a few years in a row." Zach remembers his brother "bounced back and forth positions. He played little center when Bucky pitched." Tyler Bucklin added, "Levi was the utility player for sure. He could play anywhere on the field."

One definite strength of the 1994 team was their speed. Several players could swipe a base. Zach Bowler recalls, "We had a full roster of speed. Five or six guys in the starting lineup were quick." Two speedsters who had the green light without a sign were Tyler Bucklin and Zach Bowler, but Joey Boos, Tyler Tarum, and Levi Bowler "swiped a few of our own," said Levi Bowler, and added, "Jon Hersel, Fred and Wayne could get the freight trains rolling too. Speed was definitely a strength. We didn't have any giant sluggers, but we did have guys that could put it in the gap and get that extra bag. I felt like we had some really good contact hitters, so speed, for sure, was a strength of that '94 team."

REGULAR SEASON

THE MALTA ROYALS WERE BACK IN THE EASTERN DIVISION, which had eight teams in 1994. Each team played each other four times for a 28-game conference schedule. Glendive was favored to repeat as conference champions, although Richland County had beaten Glendive in the eastern divisional tournament the year before and looked good, too. Glendive finished third at State in 1993 and had a strong program year after year, and they were well-coached with Coach Brent Diegel at the helm, now in his second year.

Coaches Meyer and Lee had several tournaments on the schedule. One of them was an annual tournament—the Curt Martin Memorial Baseball Tournament—at Burke Field in Wolf Point, and Scobey always played. The teams participating in the 1994 Curt Martin were Stanley and Tioga of North Dakota and Glasgow, Scobey, and host Wolf Point. Scobey beat Wolf Point 10-4, and then Glasgow beat Scobey in an exciting championship game to win first place. K.C. Holum of Scobey won the Offensive MVP Award, going 7 for 12 in the tournament.

Of course, one of the many tournaments the Blues played in their 53-game schedule was the annual Doc Norman Memorial Invitational, which they hosted yearly at Scobey Ball Park. This would be the 11th annual tournament following Doc's passing in 1983. Teams participating in 1994 were Glasgow, Wolf Point, Plentywood, Ray, and Grenora, and host Scobey. The Blues won three games and lost two in the tournament, with some fine pitching performances leading to their wins, including two one-hit shutouts. Wayne Linder pitched a one-hit shutout, and the Blues collected 11 big hits in getting the 12-0 win over Genora without committing an error. In the Blues' 11-6 win over Wolf Point, Zach Bowler pitched five innings allowing six runs on five hits and Ty Tarum led Scobey's 12-hit attack by going 3 for 5 at the plate. Dave Anderson threw Scobey's second one-hit shutout against Ray. He walked only two and struck out 12. Ty Bucklin pitched against Plentywood and allowed only one earned run on three hits and had 9 strikeouts but took the 5-3 loss as three errors proved costly. The Blues lost their final game of the tournament, 7-6 to Glasgow. Jamie Veis and Cody Jacobson pitched for Scobey.

In one unusual regular season game against Wolf Point at Burke Field, winds gusted at 35–40 mph, but Scobey beat Wolf Point 13-0. Tyler Bucklin got the shutout win in five innings, striking out nine Yellowjackets. I wonder how Tyler's curveball might have danced in that wind.

Scobey's regular season and conference play were stellar, as they went 21-7 in the conference (36-17 overall), taking second place behind Glendive, who dominated with a 25-3 record. Here were the complete conference standings in 1994, with conference and overall records in parentheses:

1. Glendive (25-3, 49-16)
2. Scobey (21-7, 36-17)
3. Sidney (20-8, 32-14)

Zach Bowler, in his last year of Legion baseball, was awarded the Doc Norman Memorial Scholarship. He was presented with the $250 cash award by Ann Lee and family. He attended NDSU Fargo and played baseball his freshman year, then transferred to Montana State. *Leader photo, Burl Bowler.*

Palmer Roland was the honorary tournament captain and threw out the pitch of the last game of the Doc Norman Memorial Tournament. The Blues presented Palmer with a Blues jacket. Palmer was an all-around fan, (father, grandfather and great-grandfather) to several of the Scobey Legion players over the years and is often seen helping out the umpires. He seldom misses a game. Giving him his award was his great-grandson Casey Danelson, Coach Mike Lee (Doc's grandson) and Coach Ken Meyer. *Leader caption and photo, Burl Bowler.*

4. Glasgow (18-10, 28-13)
5. Plentywood (11-17, 18-20)
6. Wolf Point (9-19, 11-24)
7. Circle (8-20, 6-22)
8. Malta (1-23, 3-25)

With their second-place conference finish and impressive 36-17 overall record, Scobey's chances to return to State by finishing in the top two in the eastern divisional tournament looked good, especially as the Blues were hosting. The Blues had had a good year—so far. But as we have seen before, the postseason is different than the regular season. Could the Blues put together a good run and play sound baseball in the Divisional tournament? Or would another successful regular season end in disappointment at home?

DIVISIONAL TOURNAMENT

SCOBEY HOSTED THE EASTERN DIVISIONAL TOURNAMENT FOR the seventh time. The last time the Blues hosted was in 1990, when they won the eastern divisional and then finished third at State, losing only to Vauxhall and Bitterroot, who finished 1-2 at regionals. In 1990, Coaches Meyer and Lee were players; now, they were trying to return the Blues to State as coaches. May the odds be ever in the Blues' favor. Opening-day matchups (with seeds) looked like this:

- Glasgow (4) vs. Plentywood (5)
- Glendive (1) vs. Malta (8)
- Sidney (3) vs. Wolf Point (6)
- Scobey (2) vs. Circle (7)

Wayne Linder started on the mound in the first-round game against Circle and pitched well. This game was close for six innings, as Scobey only led Circle 6-3 after six. But the Blues broke it open with a big seven-run seventh, winning by the 10-run rule, 13-3, giving Wayne Linder the complete-game win. He pitched a four-hitter, striking out 12 Zephyrs and walking six. Tim Vigliotti went 3 for 3 at the plate to lead Scobey's 14-hit attack. Dave Anderson also had two hits.

The win over Circle set up Scobey's second game against third-seeded Richland County, who had beaten Wolf Point 12-5 in their first game. The Blues had only finished one game ahead of Sidney in the conference standings and had close games with them during the season. This one would be a dogfight.

It was up to ace pitcher Tyler Bucklin and Scobey's defense to get Scobey to the undefeated semifinal, as they were facing good pitching from Sidney's hard-throwing Darin Nickoloff. One concerning statistic in Scobey's win over Circle was five Blues' errors. Error-contagion had portended doom for Scobey in previous postseasons, and the fielding would need to improve if Scobey was going to return to State. Tyler did his job—but the defense did not: Sidney scored all four of their runs on five Scobey errors, winning the game 4-2. Tyler scattered five hits in eight innings of work, allowed no earned runs, struck out 14 Patriots, and walked five. Bucklin's counterpart on the mound, Nickoloff, went six innings to get the win. He had control problems but only allowed two Scobey hits. Scobey finished with four hits, and Zach Bowler had two of them.

The loss pushed Scobey onto the dirt route against their old rival, fifth-seeded Plentywood, who had upset Scobey

Shortstop Levi Bowler tagged a Sidney player out in a run down after getting picked off first but then almost got run over by him too. Casey Danelson (at left in photo), along with pitcher Tyler Bucklin, started the for the Scobey Blues. *Leader caption and photo, Burl Bowler.*

countless times in previous postseasons to end their year. Could the Athletics cut short another run by Scobey in the postseason in 1994?

Usually, errors ended it for Scobey with Plentywood. The worst it had ever been for Scobey was in the 1971 state tournament, when the Blues, who clearly had a better team than Plentywood that year, committed six errors in the last two innings, leading to five unearned runs, blowing a 4-0 lead, and losing 6-5. This ended Scobey's season, who were trying to get to the championship game against Havre.

And once again, for Scobey, errors were their undoing against their old rival at home in Scobey, as seven Blues' errors "proved costly,"[12] leading to eight Plentywood runs, and Plentywood won 8-4. Brent Veis pitched the first seven innings and was relieved by Dave Anderson and Morgan Oie. K.C. Holum had two of Scobey's seven hits.

Zach and Tyler remember the two tough losses at home that ended their Legion careers. Zach said, "Sidney was always a toss-up with Nickoloff pitching. Plentywood wasn't a bad team, but that season, there should never have been a game we lost to them. Clearly, errors got us in those two games. I don't even remember how they happened." Tyler added, "Losing both of those games was tough. We all had pretty high expectations. The goal was always one get to the state tournament. The Sidney game was going to be a tight one, and Nickoloff threw better than he usually did, and we couldn't get enough runs across for the win. We never should have lost to Plentywood. I remember that we just couldn't get anything going at the plate. It was a tough loss to end on for sure."

Tim Vigliotti recalls the losses, too, but how the disappointment helped prepare the team for future years. "I remember being frustrated in that loser-out game against Plentywood. We were hitting the ball, but it was always at someone. But all those learning experiences of losing to Glendive, Sidney, and Plentywood just made us hungrier each season to get better. In Levi and my 18-year-old year, we finally got the best of Glendive, Sidney, and Plentywood."

Glendive won the championship game 11-1 over Richland County. Glendive was clearly the class of the east that year: "The new Divisional champions had the best record coming into the tourney and proved they were the best by outscoring their opponents 38-7 at Scobey Ball Park."[13]

The Blues finished the season with a 37-19 record. Like the players, Coach Meyer was unhappy with the early tournament exit. "That was a good group of kids to coach, and we had a lot of fun. Unfortunately, we shit the bed in the tourney."

Zach Bowler, Casey Danelson, Coach Ken Meyer, and Tyler Bucklin at the Eastern Divisional Tournament. *Family photo.*

For 18-year-olds Tyler Bucklin, Casey Danelson, Zach Bowler, and Wayne Linder, not getting back to State in their final year was especially disappointing, but as with many other players whose Legion careers ended with a tough loss, the disappointment did not define their baseball careers, nor did it overshadow the wonderful memories they have of playing baseball in northeastern Montana. I asked Tyler Bucklin from Outlook to share his baseball story:

Little League

My first memories of baseball were around the time that I started Kindergarten. My dad and I would play catch in the yard between our house and my grandparent's place. My aunt Carolyn was my first coach when I was 6. Through my little league years, Outlook was never really competitive until I was 12. We never had enough of the older kids to compete with Scobey, who seemed to always have a bunch of giants on their teams.

I made the Border League All-Star team when I was 11 and 12. I felt very fortunate when I was 11 to be on the team. This is when I really got to know my future summer families in Scobey. I stayed with Josh Lee that summer and what a wonderful summer it was. We played a ton of RBI baseball on the Nintendo and spent a lot of time at the pool. Ann would take us to practice and town to be able to hang out with the team. Mike was playing for the Blues at that time and that was my first real experience with legion baseball.

Scobey hosted the district all-star tournament that year. We didn't make it to State but I remember being competitive and not being able to wait for the next summer to do it all over again.

When I was 12, Outlook was at least competitive in the league. I was starting to develop as a pitcher, and we were able to win a few more games than usual. My dad was the coach for those little league teams, and it was always fun to get to ride with him to practice and talk about strategies to win the games. That year I watched a video by Oral Hershiser on how to throw a curveball. The technique stuck and I was able to throw a wicked hook. I got a little overzealous in the first game. I used my new weapon and had elbow problems for the next couple of weeks. To say the least I was a little more judicious in using the curve ball the next time.

I was once again on the Border League All-Star team, and we were pretty loaded this year. State was being hosted by Scobey, so we had an automatic bid into the tournament. This summer I stayed with Zach Bowler and family. Once again, I had the summer of my life. We had a really good tournament and ended up taking 4th place at the state tournament. I was completely hooked and continued to play baseball with my brothers at the farm throughout the summer.

Babe Ruth

Transitioning from Little League to Babe Ruth is always a large step. There are few things that I remember specifically from that year. One was all the trips from the farm to Scobey with my grandpa Bucklin. We got to spend a lot of time together during that summer, traveling back and forth, which, looking back now, was a special experience.

I never got to pitch that year in the regular season. The team that I was on was loaded with 15-year-olds, and there was a significant amount of bench time. I threw a lot of batting practice in the cage but that was about as far as it went in the season. I made the 13-year-old all-star team after the season, and the district tournament was in Glendive. My mom and I drove down in our red Bronco without AC, and holy hell, was it a hot July in Glendive. I remember Zach was sick during the tournament and he was by far and away our best hitter. The tournament didn't go very well. I did get a chance to pitch in the tournament and that was a good experience, but completely different as compared to when I was 12. Holding runners on base and then adding another 15 feet was pretty intimidating.

The tournament wrapped up, and I was still in love with the game and again looked forward to the next summer.

My 14-year-old year was my first appearance in the Doc Norman Tournament. They brought a few of us up to Legion to be able to field a team that year. A lot of the older kids were at the 8-man football all-star game. I played right field and got to cut my teeth in a Blues jersey. I remember Don telling Kevin Nelson that he wasn't going to pitch during the tournament, but he ended up throwing a little. That was the first time I had ever seen a ball move that fast. It was a really incredible experience.

I made the 14–15-year-old all-star team that year. We had tryouts in Plentywood and made the team. I don't recall a bunch but I do remember going to Forsyth for the district tournament. Josh, Zach, and I were in our dad's hotel room, and before they took us out to eat, we turned up their heater to full blast without them noticing. To say the least, they weren't happy with us the next day. We ended up placing 2nd…I think… and moved on to the state tournament in Havre. Randy Rice was our coach and we had an ok state tournament. That was the year that the movie Major League was out, so everyone was sporting the "wild thing" hair due. Burl Bowler did the honors of shaving the lightning bolt type due into the back of my head.

When I was 15, we won the league championship. We had a nice group of 15-year-olds and had a lot of experience. Ken, Karch, and Art Holum were our coaches that year, as well as our all-star coaches. I pitched a lot that year but didn't really find myself until all-star districts in Wolf Point. We were playing Glasgow, and I was holding my own. My catcher for that game was Barry Jeide (not sure if that is spelled correctly). There was a play at the plate, and Bubba McKenzie was the base runner. Bubba absolutely freight-trained Barry. I still don't know how Barry held on to the ball, but he did, and Bubba was called out. Barry left the game because of a head injury, and I was absolutely pissed. There was something that changed in me as a pitcher after that moment. I don't know how to explain what happened, but I was a completely different presence after that. I don't think I gave up another hit in that game. Larry Trangsrud was the plate ump and threw me the game ball after the game. I still have it. We took second to Sidney but moved on to the state tournament in Glendive that year.

We drew Glendive in the first round that year, and they were the favorites to win state. It was a night game, and the coaches gave me the ball after my performance against Glasgow. In my entire career it was probably the best game that I ever threw. Wade Gilbertson, from Plentywood, was my catcher, and we were completely in sync. The atmosphere was amazing. Since Glendive was playing, everyone in town was at the game. It was loud, and the energy was something that I had never experienced before. I was locked in. In the sixth inning, I had let a base runner or two on, and the coaching staff was going to replace me with Chad Shuman. I remember Karch coming out to get me, and I was so amped up that I spiked the ball off the ground. Karch grabbed me by the collar and said, "Tyler, you little asshole. You pitched a great game; now get off the mound and go play defense." I jogged out to center to play my position, still mad. I don't remember the score, but we beat the home team in a game to remember. I think that we lost the next two games and were done for the tournament.

When I got home from Babe Ruth State, Don Lekvold gave me a call and asked if I would go to Miles City with them for State Legion. Denton Field was gigantic. I had never seen a center field wall at 440 feet, but there it was. I didn't get to play a lot, but I did pitch in relief and had a great time with the older kids. I had a lot to look forward to for the next three years and couldn't wait to get into Legion full time.

Legion

In my 16-year-old year, we had a lot of 18-year-olds. These guys were highly competitive, and each of them had their own way of playing the game. Karch and Ken were first-year coaches that year and definitely did things the way they wanted them to go. You didn't ever shake off Karch when he was giving signs to the catcher. We ended up winning the district tournament that year against Glendive. I pitched in the championship game. Unfortunately, the usually rock-solid defense that year fell apart, and I ended up losing the game. I only gave up one home run in my Legion career, and it was in that game. Brent Tarum was playing left field that game. There was a shot hit to left field, and Brent had a bead on it. He caught the ball while simultaneously hitting the wall. The ball popped out of his glove and went over the fence for a home run. We ended up winning in the next game for the championship.

State was in Missoula that year so there was a long bus trip ahead of us. We played pitch all the way across the state. I don't recall if I was ahead of money or down, but we always had a great time bantering back and forth during those road trips. The tournament itself didn't go as well as we would have liked. Dillon beat us twice during the tournament and we headed back across the state for home.

Josh Lee was the only 18-year-old when I was 17. We had a super young team and were looking for our identity after losing so much leadership from the year before. Josh was the first kid in Scobey that I really got to know back when I was 11, and we had always been friends through my baseball-playing years. He was the general of that team. As usual, we had a great summer of bus trips and shenanigans off the field while improving and getting better together on the field. Kevin Nelson had replaced Karch as one of our coaches. Kevin brought a lot of knowledge to help with my pitching. That summer, he taught me how to throw a slider. It ended up being one of my better pitches.

Districts were in Sidney that year, and we were in the middle of the pack. We had a nice run during the tournament and went 3-2. I pitched against Glendive in the second game of the tournament. I pitched okay but could never really get some momentum to be able to slam the door on them. We lost a close one. I remember being disappointed that we didn't make it to State that year and vowing that we would make it the next year when we would have a little more experience.

When I was 18, Karch came back to coach with Ken. Districts were going to be hosted in Scobey that year and we were slated for a ton of games that summer. Zach, Fred, and I were the 18-year-olds who had been together for the past seven years. We spent every summer together and played a ton of baseball. We had other 18-year-olds on the team, but none of them had been teammates longer than the three of us. Zach had always been an amazing hitter. He was super quick and had a quiet way of competing at a high level. Casey Danelson (Fred) was the muscle of the operation and our first baseman. Fred was also quiet, but you knew who was in charge when he was around. Wayne Linder joined the Blues when we were 17. Wayne and I always got along and were good friends those last couple of years. We all had a lot of high expectations for that summer and the number one goal was to get back to State.

I pitched a ton that summer but in a little different capacity. Ken and Karch used me more as a reliever during the season. We would build a lead, and then I would come in and shut the door for a couple of innings. It was fun to pitch in more games and for shorter durations. We had a nice regular season and went into the tournament feeling confident but knowing that we would need to play well to make it to State. Glendive and Sidney were standing in our way. Glendive was really good that year and ended up being one error away from winning the state championship.

We beat Circle in our first-round game at districts. Which then set us up for an evening game against Sidney. I got the ball that game, and it was the last game that I ever pitched in Legion. I remember warming up on the warm July evening with Karch standing beside me and talking to me about the lineup and how to pitch to them. The bullpens had been rebuilt that summer for districts, and I was feeling really good before the game. I wanna say that Larry Trangsrud was once again the ump behind the plate, but I could be mistaken. Whoever it was, they were giving me a ball off the plate for a strike, so I lived away from the right-handers with a sinking fastball. This would then set up a hard 12-6 curveball right down the middle of the plate, with the ball ending up at the ankle of the right-handed batter. Things were going pretty well minus the errors in the field. I had zero earned runs and ended up losing the game 4-2.

The errors were not the only contributing factor to the loss that day. Darin Nickoloff threw well for Sidney, and we were not able to produce a lot of runs. In the 8th inning, I will never forget Karch coming to get me on the mound. The walk to center field was a long one, and turning around to see the cars lined up along the fence and all of the people in the grandstands was etched as a lasting memory. And something that I never got to experience as a ballplayer again.

The next morning, we lost to Plentywood. It was a bitter pill to swallow. Dreams are hard to let go of, and this one really hurt. It was the end of something that had been a part of my life every summer for as long as I could remember. It is still fun to reminisce about and even more fun when you haven't talked about it for a long time, and you listen to stories that you had forgotten about. To say the least, baseball in northeastern Montana is something that I am extremely proud of. I am so thankful for having had the opportunity to play baseball for my dad first and then all the amazing folks that I played with in Scobey throughout my years.

Although losing four starters in 1994, the future looked promising for Scobey, as several good, experienced players were returning, and a talented group of baseball players—and all-around athletes—would join the team from the Babe Ruth ranks in 1995. Yes, the sun would rise on another promising season for the Blues, and hopes would spring eternal in April for another berth at State in 1995.

STATE TOURNAMENT

THE LETHBRIDGE MINERS HOSTED THE 1994 STATE TOURNAment at Henderson Field in Lethbridge, Alberta. The Fort Macleod Royals went undefeated in the tournament, beating Glendive 13-4 in the championship. Glendive and Sidney represented the east well, finishing second and third in the tourney. Glendive beat Sidney 15-5 to make it to the championship game.

Only Fort Macleod would advance to the Northwest Regional in Missoula, as the Missoula Reds were the host team. Unfortunately for Coach Brent Diegel and the Blue Devils, their fantastic season was over, finishing with an impressive 56-18 record.

NORTHWEST REGIONAL

THE MISSOULA REDS HOSTED THE 1994 NORTHWEST REGIONAL at Lindborg-Cregg Field in Missoula, Montana. State champion Fort Macleod and the host Reds represented Montana/Alberta. The powerful Fort Macleod team, coached by Rocke Musgraves, repeated as Northwest Regional champions, beating Eagle Point, Oregon, in the championship game, 7-3. This was the third time a team from Montana/Alberta had won the tournament. Coach Rocke Musgraves of Fort Macleod was named coach of the year.

EXTRA INNINGS

ZACH BOWLER PLAYED BASEBALL AT NDSU IN FARGO DURING his freshman year. Josh Lee recalls that Zach "took one of their stud pitchers off the wall in Fargo." He transferred to MSU in his sophomore year, where he rejoined Josh and Levi on the field in the spring of 1996, playing for the MSU Bobcats Club Team.

The Blues were lucky that Tyler "Bucky" Bucklin began his baseball career playing Bambino baseball in Scobey, then Babe Ruth. Partly because of that, Tyler—and younger brothers Ben and Matt—could play Legion baseball with the Blues. Legion rules required kids from Outlook to play Legion baseball for Plentywood, as they were geographically closer: Outlook is 18 miles from Plentywood and 37 miles from Scobey. The Bucklins were the only athletes from Outlook who played for the Scobey Blues—Bluejays in winter and Blues in summer. Ironically, Plentywood eliminated Scobey from the 1994 Divisional Tournament.

At the divisional tournament, head "gatekeeper" Ronald Tande was honored for his many years working with the Legion ticket crew in a Friday evening ceremony. Gary and Bonnie Meyer were tournament managers and honored for their many years of service to area baseball on the last day of the tournament.

Other committee chairmen included Art Holum, Ken Lee, John Bucklin, Marvin Tarum, Clo Ann Danelson, Roz Bowler, and Lois Leibrand. Umpires were Kevin Nelson of Opheim, Troy Halverson of Wolf Point, Bill Linder of Sidney, Larry Trangsrud, and Jeff Jones of Peerless.

Ronald Tande was honorary captain at the Divisional Legion baseball tournament. Ron received a Scobey Blues coat from the team and was presented the award for many years of volunteer service by his grandson, Casey Danelson. Head "gatekeeper" Ronald Tande was honored for his many years working with the Legion ticket crew. *Leader photo, Burl Bowler.*

The Ken Meyer/Mike Lee Era

Gary and Bonnie Meyer were tournament managers and honored for their many years of service to area baseball on the last day of the tournament on Sunday. From left to right: Deanna, Gary, Ron, Ken, and Bonnie Meyer. Family photo.

Coach Meyer recalls a hilarious story involving left-handed pitcher Dave Anderson from Peerless that happened that season. "Dave was pitching, and there were runners on base. He stepped on the rubber to get the sign from the catcher in a full-windup stance. Karch started yelling at Dave, 'Go from the stretch, Go from the stretch!' Dave was confused/baffled and stepped off the rubber, looking at Kevin with a dumbfounded stare, and started stretching his muscles—bending down, touching his toes, pulling his arm across his chest, etc. Karch was like, 'What in the fuck are you doing!' He immediately started yelling, 'Timeout, timeout,' as he walked out to the mound to get Dave's head back in the game! I can just see Dave standing there so confused, probably thinking, *Why in hell does he want me to stretch? I've already thrown 70-plus pitches, have sweat running down my ass, and my coach wants me to stretch!* That was an all-time classic story and has been told many times over the years! Too frickin funny!"

Tim Vigliotti was catching and remembers the story, too. "I went and chatted with Karch and Dave on the mound. We had a good laugh about it during the visit." Karch Lee remembers talking about it later that week with Wallace Fladager on *Blues Review* on KCGM.

It seems the Peerless boys were providing funny stories on the field that summer. Coach Meyer recalls another incident with a Peerless player, this time Jon Hersel. "We were in Wolf Point playing, and Jon Hersel was up to bat, and I had him bunt to get a runner from second over to third. He squared around, and the pitcher threw the ball right at him. He still tried to bunt it, but it ticked off his bat and hit him square in the forehead. Knocked his helmet off (the dugout erupts in laughter.) He shook it off and ended up walking on the next pitch with a passed ball. He got on first base, and the pitcher threw one pitch to the next batter, and Jon ('Love Butt' as the kids called him) started casually walking to second base. Everyone was screaming at him to get back, but to no avail, as he just kept sauntering towards second base. The Wolf Point players were baffled at what was going on just as much as all of us. The catcher threw the ball back to the pitcher because we now had a runner on third base. The pitcher threw it to the second baseman, and he tagged Jon out, but our guy on third scored to put us up a run. Jon had no clue what was going on as he was walking back to the dugout. I was half chewing his ass, but at the same time glad we scored. It was the most unintentional way of getting into a 'run down' to score a guy from third base anyone would ever see. Back then, there wasn't any protocol on concussions, but he certainly had one. He didn't even know that he was playing in a baseball game."

Mike Lee recalls how Bud Veis's boys (Jamie and Brent) became eligible to play for the Blues that summer. "Brent Veis stayed with my parents for about a month at the end of the school year until Jamie graduated from high school. After graduation, the rest of the family moved to Scobey. Brent had to be enrolled in Scobey, or he would not be allowed to play. Something about his previous coach the year before would not sign a release or something. By the time I got home from school, he was already living in town."

It is appropriate that the only action photo of the 1994 Eastern Divisional Tournament was a pickoff play at first because Tyler Bucklin was pitching at the time, and he had a great move to first. Levi Bowler said, "Bucky had the best move to first base in Legion baseball. His leg lift and hip rotation were exactly the same whether going home or to first. His head was always locked on the catcher's mitt, barely seeing his eyes between his mitt and hat brim. He would initiate his pickoff move to first while still looking at the plate . . . and then the deadly left-hand flick. Bucky was crafty like that, a smooth operator." Josh Lee added that Bucklin's pickoff move was so deceptive that first baseman Fred (Casey Danelson) "didn't even know when it was coming" sometimes.

Tyler Bucklin's crafty pickoff move recalls another left-handed Blues pitcher, big Bill "Oscar" Thompson, who pitched for the Blues from 1959 to 1963. Bill's teammates, including Rod Tande, Charlie Mueller, and Baldy Sell, said the same thing about Bill's move to first: no one could see it coming, and the first baseman would sometimes be fooled. I wish I could have seen both moves.

Tim Vigliotti recalls the 1994 season when he moved from pitcher to catcher. "I didn't pitch much in 1994, my 16-year-old year. I took over the catching duties from Josh. I got to catch Bucklin. His fastball was very deceptive, he kept Glendive off balance each time he faced them. It was enjoyable playing with Bucky, Fred, and Zach cause I looked up to all of them. Even Wayne 'Koool' Linder got some innings in that year I believe. Levi, Joey, and I all started as 16-year-olds, so that was a lot of fun to be on the field with them growing up. We all played together, starting in T-ball and up, so it was a fraternity of sorts. You messed around with one Blues player, the whole team was right there. We were a family."

Tim Vigliotti, not known for his blazing speed, "stealthily" stole second base in a game against Wolf Point. Tim said, "I remember forgetting the count standing on first base, thinking it was ball four. It was only ball three. I jogged to second base and collected a stolen base. Probably the only stolen base of my career." Then he added, "I was stealthy."

Zach Bowler recalls the essential things about Scobey American Legion Baseball. "One of the best parts of home games was knowing you were getting a Legion burger. And that applied every year."

The famous Legion Burgers were as a part of the Scobey baseball tradition as anything. Kirby Halvorson, who works as a physical therapist in Sidney, was recently having a conversation with a patient, and she asked him where he was from. Kirby said, "I responded proudly that I was from Scobey. I asked if she knew where it was, and she quickly responded: 'Of course I do.' She went on to explain that her son played Legion baseball there in the mid to late '90s. She also mentioned that her best memories were the hamburgers they had at the concession stand! She said, 'Me and the other moms didn't really like to go there for the games, but we *loved* to go there for the burgers!'"

Former players speak highly of coaches Ken Meyer, Mike Lee, and Kevin Nelson. In my interviews across the seasons, it is common to hear the teammates needle each other, just like I did with my teammates as they did with me. However, Levi Bowler speculates that the needling of his teammates might have been induced by these coaches. "I sometimes wonder if it doesn't stem from coaches like Kevin, Karch, Ken, and Art Holum. If they chewed your ass with love behind it or made fun of some situation you were in, you could rest assured they believed in you and believed that you had more to give. If they quit chewing you out and they quit making fun of you, that's when a guy should hang it up."

But it wasn't all fun and games between these coaches and players. Levi Bowler recalls an unforgettable memory from the 1994 season. "I will never forget losing to Plentywood in Plentywood. Ken and Karch were not happy. There was no conversation at the end of the game; there wasn't a word said, just 'On the line.' We must have run 20-plus 90-foot sprints in the outfield. On the bus and out of town we went, but that wasn't enough. They dropped us off east of Scobey at the Rasmus Nelson John Deere building and said, 'Get going . . . run to Uncle Gary's' (west end of Scobey). We all met and got on the bus at Gary and Bonnie Meyer's place, so our transportation was there. I didn't have tennis shoes. I had these Nike ACG hiking boots, and I was so mad I didn't even tie them. That was a mistake. I ended up with blisters on my heels that I'm not sure healed for the rest of the season. Not a fun night. Karch hated to lose to Plentywood, and he let us feel it."

Tim Vigliotti remembers the incident, too, and why the two young coaches were so upset. "We all got drunk the night before that Plentywood game, and Karch had enough of our bullshit and messing around. Some of us didn't bring running shoes with us. After that experience, I brought shoes just in case the coaches wanted us to run home."

Zach Bowler added, "Karch, Nelson, and Meyer knew all the tricks in the book. There was no pulling the wool over their eyes. We couldn't get away with nothing. We definitely did plenty of 90-foot sprints."

Karch remembers the disciplinary action. "Losing to Plentywood was the final straw on a list of things that needed to be addressed and hopefully corrected. Ken and I could already see things were not going to end up good unless things started to move in a different direction. Kids missing practice and showing up hungover for games was getting more and more frequent and frustrating. Looking back now, making them run from John Deere was probably too excessive, but we were young and pissed off."

Levi Bowler recalls Art Holum helping the young players develop during the season. "On occasion, Art would come down to practice and help out. He'd pound balls at us. His favorite line to use was, 'My grandmother can field it better than you.' He would hit you a grounder and if you were clean, he'd rip another one harder and harder until you booted one . . . then he'd hit you with his favorite line, "My grandmother can field it better than you.' A very distinct Art Holum laugh would ring out and then on to the next guy."

The 1994 season was the 75th anniversary of the 1919 Chicago Black Sox scandal. The *Leader* ran an article on it in the "Things, Ideas, and People" section, mentioning how ironic it was that there was a player's strike that season (1994) and that the primary reason the 1919 White Sox threw the Series was because they were underpaid. Swede Risberg's $600 salary playing for Scobey in 1925 was more money than he made with the Chicago White Sox when he played with them. The 1994 player's strike was the longest work stoppage in the history of major North American professional sports leagues. The strike resulted in the cancellation of the remainder of the 1994 season, including the postseason and the World Series.[14]

While Legion teams in Northeastern Montana struggled to find volunteer coaches to take the Legion teams each summer, the Alberta teams were hiring coaches from the United States—usually California and Arizona—to coach their teams. Rocke Musgraves began coaching in Fort Macleod in 1988, coaching the Royals to the 1993 and 1994 Pacific Northwest Regional Championships. The Royals won the 1994 Montana state championship, collecting an overall record of 207-98, which led to Musgraves being named the 1994 Montana State Coach of the Year. Rocke served as an assistant coach at Pima Community College in Tucson from 1993 to 1995, where he worked with infielders and hitters, including the nation's leading hitter, Erubiel Durazo, who went on to play in the Major Leagues for the Oakland A's and Arizona Diamondbacks. In 1995, he coached in the Saskatchewan Major Baseball League (summer collegiate league), leading the Oyen Pronghorns to their first-ever championship with a 32-7 record. He likely would have coached against former Blues Rob Fladager and Derek Solberg, who were playing for the Rockglen Rats then. Rocke is currently the head baseball coach at John Melvin University. During his 36-year coaching career, he has amassed a college head-coaching record of 725-431 and an overall record of 969-561. And it all began at Fort Macleod. My favorite snippet about Rocke Musgraves is that he named his daughter Libbi Montana Musgraves.

A hired gun from the United States was also the case with the State champion Vauxhall Spurs in 1990, who hired Coach Greg Kuntz, the assistant baseball Coach at Azusa Pacific in California. Coach Kuntz took Alan Holt, Vauxhall's shortstop and pitcher, back to Azusa Pacific with him.

American Legion Baseball was growing in Montana in 1994, as there were 38 Class A teams in five divisions in Montana and Alberta. Here were the teams and divisions:

- Central A – Anaconda A's, Belgrade Bandits, Bozeman Bucks A, Butte Muckers, Deer Lodge Wranglers, Dillon Cubs, Helena Reps and Manhattan/Three Forks.
- Eastern A – Circle Zephyrs, Glasgow Reds, Glendive Blue Devils, Malta Royals, Plentywood Athletics, Scobey Blues Richland County (Sidney) Patriots, and Wolf Point Yellowjackets.
- Northern A – Fort Macleod Royals, Great Falls Sparkies, Great Falls Stallions A, Havre Northstars, Lethbridge Miners, Okotoks Expos and Vauxhall Spurs.
- Southern A – Billings Blue Jays, Billings Cardinals, Colstrip Rangers, Laurel Dukes, Lewistown Redbirds, Livingston Braves, Miles City Colts, and Roundup Miners.
- Western A – Bitterroot Bucs, Glacier Twins A, Bitterroot Red Sox, Kalispell Lakers A, Libby Loggers, Mission Valley Mariners (Polson/Ronan/St. Ignatius) and the Missoula Reds.

The Laurel Dodgers were elevated from Class A status into the Eastern AA Conference a year earlier. The Dodgers competed in Class AA for 11 years (from 1993 to 2003). During that time, their team in the Class A division was called the Laurel Dukes.

The Bitterroot Red Sox joined the Bitterroot Bucs as a second team from the Bitterroot Valley in the Class A Division in 1994. The Red Sox had been operating as a Senior Babe Ruth Senior League club since 1987. The Bucs had existed since 1983 and had already won three state championships. The two Bitterroot Valley teams consisted of players from several towns in the area, including Hamilton, Stevensville, Darby, Corvallis, Florence, and Victor. In 1994, the Bucs were based in Stevensville, and the Red Sox were in Hamilton.

All these towns are located in Ravalli County. The Bitterroot Bucs started in 1983 and were the first Legion team in the Bitterroot Valley since the Great Depression. Part of the reason Ravalli County could field one—then two—Legion teams was because the population in Ravalli County was exploding. In 1960, the population of Ravalli County was around 12,000 people; in 1990, it had more than doubled to 25,000, and by 2000 it had tripled to 36,000. It has now almost quadrupled to 48,000 people.

Why am I talking about Ravalli County baseball and the population? Because the population was changing in Daniels County, too—except it was declining. It was declining in Valley and Sheridan Counties, too. Choosing the same decades to compare to Ravalli County, the population of Daniels County in 1960 was about 3,800 people; in 1970, it had decreased to 3,000; in 1980, 2,800; in 1990, 2,300; and in 2000, just a little over 2,000 people. The population in the county is now a little over 1,600 people, a decline of three-fifths since 1960. The decrease is even more dramatic in the decades before 1960. This was a big part of the reason Scobey's Legion program was difficult to sustain and continue in the early 2000s; it was a simple numbers game. And it is one thing to field a team; quite another to be competitive.

Tyler Bucklin—an Outlook Bluejay on the hardcourt in winter and a Scobey Blue on the diamond in summer—played with younger brothers Ben and Matt on the last Outlook Bluejay basketball team in the 1994-1995 season. Josh Lee put it poignantly. "Bucky was the last Bluejay." Due to declining enrollment, Outlook and Flaxville were forced to combine in athletics for the 1995-96 season. The *Missoulian*, clear across the state of Montana, recognized the decline in an article in March 1995: "Low enrollment has forced Flaxville and Outlook to merge next fall, becoming Flaxville-Outlook. The schools couldn't agree on mascots or colors, so the Cardinal and Bluejays became the Knights, with black, purple, and gray replacing blue and red."[15]

The merger of Flaxville and Outlook in 1995 was the beginning of the end for District 1-C, once the most powerful Class C basketball conference in the state of Montana. In 1969, District 1-C in boys basketball included seven high schools. Four of them, Antelope (1980), Outlook (2005), Flaxville (2006), and Peerless (2009), have now closed. Flaxville had one student in high school when it closed in 2006; Peerless had 11 in 2009. The current enrollment at Opheim High School for the 2024-25 school year is four students. These high schools were the "farm clubs" for Scobey Blues baseball. When the enrollment dried up, the pipeline of baseball players flowing into Scobey slowed to a trickle. The first all-Daniels County Legion baseball team in Scobey was in 1968 when players from Scobey, Flaxville, and Peerless were on the team. The 1994 team also had Opheim (Valley County) and Outlook (Sheridan County) players.

The days of these feeder towns supplying the Blues' roster with baseball players were coming to an end, and this would severely impact Blues baseball. The population was declining in northeastern Montana, and though the Blues program was going strong in 1994, the sun was beginning to set on the Blues of Summer. The merger of Outlook and Flaxville in athletics in 1995 portended a time soon when the Blues program would suffer the same fate as the area high schools. If Tyler Bucklin was "the last Bluejay," a time was coming when there would be "the last Blue."

But the Blues were still vibrant in 1994, and the summer sun was shining bright. We have a lot more baseball to play before the sun sets on the Blues of Summer.

1995

The Blues Finish Third at Divisional and Get Back to the State

> *It was just amazing back then. The baseball program was exceptional, but it was the friendships that made the Scobey Blues special. I still have some really close friends from the people I played with on those teams. It was awesome; one of my favorite things to do.*
>
> —Dave Anderson, Scobey Blues pitcher (1992–95)

PRESEASON

Brent Tarum assisted head Coach Ken Meyer in 1995 (Karch coached the Billings Central Giants in Babe Ruth). Coach Meyer was missing key players when he assembled his team for the first practice, as starters Ty Bucklin, Casey Danelson, Zach Bowler, Wayne Linder, and Jamie Veis had all aged out. But Scobey was returning some good, experienced players, like 18-year-olds K.C. Holum, Dave Anderson, Tyler Tarum, Morgan Oie, and Cody Jacobson. Back for their third season were 17-year-olds Tim Vigliotti, Levi Bowler, Joey Boos, and Gordy Leibrand. That was a solid team by itself, but a bumper crop of talented 16-year-old all-around athletes joining the team from the Babe Ruth ranks would make the Blues even stronger. Rookie 16-year-olds Joel Nieskens, Jake Petersen, Spencer Frederick, Curt Ware, Jason Wolfe, Lee Farver, and Ben Bucklin rounded out this 16-man roster, loaded with talent from top to bottom. Like previous teams, Coach Meyer's job would be to meld the old with the new and make this a team. Many of the former Babe Ruthers would immediately step in and make an impact for the Blues as 16-year-olds. The future was bright for the Blues with the young talent on this roster, but every season in Scobey, the goal was to make it to State and do well there. And the 1995 team had state tournament potential.

Tim Vigliotti, Dave Anderson, Levi Bowler, and Curt Ware would be the four main pitchers, with Joey Boos, Gordy Leibrand, Morgan Oie, and Lee Farver also getting innings on the mound for Coach Ken Meyer. Sixteen-year-old Jake Petersen would become the iron man behind the plate, handling the pitching staff as the starting catcher for the next three years.

REGULAR SEASON

The young Blues had another good regular season, finishing second in the conference (29-15 overall), again behind the Glendive Blue Devils but ahead of the Richland County Patriots, who were in third place. These three teams dominated the conference at the top. A newcomer, the Froid (Homestead) Pioneers, was welcomed to the conference in 1995. Froid had a fine baseball tradition, and seeing them enter the American Legion Baseball fold was awesome. They would field a Legion team for almost a decade and host divisional tournaments at Fjeseth Field in Froid.

One regular season highlight was Levi Bowler being named Offensive MVP at the 12th annual Doc Norman Memorial Tournament, batting .545. Chad Shuman of Plentywood, who won the tournament, was named Defensive MVP.

Chad Shuman from Plentywood (second from left) was the Defensive MVP, and Levi Bowler (second from right) was the Offensive MVP, hitting .545 at the 12th annual 1995 Doc Norman Memorial Tournament. Presenting the awards were Art Holum (left) and Carl Holum (right), long-time ground crew members. *Leader photo and caption, Burl Bowler.*

The final conference standings looked like this:

1. Glendive
2. Scobey (29-15 overall)
3. Sidney
4. Plentywood
5. Glasgow
6. Wolf Point
7. Froid

Headed into the Divisional tournament in Glendive, Scobey only needed to finish in the top three to qualify for State. As Sidney was hosting the state tournament, the Montana/Alberta American Legion Committee decided the division hosting would have three teams—the host plus two—in the state tournament, making an 11-team tournament with three byes in the first round. With their second-place conference finish, Scobey's chances to return to State with a top-three finish in the eastern divisional tournament were good. However, we have all seen how good regular seasons do not necessarily transfer to winning postseasons. Hopefully, 1995 will be different.

DIVISIONAL TOURNAMENT

The eastern divisional tournament was played at Meissner Memorial Field in Glendive. Scobey played seventh-seeded Froid in their first game. Opening-day match-ups looked like this:

- Glendive (bye)
- Plentywood (4) vs. Glasgow (5)
- Scobey (2) vs. Froid (7)
- Sidney (3) vs. Wolf Point (6)

Scobey pounded Froid 26-5 in seven innings, and the starters were pulled after the third inning. Dave Anderson started for Scobey, with Gordy Leibrand and Lee Farver also on the mound after the game was out of reach. Anderson went 3 for 3 with four RBIs to lead Scobey's 14-hit onslaught, and Lee Farver had a home run and three RBIs. Scobey played well in the field, committing only one error. Defensive lapses had been a problem for Scobey in previous tournaments, so this was a good sign.

The Blues faced the third-seeded Richland County Patriots in their second game. This was a well-played game by both teams, but Sidney came out on top, 6-2. Tim Vigliotti started and went the distance for Scobey, giving up nine hits. The Blues also had nine hits but couldn't get the key hits they needed with runners on base. Levi Bowler was 3 for 5 to lead Scobey's hitting, and Jake Petersen and Joey Boos each had two hits. Both teams played well in the field, as Scobey committed only two errors while Sidney had one.

So, Scobey was relegated to the dirt route again, but this time, they wouldn't need to crawl back as far, as they only needed to finish third to advance to State. Scobey's old foe, Plentywood, was their first challenge on the dusty path to paydirt, and this one would be another classic matchup between the two old rivals, as "both teams fought for 12 innings to stay alive in the tourney."[16] With the score tied 13-13 in the bottom of the ninth, Scobey got the winning run on first base with no outs but couldn't bring the runner home. The same scenario happened again in the 10th and 11th innings, but the runner was stranded each time. Meanwhile, Dave Anderson entered the game on the mound and kept the Athletics at bay in extra innings as Scobey tried to score. Finally, the Blues broke through in the bottom of the 12th. With the winning run on base—again—Coach Meyer decided to pinch-hit Lee Farver to try to get him home, and Lee came through, lacing a double to score the winning run, and the Blues walked off with a dramatic 14-13 win, staying alive in the tournament and sending their rival home. Levi Bowler started the game on the mound, with Joey Boos and Tim Vigliotti relieving and Dave Anderson pitching the final innings to get the win, his second of the tournament. At the plate, Joey Boos had three hits, and Morgan Oie had two to lead Scobey's hitting. Each team had 14 hits in the evenly matched game. Jason Wolfe recalls the wild Plentywood game. "I remember that marathon versus Plentywood pretty well. Me and Curt's cousin, Chad Shuman, was their stud. If we had lost to them, we would never have heard the end of it. Holidays and family reunions would have been miserable. That was a great game! Plentywood was a scrappy team that year."

With the hard-fought win, the Blues moved on and needed only one more win to advance to the state tournament. The obstacle in their path was the Glasgow Reds. This was an important game for the young Blues team, as with the win, they would get to State and gain valuable experience there, which would help prepare them for the next season. And the Blues got what they needed, a one-hit gem hurled by veteran pitcher Dave Anderson, to get back to State. Dave struck out 17 Reds and allowed only one run in seven innings, and Curt Ware came in to finish with five more Ks in the final two innings as the two pitchers combined for 22 strikeouts and only one run to get Scobey back to the state tournament with a 9-1 win. This was a tense game late, as Scobey only led 4-1 in the top of the ninth inning but exploded for five runs to break it open. The Blues

1995 Scobey Blues. Back row, left to right: Coach Ken Meyer, Cody Jacobson, Ben Bucklin, Morgan Oie, Lee Farver, Jake Petersen, Tyler Tarum, Jason Wolfe, Joel Nieskens, Coach Brent Tarum. Front row, left to right: Joey Boos, Levi Bowler, K.C. Holum, Tim Vigliotti, Gordy Leibrand, David Anderson, Spencer Frederick, Curt Ware. *Leader photo, Burl Bowler.*

also played well defensively, committing only two errors. Scobey's hitting was led by Joel Nieskens, who went 3 for 5 with a triple and a double. Levi Bowler also had three hits, and Joey Boos chipped in with two as the Blues bats got it done, too, banging out 11 hits. Jake Petersen remembers how juiced the Blues were for the Glasgow game. "There was a huge adrenal rush from everyone in that game against Glasgow. I can remember that game pretty well because we had struggled with them a bit that year, mostly in the Wolf Point tournament early in the year."

With the big wins over Plentywood and Glasgow guaranteeing them a berth in the state tournament, Scobey "came out a bit flat"[17] the next day against Sidney and lost 12-2. But no matter—the young Blues were headed back to State for the first time since 1992. Ty Tarum and Joel Nieskens each had two hits. Curt Ware and Joey Boos were on the mound.

Dave Anderson, in his final year of Legion ball, was a workhorse on the mound for Scobey in the tournament. He pitched 11 and two-thirds innings, appeared in three of the five games, struck out 27, and picked up two wins. Jake Petersen recalls his performance. "Dave Anderson pitched lights out. He had everything working. My favorite pitch he used really well was his knuckle curve." Jason Wolfe added, "Dave was a workhorse! Such a big, imposing presence on the mound. When his stuff was working, he was a dynamite pitcher."

Glendive beat Sidney 7-4 in the championship game to go through the tournament undefeated and repeat as eastern division champions.

STATE TOURNAMENT

THE 1995 STATE TOURNAMENT WAS HOSTED BY THE RICHLAND County Patriots at Moose Memorial Park in Sidney. The last time Sidney hosted State was in 1981, and they won the tournament. Could they do it again? The odds were not in their favor. For one thing, Glendive dominated during the regular season, and they were the top seed in the east. But other top seeds looked tough, too: the defending State champion Fort Macleod Royals had won the north, and they were strong again; from the west, the Bitterroot Bucs were the champions, and the Red Sox had taken second. This was the first time since Bitterroot Valley split into two teams three years earlier that both Bitterroot teams were at State.

Scobey played the west champion Bucs in their first game. With 11 teams in the tournament, there were three first-round byes. Here were the complete opening-day matchups at Moose Memorial Park:

- Lewistown Redbirds (2S) vs. Bitterroot Red Sox (2W)
- Bitterroot Bucs (1W) vs. Scobey Blues (3E)
- Belgrade Bandits (2C) vs. Fort Macleod Royals (1N)
- Glendive Blue Devils (1E) Great Falls Stallions (2N)
- Helena Reps (1C), Billings Blue Jays (1S), Richland Country Patriots (2E) (byes)

The Bitterroot Bucs banged out 21 hits against Scobey and overwhelmed the Blues 24-1 in the opening game. There is little to write about here—the young Blues were outmatched against the western division champs. With the score 12-1 in the seventh, the Bucs tacked on 12 more runs to make the final score what it was. Levi Bowler collected two of Scobey's seven hits, including a triple. The jittery Blues committed six errors in the game, but the state tournament experience against tough competition was good, regardless of the outcome. Jake Petersen said the Bitterroot game was "one he'd like to forget." So, let's forget it and move on.

Scobey got off the mat in their second game, beating the Great Falls Stallions in seven innings 14-4. A two-run homer by Joel Nieskens highlighted a five-run first inning as the Blues jumped on the Stallions early. Scobey added two more runs in the second and third as K.C. Holum and Joey Boos crossed the plate to stake Scobey to a 7-0 lead after three innings. But this one wasn't over, as Great Falls closed to 7-4 with two runs in the fourth and fifth innings. Scobey responded with three runs in the sixth to get back on top 10-4, as Holum, Nieskens, and Levi Bowler scored. Scobey ended the game by the 10-run rule when they scored four runs in the seventh. Jake Petersen tripled, and Curt Ware doubled to lead the rally and get Scobey their first win in the tournament.

That pitted Scobey against defending State and two-time defending Northwest Regional champion Fort Macleod in their third game. The Royals had been shocked by an upset in their first game against the Belgrade Bandits and were snaking their way back to the championship game on the dirt route. This was a tough, experienced team, and the Royals ended Scobey's successful season with a 21-9 win in seven innings. Scobey led Fort Macleod 7-3 after their at-bat in the top of the second, but Fort Macleod scored five runs in the bottom half to take the lead back, then had a big 10-run outburst in the sixth to force the 10-run rule.

The loss eliminated Scobey from the tournament and ended their season.

TOURNAMENT SUMMARY

THE COMPETITION AT STATE WAS TOUGH, BUT THE YOUNG Blues' experience playing two good teams, the Bitterroot Bucs and Fort Macleod Royals, helped prepare them for a run at the State championship the following two seasons. These would be the final two appearances at State in the history of the Blues' storied American Legion program.

Scobey ended the season with a very respectable 33-19 record. Coach Meyer and his young team's second-place finish in the conference, third at the Divisional, and one win at State were successful accomplishments for a team preparing for better things in 1996 and 1997. However, with ace pitcher Dave Anderson aging out, the Blues would need to find some depth at pitching and improve their defense if they were going to make a run at State in 1996. There was no issue with hitting; these boys could pound the ball. The Blues would also lose K.C. Holum, Tyler Tarum, Morgan Oie, and Cody Jacobson.

Levi Bowler summed up the 1995 season. "We lost three studs in '94, which pretty much rearranged our whole lineup. It's crazy how losing veteran experience in Fred, Zach, and Bucky could make such an impact on a lineup. They each had tons of experience making an impact in Legion when they were 15-16 years old. Losing that experience and replacing it with a huge class of fresh 16-year-olds made for another year of lessons. At the end of the '95 season, I knew we had all the tools to be a great baseball team; we just needed to sharpen them. I believe it goes back to experience and pitching. Just like the year Tyler Bucklin was our dominant ace, everybody behind him lacked experience. And in '95, I felt the same way—Tim Vig and Dave Anderson couldn't pitch every game and everybody behind them just lacked experience and innings. I think more than physical preparation, it was mental preparation for our younger guys . . . trying to get these young studs to believe in themselves and that they were capable of competing at this level."

I asked the younger Blues from the 1995 team what they learned at the state tournament. Jake Petersen said, "We were such a young team. Five of our starters were first-year American Legion players. It was great experience for us to be in the state tournament. That Bitterroot game is one I would like to forget. Fort Macleod was a really well-coached team. In the offseason, their head coach lived in Arizona and coached at Pima Community College. Ken went and coached with him the next year and brought back a lot to our team from what he learned coaching in Arizona. The main takeaway for me was that the state tournament baseball was way different. You couldn't get away with errors, and every batter against opposing teams was dangerous. It wasn't like league play, where if you got to the bottom of the order, you were right on defense. It was like playing Glendive every game."

Jason Wolfe added, "The margin of error was slim. A few errors turned into an avalanche of runs, as we learned in those two blowouts. Another thing that stuck out to me was pitching depth. Something we really lacked in '95. I think Ken really focused on developing more arms in 1996

1995 Richland County Patriots, State Class A Champions. Front row, left to right: Casey Whipple, Rustin Douglas, Jason Obergfell, Robbie Johnston, Chris Free, and Jason Collopy. Back row, left to right: Head Coach Thom Barnhart, Chris Cavanaugh, Charles Meehan, Brian DiFonzo, Chad Whipple, Mike Peel, Ben Thogersen, Tracy Elletson, B.J. Neiss, Brad Kallevig, Boyd Candee, and Assistant Coach Jason Barkley. *Sidney Herald photo, Rick Schneider.*

Richland County Patriots celebrate after winning the state championship in Sidney against Fort Macleod. *Sidney Herald photo, Rick Schneider.*

throughout the season. I know he learned a ton working with those Fort Macleod coaches at Pima."

The Richland County Patriots, coached by Tom Barnhart, went undefeated through the tournament and won the State championship game over the Fort Macleod Royals 9-7 to bring the championship trophy back to the east for the first time since Wolf Point won it in 1987. Fort Macleod had traversed the dirt route with five wins—including over Scobey and the Bitterroot Bucs and Red Sox—to make it to the championship game after losing their opener to Belgrade. Cole Archibald was the winning pitcher for Sidney, and Chris Free and Kallevig each hit home runs. It was Richland County's third state championship (1966, 1981, and 1995).

B.J. Neiss connects for a hit against Fort Macleod in the championship game. Neiss was selected as the tournament's most valuable player. *Sidney Herald photo, Rick Schneider*

B.J. Niess of Sidney, who hit .429 and won two games as a pitcher, was named MVP, and Coach Thom Barnhart was named Coach of the Year.

NORTHWEST REGIONAL

Eight teams from Idaho, Montana, North Dakota, Oregon, Washington, and Wyoming played in the Northwest Regional at Wigle Field in Boise, Idaho. The Patriots were eliminated in two games. Despite the two losses, Coach Thom Barnhart said the tournament was "a great experience for the Patriots because they got to see kids from other towns play." He added, "The Patriots are at a disadvantage because they can play baseball only three to three and a half months while the other towns they competed against play baseball six months out of the year." Gotta love those Montana winters, Thom.

EXTRA INNINGS

Levi Bowler remembers Jason Wolfe's unique contribution to the Blues as a 16-year-old in '95. "Wolfe came up and made his mark. Finding his spot batting leadoff because of his knack for receiving the beanball. I don't know how many walks Wolfe had in '95, but you can bet a large percentage of those walks were due to his left arm—that year and even years ahead, from his shoulder to the back of his elbow, stayed black and blue all season. It almost became a game for him. Loved his 'do-anything-to-get-on' mentality. A minor rotation of the shoulder inward, and he'd get nailed, gently tip his bat over on top of home plate, and sprint to first. Not a flinch in him. Had to piss those pitchers off." Jake Petersen added, "So many off that left tricep for Wolfe over the years. Of course, nowadays, you don't have to be tough to take those because every freaking kid has an elbow guard." Jason was self-deprecating about his ability: "I got hit all the time. Too dumb and slow to get out of the way."

Coach Lee remembers Dave Anderson. "He was a big left-hander who could throw some gas and a great kid. He played softball with us up in Canada at the end of his senior year and caught a ball at the fence in right field. The guy tagged up from third, Dave chucked the ball, and it flew over the top of the backstop!" Coach Lee added, "Dave was a great kid, for sure! Easy as hell to coach and would do anything to help out."

Dave Anderson remembers a funny story about being asked to umpire as a player. "We were playing a nonconference game in Scobey against Williston. They came out, and we came out, and we were ready to start playing, and then Ken came up, and he goes, 'We don't have any umpires. We need you to umpire the game. Go get the gear on and call balls and strikes back there.' And I said, 'Okay, as long as it won't be a close game. Well, lo and behold, the game went down to the bottom of the seventh. We're up to bat; there were two outs, bases loaded, and the game was tied. Morgan Oie came up to bat, and he crowded the plate. He leaned into a pitch, dipped his shoulder over the plate, and got hit on the arm. I knew the pitch was probably a strike. In fact, I'm about 90% sure it was a strike, but I called it a hit-by-pitch and let him go first. He took his base, and that was the ballgame. I kind of got a little upset with him. I was like, 'Don't do that again.' He goes, 'What? That's strategy. We won the game, right?' I'm like, 'Okay, just don't do it again.' I'm sure the Williston coach wasn't too happy about that, either."

The 22 strikeouts recorded by Dave Anderson (17) and Curt Ware (5) against the Glasgow Reds at the divisional tournament were the second-most strikeouts in a game in Scobey Blues history. Jim LeProwse holds the record with 23 (in 12 innings) against the Havre Northstars in Scobey's 5-4 remarkable upset win at the state tournament in Scobey in 1985.

When I interviewed Dave Anderson from Peerless, he attributed his pitching success to the coaching he had. Dave said, "I was blessed with pitching help. Terry Puckett taught me how to pitch, not just throw the ball as hard as I could. Then, I had one season with the Blues when Kevin Nelson coached, and I learned more from him. Also went to church with Andy Stolen. God bless, I had several valuable conversations with him after church every Sunday." Terry Puckett, Kevin Nelson, and Andy Stolen as pitching coaches. You were blessed indeed, Dave—and so were the Blues.

Terry Puckett remembers teaching Dave how to pitch. "He was a very nice boy, that's why I helped him. Very big and strong!"

The Fort Macleod Royals, after playing six games in the tournament to make it to the championship game, would have had to beat Sidney twice to win it if they had won the first game. That would have made seven wins and eight games in the 11-team tournament for them—and all the games were nine innings. As it was, they played seven games. The batboys had to be pitching—nine-inning games in 11-team tournaments was not a good idea.

Pitchers Dave Anderson and Tim Vigliotti know what Jake Petersen meant when he said, "Fort Macleod was a really well-coached team." Dave and Tim pitched against Fort Macleod, and Fort Macleod Coach Len Anderson saw they were tipping their pitches off before they delivered them and relayed the pitch to the hitters. Tim said, "They knew every pitch I was going to throw before I let it go. Their third-base coach [Len Anderson] told me after the game that he could see my hand on the ball and tipped his batters. I had a little infielder's glove that season. I bought a bigger mitt for the next season. I learned to hide the ball better in my mitt. That coach recruited me to go to Pima Community College." Dave Anderson added, "I got rocked in the game. After the game, the opposing coach [Len Anderson] came out to me and said, 'We really had you timed out pretty good,' and I said, 'Yeah, it was like I was throwing batting practice out there.' He goes, 'You know what the one fatal mistake you made was? You set your fastball in your glove after every pitch. My guys knew when you were going to throw a fastball at 'em.' I was like, 'You're kidding me!' So, it was like I was just pitching batting practice. They had me timed so well. And they were just spraying the ball all over the field.' I think Kenny even came out and said, 'What do you think, are you done?' I think I pretty much told him, 'Nah, give me a little bit more, and then that was that. That game was very humbling for me. I thought, 'Okay, maybe I'm not quite as good as I thought it was.'"

The last time Sidney hosted the state tournament in 1981, they also won it, snapping Scobey's streak of five consecutive State championships (1976–80).

Bitterroot Valley teams had split into two teams three years earlier, and both the Bucs and Red Sox were appearing at the state tournament for the first time together, finishing 1-2 in the western division. At the time, the Bucs were from Florence, Carlton, Stevensville, and Victor, and the Red Sox were from Hamilton, Corvallis, and Darby.

There were an estimated 3,000 fans at Moose Memorial Park for the Fort Macleod – Belgrade Bandits game. That is remarkable.

1996

The Blues Aim for Their Ninth State Championship

> *When we had home night games, cars would line the fences down the lines. It was always electric, with the community showing up and supporting us. We had good umpires who made the game fun for us. Cliff Hagfeldt broadcast our games. Blues baseball was big-time back then.*
>
> —Tim Vigliotti, Scobey Blues (1993–1996)

1996 Scobey Blues, third at State. Back row, left to right: Coach Ken Meyer, Tracy Vatnsdal, Brent Tarum, Curt Ware, Spencer Frederick, Joel Nieskens, Levi Bowler. Middle row, left to right: Jason Wolfe, Jake Petersen, Matt Bucklin, A.J. Shipstead, Mark McElvaney, Ken Fossum. Front row, left to right: Lee Farver, Tim Vigliotti, Joey Boos, Ben Bucklin. *Leader Photo, Burl Bowler.*

PRESEASON

NO MATTER WHAT BASEBALL TEAM WAS ASSEMBLED ON the field in early spring in Scobey, the hope for every season was another run at a state championship; however, the 1996 season was different. Not since 1990—when 18-year-olds Kevin Nelson, Mike Lee, Ken Meyer (now head coach), and Terry Farver placed third at State—had Scobey's chances for a state championship been so good. The 1996 Scobey Blues were a fine collection of all-around athletes, and they knew how to win. During the 1995-96 high school sports season, Scobey-Peerless won the state championship in football, their first state title. Scobey then won their first state basketball championship since 1979 and its first track and field state championship. In an article in the *Billings Gazette* written by Vince Briggeman of the *Missoulian*, the feat was called an "incredibly rare trifecta."[18] In addition, a year earlier, in 1995, Joel Nieskens and older brother Jerod had led the Peerless Panthers to their last State Class C basketball tournament appearance and a second-place trophy. Bucky Henderson coached Scobey-Peerless to the football title and Scobey to the track and field title, and Dave Selvig coached Scobey to the basketball title. Following the third state championship in track and field in May, Head Coach Henderson said, "It's pretty unbelievable. I wish we had 'em all back next year. They're a great group of kids"[19] A lot—but not all—of those "great group of kids" would be back the following year.

The leadership of this talented, athletic, and experienced baseball team would come from three 18-year-olds—Levi Bowler, Tim Vigliotti, and Joey Boos—who had been starters for three years and were returning for their final season of Legion ball. Jason Wolfe recalls, "Having Levi back in '96 was huge for us. His experience and leadership were pivotal for our success that year. We could see how committed he was to it. We all wanted him to experience a championship." Seventeen-year-olds Joel Nieskens, Spencer Frederick, Curt Ware, Jake Petersen, and Jason Wolfe—all starters on the 1995 Blues—were also back, as were Lee Farver and Ben Bucklin. Not to be outdone by the Scobey and Peerless athletes, Ben had scored 40 points in a basketball game playing for the Flaxville-Outlook Knights in their first season of combined sports. Joining the team as rookies in 1996 were Mark McElvaney, A.J. Shipstead, Matt Bucklin, Ken Fossum, Cale Handran, Jay Hoversland, Stew Fladager, and Jedd Lekvold.

Brent Tarum again assisted Coach Meyer in 1996, and Tracy Vatnsdal joined the coaching staff. Coach Meyer, now in his fifth and final season as head coach, by season's end, arranged the talented 1996 Scobey Blues batting lineup in the following order:

- Joel Nieskens (SS)
- Levi Bowler (CF/P)
- Jake Petersen (C)
- Jason Wolfe (2B/P)
- Joey Boos (LF/P)
- Spencer Frederick (OF/3B/1B)
- Curt Ware (3B/P)
- Tim Vigliotti (1B/P)
- Ben Bucklin (RF/2B) / Lee Farver (RF/DH/P)

The offensive punch in this lineup was all there—power, average, speed. Offense was the strength of this team. However, pitching and consistent defense would be the two aspects of Scobey's game that needed to improve from 1995 if Coach Meyer and the Blues were to bring a ninth State title home to Scobey. Yes, we are talking about the real possibility of a State championship with this team—this is not a drill; repeat: this is not a drill. The 1996 Blues had the horses to do it. Coach Meyer said of his team before the state tournament, "Last year, our goal was making it to State. When we got there, it was more like we were happy to be there instead of coming to play. This year will be a different story because after all the success the players had over the last year, they'll accept nothing less than a state title."

Scobey returned all the starting pitchers from the previous season except Dave Anderson, but he would be sorely missed for the all-critical pitching. Ace pitcher Tim Vigliotti would be key to Scobey's title aspirations, but he broke his shoulder bone before the first football playoff game. He played out the football season before surgery, so he could not return to the starting rotation until early July. In his absence, Coach Meyer relied heavily on Curt Ware, his most consistent pitcher during the regular season. Ken Meyer said of his pitching staff, "We don't have any overpowering pitchers. Curt Ware is probably our most consistent pitcher as far as facing tougher competition. He is one of the main guys since Vigliotti went down. We throw him against tougher competition." The other "main guys" in Coach Meyer's starting rotation were Levi Bowler, Jason Wolfe, and Joey Boos. Lee Farver and Cale Handran also gave

Coach Ken Meyer in the 1996 Pima Baseball Program. "Coach Meyer begins his first year as an assistant coach in the Pima Baseball program. He will be working primarily with the infielder and hitting departments. Ken came to Pima from Scobey, Montana, where he has been head baseball coach for the past four years (Montana American Legion Baseball). His Scobey Blues have complied a 141-63 overall record during this stretch, including two state Tournament berths. He attended the University of North Dakota-Williston, where he was named All-State in his two years with the Tetons. He brings youth to the program along with a solid background of baseball. His two greatest influences in life still remain his parents, Gary and Bonnie Meyer." *Quote from Pima Baseball Program*

some innings to Coach Ken Meyer in the Divisional tournament. Jake Petersen would return as the starting catcher. Coach Ken Meyer said of Jake Petersen, "He catches every day and is a strong kid with determination and the will to go out and play every day. You almost have to beat him out for him not to play. He is such a great competitor. He is never slacking off. He is the hardest worker on our team."

While the Scobey Blues baseball players were busy winning three state championships in the offseason, Coach Meyer was honing his baseball coaching skills in Arizona. At the state tournament in Sidney in 1995, he met Coach Len Anderson of Fort Macleod, Alberta, the pitching coach for the Pima Community College Aztecs in Pima, Arizona. (The Alberta teams hired American coaches to coach their Legion teams.) Len invited Ken to come down to Pima Community College in Tucson, Arizona, if he helped with the coaching, so Ken went down to Pima to be an Aztec assistant coach. Ken said, "I actually stayed with him in Tucson for a few weeks before I found a place. His son Dennis, I believe, made it to AA ball. Len was a great guy." Mike Lee, who coached Wolf Point in 1996, joined Ken in Tuscon and also learned from Coach Anderson. Karch remembers, "It was a lot of fun that spring, living with Ken in Tucson, putting schedules together, and getting ready for the season."

Back from the spring warmth of Arizona to the spring chilliness of Scobey, Coach Meyer was now applying his college coaching experience to heat the Scobey Blues to win their ninth state championship.

Levi Bowler, who had an August birthday and had graduated in 1995, was back from Montana State University for his final Legion season. Like Coach Meyer, Levi also honed his baseball skills in the offseason, joining older brother Zach and Josh Lee on the Montana State club team. Levi remembers playing for the Bobcats. "I went off to college in the fall of 95 at the age of 17 and was able to return to play the '96 season as an 18-year-old. I remember really looking forward to that season. The boys weren't getting experience and building confidence in baseball per se, but they were getting a real good taste for winning and confidence in other sports. They won both State C football and State C basketball that year. That self-belief mixed with the talent coming up, I knew '96 was our chance. I missed out on those high school state championships, and I was hungrier than ever that summer for baseball. I wanted to get me one. I made Montana State University's club team and again got to join up with Josh Lee and my brother Zach to play games across the west that winter and spring. It was a great experience and a way for me to stay in the game preparing for the '96 summer."

Three state championships in one season, Head Coach Ken Meyer training in Arizona, team leader Levi Bowler playing for the Bobcats club team—the table was set for a Scobey run at another State championship in 1996.

REGULAR SEASON

COACH MEYER PLANNED AN AGGRESSIVE 50-GAME REGULAR season schedule for the Blues to develop them into a state title contender. Curt Ware recalls the difference from 1995. "I feel like our coaches realized that we needed more reps and needed more in-game experience. As all-around athletes, we didn't have the opportunities to improve and grow as players during the offseason like the sports athletes of today. Coach Meyer and Tarum filled our schedule with many more games for '96 after the '95 season. It was like a full-time summer job, and it showed in all of us." Jake Petersen added, "I think in the month of June I was home about four days. We were always traveling that summer. It made us the team we were. We played in a lot of tournaments outside of just the league games. We lived on that bus."

The schedule included several tournaments. The Blues played in an early season tournament in Belgrade and took second place, losing 7-3 in the championship game to the Missoula Mavericks A-Team. Tim Vigliotti has special memories of the Belgrade Tournament. "I won the Defensive MVP trophy that weekend. That was a fun tourney. When we were on the road, we three 18-year-olds roomed together, and Levi thought he was tough and would tap me out wrestling because I used to talk shit about his girlfriend at the time. Boos never came to my rescue. So basically, Levi always got a bed to himself, and Boos and I had to share. The only time Boos and I didn't share a bed was in Belgrade because we stayed with Belgrade players. We stayed with Dustin Huff, and a couple of years later, I played with him at Dawson."

Scobey, gunning for its ninth state title, took the first step when they won the eight-team conference for the first time since 1992. Defending conference and eastern divisional champion Glendive finished third behind Scobey and Glasgow. The 1996 Blues remember being dominated by Glendive, going back to their Little League days, but finally getting the best of them during the regular season in 1996. Jason Wolfe said, "I remember finally getting over the hump versus Glendive. We took both games of a doubleheader from them at home. For the first time, I felt like we were the better team!" Jake Petersen added, "Our biggest rivalry was always Glendive. We really struggled against them in our history all the way back to our early Little League years." Levi Bowler said, "You could say we had a chip on our shoulder; they always bested us when it mattered. Going all the way back to Little League All-Stars." Tim Vigliotti added, "I think that winning all those championships in '95-96 helped us get over the hump against Glendive in '96. I believe it was mental."

Defending state champion Sidney finished fourth. Here were the final conference standings:

1. Scobey (24-4 in conference and 39-11 overall)
2. Glasgow
3. Glendive
4. Richland County
5. Wolf Point
6. Homestead
7. Plentywood
8. Circle

After a first-place conference finish and a 39-11 overall record, the Blues were healthy for the postseason and ready to make a run at another state title. The first step was to finish in the top two in Divisional. It was time to play ball.

DIVISIONAL TOURNAMENT

THE 1996 EASTERN DIVISIONAL TOURNAMENT WAS HOSTED by the Wolf Point Yellowjackets at Burke Field in Wolf Point. The top two teams would advance to the state tournament at Cobb Field in Billings. Scobey, the number-one seed, faced eighth-seed Circle in their first game. Here were the complete opening-day matchups:

- Glendive (3) vs. Homestead (6)
- Glasgow (2) vs. Plentywood (7)
- Scobey (1) vs. Circle 8
- Richland County (4) vs. Wolf Point (5)

Scobey's march to Cobb Field started swiftly as the Blues cruised to an easy win over Circle, 14-2 in seven innings. Cale Handran and Lee Farver combined on a three-hitter. Jake Petersen and Levi Bowler drove in half of Scobey's runs. Jake had three hits with a double and three RBIs; Levi Bowler had two hits with a triple and four RBIs. Spencer Frederick also had two hits and two RBIs.

The win set up Scobey's second game against the fourth-seeded Richland County Patriots, the defending state champions. To get the Blues to the undefeated semifinal, Coach Meyer handed the ball to ace Tim Vigliotti, who was now healthy after his successful return from shoulder surgery. Tim responded with a six-hit shutout, striking out 13 Patriots, leading Scobey to a 7-0 win. Jason Wolfe had a

Coach Ken Meyer makes a trip to the mound in the eighth inning of the first Glendive game at Divisional. Left to right: Spencer Frederick, Joel Nieskens, Curt Ware (pitching), Ken Meyer, Jason Wolfe, Tim Vigliotti, and Jake Petersen. *Leader photo, Burl Bowler*

solo home run to provide Tim with the only run support he would need. Jake Petersen and Joey Boos chipped in with two hits apiece. Tim's shutout was backed up by solid defense, as the Blues committed no errors in the game. Neither did Sidney. This was a well-played game on both ends.

The Blues were moving on to the undefeated semifinal against Glendive. With one more win, the Blues' first goal—getting back to State—would be accomplished.

But it was not meant to be against Glendive in the eastern divisional.

Although Scobey had won the conference and Glendive had taken third, this was the postseason, and Glendive had always given Scobey trouble during the regular season. And they would give Scobey more trouble than they could handle in the undefeated semifinal. This game was a pitcher's duel until the top of the eighth inning, which started with the Blue Devils leading 3-2 but ended with Glendive leading 9-2, as Glendive broke it open with six runs, the big blow coming on a three-run home run by Jeremy Alley. Curt Ware, who Coach Meyer said was his go-to pitcher during the regular season against tough competition, kept the Blue Devils in check until the eighth when he got into trouble and was relieved by Jason Wolfe. The heavy-hitting Blues were limited to just six hits against Glendive's strong pitching. Joel Nieskens and Jake Petersen had two hits each to lead Scobey's hitting. Scobey's defense was not bad, as they committed three errors. The Blues were keeping the errors in check during this tournament.

The loss to Glendive pushed Scobey into the loser's bracket, where they would need to win one more game to gain a berth in the divisional championship game—and, more importantly, the state tournament. What eastern division rival would stand in Scobey's way? The answer was host Wolf Point, coached by former Blue Mike "Karch" Lee. This was interesting. Mike was Ken's childhood friend and former Blues teammate. The two had narrowly missed making it to the state championship game and going to the Northwest Regional in 1990, leading Scobey to a third-place finish. Now, here they were, two old friends and former teammates, coaching against each other on Wolf Point's home field with a berth in the state tournament at stake. Hollywood couldn't have scripted this any better. These were two Blues who you couldn't keep off the baseball field.

Which of the two childhood friends and former teammates would celebrate a state tournament berth and a shot at Glendive for the eastern divisional championship? Coach Mike Lee had already coached Wolf Point to two upset wins over higher-seeded tournament teams—Sidney and Glasgow—and was aiming for a third, this time over the Blues. The *Wotanin Wowapi* wrote, "In order to get to the state tournament, the Jackets were going to have to knock off the Scobey Blues."[20]

Who would Coach Meyer hand the ball to pitch Scobey to the promised land? When Coach Meyer brought the starting lineup to home plate, the player in the one position was Levi Bowler, who had yet to deliver a single pitch in the divisional tournament. The Jackets got to Levi with two quick runs in the first to take an early 2-0 lead. Golik and Miller each scored.

Uh-oh.

But Scobey tied the score at 2-2 after two innings. After a scoreless third, the Blues broke the game open, scoring six runs in the fourth inning. Levi's forkball and defense behind him held Wolf Point scoreless after the first inning as they won 12-2 in seven innings. Levi finished with a five-hitter—and a scoreless last six innings—to lead Scobey to the win. Levi helped his cause with a two-run homer, and Tim Vigliotti had two hits and three RBIs, and Jake Petersen chipped in with two hits and two RBIs. The Blues were near flawless in the field, committing only one error. Pitching, defense, and good hitting got the Blues to the promised land.

The *Wotanin Wowapi* recognized Mike Lee for his fine coaching performance of the 1996 Yellowjackets. "The

Levi Bowler rounds third after hitting a two-run home run against Wolf Point in the semifinal at Divisional. Levi helped his own cause with the homer, as he pitched a complete game to get the win, giving up only two runs and five hits in seven innings. *Leader photo, Burl Bowler.*

Jackets had a great tournament after their first-round loss. Finishing the season under .500, the tournament is where this team peaked and played their best baseball of the season. In his first year as head coach, Mike Lee did a great job in the tournament as well as the entire season improving the team each week."[21]

Firing on all three baseball cylinders, the Blues hoped to carry the momentum of the win over Wolf Point into the championship game against Glendive. But the Blue Devils had Scobey's number in the eastern divisional. A big second inning, in which the Blue Devils plated seven runs to take a 7-1 lead, "seemed to take the steam out of the Blues,"[22] and Glendive went on to win 11-1 in seven innings. Jeremy Alley from Glendive again did the damage at the plate, going 3 for 4 to lead Glendive's 16-hit attack. Scobey was limited to two hits by Glendive pitching—the second consecutive game Glendive pitching had silenced the Scobey bats. Tim Vigliotti, pitching his second game of the tournament, took the loss, with Lee Farver and Joey Boos coming on in relief after the game was out of reach.

But the Blues were advancing to the state tournament, where Coach Meyer and the team's goal was to bring another state championship back to Scobey—and maybe get another shot at Glendive, the team's nemesis since Little League.

Coach Meyer and these players knew how to win, but it would be crucial not to falter early in the 11-team state tournament, as the games were all nine innings. What was Montana/Alberta American Legion Baseball thinking? Eleven teams and nine-inning games? Some teams would need to win seven games to win the state tournament through the dirt route, playing eight.

Scobey had a four-man starting rotation, which was good, but winning an 11-team tournament through the dirt route would take five—maybe six. Without any "overpowering pitchers," the margin for error for Scobey to win the state tournament was razor-thin. The only viable path was sweeping their first four games to get to the championship game.

STATE TOURNAMENT

THE 1996 STATE TOURNAMENT WAS HOSTED BY THE BILLINGS Blue Jays on iconic Cobb Field in Billings. What a wonderful setting for American Legion Baseball! The *Leader* always welcomed the teams to Scobey when Scobey hosted the state tournament, but no warmer welcome was ever extended to the Blues than when they were welcomed to Billings in an article titled, "Scobey, a town for all seasons," written by John Letasky. The article reviewed Scobey's three state championships during the 1995-96 prep season in football, basketball, and track and field, and Coach Meyer talked about his team and his experience as a coach. Here is the fascinating article in its entirety:

Scobey, a town for all seasons[23]

Scobey has been a place for winners this past year.

Scobey High School has won three major state championships in boys' competition this year. The Spartans took home state class C titles in track, basketball, and football.

Now the Scobey Blues, with most of their players coming from those championship teams, are in the hunt as the State A American Legion Baseball tournament kicked off Thursday at Cobb Field.

"They have a great attitude when they step on the field. Their winning attitude is to get the job done," said Scobey coach Ken Meyer. "The team is not intimidated on the field. They have been in tough situations before. Their mental mindset gets us through a lot of games."

Two members of the Blues played on all three championship teams. Those two players were catcher Jake Petersen and left fielder Joey Boos. Peterson had a .452 average during the regular season to lead the Blues in hitting.

"Peterson catches every day and is a strong kid with determination and the will to go out and play every day," said Meyer. "You almost have to beat him out for him not to play. He is such a great competitor. He is never slacking off. He is the hardest worker on our team."

The other top hitters for the Blues are Levi Bowler, with a .395 average, and leadoff batter Joel Nieskens, with a .376 percentage. The Blues also have Spencer Frederick, who was the MVP of the Class C state basketball tournament.

The Blues were without the ace of their pitching staff, Tim Vigliotti, until early July because of a broken shoulder bone sustained just before the Spartans' first playoff game. Vigliotti then played out the season before having surgery to repair his damaged pitching shoulder. Because of the injury, other pitchers had to step it up.

"We don't have any overpowering pitchers," Meyer said. "Curt Ware is probably our most consistent pitcher as far as facing tougher competition.

"He (Ware) is one of the main guys since Vigliotti went down. We throw him against tougher competition, so his overall record may be deceiving."

Meyer, himself a former Blue, is in his fifth year coaching the team. The 24-year-old understands the way of life small-town athletes live.

"I understand all of their situations. Playing every sport throughout the year might wear on you," said Meyer. "Summer is your free time, but when you go out in a competitive sport, like baseball, the heart and desire of your own athletic ability will not let you be defeated, just because you could be doing some other extra-curricular activities."

Last winter, Meyer went down to Pima Community College in Tucson, Ariz., to be an assistant coach in baseball. The experience helped Meyer become a better coach, and Meyer is very happy to compliment the person who encouraged him to better himself.

"I owe a lot of my experience at the college level to Len Anderson, the head coach of Fort Macleod," said Meyer. "I met him at State last year, and he said I could come down there if I was willing to help out with the program. I have a lot of respect for Coach Anderson. We need more people in the game like him."

The Blues are now armed with more precise coaching know-how and gifted athletes who have been in the spotlight before and have experience winning. The Blues also want to have a better showing at State than they did last year when they finished with only one win.

"Last year, our goal was making it to State. When we got there, it was more like we were happy to be there instead of coming to play," Meyer said. "This year will be a different story because after all the success the players had over the last year they'll accept nothing less than a state title.

"In my own personal opinion, I believe that if we compete well and play up to our potential, I'll be more than satisfied. Although a state title will be a dream come true."

As for tournament favorites, the Northern division champions, the Fort Macleod Royals, who finished second to Sidney in 1995, won the state championship in 1994, and the Northwest Regional tournament in 1993 and 1994 was considered one of them. Others mentioned were the Bitterroot Red Sox, Glendive Blue Devils, and host Billings Blue Jays.

Scobey's first game was against the Libby Loggers (37-21), who had finished second in the west. Here were the complete opening-day matchups:

- Glendive (1E), Helena (1C), Billings Blue Jays (1S) (byes)
- Havre (2N) vs. Anaconda (2C)
- Fort Macleod (1N) vs. Livingston (3S)
- Scobey (2E) vs. Libby (2W)
- Bitterroot Red Sox (1W) vs. Billings Cardinals (2S)

As mentioned, Scobey's path to a state championship depended on not losing early in the tournament. Of course, this was true of every team, but some teams had a deeper pitching staff than others to endure the 11-team, nine-inning-games tourney. Coach Meyer handed the ball to his ace, Tim Vigliotti, to get the first win in the tournament. Libby scored two runs in the top of the first, but Scobey came back to tie it 2-2 in the bottom of the third. From there, Libby scored three runs in the fifth and sixth to take a 5-2 lead. Each team scored a single run in the eighth and entering the bottom of the ninth, Scobey faced a 6-3 deficit and the prospect of an opening-day loss in the tournament, something they needed to avoid.

But down three runs with two outs in the bottom of the ninth, the Blues—a battle-tested team of champions with no quit in them—rallied to score three runs to tie the game 6-6 and force extra innings. The Blues had come back!

But in the top of the tenth, Bryce Baillie of Libby hit a flat liner to center field, but the Scobey center fielder overran the ball, and the ball sailed over his head into center field for a one-out triple, scoring Dan Magone to pop Libby right back on top. Levi Bowler, who was pitching, remembers the play. "I remember it coming off the bat headed for center field. I gave a fist pump and spun around, thinking we had just got the second out. Instead, as I spun around, I saw the center fielder crashing in on the play . . . the ball sailing over his head. Damn." Coach Meyer then brought Scobey's infield in to prevent a second run from scoring, but Steve Burrell slapped a single past the drawn-in infield to give Libby a two-run lead. Scobey was only able to counter with one run in the bottom half, and the Loggers ran off the field with an 8-7 win in 10 innings, a heartbreaking loss for Scobey in their opener after coming from behind with two outs in the ninth to force extra innings. Bryce Baillie did most of the damage for Libby, going 4 for 5 with three

RBIs and two runs scored. Three of Baillie's hits went for extra bases—the triple in the tenth and two doubles. Tim Vigliotti went seven gutty innings for Scobey and was relieved by Levi Bowler in the eighth. Spencer Frederick had three hits and two RBIs, and Curt Ware had two hits and two RBIs to lead Scobey's hitting. For Scobey's extra-base hits, Spencer Frederick doubled, and Ben Bucklin tripled. Joey Boos also had two hits for Scobey.

Levi Bowler delivers a pitch in the tenth inning against Libby. *Family photo.*

Each team committed five errors, but the misjudged liner by Scobey in center field in the 10th inning proved costly, as it led to the winning run. However, Scobey's players quickly pointed out that they thought the misjudged fly ball did not cost them the game. Levi Bowler said, "More than the error, I feel like my 0 for 6 could've changed the game if I would've showed up at the plate. So, I don't fault any fielding mistakes. My plate appearances probably affected the outcome more than any error." Jake Petersen said, "I don't think anyone feels one specific mistake cost us the game. That first game was out of character for us." Jason Wolfe, a coach for 23 years, added, "It's never a single play or player or official that costs teams games. That's the beauty behind team sports. I think I was 0-5 in that Libby game. A hit here or there from me, Levi, and that play in center field doesn't matter." Tim Vigliotti said, "I could have struck more guys out or missed bats more." It's great that the team picks up their teammate like that.

After the loss to Libby, the Blues knew they had a long road ahead. Levi Bowler said, "There was a monster dirt road to get back to the chipper that year." Jake Petersen added, "We should have never lost that game. We were way better than that team. We would have set ourselves up way better to get to the championship had we won that game." Jason Wolfe knew the loss would tax their pitching, saying, "That game was tough because it meant we had to burn too many arms to try to get through the back door."

Suddenly, the calculus had changed from winning five games to winning *seven*. It would now be a dirt marathon—seven consecutive wins—for the Blues to bring a championship trophy back to Scobey. The *Leader*, in 1969, had coined the phrase "dirt route" to describe teams that had to come back through the loser's bracket to win a state championship. Scobey's first state championship team in 1969 had to do it, winning five games and playing six—but that was in a six-team tournament. Doc Norman had to use six pitchers to get the job done in 1969. Havre Coach Tom Nielson had to do the same thing when Havre won its first state tournament in 1968 after losing to Scobey in the first game. Coach Meyer had four starting pitchers—and Joey Boos as a fifth if needed—so the odds were not good. However, the goal was not to win seven games but to win one game at a time and not look past each game to the next. And slowly but surely, one win at a time, one day at a time, facing elimination in each game they played, the gritty Blues clawed their way back and went deep into the tournament.

Scobey's next game was against the Havre Northstars, coached by Micky Williams. Scobey and Havre last met in the state tournament in Scobey in 1985, when the miracle Blues upset Havre 5-4 in 16 innings. Larry Trangsrud doubled and scored the winning run on a throwing error with two outs in the 16th. Havre had entered the tournament with a 41-3 record, but behind the 12-inning, 21-strikeout performance by starting pitcher Jim LeProwse, the host Blues shocked Havre in 16 innings. The teams were more evenly matched in this game. This would be the last time these two storied Legion programs would meet in a state tournament.

In their final matchup at the state tournament, the two teams would not disappoint. The game would go back and forth, with wild eighth and ninth innings, and it would go down to the last out in the ninth on a play at the plate. It was another classic game, the final time the Northstars and Blues faced each other in a state tournament. The two teams had seen classic pitcher's duels in state tournaments; this would be a classic high-scoring context.

Coach Meyer started Curt Ware to keep Scobey alive in the tournament; Micky Williams countered with Sam Evans, the younger brother of Dude Evans, who was the starting pitcher in Scobey in 1985. This was a back-and-forth contest, as the two clubs battled between one or two runs most of the game. Havre grabbed an early lead when they scored four runs in the top of the second, but Scobey quickly responded in the bottom half with three runs to close to 4-3. Each team scored a single run in the fourth, then Scobey took their first lead in the bottom of the sixth when they scored two runs to take a 6-5 lead. It was the first time the Blues led in the tournament in the 16 innings they had played. Scobey added a run in the bottom of the seventh to take a 7-5 lead, setting up the wild eighth and ninth.

After giving up four runs in the second, Curt Ware had settled down and had only allowed one Northstar run since, but Havre rallied with three runs in the top of the eighth to jump back on top, 8-7. Oh no. Batting in the bottom of the eighth, the Blues were trailing and had six outs to avoid a two-and-out at State. But this team knew how to win, and they had a lot of fight. As they had done against Libby in the bottom of the ninth—scoring three runs to tie the game and force extra innings—the Blues, with their backs to the wall, got it done with their bats again, this time putting five runs on the Cobb Field scoreboard to take a commanding 12-8 headed into the top of the ninth. Three more outs and the Blues would live to fight another day.

But nothing ever comes easy, especially against the Northstars, and the top of the ninth came down to a critical play at the plate with two outs. Let's let Havre coach Micky Williams take it away from there. Mickey said, "In the top of the ninth, we loaded the bases with two outs. Ryan Knudson on third, Tim Harada on second, and Bert King on first. David Curtiss came up, and they changed pitchers to Tim Vigliotti, their top pitcher. David hit one in the gap. That's when I made a bad coaching error. We scored Ryan and Tim easily. I sent Bert, and they threw him out at home. I blew it. I should have held him."

Ironically, after Scobey scored 12 runs and Havre 10, it was a defensive play by Scobey that won the game. You gotta love baseball. Curt Ware got the win for Scobey, pitching eight and two-thirds innings, and Tim Vigliotti got the save. Scobey had twice as many hits as Havre, outhitting the Northstars 14 to 7. Levi Bowler was 4 for 5 and Ben Bucklin was 2 for 4 to lead Scobey's hitting. Scobey also outplayed Havre defensively, committing three errors to Havre's five.

But the only stat that mattered was the final score—12-10—and the Blues were still alive in the tournament. One game at a time.

Slowly traversing the dirt route, Scobey's next game was against the Livingston Braves. Scobey had previously played Livingston in the 1975 state tournament in Scobey when Craig Miller pitched a one-hitter to lead Scobey to a 10-1 win. It would be nice if Scobey could get a strong pitching performance like Craig's in this game. Going with this third starting pitcher, Coach Meyer handed the ball to Jason Wolfe. Coach Meyer and Scobey needed a well-pitched game to stay alive—and save precious innings on the staff.

After playing two high-scoring contests with scores of 8-7 and 12-10, how about a pitcher's duel? For seven and a half innings, Jason Wolfe and Livingston starting pitcher Justin Seanson dueled, and the Braves led 2-1 in the bottom of the eighth. The only two runs Jason Wolfe had allowed were in the first and sixth innings, and Scobey scored their only run in the first. This was another tense, tight game where Scobey never led, and they would need to come from behind in the eighth—again—to win.

In the bottom of the eighth inning, with the Braves leading 2-1, Scobey needed to get something going off Seanson—and they did. Scobey's heretofore silent bats boomed, and the Blues erupted for six runs, chasing Seanson and taking a commanding 7-2 lead into the top of the ninth. For the third straight game, the Blues had a big inning in the eighth or ninth to tie the game or take the lead. This team of champions never quit—you had to get 27 outs to drive a stake through the 1996 Blues.

Levi Bowler beats a throw to first base in Scobey's big eighth inning against Livingston. *Leader photo, Burl Bowler.*

Jason Wolfe pitched a scoreless ninth to complete his four-hit gem for the win. He needed a well-pitched game from his staff, and Coach Meyer got it from Jason. Having a fantastic tournament at the plate, Spencer Frederick again led the Blues in hitting, going 3 for 4 with a double, a triple, and two RBIs. Scobey outhit Livingston 14 to 4, and the defense was solid, committing only one error. The *Great Falls Tribune* wrote, "Scobey continued its winning ways at the State A American Legion State Tournament at Cobb Field."[24] But the winning ways would need to continue—one game at a time—if the Blues were going to go deep in the 11-team tournament.

After three games, the Blues were 2-1 in the tournament, but they needed three more wins to advance to the championship game, where they would need to win two more games to win it. One game at a time, though. One distinguishing feature of Scobey's three games in the tournament was this: they had played 28 innings and had only led in four, playing from behind or tied the rest of the time. It would be nice to get a lead and coast in a game, but that was not the way in this tournament.

Next up for the Blues was their season's nemesis, the Glendive Blue Devils, who had manhandled Scobey in the eastern divisional tournament, winning the undefeated semifinal 9-2 and then the championship game 11-1 in seven innings. Scobey had won the conference championship, but Glendive owned them in the divisional tournament. Coach Meyer started Levi Bowler, the fourth pitcher in his rotation, to beat Glendive and stay alive in the tournament. And once again, the Blues would need to battle from behind, overcoming their largest deficit of the tournament, to win.

Jake Petersen recalls how up for this game Scobey was. "I remember a lot of emotions before that game. We were so locked in! I remember talking with Wolfe before that game, and the focus we had and the emotion we played with was different than any other game of any other sport we played, including our state titles."

The Blues trailed big in this one, but it was early. After two complete innings, Glendive led 7-0, an enormous deficit to overcome. But Scobey's biggest strength—their hitting—would bring the Blues back from the dead again. Scobey had a huge rally in the top of the third, scoring six runs to get right back in the game, and they now trailed 7-6. Glendive added a run in the bottom half to take an 8-6 lead, but Scobey responded again with three runs in the top of the fifth to take a slim 9-8 lead, then added two in the sixth to hop on top 11-8. Not accustomed to playing with a lead, it seemed natural that Glendive plated three runs in the bottom of the sixth to knot the game at 11-11.

So, after six complete innings and a lot of back and forth, the two eastern division rivals were even at 11 in the "wild game."[25] Coach Meyer had brought Joey Boos in to pitch and would later bring in his ace, Tim Vigliotti, to finish the game for his third appearance in the tournament. Glendive would use three pitchers of their own in the slugfest.

Coming down the stretch, the Blues bats had more pop than the Blue Devils, which was the difference in the game. Scobey scored a single run in the eighth to take a 12-11 lead, then added two more in the top of the ninth to lead 14-11. It was the fourth consecutive game where the game was decided coming down the stretch. Tim Vigliotti held Glendive scoreless in the final three innings to get his first win in the tournament, which added to his save against Havre. The Blues had won a wild one indeed. Scobey had 17 hits in the slugfest, and Glendive had 16. It was Joel Nieskens' turn to lead Scobey at the plate, as the leadoff hitter was 4 for 6, with every one of his hits—three doubles and a triple—going for extra bases. Each team committed three errors in the game, so the fielding was even. The Blues' bats—and Tim Vigliotti's mended shoulder—kept Scobey in the tournament.

Jake Petersen recalls the end of the Glendive game. "I think Glendive had bases loaded and two outs in the ninth with one of their best hitters (Ryan Buckley) up to bat. Tim struck his ass out to send those guys home. Vig battled all year to get back from the shoulder injury. I don't remember any loss of velocity on the last fastball to Buckley. He dialed one up and blew it by him!"

All the 1996 Blues commented on how Glendive had dominated them since Little League and how important it was to beat them. The win over them in the 1996 State Tournament was huge, almost like the Red Sox beating the Yankees. Jake Petersen said that beating Glendive was "almost as good as winning the chipper!"

And the Blues were moving on—one game at a time.

The next obstacle on the long and winding dirt route to paydirt was the Fort Macleod Royals. The Royals were one of the favorites going into the tournament and had a phenomenal program. Since 1993, the Royals had won the Northern division four consecutive years, the state tournament in 1994, runner-up at State in 1993, and 1995, and they had won

Levi Bowler makes a pickoff move to first base on Glendive's Brad McPhearson. Blues first-baseman Tim Vigliotti, in foreground, finished the game on the mound and got the 14-11 win. At right is Scobey Blues third-baseman Curt Ware. Glendive Coach Brent Diegel is in the third base coaching box. *Leader photo, Burl Bowler.*

back-to-back Northwest Regional titles in 1993 and 1994. For Macleod was no stranger to the dirt route themselves. The year before in Sidney, after losing their first game to Belgrade, they won five consecutive games to make it to the state championship game against Sidney. The Royals had met Scobey on that path, and they eliminated Scobey from the tournament 21-9 in seven innings in 1995. So the Blues might have had a little revenge factor.

The Royals were coached by Len Anderson, who Coach Ken Meyer mentioned in his pre-tournament interview. Coach Meyer met Coach Anderson at the state tournament in Sidney in 1995. Over the winter, Coach Meyer went to Pima Community College in Tucson, Arizona, to be Len's assistant coach. Ken said, "I owe a lot of my experience at the college level to Len Anderson, the head coach of Fort Macleod. I met him at State last year, and he said I could come down there [Pima College] if I was willing to help out with the program. I have a lot of respect for Coach Anderson. We need more people in the game like him." How passionate was Coach Anderson about baseball? *He had a batting cage installed in his backyard for his son, Dennis.* This was an intriguing matchup from a coaching perspective. Could the student become the master?

The Scobey-Fort Macleod game would be like every game Scobey played in the tournament—another "wild one." And speaking of wild games, the Fort Macleod Royals had gotten to this game by beating the Libby Loggers 20-18 in thirteen innings. The Libby-Fort MacLeod game featured 42 hits and 19 errors and lasted nearly four and a half hours, ending at 12:15 a.m. Fort Macleod starter Craig Hann pitched 12 innings, *throwing 219 pitches*. Yes, folks, 219 pitches. This was before the pitch count era. Libby manager Andy Gideon changed pitchers eight times and used Bryce Baillie twice and Ryan Miller three times in the crazy game.

At this point in the 11-team, nine-inning tournament, it was a war of attrition with pitching arms. Pitching staffs were getting worn down, and it was now simply a matter of survival. It was expected we would see a lot of runs scored in the Scobey-Fort Macleod game, and we did. And again, the game would come down to the final two innings for the Blues.

Coach Meyer started Levi Bowler against Fort Macleod. In an odd turn of events, Scobey jumped on top in this one, scoring four runs in the bottom of the third to take an early 4-0 lead. Not comfortable playing with the lead, apparently, the four-run margin was quickly erased, as the Royals plated four runs in the top of the fourth to tie the game, 4-4. From there, the game seesawed back and forth. Fort Macleod scored a single run in their half of the fifth to take a 5-4 lead, but Scobey countered with another big inning, this time plating three runs in their half of the fifth to jump back on top, 7-5, then added a run in the sixth to lead 8-5. But the lead was again short-lived—again—as the Royals scored three runs in the seventh to knot the score, 8-8. As the seesaw continued to rock back and forth, the Blues scored in the bottom of the seventh to tilt it in their direction, only to see Fort Macleod level it again at 9-9 in the top of the eighth. It was time for another eighth-inning rally for Scobey. We had seen this movie before several times in the tournament, and almost as if on cue, the Blues did it again, scoring two runs to retake the lead 11-9. Three more outs and the Blues would win their fourth game and advance to the play-in game for the championship. Coach Meyer handed the ball to his ace, Tim Vigliotti, to get it done, and he did, holding the Royals scoreless in the ninth to notch his second win of the tournament, to go along with one save. Tim helped his cause at the plate by getting two hits. Scobey's defense—which had been sound to this point—broke down in this one, as they committed seven errors to the Royals' three. But it didn't matter. The Blues were not done. After eliminating the Eastern division and Northern division champions in their last two games, the Blues were moving further up the path following their fourth consecutive win in the tournament.

The Bitterroot Red Sox, champions of the west, were the next obstacle on the dirt marathon, but they would be a roadblock. Now playing in their sixth game of the tournament, Scobey faced a strong team that had only played four games—still a lot, but two games less than Scobey. Coach Meyer handed the ball to Curt Ware to pitch, who had three innings of eligibility left, and Bitterroot countered with Chad Ekin. Curt Ware allowed only one run in his three innings, and Coach Meyer brought in his fifth pitcher Joey Boos, who also pitched well, keeping Scobey in the game through the sixth, as he only allowed single runs in the fifth and sixth innings. But Red Sox pitcher Chad Ekin had pitched six scoreless innings, and it was 3-0 Red Sox after six. Then, as in the previous five games, the stretch innings decided it, as Bitterroot scored two runs in the seventh to take a 5-0 lead, then added three more in the eighth to take a commanding 8-0 lead into the ninth. Levi Bowler remembers the pitching arms finally giving out. "Curt Ware started, and then his arm was smoked. Boos came in early to relieve Curt and did a good job keeping us in the game. Halfway through that game, we were still only down a couple of runs, but then they went off for a couple of innings, and our gas started to run out." Jake added, "We were pretty gassed. Boos came in and was throwing

Curt Ware, left, runs down the Fort Macleod Royals' Christopher Brooks between second and third base. Scobey won the game, 11-9. Billings Gazette photo, David Grubbs.

some nasty junk, but they eventually got on him. They just threw a junk-baller at us, and we could not get solid hits."

Coach Meyer had to bring in both Vigliotti and Wolfe in the eighth to try to stop the bleeding, but the arms were done. Bitterroot added two more runs in the top of the ninth, and trailing 10-0 in the bottom of the ninth, Scobey was down to its last three outs in the tournament and running out of gas. But as always with this team, they fought to the end, breaking up Ekin's shutout with a single run, but they couldn't pull out another fantastic comeback, and the season ended with a 10-1 loss to the Red Sox. The Red Sox had eight different hitters drive in runs in their balanced hitting attack. Ekin finished with a six-hitter, with Spencer Frederick driving in Scobey's only run in the ninth, his 10th RBI of the tournament. Scobey committed four errors, and Bitterroot two.

The team of champions had left it all on the field but couldn't rally in the final three innings against the Red Sox.

1996 Scobey Blues, Third at State. Back Row, left to right: Jedd Lekvold, Mark McElvaney, Matt Bucklin, Cale Handran, Levi Bowler, Jay Hoversland, Coach Ken Meyer, Assistant Coach Tracy Vatnsdal, A.J. Shipstead, Brent Tarum, Ken Fossum. Front Row, left to right: Curt Ware, Lee Farver, Jake Petersen, Joel Nieskens, Jason Wolfe, Spencer Frederick, Ben Bucklin. *Family photo.*

TOURNAMENT SUMMARY

THE BILLINGS BLUE JAYS WON THE CHAMPIONSHIP GAME OVER Bitterroot, 21-10. The championship was the first for the Blue Jays. Blue Jay first baseman Kasey Austin, who finished the tourney with an astronomical .714 average, was named the batting champion. The Blues, who finished 4-2 and in third place, made quite an impression in the tournament, claiming two awards. The first was the sportsmanship award. There is no greater honor a coach and a team can receive than the sportsmanship award. It reflects the players' discipline and respect for their coach, respect for the other teams, umpires, and other team's coaches. The second award Scobey claimed was when Spencer Frederick was named MVP of the tournament for hitting .530, driving in 10 runs, and scoring nine. The sportsmanship trophy honored the team, and the MVP award recognized an incredible six games turned in by Scobey's Spencer Frederick.

In trying to make sense of the 1996 tournament, Scobey's path to a state tournament title—the dirt marathon—was nearly impossible after they lost their opener in 10 innings to Libby. Winning seven games in a row would be tough for any team, but it was Scobey if anyone could have done it. They took it as far as they could, winning four of the seven games they needed, but the pitching arms were just done in the last three innings against Bitterroot.

If there had ever been an award for the most dramatic game endings in a state tournament, the 1996 Blues would have won it. In every game they played, the game was decided coming down the stretch. In their first game, the Blues scored three runs in the bottom of the ninth to tie Libby and force extra innings, losing by one run in the tenth.

Against Havre, they scored five runs in the bottom of the eighth to take a 12-8 lead, then cut a man down at the plate with the bases loaded in the top of the ninth to preserve the 12-10 win. They trailed Livingston 2-1 in the bottom of the eighth, then rallied for six runs to win 7-2. They trailed Glendive 7-0 early and were tied at 11-11 in the eighth, then scored one run in the eighth to take a 12-11 lead, then more in the ninth to win 14-11. Against the Royals, they scored two runs in the bottom of the eighth to win 11-9. That marked the fourth consecutive game the Blues had won, where they scored runs in the eighth inning to either win a tied game or come from behind. Scobey's magic number in the tournament was eight. Against Bitterroot, the Red Sox scored seven runs in the stretch innings to pull away with the lead. Every game was decided at the end.

While the Blues didn't achieve their goal of bringing home another State championship, the tournament tested the will and strength of the team, and beating Glendive was a highlight for them. Tim Vigliotti said, "Beating all the teams that gave us trouble in previous seasons was satisfying. Knocking Glendive, Havre, and Fort Macleod out of the state tournament was an experience. We always seemed to get the job done, no matter what the game looked like early on. Those nine-inning games, we just grinded them out. Nothing was impossible. The baseball Gods wanted to see us come through the back door to win it. We were certainly on a mission after that Libby game. We had to dig deep in some innings just to tie games up to get to another inning. We showed a lot of heart, I believe. We took pitches at the plate that we normally would take a hack at. We grinded out at-bats, making teams go to their bullpen earlier than planned. Being able to play each year with Levi, Joey, Jake, Jason, Curt, Spencer, Joel, was the highlight of my summers. I loved every minute of it, and I loved being a Blue!"

The 1996 state tournament would be the last Legion games for 18-year-olds Levi Bowler, Joey Boos, and Tim Vigliotti. It would also be the last Blues game for Coach Ken Meyer, who would end his five-year career coaching the Blues. In his five years as head coach, Coach Meyer had won two conference championships (1992 and 1996), one eastern divisional championship (1992), three state tournament appearances (1992, 1995-96), and one third-place finish at State (1996). The 1996 Blues finished with a remarkable 46-15 record, and Ken's overall coaching record with the Blues was 187-79 (70%).

Ken reflected on his last season as head coach and his playing and coaching career with the Scobey Blues. "I knew after the 1996 Blues season that I was going to be done coaching. I had already made plans to go to college at DeVry Institute of Technology in Phoenix, Arizona. The school went through the summers, so it was not going to allow me to coach again the next summer. I would have loved to stick around and coach one more year because of the players we had coming back, but I needed to move on in life. I'm still really good friends with a lot of the players from that year, and looking back, we had a lot of good memories. Ken added, "As I reminisce about baseball growing up in Scobey, that's all we ever wanted to do. The memories and friendships made during those years definitely last a lifetime."

I asked Tim Vigliotti to share his baseball story. His story is like his dad's and his older brother Tony's, as he has followed in their footsteps as an umpire. Tim said, "I'm living my life in 17 2/3.[26] That is how I call my strike zone."

I have been involved in baseball my entire life. Growing up, I watched my brother. I remember pitching to my dad, he always had time to play catch. I spent most of my summers at the ballpark either playing or traveling as a family to tournaments that my dad umpired. My birthdays were celebrated at Regional AA tourneys.

When I played for the Blues, I enjoyed playing with all the guys I grew up with. We were all great athletes, and we played at a high level. Those days, I will never forget.

After my playing days, I followed my dad and brother to the other side and started umpiring. I wanted to give back to the game that greatly influenced my life, and it kept me close to my dad and brother. I pride myself on calling a consistent strike zone and being fair. I will be heading into my 22nd year this season. I was fortunate to be invited to 19 district tournaments, 20 State A and AA tournaments and two Regional tournaments.

Kade Vatnsdal (left) and umpire Tim Vigliotti (right) at Belgrade when Kade played for the Billings Cardinals in 2021. *Family photo.*

The Blues would miss Coach Meyer and their three starters and pitchers in 1997, but Scobey was not done. Seven returning starters—all 18-year-olds—would try again to return a state championship trophy to Scobey. Who would take the reins from Coach Meyer to guide the Blues in 1997?

TOURNAMENT STATS

Hitting

MAKE NO MISTAKE ABOUT IT, THE STRENGTH OF THIS TEAM was hitting, and except for the final game against Bitterroot, the Blues' bats were popping in the state tournament. The team averaged 12 hits and almost nine runs per game, a tremendous offensive output. Several players had three-hit games, with many hits going for extra bases. Two players—Levi Bowler and Joel Nieskens—had four-hit games, with all four of Joel's hits going to extra bases, three doubles and a triple. Spencer Frederick's bat was on fire during the tournament as he hit .530, had 10 RBIs, and scored nine runs, leading to his selection as MVP.

Spencer Frederick was named MVP of the 1996 state tourney. He had 10 RBIs, scored nine runs with a batting average of .530 in the six games the Blues played. *Leader photo, Burl Bowler.*

Pitching

COACH MEYER USED FIVE PITCHERS—TIM VIGLIOTTI, CURT Ware, Jason Wolfe, Levi Bowler, and Joey Boos—to cover the 55 innings pitched in the tournament. While Scobey's pitching was not dominant—the opposition scored an average of over eight runs per game—it was good enough to keep Scobey in every game, including the final game against Bitterroot, except for the final three innings when the arms gave out. Certainly, Jason Wolfe's four-hit complete game against Livingston was the highlight for the staff, but Tim Vigliotti was the workhorse, as he figured in 3 of the 6 decisions for Scobey. He got the save against Havre and had the wins pitching at the end of the game against Glendive and Fort Macleod. Levi Bowler took the tough loss against Libby, and Curt Ware took the loss against Bitterroot, although he only allowed one run in three innings pitched. Here were the inning counts and records by pitcher:

- Tim Vigliotti, 11.2, 2-0, S
- Levi Bowler, 11.0, 0-1
- Curt Ware, 11.2, 1-1
- Jason Wolfe, 10.2, 1-0
- Joey Boos, 10.0, 0-0

Fielding

SCOBEY'S FIELDING WAS ON PAR WITH THE OPPOSITION, AS THEY averaged the same number of errors per game—3.8—as did the teams they played. The only bad game they had defensively was against Fort Macleod when they committed seven errors, but they won, so it didn't matter. The most important thing was their defense did not cost them any games.

Scobey's pitching and defense were good enough to keep them in games because the team could score runs.

NORTHWEST REGIONAL

THE 1996 NORTHWEST REGIONAL TOURNAMENT WAS HOSTED in Powell, Wyoming. Since its humble beginnings in 1984, when only three states—Oregon, Washington, and Idaho—participated, the tournament had expanded to seven states. The seven states represented in 1996 were Oregon, Washington, Idaho, Montana, North Dakota, South Dakota, and Wyoming. Because of the expansion, only the state's champion advanced, except the host state got two.

The Billings Blue Jays went 1-2 in the tournament, losing their first game against Worland, Wyoming, beating Nampa, Idaho, then losing to host Powell. Both of their losses were by one run. Okanogan Valley, Washington, won the championship over North Jackson, Oregon.

EXTRA INNINGS

SCOBEY'S STATE CHAMPIONSHIPS IN FOOTBALL AND TRACK AND field during the 1995-96 season were the first in history, but Scobey had won its first State Class B basketball championship in 1979 when Dan Danelson and Gerry Veis let Scobey over Plentywood in the championship game. A week later, Kevin Hatfield led Flaxville to its second State

Class C championship with a win over Peerless in the state championship game. Six Blues players were dual state champions in basketball and baseball in 1979: Dan Danelson, Kelly Norman, and Kirby Halvorson from Scobey; Jesse Cook, Ron Higgins, and Gord Tryan from Flaxville. Joe, Jon Puckett, and Ray Chapman played for the state champion Blues from state runner-up Peerless. Scobey's high school enrollment in 1979 was 183 students, but due to declining enrollment, Scobey was moved down to Class C in high school sports in 1986.

The 1996 state tournament would be the last time the Scobey Blues would play on Cobb Field. The Blues had played their first game on Cobb Field 30 years earlier in 1966, when Phil Audet pitched Scobey to a 4-3 win over the Billings Scarlets.

After graduating, Tim Vigliotti joined some of his Glendive opponents playing baseball for Dawson Community College. "I played with half of Glendive's squad at DCC. Tom Ziegler was an all-around athlete. He was special. It was weird playing for Coach Diegel. I played for one year for him at Dawson."

The 11-team tournament with nine-inning games was savage on pitching arms. In the 13-inning Fort Macleod–Libby game, Fort Macleod starter Craig Hann pitched 12 innings and delivered 219 pitches. This was obviously before the pitch count era. Many Scobey pitchers, including me, threw 12-inning games and probably delivered well over 200 pitches. Havre's Dave Fanning pitched 12 innings in the State A Tournament against the Royals in 1971; Jim LeProwse threw 12 innings against Havre at State in 1985. It happened a lot. Some pitchers probably chucked well over 150 pitches in just nine-inning games with walks, hits, and errors. The Legion rule in 1996 (and when I played) only limited pitchers to 12 innings and three appearances in three days, but no pitch counts. For example, if a pitcher threw 12 innings on Thursday, he would get those 12 innings back on Sunday. As sensible as pitch counts are to us now, it took American Legion Baseball until 20 years later (2017) to institute pitch counts (and seven-inning games). The new pitch count rules established by the National Executive Committee of The American Legion in August 2017 included a maximum of 105 pitches per day, and pitchers could also only make two appearances (down from three) on any three consecutive days. The rationale for the new rules was to put American Legion Baseball more in line with high school baseball, which had always had seven-inning games. The new pitch-count rules also required the following days of rest:

- 1-30 pitches: 0 days
- 31-45 pitches: 1 day
- 46-60 pitches: 2 days
- 61-80 pitches: 3 days
- 81+ pitches: 4 days

Tracy Vatnsdal, along with Brent Tarum, was an assistant coach in 1996. He has fond memories of the season. "It was a great summer. When Ken asked me to help, I said sure I wasn't doing anything else, really. It was a great group of ball players who had a winning culture from high school sports. I was the dugout coach and made sure the boys stayed fired up and engaged in the game."

Tracy has a couple of memories of the state tournament at Cobb Field. "During infield, I would always hit the outfield pop flies. So when we made it to State at Cobb Field in Billings, I was pumped that I would get to hit balls on Cobb, but come to find out, they wouldn't let us take infield and outfield on the field. Another funny story was when we took the field in Billings, they weren't gonna let me be in the dugout because I wasn't on the roster. So, Ken ended up telling them my name was Dan Wolfe, as he was on the roster as the manager. So that was kinda comical." We'll expect your best Dan Wolfe impersonation at the reunion, Tracy.

Every team has at least one humorous anecdote about chewing tobacco and baseball. I have one of my own. But Levi Bowler's story about chewing tobacco and baseball is epic—it spans his four-year Legion career. Assistant Coach Tracy Vatnsdal told me about an incident on the bus with Levi and the dip in 1996, so I asked Levi if he remembered it. Levi replied, "Oh, do I remember. The story goes deeper. It started when I got brought up at 15. The boys made me try one. I puked all over inside my duffel bag so the coaches wouldn't know about it, and then the stench was so bad the whole bus had all the windows down. The coaches obviously found out. Every year after, I would try it again, even at the age of 18. So the next year, I tried it again. Ken did not want the bus to smell like puke, so he pulled over, and I puked my guts out in the ditch. The following year, I remember it was in Glasgow about 100 degrees. I was on the back of the bus, and the boys thought it was a good time for me to try it again. It wasn't sitting well and I wasn't gonna make it to the front of the bus, so I hung my head out the window and puked. That brings us to the year Tracy is talking about when the boys said I had to go out trying it one last time. Before I even put it in, Ken told me the bus was not stopping and that if I puked, he was going to kill me. I figured I was a big college boy now, and I wouldn't puke, so I threw one in. Couldn't handle it. Ran to the front of the bus Ken was driving. Ken yelled, "You son of a bitch, I told you the bus was not stopping!" He pulled the door open but wouldn't stop the bus, so Joel Nieskens had me hooked around the waist while I held onto the handrail. I was trying to puke out the door thinking we wouldn't get it on the bus like the last time that I puked out the window. That was a giant failure—should've gone to the back of the bus and puked out the window again. I painted the whole side of the bus . . . in fact, so bad I got a phone call from Sean Cromwell after we got home. He told me to meet him down at the bus barn because I had a bus to wash. Best thing that ever happened to me. I don't think I've ever taken a chew since."

In addition to his coaching duties, Coach Ken Meyer was also the Blues bus driver starting in 1995. Jedd Lekvold remembers a time when Coach Meyer let Levi take the wheel. Levi recalls, "All the coaches did some driving throughout the year from what I remember. But there was one particular time, and I couldn't tell you where we were as far as which highway, but we did an 'on the fly' switch. I maybe took the wheel for 5–10 minutes." Yikes!

I asked Levi to share more about his experience playing for the Bobcats. "We played some teams in Clarkson, Idaho, Moscow, Idaho, and Missoula, Montana. We went down and played in Boise, too, I remember. It was kind of a good old boys' club; we were just lucky enough to all make it. Zach had just transferred from NDSU, where he played the fall before. Josh was coming off two knee surgeries and still had the fight in him to be on the field. Because of the knee surgeries, he couldn't catch, but he held down the hotbox pretty damn well. Zach was at short, and I played left and center field. One of the greatest road trips we had was to Moscow, Idaho, driving over the pass to Coeur d'Alene in a snowstorm with that dude from Minnesota. It was pretty unorganized back in those days, but it was still fun to compete."

Josh Lee remembers playing with Zach and Levi with the Bobcats, too. "We played the other club teams in the Big Sky plus MSU-Billings before they had a sanctioned program. Had an absolute blast. I was three years removed from competitive baseball, but after the rust shook off, it was pretty damn fun. Played some ball, drank some beer, kissed some

Josh Lee (far right) crosses home plate after hitting a home run for the Montana State University Club Team. *Family photo.*

girls, and had a couple of fights. Not us in the fights, but some guys on the team. Definitely a bunch of knuckleheads."

Josh remembers one highlight of playing for the Bobcats. "I hit a three-run homer at Urbaska Field in Billings. It should have been a grand slam, but the kid in front of me swung at a 3-0 pitch to see another pitch. He should of walked to get the bases loaded. He ended up striking out. I gave him an earful. It was the same game where we found a bra in the dugout, and Levi put it on with a couple of baseballs in it. It was my total inspiration. That and he told me to swing like Johnny Love Butt. I was living in Great Falls after college and still had that home run ball. Tommy Lasorda was there, making an appearance for the Pioneer League at the time. I got that ball autographed by him. Pretty cool for me. I've been a Dodger fan my entire life."

Jake Petersen, who led the Blues in hitting with a lofty .472 batting average during the regular season and batted third in the lineup, credited his hitting success to an assistant coach. "I owed that year [hitting] to Brent Tarum. When he came back from college, he taught me some hitting strategies that really clicked with me. Really changed my swing and approach. Doc Norman tournament went well for me, especially."

Levi Bowler became a critical pitcher for Scobey during his Legion career, but he didn't come up as a pitcher. Levi recalls, "I was a catcher my whole life (8-15). I was a lot better at calling games than I was pitching! I would say I developed as a pitcher in Legion. I didn't have a lot of pitches, my curveball didn't move, I had a pretty dirty forkball, but you never knew if it was ever going to land close to the plate or not, and my fastball probably didn't top 75. But the important thing was, I could throw strikes. I was the guy Meyer put in when he just needed ground balls and pop flies." Jake Petersen agreed with Levi's assessment of his forkball. "You would never know where that forkball was going to go!" Jason Wolfe added, "But it was filthy!"

Levi's forkball recalls Danny Wang's forkball, which he used effectively to win key games for Scobey when he played from 1966 to 1970. Danny hurled his forkball at Havre for nine innings in the state championship game against Havre in 1970, keeping Scobey in the game but eventually taking the 6-1 loss. There were not a lot of fork ballers in Scobey Legion baseball history, but two notable ones were Danny Wang and Levi Bowler. Throwing strikes with movement on the ball leads to outs if fielders can make plays.

The 1996 Scobey Blues played together in Little League and Babe Ruth when they were known as the "Baby Blues." Jason Wolfe said, "The 17-and 18-year-olds had good chemistry. I think we were undefeated in Babe Ruth when I was 14.

As mentioned, going back to those Little League days, Glendive had been this team's nemesis, which made beating them in the 1996 State Tournament satisfying for them. But it wasn't all bad blood. Levi Bowler said, "Over the years I got to be friends with a few of those guys and am still really good friends with Derek Berube. I think they were a lot like us; they had a young confident coach with a little cock in his walk, backed with a bag full of talent."

Jason Wolfe remembers a hot doubleheader at Denton Field in Miles City during the 50-game regular season schedule. "I think it was 110 degrees. Jake caught both games of a doubleheader and didn't complain once. That guy was a shit-eating psycho, and we loved him for it. It cooled down to about 104 at night. Meyer made us sleep on the bus. It was so hot we all tried to sleep outside. Cotton was falling from the cottonwoods. We were all covered in cotton because it was sticking to our sweat. Longest, most miserable night ever, but I lived every minute of those road trips. Jake added, "Oh, the cotton! That was a terrible night. Played a lot of smear and hacky sack."

The Canadian coaches, in this case the head coach of Fort Macleod, were serious. They charted individual players of opposing teams, including times to second base on steals and hitting charts. Jake Petersen and Levi Bowler remember the Fort Macleod coach handing them their charts after the game. Jake said, "The Fort McCleod game was the toughest for me because their coach attended every game and scouted every player. He had hitting charts on all of us and gave it to us after the tournament. I was pretty dialed in that season [Jake led the team in hitting], and they robbed me of two hits that I would have normally had. I had to change my approach at the plate deep into that game." Levi's experience of the charts was with his baserunning tendencies, specifically his lead of third. Jason Wolfe recalls a play at third on Levi during the game. "They had a pitcher that would make this sweet balk move to third. He was picking guys off third all tournament. We had a guy on third, and that pitcher went to his move, and their third baseman wasn't ready for it. The ball caromed off his forehead and into left field. I think that led to a big inning." Levi remembers the play. "They had me dead. The coach knew I was an easy out at third. He gave me a scouting report on myself after the game. In the top left corner, circled in red, it read, 'can pick at 3B'" Amazing!

Tim Vigliotti recalls his struggle with his broken shoulder injury in football and how he had to adjust his pitching during the season. "Coming back from the shoulder injury was tough because I didn't have the velocity that I had in previous years—I had to rely more on my off-speed, curveball, and change. It was hard not to be able to throw it by guys like I used to be able to do. By the time tournaments rolled around, I had things figured out and was still able to strike guys out by hitting spots. It was a completely different approach that I learned on the fly."

I asked Ken Meyer and Mike Lee what it was like coaching against each other. They had played together as kids through Legion and coached the Blues together for two seasons; now, here they were, coaching against each other for a state tournament berth. I was intrigued by it because it reminded me of my experience of how difficult it was to compete against someone I was close to and had played with growing up. The meeting at home plate between Ken and Mike reminded when I took the court for the first time against my twin brother Jon in college basketball when we were freshmen, and it was hard. Jon was at Montana Tech, and I was at Carroll. We got in the game together and guarded each other, and I knew if I did well, he might come out, and the same applied to me. (I dominated him.) Ken said about the encounter, "I don't really remember feeling any different. It was an opposing team that, when we took the field, we wanted to beat. I suppose we might have known each other's tendencies, but it wasn't like there was extra motivation to beat Wolf Point because Karch coached. We always knew we would be in for a good game when playing them, regardless of the coach. I suppose the hardest part was seeing Karch in a black and yellow uniform! Didn't look quite right." Mike replied, "It was a little odd for me coaching against Scobey, but like Ken said, it really didn't matter who you were playing and who was coaching; you just wanted to win, and it didn't matter what you needed to do to win." (This recalls Art Holum's statement that Karch "would strike out his own grandma" if it meant winning a game.)

Karch remembers the Scobey-Wolf Point game at divisional. "I think we went up one run early in the game and then got 10-run ruled. Beating Glasgow the game before was the pinnacle of our season. Glasgow still had their number-one and number-three pitchers who hadn't thrown an inning yet; however, they decided to go with their number-four or five against us. I was fired up before the game about it and let my kids know just what Glasgow thought of them by doing that. Taking third sucked, but it really was the best we could do. Scobey and Glendive were by far deeper and more talented. They definitely were the right teams to represent the east at State."

But Karch still got to go to State anyway—with Scobey. Mike recalls, "[Ken] Meyer and the team picked me up in Wolf Point with my golf clubs on their way to Billings. I already had accepted a job in Scobey at Scobey High School starting in the fall. I knew I was going to be coaching the Scobey kids in football, basketball, track, and baseball that next year, so it was fun hanging out with them."

And Karch provided logistical support for the Blues at State. Jake Petersen said, "I am pretty much blind without glasses or contacts. One of the maids threw my contacts away at the hotel we were staying at on accident and Karch had to help me find an eye doctor that had my prescription. Thank goodness."

Pitchers Tim Vigliotti and Jason Wolfe tipped their hats to catcher Jake Petersen. Tim said, "Jake was the best catcher I ever pitched to. He knew my strengths and weaknesses. He kept me calm in all the big-time games and brought confidence to the whole team." Jason Wolfe agreed. "Jake was the best teammate! I've been coaching for 23 years and use him as an example to all of my kids on how to prepare yourself for success."

Scobey had previously played Libby in the State A Tournament in 1973 and the best-of-three playoff series in 1976, when Scobey was competing in Class B, and Libby was in Class A. Scobey had lost to Libby 6-5 in 1973 and won two out of three against the Loggers in the 1976 playoff, so the Blues were 3-2 lifetime against Libby. There was also a regular season game where Craig Audet threw the ball over first base, across the street, and into a swimming pool on the other side.

Spencer Frederick was the third Scobey Blue to be named MVP of a state tournament, following Randy Stolen in 1980 and Pat Audet in 1982. Before 1980, no MVP was selected.

Coach Len Anderson's son Dennis, who installed the batting cage in the backyard, benefited from the cage. In the 1996 high school baseball season, Anderson was Tucson's player of the year and a first-team All-State catcher. The New York Mets drafted him, but Anderson chose to play at Pima College, where he was selected to join the All-ACCAC team in 1998 and became a two-year starter for the Aztecs. In his one season at the University of Arizona in 1999, he was the starting catcher for the Wildcat team that reached the NCAA regionals. He batted .349. The Florida Marlins drafted him and, once signed, began an eight-year career in the minor leagues, in which he played in 490 games and had 1,401 at-bats. He reached Double-A and played for the Carolina Mudcats of the Southern League. Coach Len Anderson later coached Canyon Del Oro to the 2009 Arizona State baseball championship.

The 12-10 Havre-Scobey game was the last game these two storied Legion programs would play against each other in a state tournament, and the two teams went out with a bang against each other. Here is the history of the state tournament matchups between the Northstars and Blues, with the scores, winning and losing pitchers, and year:

- Scobey 7-3, WP Dick Puckett, LP Dan Morris (1967)
- Scobey 12-2, WP Dick Puckett (Terry Puckett in relief), LP Dennis Kuntz (1968)
- Havre 12-0, WP Barry Damschen, LP Dick Puckett (1968)
- Havre 7-2, Mike Hanson, LP Dick Puckett (1969)
- Scobey 8-7 (10 innings), WP Jim Hansen (in relief), LP Scott Kato (1969)
- Scobey 7-6, WP Dick Puckett, LP Barry Damschen (1969)
- Havre 6-1, WP Kurt Grimm, LP Danny Wang (1970)
- Havre 1-0, WP Dave Fanning, LP Terry Puckett (1971)
- Havre 20-5, WP Dick Clark, LP Dana Audet (1972)

- Havre 4-2, WP Mark Kato, LP Jay Hagfeldt (1974)
- Havre 1-0, WP Barry Kato, LP Mike Hagfeldt (1975)
- Scobey 5-4 (16 innings), WP Mike Roland (in relief), LP Bucky Lindstrand (1985)
- Scobey 12-10, WP Curt Ware, S Tim Vigliotti, LP Sam Evans (1996)

The two years Havre and Scobey met in the State championship game were 1969 and 1970. The 13-game "series" played between the Northstars and Blues in state tournaments ended 7-6 in favor of the Northstars. In the 10 different state tournaments, the two teams faced each other, Scobey or Havre won that state tournament six times.

1997

The Last Hurrah: Scobey's Final State Tournament Appearance

> *I had such an empty feeling when that final out of the state tournament was made, and the game was over, that this was done, and I knew I wasn't gonna ever be coaching or playing for the Blues again. There were a lot of connections with current players and previous Blues, nostalgia, and a connection with Grandpa and Grandma. It was a tough one.*
>
> —Mike "Karch" Lee, Scobey Blues batboy (1978–83), player (1987–90) and coach (1992, 1994, 1997)

1997 Scobey Blues. Front row, left to right: Ben Bucklin, Joel Nieskens, Jason Wolfe, Jake Petersen, Brian Solberg, Jedd Lekvold, Mark McElvaney, A.J. Shipstead. Back row, left to right, Head Coach Mike Lee, Assistant Coach Tim Tharp, Curt Ware, Spencer Frederick, Jay Hoversland, Cale Handran, Matt Bucklin, Lee Farver, Assistant Coach Jim Petersen. *Leader photo, Mike Stebleton.*

PRESEASON

Seven seasoned veterans—Joel Nieskens, Spencer Frederick, Curt Ware, Jason Wolfe, Jake Petersen, Ben Bucklin, and Lee Farver (all 18 years old)—were returning from Scobey's 1996 team, which finished third at State. Mike Stebleton, the newly hired *Daniels County Leader* sportswriter, captured the promising upcoming season for the Blues when he wrote the preseason article, "Don't look for the Blues to be singing the blues," writing, "The American Legion Baseball team is anchored by seven 18-year-olds who are loaded with experience, having participated in the state tournament as 16-and 17-year-olds and placing third last season."[27]

That was the good news.

The bad news was that the three starters who were not returning—Tim Vigliotti, Levi Bowler, and Joey Boos—were excellent all-around baseball players, and good pitchers, with Tim Vigliotti the ace. The three of them had logged over 30 innings for Coach Meyer at the state tournament a year earlier, with Tim getting two wins and a save in Scobey's four wins.

There were two big questions for this team: Who would coach them? Who was going to pitch? Coach Ken Meyer, who had led the Blues the past five seasons—and to a third-place finish at State in 1996—had moved on. Ken's former Blues teammate and Doc and Marge Norman's

563

grandson, Mike "Karch" Lee, who had coached the Wolf Point Yellowjackets to a third-place finish at the eastern divisional in 1996, would take the helm for Scobey in 1997.

Coach Lee's biggest challenge in his first year as head coach was pitching. Two returning starting pitchers, Curt Ware and Jason Wolfe, would anchor the staff. Each of them had won games in the state tournament in 1996: Jason Wolfe pitched a complete game four-hitter to beat Livingston; Curt Ware pitched eight and two-thirds innings in a 12-10 win over Havre. While neither pitcher was overpowering, they were good pitch-to-contact pitchers and would keep Scobey in games because Scobey would score runs with their big bats. But in 11-team state tournaments, two pitchers would not get you very far. Coach Lee said he would "have to develop a pitching staff after" Curt and Jason. That pitching staff would consist of Spencer Frederick and Joel Nieskens, who hadn't pitched much previously but would need to step up in 1997. Lee Farver and 16-year-old Cale Handran—who had seen innings in 1996 and threw a combined three-hitter against Circle in the opening game of the eastern divisional tournament—would also get plenty of innings. Rookie 16-year-olds Jay Hoversland and Jedd Lekvold—Coach Don Lekvold's son—would complete the staff. Jake Petersen would again be the rock behind home plate, handling the staff for the third consecutive year.

In his assessment of the team before the season's start, Coach Lee recognized the fine coaching the Blues had received under his predecessor, Ken Meyer, saying, "Their fundamentals—the basics, the mechanics—are superb due to the fact of the consistency of Ken Meyer' program the last five years."

Yes, pitching would be a problem for Scobey in 1997—but there were no problems with the offense. This team could pound the ball for average and power, and they had great speed on the basepaths. If I were a betting man, I would take the over *every* time on runs scored for this team.

These athletes were busy again bringing trophies back to Scobey during the "offseason" on the gridiron and hardwood. On the gridiron, Coach Larry "Bucky" Henderson led Scobey-Peerless to a repeat state championship in football, going undefeated in both seasons, winning 24 consecutive games. The team was undefeated and ranked number one on the hardwood going into State. However, a blizzard delayed the team's (and cheerleaders and fans) departure from Scobey on Wednesday, and it took four hours for them to get 48 miles to Wolf Point, leaving Scobey early Thursday morning, the day of the first game at the tournament. Private boosters then arranged for two private flights for Coach Selvig and nine players to fly from Wolf Point to Billings in time for their opening game against Seeley Swan on Thursday, which the MHSA delayed. Exhausted from the travel, the undefeated Spartans suffered a 52-51 upset at the hands of Seeley-Swan in the opening game of the state tournament, but they came back to beat them 60-50 in the consolation. During the baseball season, Curt Ware and Jason Wolfe played in the Treasure State Classic Class C All-Star football game, and Spencer Frederick and Joel Nieskens played in the Montana-Wyoming All-Stars basketball series. To give you an idea of what outstanding all-around athletes these Scobey-Peerless players were, Joel Nieskens and Spencer Frederick—who were both selected to play in the All-Star football game—chose to play in the Montana-Wyoming basketball series because it was played on the same weekend. You get the idea: these were some athletes.

Completing the 15-man roster were three 17-year-olds: Matt Bucklin, A.J. Shipstead, and Mark McElvaney—and five 16-year-olds: Jedd Lekvold, Mark McElvaney, Jay Hoversland, Cale Handran, and Brian Solberg.

Coach Lee had two assistant coaches during the 1996 season, Jim Peterson and Tim Tharp.

REGULAR SEASON

ALONG WITH THE 28-GAME CONFERENCE SCHEDULE, COACH Lee had planned another full season of competitive non-conference tournaments and games. Jason Wolfe recalls the demanding schedule. "Karch put together a great schedule for us in 97. We had a chance to see a ton of good competition, including some teams that were at the state tournament the year before." The Blues traveled to Havre and Belgrade again to participate in two early-season tournaments hosted by the Northstars and Bandits. In Havre, the Blues were a little shorthanded, as four starters were playing in all-star football and basketball games, but Jake Petersen stepped up and hit two doubles to lead Scobey over the Great Falls Stallions 6-5. Referring to the Belgrade Tournament, Jason Wolfe recalls, "The Belgrade Tournament was also full of great teams. Mike Neubauer coached Belgrade and always invited the Blues. It was an awesome tournament. They had a radar gun behind the plate and were clocking Curt in the upper 80s." In Belgrade, the highlight was when the Blues beat a good Helena Reps team, ending their 17-game winning streak with an 8-7 win in 10 innings. Jason Wolfe started, and Lee Farver got the win in relief. Jason Wolfe, Jake Petersen, and Spencer Frederick had doubles to lead Scobey's hitting. In the same tournament, the Blues lost a 17-14 slugfest to the Bitterroot Bucs.

Scobey hosted two tournaments in 1997, the Scobey Invitational Tournament and the 14th Annual Doc Nor-

Spencer Frederick put the hurt on this pitch this afternoon, sending it over the left field wall in the top of the seventh inning to give his Scobey team a 7-6 lead against Havre. But the Northstars scored two runs in the bottom of the seventh to win 8-7. *Leader photo, Mike Stebleton.*

man Memorial Tournament. Jason Wolfe recalls the Doc Norman Memorial Tournament "being loaded. It was us, Glendive, Havre, and maybe a good team from Regina and a few others." The Blues dramatically lost to Havre 8-7 at the Doc Norman. Spencer Frederick put the Blues up 7-6 in the top of the seventh inning by sending a towering home run over the left-field wall, only to see the Northstars score two runs in the bottom of the seventh to win 8-7. There always seemed to be drama when the Blues met the Northstars, whether during the regular season or in a state tournament.

Jason Wolfe remembers a first-time event at the 1997 Doc Norman. "Karch had a home run derby where each team picked two players to participate. Our selection was me and Spencer Frederick. I wasn't known for power, but I had hit a few early home runs that season, so I got in. Spencer was in for obvious reasons. He hit some mammoth home runs that year. I wanna say we won the derby 7-6 over Havre. Spence hit 7, and I hit 0."

Two special moments happened at the 14th annual Doc Norman Memorial Tournament: Jason Wolfe and Marge (Norman) Shiell received awards, and Ernie Halvorson was recognized for his many years of service to the Blues program and the community.

During the regular season, one of those "mammoth" home runs Spencer hit was a dramatic walk-off at home against the team's nemesis, Glendive. Jake Petersen recalls, "My favorite memory from the season was the one win against Glendive. Spencer and I hit back-to-back home runs in a walk-off win. Wolfe got on first in the bottom of the seventh. I came up and hit what I thought was going to be a pop-up to left field off the handle of my bat. Somehow, it went over the fence on the left. Before Jason and I were even in the dugout from the base paths, I heard a loud grunt from Spencer and looked up as the ball went over the center fielder's head and fence to walk-off Glendive." Jason recalls Spencer's walk-off home run. "Spencer's walk-off bomb hit the old curling rink!"

Jason Wolfe recalls another mammoth home run Spencer hit that regular season in Belgrade. "Spencer hit another

Jason Wolfe, center, and Marge (Norman) Shiell, right, were two awards recipients during the 14th annual Doc Norman Memorial Baseball Tournament held recently in Scobey. Wolfe was awarded the Norman Scholarship, while Shiell was presented with a Scobey Blues team jacket for her many years of supporting the Blues program. Ann Lee, left, Doc and Marge Norman's daughter, presented Wolfe with his award. *Leader photo, Mike Stebleton*

Ernie Halvorson is recognized for all his years of service with the Blues and the community of Scobey. Coach Mike Lee (right) and the team gave him a ball that the kids signed and a Blues Jacket at the Doc Norman Memorial Tournament. *Leader photo, Mike Stebleton.*

one of his moon shots in that tournament. An old-timer came up to us after the game and told us he'd seen lots of baseball at that field, and that was the farthest home run he'd ever seen!"

Circle was the cellar-dweller of the conference in 1997, and Jake Petersen recalls a game against Circle where Karch had to show mercy to get the teams off the field. "We were playing Circle in the second game of the doubleheader, and we scored either 17 or 19 runs in the first inning. Karch made me get out by purposing missing home plate. They could not get us out."

In conference play, Scobey, with a 21-7 conference record, and Glendive were again at the top, with Glendive winning the conference and Scobey in second. During the regular season, the Blue Devils owned the Blues, beating Scobey 4 of 5 games. Glasgow had a good team again in 1997 and took third, finishing one game behind the Blues at 20-8. They had finished second the previous year.

Here were the final conference standings:

1. Glendive
2. Scobey (31-17 overall)
3. Glasgow
4. Richland County
5. Wolf Point
6. Plentywood
7. Homestead
8. Circle

After their second-place conference finish and 31-17 overall record, the Blues were ready to make a run at another state title. The first step was to finish in the top two in the Divisional, hosted by the Glasgow Reds at Bill Connors Field in Glasgow.

DIVISIONAL TOURNAMENT

Scobey needed to win three games in the tournament to advance to the state tournament. Their first step would be the opening round against the seventh-seeded Homestead Pioneers. Here were the complete first-round matchups:

- Glendive (1) vs. Circle 8
- Richland County (4) vs. Wolf Point (5)
- Scobey (2) vs. Homestead (7)
- Glasgow (3) vs. Plentywood (6)

Scobey had handled Homestead easily during the regular season, and the opening game of the eastern divisional would be no different, although the game would not be without its drama—at least for two innings. The Blues' bats feasted on Homestead's pitching in the first inning as they went ahead 5-0 on a two-run double by Jason Wolfe and a three-run home run by Jay Hoversland. The Blues scored five more in the third to take a 10-0 lead, with the big blow coming on another three-run home run, this time by Mark McElvaney.

But the drama came in the bottom of the third when Homestead plated seven runs on six hits and two Scobey errors to jump back in the game, 10-7—all with no outs. It was already a slugfest, only in the third inning. With winds gusting at 30-40 mph, blowing into straightaway center field, balls were flying out of the park as if Charlie Brown were pitching on a bad day. In the top of the fourth, Jay Hoversland blasted his second home run—a line drive over the center field fence—to drive in two more runs and give Scobey a 13-7 lead. Homestead responded with three more runs of their own in the bottom of the fourth on two hits—and two more Scobey errors—to climb back to 13-10, and the slugfest was raging like the winds swirling around Bill Connors Field.

As if there hadn't been enough scoring in the first four innings, the top of the fifth went from crazy to ridiculous when Scobey plated a dozen runs to take a 25-10 lead. Spencer Frederick had a two-run double with the bases loaded, which brought Jay Hoversland to the plate. Jay had already hit two home runs in two plate appearances. Could the 16-year-old do it again? He did! Jay pounded his third home run—a line drive over the left field fence—to drive in three runs and give Scobey a 19-10 lead. At this point, Jay was 3-3 with three home runs and eight RBIs. (This is a record for home runs in a single game by a Scobey player.) Scobey continued to light up the scoreboard like a pinball machine, batting around, and the score was 25-10. So, who comes to the plate with two outs? Jay Hoversland! Mike Stebleton of the *Leader* wrote what happened next: "Finally, the third out occurred, and it was the most unlikely Blues player, on this day anyway, to get it. Hoversland, who had already smacked three pitches out of the park for eight RBIs, swung and missed on a 1-2 count, thus ending the inning of 12 runs, seven hits, and two Homestead errors."[28]

There was no joy in Scobey, for mighty Jay had struck out.

Not really. The game ended in seven innings, with Scobey walloping Homestead by a football score of 27-14. Lee Farver earned the win with three and two-thirds innings of work. Cale Handran pitched two and one-third innings, and Jedd Lekvold—in what was decidedly not a save opportunity—pitched the last inning. Jedd had pinpoint control, throwing 16 pitches, 15 of them for strikes, to the five

Jay Hoversland had a big tourney in the batter's box for Scobey, hitting at a .357 average with three home runs and a team-leading 11 RBI. He scored seven runs. *Leader photo, Mike Stebleton.*

Coach Lee, Jake Petersen, Spencer Frederick, Curt Ware (behind Spencer), and Jason Wolfe during a mound visit at the 1997 Eastern Divisional Tournament in Glasgow. *Family photo.*

hitters he faced. Hoversland led Scobey's hitting, having a career day with three home runs and eight RBIs. Mark McElvaney also hit a three-run home run. Jason Wolfe recalls the crazy game. "That was such a wild first game. Hoversland was a big, strong kid. It was awesome to see him hit those home runs." When I asked Jay to comment about the three home runs, he was humble. "The wind was blowing 50 miles an hour from right center to center," he said. "I hit what would be considered a normal day three routine pop flies. However, they happened to be just high enough and deep enough to clear the fence three times. I guess I thank the good Lord for the northeastern Montana wind." (Very humble indeed: *two* of the home runs were line drives, not "pop flies.")

The slugfest win in the swirling northeastern Montana winds was a rousing way for Scobey to start the postseason, but now it was time for the wind—and Scobey—to settle down and get about the business of winning two more games to get to State. Scobey faced the Glasgow Reds on their home field in the second game. The Reds had finished third in the conference and were playing at home, so the Blues needed to be careful in this one. In a game that started late and ended at 12:15 a.m., Coach Lee handed the ball to Curt Ware to start, and he got into trouble early. In the first inning, he gave up a leadoff double, hit a batter, then walked three consecutive hitters with two outs. Glasgow had scored two runs before Coach Lee came to the mound to make a pitching change. "I didn't want to take the chance of them having a big inning," Coach Lee said. In the huddle on the mound, Coach Lee looked at Jason Wolfe and Joel Nieskens and asked, "Who wants the ball?" Jason Wolfe grabbed it, struck out the next batter, then pitched eight innings of four-hit ball to lead Scobey to a 12-4 win. Scobey scored all the runs Jason needed in the bottom of the first, erasing Glasgow's 2-0 lead with a big six-run inning to snatch a 6-2 lead.

But this was a close game. In the bottom of the eighth, Scobey only led 7-4, but then had another classic big inning, characteristic of this heavy-hitting team. Mark McElvaney hit a booming three-run double, and Scobey scored five runs in the inning, giving Jason Wolfe a comfortable eight-run cushion to close out the ninth, which he did, pitching a scoreless inning. Jason finished the game with a four-hitter, striking out 10 Reds and walking only three.

The win propelled Scobey into the undefeated semifinal against the Glendive Blue Devils, whom Scobey had only beaten once (on Spencer Frederick's walk-off home run) in six games during the regular season. Jason Wolfe said, "Glendive was again a thorn in our side." Scobey only needed one more win in the tournament to make it back to State for the third consecutive year, but the Blue Devils again had Scobey's number, beating them 13-7. Spencer Frederick pitched a complete game for Scobey. The Blue Devils scored six runs in the second and six in the eighth and ninth to salt this one away. Offensively, Scobey left a whopping 17 runners on base—14 in scoring position!

Jason Wolfe had three hits, and Curt Ware had two to lead Scobey's hitting, but the team couldn't get the hits they needed with runners on base.

It was very clear what the stakes were in Scobey's next game against Glasgow: "Win and advance to the state tourney; lose and get a third-place trophy."[29] To whom would Coach Lee hand the ball to lead Scobey back to State? "The Blues wanted the win; Curt Ware wanted another opportunity. After his problem pitching performance against Glasgow Friday night, the Scobey 18-year-old felt he had it in him to throw well enough to keep it close and let the Blues offense score enough runs to find a way to win."[30] So, Coach Lee handed the ball to Curt Ware, and the All-State quarterback, who had led Scobey to two state championships and 24 consecutive wins on the football field, led Scobey back to the state baseball tournament. He put the rough first inning against the Reds two days earlier behind him and returned with a vengeance, taking a shutout into the fifth inning. He helped his own cause at the plate, too, as he opened the scoring with a solo home run to straightaway center field in the second inning to stake Scobey to a 1-0 lead. Scobey had a big six-run fourth to take a 7-0 lead. Glasgow got to Curt for the only two runs he allowed in the top of the fifth, but the Blues answered with three runs in the fifth and sixth innings to take a commanding 13-2 into the top of the seventh, where Curt needed only three more outs to secure a seven-inning win for Scobey. The veteran right-hander pitched a scoreless seventh, finishing with a three-hitter, and the Blues danced off the field, knowing they had secured another berth in the state tournament. Coach Lee said, "Curt kept Glasgow guessing on his fastballs and off-speed stuff. He came hard to the plate."

Jason Wolfe recalls Curt's clutch performance. "Curt threw a hell of a game in that state clincher. When Curt's command was on point, he was untouchable. He had great velocity on his fastball and complimented it with a filthy change-up. I could usually tell within the first couple of batters if he was gonna have one of those special games, and that was certainly one of them."

Defensively, Scobey played errorless ball in the "game that mattered."[31] Cale Handran at third and Ben Bucklin in right "made some fine defensive plays."[32]

Jason Wolfe remembers the pressure of the two Glasgow games. "Those games with Glasgow were intense. I remember feeling a ton of pressure to win that first one with Glasgow to preserve pitching. Glasgow had a good team. They had three really good left-handed pitchers that year. They had given us some trouble a couple of times during the regular season."

Having already secured a berth in the state tournament and facing the "extremely tough Glendive Blue Devils"[33]—who the Blues would need to beat twice to win the championship—Coach Lee made an unpopular decision with the Scobey faithful: he rested some of his starters—including catcher Jake Petersen—and rested his starting pitchers, starting Jay Hoversland on the mound. His logic? "Even if we'd have won Sunday with one of our best pitchers, we'd have had to come back again Monday and throw another one of our better pitchers to even be in the game. And then we lose another day of rest. I felt it necessary to rest our top pitcher's arms and Jake's body for the state tournament, plus giving some great tournament experience to some players who didn't see a lot of playing time in this tourney. I always feel it's important to keep looking ahead to the future of the program."

It is tough to argue with that logic; it is also not hard to see how that would have been difficult for Scobey fans to accept, ceding a championship game. Jason Wolfe agreed with Karch's decision. "I think Karch made the right decision in that chipper against Glendive. We were short on pitching and might as well save some arms. Jake caught every game and even though he was a warrior, it was good to get him some rest heading into State."

Glendive won the championship game 14-1 in seven innings as pitcher Kyle Pederson pitched a three-hitter. Jay Hoversland gave a gutsy performance, as "the youngster hung in there and did what he had to do for his team."[34]

Coach Lee flashing signs at the 1997 Eastern Divisional Tournament in Glasgow. Doc's indicator signal was skin on skin, which meant the next sequence of signals coming was a go. Doc's signs were passed down to the Don Lekvold, Ken Meyer, and Mike Lee teams. *Family photo.*

But no matter, all water under the bridge. Scobey won the game that mattered, and the Blues were advancing to their third consecutive state tournament in Helena, where they would compete for another state title. Mike Stebleton of the *Leader* summed the divisional tournament up best: "Say what you want about the Scobey Blues—there seems to be some differing opinions these days—but they won the game that counted at the Eastern A Divisional Tournament in Glasgow. And they're going to the state tourney because of it!"[35]

Scobey's bats boomed in the tournament with some eye-popping averages. Curt Ware led the way with a .538 average, followed by Jason Wolfe at .474, Spencer Frederick at .467, Cale Handran at .438, Jay Hoversland at .357, Mark McElvaney at .357, and Jake Petersen at .316. Extra-base hits popped off these bats, too, as these heavy hitters launched several home runs out of Bill Connors Field. Jay Hoversland finished with three home runs and a team-leading 11 RBIs. He scored seven runs. Jake Petersen mentioned that some younger players stepped up and contributed. "Jay Hoversland and Cale Handran played really well. I think in the first-round game, Jay hit three home runs. Cale filled a great role on the pitching staff as well."

Curt and Jason led Scobey's hitting, but for a team where "pitching was a major weakness,"[36] it was two well-pitched games by Jason Wolfe and Curt Ware that got Scobey back to State. In the first game against Glasgow, Jason Wolfe pitched a four-hitter, giving up only two runs. In the second game against Glasgow ("the game that mattered"), Curt Ware pitched a three-hitter and gave up only two runs. And Scobey's defense only committed one error in the two games. Giving up only two runs was more than sufficient for Scobey's bats to win.

The 1997 state tournament would be the last in history for the legendary Scobey Blues. It was fitting that Jason Wolfe and Curt Ware led Scobey back to State: Catcher Danny Wolfe, Jason's dad, got the game-winning hit against Havre in Scobey's first state championship in 1969, and first baseman Rocky Ware, Curt's dad, scored the winning run in the first championship game against Havre the night before to keep Scobey alive. It was also significant that Coach Mike Lee—Doc and Marge Norman's grandson—was the last coach to lead Scobey to a state tournament. Doc Norman, led by pitcher Phil Audet, coached Scobey to its first state tournament in 1967. Also, 16-year-old Jedd Lekvold, who pitched in relief in the divisional championship game, was the son of Don Lekvold, who had dedicated 15 summers as an assistant coach and head coach of the Blues. Finally, Lee Farver, son of Gary Farver (who played for Scobey Legion and Plainsmen in the 1950s and, along with brother Howard, was on the 1958 Scobey Plainsmen state championship team), was the second generation of Farvers playing for the Blues. There would be a third generation of Farvers when Martin—Terry Farver's son—donned the Blues uniform for the Blues from 2016 to 2019.

The 1997 state tournament showed that the game had been passed down to the next generation in "Baseball Country." The offspring—players and coaches—had delivered a final state tournament berth for Scobey. Baseball, more than any other sport, seems to run in families. Keith Whipple, who played on Scobey's famous 1925 town team with two former Chicago White Sox, said it best: "I don't think you ever get baseball out of your blood." In this case, it was the blood of the next generation.

In another example of what classy winners this team of champions was, Scobey won the sportsmanship trophy for the third consecutive tournament. They had won the sportsmanship trophy at divisional at Wolf Point a year earlier, at State at Billings, and now at the divisional in Glasgow. This recognition was a testament to the fine coaching of Ken Meyer and Mike Lee. This might be a good time to print the American Legion Baseball Code of Sportsmanship, which these coaches and players abided by:

I will:

KEEP the rules

KEEP faith with my teammates

KEEP my temper

KEEP myself fit

KEEP a stout heart in defeat

KEEP my pride under in victory

KEEP a sound soul, a clean mind, and a healthy body

Let's make some noise at State boys; this will be the final one—the last hurrah for Scobey.

STATE TOURNAMENT

Coach Lee sensed the gravity of the moment—the boys had earned a trip to the state tournament, and he knew this was his last year coaching the Blues. With that in mind, he decided to inject the historical tradition of the Doc Norman–era into the journey to Helena for the state tournament. He said, "I had all the kids meet at Grandma Marge's the day we left.

That's where we got on the bus and they all parked their cars. I just thought it would be a cool send-off with the team to have them all come to the house just like before when all those teams were back in the '60s, '70s, and '80s. That's where they met, converged on Grandma and Grandpa's house, parked their vehicles, loaded the bus, and took off. So that was an important thing for me that I didn't really share with anybody at the time, but I just thought it would be kinda cool for my grandma to experience that and see because she was still, at that point, totally in the mix of coming to all the games and knowin' all the kids and supporting the team every way she could. I felt really happy for her to see that. She made a bunch of signs and had 'em posted outside her steps, and she came out and saw all the kids and stuff, so it was a good send-off, not knowing at the time that was the last state tournament, so it was a bigger deal when you looked at it down the stretch—the last time Scobey packed a bus and headed off to a state tournament, they did it from Doc and Marge's house in Scobey."

The Helena Representatives hosted the 1996 state tournament on Kindrick Legion Field in Helena. The Bitterroot Red Sox, who had never won a state championship, were one of the tournament's favorites. The Sox had eliminated Scobey from the state tournament the year before in Scobey's sixth game, and they went on to take second place, losing the championship game to the Billings Blue Jays. They won the Western Conference, then swept the western division tournament in four games. Red Sox Coach Vester Wilson liked the Red Sox's chances, saying, "We're playing our best ball of the year. Our pitching is set up, and we're the healthiest we've been all year. We're better than we were last year." Other teams mentioned as favorites were the number-one seeds from the four other divisions: Fort Macleod, Glendive, the Helena Reps, and the defending champion Billings Blue Jays.

Scobey entered the tournament with a 32-15 record. Curt Ware, who pitched a three-hitter in the divisional championship game to lead Scobey to State, led the team in pitching with an 8-2 record. Curt Ware and Jason Wolfe were the top two hitters, each with .405 averages. Spencer Frederick was hitting .393 and had a .640 slugging percentage. The Blues played the Lethbridge Miners (37-21), the second-place finisher from the northern division. If the Blues won, they would play the host Helena Reps, the number-one seed from the Central, in their second game.

Here were the complete opening-day matchups:

- Missoula (2W) vs. Fort Macleod (1N)
- Livingston (2S) vs. Belgrade (2C)
- Scobey (2E) vs. Lethbridge (2N)
- Glendive (1E) vs. Anaconda (2W)
- Billings Blue Jays (1S), Bitterroot Red Sox (1W), Helena Reps (1C) (byes)

Coach Lee and the Blues take infield at the Scobey's last State Tournament at Kindrick Legion Field in Helena.

If the Blues were going to make a deep run in their last state tournament, their pitching and defense would have to be good enough to keep them in games. The bats were never an issue. Coach Lee started Jason Wolfe against the Miners, and before Jason delivered a single pitch in the bottom of the first inning, the Blues' greatest strength, their bats, popped, scoring seven runs in the top of the first inning to vault to a 7-0 lead. Five Lethbridge errors aided them in the inning. Six of their first seven batters scored in the inning. But the Miners responded with four runs in the bottom half, then added a single run in the second and two more in the third to tie the game at 7-7. Curt Ware relieved Jason Wolfe in the fourth inning, and the game seesawed back and forth from there. Scobey scored a run in the top of the fourth to take an 8-7 lead, but Lethbridge scored two runs in the bottom of the fourth to take its first lead at 9-8, only to see Scobey jump back on top 10-9 in the fifth with two runs. Lethbridge scored a single run in the bottom of the fifth to tie the game back up at 10-10. From there, Scobey scored single runs in the seventh and eighth to take a 12-10 lead, then Curt Ware drove in Jason Wolfe with what proved to be the winning run in the ninth to take a 13-10 lead. The Miners scored two runs in the bottom of the ninth to close to 13-12 and loaded the bases with two outs, but Spencer Frederick caught a long fly ball to center field for the third out, and Scobey escaped with a wild 13-12 win. Jason Wolfe and Ben Bucklin led Scobey in hitting, as each was 3 for 4, with two RBIs. Spencer Frederick had a triple for Scobey's only extra-base hit. Curt Ware picked up his ninth win of the year, pitching six innings of relief. But pitching and hitting aside, what won this game for Scobey was their defense. The Miners committed eight errors while Scobey played errorless ball and turned a double play. And the Blues were moving on to play the host Helena Reps.

The Blues had earlier in the season ended the Reps' 17-game win streak at a tournament in Belgrade by beating them 8-7 in 10 innings. Helena had received a first-round bye and was the number-one seed from the Central Divi-

Curt Ware is about to be tagged out by Helena's Mike Hoven on his attempted steal of second base. *Helena Independent Record photo, Jon Ebelt.*

Jake Petersen (left) misses the tag at home, but it didn't matter as Lethbridge's David Ferguson missed the plate and was later tagged out by Jake. *Helena Independent Record photo, Jon Ebelt.*

sion. Coach Lee used both Jason Wolfe and Curt Ware to beat Lethbridge, so he handed the ball to Joel Nieskens to start the game. This one again turned out to be a slugfest, with Scobey winning 15-8. Scobey again got out of the gate strong at the plate, jumping on Helena's starting pitcher, Joe Hancock, for nine hits and 11 runs in the first three innings, smashing out three doubles and three triples. Maybe the Scobey and Peerless boys, who almost all played football, were more comfortable with football-like scores? The *Independent Record* summed up the way Scobey won games by writing, "The Scobey Blues had a dismal day on the mound and still had little trouble finishing off the Helena Reps for a 15-8 win."[37] Scobey pitching walked 16 Representatives, but the defense was again strong, as the Blues committed only two errors—and turned three double plays—while Helena committed five errors. In the two games Scobey had won, their defense was the difference-maker. Joel Nieskens pitched five innings to get the win. Cale Handran pitched three innings of relief for the hold, and Jedd Lekvold finished the game by pitching a scoreless ninth inning. Joel Nieskens had another monster day at the plate, going 3 for 6 with a triple, driving in three runs, and scoring four more. Leadoff hitter Ben Bucklin again had a good day at the plate with two hits, one of them a double, and three runs scored. Jake Petersen and Jay Hoversland each had two hits, and Mark McElvaney drove in two runs with a triple. Scobey had four triples in the game.

The Blues, with two wins under their belts, playing good defense, and with the bats booming, advanced to play the Bitterroot Red Sox. The boys were making some noise at State.

In a "normal" eight-team state tournament, Scobey's two wins would have placed them in the undefeated semifinal. In the 11-team tournament, however, the Blues would need to win the game against the Bitterroot Red Sox to make it to the undefeated semifinal. Without a bye, Scobey would need to win five games to win the tournament. Could the pitching be good enough to advance them further in the tournament?

Coach Lee handed the ball to Spencer Frederick to pitch against the number-one seed from the west. Jason Wolfe recalls how Spencer Frederick had improved as a pitcher that year. "Spence got better as the year went on. I'd say he was our third guy. Hoversland, Handran, and Lekvold could all throw but were still developing."

The strong Bitterroot Red Sox team had eliminated the Blues in the 1996 tournament, stopping Scobey from making it to the state championship game, and finished second. They were looking for their first state championship. Scobey had eight state championships and was looking for its ninth—and first since 1982.

Red Sox Coach Vester Wilson started Chad Ekin, who had ended Scobey's run in the 1996 state tournament by stymieing the Blues with a six-hitter, allowing only one run, losing his shutout in the ninth. Allowing six hits and only one run against this heavy-hitting Scobey team was like pitching a no-hitter.

But this was a new year, a new season—and a new state tournament—and the Blues would assert themselves early in this game, as they had done the previous two games. The Blues came out of their corner swinging, jumping on

Red Sox starter Ekin for two runs in the second inning on a two-run single by Cale Handran, then batted around in the fourth to take a 6-1 lead, rattling Ekin and the Western champion Red Sox.

Scobey, winning two games and leading 6-1 in the bottom of the fourth inning of their third game, was dominating Bitterroot and cruising to the undefeated semifinal. Spencer Frederick was pitching well, the bats were booming, and the defense was holding the line. (An appropriate metaphor for this team full of football players.) All three baseball cylinders were firing. The Big Blue Machine was humming. Jason Wolfe remembers the strong start. "We came out swinging against the Bitterroot Red Sox. We took a 6-1 lead early, and it felt like we were on our way. Spencer started on the mound and was throwing a gem."

And then it all fell apart.

Freeze frame. Pause. Timeout. Stop the tape. Blue over Red. East over West. Scobey over Bitterroot. Daniels County over Ravalli County.

In the middle of the fourth inning, Bitterroot Coach Vester Wilson gave a pep talk to his team in the dugout. "I had to set a fire under them," he said.[38] Apparently, he did. The *Billings Gazette* wrote, "Coming into the bottom of the fourth, where they might have folded and quit, the Red Sox flourished. Bitterroot scored six runs on five hits and three errors, taking a lead they would not relinquish."[39]

Dammit.

Jason Wolfe remembers the pivotal inning. "Sometime in the fourth inning, Spencer took a sharp comebacker off the index finger of his pitching hand. It ripped his fingernail off. He bandaged it up and tried to keep going, but he got roughed up. By the time we made the switch, it was too late. The damage was done. I've spent a lot of time thinking about what could have been if that ball didn't hit Spence."

From there, trailing 7-6 in the fifth, things went downhill for Scobey. Chad Ekin settled down on the mound, pitching five innings of scoreless ball. Scobey, perhaps rattled by seeing starting pitcher Spencer Frederick get injured, played shaky in the field. Bitterroot got to Scobey's pitching, banging out 16 hits in the game, adding two runs in the fifth and three more in the sixth and seventh to take a 12-6 lead, which is all Chad Ekin needed to win, his 14th of the season. Jason Wolfe relieved the injured Frederick in the fifth, and Jedd Lekvold came on in the eighth. Scobey finished with 13 hits and six runs, with Jason Wolfe going 3 for 5 and Jake Petersen 4 for 5, but it wasn't enough to top the Red Sox. In addition to Spencer's injury in the fourth, the defense, which needed to stay strong to win, hurt Scobey. Jason Wolfe recalls how pivotal the Bitterroot game was. "That was a tough loss! I think it took the wind out of our sails for that Missoula game. And . . . as always, we ran out of pitching."

The loss pushed Scobey into the loser's bracket, where they faced the Missoula Mavs. We would expect another slugfest this deep into the tournament, and that's precisely what we got. The *Independent Record* wrote, "It looked more like a hailstorm than a baseball game, but when the baseballs finally quit falling from the sky, the Missoula Mavs had an 18-8 win over the Scobey Blues, and the two teams had a combined total of 31 hits."[40]

Scobey had jumped on the opposition early in their previous three games, but it was the opposite this time. Missoula batted around in the first inning, scoring eight runs to take an 8-0 lead. But as usual, this team didn't quit; they were never truly out of a game, no matter the score. "The eight runs Missoula put up didn't intimidate the Blues."[41] Scobey gradually began chipping away at Missoula's lead, scoring two runs in the second on a two-run homer by Curt Ware, one in the third, and combined for four more in the fifth and sixth innings—the big blow coming on a two-run double by Lee Farver—to claw their way back into the game at 10-7 at the end of the sixth inning. These kids never quit.

But the pitching and defense couldn't hold, and the bats couldn't outslug Missoula. Missoula batted around again in the seventh inning, scoring four runs on four hits and three Scobey errors to take a commanding 15-7 lead entering the eighth.

Did Scobey have one last hurrah left in them?

Yes, they did. Helena *Independent Record* Assistant Sports Editor Sandra Kelly recognized the fight in this team. She wrote, "Though behind, the Blues didn't throw in the towel. Jay Hoversland drilled a double to right field, advanced to third when Lee Farver hit a single to center field and reached home when Cale Handran hit a slow curve into left field."[42]

But that was the last hurrah for Scobey in a state tournament. Missoula scored three runs in their half of the eighth to walk off the field with an 18-8 win, ending Scobey's season and run in the state tournament.

Missoula pitcher Chad Hines went the distance for the Mavs and gave up only five earned runs. He didn't walk a batter. Coach Lee used four pitchers in the game, starting Lee Farver, who went two innings and took the loss, relieving with Jay Hoversland and Curt Ware, and finishing again with Jedd Lekvold. Scobey had 12 hits, led by Curt Ware, who homered and had two hits. Jason Wolfe, Spencer Frederick, Jay Hoversland, and Lee Farver each had two hits, with Wolfe and Farver each driving in two runs. Joel Nieskens, Lee Farver, and Jay Hoversland doubled.

With their 2-2 record, the Blues finished fifth in the 11-team tournament and had another great year at 36-21. In an eight-team tournament, their first two wins would have placed them in the undefeated semifinal and guaranteed them a third-place finish; however, without a bye, they needed to win five games to win the championship. In their last state tournament appearance, the Blues won their first two games and fought hard to the end, showing the state of Montana what the Scobey baseball tradition, "Baseball Country," was all about.

TOURNAMENT SUMMARY

THE BITTERROOT RED SOX WENT ON TO WIN THEIR FIRST STATE championship, beating Glendive in the undefeated semifinal 15-10 and again in the final, 6-5 in 10 innings. As they did against the Blues, the scrappy Red Sox team came from behind in both games to beat Glendive. In the undefeated semifinal, the Red Sox trailed Glendive 9-1 before coming back to win it. Derek Ihde, Bitterroot's ace pitcher, won the batting title, hitting .647, and Missoula Mavs' Todd Schaelbitz was named MVP. Glendive was awarded the sportsmanship trophy. Bitterroot and Glendive both advanced to the Northwest Regional in Eagle Point, Oregon.

The bottom of the fourth inning of the Scobey-Bitterroot game, when Spencer got injured and Bitterroot scored six runs to overcome a 6-1 deficit and take a 7-6 lead, was not only a pivotal moment for Bitterroot in the game and the tournament but was also a pivotal moment in the history of Montana Class A/B American Legion Baseball. The Bitterroot Bucs eliminated Scobey in 1990, and the Bitterroot Red Sox eliminated Scobey in 1996, both times thwarting Scobey from the state championship game. In 1997, the Red Sox stopped Scobey's drive to the undefeated semifinal. Scobey finished their run of state tournaments with eight state championships, including five in a row between 1976 and 1980. Scobey never returned to the state tournament after 1997.

The fall of one dynasty coincided with the rise of another. It was appropriate that Bitterroot beat Scobey in 1997, as they went on to win the championship, winning five state championships in seven years (1997–2003), creating another dynasty. The Bitterroot Bucs had already won three state championships in 1988-89 and 1991. That made eight state championships for the Bucs and Red Sox between 1988 and 2003, a dominance unmatched since Scobey's five consecutive state championships between 1976 and 1980 and eight between 1969 and 1982. The Red Sox then won three consecutive state championships between 2015 and 2017, tying Scobey with eight state championships.

The 1997 state tournament cemented the changing of the guard for baseball supremacy in Class A/B baseball and the transfer of power from Daniels County to Ravalli County, from East to West, and from Blue to Red.

Following the season, Bitterroot Red Sox Head Coach Vester Wilson III was named the 1997 Montana/Alberta American Legion Class A Coach of the Year. Head Coach Vester Wilson, III, and the 1997 Bitterroot Red Sox, in one pivotal fourth inning against Scobey, altered the course of Montana/Alberta American Legion Baseball.

Vester Wilson, pictured here in May of 2000 with the championship banners behind him at Hamilton Athletic Field. Following his death in September 2000, the field was renamed Vester Wilson Athletic Field, honoring his years of coaching and financial support to baseball in the Bitterroot Valley. *Ravalli Republic photo, Jenny Jones.*

Every sports dynasty has a passionate individual who can be attributed to the program's success. For Bitterroot Valley baseball, that was Vester Wilson, III, whom I will dub the "Doc Norman of Bitterroot Valley." He contributed to the two Bitterroot Legion teams on the field with coaching and off the field with financial support. Like Doc, Vester's life was cut short by a debilitating disease—this time it was cancer—and he was gone before his time. And like Doc, you couldn't keep him off the field, even with the disease. After Vester's death from cancer at only 59 years old, three years later, in September 2000, Jenny Johnson, a staff reporter for the *Ravalli Republic*, wrote this about Vester:

```
Wilson initiated American Legion Baseball in
the Bitterroot. A fanatic as a child, Wilson
has never been separated from the sport. After
he played, he coached. He was the manager of
the Bitterroot Bucs since their inception, win-
ning three state championships before the Bucs
moved to Florence and the Red Sox Legion team
started in Hamilton.

In his final months, Wilson saw the Bitterroot
Red Sox, Hamilton's American Legion Baseball
```

team he has mentored for so many years, win a third Class A state championship. The Red Sox won two state titles under Wilson, and this year's [2000] triumph was managed by his son Jesse Wilson.

Four days after his first cancer surgery, Wilson was on the field with the Red Sox. Lots of things in the Wilson family are figured in baseball time. Wilson's cancer diagnosis came the year the Red Sox swept the regional tournament, for instance.

Wilson's legacy is baseball—all the boys who learned the game under his instruction, stood under the lights that Wilson installed at Hamilton Athletic Field and practiced in the batting cages Wilson paid for. Wilson was a driving force behind Legion baseball in the valley. Catcher Chad Lawrence, 18, had Wilson as his coach on the Red Sox for two years. "He taught me the game of baseball, and he's the best coach I ever had," said Lawrence Wednesday. "He has a world of knowledge of baseball.

In tribute to Wilson's dedication to baseball and its growth in Hamilton, Mayor Laurel Frankenfield suggested to city council members that Hamilton Athletic Field be renamed Vester Wilson Athletic Field. The council will likely approve the name change at Tuesday's meeting.

A memorial service at 1 p.m. Saturday is aptly located at Hamilton Athletic Field. The family suggests memorials to the Vester Wilson scholarship fund for local outstanding American Legion Baseball players.[43]

Later that week, the council approved renaming Hamilton Athletic Field to Vester Wilson Athletic Field. A ceremony officially naming the field was held at the first Bitterroot Red Sox baseball game the following spring.

The 1997 State Tournament was the last season for Jason Wolfe, Curt Ware, Spencer Frederick, Joel Nieskens, Jake Petersen, Lee Farver, and Ben Bucklin. Jason Wolfe reflected on his three-year career with the Scobey Blues. "Playing for the Blues gave me some of my fondest memories. I think back on those years often. Loved every minute of the practices, games, trips, and tournaments. Lots of those guys are still my best friends today. I try to keep in touch with many of my teammates at least a couple of times per year." Curt Ware added, "Most of the memories I have are the camaraderie we had as a group. I enjoyed each and every person on our teams. Just wanted to get better and perform our best for each other." I asked Ben Bucklin from Outlook to share his memories of playing for the Blues, and he offered this letter:

> *Being from Outlook, I spent half of each year competing against my Blues teammates . . . and they almost always got the best of us. I loved the challenge of playing basketball and running track against them, but I always looked forward to spring when baseball started, and I could reconnect with the guys. A lot of us had been playing together every summer since we were nine years old, and we had a pretty good track record of making state tournaments. I graduated in '96 and had gone to school in Missoula and wasn't sure if I would come back for the '97 season. I don't know who pulled the strings, probably Karch, but I ended up getting a job with the city of Scobey for the summer. I worked with Art, Louie, and Spencer, and I'm pretty sure it was the most fun I've ever had at "work." Spence and I even made the front page of the Leader when we burned up the city pickup in front of Cromwells. Wolfe's generously put me up in their basement that year, and I'm sure there were days when they regretted it. We had a lot of fun that summer.*
>
> *In '97, we were a talented group with a ton of experience, and it felt like Karch kept it pretty loose, not having to crack the whip too much on us. I think the only thing that held us back in '97 was we didn't have great pitching. In the '96 team with Vig, Levi, and Joey, we had depth, but in '97, outside of Curt, I don't think we had a lot of consistent pitching. My brother Tyler could really pitch, but for some reason, it didn't get passed on to me.*
>
> *I don't have a lot of specific memories of individual games that year, but I remember always battling with Glendive. They had our number since we were 9–10-year-old all-stars. Knocking them out in '96 probably helped our confidence in '97 because I don't remember feeling like they were going to beat us every time we went toe to toe that year.*
>
> *Playing baseball in Scobey was such a great experience. I don't think I ever truly appreciated the legacy of the Blues while I was playing, what 16–18-year-old ever does.*
>
> *Baseball is such a beautiful game, and what most people never realize is half the time you are in the dugout with your buddies, goofing off and flipping each other shit. Those are the lasting memories of my days with the Scobey Blues.*

Coach Mike Lee moved on the following year, too. I asked Karch to reflect on his final season as head coach of the Blues, the last coach to lead Scobey to a state tournament. He said, "I had such an empty feeling when that final out was made, and the game was over, that this was done, and I knew I wasn't gonna ever be coaching or playing for the Blues again. There were a lot of connections with current players and previous Blues, nostalgia, and connection with Grandpa and Grandma. It was a tough one. For me, it closed the chapter on my Blues' history, you know, from being a batboy to coaching. I knew I would never put on a Blues uniform again, so I remember it being tough. I . . . I was pretty bummed out for, oh . . . quite a while there afterward, just kind of just reminiscing and thinking about things and then packing my bags and moving down to Billings."

Mike then reflected on his 1997 team. "I felt bad for all the 18-year-olds because they were all such a good group of kids, but to me, Jake Petersen really amplified that toughness and that willingness to be completely in. And Jason Wolfe . . . I can't say enough good things about him, with his dad [Dan Wolfe] and his history playing for Grandpa Doc. Dan installed a pitching mound in the gym during the winter of 1997, and Jason had the willingness to come out and work in the offseason, when a lot of the other kids didn't. He was taking ground balls, hitting into a net, and throwing. He took baseball real, real serious. They [Jake and Jason] are friends of mine now, and at the time, they were as close to a friend as a player-coach could get. We didn't hang out, but I trusted them. I knew they would give you everything they've got."

Losing the seven 18-year-olds in 1997 gutted Scobey in 1998. Scobey had always been able to recover from losing good players before, but the loss of this bunch would be tough to overcome—this was a generational collection of athletes. Karch Lee also moved on, so there would be a new head coach for Scobey in 1998.

The good news was that seven Blues—Cale Handran, Jay Hoversland, Mark McElvaney, Matt Bucklin, A.J. Shipstead, Jedd Lekvold, and Brian Solberg—who saw action at the divisional and state tournaments were returning, and Cale, Jay, and Jedd had pitched in the divisional and state tournaments as 16-year-olds.

TOURNAMENT STATS

Hitting

THE 1997 SCOBEY BLUES' GREATEST STRENGTH WAS THEIR hitting, and they were by far the best-hitting team in the tournament. In four games, the Blues had an incredible 0.372 team batting average, averaging 14.5 hits and 10.5 runs per game. Individually, Jason Wolfe led the team in hitting and RBIs, batting an astronomical .625 and driving in nine runs. Jason was second in the batting title to Derek Ihde of the Bitterroot Red Sox, who hit .647. Jason was followed by Jay Hoversland (.462), Joel Nieskens (.421), Mark McElvaney (.417), Jake Petersen (.368), Cale Handran (.333), and Curt Ware (313). The heavy-hitting Blues also had several extra-base hits: Curt Ware homered, Spencer Frederick had two triples, and Jay Hoversland had two doubles. It could be safely stated that Scobey's last team to appear in a state tournament was one of the best-hitting teams in Scobey American Legion Baseball history.

Pitching

AS UNBELIEVABLY DOMINANT AS THE HITTING WAS, THE PITCHING was the opposite. As Mike Stebleton of the *Leader* wrote in his divisional tournament wrap-up, "Pitching was a major weakness."[44] Jason Wolfe said, "Pitching depth was always our Achilles heel. I thought we were a couple of good pitchers away from a State championship in '96 and '97." The Blues had a team ERA of 10.16 in four games and a WHIP of 2.85. Jason Wolfe got the win against Lethbridge, and Joel Nieskens got the win against Helena. Spencer Frederick, affected by the comebacker, took the tough loss against Bitterroot and Lee Farver against Missoula. One bright spot on Scobey's staff was 16-year-old Jedd Lekvold, who appeared in three games, pitched two and two-thirds innings, and didn't allow an earned run, striking out two and issuing only one walk. Coach Lee used eight different pitchers in the four games, spreading their innings out as follows:

- Curt Ware, 6.2 (1-0)
- Jason Wolfe, 6.0
- Joel Nieskens, 5.0 (1-0)
- Jay Hoversland, 4.1
- Spencer Frederick, 4.0 (0-1)
- Cale Handran, 3.0
- Jedd Lekvold, 2.2
- Lee Farver, 2.0 (0-1)

Bitterroot Red Sox ace left-hander Chris Rennaker was the workhorse of the tournament, pitching 19 innings, including 12 innings in back-to-back days, and figured prominently in their championship.

Fielding

WITH SCOBEY'S ENTIRE STAFF PITCH-TO-CONTACT PITCHERS, Scobey's defense needed to be good, and for the first two games, it was. In fact, it wasn't just good—it was great. Scobey played errorless ball in the field against Lethbridge and committed only two errors against Helena. Of the 20 runs Scobey allowed in the first two games, only two were unearned. That's as good as it gets. Not only that, but they also turned *four* double plays. The strong defense continued in the first three innings against Bitterroot, but it broke down after Spencer's injury in the fourth. Errors are contagious, and the error contagion hit Scobey. The mistakes enabled Bitterroot to score five unearned runs, which was the difference in the game. The error contagion continued in their final game against Missoula, as the Blues committed five errors. That pivotal fourth inning against Bitterroot was the turning point in the tournament for Scobey defensively—pitching and fielding—and their fortunes declined after that. Scobey's defense was on par with the opposition for the tournament, but it needed to be better to win.

NORTHWEST REGIONAL

The 1997 Northwest Regional Tournament was played in Eagle Point, Oregon. Bitterroot eliminated Glendive 11-2—their third win over Glendive in a week—to take fourth place. Bitterroot finished 2-2 in the tournament, and Glendive was 1-2.

EXTRA INNINGS

Jay Hoversland's three home runs against Homestead in the opening game of the 1997 Divisional Tournament broke Rob Fladager's record of two home runs in one game. Rob's two home runs were also hit in the opening game of a divisional tournament (1991 against Sidney at Plentywood). Later in his career, Jay hit two home runs and had a six-RBI game.

Following their prep careers, several 18-year-old multi-sport athletes on the 1997 team continued their athletic careers at the collegiate level. Some played football, some basketball, and some baseball:

- Spencer Frederick played football for the University of Montana Grizzlies. He was named second-team All-Big Sky Conference as a junior and first-team All-Big Sky Conference as a senior. He played in two national championship games with the Grizzlies, winning the title with his team his senior year. He was signed as an undrafted free agent by the New Orleans Saints in 2002 and played until a second ACL injury ended his football career. He was inducted into the MHSA Athlete's Hall of Fame in 2022.
- Curt Ware played two years of baseball for the University of Mary Marauders in Bismarck, North Dakota, then joined the Air National Guard and got his pilot's license.
- Jason Wolfe went to MSU Billings (formerly Eastern Montana College). They had club baseball then, and Jason played one year of club ball for the Yellowjackets. He also was a student assistant on the men's basketball team. "That's what got me into coaching," he said. In his 23rd year coaching the Scobey High School boys' basketball Spartans, Jason has led Scobey to eight State C tournaments, winning three (2011, 2020, and 2021) and third in 2017 and 2019. Jason said, "We've had some good runs. I've been blessed with some great players up here. I always hoped that we could build a basketball legacy that would compare to what the Scobey Blues of the '70s and '80s were!" I'd say you're doing it, Jason.
- Joel Nieskens played basketball for three years (redshirted one) at MSU Billings, then transferred to play for the Jamestown College Jimmies in the Dakota Athletic Conference (DAC) his senior year, where he was named Honorable Mention All-American.
- Jake Petersen had one year of high school remaining after the 1997 baseball season, then played football for the University of Mary Marauders and baseball for one season there. After his senior season, he also spent a year at the University of Mary as an assistant coach. He returned to Scobey to coach the 2002 Scobey Blues (more on that later). He has been coaching football for the past 20 years and is currently the head coach at Valley Christian High School in Chandler, Arizona, where he joined the staff in 2014.

The 1997 State Tournament was the last for Scobey. The first appearance came in 1967, when Phil Audet, in his final season, led Scobey to the promised land. Between the 31 seasons from 1967 to 1997, Scobey qualified for the state tournament 23 times, winning eight (1969, 1973, 1976–80, 1982), taking second once (1970), and third four times (1971, 1985, 1990, 1996).

I asked three 16-year-olds—Jedd Lekvold, Jay Hoversland, and Cale Handran—what the experience was like playing in their first state tournament with the seven seasoned veterans. Jedd Lekvold said, "The experience was awesome and a little nerving for me. We had a good team and lots of kids who could hit. I wasn't one of them, though. My contribution and role was to pitch an inning or two and throw strikes. Against Helena, I got to pitch towards the end of the game. If I recall, I remember our coach, Mike Lee, getting upset with our inability to throw strikes that game [Scobey pitching had 16 walks in the game]. I think we had a comfortable lead, but we weren't closing out the game like Coach wanted. In the dugout, I remember Coach making the comment, 'Is there anybody on this team who can throw a strike?' (He might not have said it that nice.) As I took the mound when I got in for relief, I just remembered him saying that, and I really didn't want to go out there and be inconsistent with my pitches. We had really good 18-year-old olds, and I didn't want to let those guys (and the rest of the team and coaches) down either." (Jedd threw one inning of scoreless relief to close the game, giving up one hit and not walking a batter.)

Jay Hoversland, Scobey's second-leading hitter in the tournament with a .462 average, agreed with Jedd. "We had a lot of good 18-year-old players on that team, and we didn't want to let them down; I was just happy to be on the field and hoped to contribute positively in any way I could. That was a great experience, and we were able to see a lot of good baseball played. I would like to think the Blues played some of that good ball. Great times and great memories made for sure."

Cale Handran, who hit .333 in the tournament, responded similarly to Jedd and Jay. "My best memory of playing in the state tourney was doing my best not to mess up. The 18-year-olds on that team held a pretty high standard to compete at a high level. Trying to control nerves and emotions, the 16-year-olds did a pretty damn good job of holding up the expectations of the 'veterans' on the club. Coach Karch relied on the 16-year-olds a lot. It was pretty awesome playing at that level and being a Scobey Blue."

Terry Farver (Blues 1988–90) recalls what a great team player Jake Petersen was. "I was driving the bus home from the state track meet. The bus was pulling into Scobey, and Jake asked if I could drop him at the ball field, so I just pulled in and let them off. That was the Sunday of Memorial Day weekend. By the time I got the rest of the team unloaded and the bus put away, Jake was behind the plate calling the shots. Jake was a stud, the best team player I've probably ever had the privilege to coach in track and watch in his other sports. In football, he was feared by several running backs; he was a linebacker and ended up playing at the University of Mary in Bismarck, North Dakota. What a kid!"

A Scobey pitcher—who surrendered three home runs to one batter in the same game during the regular season—humorously requested to remain anonymous, saying, "No need to put this in the book, Joe, but I was pitching against Glendive, in Glendive, and they had a great player named Tom Ziegler. He hit three home runs off me in one game! Karch reminds me that when the game was out of hand, he relieved me with one of our 16-year-olds who came in and struck Ziegler out his next at-bat."

Reading about the Bitterroot Red Sox winning their first state championship in 1997 reminded me of the excitement that swirled around Daniels County when Scobey won its first state championship in 1969. I was eight years old and was there, and I have some great memories of the tournament. It was a *big* deal. What made it even more special was the dramatic fashion in which Scobey won it, and it was at home. In an end-of-season article titled, "Sox end a memorable season," in the *Ravalli Republic*, Francis Davis captured the excitement of how special the first state championship was for the team and community, writing, "In the end, what will never be lost is the special memories of all the players who played for the 1997 Bitterroot Red Sox. Championships of any kind are rare, and state championships are something you never forget. Recently, I had the honor of talking to a team member of the 1947 state champion Hamilton Broncs basketball team who still teared up when he spoke about those special days 50 years in the past. I'm sure some of the Bitterroot Red Sox players will get a tear or two in the eye when they recall what happened in 1997 in, say, 2047. Way to go, boys—you made the community proud."[45]

In 1969, no one had any idea that Scobey would win another seven state championships, just as in 1997, no one would have thought the Red Sox would win seven more. But Francis Davis thought the Red Sox might win at least *one* more, as several key starters were returning. He wrote, "The good news for the Sox, aside from their diamond-of-a-season, is the potential to do the same next year."[46]

Boy was Francis right.

The Ken Meyer/Mike Lee Era

The first state championship sign for the Bitterroot Red Sox was hung at Hamilton Athletic Field in 1997. Vester Wilson coached the Red Sox. *Ravalli Republic photo, Kim Eiselein.*

The 1997 Scobey Blues were the last Blues team to make it to the state tournament. Between 1969 and 1982, the Blues won eight state championships under Coach Doc Norman. *Family photo.*

The Bitterroot Red Sox have now won eight state championships, and the Bitterroot Bucs four. The signs hang at Vester Wilson Athletic Field in Hamilton. The field was named in honor of Vester Wilson, who started the Bitterroot Bucs Legion program in 1983, the first Legion program in the Bitterroot Valley since the Great Depression. He later started the Red Sox Senior Babe Ruth program in 1987, then the Legion program in 1994, and coached the Red Sox to their first two state championships in 1997 and 1998. His son Jesse coached the third Bitterroot Red Sox state championship in 2000, and Vester was able to see it before his death in September 2000. *Family photo.*

Dan Wolfe (left) caught Dick Puckett in the decisive state championship game in Scobey in 1969 and drove in the game-winning run. Dan passed the game down to his son, Jason Wolfe (right), who was a key player on the 1997 Scobey Blues, the last Blues team to qualify for the State Tournament. Dan is pictured here receiving the 2008 Frank Morrison Memorial Award, presented to an area citizen for outstanding community service in the field of sports. Making the presentation was Wolfe's son, Jason, and his grandson, Braxton. *Leader photo, Mike Stebleton.*

SECTION NOTES

1. "Blues Repeat; Win District Tourney," *Daniels County Leader*, July 23, 1992.
2. Ed West, "Dog fight expected at State A Legion showdown," *Billings Gazette*, July 25, 1992.
3. Ibid.
4. Ibid.
5. Ibid.
6. Ibid.
7. "Cubs fifth at State," *Dillon Tribune*, July 29, 1992.
8. Steve Stiffarm, "Wolf Point 'Lights Up Burke Field,'" *Wotanin Wowapi*, May 23, 1991.
9. "Scobey Blues 3rd At Divisional 'A' Tourney in Sidney," *Daniels County Leader*, July 29, 1993.
10. "Bowker receives scholarship," *Dillon Tribune*, July 7, 1993.
11. J. P. Plutt, "Cubs take dream to Yakima, no further," *Dillon Tribune*, August 18, 1993.
12. *Daniels County Leader*, "Glendive, Sidney on to Legion State 'A'," July 28, 1994.
13. Ibid.
14. "Things, Ideas, and People," *Daniels County Leader*, October 6, 1994.
15. "Trivia," *Missoulian*, March 21, 1995.
16. "Blues Heading to State Tourney; 3rd at Divisional," *Daniels County Leader*, July 27, 1995.
17. Ibid.
18. Vince Briggeman of the *Missoulian*, "Scobey pulls off sports trifecta," *Billings Gazette*, May 26, 1996.
19. Ibid.
20. "Yellowjackets save best for last; 3rd place," *Wotanin, Wowapi*, August 1, 1996.
21. Ibid.
22. "Blues Earn Berth at State with Divisional 2nd," *Daniels County Leader*, August 1, 1996.
23. John Letasky, "Scobey, a town for all seasons," *Billings Gazette*, August 2, 1996.
24. "State A Legion," *Great Falls Tribune*, August 5, 1996.
25. "Scobey scores wild win," *Billings Gazette*, August 5, 1996.
26. The strike zone is 17 inches wide and 17 2/3 inches deep.
27. "Don't look for the Blues to be singing the blues," *Daniels County Leader*, May 29, 1997.
28. "Blues Take 2nd, Head to Helena for State Event," *Daniels County Leader*, July 24, 1997.
29. Ibid.
30. Ibid.
31. Ibid.
32. Ibid.
33. Ibid.
34. Ibid.
35. Ibid.
36. Ibid.
37. Scott Farley, "Scobey downs Reps, 15-8," *Independent Record*, July 27, 1997.
38. "Glendive, Hamilton in finals," *Billings Gazette*, July 29, 1997.
39. Ibid.
40. Sandra Kelly, "Missoula gives Scobey the Blues with 18-8 thumping, *Independent Record*," July 29, 1997.
41. Ibid.
42. Ibid.
43. Jenny Johnson, "Bitterroot baseball coach, businessman Vester Wilson dies," *Ravalli Republic*, September 14, 2000.
44. Ibid.
45. Francis Davis, "Sox end a memorable season," *Ravalli Republic*, August 15, 1997.
46. Ibid.

The Last Year
1998 – 2003

1900 – 1924
The Homesteaders
and Early Town Teams

1930 – 1945
The Sons of
the Pioneers

1957 – 1968
The Baseball
Renaissance

The Scobey
Giants
1925 – 1929

Baseball is Back
in Daniels County
1946 – 1956

The D
Cham
1969 –

s

1983 – 1991
The Don Lekvold Era

2016 – 2019
The Revival

rman
hip Era

The Ken Meyer/Mike Lee Era
1992 – 1997

The Long Winter
2004 – 2015

The Froid Bulls
2020 – 2024

1998

The Blues Reload, Rebuild, and Renew

> *We missed the group of 18-year-olds from the year before, but now it was getting to the point when we had to start stepping up to lead the ball club. I just remember it was a year of highs and lows. We still had a competitive ball team, but for how many more years?*
>
> —Cale Handran, Scobey Blues (1996–99)

PRESEASON

"For every season, there is a time," and for the Scobey Blues, the spring of 1998 was a time to reload, rebuild, and renew. Gone were big guns Joel Nieskens, Spencer Frederick, Curt Ware, Jason Wolfe, Jake Petersen, Lee Farver, and Ben Bucklin, who had played on three consecutive Blues teams that qualified for the state baseball tournament (1995–97), finishing third in 1996. But seven ballplayers—Cale Handran, Jay Hoversland, Mark McElvaney, Matt Bucklin, A.J. Shipstead, Jedd Lekvold, and Brian Solberg—were returning, and Cale, Jay, and Jedd had pitched in the divisional and state tournaments as 16-year-olds.

Completing the Scobey Blues roster in 1998 were Mike Rider, Kelly Nieskens, Matt Stentoft, Travis Skar, Tyler Pittenger, and Kenny Fossum.

In this season of renewal, there would also be a new head coach for the Blues, as Coach Lee had moved on after the 1997 season. Mike Flamm, a teacher at Outlook from 1996-2000 and the athletic director and girls' basketball coach at the Flaxville-Outlook Knights Coop, would take the reins for the Blues in 1998 and would remain as head coach for three years, coaching through the 2000 season. Not recognizing the name "Flamm," I asked three Blues to comment on him as a coach, and they were all positive. Jedd Lekvold said, "Flamm knew the game. You could tell he was passionate about baseball. He wanted us to be good." Jay Hoversland agreed. "Yeah, he knew the game. He wanted us to be good, and he put a lot of time into it." Cale Handran added, "He was good, not being from around the area [he graduated from Huntley Project and went to Dickinson State], he still recognized the importance of Blues baseball and did what he could to help keep the program running."

The pitching staff for the Blues would include A.J. Shipstead (the lone lefty), Jedd Lekvold, Cale Handran, Jay Hoversland, and Kelly Nieskens. Brian Solberg assumed most of the catching duties and would occasionally pitch.

REGULAR SEASON

One highlight of every regular season was the Doc Norman Memorial Tournament. The 1998 season would be the 15th iteration of the tournament. I asked some of the players to comment on their memories of the tournament. Jay Hoversland said, "I personally remember the Doc Norman tournament all throughout my childhood and when I was able to play in it. As a kid, as a lot of us did, we spent our summer days at the pool and our nights at the ballpark watching Blues baseball, chasing down foul baseballs for baseball bubble gum. Then, when I played, it was one of those rights of passage; you were playing in this tournament that was known all through the area and beyond, and it was a pretty humbling experience. Just a lot of fun meeting new kids and playing under the lights." Jedd Lekvold added, "The Doc Norman was a big deal growing up in Scobey. I remember it back when I used to be a batboy. Growing up in my house, my dad would talk about Doc Norman a lot. I thought he was some sort of mythical legend as often as I heard his name."

In the rebuilding year, the Blues finished fifth in the conference with a record just below .500 (13-15) with an overall record of 15-19. Glendive—dominant in the east as they had been for several years—again won the conference.

Here were the final conference standings:

1. Glendive
2. Glasgow
3. Plentywood
4. Sidney
5. Scobey (13-15 and 15-19)
6. Froid
7. Wolf Point
8. Circle

The week before the divisional tournament, the Blues were swept by Glasgow and Sidney in two doubleheaders, and Coach Flamm recognized that the team needed to turn it around quickly, saying, "We can't play like we played last week. Hopefully, that was our bad streak." He added, "We have to be more aggressive. I really don't think we are a fifth-place team."

Let's see if Coach Flamm and the Blues can turn it around at the divisional tournament.

DIVISIONAL TOURNAMENT

THE 1998 EASTERN DIVISIONAL TOURNAMENT WAS HOSTED for the first time by the Homestead Pioneers at Fjeseth Field in Froid. Opening day matchups were as follows:

- Glendive (1) vs. Circle 8
- Sidney (4) vs. Scobey (5)
- Glasgow (2) vs. Wolf Point (7)
- Plentywood (3) vs. Froid (6)

Scobey's first game was against fifth-seeded Sidney, who had swept Scobey in a doubleheader in Sidney four days earlier by scores of 8-1 and 7-4. Coach Flamm's statement—"I don't think we are a fifth-place team,"—proved prophetic as the Blues stomped Sidney 12-5. Sidney led by one run in the middle innings, but a squeeze bunt by Brian Solberg scored Mike Rider to tie the game. Coach Flamm said, "That play seemed to get us going." Then, Scobey had a big six-run eighth inning to run away with the game. Jay Hoversland, Cale Handran, and A.J. Shipstead shared duties on the mound to get the win.

The opening-day win was a great start to the tournament, but top-seeded Glendive, who had taken second at State the year before, loomed on the horizon for Scobey in their second game.

Against Glendive, it looked like Coach Flamm's statement that Scobey was not a fifth-place team should have been changed to, "We are a first-place team," as the Blues jumped all over the top-seeded Blue Devils, scoring six runs in the first inning to take a 6-0 lead and later led by a whopping score of 10-2. "We came out hot," Coach Flamm said. "We hit the ball hard and hit the gaps. Glendive had a couple of uncharacteristic errors." It appeared Scobey was headed to the undefeated semifinal and a possible fourth consecutive berth in the state tournament, but the Blue Devils came back with a vengeance, outscoring the Blues 21-3 the rest of the way to win a 23-13 slugfest.

But after blowing the big lead against Glendive, the Blues were not done yet. In their next game against Wolf Point, they again jumped to a big lead early (8-2), then held on for a 17-9 win.

In their first three games of the tournament, Scobey scored 12, 13, and 17 runs for an average of 14 runs—two converted touchdowns—a game. That's phenomenal and normally would be enough to sail a team through a tournament. Like the 1995–97 Blues before them, this team could score runs. But could the pitching be good enough for two more wins to return to State?

No. It could not.

In their next game against Plentywood, the Blues scored 16 runs—but lost the game 19-16 in another slugfest, and the Blues' old nemesis Plentywood again eliminated Scobey from postseason play. In the end, Scobey could not slug their way to another state tournament berth, even though they averaged 14.5 runs per game in the tournament.

Scobey finished 2-2 in the tournament, good enough for fourth place, and technically making Coach Flamm's statement that the Blues were not a fifth-place team accurate—but Coach Flamm and the Blues wanted more.

Glasgow pushed Glendive to the limit for the championship, getting 20 hits to win the first championship game 12-5 and force a second game, but Glendive proved they were the team to beat in the east, pounding Glasgow 20-9 in the second championship game.

Scobey finished their rebuilding year with a 17-21 record, which wasn't bad. The divisional tournament in Froid was the last for 18-year-olds A. J. Shipstead, Mark McElvaney, Matt Bucklin, and Kenny Fossum.

I asked three of the 17-year-olds to reflect on the 1998 season. Jay Hoversland said, "It was tough losing a group of 18-year-olds that large and having that much skill. I think our biggest adjustment besides playing for a new coach was finding leadership within our team. We had lost so many the year before, and in a way, I think some of that responsibility fell on us (the now 17-year-olds). During the regular season and postseason, we were competitive in most games, probably winning the ones that we should. We just didn't have the bats and arms depth needed to make a deep run in the postseason." Jedd Lekvold said, "I remember that year that Glendive and Glasgow were obviously the best teams. After that, it just kind of depended on the night. Those two teams had a lot of baseball talent, and they kind of separated themselves from the rest of the conference. I felt like, on a given night, we could beat any other team in the conference. We would have had to play perfect baseball to beat Glendive or Glasgow, and I'm not sure we had a win against either of them that year." Cale Handran added, "There was no doubt that we missed the group of 18-year-olds from the year before, but now it was getting to the point when we (the 17-year-olds) had to start stepping up to lead the ball club. I just remember it was a year of highs and lows. We still had a competitive ball team, but for how many more years?"

But for how many more years? For how many more years? The summer sun was beginning to set on the Scobey Blues—there was a touch of autumn in the summer air in 1998.

But several veteran players, including starters Jay Hoversland, Jedd Lekvold, Cale Handran, Brian Solberg, and Mike Rider, would return in 1999, and Scobey's chances to return to State looked promising.

STATE TOURNAMENT

THE 1998 STATE CLASS A AMERICAN LEGION TOURNAMENT was hosted at Hamilton Athletic Field in Hamilton by the defending champion Bitterroot Red Sox, who were favored to repeat—and did. The Red Sox, coached by Vester Wilson, swept the tournament in four games, beating the Vauxhall Spurs 19-8 in the championship game on their home field. They were the first team to repeat as state Class A champions since the Bitterroot Bucs did it 10 years earlier in 1988-89. Bitterroot Coach Vester Wilson was named Montana/Alberta Class A American Legion Coach of the Year for the second consecutive year. The Glendive Blue Devils represented the east well at State again, this time finishing third place. Glasgow went 1-2 in the tournament.

NORTHWEST REGIONAL

THE BITTERROOT RED SOX WON THE NORTHWEST PACIFIC Class A Regional American Legion Baseball Tournament in Yakima, Washington, by beating Aberdeen, Washington, 13-8 in the championship game. Along the way, they beat Marsh Valley, Idaho, 20-1; Yakima, Washington, 18-10; Aberdeen, Washington, 15-9; and Worland, Wyoming, 14-1. The Class A regional championship was the first for a Montana/Alberta League team since the Fort Macleod Royals did it in 1993 and the first for a Montana team since the Bitterroot Bucs in 1992.

EXTRA INNINGS

GLASGOW'S BERTH IN THE STATE TOURNAMENT WAS THEIR FIRST since 1985. The Reds, perennial also-rans in the eastern division, were up-and-coming in 1998 and would see some good teams in the following years.

1999

The Blues Falter at Divisional and the North Star Rises One More Time at State

> *I will always remember and cherish the days of the Blues. There's just something about playing on a hot summer night under the lights, along with those bus trips with every window being cracked open.*
>
> —Jedd Lekvold, Scobey Blues (1996–99)

1999 Scobey Blues. Back row, left to right: Assistant Coach Don Lekvold, Assistant Coach Tim Tharp, Brian Solberg, Matt Stentoft, Jay Hoversland, Cale Handran, Jedd Lekvold, Head Coach Mike Flamm. Middle row: Pat Fouhy, Tyler Pittenger, Phil Wahl, Neal Levang, Mike Rider, Kelly Nieskens, Curt Holum. Front row, left to right: Casey Cote, Neill Crandell, Scott Sterrett, Kevin McElvaney. Not pictured are Jared Petersen and Cory Cromwell. *Leader photo, Borderland.*

PRESEASON

The 1999 Blues had the potential for another return to the state tournament, as five 18-year-olds—Jay Hoversland, Cale Handran, Jedd Lekvold, Matt Stentoft, and Brian Solberg—were playing in their final season. Several of these players were experienced and had played at the state tournament as 16-year-olds in 1997. Also rostered were three 17-year-olds—Kelly Nieskens, Mike Rider, and Phil Wahl—and five 16-year-olds: Neal Levang, Eli Harmon, Tyler Pittenger, Jared Petersen, and Pat Fouhy. Duel-rostered from the Babe Ruth team was a talented group of 15-year-olds—Kevin McElvaney, Cory Cromwell, Neill Crandell, Casey Cote, Scott Sterrett, and Curt Holum—who formed the backbone of the future Scobey Legion program.

The Blues had several players who could pitch in 1999. Leading the way were Cale Handran, Jedd Lekvold, and Jay Hoversland, all of whom had pitched in the state tournament as 16-year-olds in 1997. Kelly Nieskens, Mike Rider, Eli Harmon, Tyler Pittenger, Neal Levang, and Curt Holum also saw innings. Brian Solberg and Ty Pittenger anchored the staff behind the plate.

Coach Mike Flamm returned for his second season as head coach. Don Lekvold, who was the assistant coach to Doc Norman (1977–82) and head coach (1983–91), joined Tim Tharp on the coaching staff as an assistant coach in 1999. I asked Don to describe the experience of returning to the field to coach after leaving the field following the 1991 season after six years as Doc's assistant and nine years as head coach of the Blues. He said, "It was quite different coming back as an assistant coach. I was used to coaching practices and games my way—Doc's way. So, I offered suggestions to coach Flamm on how I thought things should be done. Some things he considered and did, and some things not so much. But it was my intention to support the new coach and build a positive relationship with him and all the players, and that's what I did."

REGULAR SEASON

THE BLUES TRAVELED TO A REGULAR SEASON TOURNAMENT TO play at Henderson Field in Lethbridge, Alberta. Scobey played the Mission Valley Mariners from Polson, Montana, for the first time in the Scobey American Legion history. The Mariners were among 42 teams in the Montana/Alberta Class A League in 1999, a growing league, mostly with teams from Western Montana. The Blues led the Mariners 4-3 in the bottom of the seventh, but Mission Valley walked it off with two runs to win it 5-4.

Jedd Lekvold and Jay Hoversland remember what gracious hosts the Canadians were and what a unique experience it was playing on Henderson Field in Lethbridge. Jedd said, "The field we played on was really nice." Jay Hoversland added, "I remember the people being very generous, feeding us potluck after our first game. And being very welcoming. Their facilities were top-notch." The Blues hoped they would return to Henderson Field in August, as the Lethbridge Miners were hosting the State Class A Legion Tournament that year.

But both Jedd and Jay added that the tournament was a "very interesting experience, to say the least."

How "interesting" of an experience?

Jedd Lekvold recalls the story. "The drinking age in Alberta was 18 at that time. Coach Flamm gave us a talk before we got settled into our hotel rooms about not drinking. Well, we 18-year-olds had already made up our minds we were going to have a good time since we could do it legally. We walked to a nearby bar or two, had some drinks, sang some karaoke, and whooped it up. Coach Flamm got wind we were loose, tracked us down, and that was it for us 18-year-olds for the remainder of the Lethbridge tournament. We played one game [against Mission Valley] and got benched. Good on coach. We deserved it." Jay Hoversland added, "It was not my proudest moment."

I asked Jedd if he remembered what karaoke song he had sung in the bar. He replied, "Damn right. Beastie Boys. 'Fight for Your Right.'" Jay Hoversland added, "I can fact-check that—that is accurate." Well, if you're going to get benched for drinking legally but breaking the coach's training rules, the Beastie Boys' "Fight for Your Right" was a good choice. Jedd Lekvold fought for his right to party and—although a pitcher—went down swinging in Lethbridge, Alberta. In the end, the coach busted in and said, "What's that noise?"

The Blues completed the regular season by winning 4 of their last 7 games, sweeping a doubleheader—13-3 and 13-10—from the Homestead Pioneers in Froid in their final two games. Jay Hoversland had a big day, hitting two home runs and driving in six runs, while Brian Solberg and Neal Levang also hit home runs in the first game. Levang hit another home run in the second game. Cale Handran pitched all five innings of the first game to earn the win, scattering eight hits and issuing only two walks. Jedd Lekvold pitched six and two-thirds innings in the second game to get the win, with Jay Hoversland pitching the final two-thirds to earn the save. The doubleheader highlighted the key pitching and hitting the Blues would need to carry over into the divisional tournament.

The Blues finished third in the conference with a .500 record (12-12) and were 14-21 overall. Final conference standings looked this this:

1. Glendive
2. Glasgow
3. Scobey (12-12 and 14-21)
4. Homestead
5. Plentywood
6. Sidney
7. Wolf Point

The Blues would need to beat one of the higher seeds (Glasgow, Glendive, or both) to finish in second place and advance to the state tournament, but it would be tough. Glendive and Glasgow had separated themselves from the rest of the pack during the past two seasons, and it would be difficult for any of the other five teams to knock one of them off.

Let's go knock one of them off, boys.

DIVISIONAL TOURNAMENT

THE PLENTYWOOD ATHLETICS HOSTED THE 1999 EASTERN Divisional Tournament at Sportsman Park in Plentywood. Opening day matchups were as follows:

- Glendive (1) (bye)
- Homestead (4) vs. Plentywood (5)
- Glasgow (2) vs. Wolf Point (7)
- Scobey (3) vs. Sidney (6)

Scobey sprinted out of the gate in the tournament, racing to an 8-0 lead in the first inning against Sidney. Tyler Pittenger led off with a base on balls, and Cale Handran, Mike Rider, and Jay Hoversland followed with singles and scored for a 4-0 lead. With two outs, Scobey's next four batters scored, including Brian Solberg (walk), Neal Levang (single), Jared Petersen (walk), and Tyler Pittenger (batting around) for the 8-0 lead. Scobey never looked back after the first inning, winning 13-6. Coach Flamm started Jedd Lekvold on the mound, and he pitched six and one-third innings, scattering six hits and striking out six Patriots to get the win. Tyler Pittenger and Jay Hoversland finished on the mound for Scobey.

The win propelled Scobey to a key second-round matchup against Glasgow, who they would have to beat (maybe twice) if they wanted to advance to State. The Blues got off to a good start again, leading 4-3 after four complete innings. The big three-run inning in the fourth staked them to the lead as Jay Hoversland, Kelly Nieskens, and Brian Solberg scored.

But Glasgow came back in the bottom of the fifth to take a 5-4 lead and added four more in the seventh for a 9-4 advantage, which is how the game ended. The disappointing loss for Scobey, after leading early, now relegated them to the dirt route for the remainder of the tournament.

The Blues paired up against Homestead in their next game. The Blues had swept Homestead in a doubleheader at the end of the regular season, but Homestead eliminated Scobey from the tournament, pounding them 14-4 in seven innings. The game was tied 3-3 after three innings on runs scored by Levang, Petersen, and Lekvold, but Homestead scored a run in the fourth when Brock Aasheim tripled and later scored. The Pioneers added five runs in the fifth to take a commanding 9-3 lead and never looked back. Homestead pounded out four home runs in the game.

For the second consecutive year, the Blue Devils broke the Reds' hearts, denying Glasgow their first eastern divisional championship since 1952, when coaches Bunky and Sully Sullivan led Glasgow to the eastern division title. Glasgow was sitting in the driver's seat after beating Glendive 6-4 in the undefeated semifinal when Michael Falcon hit a clutch two-run single in the top of the ninth to give the Reds the win. But in the first championship game, Glendive came from seven runs down to beat Glasgow 11-8, then shocked Glasgow with a seven-run seventh in the second championship game to claim the title with a 7-5 win. Both teams advanced to the state tournament in Lethbridge, Alberta.

Scobey finished 1-2 in the tournament and 15-23 on the season.

After tasting the excitement and competition of a state tournament in Helena when they were 16, three of the 18-year-olds reflected on their disappointing final season. Losing to Homestead—who they had handled easily during the regular season—was a tough way to end their Legion careers. Jedd Lekvold said, "It was a disappointing season in 1999. I thought we were a better team than .500, but we didn't play like it. I remember that first game in the divisional tournament. I figured we would beat Sidney the first game, but I really wanted to pitch against Glasgow in the next game. They had our number (along with Glendive) over the 1998 and 1999 seasons. Coach Flamm started me on the mound against Sidney, and I think he could tell I was upset because I recall him pulling me aside and saying, "I want to make sure we don't slip up this first game. We get the Reds tomorrow, and Handran will pitch." That made me feel better, as it gave me confidence that I'd go out there and perform. Plus, Cale was our best pitcher, and we'd have him for our most important game. It didn't work out the next game obviously, and I don't remember how it went. I do remember I ended that game striking out, looking on an outside curve ball. I don't remember the Homestead game, but wow, not a good way to go out.

"Looking back on it now, I wish we could have taken it more seriously playing baseball for the Blues. Playing as a 15-and 16-year-old, I always thought the Blues were going to win. We had great players who I looked up to. And those guys could really play. Then, as a 17-and 18-year-old, I guess we just didn't have as good players that ran through that program. That's not a knock against anyone, but more of a tip of the cap to the guys before us. I will always remember and cherish the days of the Blues. Some of my best memories growing up. Many relationships were formed during this time. There's just something about playing on a hot summer night under the lights along with those bus trips with every window being cracked open."

Jay Hoversland agreed with Jedd. "The 1999 season was one that I do feel we underachieved. We had talent on our team. If I remember right, we played Glasgow pretty tough in the regular season; I thought we at least split with them. So, we could play pretty good ball but consistently was another story. And going into the divisional tournament, that lack of consistency showed up. We were just as good as any team there on any given night, but man, we certainly didn't show it.

"Playing for the Blues, man, that was the pinnacle of baseball in my mind. As we all did, as a kid, spending nights watching the Blues eating Legion burgers (which still get talked about quite a bit). Running around emulating swings, hanging on fences, sitting on the bench on the walkway between the backstop and grandstand (best seat in the house). Just awesome memories that added fuel to the fire of the desire to be part of the Scobey Blues. Playing for the Blues, is an experience/opportunity that I will forever be grateful for. Like Jedd said, the bus trips playing cards, hanging out in the clubhouse under the grandstands before/after games, and practice. It was pretty beat up by the time we were in there, but we still thought we were cool and loved it. Playing under the lights. These are all experiences that I think I took for granted at the time, but wow, those memories have really stuck with me. Blues Baseball carried its own aura, and it was pretty damn special. My son asked about me playing baseball, and my answer is almost always the same:" 'I was lucky enough to play with some of my closest friends; we were pretty good for a few of those years. And playing for the Blues was one of my greatest memories growing up.' The Legion burgers were dynamite. And how could I forget about the clubhouse? Felt like you were in a special club being down there."

Cale Handran added, "We no doubt underachieved with our last couple of seasons. But there was nothing better than representing Blues baseball living in our community as a whole. Nothing better than having that brotherhood with all the other Blues."

The 1999 season would be the last for veterans Jay Hoversland, Cale Handran, Jedd Lekvold, Matt Stentoft, and Brian Solberg, but the future for the Blues looked promising: three 17-year-olds would return in 2000 along with six 16-year-olds. And climbing further down the age ladder, the Hi-Line Babe Ruth All-Star and the Border League Bambino teams and did well that summer. The 14-15 Hi-Line Babe Ruth All-Star team, coached by Morgan Oie (Blues 1992–95) and Cody Jacobson (Blues 1993–95), did even better, finishing third at State, winning two and losing two. The team featured seven players from Scobey's 14-1 Babe Ruth team: Zach Audet, Chris Cromwell, Casey Cote, Neill Crandell, Cory Cromwell, Kevin McElvaney, and Scott Sterrett. And the 11-and 12-year-olds, the Border League Bambino All-Star Baseball Team, consisting of players from Scobey and Flaxville and coached by Jim and Craig Miller of Flaxville (both former state champions for the Blues in 1969 and 1976) and Mike Nelson of Scobey, took fourth at the state tournament, winning two games and losing two. Pitcher Chauncy Handran, 12, won both games in the tournament, pitching complete games in both outings. Four players for Scobey—Chauncy Handran, Cory Graff, Josh Miller, and Tyler Thievin—were named MVP by the opposing team in the four games.

Jedd Lekvold remembered the 1999 Scobey Babe Ruth team. "Those guys were all 15 and got brought up when their Babe Ruth season was over. Pretty talented group. I think they won quite a few games when they got older. Crandell was pretty decent at that young age, and he continued to get better as he got older. After these guys moved on, the program pretty much folded, from what I remember."

Jedd was right: the program did fold after this "talented group" moved on. But we have some more baseball to play before that happens.

STATE TOURNAMENT

THE LETHBRIDGE MINERS HOSTED THE ELEVEN-TEAM 1999 Montana/Alberta Class A American Legion State Tournament at Henderson Field in Lethbridge, Alberta. Representing the east were Glendive and Glasgow. The Havre Northstars, champions of the northern division and coached by Micky Williams, swept the tournament in four games, beating both eastern division teams along the way. The state championship was the first for the Northstars since 1984.

The Northstars beat Livingston 11-8 in their first game, then shut out Glasgow 11-0. Havre's two wins set up the critical undefeated semifinal against eastern division champion Glendive, who had upended two-time defending champion Bitterroot 12-11 and beat Gallatin Valley 9-7 to advance.

A gutsy call by Havre coach Micky Williams proved the difference in the game. Trailing Glendive 6-4 in the top of the ninth and three outs away from the dirt route, Havre loaded the bases. Williams then called for a squeeze bunt by Josh Lybecker that scored a run, and an error was committed on the play that brought home a second run to tie the game 6-6. Mace Mangold followed with a two-RBI single, and the Northstars added another run to take a 9-6 lead entering the bottom of the ninth. They held Glendive in the bottom of the ninth to advance to the championship game with the ninth-inning 9-6 win. Northstar pitcher Dan Danielson held the Blue Devils to four hits in seven-plus innings, and Dustin Fulwiler pitched the final two innings to get the win in relief. Catcher Steve Fanning (Dave Fanning's son) had three hits to lead Havre's hitting. It was uncanny that 28 years earlier, Steve's father, Dave, also had three hits (and scored the winning run) to lead Havre's hitting against Terry Puckett in the undefeated semifinal in Havre's 1-0 win in Scobey. Nate Baltrusch added two hits for Havre.

I asked Coach Williams to comment on the squeeze bunt call. "I recall thinking at the time that I needed two more runs. Josh Lybecker was a great pitcher but not a great hitter. I sometimes took chances on kids like him just to take away a double play. He was also a very slow runner, but boy, could he pitch. [He won two games in the tournament and was the MVP.] I think they had trouble covering bunts in earlier games we played Glendive, so I just took a chance, and fortunately, it worked out for us. Was a very exciting game."

The heart-breaking three-run loss for Glendive pushed them into a playoff game with Gallatin Valley to get back to the championship game, and Coach Diegel and the Blue Devils had their hearts broken in the ninth inning again—this time in the bottom half. With Glendive leading Gallatin Valley 9-6 in the bottom of the ninth, the Outlaws scored four runs to steal a 10-9 victory from the Blue Devils.

Havre then beat Gallatin Valley 14-4 in eight innings to win their first state championship in 15 years. Josh Lybecker got the win, while Alan Mapes provided the big blow at the plate with a grand slam home run in the fourth inning and went 3-for-4 with five RBIs. On his home run, Mapes said, "I hadn't hit very good all tournament. I just wanted to hit the ball hard." Jake Ingram was 4-for-5—including a double and a triple—and had two RBIs for Havre. Havre pitcher Josh Lybecker, the winning pitcher in the championship game and 2-0 in the tournament, earned MVP honors. Bret Clampitt of Glasgow won the batting championship, hitting .667 in Glasgow's five games. The Glasgow Reds, coached by Ryan Malmin, were awarded the Sportsmanship Trophy.

Mapes's reflected on winning the state championship. "It felt good. Winning this is something that I've wanted all year. We've all played together as a team since 12-year-old All-Stars. This is something we can always look back on."

As with most teams who win state championships, pitching was key. Coach Williams said, "Pitching was our strength. When somebody didn't do it, somebody else did." He added, "There's not one kid on this team who didn't contribute to any of these wins. I can't say enough about them."

Coach Williams was selected as the 1999 Montana/Alberta Class A American Legion Baseball Coach of the Year.

Twenty-five years later, I asked Coach Williams to reflect on his 1999 state championship team. "I wasn't even thinking about a state championship when the 1999 season started. Like every year, we would just hope that we could get to the state and see what happened from there. We didn't have a very successful 1998 season, so in 1999, I really didn't have a lot of confidence at the beginning of the season. The difference between the 1999 season and some of the prior ones is that these kids liked each other and played together as a team. We were fortunate to have a lot of talent that wasn't super but very consistent, and I had a bench just as reliable as the people on the field. They were very fun to coach, and it was a great year as things progressed. I started having a little bit more confidence and it was just a special season how it ended up. The major difference also, was I had very strong pitching. I actually had a five-man rotation, and four of them did little else but just pitch, and I had good alternatives from the field if I needed to get some innings."

Glendive and Glasgow made fine showings at State and respectfully represented the east. Coach Brent Diegel's Blue Devils finished third after losing leads in the ninth inning to Havre and Gallatin Valley. Glasgow won three games and lost two to finish in fourth place, also being eliminated by Gallatin Valley.

Havre's sweep of the state tournament completed a perfect 8-0 run in the postseason. After finishing 23-3 in the northern conference, they carried a sparkling 42-10 record into the Northwest Pacific Class A Regional Tournament.

NORTHWEST PACIFIC REGIONAL

THE GLENDIVE BLUE DEVILS HOSTED THE EIGHT-TEAM Northwest Pacific Class A Regional Tournament at Meissner Memorial Field in Glendive, Montana, for the first time. Glendive Head Coach Brent Diegel had built a perennial eastern division champion and state championship contender in the 1990s with the Blue Devils and was also the head coach for the Dawson Community College Buccaneers baseball team, beginning in 1997. Coach Diegel stepped down from Legion coaching following the 1999 season to concentrate year-round on building the Dawson CC Bucs baseball program. Before the regional tournament, Coach Diegel said, "Hopefully, the kids will give me a nice going-away present by winning the regional. That would be a great way to go out."

Coach Diegel said the Blue Devils (36-15) and Northstars (42-10) both had a chance to win the regional championship. Following the state championship, Coach Williams said, "We're going to go down there [Glendive] with the idea of winning. We can't sit down and be satisfied with participating. We've got to go in and win that one, too."

The 1999 Blue Devils, as was the case with Scobey throughout their championship years, were aided by players from surrounding towns, as John Stickel (Terry), Brent Nellermoe (Wibaux), and Brent Sukut (Circle) were key players on Glendive's team.

Havre made a fine showing in the tournament, finishing third, beating Douglas, Wyoming, 5-4, Glendive 12-2, Salem, Oregon, 6-4, but losing to Burley, Idaho, 12-2, and 14-9. Glendive lost to Aberdeen, Washington, 9-4, beat Anchorage, Alaska, 11-10, and were eliminated by Havre 12-2.

Burley, Idaho, beat Salem 4-3 for the regional championship.

Coach Diegel signed three 1999 Northstars—Josh Lybecker, Alan Mapes, and Jake Ingram—who played at the Northwest Regional to play baseball for his Dawson Community College Bucs the following baseball season.

EXTRA INNINGS

THE BLUE DEVILS DID NOT DELIVER THE GOING-AWAY PRESENT Coach Diegel had hoped for at the Northwest Regional, but his nine-year stint as head coach between 1991 and 1999 was a dynasty in the east. During the nine seasons when Diegel was head coach, the Blue Devils—the "Beast from the East"—were dominant, as all nine of his teams qualified for the state tournament, finishing second twice and third three times. They won the eastern divisional tournament for six consecutive years (1994–1999). During the 1990s, Glendive and Scobey won 9 of 10 of the eastern division championships (Scobey won three), and they met four times for the eastern divisional championship, with each team winning two championships. In the 1990s, Sidney was the only team other than Glendive or Scobey to win an eastern division championship (1994), but they were the only team in the east to win a state championship (1995).

Coach Williams had a tremendous amount of respect for Coach Diegel, saying, "I loved coaching against Coach Diegel. He is one of the good ones and we became pretty good friends." After "retiring" from Legion coaching in 1999, Coach Diegel returned to coach the Blue Devils' Legion program.

Coach Diegel had ties to the Blues in the form of Jim LeProwse, as Brent recruited Jim to coach the Dawson Community College Lady Bucs softball team from 2011–2021. While in Glendive, Jim assisted Coach Diegel with the Legion team.

Coach Diegel helped get baseball started at Dawson Community College in 1997. He was the first coach and recruited their first team. He served as the head coach for 14 years (1997-2006; 2007-2011; and 2016), winning the Mon-Dak Conference in their first 3 seasons (1998, 1999, and 2000) and two other times (2002 and 2004). They won the Mon-Dak Conference Tournament three times, including in 1999 and 2001, and then again in 2016, when he returned to fill in as the interim coach for one season after being away for five years. They finished as runners-up in the Region XIII tournament three times (1999, 2000, and 2004). Diegel was named American Baseball Coaches Association NJCAA Division III Regional Coach of the Year five times. In the Buccaneer's most memorable season, the 2001 team won the Mon-Dak Conference Tournament and the Region XIII Tournament and then finished in 7th place at the NJCAA Division III World Series. While at DCC, Diegel coached five All-Americans and four Mon-Dak Conference Players of the Year. He also coached the USA team to a 1st place finish in the European International Tournament in 2001. He was inducted into the Dawson Community College Athletics Hall of Fame in 2023.

The Laurel Dodgers, who had moved up to Class AA in 1993, qualified for their second State AA Tournament in 1999 as the fourth seed in the Eastern AA Division. The Dodgers would return to the Class A ranks in 2004. During the time the Dodgers competed in AA, the Laurel Dukes competed in Class A and made it to the State A Tournament in 1993 and 1994.

I asked Jedd Lekvold what playing for his dad in his final season was like. He said, "Playing for my dad is something I'll always remember. Growing up as a bat boy and getting to ride the bus as he drove the team to other towns, I just recall I couldn't wait to be playing for the Blues someday. He was in quite a different role as an assistant when I got up there to play. He coached Cale and me (along with Cale's dad, Dave) in Little League, so we had him as a coach before. I felt he was a good assistant to Flamm. It was Flamm's team, and Flamm was the head coach. That was obvious. He would give little pointers here and there to players, but I think he was perfectly fine with his role for the Blues. I just wish we could have done better as a team for him and Flamm. I feel like they put everything they had into us. They were invested."

Glasgow's three wins in the state tournament and fourth-place finish was their best performance in the program's history. Glasgow played for the state championship in 1952, but this was before there was a state tournament, and the Legion teams competed in a best-of-three playoff format. In 1952, Glasgow lost the state championship—their only state championship appearance—in a best-of-three series to Fairfield in two games.

Scobey-Peerless's run at another state title in football fell short in the fall of 1998 when they lost to Chester in the semifinals. Before the loss to Chester, the second-ranked Spartans were undefeated at 10-0.

Havre's state championship in 1999 was their seventh in team history. Their last state championship came in 1984 when they were coached by Tom Nielson, who revived Havre's Legion program in the mid-1960s, coached Havre to its first state tournament in 1967, and its first state championship in 1968. Micky Williams played on Havre's first state championship team in 1968. He played with left-handed ace pitcher Dave Fanning on Havre's 1970 state championship team when Havre beat Scobey 6-1 for the state championship in Havre. Dave Fanning pitched against Terry Puckett in the epic 1-0 pitcher's duel in the undefeated semifinal in 1971 when Havre repeated as state champions at Scobey Ball Park. Mickey was the assistant coach to Tom Nielson on Havre's last state championship team in 1984 and was Tom's assistant in Scobey in 1985 when the infamous "chalkgate" incident occurred. Scobey upset Havre 5-4 in 16 innings in the tournament's first game.

Havre's first state championship in 15 years recalled Havre and Scobey's great dynasty between 1968 and 1980 when the two teams won 12 of 13 state championships. The only team to spoil a perfect 13 for 13 sweep for the two storied Legion programs was the Billings Scarlets in 1974. The Scarlets moved up to Class AA the following year. Extending the timespan to Havre's last state championship in 1984, Scobey and Havre won 14 of 17 state championships.

Scobey and Havre's programs during those years mirrored each other in many ways. Like Doc Norman, Coach Tom Nielson had revived Havre's Legion program in the mid-1960s and led Havre to its first state tournament in 1967, which was Scobey's first year. I asked Mick Williams and Dave Fanning, who both played for Coach Nielson, to comment on Tom as a coach. Mick said, "Playing for Tom was an experience I will never forget. He worked so hard. He stressed the fundamentals, and he made sure that you had fun and were accountable for everything you did. I certainly did use his influence and philosophy when I started coaching and I believe everything I learned was from him. It was a great experience, and I wished every kid had the opportunity to play for Tom. He was a top individual and a mentor, and I surely miss him to this day." Dave Fanning added, "Tom was one of the best coaches I ever played for. He was very fundamental-oriented like Mick, but he trusted his players. He very rarely raised his voice, even though one time in '71, he chewed my ass for not sliding at second on a double play. It was a hard grounder up the middle. The shortstop had about two steps to second. So I just veered off to the right. I was out by 15 feet. The only time I can ever remember him raising his voice at me. We had a very good relationship. Very good situational coach. He would play small ball and expect a number-four hitter to bunt if he called on him. Then, he would open it up when the situation was there. The only thing that bothered me, I never got to pitch a championship game. I whined to him one time about that. He said, 'Dave, we have to get there. With you pitching the second game, we'll get there. Gotta look at the big picture.' Great coach. The older I got, the better friend he became. The one regret I had is that I never talked to him before I signed my pro contract. Tom always had sensibility. Never wavered, great Man."

Mick Williams played on two state championship teams at Havre (1968 and 1970) and won two as a coach (in 1984, he assisted Tom Nielson)—a rare combination. I was interested to hear his perspective on the difference between playing on and coaching a championship team. He said, "I think the difference between winning as a coach versus a player is as a coach, you are responsible for all the kids or players on the field on what they can do and what you expect of them. As a player, you only kind of think about yourself and you just play to have fun. I don't think as a player the pressure is on you as much as the coach, but being both a player and a coach winning state championships is one of the most memorable things in my life and something you never forget. Having the chance to win multiple state championships as a player and a coach and assistant coach is something that I am very proud of, and I think kept me coaching as long as I have."

Dave Fanning offered his perspective of playing on two state championships (1970-71) and as a parent of one of the Northstars (catcher Steve Fanning) on the 1999 state championship team. "I was very proud of our state championships in 1970-71. But you have to realize I was a transplant [from Klamath Falls, Oregon]. I made dear friends like Mickey. Been a friend for 55 years. But it was different. The '99 team . . . I watched them all grow up. Coached most of them at one time or another. The whole team seemed like my boys. The two years 1970-71 were like a fleeting moment. I played with a kid in Oregon, Dave Selinsky. We played Little League, Babe Ruth, one year of Legion, and high school ball. Then I got to play with him [for the Phillies] in '73 at Spartanburg, South Carolina. We were roommates. Very close friend. A lot different than two years. I just think the '99 team was buddies from grade school till high school graduation. Just like Mick says, they were all friends."

It was rumored in the *Havre Daily News* that Coach Williams was retiring from Legion coaching following the 1999 season, but he hung in there for several more years. He couldn't walk away, even after winning a state championship. He said, "I ended up coaching until 2003 or 2004; it might've been longer than that. The kids just kept coming

The Last Years

up and I kept having fun. Some of the teams I had after that '99 season were as good or even better than the '99 team but we just came up short a couple times and I did end up retiring. I did come back twice after that, and then I finally did hang up, but it was it experience I would never pass up and I have benefited by the association with coaches, players, sponsors, and parents—something that if not going through it people don't understand how enjoyable and the pleasure it can give somebody."

I asked Coach Williams to comment on the difference between the kids he played with in the late 1960s and the kids he coached in 1999. "I don't think there was much of a difference. I know each generation is a little different. We had nothing else to do in the summer but play baseball. We didn't have football camps, basketball camps, video games, much of anything but baseball, so that was probably the main difference. The kids in the 1990s and after, they had to be pretty dedicated to baseball because they played probably twice the games as when I was a player, and they had many things that they were also involved with such as the camps, etc. But as far as the players and the kids I coached and played with, we all loved the game, we loved competing, and the experience we had could not be done with anything else except with some sort of competition through sports and athletics."

I also asked Dave to weigh in on the difference between the two generations of baseball players, and he agreed with Mick. "I don't think there is much difference. The '70-71 teams were guys that played because they loved the game and enjoyed being around the guys. The '99 team was the same way—they *loved* playing baseball and really enjoyed being around each other. I know the '70 team made me feel at home. They made me feel like a good friend. One of the first guys I met in Havre was Mickey, all he could talk about was baseball. But the difference between the teams I played on and my son's team was I felt so proud of them boys—they played unselfishly. They did what Mick told them to do. Sometimes they didn't like it—sometimes I didn't agree with it either—but that's what good *teams* do."

I also asked the two old teammates and friends to comment on the difference between the game when they played in the late '60s/early '70s and 1999. They didn't see much difference there either. Dave said, "I don't know if there are any major differences. You still have to throw the ball, catch the ball, and hit the ball. I think one of the differences is the bat. When we played you had exclusively wood bats. One time a guy broke my favorite bat in batting practice. I was pretty disappointed. So after that, I wouldn't bring my good bat to practice."

As both Mick and Dave played against Scobey during the heyday of Scobey baseball, I wanted to hear their perspectives on playing against Scobey, playing in the state tournament in Scobey, and any memories they had of Doc Norman. Coach Williams said, "Playing and coaching against Scobey is one of the highlights of my playing and coaching careers. I remember as a player going to Scobey during the '69 state tournament and arriving to town, checking into the motel, and getting something to eat. All the signs of the businesses said, 'GONE TO BALLGAME BE BACK LATER.' Nothing truer or greater than support from the community. I remember Coach Nielson always had admiration for Doc Norman. Whether we were in school or later in life, it was just a tremendous experience, and I just wish today's generation and kids could have the same experience we did with two phenomenal coaches and individuals like Tom Nielson and Doc Norman. Nobody could be better than those two in my opinion."

Dave Fanning added his thoughts of playing against Scobey and Doc Norman. "It seems that when I played Scobey or in Scobey it brought the best out of me. The '71 state tournament was a great tournament for me. We won the 1-0 game against Scobey. [Terry Puckett pitched for Scobey.] Scored the winning run, got some [three] hits. On top of that won the state championship. Also won the tournament batting title. What more could you ask for? In '70, we played Scobey at home in a two-game stand. I pitched one of the games. We won, I think I struck out 17 Blues. They brought the best out of me. Because they were tough competition, and you had to bring your A-game. I don't think I pitched against them at State in '70. My memories of Doc were all great. After the games I pitched, he was the first to congratulate me. When I moved to Havre, and we played the Blues at home, after the game, we were chatting. Doc asked me where I was from. I told him, and also told him my sister and I were going to live with my grandmother till we graduated high school. My mom put a stop to that. He told me that if he was the coach in Klamath Falls, there was no way he would have let me leave. I thought that was kinda funny. I always enjoyed Doc. After the game against the Billings Royals in Billings at the '71 State A Tournament [Dave struck out 25 Royals in 12 innings, and Havre won the game in 14 innings], he called me at the motel and congratulated me and the team. The man loved baseball; a real gentleman."

Since one of the book's themes is how baseball tends to run in families and is passed down to the next generation, I asked Dave to comment on that experience with his kids. He fondly recalled his memories. "I coached my boys from

Little League and Babe Ruth, then handed them off to Mick. I even coached my daughter in softball. I think that was the funnest times. I loved playing, but coaching the kids and seeing how they matured and improved, thinking you might have had something to do with that . . . I still get choked up thinking about those days. My son Brian was right next to me the whole time. Really enjoyed it, coaching the city league teams, the all-star teams. The only regret I have was not coaching Scott, my middle son's Babe Ruth all-star team, when they won the state championship when he was 15. Then went to regionals in Oregon. That would have been special. I coached Steve's 13-and 15-year-old all-stars. Very special times."

One of the themes of *The Blues of Summer* is how the passion for baseball tends to run in families and how the game is passed down to the next generation. With that in mind, I interviewed Dave's son, Steve, to get his perspective on his experience growing up in a baseball family and town.

Joe: "What are your first memories of playing baseball with your dad?"

Steve: "Growing up I just remember being at the baseball park quite a bit. Can't remember exactly, but there were a few seasons that my dad assisted Mickey, and I tagged along as the bat boy. That was my introduction to legion baseball; I was hooked. Learned a lot as a youngster during those doubleheaders in the dugout.

"Being a baseball fan, obsessed with the game, I would always wait until after he got off work, bugging him to go play catch in the yard. As a young kid it was like playing catch with Nolan Ryan. Always had a heavy ball, even when just warming up. Would throw a knuckleball or two, just to mess with me.

"Havre was very proud of their "alumni games" and those are some of my fondest memories of getting to watch my dad actually play baseball. I watched a lot of him playing fast-pitch softball and slow-pitch, but this was when I got to be a spectator of the lefty on the mound. It was great. You would have 17-and 18-year-old ballplayers step up to the plate, not really knowing what they were getting into, most of whom were cocky and wanted their shot at Dave. Early on, they didn't have a sniff. Dave would muster up the strength to throw a few scoreless innings, mainly with strikeouts, then he would find the dugout and probably enjoy a couple cold ones. Let's just say by the end of the contest he had earned their respect. As I grew older and was myself a Legion baseball player, I would too get to step in and take a few hacks off the old man. Knowing me, I probably tried to lay down a bunt or two. I had no shot."

Joe: "Describe how your dad influenced your baseball career."

Steve: "I don't know if it was the lore of my dad or just being at the park so much, but baseball was my passion. I played other sports, but baseball always came first for me. My dad started coaching me in T-ball and did so up to Legion ball. He helped or was the head coach for all-star teams as well. He would show up throughout my Legion years to work with pitchers and help Mickey with other things. I can say that I always felt confident facing lefties due to the hours and hours spent in the cage with Dave tossing to me. Just was my normal. My dad pushed me. He was not an easy coach and no doubt we had our battles. But I know that this made me the player I was and the man I am now.

"The summer after my senior season, I jumped into being an assistant for the Legion program, mainly helping with the feeder B program. I continued coaching for approximately 10 more years, eventually taking over for Mickey and being the head Northstar coach for a few years.

Throughout this time, Dave was there. Watching games, helping at practice, pitching in with field work, and, at times, putting the uniform on and filling in to coach first base. He still loved the game."

Joe: "Were you aware growing up that your dad had been drafted to play professional baseball?"

Steve: "My parents (probably my mom/grandparents) did a great job of keeping a scrapbook together with all of my dad's articles, achievements, etc. I spent hours looking at that thing. Just unbelievable. I remember many baseball fans borrowing the scrapbook just to check it out and take a walk down memory lane. My dad would always make a point to share when he was getting accolades for his work at the plate. Would always say he wasn't just a pitcher. It is always great to hear the stories from both my mom and dad about their days as a young couple in the minor leagues. If only to be a fly on the wall back then. Stories of living off the small wages from playing ball. Getting by on free hot dogs after the games, stealing watermelons out of farm fields. Crazy days."

Joe: "What are your memories of playing Little League and Babe Ruth baseball in Havre?"

Steve: "As I mentioned, Dave was always my coach growing up and playing ball in Havre. By the time I was in Babe Ruth, he had me pitching and catching, seldom playing another position in the field. I still blame him for blowing out my arm. I would finish pitching five innings and jump into the catcher's gear. During my time in Babe Ruth, I felt that Havre always had a strong league. There would even be some teams from the surrounding area in the league. Always competitive baseball. This would then lead to some pretty darn good all-star teams, then quality legion teams. I am a firm believer that Havre baseball in the late '90s and into the 2000s was as good as anywhere in the state. So much talent coming through there. I will say that thanks to guys like Dave and other dads, we were able to build a strong youth baseball program, thus contributing to teams that were solid at the legion level."

Joe: "What are your memories of playing in the 1999 state tournament in Lethbridge?"

Steve: "We knew we were going to be good—such a strong group of ballplayers, a special comradery for sure. But I don't think any of us thought we would be that good. Being young players who were around and competed with players from the '97 team, we didn't know what to expect. That '97 team was loaded. More talent than any other team in the state, bar none.

"They didn't even earn a chance to compete at the state tournament that year. Sadly, things fell apart for them that season. Having seen them fail to achieve their season goal, I was a bit nervous as I didn't feel we had the talent they did. But, we were a tight-knit team, and I say to this day that is what brought that championship home to Havre; we were a team, not individuals.

"We had a great season that summer. I don't recall our record [it was 42-10], but it was pretty salty. Mickey knew this was going to be the case and scheduled appropriately. We battled some of the top AA teams in the state that year, going blow for blow with Great Falls and Lethbridge (eventually AA champ), both being great teams that year. We also had a full schedule of competitive tournaments. The schedule that Mickey put together prepared us for the state and regional tournaments. We had played in Lethbridge many times before, and we were ready, not cocky, but definitely a swagger; we were the team to beat. I believe what made that team different was the way that Mick built that roster. Most of our pitchers were only pitchers, seldom playing a position. This kept our defensive roster in check with very few changes having to be made. Our pitching staff was loaded, and we could hit: 1–9, we could swing it. Each game could have a different clutch hitter."

Joe: "Describe what it was like playing in the championship game and winning it."

Steve: "In the chipper, we went up against GVO [Gallatin Valley Outlaws]. I believe this was when GVO started to become regular attendees of the state tournament. We had heard they had some studs, but we were rolling. I believe we ten-runned them to close things out. [Havre won 14-4 in eight innings.] Josh Lybecker was the tournament MVP. Pitched well, if I remember correctly, and came away with two wins. Everything had come together, and wow, what a moment. So proud of that team. Pretty awesome feeling. Twenty-five years later, still gives you chills. Havre hasn't seen a title since. Makes you realize how big of a moment it was—just a dream summer.

"We had fun advancing to regionals and got to show that we could hang with anyone. We were short a couple of players who had to leave for college football, so who knows what we could have done. One Idaho team [Burley] had our number, and we just couldn't get by them."

Joe: "What do you think of when someone mentions the Scobey Blues?"

Steve: "I always knew there was a history there. Heard of the rivalries from Dad and Mick. Heard stories and some bragging about the program from the Vigliotti family. They were always connected to baseball in Havre, from Pat and Tony umpiring and then Tim."

Joe: "Have you heard of legendary Coach Doc Norman?"

Steve: "Heard about the program he built in Scobey. I have a lot of respect for people who do it that long and can still maintain a competitive program. Guys like him and Tom Nielson, Micky Williams, Dewey Scott (GVO), they don't make them like that anymore. Have to really admire their dedication to their communities and to those kids. Jealous really. I loved my stint in coaching baseball. *If* not for coaching my boys and following them in their sports, I would probably still be doing it today."

Dave Fanning spoke about his son Brian "Bub" Fanning, who had Down's syndrome and died of a brain abscess on June 29, 2000, just 10 months after Havre's state championship. Brian was only 23 years old when he died. Dave said, "You notice Brian was in the picture, too. [He is holding up his two index fingers, signaling number one.] Mick always called him his 'bench coach.' One time, he

1999 Havre Northstars, Montana/Alberta Legion State Class A Champions. Top row, left to right: Assistant Coach Bob Evans, Mike Holden, Jake Ingram, Dusty Fulwiler, Alex Crosby, Bryon Thompson, Josh Lybecker, Ryan Evans, Mace Mangold, Dave Heberly, Head Coach Mick Williams. Bottom row, left to right: Steve Fanning, Nate Baltrusch, Alan Mapes, Jarrod Wirt, Ricky Brown, Brian Fanning, Dan Danielson. *Family photo.*

even let him write the lineup. Great times; he was loved by everyone. They started a memorial for him, 'Brian's Light Fund.' That's how we got lights on Legion Field. Oh boy, a lot of emotions. When we all got together, we figured it would take five years to raise the money. It took 6 to 8 months. Absolutely crazy! We put them in with help from Northwestern Energy, BNSF, and many other electrical people. Boy, was it fun. Brian passed away on June 29, 2000. I think we started putting up lights in March 2001."

The inspiration for *The Blues of Summer* is the nostalgic book *The Boys of Summer* by Roger Kahn. In the book, Roger Kahn follows the lives of the Brooklyn Dodgers after their heyday of playing baseball in Brooklyn in the 1950s. One of those players was Dodgers pitcher Carl Erskine, who, like Dave Fanning, had a son (Jimmy) with Down's syndrome. The most inspirational story in Roger Kahn's book is the story of Carl Erskine and his son Jimmy. Following his career with the Dodgers, Carl was deeply involved with the Special Olympics and charities that aimed at helping people with developmental difficulties, such as his son Jimmy. In 2023, the National Baseball Hall of Fame and Museum awarded Erskine the Buck O'Neil Lifetime Achievement Award for his charity contributions and work towards the Special Olympics. Erskine died in 2024 and was the last surviving member of the "Boys of Summer" Brooklyn teams of the 1950s.

Brian Fanning, who was with Dave Fanning on the bench all the years he coached and was Mick Williams's 'bench coach,' is the Jimmy Erskine of *The Blues of Summer*. Dave said this about Brian, "He loved baseball. When I coached Little League and Babe Ruth, he was right there. Thought he was a coach." In the picture of Brian, he was giving the Havre Legion team a pitching clinic. When Dave shared the picture, I mentioned that Brian's leg kick looked exactly like his in Scobey in 1971. Dave said, "Yeah, he was proud of that. Doing it just like Dad!" That would have been like the leg kick Donnie Higgins saw as he was ready to break toward second base, except from a left-handed pitcher.

Mick Williams, Dave Fanning, Brian Fanning, and Steve Fanning all share a passion for baseball. And where passion is found is where the story of *The Blues of Summer* lives.

Brian "Bub" Fanning (1977–2000) giving a pitching clinic to the Havre Northstars. Dave said, "He loved baseball. When I coached Little League, Babe Ruth, he was right there. Thought he was a coach." *Family photo.*

2000

Coach Flamm and the Young Blues Try to Get Back to State

> *Scobey was a great community, and the Blues program still holds a special place in my heart. There was an amazing baseball and basketball culture up there, and it shaped a lot of what I've done over the years.*
>
> —*Mike Flamm, Scobey Blues head coach (1998–2000)*

2000 Scobey Blues. Back row, left to right: Coach Mike Flamm, Kevin McElvaney, Scott Sterrett, Mike Rider, Neal Levang, Neill Crandell. Front row, left to right: Cory Cromwell, Jared Petersen, Casey Cote, Kelly Nieskens, Tyler Pittenger, Eli Harmon. Not pictured is Curtis Holum. *Leader photo, Mike Stebleton.*

PRESEASON

COACH FLAMM WAS NOW IN HIS THIRD AND FINAL YEAR as head coach of the Blues, and he would have a challenge in 2000, as the 12 players who gathered around him at his first spring practice were young. This would be Scobey's youngest team in recent memory. Several experienced players, many who saw action at the state tournament in 1997—Scobey's last team to make it to State—were gone, as Jay Hoversland, Cale Handran, Jedd Lekvold, Matt Stentoft, and Brian Solberg had all aged out. Only two 18-year-olds—Kelly Nieskens and Mike Rider—were on the roster. Neal Levang, Eli Harmon, Tyler Pittenger, and Jared Petersen returned as the four 17-year-olds. The roster was weighted young as six 16-year-olds—Kevin McElvaney, Scott Sterrett, Neill Crandell, Cory Cromwell, Casey Cote, and Curtis Holum—formed 50 percent of the team. This talented group had played on Hi-Line's Babe Ruth All-Star team (coached by Morgan Oie) and finished third in the state a year earlier. This was the "talented" group Jedd Lekvold referred to a year earlier, and after they had aged out, "the program pretty much folded."

Kelly Nieskens, Tyler Pittenger, Mike Rider, Neal Levang, Neill Crandell, Eli Harmon, and Kevin McElvaney would all see action on the mound for Coach Flamm, with Jared Petersen and Cory Cromwell sharing catching duties.

The 16-year-olds on the team mentioned the difficulty in adjusting to a new coach during their first year in Legion. Of Coach Flamm, Kevin McElvaney said, "He was tough but fair. We were a tough group; we spent lots of time screwing off." Neill Crandell added, "It was challenging since he was a new teacher in the area, and it was his first year with all of us. We barely knew who Coach Flamm was at the time, and it showed in our lack of trust between us." Cory Cromwell said, "We were talented but young

Kevin McElvaney beats a pickoff throw back to first base during a regular season game against Glasgow. *Leader photo, Mike Stebleton.*

and needed direction and some depth, which we didn't have either."

Everyone on this 12-man roster would need to play up to their potential if Coach Flamm and the Blues hoped to go deep into the divisional and return to the state tournament.

REGULAR SEASON

THE BLUES FINISHED THE REGULAR SEASON WITH A 14-24-1 overall record and placed fifth in the conference, which was dominated again by Glendive and Glasgow, who repeated as the top two teams. The final conference standings looked like this:

1. Glendive
2. Glasgow
3. Sidney
4. Wolf Point
5. Scobey (14-24-1 overall)
6. Homestead
7. Plentywood

DIVISIONAL TOURNAMENT

THE 2000 EASTERN DIVISIONAL TOURNAMENT WAS HOSTED by the Richland County Patriots at Moose Memorial Park in Sidney. Scobey's first game pitted them against fourth-seeded Wolf Point, who finished one place ahead of Scobey in the final conference standings. Scobey lost to Wolf Point 16-6, as the Yellowjackets raced to an early, and Scobey couldn't recover. Scobey threatened to score several more runs but left the bases loaded in three innings and came up empty-handed each time, stranding 14 runners for the game. Mike Rider led the hitting, going 3-for-5 with 2 RBIs. Mike Rider, Neal Levang, and Eli Harmon pitched for Scobey.

The loss pushed Scobey into the loser's bracket, where they faced Plentywood. The Blues avoided another season-ending loss to the Athletics in the divisional tournament, beating Plentywood 12-8. The Blues' bats came alive, as all of Scobey's starters had at least one hit, and all but one scored a run. Tyler Pittenger and Casey Cote each had three hits, and Kelly Nieskens homered and had two hits to lead Scobey's hitting. Mike Rider and Kevin McElvaney chipped in with two hits each. Kelly Nieskens started on the mound, with Kevin McElvaney and Tyler Pittenger relieving. Kevin McElvaney earned the win in relief.

With the win to stay alive, the Blues faced Wolf Point again, the winner moving into the third-and-fourth-place game and the loser eliminated. The Yellowjackets beat Scobey again, this time 8-5. Coach Flamm commented that the close loss symbolized Scobey's season, saying, "This game was typical of how our season went. We have an inning that hurts us, and we have to play catch-up the rest of the way. We definitely had our chances with 16 guys left on base, but we typically came up short in the end." Neill Crandell led Scobey's hitting with three hits, with Mike Rider and Kelly Nieskens adding two hits apiece. Neill Crandell started on the mound and took the loss, relieved by Tyler Pittenger.

In the two losses to Wolf Point, the Blues couldn't get the big hit when needed, as they stranded 30 baserunners in the two games.

Scobey finished fourth in the tournament with a 1-2 record, ending their season 15-26-1.

Top-seeded Glendive won the championship with a 19-13 decision over Sidney, a slugfest featuring 21 hits by Glendive and 17 by Sidney. Those two teams, along with the Glasgow Reds, who entered the tourney as the number two-seeded team but lost twice, advanced to the state tournament at Bill Connors Field in Glasgow. Wolf Point placed third after losing 5-3 to Sidney.

Coach Flamm reflected on the 2000 team. "Despite the frustration of losing so many close ball games, this truly was a special team. They never gave up and fought to the end. I appreciate the efforts they put into this season and wish them the best of luck in the future."

I asked some of the players to reflect on the tough season. Neill Crandell said, "We were an extremely young team with little consistency in anything, whether it was pitching or hitting. Our talent showed through at times, but we couldn't sustain it for nine innings normally. That's where the bad inning comment from Flamm came from. We'd play a lot of good innings, and then the wheels would fall off quickly." Cory Cromwell added, "It was a long season with only a couple of pitchers."

STATE TOURNAMENT

The Glasgow Reds hosted the State Class A Legion Tournament at Bill Connors Field for the first time. The Reds had finished second in the conference to Glendive but were upset by seventh-seeded Plentywood (they did that a lot) in their first game at divisional. They beat Homestead but were eliminated by fourth-seeded Wolf Point, going 1-2 and finishing a dismal fifth. But as the Reds were the host, they had an automatic bid. The Reds, coached by Ryan Malmin and led by 18-year-olds Bret Clampitt, Michael Falcon, Ben Radakovich, and Deron Galston, had qualified for the state tournament the previous two years (finishing fourth in 1999), but the Reds wanted to prove that they belonged at State again—and they did.

The Bitterroot Red Sox, coached by Jesse Wilson, Vester Wilson's son, also had something to prove—that they were unbeatable. They were the prohibitive favorites to win the tournament, as they swept the western divisional tournament in four games and entered the tournament with a formidable 43-7 record. Northern division champion Havre, the defending state champions, and southern division champion Livingston were also in the running, but the Red Sox were the team to beat and were gunning for their third state championship in four years. They carried the same aura of invincibility the Blues once did. Mission Valley Manager Travis Devore said of Bitterroot, "When you play the Red Sox, you're not just playing the Red Sox, you're playing their whole mystique."

The tournament's story was the Red Sox' mystique and the Reds' resilience. Bitterroot swept the tournament in four games, beating Helena 14-0, Glasgow 10-0, Livingston 10-9, and Glasgow 13-1. Glasgow won four games—three by one run—to finish second, their two losses coming against Bitterroot, who overpowered them in both games. Glasgow's wins were 9-8 over Medicine Hat, 20-15 over Havre, 12-11 over Medicine Hat, and 11-10 over Livingston.

Glasgow's second-place finish was their best since 1952 when coaches Bunky and Sully Sullivan led the Reds to the best-of-three state championship series against Fairfield, which they lost in two games. The Reds finished second at State again in 2012, beating Mission Valley in their first game of the tournament 4-3 but losing twice to them in the championship games after Mission Valley came back through the dirt route. The Glasgow Reds are still seeking their first state championship.

2000 Glasgow Reds, State Runners-Up. Back row, left to right: Coach Ryan Malmin, A.J. Mock, Bret Clampitt, Deron Galston, Michael Falcon, Ben Radakovich, Justin Traeger, Coach Chad Maczka. Front Row, left to right: Steve Hall, D.J. Elletson, John Grimes, Nate Meiers, Drew Henry, Steven Falcon, Tyson Schlabs. *Image Photography.*

Mark Falcon, a sportswriter for the *Glasgow Courier*, captured the pride of the Glasgow community for the home team's fine showing at State. "The Glasgow Reds had an awesome tournament. They pulled together as a team offensively as well as with the defense and pitching. For a team that finished fifth in their own district tournament to a second-place finish at State shows a lot of character and team unity. The *Glasgow Courier* and our entire community salute the Reds for an outstanding season, and congratulations on your second-place finish in the State American Legion Tournament."[1] The article contains resonances of the community pride the *Leader* trumpeted in its summary of the first state tournament Scobey hosted in 1969.

In an article titled "End of an Era," Mark Falcon also honored the four 18-year-olds who had played in three consecutive state tournaments and finished second at State for the first time in almost 50 years. "The four Glasgow Reds seniors have enjoyed much success playing baseball in Glasgow. With a second-place finish at last week's State American Legion Tournament, Ben

2000 Glasgow Reds seniors. From left: Bret Clampitt, Michael Falcon, Coach Ryan Malmin, Ben Radakovich, and Deron Galston. Image Photography.

Radakovich, Deron Galston, Bret Clampitt, and Michael Falcon have compiled quite an impressive record playing baseball. Taking third place at the Pacific Northwest regional when they were 12 and last week's runner-up finish at State top the list of their many accomplishments. With third-year head coach Ryan Malmin, they have a record of 107 wins and only 37 losses, while playing American Legion Baseball the last three years. Ben Radakovich plans to attend Montana State University this fall. Deron Galston is going to Jamestown this fall and will participate in track. Bret Clampitt is also going to Jamestown and will do both football and baseball. Michael Falcon will be attending the University of North Dakota and playing baseball."[2]

Mark's article eerily foreshadowed the "end of an era" three years later, one hundred miles to the north and east, when Scobey's Legion program would fold.

NORTHWEST PACIFIC REGIONAL

THE BITTERROOT RED SOX TRAVELED TO LEWISTON, IDAHO, to represent Montana/Alberta in the Northwest Pacific Regional for the third time in four years. The Red Sox won the regional title in 1998 and finished third in 1997.

The Red Sox went to Lewiston to win it, and they got off to a fast start, winning their first two games, 10-7 over Lebanon, Oregon, and 4-0 over Lakeside, Washington. But they lost a close game to Marysville, Washington, 12-11 in the undefeated semifinal. They eliminated host Lewiston 8-6, then lost again to Marysville 8-5 to finish second at regional, giving them gold, silver, and bronze in their three appearances in four years. Hats off to the Bitterroot Red Sox for representing Montana with pride at the regional and building another baseball dynasty in Class A/B American Legion Baseball in Montana.

EXTRA INNINGS

COACH MIKE FLAMM BEGAN HIS CAREER TEACHING SCIENCE at Outlook and serving as the athletic director and girls' basketball coach at the Flaxville-Outlook Co-op. Following the 2000 baseball season, Mike moved to Fairfield to teach and coach and is now the principal at Hardin Middle School, where he has been for the past 19 years. I was intrigued to learn about Mike's experience coaching the Blues as he was not from Scobey, so I asked him a few questions. Here is the resulting interview:

Joe: "When you took the head coaching job for the Scobey Blues, were you aware of the program's tradition with its eight state championships under legendary Coach Doc Norman?"

Mike: "In the summers during high school I would live with my mom in Circle so that I could continue playing baseball. I graduated from Huntley Project, but in order to play ball, I would have had to go to Billings to play, and I didn't have any way to drive in each day. My 16-and 17-year-old years we would get beat pretty good by the Blues. Mike Lee is the grandson of Doc Norman, and we would stay in Scobey during our regular season games, where we'd play Scobey and Plentywood. After the games, we'd hang out with the Scobey guys and go under the grandstand at the ballpark. There were a lot of good times there, and we learned quite a bit about the history of the program. We became pretty good friends with Mike and the Scobey players. I played college baseball with Kevin Nelson who was one of the best pitchers I faced in high school. In our 18-year-old year (1991), we actually were the best team in the east (pretty unusual for Circle), but ultimately, we pissed down our leg at the tournament and lost to Plentywood in the first round and had to go backdoor all the way to the 2nd/3rd place game vs. Scobey. We beat them all four times during the season, but they pitched someone [Steve Stephenson] who just kept chucking curveballs at us and beat us 5-2. That was my last Legion game. I think we went to the Doc Norman tournament during my 17-and 18-year-old years and stayed in the old high school gym. Lots of stories from those trips but none that I should give details to."

Joe: "What were the highlights of your three years coaching the Blues?"

Mike: "I was fresh out of college and got a teaching job in Outlook teaching science and I was the head girls basketball coach for the Flaxville/Outlook Co-op. I heard there was an opening for the Blues coaching job, so I went over and met with the board and got the job. Mike Lee had coached them the year before, so I had a little insight into what I was going into. I drove a lot of miles the three years that I coached, just going back and forth to Scobey. I remember driving my little hatchback in the dark, listening to 660 Keys Country or scanning channels on the AM dial and picking up Colorado Rockies games or some channels in other languages. I loved the small-town atmosphere and how the town got behind supporting the team. We had a big basketball tournament in the winter that raised a lot of money. I remember when there would be a soaked field on game day, having people come down and help me get everything ready for the evening games. I was only 24 years old, and I was coaching kids that were pretty close to my age, so I probably have a few regrets about the way I handled some things, but I've run into a lot of the guys over the years, and it's pretty cool considering them friends now. They made me a small bat from shop class, and they all signed it, and it hangs on the wall in the basement still. They burned in 'Wonderboy' on the bat because I loved the movie *The Natural*. A personal highlight for me was that Mike Stebleton was the reporter at the Scobey *Leader*, and when I was a kid, we lived in Glasgow, and Mike was my coach in Little League. He was a real influence on me at an early age when it came to playing baseball and not turning into a punk. I wish I could say that winning was a highlight during my coaching tenure, but we didn't qualify for a state tournament during my three years. That was frustrating, but I did learn a lot from Don Lekvold, which has helped me in my coaching career."

Joe: "How did coaching the Blues baseball team differ from other coaching assignments you have had?"

Mike: "When we moved from Outlook, we ended up in Fairfield. I continued to coach girls' basketball, and in the second year I was there, an opening with the Great Falls Electrics came open to be the head coach of the Sparkies, their Class A feeder program. I got the job, and similar to Scobey, I was driving 40 miles in my hatchback to get to practice. I learned right away in Great Falls how good we had it in Scobey. I was frustrated by May with the program. Most of my frustration was based on the team that I inherited. In Great Falls the only qualification to make the Sparkies was $600. I ended up with a lot of kids that should have been playing a level down, and the parents were really tough for me to deal with. There was no community feel to what I was doing, and I was sure early on that I'd only do one year of this.

I'm a small-town kid who missed the small-town feel where everyone makes the team, and you make things work with the hand you are dealt."

Joe: What do you coach now at Hardin?

Mike: "This is my 19th year in Hardin. I've been the head football, head girls' basketball, assistant football, assistant boys' basketball coach, and assistant golf coach. My number one sport became tennis the year after I got out of the Sparkies program. I begged my superintendent in Fairfield to let me coach tennis because I knew they would want me to coach track once I was done with baseball. I always hated track. He asked what I knew about tennis, and I told him absolutely nothing, but it looked like a cool sport. I've been fortunate to build a program in Hardin that is competitive every year at a state level. My teams have won three state championships, I think we've won 14 divisional championships, and I've been able to coach both of my daughters in the program.

"I do miss baseball but that last year in Great Falls did sour me on it. Scobey was a great community, and the Blues program still holds a special place in my heart. I've warned my wife that it would be a great place to retire in with the home prices and great golf course. It won't happen, but we still have a lot of friends in the northeast corner of the state. There was an amazing baseball and basketball culture up there, and it shaped a lot of what I've done over the years."

2001

The Blues Host the Eastern Divisional Tournament for the Final Time

> *Very few kids were serious about baseball; it was just something they did on the side. Numbers were getting low because there wasn't much of anyone to run the Little League or Babe Ruth programs anymore. There were no teams in Peerless, Flaxville, or Outlook. Baseball was barely hanging on."*
>
> —*Jake Petersen, Scobey Blues assistant coach (2001)*

2001 Scobey Blues. Back row, left to right: Assistant Coach Jake Petersen, Patrick Fouhy, Casey Cote, Neal Levang, Eli Harmon, Neill Crandell, Scott Sterrett, Head Coach Morgan Oie. Front row, left to right: Ryan Baldry, Chris Jensen, Tyler Pittenger, Curt Holum, Jared Petersen, Cory Cromwell. Not pictured is Chauncy Handran. *Leader photo, Mike Stebleton.*

PRESEASON

CHANGE WAS IN THE AIR ON THE SCOBEY BALLFIELD IN the spring of 2001, as Head Coach Mike Flamm had moved on, and the Blues would have a new head coach. Morgan Oie (Blues 1992-95) would take the reins, assisted by Jake Petersen (Blues 1995–97). As players, Morgan and Jake had been teammates in 1995 and played together at the state tournament in Sidney. Morgan had played in two state tournaments (1992 and 1995), and Jake played in state tournaments in all three years he played. Morgan had coached several of the 2001 Legion players on the 1999 Scobey Babe Ruth team when he and Cody Jacobson led the team to a 14-1 record and a third-place finish at State for the Hi-Line All-Stars. Like the Hi-Line All-Star team in 1999, the goal for Morgan and Jake would be to get the Scobey Blues back to the State Class A American Legion Tournament, where they had experienced that thrill as players.

The Blues would miss Kelly Nieskens and Mike Rider, who had aged out, but five 18-year-olds—Eli Harmon, Pat Fouhy, Jared Petersen, Tyler Pittenger, and Neal Levang—were back for their final season. Returning for their second season were 17-year-olds Casey Cote, Neill Crandell, Scott Sterrett, Cory Cromwell, and Curt Holum. The Blues would sorely miss 17-year-old Kevin McElvaney (a tremendous all-around athlete) on the diamond in 2001, as he worked two jobs during the summer months to play in the "Down Under Bowl" football game the following summer in Australia. Ryan Baldry and Chris Jensen joined the team for their first season with the Blues.

For pitching, Eli Harmon, Tyler Pittenger, Neal Levang, Curt Holum, Neill Crandell, Scott Sterrett, and Cory Cromwell would all see mound time, with 14-year-old Chauncy Handran getting "called up" from Babe Ruth to get some innings. Cory Cromwell and Jared Petersen shared the catching duties.

REGULAR SEASON

ALTHOUGH THE BLUES DID NOT HAVE MUCH OF A TRAVEL budget in the later years, they did travel to play in the Ed Gallo Tournament in Whitefish, Montana, staying at the KOA Campground. The Blues played well in the tournament, slamming the Great Falls Sparkies 17-2 in one game, with Eli Harmon going the distance to get the win, pitching a four-hitter. Scott Sterrett had three hits, including a home run, and Neill Crandell also homered for Scobey. Casey Cote, Jared Petersen, and Neal Levang chipped in with doubles.

Cory Cromwell remembered the tournament. "It was a fun tourney. We played pretty well against some of the big-city teams. Stayed at a KOA in tents due to our budget. I remember Scott [Sterrett] and Casey [Cote] driving the bus on the way there. Pretty sure Neill got some *Playboys* and *Hustlers* at a gas station."

Neil Crandell remembered the tourney, too. "Fun tourney, as Cory said, and we played pretty well; Scott and I made one of the tournament all-star teams. That damn bus was sweltering on that trip, too; think we all had heat exhaustion in that cracker box." He added a funny—but not at the time—story. "The interesting part was after that game, the team bus left me at the stadium. I had no clue what to do once everyone had cleared out and watched me try to chase the bus down; I'm pretty sure the other busses were laughing pretty hard, so I just started hoofin' They didn't realize they had left me until they ran into my family at the grocery store and asked where I was. I walked most of the way back to our campsite in my uniform and cleats. Coach Peterson drove the bus back to find me, and the bus caught up with me about a half mile from camp, but I was so pissed I just finished walking. It was pretty comical after the fact." Neill added, "Hacky sack was a favorite campsite game amongst the team, and Jared tried to float out onto the lake in a one-man raft that was half-inflated.

Another regular-season highlight included a doubleheader sweep of Malta at home a week before the divisional tournament. In the first game, 14-year-old Chauncy Handran pitched a two-hitter and struck out 11 Royals in Scobey's

Chauncy Handran handcuffed Malta with a six-inning complete game by surrendering only two hits and fanning 11 in an 11-1 Scobey triumph. *Leader photo, Mike Stebleton.*

11-1 win. The youngster demonstrated he would be a serious pitcher in the years to follow, but he would not be able to complete his Legion career at Scobey. Casey Cote went 2-2 with an RBI, Ryan Baldry was 1-3 with three RBIs, and Tyler Pittenger was 2-3 with two RBIs to lead Scobey's hitting.

The Blues won the second game 17-11, as Cory Cromwell, "sporting a sore arm like the rest of the Scobey pitching staff,"[3] was the winning pitcher. Coach Oie said of Cory, "He said he could do it, and he stepped up and got the job done." Leading Scobey's 17-run outburst were Casey Cote (3-3 with three RBI), Cory Cromwell (2-3 with two RBI), Ryan Baldry (2-3 with three RBIs), and Tyler Pittenger had a solo home run.

After the doubleheader sweep of Malta in the final week of the season, the Blues finished 9-15 in the conference (14-23 overall), placing them in fifth place, the same as the previous season. Glendive and Glasgow, as they had done for the past four years, finished 1-2 and remained the class of the eastern division. The final conference standings looked like this:

1. Glendive
2. Glasgow
3. Wolf Point

4. Sidney
5. Scobey (9-15, 14-23)
6. Plentywood
7. Malta
8. Homestead

DIVISIONAL TOURNAMENT

The 2001 Eastern Divisional Tournament was hosted for the eighth—and final—time by the Scobey Blues at Scobey Ball Park. The last time Scobey had hosted the divisional tournament was in 1994. Glendive and Glasgow were favored to go 1-2 and advance to State together for the fourth consecutive year, but Wolf Point, coached by Jack Sprague and assisted by Noel Sansaver, had other ideas and was looking to crash the party as the three seed. Scobey would have to amp the game up to upset some higher seeds and advance. First-round matchups looked like this.

- Wolf Point (3) vs. Plentywood (6)
- Glasgow (2) vs. Malta (7)
- Glendive (1) vs. Homestead 8
- Sidney (4) vs. Scobey (5)

In their first game, Scobey lost a tough "see-saw battle"[4] to Sidney 11-9. The score was knotted 6-6 after five innings, but Sidney erupted for four runs in the top of the sixth to

Neill Crandell slides into third base during the 2001 Class A Eastern Divisional American Legion Baseball Tournament at Scobey Ball Park. Scobey lost to Sidney 11-9 in the opening game. *Leader photo, Mike Stebleton.*

take a 10-6 lead. Neal Levang batted 3-4 with two RBIs, Tyler Pittenger was 3-5, and Casey Cote was 2-3 to lead Scobey's hitting. Eli Harmon and Neill Crandell pitched for Scobey, with Harmon taking the loss.

The loss pitted Scobey against eighth-seed Homestead in their second game. This one was a nail-biter for Scobey, and they narrowly escaped a two-and-a-BBQ tournament with a walk-off win in the bottom of the ninth. With the Blues leading the Pioneers 11-8 in the top of the seventh, Homestead scored four runs (aided by three Scobey errors) to snatch the lead at 12-11. The Blues came back to score a single run in the bottom of the eighth to tie it 12-12, setting up Cory Cromwell's dramatic walk-off game-winning RBI in the bottom of the ninth. Cory remembers the at-bat: "I used to get really nervous at the beginning of every game. After the first at-bat, I'd settle it. I remember just thinking, *I have to find some grass*. I went with an outside pitch and hit a line drive into right center." Cromwell led Scobey's hitting, going 2-5 with three RBI (including the game-winner.) Eli Harmon (3-3, two RBI), Tyler Pittenger (2-3), and Jared Petersen (2-3, one RBI) were Scobey's other key hitters in the game. Tyler Pittenger got the win in relief of Scott Sterrett.

The win against Homestead kept Scobey alive in the tournament, and they faced second-seeded Glasgow in their next game, which resulted in a "wild"[5] 24-18 loss for the Blues. Glasgow scored 10 runs in the third and was pounding Scobey 19-1 through the top of the sixth, but Scobey didn't give up and came very close to staging the biggest comeback in Blues history. Scobey banged out nine consecutive hits and scored five runs in the bottom of the sixth to trim the deficit to 19-6.

The Blues were not going away. Head Coach Morgan Oie said of his team, "These guys can never be accused of rolling over and dying. All Glasgow had to do was throw some dirt on the coffin, and it was all over, but our guys came to life by getting nine consecutive hits and getting back into it. There's no quitters on this team."[6]

Glasgow plated another run in the top of the seventh to make it 20-6 and needed to hold Scobey to "only" four runs in the bottom of the seventh to win by the ten-run rule. But the Blues were not going to go gentle into that good night. Rallying again to stay alive, Scobey scored eight runs in the bottom of the seventh to close to 20-14. Glasgow scored four more runs in the top of the eighth and ninth innings to make it 24-14, but Scobey refused to quit and scored four more runs in the bottom of the ninth to make the final score 24-18. Glasgow had 22 hits, and Scobey had 18 in the slugfest. Wild indeed.

Scobey didn't quit and fought till the end, but in the end, a lack of pitching doomed the Blues. Scobey averaged over

13 runs per game in the three games they played in the tournament—but lost two of those games.

After the two losses at Divisional, Scobey finished the season 15-25.

Glendive won the championship 4-3 over Wolf Point, and both teams advanced to State. Coach Jack Sprague led the Yellowjackets back to the promised land for the first time in 12 years (1989), when Coach Mike Neubauer led Wolf Point to three consecutive state tournament appearances (1987–89), winning it all in 1987 and placing third at regionals.

Coach Morgan Oie reflected on the season in the *Leader*. "I'm pleased with the way our season went. It would have been nice to make it to State, but that's the breaks. This is a great group of kids. They're fun to be around and associated with. It was tough to gel as a team down the stretch because we had a few kids gone for different reasons and had to go with only nine players for a few weeks. If we could have had the whole team together for the whole season we would have been a more complete team. I'd like to say a special thanks to the team's 18-year-olds, Eli (Harmon), Pat (Fouhy), Jared (Peterson), Tyler (Pittenger), and Neal (Levang). It was great working with them and I wish them all the best of luck."[7]

I asked one of the five 18-year-olds on the 2001 team, Neal Levang (who coached the Blues in their final season in 2003), to reflect on his final season. He said, "One of the things I seem to remember about my last year was that we came out playing well that year. I think we had played about the first half of the conference games and only had one or two conference losses. Everyone on the Scobey High football team had a week-long football camp at Rocky in Billings that summer. For whatever reason, when we got back from that football camp we struggled to get back in the swing of things. We struggled through the second half of the conference games and ended up in the middle of the pack. Divisionals were in Scobey that year, and we never made it out."

I asked Coach Oie about his thoughts on the Rocky Mountain College football camp in the middle of the season and how it might have affected his baseball team. He said, "That one was tricky as I was coaching football as well at the time. Of course, 'baseball me' didn't think highly of a football camp during baseball season. It's just not something we would have done when I played."

Coach Oie also thanked all the hard-working volunteers who made Scobey's final divisional tournament happen. "Thanks to Art and Carl Holum for the excellent job they did on the grounds during the tournament and to Lee Cook, Kent Cromwell, and Orville Germaine for the great job they did running it. And thanks to all the parents and volunteers for all their work. It was a good showing for the program."[8]

KCGM covered all the games in the tournament, as it did at every divisional and state tournament in Scobey, beginning in 1971.

The loss of the five 18-year-olds would hurt Scobey in 2002, but a talented group of 18-year-olds was returning for their final season with the Blues in 2002 when the Blues would try to get back to State one more time. However, the late summer sun was arching downward in the western sky in Scobey, and a long Montana winter was soon coming for *The Blues of Summer*.

STATE TOURNAMENT

THE 2001 MONTANA/ALBERTA STATE CLASS A STATE TOURnament was hosted for the first time by the Belgrade Bandits, one of the many newer teams in the league. The Bitterroot Red Sox (41-16), the defending state champions, were one of the favorites, but Red Sox co-manager Jesse Wilson deferred to two other teams in the tournament, saying, "Glendive is an older team. Havre (43-17) played against us very well. Glendive is the 'beast from the east' this year. Whoever comes out of the east as the winner is always tough." The Bitterroot Bucs (45-17) were the second seed from the west and were also in the hunt, but they were not mentioned because they had played second fiddle to the Red Sox the entire season.

The Red Sox repeated as State champions and won their fourth in five years, but Micky Williams's Havre Northstars beat them in the first championship game. Bitterroot won 11-1 over Gallatin Valley, 13-2 over Beartooth, and 9-8 over Lethbridge to make it to the championship game undefeated but lost to Havre 5-4 in the first championship game. They came back to beat Havre 12-2 in the second championship game, as Havre ran out of pitching in its seventh tournament game. Havre lost their first game to Gallatin Valley 15-6, then proceeded to win five consecutive games along the dirt route, making it to the championship game. Glendive went 1-2, and Wolf Point went 1-2 in the tournament.

Duwayne Scott from Gallatin Valley was named Coach of the Year in 2001.

NORTHWEST REGIONAL

THE 2001 NORTHWEST PACIFIC REGIONAL WAS HOSTED IN Powell, Wyoming. The Montana/Alberta champion Bitterroot Red Sox made another fine showing in the tournament, going 2-2 to finish in third place. In their four regional appearances, the Red Sox won it once, took second once, and third place twice. LaGrande, Oregon, beat Burlington, Washington, for the championship.

EXTRA INNINGS

I asked Head Coach Morgan Oie, who played for the Blues from 1992 to 1995, how "he got the job" as head coach of the Scobey Blues in 2001. He said, "I think because I had coached those boys in Babe Ruth [in 1999], the board felt that I should continue with them after Mike [Flamm] moved on."

I was interested in getting Morgan's perspective on the changes in the program he observed from when he played in the early 1990s when he coached. He said, "The conference was the same as far as opposing teams. I would say the biggest change—and I don't want this to sound negative—was the enthusiasm from the community. The shift was going away from baseball at that time. Fewer boys going out for the team. In 2000 or 2001, we had 10 players of age. We had to pull up 15-year-olds just to field teams. I remember cutting the schedule down to basically the conference games and the Doc Norman. At the Doc Norman Memorial Tournament, we were short guys because of the 8-man All-Star Football Game. That might have been the year we had an alumni team. The tournament was a shell of what it once was. Baseball had almost become an inconvenience. I think in my 17-year-old year [1994], we played close to 70 games; in 2001, we played 28 or so. The budget was also reduced from when I played. It was kind of a vicious cycle: fewer games and fewer people attending the games equals less gate money. The baseball board didn't want to charge players to play. We tried a few fundraising ideas. The program was financially poor. When I started umping in 2002 or whenever I was paid a hamburger for a doubleheader."

I asked Morgan why he didn't return to coach in 2002, and he said the lack of commitment to baseball from the multi-sport athletes was "one of many reasons that I stepped down. I knew Jake Petersen was a more qualified coach. I was hoping he could resurrect the program. It was hard to admit that baseball was no longer the game in Scobey. To this day, I meet people around the state and am asked what happened. Scobey was such a baseball town. I still don't have an answer. A lot of things changed. I remember in the mid-80s going to the ballpark and thinking the whole town must be there. I wanted baseball to stay king."

I asked Assistant Coach Jake Petersen to comment on what had changed since his last season in 1997 and 2001. He said,

"In 2001 you had to recruit kids to play. Kids were more concerned with having a job to make money than playing baseball. I think the constant change in coaches played a big role as well. Very few kids were serious about baseball—it was just something they did on the side. Lots of kids that didn't play for a few years and then came back and played, not that many that played all the way through. I think the region as a whole got weaker, too. Glendive seemed to be the only team really that was very good to compete at the state level, and even they weren't as good because [Brent] Diegel was not coaching anymore."

I also asked Jake—a multi-sport athlete and former Blue (1995–97)—if seeing the decline in interest in baseball in Scobey was one of the reasons he was drawn to coach the Blues. His answer was yes. "That's why I came back to coach the two years I did. I couldn't stay doing it, though, and there was no talent coming up at all. Don't know if they even had a Babe Ruth team the next year. Numbers were getting low because there wasn't much of anyone to run the Little League or Babe Ruth programs anymore. There were no teams in Peerless, Flaxville, or Outlook. Opheim was down to one team, and Scobey was down to two teams. Baseball was barely hanging on."

Hearing from both coaches about their perspectives on the 2001 season and what was changing with baseball in Scobey, I asked Neal Levang, one of the 18-year-olds on the 2001 team, for his perspective. He sent me this letter:

I grew up on a farm and ranch several miles outside of Scobey, so I wasn't always in town in the evenings as a kid to watch the Blues games like some of the other kids my age. I always knew there was a storied history that went along with Blues baseball (Don Lekvold used to talk about the history of the program a lot in the first couple of years I played with the Blues when he helped coach), but I didn't have some of the same experience of watching the Blues in their heyday . . . I just loved playing the game. I felt there was always a different level of camaraderie that existed in baseball when I was playing for the Blues. Most of the opponents we played were further away than other sports with much longer bus trips and lots of overnight stays that were usually done very economically. I remember staying on the floor of the armory one year when we played in a tournament in Havre. We camped at a campground for several nights in Whitefish one year for a tournament. There were many hours spent with teammates playing cards and hanging out, that wasn't the case when traveling for other sports.

My last season we were fairly limited in 'seniors' that year and knew that many from the 'junior' class would need to be major contributors. (I put those in quotes as those juniors in baseball were in my class for school, but because of the July cutoff date,

The Last Years

three of us were playing in our final year when the others had one more season of eligibility in baseball.) For our 2002 graduating class, we were probably more focused on making a run at winning the state football championship the following year (which we ended up losing in the championship game) than winning the state baseball championship. We all loved the game of baseball, but football was the sport we all wanted to win the most, and at that point, football/basketball had a much more significant following from the community than baseball games.

In my final year, I think we all thought that we were up against pretty steep competition playing against much bigger towns and teams. Glendive and Glasgow had put together pretty solid programs by that point and were always tough for us to complete with. Our class was very competitive, though, and we knew we would have to play very well to have a shot at making the state tournament. Our pitching that season was limited, and with most of the games being doubleheaders and oftentimes on back-to-back days without much rest . . . our pitchers relied on a lot of Advil and Icy Hot to push through.

To answer the question of 'What it meant to me to be a Scobey Blue,' for me it was less about the storied history of the program and the past championships, and more about the experience of playing baseball with your friends and teammates. Representing our small Class C town against larger Class A schools and trying to compete to win games.

For the most part, we were able to play with the bigger towns, but the expectation at the beginning of the season that the Blues were a contender to win the state tournament was dampened this year by a desire that we could make it to the state tournament. We knew we'd have to knock off Glendive or Glasgow to make the state tournament and thought with the Divisionals being hosted in Scobey, with single nine-inning games being played in the tournament rather than seven-inning doubleheaders, our limited pitching compared to the larger towns may be less of an issue than it was in the season games."

The Beartooth Bighorns, comprised of players from Columbus, Red Lodge, and Absarokee, made their first appearance in the state tournament in 2001. Columbus is where Doc Norman started his coaching career in the early 1950s.

In its storied history, Scobey hosted the divisional tournament eight times (1958, 1965, 1974, 1978, 1988, 1990, 1994, and 2001). In 1958, Scobey hosted the best-of-three eastern division championship series between Roundup and Flaxville, which Roundup won in three games. Although home field is typically an advantage, Scobey was only able to win the divisional twice at home (1978 and 1990), and only one other time (1974) did the Blues advance to State hosting the divisional tournament at home.

The Scobey-Peerless Spartans football team, led by Coach Larry Henderson, was a perennial top-ranked team and state championship contender. In the fall of 2000, the Spartans finished 6-2 but lost to Wibaux, the eventual state champion, in the first round of the playoffs. Most of the key players from the 2000 team would return for their senior season in the fall of 2001, where they would gun for Scobey-Peerless's third state championship. The same talented group of all-around athletes were also contenders for the state basketball championship, and many competed in track and field as well.

2002

The Blues Struggle During the Regular Season but Play Well at Divisional

> *The Scobey Blues proved they were a better American Legion Baseball team than a number seven seed out of eight by capturing fourth place at the Eastern Class A Divisional Tournament.*
>
> —Mike Stebleton, Daniels County Leader, August 1, 2002

2002 Scobey Blues. Back row, left to right: Assistant Coach Mike Rider, Scott Sterrett, Chauncy Handran, Zach Audet, Neill Crandell, JD Matternach, Casey Cote, Head Coach Jake Petersen. Front row, left to right: Kevin McElvaney, David Leibrand, Jude Chabot, Matt Selvig, Curtis Holum, Chance Hammer. *Leader photo, Mike Stebleton.*

PRESEASON

MORE CHANGES WERE IN THE SPRING AIR FOR THE Scobey Blues program in 2002. Head Coach Morgan Oie had stepped aside, allowing Jake Petersen, his assistant the previous year, to take over as head coach. Morgan stepped aside for several reasons, but his priority was the survival of the Blues program. He said, "I knew Jake Petersen was a more qualified coach. I was hoping he could resurrect the program." Mike Rider (Blues 1998–2000) would assist Jake on the diamond.

If Jake was going to resurrect the program, he would have to do it without five 18-year-olds—Neal Levang, Eli Harmon, Pat Fouhy, Jared Petersen, Tyler Pittenger—who had aged out, and Neal, Eli, and Tyler were pitchers. But Jake inherited a talented crop of multisport athletes, as back for their final seasons were 18-year-olds Kevin McElvaney, Neill Crandell, Scott Sterrett, Casey Cote, and Curtis Holum. This group had played on Morgan Oie's Scobey and Hi-Line Babe Ruth All-Star teams, finishing 14-1 in conference and third at State in 1999. Catcher Cory Cromwell was part of this age group but couldn't play because he had surgery on his ankle after breaking it and tearing ligaments during track that year. The Blues would miss Cory in 2002—and Cory would miss the Blues, saying, "I was disappointed I didn't get to play my last year and jealous I didn't get to play with that group of guys. Would've been a great summer and a great team to end with."

And for the first time in 19 years (1983), an Audet was on a Scobey Blues roster, as 17-year-old Zach Audet joined the team. Zach's uncle, Pat Audet, played from 1979 to 1983 and was on three state championship teams (1979-80 and 1982). Pat was the last in a series of five Audets who played for Scobey during the championship era. Phil (1963–67) pitched Scobey to its first state tournament in 1967; Craig (1965–69) played on the 1969 state championship team; Dana (1971–74) in 1973; Allan (1975–78) in 1976-78, and Pat (1979–83) in 1979-80 and 82. Except in 1970, there was an Audet on the Scobey Legion roster every year from 1963 to 1983, and an Audet played on all eight state championship teams.

When he played in 2002, Zach was the last Audet to play for Scobey. Since I watched Phil, Craig, and Dana play, and I played with Allan and Pat, I was interested in talking a little baseball with Zach, so I asked him a few questions:

Joe: "Do you remember who taught you how to play baseball in Little League?"

Zach: "Oh yeah. I was a Red Sox lad. My dad [Dan] coached. Uncle Pat Harold coached. And Uncle Pat Audet would come up. All three showed me the ropes."

Joe: "Were you aware of the storied history of the Scobey Blues?"

Zach: "Oh yeah. I've heard the stories. You guys were tough."

Joe: "You were the last Audet to play for the Blues. Did you feel connected to the previous generation of Audets who played before you for Scobey?"

Zach: "Yeah, I was the last, but no, I didn't feel connected. I mean, we were good but never came close to winning a chipper, which was weird because we went to State every year in Babe Ruth. Came close a couple of times. But when we got to Legion, most of us were more focused on lifting and dominating football. We did that, at least."

Joe: "I'm tracking the only year you played Legion was in 2002 when you were 17. Why didn't you play when you were 15, 16 and 18?"

Zach: I was still playing Babe Ruth when I was 15 [in 2000]. The next year [2001], [Kevin] McElvaney and I just focused on football most of the summer. One of those summers, a bunch of us forked out a pretty penny to go to Australia [2002] to play in some football tourney [the Down Under Bowl], but I didn't do that. I didn't play in the summer of 2003 because I took that summer training for football. That was going into my freshman year at Rocky Mountain College. I couldn't play anyway because I had to report to Rocky at the beginning of July. We all did love baseball. But I was really the only one in my grade that played. I was always playing with everyone above me."

Also on the 2002 roster for their first full year were Jude Chabot (18), JD Matternach (17), and 15-year-old Chauncy Handran, who was "called up" from Babe Ruth as a 14-year-old the previous year. Chauncy was a talented baseball player who had pitched a two-hitter and struck out 11 Malta Royals as a 14-year-old in 2001. He was joined by fellow 15-year-old rookies David Leibrand, Matt Selvig, and Chance Hammer.

Neill Crandell, Chauncy Handran, Kevin McElvaney, Scott Sterrett, and Zach Audet would be the primary pitchers, with Matt Selvig, Chauncy Handran, and Neill Crandell sharing the catching duties, as Cory Cromwell couldn't play due to his injury.

Many 2002 Blues (and former 2001 Blues) played on Coach Larry Henderson's Scobey-Peerless powerhouse football team, who made it to the state championship game undefeated at 11-0 but lost to Wibaux 42-30. They were also teammates on Coach Dave Selvig's Scobey Spartans basketball team that played Saturday night at the State Class C Basketball Tournament. They took fourth place after losing to Manhattan Christian, finishing the season 23-4. Finally, many of these multisport athletes were part of Scobey's track and field team that brought home hardware from the State Class C Track and Field Meet, finishing in second place. Kevin McElvaney led the team with wins in the pole vault and 110 hurdles, placing sixth in the long jump.

No strangers to winning on the gridiron, hardwood, and track and field, this talented group of multisport athletes would try to apply their winning ways to baseball, where Coach Peterson and the Scobey Blues hoped to get back to the state tournament one more time.

REGULAR SEASON

THE BLUES WERE SWEPT IN AN EARLY SEASON DOUBLEHEADER against Coach Jack Sprague's Wolf Point Yellowjackets (who made it to State in 2001), but Scobey's pitching looked good, as Neill Crandell went the distance and pitched well in the first game in a 7-5 loss, and 15-year-old Chauncy Handran pitched a complete game in the second game, but Wolf Point won 5-1. The *Wotanin Wowapi* recognized the talent of young Handran, writing, "Handran proved to be a very bright prospect for the Blues but was given very little support at the plate or in the field."[9] Little did the *Wotanin Wowapi* know that Chauncy would indeed turn out to be "a very bright prospect"—but for the Yellowjackets. Chauncy played for Wolf Point in 2004 and 2005 after Scobey's Legion program folded in 2003.

I asked Coach Peterson if he saw the potential in Chauncy Handran at that age. He laughed at my question. "I knew Chauncy was D1 [he pitched for the University of Minnesota Golden Gophers] when he was a fourth grader! He was a special kid. He and I have a great relationship. We still stay in touch from time to time. I remember him calling me right after he threw his first no-hitter in college. I hated that he had to go to Wolf Point to play, but Jack [Sprague] was a good coach. I had been coaching Chauncy in various sports since he was 10 years old. Our families had a close relationship because his mom babysat one of my brothers for a couple of years before he started school, and his two older brothers were friends of mine."

Coach Peterson remembered two unique aspects of the Doc Norman Memorial Tournament in the two years he coached in 2001 and 2002: it was a wooden bat tournament and had an alumni team due to cancellations. It was cool that the Doc Norman Tournament had wooden bats, as all of Doc's first teams, beginning in 1959 and his first two state championship teams in 1969 and 1973, were exclusively wooden bat teams. Doc continued to buy wooden bats for the team after aluminum was approved for Legion after 1973, and the 1976-80 state championship teams still had wooden bats along with aluminum.

The Blues were missing key players at practices and games during the regular season for various reasons, which made it difficult to develop the team. Coach Peterson recalls, "We always had people missing for something." Scobey finished seventh place (8-20) in the conference and was 12-25 overall, but this team was much better than their record indicated. Glasgow and Glendive were again the top dogs in the east, but this year, Glasgow finally knocked off Glendive for the top seed. The final conference standings looked like this:

1. Glasgow (24-4)
2. Glendive (23-5)
3. Wolf Point (16-12)
4. Sidney (15-13)
5. Homestead (11-17)
6. Plentywood (10-18)
7. Scobey (8-20, 12-25)
8. Malta (4-24)

Having the whole team together for the divisional tournament, Coach Peterson and the Blues hoped to make a deep run in the tournament and get back to State, despite being the seventh seed.

DIVISIONAL TOURNAMENT

THE GLENDIVE BLUE DEVILS HOSTED THE 2002 EASTERN Divisional Tournament at Meissner Memorial Field in Glendive. First-round matchups were as follows:

- Glasgow (1) vs. Malta 8
- Sidney (4) vs. Homestead (5)
- Wolf Point (3) vs. Plentywood (6)
- Glendive (2) vs. Scobey (7)

Against host Glendive, Scobey took a 2-0 lead in the first inning as Casey Cote and Neill Crandell had RBI singles, but the Blues could not plate any more runs off Glendive starter Chase Downs. Meanwhile, Neill Crandell pitched well for Scobey, hurling a four-hitter in nine innings, but some walks and four fielding errors led to several unearned Blue Devils runs, and Scobey couldn't upset Glendive, losing 8-2.

The first-round loss pushed Scobey into the loser's bracket, where they faced third-seeded Wolf Point in their second game, as Wolf Point had been upset by Plentywood 6-3 in their first game. The Blues responded against the higher seed, eliminating Wolf Point 10-7. Kevin McElvaney started on the mound and went five innings to get the win, with Zach Audet earning a four-inning save, allowing only three hits and one run in four innings of work to preserve Kevin's win, striking out five Yellowjackets. Matt Selvig led Scobey's hitting, going 2-4 with three RBI. Zach Audet and Neill Crandell each chipped in with two hits and two RBIs, while Kevin McElvaney added two hits.

The win propelled Scobey to another elimination game against a higher seed, this time fourth-seeded Sidney. Proving once again they were better than their regular season indicated, the Blues eliminated Sidney 13-12 in a dramatic ninth-inning walk-off win. Trailing 12-10 in the bottom of the ninth, Scott Sterrett drew a leadoff walk but was forced out at second on a fielder's choice by Cote. Neill Crandell followed with a single, but Zach Audet flew out to left, leaving Scobey down to their last out. Then, July Madness began. Chauncy Handran put a grounder in play to the shortstop, which looked like it might be the third out, but the ball rolled between his legs for an error, scoring Cote to get to 12-11. With Selvig batting, Crandell tied the score on a passed ball. Then, on a 1-2 pitch, Matt Selvig laced a double down the left-field line to the warning track to score Handran for the "line-hugging, game-winning hit."[10] Jake Petersen said of Selvig's hit, "He crushed it."[11] Selvig finished 2-5 with five RBIs, including the game-winner. Neill Crandell was perfect at the plate, going 4-4 with one RBI. Chauncy Handran pitched a complete game for the win, striking out four.

With two wins over higher seeds, Scobey aimed for a third "upset" (Scobey belonged on the field with anyone in the tournament) to survive. This time, they were pitted against fifth-seeded Homestead. Kevin McElvaney got Scobey off to a great start by leading off the third inning with a solo home run, staking Scobey to a 1-0 lead. Kevin remembers the home run. "Kyle Ryder left a changeup high, and I hit it over center field." But Homestead got to Scobey starter Scott Sterrett for two runs in the bottom half of the inning to take the lead 2-1. Scobey tied the game 2-2 in the sixth, then added a run in the seventh to reclaim the lead 3-2, but the Pioneers scored three runs in the bottom of the eighth to take a 5-3 lead.

To stay alive in the tournament, Scobey needed to rally in the top of the ninth, and they threatened, placing runners on first and second with one out, but the rally was snuffed out on a double play. Coach Peterson remembers what happened. "Neill Crandell, arguably our best all-around player, was on deck. Ground ball to the middle infield. The throw went to first, and the runner rounded third and tried to take home and got thrown out at home. Game and season over. That was a tough one because I thought we were going to get to State that year even though the record wasn't good."

Scott Sterrett took the tough loss for Scobey, pitching a strong seven and one-third innings, allowing only four hits and four runs, keeping the Blues in the game. Zach Audet came on in relief and gave up one hit and one run in two-thirds of an inning.

The Blues finished 2-2 in the tournament, good enough for fourth place, but it was a disappointing end of the season for Coach Peterson and the team as they wanted more. Coach Peterson lamented the last game against Homestead: "What hurt us was leaving 10 guys on base. We had runners on first and second with one out in the top of the ninth."[12] When asked by the *Leader* about moving from the seventh seed to a fourth-place finish in the divisional, Coach Peterson's response was also disappointment. "The guys pretty much expected to do that, but they expected to do even better. They were really disappointed in losing to Homestead, but when you leave 10 on base . . ."[13]

I asked Coach Peterson to reflect on the 2002 season. "We had talent, but it took a while to get it together. Kevin, Jude, and Zach were great athletes, but it took them a little bit to get in the rhythm of baseball again. We lacked baseball smarts at times because of it. Things seemed to be coming together at the end of the season. It was crazy how we would have a big upset of a team ahead of us and then get blown out the next game by the same team. We were capable of beating anyone that year we just couldn't keep it together for a string of games. I really loved that group of kids, though. The team speed was crazy."

Glasgow proved they were the best team in the east, as they beat Glendive 4-1 in the semifinal and 16-6 for the championship on Glendive's home field. Both teams advanced to State. Was this the year Glasgow could break through for their first state championship? Or, would Glendive, the perennial "Beast from the East," recover from its two losses to Glasgow at home and make a run in the state tournament as a Cinderella team?

STATE TOURNAMENT

The 2002 Montana/Alberta State Class A State Tournament was hosted by the Bozeman Spikes on Legion Field in Bozeman. The Gallatin Valley Outlaws, coached by Duwayne Scott, were favored to win the tournament, as they won the Central Division championship and were riding a 32-game winning streak into the tournament, sporting a 52-10 record. But Coach Jesse Wilson's Bitterroot Red Sox—two-time defending state champion (and four out of the last five years)—and Coach Micky Williams's Havre Northstars were considered equally capable of winning it. Each had won their respective division and had sparkling records of their own. As always, the Bitterroot Bucs were given honorable mention, but only because they played second fiddle to the Red Sox in the west. Glasgow, the champion from the east, was not mentioned, nor was the East's second seed, Glendive.

The 2002 State Tournament won the award for the worst first-round seeding in tournament history, as Bitterroot and Gallatin Valley, two favorites to win the tourney, faced each other in the first round. But Red Sox Head Coach Jesse Wilson was matter-of-fact about it, saying, "We're not dissatisfied with the seeding. For us, it's not a big deal. You've got to beat the best to be the best, and that's what we plan on doing." I like your style, Jesse. Bitterroot beat Gallatin 15-13 in the first game.

But it wasn't any of the top three favorites who won the 2002 state tournament. It was the perennial "Beast from the East," the Glendive Blue Devils, who were uncharacteristically wearing the Cinderella slipper in 2002 Bozeman. The Blue Devils were led by first-year coach, 23-year-old Chad Jones from Forsyth, Montana. Glendive swept the tournament in five games, beating Belgrade (9-7), the Billings Blue Jays (6-4), Lethbridge (20-9), and the Bitterroot Red Sox twice (17-11 and 12-4). In the undefeated semifinal, Glendive scored seven runs in the top of the ninth inning to upend the defending champs 17-11. Following the victory in the undefeated semifinal, Greg Ford, who picked up his third win of the tournament, said, "We're not surprised to be here. It's like Coach Jones told us, 'Respect the team, but don't fear them.'" In the 12-4 state championship win over Bitterroot, Blue Devils' 16-year-old Chase Downs from Lindsay, Montana, pitched a complete game to get the win. He threw only 102 pitches and got stronger as the game went on, retiring the last 11 of 12 Red Sox he faced. Of his 16-year-old pitcher, Coach Jones said, "I can't ask for anything more out of a 16-year-old. I knew he had it in him." Center fielder Greg Ford gave Chase all the support he needed at the plate, going 3-for-4 with two doubles, a triple, and six runs batted in. Leadoff hitter Tim DeKaye, the veteran second baseman in his fourth year with the Blue Devils, chipped in with a 4-for-6 day and a double. Greg Ford's older brother Derek was named MVP of the tournament, hitting .440. The Blue Devils, normally one of the tourney favorites, had something to prove at the tournament. Greg Ford said, "Some people predicted we'd be two and a barbecue. I think we proved them wrong."

Chad Jones—who was hired by Coach Diegel as his assistant at Dawson Community College and recently played baseball at Mayville State, North Dakota—became emotional after the game as his players mobbed him and each other. He said, "I love these kids. I told them they are my boys."[14]

After winning the state championship, Coach Jones was named Montana/Alberta Legion Coach of the Year. He joked that winning the state championship saved his job as head coach of the Glendive Blue Devils, as the community wanted to fire him after he lost two games to Glasgow at home on Meissner Field a week earlier in the eastern divisional.

Glendive's state championship was their first since 1985 when they won the state championship in Scobey, and third overall, as the Blue Devils won their first state championship in 1964. The title was also the first for the eastern division since Sidney won it in 1995. Coach Chad Jones would also lead Glendive to its fourth state championship in 2004, the last state championship for a team from the former eastern division in Montana.

Glasgow lost a tough one-run game to Lethbridge in their first game as the Miners scored two runs in the bottom of the ninth to walk it off, then were eliminated by Livingston 23-11.

NORTHWEST REGIONAL

LA GRANDE RAIN ROOFING HOSTED THE NORTHWEST PACIFIC Regional at Optimist Memorial Field in La Grande, Oregon. Glendive carried a 31-7 record into the tournament. The young Blue Devils were eliminated in two games, losing a tough one-run game to Cheyenne, Wyoming, 8-7, and La Grande, Oregon, 15-4. But Glendive would be a force to be reckoned with for at least the next couple of years. Coach Jones said, "It was a great experience for the kids. Everybody got to see some time. We only lose two kids, so hopefully [Glendive] will be there for years." (They would.)

EXTRA INNINGS

WHILE NEILL CRANDELL, KEVIN MCELVANEY, AND CASEY COTE wore blue baseball uniforms that summer, they wore red football jerseys in the 19th Annual Treasure State Class C All-Star game. The three former Scobey-Peerless football standouts led the Red Team to a 42-10 win over the Blue Team, as quarterback Neill Crandell, named the MVP for the Red Team, passed to Kevin McElvaney for one touchdown and ran for another, and Kevin scored three touchdowns in the game. "Speedy" safety Casey Cote caught Blue Team's Brian Bachmeier from behind and saved a touchdown. The three also participated in the Down Under Bowl in Australia, and Kevin McElvaney played in the 56th Annual East-West Shrine game.

The 32-game winning streak Gallatin Valley had entering the state tournament broke the previous record (31 consecutive wins) set by the 1978 Scobey Blues. Our streak was broken when we were beaten 6-3 by the Glendive Blue Devils in the first state championship game in Cut Bank. We started a new streak the next day, though, winning the state championship 8-6 over Glendive. Gallatin Valley's 32-game winning streak was ended by (who else) the Bitterroot Red Sox in the first game of the tournament, as the Red Sox beat the Outlaws 15-13.

One record the Scobey Blues still retain today is the number of consecutive State A/B Legion State championships (five) from 1976 to 1980. We can thank Micky Williams from Havre and Chad Jones from Glendive, as they stopped the Bitterroot Red Sox from winning state championships in 1999 and 2002. Otherwise, Bitterroot would have won six consecutive state championships between 1997 and 2002.

Glendive Head Coach Chad Jones played Legion ball for the Colstrip Rangers from 1994 to 1997. He remembers playing against the "tough" Scobey Blues teams that made the state tournament from 1995 to 1997. He specifically mentioned Spencer Frederick as one of those tough players from Scobey. After his Legion career, Chad played for Coach Diegel (along with Tim Vigliotti) at Dawson and was hired by him as an assistant in 2002 after his playing career at Mayville State. After hiring Chad, Brent suggested Chad apply for the summer Legion job.

Chad needed a summer job, so he applied and was chosen as the head coach among five applicants. He coached for five years at Dawson and the Glendive Blue Devils before moving to Kansas City, Missouri, after the 2006 season. Chad credited Coach Diegel as his mentor. "I took a lot from Brent. He was just a true baseball guy, just one of the old heads. He just had a knack for finding out how to win baseball games, and that's something that I gathered from him—just a calming influence on the baseball field. And just brought a wealth of knowledge and always had a great message for his team. It's a testament to him that he always had winners. I mean, he just found ways to develop guys—just a great overall friend and mentor. I basically incorporated a lot of what he taught, and I think that's what makes good coaches—they take the best bits and pieces of what they've gathered from guys that they played for, and, you know, obviously, they incorporate some of their own with that. You have to have great kids, too, who are willing to buy in, and I think Brent always had a knack for recruiting that kind of kid."

The young team that Chad Jones had (only two 18-year-olds) that won the state championship in 2002 reminded me of our 1977 state championship team, which had no starter who was 18 and an average age of less than 16. Also, Chase Downs's win as a 16-year-old in the state championship game recalled Scobey's Jon Puckett and Kelly Norman, who were two Blues 16-year-olds to win state championship games. Jon accomplished the feat in 1977, pitching a complete game to beat Sidney 13-3 for the state championship. Kelly did it in 1978, pitching six and two-thirds innings against Glendive to get the win.

I asked Coach Jones how he was able to win the state championship with such a young team in 2002. He said, "The kids bought in and got to work. My philosophy—and I got this kind of philosophy from my Mayville State, Scott Berry, who's a Hall of Fame coach and one of the all-time leading coaches in college baseball—ever. His philosophy was, 'You don't win championships with your seniors,' he goes. 'You need to learn to develop your freshman and sophomores and get them on the level of your seniors, and then you'll have something. If I've done my job by the time they're senior, they should have been bought in, understand what the expectation is, and be ready to go. So, the sooner I can get my freshman to be like a senior, that's how programs are built. You have an expectation and a standard.' So that's kind of what I what I did. I was fortunate and blessed enough to be able to pull a lot from him and then obviously try to create my own identity with them. And don't get me wrong, it was a lot of the hard work they put in because I did have some good, good young players. Obviously, anytime you can have the Ford brothers from Wibaux and Chase Downs from Lindsay, that makes your life a little bit easier as a coach."

Coach Jones's model of developing younger players to win the championship could have been taken from Doc Norman, whose model for success was "drafting" young Babe Ruth talent and bringing them up to play Legion ball as early as 13 years old. He would often start the younger players and not only develop them against stronger competition but also win state championships with them. In an interview in the *Gazette* with Dennis Gaub in 1981, Doc said, "Kids can play Legion ball for 5-6 years. By the time they're 17 or 18, they're pretty good. The only trouble is we can't have a team of all 17-or 18-year-olds."[15] Examples of Doc's successful model include Greg Stolen, the starting right fielder for the 1979 state championship team, who was 13 years old. There were also many 14-year-olds who started on Doc's state championship teams, including Rick Danelson (third base) and Terry Puckett (a pitcher) in 1969. All of Doc's eight state championship teams had at least one 15-year-old as a starter. All of the Blues 15 years old or less who played in state championships later played on state championship teams when they were older.

Chad also mentioned three other legendary coaches from Montana Class A American Legion whom he is friends with today: Micky Williams (Havre Northstars), Jesse Wilson (Bitterroot Red Sox), and Duwayne Scott (Gallatin Valley Outlaws), whom he described as "one of his best friends." This is good company to keep: Chad, Mickey, Jesse, and Duwayne have each been named Montana/Alberta Class A American Legion Coach of the Year, and they each have won multiple state championships as coaches. Chad's connection with these three coaches is another good example of the saying, "Montana is one big, small town with really long streets."

Coach Scott Berry, who Chad Jones played for at Mayville State and said was "one of the all-time leading coaches in college baseball—ever," is a legend of his own. "One of the most heralded and respected baseball coaches in America, Scott Berry, runs one of the nation's most outstanding college baseball programs (Mayville Comets website)." He has been the head coach of the Mayville Comets since 1982 and is a member of seven halls of fame. His teams have won 23 regular season conference championships (including 17 in a row from 1986—2002) and 23 conference tournament championships and have made 29 appearances in the NAIA national playoffs. The Mayville State University Comets have won three NAIA regional titles under Scott Berry, the 2002 Plains Super Regional title, and finished 5th place at the NAIA World Series in 2002. His career record as head coach after 41 years in the NAIA stands at 1172-674 -1. He has been named Conference Coach of the Year 24 times, District 12 Coach of the Year 12, and NAIA Region Coach of the Year four times. Two of the seven halls of fame Berry has been inducted into are the American Baseball Coaches Association Hall of Fame (2017) and the North Dakota Sports Hall of Fame (2018).

Coach Berry was the assistant at Mayville in 1981 when I played shortstop for the Minot State Beavers.

While I had Chad "on the line," I asked him how he handled multisport athletes on his team, knowing that the Ford brothers from Wibaux played for him. He said, "I had multiple kids like the Ford brothers from Wibaux and kids from Circle who obviously took their football very, very seriously. So, there were times when I would have to get creative with the schedule because they weren't gonna miss a camp like the Rocky Mountain Football Camp that they would always go to, and I understood that. I promoted multisport baseball athletes. I loved it, and that's just the way it was in Montana—you played multiple sports because we grew up in small towns, and there wasn't anything else to do. So, you did sports, and that was it, and you had to get creative as a coach. And I felt like if you promoted that [multiple sports] within your own program that was okay. So going to these camps was no big deal. I feel like in today's day and age, though, it's getting tougher and tougher to be a multisport athlete. It's getting more specialized and stuff like that. My son plays quarterback for a 6-A school year in Kansas City, and he also plays baseball, and a lot of the football coaches initially will say, 'We love multisport athletes,' but when it comes down to time to do some things, they don't. They're kind of passive-aggressive about it, is the way I look at it. It's like they'll say, 'You know we're okay, but then kind of give you a guilt trip, you know, like, 'Hey, you need to be at that,' and it's kind of one of those things that everybody's obviously fighting for their own program when you get to a big school. So, I understand it, but it's getting tougher and tougher to be a multisport athlete. In my eyes, it's getting more specialized and stuff like that. But my son's gonna play as many sports as he wants for as long as he can."

2003

The Blues Go Winless and the Sun Sets on the Blues of Summer

> "As far as crowd support, I remember there being only a handful of parents at the games. But when you went to a basketball game, the stands were full; you went to a football game, and there were vehicles lining Plainsmen Field, and the whole community and school supported it. With baseball, it was pretty much just the parents there watching.
>
> —Neal Levang, Scobey Blues head coach (2003)"

PRESEASON

THERE WERE MORE CHANGES FOR THE BLUES IN 2003, as Scobey had a new head coach for the fourth consecutive year. Neal Levang (Blues 1999–2001) took over from Jake Petersen, who had moved on. Neal coached the team for what would prove to be its final season in the Montana/Alberta Class A American Legion Baseball League. I asked Neal how he had become the head coach. He said, "I came back from going to college at Havre, where [Neill] Crandell and I were playing football. We were going to work for his grandpa, Ron Tade, for the summer. I had no thought of coaching. Glenda called me and said, 'We're struggling to find someone to coach. Would you want to do it?'" Neal told her that if they couldn't find anyone else, he knew enough about baseball to be the fallback so they could play. The search was empty for another coach, so Neal told Glenda he would do it. He added, "I wasn't actively searching to be the coach."

Neal initially didn't have an assistant but soon realized he needed one. "I started coaching by myself, but in one of the first games we played in Sidney one of the players (David Leibrand) was fielding a pop fly in warmups and missed it and broke out his top two front teeth. I postponed the game to run him to the hospital since I didn't have an assistant. I then realized I needed one and twisted my good friend Neill Crandell's arm into being my assistant for the rest of the season with me."

Neal and Neill would inherit a depleted roster in 2003. The Blues were losing seven starters, six to age eligibility and one (Zach Audet) to football, as Zach had signed a letter of intent to play for Rocky Mountain College and needed to report on the first of July. There were only 10 players on the roster in 2003, and all but one—17-year-old Kyle Nelson—were 16 years old. Assistant Coach Neill Crandell remembers many games when the Blues struggled to get nine players on the field. Chauncy Handran, David Leibrand, Matt Selvig, and Chance Hammer were 16 and returned from the 2002 team that finished fourth at divisional, as they played Legion when they were 15. Completing the 2003 roster were rookie 16-year-olds Cory Graff, Tyler Thievin, Seth Nelson, Jeff Jones, and Travis Ollers.

For pitching, Chauncy Handran was the ace, with Matt Selvig, Cory Graff, Jeff Jones, and Tyler Thievin rounding out the staff. Matt Selvig and David Leibrand shared the catching duties.

REGULAR SEASON

NOT ONLY DID THE BLUES HAVE A DEPLETED ROSTER, BUT THEY also had a depleted budget and schedule, as they only played three nonconference games, all coming in a tournament hosted by the Great Falls Stallions. Neal Levang remembers a funny story about the Great Falls Stallions Tournament: the opposing coaches thought they were players because they were so young. The Blues lost their first game of the tourney to the Belgrade Bandits, then to the Tri-City Cardinals (coached by former Blue Tyler Bucklin) 11-7. I asked Tyler Bucklin (Blues 1991–94), who had started the Tri-County Cardinals program a year earlier, what it was like coaching against his former team. He said, "I don't remember a lot about the game itself, but I do remember thinking that the Blues program wasn't the same as it used to be. Tri-County was still a pretty new team, and we weren't very good yet but were still able to handle Scobey pretty easily. It seemed to me that the Blues program had lost a little of their swagger and they definitely didn't have the older talent that always seemed to guide them in the past. It was nice to beat them with my young club, but at the same time, I felt saddened by the state that the Blues were in." The Blues came close to winning their third game, losing 6-5 to the Helena Reps, with Jeff Jones taking the tough one-run loss. The Lewistown Redbirds won the tournament with a 4-0 record. One bright spot for the Blues was that Chauncy Handran was selected for the all-tournament team.

There was no 20th Annual Doc Norman Memorial Tournament in Scobey in 2003. It was just as well; the tournament had been in decline for several years. Coach Morgan Oie said in 2001 that the tournament "was a shell of what it once was." Following Doc's death in 1983, the Doc Norman Memorial Tournament was held every year beginning in 1984. It was appropriate that the year the Scobey Legion program folded, the Doc Norman Memorial Tournament was not held. It was symbolic of the end of the program.

The Blues went 0-24 in conference and were 0-27 overall. Defending state champion Glendive won the conference with a 20-2 record, followed by Glasgow at 20-4. This was the sixth consecutive year Glendive and Glasgow finished in the top two teams in the standings. Here were the final conference standings:

1. Glendive (20-2)
2. Glasgow (20-4)
3. Plentywood
4. Wolf Point (12-12)
5. Sidney (9-15)
6. Homestead (7-17)
7. Scobey (0-24, 0-27)

It was a tough way for it to end for the Blues. Coach Levang remembers "maybe a handful of parents" were at the regular season home games and the last home game.

DIVISIONAL TOURNAMENT

THE 2003 EASTERN DIVISIONAL TOURNAMENT WAS HOSTED by the Wolf Point Yellowjackets at Burke Field in Wolf Point. Here were the first-round matchups:

- Glendive (bye)
- Wolf Point (4) vs. Sidney (5)
- Plentywood (3) vs. Homestead (6)
- Glasgow (2) vs. Scobey (7)

Against Glasgow, the Blues trailed 11-3 after three innings but mounted a bit of a comeback in the top of the fourth, scoring four runs to close to 11-7. However, Glasgow responded with four runs in the bottom of the fifth and three more in the bottom of the sixth to salt the game away, and the game ended 18-7 after seven innings. Glasgow had 12 hits, and Scobey five. Tyler Thievin took the loss for Scobey. Neither team played well defensively, as Glasgow had seven errors and Scobey eight.

Sixth-seeded Homestead, who played well in the tournament, finishing third and winning the sportsmanship trophy, eliminated the Blues 12-2 in another seven-inning mercy rule, ending Scobey's final season with a 0-29 record. Chauncy Handran took the loss for Scobey on the mound. It was Chauncy's last game as a Blue—and Scobey's last game as the Blues for 13 years.

Losing to the Homestead Pioneers (based in Froid) in their last game was significant, as three Blues went to play for Homestead when the Scobey Legion program folded for the second time after the 2019 season. In the summer of 2024, three Scobey boys went to play for the Froid Cardinals, their only choice if they wanted to play Legion baseball. Legion baseball was alive in Froid in 2003 and still is as of the summer of 2024. It was symbolic that the Blues would lose their last game to a team named the "Homestead Pioneers," as the homesteaders brought the game to Daniels County in the early 1900s when baseball was the only game in town.

Second-year Coach Chad Jones's Glendive Blue Devils beat the Glasgow Reds 12-6 for the championship, with both teams advancing to the state tournament, where the Blue Devils, who had all but two starters returning from the 2002 state championship team, hoped to repeat.

I asked Coach Levang if he remembered anything about the 0-29 season that made him smile. He asked me if I asked Chauncy Handran that same question and his response, but I didn't ask Chauncy that question. He thought about it momentarily and said, "We were playing Sidney in Scobey in the second game of the doubleheader, and Matt Selvig started it. It must have been the bottom of the seventh, and we were up by a run. Crandell and I talked and said this might be our only chance of getting a win, so we let Matt try to gut it out in the seventh because he'd been there for six innings and had given up only four or five runs. Sidney started having some success, and we said, let's pull him and put Chauncy in and just try our damndest to get a win. We can't hold back anything to get a win and get these kids going. And lo and behold, they scored two runs on Chauncy to get the win. So that was our one game that I remember we had a shot at winning and we just couldn't quite make it happen."

Neal added, "And Chauncy couldn't save it. Goes on to pitch Division 1." Who can resist smiling at that irony? That's just how 0-29 seasons go. It was such a striking contrast that in the darkest hour of Scobey baseball, a sparkling, bright young star was shining in the form of 16-year-old Chauncy Handran, who had pitched a two-hitter for the Blues two years earlier when he was only 14 years old. When he was 15, after pitching a complete game against Wolf Point in a 5-1 loss, the *Wotanin Wowapi* wrote, "Handran proved to be a very bright prospect for the Blues."[16] After the Scobey Blues program folded in 2003, Chauncy played for Wolf Point in 2004 and 2005. Knowing that he went on to play baseball for Miles City Community College and then the University of Minnesota Golden Gophers, I was intrigued to hear Chauncy's baseball story, so I interviewed him. Here is that interview:

Joe: "When you think about playing for the Scobey Blues, what do you remember most about the experience?"

Chauncy: "I was pretty young and it was quite the dichotomy 2002 versus 2003. In 2002, we were actually decent, well-coached by Jake, and competed in almost every game. I will never forget the road trips, particularly going to Havre, where we stayed at the Armory. The young guys had to bear crawl to the bathroom so we wouldn't get shot by the air guns. Hilarious! 2003 was a different story, not winning a game and not competing at all. It was emotional, and it became normal to lose; it was terrible."

Joe: "The last season in 2003 was rough for the Blues. Although the team struggled, what stands out about that season when you think about it?"

Chauncy: "Going 0-30 (or whatever it was) was embarrassing. It was as though we showed up to lose every game. No one had expectations, and it was a waste of a summer of baseball."

Joe: "What was your feeling when you learned there would be no Scobey Blues team in 2004?"

Chauncy: "After the 2003 season, unfortunately, it was almost a relief that we weren't going to have a team. It was so challenging fielding teams that were competitive in 2003-04 that it was honestly a breath of fresh air being able to move on from it."

Joe: "What was your process for finding another team to play for? How did it happen that you became a Wolf Point Yellowjacket?"

Chauncy: "Going to Wolf Point was a no-brainer, but it was not an easy one. Based on the guidelines/rules I was supposed to play for Plentywood based on the distance of Scobey to Plentywood versus to Wolf Point. Two things were important in me going to Wolf Point: Number one was that my aunt and uncle owned a candy/tobacco distribution company (Hi-Line Wholesale) so that I would have a summer job and could live with them; the second was Jack Sprague. He was a tremendous coach that I had known from the prior seasons. I knew he was someone I wanted to learn from (no one loves baseball more than that man) and would teach me a *ton* about the game. Playing for the Yellowjackets was great and a relief from the prior year of 2003."

Joe: "What was the adjustment you went through integrating with the Yellowjackets coach and team? Was it difficult? Was it natural?"

Chauncy: "Playing for Wolf Point was an easy transition. The guys took me in immediately. Being able to live there for the entire summer, I was able to really get to know them, and they became some of my best friends. In fact, Kyle Vine was my roommate at MCC during my first year."

Joe: "As you continued your Legion career with the Yellowjackets in 2004 and 2005, did you miss donning the Scobey Blues uniform?"

Chauncy: "Not being able to play for Scobey certainly crossed my mind on occasion, but being able to play at a high level for the Yellowjackets eased that for sure."

Joe: "What was your experience playing for the Yellowjackets in 2004 and your first state tournament in 2005?"

Chauncy: "I didn't pitch that much in '04 and started to pitch some in '05. My greatest memories of 2005 were my ups and downs learning how to pitch. (I was very, very raw; Sprague taught me a *ton*.) In fact, I think I had two pitches (a fastball, a faster fastball, and a weak slider), haha. Beating

Glendive at Glendive and striking out some guys from the Bitterroot Red Sox at State were memorable. Three of the Bitterroot guys ended up being my teammates at MCC!!"

Joe: "Following your Legion career, you played at Miles City Community College (MCC) and the University of Minnesota. What do you remember most about your experience playing baseball at the collegiate level?"

Chauncy: "I was torn to play baseball in college, actually! I really wanted to play football and had a preferred spot at MSU. It wasn't until Coach Sprague had a sit-down with me that he helped me realize I could potentially go far in baseball, perhaps even play professionally. After much discussion with family, friends, and coaches, I committed extremely late to MCC. (I think it was late spring, right before summer.) I can recall Rob Bishop (MCC coach) being pretty damn happy. After my second year at MCC, I had a chance to sign with the Rockies after an early summer tryout in Denver. After this tryout and playing summer baseball in Kansas (with coach Chad Jones – Glendive coach), I had a ton of D1 offers. The one that made the most sense was Minnesota, as it was nearest to home and had a very strong baseball program. I was at another junction in decision-making, but ultimately, after much deliberation, I decided to forgo playing with the Rockies and signed with Minnesota. This ended up being a great decision as I knew I was beginning to consider medical school."

Chauncy Handran of the University of Minnesota pitches against Baylor in the NCAA men's college baseball tournament regional in Baton Rouge, Louisiana, in 2009. *AP photo.*

Joe: "Do you remember the last game you played as a Scobey Blue? When you left the field, did you know that that was it for the Blues?"

Chauncy: "I don't recall the last game as a Blue. But I did consider 2003 the end of the Blues."

STATE TOURNAMENT

THE BITTERROOT RED SOX—ONE STATE CHAMPIONSHIP AWAY from an undisputed dynasty—hosted the 2003 Montana/Alberta State Class A State Tournament on their home field, Vester Wilson Athletic Field, in Hamilton, Montana. According to many pre-tourney reviews, there was no clear favorite to win the tournament. Bitterroot Bucs Manager Mitch Messer said, "I honestly think all 11 teams could win this tournament." The host Red Sox (47-19) tied for the conference championship with the Bitterroot Bucs but finished sixth at the western divisional tournament—so what; they were automatically in as host. John Kasper of the *Missoulian* wrote that they "shouldn't be taken lightly. They've been to State every year since 1995 and have won four of the last six state titles."[17] Homefield advantage would also favor the Red Sox, as Bitterroot co-manager Dan Wolsky said, "We think being at our home park and sleeping on our own beds and having the huge crowds will help."

Although there was no clearcut favorite, Chad Jones's defending champion Glendive Blue Devils, champions

Chauncy Handran of the University of Golden Gophers hanging with the kids at Twinsfest in 2009. At that point in the season, Chauncy was 3-1 with a 3.00 ERA. *Minnesota Star Tribune photo, David Joles.*

from the east, were mentioned, as all but two starters were returning from the state championship team. Western division champion Mission Valley was considered in the hunt, as was the second-place finisher, the Bitterroot Bucs. Havre was also up there, another perennial state championship contender and third-place finisher at State the year before. Coach Williams's northern division championship team was strong again, led by Daine Solomon, who was hitting .500, had belted 14 home runs, and driven in 83 runs. That's insane. Speedster Steve Heberly, who set an all-class record in the 100-meter dash earlier that spring, was batting .400. Power and speed in two players. A bit of a dark horse but very capable were the Billings Cardinals, 40-10, and southern division champions.

If the Red Sox won, it would mark their fifth state championship in seven years. That could safely be labeled a dynasty, the likes of which the Montana State Class A/B Legion had not seen since Scobey's five consecutive state championships from 1976 and 1980, winning again in 1982 for their sixth in seven years.

Number-one seeds Mission Valley and Glendive were paired against each other in their first game. Another questionable seeding in a state tournament, but such was the way of things in an 11-team tournament. Glendive's Greg Ford pitched Glendive to an 8-1 first-round win, hurling a four-hitter and striking out 21 Mariners, a record for a nine-inning game at the State A/B Tournament. Jim LeProwse (Blues 1983–85) holds the record for an extra-inning game, striking out 23 Northstars in 12 innings in Scobey's stunning 5-4 upset of Havre in 16 innings in the first round of the 1985 State Tournament in Scobey. At the State AA/A level, Havre's Dave Fanning holds the record as he struck out 25 Royals in 12 innings at the 1971 State A Tournament in Billings. That was the week after he outdueled Terry Puckett 1-0 in the undefeated semifinal at the State Class B Tournament in Scobey.

The story of this tournament was the strength of Class A Legion baseball in the Bitterroot Valley in Ravalli County, as the Red Sox and the Bucs showed the state of Montana where the epicenter of baseball was in 2003. The host Bitterroot Red Sox did not receive a first-round bye as host. They won their first game by pounding Fort Macleod 17-1 but lost to the Billings Cardinals 11-3 in their second game. What happened next was astounding, historical, and a testament to the depth of the Bitterroot Red Sox—and the ridiculousness of an 11-team tournament. After losing to the Cardinals, the Red Sox won *seven* consecutive do-or-die games—*eight* total wins for the tournament—to win their fifth state championship in seven years on the dirt route.

They beat seven of the 10 other teams in the tournament (almost playing a round-robin), including two wins over the Bitterroot Bucs: 8-7 in a walk-off in 10 innings and 6-3 in the championship games. The Red Sox and Bucs facing each other in the state championship was the first in the 20-year history of the two teams from Bitterroot Valley.

Head Coach Jesse Wilson said of his team's historic run, "We were on a tremendous roll. You see teams come through the loser's bracket and they're a little beat up and tired. Our kids worked. They were fresh and they were ready to play. They were confident that they were going to win every game."

On the same year the Scobey Legion program folded, the Scobey Blues, owners of a Legion baseball dynasty during the golden age of Scobey baseball, tip their hats to Coach Jesse Wilson and the Bitterroot Red Sox, the creators of a new one. The cycle was complete.

Brett Henry of the Red Sox was named MVP, as he pitched the tournament's only shutout, hit .500, and had four homers. Kevin Locken of the Red Sox was named the offensive MVP, hitting .516 and five home runs.

After Greg Ford's four-hit, 21-strikeout gem against Mission Valley, Glendive lost their next two games, 8-6, to the Billings Cardinals, and then were eliminated by the Dillon Cubs 5-3. The Cubs chased Glendive starting pitcher Greg Ford—who was consistently clocked at 92 mph against Mission Valley—in the fourth inning after six hits, a walk, and a hit batter. Ford's fastball against the Cubs was in the low 80s. But Chad Jones and the Blue Devils would be back in 2004, bringing home the last state championship for the former eastern division and Glendive's fourth overall.

Glasgow was eliminated in two games.

Coach Randy Rice of Plentywood was named Montana/Alberta Class A Legion Coach of the Year for his fine work with the Athletics that year, leading them to third place with a 14-8 record behind Glendive and Glasgow in the standings. That's quite an honor for a coach.

NORTHWEST REGIONAL

THE 2003 NORTHWEST PACIFIC REGIONAL WAS HOSTED BY Shadle Park, Washington, in Spokane, Washington. On his approach to the regional, Bitterroot Red Sox Head Coach Jesse Wilson said, "Nobody wants to go there and be embarrassed. We want to win this tournament. The regional tournament, that's like our World Series. We take that very seriously. It's as far as we can possibly advance."

The Red Sox did not win it, but they certainly did not embarrass themselves, winning three games to finish in third place.

EXTRA INNINGS

AT THE TIME OF *THE BLUES OF SUMMER* PUBLICATION, THE Bitterroot Red Sox are tied with Scobey for the most state championships (eight) in Montana/Alberta State Class A/B American Legion history, as the Red Sox won three consecutive state championships between 2015 and 2017 to add to their previous five. No doubt their ninth will be coming sometime soon. Maybe the Blues will see the Red Sox on the Field of Dreams in the far future? Perhaps it could be "settled" there. That would be fun—and competitive.

The Laurel Dodgers broke Scobey's record for the most Class A/B state championships when they won their ninth state championship in 2013.

The Havre Northstars are fourth in total state Class A/B championships with seven, their last coming in 1999 when Coach Williams led them to the title, his second as a coach (1984 as assistant to Tom Nielson and 1999 as head coach), and he had two as a player (1968 and 1970). Mickey might be the only player/coach with two titles as a player and two as a coach with the same team. Scobey's two dramatic one-run wins over Havre in the championship games in the 1969 State Tournament in Scobey prevented Havre from winning five consecutive state championships, as Havre won in 1968 and 1970–72.

Ironically, in the same school year that the Scobey Blues program went winless and was at its bottom, the Scobey football program won its third state championship and was at its zenith. In the fall of 2002, first-year head coach Jon Baker and the Spartans pummeled the top-ranked Longhorns 50-6 at Plainsmen Field in Scobey, ending Wibaux's 34-game winning streak. (Coach Baker had slipped into the head coaching job after Larry Henderson had moved to coach Plentywood.) The win avenged an earlier-season 26-14 loss to Wibaux and a 42-30 loss to them in the 2001 state championship, also at Scobey. Jude Chabot ran for 146 yards and two touchdowns, and quarterback Zach Audet ran for 114 yards and three touchdowns and threw another to Matt Selvig to lead the Spartans. Eric Haddenhorst also scored a touchdown for Scobey.

In our interview, Coach Chad Jones talked about his pitcher, Greg Ford, who struck out 21 Mariners in Glendive's 8-1 win over Mission Valley. He said, "Believe it or not, Greg was as high as 95 on the gun and sat probably about 88 to 91. He was just one of those big, strong farm kids from Wibaux who just had God-given ability. God blessed his arm, and he was able to throw it." While talking about Wibaux pitchers, Coach Jones also mentioned Joe Bakken. "He was just a natural, thin, good athlete who probably threw mid-to-upper 80s. I was blessed with a pretty good pitching staff from 2002 to 2004." Chase Downs from Lindsay was another small-town boy with big-time pitching skills on Chad's staff those three years. Chase won the state championship game in 2002 as a 16-year-old.

A dark cloud hung over Montana American Legion Baseball at the state tournament in 2003, as two recent deaths—one of an old coaching legend and one of a young Legion player—happened a week apart just before the tournament. The cloud was darkest over Billings and Miles City. Legendary Billings Royals Coach Ed Bayne passed away two weeks before the first game of the tournament, and a week later, 18-year-old Mavericks pitcher Brandon Patch died after being struck in the head by a line drive in a Senators-Mavericks game at Kindrick Legion Field in Helena. Members of the Helena Senators traveled to Denton Field at Miles City to attend Brandon's funeral three days later. The incident fueled the debate about "hot bats" and whether metal is more dangerous than wood.

Second-year Billings Cardinals head coach Brian Smith felt the weight of both deaths but saw some light in the darkness. "To have somebody die so young on the baseball field, it's terrible. All the events that have happened in the last 11 days with Legion Baseball, it's a real upbeat thing that we can go on and do something positive and show that regardless of what has happened, other people's contributions to Legion Baseball will go on." Coach Smith knew his team was representing Billings baseball at the State Class A Tournament and felt the moment's gravity. He said, "At state tournament time, everything changes. You realize that you're really playing for something when you're there. Anybody who can get there, it's a credit to that program."[18]

In an article titled "Longtime Legion coach Bayne passes away," *Gazette* sportswriter Ed West wrote, "Bayne coached in the [Billings Legion] program for nearly 30 years. He first took over as head coach in 1948 and then served as an assistant on state championship teams in 1950 and '51. He became the head coach again in 1952 and led Billings to two decades of unprecedented success. From 1952-73, Bayne's teams won 18 state championships, including 14 in a row (1954-67), and advanced to the Legion World Series four times."[19]

The last year Ed Bayne coached the Billings Royals to a World Series was 1962. Fast forward 62 years to 2024, when the Billings Scarlets and Kade Vatnsdal—grandson of Phil Audet, who pitched Scobey to a 4-3 win over the Billings

The Last Years

Kade Vatnsdal of the Billings Scarlets makes an off-balance throw to first base. *Family photo*

Scarlets at Cobb Field in 1966—won the Northwest Region 7 by defeating Eugene (Oregon) 5-4 and 7-0 at Dehler Park. The Scarlets had come back through the dirt route to win five consecutive games after losing their first game of the tournament. Kade pitched the final two innings of the championship game as Papa Phil proudly watched from the Dehler Park stands, remembering when he had pitched against the Scarlets at Cobb Field in 1966. The passion for the game had been passed down to the third generation. At the time of *The Blues of Summer* publication, Kade will be playing in his final season with the Scarlets.

Ed Bayne's son, Ed Bayne Jr., was the first coach for the Scarlets when they were a B team and was the coach when they received their nickname. Ed Bayne Jr. said, "Dad named them [the Scarlets]. He didn't like the kids being called the B squad. The Royals and Scarlets' names were chosen because the monikers were 'patriotic.'" The Scarlets split off from the Royals as a second upper-level Billings team after the 1974 season. (The 1974 Scarlets won the eastern division Class B championship in Scobey and the State Class B championship in Havre that year. During the 13 years from 1968 to 1980, the Scarlets were the only team other than Scobey and Havre to win the State Class B championship.)

Following the regional championship game, *Gazette* Sports Editor John Letasky interviewed Ed Bayne Jr. and Jack Bayne, sons of legendary former Billings Post 4 coach Ed Bayne, and wrote an article in *406 MT Sports* titled "Sons: Legendary coach Ed Bayne is 'jumping up and down in heaven' celebrating Scarlets' regional title."[20] Naturally, the Bayne brothers were emotional. "'He's ecstatic,' said Ed Bayne Jr., as he wiped away a tear, when asked what his father would be feeling after the Scarlets came back from a first-round loss to win five straight, including two over previously undefeated Eugene on Sunday. 'Dad is in heaven jumping up and down.'"[21]

Jack Bayne added, "He's jumping up there (in heaven) right now. He'd be so proud and beaming from ear to ear. He is proud."[22]

In the interview, Ed Bayne Jr. said Kade Vatnsdal was his nephew through his wife's side of the family. "I'm really happy for him, just because he's a good kid," said Bayne Jr. "We text back and forth. He's an awfully good kid and a competitor."[23]

Kade is the son of Tracy Vatnsdal (assistant coach for the Blues in 1996) and Arlee Audet of Scobey. (Yes, Kade wears Scarlet red, but his blood is Scobey blue.) I asked Tracy Vatnsdal how Kade was related to Ed Bayne Jr. He said, "That is a funny story. Ed says because Phil and Myrna (French) Ferestad are together that makes us all family since his wife Diane was a Ferestad and calls Kade his nephew. So, really, he isn't, but Ed has taken Kade under his wing and calls and texts Kade weekly to see how baseball and his grades are doing at Dickinson State. We are really good family friends."

Kirk Dehler, son of Jon Dehler, pitched for the Billings Cardinals at the 2003 State Class A Tournament in Hamilton, hurling two and one-third innings of hitless relief against Glendive to get the save in the Cardinals' 8-6 win over the Blue Devils. Dehler Park in Billings was named by Billings businessman Jon Dehler, who purchased the naming rights in 2007 to honor his father, Billy Joe Dehler. Dehler Park opened in 2008, replacing Cobb Field.

2003
The End of an Era

> *Baseball breaks your heart. It is designed to break your heart. The game begins in the spring, when everything else begins again, and it blossoms in the summer, filling the afternoons and evenings, and then as soon as the chill rains come, it stops and leaves you to face the fall all alone. You count on it, rely on it to buffer the passage of time, to keep the memory of sunshine and high skies alive, and then just when the days are all twilight, when you need it most, it stops.*
>
> —**A. Bartlett Giamatti, Take Time for Paradise: Americans and Their Games, 1989**

WHAT HAPPENED?

For the first time in 49 years (1955), Scobey did not field an American Legion team in 2004. A long 12-year winter was setting in for the Scobey American Legion program, as the Blues were not revived again until 2016. Baseball in the county continued at the Little League and Babe Ruth levels but not American Legion.

For those of us who share a passion for baseball and have all the memories of playing, coaching, umpiring, or watching baseball in northeastern Montana as children, adolescents, and adults, it was difficult to accept the demise of the Scobey Legion program. Many people I interviewed commented on this. Kirby Halvorson said, "When the program died, it hit me like it was death in the family." Craig Price, head coach of the Richland County Patriots from 1976 to 1978 and team manager in the years to follow, said, "The Scobey Blues were the trademark team of eastern Montana, so when that fell off, that was hard for all of us to take because when one of the teams falls off in our area, that's not good for baseball. Wolf Point also had its struggles. When Scobey lost their team, and Wolf Point couldn't field a team, that was a hard thing for baseball in eastern Montana."

The Blues of Summer celebrates the memory of one of the most successful American Legion Baseball programs in Montana American Legion Baseball history but also tells the story of how—and why—the illustrious program fell into decline and eventually folded. A steep performance drop is evident in the final years of Scobey Legion baseball. Learning the causes of that decline helps to understand why the program was so successful in its heyday because, in many cases, they are the flip side of the same coin: for every reason for the decline, the opposite held for the ascent.

From the perspective of history, the decline and fall of the Blues program was inevitable. I began the story of *The Blues of Summer* in the early 1900s when the homesteaders brought the game to northeastern Montana because, in those early days, baseball was the only game in town (and on the farms and ranches), but the enormous popularity of the game did not survive the multiple generations—and population decline—in Daniels County. Notably, baseball's popularity in America declined during the same period; Daniels County was simply a microcosm of a national trend. The decline in the popularity of baseball and population in Daniels County was a one-two punch that knocked out Legion baseball.

Declining popularity and population were undoubtedly two of the causes of the decline of the Blues; however, it was more complicated than that. Many other factors contributed. But one word is at the root of the decline: passion. The county-wide passion for baseball was there initially and in the middle, but not in the end. That is not a judgment but an observation. And there was nothing unique about Daniels County—what happened in Daniels County happened in our nation. In a 1948 Gallup poll, 39% of Americans identified baseball as their favorite sport; football was second at 17%; basketball was 10%.[24] In the latest Gallup poll in 2024, football was number one at 41%, baseball at 10%, and basketball at 9%. In the 18–29-year-old age group, only 5% identified baseball as their favorite sport.[25]

As an example of how popular baseball was in Scobey in 1948 when the first Gallup poll was taken, there were three flavors of baseball: high school (the Spartans), Junior American Legion (the Legionnaires), and the town team (the Plainsmen). In 1949, 45 boys from Scobey High School signed up to play high school baseball for Bill Cullen.

In our discussion about the decline of Scobey baseball, Morgan Oie, who played for the Blues from 1992 to 1995 and coached in 2001, said, "To this day, I meet people around the state and am asked what happened. Scobey was such a baseball town. I still don't have an answer. A lot of things changed." Kirby Halvorson had the same question. "I've always wondered why," he said. "Disinterest? Sport specialization with mandatory camps, lifting, etc.? Other?" Terry Farver, who was there when the second iteration of the Blues were unable to field a team in 2020, said, "Just couldn't talk the kids into playing, for the life of me, I can't tell you why."

"I still don't have an answer."

"I've always wondered why."

"I can't tell you why."

I will attempt to answer Morgan's, Kirby's, and Terry's questions. Based on interviews, research, and analysis, here is my take on the nine (one for each inning of a baseball game) major causes of the fall of the Scobey Blues:

The Decrease in Population in Northeastern Montana

As a result, the pipeline of players coming from former Little League and Babe Ruth programs in Peerless, Flaxville, Opheim, and Outlook had dried up, and fewer players were playing Little League and Babe Ruth in Scobey, too. Consequently, there was less talent to draw from across Valley, Daniels, and Sheridan Counties. As the population was dwindling, the high schools where the Legion players came from eventually closed: Outlook High School (2005), Flaxville (2006), and Peerless (2009). Flaxville had one student in high school when it closed in 2006; Peerless had 11 in 2009. The current enrollment at Opheim High School for the 2024-25 school year is four students. These high schools were the "farm clubs" (literally) for Scobey Blues baseball.

Dick Puckett from Peerless started playing for Scobey in 1965. Since Doc started coaching in Scobey in 1959, he had been trying unsuccessfully for almost a decade to get the Flaxville players to come to play in Scobey, but Flaxville continued to field Legion teams through 1967. The first all-Daniels County Legion baseball team in Scobey was formed in 1968 when players from Scobey, Flaxville, and Peerless congregated on the team. Doc's first state championship followed in 1969. The 1991 state tournament team Derek Solberg played on had players from five towns and three counties. It was always the "Daniels County" or "Daniels-Valley" County Blues who were competitive in state tournaments, and the teams in the 1990s could have been called the "Tri-County" Blues when the Bucklins from Outlook joined the team. When the farm clubs from the smaller towns in northeastern Montana dried up, the program could not sustain itself.

Lack of Interest in Playing Scobey Blues Legion Baseball

Several players from the 2000 team commented on this. Neill Crandell said, "[Tyler] Pittenger traveled from the Opheim area every day to practice and play. There were other talented guys around, but they didn't seem to want to come to play in Scobey compared to the teams we saw in the heyday that had players from the surrounding towns." Cory Cromwell added, "Our 15-year-old All-Star team was loaded; if we would have had those guys join the Legion team, we could have been as good or better."

Multisport Athletes Specializing in Their "Chosen" Sport During the Summer

During the heyday of Scobey Legion baseball, all the players were multisport athletes, but baseball was the priority in the summer. Kevin McElvaney, a tremendous all-around athlete on the 2000–02 teams, said, "We had a good time, but it [baseball] wasn't as serious for most of us as the other sports we played." Fast-forwarding to the year 2020 and the Blues 2.0 (2016–19), Terry Farver experienced the same issue, but this time, basketball trumped baseball during the summer months. When putting the schedule together for the 2020 season, Terry said, "We couldn't field a team. I was trying to put that '20 team and schedule together, but too many kids wanted to play basketball instead. [My son] Martin was doing summer basketball in June, too; I just scheduled around it in June and did more games in July. Just couldn't talk the kids into playing; for the life of me, I can't tell you why."

Success Breeds Success

The Scobey Legion teams that won eight state championships between the years 1969 and 1982 had the best baseball players in Daniels County on them. Good athletes are attracted to good coaches, and Doc attracted (and recruited) the best. The kids coming up saw the packed grandstands and the state tournaments hosted in Scobey and watched them win state championships; they wanted to be on the field someday to do the same thing. I was one of those kids. I watched Scobey win two state championships in Scobey (1969 and 1973), then played on four (1976–79). I wanted to be a Scobey Blue from the moment I first saw them play. They were the best. Doc was the best. The roar of the Scobey crowd on a big play at State was electric.

The Scobey Blues American Legion Budget was Declining

AS A RESULT, THE NUMBER OF REGULAR-SEASON GAMES WAS reduced. The teams in the 1990s played well over 50 games a year, including traveling to several statewide tournaments, but the 2003 team only played a 27-game regular season schedule. Kevin McElvaney (Blues 2000–02) said, "We definitely didn't have the budget the teams in the 1990s (like my brother's teams) had, and it showed by how many games we played or tournaments we went to." Cory Cromwell added, "We didn't have much of a budget to travel. I do remember playing in Poplar a few times. Pretty chippy."

On the flip side, when Doc Norman ran the program, he funded a large portion of the program out of his personal coffers. Charlie Mueller (Blues 1960–63) said, "The years we played for Doc, we were very blessed to have all that we wanted throughout our career. Our budget was pretty much substantially supported by him. How blessed we were!" How blessed indeed. Following the state championship game against Laurel in Scobey in 1979, I had a conversation on Scobey Main Street with some Laurel Dodgers. They talked about how many bats we had—including wooden bats—outside our dugout. "Wow, you guys have all those bats," they said, adding that they had only two or three aluminum bats for the entire team to share. Part of Scobey American Legion Baseball's success was the personal financial resources Doc shared with the team. As Larry Bowler used to say, "Doc ran a champagne program on a beer budget." Doc paid for the champagne.

Lack of Continuity in the Coaching Position

THIS PHENOMENON WAS REFERRED TO AS A "MERRY-GO-ROUND of coaches" by Kelly Norman, and it led to the loss of culture and made it difficult to build a program. The final four years of Scobey's program (2000–2003) saw four different head coaches. In many cases, it can take years for a coach to build a successful program. In Scobey, for example, Doc Norman started coaching in 1959 but didn't win his first state championship until his 10th season of coaching in 1969. He then led the Blues to seven more after that, creating a dynasty. Coach Lekvold had his best season (third at State) in his eighth season as head coach in 1990, a year before he stepped down in 1991. Coach Meyer's best season was his fifth and last season in 1996 when the Blues finished third at State again. All the players I've interviewed have generally positive comments about their coaches, but building a program without continuity is difficult.

Coaching continuity was also missed at the "farm clubs," as Dad coached Peerless Peewee, Little League, and Babe Ruth in the late 1950s through 1976, Andy Stolen from Glentana was Dad's assistant and pitching coach in the early 1970s. In Flaxville, Mike Gunderson (Blues 1973–75) remembers the Miller family. "Joe Miller and his wife Marian, who was the 'Marge' equivalent for us Flaxville kids, ran that successful program in much of the 1960s and '70s, which turned out many Blues players. Doc Miller, and the rest of the seven brothers were also active in the program." Dallas Gaines coached the Flaxville Legion team in the 1960s, so he developed players at that level, like Randy Legare, Jack and Don Higgins, and the Miller brothers, who came to Scobey to play in 1968 and helped Scobey win its first state tournament in 1969. Don Tryan also developed many Flaxville players who came to play in Scobey in the late 1970s and early 1980s. The pipeline in Daniels and Valley Counties was flowing with baseball players then. Dad and Andy Stolen were running them off an assembly line in Peerless and Opheim, and the Flaxville coaches were doing the same in Flaxville.

Regarding continuity in the coaching position, it's hard to resist comparing how the Scobey-Peerless football program and the Scobey American Legion Baseball program were moving in opposite directions in the late 1990s. Coach Henderson required time to build his football program, too. He started coaching football at Scobey in the fall of 1985, and Scobey's first appearance in a state final was in 1989. Scobey-Peerless Co-Op in football began in 1990, and his first state championship came with Scobey-Peerless in his 11th year as head coach in 1995 and repeated as champs in 1996. Like Doc's Legion baseball program in 1968—when the first all-county team combined with players from Scobey, Peerless, and Flaxville—Scobey's football program benefited from the athletes from Peerless when the co-op began in 1990.

Basketball is another sport where Scobey is a perennial state tournament contender. Jason Wolfe, now in his 23rd year coaching the Scobey High School boys' basketball Spartans, has led Scobey to eight State C tournaments, winning three (2011, 2020, and 2021) and third in 2017 and 2019. Jason said, "I always hoped that we could build a basketball legacy that would compare to what the Scobey Blues of the '70s and '80s were!" He has. And it took time.

Speaking of continuity in coaching, Jack Higgins from Flaxville, who batted leadoff and was the center fielder on Doc's first state championship team in 1969, said, "I think the most important reason for much of the sporting success in Daniels County was Doc Norman. He taught us how to win and to be excited about being on a winning team. I think this started with the 1969 State championship and carried over to many more State baseball championships, plus this winning mentality carried over to the winning teams in basketball and football. I believe this 'taught us how to win' carried over to players and coaches over the years in several generations and was the single most important reason for sports success in Daniels County. Winning is contagious." Dan Wolfe, who was the catcher on the 1969 state championship team and drove in the winning run in the championship game, said, "There's something to be said about the first one in 1969; it kind of opens up like floodgates and shows everybody the thing can be done." Amen, Jack and Dan.

Scobey Stopped Hosting State Tournaments

BETWEEN 1969 AND 1985, SCOBEY HOSTED SEVEN STATE tournaments (1969, 1971, 1973, 1975, 1977, 1979, and 1985). Volunteers from the entire community of Scobey and Legion Post 56 were involved in hosting those state tournaments, but Marge Norman was the chief of staff for all of them. The Scobey Legion program missed Marge as much as Doc. Of the seven state tournaments Scobey hosted, the Blues won four (1969, 1973, 1977, and 1979).

Home-field advantage was a contributing factor in those championships. The Glasgow Reds hosting the 2000 State Tournament was a good example of how the home field can help. The Reds won four games on their home field to take second place at State after finishing fifth at Divisional a week earlier. In an article previewing the 2000 State Tournament, *Glasgow Courier* sportswriter Gregg Fromdahl captured it. "The Reds have an excellent chance of winning this tournament. Home-field advantage benefits the Reds in more ways than just playing on their home field. The Reds have no traveling to do; they get to sleep in their own beds and should have massive fan support."[26] Of course, the home-field advantage will not win you a championship; teams do that. For example, the home field could not help the Reds overcome the powerful Bitterroot Red Sox, who outscored them 23-1 in two games.

Baseball is the Ultimate Technique Sport

BASEBALL, MORE THAN ANY OTHER SPORT, IS A TECHNIQUE sport. Pitching, hitting, and fielding take several years to learn and a career to master. You can't "trick" baseball and pick it up in a year or two and be good. Michael Jordan taught us that.[*] (But Bo knows baseball.)[†] Natural athletic ability can only take you so far in any sport, but of all sports, baseball requires technique. Martin Farver (Blues 2016–19)—a talented four-sport athlete—put it best: "Baseball doesn't care about your athleticism." Or, as Yogi Berra said, "Baseball is 90 percent mental and the other half is physical."

Many baseball pundits say, "It's hard to hit a baseball." That's true—but it's also hard to pitch one. Pitching was the one area that suffered the most in the last years of the program. The latter Blues teams could always hit and score runs, were fast and could steal bases, and their fielding was generally on par with the opposition, but the pitching depth was not there. In a 1981 interview with Doc Norman titled "Scobey loses a doctor but keeps a coach," written by *Billings Gazette* sportswriter Dennis Gaub, Doc said, "If there's a secret to our success, it's that we have had top-notch batteries over the years. I think that's the single most important thing, the catching and pitching, that's kept us in business."[27]

Baseball is Predominately a Family Sport

WE FINISH WHERE WE STARTED—WITH THE HOMESTEADERS and their passion for the game. However, as was the case for America's favorite pastime, Daniels County's favorite pastime survived families but not the generations.

When I asked the coaches about their take on the decline in the end, one coach said, "A lot of those guys didn't have parents who were really into baseball, so it was an afterthought for them, and that's the way they approached it, sadly. The guys I played with, for the most part, all had dads who were also big baseball guys."

Another coach said, "I would say the biggest change was—and I don't want this to sound negative—enthusiasm from the community. The shift was going away from baseball at that time."

A third coach added, "There just was zero support from the community for baseball versus you go to a basketball game, the crowds were, you know, the stands were full. You

---

[*] In 1994, Michael Jordan played for the Birmingham Barons, a Double-A minor league affiliate of the Chicago White Sox, after his first retirement from professional basketball in 1993.

[†] "Bo Knows" was an advertising campaign for Nike cross-training shoes that ran in 1989 and 1990 featuring professional baseball and American football player Bo Jackson. Jackson was the first athlete in the modern era to play professional baseball and football in the same year.

went to a football game; there were vehicles lining Plainsmen Field. There was just the whole community support and school support, but not for baseball. It was pretty much just the parents there watching and that was about it; it was the opposite. Some of the parents wouldn't even go, so it was that lack of support."

Kelly Norman (Blues 1976–80) said, "A lot of kids then didn't have ties to baseball, and they didn't have Tiny [Puckett] and Dad coaching Little League on up. There was the loss of baseball culture."

Terry Farver, frustrated at being unable to assemble a team for his son Martin's final season in 2020, said, "Maybe [it was] dads that didn't play baseball as kids, so they don't know what they are missing."

Kirby Halvorson (Blues 1976–1980) said, "Sidney's program died a few years ago and was resurrected. We were losing kids for multiple reasons. Having the high school baseball program has sparked some interest." But there was plenty of "interest" in baseball in Sidney when Craig Price coached the Richland County Patriots in the late 1970s. In my interview with Craig, he said, "There was a kid named Jerry Lassie from Fairview who came into play with me and the Legion team. They had a big farm, an irrigated farm, but I'll tell you what, that kid never missed a practice because his dad was a baseball enthusiast. He wanted to let Jerry have that same experience he had as a boy. Every day, they would get up early, get their work done, and then be at baseball practice. There was a lot of that sort of thing for a basis for a program. I had some athletes later on out of Lambert, the Irigoins. Same situation. They were farm kids, but their dads had played ball, and they wanted their sons to play ball, so they came in and played. It was that rich history from the past."

The Last Years

SECTION NOTES

1. Mark Falcon, "Reds Second in State Legion Tourney," *Glasgow Courier*, August 10, 2000.
2. Mark Falcon, "End of an Era," *Glasgow Courier*, August 10, 2000.
3. "Blues to Host Rest of League in Tournament," *Daniels County Leader*, July 26, 2001.
4. "Blues Finish with 15-25 Record, Glendive, Wolf Point Advance," *Daniels County Leader*, August 2, 2001.
5. Ibid.
6. Ibid.
7. Ibid.
8. Ibid.
9. "Yellowjackets open long-awaited season," *Wotanin Wowapi*, May 30, 2002.
10. "Blues Play Well to Move From Seventh Seed to Finish Fourth," *Daniels County Leader*, August 1, 2002.
11. Ibid.
12. Ibid.
13. Ibid.
14. "Glendive 'Downs' Sox," *Billings Gazette*, August 8, 2002.
15. Dennis Gaub, "Scobey loses a doctor but keeps a coach," *Billings Gazette*, June 10, 1981.
16. "Yellowjackets open season," *Wotanin Wowapi*.
17. John Kasper, "Mission Valley gets tough draw at state tourney," *Missoulian*, August 1, 2003.
18. "Cardinals look to stay hot against State A tourney foes," *Billings Gazette*, August 1, 2003.
19. Ed West, "Longtime Legion coach Bayne passes away," *Billings Gazette*, July 21, 2003.
20. John Letasky, "Sons: Legendary coach Ed Bayne is 'jumping up and down in heaven' celebrating Scarlets' regional title," *406 MT Sports*, August 11, 2024.
21. Ibid.
22. Ibid.
23. Ibid.
24. Jeffrey M. Jones, "Football Retains Dominant Position as Favorite U.S. Sport," *GALLUP News*, February 7, 2024.
25. Ibid.
26. Gregg Fromdahl, "Reds get ready for State Tournament," *Glasgow Courier*, July 27, 2000.
27. Gaub, "Scobey loses doctor."

The Long Wi...
2004 – 2015

1900 – 1924
The Homesteaders
and Early Town Teams

1930 – 1945
The Sons of
the Pioneers

1957 – 1968
The Baseball
Renaissance

*The Scobey
Giants*
1925 – 1929

*Baseball is Back
in Daniels County*
1946 – 1956

*The D...
Cham...*
1969 – ...

ter

| 1983 – 1991 | 1998 – 2003 | 2016 – 2019 |
| The Don Lekvold Era | The Last Years | The Revival |

rman hip Era | The Ken Meyer/Mike Lee Era 1992 – 1997 | | The Froid Bulls 2020 – 2024

2004–2015

A Long Montana Winter Sets in for Scobey American Legion Baseball

WHILE AMERICAN LEGION BASEBALL DID NOT continue in Scobey from 2004 to 2015, Little League and Babe Ruth baseball were still being played in Daniels County, so the youngsters were still getting to play America's favorite pastime (I'm still going to call it that) and make some lifelong memories. At the end of the day, baseball is fun—how competitive and serious it is taken is the player's choice. Some Scobey boys who were serious about their game and took it beyond Babe Ruth were players like Mike Crandell, who followed in Chauncy Handran's footsteps and played for Jack Sprague and the Yellowjackets in Wolf Point. Mike said, "I went to play for Wolf Point when I got to Legion. I went alone for the first couple of summers, and then Kray Buer and Drew Baldry came down to play as well. Cole Cook, I believe, went to play for Plentywood. He would've graduated high school in 2006."

Jack Sprague, who played for Coach Mike Neubauer from 1988 to 1990 and was his assistant coach at Belgrade from 1996 to 1998, was the head coach of the Wolf Point Yellowjackets from 1999 to 2010. He remembers the quality players that came from Scobey to play for him. He said, "Every Scobey player that came down to play was a starter. They were committed to the program if they traveled over 50 miles one way to play every day. Chauncy had talent, heart, and work ethic. It was all about getting better for him, not about pride. When he first came down, I told him, 'We have a lot of work to do if you want to play at the next level.' I taught him how to pitch. His fastball had more run on it than any I had ever seen. His spin rate was incredible. If he threw it at a left-handed hitter's hip, it would move over the plate for a strike. He threw one fastball down the center of the plate, and it broke inside so far it hit the right-handed batter. Michael Crandell was an unbelievable athlete. Pure talent. He was a left-handed hitter, and his hand-eye at the plate was incredible. He roamed center field so gracefully that when a ball was hit to center, it looked like he would lope after it like he was lazy, but he would always get to the ball, even if it was on the warning track. It was effortless. Some other players I remember coming to play besides Chauncy Handran and Michael Crandell were Drew Baldry, Ethan Aldrich, Kray Buer, and Joe Miller. They were all starters; they always helped us win games."

The Montana/Alberta Baseball Class A Baseball League, I am sure, turned an eye when it noticed that the Scobey Blues did not submit a roster in 2004. Scobey dropping out of the league was one of the reasons for an eventual restructuring of the divisions in the Class A League in 2006. While Scobey's Legion program did not continue from 2004 to 2015, some significant events related to eastern Montana Legion baseball and the Scobey Blues legacy happened. This chapter highlights a few of those events.

2004

COACH CHAD JONES AND THE GLENDIVE BLUE DEVILS WON their second state championship in three years, and it was pitching that did it, as Coach Jones got four well-pitched games from four different starters to sweep the tournament in four straight games:

- **Greg Ford** went the distance in the first game, allowing one run on five hits to lead Glendive to a 6-1 win over Belgrade. Ford struck out 16 Bandits.
- **Chase Downs** pitched a two-hit shutout in Glendive's second game as the Blue Devils 10-run-ruled Lethbridge 10-0 in seven innings. Downs was also 3-5 at the plate, driving in three runs and scoring one.
- **Joe Bakken** got the ball in game three in the undefeated semifinal against Libby, and he pitched eight strong innings to lead Glendive to a 7-4 win, getting help from Greg Ford in the ninth. Bakken earned the win, allowing four runs
- on six hits in eight innings. Greg Ford retired the side in order in the ninth to earn the save.
- **Jason Erickson** scattered five hits in seven and two-third innings and didn't allow a run to lead Glendive to a 1-0 win against Libby in the state championship game. Greg Ford pitched the last one and one-third

innings to earn his second save, preserving Glendive's 1-0 win in a rare pitcher's duel in the state championship game. Glendive's scored in the fifth when Erickson drove home Collin Radakovic with the game's only run.

Glendive Head Coach Chad Jones was selected Montana/Alberta State Class A American Legion Coach of the Year for the second time.

Glendive's state championship was significant because it was the last state championship for the old Class A/B eastern division that Scobey played in. Glendive has not won a state championship since 2004.

The Blue Devils went on to win their first game at the Northwest Regional hosted by the Gallatin Valley Outlaws in Bozeman, beating Alaska 5-0 on a four-hit shutout by Greg Ford, but lost their next two games. They finished their outstanding season 46-9.

The Laurel Dodgers, who had moved up to Class AA in 1993, returned to the Class A ranks in 2004. During the 11 years the Dodgers competed in the Class AA eastern division, they qualified for the State Class AA Tournament twice (1994 and 1999). The Laurel Dukes, Laurel's second team during this period, competed in the Class A southern division. The Dukes qualified for the State A Tournament in 1993 and 1994.

The Homestead Pioneers, who had been members of the Eastern Class A Division since 1995, folded following the end of the season. The program would reemerge as the Froid Bulls in 2020.

2005

THIS WAS THE LAST YEAR SIDNEY HOSTED THE STATE TOURNAment at Moose Memorial Park. This was also the final season the Montana/Alberta Class A League consisted of five divisions, and the last time the state tournament consisted of 11 teams. (The pitchers and coaches say thank you.) The Wolf Point Yellowjackets qualified for the state tournament for the last time in the program's history.

Another sport that was struggling in Montana in 2005 was men's fast-pitch softball. In an article titled "Last of a Dying Breed," appearing in the *Havre Daily News* in August 2005, Ryan Divish wrote, "Men's fast-pitch softball has seen a steady decline in the number of teams, the number of players, and the number of tournaments across the state. We have a fading tradition. Take Havre, for example. The strong tradition of men's fast pitch here in Havre, particularly its summer league, is slowly disappearing. Growing up, fast-pitch league nights were an event with at least six different teams competing on a night. Now, we have three teams in the league. As a kid growing up, I knew I would play fast pitch when my baseball days were over because that's what my dad did. That's what everyone did."[1]

2006

DUE TO THE DECLINE IN THE NUMBER OF TEAMS, THE Montana/Alberta State Class A Legion League shifted to four divisions (the central division was eliminated), and the former eastern division was combined with teams from the southern division. The postseason changed as well, as only eight teams qualified for the state tournament, and only the host plus one qualified.

The Plentywood Athletics hosted the eastern division tournament for the last time. The Glendive Blue Devils won the championship, as Jason Erickson pitched a complete-game six-hitter to beat the Billings Blue Jays 11-1. This was the last season for Coach Chad Jones at Glendive, who moved to Kansas City.

Head Coach Micky Williams of the Havre Northstars retired from Legion coaching. Mickey finished his Legion career with four state championships, two as a player (1968 and 1970), one as an assistant coach to Tom Nielson (1984), and one as head coach (1999), all with the Northstars. His career with the Havre Northstars as a player and a coach spanned 38 years. Mickey also served in the United States Air Force for four years. Thank you for your service, Mick. Steve Fanning, Dave Fanning's son and a member of Havre's 1999 state championship team, picked up the reins to coach the Northstars for the next four years.

Chauncy Handran of Scobey was 2-for-4 with a double as the Miles City Community College (MCC) Pioneers won the NJCAA Region 13 baseball tournament, beating Madison Area Tech of Wisconsin 7-1 in the championship. It was the first regional championship for Miles City.

2007

CHAUNCY HANDRAN, "THE LAST BLUE," PITCHED THE MCC Pioneers to a 1-0 win over the Iowa Central Tritons for the northwest district championship, qualifying Coach Rob Bishop and the MCC Pioneers for their first national junior college Division II World Series. Chauncy allowed five hits in eight innings. Tony Campbell saved the game in the ninth, as he got the last three outs after Chauncy hit the leadoff hitter. The win came despite getting no-hit by Iowa Central, as MCC scored the only run of the game in the fourth inning on a walk and a sacrifice fly. The following week at the World Series, Chauncy started the first game and pitched into the eighth inning, yielding only one run and three hits, but was on the losing end of another pitcher's duel as the Pioneers lost to Longview Community College 1-0.

Chauncy finished the season 5-1 with an NJCAA Division II-leading 1.37 earned-run average for the MCC Pioneers. He also hit .299 with six home runs and 33 RBI. He signed a letter of intent to play for the University of Minnesota Golden Gophers. In an interview with Ben Catley of the MCC Sports Information Services, Chauncy said, "It's unbelievable to me to be able to continue the dream." Chauncy credited Head Coach Jack Sprague of the Yellowjackets with his decision to choose baseball over football at the collegiate level. He said, "I was torn to play baseball in college, actually! I really wanted to play football and had a preferred spot at MSU. It wasn't until Coach Sprague had a sit-down with me that he helped me realize I could potentially go far in baseball, perhaps even play professionally."

Coach Sprague was modest about taking any credit for Chauncy's decision to play college baseball. "The only credit I deserve is that when he first came to Wolf Point, I made him understand what he was committing to. I told him that if he wanted me to push him to get better, I would do that, but that it was going to take a lot of work to get him to that next level."

In another example of the saying, "Montana is a small town with long streets," Chauncy pitched for Coach Chad Jones and the Topeka Golden Giants in the Kansas summer league before heading to Minnesota in the fall. Chad had been Coach Brent Diegel's assistant at Dawson Community College when Chauncy pitched for Miles City.

The Richland County Patriots beat the Laurel Dodgers to win their first eastern division championship in 13 years, qualifying for their first state tournament in seven years. The Patriots, with only 10 players on their roster, went on to place second at State, beating the Great Falls Stallions 20-9, the Dillon Cubs 8-7 (10 innings), and the Vauxhall Spurs 8-4, but then losing twice to the Polson-based Mission Valley Mariners, 11-2 and 15-4.

The state championship was the first for the nearly 20-year-old Mariner program. Tournament MVP Brandon "Moose" Thompson knew the Mission Valley program took time to build. "It's been a long time waiting. The first year (the Legion program) started out, we didn't win at all. Then, after that, we started winning more and more games. I got here four years ago, and we never lost a conference championship. We lost the district championships, but we never lost a conference championship. But we won the district this year for the first time ever. Now we're state champs for the first time ever."

The Mariners were representative of how small-town kids contributed to winning state championships, as in addition to seven kids from Polson, three Mariners were from Ronan, three from Plains, two from Charlo, and two from Arlee. Mariner's fourth-year coach, Jami Hanson, said, "They are spread out throughout the valley. I hope everyone sees that."[2] Hanson, who was named Coach of the Year, grew up playing for the Mariners in the early 1990s.

2011

IN ADDITION TO SCOBEY'S LEGION PROGRAM SHUTTING DOWN following the 2003 season, two more Legion programs in the former eastern division—the Plentywood Athletics and the Wolf Point Yellowjackets—folded before the start of the 2011 season. Coach Jack Sprague, who had been the head coach at Wolf Point since 1999, experienced the same problem fielding a Legion team in Wolf Point in 2011 as did Scobey in 2004, but in his case, the multisport athletes chose basketball over baseball in the summer months. The Wolf Point Wolves, led by Head Coach Kelly Nieskens (Blues 1998–2000), completed a perfect 25-0 season by beating Columbus 50-44 for the State Class B basketball championship, the first for Wolf Point since 1968. Four of Jack's best baseball players would be gone for three weeks during the summer playing basketball, and with only a seven-week regular season, Jack could not find enough players to field a team. That was it for the Yellowjackets program.

To add insult to injury for the Yellowjackets in 2011, the Missouri River flooded Bill Connors Field in Glasgow, so the Reds had to come to play their season at Burke Field in Wolf Point. Coach Sprague remembers prepping the field for the Reds' "home" games in Wolf Point.

Coach Jason Wolfe led the Scobey Spartans to their third state basketball title in 2011 as Scobey beat Arlee 55-47 for the state championship. Scobey finished the year 23-3.

2012

KNOWING THAT THE WOLF POINT YELLOWJACKETS PROGRAM HAD folded, the Glasgow Legion board approached Coach Jack Sprague to take the head coaching job for the Glasgow Reds. Jack said, "I told them I'll come and coach if you want me to, but I don't know any of the players, and I will only take the best players at the tryout, so I might need to make some cuts." The board agreed, and Jack was hired. Jack said he had "12 to 14 kids at tryouts," so he didn't need to make any cuts. He had two players from Lustre, one from Nashua, and he brought three kids from Wolf Point. The rest were from Glasgow.

In our interview, Coach Sprague said, "In 2012, nobody thought we could get to State or win the state tournament. In the last six years I was coaching, a whole bunch of teams in the east were just struggling to hang on. I was giving the kids I had coached an opportunity to play."

After upsetting higher-seed Lewistown twice to win the eastern division championship, Coach Sprague and the upstart Reds then made a run at the state title. In a pre-tournament interview with Scott Mansch, *Great Falls Tribune* sports editor, Jack said his team was not "the most talented" but that they "have a lotta pride and a lotta fight. They root for each other, and that's a big deal. It's a group of guys that didn't have a lot of expectations, plus they had to deal with me as a first-year coach. So they had to go through a lot of change. But they realized that if they could do it without quitting, it would make them tougher. They stuck it out, and they came together. Our guys realize the team is much bigger than one guy. I think they'll do well this weekend."[3]

The Reds did do well that weekend. They beat the Mission Valley Mariners 4-3, the Gallatin Valley Outlaws 3-2, and the Libby Loggers 16-6 to reach the title game undefeated. But Mission Valley came back through the back door and beat Glasgow twice (11-3 and 13-4) to deny the Reds their first state championship. It was Glasgow's third time taking second place at State, as they lost to Fairfield in a best-of-three series in 1953 and the Bitterroot Red Sox in 2000 in Glasgow.

Coach Sprague was selected as Montana/Alberta Class A Coach of the Year, and the Glasgow Reds were awarded the Team and Fans Sportsmanship Award.

The Reds won two games at the Northwest Regional and took fourth place, finishing Coach Sprague's first season at 43-22. But more importantly, a lot of boys were given an opportunity to play competitive baseball that otherwise would not have had the chance. Mission Valley and veteran coach Jami Hanson won the regional tournament. The Mariners finished the season with an incredible 55-8 record.

Coach Sprague said of his 2012 team, "That first year, I don't think we could have duplicated it. They bought in

2012 Glasgow Reds, State Runners-up. Back row, left to right: Coach Jack Sprague, Wacey Ortman, Gage Legare, Grant Legare, Walt Dalbey, Zach Rodgers, Jared Smith, Jess Hanks, Tom Leland, Robbie Henville, Coach Jeff Irving, Coach Spencer Marsh. Front row, from left to right: Griffin Bengochea, Dylan Guttenburg, Andy Gardner, John Koessl, Blayd Sanders, Jacob Renner, Parker Kulczyk. *Lisa Legare photo for the Courier.*

without hesitation. No quit. No ego. Nobody thought they were the stud of the team." As I heard Coach Sprague tell me this, I thought about how special American Legion Ball is, especially compared to select travel baseball programs, which focus more on individual performance and exposure to college recruiters and pro scouts and less on the team. I was talking to a neighbor about this the other day, and he told me select travel programs are ruining high school sports in northern Virginia. He said that he is noticing that players are bringing the individual performance emphasis into prep sports, and you can spot the athletes from these programs, as their play is more individual and less team. A good coach can handle that, of course, but the culture of showcasing individual talent versus team togetherness and winning is tough to overcome once it is ingrained in a player. He also told me that players are hopping from high school to high school to get better exposure playing on better teams, which also affects individual versus team play. I played on the same team in Little League All-Stars through Legion and the Plainsmen, a special experience I wouldn't trade for anything. I can't imagine playing competitively with an eye toward a scout or a recruiter in the stands. My dad always told me, "Keep your nose to the grindstone, and good things will happen." Young athletic careers are so carefully managed now. I'm glad I missed that.

Zach Rodgers, one of the players Coach Sprague brought from Wolf Point, played on the last Yellowjacket team in 2010. He rode 50 miles with Coach Sprague daily for practice to play in Glasgow. He missed the 2011 season because Wolf Point could not field a team. He was happy to be playing baseball again. In the first game against Mission Valley, he sparked a three-run seventh-inning rally with a leadoff hit-by-pitch to lead the come-from-behind win. After the game against Mission Valley, Zach said, "I definitely want to go out with a win, and I want to be remembered. I want to go home having won the whole thing. We want to bring home the bacon."

Although you did not win a state title, Zach, you are remembered. The story of *The Blues of Summer* is about your love of the game.

2013

THE LAUREL DODGERS BEAT THE BELGRADE BANDITS 10-7 to win their ninth state title, breaking Scobey's record of eight state titles. The state title was the fourth in five years for the Dodgers, clearly a dynasty. The only team record that survives for the Scobey Blues is the five consecutive state championships from 1976 to 1980. The Blues' record of 31 straight wins was broken by the Gallatin Valley Outlaws in 2002 when they won 32 games in a row heading into the state tournament.

Coach Jack Sprague's Big Red Machine repeated as Eastern A Division champions and took third at State, finishing the season with a 53-11 record. In Coach Sprague's first two seasons at Glasgow, the Reds had over 96 victories, a second and third-place finish at State, and a fourth-place finish at regional.

The Reds won the Team and Fans Sportsmanship Award for the second straight year at State. Coach Sprague was prouder of this than the wins. He said, "Wins are great, and as a coach, if you get the players better, that's great—but if you make them better citizens, that's even better."[4]

From 2004 to 2015, there was no Legion baseball team in Scobey, but Scobey baseball was active at the Little League and Babe Ruth levels. On June 13, 2013, Mike Stebleton of the *Leader* wrote, "Scobey Ball Park is going to be a busy place from Thursday, June 13, to Tuesday, June 18, 2013, as there are baseball games scheduled every day. On the big field, the Babe Ruth Scobey Giants host the Wolf Point Mosquitos Friday at 5 p.m. and 7 p.m. and Glasgow Coca-Cola Sunday at 2 p.m. and 4 p.m. On Lions Field, the Cal Ripken kids (ages 9-12) have a game tonight, six with Glasgow teams on Saturday starting at 9 a.m., one on Monday, and another on Tuesday. The concession stand at the big field will be open for all the games, so stop by. Enjoy the games!"[5]

On July 3, 2013, 27 of Doc's former players and coaches (and batgirl DeeAnn Lekvold) gathered at Marge Shiell's Scobey home to celebrate the Blues tradition and Marge, the matriarch of Scobey Blues baseball. Players on Doc's first team in 1959 through his last team in 1983 were there. It was a special day for Marge, as she was the bedrock upon which the storied Blues tradition was built. Danny Wolfe (Legionnaires 1968–71) remembers Marge's contribution to the Blues this way: "They say that behind every successful baseball coach is a 'Sami.' That was Doc's pet name for Marge. All Doc did was coach, while Marge wore many hats. She was a travel agent, a chauffeur, an equipment manager, a laundry lady, an office manager, a chef, a seamstress, a bed check lady, and a nurse. Most of all, when we were on the road, she was our mom away from home. She made us all feel special."

I have many fond memories of Marge, but my favorite is when we were playing the Kalispell Lakers at the State A (now AA) tournament in Butte/Anaconda in 1979. We were playing in Anaconda, and the game didn't start until ten at night. There weren't many fans in the stands, but this made it easier to hear the Scobey fans, including Marge. I remember hearing her voice come out of the darkness often throughout that night in the stands, cheering us on. It made me feel like I was back in Scobey and gave me confidence. She was our number-one fan and supporter.

2014

THE GLACIER TWINS WON THEIR FIRST STATE CLASS A LEGION championship.

2015

THE BITTERROOT RED SOX WON THEIR SIXTH STATE CLASS A Legion championship and would repeat as state champions in 2016 and 2017, tying Scobey with eight state titles.

Marge (Norman) Shiell Reunion. Doc's players and coaches from 1959 to 1983. Kneeling from left: Phil Baker, Jesse Cook, Lee Cook, Barry Higgins, Brad Henderson, DeeAnn (nee: Lekvold) Howard, Marge Shiell, Jim Lekvold, Don Higgins, Terry Veis, Larry Henderson. Standing from left: Dan Wang, Ron Higgins, Jack Higgins, Pat Anderson, Randy Peck, Kirby Halvorson, Dan Wolfe, Mike Gunderson, Phil Audet, Doug Hagfeldt, Kelly Norman, Don Hagfeldt, Pat Audet, Duke Trangsrud, Don Lekvold, Terry Puckett, Dwain Sell. Leader photo, Mike Stebleton.

THE WAY OF THE DODO BIRD

Only three Legion programs (Glendive, Sidney, and Glasgow) from the former Eastern Montana Division still exist; all the others have folded. Here is a list of those northeastern Montana Legion programs that have gone the way of the dodo bird:

Scobey Blues

The program folded following the 2003 season, then was revived in 2016–2019, participating in the Montana/Alberta Class B Division in 2016 and 2017, then the North Dakota Class A and B Divisions in 2018 and 2019. The program folded again following the 2019 season. The Blues won eight state championships (1969, 1973, 1976–80, 1982).

Plentywood Athletics

The program folded following the 2010 season. The Athletics won one state championship (1954). Through the 1967 season, when Plentywood beat Scobey for the Divisional championship and then eliminated Scobey at State, Plentywood had the upper hand on Scobey in baseball, but from 1968 on, it was all Scobey. However, Plentywood had a knack for upsetting its rival Scobey in the postseason. It was rumored that Plentywood's upsets of favored Scobey in the postseason dated to a curse that was put on the town of Scobey by pitcher John Donaldson following a game in Plentywood on June 14, 1925. Donaldson was a noted pitcher with the All-Nations League who Keith Whipple said "would have been a big-league pitcher if colored men had been accepted in those days." Swede Risberg, who played shortstop for the Chicago White Sox, outdueled Donaldson 4-1 in 10 innings to win the game for Scobey in Plentywood that day, in a game witnessed by 3,500 people. Plentywood businessmen lost a ton of cash in the loss, and Donaldson was embarrassed he got beat by a former mediocre shortstop in the big leagues. After the game, Donaldson put a curse on Scobey that whenever Scobey was favored in big games against Plentywood, Scobey would implode in the field in the late innings and take an embarrassing loss.

Wolf Point Yellowjackets

The program folded following the 2011 season, had Class B teams in 2016 and 2017, was revived from 2019 to 2021, then folded again. Jack Sprague observed the decay of baseball skills in Wolf Point when the program was revived in 2019, saying, "Some of the players at tryouts didn't know what hand they were." The Yellowjackets won two state championships (1965 and 1987). Scobey beat Wolf Point in two state championship games, in 1973 and 1976.

Richland County (Sidney) Patriots

The program folded for three years (2019–2021) following the 2018 season but has since been revived, as the Patriots competed in the eastern division in 2022–2024. The program has three state championships (1966, 1981, and 1995).

Circle Zephyrs

The program folded following the 1997 season. The best season Circle had was in 1991 when they won the Eastern Conference, but Scobey and Steve Stephenson's knuckle curve eliminated them from the divisional tournament in Plentywood. Coach Mike Flamm (Blues 1998–2000) played on that Zephyrs team.

Homestead Pioneers

The Homestead Pioneers folded following the 2004 season. They participated in the eastern division from 1995 to 2004. The program was revived as the Froid Bulls in 2020–2021, participating in the Eastern Class A Division, with Scobey players Colter and Jackson Oie traveling to play for the Bulls when Scobey's program folded for the second time in 2019. The Bulls fielded a team in 2024, but not in the Montana Class A eastern division. Three Scobey players went to play for Froid in 2024.

Malta Royals

The Malta Royals sporadically fielded teams in the former eastern division throughout the 1990s, but the program folded following the 2002 season. The program was revived for one season in 2019 when the Royals competed in the eastern division again.

Miles City Colts

The Miles City Colts were the second team for the Miles City Mavericks when the Mavericks competed in Class AA/A, but following the 2010 season, the Mavericks were no longer able to compete at the Class AA level and moved down from Class AA to Class A. Miles City has a fine baseball tradition playing at historic Denton Field. The Mavericks have won 11 state championships (1931-32, 1934-35, 1937, 1939-40, 1944-45, 1947, and 1996). Scobey lost to Miles City in a one-game playoff for the eastern division championship in 1946, when there was only one baseball division in Montana. In 1947, Scobey also lost to Miles City in the playoffs, this time in a best-of-three series. Miles City won the state championship in 1947.

Fort Peck

Fort Peck Legion Post No. 83 played their last season in 1962. Fort Peck won several district championships in the 1950s and the state championship in 1953. Doc Norman's first team in 1959 beat Fort Peck for the district championship in a best-of-three series.

Poplar Indians

The Poplar Post No. 55 Indians played their last season in 1978. The highlight of Poplar's Legion baseball program was when they beat Scobey 1-0 in a pitcher's duel for the eastern division of the District 4 championship in 1951. Keith Sell pitched a 4-hitter but was outdueled by Poplar's Engles, who pitched a 2-hitter. Head coach Babe Holyk of Scobey stated in the *Leader* that "We wuz robbed,"[6] referring to a close call at the plate when Lekvold was called out, and Poplar won 1-0. The *Leader* said the locals described the pitcher's duel as "one of the tightest Junior Legion ballgames ever witnessed in the area."[7] Poplar then lost to Glasgow for the district championship. Hitting-wise, Poplar's highlight against Scobey was when Dorn Steele hit a moonshot home run off Kirby Halvorson in 1977.

Flaxville-Whitetail

American Legion Post No. 121 (Whitetail) fielded Flaxville-Whitetail American Legion teams in the 1950s and 1960s, the last coming in 1967. Flaxville-Whitetail won the district championship in 1958 and lost a best-of-three series against eventual state champion Roundup in Scobey.

Peerless

Peerless American Legion Post No. 107 (the Elwood Lien post) fielded Legion teams from 1954 to 1960. The best year Peerless had was 1959, when they were the only team in the conference to beat Doc Norman's first Scobey Legion team, 5-4. The Scobey Legionnaires would have been undefeated in the conference but for the loss to Peerless. Dad came razor-close to fielding a Legion team in Peerless in 1977 after he had developed a strong team from Peewee through Little League and Babe Ruth from 1967 to 1976.

Outlook

Outlook American Legion Post No. 72's last season fielding a Legion team was in 1965. Following the folding of their program, Outlook baseball players always played in Plentywood until Tyler Bucklin played with Scobey in 1991. Kenny Selvig from Outlook helped Plentywood finish second at State in 1966.

Opheim

Opheim Legion Post No. 122 fielded their last team in 1959. The highlight of Opheim's Legion program came in 1949, when Opheim, led by pitchers Andy Stolen and Leo Zimmer, won the Junior Legion District 4 championship in Plentywood. In Opheim's 8–2 win over Plentywood in the District 4 semifinals, the *Plentywood Herald* wrote, "Little Andy Stolen, picked two years in succession as all district pitcher, limited Plentywood to three hits as Opheim took the locals in the first-round competition."[8] Opheim then won the title game 10–9 against Fort Peck.

Culbertson

Culbertson fielded their last Legion team in 1955. In a regular season game against Culbertson in 1952, Scobey Legion won 50-4 in seven innings, likely the record for runs scored by a Scobey Legion team. Pete Hagfeldt, Terry McIntyre, Ordean Wangrud, and Donny Hansen all hit home runs for Scobey. Keith Sell pitched six innings of one-hit ball, and Cliff Hagfeldt pitched the seventh (but it was not a save opportunity).

Saco

The only record of Saco fielding a Legion team was the first year after World War II in 1946; however, in the district championship game played at Bob Cross Memorial Park in Glasgow in 1952, Kenny O'Brien from Saco pitched a one-hitter for Glasgow to lead them to a 10-0 win over Scobey for the district championship. This was Glasgow's third consecutive district championship under Bunky and Sully Sullivan and the fifth straight title for Valley County.

Scobey Plainsmen

It would be too long of a list to mention all the town teams who used to participate in the Northeastern Montana League, Eastern Montana League, and the Big Muddy League in the late 1930s, 1940s, 1950s, and 1960s. The last Plainsmen team Scobey fielded that played a regular season and in tournaments was in 1982; the last Plainsmen game was played on Doc Norman Day in 1983.

SECTION NOTES

1. Ryan Divish, "Last of a dying breed," *Havre Daily News*, August 5, 2005.
2. Carl Hennell, "Sweet trip to state, Mission Valley win Class A American Legion title," *The Daily Inter Lake*, August 6, 2007.
3. Scott Mansch, "Laurel seeks fourth straight title," *Great Falls Tribune*, July 26, 2012.
4. Jim Orr, "Reds Return To Top 3 At State," *Glasgow Courier*, August 7, 2013.
5. "Scobey Ball Park and Lions Field," *Daniels County Leader*, June 13, 2013.
6. "Poplar Wins East Division," *Daniels County Leader*, July 5, 1951.
7. Ibid.
8. Robert Carbone, "Opheim Cops First in Junior Legion Tournament," *Plentywood Herald*, July 14, 1949.

The Revival
2016 – 2019

1900 – 1924
The Homesteaders
and Early Town Teams

1930 – 1945
The Sons of
the Pioneers

1957 – 1968
The Baseball
Renaissance

The Scobey
Giants
1925 – 1929

Baseball is Back
in Daniels County
1946 – 1956

The D
Cham
1969 –

| 1983 – 1991 | 1998 – 2003 |
| The Don Lekvold Era | The Last Years |

| ...rman ...hip Era | The Ken Meyer/Mike Lee Era 1992 – 1997 | The Long Winter 2004 – 2015 | The Froid Bulls 2020 – 2024 |

2016
The Sun Rises Again on the Scobey Blues

> *Those boys wanted to restart it more than anybody. They wanted a place to go play, they wanted to be a Blues player, they understood the legacy of what it was to be a Blues player, and they came together. We weren't the most talented team by any means, but they had determination.*
>
> —Chuck Nelson, Scobey Blues head coach (2016)

PROLOGUE

Lo, and it was written in *The Book of Blues Revelations* by the prophet Jack Reiner, who christened Daniels County as "Baseball Country" in the 1960s: "After a 13-year winter for Scobey American Legion Baseball, a mountain man from the west will come to where the plainsmen roam and bring his passion for the game of baseball with him and become the new leader of the lost tribe of Blues. And the *Daniels County Leader* will trumpet his arrival in winter, announcing that a second coming of American Legion Baseball will come to the east later in the spring. The Opening Day game at Scobey Ball Park will be played against an old rival named after the North Star, who played against Scobey during the era when Scobey baseball was as golden as the wheat fields surrounding the ballfield at harvest time. The matriarch of Scobey baseball will throw the first pitch to bring forward the glorious tradition that once was the Scobey Blues, for the flame that had burned like the fire of a thousand suns that had been extinguished 13 years earlier will burn bright again. And the Great Doctor in the Sky will look down from heaven and smile, as Scobey will be Baseball Country once more."
—From the prophet Jack in *The Book of Blues Revelations*

And thus it was written . . . and came to pass.

PRESEASON

In 2015, Chuck Nelson from Eureka, Montana, who played American Legion Baseball for the Glacier Twins in Whitefish from 1995 to 1998, moved with his family to Williston, North Dakota, for work. Because he still wanted to be able to hunt elk in Montana, he lived in Plentywood to keep his Montana residency. As soon as he arrived in Plentywood, he was recruited to coach Little League baseball by Arlin Kaul (Blues 1986–89), so he coached the Plentywood Little League team and was chosen to coach the Big Muddy All-Stars Little League team. In our interview, Chuck said, "I cut my eight-year-old boy from the All-Star team. That didn't go too well at home with the wife and stuff, but he was still able to practice with us. Everyone was just appalled and amazed that I cut my own kid to a coach. But I wasn't about to give my boy a spot because he was my boy. The other 10-, 11-, and 12-year-olds were better and should have played. So, I told my boy to work hard in practice, but he can't play any games. He's 18 now and has one of the best work ethics ever. And I think it all came from that. He's not afraid. Work ethic is something I teach, whether it be Little League or Legion ball, so, yeah, it worked out good."

Sounds like this guy might have the potential to coach the Scobey Blues—any coach who cuts their own son in Little League All-Stars can't be all bad.

I asked Chuck how he became the head coach of the Scobey Blues. He said, "Coaching Plentywood Little League in 2015 is what kind of what got me into coaching for the Blues. The word got out that, 'Hey, there's this guy who likes baseball and coaches,' and the community was happy with how I coached. You gotta get the community's approval, you know? I coached Arlin's boy in Little League, and somehow, Jedd Lekvold got ahold of Arlin and asked him, 'Hey man, we're trying to start this legion program, and we're looking for a coach,' and somehow it got to me. So, Jedd gave me a call and said, 'You wanna coach this Legion team that we haven't had in forever.' I said, 'Sure, but there's a whole lot involved with that. We gotta get schedules and do all this other stuff,' so let me chew on this for a day and make sure it's okay with my wife." She was alright with it, so I decided to coach and it just started from there."

So Jake and Elwood Blues (Jedd Lekvold and Chuck Nelson) got the Blues Brothers band back together again.

Because the deadline had passed, Chuck could not register Scobey into the sanctioned Class A Montana/Alberta League, so the team played an ad hoc schedule in the unsanctioned Class "B" league. I asked Chuck about some challenges he had reviving a program after being dormant for 13 years. He said, "Well, I did a little bit of research and found out what the Scobey Blues were, and it's not your average Legion team. The history of this goes way back I was like, 'Man, if I do this, I gotta do it right. This is a legacy team that goes back so far.' So the first steps were I met with Terry Farver and Jedd, and we went out to the field, and it was just a mess. It hadn't been played on and if we were going to host games here we had to get this thing ready. They took out the mound at one point. Had to totally rebuild the mound. Went through the dugouts and fixed the fencing. I think we spent a week with heavy equipment and a ton of volunteers just getting the field ready again in early spring. We did everything from fixing fields."

The Blues needed money to get the program back going again. Kirby Halvorson, who played on five straight state championship teams for the Blues from 1976 to 1980, knew this, so he posted his picture with his Blues uniform on and wrote this letter on Facebook in May 2016:

Kirby Halvorson crawled into his old Blues jersey to announce the second coming of the Blues. *Family photo.*

It's been over 30 years since I've worn these colors, but I will always bleed blue! And at the risk of being melodramatic or cheesy, I am proud to squeeze into this jersey to once again go to bat for the Scobey Blues.

I was blessed to be associated with the program forged on the talents of names like Audet, Danelson, Hagfeldt, Higgins, Puckett, Stolen, and Tryan, to name a few. The Blues won American Legion State Championships in 1969, 1973, 1976-1980, and 1982. This dynasty was built by one of the greatest men I have ever known, Dr. Clyde H. "Doc" Norman, supported by his incomparable wife, Marge.

Around 2003, the program folded due to lack of numbers and support. This was an unfortunate situation that happened in many small towns. I felt at that time like there was a death in my family. However, due to the dedication of many Scobey people, the program is being resurrected. The start-up costs for this endeavor will be considerable (likely thousands of $$), and the financial support of the community is vital. If you grew up in Scobey, you know it is a CAN DO community. Just witness the efforts behind the school gym and pool projects, for example. But in the current economic climate, the determined folks of Scobey can use our support.

So, the primary purpose of this post is simple. I am challenging my Scobey-related Facebook friends, but especially my baseball brothers (Doc's Boys) and all other Blues Alumni, to consider helping out. I have made a humble commitment to the program and volunteered to post this appeal.

Although none of us could truly pay Doc back, I look at it as a way to honor him (and Marge) by paying it forward to the next generation. Also, with this pledge, I honor my dad, Ernie, who kept the ballpark in shape for many years as a volunteer groundskeeper. I sincerely hope you consider contributing for your own reasons.

Please, please give if you can. Remember if a lot give a little it still adds up to and means a lot! If you need further information you can contact Jedd Lekvold in Scobey.

Thank you for your consideration. And please share this post.

And to the next generation of Blues, I offer Doc's inimitable words: "Listen up, you little peckerheads, let's go out and shoot some baseball!"

Sincerely,
Kirby Forever #13

(Rick Lee commented on Kirby's post: "Grandma Marge said that is awesome and brings tears to her eyes!")

When the program folded in 2003, the shrinking budget was one of the problems. Regarding the budget, Chuck said, "We were on a tight budget. Everyone asked me. 'Hey,

The Revival

2016 Scobey Blues. Kneeling, left to right: Kole Ralston, Spencer Rush, Trey Girard, Tyler Weeks, Trevor Girard, Peyton Nieskens. Standing, left to right: Kobe Ralston, CJ Nelson, Lane Knudsen, Jace Schumacher, Brandon Meade, Tanner Weeks, Head Coach Chuck Nelson. Not pictured is assistant coach Brad Lamb. *Leader photo, Mike Stebleton.*

what's it going to take to run a program; we need to raise some money.' And Scobey being such an amazing place, on top of putting a lot of my own money in and getting things going, I said I think we need $30,000 to run a team, bare minimum at that point in the game. And I kinda thought that was going to squash it. And I don't know how we got it, but four days later, there was an account with close to $30,000 in it to run a budget and run a team on. And that blew me away about the community, really. However they did it, they did it. But it's the Blues, and I think people in Scobey and people in that area, really, the history goes so far back, you know, looking back, it doesn't surprise me, but at the time, it really surprised me."

Taking the field for the 2016 Scobey Blues were Kole Ralston, Spencer Rush, Trey Girard, Tyler Weeks, Trevor Girard, Peyton Nieskens, Kobe Ralston, CJ Nelson, Lane Knudsen, Jace Schumacher, Brandon Meade, and Tanner Weeks. At the end of the season, after the Babe Ruth season was over, Kole Ralston, Martin Farver, Jackson Oie, Anders Knudsen, and Devin Halverson joined the team. Let's call them all rookies, as it was their first year of Legion ball. Two of the boys had never played baseball before, and two boys who came over from Plentywood quit early in the season, but Scobey was able to field a team, playing many games with just nine players.

In the remarkable team photo of the Scobey Blues taken by Mike Stebleton (hands down the coolest Blues team photo ever), the sun was setting in the west behind the Blues, but the sun was rising on the program. The cold of a 13-year Legion baseball winter was over, and the warmth of another Legion baseball summer was coming to Scobey.

In a preseason article enthusiastically titled, "Blues Are Back! American Legion Team to Occupy Diamond in '16,"

Mike Stebleton of the *Leader* asked Coach Nelson what interested him in the job. "Baseball," Chuck said. "I have a passion for the game of baseball."[1]

Thanks for your passion, Chuck. It helped bring Legion baseball back to Scobey. Now let's play ball!

REGULAR SEASON

CHUCK DROVE FROM WILLISTON TO SCOBEY EVERY NIGHT (TWO hours) to coach the Blues, then back to Plentywood to his home. He said the boys arrived at practice before he arrived and would want to stay late to work on their skills. No one was late for practice. Chuck and the boys were committed to improving and making it a good season.

Chuck Nelson works with a youngster during the Blues Baseball Camp held at the Scobey Ball Park in May, which attracted 37 youngsters. A Blues camp in Plentywood earlier in May had 24 kids attending. *Leader photo, Mike Stebleton.*

The excitement was building for Scobey's Opening Day against Havre on May 30, 2016 (Memorial Day). Mike Stebleton, in an article in the *Leader* titled "Blues Play Ball Again Monday for First Time in 13 Seasons," reprinted the famous song, "Take Me Out to the Ballgame," written by Jack Norworth in 1908:

> *Katie Casey was baseball mad.*
> *Had the fever and had it bad;*
> *Just to root for the hometown crew,*
> *Ev'ry sou Katie blew.*
> *On a Saturday, her young beau*
> *Called to see if she'd like to go,*
> *To see a show but Miss Kate said,*
> *"No, I'll tell you what you can do."*
> *"Take me out to the ball game,*
> *Take me out with the crowd.*
> *Buy me some peanuts and cracker jack,*
> *I don't care if I never get back,*
> *Let me root, root, root for the home team,*
> *If they don't win it's a shame.*
> *For it's one, two, three strikes, you're out,*
> *At the old ball game."*
> *Katie Casey saw all the games,*
> *Knew the players by their first names;*
> *Told the umpire he was wrong,*
> *All along good and strong.*
> *When the score was just two to two,*
> *Katie Casey knew what to do,*
> *Just to cheer up the boys she knew,*
> *She made the gang sing this song:*
> *"Take me out to the ball game,*
> *Take me out with the crowd.*
> *Buy me some peanuts and cracker jack,*
> *I don't care if I never get back,*
> *Let me root, root, root for the home team,*
> *If they don't win it's a shame.*
> *For it's one, two, three strikes, you're out,*
> *At the old ball game."*

Mike wrote, "You, too, can be at the old ball game Monday, May 30, when the Scobey Blues make their long-awaited return to the diamond following a 13-year hiatus."[2]

The local Color Guard presented the colors on Memorial Day in the opening ceremony, and then it was time for the first pitch. Marge Shiell, symbolizing the past Blues tradition and beaming with vibrant energy, threw the first pitch to catcher Trevor Girard. Trevor said, "It was an honor to catch that ball that day. True blues fan." Coach Nelson added, "It was one of the most memorable baseball moments in my life that night. It was a pleasure to be a part of it." After Marge threw the first pitch, the Scobey Blues flocked to her because they knew what Marge represented. Somehow, they knew. The excitement of playing their first Legion home game was bursting from the Scobey nine. Although the weather was damp, cold, and rainy, nothing could dampen the spirits of these boys and the town of Scobey on Opening Day.

Marge (Norman) Shiell moments after throwing the first pitch to Trevor Girard on Opening Day, May 30, 2016.

Havre won the game 11-9, but that didn't matter. The Blues were back. American Legion Baseball was back in Scobey.

The Blues, trying to wake up after a 13-year slumber, got off to a rough start and struggled to get in the winning column. The Scobey Legion program carried a 30-game losing streak into the 2016 season, dating to the loss to Homestead at Divisional on July 27, 2002, as the Blues went 0-29 in 2003. Coach Nelson talked about the team's major weakness: "Game-time experience at this level of baseball. Defensive shifts and communication are also some things we need to get used to." After the opening-day loss to the Havre B team, the Blues lost 18-6 to the Glendive B team in the first game of a doubleheader, extending the losing streak to 32 games.

But it was only a matter of time before this hard-working coach and team broke through, and in the second game against Glendive B, the Blues "kicked the nearly 14-year skid to the curb"[3] with a 10-0 win. The Blues followed their win over Glendive B with a 13-12 loss to the Miles City Mavericks B team at historic Denton Field but then proceeded to reel off five consecutive wins, beating Miles City in the second end, then sweeping the Richland County

Patriots B team and Colstrip Rangers, in doubleheaders. Although the Blues were playing in the unsanctioned "B League" and not in the Eastern A division and were playing the team's junior varsity squads with a few varsity players dropping down, no one (except perhaps Chuck Nelson and the Blues) expected the team to be 6-3 after nine games and riding a five-game winning streak into the Havre Jamboree.

The Blues took their knocks at the Havre Jamboree, losing to the Electric City Outlaws, the Kootenai Valley Rangers, the Fort Macleod Royals, and the Medicine Hat Majestics. In talking about the tournament, Coach Nelson said, "We didn't win any games, but I told the boys, 'Yeah, we love to hit and do all those fun things, but we're going to back and work on the things we suck at, which isn't always fun.' But they worked hard, and it showed. We practiced sometimes late in the day, almost till dark sometimes. A lot of those boys drove themselves or lived right there in town, and I was like, 'Hey, man, if you want to be here, I'll be here, and we'll work on stuff, and we'll get better.' And they did. They put in the work and the effort, and they got better."

Next up for the Blues was the 27th Annual Ed Gallo Wood Bat Tournament hosted by the Glacier Twin in Whitefish, Montana, in Chuck's former neck of the woods. Chuck called in late and said Whitefish was "gracious" and let them in the tournament, making a ninth team. The family that had hosted Chuck when he played for the Glacier Twins hosted the entire Scobey Blues team at their house on Whitefish Lake for the tournament. Chuck said, "It was great for these boys from Scobey. We went out on Whitefish Lake, we swam and had a good time, did a lot of teambuilding exercises, knowing that we were going to go over there and face some very good teams. We played Olympia, Washington. There was a reporter from Olympia there covering the team, and I told him how many people lived in Daniels County. He said, 'Holy cow, we graduate more seniors than that in our high school!'" CJ Nelson pitched against Olympia, and Chuck said "he had a good day. They were hitting him early. They were hitting his fastball, so I went out and told him to mix it up a little. He started throwing his slider [CJ's dad Kevin's money pitch was his slider], and they were chasing it. Sometimes, he would throw three straight sliders to a hitter because he could control it, then close with a high fastball. He chewed through that lineup after that. We were in that game until the last inning, and we lost by four runs, all unearned, just some errors and mistakes, but we really competed, and that was a big stepping stone for the guys, even though we lost. I wouldn't let them hang their heads. This was definitely a big boost for us. To go to the Ed Gallo in year one and compete was huge."

After the rough first inning, the Blues stayed on the field with Olympia, losing 5-1. CJ Nelson (who was only 16 years old then) remembers pitching against Olympia. He said, "They were a very good team. We were a little shaky to start; we had a couple of errors that they scored on in the first inning or two, and if I remember correctly, they didn't score again. We played a great game! It was definitely one of the better games I pitched, outside the first inning, especially against that kind of talent. It was always a little more fun pitching well against better teams. I know I started out that game not throwing a ton of off-speed; I'd say about the third inning, I really started mixing it up and found a lot of success in that. I was able to get a fair amount of strikeouts, and the guys made a lot of great plays in the field! And like I said earlier, we played a hell of a game and just couldn't put runs on the board. I know a couple of times we had guys in scoring position but just couldn't capitalize."

The Blues also played up to their competition in games against the Belgrade Bandits and Glacier Twins, giving them some much-needed confidence heading into the unofficial State Class B Tournament in Lewistown in July. Chuck and the boys had worked hard after the Havre Jamboree and were improving with every day and every game. They stayed on the field with some really good teams in Whitefish.

And the Blues got to go swimming in Whitefish Lake, too.

STATE TOURNAMENT

SOME SCOBEY BABE RUTH PLAYERS JOINED THE BLUES for the unofficial state Class B Tournament in Lewistown after the Babe Ruth All-Star Tournament in Miles City. Two players who got "called up" were Martin Farver and Jackson Oie, both third-generation baseball players from Scobey. Martin's grandfather Howard played for the Scobey Legion and High School teams in the early 1950s and was a member of the 1958 Scobey Plainsmen team that won the state AAU championship. Martin's dad, Terry, played for the Blues from 1988 to 1990 and was a member of Don Lekvold's 1990 team that took third at State, narrowly missing an opportunity to play in regionals. Jackson's grandfather, Don Oie, played on Doc Norman's 1960 Legion team, and his dad, Morgan, played for the Blues from 1992 to 1995. I asked Martin if he remembered his first game as a Blue in Lewistown. He said, "Yeah, I do. The first Legion game I ever played would have started at about 11:30 p.m. because of rain delays. Through Little League and Babe Ruth, I never really expected to get a Legion team back. A lot of the guys my age and the next two and three years in front of me were really focused on basketball at the time, and that's still really common around town, but it was exciting to play my first Legion game." (Martin's comment about athletes focused on basketball surfaced a lot in my interview with him. He made no effort to conceal his frustration with multisport athletes prioritizing basketball over baseball in the summer months, but the same was true in 2003 with football when the program folded. The Scobey Legion program faced the same headwinds 13 years later.)

The Blues fared excellently in Lewistown, losing one game and winning four to take third place. They beat B teams from Great Falls 6-5, Medicine Hat 7-5, Lewistown 7-5, and Cranbrook, British Columbia, 2-1 in four innings before a hailstorm ended the game.

Scobey finished their first year back with a 20-16 overall record and a third-place finish at the Lewistown Tournament, which is outstanding considering the program was inactive for 13 years. Most importantly, the boys who wanted to play Legion ball got the opportunity to play and improved throughout the season.

2016 Scobey Blues, third place at Lewistown Tournament. Back row, left to right: Coach Nelson, Kole Ralston, Spencer Rush, CJ Nelson, Peyton Nieskens, Lane Knudsen, Kobe Ralston, Brandon Meade (from Medicine Lake), Jace Schumacher. Front row Martin Farver, Jackson Oie, Anders Knudsen, Devin Halverson. *Family photo*

I asked Chuck to reflect on the 2016 season. He said, "That group of kids, man, . . . those boys wanted to restart it more than anybody. They wanted a place to go play, they wanted to be a Blues player, they understood the legacy of what it was to *be* a Blues player, and they came together. We weren't the most talented team by any means, but they had determination.

Nobody missed practice. Everyone showed up all the time. They would put extra time in. I had to travel from Williston to Scobey every night for practice. We practiced a little late because of that, but they were there before I was, and they begged me to stay late. Those boys were dedicated. I give all the credit to them."

Unfortunately, Chuck had to move due to personal family matters and could not return to coach the Blues in 2017. Nine years later, he is still involved with Legion baseball, but he said, "I've learned not to coach my boys, so I've taken a hiatus on coaching." He recently attended the American Legion Coaches Association in Washington, DC, and he is involved with the Tri-City Cardinals, who are hosting the 2025 State Class Montana/Alberta Legion Tournament in Conrad from July 31 to August 3. His 15-year-old son Wes will be playing his first year of Legion baseball and in uniform for the host Cardinals at the tournament, as will Tyler Bucklin's son Nick. Two sons of Blues will be playing for the Cardinals at the State A Tournament in Conrad.

EXTRA INNINGS

LANE KNUDSEN REMEMBERS THE 2016 ED GALLO TOURNAment in Whitefish. "We were, for a lack of words, kind of a 'Bad News Bears' team that year. We were accepted by the host team (the Glacier Twins) through Chuck Nelson. They, in a sense, took us under their wing during that tournament. One of their coaches even welcomed us into their home through the tournament. One of my favorite memories from that tournament was one night when we stayed up a little later than we probably should have the night before a morning game playing poker and sharing jokes with those guys."

The Kootenai Valley Rangers, who the Blues played at the Havre Jamboree, were from Chuck's hometown of Eureka, Montana. Eureka started a Legion program there the year after he graduated in 1999, which ran through 2021.

Chuck Nelson is a Cubs fan, so the 2016 season was a good baseball year for Chuck. In addition to helping revive the Blues program in 2016, leading the Scobey Blues to a 20-16 season and a third-place finish at State, the Cubs won their first World Series in 108 years (1908) in 2016, beating the Cleveland Indians 8–7 in 10 innings in Game 7.

Knowing that Chuck has a passion for baseball, I asked him how he got his start in baseball as a boy. He said, "I was born and raised in Eureka and started Little League there. I was a troubled kid, and they wanted me to do something to occupy my time and exert some energy, so they signed me up for baseball. And for years and years, I lived, ate, and breathed baseball, and it still hasn't quit." That is the most amazing story I've heard about how a kid got his start in baseball and how it became his passion.

Montana Legion Classifications

FROM 1928 TO 1948, MONTANA PLAYED IN A SINGLE LEAGUE. In 1949, Montana created a second league called "Class B" (now called "Class A"). From 1949 to 1986, teams played as either Class A or Class B teams. Starting in 1987, Montana teams changed to play as Class AA and Class A teams. The reason for the change stated on the Montana/Alberta Legion Baseball website was because "high school enrollments grew," but that doesn't make any sense—the same teams competing in Class B (like Scobey) "moved up" to play in Class A and likewise, for the former Class A teams, who competed in Class AA. For one year in 1969 (Scobey's first state championship), Montana Legion Baseball changed to Class AA and Class A designations, so the patches for Scobey's first state championship have Class A on them; the remaining seven have Class B. But the same teams were competing in each league. On the Montana/Alberta website, the current requirements to participate in Class AA, Class A, and Class B read as follows:

- **Class AA:** Senior (19 years old and under) league comprised of teams whose players come from high schools with a combined, or total, enrollment of more than 1,000 students.
- **Class A:** Also a senior league, but comprised of teams whose players come from high school that do not combine, or total, 1,000 students.
- **Class B (the unsanctioned league Scobey played in 2016):** Primarily a junior league (17 years old and under). New legion teams typically play and register as Class B junior or senior teams if 18-year-olds are going to be on the roster. Many Class B invitational tournaments are around Montana each summer, but there is no officially sanctioned state tournament for this level.

2017

Coach Josh Rustad and the Blues Keep It Going

> "We were committed to holding our end of the deal to revive the sport for Scobey. That group of guys all loved baseball and wanted to keep playing after the Babe Ruth days were over, and we made it happen. Sadly, it was short-lived once we graduated high school, and I truly hope it comes back to Scobey in time.
>
> —Jace Schumacher, Scobey Blues (2016-17)"

2017 Scobey Blues. Standing, left to right: Josh Rustad, Preston Baldry, Spencer Rush, Seth Myhre, Adler Morgan, Lane Knudsen, CJ Nelson. Front row, left to right: Martin Farver, Tanner Weeks, Devin Halverson, Anders Knudsen, Jace Schumacher, and Trey Girard. Jackson Oie, Preston Baldry, and Kenny Hammerly are not pictured. *Leader photo, Mike Stebleton.*

PRESEASON

Scobey found itself in a familiar situation in 2017—they needed a new head coach. For the sixth consecutive season that the Blues had fielded a team, dating to 2000, a search for a new leader would happen for the Blues. And like how it played out in 2016, a former Scobey Blues player would help find the coach. In 2016, it was Arlin Kaul (Blues 1986–89); in 2017, it was Jim LeProwse (Blues 1983–85). Jim was coaching softball at Dawson Community College and assisting Brent Diegel with the Blue Devils Legion team, and reached out to Josh Rustad about taking the job, as Josh was coaching at Dawson and Lake Region State at the time.

Thankfully for the Blues, Josh said yes, and the Blues had another new head coach. Josh brought a wealth of baseball knowledge with him, both as a player and coach. Like Chuck Nelson, he was from western Montana and was passionate about baseball. He played Legion ball for the Mission Valley Mariners (based in Polson) from 2008 to 2011 and college baseball for the Dawson Community College Buccaneers, where he pitched a no-hitter against Bottineau, North Dakota. He was the pitching coach at Dawson and later at Lake Region State College in Devils Lake, North Dakota.

Scobey returned nine players who had seen action on the 2016 team, including CJ Nelson, Jace Schumacher,

CJ Nelson delivers a pitch with classic form at the Havre Jamboree. *Family photo.*

Lane Knudsen, Spencer Rush, Tanner Weeks, Trey Girard, Martin Farver, Jackson Oie, Anders Knudsen, and Devin Halverson. Some had been called up from Babe Ruth late in the season but still had some Legion experience. Preston Baldry, Seth Myhre, Adler Morgan, and Kenny Hammerly joined the Blues for their first year of Legion baseball.

REGULAR SEASON

As they did in 2016, the Blues played in the unsanctioned Class B League in Montana in 2017. There was no regular season conference schedule, so the Blues traveled to several tournaments, including the Havre Jamboree in Havre, the Harold Gjerde Memorial Tournament in Lewistown, the Ed Gallo Memorial Wooden Bat Tournament in Whitefish, and the Culli Tournament in Glendive.

Here were some highlights for the Blues during the 2017 season:

- Wolf Point also had a B team in 2017, and the Blues played the Yellowjackets in a game at Burke Field in Wolf Point. Nice to see the two old "rivals" back on the field together. Scobey won the game, but it was a big win for both towns to have players on the field playing against each other.
- After two tough losses at the Havre Jamboree, the Blues picked up a big 14-2 win over Havre B. After the game, Jason Polk from Plentywood said, "Great to see the Blues again. Has been such a great program."
- In their first game of the Harold Gjerde in Lewistown, Martin Farver pitched a complete game to lead the Blues to a 13-3 win over the Powell (Wyoming) Pioneers. Lane Knudsen hit a solo home run to lead Scobey's hitting.
- On the final day of the Harold Gjerde, Lane Knudsen came up with a big two-out hit in the bottom of the seventh to walk it off for Scobey against the Tri-City Cardinals. The Blues split their games and took fourth place in the tournament.
- In a creative fundraiser intended to inspire young boys in Scobey to become "Future Blues," the Blues hosted "Meet the Blues Day!" for area youth on the day of a home game against the Glasgow Reds. The fun started with a Wiffle ball game, followed by a minicamp hosted by Coach Rustad and the Scobey Blues players. The youngsters were invited to stay for hot dogs/root beer floats and sit together near the dugout during the game with Glasgow that night. (Unfortunately, the youngsters would not become "Future Blues," as the program folded for the second time following the 2019 season.)
- At the home game against the Glasgow Reds on "Meet the Blues Day," Andy Stolen was spotted in the crowd, and a photo was snapped of him. His presence at the game recalled the storied Scobey baseball tradition, both the Scobey Plainsmen and the Scobey Blues. Andy pitched for Opheim on the 1949 district champion Legion team and the two Scobey Plainsmen state championship teams in 1958 and 1960, and his sons Randy and Greg played on five of the eight state championship teams between 1977 and 1982. He coached Little League and Babe Ruth with Dad in Peerless and taught Jon and me how to throw our curve balls and Ray Chapman how to throw his knuckleball. When his picture was posted on the Scobey Blues Baseball page, several comments popped up, including, "I remember him and the Plainsmen. I spent a lot of time watching them" (Sue Dalbout) and "I remember him being a good left-handed pitcher" (Doug Zeitner). Look at the smile on his face watching the Blues play baseball again in Scobey. Can you imagine what his eyes had seen on that field in almost 70 years as a player, umpire, and fan? He had seen it all, and now he got to see the Blues play against the Reds one more time.
- At the Culli Tournament in Glendive, the Blues beat the Glendive All-Stars and Watford City. They ended their season with a nice four-game winning streak, carving out a 9-15 overall record in their second year back from the long slumber.

At the end of the season, Jace Schumacher honored Coach Rustad with a post on the Blues Facebook page: "[I] would like to thank our coach, Josh Rustad, for all that he has done this year. It means so much to the kids and this town. I'm proud of my teammates this year. I wish I could have finished out the season, but there was a calling for me to be elsewhere. Thank you all. Until next year!"

Coach Rustad summed up his first year coaching the Blues. "I couldn't have been more proud to coach a great group of guys! The strides we made as a team and as individuals can't even be put into words. Thank you to my seniors for laying the foundation and showing these guys how to put in the work for what is an outstanding baseball team! You will always have a place in this program! (Once a Blue, always a Blue.) I can't wait to re-up and do this thing again next year!

Thanks for giving me an opportunity to be your coach. Bring on the high expectations and lofty goals to be the best Class B program in the state! Good luck boys, on your future endeavors!"

The 2017 season was the last for Lane Knudsen, Preston Baldry, Spencer Rush, Jace Schumacher, and Seth Myhre. I asked Lane Knudsen what he remembered most about the two years he got to play for the Blues. He said, "One of the things I remember most was getting to go on the road trips to the tournaments. We had a good group of guys, and it made for a lot of fun. Another thing that stands out in my head is the 2016 season. There were a few of us who had taken a couple of years off from baseball because of the lack of a legion team in Scobey to bump up to from Babe Ruth ball. When a couple of us got word that we might be getting a team going, we were pretty excited to play again. It was a lot of fun! I remember there was a lot of community help and Blues alumni that helped get the ball rolling!"

I also asked Jace Schumacher what he remembered about the two summers he got to play for the Blues. He said, "What comes to mind first is the memories we all made as friends and teammates in those two summers, traveling across the state of Montana from Glendive to Whitefish and all in between. The hours spent together and the experiences we shared are so ingrained in all of us that when we get together we always talk about those summers. I know all those guys, and I just enjoyed the experience and bringing back baseball to Scobey. I also think about many of us would have lost the ability to play baseball at a high school level, and there was a certain group of us that wanted to revive that, and we were all willing to travel between Scobey and Plentywood in our own vehicles to get any type of practices in that we could. We were committed to holding our end of the deal to revive the sport for Scobey. That group of guys all loved baseball and wanted to keep playing after the Babe Ruth days were over, and we made it happen. Sadly, it was short-lived once we graduated high school, and I truly hope it comes back to Scobey in time."

EXTRA INNINGS

I ASKED MARTIN FARVER WHAT HE REMEMBERED ABOUT THE 2017 season. He said, "Funny enough, if you can imagine, in Montana, it's sparse when it comes to finding a Class B baseball team. We played Wolf Point a few times that year. They pieced together a B team, but they didn't have a great squad. There weren't a lot of B teams out there. I think most programs were kind of going through what Scobey was, just struggling for numbers. And a lot of those teams just weren't able to field B teams, because they only had 12, 13, maybe 14 kids."

Andy Stolen on "Meet the Blues Day!" *Family photo.*

Andy Stolen with Marge Shiell and Randy Stolen on "Meet the Blues Day!" Family photo.

The Revival

2017 Scobey Blues on the road with the Blues van. Left to right: Kenny Hammerly, Adler Morgan, Martin Farver, Jackson Oie, Preston Baldry, Devin Halverson, Anders Knudsen, CJ Nelson, Spencer Rush, Trey Girard, Jace Schumacher, Seth Myhre. Lane Knudsen and Tanner Weeks are not pictured. *Family photo.*

Martin said most of the games in 2017 were played at tournaments. He said, "We played three tournaments in three straight weekends in Havre, Whitefish, and Lewistown, and we played in a Class B tournament in Glendive." I asked Martin if he remembered any funny stories about those tournaments because I know all the Blues teams that traveled always had tales to tell about the road trips, some of which can be printed. Martin laughed at my question. "Oh, man," he said. "We did those three tournaments in a 15-passenger van. And the longest one of all, Whitefish, we did not have air conditioning on the way down or on the way back. Thirteen boys in a van that small, well . . . you can imagine. The program wasn't overly well funded, so we were finding different places to stay. In Havre, we stayed in their wrestling room, which was a great time. We had a Tee-ball field set up in the wrestling room. Any time we weren't at the field, we were playing tee ball. And then we did the same thing in Columbia Falls for the Whitefish Tournament. We ended up staying in the wrestling room again at the school. And I think both times after we'd been playing baseball for four days straight, the last night we stayed up playing Tee-ball in the wrestling room until about three in the morning, the whole team. Those are some of my favorite memories playing baseball."

Martin and I talked about the bonds that are formed with the other players in baseball, how spending so much time together on the road trips, in the dugout, and at practices forges a camaraderie with the other players that is not quite the same as in the other sports. Martin added, "I think it [the camaraderie] has to do with time spent together, but also, the atmosphere is a lot more laid back in baseball in the summer than the school sports, like football, basketball, and track. In school sports, you know, it was like, 'We have to win, we have to win, we have to win.' Trust me, I don't enjoy losing by any means, but baseball was always a lot more laid back; it was a very different environment. Everybody's there to win, but having fun was *as* important when we were playing baseball as anything else was, and I can't say that for any of the other sports I played in at the time."

It was an amazing comeback story for CJ Nelson to play baseball in the summer of 2017. In November 2016, CJ suffered a broken neck in a playoff football game against Ennis. Three months later, he was back on the basketball floor, leading Scobey to the state tournament and a third-place finish. In the state consolation game, CJ scored 28 points and hit the game-winning free throws with 17.5 seconds remaining to give the Spartans third place over Hays-Lodgepole, 74-72. I asked CJ to comment on the challenges he faced coming back from his injury and what helped him get through it. He said, "Well I guess I was just happy to be there and competing again! It definitely felt like a long wait to finally get back out there playing. It was extremely hard going to basketball practices and not being able to participate then the games started and it was even more difficult. Mentally for me just not being able to compete with all my friends was the most challenging. Physically I'd say just not being able to do anything basically for three months losing all my conditioning and muscle it took a while after I was cleared to finally feel more normal. But I'd just say my family, friends, and coaches, all being positive really helped me get through it all. Scobey and Opheim just being the communities that they are also played a big role in helping me get through it all. Everywhere I'd go people were always smiling and giving words of encouragement!"

Jace Schumacher remembers a couple of funny stories from the long road trips. "We pranked one of our teammates at the Whitefish tournament. At night, we went and collected a bunch of crayfish and put them all over his sleeping bag, and he didn't even notice them until morning. Another funny story was we had full access to a couple of high schools we stayed at for a tournament weekend. We would sleep in their wrestling rooms, and the entire school was open for us, and we would run around playing dodgeball or basketball until three o'clock in the morning, knowing we had to be at the field at eight o'clock. One of those nights, a teammate of ours, Spencer Rush, had brought his entire camping grill set and made us burgers and hot dogs at two or three in the morning after a game."

2018

The Underdog Blues Compete in North Dakota Northwest Region Class A

> *For the Scobey Blues, as the sixth-seeded team out of six squads, they knocked off No. 3 and No. 4 and lost to No. 1 and No. 2 to finish fourth. Any way one slices it, that's not a bad way to end a campaign for a program just three seasons into a reboot after being idle for 13 years.*
>
> —Mike Stebleton, from the article "Blues Did Not Win It All But Sure Tried To," *Daniels County Leader*, August 2, 2018

PRESEASON

When second-year Head Coach Josh Rustad assembled his 2018 team in the spring, several experienced players were returning, including ace pitcher and shortstop CJ Nelson, Devin Halverson, Jackson Oie, Martin Farver, Anders Knudsen, Kenny Hammerly, Brandon Meade, and Trey Girard. The Blues were building a little experience after two years on the diamond and would be stronger in 2018—but they would also be playing stronger competition. Joining the Blues for their first Legion seasons were Kannon Ferestad, Walker Ator, Isaac Johnson, Prewitt Leibrand, Payton Leibrand, Ayden Hobbs, Colter Oie, and Josh Hammerly.

This was a young team, as only CJ Nelson and Trey Girard were in the final year of eligibility with the Blues. Three players—Brandon Meade, Walker Ator, and Isaac Johnson—were from Medicine Lake.

The previous two seasons had been fun, but something had been missing—a competitive regular-season conference league with standings and a postseason tournament. That would change in the 2018 season when the Blues competed in the six-team North Dakota Northwest American Legion Class A Conference. (North Dakota has three sanctioned American Legion Baseball leagues: Class AA, Class A, and Class B.) So, for the first time in the history of Scobey American Legion Baseball, the Blues would be playing in the northwest corner of the state—of North Dakota. The Blues were able to enter the league when the Velva 39ers dropped down to Class B. Unlike the previous two seasons when they played ad hoc schedules against Montana B Legion teams with no postseason tournaments, the Blues would play a conference schedule and compete in a postseason regional tournament, where if they won, they could advance to State. Baseball is fun, sure, but there's nothing like competition, and the competitive juices were flowing again in Scobey in 2018.

REGULAR SEASON

The Blues played a league schedule against the five Class A North Dakota teams and some nonconference games against B teams in Montana. During the regular season, Scobey had a win over Glendive B and three wins over the Miles City B Outlaws. The week before the regional tournament in Watford City, the Blues played in the Glendive Culli Class B Tournament and had three wins—two over Wolf Point B and one over Glendive B. It was a good warm-up for the regional tournament the following week.

Martin Farver and the team enjoyed the structured competition the North Dakota Class A League offered, playing home-and-home doubleheaders with the teams in the league and a postseason tournament. Martin remembers a big conference win over the Williston Oilers at home in Scobey. "They thought they were pretty special. I think most of those kids were upset they weren't on the double-A Keybirds team, would be my guess. I remember when we beat them in Scobey, they were pretty upset they lost to a team with a thousand people. I'm guessing that bus ride home wasn't very fun."

The Blues took their knocks playing in the North Dakota Class A league during the regular season, but they also improved by playing against stronger competition. Scobey played a 12-game conference schedule in the North Dakota Northwest region, playing four doubleheaders on the road and two at home. The Blues mustered three wins in conference action, and the final standings looked like this:

1. Beulah Cyclones
2. Watford City Walleyes
3. Minot Metros
4. Williston Oilers
5. Surrey Blue Sox
6. Scobey Blues

But final standings can be deceiving. The Blues had some pitching and were looking to surprise a few people at the regional tournament in Watford City. Colter Oie said, "We had confidence going into the tournament; we knew we could play with those teams, and we were playing our best ball at tournament time."

Playing as an underdog is always an advantage: lower expectations from your opponent and higher expectations of yourself. Let's see if the underdog Blues can make some noise at the regional tournament in Watford City.

REGIONAL TOURNAMENT

THE WATFORD CITY WALLEYES (HOW COOL OF A NAME IS THE Walleyes?) hosted the 2018 North Dakota Northwest Class A Regional Tournament at beautiful Rough Rider Center Field in Watford City, North Dakota. Opening day match-ups were as follows:

- Williston (4) vs. Surrey (5)
- Minot (3) vs. Scobey (6)
- Beulah (1) and Watford City (2) had byes.

2018 Scobey Blues at Northwest Regional in Watford City. Left to right: Kenny Hammerly, Jackson Oie, Devin Halverson, Prewitt Leibrand, Anders Knudsen, Colter Oie, Martin Farver, Trey Girard, CJ Nelson, Isaac Johnson, Walker Ator. *Family photo.*

Martin Farver remembers how special it was playing in a season-ending tournament that meant something. He said, "I think all of us really enjoyed having something to play for now, other than just, 'Well, the season's over, now everyone go home.' I really enjoyed playing in the regional tournament in Watford City. It was way more organized."

Colter Oie remembers the competitive tournament. "It was really tough competition. Watford was huge. I remember every player in their lineup was big, and most of them were 18. Beulah was a good team, and they had an 18-year-old NDSU commit who was a stud."

And the Blues played up to their competition.

Coach Rustad handed the ball to ace pitcher CJ Nelson to pitch against the third-seeded Metros, who had beaten Scobey 9-6 and 16-9 during conference play. But the post-season was different, and the Scobey Blues played sparkling baseball in all three phases to claim a huge 14-1 upset. CJ pitched well, hurling 103 pitches and scattering seven hits, striking out 10 Metros and walking only one, handcuffing Minot by only allowing one run in seven innings. Coach Rustad beamed about CJ's performance. "One inning, he had runners on second and third with no outs, and he found a way to pitch his way out of it."

Scobey's bats boomed with 14 hits, providing CJ with more than enough run support as the Blues plated 14 runs. Several Blues had a day at the plate: Isaac Johnson was 3-for-5 with a double, two runs scored, and an RBI; Martin Farver was 1-for-2 with two runs and an RBI; Devin Halverson was 2-for-5 with two runs and two RBIs; Colter Oie was 3-for-3 with four runs scored and two RBIs; Jackson Oie was 2-for-4 with a double and two RBIs, and CJ Nelson scored two runs and had an RBI. Coach Rustad said, "Everybody was big. Everybody was 2-for-4 or 2-for-5."

Defensively, Scobey was near-perfect in the field, as they committed only one error in seven innings.

Mike Stebleton of the *Leader* lauded the first-round upset, writing, "Metros? Never heard of them. It's a guarantee the Minot Metros have now heard of the Scobey Blues after the northeastern Montana boys punched them in the chops with a 14-1 haymaker."[4]

The upset over the three-seed vaulted Scobey into the winner's bracket against host Watford City. Scobey's defense stayed solid against the Walleyes (they played errorless ball in the field), but the bats were silenced, and Watford City won 8-1. Coach Rustad said, "Not once did we put together back-to-back hits. We could never piece together one inning of good offense."[5] But Coach Rustad got an excellent performance on the mound from 15-year-old Walker Ator from Medicine Lake. "For a 15-year-old, he pitched extremely well for us. I couldn't ask for a better outing from him. We just couldn't get anything going on offense to help him."⁶ Isaac Johnson was 1-for-4 and drove in the lone run for Scobey.

The loss pushed Scobey into a loser-out game against the fourth-seeded Williston Oilers, and the Blues hoped to snatch another upset against a higher seed to stay alive in the tournament. The Oilers had won 3 of 4 games against Scobey during conference play. Coach Rustad started Martin Farver on the mound in the third game for Scobey, and the Blues jumped on Williston for an early 5-0 lead, but the Oilers came back to tie it 5-5 in the fifth. Coach Rustand said a defensive lapse (one costly error) led to several unearned runs in the fifth, but Scobey shored up the defense after that. From then on, it was all Scobey, as the Blues scored four runs in the sixth and added two more in the seventh to garner their second win of the tournament, 11-5. Martin Farver pitched five strong innings, getting relief help from Anders Knudsen, who pitched scoreless ball the final two frames to earn the win. Coach Rustad was pleased with his pitching again. "He [Anders Knudsen] was huge to shut the door for us." Farver and Knudsen scattered seven hits between them. Scobey's bats again popped, as the Blues banged out 13 hits with several hitters contributing to the 11 runs: CJ Nelson was 2-for-4 with a double and scored two runs; Isaac Johnson was 2-for-5 with a double and four RBIs; Martin Farver was 2-for-5 with two RBIs; Walker Ator was 3-for-4 with a run scored; Anders Knudsen was 2-for-4, with a double, three runs scored and an RBI; Jackson Oie was 1-for-4 with a double and a run scored. Coach Rustad said, "Everyone came through on offense where we had some timely hits."

One of Martin Farver's favorite memories of the 2018 season was beating Williston again in the loser-out game of the regional tournament. He said, "There were points during that game where the people in the stands were saying, 'Who the hell is this team? Where are they from? Where the hell is Scobey? What the hell is Scobey?' I enjoyed that a lot. That was a pretty fun game." It's fun to be the underdog and stick it to the home crowd.

Sixth-seeded Scobey, now with two upsets against higher seeds under its belt, now faced top-seeded Beulah. The winner would advance to the semifinal, and the loser would finish in fourth place. Another 15-year-old from Medicine Lake, this time Isaac Johnson, started on the mound for Scobey. It was the fifth pitcher Coach Rustad had used in the tournament. The Blues took a quick 1-0 lead when CJ Nelson stole home (that's rare), and the score stayed that way until the bottom of the third when the Cyclones scored some runs and pulled away for an 11-1 win in six innings. Coach Rustad was upbeat after the season-ending loss. "A couple bounces didn't go our way, but we had that underdog mentality and kept trying. That's the mentality we took on the whole season."⁷ Coach Rustad was once again proud of his 15-year-old's performance on the mound. "He [Isaac Johnson] pitched his butt off." CJ Nelson was 2-for-3 with a run (stealing home) to lead Scobey's hitting in his last game as a Scobey Blue.

Top-seeded Beulah went on to beat Watford City but lost to Surrey in the championship game. Only Surrey advanced to the state tournament, as the Williston Oilers—who Scobey had eliminated—had an automatic bid as host.

Colter Oie credited the Blues' pitchers with their success in the tournament. "Our pitchers that tournament threw really well; we didn't have a very deep bullpen, so to make it four games deep is tough without considering how good the competition was."

Mike Stebleton summed up the successful regional tournament for Scobey: "For the Scobey Blues, as the sixth-seeded team out of six squads, they knocked off No. 3 and No. 4 and lost to No. 1 and No. 2 to finish fourth. Any way one slices it, that's not a bad way to end a campaign for a program just three seasons into a reboot after being idle for 13 years."⁸

After winning two games and finishing fourth place at the regional tournament in Watford City, the Blues ended the 2018 campaign with an overall record of 12-16. They lost just two players—CJ Nelson and Trey Girard—to eligibility for the 2019 season, but these would be four big cleats to fill, and CJ's arm on the mound would be difficult to replace.

I asked CJ Nelson to share his experience playing for the Scobey Blues. He offered this letter:

My mom was my coach, so I had been around the team and at practices previous years. I started Little League early due to Opheim not having enough players out for the team—I was a first-grader. I was so excited that I was finally getting to play

Coaches with 2018 Individual Award Winners. Left to Right: Josh Johnson, Martin Farver, CJ Nelson, Trey Girard, and Head Coach Josh Rustad

baseball. I had my parents out in the yard playing catch, hitting me grounders and pop-ups, pitching to me as much as I could get them out there. Obviously, there were some pretty big guys we played against, and I remember getting hit a couple of times while I was up to bat, and that wasn't real fun for me. I also remember catching my first fly ball. We were in Lustre, and I caught a fly ball and was just so excited I caught it that I didn't throw the ball in, and their players all tagged up and took off running, and I just sat there, shocked/excited while everyone was yelling at me to "throw it in." Definitely learned a lot that year.

Then, going on, we weren't the best team; we took our fair share of losses throughout my Little League career. I don't remember winning many games, maybe a couple of games a year. My 12-year-old year of Little League we were a little better; we won a few games that year; I'd say we were around .500. I made all-stars two or three years we always could compete with a couple teams, but didn't really win any games. I think we had one year when we won a couple of games, but it was still lots of fun playing with all those players. This was well before I had moved to Scobey so I would say a lot of my friendships started through baseball and all-stars in Scobey. I then played for the Scobey Giants in Babe Ruth where we were pretty successful. My 13-year-old year was our worst year, but we still won a fair amount of games. My 14-year-old year, we were really good; we won the tournament in Wolf Point. And then my 15-year-old year, we made it to the championship but lost, so we got second that year. I made it to all-stars all three years, where we had lots of success there as well. My 13-year-old year, we played in Havre. Then my 14-year-old year we played in Butte, where we did very well. I believe we had 6 or 7 guys that made it just off our Scobey team. We ended up losing our first game of the tournament in a close game then we battled back and won 3 or 4 games and ended up getting third place. The team we lost to in our first game we ten-run-ruled later on. The field we were playing on didn't have any lights and I remember one of our games ended up getting postponed until the next morning, which worked out pretty good for me because by rule I was eligible to pitch again that morning, so I got to finish the game. That was probably one of the best if not the best and most fun teams I played on. Then my 15-year-old year we played in Conrad where we also ended up taking third. I thought that was going to be the end of my baseball, but after I signed to Dawson Community College for basketball when I was down there the baseball coach asked me if I'd like to play. So, I thought I would try it out, so I ended up right after basketball was over, I went on a trip with the baseball team to Arizona where I ended up pitching in a couple games. After that trip when we got back, I decided to just stick to one sport so I could just focus on that and train to get better there rather than bouncing back and forth. Not practicing baseball at all since the previous summer of my senior year of high school made it difficult, and ended up making the decision to stick to basketball fairly easy.

EXTRA INNINGS

THEY PLAY BASEBALL IN NORTH DAKOTA. EVERY TEAM THAT Scobey played in their conference and at the regional tournament in 2018 had been playing baseball since March, when the North Dakota High School Activities Association (NDHSAA) baseball season in North Dakota started. There are 24 Class A teams and 56 Class B teams competing in North Dakota High School baseball (80 teams). In American Legion Baseball, there are three sanctioned divisions—Class AA (10 teams), Class A (20), and Class B (48). At the collegiate level, there are teams at the NCAA D1, D2, and D3 levels, several NAIA teams, and five junior colleges. Amateur town-team baseball still thrives in North Dakota as well. The North Dakota Amateur Baseball state tournament is played yearly at Jack Brown Stadium in Jamestown with four divisions: Masters, A, AA, and AAA.

In writing about Scobey's upstart performance in the 2018 Northwest Regional in Watford City, Mike Stebleton mentioned that the Blues were "behind the 8-ball from the get-go"[9] regarding high school baseball in North Dakota. He wrote, "While the boys of the Beulah Cyclones, Minot Metros, Surrey Blue Sox, Watford City Walleyes, and Williston Oilers were starting their North Dakota High School baseball season March 15, the Scobey Blues were still the Scobey Spartans and Froid-Lake Redhawks starting their high school golf and track/field seasons. While the five aforementioned North Dakota teams were running the bases and throwing curve balls, the soon-to-be Blues were watching tee shots and putts run and rounding the final curve of the (pick-a-number)-meter dash/run."[10]

In the previous season (2017), new pitching rules went into effect for American Legion Baseball, limiting pitchers based on the number of pitches thrown rather than on number of innings pitched. The maximum pitch count rule in 2017 for one day was 120 pitches, but the new rule in 2018 reduced it to 105. Additional significant changes were made for the 2018 American Legion Baseball season:

National Tournament Play Will Feature Seven-inning Games

LEAGUES WOULD STILL HAVE THE OPTION TO PLAY NINE-INNING games during the regular season; however, beginning at the state tournament and through the American Legion World Series, games would be seven innings.

Changes to Pitch Count

AFTER THE FIRST SEASON (2017) WITH PITCH COUNT RULES under the PitchSmart program, the Legion Baseball Committee adjusted the pitch count chart ahead of the 2018 season to be more in line with the suggestions from Major League Baseball and USA Baseball:

Pitchers would have a maximum of 105 pitches daily, down from 120. Pitchers could only make two appearances in any three consecutive days. Required rest would be as follows:

- 1-30 pitches: 0 days
- 31-45 pitches: 1 day
- 46-60 pitches: 2 days
- 61-80 pitches: 3 days
- 81+ pitches: 4 days

Regarding the pitch count rule change, Gary Stone, chairman of the Legion Baseball Committee, stated, "The first year of PitchSmart in American Legion Baseball was a resounding success, and we continue to make adjustments to improve our implementation of the program. These changes, along with shortened games in tournament play, put more of a focus on player safety for our program while still letting coaches manage games effectively."[11]

Courtesy Runner and Re-entry

IN REGULAR-SEASON PLAY ONLY, LEAGUES COULD ALLOW FOR courtesy runners and re-entry. Courtesy runners were permitted for pitchers or catchers. Leagues allowing re-entry may permit players to be substituted and return to the game once, provided the player returns to the same slot in the batting order.

Graduate Rule

LANGUAGE WAS REMOVED FROM THE RULE BOOK THAT REQUIRED 19-year-olds to be former Legion players. Any interested 19-year-old could now play for their previous Legion team (if applicable) or the team closest to their domicile.

To illustrate the effect of the rule change on pitching, CJ Nelson was done after his 103-pitch seven-inning performance in the first game of the regional tournament. In the old rule (12 innings in three days), CJ would have had five innings of eligibility left and would have gotten his seven innings back after two days of rest. With the rule change, he was done, as throwing 103 pitches against Minot required four days of rest. He was also two pitches away from his maximum (105) in one day. No more 12-inning, 219-pitch games like Fort Macleod starter Craig Hann pitched in the 1996 state tournament the game before the Royals played Scobey.

Coach Jack Sprague, head coach of the Wolf Point Yellowjackets (1999–2010) and Glasgow Reds (2012–23), said the new pitch count rules made it more difficult for the smaller towns to compete against the larger towns in the regular season and postseason tournaments, as the larger towns typically had more pitching depth simply due to numbers. The switch to the seven-inning games somewhat offset the new pitch count rules. Before the pitch count, the smaller towns could ride the arms of three good pitchers and win a tournament. A coach could get 36 innings in three days out of three pitchers. For example, Jon Puckett pitched over 20 innings and made three appearances in four days in the 1977 state tournament, winning two games and saving one. With the pitch count, he likely would not have been able to complete his first start in the tournament and would have needed four days of rest before pitching again.

Doc was not a big fan of pitch counts. He butted heads with Assistant Coach Gene Thompson, who was the pitching coach for Scobey's 1969 state championship team and was big into pitch counts before they were even really a thing. Danny Wolfe remembers Gene Thompson counting pitches in the dugout in 1969, but Doc would have none of it. Danny said, "When Gene came, he set up a pitch count—and this was the first time I'd ever heard of it. He kept track of the pitches in the dugout, and when a guy got to a hundred pitches, that was it. Gene would say, 'He's got a hundred pitches,' but Doc would say, 'Well Jesus Christ, he can finish off the game,' and the two would argue about it. That's the first time I ever saw anybody do a pitch count." Gene was ahead of his time. This was 1969.

The head coach of the Blues also had to double as a van driver, which was a greater responsibility than drawing up lineup cards, making pitching decisions, and flashing signals on third base. Driving home to Scobey after a doubleheader against the Minot Metros, Coach Rustad's quick thinking saved the day when a deer jumped out in front of the Blues van and trailer at 12:30 a.m. He didn't swerve and got the van stopped quickly. Everyone was wearing their seat belts, and no one was hurt. Naturally, the parents were relieved, as one posted, "Thanks, Josh Rustad, for taking care of our Boys of Summer!"

Marge Shiell passed away on August 13, 2018. On the Scobey Blues Baseball Facebook page, the following post was made in her memory: "After Marge threw the first pitch on a Blues home game after 13 years without a Legion program in 2016, she rarely missed a game after that. The smile never left her face, and she never quit cheering. She will be greatly missed, but her spirit and love for the game and her Blues lives on!" Marge's nephew, Jim Sampson, posted this on Marge's obituary website: "Aunt Marge was a great family matriarch and probably our favorite relative of all time. She was also a favored Scobey icon. I'm not sure if Uncle Clyde or Aunt Marge was more important to Scobey baseball."

So many Scobey Legion players have a special memory of Marge. Here is Mike Gunderson's. "I recall one time in my life I was going through a tough time. I saw Marge in the store. Without saying a word, she came up to me and gave me a long hug. She then said, 'Mike, you are one of my favorite people.' I felt truly blessed. Then I started thinking, she probably says that to everyone. But you know what? It didn't matter because she totally meant it to everyone she said it to. Loved that beautiful lady."

The picture of Marge with the eight state championship Scobey Blues trophies was taken in August 2016; the summer Legion Baseball started back up in Scobey after 13 years. The caption that Mike Stebleton wrote for the picture reads as follows:

Marjorie Shiell, aptly described in the August 3, 1978, Daniels County Leader as the "always dependable chief of staff" of the Scobey Blues American Legion Baseball Program, poses with all eight state championship trophies the team won in a 14-season span from 1969 to 1982. She was involved in all eight as her husband, Dr. Clyde H. "Doc" Norman, was the head coach of all eight. She washed uniforms, set up where the team would eat and sleep while on the road, plus a myriad of other things it takes to make a baseball program run smoothly, including "keeping them out of mischief," she said. "I was the gopher and I loved it." Besides "Marge" and Doc, the only other person involved in all eight state championships, to the Leader's knowledge, was their son, Kelly Norman, who was a batboy (1969, 1973), player (1976-80) and assistant coach (1982). All eight state championship trophies are on display at the Daniels County Museum Association building on the west end of Scobey.

The picture of Kelly and Marge hugging each other in front of the "IN HONOR OF *Coach Doc & Marge Norman* & ALL THEIR BOYS OF SUMMER" sign on the Scobey Ball Park outfield wall was taken in July 2017, the summer before Marge passed away.

Marge Shiell poses with all eight state championship trophies the team won in a 14-season span from 1969 to 1982. *Leader photo, Mike Stebleton.*

Kelly and Marge at Scobey Ball Park in July 2017, the summer before Marge died. *Family photo.*

2019

The Blues Compete in North Dakota Class B League District 2

> *I've run track from Alabama to God only knows where. I played four sports, but baseball is my favorite sports atmosphere there is.*
>
> —Martin Farver (Blues 2016–19)

2019 Scobey Blues. Top row, left to right: Payton Leibrand, Walker Ator (Medicine Lake), Martin Farver, Jackson Oie, Austyn Fishell. Bottom row, left to right: Chris Hagan (Plentywood), Prewitt Leibrand, Colter Oie, Anders Knudsen, Isaac Johnson (Medicine Lake). Devin Halverson and Gage Southland (called up later from Babe Ruth) are not pictured. *Leader photo, Mike Stebleton.*

PRESEASON

Coach Josh Rustad returned for his third season as head coach for the Blues, who hoped to build on their strong fourth-place finish at the Northwest Class A Regional in 2018. Gone from the 2019 roster were CJ Nelson and Trey Girard, who were lost to age eligibility, but the Blues returned nine players with Legion experience, including some who were now in their fourth season, as they had played for the Blues since the program rebooted in 2016. Coming back for another baseball season in 2019 were Martin Farver, Jackson and Colter Oie, Anders Knudsen, Devin Halverson, Prewitt and Payton Leibrand, Isaac Johnson (Medicine Lake), and Walker Ator (Medicine Lake). Joining the team for their first year were Chris Hagan (Plentywood), Austyn Fishell, and Gage Southland (called up from Babe Ruth late in the season).

Josh Johnson assisted Head Coach Rustad in 2019.

REGULAR SEASON

After playing in 2016 and 2017 in the unsanctioned Montana Class B "league" and in the North Dakota Class A League in 2018, the Blues played in the North Dakota Class B League in 2019. They were part of District 2 and played a regular season conference schedule against three teams—Stanley, Crosby, and Burlington. The small towns in North Dakota still play competitive American Legion Baseball, as in 2019, there were seven districts with 43 teams competing in the North Dakota Class B league with postseason district tournaments and an eight-team state tournament. In 2025, there will be 48 teams competing in seven Class B districts.

The Blues played a sparse schedule in 2019, as their only nonconference games were against Glendive B in home-and-home doubleheaders and a single game against Malta. After sweeping a doubleheader in Crosby (12-7 and

Coach Rustad with Payton Leibrand at a doubleheader in June 2019 on Meissner Memorial Field in Glendive. *Family photo.*

14-3), the Blues won the District 2 title and earned the number-one seed in the district tournament in Burlington. They finished the regular season with a 7-5 overall record.

DISTRICT TOURNAMENT

The district tournament was hosted in Burlington, North Dakota, where the Blues entered as the number-one seed. If they won the tournament, they would advance to the North Dakota State Class B Tournament in Hazen, North Dakota. Naturally, the team aimed to win it and return to a state tournament. First-round matchups looked like this:

- Scobey (1) vs. Crosby (4)
- Stanley (2) vs. Burlington (3)

Scobey took care of business in their first game by beating Crosby but was upended by host Burlington in their second game. They then beat Crosby in a loser-out game to make it to the title game against Burlington, but the Titans stopped the Blues 16-6 in the championship game, ending their season. The team was disappointed not to win the tournament and advance to the state tournament, but Coach Rustad was positive about the season and the tournament, saying, "They played hard and worked hard, and in the end, it just wasn't quite enough. The Blues are coming home with a second-place finish in their region and an end to the 2019 season. They're still always number one in our eyes though!"

Burlington advanced to the state tournament in Hazen, where they lost out in two games.

The last post on the Scobey Blues Facebook page in 2019 was from Judy Wilemon Niederhauser, who wrote, "Was so fun to watch you guys play. Hope to see some games next year. Proud of you and your hard work, including the coaches. Thank you." Everyone hoped to see the Blues back on the field in 2020, but it wasn't meant to be.

EXTRA INNINGS

I asked Martin Farver, another third-generation baseball player from Scobey whose grandfather Howard played for the 1958 Scobey Plainsmen state championship team, what he remembered most about the four years he got to play for the Blues. He paused for a moment and said, "Definitely, my friends. You know, getting to spend more time with them." He paused and chuckled a second before adding, "All the shenanigans. The last two years I played, Anders Knudsen was with us, from south of Scobey there. He played all the way through. He was one of those kids who loved the game. I mean, you could have never made him quit playing; he was right there with me. We got into a

Anders Knudsen is at the center of some shenanigans with Austyn Fishell (right) and Chris Hagan from Plentywood (left). *Family photo.*

habit the last two years: every home game, he would burn a baseball in the dugout as a sacrifice to the baseball gods. There were so many damn shenanigans. That was probably my favorite thing of it." Martin paused for the third time and added, "A July Friday night under the lights. I've run track from Alabama to God only knows where. I played four sports, but baseball is my favorite sports atmosphere there is."

Time with friends, shenanigans, July Friday nights under the lights . . . memories for Martin to last a lifetime.

I asked Jackson and Colter Oie, whose grandpa Don Oie played Legion baseball for Doc Norman in 1960, to share their stories of playing for the Blues after the program had been dormant for 13 years. Jackson said, "I remember being excited to get to play for the Blues, especially since I was only 14 the first summer [2016] I played with them. It was fun to get to play up like that, but it was definitely a challenge to play up to that level so young. I remember being glad I could keep playing baseball after All-Stars ended in July. I also remember being honored to play on the 'first' Blues team after the 13-year break, and it was even more cool because Dad [Morgan] played for the Blues back in his day [1992–95]. Getting to play Legion Ball in the same program as he did was really fun for me."

Colter was only 11 years old and playing Little League when the Blues rebooted in 2016. He said, "I remember the first couple of years the program came back, seeing those huge Legion players show up to practice as our practice was getting over, and I thought it was way too late to have practice because it started so close to supper time. If I was ever waiting for a ride or anything after practice, I was eyeballing the big field. I thought it was super cool that my brother played up like that, and I wanted to do the same thing. As soon as Jackson could drive, he was my ride. So I watched a lot of their practices, and I couldn't wait to play with them."

Morgan Oie, father of Jackson and Colter, remembers the last season in Scobey for his sons Jackson and Colter, who, like Martin Farver, were third-generation baseball players in Scobey. "I loved and still love baseball. I umpired right up until the last team the Blues had, often doing both games behind the plate. It was fun. The budget wasn't much, so I got paid in Legion burgers to ump. Colter was the catcher, and Jackson pitched. So I definitely got to see them play."

I asked Colter if he remembered catching Jackson with his dad umpiring behind home plate. He did, and it is a fantastic story. Colter said, "I believe we were playing Crosby, and I think Jackson started game two. I loved catching for Jackson no matter where or when, but it was extra special when Dad was umping. We would chit-chat and make comments to each other when we were out of earshot of other people. Things like, 'Jeez, Jackson, don't leave a fastball right there.' All in good fun, of course. That game was tied going into the last inning. We were batting in the top of the seventh (we were away in game two). With runners on second and third with two out, I had a five-or six-pitch at-bat with an 0-2 count the whole AB. The whole time, I was thinking, *Anything close, and Dad is gonna ring me up*. I ended up hitting a go-ahead two-run single over shortstop. It felt good to give Jackson some run support after he threw lights out all game. I can, without a doubt, say that the most fun I ever had playing ball was catching for my brother with my dad behind the plate. It was just a special experience."

Jackson added, "I always enjoyed pitching to Colter because he took his job very seriously. Catching isn't easy, and he would put in the work to get good at it before it mattered in the game. He knew how to set up spots, could block about anything I put in the dirt, and threw guys out at second on a regular basis. It made pitching that much easier. I usually enjoyed playing when Dad umpired, but sometimes he could get on my nerves when I thought he missed a call. But overall, I loved it too! It was always so fun to ride home after the game and talk about it. We all loved to analyze baseball, so we enjoyed talking it over afterward."

A while ago, I interviewed Ryan Oie (Blues 1990–1992), Morgan's older brother, who played Legion ball with Morgan for one year in 1992. Ryan is Jackson's and Colter's uncle. Ryan was talking to his dad, Don, who remembers a funny story about playing slow-pitch softball with me in 1980—except it wasn't me; it was my brother Jon. Ryan asked me, "Do you remember you played softball with my pop, and they called you 'Whiff'?" Realizing my reputation was on the line, I quickly replied, "No, that wasn't me. That was my brother, Jon." Ryan said, "Oh. My pop thought it was you, but don't worry, I'll let him know it wasn't you!" In case you missed it, Jon Puckett's "The Epic Story of Whiff" story appeared in the 1980 chapter of *The Blues of Summer*.

SECTION NOTES

1. "Blues Are Back! American Legion Team to Occupy Diamond in '16," *Daniels County Leader*, January 14, 2016.
2. "Blues Play Ball Again Monday for First Time in 13 Seasons," *Daniels County Leader*, May 26, 2016.
3. "Blues End Long Skid and Take 5-Game Win Streak into Havre," *Daniels County Leader*, June 9, 2016.
4. "Blues Did Not Win It All But Sure Tried To," *Daniels County Leader*, August 12, 2018.
5. Ibid.
6. Ibid.
7. Ibid.
8. Ibid.
9. Ibid.
10. Ibid.
11. "American Legion Baseball Announces Major Rule Changes," legion.org, October 12, 2017.

The Froid Bu[...]

2020 – 2024

1900 – 1924
The Homesteaders
and Early Town Teams

1930 – 1945
The Sons of
the Pioneers

1957 – 1968
The Baseball
Renaissance

The Scobey Giants
1925 – 1929

Baseball is Back in Daniels County
1946 – 1956

*The Do[...]
Champ[...]*
1969 – 1[...]

s

983 – 1991
he Don
ekvold Era

1998 – 2003
The Last Years

2016 – 2019
The Revival

han
o Era

The Ken Meyer/Mike Lee Era
1992 – 1997

The Long Winter
2004 – 2015

2020–2024

"Legion Baseball Still Exists for Scobey Boys but It's Based in Froid"

> *The history of baseball runs deep in Daniels County, starting with the Chicago Black Sox controversy over a century ago when two of those players made a short pitstop in Scobey. Then there were the Doc Norman days, when the coach led the Scobey Blues American Legion teams to multiple state championships.*
>
> **—Mike Stebleton, Daniels County Leader**

THE FINAL FIVE YEARS

Following the 2019 season, Scobey Blues American Legion Baseball folded a second time, as the program faced the same headwinds when it folded following the 2003 season and couldn't sustain itself. Terry Farver tried in vain to build a schedule for the team and his son Martin to play his final year in 2020, but he couldn't find a way to get it done. Terry said, "We couldn't field a team. I was trying to put that 2020 team and schedule together, but too many kids wanted to play basketball instead. I just scheduled around it in June and did more games in July. Just couldn't talk the kids into playing, for the life of me, I can't tell you why. Maybe dads who didn't play baseball as kids, so they don't know what they are missing. I do wish I could have watched Martin steal bases that 19-year-old summer. Catchers would have hated him."

Although the stubborn northeastern Montana headwinds that halted a Legion Baseball comeback in Scobey will not be rehashed here, I will mention that chasing athletes to play baseball to field a team is a symptom, not a problem. You can't squeeze blood out of a rock. Either the passion to play baseball is there—or it's not. In our interview, Coach Jack Sprague (Wolf Point and Glasgow) talked about what he called the "50% rule": if he had 12 boys in Little League, six would take it to the next level in Babe Ruth, and three would be serious about playing Legion baseball. He'd start with 12 and end with three. That is not enough to field a team, let alone be competitive. Another consideration is that those three baseball players who are serious about the sport deserve to play competitively on a team with other baseball players who share the same passion. Chauncy Handran—who played in Wolf Point after the Scobey Legion program folded in 2003—and Jackson Oie, and Colter Oie—who played in Froid—all said they missed playing for the hometown Blues, but they were happier to be playing with other baseball players who were committed to the sport like they were, even if it was in another town.

Although Scobey was not able to field a Legion baseball team in 2020, it wasn't due to a shortage of athletes, as the Spartan trophy case was crammed full with additional hardware during those years: Scobey took third at the state basketball tournament in 2019; won the state track and field state championship in 2019; lost to Drummond for the state championship in football in 2020 and won back-to-back state basketball championships in 2020 and 2021. That's a lot of hardware coming back to Scobey. But as Martin Farver said, "Baseball doesn't care about your athleticism," and his dad Terry couldn't coax some of those athletes to play baseball in the summer. That's not a dig on those athletes; it is what it is. They were passionate about playing their chosen sport, and many went on to successful athletic collegiate careers, including Martin Farver in track and field at Dickinson State.

The history of American Legion Baseball in Scobey began in *The Blues of Summer* with Scobey's first American Legion Baseball team in 1930 and ended with the last team in 2019; however, several Scobey boys have continued to play baseball following the 2019 season, just in another town—Froid. Morgan Oie remembered what happened when his boys were not able to play for Scobey in 2020. "In 2020, when Scobey decided to end the program, they went to Froid to play. Froid had a team consisting of players from Medicine Lake, Froid, Plentywood, Culbertson, Bainville, Sidney, Scobey, and Peerless. It was quite a bunch. They played American Legion in Eastern A in Montana for two years. Then, they became independent, like a travel team."

After the Blues program folded, I asked the Oie boys what playing for the Post 49 Froid Bulls was like. Jackson said, "The 2020 year was probably the most fun I ever had playing baseball. There was something unique about kids who really wanted to play from all over Eastern Montana (and even one from Ray, North Dakota) getting together to play ball all summer.

Everyone was that much more committed to the team, and it really made for a fun environment. We were underdogs in every aspect of the game, and we didn't mind it one bit! We had a solid season for sure, got a couple of eastern A divisional tournament wins, and had a blast the whole time. Everyone got along really well and we made some great friends. A lot of the 'city kids' got to come to Froid and play baseball next to a decades-old grain elevator and across the road from our buddy's mom's cow pasture. Little different than Pirtz Field in Billings! You can't talk about that season without mentioning the Crain family, though. Scott worked his tail off to set that program up, get the field ready, find umpires, and everything else it takes. He also was the head coach. His mom, Sheri, did tons and tons of cooking and cleaning in the concessions and lots of other behind-the-scenes work to get baseball to Froid. They made it happen for us. They gave me and Colter another

Jackson Oie coaching first base for the Froid Bulls in 2021. *Leader photo, Mike Stebleton.*

opportunity to play baseball in our neck of the woods and I'm so grateful for that."

Colter added, "It was awesome. There is definitely something special about playing for and in your hometown, but the Bulls were still a very fun team to play for. I had been playing baseball with most of the guys on that team for a long time. From the time I was 11, and our little league team joined the Big Muddy League through Babe Ruth, I played against them and then played in all-star tournaments with them. So, I was very good friends with quite a few of them already. There were kids from nine different towns on the team up to two hours away from Froid. So it was a group of guys who would do about anything to play baseball. We all shared a love of the game that brought us pretty close. When we went over there to play, it really broadened my horizon. It made me realize that there are good people all over and that baseball was a passion that I wanted to pursue. I can't believe how many amazing, generous people we met because of how diverse the team was (not that Scobey didn't have great people involved in the program). Playing for different coaches in different towns erased any doubts I had about my desire to play college ball."

Only the Oie brothers traveled from Scobey to Froid to play in 2020, but former Blues Walker Ator and Isaac Johnson from Medicine Lake also joined the Bulls in 2020. Jackson played for one season at Froid, then helped coach for the Bulls and Colter his last two seasons in 2021 and 2022. Scobey's Cooper King joined the Bulls in 2021 after finishing his season with the Scobey Giants of the Babe Ruth League. Josh Johnson, an assistant coach with the Scobey Blues under head coach Josh Rustad, was also one

Colter Oie playing catcher for the Froid Bulls against the 406 Flyers in 2021. *Leader photo, Mike Stebleton.*

of the coaches with the Bulls in 2021. Other Scobey boys followed on the heels of the Oies and Cooper King, including Ty Leischner, Aiden Leibrand, and Alex Moreno. As *The Blues of Summer* has relied so heavily on the *Daniels County Leader* to tell the Scobey baseball story, I'll hand the reins over to Mike Stebleton, *Daniels County Leader* Sports Editor, to bring us home on Legion baseball in Scobey (Froid). On June 20, 2024, Mike wrote the following article in the *Daniels County Leader*:

Legion Baseball Still Exists for Scobey Boys but It's Based in Froid[1]

Take me out to the Bulls' game, Take me out for some fun, I'll watch Alex, Coop & Ty play, I don't care whatever the day.

The history of baseball runs deep in Daniels County, starting with the Chicago Black Sox controversy over a century ago when two of those players made a short pitstop in Scobey.

Then there were the Doc Norman days, when the coach led the Scobey Blues American Legion teams to multiple [eight] state championships.

Following decades of success the unheard of happened: the Blues shut down operations in 2003 following an 0-29 overall season record. Legion Baseball was done in Scobey.

Or was it? The program was resuscitated in 2016 with Head Coach Chuck Nelson leading the way. On Monday, May 30, the locals hosted the Havre Northstars in a Memorial Day doubleheader. The Blues posted a 20-16 overall record, which is very good considering the program was inactive for 13 years.

Nelson had to move away from Daniels County and Josh Rustad became the head coach.

The Blues carved out a 9-15 overall record in 2017, ending the season with a 4-game winning streak. Following were 12-16 and 9-7 overall records in the 2018 and 2019 seasons, respectively.

Then the program was done again, with the 4-season comeback equating into a 50-54 (.480) overall record.

Five baseball seasons later the Scobey Blues are still on the shelf waiting for the next comeback attempt, as is the Babe Ruth program for those ages 13-15.

However, it doesn't mean Scobey kids wanting to play American Legion Baseball don't have the opportunity, because they do, and three young men are taking full advantage of such an opportunity this 2024 season.

Cooper King, Tyler Leischner and Alex Moreno, all of them graduating from Scobey High School 25 days ago from today's publication date of June 20, 2024, are on the roster of the Froid Bulls.

This is one of the more interesting baseball teams around these parts, a who's who of northeast Montana.

For instance, take Jaydeen Henshaw, who moved with his family to Hinsdale a few years back. He's a Froid Bull. It's 145 miles from Hinsdale to Froid, or 290 miles round-trip. He's putting on the most miles of anybody on the team.

The rest of the hodgepodge roster looks like this: Brooks Solem and Plenny Williams call Culbertson home; Trent Williams and Rylan Young are the two hometowners from Froid; Kash Ator hails from Medicine Lake; Henry Kukowski calls Plentywood home; Logan Brown and Mitch Brown are Poplar guys; Preston Swenson is from Wolf Point.

Thirteen young men stretching from Hinsdale to Scobey to Plentywood, down to Medicine Lake, Froid and Culbertson, and then back west to Poplar, Wolf Point and Hinsdale. That's a big swath of landscape!

Even one-third of the coaching staff has to do some major traveling throughout the season.

Phil King, Cooper's father, is an assistant coach on the team, as is Ryan Young of Froid, he the husband of Laurie (nee: Handy), a 1997 graduate of Scobey High School.

The head coach is Scott Crain of Froid, who this writer met for the first time Saturday, June 15, at Vournas Field, located in the southwest corner of the lovely community of Crosby, North Dakota. He told the Daniels County Leader Sports Editor he used to play baseball with the Bowler brothers, Zach and Levi, whose parents, Burl and Roz, own the newspaper you are reading at this very moment.

I remember at one point in the first game of the doubleheader, Crain was coaching in the third-base box, I was on the other side of the fence, and we were talking in between a pause of the game. I said something like "later I need to get the names of all the kids on the roster." Crain whips out his cell phone, presses a couple of "buttons," and hands me the phone over the top of the fence and walks back over to the third-base box. On the screen was the roster of the entire team.

Now that's service!

Two days later, on Monday the 17th, the three Bulls from Scobey knew the Daniels County Leader would be telephoning around noonish to get a little more insight on their time as Froid Bulls.

In last-name alphabetical order, King received the first call, and the first question was: how long have you been playing with the Bulls? The answer was surprising: four and one half-seasons.

"I was going into my freshman year of high school and called the coach and he said yes, so I've been with the team for four and a half seasons," said King, who, in addition to his catching duties, which he loves, has also played third base, second base, pitcher and all three outfield positions.

Asked what he was looking forward to as the season begins winding down, he said: "Just having fun, make some good plays, sticking together as a team and make the best of it that we can."

Asked what was it like to have his father as a coach the past three seasons, King commented: "It's amazing. So nice. We've been playing baseball together since I was five." The usual starting catcher said the most fun with the team is when they are traveling to and from games. "Scott will come back and talk with us and we have some good laughs. It doesn't get any better than that."

King said he will attend Miles Community College in Miles City, Montana, this fall to earn a degree in Livestock Management.

He will head down to grandpa's place in South Dakota and eventually start building his own herd of livestock.

Leischner is in his second and final season with the Bulls and just wants to have some fun to close out his senior year of high school.

"I'm having a lot of fun this season," he said. "I love it."

In his two years with the Bulls he has "played in the outfield, pitched, played shortstop once, a left-hander at shortstop is no good, played third base once last year. I haven't played at first, second or catcher." Asked what was the most fun he had this season with the team, his answer was: "When we won our first game. It was a good moment. We were all just jumping up and down."

"I love them because they do a good job," he said when asked about his thoughts on the coaching staff. "Scott knows what he's doing. He keeps our heads up."

Moreno is in his first season with the Bulls and he told the Leader he "is having a lot of fun."

His baseball career began with the Scobey White Sox of Coach Jason Wolfe as a 9-10-year-old, then graduated to the 11-12-year-old Scobey Red Sox.

"I'm just looking to improve the rest of the season, need to get better at pitcher," he said.

In addition to pitching, he has also played at second and third base, shortstop, and center field.

Asked about his head coach Crain, Moreno responded with: "He's crazy good, great personality and just a great coach. And Phil and Ryan, I love them all."

Moreno is eligible to play with the Bulls next year but at this point he says "it's 50/50." He plans on eventually moving to the Dickinson, North Dakota region at some point and work in the oil patch.

Bottom line, these three are having a ball, and that's no bull!

In this article, Mike Stebleton wrote, "Five baseball seasons later, the Scobey Blues are still on the shelf waiting for the next comeback attempt, as is the Babe Ruth program

Scobey members of the Froid Bulls American Legion Post 49 baseball team in 2024. From left, Tyler Leischner, Cooper King, and Alex Moreno. *Leader photo, Mike Stebleton.*

for those ages 13-15."[2] Little League baseball is still being played in Scobey, but nothing above that level.

What would it take to bring the Blues program back and sustain it? The Tri-County Cardinals model is the proven solution for a sustainable program. Tyler Bucklin (Blues 1991–94) started the Tri-County Cardinals baseball team in 2002, and 23 years later, it is still going strong. In the letter he wrote about his experience playing for the Blues, he recalls how the program began:

> *I had just moved back to Montana in July of 2001 after living in Las Vegas for four years. I was finishing up my student teaching, and at that time, my wife, Vanessa, and I were living with her parents until we could get our own place. I was coaching JV girls' basketball for the first time and just trying to figure out where I fit in the community of Conrad. The inception of the Tri-County was solely David Brown. He was a Texan who lived in Conrad to oversee his family's interests in the oilfields in the Golden Triangle. He had a son who was 14 or 15 years old, and David wanted him to continue playing after Babe Ruth. Somehow, he had heard that I had played baseball along the way and asked me to help him get the program off the ground and be the head coach. I accepted and had no idea how hard it was going to be to get the program back.*
>
> *The Cut Bank Cardinals had closed their doors in '98 or '99. They didn't have enough kids to continue the program. David's idea was to have Conrad, Shelby, and Cut Bank kids play together to get enough players. I could get on board with this since the Blues teams that I played on were made up of so many different communities. We would have a baseball board of members from each community, and they would oversee the operational side of the team, and I would take care of the players.*
>
> *We had a lot to figure out in those early years. Each town had a field to play on and each of them were in need of repair. We practiced in each town on a weekly rotation to try to eliminate travel for the kids. Conrad and Shelby were willing to put money into their fields, but in the end, it was David who made sure that Conrad's field was by far and away the best field. By the middle of my coaching years, we were practicing and playing all our games in Conrad.*
>
> *I ended up coaching the Tri-County Cardinals from 2002–2014. Besides my first year, I coached all of those years with Tyson Anderson from Glendive. He brought a lot of knowledge to the team, and we worked well together. As a club, we really didn't get very competitive until 2004. We had some kids that really bought into the program, and we made large leaps that summer. From 2004–2010 we were always contenders in the northern division. We won districts in 2009 and finally made it state. My wife, Vanessa, was pregnant that summer with our second child. Everyone all summer said that she would have it during state, and they were right. My son Nick was born on the first day of state. I listened to the game on the radio, and we won our first game. I made it to the tournament for days two and three, but we ended up losing both.*
>
> *By the time I finished coaching in 2014, I had many players go on to play college ball and many others that should have. I am still in touch with many of them as they have become fathers and are teaching their own kids how to play. My son Nick is 15 this year and will get to double roster the same as I did in 1991. He will also get to play in a state legion tournament, as Conrad is hosting the tournament this summer. I am really proud of the work that I did to bring the program back to life and to help build a program that is sustainable and thriving.*

Interestingly, the name "Tri-County" (Pondera, Glacier, and Toole Counties) is what the Scobey Blues could have been called (Tri-County Blues) when Tyler played as players from Opheim (Valley), Scobey, Peerless, and Flaxville (Daniels), and Outlook (Sheridan) were on the Scobey Blues teams Tyler played on from 1991 to 1994. Beginning in 1968, the Scobey Legionnaires could have been called the Daniels County Legionnaires when players from Scobey, Flaxville, and Peerless comprised the first all-county team for Coach Doc Norman.

For small towns in Montana to sustain a Legion program, it would take more than a village—it would take several. In addition to Conrad, Cut Bank, and Shelby, the Tri-County Cardinals have had players Sunburst, Choteau, Fairfield, Brady, Dutton, Power, Chester, and "even a kid or two from Milk River Alberta. Just depends on who is interested." Scobey's teams from 2016 to 2019 had players from Scobey, Opheim, Plentywood, and Medicine Lake on the roster. The Tri-County model is currently happening in Froid, as players from several small towns, including Scobey, travel to Froid to play for Scott Crain. The 2024 Bulls's roster had players from eight towns; Colter Oie's 2021 had players from nine.

Tyler's 12 years of dedication to the Tri-County Cardinals baseball program enabled it to get off the ground and sustain itself, even winning a district championship, and it has allowed many small-town boys to play Legion baseball who wouldn't have otherwise had the opportunity, including his son Nick. It takes the commitment and continuity of a Tyler Bucklin in a small-town community to sustain a baseball program. Doc and Marge Norman did this in Scobey for 25 years, from 1959 to 1983. I was one of the lucky boys who had the opportunity to play Legion baseball because of Doc and Marge.

When Tyler's son Nick plays in the 2025 Montana/Alberta State Class A American Legion Tournament in Conrad from July 31 to August 3, the spirit of *The Blues of Summer* will be there in the small town of Conrad, Montana, as former Blue Tyler Bucklin from Outlook ("the last Blue Jay") has passed the game down to the next generation—not only to his son but to multiple small towns in Montana.

The Scobey Legion program has a history with the former Cut Bank Cardinals and Conrad. The Cut Bank Cardinals won the state championship in Scobey's first state tournament appearance in 1967. Scobey beat Conrad 2-1 in the first game of the 1971 tournament, and the Blues played Cut Bank several times in state tournaments when I played, including in 1976 and 1977. The Cut Bank Cardinals hosted the State Class B Tournament in 1976, 1978, and 1980, and Scobey won the state championship there all three years. Cut Bank won state Class B state championships in 1957, 1963, and 1967. Conrad lost to Plentywood in the best-of-three championship series in 1954, as Plentywood's only state championship denied Conrad theirs. Shelby played under the "Toole County Can-Ams" moniker in 1971, an international team with players from northern Montana and southern Alberta. Players came from Shelby, Milk River, Warner, Coutts, Sunburst, and Kevin.

EXTRA INNINGS

The Froid Bulls play their home games on Fjeseth Field in Froid. One of the first Peewee games I remember playing for the Peerless Pirates was against Froid when I was seven or eight years old in 1968 or 1969. It was one of our first "road trips" past Scobey, Opheim, Flaxville, or Outlook, and I remember it being so much fun to travel that far to play a baseball game with all my friends. A player named Yogi Fjeseth was pitching for Froid. Mom and Dad were huge Yogi Berra fans, and I heard them calling out "Yogi" a lot during the game and talking about it when we got home. When we were batting, Dad would talk to Yogi on the pitcher's rubber from his third-base coaching box. Froid's baseball field is named after Gustav "Gus" Fjeseth, Yogi's father, who died untimely in 1968. I played against Yogi throughout Little League and Babe Ruth and played with him for two years on the 1974 and 1975 Mon-Dak Babe Ruth All-Star teams, and Dad got to coach Yogi. Yogi's family moved to Dillon following the 1975 Babe Ruth season.

SECTION NOTES

1 "Legion Baseball Still Exists for Scobey Boys but It's Based in Froid," *Daniels County Leader*, June 20, 2024.

2 Ibid.

2025: Epilogue

ONE OF THE QUESTIONS I ASKED EVERY PLAYER during the interview process for *The Blues of Summer* was, "When you think about playing Legion baseball for Scobey, what do you remember most?" Kevin Sell, who was a batboy for the Plainsmen in 1952 and played baseball for the Scobey Legion team from 1957 to 1959 (Doc Norman's first season), said, "After almost 64 years, that summer of 1959 remains, not just a good baseball memory, but a great life memory. And at the center of it all is my mentor, my manager, and my lovable friend, Doc Norman." Kevin Sell, on behalf of all the players, presented a plaque—in the shape of the state of Montana with a baseball on it—to his mentor and friend Doc at the Scobey Legion Baseball Reunion in 1983. The plaque had the following inscription:

Dear Doc,

> *We were truly the "Boys of Summer." We lost and we won,*
> *Best of all we had fun.*
> *If winning wasn't everything Then playing for you was!*
> *Thanks for putting us on the map.*
> *With every best wish*
>
> *From*
> *Your boys*

"We lost and we won / Best of all we had fun." Friendship and fun were common themes in the responses I received from every player I interviewed, from Kevin Sell in 1959 to the last Blue, Martin Farver, who played from 2016 to 2019. Martin answered the question this way: "Definitely, my friends. You know, getting to spend more time with them." He added, "Everybody's there to win, but having fun was *as* important when we were playing baseball as anything else was." Both players—spanning over 60 years of Legion baseball—mentioned their friends and having fun, as did every player between Kevin and Martin.

To the same question, Kirby Halvorson replied, "That's easy. Building friendships that have lasted a lifetime." Kelly Norman added, "Playing with my best friends who are still my best friends and brothers is at the top, and that starts from Little League, Babe Ruth till the end." Ray Chapman said this: "We all got to play the amazing game of baseball together while making lifelong friends and starting our journeys of life in the world outside our blessed northeastern Montana. We were friends who had a helluva lot of fun together and were lucky to be part of something far greater than each one of us individually. We were a team, each one of us made better as individuals because of our bond of brotherhood, a bond which lasts forever."

I could go on.

After hearing all these similar responses to question, "What do you remember most about playing for the Blues?" I reflected on how I would answer that question myself. As I contemplated my response, I considered how blessed I was to play on four Blues state championship teams. Coming from a culture of winning in Peerless—ingrained in me by my dad—I fell in on another winning tradition with Doc Norman and the Blues. In Peerless basketball, I played on a team that lost the state championship game my senior year, which crushed me. It had been a lifelong dream for Jon and me to win it for our small town, and it took me years to recover; to this day, it still bothers me when I think about it. But when I wrote *The Dream: The Story of the 1978 and 1979 Peerless Panthers*, I ended the book with a memory of being in the Peerless Gym after graduating high school. I was looking at the banners on the walls and did not see a state championship banner hanging there, and it saddened me. But reflecting on that memory, I ended *The Dream* this way: "Now that I think about it, when Peerless Schools closed its doors forever in June 2009, there was not a state championship banner hanging in the gym, but it didn't matter; that's not what it was about. It was about all the fun we had playing basketball together growing up, the memories we still have of that time of our lives. And it was about how basketball was the one thing, the glue, the gravity, that brought us all together."

Counter to not seeing a state championship banner hanging in the Peerless Gym, every time I drove into Scobey from Peerless, I would see the sign outside the Scobey Ball Park that listed the eight Scobey Blues state championships, and I felt proud. I still feel proud today, but now that I reflect on that memory, I realize that there was something more enduring than winning and losing state championships and that the ending for *The Blues of Summer* is the same as *The Dream*, substituting the word "baseball" for "basketball," and the season of summer for winter:

Now that I think about it, when the Scobey Blues folded for the second time in 2020, the program had eight state championships, but it didn't matter; that's not what it was about. It was about all the fun we had playing baseball together growing up, the memories we still have of that time of our lives. And it was about how baseball was the one thing, the glue, the gravity, that brought us all together.

ONE MORE TIME

Lo, and it was written in *The Book of Blues Revelations* by the prophet Jack Reiner:

"On the 100th anniversary of the year of the founding of American Legion Baseball in Milbank, South Dakota, and when Swede Risberg and Happy Felsch from the Chicago White Sox came to play baseball in Scobey, former Scobey Legion and Plainsmen coaches, players, batboys, batgirls, umpires, and supporters will congregate in the town of Scobey to celebrate the memory of 'Baseball Country.' They will make a pilgrimage to Scobey from all parts of the United States. A former Legion and Plainsmen player from Peerless will scribe the story of baseball in Baseball Country titled *The Blues of Summer: The True Story of Baseball in Daniels County, Montana*. The written word will tell the story of Baseball Country from when the homesteaders brought the game to the area in the early 1900s to when the last Legion team in Scobey took the field in 2019. It will contain the stories of the coaches, players, and teams who roamed the eastern plains of Montana every summer, playing the game they loved. On that weekend, the spirits will flow freely, and there will be great rejoicing, dancing, and the honking of horns in the streets, for the lovers of the game of baseball shall get together one more time."
—From the prophet Jack in *The Book of Blues Revelations*

And thus it was written . . . and so it shall come to pass.

At the time of *The Blues of Summer* publication in late June 2025, a Scobey Blues baseball reunion is planned to celebrate the storied Daniels County baseball tradition. The reunion consists of two major events: "This is Baseball Country," at the Richardson Theater on Friday, June 27, and the "Field of Dreams'" at Scobey Ball Park on Saturday, June 28. The glue and gravity of baseball will bring us back together . . . one more time.

Here are the descriptions of the two events:

"This Is Baseball Country," Friday, June 27, 2025, 2:00 p.m. – 5:00 p.m., Richardson Theater: On the first day of the 1969 State Legion Baseball Tournament in Scobey, an article titled "Baseball Country" appeared in the Daniels County Leader, proudly announcing to all the visiting teams that Daniels County was historically baseball territory. This three-hour walk down memory lane will include pictures on the big screen and will revisit the glorious baseball past in Daniels County, starting with the first Scobey town team in 1914, the 1925 team with two former Chicago White Sox players, Scobey's first American Legion team in 1930, the great Scobey Plainsmen teams of the 1950s and 1960s, the Scobey Blues teams that won eight State championships between 1969–82, and all the great Blues teams that came before and after the championship era, including Doc Norman's first team in 1959, the Don Lekvold teams from 1983–1991, through the year the program folded in 2003, ending with the Blues 2.0 from 2016–2019. Facilitated by Joe Puckett, former players, coaches, umpires, and opponents will be invited to share their stories and celebrate their memories of Baseball Country.

"Field of Dreams," Saturday, June 28, 2025, 1:00 p.m. – 4:30 p.m., Scobey Ball Park: "You know what we get to do today? We get to play baseball!" (From the movie *The Rookie*.) Bring your gloves! (Or just come and watch the fun.) Former players are invited to Scobey Ball Park for an afternoon of fun, continuing the celebration of Scobey baseball memories from the Richardson Theater on Friday. The event will open with a ceremonial first pitch. Then players can find their favorite teammate to play catch with and get warmed up to take infield and maybe hit some balls, whatever the old body feels capable of, or just watch the fun and talk to former players and fans across the years and share your favorite memories of the Scobey Ball Park. Pitchers can try to snap one last curve ball off if they can find a catcher to catch them. The famous Legion Burgers will be sizzling! The afternoon will conclude with the "Honking of the Horns," remembering the cheering cars parked around the ballpark that would applaud the great plays and wins all those years ago.

⚾ ⚾ ⚾

Speaking of the Field of Dreams, Doc Norman has recently been spotted on the heavenly Field of Dreams in Dyersville, Iowa, coaching former Scobey Legion players who have passed on and who want to play baseball in heaven. How could Doc and the boys be kept away? Andy Stolen, who recently joined Doc in heaven, immediately took to the baseball field with some former Scobey Plainsmen and ran into Doc on the Field of Dreams. While they were getting caught up on old times, Andy told Doc that the Laurel Dodgers now had more state Legion championships (nine) than the Scobey Blues, the Bitterroot Red Sox were tied with eight, and Havre was fast on his heels with seven.

---

* *Field of Dreams*, directed by Phil Alden Robinson, Universal Pictures, 1989.

Epilogue

Doc was mad when he learned his record of eight state championships had been broken and tied. He said, "The Laurel Dodgers? We beat them 11-0 in the 1979 state championship in Scobey. And who the hell are the Bitterroot Red Sox? What about our 31-game winning streak in 1978? Does that record still stand?"

Andy said, "No, the Gallatin Valley Outlaws stole that in 2002 when they won 32 games in a row."

That set Doc off even more. "Who the hell are the Gallatin Valley Outlaws? What about the five consecutive state championships? You better not tell me some outlaws stole that, too!"

"There's been a lot of changes since you left, Doc," Andy said. "There are a lot more teams from western Montana now, and even Alberta, but no one has won five in a row."

Doc was relieved to hear that one of his records was still intact, but it wasn't enough to offset his anger at learning his record of eight state championships had been broken. To settle who the best Legion program in the history of Montana Class A/B American Legion Baseball is, Doc is coordinating with management at the Field of Dreams in Iowa to schedule a four-team winner-take-all tournament with the Laurel Dodgers, Bitterroot Red Sox, Havre Northstars, and the Scobey Blues on the Field of Dreams. Legion All-Stars from the four teams will be selected and meet on the Field of Dreams in the far future. (We all have to pass on to be eligible to play.)

The best-of-seven opening-round series looks like this:
Scobey Blues (1E) vs. Havre Northstars (1N)
Bitterroot Red Sox (1W) vs. Laurel Dodgers (1S)

The winners of the first two series will meet in the final best-of-seven series.

Once Doc got the field reserved, Doc, Tiny Puckett (taking a break from playing with the Peerless Pirates on the basketball court in heaven), and Andy set to work immediately on building a roster for Scobey's All-Star team, but there was a glitch right out of the gate—Tiny wanted to field a Legion All-Star team from Peerless. Dad told Doc, "And I get the Opheim boys, too."

Doc said, "Goddammit, Tiny, haven't we been through this before in 1977? If we're going to beat the best from Bitterroot, Havre, and Laurel, we've got to combine the best in the county." Dad reluctantly agreed that Doc was right (again) but said he'd only go along with it if Doc started Terry Puckett from Peerless in game one against Havre. Doc had already planned on starting Terry in game one, so it didn't matter. Imagine if Tom Nielson from Havre starts Dave Fanning in game one—we'd all get to see a rematch of the 1-0 pitcher's duel in the 1971 state semifinal in Scobey on the Field of Dreams in Iowa.

Once Doc settled Tiny down with the threat of fielding a separate team, he was approached by shortstop Swede Risberg and center fielder Happy Felsch from the Chicago White Sox, who had been playing on the Field of Dreams since it opened. They argued with Doc that since they had played baseball in Scobey in 1925, they should be eligible to play in the Legion series. Doc told Swede, "I got three shortstops in front of you right now, Swede, so you just go back to playing with the White Sox. Besides, you led American League shortstops in errors with 61 in 1917, and you had 45 errors in your last year in 2020. I'll take my boys in front of you any day."

"Well, I can pitch, Doc. I beat John Donaldson in Plentywood in 10 innings in 1925. He pitched in the Negro Leagues. I made a lot of businessmen in Scobey happy that day with the money they made on their bets."

"You're gonna bring up some glorified pick-up game in Plentywood to get on my staff? And you're gonna talk gambling after you got booted from baseball? I got five right-handed starting pitchers off the top of my head in front of you. I don't even need you as a spot reliever."

That was it for Swede.

Happy Felsch laughed. "Yeah, but you'll take me, won't you, Doc? I was the best goddamn center fielder in baseball when I played."

Doc told Hap Felsch, "Jack Higgins from Flaxville is a better center fielder than you are, so you go play with Swede."

Hap laughed again. "Okay, put me in left then."

"I got Randy Stolen playing there. And don't even ask me about right field. I got plenty of outfielders in front of you there, starting with Jay Hagfeldt. I started Randy's younger brother Greg there as a 13-year-old in 1979, and he's better than you. I got my boys, Hap. You go play with the White Sox."

It's going to be a great tournament on the Field of Dreams someday.

Acknowledgments

ORIGINALLY CONCEIVED AS A MEMOIR ABOUT MY LIFE PLAYING baseball in northeastern Montana in the 1960s and 1970s, *The Blues of Summer* expanded in scope to become a comprehensive history of baseball (and softball) in Daniels County. A massive undertaking that, without the help of many people, could never have come to fruition. To put it all together, there were six principal sources I drew from to write the book: the *Daniels County Leader* newspaper archive, the *Daniels County History* book, the *1913–1948 Anniversary Album of the Scobey Community* book, Daniels County History Museum artifacts, online newspaper archive at newspapers.com, and interviews and chats with former players and coaches.

There are many people to thank who helped me along the way. Without them, the book would not exist.

First and foremost, I would like to thank Burl Bowler, Publisher/Editor in Chief of the *Daniels County Leader*. When I initially called Burl to discuss the project, he offered me unlimited access to the *Leader* archive and volunteered to digitally scan photo negatives to provide higher quality images in the book. On his own time, he went into the office and digitally scanned countless photos, catalogued them, and uploaded them to a shared platform where I could download the images, which provide windows to the baseball past of Daniels County. Roz and Burl Bowler and the *Daniels County Leader* represent the community of Scobey and Daniels County. As a result of their effort, the wonderful articles that were written by the previous generation of Bowlers—Burley and Larry—live on in these pages for all to read.

After Burl offered me unlimited access to the hardcopy archive of the *Leader*, I asked Ray Chapman, my childhood friend and former Blues teammate, to go into the *Leader* office and take digital photos of all the articles I needed. On his own time on the weekends, Ray went into the office and painstakingly snapped digital photos, catalogued them, and uploaded them to a shared platform where I was able to access the articles. Without Ray's help, I would not have gotten far on the project.

Another person I need to thank at the *Leader* is Mike Stebleton. Towards the end of the project, I needed access to articles that I did not initially request, and Mike offered his help to provide me with those articles. He made several copies of articles and mailed them to me at his own expense, allowing the story of Daniels County baseball to be told through the end of the Legion program.

A huge thank you is due Brenda Cook at the Daniels County History Museum. After I contacted her to request digital photos of the archive—especially the material related to the 1925–28 Scobey Giants—she mailed me the entire archive so that I could scan what I needed myself. Without Brenda's help, the story of the wild baseball years of the 1920s could not have been told. There were two artifacts Brenda mailed me from the baseball archive of the Daniels County Museum that were invaluable in telling the story of the Scobey Giants: Dave Walter's article, "Pitched Battles on the Diamond, 1925-26," from *Montana Magazine*, and Gary Lucht's article, "Scobey's Touring Pros: Wheat, Baseball & Illicit Booze," from *Montana The Magazine of Western History*. I quoted liberally from each article and am indebted to both authors for their exhaustive research and colorful writing.

In my experience of writing this book, I learned there are some people who share a passion for baseball history like I do, and John Murphy from Scobey is one of those people. Early in the project, when he recognized that I was attempting to travel back in baseball time to the 1920s and earlier, he mailed me a copy of a little gem of a book, the *1913–1948 Anniversary Album of the Scobey Community*. The raggedy book contained priceless baseball photos and information about the earliest baseball teams in the county, beginning in 1913, when the town of Scobey was established. My favorite photo in the book is the baseball game played in Whitetail on Christmas Day in 1928. Thanks, John, for sharing your passion—and your book.

While there is no one to thank specifically for the *Daniels County History* book (published in 1977), I must mention what a treasure-trove of baseball history this book is. It is amazing the baseball stories I was able to extract from this book, going back to the homesteaders in the early 1900s continuing through Scobey Giants in the 1920s, the Plainsmen of the 1940s, 1950s, and 1960s, through Doc's Legion teams in the mid-1970s. The *Daniels County History* book enabled me to tell the story of the homesteaders, the earliest baseball players in northeastern Montana.

For anyone planning extensive research on a project where newspaper articles are a primary source, I highly recommend the online newspaper archive at https://newspapers.com. This online platform enabled me to access articles from all the major Montana newspapers, from the early 1900s through the present day. Its search capabilities are fast and enabled me to find the articles I needed.

Acknowledgements

In addition to the help I received from the *Leader*, I requested articles and pictures from several other small-town newspapers in Montana and was not surprised at the warm welcome I received when I contacted each of them and how eager they were to help. I was not surprised because I come from a small town and know that the people who live in small towns are willing to help when asked. I received fast and courteous assistance from the following wonderful people in Montana:

- **Jaci Webb**, Editor, *Laurel Outlook*. Jaci helped me with access to the 1959 Scobey-Laurel eastern divisional championship series game details and took the time to share some stories about baseball and Laurel, a great baseball town like Scobey.
- **Dawn Texidor**, Advertising, Ponderosa Publications, Cut Bank *Pioneer Press*. Dawn scanned and emailed articles from the *Pioneer Press* archive for the 1976, 1978, and 1980 State Class B tournaments, hosted by the Cut Bank Lobos.
- **Samantha Lyle**, Multimedia Account Executive, *Sidney Herald*. Samantha helped me with numerous articles and photos I requested from the *Sidney Herald*, going back to the Sidney Gems Montana AAU championship in 1959, Sidney Majestics state Legion championship in 1966, through Sidney's last State American Legion championship in 1995.
- **Jamie Ausk Crisafulli**, Managing Editor, *Glendive Ranger-Review*. Jami helped with the articles and photos of the 1990 State Class A Legion Tournament, played at Meissner Memorial Field in Glendive. She shared a wonderful photo of Kevin Nelson pitching in the classic game between Scobey and Laurel, which Scobey won 3-2 in 11 innings.
- **Leta Godwin**, Supervisor, Valley County Pioneer Museum. Leta and her team at the museum were invaluable in scanning over 100 *Glasgow Courier* articles and photos from issues dating to the 1940s when Andy Stolen played Legion baseball for Opheim, through the 2000 and 2012 state tournaments hosted at Glasgow. Leta uploaded the files to an online platform where I was easily able to download them.
- **Arlin Kaul**, former Scobey Blue, helped me by taking several digital photos of articles and pictures from the *Plentywood Herald* archive at the Plentywood Library, including from the 1965 State Class B Legion Tournament won by Wolf Point, and the 1967 Eastern Divisional Tournament, when Scobey qualified for the state tournament for the first time.

I need thank all the former Blues players and coaches—and players and coaches from opposing teams—for your patience enduring my incessant texts and phone calls requesting your memories, letters, interviews, and inputs on games from—in the case of Ron Fjeld—almost 80 years ago. Your comments have made the book what it is—a testament to the players and coaches who roamed the fields of northeastern Montana all those summers ago. For the same reason, I also need to thank the former players of the Peerless Hellcats for their willingness to provide me their tales and history, which enabled me to write their story.

The images in *The Blues of Summer* of the "Brave and the Bold: Gorillas Wonders of the Diamond" from *DC Comics*, "The King is a Fink" from *The Wizard of Id*, and Snoopy from *Peanuts* playing baseball are used solely for the purpose of telling my childhood baseball story and nothing else.

Thank you to my eldest daughter Cosette Puckett, who I loaded up with the most difficult book layout in history, complete with footnotes, images, references, and index. I cannot thank you enough for your quality work. And thank you to my youngest daughter Emma for helping me generate the index automatically, saving me a good deal of time and effort.

Finally, to my dear wife, Vonda, who has endured my obsession with this gargantuan project for over the past two and a half years. Your patience with me is beyond understanding. Thank you for letting me run with my passion. You may not understand the attachment I have to my baseball past in small-town Montana, but you understand how important it is to me.

References

1913–1948 Anniversary Album of the Scobey Community, Daniels County, Montana: A Picture Story of Its Pioneers, Its Progress, Its Present, Junior Chamber of Commerce of Scobey Montana, 1948.

"1973 Peerless Tournament. Chinook Gets First In 2-Day Series." *Daniels County Leader*, June 14, 1973.

1979 State Class B Legion Baseball Tournament Program, July 1979.

"20-20 Legion Tie." *Billings Gazette*, July 27, 1975.

"28th straight win gives Scobey title." *Billings Gazette*, July 24, 1978.

"4 Wins, 1 Loss for Blues in Past Week." *Daniels County Leader*, July 13, 1978.

"7-1 Blues Run at Season End." *Daniels County Leader*, July 19, 1990.

"81-Year-Old Man Digs Own 105-ft. Sewer Ditch." *Daniels County History*, 1977.

Marshall, Penny. *A League of Their Own*. Columbia Pictures, 1992.

Akin, William E. *American Legion Baseball: A History, 1924-2020*, McFarland, 2021.

"Amazing Comeback by Scobey Wins Marathon State Tourney." *Daniels County Leader*, August 5, 1976.

"American Legion Baseball Announces Major Rule Changes." legion.org, October 12, 2017.

American Legion website. legion.org, retrieved on 28 Feb 2025.

Anderson, Jim. "Scobey scoring twins." *Miles City Star*, June 27, 1980.

"Area Baseball History." *State Class B Legion Tournament Program*, 1971.

Associated Press. "Electrics, Scarlets battle in game of undefeateds." *Helena Independent Record*, August 16, 1976.

Associated Press. "NeMont League Opens Regular Season May 18." *Great Falls Tribune*, May 5, 1958.

Associated Press. "Possible Record in 33-27 Game." *Great Falls Tribune*, May 24, 1958.

"At The Scobey Ball Park." *Daniels County Leader*, June 18, 1959.

"Athletic Club Plans Expanded Babe Ruth, L-L." *Daniels County Leader*, March 9, 1961.

"Audet's homer gives Scobey Class B title." *Great Falls Tribune*, August 1, 1978.

"B Legion Tourney Set." *Billings Gazette*, August 2, 1968.

Balock-Hamilton, Rita. "Time-Out with Rita." *Havre Daily News*, August 8, 1984.

Bartley, Bruce. "Royals Aren't Quite the Same without Bayne." *Great Falls Tribune*, July 3, 1974.

Barzun, Jacques. *God's Country and Mine: a Declaration of Love Spiced with a Few Harsh Words*. Atlantic Little Brown, 1954.

"Baseball at Flaxville Sunday, August 26th." *Daniels County Leader*, August 23, 1934.

"Baseball Boys Organize Club; All Home Team." *Daniels County Leader*, May 2, 1929.

"Baseball Club of 1913 Was Fast Aggregation." *Glasgow Courier*, August 6, 1953.

"Baseball Not Over Here Yet." *Daniels County Leader*, August 6, 1980.

"Big weekend ahead for sports buffs." *Pioneer Press*, July 23, 1980.

"Billings has had baseball since the 1880s. Here are some of the city's ballparks." 406mtsports.com, June 18, 2017.

"Billings, Wolf Point, and Scobey Head to State." *Daniels County Leader*, July 25, 1974.

Balock-Hamilton, Rita. "Title possible for Havre." *Havre Daily News*, July 30, 1981.

"Blues Action at Sidney." *Daniels County Leader*, July 28, 1988.

"Blues Are Back! American Legion Team to Occupy Diamond in '16." *Daniels County Leader*, January 14, 2016.

"Blues Breeze to Championship; 4th in a Row for 'Doc's Boys,'" *Daniels County Leader*, August 2, 1979.

"Blues Did Not Win It All But Sure Tried To." *Daniels County Leader*, August 12, 2018.

"Blues Earn Berth at State with Divisional 2nd." *Daniels County Leader*, August 1, 1996.

"Blues Easily Win Tourney; MVP Stolen." *Daniels County Leader*, July 24, 1980.

"Blues Easily Win Tourney; MVP Stolen." *Daniels County Leader*, July 24, 1980.

"Blues End Long Skid and Take 5-Game Win Streak into Havre." *Daniels County Leader*, June 9, 2016.

"Blues Finish with 15-25 Record, Glendive, Wolf Point Advance." *Daniels County Leader*, August 2, 2001.

"Blues Heading to State Tourney; 3rd at Divisional." *Daniels County Leader*, July 27, 1995.

"Blues Hitting Good; Defense Bad at Class A." *Daniels County Leader*, August 7, 1980.

"Blues in Big Holiday Tourney." *Daniels County Leader*, June 28, 1979.

"Blues Keep Rolling On." *Daniels County Leader*, June 26, 1980.

"Blues Look to Three-Repeat." *Daniels County Leader*, April 20, 1978.

"Blues Make Good Showing in 'A' Tourney." *Daniels County Leader*, August 16, 1979.

"Blues Play at State Tourney." *Daniels County Leader*, August 1, 1991.

"Blues Play Ball Again Monday for First Time in 13 Seasons." *Daniels County Leader*, May 26, 2016.

"Blues play dbh, Glendive tonight." *Daniels County Leader*, July 14, 1983.

"Blues Play Well to Move From Seventh Seed to Finish Fourth." *Daniels County Leader*, August 1, 2002.

"Blues Repeat as Division Champions." *Daniels County Leader*, July 25, 1991.

"Blues Repeat Divisional Champs." *Daniels County Leader*, July 26, 1979.

"Blues Repeat; Win District Tourney." *Daniels County Leader*, July 23, 1992.

"Blues Runner-Up at Divisional; to Glendive." *Daniels County Leader*, July 30, 1981.

"Blues Sharp; Postseason Begins." *Daniels County Leader*, July 20, 1989.

"Blues Start Season." *Daniels County Leader*, May 26, 1983.

"Blues Suffer First Conference Loss to Wolf Point." *Daniels County Leader*, July 12, 1979.

"Blues Sweep Divisional in Four Games." *Daniels County Leader*, July 26, 1990.

"Blues Sweep Divisional in Four Games." *Daniels County Leader*, July 26, 1990.

"Blues Sweep State Tourney; 5th Straight." *Daniels County Leader*, July 31, 1980.

"Blues Take 2nd, Head to Helena for State Event." *Daniels County Leader*, July 24, 1997.

"Blues Take 3rd in East Tourney." *Daniels County Leader*, July 28, 1977.

"Blues to Host Rest of League in Tournament." *Daniels County Leader*, July 26, 2001.

"Blues Win Four Straight Games; Keep State Legion Title Here." *Daniels County Leader*, August 4, 1977.

"Blues Win; 'Iron Man' Pederson." *Daniels County Leader*, July 29, 1982.

Boe, R. L. "Scobey Beats Wolves 9-8." *Wolf Point Herald*, August 1, 1930.

Bourassa, Horace J. "Mr. and Mrs. Horace Bourassa, Sr." *Daniels County History*, 1977.

"Bowker receives scholarship." *Dillon Tribune*, July 7, 1993.

Bowler, Burley. "The Off Colored Sox." *Daniels County History*, 1977.

Bowler, Printer. "Scobey Legion Seeing Plenty of Action." *Daniels County Leader*, June 18, 1959.

Bragg, Addison. "Players will pay to play in whacky game." *Billings Gazette*, July 30, 1980.

Brenden, Alice. "Flaxville Baseball Teams." *Daniels County History*, 1977.

References

Briggeman, Vince. "Scobey pulls off sports trifecta." *Billings Gazette*, May 26, 1996.

Shelton, Ron. *Bull Durham*. Orion Pictures, 1988.

"BULLETIN." *Billings Gazette*, August 14, 1971.

"Bundren's Homer with Bases Full Beats Wildcats." *Daniels County Leader*, May 18, 1950.

"Busy Sports Weekend Starts Friday." *Daniels County Leader*, August 14, 1986.

Carbone, Robert. "Opheim Cops First in Junior Legion Tournament." *Plentywood Herald*, July 14, 1949.

"Cardinals look to stay hot against State A tourney foes." *Billings Gazette*, August 1, 2003.

Cassidy, Charles. "Baseball." *Daniels County History*, 1977.

Cassidy, Charles. "Scobey Post 56, American Legion." *Daniels County History*, 1977.

"Champion Plainsmen Play Here Sunday." *Daniels County Leader*, August 11, 1949.

"Cinderella Juniors in State Play." *Daniels County Leader*, July 27, 1967.

"Claude and Alice Hanrahan." *Whitetail, Daniels County History*, 1977.

"Clifford Hanson." *Scobey, Daniels County History*, 197, 1977.

"Cubs fifth at State." *Dillon Tribune*, July 29, 1992.

"Cut Bank Legion takes third in state baseball." *Pioneer Press*, August 4, 1976.

"Cut Bank Wins B Junior Title." *Billings Gazette*, July 22, 1963.

"Cut Bank, Sidney, Scobey Win Legion B." *Great Falls Tribune*, July 29, 1967.

Daniels, Else. "American Legion Auxiliary No. 56." *Daniels County History*, 1977.

Davis, Francis. "Sox end a memorable season." *Ravalli Republic*, August 15, 1997.

Diamond in the Rough Jubilee, Peerless, Montana, 1987.

Divish, Ryan. "Last of a dying breed." *Havre Daily News*, August 5, 2005.

"Division Champs to Host Legion B." *Laurel Outlook*, August 5, 1959.

"Doc Norman Classic Sees Laurel Win." *Daniels County Leader*, June 22, 1989.

"Doc Norman Day." *Daniels County Leader*, June 30, 1983.

"Don't look for the Blues to be singing the blues." *Daniels County Leader*, May 29, 1997.

"Double Bill Is Schedule Here this Sunday." *Daniels County Leader*, June 14, 1951.

"Doubleheader Baseball Game this Sunday." *Daniels County Leader*, June 10, 1954.

"Duke No-Hits Plentywood." *Daniels County Leader*, June 12, 1975.

"Early Dope for the Hot Stove League." *Daniels County Leader*, August 29, 1946

"East Divisional Legion Tourney Here." *Daniels County Leader*, 20-23, July 20, 1978.

"Ed Gallo Memorial Tourney starts Thursday in Whitefish." *The Daily Inter Lake*, June 16, 2017.

"Edwin and Norma Puckett." *Daniels County History*, 1977.

Sayles, John. *Eight Men Out*. Orion Pictures Corporation, September 2, 1988.

"Electrics Blast Their Way into State Tourney." *Great Falls Tribune*, August 13, 1969.

"Electrics, Scobey play this weekend at Optimist." *Great Falls Tribune*, July 31, 1980.

Falcon, Mark. "End of an Era." *Glasgow Courier*, August 10, 2000.

Falcon, Mark. "Reds Second in State Legion Tourney." *Glasgow Courier*, August 10, 2000.

"Fanning's 1-hit win puts Havre in finals." *Billings Gazette*, August 14, 1971.

"Fans See Some Good Baseball." *Daniels County Leader*, July 8, 1965.

Farley, Scott. "Scobey downs Reps, 15-8." *Helena Independent Record*, July 27, 1997.

Field of Dreams, directed by Phil Alden Robinson, Universal Pictures, 1989.

Field, Jeremy. "In 1925, American Legion Baseball was born of a need to strengthen young people and the nation." *The American Legion Magazine*, July 18, 2019.

Fladager, Lois. "Peerless News." *Daniels County Leader*, August 9, 1962.

"Flaxville Beats Wolf Point, 6-2." *Daniels County Leader*, July 15, 1948

"Flaxville Club Brings Strong Team Here." *Daniels County Leader*, July 7, 1949.

"Flaxville Undisputed Title Holders; Drub Poplar 10 To 1 On Foreign Diamond; Win Both Halves." *Daniels County Leader*, September 1, 1938.

"Former Pitching Star Revisits Scobey Scene." *Daniels County Leader*, Aug 04, 1949.

"Fred and Evelyn Hanson." *Eagle Creek, Daniels County History*, 1977.

French, Brett. "Red Sox: the new kids on the block." *Ravalli Republic*, May 22, 1987.

Fromdahl, Gregg. "Reds get ready for State Tournament." *Glasgow Courier*, July 27, 2000.

Funderburke, Al. "Little League Craze in Scobey Is Spark for Town Action (Curling Too)." *Billings Gazette*, September 14, 1959.

Gardner, Charles. "Scobey blue as Elects rally twice for victories." *Great Falls Tribune*, August 3, 1980.

Gaub, Dennis. "Scobey loses a doctor but keeps a coach." *Billings Gazette*, June 10, 1981.

Geise, George. "Chargers sweep Scobey, make tourney." *Great Falls Tribune*, August 7, 1978.

Geise, George. "Chargers-Scobey Clash: no Championship today." *Great Falls Tribune*, August 6, 1978.

Geise, George. "Dick Kloppel Named Coach of the Year." *Great Falls Tribune*, May 1, 1983.

Geise, George. "Just call him a Goliath among a whole lot of Davids." *Great Falls Tribune*, August 8, 1978.

Geise, George. "Mavs out, Lakers advance." *The Daily Inter Lake*, August 9, 1976.

"George and Ruth Severson." *Eagle Creek, Daniels County History*, 1977.

"George W. Johnson Family." *Scobey, Daniels County History*, 1977.

Giamatti, A. Bartlett. "Going Home." 1989, taken from James Preller Blog, April 15, 2015.

Giamatti, A. Bartlett. *Take Time for Paradise: Americans and Their Games*. Bloomsbury USA, 2011.

"Glendive 'Downs' Sox." *Billings Gazette*, August 8, 2002.

"Glendive Coach Issues Statement." *Billings Gazette*, July 29, 1966.

"Glendive Takes State Title Going Away." *Daniels County Leader*, August 1, 1985.

"Glendive Upsets Scobey." *Great Falls Tribune*, July 31, 1978.

"Glendive Upsets Scobey." *Montana Standard*, July 31, 1978.

"Glendive, Hamilton in finals." *Billings Gazette*, July 29, 1997.

"Glendive, Sidney on to Legion State 'A.'" *Daniels County Leader*, July 28, 1994.

"Goodwill via baseball." *Great Falls Tribune*, July 4, 1971.

Grant, Bob. "Herbert Grant." *Daniels County History*, 1977.

"Greenhorns Are Softball Champs." *Daniels County Leader*, August 31, 1961.

"Greenhorns Runners-up at Tourney." *Daniels County Leader*, September 10, 1964.

"Greenhorns Will Play in Tourney in Williston." *Daniels County Leader*, August 27, 1964.

"Greenhorns Win Championship at Plentywood." *Daniels County Leader*, September 3, 1959.

"Greenhorns Win First at Glendive." *Daniels County Leader*, July 16, 1964.

"Gullick and Anna (Horvick) Fadness." *Pleasant Prairie, Daniels County History*, 1977.

Gunderson, Milton. "Scobey, Pioneer Country." *Daniels County History*, 1977.

Halverson, Dixie. "Slighted by Class B coverage." *Billings Gazette*, August 4, 1985.

Hanrahan, Ruth A. "Enjoying Life – Pioneer Style." adapted from Richard C. Davids, in Farm Journal, Scobey, Daniels County History, 1977.

"Happy Felsch and Several Players Already in Town." Scobey Sentinel, April 30, 1926.

"Happy Felsch Says He Plays with Havre This Year." Havre Daily News, May 10, 1928.

"Harry and Mayme Cottingham." Westfork, Daniels County History, 1977.

"Harry J. and Laura M. Hansen." Daniels County History, 1977.

"Havre Beat Royals in 14th." Billings Gazette, July 11, 2010.

"Havre Champs in State Legion Tourney Here." Daniels County Leader, August 7, 1975.

"Havre Eyes 2nd Title." Great Falls Tribune, August 12, 1971.

"Havre loses opener." Havre Daily News, July 31, 1987.

"Havre Out of Tourney." Montana Standard, August 22, 1970.

"Havre Shooting for Fourth Legion B Title." The Daily Inter Lake, August 1, 1973.

"Havre Wins Opener." Billings Gazette, August 13, 1971.

"Havre Wins State Class B Tourney Here." Daniels County Leader, August 19, 1971.

Hellickson, Laverne Holmberg. "Line Coulee School in the Late 20s." Daniels County History, 1977.

"Help Wanted, Men." Missoulian, July 20, 1958.

Hennell, Carl. "Sweet trip to state, Mission Valley win Class A American Legion title." The Daily Inter Lake, August 6, 2007.

"High School Baseball Will be Played in Two Classes Next Year." Havre Daily News, May 18, 1949.

"History of Peerless Auxiliary." Peerless, Daniels County History, 1977.

"History of the James R. McIntyre Family." Scobey, Daniels County History, 1977.

Hogan, Mark. "Delgado: Family outshines diamonds." The Daily Inter Lake, August 16, 1987.

"How It Went at Tourney." Daniels County Leader, August 8, 1968.

"Impossible dream ends in nightmare." Billings Gazette, Norm Clarke, August 21, 1971.

Jacobson, H.J. "The Life and Times of the Carl Jacobson Family." Daniels County History, 1977.

"John (Jack) and Nettie Higgins." Smoke Creek, Daniels County History, 1977.

Johnson, Jenny. "Bitterroot baseball coach, businessman Vester Wilson dies." Ravalli Republic, September 14, 2000.

Johnson, Norman and Hilda. "Four Buttes." Daniels County History, 1977.

Jones, Jeffrey M. "Football Retains Dominant Position as Favorite U.S. Sport." GALLUP News, February 7, 2024.

Jones, Lalon. "Butte Creek Community." Daniels County History, 1977.

"July Fourth Brings Biggest Crowd Ever Seen At Scobey." Daniels County Leader, July 5, 1928.

"Junior Leaguers Wallop Opheim." Daniels County Leader, June 20, 1946.

"Junior Legion Club Defeats Scobey 8-4." Billings Gazette, August 1, 1930.

"Junior Legion Meets Big-Time Competition." Daniels County Leader, June 11, 1959.

"Junior Legion Series for N.E. Title Here July 17." Daniels County Leader, July 16, 1959.

"Juniors Defeat Outlook 12-3." Daniels County Leader, June 9, 1949.

"Juniors Downed in Regional Contest." Daniels County Leader, July 25, 1946.

"Juniors Have Heavy Going at Tourney." Daniels County Leader, July 23, 1964.

"Juniors Trample Plentywood Nine." Daniels County Leader, June 19, 1947.

"Juniors Win an Exciting Game Sunday." Daniels County Leader, July 31, 1930.

Kahn, Roger. The Boys of Summer. Harper & Row, 1972.

Kasper, John. "Mission Valley gets tough draw at state tourney." Missoulian, August 1, 2003.

"Kato and Kato help Havre edge Scobey." Billings Gazette, August 2, 1975.

Kelly, Sandra. "Missoula gives Scobey the Blues with 18-8 thumping," Helena Independent Record. July 29, 1997.

"Late Rally by Peerless Is Not Enough." Daniels County Leader, July 27, 1950.

"Laurel Legion Team Takes Second Place." Laurel Outlook, July 25, 1962.

"Legion Ball 'Iron Men' End Season." Daniels County Leader, August 19, 1976.

"Legion ball opens today." Ravalli Republic, May 25, 1983.

"Legion Baseball Still Exists for Scobey Boys but It's Based in Froid." Daniels County Leader, June 20, 2024.

"Legion Club Takes In State Series." Daniels County Leader, August 16, 1973.

"Legion Juniors Beat Scobey, 5-4 and 13-2." The Missoulian, July 3, 1959.

"Legion Kids Win Rubber at Libby." Daniels County Leader, August 12, 1976.

"Legion Retains Lead; Splits Weekend Games." Daniels County Leader, June 11, 1959.

"Legion tourney looks 'close as a clone,'" Great Falls Tribune, August 11, 1979.

"Legionnaires Drop Two To Flaxville, Circle." Daniels County Leader, May 14, 1959.

Letasky, John. "Scobey, a town for all seasons." Billings Gazette, August 2, 1996.

Letasky, John. "Sons: Legendary coach Ed Bayne is 'jumping up and down in heaven' celebrating Scarlets' regional title." 406 MT Sports, August 11, 2024.

"Little Scobey Boys Are Learning To Play Baseball." Daniels County Leader, July 16, 1946.

"Local Legion Drops Scorcher to Scobey." Missoulian, June 15, 1969.

"Local Marine Found Japs, Sharks Both Troublesome in Yank Raid on Makin Island." Billings Gazette, October 9, 1942.

"Locals Lose; Wolves Here for Sunday." Daniels County Leader, July 7, 1938.

Lockrem, Orville. "The Henry & Orville Lockrem History." Daniels County History, 1977.

Lucht, Gary. "Scobey's Touring Pros: Wheat, Baseball & Illicit Booze." Montana The Magazine of Western History, Vol. 20, No. 3, Summer 1970.

Machart, Mary. "Peerless Ball Field Dedicated." Daniels County Leader, July 2, 1998.

"M.J. and Auget Walker."Daniels County History, 1977.

Mansch, Scott. "Laurel seeks fourth straight title." Great Falls Tribune, July 26, 2012.

"McNally voted MVP." Montana Standard, August 18, 1979.

"Meissner Memorial Field Dedication Slated Tonight." Glendive Ranger-Review, July 14, 1963.

"Men's baseball returns to Wales with Welsh Baseball Union Cup final." BBC Sports, August 5, 2021.

Middlebrook, William. "William T. Middlebrook." Daniels County History, 1977.

"Miles City Eliminates Scobey; To Meet Billings in Semifinal." Billings Gazette, July 22, 1946.

Moe, Sig and Erickson, Ida. "Peder Moe." Daniels County History, 1977.

Mohn, Ellen R. "The Thomas Mohn Family." Daniels County History, 1977.

"Mohn's Speed Paces Flaxville; Notre Dame University Hounds Fall Prey to League Leaders." Daniels County Leader, July 14, 1938.

"Molnor Upsets Flaxville; Nashua Hurlers Speed ball, Hooks And Drops Halt Flaxville Hopes." Daniels County Leader, September 15, 1938.

Miller, Bennett. Moneyball. Columbia Pictures 2011, based on Moneyball: The Art of Winning an Unfair Game by Michael Lewis.

"Monsignor (Père) Athol Murray 1892-1975." Heritage Toronto, archived from the original on August 19, 2019.

Montgomery, Sam. "Sam Montgomery." Daniels County History, 1977.

Mouat, Marty. "Blues oust Senators." Helena Independent Record, August 6, 1979.

References

Nash, Ada. "Raymond Is the Winner of BB Tourney." *Plentywood Herald*, October 18, 1951.

Nash, Ada. "Redstone." *Plentywood Herald*, October 11, 1951.

Nash, Ada. "Redstone." *Plentywood Herald*, October 18, 1951.

Nelson, Melvin. "Melvin Nelson recalls early homesteaders." *Daniels County History*, 1977.

"New Baseball League Is Organized." *The Nashua Messenger*, June 16, 1938.

"Norman Honored by Former Players." *Daniels County Leader*, July 7, 1983.

"Norman, Audet lead Scobey to B crown." *Billings Gazette*, August 1, 1978.

"Old Cronies." *Daniels County Leader*, August 5, 1965.

"Opheim Radars Bow 15-7 to Plainsmen." *Daniels County Leader*, July 26, 1951.

Orr, Jim. "Reds Return To Top 3 At State." *Glasgow Courier*, August 7, 2013.

"Outlook Wins Here Sunday Over Scobey." *Daniels County Leader*, June 24, 1954.

"P'Wood Juniors Win Second in District Meet, *Plentywood Herald*, July 22, 1948.

Pace, Roy. "Blues, Senators split; deciding game today." *Helena Independent Record*, August 5, 1979.

Pauley, Dooley. "Vauxhall wins berth in state championship game." *Glendive Ranger-Review*, August 1, 1990.

"Peerless Beats Ossette Sunday on Pirate Field." *Daniels County Leader*, August 1, 1940.

"Peerless Gets Revenge Sunday; Beats Scobey 6-5; Second Game Goes Ten Innings At Scobey Park" *Daniels County Leader*, July 4, 1940.

"Peerless Seeks Revenge Over Flaxville." *Daniels County Leader*, July 11, 1940.

"Peerless Softball Tournament." *Daniels County Leader*, August 1, 1963.

"Plainsmen Cop League Trophy." *Daniels County Leader*, August 9, 1956.

"Plainsmen not in National Competition." *Daniels County Leader*, August 21, 1958.

"Plainsmen Open Here Sunday Night." *Daniels County Leader*, June 11, 1964.

"Plainsmen Place 2nd at Tourney in Coronach, Sask." *Daniels County Leader*, May 26, 1955.

"Plainsmen Show Excellent Wares at Ball Meet." *Daniels County Leader*, September 8, 1949.

"Plainsmen This Year, New Arrangement." *Daniels County Leader*, July 2, 1964.

"Plainsmen Will Play Exhibition with Regina Here; Benefit for Trip to National Finals." *Daniels County Leader*, August 11, 1960.

"Plainsmen Win Ball Tourney." *Daniels County Leader*, July 6, 1961.

"Plainsmen Win from Outlook." *Daniels County Leader*, August 13, 1953.

"Plainsmen Win In Overtime From Wolves." *Daniels County Leader*, August 9, 1951.

"Plainsmen Win Over Brockton." *Daniels County Leader*, July 2, 1953.

"Plainsmen Win Plentywood Tournament." *Daniels County Leader*, September 9, 1948.

"Plainsmen Win Thriller from Opheim Radars." *Daniels County Leader*, July 19, 1951.

"Plainsmen Win Two Games; Rebs Leave Hungry." *Daniels County Leader*, July 20, 1961.

"Plans Completed for July 3 and 4 Celebration Here." *Daniels County Leader*, June 17, 1926.

"Plentywood Nine Bewildered." *Billings Gazette*, July 28, 1966.

"Plentywood Pirates Would Pilfer Game When Pitcher Fails." *Scobey Sentinel*, June 11, 1926.

Plutt, J. P. "Cubs take dream to Yakima, no further." *Dillon Tribune*, August 18, 1993.

"Police Creek Baseball Team." *Kahle-Silver Star, Daniels County History*, 1977.

"Poplar Wins East Division." *Daniels County Leader*, July 5, 1951.

Price, Craig. "Patriots left out in the cold, after outstanding tourney performance." *Sidney Herald*, August 3, 1978.

Puckett, George and Faustine. "Peerless Peewee, Little League, and Babe Ruth Baseball, 1967-1975." *Daniels County History*, 1977.

Puckett, Joe. *The Dream: The Story of the 1978 and 1979 Peerless Panthers*. Aubade Publishing, 2010.

"Radar Players Lost to GFAB in Fatal Eighth." *Glasgow Courier*, August 4, 1955.

"Randy Stolen." *Daniels County Leader*, August 13, 1980.

"Recalling When Havre Hurler Fanned Foes with Regularity." *Great Falls Tribune*, Scott Mansch, July 11, 2010.

Rickey, Les. "Profound apologies are due to some dedicated kids." *Havre Daily News*, July 29, 1976.

Ring, Glenn. "Glenn Ring." *Daniels County History*, 1977.

Robertson, Hilda. "M. M. Robertson." *Daniels County History*, 1977.

Roby, Tim. "Electrics oust Scobey." *Great Falls Tribune*, August 10, 1982.

Rocene, Ray T. "Sport Jabs." *Missoulian*, June 7, 1959.

"Rush Pitcher by Plane in Effort to Score Victory." *Helena Independent Record*, June 1, 1928.

Rustebakke, Dorothy. "Prairie baseball in 1920s featured pro players." *Billings Gazette*, March 24, 1987.

Sandon, Fern Wiley. "J. L. Wiley." *Whitetail, Daniels County History*, 1977, 1977.

Sayler, Bruce. "Electrics, Royals win in first round." *Montana Standard*, August 12, 1979.

Sayler, Bruce. "Mavericks declared ineligible for state." *Missoulian*, August 9, 1976.

"Scholars End Season Sunday with Plainsmen." *Daniels County Leader*, May 17, 1951.

"Schuster Fans 15; Tops Scobey." *Billings Gazette*, July 30, 1969.

"Scobey Again Hosts State Legion Ball." *Daniels County Leader*, July 26, 1979.

"Scobey Ball Park and Lions Field." *Daniels County Leader*, June 13, 2013.

"Scobey Ball Park Scene of Lively Action." *Daniels County Leader*, May 13, 1965.

"Scobey blanks Laurel for State B Legion title." *Billings Gazette*, July 31, 1979.

"Scobey Blues 3rd At Divisional 'A' Tourney in Sidney." *Daniels County Leader*, July 29, 1993.

"Scobey Blues are State Champs Once Again." *Daniels County Leader*, August 3, 1978.

"Scobey Blues Do It Again; 8th State Title." *Daniels County Leader*, August 5, 1982.

"Scobey Blues seek fourth straight title." *Great Falls Tribune*, July 26, 1979.

"Scobey Captures B Title Defeats Glendive 8-6." *Cut Bank Pioneer Press*, August 3, 1978.

"Scobey Commissioner Blames Technicalities." *Billings Gazette*, July 30, 1966.

"Scobey Defeats Plentywood 4-1." *Scobey Sentinel*, June 19, 1925.

"Scobey Earns Tourney Berth." *Billings Gazette*, July 27, 1966.

"Scobey Gets 4th in 'B' State Play." *Daniels County Leader*, August 3, 1967.

"Scobey Handed 1st Loss." *Billings Gazette*, July 24, 1967.

"Scobey Has Young Team." *Daniels County Leader*, June 16, 1977.

"Scobey Hosts 7th State B Legion Tourney." *Daniels County Leader*, July 25, 1985.

"Scobey Hosts Eastern Divisional Tournament." *Daniels County Leader*, July 18, 1974.

"Scobey Hosts State Tourney . . . Starts Today." *Daniels County Leader*, August 12, 1971.

"Scobey Junior Legion Seeing Plenty of Action." *Daniels County Leader*, June 18, 1959.

"Scobey Junior Legion Wins District Title." *Daniels County Leader*, July 18, 1946.

"Scobey Juniors Enjoy Tour; Nip Billings, Miles City." *Daniels County Leader*, July 21, 1966.

"Scobey leaves Northstars singing 'blues,'" *Havre Daily News*, July 26, 1985.

"Scobey Legion Juniors Down Poplar Rivals." *Wolf Point Herald*, July 31, 1931.

"Scobey Legion Wins Div. 2nd; On to State." *Daniels County Leader*, July 29, 1976.

"Scobey Loses at Plentywood." *Daniels County Leader*, July 18, 1940.

"Scobey Loses in 11 Innings to Old Rivals." *Daniels County Leader*, July 31, 1941.

"Scobey Loses to Billings 8-4." *Daniels County Leader*, July 31, 1930.

"Scobey Opens Play Sunday on Peerless Diamond." *Daniels County Leader*, June 13, 1940.

"Scobey Ready for State Tourney Here." *Daniels County Leader*, August 7, 1969.

"Scobey scores wild win." *Billings Gazette*, August 5, 1996.

"SCOBEY SLUGGERS WIN." *Great Falls Tribune*, July 7, 1928.

"Scobey Splits Sunday Tilts, Loses Tuesday." *Daniels County Leader*, June 17, 1954.

"Scobey Stuns Sidney." *Billings Gazette*, July 23, 1967.

"Scobey Takes Eastern District 'B,'" *Miles City Star*, July 30, 1973.

"Scobey topples Reds, 7-2." *Missoulian*, July 27, 1980.

"Scobey Upsets Glendive." *Billings Gazette*, July 22, 1967.

"Scobey Wins Area's First Baseball Title." *Daniels County Leader*, August 14, 1969.

"Scobey Wins Divisional at Miles City." *Daniels County Leader*, August 2, 1973.

"Scobey Wins Eastern Division." *Daniels County Leader*, August 10, 1972.

"Scobey Wins Second, State Legion Tournament." *Daniels County Leader*, August 20, 1970.

"Scobey Wins State Title in Thriller." *Daniels County Leader*, August 9, 1973.

"Scobey, Wolf Point win." *Billings Gazette*, July 22, 1979.

"Scobey: Legion Team to Beat." *Billings Gazette*, August 6, 1969.

"Scobey's Danelson one-hits Royals, 2-1." *Billings Gazette*, July 3, 1979.

"Scobey—as predicted—is Class B Legion champ." *Pioneer Press*, July 30, 1980.

"Scramble in Offing for Best Legion B Team." *Great Falls Tribune*, August 2, 1972.

"Scramble in the Offing for Best Legion B Team." *Great Falls Tribune*, August 9, 1972.

Seals and Crofts. "Summer Breeze." *Summer Breeze*. Warner Bros. Records, 1972.

"Sealy Stars on Mound." *Daniels County Leader*, May 31, 1928.

"Season Ends." *Daniels County Leader*, August 31, 1961.

Seger, Bob. "Night Moves." *Night Moves*. Capitol, 1976.

Sell, Keith. "Poplar Trounces Scobey 12-2." *Daniels County Leader*, May 19, 1955.

"Senators sweep Scobey, head for state tourney in Great Falls." *Helena Independent Record*, August 7, 1977.

"Senators Win, 17-2." *Helena Independent Record*, June 6, 1972.

"Services held Thursday for Sgt. Elwood Lien of Peerless." *Daniels County Leader*, August 16, 1945.

"Sidney Defeats Plainsmen for Montana Title." *Daniels County Leader*, August 6, 1959.

Smith, Clausie. "Should Boost Legion Age Limit." *Ottawa Herald*, August 23, 1958.

Smith, Phil. "Electrics host powerful Blues." *Great Falls Tribune*, August 2, 1980.

Smith, Phil. "French, Electrics blank Scobey." *Great Falls Tribune*, August 12, 1979.

Smith, Phil. "Predictably, the Legion tournament was unpredictable." *Great Falls Tribune*, August 17, 1979.

Smith, Phil. "Scobey upsets Kalispell in state Legion tourney." *Great Falls Tribune*, August 15, 1979.

Southland, Phyllis. "American Legion Post." *Daniels County History*, 1977.

"Sports Chatter." *Great Falls Tribune*, May 23, 1948.

"State A Legion." *Great Falls Tribune*, August 5, 1996.

"State American Legion Class B Tourney Opens Here Today." *Daniels County Leader*, July 31, 1975.

"State Class B Tourney Off to Colorful Start." *Havre Daily News*, August 11, 1972.

"State Corner Ball League Starts Play." *Daniels County Leader*, June 2, 1938.

"State Legion B-B Tourney Starts Here Today." *Daniels County Leader*, July 28, 1977.

"State Tourney on Here Today." *Daniels County Leader*, August 2, 1973.

Stiffarm, Steve. "Wolf Point Lights Up Burke Field,'" *Wotanin Wowapi*, May 23, 1991.

Stiffarm, Steve. "Yellowjackets win three of five at State A." *Wotanin Wowapi*, August 3, 1989.

"Strong Third at State for Blues." *Daniels County Leader*, August 9, 1990.

"Sweep by East in Legion." *Billings Gazette*, July 28, 1978.

Tanner, Jack. "1983—The year of the Bucs." *Ravalli Republic*, December 30, 1983.

"Team Transportation." *Havre Daily News*, July 26, 1974.

"The Conboy History." Carbert or Coal Creek, *Daniels County History*, 1977.

"The End of an Era; Clyde H. Norman, 1920–1983." *Daniels County Leader*, November 24, 1983.

Hancock, John Lee. *The Rookie*. Walt Disney Pictures, 2002.

Evans, David Mickey. *Sandlot*. Island World, 1993.

"Things, Ideas, and People." *Daniels County Leader*, October 6, 1994.

Thorpe, Randall and Christianson, B. Family. "Carbert Store and Post Office." *Daniels County History*, 1977.

"Tired Scobey Club Loses to Great Falls." *Daniels County Leader*, August 14, 1969.

"Trangsrud hurls Legion no-hitter." *Billings Gazette*, June 9, 1975.

"Trivia." *Missoulian*, March 21, 1995.

Trower, Fern E. "James A. (Jim) and Rosa Trower." *Daniels County History*, 1977.

"Two Players Ejected as Whitetail Wins." *Plentywood Herald*, August 12, 1954.

Walter, Dave. "Pitched Battles on the Diamond, 1925-26." *Montana Magazine*, May/June 2001.

"War Amputee to Hurl Game." *Billings Gazette*, June 22, 1947.

Weiskopf, Donald and Alston, Walter. *The Complete Baseball Handbook*, 1972.

West, Ed. "Bitterroot gunning for 3rd title." *Billings Gazette*, July 28, 1990.

West, Ed. "Dog fight expected at State A Legion showdown." *Billings Gazette*, July 25, 1992.

West, Ed. "Legion tournament has no favorites." *Billings Gazette*, August 11, 1979.

West, Ed. "Longtime Legion coach Bayne passes away." *Billings Gazette*, July 21, 2003.

West, Ed. "Scobey's Doctor is a lot like Eddie Bayne." *Billings Gazette*, July 1, 1979.

West, Ed. "Wolf Point Wearing Its First Legion Crown." *Billings Gazette*, August 3, 1987.

Wester, C.O. "Dodgers play in state tournament." *Laurel Outlook*, August 1, 1990.

"What it was was baseball." *Billings Gazette*, August 8, 1971.

"What's Uniquely Different About This Ball Club?" *Daniels County Leader*, June 14, 1979.

"Whitetail Cops NeMont Ball Event." *Plentywood Herald*, August 4, 1955.

"Whitetail." *Plentywood Herald*, August 12, 1954.

Whitworth, Kevin. "Legion teams converge on Dillon." *Dillon Tribune*, June 6, 1990.

References

"Williston Takes Tournament; Scobey 2nd; Blue Moon is 3rd." *Plentywood Herald*, September 3, 1959.

Willse, Hudson. "Vauxhall, Bitterroot clash for Legion title." *Montana Standard*, August 15, 1990.

"With People Making News." *Daniels County Leader*, April 13, 1950.

"With People Making News." *Daniels County Leader*, July 31, 1958.

"With People Making News." *Daniels County Leader*, May 14, 1953.

"Wolf Point Division Champs Over Sidney." *Daniels County Leader*, July 30, 1987.

"Wolf Point Outlasts Scobey 24-23 for District Title." *The Herald-News*, July 31, 1975.

"Wolves Win Class B Tourney." *Daniels County Leader*, July 22, 1965.

"Yellowjackets open long-awaited season." *Wotanin Wowapi*, May 30, 2002.

"Yellowjackets save best for last; 3rd place." *Wotanin Wowapi*, August 1, 1996.

Yuill, Grace. Madoc, "A.B. Yuill Family." *Daniels County History*, 1977.

Index

A

Aafedt, Ardean, 320–21, 328, 402
Aasheim, Brock, 587
Abar, Mike, 268, 276, 290, 297
Ackerman, Leroy, 68
Ackerman, Ted, 332
Ackerman, Todd, 332, 335, 339, 395, 397–98
Adkins, Jason, 434
Adkins, Wasyl, 67
Ahlberg, Dave, 132
Akin, William E., 30, 32
Albert, Shannon, 467–68, 473
Alden, Phil, 672, 677
Alderson, Justin, 524
Aldrich, Ethan, 630
Aldrich, Tom, 463, 467–68, 480, 483–85
Aldridge, Joe, 364
Allen, Pokey, 100
Alley, Jeremy, 548–49
Alston, Walter, 320, 356, 428
Altman, Dutch, 13
Anders, Dave, 74, 76
Anderson, Andy, 78, 315
Anderson, Dave, 499, 512, 514, 520–24, 527–30, 534, 538–43, 545
Anderson, Ernie, 122, 126
Anderson, Gary, 58
Anderson, Harvey, 81
Anderson, Jay, 179
Anderson, Jim, 384–85, 429
Anderson, Joe, 93, 95–96, 99, 106, 112–13, 116, 153, 155, 172, 220, 426, 476
Anderson, Len, 543, 546, 550, 554, 561
Anderson, Les, 81
Anderson, Mike, 279
Anderson, Mitch, 295, 300
Anderson, Norm, 107, 112–13, 116–17, 124
Anderson, Pat, 144, 152, 160, 205, 210, 216–17, 390, 634
Anderson, Russ, 178–80
Anderson, Scott, 353
Anderson, Ted, 203, 220
Anderson, Tyson, 668
Antonson, Chris, 470
Archdale, Ginny, 495
Archibald, Cole, 542
Armstrong, Neil, 3
Arredondo, Dan, 362
Arthur, Maybelle, 489–90, 500, 502
Ashley, Mayo, 162
Asinof, Eliot, 29
Askelson, Roger, 188
Ator, Kash, 666
Ator, Walker, 652–54, 658, 665
Atwood, Dick, 265, 276, 280, 282, 290, 298, 303, 306, 312, 319, 344, 361, 372

Audet, Allan, 216–17, 251, 255, 261, 265, 268, 276–78, 280–82, 285, 289–93, 295–97, 299–304, 306–7, 309–13, 315, 317, 319, 336, 378, 423
Audet, Arlee (Vatnsdal), 620
Audet, Art, 220, 293, 338
Audet, Craig, 62, 126, 130, 133–34, 140, 144, 152–55, 158, 160, 162, 164, 166, 169, 182, 184, 190, 202, 217, 234, 383, 385, 388, 422, 471, 561
Audet, Dana, 63, 133, 136, 140, 142, 146, 163, 172, 176–79, 185–89, 191–201, 203, 205–11, 213, 216–17, 266, 283–84, 312, 328, 332, 340, 348, 375, 383, 426, 561
Audet, Danny, 126, 163, 213
Audet, Maury, 185, 438
Audet, Mazel, 179, 293, 301, 439
Audet, Michelle, 375, 379, 384–85, 392, 404, 406, 434
Audet, Pat, 213, 319–20, 329, 334, 337–38, 360–61, 368, 373–76, 378–84, 386, 392, 394–96, 398, 404–16, 422–25, 433–37, 444, 447, 450, 501, 561, 607–8, 634
Audet, Patti, 213, 411
Audet, Phil, 62, 122–23, 126–27, 130–31, 133–35, 139–42, 144, 154, 164, 186, 189–91, 197, 202, 205, 210, 220, 283, 293–94, 298, 312, 328, 331, 338, 383, 422, 435–36, 440, 443, 519, 524, 558, 569, 576, 619, 634
Audet, Richard, 67, 70, 74
Audet, Zach, 588, 607–10, 614, 619
Ault, Troy, 470
Ausk, Jamie, 675
Ausk, Jim, 139
Austin, John, 112
Austin, Kasey, 555
Azure, Kenny, 470, 475, 482

B

Babb, Lavina, 39
Bachmeier, Brian, 611
Baggs, Kelly, 120
Baillie, Bryce, 550, 554
Baker, Dennis, 94, 105
Baker, Jon, 619
Baker, Kayli, 477
Baker, Loren, 390
Baker, Phil, 99, 101–2, 111, 115, 120, 122, 127–28, 634
Bakken, Joe, 619, 630
Bakken, Shane, 448
Baldry, Alvie, 184
Baldry, Buck, 82, 115
Baldry, Drew, 630
Baldry, Kevin, 245, 251
Baldry, Myrna, 227–31, 233, 440
Baldry, Preston, 647–50
Baldry, Ryan, 601–2

Baldry, Terry, 257, 302–3, 308, 313, 330, 333, 340, 375, 389
Baldry, Todd, 406
Baldwin, Jim, 398
Ball, Chuck, 208
Ballantine, Craig, 285, 294, 301, 307, 312–13
Ballard, Jeff, 362, 364
Balock, Rita, 397, 429, 446, 509
Baltrusch, Nate, 588, 595
Bandy, Tom, 188
Banko, Donnette, 128
Bantz, Lloyd, 144
Barkley, Fred, 386
Barkley, Jason, 541
Barnes, Tony, 397
Barnhart, Harry, 10–11
Barnhart, Ken, 288, 291, 303
Barnhart, Russ, 335, 396
Barnhart, Tom, 397–98, 408, 413–14, 472, 542
Barr, Austin, 470, 475, 482
Barstad, Dale, 216–17, 255, 259, 264–65, 276, 341
Barstad, Mark, 251
Barstad, Mike, 130, 140
Bartel, Dan, 189, 191, 193–96, 198, 200, 203
Bartels, Billy, 418
Bartley, Bruce, 214, 427
Bartole, Bill, 205, 207, 216–17, 249, 255, 257, 259–60, 264–66, 268, 276
Bartsch, Mike, 343, 346
Barzun, Jacques, 36
Battleson, E.W., 30
Bauer, Jay, 434
Bayne, Eddie, 38, 321, 329, 428, 680
Bayne, Jack, 620
Beardsley, Bob, 68
Beatty, Bob, 113
Beauchamp, Joe, 10
Bechtold, Brian, 154, 165, 171, 192
Bechtold, Dennis, 168, 171
Beck, Jay, 250
Becker, Keith, 425
Bedwell, Jesse, 73–74
Beesley, Dianne (Puckett), 82, 241, 244, 267
Beliveau, Carole, 119
Bell, Lindsay, 448
Belling, Ray, 273
Belling, Sam, 101–2
Bench, Johnny, 287, 419, 471
Bengochea, Griffin, 633
Benjamin, Dan, 208
Benjamin, Jeff, 358
Benn, Ted, 362
Benson, Cory, 279, 281
Benson, Darrell, 80–81
Benson, Don, 81
Bergen, Wayne, 132
Bergenheier, Don, 220
Berger, Paul, 72, 74

Index

Berland, Larry, 279
Berna, Jim, 397
Bernhart, Bill, 493, 500
Berra, Yogi, 270, 624, 669
Berry, Scott, 612–13
Berube, Craig, 513
Berube, Derek, 560
Bicha, Benji, 505
Biering, Troy, 353
Bies, Kenny, 247
Billehus, Dave, 341
Bingham, Doreen, 15
Birdsbill, Carmen, 188–89, 191–95, 197–201, 203, 282, 369
Bishop, Rob, 617, 631
Black, Bill, 76
Boe, R.L., 37, 50
Bolin, Brent, 358
Bonds, Barry, 93
Boos, Don, 268, 276, 290, 297
Boos, Joey, 520, 524, 527–28, 538–41, 544–45, 548–49, 551, 553–54, 556–57, 563
Borchert, Laroy, 220
Borchgrevink, Delno, 22
Bourassa, Horace, 16, 676
Bowker, Chris, 503, 514–17, 524
Bowler, Burl, 20, 23, 27, 32, 213, 250–51, 341, 373, 457, 463, 476–77, 497, 521, 527, 529–31, 533, 538, 540, 544, 547–48, 552–53, 557, 674
Bowler, Burley, 20, 23, 27, 32
Bowler, Larry, 2, 29–30, 37–38, 155, 160, 184, 316, 339, 459–60, 623
Bowler, Levi, 520, 523–24, 527–28, 530, 534–35, 538–42, 544–60, 563
Bowler, Printer, 100, 148, 180
Bowler, Roz, 508, 533
Bowler, Zach, 502, 505, 507–8, 512–16, 520–24, 527–31, 533, 535, 538
Bowman, Chuck, 84–85, 95–96
Boyd, Lou, 8, 14, 37, 418, 460
Boysun, Grant, 218, 256, 258–59, 261–62, 265–66, 279
Braaten, Norm, 256, 259, 266
Brackee, Lita, 231
Bradley, Beaumont, 448
Bragg, Addison, 391, 429
Brandt, Carissa, 231
Brasen, Don, 63–64, 66–67, 70–71, 79, 83
Brasen, Larry, 82
Brastrup, Gary, 314, 316
Brayko, Don, 54–56, 58, 60, 64–65, 68–69, 71–72, 75
Brekke, Dale, 194
Brekke, Norm, 197
Brenden, Alice, 16, 42
Brenden, Gary, 94, 105, 127, 133
Brenden, Loyal, 41–42, 222, 293, 478
Brett, George, 270, 440
Bretzke, Lou, 13
Brien, Pete, 13
Briggeman, Vince, 544, 579
Brockett, Jay, 496, 503, 506

Broeg, Bob, 93
Brogdon, Wade, 352, 362
Brokevic, Irv, 80
Bronson, Bob, 188
Brooks, Chet, 68, 76
Brooks, Christopher, 555
Brooks, Eddie, 67, 70, 74, 76, 79
Brothers, Moe, 9–11
Brown, David, 668
Brown, Gene, 77–78, 80, 84, 393
Brown, Jack, 655
Brown, Logan, 666
Brown, Mitch, 666
Brown, Ozro, 10, 61
Brown, Ricky, 595
Brozovich, Dan, 448
Brunet, Blanche, 39
Brunet, Fay, 39
Bryan, Andy, 342–43, 346
Bryant, John, 159–60, 169, 175, 179–80
Bublitz, Dan, 515
Buchanan, W.D., 83
Buck, Arthur, 153
Buckles, Dana, 241
Buckles, Melvin, 97
Buckley, Ryan, 553
Bucklin, Ben, 538, 540, 544–45, 551–52, 555, 563, 568, 570–71, 574, 582
Bucklin, John, 533
Bucklin, Matt, 544–45, 555, 563–64, 575, 582–83
Bucklin, Tyler, 502, 505, 512–14, 520–24, 527–30, 534, 537, 541, 614, 636, 645, 668–69
Buckner, Bill, 253
Buer, Joan, 118
Buer, Kray, 630
Bummer, Leland, 71, 74
Bundren, Doug, 63–64, 66, 68–69, 71–72
Bunse, D., 41
Burke, Mike, 84
Burkett, John, 487
Burnett, Arnie, 94, 115
Burns, Dan, 76
Burns, Tom, 76
Burrell, Steve, 550
Burt, Jim, 95
Bush, Bob, 362
Bush, Harvey, 140
Bushly, Tom, 351
Butner, Jerry, 179, 400, 472
Butner, Lance, 398, 414
Butner, Troy, 303
Butzlaff, Henry, 116, 127
Byrne, Tim, 333, 336–39
Bystrom, Amelia, 39
Bystrom, Lillian, 39

C

Caldwell, Bill, 338–39
Callen, Jerry, 305, 330, 340
Calvin, Ebby, 266
Campagna, Joe, 416
Campbell, Anthony, 458

Campbell, Kahle, 458
Campbell, Kevin, 437
Campbell, Scott, 291
Campbell, Tony, 459, 631
Candee, Boyd, 541
Canseco, Jose, 513
Cantrell, Leon, 130
Caray, Harry, 426, 440
Carbo, Bernie, 197, 253
Carbone, Robert, 86, 637
Carew, Rod, 417
Carlson, Evans F., 46
Carney, Betty, 93
Carney, Jack, 9, 11, 130
Carranza, John, 107
Carranza, Tom, 139
Carroll, Will, 203
Casey, David, 293
Casey, Dennis, 153
Casey, Katie, 643
Casey, Tim, 220
Cassidy, Charles, 16, 32, 50, 153, 174, 179, 214, 220, 293, 338, 408
Cassidy, Jack, 201
Castle, Scott, 83
Catley, Ben, 632
Cavanaugh, Chris, 541
Cerrano, Pedro, 519
Chabot, Jude, 607–8, 619
Chabot, Mark, 213
Chadwich, Jerry, 284
Chapman, Janet, 226
Chapman, Jim, 205, 208, 249
Chapman, Ray, 48, 161, 230, 235–37, 239–40, 242, 247–48, 250–51, 256, 268, 273, 276–78, 284, 289–90, 292, 296–99, 302–3, 306–7, 310–11, 313, 316, 319–20, 325, 328–30, 332, 335, 337–38, 342–45, 347, 349, 353, 355, 357, 360, 368, 370, 373–74, 486–87, 500, 558, 648, 671, 674
Chapman, Ross, 216–17, 235–37, 239, 243, 248, 272–74
Chapman, Roy, 411–14
Chelgren, Ruth, 39
Chenoweth, Harland, 163
Chenoweth, Hulda, 39
Chenoweth, Jim, 160, 169
Chenoweth, Lynn, 160, 163, 169, 171
Chilton, Bob Sr., 344
Chilton, Bob, 292, 344
Chouinard, Lee, 13
Christensen, Craig, 80–81, 92
Christensen, Don, 40, 54–56, 58, 60, 64, 66–68, 71–72, 74, 79
Christensen, Ken, 12
Christensen, Ronnie, 70
Christensen, Tom, 179
Chumrau, William, 84
Clampitt, Bret, 589, 598–99
Clark, Dick, 169, 179, 189, 561
Clark, Torrence, 485
Clark, Will, 367

Clarke, Norm, 181, 182, 427, 678
Cleland, Troy, 485, 495–99, 501, 517
Clemens, Bob, 60
Clemens, Roger, 93, 203
Clemmensen, Kurt, 321–22
Clump, Bob, 301–2, 307, 312, 316
Clyde, Kelly, 389
Cobb, Bob, 62
Cody, Tim, 188, 191, 196, 198
Cody, Troy, 470, 476, 482
Cole, Dan, 160, 169
Cole, Dave, 169, 175, 179, 188–89
Collopy, Jason, 541
Combs, Bernard, 68
Conboy, Agnes, 39
Conboy, Dick, 54–55, 57
Conboy, Harrison, 37
Conboy, Jack, 20, 29
Conboy, Tom, 15, 22, 54–55, 57
Conger, Bart, 483, 487
Conger, Ray, 477
Connors, Bill, 566, 569, 598, 632
Connors, Bob, 397
Connors, Jimmy, 426
Conroy, Patti, 227
Cook, Brenda, 674
Cook, Cole, 630
Cook, Jesse, 81, 251, 319, 334, 337–38, 361, 373–76, 379, 381, 386, 394, 558, 634
Cook, Lee, 81, 186, 188, 191–93, 197, 201, 205–7, 209–12, 214, 249, 369, 439, 466, 604, 634
Cook, Luke, 38
Corey, David, 297, 303, 305, 311, 319, 329
Cornell, Scott, 174
Cornwell, George, 54–56, 58, 60
Cornwell, Gordon, 111, 115
Correll, Dick, 82
Coryell, Mark, 219
Cossette, Bert, 41, 43
Cossette, Clifford, 41–42
Costner, Kevin, 355
Cote, Casey, 585, 588, 596–97, 601–3, 607, 609, 611
Cottingham, Delno "Cotty", 15, 20–21, 30
Cottingham, Mayme, 32, 678
Coughlin, R.J., 27
Courchene, Chappie, 41–42
Crain, Scott, 666, 668
Crandell, Grace, 93, 96
Crandell, Jay, 295
Crandell, Michael, 630
Crandell, Neill, 585, 588, 596–98, 601–3, 607–11, 614, 622
Crawford, Bob, 212
Cromwell, Chris, 588
Cromwell, Cory, 527, 585, 588, 596, 598, 601–3, 607–8, 622–23
Cromwell, Kent, 604
Cromwell, Sean, 559
Crosby, Alex, 595
Cross, Bob, 75, 83, 636
Crow, Chief, 41
Crowe, Scott, 458

Crowe, Warren, 191, 198
Crum, Taylor, 37
Cullen, Bill, 59, 63–66, 69–70, 622
Cummings, Craig, 220–21
Cuplin, Tracy, 84
Curtis, Jamie Lee, 332
Curtis, Kip, 466
Curtiss, David, 552

D

Dahl, Lura, 39
Dahl, Walter, 68
Dalbey, Walt, 633
Dalbout, Sue, 648
Dale, Bill, 122, 126, 130, 140
Dallas, Len, 54–56, 60
Dallas, Porky, 15, 20–23, 25
Damm, Bobby, 327
Damon, Johnny, 253
Damschen, Barry, 146, 154, 158, 160, 188, 212, 294, 561
Dana, Chris, 259
Danelson, Ben Lee, 109
Danelson, Ben, 171, 179, 421
Danelson, Casey, 512, 514, 520–22, 524, 527, 529–30, 532–34, 538
Danelson, Clo Ann, 533
Danelson, Dan "Dano", 63, 152, 160–61, 186, 192, 197, 203, 216–17, 247, 249, 251, 255–56, 258, 260, 264–68, 272, 276–80, 285, 290–92, 294, 297–99, 301–4, 306–7, 311, 313–14, 318–19, 324, 326–27, 329–31, 334–35, 337, 339, 341–42, 350–51, 355, 360, 362–63, 366, 373–75, 381, 384, 394, 402, 418–19, 421, 423, 434, 436–37, 444, 447, 449, 451, 487, 499, 557–58
Danelson, Delores, 293, 338, 439
Danelson, Jerry, 463, 467–68, 473, 480, 501
Danelson, Rick, 3, 48, 144, 152, 155–56, 158, 160–61, 163, 165–67, 170–72, 175–76, 179–80, 186–88, 190–93, 195–202, 205, 209–10, 364, 383, 386, 419, 500, 612
Daniels, Else, 50, 153, 179
Daniels, Justin, 515
Danielson, Dan, 219, 221, 588, 595
Dantic, Brad, 335, 338–39
Dantic, Matt, 338, 340
Darchuk, Carl, 122, 130, 133
Darchuk, Jim, 144, 166–67
Darchuk, Pete, 111–12, 115, 122, 185
Davenport, Davie, 26
Davids, Richard C., 16, 678
Davies, Gary, 82–84, 92, 106, 116, 486
Davis, Estelle, 39
Davis, Francis, 577, 579
Davis, Irving, 14, 37–38, 44, 103, 460
Davis, Laura, 39
Davis, Marty, 404–5, 407, 409, 414, 433
Davis, Mary, 39
Davis, Mike, 458
Davis, Wayne, 525
Dawson, Gene, 76, 79, 82
Day, Mike, 298, 323, 325, 327–28, 364

Dean, Blaine, 26
DeBolt, Larry, 362
Deem, Glyn, 132
Deer, Todd, 250
Dehler, Billy Joe, 620
Dehler, Jon, 620
Dehler, Kirk, 620
Del, Canyon, 561
Delgado, Julio, 471
Demick, Karen, 128
Demieux, Lional, 72
Denning, Steve, 354
Dent, Bucky, 253
Denton, Doug, 40
Denton, Glenn, 293
Derheim, Bodean, 446
Devereaux, Mike, 324
Devore, Travis, 598
Dickinson, Howard, 172, 437
Dickman, Larry, 130
Dickson, JoAnn (Mutt), 227
Dickson, Pete, 3, 144, 160, 166
Dickson, Sue, 226–28
Diegel, Brent, 458, 460, 504, 528, 533, 553, 558, 589–90, 611–12, 632, 647
Dighans, Bernie, 119
Dighans, Helen, 93
Dighans, Jim, 82
Dighans, Patti, 223, 227–28
Dighans, Pete "Oil Can", 463, 467–69, 471, 473, 481
Dighans, Scott, 242
Dishman, Mike, 84, 106–7
Divish, Ryan, 631, 637
Dixon, Pete, 152
Dixon, Sue, 226, 228
Dobie, Darrin, 458
Dobner, Billy, 84
Domenech, Ivan, 433, 444–46, 452–53, 457, 463–64, 466–67
Donaldson, John, 21–24, 30, 635, 673
Dooley, Rick, 220, 259
Dorwin, Art, 11
Dorwin, Jim, 9–11, 16
Doucette, Allie, 108, 114, 118, 128
Doucette, Karlene, 128
Dougherty, Brad, 459
Dougherty, Brian, 457–59, 471
Douglas, Rustin, 541
Downs, Chase, 609, 611–12, 619, 630
Downs, Jim, 122, 126–27
Downs, John, 111, 115, 125
Doyle, Denny, 253
Drapak, Mike, 200, 202
Drapak, William, 202
Driscoll, Jon, 366
Drummond, Darla, 231, 255
Drummond, Frances, 93, 96
Drummond, Jacky, 231
Drummond, Mary, 231
Drummond, Susan, 227–28
Dryden, Pat, 354
Dunlap, Clay, 124, 127

Index

Durazo, Erubiel, 536
Duval, Gary, 94
Dwyer, Jim, 132

E

Eastman, George, 12, 20–22
Ebelt, Jon, 571
Eckelberry, Rick, 355, 362, 366
Eckerdt, Ken, 179
Eckersley, Dennis, 296, 364
Edington, Dave, 401
Edwards, Alvin, 72
Edwards, Jerry, 68
Eichhorn, Charles, 54
Eichhorn, Elsie, 39
Eichhorn, George, 449
Eichhorn, Patty, 449
Eide, Harvey, 54–56, 58, 60, 64
Eiselein, Kim, 578
Ekin, Chad, 554, 571–72
Ekness, Lyle, 81
Elfring, Danny, 304
Eliason, Andy, 374–77, 379, 381, 384, 392, 394–96, 398, 400, 405
Eliason, Glenn, 400
Elletson, D.J., 598
Elletson, Tracy, 541
Elliot, Dean, 179
Emming, Charlie, 13–14
Emter, Wayne, 312
England, Gertrude, 39
Erickson, Ida, 16
Erickson, Jason, 630–31
Erickson, Tony, 256, 259, 269
Erskine, Carl, 595
Erskine, Jimmy, 595
Estenson, Lester, 43, 55
Ethier, Dorothy, 15
Evans, Alan, 454
Evans, Bob, 595
Evans, Dude, 454–55, 464, 466, 551
Evans, Ryan, 595
Evans, Sam, 551, 562
Evers, Lloyd, 184
Evinrude, Russ, 140
Ewing, Ron, 179, 182, 212, 293–95, 403
Eyer, Larry, 170

F

Faanes, Len, 58
Falcon, Chad, 512, 514
Falcon, Mark, 598, 626
Falcon, Michael, 587, 598–99
Falcon, Steven, 598
Fanning, Brian, 595
Fanning, Dave, 62, 163, 168–73, 175, 177, 179–81, 183–84, 187–88, 190, 198, 203, 212, 215, 219, 282, 333, 336, 364, 369, 380, 386, 420–21, 449, 453, 501, 516, 558, 561, 588, 591–92, 594–95, 618, 631, 673
Fanning, Steve, 588, 591, 595, 631
Farley, Scott, 579
Farmer, Bob, 436
Farrell, Tommy, 68
Farry, Kevin, 345–47
Farver, Gary, 82–83, 92, 95, 106, 116, 569
Farver, Howard, 63, 67, 70–71, 76, 79, 85, 92, 95, 106, 116, 476
Farver, Lee, 538–40, 544–45, 547, 549, 555, 563–64, 566, 569, 572, 574–75, 582
Farver, Martin, 624, 642, 644–45, 647–50, 652–54, 658–60, 664, 671
Farver, Terry, 459, 472–73, 475, 478, 481, 483–85, 488–91, 493–99, 502, 544, 569, 577, 622, 625, 641, 664
Fassett, Ancel, 14
Feller, Bob, 47
Felsch, Happy, 1, 20–22, 24–30, 32, 155, 172, 216, 241, 304, 477, 672–73, 678
Feltis, Steve, 235
Feltis, Tim, 235
Ferestad, Kannon, 652
Ferguson, Aubrey, 117, 476
Ferguson, David, 81, 571
Ferguson, Larry, 81, 113, 133
Feser, Paul, 113, 117
Feuerbacher, Fred, 492, 505, 514
Fiechtner, Scott, 362
Fingers, Rolly, 479
Fink, Greg, 453
Fischer, Gene, 345
Fischer, John, 480, 482
Fish, Joel, 353–54
Fishell, Austyn, 658–59
Fishell, Dale, 140
Fishell, Royce, 140
Fisher, Richard, 448
Fisk, Carlton, 253
Fiske, Ole, 61
Fitz, Merle, 440
Fjeld, Clark, 480–81
Fjeld, Greg, 160, 191–92, 196–99, 201, 203, 205–7, 209–10, 216–19, 249, 255–56, 258–59, 261–62, 264–68, 271, 276, 295, 348, 383, 470
Fjeld, Larry, 37–38, 41–43, 114, 459–60
Fjeld, Ron, 54–55, 57–58, 61, 64, 68, 72–74, 77, 79–81, 90, 95–96, 106–7, 112, 201, 220, 329, 675
Fjeld, Scott, 247, 251
Fjeld, Stub, 41–42
Fjeseth, Yogi, 669
Fladager, Armand, 404–5
Fladager, Bill, 235–37, 245, 250, 272–74
Fladager, Bruce, 82, 437, 499
Fladager, Daryl, 166–67
Fladager, Donna, 224–29, 231–32
Fladager, Karen, 226, 233
Fladager, Kathleen, 223
Fladager, Lois, 148
Fladager, Lorna, 226
Fladager, Lorraine, 93, 96
Fladager, Majorie, 15
Fladager, Marshal, 520–21, 525
Fladager, Nola, 225
Fladager, Rob, 424, 488–89, 497, 502–6, 508, 512–20, 525, 536, 576
Fladager, Scott, 467–69, 480
Fladager, Stew, 545
Fladager, Wallace, 534
Fladager, Willard, 235–36, 248, 272
Flamm, Mike, 582–83, 585–87, 596–99, 601, 635
Flint, J., 121
Floyd, Len, 392, 394–96, 404–7, 409, 414, 416, 423, 425–26, 433, 450
Foli, Tim, 184
Forberg, Illa Mae, 93, 96
Forbregd, Herman, 10
Forchak, Terry "Turk", 99, 109, 111
Ford, Greg, 611, 618–19, 630–31
Forman, James, 84
Forte, Aldo, 441
Fortmann, Brian, 378
Fossen, Eddie, 70, 83
Fossum, Justin, 483–84, 488–89, 491–92, 496–98, 502, 508
Fossum, Ken, 544–45, 555, 582–83
Fought, Mike, 382, 384
Fouhy, Annabelle, 93, 96, 224, 230, 233
Fouhy, Bitsy, 224
Fouhy, Bob, 223–24, 231, 253
Fouhy, Bonnie, 224
Fouhy, Helen, 93
Fouhy, Jeannie, 226–31
Fouhy, Judy, 231–32
Fouhy, Laura, 225, 228–29, 231, 233
Fouhy, Mary Kay, 93, 223–24, 226–30, 232
Fouhy, Matt, 224, 235–37, 239, 245, 250, 272
Fouhy, Pamla, 223, 226–30, 232–33
Fouhy, Pat, 224–31
Fouhy, Patrick, 585, 601, 607
Fouhy, Patsy, 225–31
Fouhy, Shauanna, 223–29
Fouhy, Taunya, 223, 226–28
Fouhy, Vicki, 225, 231
Fox, John, 505
Fox, Nellie, 164
Frandsen, Travis, 414, 448
Frank, Ervin, 138–39
Frankenfield, Laurel, 574
Frasier, Jim, 130
Frazee, Warren, 134
Frederick, Charles, 471
Frederick, Spencer, 63, 538, 540, 544–45, 547, 549, 551–52, 555, 557, 561, 563–67, 569–72, 574–76, 582, 612
Fredriksen, Art, 67
Free, Chris, 541–42
Free, Pat, 518
Freeman, John, 107, 109
French, Alvida, 41, 114
French, Bert, 72
French, Brett, 472, 509
French, Charlotte, 121, 128
French, Chick, 71–72
French, LuAnne (Puckett), 121, 128
French, Paris, 122, 130, 133–34, 140–41, 190
French, Shawn, 240

685

The Blues of Summer

French, Sherry, 118
French, Skip, 351–52, 362
Frenzel, Dan, 249
Frenzel, Doug, 257, 260, 281, 283, 285, 291, 299–300, 302–3, 307–10, 312–13, 316, 369–70, 388
Frenzel, Tawn, 458
Frickey, Russ, 501
Froelich, Leo, 132
Fromdahl, Gregg, 624, 626
Fuchs, Dan, 208
Fudge, Sam, 362
Fugere, Paul, 425
Fugere, Tom, 444–45, 452–53, 457, 463–64, 466–67
Fuhrman, Todd, 502
Fulwiler, Dustin, 588, 595
Funk, Selma, 39
Fuqua, Hunter, 458

G

Gaines, Dallas, 60, 64, 68–69, 71, 75–76, 84, 95, 106, 118, 130, 134, 476, 478, 623
Gallagher, Pat, 66
Galloway, Layton, 10–11
Galston, Deron, 598–99
Gampp, Ernie, 10, 61
Garagiola, Joe, 266, 269, 304, 415
Garberg, Justin, 463
Gardiner, Trent, 448
Gardner, Andy, 633
Gardner, Charles, 382, 429
Garrick, Clair, 120
Garvey, Steve, 480
Gaub, Dennis, 392, 395, 401–2, 404, 409–10, 429, 612, 624, 626
Gear, Mike, 139, 145, 212
Geise, George, 267, 317, 319, 428, 509
Gene, Kelly, 120
Generud, Pearl, 39
George, Ron, 105
Germaine, Orville, 604
Germann, Cory, 331
Giamatti, A. Bartlett, 4–5, 621
Gideon, Andy, 554
Gilbert, Brad, 452, 457, 463–64, 467–69, 473–75, 481, 483
Gilbert, Brian, 392, 394, 404–6, 409, 414, 433–34, 436, 444
Gilbertson, Terry, 122–23, 126–27, 133
Gilbertson, Wade, 524, 531
Gilchrist, Clay, 54–55, 61, 63, 68, 79
Gilchrist, Dennis, 82
Gilchrist, Elmer, 60–61, 64
Gilchrist, Tim, 235–36
Gile, Elmer, 11
Gilluly, Bob, 67–68
Gilman, Brett, 470, 476
Ginger, Jerry, 127
Girard, Jerry, 228–29
Girard, Joey, 143, 392, 394–95, 405–7, 409, 412, 414, 416, 422, 424, 433–35, 437, 444–46, 448–50, 452

Girard, Robert, 71, 74, 82–83
Girard, Trevor, 642–43
Girard, Trey, 642, 647–48, 650, 652–54, 658
Gjerde, Harold, 648
Gjerde, Stephen, 448
Glasser, Todd, 458, 465
Goddard, Butch, 129, 441
Godwin, Leta, 675
Goldrick, Brent, 219, 221
Goligoski, Jason, 486, 501
Goller, Ruth, 108, 114, 118
Goltz, Jim, 520
Goosevski, Bill, 83
Gord, Art, 11
Grace, C.F. (Chet), 13, 42
Graff, Cory, 588, 614
Graham, Tom, 76
Grant, Bob, 16
Grant, Herbert, 9, 16, 677
Gratz, Rob, 398, 414
Gray, Mike, 425
Gray, Stephanie, 425
Grayson, Edith, 108, 114, 118, 128
Grayson, Grant, 493
Grayson, Larry, 152, 160, 166, 172–73, 177, 186–87
Grayson, Muriel, 108, 114, 118, 128
Grayson, Reid, 104, 108, 114, 118–19, 122, 128–29, 179
Greany, Lisa, 425
Green, Bob, 365
Green, Mike, 191, 198
Greengard, Bert, 39
Greengard, Bertha, 39
Greengard, Ralph, 44
Gregerson, Bart, 502, 504
Grendal, Oscar, 72
Grendal, Smokey, 115–16, 120, 123
Griffin, Barry, 445–46, 448–49, 501, 517
Griffith, John L., 31
Grimes, John, 598
Grimm, Kurt, 156, 158, 160, 169, 173, 175–76, 178–81, 187, 188, 561
Gritz, Johnny, 13
Grondahl, Larry, 321, 328
Grotjohn, Carol, 108
Grove, Dale, 179
Grove, Jennie, 15
Grove, Lefty, 332, 440
Grubbs, David, 555
Gunderson, Mike, 191–93, 197, 205, 207–9, 216, 220, 249, 296, 623, 634, 657
Gunderson, Milt, 32, 50, 172, 174, 178–80, 205, 207–8, 212–14, 216, 218, 220–22, 288–92, 295, 300, 303, 313, 319, 334–36, 338–39, 438–40, 456, 458, 467, 499
Guttenburg, Dylan, 633
Guy, Ronnie, 72
Guyer, Honey, 20–23
Gwynn, Tony, 93

H

Haagenson, Ben, 102
Hackman, Jason, 502
Hackman, Lee, 488, 497, 502, 504, 512, 514–15, 520
Hackmann, Dallas, 94, 100, 102
Haddenhorst, Eric, 619
Hagan, Chris, 658–59
Hagan, Stacy, 471
Hagen, Art, 11
Hagfeldt, Cliff "Finley", 70–71, 74–76, 79, 83, 92, 95, 97, 106, 112–13, 116–17, 124, 127, 153, 161, 174, 179, 184, 187, 208, 215, 217, 220, 271, 299, 345, 349, 374, 390, 402, 419, 439, 544, 636
Hagfeldt, Dallas, 67, 167, 172–73, 177–79, 186–88, 191–200, 202, 205, 210, 217, 327, 405, 410
Hagfeldt, Don, 205, 216–17, 249, 255, 259, 264–65, 276, 418–19, 634
Hagfeldt, Doug, 186, 188, 191–92, 197, 205–6, 210, 332, 634
Hagfeldt, Jay, 49, 63, 186–89, 191–94, 196–200, 205–7, 209–11, 214, 216, 269, 298, 348, 390, 499, 562, 673
Hagfeldt, Marge, 121, 214, 439
Hagfeldt, Mike, 161, 205, 207, 209–12, 216–17, 219, 221–22, 249, 255–57, 259–63, 265–70, 276, 282, 316, 332, 365, 369, 385, 389, 403, 418–20, 439, 453, 499, 501, 562
Hagfeldt, Pete, 74–76, 220, 636
Hahn, Johnny, 76
Hahn, Tim, 358, 362, 366
Hall, Fred, 72
Hall, Steve, 598
Halverson, Devin, 642, 645, 647–48, 650, 652–53, 658
Halverson, Dixie, 460–61, 509
Halverson, Troy, 470, 533
Halvorson, Alice, 108, 114, 338
Halvorson, Ernie, 43, 338, 421, 565
Halvorson, Glen, 122, 126–27, 130–31
Halvorson, Indy, 43, 55, 60, 64, 68–69, 71, 79, 83, 97–98
Halvorson, Kirby, 186, 192, 197, 203, 247, 251, 255–58, 262, 265, 267–68, 276–79, 281, 284, 289–90, 292, 294–97, 299, 302–3, 305–7, 311–12, 314, 319–21, 323, 328–29, 331, 335–39, 342, 345, 347–48, 355, 368, 372–82, 384, 386–87, 394, 402, 404, 406, 409, 418, 420, 422–23, 437, 447, 450, 486–87, 499–500, 535, 558, 621–22, 625, 634, 636, 641, 671
Halvorson, Lynette, 128
Halvorson, Ric, 43
Hames, Bill, 231
Hames, Debbie, 226
Hames, Mae, 93
Hames, Wally, 437
Hames, Wanda, 223, 226–27, 229
Hames, Win, 227–229, 231
Hamill, Henry, 132
Hammer, Chance, 607–8, 614
Hammerly, Josh, 652

Index

Hammerly, Kenny, 647–48, 650, 652–53
Hancock, Joe, 571
Handran, Cale, 545, 547, 555, 563–64, 566, 568–69, 571–72, 575–77, 582–88, 596
Handran, Chauncy, 588, 601, 602, 607–10, 614–17, 630–31, 664
Handy, Chris, 304
Handy, Donnette, 128
Hanger, Phyllis, 114
Hanks, Jess, 633
Hann, Craig, 554, 558, 656
Hanrahan, Alice, 16, 677
Hanrahan, Claude, 9
Hanrahan, Ruth A., 16
Hansen, Dave, 437
Hansen, Don, 71, 74–75, 636
Hansen, Doug, 78
Hansen, E. Helen, 39
Hansen, Gene, 448–49
Hansen, Greg, 398
Hansen, H.J., 22–23
Hansen, Harry, 21–22, 30
Hansen, Helen, 39
Hansen, Jim, 130, 140, 144, 152–54, 156, 160–62, 164, 166–70, 172–73, 175, 177, 179–80, 185–88, 190, 202, 418, 561
Hansen, Kenneth, 106, 112-113, 116–17, 127, 476
Hansen, Laura M., 32, 678
Hansen, Luverne, 113, 115
Hansen, Rick "Fireball", 249
Hanson, Arlen, 169–70, 173, 176–77, 179–81, 187, 189
Hanson, Cliff, 179, 214, 220, 293, 300, 338, 384, 408, 421, 428, 439, 677
Hanson, Eric, 466
Hanson, Evelyn, 16, 677
Hanson, Fred, 9, 11
Hanson, Harold, 42
Hanson, Jami, 632–33
Hanson, L.V., 11
Hanson, Mike, 154, 160, 168–70, 188, 561
Hanson, Ogden, 81
Harada, Tim, 552
Harcharik, Kip, 241, 256–58, 261–66, 270, 279, 302, 305, 307–8, 313, 330–31, 333, 339, 370
Harcharik, Ron, 241, 257
Hardy, Bob, 72
Harmon, Barry, 122, 126–27
Harmon, Eli, 585, 596–97, 601–3, 607
Haroldson, L., 41
Harris, John, 472
Harris, Lee, 398
Harris, Mike, 145
Harrison, Shawn, 525
Harsager, H., 43
Hartgrove, Della, 108
Hash, Marvin, 227, 251
Hatfield, Kevin, 247, 557
Hauck, Phil, 342–43, 345–46, 350, 366
Hauer, Rod, 175
Hauer, Ron, 180
Haugen, Jim, 41, 107, 212
Haugen, Joe, 41

Hawbaker, Dave, 84
Hawbaker, Doc, 85
Hawbaker, Jim, 78, 80
Hawbaker, Levi, 82
Hawbaker, Marcia, 82, 92
Hawthorne, John, 458
Hayes, Dave, 127
Hayes, Tom, 61, 63, 67, 70–71, 85
Healy, Pete, 83
Heath, George, 130–31, 133–34, 140, 144, 146
Heaton, Jim, 341
Heaton, Mike, 433, 444, 452, 457–58, 463
Heberly, Dave, 595
Hedges, Edna, 108, 114, 118
Heidinger, Mark, 448
Heisler, Rod, 420
Heit, Steve, 303, 333, 339
Heit, Terry, 398, 407, 414
Helland, Peter, 448
Hellickson, Jim, 123
Helmer, Warren, 362
Henderson, Brad, 247, 251, 256, 268, 276, 290, 297, 437, 634
Henderson, Darlene, 118
Henderson, Larry "Bucky", 107–8, 437, 478, 480, 544–45, 606, 608, 619, 623, 634
Hendricks, Elrod, 370
Hennell, Carl, 637
Henry, Brett, 618
Henry, Drew, 598
Henry, Paul, 37–38
Henshaw, Jaydeen, 666
Henville, Robbie, 633
Heppner, Ron, 81
Herbert, Alan, 398
Herman, Lonnie, 289
Hersel, Aquina, 225–26
Hersel, Jon, 512, 514, 520–21, 527–28, 534
Hersel, Neil, 527
Hershiser, Oral, 531
Hershkivitz, Joe, 9, 11
Heskett, Dave, 156
Hess, Kevin, 518
Hester, Herb, 27
Hewitt, Frank, 10–11
Hewitt, Harold, 41–42
Hewitt, Harvey, 41
Hexom, Adolph, 41–43
Hexom, Phil, 41, 43, 55
Hickethier, Jeff, 380
Hicks, Harvey, 41
Hicks, Marlowe, 42
Higgins, Barry, 166–67, 171–72, 179, 186, 188–89, 191, 634
Higgins, Don, 72, 140, 152, 160, 166–68, 170–73, 175–77, 179–80, 184, 186, 190, 212, 293, 421, 447, 595, 623, 634
Higgins, Grandpa Jack, 9
Higgins, Iris, 398, 439
Higgins, John "Jack", 130, 140, 144–46, 152, 154, 156, 158–60, 162, 164–66, 169, 171, 183, 190, 202, 328, 375, 383, 390, 417, 424, 439, 447, 624, 634, 673

Higgins, John, 174, 179–80
Higgins, Mitch, 130–31, 140
Higgins, Nettie, 16, 678
Higgins, Ron, 297, 303, 311, 319, 329, 334, 337–38, 353, 361, 365, 373–75, 379, 384, 392, 394–96, 398, 405, 486, 558, 634
Hill, Dennis, 84
Hillstrom, Gordon, 82
Hillstrom, Vic, 21
Hillukka, Warren, 362
Hinden, Wally, 20–22
Hines, Chad, 572
Hinman, Mike, 344
Hinnershitz, Stephanie, 47
Hirst, Joe, 448
Hobbs, Ayden, 652
Hober, Floyd, 84
Hober, Terry, 84, 152
Hodges, Michael, 448
Hoe, Walt, 84
Hogan, Bill, 401
Hogan, Mark, 471, 509
Holden, Mike, 595
Holle, Doug, 94
Holle, Jimmy, 72
Holmberg, Laverne, 16, 678
Holmes, George, 10
Holt, Alan, 495–97, 499, 501, 536
Holt, Kim, 230
Holtan, Duane, 179
Holum, Art, 92, 508, 522, 531, 533, 535, 538, 561
Holum, Carl, 538, 604
Holum, Curt, 585, 596, 601–2, 607
Holum, K.C., 520–21, 527–28, 530, 538, 540–41
Holum, Kevin, 527
Holyk, Babe, 40, 68, 70–71, 74–76, 79, 163, 636
Holyk, Don, 179, 251, 268, 276, 290, 297
Hons, Duane, 480
Hood, Terry, 281
Hoppel, Monte, 337–39
Hopson, David, 218, 256, 265
Hopstad, Alan, 256, 259, 266, 269, 279–280, 369, 386
Horn, Ken, 75
Hotvedt, Carl, 132
Hoven, Mike, 571
Hoversland, Alan, 218, 265
Hoversland, Ben, 488–90, 497, 502, 504–5, 507–8, 512, 514–15, 520
Hoversland, Jay, 508, 545, 555, 563–64, 566–69, 571–72, 575–77, 582–88, 596
Howard, Marion, 15
Hoy, Richard, 349
Huber, Dale, 84
Hudyma, John, 122
Hudyma, Rod, 444, 452, 457, 463, 467–68, 473, 475, 480–81, 483
Hueseman, Young, 61
Hueth, Darrel, 76
Huff, Dustin, 546
Hughes, Don, 114
Hughes, Grant, 375, 486
Humbert, Bob, 9, 11

Humbert, Roy "Jiggs", 59, 64–65
Hurly, Leo, 13
Hustava, Andy, 448
Huwe, Mark, 452, 457

I

Icenhower, Barry, 212
Ihde, Derek, 573, 575
Illman, Johnny, 13
Ingram, Doug, 361–62
Ingram, Jake, 589–90, 595
Innocenti, Jason, 455, 458, 461, 465
Ivers, Larry, 154

J

Jackson, Kurt, 172
Jackson, Phil, 112
Jacob, Elwood, 14
Jacobs, Mike, 79
Jacobson, Carl, 16, 678
Jacobson, Cody, 520–21, 523, 527–28, 538, 540–41, 588, 601
Jacobson, Don, 208
Jacobson, H.J., 16
Jacobson, Irv, 72
Jacobson, Oscar, 37
Jaffe, Jay, 203
Jager, Duane, 68
Jakanowski, Scott, 396
James, Mable, 39
Jeide, Barry, 531
Jensen, Bud, 92, 114, 476
Jensen, Carol, 230
Jensen, Chris, 601–2
Jensen, Dan, 301, 313, 330, 338, 340
Jensen, Dixie, 114, 118
Jensen, Gus, 42
Jensen, Mike, 398, 414
Jensen, Sonny, 73
Jerome, Lorraine, 108, 114, 118, 128
John, Tommy, 203
Johnson, Bryon, 303, 414
Johnson, Dave, 189, 191, 194, 198–99, 209
Johnson, George, 22, 32
Johnson, Hilda, 16
Johnson, Isaac, 652–54, 658, 665
Johnson, Jack, 401–2
Johnson, Jenny, 573, 579
Johnson, Jim, 103
Johnson, Josh, 654, 658, 665
Johnson, Mark, 418
Johnson, Mary, 230
Johnson, Myron, 37–38, 103
Johnson, Norma, 128
Johnson, Pete, 42
Johnson, Sam, 43
Johnson, Scott, 335, 397–98
Johnson, Steve, 179, 398, 411, 414
Johnston, Chuckie, 76
Johnston, Jim, 76
Johnston, Robbie, 312, 541
Johnstone, Bill, 65

Joles, David, 617
Jones, Brian, 191–92, 194, 196, 198–200, 266
Jones, Chad, 610–12, 615, 617–19, 630–32
Jones, Del, 208, 212
Jones, Garnet, 226
Jones, Jeff (Peerless), 386, 452, 457, 463, 467–69, 472–75, 478–81, 483, 501, 506, 533
Jones, Jeff (Scobey), 614–15
Jones, Jeffrey M., 626
Jones, Jenny, 573
Jones, Lalon, 42, 50
Jones, Mike, 281, 302, 307, 309–10, 312, 316, 369–70
Jones, Rob, 448
Jones, Ruppert, 270
Jordan, Michael, 624
Joy, Jane, 349
Joyner, Wally, 388–89

K

Kahn, Roger, 4–5, 595
Kaiser, Audrey, 93, 96
Kaline, Al, 210
Kallevig, Brad, 541
Kampsher, Norm, 116–17
Kaneski, Jim, 68
Kangas, John, 362
Kanning, Ralph, 130
Kanning, Scott, 473, 483
Karlsrud, Quentin, 55–56, 60
Kasper, John, 617, 626
Kasseth, Jimmy, 43
Kasuske, Chris, 437
Kato, Barry, 219–22, 282, 401, 453, 562
Kato, Johanna, 222
Kato, Mark, 209, 211, 219–20, 562
Kato, Ray, 222
Kato, Scott, 154, 156, 158, 160, 169–70, 173, 175, 179–81, 187, 561
Kaul, Arlin, 463, 467, 473, 480–81, 483, 485, 487, 640, 647, 675
Kaul, Buddy, 487
Kazebier, Jim, 472
Kegel, Percy, 184, 215
Keistling, Walt, 28
Keller, Scott, 181
Keller, Steve, 480
Kelly, Ken, 314
Kelly, Sandra, 572, 579
Kemmiss, Scott, 303
Kennedy, Kevin, 437
Kessler, Mae, 108
Kestin, Llewellyn, 63
Keto, Roger, 221
Killebrew, Harmon, 162, 320, 386, 417
Kindrick, Ace, 350
King, Bert, 552
King, Cooper, 665–67
King, Otto, 30
King, Phil, 666
King, Steve, 312
Kingsley, Milo, 10
Kiraly, Karch, 471, 500

Kissel, Pat, 380
Kittelson, Kit, 208
Kitzenberg, Lee, 178–79
Kjensmo, Arletta, 114, 118
Kleeman, Pete, 102
Kleppelid, Darrel, 304
Kleppelid, Dave, 458–60
Klofstad, Gordon, 81
Kloppel, Dick, 401, 509, 677
Klos, Mike, 94
Klunder, Tom, 362
Knight, Duane, 82–83, 92
Knowles, Bucko, 13
Knudsen, Anders, 642, 645, 647–48, 650, 652–54, 658–59
Knudsen, Lane, 642, 645, 647–50
Knudson, Dave, 115
Knudson, Ryan, 552
Knudsvig, Gary, 81
Knudtson, Jim, 207–8, 212
Koessl, John, 633
Kolstad, Jon, 470
Koski, Joe, 464
Koufax, Sandy, 437
Kovik, Loren, 208
Kowcun, Pete, 76
Krassin, Doug, 94, 105, 124
Krause, Brad, 337–38
Krivec, Jim, 362
Krivee, Mike, 208
Kronick, Molly, 39
Krumm, Dan, 84
Krumm, Don, 101
Kubo, Carl, 134
Kuka, Paul, 212
Kukowski, Henry, 666
Kulczyk, Parker, 633
Kuntz, Dale, 188–89, 199
Kuntz, Dennis, 146, 561
Kuntz, Dirk, 464, 470–71
Kuntz, Greg, 495, 501, 536
Kuntz, Kirk, 475
Kurokawa, Barry, 132
Kurtz, Bob, 72
Kurtz, Dennis, 94
Kurtz, Greg, 140
Kurtz, P.R., 11
Kurtz, Pete, 41–42, 214, 421

L

Lagerquist, John, 178–79
Lake, George, 122
Lake, Harvey, 448
Lamb, Brad, 642
Lammerding, Dennis, 220
LaMotte, M.A., 61
LaMotte, Marion, 10, 61
LaMotte, Tony, 63–64, 71, 75, 391
Lancaster, Ronnie, 218
Landis, Kenesaw Mountain, 31
Lane, L.P., 28
Langager, Harvey, 194, 198, 256
Lannon, Dick, 406, 423

LaPierre, Jerry, 133, 140-141, 152, 154, 156, 158, 160, 162, 166-170, 182, 190, 439
LaPierre, Nellie, 222
LaPierre, Ray, 171
Lapke, Gene, 11
Lapke, Mike, 319, 425
Lapke, Steve, 444–45, 452, 456–59, 463, 467–69, 471, 473, 480–81, 500, 507–8
Larkin, Barry, 367
LaRoche, Gene, 40
LaRoche, Hazel, 39
Larsen, Bryce, 288, 291–92
Larsen, Jeff, 249–50
Larson, Bob, 227
Larson, George, 93, 224, 275, 476, 478
Larson, Greg, 467, 473, 480
Larson, Harry, 36, 60, 64–65, 68–69, 71, 75, 80, 85, 92, 95, 99, 106
Larson, Ken, 36, 43, 55, 60–61, 64, 68–69, 71–72, 75–76, 114
Larson, Kenny, 43, 114
Larson, Marie, 163
Larson, Mark, 11
Larson, Millie, 93, 96
Larson, Roll, 9
Lasorda, Tommy, 559
Lassie, Jerry, 625
Laurel, Bill, 493
Lebsock, Jeff, 257, 282, 285, 288–89, 291, 294, 301–3, 307–8, 313, 369–70, 407, 414
Ledbetter, Brian, 260, 284, 308
Lee, Ann (Norman), 104, 153, 114, 157, 432, 529, 565
Lee, Bill, 253
Lee, Craig, 397
Lee, Dennis, 132
Lee, Gary, 178–80
Lee, Harvey, 219
Lee, John, 427, 680
Lee, Josh, 203, 337, 392, 404, 406, 409–10, 421, 433–34, 502–5, 508, 512–14, 516, 518, 520–25, 527, 530, 532–34, 537, 546, 559
Lee, Keith, 191, 198
Lee, Ken, 198, 218, 221, 261, 265, 410, 512, 514, 518–21, 533
Lee, Mike "Karch", 6–7, 18–19, 34–35, 52–53, 88–89, 150–51, 298, 315, 319, 326, 337, 361, 375, 379, 410, 430–31, 463, 466–68, 471, 473–75, 477, 480–86, 488–502, 507, 510–12, 514, 516–18, 522–78, 580–81, 599–600, 628–29, 638–39, 662–63
Lee, Pearl, 293
Lee, Rick, 197, 203, 276, 290, 303, 311, 319, 337, 375, 392, 394, 641
Lee, Steve, 267
Lee, Terry, 177–80
Legare, Gage, 633
Legare, Grant, 633
Legare, Leo, 72
Legare, Lisa, 633
Legare, Patty, 142

Legare, Randy, 130, 140, 144, 152, 154–55, 158–62, 164, 166, 169, 172, 203, 340, 375, 383, 417, 447, 623
Lehman, Kenny, 78
Leibach, Brent, 249, 279, 281
Leibrand, Aiden, 666
Leibrand, David, 607–8, 614
Leibrand, Fred, 55, 64
Leibrand, Garry, 70
Leibrand, Gordy, 527, 538–40
Leibrand, Lois, 533
Leibrand, Payton, 652, 658–59
Leibrand, Prewitt, 652–53, 658
Leibrand, Richard, 74, 82–83
Leininger, Lance, 268
Leininger, Tim, 361–62
Leischner, Tyler, 666–67
Leister, John, 314, 316, 517
Lekvold, B.J., 10, 44, 61, 291
Lekvold, DeeAnn, 276, 290, 298, 303, 311, 319, 328, 360-361, 368, 375, 384, 634
Lekvold, Don, 6–7, 18–19, 34–35, 52–53, 88–89, 150–51, 217–18, 221, 256–59, 265, 269, 276, 284, 290–91, 295, 298, 303, 307, 311, 313, 319, 325–26, 337, 344, 361, 372, 374–75, 378–79, 384, 392, 394, 404–6, 409–11, 414, 416–17, 423–26, 430–31, 433–36, 438–508, 510–12, 532, 564, 568–69, 580–81, 585, 600, 605, 623, 628–29, 634, 638–39, 644, 662–63, 672
Lekvold, Jedd, 545, 555, 559, 563–64, 566, 569, 571–72, 575–76, 582, 584–88, 590, 596, 640–41
Lekvold, Jim "Sneed", 319, 334, 337–38, 361, 373–75, 378–79, 381–84, 392, 394–96, 398, 404–10, 412, 414–15, 422–24, 433, 435–38, 444, 450, 460, 472, 501, 507, 634
Lekvold, JoAnn (Loendorf), 269, 276, 368
Lekvold, Ken, 63, 67, 70–71, 75–76, 85, 92, 106, 112–13, 116–18, 124, 127, 422
Lekvold, Laura, 39
Lekvold, Louis, 116
Lekvold, Morgan, 502
Leland, Tom, 633
LeProwse, Jim, 78, 433–34, 436, 444–46, 450–60, 463, 499, 543, 551, 558, 590, 618, 647
LeProwse, Judy, 465
Letasky, John, 549, 579, 620, 626
Levang, Neal, 585–87, 596–97, 601–5, 607, 614–15
Lewis, Craig, 307, 313
Lewis, Doug, 358, 362
Lewis, Mark, 260, 284
Lewis, Mike, 291
Liebman, Ron, 95
Lien, Ben, 476
Lien, Elwood, 14, 16, 102, 255, 636, 680
Lightfoot, Gus, 76
Lighthizer, Jimmy, 251
Linder, Bill, 533
Linder, Eric, 520–21
Linder, Gary, 115, 123
Linder, Karen, 114

Linder, Ryan, 3, 473, 483–84, 488–91, 493, 495–98, 502–8
Linder, Wayne, 520–21, 523–24, 527–30, 532, 538
Lindler, Bert, 315
Lindsey, Toby, 323–24, 327, 434
Lindstrand, Bucky, 455, 464–66, 562
Linebarger, Clayton, 76
Linville, Ken, 38
Locken, Kevin, 618
Lockrem, Orville, 16, 678
Loendorf, Dennis, 209, 218, 256, 259, 262, 265–66, 269, 364, 369
Loendorf, Lenny, 131–32, 269
Loendorf, Ron, 132
Lofing, Alex, 77–78
Lohman, Clint, 312, 316
Lolich, Mickey, 419
Lonborg, Jim, 252
Loucks, Bob, 131–32
Loucks, Dut, 73
Loucks, Phil, 73
Love, Johnny, 559
Lovegren, Robert, 414
Lowes, Allan, 113
Lowry, Bobby, 112
Lucht, Gary, 21, 25, 32, 674
Luck, Andrew, 203
Luckman, Jerry, 68
Luft, Alan, 95, 99, 111
Luft, Curtis, 111, 122
Luft, Vic, 90, 92, 106, 117
Lund, Beverly, 293
Lupe, Joe, 15, 20
Luscombe, Doug, 208
Lusty, Scott, 445
Lybecker, Josh, 588–90, 594–95
Lyle, Samantha, 675
Lystad, Della, 223, 227, 231
Lystad, Lena, 128
Lystad, Mary, 223, 226–30
Lystad, Maynard, 224, 226
Lystad, Ralph, 122, 126
Lystad, Ray, 126–27

M

Machart, Bernice, 15
Machart, Bobby, 79, 124, 225
Machart, John, 235, 237
Machart, Mary, 273, 428
Machart, Ruth, 15
Machart, Virginia, 15
Mack, Connie, 393, 402
Mack, Earl, 59
Maczka, Chad, 518, 598
Madison, Dave, 189
Madsen, Bruce, 380
Magone, Dan, 550
Mahar, Chad, 523
Maher, Bernie, 126
Maher, Greg, 458
Mahler, Karen, 118
Mair, Doug, 132
Malloney, P.J., 434

Malmberg, Steve, 179
Malmin, Ryan, 589, 598–99
Malone, Russ, 406
Maloney, Ryan, 493
Maney, Kevin, 487
Mangold, Mace, 588, 595
Mann, Jeff, 374–75, 379, 392, 394–96, 433, 436–37, 444, 486
Manning, Chief, 11
Manno, Bruce, 361
Mansch, Scott, 181, 427, 633, 637, 679
Mapes, Alan, 589–90, 595
Maris, Roger, 437–38
Markovich, Nick, 333, 338–39
Marlenee, Allison, 375, 379, 384–85, 392, 404, 406, 434
Marlenee, Ron, 438–39
Marley, Gene, 197, 214, 220, 289–90, 293, 300, 338, 408, 468
Marley, Patty, 214, 293
Marman, Jack, 108
Marriage, Dennis, 94, 114
Marriage, Rick, 130–31, 139
Marshall, Bob, 21
Marshall, Dan, 342–43
Marshall, Jerry, 293
Martin, Billy, 270, 344, 393, 402
Martin, Curt, 528
Martin, Gene, 75
Martin, J.D., 11
Martin, John, 43, 207–8
Masters, Art, 76
Matternach, JD, 607–8
Matternach, Oscar, 57
Mattick, Steve, 20
Mattson, Jeff, 437
Maxwell, Hugh, 380
Maybelle, Arthur, 505
Mayer, Kendal, 470
Mayers, Chuck, 339, 382
Mays, Willie, 49
McCann, Joyce, 108
McCann, Lee, 9, 11
McCann, Pat, 134
McCarren, 116
McCarrow, Cecil, 113
McCarvel, Russell, 448
McChesney, Bob, 131, 139
McClure, Paul, 167, 181
McConnen, Dick, 9
McCormick, Frank, 31
McDaniel, Olive, 39
McDowell, Oddibe, 367
McElvaney, Kevin, 585, 588, 596–97, 601, 607–11, 622–23
McElvaney, Mark, 544–45, 555, 563–64, 566–67, 569, 571, 575, 582–83
McEnroe, John, 426
McGeshick, James, 396
McGeshick, Rick, 218, 256, 261, 265, 279
McGovern, Todd, 316
McGowan, Jack, 80–81
McGraw, John, 23

McGregor, Bob, 361
McGuire, Dan, 448
McGuire, Mark, 367
McIntyre, Jack, 156
McIntyre, Jim, 22
McIntyre, Lydia, 39
McIntyre, Terry, 61, 63, 67, 70–71, 74–75, 636
McKenzie, Brett "Bubba", 518, 531
McKnight, Carter, 292
McKnight, Ken, 416
McLaughlin, Glenn, 361
McLaughlin, P.R., 103
McLaughlin, Selma, 39
McLean, Mike, 179–80, 348, 418
McLean, Zoonie Jr., 140–41
McLean, Zoonie, 81, 140–41, 248, 252, 328, 348, 417
McLoughlin, Preston, 37, 460
McMahon, Joe, 345–46
McMaster, Jon, 191, 196, 198
McNally, Dave, 111-112, 181, 214, 359, 364, 370, 401, 440
McNary, Kelly, 299
McNulty, Dick, 81
McPhearson, Brad, 553
McRae, Travis, 458
Meade, Brandon, 642, 645, 652
Meehan, Charles, 541
Meiers, Nate, 598
Meissner, Steve, 124
Melby, Mitch, 294, 414, 421
Melcher, Scott, 338
Melin, Ron, 414
Melvin, John, 536
Merell, Vick, 11
Merkle, Fred, 422
Messer, Mitch, 617
Metts, Brad, 425
Meyer, Bonnie, 438, 492, 533–35, 545
Meyer, Deanna, 534
Meyer, Gary, 439–40, 473, 477, 481, 483, 501, 512, 520
Meyer, Ken, 6–7, 18–19, 34–35, 52–53, 63, 88–89, 150–51, 185, 326, 430–31, 438, 463, 466–68, 471, 473–75, 478, 480, 482–86, 488–502, 507, 510–78, 580–81, 623, 628–29, 638–39, 662–63
Meyer, Ron, 185, 437–38, 467, 473, 475, 480, 483
Meyer, Sue, 230
Meyers, Johnny, 20–23, 28, 30
Michel, Madonna, 114, 118
Middle, Hardin, 599
Middlebrook, William, 16
Milbrandt, Bruce, 313
Milford, Paul, 11
Milford, Stan, 10–11
Millar, Korab, 39
Miller, Bennett, 428
Miller, Brian, 338
Miller, Chuck, 145
Miller, Craig, 140, 205, 207, 210, 216–19, 221, 237, 249, 255–59, 262, 265–67, 271, 276, 507, 552, 588

Miller, Darin, 490
Miller, Dennis "Doc", 140, 160, 166, 447, 623
Miller, Greg, 353–54, 365
Miller, Jim, 140, 160, 414, 447
Miller, Joe, 210, 623, 630
Miller, Josh, 588
Miller, Kevin, 312, 380
Miller, Marian, 623
Miller, Perry, 139
Miller, Roger, 76
Miller, Ron, 221
Miller, Ryan, 489, 554
Miller, Steven, 328
Miller, Ted, 445, 448, 465
Miller, Udell, 76
Mills, Les, 416
Mills, Tim, 352, 362
Mock, A.J., 598
Modler, Glen, 505
Moe, Peder, 9, 11, 16
Moe, Sig, 10, 16
Mogen, Greg, 337–38
Mohn, Burnie, 41–42
Mohn, Don, 41–42
Mohn, Ellen R., 50
Mollerstuen, Bob, 72
Mollerstuen, Elvin, 42
Monahan, Mickey, 287, 293, 314
Monahan, Mike, 362
Monson, Larry, 191, 197–99
Monson, Orris, 42
Montana, Libbi, 536
Montgomery, Ron, 122
Montgomery, Sam, 16, 678
Mooney, Jerry, 338
Moran, Bob, 330, 339
Moran, Dennis, 168
Moran, Jerry, 218–19, 221, 256–58, 260–62, 265–66, 269, 279, 369
Moran, Travis, 493, 500
Morasko, Todd, 303
Mordabito, Mae, 500
Moreno, Alex, 666–67
Morgan, Adler, 647–48, 650
Morgan, Tom, 208
Morganthaler, Wilfred, 83
Moriarity, Todd, 306
Morris, Corky, 158, 160
Morris, Dan, 561
Morris, W.R., 116
Morrison, Brent, 448
Morrison, Frank, 578
Morrison, John, 122, 130–31, 133–34
Morrison, Perry, 208
Morrow, Bill, 41–42, 60
Morrow, Grace, 39
Morvik, Emil, 42, 72
Moser, Larry, 171
Mouat, Marty, 348, 429
Mueller, Art, 460
Mueller, Charlie, 111–12, 115–16, 120, 122–23, 125–28, 130, 133, 153, 294, 534, 623
Mueller, Mick, 488–90, 492, 497

Index

Mueller, Vicki, 499
Mulder, Mark, 203
Mulholland, Mickey, 398
Mulholland, Tim, 414
Munoz, Mike, 437
Munson, Jody, 321
Munson, Larry, 194
Munson, Thurman, 270
Murphy, Jack, 479
Murphy, Jere, 302
Murphy, John, 81, 122, 126–27, 153, 179, 183, 185, 190, 198, 202, 674
Murphy, Pat, 21
Murray, Brad, 144, 166–70, 190
Murray, Don, 172, 174, 179
Murray, Father Athol, 41–42, 50, 60, 678
Musgraves, Rocke, 533, 536
Myers, John, 15
Myhre, Seth, 647–50

N

Narveson, Esther, 293
Nash, Ada, 73, 86
Nash, Hazel, 39
Nash, Willard, 73–74
Neal, Jim, 107
Nees, David, 463
Nefzger, Darrell, 218
Neiskens, Kenny, 76
Neiss, B.J., 541–42
Nellermoe, Brent, 589
Nelson, Arden, 101–2
Nelson, Art, 11
Nelson, Bruce, 146, 159–60
Nelson, Chuck, 640–42, 644–45, 647, 666
Nelson, CJ, 642, 644–45, 647–48, 650, 652–54, 656, 658
Nelson, H.C., 21
Nelson, Jim, 140
Nelson, John, 54–56, 58, 60–61, 103, 126, 133, 140, 144
Nelson, Kevin, 472–75, 477, 481, 483–86, 488–502, 506, 519–21, 531–33, 535, 543–44, 599, 675
Nelson, Kyle, 614
Nelson, Melvin, 21, 32, 679
Nelson, Mike, 588
Nelson, Rasmus, 21, 535
Nelson, Ryan, 520–21, 527
Nelson, Scott, 488–90, 497, 502–5
Nelson, Selmer, 10, 57
Nelson, Seth, 614
Nesper, Delmar, 108, 332, 386
Nesper, Jay, 281, 288
Nesper, Jeff, 279, 285, 288–89, 291, 301–3, 316, 330, 339, 364, 421
Neubauer, Jeff, 191, 194, 198, 218, 470
Neubauer, Mike, 63, 198, 218, 241, 256, 259–60, 262–66, 269–70, 279, 286, 294, 300, 303–4, 307, 338, 369, 385, 388, 403, 420, 467, 469–71, 475–77, 482, 485–86, 489–92, 525, 564, 604, 630

Neumiller, Bill, 207, 209, 218–19, 221, 256–57, 262–63, 265–66, 369
New, Russell, 82
Nickerson, Geoffe, 514
Nickola, Albert, 114
Nickoloff, Darin, 529, 533
Nicks, Stevie, 283
Nielsen, Allen, 70
Nielsen, Sue, 230
Nielson, John, 455, 466
Nielson, Tim, 356, 446, 448
Nielson, Tom, 40, 134, 145, 158, 160, 166–70, 173, 175–76, 178–79, 181–82, 190, 401, 445–46, 448–49, 453–56, 460, 464–66, 470, 551, 590–92, 594, 619, 631, 673
Nieskens, Dennis, 126
Nieskens, Gary, 166–67, 171
Nieskens, Jeannette, 231
Nieskens, Joel, 538, 540–41, 544–45, 547–49, 553, 555, 557, 559, 563–64, 567, 571–72, 574–76, 582
Nieskens, Kelly, 582, 585, 587, 596–97, 601, 632
Nieskens, Marcae, 231
Nieskens, Peyton, 642, 645
Norden, Dick, 139
Norman, Ann (Lee), 104, 153, 114, 157, 432, 529, 565
Norman, C.L. Mr. and Mrs., 46
Norman, Clyde H. "Doc", 2–3, 6–7, 18–19, 34–35, 38, 40, 45–49, 52–53, 58, 75, 77, 80, 82, 84, 88–89, 92, 97, 99, 101–2, 104–5, 111–12, 122, 124, 126, 134, 136, 139, 141–42, 144–46, 150–51, 154–56, 158–64, 166–68, 170, 172, 174–84, 186, 188–214, 216, 218–70, 274, 278–390, 392, 394, 396, 398, 400, 402, 404, 406–28, 430–33, 437–44, 447–48, 464–66, 468, 471, 475, 483, 487, 489, 492, 497, 500, 502, 506, 509–12, 520–22, 524–26, 528–29, 531, 538, 551, 559, 565, 569, 573, 575, 578, 580–82, 585, 591–92, 594, 599, 605–6, 609, 612, 615, 623–24, 628–29, 636, 638–39, 644, 660, 662–64, 666, 668, 671–72, 677, 680
Norman, Kelly, 2, 46, 140, 142, 144, 152, 155, 160–61, 165–66, 176, 186, 192, 197, 201, 203, 205, 215–17, 234, 245, 247, 249, 251, 255–57, 264–66, 268, 270, 276–79, 287, 289–91, 294, 297, 299, 301, 303, 307–9, 311, 313, 319, 323–25, 328, 330, 332–33, 335, 337–40, 343–44, 353, 360, 362–63, 366, 373–82, 384, 387, 394, 402–4, 406, 409–10, 414–15, 418–19, 423, 425, 433, 435–37, 439, 447–48, 450, 487, 558, 612, 623, 625, 634, 657, 671
Norman, Marge (Shiell), 48, 114, 139, 141, 153, 162, 179, 293, 338, 355, 361, 373, 410, 439, 442, 492, 495, 521–22, 563, 565, 569, 624, 634, 641, 643, 649, 656–57, 668
Norman, Mike, 84, 98–99, 104–5, 109, 111, 115–16, 125, 127–28, 133, 401, 410
Norman, Myrtle, 441
Northelfer, Bill, 10
Norworth, Jack, 643
Notholfer, Bill, 41
Nuhring, Anna Mae, 118

Nuhring, Rosie, 128
Nyquist, Father Ray, 157

O

Oakland, Brent, 307, 312–13, 316
Oaks, Don, 290
Obergfell, Jason, 541
Ofstedal, Clara, 153
Oie, Andy, 43
Oie, Colter, 652–54, 658, 660, 664–65, 668
Oie, Don, 111, 115, 644, 660
Oie, Jackson, 635, 642, 644–45, 647–48, 650, 652–54, 658, 664–65
Oie, Morgan, 3, 512, 514, 520–21, 523–24, 527, 530, 538–41, 543, 588, 596, 601, 603–5, 607, 615, 622, 660, 664
Oie, Ryan, 488–92, 497, 502–5, 507, 512–16, 518–20, 660
Oikawa, James, 448
Oldenburg, Earl, 67
Oliver, Jim, 83
Olivia, Tony, 417
Ollers, Travis, 614
Olmstead, Chuck, 284
Olness, Ernie, 108
Olsen, Aaron, 295
Olson, Bob, 160
Olson, Elmer, 10, 61
Olson, Greg, 364, 473, 483–84, 489
Olson, Gregg, 364
Olson, Jim, 120, 123, 127–28, 132–33
Olson, John, 456
Olson, Marshall, 139
Olson, Nancy, 227, 229
Olson, Victoria, 39
Orr, Jim, 637
Ortman, Wacey, 633
Osborne, Bill, 362
Overby, Duane, 67, 70
Owen, Bruce, 130
Owen, David, 130–31
Owen, Gerry, 80, 94, 130

P

Pace, Roy, 344, 347–49, 429
Page, Cliff, 93, 120, 307
Page, Greg, 500–501
Page, Mark, 396, 406, 436
Page, R.C., 484
Paige, Satchel, 93
Painter, Bob, 76
Paladichuk, Brian, 414
Paladichuk, Tom, 259, 261, 266, 282, 288, 291, 300–303, 305, 307, 313, 364
Palmer, Greg, 328
Park, Shane, 471
Parker, Brant, 255
Parsley, Bob, 120
Parsley, Dave, 132, 470, 475–76
Partyka, Brad, 298
Pasquarello, Bob, 181
Patch, Brandon, 619

The Blues of Summer

Pattison, Lois, 222
Pattison, Patricia, 222
Pauley, Dooley, 493, 509
Paulson, Don, 81, 106, 122, 126–27, 130–31, 133, 258–59, 279
Paulson, Frances, 114, 118
Paulson, Wanita, 228
Pearce, Randy, 452, 457, 463–65, 467
Peaton, Neal, 493–94, 498–99
Peck, Brian, 353–54, 362
Peck, Randy, 122, 126–27, 130–32, 634
Pederson, Gary, 135
Pederson, Kyle, 568
Pederson, Randy, 124, 332, 395–96, 404–17, 422–24, 426, 433, 435–36, 450
Peel, John, 474
Peel, Mike, 541
Pelly, Mike, 313
Penrose, Jim, 10
Peres, Fred, 285, 291, 362
Perkins, George, 75
Perry, Gaylord, 479
Pertuit, Don, 293, 303
Pesky, Johnny, 57, 253
Peters, Florence, 39
Peters, Jim, 112, 135, 212, 563–64
Petersen, Jake, 538–49, 551, 553, 555, 559–61, 563–69, 571–72, 574–77, 582, 601, 605, 607, 610, 614
Petersen, Jared, 585, 587, 596, 601–3, 607
Petersen, Jim, 563, 564
Peterson, Cliff, 28
Peterson, Dick, 208
Peterson, Greg, 208, 401
Peterson, Jim, 112, 212
Peterson, Shane, 470–71, 476
Peterson, Willard, 37
Petrino, Bobby, 350, 401
Pickthorn, Lane, 191, 194, 197–200, 208
Pierce, Randy, 480
Pischel, Marvin, 76
Pittenger, Gerald, 61
Pittenger, Tyler, 582, 585, 587, 596–97, 601–3, 607
Plank, Bob, 212
Plante, Bev, 293
Plutt, J.P., 525, 579
Polberg, J.H., 13
Poleski, Steve, 380
Polesky, Gerry, 458
Polesky, Jerry, 458, 465
Polk, Harry E., 108
Polk, Harry E., 108
Polk, Jason, 648
Polk, Stuart, 179
Pollack, Jeff, 353
Popp, Rick, 208
Popson, Darren, 456, 458–59
Powell, Mike, 362
Poyner, Millie, 108, 114, 118
Pramenko, James, 84
Pratt, Brad, 245, 247, 249, 385
Preller, James, 5, 677
Prewitt, Patty, 93, 96

Price, Bill, 139
Price, Craig, 107, 117, 288, 301, 303, 305, 308, 340, 407, 428, 432, 621, 625
Price, Mark, 396–98, 412, 414
Price, Matt, 303
Pride, Charlie, 104
Prior, Mark, 203
Prough, Irv, 80
Puckett, Bill, 57, 82, 92, 101-102, 252, 267, 447
Puckett, Cosette, 240, 254-255, 675, 684-685
Puckett, Dianne (Beesley), 82, 241, 244, 267
Puckett, Dick, 3, 82, 126, 130, 133–34, 140–42, 144–46, 152–54, 156, 158–66, 169, 182, 188, 190, 195, 202, 212, 220, 222, 256, 261, 283, 293, 303, 340, 367, 375, 383, 385, 388, 393, 423, 447, 454, 461, 478, 561, 578, 622
Puckett, Don, 152, 160–61, 166–67, 170–72, 184, 186, 191–93, 196–98, 203, 205, 207–10, 216, 235, 282, 367, 459, 507–8
Puckett, Eddie, 327
Puckett, Emma, 253–254, 675, 684
Puckett, Faustine (Sparagno), 48, 86, 253, 272, 341, 369
Puckett, Forgey Reese, 46, 274–275
Puckett, George "Tiny", 45, 47, 157, 227, 235–37, 247, 250–52, 272, 278, 281, 338, 345, 365, 391, 673
Puckett, Gerri (Girard), 82, 92–93, 223, 227–28
Puckett, Gordie, 79
Puckett, Joe, 5, 235–38, 243–44, 247, 250, 255, 265–66, 268, 272, 276–77, 280–81, 290–91, 297, 299, 303, 308, 311–13, 319, 329–31, 333–34, 337, 339, 352, 356, 362–63, 365, 369, 373, 394, 447, 499, 507, 672, 684
Puckett, Jon, 161, 235–38, 246–47, 250–51, 255–57, 259, 263–66, 268, 271, 273, 276–80, 284–85, 290–91, 295, 297, 299, 301–4, 307, 311, 313, 315, 317–20, 323–25, 329–30, 333–35, 337, 339–40, 342–43, 349–51, 353, 356, 360, 362, 366, 373–74, 389–90, 419, 487, 558, 612, 656, 660
Puckett, Lauretta (Fouhy), 93, 96, 156–57, 271, 296
Puckett, Norma, 15, 93, 223, 428, 677
Puckett, Reese Jr., 92, 101–2, 105, 123, 447, 506
Puckett, Reese Sr., 43, 68, 82, 101, 156–57, 175, 179, 183–84, 203, 271, 273
Puckett, Terry, 62, 125, 144–46, 152–53, 160–68, 170–73, 175, 177, 179, 181–84, 186–88, 190–94, 196–98, 200, 202–5, 210, 212, 215, 217, 219, 249, 282, 305, 328, 333, 336, 341–42, 348, 364–65, 369, 383, 387, 393, 418–21, 424, 434, 439, 453, 499–500, 507, 543, 561, 588, 591–92, 612, 618, 634, 673
Puckett, Vonda, 1, 675, 684

Q

Quick, Warren, 448
Quilling, Ron, 108, 112–13
Quilling, Tom, 107, 112–13

R

Radakovic, Collin, 631
Radakovich, Ben, 598–99
Raeth, Bob, 401
Raisl, Dale, 312
Ralston, Kobe, 642, 645
Ralston, Kole, 642, 645
Ramsbacher, Charles, 76
Ramsbacher, John, 76
Randall, Earl, 42, 214, 421
Rapkoch, Mark, 448
Rasmussen, J.R., 396
Rasmussen, Tom, 90, 94, 112
Rausch, Dan, 381–82
Rauthe, Mike, 355–56
Ray, Doug, 284
Ray, John, 436
Reagan, Ronald, 438-439
Redekopp, Jim, 470, 475
Redpath, Randy, 343
Reed, Willie, 353
Reemsnyder, Frank, 153, 155, 220
Reiner, Jack, 2–3, 60, 64, 68–69, 71–72, 75–76, 79, 85, 92, 95, 97, 104, 106, 109, 111–12, 116–17, 124, 127, 133, 153, 160, 174–75, 179, 212, 214, 220, 283, 293, 338, 411, 453, 476–77, 486, 640, 672
Reiner, Mark, 126
Renfro, Rolly, 164
Rennaker, Chris, 575
Renner, Jacob, 633
Rensvold, Dave, 470
Ressmeyer, Don, 256
Retz, Howard, 349
Reyes, Robert, 448
Rhoads, Fred, 218, 256, 265
Rhodes, Bob, 10, 61
Rhodes, Burnell, 61, 70
Rhodes, Jim, 10, 61
Rhodes, Rex, 10, 61
Rhodes, Robert, 61
Rice, Randy, 531, 618
Richardson, Bill, 95, 153
Richardson, Clint, 9, 11
Richardson, Cubby, 402
Richardson, Edgar, 29, 261–62, 264
Richardson, Jeff, 166, 172, 205–6, 216–17, 219, 249, 258, 261–65, 268, 271, 276, 293, 303, 342, 378
Richardson, John Ray, 457, 480–81, 483–85
Richardson, Leona, 93
Richardson, Nola, 226
Rickey, Les, 401, 429
Rider, Mike, 582–85, 587, 596–97, 601, 607
Riecker, Alan, 342–45
Riley, Dave, 139
Ring, Glenn, 16, 679
Ripken, Cal, 634
Risberg, Charles "Swede", 1, 20–23, 26, 29–30, 155, 172, 216, 241, 304, 477, 536, 635, 672–73
Ritter, Chuck, 398, 414, 423
Ritter, Ted, 412

Rivers, Mickey, 295, 419
Rizzuto, Phil, 370
Robbins, Dwight, 307, 309, 312
Robertson, Hilda, 16
Robinson, Howie, 480
Robinson, Jennifer, 121
Robinson, Jim, 171
Robinson, Roy, 72
Roby, Tim, 416, 429
Rocene, Ray T., 148
Rodgers, Zach, 633
Roe, Dana, 220
Rogers, Jim, 181
Rogers, Wes, 268
Rogers, Will, 46
Roland, Bob, 74–75, 99–101, 103–5, 111
Roland, Donna, 465
Roland, Mike, 276, 290, 298, 303, 319, 337, 361, 375, 444–46, 452, 455–57, 459, 463–64, 467–69, 471, 473, 480–81, 483, 488, 492, 497, 499, 562
Roland, Palmer, 529
Roland, Richard, 54–55, 85
Roland, Rip, 56, 60, 75
Rollnis, Bob, 139
Roosevelt, Franklin Delano, 40
Rose, Pete, 504
Rosich, Grace, 443
Ross, Craig, 247
Rowe, Dave, 351, 362
Rowe, Jim, 448, 459
Rowe, Larry, 333
Rowe, W.E., 44
Rule, Cliff, 13–14, 422
Rush, Spencer, 642, 645, 647–51
Russell, John, 135–36, 156, 160, 167, 179–80
Rust, Rod, 395
Rustad, Josh, 647–49, 652–54, 656, 658–59, 665–66
Rustad, Mert, 162
Rustebakke, Dorothy, 29, 32
Rustebakke, Ted, 10, 61
Ruud, Herman, 72
Ryals, Connie, 230
Ryan, Bill, 401
Ryan, Jay, 170
Ryan, Nolan, 487, 593
Ryan, Tom, 458
Ryder, Jeff, 249
Ryder, Kyle, 610
Ryerson, Alvin, 11

S

Safty, Delmer, 72
Safty, Ronny, 80
Safty, Selmer, 80
Sagen, George, 13
Sain, Johnny, 135
Salisbury, Rodney, 27
Sampsen, Rick, 190, 202
Sampson, Jim, 657
Sampson, Kelvin, 366, 684
Sampson, L.R., 62
Sampson, Tim, 139, 145
Samuelson, Lori, 230
Sandau, Joel, 470
Sandefur, Dirk, 382
Sanders, Blayd, 633
Sansaver, Noel, 603
Sayler, Bruce, 267, 352, 428–29
Sayler, Todd, 483
Sayles, John, 29, 32
Scanson, Dave, 315
Scarseth, Lydia, 39
Schaefer, Berniece, 386
Schaefer, Bob, 37–39, 84, 103, 119, 141, 153, 386, 486, 507
Schaefer, Howard, 42
Schaefer, Jim, 115
Schaefer, Larry, 82–83, 386
Schaefer, Steve, 374, 379, 386, 392, 394–96, 404–5, 407, 409, 414, 416, 421, 433, 444, 446–47, 452
Schaelbitz, Todd, 573
Schaff, Jeff, 464
Schammel, Alfred, 54, 64
Schellinger, Dan, 68
Schend, Frank, 190
Scheuffele, Mark, 312
Schilling, Curt, 203
Schillinger, Don, 132
Schillinger, Doug, 120, 127–28, 133
Schillinger, Jaron, 335
Schillinger, Roger, 132
Schindler, Kent, 256
Schlabs, Tyson, 598
Schlenker, Leo, 139
Schlenker, Todd, 414
Schlepp, Bill, 174–75
Schmitt, Erwin, 107–8
Schmutzler, Darren, 338
Schneider, Rick, 541–42
Scholtz, Lloyd, 42
Schrader, Cody, 520
Schultz, Mark, 448
Schumacher, Jace, 642, 645, 647–51
Schuster, Jerry, 62, 153, 434
Scott, Dewey, 594
Scott, Duwayne, 604, 610, 612
Scott, John, 72, 80
Scott, Johnny, 80
Scott, Ron, 164, 390
Scully, Vin, 3–4
Sealy, Chief, 27–28
Seanson, Justin, 552
Seaver, Tom, 93
Sebring, Bill, 208
Secord, Wes, 362
Seeberger, Dave, 312
Seger, Ross, 37
Seiler, Dick, 11
Seiler, Harry, 40, 42
Seiler, Walt, 11
Selinsky, Dave, 591
Sell, Caden, 350
Sell, Dwain "Baldy", 99, 101, 103, 109, 111–12, 115–16, 119–20, 122–25, 127–28, 133, 294, 401, 439, 534, 634
Sell, Ernie, 125
Sell, Keith, 71, 74–77, 79, 82–83, 86, 104, 132–33, 350, 636
Sell, Kevin, 75, 90, 99–103, 105, 108, 111, 116, 119, 124, 306, 401, 437, 439–40, 443, 486, 671
Sell, Mike, 350
Selvig, Dave, 256, 544, 564, 608
Selvig, Dawn, 230
Selvig, Doug, 376, 395–96, 405, 418
Selvig, Kari, 230
Selvig, Kenny, 131, 140, 636
Selvig, Matt, 607–9, 614–15, 619
Selvig, Roald, 75, 79, 84, 153
Severson, Ruth, 16, 677
Shaffer, Clark, 170, 182, 367
Shaffer, Paul, 452, 457, 463, 467–69, 473–75, 478, 481, 483, 506
Shamley, Jack, 132
Shane, Rusty, 205
Sharp, Bill, 107
Shaw, Bob, 195
Shaw, Hazel, 39
Shelton, Ron, 428
Shennum, Christine, 108, 114
Shennum, John, 448
Shepard, Bert, 59
Sheppard, Jere, 83
Shepphard, Doug, 134, 146
Sheridan, Mike, 220
Sheridan, Tom, 145
Sheron, Bink, 99, 111–12
Sheron, Moose, 82
Sherrill, Mike, 219, 221
Shipstead, A.J., 544–45, 555, 563–64, 575, 582–83
Shipstead, Oscar, 10
Shook, Harry, 30
Shortle, Harold, 75
Shuland, Cub, 448
Shumacher, Cora, 39
Shuman, Chad, 532, 538–39
Shuman, Gary, 82
Shuman, Tom, 122, 126–27
Shutz, Roger, 506
Sickels, Howard, 84
Sifuentes, Eddie, 398
Sinner, Wally, 112–13
Siring, Rodney, 448
Skar, Travis, 582
Skjerven, Gordon, 112–13, 116–17, 124, 133
Slaughter, Enos, 57
Sletten, Donna, 223
Slezak, Mark, 220–21
Slezak, Wayne, 266, 284, 291
Smith, Billie Lou, 138, 163
Smith, Brian, 619
Smith, Charlie, 14, 20–21, 30
Smith, Clausie, 97, 148
Smith, Craig, 301, 303, 335, 339
Smith, Curt, 160, 163, 168–69, 171

Smith, Dan, 62, 99, 101, 126, 130–31, 133–35, 138, 140, 142, 163, 298
Smith, Darryl, 159–60, 168–69
Smith, Dean, 200
Smith, Frank, 163
Smith, G., 338
Smith, G., 338
Smith, Hazel, 254
Smith, Jared, 633
Smith, Joel, 527
Smith, Margaret, 39
Smith, Ozzie, 93, 479
Smith, Phil, 351–52, 361–62, 365, 381, 429
Smith, Randy, 99–102, 105, 111, 115–16, 122, 124, 127–28, 130–31, 220
Smith, Sidney, 37–38, 103
Smith, Tony, 267
Snare, Jack, 237
Snare, Pixine, 223–29, 232–33
Snyder, Cory, 388–89
Sohm, Gary, 179, 181
Solberg, Brian, 563–64, 575, 582–88, 596
Solberg, Derek, 488–90, 497, 502–5, 512–20, 536, 622
Solem, Brooks, 666
Solomon, Daine, 618
Sorenson, Dave, 256
Sorte, Jim, 58, 61
Southland, Gage, 658
Southland, Phyllis, 16
Southland, Van, 130–31
Spahn, Warren, 135
Sparagno, Angelo, 43–44, 55
Spawn, Kelly, 343
Spear, Ober, 68
Spoonheim, Lorraine, 121
Sprague, Jack, 485, 490, 603–4, 608, 616–17, 630, 632–35, 656, 664
Sprague, Steve, 122
Squires, Leon, 76
Stafne, Art, 41–42
Stage, Tom, 84
Stageberg, Truman, 81
Stahl, Glenn, 70
Stahlecker, Harlan, 116–17
Stanley, Mark, 152
Stark, Bill, 456
Stebleton, Mike, 563, 565–67, 569, 575, 578, 596–97, 600–603, 607, 634, 642–43, 647, 652–55, 657–58, 664–67, 674
Stedman, Jim, 164
Steele, Dorn, 295, 385, 636
Steele, Fred, 299
Steele, Harold, 83
Stein, Jim, 218
Stengel, Casey, 81
Stengel, Dave, 191, 194, 196–200, 266, 369
Stenglein, Dan, 162
Stentoft, Matt, 582, 585, 588, 596
Stephens, Bill, 27
Stephenson, Dan, 452, 455, 457, 459
Stephenson, Steve, 488–91, 495, 497–98, 502–5, 512, 514–17, 520, 599, 635
Sternhagen, Chuck, 67–68
Sterrett, Lonnie, 80
Sterrett, Scott, 585, 588, 596, 601–3, 607–10
Stetson, Kirk, 189–90, 194, 211, 220–21, 270
Stevens, Mark, 249
Stevens, Ray, 213
Stickel, John, 589
Stiffarm, Steve, 486, 509, 579
Stinglien, Brian, 468
Stoe, Donna, 114
Stoick, Dave, 355–56
Stolen, Andy, 64, 72, 83, 95, 106–7, 112–13, 116–17, 121, 124, 127, 153, 179, 220, 241–42, 245–47, 252, 277, 324, 331, 368, 371, 385, 422, 476, 543, 623, 636, 648–49, 672, 675
Stolen, Carol, 115
Stolen, Gertrude, 400
Stolen, Greg, 235, 247–50, 272, 276, 319–21, 329, 337–38, 341–46, 349, 352, 354–55, 363–64, 373–85, 392, 394–98, 400, 404–9, 412–16, 425, 433, 435–36, 444, 450, 499, 612
Stolen, Randy, 161, 241, 245, 247–50, 256, 268, 273, 276–78, 281, 284, 289–92, 296–97, 299, 301–3, 307, 310–12, 314–16, 319–21, 326, 328, 330–31, 334–35, 337–39, 342–44, 347, 353, 355, 357, 359, 362–63, 373–82, 384, 386–90, 394, 402–4, 406, 409–11, 413–14, 418–19, 429, 437, 439, 447, 450, 481, 487, 499–500, 561, 649, 673, 679
Stolte, Jim, 380
Stone, Gary, 656
Street, Jim, 401
Strickland, Rusty, 339, 381
Strobel, Raleigh, 522
Stroh, Marsha, 128
Stubbs, Todd, 352, 362
Stuber, Mike, 397
Suess, M., 121
Sukut, Brent, 589
Sukut, Jeff, 300
Sukut, Joe, 207
Sukut, Kevin, 300, 302, 333, 339
Sukut, Wade, 194, 199, 207
Sularz, Allen, 84
Sullivan, B.T. "Sully", 68, 71, 75, 279, 587, 598, 636
Sullivan, Bernard "Bunky", 64, 74
Sullivan, Ella, 39
Sullivan, Jim "Sly", 400
Sullivan, Jim, 68
Summitt, Pat, 359
Sutton, Don, 93
Swenson, Clayton, 61, 63, 67, 70–71
Swenson, Preston, 666
Swenson, Tony, 11
Swenson, Wilbur, 40–41
Sylstine, Bill, 83
Syme, Rick, 179–80

T

Tade, Jacki, 276, 290, 298, 303, 311, 319, 343, 360, 375, 384
Tade, Kathie, 450
Tade, Ron, 614
Tadvick, Brad, 496, 500
Tande, Bob, 40, 43–44, 55–58, 60, 99, 101, 103–6, 115–16, 119, 123, 338, 447
Tande, Carl, 99, 102, 111, 115, 122
Tande, Claude, 57
Tande, Lillian, 104
Tande, Lona Rae, 104
Tande, Rod, 55, 92, 99–100, 102–3, 105, 108–9, 111, 115–16, 120–22, 124, 160, 191, 202, 210, 251, 283, 379, 383, 401, 418, 534
Tande, Ronald, 533
Tange, Jerry, 120
Tanner, Jack, 436, 509
Tarum, Brent, 488–91, 497, 500, 502–5, 512–16, 518–20, 532, 538, 540, 544–45, 555, 558–59
Tarum, Marvin, 533
Tarum, Tyler, 512, 514, 520–21, 524, 527–28, 538, 540–41
Teigen, Marla, 121
Terry, Morey, 448
Texidor, Dawn, 675
Tharp, Tim, 563–64, 585
Thievin, Tyler, 588, 614–15
Thilmony, Bob, 414
Thode, Joey, 235–36
Thogersen, Ben, 541
Thogerson, Jim, 139
Thogerson, Tim, 288, 291–92, 294, 303, 307–8, 313, 328, 330, 332–33, 335–36, 340, 369–71
Thomas, Dale, 138–39
Thomas, Dylan, 3–4
Thomas, Hayden, 10
Thomas, Rick, 291, 293, 351, 362
Thompson, Anna, 39
Thompson, Bill "Oscar", 99–102, 105, 111, 115–16, 120–23, 127–28, 294, 383, 388, 401
Thompson, Bob, 111, 126–27
Thompson, Bryon, 595
Thompson, Gene, 97, 101, 105–6, 116, 120, 152, 160, 162–64, 364, 656
Thompson, Larry, 126, 133
Thompson, Oscar, 179
Thompson, Terry, 256, 265
Thorpe, Jim, 27
Thorpe, Randall, 16
Timmerman, Shorty, 73
Tkachyk, Jim, 122, 126
Tkachyk, Ralph, 63, 67
Tokerud, Eric, 249
Tollefson, Pete, 382
Tollefson, Scott, 351
Tonjum, Ken, 63, 67, 70–71, 74, 76, 79
Tonjum, Mons, 54
Torgerson, Buzz, 106–7, 112, 124
Torgerson, Marvin, 106
Torre, Joe, 112
Towberman, Dennis, 458
Traeger, Justin, 598
Trang, Kelly, 235–37
Trang, Lalon, 227
Trang, Roger, 231, 235–37, 248, 250–51, 272
Trang, Tom, 404–5

Index

Trangsrud, Dallas, 161, 189, 191–92, 197, 205, 207–8, 210, 249, 437
Trangsrud, Duke, 186, 191–92, 194, 196–200, 205, 207–10, 212, 215–17, 219–20, 242, 296, 303, 338, 348, 365, 486, 507, 634
Trangsrud, Helen, 15, 93, 96, 265
Trangsrud, Larry, 392, 394, 404–5, 409–10, 414, 433, 444–46, 451–55, 457, 459, 463–67, 472, 478, 494, 531–33, 551
Traynor, Jan, 227–28
Traynor, Mike, 182
Triplett, Ken, 95, 106
Trower, Donald, 10
Trower, Fern E., 16
Trower, Jim, 10
Trower, Ramon, 54–55, 58, 60
Trower, Ray, 75
Trower, Rosa, 16, 680
Trudnowski, Jim, 341
Tryan, Audrey, 315
Tryan, Bob, 404–5, 409, 414, 433, 436, 444
Tryan, Cory, 417
Tryan, Dan, 126–27, 131, 140, 142–43, 417, 422, 447
Tryan, Don, 72, 77, 107, 117, 121, 124, 142–43, 237, 417, 446–47, 623
Tryan, Donette, 121
Tryan, George, 42, 417, 420
Tryan, Gord, 237, 319, 334, 337–38, 361, 373–77, 379–84, 392, 394–96, 400, 404–9, 414–17, 420, 423, 426, 433, 447–48, 486, 558
Tryan, Jack, 49, 171, 191–92, 196–98, 205, 210–11, 348
Tryan, Mike, 374, 379, 392, 394–96, 404–9, 414, 425, 433, 444–46, 448–50, 452
Tryan, Phyllis, 446–47
Tryan, Tully, 205, 216–17, 240
Tryan, Wade, 160, 171, 206, 216–17, 247, 251, 255, 261, 264–65, 267–68, 276–78, 280–81, 283, 290–92, 297, 300–301, 303, 307–8, 311–12, 319, 324–25, 329, 334–35, 337, 339, 342–44, 346, 353, 360, 363, 373–74, 418–19
Tryan, Wendy (Danelson), 202
Tucker, Pete, 382
Turnquist, Jay, 448
Tweeten, Hank, 146, 154, 159–60, 179
Tyler, Bob, 122
Tymofichuk, Frankie, 202

U

Ueland, Kurt, 184, 215
Unsworth, Don, 70–72
Urquhart, Diane, 128

V

Vachal, Jim, 341
Van Gorden, Charles, 92
VanAtta, Larry, 132
Vance, Randy, 381
Vandeberg, JoAnn, 108
Vandenberg, Harry, 11
Vandenburg, Esther, 237
Vanderpan, Gordon "Dike", 54–56, 60, 103
Varnes, Kelly, 208
Vatnsdal, Kade, 556, 619–20
Vatnsdal, Tracy, 544–45, 555, 558, 620
Veis, Brent, 527, 530, 534
Veis, Bud, 111, 122, 126–27, 534
Veis, Cary, 182
Veis, Chris, 10, 43, 55, 57, 61, 78, 84
Veis, Doug, 172
Veis, Gerry, 185, 222, 245, 328, 557
Veis, Jamie, 527–28, 538
Veis, Kelly, 228
Veis, Larry, 99–101, 103–5, 111, 115–16, 120, 122–24, 127, 133
Veis, Richard, 10
Veis, Terry, 99–101, 105, 109, 111, 115, 122, 125, 634
Veis, Vern, 54–55, 58, 61, 64, 66, 68, 78–79, 92, 153, 176, 179, 220, 486
Verlander, Justin, 487
Vigliotti, Anthony, 449
Vigliotti, Pat, 472, 501
Vigliotti, Tim, 450, 520, 522–24, 527–30, 534–35, 538–40, 543–54, 556–58, 560–63, 612
Vigliotti, Tony, 374, 379, 392, 394–96, 402, 404–10, 414, 416, 433–34, 436–37, 444–50, 452, 505
Vincent, Jerry, 208
Vine, Kyle, 616
Vine, Lenny, 191, 198
Vink, Leendert, 153
Vinson, Earl, 83
Voight, Peter, 82
Volk, Chris, 414, 448
Volosick, Tony, 77
Von Kuster, Kate, 39

W

Wagar, Sharon, 128
Wagner, Hans, 28
Wahl, Lillian, 108, 114, 118, 121
Wahl, Phil, 585
Waldron, Matt, 487
Walker, Auget, 32, 678
Walker, Fred, 76, 79, 81, 83–85, 92, 95, 476
Walker, Harry, 57
Walker, Jack, 398
Walker, Joe, 11, 15, 20–22, 26, 29–30, 38
Waller, G.J. (Gus), 97
Waller, Leverne, 108
Waller, Raymond "Whitey", 37, 460
Walter, Dave, 20, 27, 32, 674
Wang, Danny "Charlie", 133, 140, 144, 152, 154–56, 159–64, 166–70, 172–73, 181–83, 190, 220, 283–84, 437, 560–61, 634
Wang, Johnny, 171
Wangerin, Randy, 48, 279, 281, 294, 298, 421
Wangrud, Butch, 75
Wangrud, Larry, 67, 70–71, 75, 95, 106, 117
Wangrud, Ordean, 67, 70, 74–76, 79, 83, 85, 92, 95, 106, 116, 636
Wangrud, Ron, 106
Ward, Jeremy, 438
Ware, Curt, 538–41, 543–49, 551–55, 557, 562–64, 567–72, 574–76, 582
Ware, Rocky, 114–15, 122, 126–27, 130, 133, 140–41, 144, 147, 152, 154–56, 158–60, 162, 164, 166, 169, 190, 202, 283–84, 303–4, 338, 383, 440, 443, 569
Ware, Walt, 115, 119
Warken, Rita, 81
Wasser, Bernie, 235–37, 239, 243, 245, 250, 256, 268, 273, 275–76, 290, 293, 297, 360
Wasser, Donna, 223, 227–28
Wasser, Rick, 234–35, 237, 272
Waterman, Jay, 179, 189
Watkins, Todd, 335, 337–38
Weaver, Doug, 83
Weaver, Hank, 219
Webb, Jaci, 103, 675
Webb, Virgil, 83
Webster, Bill, 251
Wednes, Lawrence, 574
Weeks, Tanner, 642, 647–48, 650
Weeks, Tyler, 642
Weidner, Curley, 114
Weier, George, 378
Weinberger, Bob, 134–36
Weiskopf, Donald, 428
Welch, Harvey, 190
Welch, Mike, 169, 179
Welk, Jerry, 358–59, 362
Welsch, Jeff, 447
Welzenbach, Tony, 132
Wensloff, Dave, 106
Werleu, Willie, 83
West, Dick, 236
Wester, C.O., 493, 509
Wetteland, John, 437
Whaley, Pat, 180
Whelan, Jack, 267, 351
Whipple, Casey, 541
Whipple, Chad, 541
Whipple, Gussie, 43
Whipple, Keith, 11, 20–21, 25, 28–29, 66, 74–75, 477, 569, 635
Whitlow, Ada, 108, 114, 118, 128
Whitmus, John, 470
Whittelsey, Rick, 132
Whitworth, Gail, 465–66, 505, 524–26
Whitworth, Kevin, 509
Wholery, Marc, 491
Widerholdt, Dick, 443
Wier, Jim, 471, 474
Wilcoxen, Harry, 10
Wilcoxon, Sherd, 10, 61
Wilemon, Judy, 659
Wiley, Dallas, 81
Wiley, Fern, 8, 16, 679
Wiley, Floyd "Skeg", 72–74, 77, 80–81
Wiley, Jesse Lee, 8, 80–81, 214, 421
Wiley, Merle, 80
Wiley, Mickey, 186–87
Wiley, Pete, 72, 77, 80, 90
Wilkes, Art, 10, 41

Wilkinson, Bill, 416, 421, 423–24, 434, 449, 452, 501, 516
Wilkinson, J.L., 22
Wilkinson, Jim, 351, 353
Wilkinson, John, 382
Willard, Alan, 114, 126
Willard, Bob, 60, 68, 71, 75, 114, 476
Willard, Buddy, 114
Willard, Larry, 114
Williams, Mick, 154, 158, 160, 169, 173–74, 453–56, 461, 470, 487, 551–52, 588–92, 594–95, 604, 610–12, 618–19, 631
Williams, Plenny, 666
Williams, Robin, 365
Williams, Ted, 47, 57
Williams, Trent, 666
Willse, Hudson, 496, 509
Wilson, Dick, 107, 112, 116, 120, 155
Wilson, H.M. (Orpheum), 13
Wilson, Jesse, 448, 574, 598, 604, 610, 612, 618
Wilson, Vester, 436, 570–74, 578–79, 584, 598, 617, 678
Wilson, Warren, 75
Winfield, Dave, 479
Winkler, Marsha, 128
Wirt, Jarrod, 595
Wirtzberger, Bucky, 81
Witt, Bobby, 367
Wojick, Jeff, 338
Wolf, Gregory H., 57
Wolfe, Danny, 125, 144, 152, 158–60, 163, 166–73, 177–79, 182–83, 185–87, 190, 202, 212, 220, 282–84, 293, 340, 390, 402, 418–20, 438–40, 443, 518, 558, 569, 575, 578, 624, 634, 656
Wolfe, Jason, 538–42, 544–48, 551–52, 555, 557, 560–61, 563–72, 574–76, 578, 582, 623, 632, 667
Wolfe, Joyce, 179
Wolfe, N.C., 90, 153, 162-163, 182
Wolfe, Perry, 222, 293, 341, 439
Wolsky, Dan, 617
Wood, Wilbur, 277, 371
Woods, Kevin, 261
Working, F., 11
Worley, Mark, 490
Worthington, Jim, 80
Wright, Bill, 61
Wright, Tom, 64

Y

Yeager, Jim, 208
Yegen, Charlie, 181
Yoakam, Mark, 256, 259, 269, 279, 401
Young, Ralph, 83
Young, Ryan, 666
Young, Rylan, 666
Yuill, Grace, 16

Z

Zeidler, Ben, 145
Zeitner, Doug, 648
Ziegler, Tom, 558, 577

Zieske, Clarence "Clip", 84, 114, 144
Zieske, Keith, 191–92, 197
Zimmer, Bill, 256, 260, 264–65, 279, 307
Zimmer, Jim, 458
Zimmer, Leo, 64, 68, 72, 80, 85, 95–97, 106, 109, 116–17, 636
Zimmer, Michael, 448
Zimmer, Vince, 85, 90, 92, 112, 116–17, 124
Zuroff, Mel, 333

About the Author

Joe Puckett as the head coach for his daughter's recreational softball team in 2012 in Stuttgart, Germany, where the family lived when his daughters Cosette and Emma were growing up from 2007 to 2018.

JOE PUCKETT is the chief editor of Aubade Publishing, a small family publishing business specializing in literary and historical fiction, poetry, and sports memoirs. He was born and raised in a small town in northeastern Montana, where he, along with his twin brother Jon, learned how to play basketball and baseball from their dad, George "Tiny" Puckett. His youth in the 1960s and 1970s was spent on baseball fields in summer and basketball courts in winter. *The Blues of Summer* is his second nostalgic memoir about small-town sports, as he previously published *The Dream: The Story of the 1978-79 Peerless Panthers*, which tells the story of how the 1978 Peerless Panthers were the first team to qualify for the state basketball tournament in the high school's history. He is planning a third book, *Out of the Ashes: How Kelvin Sampson Resurrected the 1981–85 Montana Tech Orediggers*, which is scheduled for publication in 2028. Joe currently resides in Ashburn, Virginia, with his wife Vonda and daughters Cosette and Emma, who are all part of the family publishing business.

About the Book Designer

Cosette Puckett (right) and her teammate Shannon Nam (left) playing in a game for Stuttgart Select, a team her dad founded in Germany with both American and German players. Cosette (third base) and Shannon (shortstop) shared a laugh after bumping into each other going after the same fly ball (which, fortunately, Cosette still managed to catch).

COSETTE PUCKETT wears many hats as book designer, cover designer, illustrator, copyeditor, and manuscript reviewer for Aubade Publishing, her family's publishing business. Graduating from University of St Andrews in Scotland in 2019 with a degree in English, Cosette is a technical writer by day, book publisher by night. Growing up, her dad Joe instilled in her the same love of sports (and no small amount of competitiveness) his own dad had given him, particularly for softball and basketball. Cosette shares several things in common with her dad: both graduated from high schools that are now closed (Cosette graduated from Patch High School on Patch Barracks in Germany), played basketball and baseball/softball in high school, lost their basketball championships in their senior year, but won their championships for baseball/softball. She dearly loved playing sports growing up and remembers best the friends she made, the fun times she had, and those magical moments when you hear the roar of the crowd and execute the perfect play—though her memories don't quite have the same exhaustive detail as her dad's (who can seemingly remember exactly what he was doing during every game he's every played).

Cosette was lucky enough to have her dad as her coach in her formative years, during which he didn't just share his deep knowledge and passion for sports, but also taught her about leadership, dedication, and the importance of teamwork. She treasures every memory and minute they spent having fun together in her (relative) youth, and now working together in the family business, throwing a ball around or shooting a few hoops, hitting the slopes for some skiing (her dad and sister) and snowboarding (Cosette), or catching a game. Cosette lives and works in Virginia with her parents, sister, and their very beloved, very spoiled dog, Baby.